THE PAST ALL AROUND US

THE PAST ALL AROUND US
was edited and designed by
The Reader's Digest Association Limited,
London

First Edition
Copyright © 1979
The Reader's Digest Association Limited,
25 Berkeley Square,
London W1X 6AB

® READER'S DIGEST is
a registered trademark of
The Reader's Digest Association, Inc.
of Pleasantville, New York, U.S.A.

Typesetting
Brown Knight and Truscott Ltd, Tonbridge
Separations
Hilo Offset Ltd, Colchester
Printing
Alabaster Passmore & Sons Ltd, Maidstone
Binding
Hazell, Watson and Viney Ltd, Aylesbury
Paper
C. Townsend Hook Paper Co. Ltd, Snodland
Bowater Paper Sales Ltd, Sittingbourne

The main text in THE PAST ALL AROUND US
is typeset in 9 pt Monophoto Bembo

Printed in Great Britain

THE PAST ALL AROUND US

AN ILLUSTRATED GUIDE TO THE RUINS,
RELICS, MONUMENTS, CASTLES, CATHEDRALS,
HISTORIC BUILDINGS AND INDUSTRIAL
LANDMARKS OF BRITAIN

PUBLISHED BY THE READER'S DIGEST ASSOCIATION LIMITED
London   New York   Montreal   Sydney   Cape Town

CONTENTS

(CONTENTS CONTINUED OVERLEAF)

CONTENTS

VISITING THE PLACES IN THIS BOOK

Part Two of THE PAST ALL AROUND US
*contains descriptions of buildings and locations
that reflect in some way the life of the British people – from the
earliest identifiable dwellings where Stone Age
families lived in the last Ice Age, to the steam-engines
and mines of the Industrial Revolution and beyond.*

*In nearly 2,000 different locations, under different ownership,
visiting times vary greatly. Some places are open
throughout the year, others only during the summer.
Many restored engines and mills are run by amateur groups
who might only open at weekends.
All the places in Part Two are open to the public for a reasonable
time of the year, unless the description states otherwise.
But before travelling long distances it is advisable
to check opening hours first.
Most places are listed in the local telephone book.*

*Some of the sites that figure in the story of
the Industrial Revolution have now become derelict.
Great care should always be taken in exploring them, as there
could be open mine shafts, or old buildings might be dangerous.
Road and rail bridges and canal aqueducts have been included
and in many cases they can be crossed by foot
on the road or towpath, but railway bridges are
closed to the public.*

*Churches may sometimes be closed, but notices often tell
visitors where a key can be obtained.*

*Locations have been given for each entry, but to find some of
the more out-of-the-way sites a good road atlas such as*
READER'S DIGEST/AA NEW BOOK OF THE ROAD *will be helpful.*

ACKNOWLEDGMENTS

The following people played a major part in making
THE PAST ALL AROUND US

CONTRIBUTORS
Professor Keith Branigan, *University of Sheffield*
Anthony Burton · Gillian Darley · Bryn Frank
Plantagenet Somerset Fry · Nigel Harvey · Frank E. Huggett
J. Kenneth Major · Donald Lamond Macnie · David Owen
John Physick F.S.A. · Shirley Toulson
Dr Roger J. A. Wilson, *Trinity College, University of Dublin*

ADVISER ON COSTUME
Pegaret Anthony

ARTISTS
Richard Bonson · Barbara Brown · Roy Castle
Brian Delf · Ivan Lapper
Jeffery Matthews · Robert Micklewright · Stanley Paine
Charles Pickard · Marjorie Saynor · Les Smith

PHOTOGRAPHERS
Malcolm Aird · Clive Coote · Mike Freeman
Michael Holford · Lucinda Lambton · Colin Molyneux
Tom Scott · Patrick Thurston · Eileen Tweedy

The publishers also wish to thank
the many people who checked and advised on the great
variety of material – both written information and illustrations –
that makes up THE PAST ALL AROUND US

PART ONE

The man-made Landscape

A JOURNEY ACROSS THE COUNTRYSIDE AND THROUGH TIME
BEGINS IN 3500 BC WHEN THE FIRST FARMERS
BEGAN CHANGING THE FACE OF THE BRITISH LANDSCAPE.
EVER SINCE, MAN HAS LEFT HIS MARK ON THE LAND
AS HE HAS TRAVELLED DOWN THROUGH THE AGES

Farmers of pre-history

STONE AGE MAN CARVED HIS FIRST MARK ON THE
LANDSCAPE WITH FLINT AXES AND WOODEN PLOUGHS, AND
LEFT BEHIND THE REMAINS OF HIS STONE HOUSES

When the first Stone Age hunters ventured into Britain about
300,000 BC, crossing on dry ground from the Continent, the land
was a treeless plain in the midst of the Ice Age. When the ice finally
retreated around 10,000 BC, trees grew, and by about 5000 BC a
thick blanket of deciduous forest covered most of Britain.

Stone Age man made no real impact on the landscape until the
first farmers arrived from France and Belgium by sea about 3500
BC. They brought with them wheat and barley, and probably
domesticated sheep and cattle. They began to cut down the forest
with polished stone axes and cultivate the soil with primitive ploughs
made of forked branches. By 3000 BC parts of the chalk downlands
of southern England had been cleared of woodland for ever.

The flint for making axes, sickles and knives was dug from flint
mines on the chalklands. At Grime's Graves in Norfolk and Cissbury
in West Sussex, old mines still pock-mark the land. From these
mines the flint was carried along the first English trackways to
communities hundreds of miles away. The Berkshire Ridgway and
the Icknield Way still roll across England, in some places marking
parish boundaries, in others still used by traffic.

The end of Stone Age technology
Around 2000 BC, new migrants, called the Beaker People after their
pottery, were reaching Britain from the Netherlands and the
Rhineland of Germany. Their arrival heralded the end of the Stone
Age cultures, for they brought with them the revolutionary
knowledge of how to make tools and weapons from copper.

On the downlands of southern England, the Beaker People
divided their farmland into blocks of small fields, roughly square and
each about an acre in size. An example can still be seen at
Cheselbourne in Dorset.

As the Beaker People arrived, the climate was becoming warmer
and dryer, and farmers began cultivating hilly areas that had
previously been ignored. Dartmoor was cleared of its forests and
parcelled up into fields with long stone walls called reaves, which can
still be seen. Stones were cleared from the fields and dumped in
heaps, or cairns, which dot the landscape of upland Britain today.
The remains of farming villages still exist – such as Grimspound on
Dartmoor where a community lived in 20–30 circular stone huts.

The clearing of the trees and grazing of the pastures exposed the
uplands to severe erosion. As the climate became wetter and colder
again around 1200 BC, moss blanketed the impoverished wet soil
and turned large areas into the empty lonely moors of today.

BRONZE AGE VILLAGE *The stone wall around Grimspound village on
Dartmoor was built about 1500 BC when the area had been cleared of trees.*

OLDEST FIELDS
*Some of the earliest fields in
Britain show up in aerial
photographs of southern
England. Small square fields
were farmed through the
Bronze and Iron Ages, as at
Crowhill, near Abbotsbury,
Dorset. The downward drift
of soil built up ridges on
the lower boundaries.*

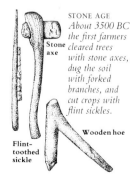

STONE AGE
About 3500 BC the first farmers cleared trees with stone axes, dug the soil with forked branches, and cut crops with flint sickles.

Stone axe

Flint-toothed sickle

Wooden hoe

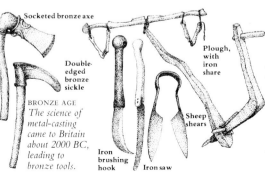

Socketed bronze axe

Double-edged bronze sickle

BRONZE AGE
The science of metal-casting came to Britain about 2000 BC, leading to bronze tools.

Iron brushing hook

Iron saw

Sheep shears

Plough, with iron share

IRON AGE *In the 7th century BC, iron became available to farmers for the first time. They used it to make tougher points (or shares) for their simple ploughs, as well as for saws, brushing hooks for trimming hedges, and sheep shears.*

The arrow-straight lines of Roman Britain

FOUR CENTURIES OF ROMAN OCCUPATION LEFT BEHIND A ROAD NETWORK THAT STILL CARRIES TRAFFIC TODAY

Only 50 years before Julius Caesar invaded Britain in 55 BC, Celtic tribes from Belgium came to the south-east of England and built Britain's first towns. Caesar called the towns *oppida*. Inside their massive banks and ditches were fields, craft centres, and timber houses for hundreds and perhaps thousands of people. The remains of *oppida* defences can still be seen at Colchester in Essex, the capital of pre-Roman Britain, and Winchester, in Hampshire.

The *oppida* were the capitals of the eight tribal kingdoms of southern England, and coins were minted there for use throughout each territory. A permanent memorial to the Belgic culture still shines from a chalk hillside in Berkshire. The 374 ft long White Horse of Uffington is probably the same galloping-horse that the Atrebates tribe depicted on their coins.

When the Romans conquered Britain nearly 100 years after Caesar's first visit, they began a formidable campaign of road building. In 400 years, 6,000 miles of roads were built, slicing across the country in long straight lines, many of which are the routes of modern roads. Watling Street ran from Dover to London (now the A2) and then on past Birmingham (now the A5). Foss Way ran diagonally across the country, from Bath through Cirencester to Lincoln (now including the A429 and A46). Ermine Street ran north from London to the Humber estuary (now sections of the A10, A1 and A15).

By AD 80, the military conquests had carried the roads and forts into Scotland, and led to the most famous Roman landmark in Britain, Hadrian's Wall.

Food for the towns of Roman Britain
The new Roman civilisation created a demand for craftsmen to provide its high standard of living – builders, metal-workers, jewellers and potters. The new crafts became concentrated in the towns, and to supply food for the townspeople farming estates were established in the countryside. The nucleus of each estate was a villa, such as Chedworth villa in Gloucestershire. The estates – 1,000 acres or more – often included native farmsteads, and sometimes small villages, but the whole estate was organised from the villa.

One of the permanent changes to the landscape made by the Romans took place in the Fens. Dykes and canals were dug to drain the land and make it suitable for farming. It was the first chapter in the story of man's long battle against the sea in lowland England.

ROMAN ROAD
King Street ran in an almost straight line from the Roman town of Durobrivae in Lincolnshire to Bourne, 15 miles north. It is now a minor road running through West Deeping, east of Stamford. In the foreground the road kinks after crossing the River Welland.

FENLAND FIELDS *A pattern of Roman ditches and droveways in the fens near Spalding, Lincolnshire, shows up as dark green lines in the crops.*

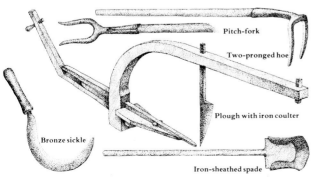

VILLA FARMING *Estates were cultivated with ploughs that had an iron coulter, or vertical blade, to cut the soil in front of the ploughshare. The soil was also dug with wooden spades sheathed with iron, and with two-pronged hoes. Grain might be reaped with sickles, which were swung by the farmer, or with reaping hooks, which were pulled through the grain as it was held in the left hand. Hay and straw were moved with pitch-forks.*

Pitch-fork

Two-pronged hoe

Plough with iron coulter

Bronze sickle

Iron-sheathed spade

The ridged fields of the Anglo-Saxons

MOST OF ENGLAND'S VILLAGES WERE FIRST BUILT BY ANGLO-
SAXON FARMERS WHOSE PLOUGHS HAVE LEFT A
RIDGE-AND-FURROW PATTERN ON THE COUNTRYSIDE

Roman troops were finally withdrawn from Britain in AD 407 to
defend Rome itself from barbarian attack. As the last Roman ship
left, the native British south of the Tyne found themselves
responsible for running their own country and defending themselves
against foreign invaders for the first time in 400 years.

The country entered a period of chaos, the details of which are so
confused that it is called "the Dark Ages". While rival factions
struggled for power, Britain was attacked by marauding bands of
invaders from almost every side – Scots from Ireland, Picts from
Scotland, and Anglo-Saxons from the north-west coast of Europe.

In these troubled years, parts of the Roman landscape reverted to
wilderness or scrub, and towns and villas fell into ruins. But by AD
600 the Anglo-Saxon invaders had settled in most of England, except
for the far west, and were making a unique contribution to the face
of Britain. The Saxon settlement was, above all else, a time of
building villages. Almost every village on the modern map of England
had been created before the Norman Conquest in 1066.

Street villages and green villages

Some villages still preserve their Saxon plan, as either a "street
village" or a "green village". "Street villages" were built as a string
of houses along both sides of a single street with a church at one end.
The more picturesque "green villages" were built around a village
green, usually containing the church and a well. The circular
arrangement of the houses may have been a means of defending
livestock against attacks by wolves or marauders.

Every Saxon village was surrounded by two or three huge "open
fields" each covering hundreds of acres. The fields were divided into
blocks, or furlongs, each containing dozens of long narrow strips.
The standard size of a strip was 1 acre – the amount of land one man
could plough in a day. Each farmer in the village worked about 30
acres scattered throughout the fields. The system ensured that each
farmer had a fair share of good and poor land.

As the plough went up and down the strips the soil was thrown
inwards, building up a ridge on the strip with deep furrows on each
side. In parts of the country, particularly the Midlands, where the
land has been turned over to grazing, the "ridge and furrow" strips
can still be seen, preserved under the grass. And in Laxton,
Nottinghamshire, the fields are still farmed in the old way.

FURLONGS *Strips owned by individual farmers were grouped into blocks called
furlongs (furrow-long), which are still visible near Barley, Lancashire.*

RIDGE AND
FURROW
*Ridges in the soil created by
Saxon farmers near Westcote,
Gloucestershire, are still
visible from the air in the late
afternoon when shadows are
long. In Saxon times the
British landscape was still
mostly forest, interspersed
with fields and villages.*

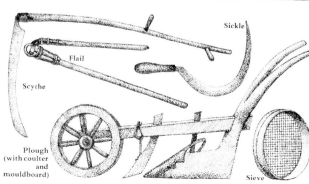

TOOLS OF THE SAXON FARMERS
The strip farms of the Saxons were cultivated with wheeled ploughs fitted with a coulter to cut the soil and a mouldboard to turn it. At harvest time, the crops were cut by hand with sickles and scythes. The grain was then separated from the chaff by being beaten with flails on the floor of the barn; breezes through the barn helped the process. Weed seeds were sifted from the corn with a wooden sieve.

Sickle

Flail

Scythe

Plough
(with coulter
and
mouldboard)

Sieve

A land of wool and spires

LAND RECLAIMED FROM THE EASTERN MARSHES HELPED TO
BUILD THE WOOL–WEALTH OF MEDIEVAL ENGLAND, BUT THE
TRAGEDY OF THE BLACK DEATH LEFT HUNDREDS OF VILLAGES
ABANDONED AND LIFELESS

When William the Conqueror invaded England in 1066 he set about
turning his new kingdom into a great private hunting ground. The
forests became Royal game preserves, governed by repressive Forest
Laws that forbade anyone from taking deer or wild boar or the
vegetation they fed on. Forest courts inflicted savage penalties on
poachers. In William's reign, says the Anglo-Saxon Chronicles,
"whoever killed a hart or a hind should be blinded". Under later
Norman kings poachers were put to death.

William created the New Forest in Hampshire by destroying
farms and villages, and turning them over to woodland. The whole
of Essex and great tracts of the Midlands were also the king's
preserve.

In the 12th and 13th centuries a rash of new boroughs were
created by royal charter, a form of land speculation in which the
great landowners sub-divided parts of their land to create towns.
Many of the new towns failed to grow, but others thrived – the first
planned settlements since the Roman conquest. Salisbury, Ludlow
and Stratford-upon-Avon were three of the new towns, and at
Salisbury the regular grid of medieval streets still largely survives.

Medieval dikes that carry today's cars

From about 1200, thousands of acres of farmland were created in the
low-lying areas of Lincolnshire, Kent and Somerset. Ditches were
dug to drain marshes and fens, continuing work that the Romans
had begun 1,000 years before. Around the Wash, farmers banded
together to build 6 ft high dikes that today carry roads. Hardy sheep
were sent out to forage on the reclaimed marshland. The prosperity
of the medieval wool industry is still reflected in the grandeur of the
churches that were built from its revenues in wool counties such as
Norfolk and Suffolk. It was in the 13th century that the church
steeple first made its appearance on the English landscape.

In the middle of the 14th century the Black Death ravaged
Britain, killing between one-third and a half of the population. In
the years that followed, villages in the marginal lands were deserted
as farmers moved to vacant land in better areas. There are more than
1,300 deserted medieval villages in England, many of them resulting
from the years of the Black Death. They are now usually no more
than ridges in the grass marking the foundations of the long-
forgotten houses, and depressions where the village streets once
carried their medieval traffic.

MARSH FIELDS *Great areas of fen and marsh land were reclaimed in the
Middle Ages. Around Rye in Kent, nature helped by silting up the coast.*

HILL FIELDS
*In the hill country of the
north and west most fields
were carved from the forest
by individual farmers. The
lanes that wound from farm
to farm in the Middle Ages
now carry today's traffic.
And patches of the original
forest remain, as in the area
near Manaton, Devon.*

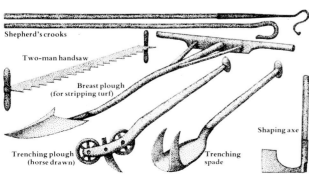

MANUAL LABOUR *In medieval Britain most work was still done by hand, as it had been since the Stone Age. Timber was cut and shaped with saws and axes; land was stripped of turf manually before ploughing; drainage trenches were dug by hand (with some help from horse-drawn ploughs). And the sheep that grazed the land were tended by shepherds equipped with little more than wooden or iron crooks, for gripping the sheep by leg or neck.*

Shepherd's crooks

Two-man handsaw

Breast plough
(for stripping turf)

Trenching plough
(horse drawn)

Trenching
spade

Shaping axe

The new face of England

THE AGRICULTURAL REVOLUTION OF THE 18TH CENTURY TRANSFORMED THE HUGE OPEN FIELDS OF THE SAXONS INTO THE PATTERN OF SMALL FIELDS THAT EXISTS TODAY

In the 18th century a revolution took place that altered the face of England. At the beginning of the century there were still millions of acres of land farmed in great open fields that had stood unchanged for 1,000 years.

But new ideas of farming were introduced by two Norfolk farmers, Viscount "Turnip" Townshend and Thomas Coke. Their methods involved a four year crop rotation system which gave greater yields and reduced pests and diseases, but it meant the land had to be enclosed into fields to keep livestock away from crops.

Farmers rapidly became converted to the new ideas, and by the mid-18th century the open fields were being swept away by a wave of parliamentary enclosure acts. Throughout central England, where the open-field system had been most widely used, a new network of fields was created. Each field was about 10 acres in size, more or less square, and enclosed by hawthorn hedges or stone walls.

Between 4 million and 5 million acres of rural England were remoulded in this way between 1750 and 1850, creating the rural pattern of small hedged fields that has existed up to the present day.

Classical landscapes in noble parks

The 18th century also saw a second innovation in rural Britain that left a permanent mark on the landscape. Foreign travel had introduced wealthy landowners to the culture of Europe, and a fashion arose for landscaped parks. The parks attempted to imitate classical landscapes painted by the Italian artists Claude and Poussin. Designers such as William Kent and "Capability" Brown altered the appearance of hundreds of square miles of land to create noble settings for great houses such as Chatsworth in Derbyshire and Longleat in Wiltshire. Some of the parks, including Woburn in Bedfordshire, occupied more than 2,000 acres, and others involved the destruction of entire villages to remove them from the landowner's view. The farming village of Nuneham Courtenay in Oxfordshire was rebuilt a mile away, and was immortalised by Oliver Goldsmith in his poem *The Deserted Village*. Parks continued to be created until cheap food from the New World brought the agricultural depression of the 1880s.

In Scotland, the 18th century saw the beginning of the brutal Highland Clearances, during which whole communities of farmers were evicted to make room for sheep. Between 5,000 and 10,000 tenants were expelled from the land of the Duchess of Sutherland alone. The farmers moved into crofts in marginal areas while the deserted villages decayed into heaps of stones.

WALLED FIELDS *In upland areas, such as Monsaldale, Derbyshire, the new fields were enclosed by miles of straight, dry-stone walls.*

HEDGED FIELDS
Between 4 and 5 million acres of central England, like the area around Gumley, Leicestershire, were enclosed into squarish fields in the 18th century. Each field was about 10 acres, bounded by a hawthorn hedge. The thousands of new hedges attracted millions of birds.

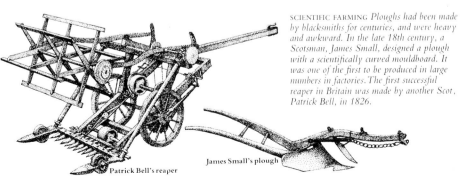

SCIENTIFIC FARMING *Ploughs had been made by blacksmiths for centuries, and were heavy and awkward. In the late 18th century, a Scotsman, James Small, designed a plough with a scientifically curved mouldboard. It was one of the first to be produced in large numbers in factories. The first successful reaper in Britain was made by another Scot, Patrick Bell, in 1826.*

Patrick Bell's reaper

James Small's plough

Moonscapes of industry

AWESOME MOUNTAINS MARKED THE LANDSCAPE OF THE
18TH AND 19TH CENTURIES, MADE OF THE WASTE FROM THE
RAW MATERIALS THAT FED BRITAIN'S FACTORIES

The Industrial Revolution of the 18th and 19th centuries created its
own landscape, ranging from white moonscapes in Cornwall to
black mountains in Wales and the north of England.

When Josiah Wedgwood set up his own pottery business at
Burslem, Staffordshire, in 1759, he made a decision that was to affect
the countryside more than 200 miles away. To capture the
fashionable market, Wedgwood used the white china clay of
Cornwall rather than the red clay of Staffordshire that had been the
basis of the pottery industry for centuries. His innovation caused a
boom in the china clay industry, and great white spoil heaps grew up
around St Austell, to stand out eerily on the Cornish landscape.

On the bleak moorlands of Cornwall the remains of another
industry stand remote and deserted. Tin and copper had been mined
in Cornwall since prehistoric times, but by the 18th century the
mines had reached such depths that they were constantly being
flooded. The invention of the steam pumping engine provided the
answer. The engines were built into granite engine-houses, with high
chimney stacks. Hundreds of engine-houses grew up from one end
of the county to the other, and they still dominate the countryside
east of St Day, near Camborne.

Bell pits, like giant doughnuts

It was the fuel that powered the Cornish mining engines that
probably had the greatest effect on the British landscape during the
Industrial Revolution. Until the invention of the steam-engine coal
had been used only for heating. Some of the early coal-mines were
known as bell pits, from their shape. A shaft was dug down into a
coal seam and the miners excavated outwards from the bottom of
the shaft. When the pit threatened to collapse they dug another.
Remains of 18th-century bell pits, like giant doughnuts, still scar the
countryside on the old Scottish coal-fields around Muirhead and
Glenbuck, 25 miles south of Glasgow.

As the Steam Age arrived in the early 19th century, requiring
great amounts of coal, new mining villages grew up in Wales, the
north of England and the lowlands of Scotland. And they created
their own landscapes around them. Mountainous heaps of black
waste marked every coal community, looming over the miners'
houses.

A tragic aftermath of the Industrial Revolution occurred in
October 1966, when an old spoil heap slid down the side of a valley
in Wales, engulfing the village school of Aberfan and more than 100
of its children under 45 ft of slag and mud.

CANAL AGE *Pontcysyllte Aqueduct which carries canal boats over the River
Dee in Clwyd is one of the industrial achievements of the 19th century.*

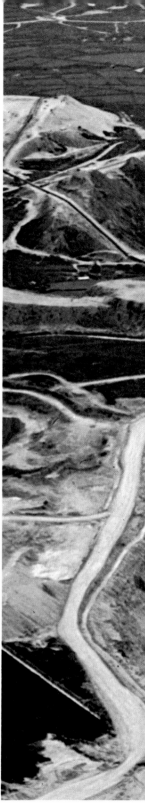

"CORNISH ALPS"
*For more than 200 years
Cornish miners have dug
china clay for the potteries of
Staffordshire. Eight tons of
soil must be excavated to
produce 1 ton of usable china
clay, and the gleaming white
waste has piled up into
mountainous cones around St
Austell and on Bodmin Moor.*

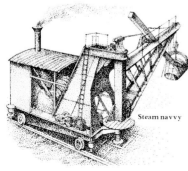

Steam navvy

STEAM AND MUSCLE *In the late 19th century, machines called steam navvies (left) shifted 3,000 tons of earth a day to excavate cuttings for new railway lines. But in the Cornish china-clay mines most of the work was still done with hand tools (right). Clay was dug with dubbers and broken up with biddicks; washed clay was moved with ladles and dried clay was scooped up with banjo shovels.*

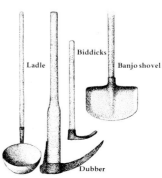

Ladle

Biddicks

Banjo shovel

Dubber

The landscape of the Transport Age

The two vital transport systems of the Industrial Revolution – the canals and the railways – created their own permanent marks on the British landscape.

In the second half of the 18th century a canal was built from Worsley to Manchester to carry coal to the growing city. The engineer responsible was James Brindley, a millwright, who went on to become one of the great figures of the Canal Age. Brindley's canals meandered leisurely through the countryside, following the contours of the land. This method was cheaper than building aqueducts over valleys and tunnels through hills, but a second generation of canal builders, including the engineer Thomas Telford, used new techniques. Their canals sliced across the landscape over soaring structures such as the Pontcysyllte Aqueduct in North Wales, and through vast tunnels, such as the 3 mile long Standedge Tunnel on the Huddersfield Canal.

The end of the canal boom was heralded in the 1820s by the clatter of the first passenger trains running on iron tracks in the north of England, at first between Stockton and Darlington, then from Liverpool to Manchester. In the 10 years between 1840 and 1850, 4,600 miles of railway lines were built across the nation, carried over viaducts and embankments, and through deep cuttings and long tunnels with magnificently designed entrances.

It was another century before the landscape was to feel such an impact from a transport boom. Then the Motorway Age arrived.

RAILWAY AGE *A disused viaduct, one of hundreds built in the railway era, stands deserted in the Galloway hills of southern Scotland.*

PART TWO

Discovering the Past

A SELECTION OF NEARLY 2,000 PLACES
WHICH EACH TELLS PART OF THE STORY OF OUR PAST—
FROM THE CAVES OF STONE AGE BRITONS TO THE FIRST
NUCLEAR POWER STATION

A

Abbeydale *S. Yorks.*   *Map: 393 Gf*
INDUSTRIAL HAMLET One of the country's best-preserved industrial monuments, where steel scythes and other cutting tools were made in the 18th and 19th centuries. The works closed down in 1933, but have now been restored and regular

demonstrations are given (see below).

Abbeydale was not without industrial strife. In 1842 the grinding shop was blown up because non-union labour was being employed. No casualties were recorded.

Location: 3½ miles SW of Sheffield on A621.

Scythe-making by water power

AT ABBEYDALE, MEN LABOURED IN THE HEAT OF THE FURNACE, THE NOISE OF THE
FORGE AND THE DUST OF THE GRINDSTONES TO SHAPE FARMERS' SCYTHES

Before the days of steam-engines, water was the chief source of industrial power. An 18 ft water-wheel drove Abbeydale's two huge tilt-hammers which shaped scythe blades from a sandwich of steel between two layers of iron.

The steel for the cutting edge was made in the crucible steel furnace. The raw material – iron and charcoal – was carefully weighed out and placed in special clay pots, then melted for three or four hours in intense heat.

The amounts of steel and iron for making the blades were crucial; the details were jealously guarded by the forgers as a form of job insurance.

The sandwich of iron and steel was heated in the forge hearth then drawn out under the steeling hammer which gave 126 blows a minute. Then the length of metal was cut into two with shears and each part re-heated and shaped into a blade under the plating hammer, working at about 66 blows a minute.

WHERE THEY WORKED

Raw materials for the steel were melted in pots in a furnace at a temperature of 1550°C. The cellar lad who controlled the draught also kept the furnace men supplied with cooling beer.

CRUCIBLE FURNACE *The men wore water-soaked leather sacking to protect them from the heat.*

GRINDING SHOP *Each grinder sat astride a wooden "horse" in front of a 6 ft revolving sandstone.*

TILT FORGE *Iron and steel were welded by the steeling hammer (right, foreground).*

Abbotsford *Borders*   *Map: 389 Fc*
The home of Sir Walter Scott, one of the most popular novelists of all time and originator of the historical novel. He built Abbotsford, his dream home, on land bought in 1811, completing the baronial mansion in 1824. Here he wrote prolifically, including the Waverley series of novels, and entertained with great hospitality, and also built up a large collection of books and historical relics.

After involvement in a financial crash in 1826,

Scott spent the last six years of his life endeavouring to pay off the debt, but his health failed and he died at Abbotsford in 1832.
Location: 3 miles W of Melrose off B6360.

Abercynon *Mid Glam.*   *Map: 393 Da*
PENYDARREN TRAMWAY The horse-wagon tramway – gauge 4 ft 2 in. – was the first track in Britain to carry a steam train. Richard Trevithick used it in 1804 to show that a steam locomotive could be used for haulage on a railed

---

Blades that had been roughly forged under the hammers were re-heated and tempered in small hand forges, then passed to the grinding shop for sharpening. Each grindstone revolved in a water trough to keep the blades cool.

In the boring shop the scythe blade was drilled with a hole to which a strengthening stay could be riveted when the handle was fitted. Handles and stays were not fitted at Abbeydale; completed blades were stored in the warehouse.

POT-MAKER *Pots in which the steel was smelted were made from a mixture of clays and coke dust. Only the pot-makers knew the proportions. They trod the clay for five to six hours in bare feet to remove air-pockets.*

GRINDER *Sharpening the scythe blades was dangerous work. The stones could split and fly from their mounts, and the dust caused lung damage – although wet-grinding helped to keep down dust at Abbeydale.*

HOMES FOR CRAFTSMEN

Abbeydale was a community of craftsmen. The workers lived next to the scythe works in terraced cottages that were of high standard for the times. The count house (office) and manager's house were close by.

MANAGER'S KITCHEN IN THE 1890s *Meat could be roasted in the oven of the Yorkshire range. Water was available from a pump beside the sink.*

MANAGER'S PARLOUR *Only the manager's house had a parlour as well as a living-room. It was rarely used – only on family occasions or to receive visitors.*

WORKER'S BEDROOM *The weary craftsman slept in a simple room with a brass bedstead and feather bed. The bare boards were softened by a bedside rug.*

WORKER'S KITCHEN IN THE 1830s *The coal stove had no oven, so meat was cooked on a spit. Water had to be fetched from the pump in the works' main yard.*

track. The tramway ran for $9\frac{1}{2}$ miles from Penydarren Ironworks to the canal (now filled in) at Abercynon. Parts of the stone sleepers are visible. The route can be followed from the Navigation Hotel on A4059 near the junction with A470.
Location: $3\frac{1}{2}$ miles N of Pontypridd on A470.

Aberdare *Mid Glam.*   *Map: 392 Db*
TRAMWAY BRIDGE The oldest surviving tramway bridge, dated 1811, crosses the Cynon river just north of Robertstown, Aberdare. In the 19th century, horse-wagon tramways were used extensively in this coal-mining area. They converged on the Aberdare Canal, a small part of which is now preserved at Canal Head, between Aberdare and Cwmbach.
Location: 10 miles NW of Pontypridd (A470, A4059).

Aberdeen *Grampian*   *Map: 387 Fb*
HARBOUR A fishing village from prehistoric times, Aberdeen developed as a port chiefly through its trade in fish and in granite from the nearby Grampian mountains.
    Its fine harbour on the River Dee was built about 1770–1810 by the engineers John Smeaton and Thomas Telford. Their task was made difficult by the shifting sandbanks of the estuary. The grand Customs House on Regent Quay was once an 18th-century private house.
Location: Off Market St.
PROVOST ROSS'S HOUSE Built in 1593, the house stands in Ship Row leading up from the harbour to Castlegate, the oldest part of the city. It was bought by John Ross of Arnage in 1702. He was provost (mayor) from 1710 to 1712.
PROVOST SKENE'S HOUSE The oldest surviving house in the city, with parts dating back to 1545. It was bought in 1669 by Sir George Skene of Rubislaw, provost from 1676 to 1685.
    A later occupant for a few weeks before the Battle of Culloden was the Duke of Cumberland, the English commander, whose officers made free with the goods of the owner, Alexander Banchory.
Location: Broad St, off Union St.

Aberdour Castle *Fife*   *Map: 389 Ee*
The L-shaped castle began as a 14th-century tower house built by Thomas, Earl of Moray, nephew of Robert Bruce. It once belonged to George, Earl of Morton, probably one of the murderers at Holyrood Palace in 1566 of David Rizzio, secretary and favourite of Mary, Queen of Scots.
Location: Overlooking Aberdour harbour.

Aberedw *Powys*   *Map: 393 Dc*
CHURCH OF ST CEWYDD The small 13th-century mountain church still has a fine 14th-century rood screen. A medieval pitch-pipe blown by the choirmaster to give his singers the correct pitch is on display. Until the 17th century, villagers used to gather round the ancient yew trees by the porch for the start of the annual sports gathering.
    It was here that Llewelyn the Last, native-born Prince of Wales, took his last Communion in December 1282, before he was killed in a skirmish with Edward I's soldiers. He is buried in Abbeycwmhir churchyard, 15 miles north.
Location: 3 miles SE of Builth Wells off B4567.

Aberfeldy *Tayside*   *Map: 388 Df*
GENERAL WADE'S ROAD BRIDGE Between 1726 and 1737, the English general George Wade undertook a major road-building programme as part of a plan to pacify the Highlands after the 1715 Jacobite uprising.
    The route from Crieff to Fort Augustus crossed the River Tay at Aberfeldy. Wade asked the architect William Adam to help him to design the five-arched bridge, completed in 1733.
Location: On B846 to Kinloch Rannoch.

Abergavenny *Gwent*   *Map: 393 Eb*
CASTLE Hamelin de Balun, one of William the Conqueror's barons, pressed the local people into building a motte-and-bailey castle about 1090. By about 1300 it had high walls and towers dominating the town. More than once attacked by the Welsh, the castle was held for a time by the Welsh prince Llywelyn the Great (died 1240).
Location: Castle St.
CHURCH OF ST MARY Once part of a Benedictine priory, the church has outstanding effigies. They include that of a mail-clad warrior, George de Cantilupe, who died at the age of 20 in 1273.
Location: Monk St.

Aberlemno *Tayside*   *Map: 389 Ff*
PICTISH STONES Skilled masons carved these sculptured stones in the 6th–8th centuries. One in the churchyard bears a richly decorated Christian cross and a graphic battle scene. Two other carved stones stand by the roadside.
Location: 5 miles NE of Forfar on B9134.

Aberystwyth *Dyfed*   *Map: 392 Cd*
CASTLE A huge concentric structure with two diamond-shaped rings of walls, the castle was built between 1277 and 1289 by Edward I after the first of two Welsh campaigns. Master James of St George, the king's chief military engineer, supervised the later stages of construction.
    Owain Glyndwr held the castle from 1404 to 1408 during his uprising against English rule, but it finally fell to the cannons of Prince Henry (later Henry V). In 1637 Charles I allowed a mint to be set up at the castle, using silver from local mines. The profits were sufficient to raise and equip a regiment of miners for him in the Civil War (1642–7).
    After surrendering to Cromwell's forces in 1646, the castle was blown up in 1649. Local builders used the remains to such an extent that in 1739 a fine of £5 was imposed for removing stone.
Location: Promontory on sea-front.
VALE OF RHEIDOL RAILWAY The narrow-gauge (1 ft $11\frac{1}{2}$ in.) railway is the last-remaining regular steam service run by British Rail.
    It was opened in 1902 as a freight line, but is now a tourist attraction, running $11\frac{3}{4}$ miles to the beauty spot of Devil's Bridge. The tiny locomotive burns half a ton of coal on the steep $4\frac{1}{2}$ mile ascent from Aberffrwyd.
Location: Terminus at Aberystwyth Station.

Ackling Dyke *Dorset*   *Map: 398 Ab*
This broad, straight embankment, 40 ft wide and 6 ft high in places, is one of the finest stretches of Roman road in Britain.
    From B3081, which crosses it, you can walk along the road for about 8 miles across downland

to the Iron Age hill-fort of Badbury Rings.
Location: 13 miles SW of Salisbury; turn left off
A354 along B3081 for ¼ mile.

Acle *Norfolk* *Map: 395 Ga*
STRACEY ARMS WINDPUMP A brick-built tower
pump of 1883, used to draw off surplus water
from flat marshland sunk below sea-level. A
turbine pump lifted water 7 ft to the River Bure.
Location: 2 miles E of Acle beside A47. Park next
to public house and walk along towpath.

Acorn Bank *Cumbria* *Map: 391 Ed*
WALLED GARDEN A traditional herbaceous
garden, kept as close as possible to its likely
appearance in the 1600s. It has a collection of
more than 150 herbs. The house is not open to the
public.
Location: 6 miles E of Penrith (A66, B6412).

Acton Burnell *Salop* *Map: 393 Ed*
CASTLE Acton Burnell was the seat of Robert
Burnell, descendant of a Shropshire landowner,
who was clerk to Prince Edward (later Edward I)
and rose to become Chancellor of England and
Bishop of Bath and Wells. Edward wanted to
make him Archbishop of Canterbury, but this
was vetoed by the Pope. Burnell's manor was
rebuilt and fortified in 1284.
Location: 8 miles SE of Shrewsbury off A458.

Acton Round Hall *Salop* *Map: 393 Ed*
A handsome, compact early-Georgian house of
1715, the Hall was built by Sir Edward Acton as a
dower house (endowed upon a widow or other
relative) to Aldenham Park.
Location: 6 miles W of Bridgnorth off A458.

Adlington Hall *Cheshire* *Map: 393 Ff*
Two oak trees supporting the east end of the
15th-century Great Hall are the remains of an
original Saxon hunting lodge. Between them is a
17th-century Bernard Smith organ played by
Handel, the composer, on visits to the Hall in
1741 and 1751.
Partly half-timbered and partly Georgian red
brick with a massive porch, the Hall has been the
home of the Legh family for over 650 years.
Location: 5 miles N of Macclesfield off A523.

A La Ronde *Devon* *Map: 397 Ec*
The Byzantine church of San Vitale, Ravenna,
inspired the design of this round house, built in
1798 by two cousins, Mary and Jane Parminter.
The rooms radiate from a 35 ft high octagonal
hall with a gallery above.
The gallery walls are covered with a mosaic of
shells worked by the two cousins. They also
worked the drawing-room frieze of feathers.
Location: 1 mile N of Exmouth in Summer
Lane, off A376 Exeter road.

Albury Park *Surrey* *Map: 398 Db*
The diarist John Evelyn, who also wrote *Sylva*
and *Pomona*–pioneering works in tree and fruit-
growing–laid out the terraced gardens with his
brother George for the Duke of Norfolk in
1655–8. The terraces are retained by walls for
fruit-growing, with shelter hedges of yew.
The original mansion was the retreat of Lord
Arundel (1585–1646), England's first great art
collector. It was re-fashioned in Tudor style by

A. W. Pugin in 1846. The estate, which was
originally known as Elderberry, was recorded in
the Domesday Book.
Location: 7 miles W of Dorking off A25.

Aldborough *N. Yorks.* *Map: 394 Be*
ROMAN TOWN From the 2nd century,
Aldborough was a small Roman town, the
administrative centre of the Celtic tribe of
Brigantes, who occupied much of northern
England.
A part of the south-west corner of the Roman
defences still remains, and two mosaic
pavements–one very well preserved–belonging
to a Roman town house can be seen in their
original position near the small site museum.
Location: 17 miles NE of York (A59, B6265).

Aldbourne *Wilts.* *Map: 398 Bc*
CHURCH OF ST MICHAEL The nave houses the
village's two 18th-century fire-engines–*Adam*,
manned by six to eight men, and *Eve*, a hand-
operated machine. They were retired in 1924.
Location: 9 miles SE of Swindon on A419.

Alderley Edge *Cheshire* *Map: 393 Ff*
ALDERLEY NETHER MILL The moat of Alderley Old

MYSTERIOUS SYMBOLS
*No one is certain of the meaning of the symbols on this
Pictish stone of the 7th or 8th century at Crosstown,
Aberlemno. Engraved in outline are a serpent, a
double-disc and Z, and a mirror and comb.*

Hall served as the mill-pond for this stone-built 15th-century grain mill, used until 1939.

The mill nestles into the dam wall, and the dam height allows the unusual arrangement of two stepped water-wheels, the water from the upper wheel driving the lower. Each wheel drove two pairs of millstones.
Location: 1½ miles S of Alderley Edge on A34.

Alexandra Palace *Greater London Map: 399 Dc*
The world's first public television broadcast was transmitted from BBC studios here on November 2, 1936. The radius of coverage was about 35 miles.

Built as an exhibition and concert hall, the Palace was intended as a north London equivalent of the Crystal Palace at Sydenham. It drew over 100,000 visitors after its opening in 1873, but only 16 days later it was destroyed by fire. It was rebuilt and reopened in 1875.
Location: Alexandra Park, Wood Green N22.

Alford Windmill *Lincs.* *Map: 395 Ec*
A five-sailed windmill with a 95 ft high six-storey tower built in 1813. There is a bakehouse attached, for the miller was also a baker, as was common in Lincolnshire.

Before 1796 millers could be paid with a proportion of the ground grist, but since then payment has, by law, to be made with money. In 1872 the grinding charges at Alford were 9d per measure for wheat and 4½d for barley.

A pair of very hard French stones was used to grind wheat into flour. Three other pairs ground cereals for livestock. The mill is still worked on open days in summer and can grind 4–5 tons of corn a day.
Location: At A1104/A1111 junction.

Alfriston *E. Sussex* *Map: 399 Ea*
DRUSILLAS ZOO PARK Longhorn cattle, now rare, were one of the commonest breeds in England until the mid-18th century. There are some at this zoo, which specialises in rare breeds, including cattle, sheep and pigs.

Sussex ox-wagons and harness, and other old farm equipment, are displayed in a rural museum.
Location: 3 miles W of Polegate on A27.
OLD CLERGY HOUSE A medieval priest's house built in the late 14th century, with a self-contained apartment for the housekeeper. The hall of the timber-framed house is open to the roof, and the timbers are blackened from the smoke of the central hearth.

In the priest's time, the rammed-chalk floor was spread with rushes and sweetening herbs.
Location: 4 miles NE of Seaford on B2108.

Allington Castle *Kent* *Map: 399 Ec*
Sir Thomas Wyatt, the poet who introduced the sonnet form into England, lived here in the 16th century. The moated castle by the Medway dates back to the 13th century.

Thomas Wyatt the younger was a leader of the unsuccessful Kent rebellion in 1554, aimed at preventing Queen Mary from marrying Philip of Spain. Rebels taken by the royal troops were imprisoned at the castle. Wyatt was executed.

The castle now belongs to the Carmelite Order and is run as a Christian centre.
Location: 2½ miles N of Maidstone off A20.

Alloway *Strathclyde* *Map: 388 Cc*
BURNS COTTAGE Robert Burns, Scotland's renowned poet, was born in 1759 in this "auld clay biggin" built by his father, a market-gardener. Here Burns lived until he was seven years old.

Alloway, with its old kirk and bridge over the Doon, was featured by Burns in his poem *Tam O'Shanter*. The Burns Museum is beside the cottage, the Burns Monument near the bridge.
Location: 2 miles S of Ayr on B7024.

Almondbury *W. Yorks.* *Map: 391 Fa*
WEAVERS' HAMLET On the edge of open moorland, the weavers' hamlet (all private houses) is a relic of the 18th-century cloth trade.

The clothier lived in the grand, stone-built merchant's house, from where he distributed wool to be spun and woven by the workers in their cottages across the lane. Looms were worked on the upper floors, which have many windows to let in plenty of light.
Location: 2 miles SE of Huddersfield centre off A629, at Lumb Lane, Almondbury.

Alnwick Castle *Northld.* *Map: 391 Ff*
Most formidable of the northern Border castles, Alnwick was originally built by the Normans. Many clashes between English and Scots took place near its walls. A cross marks the spot where Malcolm Canmore, King of Scotland, was killed in 1093, and a stone the place where King William the Lion was captured in 1174.

In 1309 Alnwick became the stronghold of the powerful Percy family, who in medieval times ruled the north-east like kings. Like many great lords of the time, the Percies moved from castle to castle as supplies for their retainers ran low. The *Northumberland Household Book* of about 1520 sets out the 5th earl's accounts and regulations. Instructions for wagon loading during moves reveal that the clergy and servants had to sleep two to a bed.
Location: N side of town, overlooking R. Aln.

Alperton *Greater London* *Map: 398 Dc*
AQUEDUCT Few motorists on London's busy North Circular Road (A406) realise they are passing under a canal ½ mile east of Hanger Lane junction.

The modern aqueduct carries the Paddington arm of the 19th-century Grand Junction Canal – now the Grand Union Canal – over the road.
Location: E along towpath from Water Rd.

Althorp House *Northants.* *Map: 398 Ce*
Charles I was playing bowls at Althorp on June 3, 1647, the day troops arrived to escort him to more secure imprisonment. He was on a visit from nearby Holdenby House, where he had been held in easy-going custody for four months.

The manor house of Althorp, which has a fine private art collection, has been the home of the Spencer family since 1508, when it was bought by John Spencer, a wealthy sheep farmer. In 1765 his descendant became the 1st Earl Spencer.

In the 1830s, Lord Althorp (later the 3rd earl) was Leader of the House of Commons. He was chiefly responsible for piloting through Parliament the 1832 Reform Bill and also in 1833 the first effective Factory Act, which limited the working hours of children.

ALNWICK'S ARMY

Many county regiments were raised in the 1790s, when invasion by Napoleon seemed imminent. In 1798 the 2nd Duke of Northumberland raised and equipped 1,500 men from his estates. They were known as the Percy Tenantry Volunteers; the cavalry were called Yeomanry.

DUKE'S SABRE *In 1807 the Percy Tenantry Volunteers presented a sabre (right) to their 22-year-old Lieutenant-Colonel, Hugh, Earl Percy – later the 3rd Duke of Northumberland.*

PERCY HOME-GUARD WEAPONS *The sabres and pistols (below) on display at Alnwick Castle once belonged to the Percy Tenantry Yeomanry, disbanded about 1820. The armour dates from the Civil War.*

PERCY TENANTRY UNIFORM *A portrait at Alnwick Castle shows Hugh Percy, aged about 14 years, in the uniform of the Percy Tenantry Yeomanry. In 1817 he became the 3rd Duke of Northumberland.*

Location: 5 miles NW of Northampton off A428.

Ambleside *Cumbria*   *Map: 391 Dc*
GALAVA A stone-built 2nd-century Roman fort on the slopes above Lake Windermere. Outlines of buildings and part of the defences can be identified with the help of a display board.
Location: At Borrans Field, signposted from Borrans Rd between A591 and A593.

Anderton *Cheshire*   *Map: 393 Ef*
BOAT LIFT The Trent and Mersey Canal is 50 ft above the River Weaver at Anderton. The two are joined by a boat lift completed in 1875. From the canal, boats reach the lift along a short aqueduct and float into one of two metal caissons

that each take two 70 ft narrow-boats.
    Originally the lift operated hydraulically, and one caisson went up to the canal as the other went down to the river. Electric power was installed in 1908, and each metal caisson now works independently.
Location: 1 mile NW of Northwich off A533.

Ann Hathaway's Cottage see Shottery

Anstey *Herts.*   *Map: 399 Ee*
CHURCH OF ST GEORGE Military-style graffiti on the chancel walls date back to the 13th century, and were probably drawn when the stones were part of the demolished castle. Carvings on the 13th-century misericords (tip-up seats) show men in the headgear fashionable at the time –

A "FIFIE" HERRING BOAT

This model of a "Fifie" 70 ft sailing boat of 1912 shows the straight bow and stern that distinguished the "Fifies"—seven or eight-man herring boats. A restored "Fifie", Reaper, is on show at Anstruther.

a hood with the point low down at the back.

The Norman font is carved with mermen, and part of the 15th-century lich-gate was bricked up and converted into the village lock-up in 1831. Location: 7½ miles SE of Royston (B1039, B1368 then minor roads).

Anstruther *Fife*   *Map: 389 Fe*
SCOTTISH FISHERIES MUSEUM In 1318 St Ayles Land, the site of the museum, belonged to the Abbey of Balmerino, which leased booths to local fishermen. The oldest part of the museum buildings is the 16th-century Abbot's Lodging.

The museum shows the history of Scotland's fishing industry from the early days of sail. Location: 10 miles S of St Andrews on A959.

Antonine Wall *Strathcl.-Central Map: 388 Dd*
Hadrian's Wall was not the only frontier line built by the Romans in Britain. In about 141, less than 20 years after that massive barrier had been built, the new emperor Antoninus Pius ordered a fresh advance and the building of a new wall roughly 100 miles further north.

The Antonine Wall ran for 37 miles from Bridgeness on the Firth of Forth to Old Kilpatrick on the River Clyde. Built of cut turves laid to a height of at least 9 ft, it was about 14 ft wide on its stone foundations and about 6 ft wide at the top, which was surmounted by a timber walk and breastwork about 5 ft high. On the north side was a formidable ditch.

On the south side of the wall there were about 19 forts, spaced at intervals of roughly 2 miles, with a communications road between them. A few small fortlets have also been found, and six platforms for signal beacons.

Skilled Roman legionaries built the wall, and distance slabs were set up to mark the stretches completed by different working parties. The 6,500 or so men who manned the wall were mostly from auxiliary cohorts—men from Spain, Germany and Gaul and archers from Syria gradually giving way to local recruits.

The Antonine Wall had a short life. There were two periods of occupation, the first lasting about 13 years until a serious uprising among British tribes to the south caused troops to be withdrawn. The wall was garrisoned again from 159 to 163, when it was finally abandoned.

Location: The best-preserved remains lie 4 miles west of Falkirk, and include the small fort known as Rough Castle. Turn off A803 on to B816 at Bonnybridge, and after crossing the canal take the lane on the left (signposted). Beyond the railway line the wall and ditch are clearly visible to the left. Just before the car park there is a beacon-stance about 18 ft square, and from the car park there are good views of the wall—here still about 5 ft high—and the huge ditch. Beyond the stream are the prominent earth ramparts that defended Rough Castle.

About 20 yds north of the ditch there are a number of small rectangular pits. These—described as *lilia* (lilies) by Roman writers—were traps filled with pointed stakes and covered with brushwood and leaves.

The most impressive stretch of ditch—which is about 40 ft wide and 15 ft deep—is at Watling Lodge. This also lies off B816, just off Lime Rd, Camelon, 1 mile west of Falkirk.

Antony House *Cornwall   Map: 396 Cb*
The finest Queen Anne House in Cornwall, Antony was built from 1711 to 1721 of silvery Pentewan stone for Sir William Carew.

The family is still at Antony, and has changed the house very little in 250 years. Small panelled rooms lead one into the other in the manner of the time, and much of the furniture is original. Location: 2 miles NW of Torpoint, N of A374.

Appleby-in-Westmorland *Cumbria   391 Ed*
APPLEBY CASTLE CONSERVATION CENTRE The 80 ft high Norman tower known as Caesar's Tower was probably built by Ranulf de Briquesart, called le Mesquin (the wretch)—a Norman who held the lordship of the north-west from about 1100.

Today the tower overlooks a Rare Breeds Survival Centre. The rare domestic species include Soay sheep (the oldest breed in Britain), four-horned Hebridean and Manx sheep, cattle, pigs, and Bagot goats, a Swiss breed brought back by Crusaders. (See p. 114.) Location: 13 miles SE of Penrith on A66.

Appuldurcombe House *IOW   Map: 398 Ba*
In the 1700s, Tudor and earlier architecture was considered uncivilised or "Gothic". So in 1710 Sir Robert Worsley replaced the beautifully situated Tudor mansion of his ancestors with the great Renaissance mansion partly remodelled in 1772. Now a ruin, the house was damaged by a German landmine in 1943. Location: ½ mile W of Wroxall off B3327.

Arbor Low *Derbys.   Map: 394 Ab*
The Beaker people, who reached Britain from the Continent about 2000 BC, probably built this stone circle on a remote hill-top. It is enclosed by a 250 ft diameter ditch and bank, with entrances at the north and south.

The site may have been used for religious rites. It is in the centre of an area thickly strewn with later Bronze Age burial mounds, which could well have been grouped there to share the prestige of the henge. Location: 9 miles SE of Buxton off A515.

Arbroath Abbey *Tayside   Map: 389 Ef*
Founded in 1178, the abbey was for 400 years one

ELIZABETHAN WOMEN'S AIDS TO BEAUTY

A jewelled toothpick of about 1600.

The lily and the rose – medieval emblems of romantic chivalry – represented the Elizabethan idea of a perfect complexion.

Influenced by the women of Renaissance Italy, the Elizabethans were the first to make great use of cosmetics in England, particularly in London and at court. They used mainly white powder, rouge and lip colouring.

The queen and her maids-of-honour – such as Mary Fitton, pictured below – would first cover their faces with white powder made from lead. Although this dried the skin, turned hair snow white and poisoned the system, it remained the chief cosmetic base for many years.

Cheeks were rouged with red ochre or a red dye made from cinnabar (mercuric sulphide) – also dangerous to the user. Lip colouring was made from a mixture of cochineal, egg white, milk of green figs, alum and gum arabic. This was mixed into a paste with powdered plaster of Paris or ground alabaster, rolled into a crayon, then dried in the sun to make a lip pencil.

To prevent make-up rubbing off, it was given a protective glaze of egg white. Out of doors, ladies wore a mask – held by a button between the teeth – to guard against sun-tan spoiling their milk-white complexions. Hands were kept lily-white by wearing gloves. A high, broad expanse of white forehead was considered most desirable, and eyebrows and low-growing hair were carefully plucked. Queen Elizabeth even painted artificial veins on her brow to give the impression of a pale, translucent skin. At night, ladies tied a cloth round the forehead to prevent the brow wrinkling.

Toothbrushes were unknown. Teeth, which were often bad, were cleaned with a toothpick or rubbed with a piece of mallow root or a piece of linen.

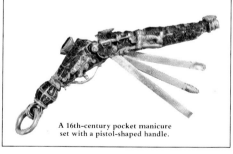

A 16th-century pocket manicure set with a pistol-shaped handle.

Newdigate Poetry Prize at Oxford University. Sir Roger spent over 50 years (1750–1805) converting the Hall into a castellated mansion in the Gothic Revival style.

The novelist George Eliot (Mary Ann Evans) was born on the Arbury estate in 1819.
Location: 3 miles SW of Nuneaton off B4102.

Ardoch Fort *Tayside*   Map: 388 De
One of the most spectacular of the Roman sites in Britain, the fort has a very well-preserved earth rampart and multiple ditches on its north and east sides. In the 2nd century it was an outpost of the Antonine Wall. (See p. 30.)
Location: To E of bridge over R. Knaik in Braco village, 12 miles N of Stirling on A822.

Arlington Court *Devon*   Map: 396 Dd
The neo-Grecian house in a thickly wooded estate dates from 1820. The estate was the home of one family from 1384 until 1949.

The last of the line, Miss Rosalie Chichester, made the park a nature reserve. The house contains her extensive collections, including sea shells, model ships and pewter.
Location: 7 miles NE of Barnstaple off A39.

DARK LADY?

Mary Fitton, who became a maid-of-honour to Elizabeth I in 1595 when 17 years old, is thought by some to be the fickle "dark lady" of Shakespeare's sonnets. But it is uncertain whether they ever met. The sister-in-law of Sir John Newdegate, her portrait hangs in the dining-room at Arbury Hall.

of the richest and most influential in Scotland. The Declaration of Arbroath of 1320 was a proclamation of national independence.

The abbey is now a ruin. A circular window in the surviving south transept used to be illuminated at night as a beacon for ships.
Location: At the top of High St, Arbroath.

Arbury Hall *Warks.*   Map: 398 Bf
John Newdegate acquired Arbury Hall, an Elizabethan mansion built on the site of an old Augustinian monastery, in 1586. Sir Roger Newdigate, his descendant, founded the

Arnol *Lewis, Western Isles*   *Map: 386 Bd*
The long, low blackhouse preserved in its original state (No. 42) is typical of a 19th-century crofter's house in Lewis and Harris.
Location: 14 miles N of Stornoway (A857, A858).

ARNOL BLACKHOUSE

Building materials were stone, driftwood and thatch. The peat fire was in the middle of the clay floor, smoke filtering out through the thatch. Pots and kettles were suspended above the fire on a chain from the roof. Byre and barn were part of the same building.

A LEWIS CROFTER'S YEAR

Highland crofts date from the 19th century when wool prices soared and the great landowners pushed the remaining small farmers off the fertile land to make way for *na caoraich mora* – the big sheep.

Large-scale sheep-farming had been spreading across the Highlands since 1745, for after the defeat of Prince Charles Edward Stuart, the lairds no longer needed fighting men on their lands. Sheep-farming was more profitable than leasing to tenant farmers.

Crofts were unfenced individual holdings on less-fertile land, where crofters could grow a few crops and graze their flocks on common pasture. To gain a livelihood – and cash for the rent – they also relied on seasonal work, mainly fishing and lowland harvesting.

Ploughing, peat-cutting, herding
April, when the ground became workable, was the time for ploughing. A light wooden plough worked with the foot – the *cas chrom* – could be used where no horse could go. In coastal districts, seaweed was spread in rows to rot down for the potato beds.

Peat-cutting for fuel followed in late April and early May. Each croft had cutting rights in the local peat deposits. Blocks were cut out with a special spade and dried in the sun and wind. Black, bottom peat was best, giving a bright, almost smokeless flame.

When the lambs were big enough in May, the sheep and cattle were moved from the townships to graze on outlying land, then from there to the shielings, or summer grazing, in the hills. In the shielings they were herded by the women and children, who lived in small tent-like huts of stone and turf, with heather beds. Here the women made cheese and a little butter, and the girls learned to use a hand-worked spindle to spin wool yarn. Weaving was done mostly in winter, chiefly for home and family use.

Some of the men and women left for the herring fishing from Stornoway in May and June, and from Wick in July. The men worked on the boats and the women in the gutting and packing stations.

Sowing, sheep-shearing, harvesting
While the animals were in the hills, the bere (a form of barley) and oats were sown. Fields were manured with the winter's dung from the byre, a gable-end of the blackhouse often being broken open to remove it.

The potatoes were planted in seaweed-manured beds, and the sooty thatch laid on as a top-dressing. The roof was re-thatched with straw from last year's crop.

Sheep were sheared in June and July. About July also, the beef cattle, then in prime condition, were brought down from the shielings for market. The rest of the flocks were brought back in August, when the women and children, and also the herring fishers, returned for the harvest. At the end of October, some might go off again for the east coast fishing.

From mid-November onwards, the surplus sheep were slaughtered – some for fresh meat, the rest being salted down. Barrels of salted herring were also got in for the long Highland winter.

Using a foot-plough   Cutting the peat   Milking at a shieling

Spinning and carding wool yarn   Sowing the bere   Off to the herring fishing

Arreton Manor *Isle of Wight*   *Map: 398 Ba*
Mellow stone walls, panelled rooms and polished
wood floors make this the perfect English manor
house. The manor dates back to the 9th century
and once belonged to Alfred the Great. The
present E-shaped house was built 1595–1612.
Location: 3 miles SE of Newport off A3056.

Arundel Castle *W. Sussex*   *Map: 398 Da*
Built in a commanding position overlooking the
Arun valley, the castle was part of the south-coast
defences in Norman times.
   Henry II built the stone shell keep on the
original motte in the 12th century. Little of the
early structure now remains. The castle was
pounded by Cromwell's cannons in 1643–4, and
was rebuilt in the 18th and 19th centuries.
   The 1st Earl of Arundel, Richard Fitzalan,
died in 1302. In 1580 the title passed by marriage
to the Howard family, dukes of Norfolk.
Location: Entrance in Mill Rd, Arundel.

Ashbourne *Derbys.*   *Map: 394 Ab*
CHURCH OF ST OSWALD Among the many family
monuments in the medieval church is the marble
effigy of a sleeping child, Penelope Boothby,
who died in 1791 when six years old.
   It was carved by Thomas Banks, and the
naturalistic style was condemned by Sir Joshua
Reynolds. The figure was exhibited in 1793 and
is said to have moved Queen Charlotte to tears.
Location: Mayfield Rd (A52 to Stoke-on-
Trent).

Ashby de la Zouch *Leics.*   *Map: 394 Ba*
CASTLE A manor house in Norman times, Ashby
gained the suffix de la Zouch from the
descendants of a Breton nobleman, Alan la
Zouch, who became the owner in 1160. In 1464
Edward IV gave the manor to his Lord
Chamberlain, Lord Hastings, who fortified it.
   A 14th–15th century development in castle
building was a great tower that could give the
lord and his family comfort and privacy in the
upper storeys–and security from their own
mercenary troops if necessary. The ruined
Hastings Tower is a good example of a 15th-
century great tower. A private well ensured that
the lord's water supply could not be poisoned.
Location: Entrance off South St.
CHURCH OF ST HELEN Monuments in the 15th-
century church include a rare wooden effigy of
1623. It is of a Mrs Margery Wright, dressed in a
steeple hat and ruff. The inscription states that she
gave "£43 to provide Gowns for ever to certain
aged and poor people".
Location: Off South St.

STOCKS *Up to 1837,
anyone who fell
asleep or misbehaved
in St Helen's Church
might have to spend
the rest of the service
in the finger stocks.*

Ashdown House *Oxon.*   *Map: 398 Bc*
In a high and lonely spot on Lambourn Downs,
the tall white house was built by the wealthy Earl
of Craven not long after 1660. The earl was
devoted to Elizabeth of Bohemia, the sister of
Charles I, and spent many years in her service.

Elizabeth was known as the Winter Queen,
she and her husband, the Elector Palatine, having
reigned in Bohemia for one year (1619–20)
before being ousted by the Habsburgs. Lord
Craven helped Elizabeth when she needed
money, and it is possible that he built Ashdown
as a refuge for her from plague-ridden London.
But she died of the plague in 1662, and never saw
the house.
Location: 3½ miles NW of Lambourn on B4000.

Ashley House *Devon*   *Map: 396 Dc*
COUNTRYSIDE COLLECTION All the rare breeds of
sheep can be seen on this working farm. There is
also a large collection of old farm and farmhouse
equipment and rural craft tools, including 12
different types of horse plough.
Location: 21 miles NW of Exeter (A377 then
B3220 – turn off at Berner's Cross 1 mile N of
Winkleigh).

Ashton *Devon*   *Map: 397 Dc*
CHURCH OF ST JOHN THE BAPTIST A characteristic
example of 15th-century Perpendicular architecture, the church has some splendid figure paintings on the north parclose screen and aisle screen.
Location: 9 miles N of Newton Abbot off
B3193.

Ashwell *Herts.*   *Map: 399 De*
CHURCH OF ST MARY Fascinating medieval graffiti
have been scratched on the walls and pillars of the
large 14th-century church.
   One Latin inscription makes a chilling
reference to the Black Death: "1350 Pitiable,
fierce, violent, the dregs of a people survive to
witness. . . ." Another, perhaps the scrawling of a
mason, states: "The quoins (corner stones) are
not jointed aright–I spit at them." A third is a
detailed sketch of Old St Paul's Cathedral. The
church has the tallest tower in the county – 176 ft.
Location: 6 miles E of Royston off A505.

Asthall *Oxon.*   *Map: 398 Bd*
COTSWOLD FOLK AND AGRICULTURAL MUSEUM A
horse-drawn float for taking bulls to market is
among the old farm equipment on display. A
saddler's shop, shepherd's hut and farm kitchen
have been reconstructed, and there are documents relating to the founding of the Union of
Agricultural Workers in the Cotswolds in the
1870s.
Location: 3 miles E of Burford off A40.

Astley Hall *Lancs.*   *Map: 391 Ea*
The shovel-board table in the Long Gallery at
Astley is 23½ ft long with 20 legs, and probably
dates from 1666. Shovel-board, or shove-groat,
was a popular game similar to shove-ha'penny.
   The earliest part of Astley Hall was built in
1600. Oliver Cromwell is said to have slept at the
house in 1648, in the fine, carved Elizabethan
four-poster. The house was on his route on the
stormy night of August 18 after he defeated the
Duke of Hamilton's force at Preston.
Location: 1 mile NW of Chorley off A6.

Aston Hall *W. Midlands*   *Map: 393 Fd*
The imposing Jacobean manor house was built
by Sir Thomas Holte early in the 17th century.
Sir Thomas was an ardent Royalist, and the
finely carved great staircase still bears the scars of

33

cannon shot from a three-day siege by Parliament troops in 1643 during the Civil War.

In the kitchen, the open fire has an 18th-century smoke jack to turn the roasting spit. It was operated by a fan that turned in the hot-air current rising in the chimney.
Location: 2 miles N of Birmingham off A34.

Athelhampton *Dorset*   *Map: 397 Gc*
A battlemented medieval manor house surrounded by walls and courts. In the gardens there are fishponds, fountains, a dovecot, clipped yews and pleached (interlaced) limes.

The 15th-century Great Hall is one of the finest still in existence, with its timber roof, brass chandelier, linenfold wall panelling, minstrels' gallery and heraldic window glass.

Sir William Martyn, a Lord Mayor of London, built the house about 1485. His crest, a chained ape holding a mirror, is on some windows.
Location: 5 miles NE of Dorchester on A35.

Atherington *Devon*   *Map: 396 Dd*
CHURCH OF ST MARY Devon churches are noted for their screens, and St Mary's still has its beautifully carved 16th-century rood screen. Above it is the only original rood loft left in Devon.

Outside, beneath the lich-gate, is a stone coffin table where the parish coffin, hired out for funerals, rested while the shrouded corpse was removed for burial. Only the wealthy could afford to be buried in a coffin.
Location: 7 miles S of Barnstaple (A377, B3217).

Attleborough *Norfolk*   *Map: 399 Ff*
CHURCH OF ST MARY The finest rood loft and screen in England, one of the few that survived the Reformation intact, spans the nave and aisles. The church dates mainly from the 15th century.

On the wall behind and above the loft there are fragments of a medieval wall-painting depicting, among other subjects, Moses and David.
Location: 14 miles SW of Norwich on A11.

Auchindrain *Strathclyde*   *Map: 388 Be*
MUSEUM OF COUNTRY LIFE Joint-tenancy farms were once common in Scotland. Most were swept away during the clearances of the 18th and 19th centuries, but such a holding continued at Auchindrain into the early 20th century.

About a dozen families worked the ground as a group, paying a common rent to the landlord (in this case the Duke of Argyll). They shared the arable ground by lot and held the grazing ground in common.

The original dwellings are now being restored and furnished to show what life was like in this part of the Highlands from 1790 to 1914. The houses include the one-roomed Puir House, given rent free to an elderly widow. She visited each house in turn for a midday meal, and acted as a midwife, baby-sitter and general help.

The ground is being cultivated in the traditional manner, and there are demonstrations and displays showing the traditional way of life.
Location: 5½ miles SW of Inveraray on A83.

Auchinleck *Strathclyde*   *Map: 388 Cc*
BOSWELL MUSEUM Auchinleck was the family name of the Boswells, whose most famous member was James Boswell (1740–95), the biographer of Dr Johnson. The old parish church where the family worshipped is now a Boswell Museum, containing books, manuscripts and portraits.
Location: Church Hill off A76.

Auchtermuchty *Fife*   *Map: 389 Ee*
WEAVERS' COTTAGES Linen cloth was woven on hand looms in the tiny thatched cottages in Cupar Road, built in the late 18th century. The large windows allowed plenty of light to fall on the loom. The cottages are now private houses.

Audley End *Essex*   *Map: 399 Ee*
Audley End took 13 years to build, and once rivalled Hampton Court Palace in size and splendour. It was begun early in the 17th century by Thomas Howard, 1st Earl of Suffolk, who inherited the estate on the site of Walden Abbey from his father-in-law, Sir Thomas Audley.

The earl was Lord Chamberlain at the time of the Gunpowder Plot to blow up Parliament in 1605, and it was largely due to his alertness that the plot was uncovered. He was made Lord High Treasurer of England in 1614, but his extravagances led to his downfall. In 1618 he was committed to the Tower of London on charges of embezzlement, and fined £30,000.

When James I first saw Audley End, he is said to have commented: "Too large for a king, but might do well for a Lord Treasurer." The house surrounded two courtyards and had a grand gatehouse with four towers.

But Audley End was destined to become a royal palace, for Charles II took a fancy to it and bought it in 1669 for £50,000. Known as the New Palace, it became the occasional residence of Charles II, James II and William and Mary. Their ciphers on the heads of rainwater pipes are relics of royal occupation. Early in 1701 Audley End was returned to the 5th Earl of Suffolk in lieu of the balance of purchase money still owing.

The upkeep of such a large residence was beyond the resources of succeeding earls, and parts were demolished during the 18th century, leaving only the Great Hall and two wings. The present building is largely the work of Sir John Griffin Griffin, later Earl of Braybrooke, who inherited it in 1762 and had it extensively repaired and redecorated.

The Jacobean stable block survives, and now houses an exhibition of farm implements and techniques, and a carriage collection.
Location: 1 mile W of Saffron Walden off A11.

Avebury *Wilts.*   *Map: 398 Ac*
AVEBURY STONE CIRCLE High Street, Avebury, runs through the centre of one of the largest prehistoric stone circles in Europe, about four-fifths of a mile in circumference. It is much larger than Stonehenge, although the stones are smaller and are natural, unhewn blocks.

Between 3000 and 1500 BC, this prehistoric temple was perhaps the ceremonial centre for 5,000–10,000 people, who gathered maybe once or twice a year to join in religious rites or to pledge loyalty to their chieftain.

Pagan rites seem to have been practised at the circle as late as the 14th century, for at this time local Christians considered it their duty to fell and bury many of the stones.

One of the Christians was crushed to death by a stone as it fell. His skeleton was found in the 1930s, pinned against the side of a burial hole. The contents of the purse he was wearing, still intact (see below), showed him to be a barber-surgeon. The stone, in the south-west of the circle, has now been raised and is known as the Barber's Stone.

In the 17th and 18th centuries, the circle was further destroyed by local builders looking for stone and by farmers wanting to clear the land. Stones were felled into pits filled with straw, which was set alight. When the stones were well heated, cold water was poured over them. They cracked and were then easy to break up.

Avebury stone circle is surrounded by a bank and ditch with a diameter of about 500 yds, enclosing about 28 acres. Its prehistoric builders must have had a social organisation comparable to that of the Middle Ages, or even surpassing it, for 1½ million man-hours would have been needed to build the great monument.

The huge bank of earth, still 20 ft high in places, was made of material dug out from the ditch on its inside, and four causewayed entrances were left at north, south, east and west. The ditch, up to 30 ft deep, was dug from the chalk with picks made from antlers and shovels made from ox shoulder-blades. Discarded tools have been recovered from the ditch bottom.

CENTRE OF PAGAN RITUAL

Between about 3000 and 1500 BC, Avebury stone circle was a ritual centre for one of the most densely populated areas of Britain. Within a 3 mile radius are several other outstanding prehistoric monuments (right). The 1½ mile stone-lined avenue leading to The Sanctuary may have been used for processions. The two stones known as the Cove (above) form the centre of the northern inner circle. A third stone, the third side of a square, fell in 1713.

THE BARBER'S TOOLS *In medieval times, barbers also acted as dentists and surgeons. The scissors and probe shown above belonged to the barber-surgeon crushed to death by a stone at Avebury in the 14th century.*

THE BARBER'S MONEY *Two coins (right) found in the barber's purse were pennies of the time of Edward I, issued at Canterbury between 1300 and 1307. They are now displayed at the Alexander Keiller Museum at Avebury.*

About 100 stones formed the circle, which is situated about 20 ft from the inner lip of the ditch. About 25 stones are now standing. They are of sandstone, but have long been known as sarsen stones, sarsen being derived from the word "saracen", which after the Crusades was used to mean foreign or heathen.

The great stones, some weighing up to 60 tons, had to be manhandled from the nearby Marlborough Downs. They were probably rolled on tree trunks, then set upright in the chosen positions with levers, ropes and the careful use of packing stones.

Inside the great stone circle there were two smaller stone circles, of which only a few traces remain. Originally each of them had about 30 stones and was about 330 ft in diameter. These two inner circles were probably the work of the Beaker people, about 2000 BC. The massive earthworks and outer stone circle may well have been laid out some centuries earlier.
Location: 10 miles south of Swindon on A361.
AVEBURY MANOR The gabled, stone-built manor house of 1557 was probably built for Sir William Sharington, who financed it from profits made while in charge of Bristol mint. It has fine panelling, ceilings and antique furniture.
Location: Off Avebury High St, near church.

Aveline's Hole *Avon* *Map: 397 Fd*
A shallow but steeply sloping cave used as a home and burial place by Stone Age men about 10,000 BC. Near by is the rock cleft where in 1775 the Rev. Augustus Toplady sheltered during a storm. It inspired him to write the hymn *Rock of Ages*.

Location: 11 miles E of Weston-super-Mare (A371, A368 and B3134 in Burrington Combe).

Avoncroft Museum of Buildings see Bromsgrove

Aylesford *Kent* *Map: 399 Ec*
THE FRIARS One of the earliest Carmelite priories in Europe, founded in 1242 and dissolved in 1538. It was re-occupied by Carmelite friars in 1949.
Location: 3 miles NW of Maidstone off A20.

Aylestone *Leics.* *Map: 398 Bf*
PACK-HORSE BRIDGE Nearly 50 yds long but only 4 ft wide, this medieval bridge over the River Soar was built for the use of pack-horse trains, for centuries the chief transport for merchandise.
Location: 2⅓ miles S of Leicester. Turn right off A426 to B5418.

Ayot St Lawrence *Herts.* *Map: 398 Dd*
SHAW'S CORNER The playwright George Bernard Shaw lived here from 1906 until 1950. The house remains much as it was in Shaw's lifetime.
Location: 4½ miles NE of Harpenden off A6129.

Aysgarth *N. Yorks.* *Map: 391 Fc*
YORE MILL Red cloth for the shirts worn by Garibaldi, the Italian nationalist leader, and his men, was woven here in the 19th century. When the cloth trade declined the mill became a corn mill, and was grinding until 1968. It now houses a carriage museum.
Location: 1 mile E of Aysgarth on A684, by the stone bridge close to Aysgarth Falls.

B

Baconsthorpe Castle *Norfolk* *Map: 395 Fb*
In England, during the Middle Ages, a licence was needed to build a large manor house. John Haydon, a tough and wealthy lawyer, ignored the law and built Baconsthorpe Castle in the mid-15th century, complete with gatehouse.
Location: 5 miles S of Sheringham (A1082, A148 then minor roads).

Badbury Rings *Dorset* *Map: 397 Gc*
An Iron Age hill-fort enclosing 18 acres of land within three concentric rings of banks and ditches. The outer ring may have been added shortly before the Roman invasion of AD 43.
Location: 3 miles NW of Wimborne off B3082.

Badminton House *Avon* *Map: 397 Ge*
A Palladian mansion that gave its name to a game. Guests on a wet afternoon in the 1860s found in the nursery battledores and shuttlecocks – crude rackets and corks with feathers in them, used by children. A string was stretched across the hall as a net, for a game of indoor tennis, and badminton was born.

The house was built for the 1st Duke of Beaufort between 1665 and 1700. In about 1740 the house and park were remodelled by William Kent and little has changed since. Horse trials are now held annually in the park.
Location: At Great Badminton, 6 miles E of Chipping Sodbury (A432, B4040).

THE BIRTH OF BADMINTON

The rudimentary game of badminton was started during the 1860s by weekend guests at Badminton Hall. One of the guests took the game to India where, in Karachi in 1877, the first set of formal rules was drawn up.
In the early years, the long-handled rackets were used with shuttlecocks for indoor games, but with small rubber balls for games outside.
The Badminton Association was formed in 1899 and only indoor games with the regulation shuttlecock – or bird – are now recognised. It is a game for two or four players.

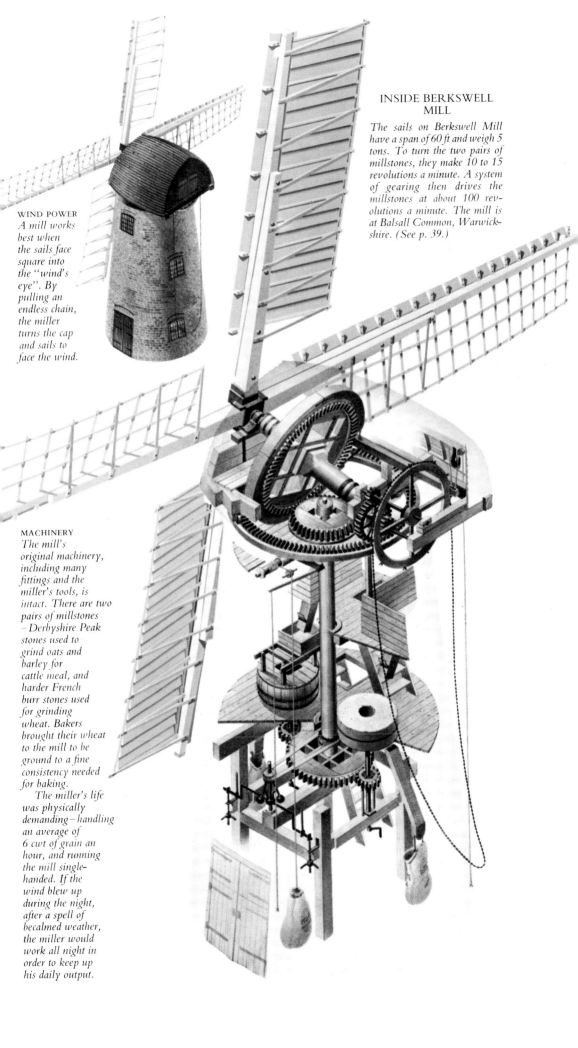

INSIDE BERKSWELL MILL

The sails on Berkswell Mill have a span of 60 ft and weigh 5 tons. To turn the two pairs of millstones, they make 10 to 15 revolutions a minute. A system of gearing then drives the millstones at about 100 revolutions a minute. The mill is at Balsall Common, Warwickshire. (See p. 39.)

WIND POWER
A mill works best when the sails face square into the "wind's eye". By pulling an endless chain, the miller turns the cap and sails to face the wind.

MACHINERY
The mill's original machinery, including many fittings and the miller's tools, is intact. There are two pairs of millstones – Derbyshire Peak stones used to grind oats and barley for cattle meal, and harder French burr stones used for grinding wheat. Bakers brought their wheat to the mill to be ground to a fine consistency needed for baking.

The miller's life was physically demanding – handling an average of 6 cwt of grain an hour, and running the mill single-handed. If the wind blew up during the night, after a spell of becalmed weather, the miller would work all night in order to keep up his daily output.

FRESH MEAT ALL WINTER LONG

Erddig – Clwyd

Dovecots – doocots in Scotland – were popular in crop-growing areas in the late 15th century, as a means of providing fresh meat during the winter months. The only other meat available at this time would have been beef – slaughtered and salted during the autumn.

East Linton – Lothian

Basing House – Hants

Direlton – Lothian

Lady Kitty's Doocot – Lothian

Penmon – Anglesey, Gwynedd

Legal obligations
During the 16th century, in Scotland, Acts of Parliament were passed, first making it obligatory for a laird or landowner to build a doocot, and then, later, to have a licence to do so. In England a lord of the manor could build a dovecot without a licence; but he was the only one so privileged. The birds were rock doves or pigeons, which normally mate for life, so a dovecot with 900 nest boxes could house 1,800 adult birds when full. The adults were expected to forage on their owner's land but often strayed and damaged neighbour's crops. The meat supply came from squabs (pessers, in Scotland) – the young unfledged birds. Reared on pigeons' milk – partly digested food regurgitated by the parents – they reached a considerable size before being able to fly. Squabs were collected from the nests by means of a ladder revolving around a central pole. Surplus eggs were eaten as a great delicacy.

Dovecot design
The shape of dovecots varied greatly, depending upon the whim of the landowner or the masons who built them. Some dovecots were cylindrical and turreted; some with a horseshoe-shaped or conical roof.
The introduction of turnips, during the 18th century, made the winter-feeding of livestock practicable, and with developments in cold-storage techniques, the need for pigeon meat vanished.

Baginton Roman Fort *Warks.*   *Map: 398 Bf*
"The Lunt" is a fascinating reconstruction of a turf-and-timber Roman fort, built after the Boudicca uprising in AD 60. The reconstructed portions include a granary, a portion of the eastern defences and the east gate.
   The unique stockade is thought to have been a training ground for military horses.
Location: 2 miles S of Coventry off minor road to airport.

Bakewell *Derbys.*   *Map: 394 Bb*
OLD HOUSE MUSEUM This house, built in 1534 and with later additions, now contains collections of costumes, toys and craftsmen's tools, relating to the history of the Peak District.
Location: Off Church Lane.

Bala *Gwynedd*   *Map: 392 De*
BALA LAKE RAILWAY A narrow-gauge railway, running from Llanuwchllyn Station to within half a mile of Bala town centre, on the trackbed of the old Great Western Railway. Both steam and diesel locomotives are in use, as well as rolling stock from various slate quarries.
Location: 5 miles SW of Bala off A494.

Balcombe Viaduct *W. Sussex*   *Map: 399 Db*
A brick-and-stone viaduct, 96 ft high, strides across the Ouse Valley on 37 slender arches, carrying the London-to-Brighton railway. Built in 1839 by John Rastrick, it proved the resourceful engineer, John Rennie, to be right. He had surveyed the line and favoured this direct route through the Downs, which his colleague, Robert Stephenson, considered impossible.
Location: S of Balcombe on B2036 to Cuckfield.

Balerno *Lothian*   *Map: 389 Ed*
MALLENY DOOCOT AND GARDEN The doocot (or dovecot) in the grounds of the 16th–17th-century house has 915 nest-boxes, which once provided accommodation for 1,830 birds.
   The gardens are known for their shrub roses, and until 1961 there were 12 large yew trees, said to have been planted in 1603 to represent the Twelve Apostles. To admit light to the house

BALERNO DOOCOT
This handsome doocot at Malleny, with a saddleback – or pitched – roof, and stepped gables at each end, has entrance holes in the northern rather than the more normal southern side of the roof. This may have been due to the limitation of the site.

they were reduced to the Four Evangelists.
Location: 7 miles SW of Edinburgh off A70.

Ballaugh *Isle of Man*   *Map: 390 Bc*
CHURCH OF ST MARY There are two churches of
this name in Ballaugh. The Old Church, near the
shore, has a 10th-century cross. An inscription
reveals that it was erected by Olaf Ljotulfsson, a
Viking prince or lord, in memory of his son, Ulf.
Ljotulfsson is connected, linguistically, with the
name Corlett–a family that still lives and
worships in the parish.
Location: 7 miles W of Ramsey on A3.

Ballindalloch *Grampian*   *Map: 387 Ec*
GLENFARCLAS DISTILLERY Malt whiskies made in
the Highland regions of the River Spey are
world-renowned for their quality and distinctive
taste. This is partly due to the peat streams
flowing from the Grampian Hills, and the use of
peat fires for drying barley–the smoke adds extra
flavour.
    Glenfarclas is typical of many distilleries in the
region producing malt whisky, and caters for
visitors with exhibits and guided tours.
Location: On A95, 20 miles S of Elgin.

Balsall Common *Warks.*   *Map: 398 Bf*
BERKSWELL MILL A four-storey brick tower mill
was built in 1826 and stands on a mound where
there was once a 16th-century post mill. The mill
sails–one pair has common sails and one pair
shuttered sails–drove two pairs of millstones. A
diesel engine was used after 1933 when a gale
destroyed the mill's sails.
    The windmill–last used for grinding corn in
1948–has recently been restored. (See p. 37.)
Location: Windmill Lane, off A452 end of
Balsall Common.

Balvenie Castle *Grampian*   *Map: 387 Ec*
A late-13th-century quadrangular enclosure of
high stone walls. It had two corner towers and
was encircled by a wide ditch lined with stone.
Location: 1 mile N of Dufton off A941.

Bamburgh *Northld.*   *Map: 389 Gc*
CASTLE When William II came to
Northumberland in 1095, an Anglo-Saxon fortress occupied Bamburgh Rock. He built a
wooden fortress outside its walls from which to
mount an assault, but found it a formidable castle
to conquer.
    During the 14th century, the Norman castle
fell into the hands of the Percies–a powerful
family of Northumberland earls–and was a
constant menace to the medieval kings.
Location: 15 miles N of Alnwick (A1, B1341).
CHURCH OF ST AIDAN The church is mainly 13th
century with a superb chancel and vaulted crypt.
The breastplate, helm and gauntlets of Fernando
Forster MP hang in the chancel. He was an
unpopular man, killed in a local brawl in 1701.
    Grace Darling's grave is in the churchyard.
GRACE DARLING MUSEUM In 1838, during a storm,
the SS *Forfarshire* was wrecked on rocks near the
Longstone Lighthouse. The 22-year-old Grace
Darling, with her father the lighthouse keeper,
rowed five people to safety and became a national
heroine.
    She died of tuberculosis only four years later.
The boat, renamed *Grace Darling*, is in the
museum, with some of her clothes and personal
effects.
Location: Next to Bamburgh church.

Banavie *Highland*   *Map: 386 Cb*
NEPTUNE'S STAIRCASE This spectacular group of
locks on the Caledonian Canal was built to help
save ships the long passage round the north coast
of Scotland. Begun in 1803 under Thomas
Telford, it was completed in 1822.
    Eight locks form a staircase, with boats passing
directly from one lock into the next, rising 64 ft
in a distance of 1 mile.
Location: 3 miles N of Fort William (A82 then
A830).

Banff *Grampian*   *Map: 387 Fc*
DUFF HOUSE The Georgian mansion was designed
by Robert Adam's father, William, for the 1st
Earl of Fife in 1735. During the Second World
War it was used to house German prisoners.
Location: ½ mile S of Banff off A98.

Bannockburn *Central*   *Map: 388 De*
The Battle of Bannockburn on June 23 and 24,
1314, was decisive in British history, restoring
Scotland's independence and finally establishing
Robert Bruce as king.

THE BANNOCKBURN BATTLE

*A 15th-century illustration of the Battle of Bannock-
burn where, in 1314, Robert Bruce crushed the
English, won Scotland her independence, and established himself as king.*

Robert Bruce routed Edward II's army of 20,000 soldiers, with a hastily assembled force of 5,500 of whom 2,000 were "small folk" – artisans, shopkeepers and crofters who had volunteered to strike a blow for Scotland.

Edward I had virtually overrun Scotland during his reign, but Robert Bruce won most of it back. The last major stronghold of the English was Stirling Castle, held under siege by his brother, Sir Edward Bruce, and occupied by its English governor, Sir Phillip Mowbray. If the castle was not relieved by Midsummer's Day, June 24, Mowbray agreed to surrender it.

Edward II assembled a force at Berwick to relieve Stirling and crush Scotland for ever. Robert Bruce, meanwhile, chose his ground brilliantly, making full use of the tidal Bannock Burn to the east, and woods and moorland to the west.

The first day's fighting was inconclusive. But Bruce raised Scottish morale when, unarmoured, and mounted on a pony, he slew an English cavalry leader, Sir Henry de Bohun. When reproached for the risk he had taken, Bruce commented: "Alas, I have broken my good battleaxe."

Next day, the English cavalry were confused by the Scot's use of the "hedgehog" – a formation with spears thrust out in all directions. More Scots joined, until the English disintegrated. Edward, realising the day was lost, made his escape. The rout was completed with hundreds of English perishing in the Bannock Burn and the River Forth.

An equestrian statue of Robert Bruce overlooks the area where the conflict took place.
Location: 1 mile SE of Stirling off A905.

Barclodiad-y-Gawres *Gwynedd* Map: 392 Bf
A small passage grave that stands on a headland above a sheltered beach on the west coast of Anglesey. A stone-lined passage leads to burial chambers in which cremated human remains were found – including those of two young men – during excavations in 1953. They are probably of people who crossed the Irish Sea before 2000 BC.
Location: 2 miles NW of Aberffraw off A4080.

Barfreston *Kent* Map: 399 Gc
CHURCH OF ST NICHOLAS An outstanding example of Norman architecture, celebrated for its wealth of decorative stone carvings. Much of the carving – influenced by French craftsmen who crossed the Channel – is symbolic.

The masons drew inspiration from a variety of sources, including the Bible, *The Lives of the Saints*, and the *Bestiary* – morality tales related to real and mythical animals.

The south doorway is a brilliant display of the stone-carver's art. There are also seven "scratch" or "Mass" dials on it. These are thought to have been a form of sundial, with a hole in the centre in which a stick was placed to cast a shadow on the rim, indicating the time of Mass.
Location: 8 miles NE of Dover off A256.

Barmouth Viaduct *Gwynedd* Map: 392 Cd
One of the few wooden railway viaducts to have survived in Britain, Barmouth Viaduct is also used as a footbridge.

Built in 1867 for Cambrian Railways, it is half a mile long with an iron swingbridge at one end.
Location: Across the Mawddach Estuary.

Barnard Castle *Durham* Map: 391 Fd
CASTLE The 11th or 12th-century castle is on a 100 ft high precipice over the River Tees. The castle is now in ruins. It originally belonged to the Baliol family – one of whose members became King John Baliol of Scotland in 1292 – and passed to the Beauchamp family the following century.

An 11-day siege was resisted during the Rising of the North in 1569, by Sir George Bowes. The castle held firm but ultimately fell due to treachery of the townsfolk from within.

Barton-upon-Humber *Humber.* Map: 394 Dd
There are two fine churches: the older – St Peter's – has a Saxon tower, 70 ft high, dating from before 1000. St Mary's was a "chapel of ease" – a subordinate church, built in Norman times for the convenience of parishioners who lived too far from the main church.
Location: S bank of R. Humber, 14 miles NE of Scunthorpe.

Barton-upon-Irwell *G. Manchester* Map: 391 Ea
BARTON SWING AQUEDUCT A revolutionary piece of machinery that carries the Bridgewater Canal over the Manchester Ship Canal. Built in 1894 by Edward Leader Williams, it is centred on an island in the Ship Canal and pivots to allow ships to pass. Gates at each end close to form a steel tank, 7 ft deep, 18 ft wide and 235 ft long.
Location: 5 miles W of Manchester, near B5211 across the Manchester Ship Canal.

Bateman's *E. Sussex* Map: 399 Eb
This stone-built ironmaster's house was built in 1634, and bought by Rudyard Kipling in 1902. The study – with his desk and writing materials – remains as he left it at his death in 1936.
Location: 1 mile S of Burwash off A265.

Bath *Avon* Map: 397 Ge
ABBEY CHURCH OF ST PETER AND ST PAUL England's last great abbey church, the Benedictine "Lantern of the West", was founded in 1499 by Bishop King, Henry VII's chief secretary. The abbey's completion was interrupted by the Dissolution of the Monasteries in 1536–40; in the next 40 years the stained-glass windows and lead were plundered, and the abbey left to decay.

Restoration work started in the 16th century, following a public subscription ordered by Elizabeth I, and the abbey – largely Perpendicular in style – was finished by the 17th century.

In addition to a great many monuments, the abbey has a rare wooden and portable font, four 17th-century alms boxes and, in the Library, a book reprinted by Caxton's successor, Wynkyn de Worde, in 1493.

Richard "Beau" Nash – the 18th-century "King" of Bath – is buried in the nave.
Location: Near Pulteney Bridge, between the Roman Baths and the Guildhall.
ASSEMBLY ROOMS Built between 1769 and 1771 by John Wood the Younger for £14,000, the Assembly Rooms are housed in two large and elegant blocks that contain a magnificent collection of rooms.

Here, fashionable society mingled with men and women of letters and music; gossiped over

RELICS FROM AN AGE OF ELEGANCE

Exhibits in the town's museums help to create a vivid impression of life in Bath, when the town was the glittering centre of fashion and elegance.

TOMPION'S CLOCK *The equation clock and sundial were presented to Bath by Thomas Tompion, the celebrated clockmaker, in 1709. Both are in the Pump Room. Sundials were used to check clocks.*

EMBROIDERED DOUBLET *A lady's doublet, about 1610–20, from the Museum of Costume in the Assembly Rooms. It was similar to a waistcoat.*

CHARABANC *Built about 1840 by John Marson of Birmingham, the charabanc could carry 20 passengers, in addition to the driver. It was drawn by a pair or a team of four horses, and was in regular use until ten years ago. Charabancs were intended for holiday excursions, such as day trips to the coast. The charabanc is in the Carriage Museum.*

HEARSE *This splendid vehicle has been used for funerals of many of the city's dignitaries—and is still in occasional use. It was built in 1860 by C. Porter and Sons of Liverpool, and is drawn by a pair or a team of four horses. The coffin is held in place by silver metalwork, and the ceiling above it is elaborately painted. The hearse is in the Carriage Museum.*

breakfast in the Tea Room; danced in the 100 ft long Ballroom; or played a rubber of bridge, whist or backgammon in the adjoining Card Room.

Location: Bennet St and Alfred St.

BRIDGES Pulteney Bridge across the River Avon was designed in 1771 by Robert Adam, and is the only example of his work in Bath. Inspired by the Ponte Vecchio in Venice, Adam lined it with shops.

A walk down Great Pulteney Street to Sydney Gardens leads to the Kennet and Avon Canal with its elegant 19th-century bridges designed by the engineer John Rennie.

Follow the towpath past the locks and the old pumping-engine house at Widcombe locks, to the junction with the Avon. The Victoria Suspension Bridge spanning the river was built in 1836. The suspension rods incline towards the piers—an unusual method of construction patented by the designer J. Dredge.

CARRIAGE MUSEUM Tucked away in a mews is one of the most comprehensive and fascinating carriage museums in the country.

The museum is in the coach houses and stables built by John Wood the Younger in 1759 for the use of residents living in the Circus. There are more than 30 vehicles displayed, including the Duke of Somerset's State Coach, used at several coronations. There are also many prints and documents relating to coaching.

Location: Circus Mews.

PRIOR PARK A Palladian villa built in 1735–48 by John Wood the Elder for Ralph Allen, who wished to proclaim in the grand manner the merits of stone used from his quarry at Combe Down. Allen had amassed a fortune in promoting an efficient postal system and, with "Beau" Nash and John Wood, was responsible for transforming Bath from a health resort to a centre of fashion. Prior Park helped to promote the beauties of Bath stone and its use throughout the city.

Occupied as a school since 1830, the house can be visited during holidays. A chapel in the house and the park, with its celebrated Palladian Bridge, are open at all times.

Location: 1 mile SE of Bath between A367 and A36.

PUMP ROOM Society people coming to 18th-century Bath visited this elegant building as part of their daily routine. To a background of music and gossip, they drank three glasses of the warm medicinal spring water before lunch, and three more after it. One frequent visitor was Queen Charlotte, George III's neglected wife, who lived near by in Sydney Place.

The Pump Room, built between 1789 and 1799 by Thomas Baldwin, has two original sedan chairs.

Location: Entrance in Abbey Churchyard.

ROMAN BATHS The principal bathing station of Roman Britain was in use for more than 300 years. The buildings include a museum with finds from the site. (See opposite.)

Location: Entrance in Abbey Churchyard.

ROYAL CRESCENT A great half-circle of terraced houses, begun in 1767 by John Wood the Younger—the first of its kind to be built in the world. Number One has been restored and refurnished.

Location: W of The Circus.

Where Romans relaxed

THE HEALING SPRINGS OF BATH, AND ITS GRANDIOSE BUILDINGS, ATTRACTED THE RICH AND ELEGANT ROMANS IN ENGLAND AS WELL AS VISITORS FROM EUROPE

When the Romans discovered warm therapeutic springs at Bath, they established one of the most celebrated bathing stations in the country—designed on an elegant and ambitious scale. By the end of the 1st century the baths had acquired an international reputation. Visitors from all over the Roman world included a sculptor from Chartres in northern France, a lady from Metz and a man from Trier in Germany.

The most impressive feature is the Great Bath—a swimming pool still fed with hot springs and with its Roman lead lining intact. The Bath was originally roofed—first with timber, then with a concrete semicircular vault.

A swimming pool was not an essential in a Roman bathing system, but an optional extra—the only other municipal one known in this country is at Wroxeter.

Roman bathing was similar to a modern Turkish bath, with the bather normally proceeding from the changing room into a cold room, then into a warm room and finally a hot room. Here he would sweat profusely, scrape off the sweat and dirt with a strigil (see opposite) and then take a hot dip (the springs at Bath gush out at 120°F). The procedure was then reversed, ending with a cold-water plunge to seal the pores of the skin.

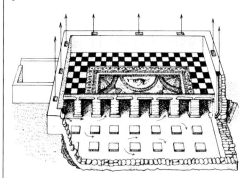

HYPOCAUST HEATING *The hypocaust was an ingenious method of heating rooms, with the floors raised on a number of short pillars, and the walls built with hollow tiles in them to act as flues. Hot air from an underground furnace—burning brushwood and charcoal—circulated through the hollow floor space and rose through flues to the outside air, heating both floor and walls simultaneously.*

SACRED CURSE *A sheet of lead in the Roman Museum has a curse scratched on it. "May he who carried off Vilbia from me become as liquid as water."*

A curse was a popular way of expressing a grievance.

A PLACE FOR GOSSIP

Solinus, a Roman writer, described Bath as the most excellent town in Roman Britain "furnished luxuriously for human use". But the baths were the main attraction – a place in which to cleanse the body and spirit, relax and gossip.

HOW THE ROMANS WASHED

There was no soap in Roman Britain – dirt and moisture were scraped from the skin, and after further baths the body was massaged with perfumed oils.

TOILET EQUIPMENT *The strigil (left) was used to scrape the body clean; the glass flask (below) contained perfumed oil. These may have been carried on a ring with tweezers, ear-scoops and nail cleaners.*

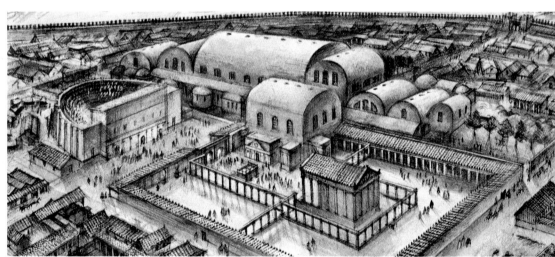

WHEN ROMAN BATH FLOURISHED *A reconstruction of Aquae Sulis, as Roman Bath was then known, during the 2nd century AD. The massive semicircular roofs cover the bathing areas – the largest spanning the Great Bath or swimming pool. The Temple of Sulis Minerva in the foreground was dedicated to the guardian goddess of the springs. Opposite it is a theatre, and between them – outside the entrance to the baths – an altar where sacrifices were offered.*

THE HEAD OF MEDUSA *One of the sculptured blocks that came from an elegant temple in the bath complex. The temple has since gone. The local sculptor has portrayed Medusa – one of the female Gorgons who had snakes for hair – as a craggy-faced Celtic male.*

Life when coal was king

The North of England Open Air Museum at Beamish in Durham illustrates the industries that helped to shape the life of the north-east – such as farming, coal mining, railway and heavy engineering.

A Victorian colliery has been built, dominated by a winding engine in its tall engine-house. A replica of George Stephenson's *Locomotion*, which ran on the Stockton and Darlington Railway in 1825, runs to the pit-head.

A station from Rowley in Durham has been furnished as it was in 1910. An electric tramway connects the station with the main transport collection, which includes a locomotive built by George Stephenson in 1822. There is also a massive steam shovel.

EARLY RAILWAYS *A replica of Stephenson's 1825 Locomotion (above). The booking office (right) is from Rowley Station, built in 1867. In 1914 it was snowbound with a trainload of passengers, and thereafter was known as Cold Rowley.*

FIGHTING FIRE WITH FIRE *Horse-drawn fire-engines with pumps driven by steam were developed in the 1860s. The engines brought a romantic appeal to fire-fighting. As they raced through the streets they often belched sparks and flame from the boilers, and onlookers cheered them on their way. The engine at the Beamish museum could pump 350 gallons of water a minute. Steam could be raised from cold water to the working pressure in less than ten minutes while the engine was on its way to the fire. The captain rode on the raised seat with the driver, and the nine-man crew sat back-to-back on the open body. Bells attached to the horses' harness sounded a warning.*

Bathampton *Avon*　　　　*Map: 397 Ge*
TOLL BRIDGE This bridge, built in 1863 across the River Avon, was a vital link in the old turnpike road system – special tolls were collected to recoup the cost of construction. The toll house is still standing and tolls are still payable.
Location: 2 miles NE of Bath on minor road linking A36 with A4.

Battle *E. Sussex*　　　　*Map: 399 Eb*
BATTLE ABBEY The Benedictine abbey was built on the ridge of Senlac Hill where William the Conqueror defeated the English in 1066. According to tradition, William vowed that if he were victorious in battle he would found an abbey as an expression of his thanks to God. The High Altar was placed over the spot where Harold was fatally wounded.

The abbey was largely pulled down after the Dissolution of the Monasteries (1536–40) but impressive ruins have survived.
Location: 6 miles NW of Hastings on A2100. The abbey is off A2100 S of town centre.
CHURCH OF ST MARY After the Battle of Hastings, a small community settled, using the abbey for worship. Since this infringed the rules of the Benedictine Order, St Mary's was built to the north of the abbey, in 1115, for parish use.
Location: The church is in the town centre.
STATION Built by William Trees in 1852 for the

A HARDWARE SHOP AND A CHEMIST'S *A Victorian hardware shop (above) has cane carpet-beaters hanging from the ceiling, and a knife polisher in front of the counter—everyday objects that have since become collectors' items. The chemist's shop (right) came from Finkle Street, Stockton on Tees, and belonged to William Hardcastle. Many of his gilt-labelled bottles have their original contents. The shop also has some contents from the shop of John Walker—a well-known Stockton chemist who invented the friction match in 1826.*

COTTAGES OF A MINER AND FARM-WORKER *Some of the cottages that were built for workers on the Beamish estate have been refurnished with their mid-19th-century fittings. The miner's cottage (left) has the traditional tin bath, used in front of the fire during winter months. Life in the farm-worker's cottage revolved about the central fireplace, where food was cooked and washing dried.*

South Eastern Railway, the station is a fine example of the romantic Gothic style applied to Victorian railway architecture.
Location: SE of the town centre.
SENLAC HILL On the ridge of Senlac Hill, on October 14, 1066, King Harold of England and his troops faced the advancing Normans, led by William, Duke of Normandy.

The combined armies amounted to 16,800 men, fairly evenly divided between them. Less than one-third of Harold's men were well equipped—the remainder wielding an assortment of weapons that included clubs and stones. They were also battle-weary, having fought off Norwegian invaders at Stamford Bridge in north Yorkshire and marched 250 miles to the south.

William's army included 3,000 cavalrymen, and men armed with chain-mail, swords and bows and arrows.

At first the Saxons held their ground in hand-to-hand combat. But a rumour that William had been killed gave them false hopes. In a wave of wild enthusiasm they swept down the hillside towards the enemy cavalry. The Normans maintained their discipline, broke through the disorganised Saxons and cut them to pieces from the rear. Four knights cornered Harold and butchered him.

William the Conqueror's reign had begun.
Location: SW of town centre off A2100.

Bayham Abbey *E. Sussex*   *Map: 399 Eb*
Bayham Abbey was suppressed in 1525 by Cardinal Wolsey, to help him finance Christchurch College, Oxford. Towards the end of the 18th century the ruin was "tailored" to suit the romantic mood of the time by the fashionable landscape gardener Humphry Repton.
Location: 5 miles E of Royal Tunbridge Wells, off B2169.

Beacon Hill *Hants.*   *Map: 398 Bc*
This prominent Iron Age hill-fort, 800 ft above sea-level, has traces of more than a dozen circular huts and many storage pits within a single line of defences. The fort includes the tomb of Lord Carnarvon (he and Howard Carter uncovered Tutankhamun's tomb in 1922), who wished to be buried at the top of the hill overlooking Highclere, the place where he was born.
Location: 7 miles S of Newbury off A34.

CONCENTRIC CASTLE

Beaumaris is the best-preserved concentric castle to have survived. It was started in 1295 but was never completed. No shot was ever fired in its defence. The moat is fed by the sea and originally encircled the castle, making it a formidable stronghold. The acme of military architecture in mediéval Britain, Beaumaris used a design that had long been basic in the Byzantine Empire.

GARDEROBE *The outlet from one of four groups of garderobes or latrines in Beaumaris Castle. Each group was accessible from the wall-walks at parapet level, and discharged into the moat.*

Beaminster *Dorset*   *Map: 397 Fc*
PARNHAM HOUSE A Tudor house rebuilt in 1585 by its owner, Sir Robert Strode. His widow, Lady Anne, was murdered in the Great Hall by Cromwell's men for supporting the Royalists' cause during the Civil War.
Part of the house is now used as the John Makepeace Furniture Workshops – open to the public.
Location: 5 miles N of Bridport on A3066.

Beamish *Durham*   *Map: 391 Fe*
NORTH OF ENGLAND OPEN AIR MUSEUM A museum showing principal features of the economic and social life of the region. (See pp. 44–45.)
Location: 2 miles E of Stanley on A693.

Bearley Aqueduct *Warks.*   *Map: 393 Gc*
The Bearley, or Edstone, Aqueduct is 475 ft long – the longest iron aqueduct in England. It was built in 1813, to carry the Stratford-upon-Avon Canal across the valley of a tributary of the River Alne. The aqueduct also crosses a minor road and a railway line.
Location: 4 miles N of Stratford-upon-Avon, on minor road to W of A34.

Beaulieu *Hants.*   *Map: 398 Ba*
ABBEY AND PALACE HOUSE A Cistercian monastery founded by King John in 1204, and now largely in ruins. The well-preserved refectory, however, is still used as the parish church.
The two-storeyed 14th-century gatehouse was converted into a private house in 1538. In the upper rooms there are two piscinas – niches for washing sacred vessels – indicating where there were once two chapels, side by side. One chapel was for outside worshippers, the other for dependants of the abbey.
Location: 6 miles NE of Lymington off B3054.
NATIONAL MOTOR MUSEUM In 1952 the museum started with a modest collection of veteran cars displayed in the entrance hall of Palace House, Beaulieu Abbey. The separate museum in the grounds now has more than 200 vehicles, illustrating the story of motoring from the pioneer days of the late 19th century to cars of the 1970s.
There are racing cars, family cars, commercial vehicles and motor cycles. There are also world-record breakers, including the 350 hp Sunbeam, in which Sir Malcolm Campbell broke the land-speed record in 1925 – the first car to travel at over 150 mph, and the 1,000 hp Sunbeam of 1927 – the first car to travel at more than 200 mph.
Many vehicles are regularly on view at such events as the London to Brighton run and the Vintage and Veteran Racing Car meet.

Beaumaris *Anglesey, Gwynedd*   *Map: 392 Cj*
CASTLE Beaumaris was the last of the ten new castles built by Edward I during and after his conquest of Wales. It guards the Menai Strait – once easy to cross at low tide.
Designed in 1295 by Master James of St George, Edward I's principal military engineer, the castle is almost perfectly concentric. Two rings of walls and flanking towers are surrounded by a moat fed from the sea.
Location: 4 miles NE of Menai Bridge on A545.
GAOL In 1823 the Gaol Act was passed, stipulating new standards to be observed in prison design,

A model Victorian prison

BEAUMARIS GAOL WAS A HUMANE PRISON, WITH SEXES SEGREGATED AND PLENTY OF LIGHT AND AIR. BUT THE TREADMILL AND SCAFFOLD WERE STILL USED

The gaol was built in 1829 by the architect Joseph Hansom, inventor of the Hansom Cab.

Despite the gaol's forbidding appearance, it was a well-built modern prison, an example of how a prison of the day was planned. In 1867 a model wing was added incorporating great improvements. Larger cells – 10 ft by 6 ft – were equipped with bed board and straw or hammock, an enamel wash bowl, running water and a flush lavatory. There was gas lighting and a crude form of warm-air heating.

Visitors see the gaol as it was when it closed in 1878, and the prisoners were transferred to Caernarfon.

WEIGHING-IN *Prisoners were weighed on entering and exchanged their clothes for prison wear. Convicted prisoners wore different colours to those awaiting trial.*

CELLS AND THE SCAFFOLD

Prisoners rose at 6 a.m. in the summer and 8 a.m. in the winter and worked ten hours a day, returning to their cells at 8 p.m. for the rest of the night. Inmates were divided into groups, and did jobs varying from breaking stones and picking oakum, to shoe-making, mat-making and spinning and weaving cloth for shirts. The goods were sold and the money used to help run the prison.

The condemned cell was linked to the scaffold on an outside wall by a corridor. Executions were witnessed by the public – the last, in 1862, was of a man who attempted to murder his wife.

TYPICAL CELL *Each prisoner spent 10–12 hours a day in his cell.*

SANITATION *Each cell had a lavatory, flushed by water from the basin.*

ALARM SYSTEM *A warder could be called by a bell-pull in each cell.*

SIGNATURES *Prisoners' initials carved on the male-workroom floor.*

THE LAST WALK *The route from the condemned cell to the gallows.*

THE GALLOWS' DOOR *A scaffold stood outside the door under the gallows.*

SOLITARY CONFINEMENT AND HARD LABOUR

For such offences as swearing, insolence or refusing to work, a prisoner would spend a day or more in the sound-proofed punishment cell in total darkness.

Those prisoners serving a sentence of "hard labour of the first class" spent six to eight hours a day on the treadmill. Periods of 15 minutes on the wheel alternated with 15 minutes' rest.

In some prisons the power produced was used to grind grain or – as at Beaumaris – pump water to a distribution tank. When water overflowed it was fed back to the well to make the work a never-ending task. Six prisoners could be on the wheel at a time.

The treadmill is the only one still in place.

THE TREADMILL *Where prisoners did hard labour.*

PUNISHMENT CELL *Only bread and water were provided in here.*

LEG IRONS *These were rarely used – generally to restrain the violent.*

NURSERY *Mothers working below pulled a rope to rock the cradle.*

TREADMILL *A prisoner gripped the handle and "walked" up the stairs.*

such as segregating sexes and building brighter and lighter cells. Beaumaris Gaol was built in 1829 and a wing was added in 1867, incorporating these improvements.

The gaol closed in 1878 and has been preserved as a museum of 19th-century prison life. There is also an exhibition of documents describing crime and punishment in Gwynedd.
Location: The gaol is in centre of town.

Bedale Hall *N. Yorks.*   *Map: 391 Fc*
A Georgian house overlooking the countryside at the front and a busy market place at the back–adjoining other houses of the same period.

There is a museum of domestic arts and crafts.
Location: 7½ miles SW of Northallerton on A684.

Beddington *Greater London*   *Map: 399 Dc*
CHURCH OF ST MARY A large Early English and Perpendicular church that once served a small village but is now set in parkland.

The interior was lavishly decorated during the late 19th century. The organ gallery has painted panels of flowers and figures by William Morris.
Location: Church Rd, Wallington, 2 miles W of Croydon off A232.

Bedford *Beds.*   *Map: 398 De*
CASTLE A 15 ft high mound, 160 ft in diameter, is all that survives of a motte-and-bailey castle enlarged by Hugh de Beauchamp in the 12th century.

In 1224 the new owner of the castle, Falkes de Breaute, seized and imprisoned a judge who had come to hear a case against him. Henry III, outraged by de Breaute's action, raised a siege, and took command in person.

After ten weeks of day-and-night bombardment with heavy stones, the garrison surrendered. The judge was freed and the rebels hanged.
Location: E of town centre by Castle Close Gardens.
BUNYAN MEETING HOUSE MUSEUM John Bunyan, son of a tinker, was born at Elstow, 1½ miles south of Bedford. After service in the Parliamentary Army, he became a vigorous Puritan teacher, and at the Restoration in 1660 was imprisoned as a religious dissenter and "common upholder of several unlawful meetings". An inscription at the corner of Silver Street marks the site of the gaol, in which he wrote the first part of *Pilgrim's Progress* in 1678.
Location: The museum is in Mill St.

Beeston Castle *Cheshire*   *Map: 393 Ee*
The castle, built in 1220 by Ranulf, Earl of Chester, and perched on a 500 ft high rock of red sandstone, is now largely in ruins. It had an inner and outer enclosure, with gatehouse, drawbridge and cylindrical towers.
Location: 10 miles NW of Nantwich (A534, A49 and minor road).

Beetham *Cumbria*   *Map: 391 Ec*
HERON CORN MILL This site was chosen for a watermill because of a natural stone dam in the River Bela. Four pairs of millstones stand on a timber table in the middle of the entrance floor. Grain was stored in sacks on the top floor and fed to hoppers above the millstones.

There is also a kiln, the floor of which is made of perforated tiles supported over a low smokeless fire. Oats were dried out on this, before being crushed.
Location: 6 miles N of Carnforth on A6.

Belas Knap *Glos.*   *Map: 393 Fb*
This neolithic barrow, or burial chamber, nearly 1,000 ft long, encloses four small chambers. They may have been separate tombs in a small cemetery dating back to beyond 3000 BC.

The chambers–built of dry-stone walling–contain the remains of between 30 and 40 men, women and children. But a man and five children were buried–possibly sacrificially–behind an impressive false entrance at the broad end of the mound; this may have been to mislead tomb-robbers or evil spirits.

The mound covering the site may have been built about 2000 BC.
Location: 7 miles NE of Cheltenham (A46, then minor road to Charlton Abbots).

Belle Isle Lodge *Cumbria*   *Map: 391 Dc*
An 18th-century house on a 38 acre island–also named Belle Isle, the largest island in Lake Windermere. Based on the Villa Vicenza in Rome, the house has a circular plan, with a domed roof and an elegant columned portico.
Location: 1½ miles S of Windermere on A5074.

Belper *Derbys.*   *Map: 394 Bb*
The town where Richard Arkwright's partner, Jebediah Strutt, established his cotton works in the late 18th century. Strutt built the town up around his mills, with dignified houses for his workers–notably the terraces of Long Row –and the cottage hospital near the road bridge. The bridge had gun embrasures cut in it– reminders of a time when the owners could expect rioting to occur among the unemployed –so that it could be used as a point of defence.
Location: 8 miles N of Derby on A6.

Belton House *Lincs.*   *Map: 394 Cb*
This 17th-century house–built by an unknown architect in the style of Christopher Wren–is regarded as "the finest surviving example of its class". It has been the ancestral home of the Brownlow family for 300 years.

The house and its contents reflect the life of a nobleman's family through the centuries. There are rose gardens, a deer park and an orangery.
Location: 2 miles NE of Grantham on A607 Lincoln road.

Belvoir Castle *Leics.*   *Map: 394 Cb*
A late-Norman castle that was held by the Lancastrians during the Wars of the Roses and successfully besieged in 1464 by Lord Hastings, the Yorkist commander.

The present castle, owned by the Rutland family since Henry VIII's reign, was reconstructed during the 19th century. It has many exhibits of historical interest, including a bugle sounded at the Charge of the Light Brigade in 1854.

On most Sundays there are regular displays, which include a medieval jousting tournament, a mock battle–complete with cannons and small arms; and falconry.
Location: 6 miles SW of Grantham off A607.

Bembridge Windmill *IOW*   *Map : 398 Ca*
The four-storeyed stone tower mill was built in 1746. The sails are turned into the wind by means of a chain and wheel at the rear of the cap on top of the tower.

The mill has two pairs of millstones, and was in use until the harvest of 1913. The method of altering the space between the millstones–a critical factor determining the quality of the milled product–is unique at this mill.

Models and drawings of mills are displayed.
Location : 4 miles SE of Ryde on B3330.

Beningbrough Hall *N. Yorks.*   *Map : 394 Be*
A large red-brick house, thought to have been built in 1716 by William Thornton, a joiner-architect. This may account for the house having the finest wood carving in the north of England–on the staircase and in several of the rooms.
Location : 8 miles NW of York off A19.

Benthall Hall *Salop*   *Map : 393 Ed*
During Elizabeth I's reign the Benthall family were Roman Catholics–a dangerous faith to hold at the time. Since plots to replace the queen with a Catholic monarch were rife, Catholics used signs known only to sympathisers.

On the south wall of the entrance porch there are four stone discs–a fifth is missing–symbolising the stigmata or the wounds inflicted on the body of Christ at the Crucifixion, a sign to a Catholic that he would find safety at the Hall.

Built about 1583, the house was occupied and damaged by Parliamentarians in the Civil War.
Location : 4 miles NE of Much Wenlock (B4376, B4375).

Bere Regis *Dorset*   *Map : 397 Gc*
CHURCH OF ST JOHN THE BAPTIST A 12th-century church with a carved and gilded timber roof.

A pair of 17th-century fire hooks are in the porch. In case of fire in the village they could be used to pull burning thatch from a roof.
Location : 12 miles W of Poole on A35.

Berkeley Castle *Berks.*   *Map : 397 Fe*
It was in Berkeley Castle that Edward II was murdered in 1327, allegedly "with a hoote brooche put thro the secret place posteriale"–a gruesome end for the homosexual monarch. The king, turned off his throne by his wife and her lover–and confined for months at Berkeley–paid a terrible price for his ineffective rule and his injudicious choice of friends.
Location : 16 miles SW of Gloucester off A38.

Berkhamsted Castle *Herts.*   *Map : 398 Cd*
One of the earliest motte-and-bailey castles in England, built soon after 1066 by William the Conqueror's half-brother, Robert of Mortaine.

A stone shell keep was built on the motte during the 12th century by Thomas Becket, who was later to become Archbishop of Canterbury.

The buildings have now vanished but the motte and bailey are much as they were in Robert's day.
Location : 4 miles NW of Hemel Hempstead off A41.

Berkswell *W. Midlands*   *Map : 398 Bf*
CHURCH OF ST JOHN THE BAPTIST The best Norman church in the county. The upper floor of the Tudor porch is the vestry. In it there is a 17th-century communion table ; a three-volume set of Foxe's *Book of Martyrs*; and a "hobby horse" stool, used by a 19th-century rector. He claimed he could preach best when astride it in the pulpit.

The village green has stocks with five holes–the purpose of the fifth hole is conjectural. Some say it was for a regular 18th-century offender–a one-legged soldier.
Location : 6 miles W of Coventry off A4023.

Berrington Hall *Heref. & Worcs.*   *Map : 393 Ec*
Thomas Harley, a banker and government contractor, bought the estate with "Capability" Brown's advice, in 1775. Brown redesigned the 450 acre parkland, and his son-in-law, Henry Holland, built the mansion between 1778 and 1781.
Location : 4 miles N of Leominster off A49.

Berry Pomeroy Castle *Devon*   *Map : 397 Db*
A quadrangular building, with an unusual gatehouse of twin towers, built in the late 12th century. The powerful Edward Seymour, Duke of Somerset and Lord Protector, obtained the castle in 1548. His descendants built an Elizabethan mansion in the quadrangle, out of character with the castle. Both are in ruins.
Location : 2 miles NE of Totnes off A385.

Berwick-upon-Tweed *Northld.* *Map : 389 Gd*
BERWICK CASTLE AND TOWN FORTIFICATIONS When Edward I and John Baliol, King of Scotland, went to war in 1296, Edward captured and fortified Berwick with a stout wall and towers, and improved the castle's defences. Modifications were made later, and Elizabeth I reorganised the defences completely.

The result of Elizabeth's plan is the present system of ditch and bastions, and connecting ramparts which are of earth faced with masonry. The ramparts are among the best artillery defences of the 16th century.
Location : Castle ruins are near station.
BRIDGES Two of the three bridges crossing the Tweed are of historical interest : the Old Bridge and the Royal Border Railway Bridge.

The Old Bridge was built between 1610 and 1634, has 15 arches, is 45 ft high and 1,164 ft long.

The Royal Border Railway Bridge was built by Robert Stephenson and opened by Queen Victoria in 1849. It rises to a height of 126 ft.

Bestwood Colliery *Notts.*   *Map : 394 Bb*
An unusual winding engine, used to move men and material up and down the shaft, still stands at the colliery. Instead of the conventional beam engine, which has the piston rod attached to one end of the beam and the crank to the other, this engine dispensed with the beam altogether. The cable drum is placed immediately above the cylinder of the steam-engine, and the crankshaft is powered directly by the piston.

Built in 1873, the engine stands in its original house–recently restored.
Location : 4 miles N of Nottingham off A611.

Bethesda *Gwynedd*   *Map : 392 Cf*
PENRHYN SLATE QUARRY This is one of the largest quarries in Britain, more than 600 ft deep, and still in use after two centuries.

Water-balanced hoists were once used to haul blocks of slate up from the galleries where they were cut. The quarry, including the hoists, can be seen from the roadside.

The quarry is not open to the public.
Location: 5 miles SE of Bangor on A5.

Betws-y-coed *Gwynedd   Map: 392 Ce*
WATERLOO BRIDGE A cast-iron bridge, built by Thomas Telford in 1815, carries his Holyhead Road (A5) across the River Conwy. An inscription on the bridge states: "This arch was constructed in the same year as the Battle of Waterloo was fought."
Location: 9 miles SE of Bangor on A5.

Beverley *Humberside   Map: 394 Dd*
THE MINSTER (CHURCH OF ST JOHN THE EVANGELIST) The largest parish church in England is a mixture of Early English, Decorated and Perpendicular.

Beverley Minster has a wealth of fine carvings in wood and stone, including the celebrated 14th-century Percy tomb; an abundance of carvings depicting medieval minstrels; and 16th-century misericords – brackets on hinged seats.

There is also a pre-Conquest sanctuary seat, used by officials investigating fugitives' pleas for sanctuary. Records show that 469 self-confessed criminals sought sanctuary from 1478 to 1539.
Location: S end of town's main street.

Bewcastle Cross *Cumbria   Map: 389 Fb*
The surviving shaft of a late 7th-century cross, 14 ft 6 in. high, stands in St Cuthbert's churchyard. The cross is carved with interlaced patterns, birds, beasts and figures. An inscription commemorates King Alcfrith, son of Oswi the Northumbrian king.
Location: 10 miles NW of Haltwhistle (A69, B6318).

VICTORIAN GROCER'S SHOP
William Inglis's grocery shop, dating from about 1879, and originally in Biggar, has been rebuilt in the Gladstone Court Museum. The counter displays contemporary price lists and advertising leaflets.

THE BIRTH OF THE BICYCLE

As far back as the 15th century, men were experimenting with crude foot-operated, four-wheeled vehicles. In 1818 a French engineer designed the hobby-horse, ushering in the era of the bicycle. At first it was a novelty enjoyed by a few, but by the 1880s it was a sophisticated machine, popular among all classes with over 230 cycling clubs in Britain alone.

HOBBY-HORSE
First used in 1818, the "Draisienne" hobby-horse was propelled by the rider leaning on the arm-rests and thrusting at the ground with his feet. It lasted until about 1820.

"BONE-SHAKER"
The English bone-shaker, the 1869 Hedges' velocipede, was operated by pedals, and had a rubberised saddle. Leg-rests were used for cruising down hill, and a candle-lit lamp for night riding.

PENNY-FARTHING
The Bayliss-Thomas penny-farthing bicycle of 1890. The larger the front wheel, the greater the distance the rider could cover with one turn of the pedals. Different wheel sizes were made.

SAFETY BICYCLETTE *One of the early machines, made in 1879, incorporated major features in the design of the safety bicycle. It had rubber tyres and a rear wheel driven by a chain and sprockets.*

LADIES' SAFETY BICYCLE *The 1895 Elswick bicycle in a form that survived for the next three decades. It had pneumatic tyres, a tubular frame, and guards to protect the riders' full-length skirts.*

BIGGLESWADE: FROM TWO-WHEELERS TO THE AGE OF FLIGHT

Bicycles at the Shuttleworth Collection illustrate 70 years of development – from a hobby-horse of 1818 to a safety bicycle of 1890. The Avro 504 (right), in the aircraft section of the museum, was designed in 1910, and used extensively as a tutor aircraft. It is still considered to be the world's best trainer, and its design was a prototype for such machines as the Anson, Lancaster and Vulcan.

Bewdley Museum *Heref.*   *Map: 393 Fc*
A craft museum is housed in the 18th-century Shambles, or market, behind the Town Hall.

Among the exhibits are reconstructed workshops which include displays of charcoal burning, basket-making, coopering and other local crafts. Demonstrations of glassblowing, pottery and lace-making can often be seen here.
Location: 3 miles W of Kidderminster on A456.

Bexley see Red House

Bibury *Glos.*   *Map: 393 Gb*
ARLINGTON MILL A large 17th-century water-driven corn mill that was restored and enlarged in 1859. The original machinery was removed in 1914. Machinery from another mill was fitted in 1966 and visitors can see it turning.

At one time the mill was also used for fulling – cleaning and thickening the weave of newly woven cloth by beating it under water with wheel-operated hammers.
Location: 7 miles NE of Cirencester on A433.

Bickleigh Castle *Devon*   *Map: 397 Ec*
The first stone castle on this Norman motte and bailey was destroyed by King Stephen in the 1140s. Only the chapel has survived.

The second castle, built during the Tudor period, was largely destroyed during the Civil War by Parliamentarians.
Location: 4 miles S of Tiverton off A3072.

Bicton Gardens *Devon*   *Map: 397 Ec*
JAMES COUNTRYSIDE MUSEUM Bicton Gardens were planned by Lord Rolle in the mid-18th century, from designs said to have been drawn by André le Nôtre – who landscaped Versailles.

The museum illustrates the seasonal activities of the farming year, with hand-tools, agricultural machinery and horse-drawn implements.
Location: 3 miles N of Budleigh Salterton off A376.

Biggar *Strathclyde*   *Map: 389 Dc*
At Burn Braes an open-air museum is being developed to re-create aspects of the region's cultural and economic history. Among the exhibits approaching completion are the town's early-Victorian gas-works and a 17th-century farmhouse, which has been brought from Wiston, 9 miles away. The Gladstone Court Museum near by, in a 19th-century coachworks, shows reconstructions – through shops and shop windows – of local Victorian life.
Location: 13 miles SE of Lanark (A73, A72).

Biggleswade *Beds.*   *Map: 398 De*
THE SHUTTLEWORTH COLLECTION One of the finest collections of old aircraft in the world. Many of the historic aeroplanes are regularly flown.

The oldest British flying exhibit is a Blackburn monoplane of 1912. Machines also to be seen on flying days include the Hurricane and Spitfire.
Location: 3 miles W of Biggleswade off A1.

Bignor *W. Sussex*   *Map: 398 Cb*
The Roman villa at Bignor, found in 1811, is one of the largest to be unearthed in Britain. It was a 4th-century courtyard villa, a grandiose successor of earlier more modest houses.

The main feature is the spectacular set of pavement mosaics, of which there are several, including 80 ft of corridor mosaic.
Location: 12 miles NE of Chichester off A285.

Billing Mill see Little Billing

Binchester Fort *Durham*   *Map: 391 Fd*
A Roman cavalry fort with well-preserved hypocausts (see p. 42) that heated two rooms, probably the commanding officer's bath suite. In one room, the concrete floor is intact, supported on brick piers, some stamped with the name of the army unit that made them.
Location: 1½ miles N of Bishop Auckland on minor road.

Bingley Five Rise *W. Yorks.*   *Map: 391 Fb*
The most spectacular lock staircase in England is at the north-western edge of Bingley. The five inter-connected broad locks drop the Leeds and Liverpool Canal by 60 ft from the summit, within a length of about 100 yds.
    The lock was opened in 1774.
Location: 6 miles NW of Bradford on A650.

Binham Priory *Norfolk*   *Map: 395 Fb*
Founded as a Benedictine Priory in 1091, it owes its fame to Richard de Pasco, who was prior from 1226 to 1244. He built the magnificent west front—a rare example of Early English in East Anglia.
    The priory was never very prosperous and Pasco's successor, William de Somerton, sold its few treasures to raise money for his research work as an alchemist. Having impoverished the priory he fled to Rome, leaving a deficit of £600.
    The priory was dissolved in 1540.
Location: 5 miles SE of Wells, off B1105.

Birmingham *W. Midlands*   *Map: 393 Fd*
CURZON STREET GOODS STATION The Greek Revival portico, designed in 1838 by Philip Hardwick, marks the end of the London to Birmingham railway. Based on an ancient Greek triumphal arch, the portico has four Ionic columns, 50 ft tall.
Location: Facing New Canal St.
FARMER'S BRIDGE Birmingham is the centre of the Midlands' canal network–the Birmingham Canal Navigations.
    At Farmer's Bridge, three canals meet: the Worcester and Birmingham Canal; the Birmingham and Fazeley, via a flight of locks; and the Birmingham Canal. Many old buildings preserved include the canal toll-house.
Location: St Peter's Place, off Broad Street, W of city centre.
RAILWAY MUSEUM In a new steam shed with workshops, the museum has locomotives ranging from a tank engine built in 1889 for the Lancashire and Yorkshire Railway to *Clun Castle*, one of the celebrated Great Western Railway locomotives.
    Rolling stock includes replicas of the Liverpool and Manchester Railway coaches of 1836 and a number of Pullman coaches.
    Visitors can see engines regularly steamed.
Location: 3 miles SE of city on A41.
ST CHAD'S ROMAN CATHOLIC CATHEDRAL The first Roman Catholic cathedral to be built in Britain after the 16th-century Reformation (1538–88). Designed by Augustus Welby Pugin–who, with Charles Barry, designed the Houses of Parliament–the cathedral was built between 1839 and 1841. This astonishing speed is perhaps a reflection of Pugin's fanatical energy–he died, insane, when 40.
    The cathedral has a superb 15th-century oak pulpit, thought to have been brought from the abbey of St Gertrude at Louvain in Belgium. There is also a 15th-century bishop's throne.
Location: Shadwell St, NW of city centre.
ST PHILIP'S ANGLICAN CATHEDRAL St Philip's was built as a parish church in 1709–25 by Thomas Archer–a pupil of Sir John Vanbrugh–and raised to the status of a cathedral in 1905.
    There are four stained-glass windows by Sir Edward Burne Jones and William Morris– leaders of the Victorian pre-Raphaelite movement. Three of the windows are in the chancel; the fourth in the baptistry.
Location: Colmore Row in centre of city.

Blackheath see Ranger's House

Blackmore *Essex*   *Map: 399 Ed*
THE PRIORY CHURCH OF ST LAURENCE The church has one of the finest of the few wooden belfry towers left in Essex.
    Linked to the nave of the 12th-century church–all that remains of a former priory–the 15th-century tower rises in a series of pagoda-like steps, terminated by a shingled-broach spire. Strutted, braced and jointed together, a complex framework of timbers forms a rigid structure, capable of resisting the erratic strains imposed by the swing of the bell or gale-force winds–clearly owing much to the combined skills of continental invaders and medieval shipwrights.
    There is a rare cresset stone in the tower. Used as night-lights in monasteries, cresset stones had cup-like hollows in them, filled with oil and a floating wick.
Location: 8 miles SW of Chelmsford off A122.

Blackpool Mill *Dyfed*   *Map: 392 Ab*
This large water-driven flour mill was built in 1813–refitted with machinery in 1901. It has since been restored and can be seen in motion.
Location: 8 miles E of Haverfordwest (A40, A4075 for 200 yds, then minor road).

Blackstone Edge *G. Manchester*   *Map: 391 Fa*
A fine stretch of Roman road, 16 ft wide and paved with stone setts, or paving blocks, unlike most Roman roads in Britain which had rammed-gravel surfaces. A groove in the centre of the road was intended for the brake-pole on carts, to help drivers keep control while going downhill. The road is obscured in parts by vegetation.
Location: 5 miles NE of Rochdale on A58. (The Roman road traverses Blackstone Edge.)

Blaenau Ffestiniog *Gwynedd*   *Map: 392 Ce*
SLATE QUARRIES Blaenau Ffestiniog is at the centre of the most extensive slate-working complex in Wales, surrounded by vast hills of debris from slate quarries and mines. The industry was at its height during the 19th century, producing slate for the building trade; and some of the quarries are still in use.
    Gloddfa Ganol is the site of the largest slate mine in the world, and has 42 miles of tunnels. A whole range of activities connected with the slate industry can be seen at the Mountain Tourist Centre, and there are conducted Land Rover tours through the old mine workings.
    Craftsmen can be seen at work, splitting slate blocks, and cutting and shaping them at the former Oakeley Slate Mill–where monuments were once manufactured. The mill was originally steam-powered through overhead shafting and part of the old belt-driven machinery has been preserved. The products of the mill are sold at the museum shop.
    To save the long trudge up the hill to the quarries, some of the quarrymen had homes on the site. A number of these houses have been preserved and are furnished to show how they

SYMBOL OF A SLATE QUARRY

One of the original wagons at the slate quarries in Blaenau Ffestiniog, used during the middle of the 19th century. Wagons like this were either horse-drawn or manhandled up gentle gradients from the quarries to the saw benches, some of which were 1,500 ft above sea-level. Some were wound up inclines by stationary steam-engines, which can still be seen. The mountain of rubble in the background was the typical by-product of the quarries, with 13–20 tons of waste material for every ton of dressed – or prepared – slates produced.

would have looked at different periods of the quarries' history – from early Victorian to mid-1930.

At Llechwedd Slate Caverns near by, there are 16 different tunnel-levels – each leading to vast chambers where the slate was cut from the living rock. A number of tableaux along the route taken by visitors vividly demonstrates the working life of the miner during the 1850s. One of the caverns – the Victorian demonstration chamber – was excavated solely by two men, working by candlelight.

Some of the chambers were worked by the same groups of men for as long as 15 years, excavating caverns 50–60 ft long and 60–80 ft high. One, known as The Cathedral, is 200 ft high.
Location: Gloddfa Ganol is 4 miles N of Blaenau Ffestiniog; Llechwedd Slate Caverns 3 miles N – both on A470.

Blaenavon Ironworks *Gwent*   Map: 393 Db
The best-preserved example of an 18th-century ironworks in the whole of Wales stands on the western edge of the town.

Three English ironmasters came to Blaenavon in 1789, then a quiet farming hamlet, attracted by the abundance of raw materials, such as iron ore, limestone and coal. They leased the site from the Earl of Abergavenny, and built furnaces and houses for up to 350 workers. As the works expanded, more houses were built, forming the nucleus of the present town.

The surviving ironworks occupy three sides of a square, built to follow the contours of the land. Two of the casting houses still stand. Here, the furnace was tapped and the molten metal run into moulds made of sand and set in the floor of the casting houses. At the end of the row of furnaces are the remains of an engine-house.

The second side is dominated by a vast stone water-balance tower, and along the third side are the workers' houses, built within the heat, dirt and sound of the works. One of the houses was used as the company shop – the first of its kind

where workers could spend tokens, which formed part of their wages.

A tramway over a viaduct linked the furnaces to the forge at Garnddyrys, 2 miles to the north.

The ironworks went out of business in the 1860s when more modern works were built near by at Forgeside. Until about three or four years ago, the ironworks at Blaenavon was used as a foundry and a coalyard, and the houses were still occupied. Since then the site has been abandoned.
Location: 6 miles N of Pontypool off A4043.

Blair Atholl *Tayside*   Map: 387 Da
BLAIR CASTLE The oldest part of the castle is the 13th-century square great tower. In the second Jacobite rebellion (1745–6) the castle was occupied by Charles Edward Stuart – "Bonnie Prince Charlie" – a friend of its owner the Duke of Atholl. The castle was occupied by government forces when he abandoned it, and then unsuccessfully besieged by Atholl after the prince's defeat and escape. This was probably the last siege of a castle in Britain.
Location: 7 miles NW of Pitlochry off A9.
TILT VIADUCT The viaduct was built by Joseph Mitchell in 1861 to carry the Highland Railway across the River Tilt. It is a fine example of a lattice-girder bridge, with a main wrought-iron girder 150 ft long. The viaduct is an outstanding feature on a line having the highest mainline summit in the country – 1,507 ft.
Location: 7 miles NW of Pitlochry off A9.

Blaise Hamlet *Avon*   Map: 397 Fe
BLAISE CASTLE AND HAMLET The castle was built in 1796 for John Scandrett Harford, a Quaker banker, and is appropriately plain and sober. Now used as a museum of social history, it looks across a deep gorge, landscaped by Humphrey Repton, towards a mock castle on the opposite crest. The castle is now in ruins.

Blaise Hamlet consists of cottages designed in 1811 by John Nash – George IV's favourite architect – dotted haphazardly around a village green. The cottages were built for estate

pensioners – each dwelling detached and individual.
Location: 4 miles NW of Bristol off A4018.

Blantyre *Strathclyde*   *Map: 388 Cd*
DAVID LIVINGSTONE CENTRE The great missionary-explorer was born here in 1813, and sent to work as a boy in the nearby cotton-spinning mill.

The three-storey tenement, built in the 1780s, consists of 24 one-roomed dwellings to accommodate the workers and their families. It is now preserved as a memorial to Livingstone, containing a vast collection of personal relics. On display are Livingstone's battered despatch case, saved from a river by H. M. Stanley – the American journalist who found him; the explorer's surgical instruments; and the pocket Bible he carried.

The Centre includes a social history museum of 19th-century Scotland.
Location: 3 miles NW of Hamilton off A724.

Blenheim Palace *Oxon.*   *Map: 398 Bd*
"We have nothing to equal this!" was the response of George III to his first sight of Blenheim Palace. A gift from the nation to the Duke of Marlborough for his victory over the French at Blenheim in 1704, it is England's Versailles; a Renaissance monument to the glory of England and Queen Anne, and only secondly a home.

Though these priorities were clear to the duke and his architect, Sir John Vanbrugh, from the day of their first survey of the old Royal Manor of Woodstock in 1705, they were never accepted by the duke's formidable wife. "I mortally hate all gardens and architecture," she once said. At Blenheim all she required was "a clean sweet house and garden be it ever so small".

Querulous, combative, philistine and parsimonious, the duchess fought against every stage of Vanbrugh's unfolding design. "I made Mr Vanbrugh my enemy," she wrote, "by the constant disputes I had with him to prevent his extravagance." The extravagances of which she particularly complained were the provision of covered ways for servants, the use of the best stone for the service court, and the scale of the Grand Bridge across what is now the lake. In the bridge she scathingly counted "33 rooms and a house at each corner".

The park is one of "Capability" Brown's most successful creations. Commissioned in the 1760s by the 4th duke, he swept away the Grand Parterre and the rest of the formal setting which Henry Wise, Queen Anne's gardener, had provided for Vanbrugh's palace and brought the greensward up to the walls. He dammed the River Glyme to make an immense serpentine lake, half submerging and greatly improving the appearance of the controversial bridge.

West of the Great Hall lies a suite of rooms, once occupied by the 1st duke's domestic chaplain. Their low ceilings and lack of architectural embellishment are in striking contrast to the great sequence of state rooms near by. In one of them in November 1874, Winston Churchill was born. "At Blenheim," he wrote, "I took two very important decisions: to be born and to marry. I am happily content with the decisions I took on both those occasions." About the circumstances of his birth there are conflicting traditions: one records that immediately before it his mother had been dancing at a ball in the Long Library; the other that she was accompanying the guns at a shoot in the park. When asked which was true, Churchill replied: "I believe the latter to be true, but although present on that occasion, I have no clear recollection of the events leading up to it."
Location: 8 miles NW of Oxford off A34.

Bletchley *Bucks.*   *Map: 398 Ce*
RAILWAY BRIDGE One of the very few bridges on Robert Stephenson's London and Birmingham Railway to survive virtually as it was built. It is a skew metal bridge – one that crosses the road at an angle – built in 1838.
Location: On A5, 14 miles NW of Dunstable.

Blickling Hall *Norfolk*   *Map: 395 Fa*
The existing 17th-century red-brick Hall, with turrets and attractive Dutch gables, was designed by Robert Lyminge – architect of Hatfield House – between 1616–24, for Sir Henry Hobart, Lord Chief Justice.

The Hall was remodelled in the next century by Thomas Ivory, when a superb staircase was raised in the Great Hall. Niches in the wall have life-size wood carvings of Elizabeth I, and her mother, Anne Boleyn. The estate once belonged to Anne Boleyn's grandfather, although the Hall was built 80 years after Anne's death.

Another earlier owner of the estate was Sir John Fastolf, whom Shakespeare is thought to have used as his character Falstaff.

Bedrooms now portray different periods up to Edwardian times. There are formal gardens and a workshop for the conservation and repair of tapestries and fabrics throughout East Anglia.
Location: 14 miles N of Norwich (A140, then B1354).

Blisland *Cornwall*   *Map: 396 Cb*
CHURCH OF ST PROTUS AND ST HYACINTH This parish church on the edge of Bodmin Moor is largely Norman with a 15th-century tower.

Characteristic of churches found inland in Cornish towns and villages, it is built of local granite and slate. The splendid wagon roof, with timbers resembling the interior of a covered wagon, has the ends carved to resemble angels.

The interior, with a screen and rood, richly gilded and glowing with colours, is unusually decorated – the result of Victorian restoration.
Location: 6 miles NE of Bodmin off A30.

Bluebell Railway see Sheffield Park

Blyth *Northld.*   *Map: 391 Ge*
One of the main coal ports, serving the many collieries and open-cast sites in the region.

Along the banks of the estuary at North Blyth, the coal chutes can still be seen – stout wooden structures down which coal was emptied into the waiting coasters. Transport to the chutes was originally by horse-drawn trucks.

One of the 19th-century colliery stable blocks survives beside A193, near its junction with A189. A two-storeyed brick and stone building, it has attractive iron-traceried windows. The upper floor, with an outside staircase, was the hay loft and the ground floor, the stables, fitted with stalls – that are still in place – for 16 horses.
Location: 9 miles N of Tynemouth on A193.

THE IMAGE-BREAKERS

In 1525 Cardinal Wolsey—the most powerful man in England after Henry VIII—dissolved a handful of small and impoverished monasteries. He sold the land, and with the money endowed Christ Church College, Oxford. It was a hint of things to come—a device for raising funds that heralded the end of the monastic era.

Nine years later, in 1534, Henry finally usurped the authority of the Pope and declared himself to be Supreme Head of the English Church. It gave Thomas Cromwell, the King's Vicar-General, a chance to boost the Crown's ailing finances. Within four years more than 800 monasteries were dissolved, and nearly 10,000 monks were dispossessed.

Licensed vandalism

As valuables were transferred to London and the land sold to eager speculators, Cromwell's men worked with ruthless efficiency. The fanatical anti-papists among them defaced or destroyed any "monuments of idolatry" they encountered, as symbols of the Pope and Roman Catholicism. Many, less motivated by ideals, abandoned themselves to licensed vandalism. The result was the destruction of countless works of art as fonts, shrines, tombs and statues were smashed or mutilated.

Becket's tomb

Henry VIII, who never personally abandoned his Catholic faith, even ordered Thomas Becket's shrine in Canterbury Cathedral to be desecrated. Stripped of its jewels, gold and silver plate—it took 26 cartloads to transfer them to London—the shrine was levelled.

A second, more vigorous wave of iconoclasm—or image-breaking—followed a century later. Puritans regarded the representation of Christ, saints and other religious figures as blasphemous. An order from the House of Commons in 1641 instructed Oliver Cromwell's men "to demolish and remove out of churches and chapels all images, altars, or tables turned altar-wise, crucifixes, superstitious pictures and other monuments of idolatry".

Puritanical fury

The Puritans did their work with relish—rood screens and crosses were torn down or defaced . . . vestments, books and manuscripts burned . . . murals whitewashed and tapestries slashed . . . stained-glass windows stoned . . . organs destroyed . . . brasses defaced. Little was spared. Churches were sometimes used as barracks, stables or prisons.

With the restoration of the monarchy in 1660, the destruction came to an end. Today, few cathedrals or churches are without a damaged statue, tomb or carving—grim testaments of extreme religious intolerance.

IMAGE-BREAKERS AT WORK *A contemporary engraving depicting soldiers during the Commonwealth era—1649–60—"pulling down Popish pictures" and tearing down the altar rails and altar in a church.*

MEDIEVAL ANGELS IN WOOD

The roof of Blythburgh church is held together with wooden pegs—one of the skills of the medieval carpenter. It is also rich in carving. In 1644, William Dowsing and his Puritan troops damaged many of the wooden angels with gunshot. He defaced scores of churches to purge them of "superstitious idols".

Blythburgh *Suffolk*   Map: 399 Gf
CHURCH OF THE HOLY TRINITY This mid-15th-century church—unexpectedly large for the size of the village—was built when Blythburgh was a prosperous port. Soon after, the River Blyth silted up and ships were no longer able to come inland.

Holy Trinity has a 15th-century font, a Jacobean pulpit and benches carved with the Seven Deadly Sins, instead of the usual poppy-head common to Suffolk churches.

In 1577 the church was struck by lightning—the spire crashing through the roof and killing two members of the congregation. In 1644 the interior of the church was ravaged by William Dowsing, the infamous Puritan whose horses damaged brickwork on the floor of the nave.

The church has a rare Jack-o'-the-clock—a painted wooden figure, in armour, with a hinged arm holding a hammer. A cord is pulled to strike a bell at the start of Divine Service.

A case beneath the west window holds an alms box, dated 1473, and a First Edition James I Bible, dated 1611 and 1613.
Location: 13 miles S of Lowestoft off A12.

Boat of Garten *Highland*   *Map: 387 Eb*
STRATHSPEY STEAM RAILWAY The station, on the
old Highland line axed by the Beeching Report
in 1963, has since been restored.

The rolling stock on display has also been
restored, and includes locomotives from the
London, Midland and Scottish Railway.
Location: 9 miles SW of Grantown on B970.

Bodiam Castle *W. Sussex*   *Map: 399 Eb*
Few English medieval castles look now as they
did in their heyday. Bodiam is one, and when
you get close to its marvellous water-girt
surroundings, it needs little imagination to slip
back six centuries in time and to wait for the
portcullis in the huge twin-towered gatehouse to
grind upwards on its rollers, allowing a party of
mounted retainers out to exercise their horses.

Bodiam Castle was built by Sir Edward
Dalyngrigge, a knight and veteran of Edward
III's wars in France. Dalyngrigge was granted a
royal licence in 1386 to fortify his house against
invasion from France. The nearby town of
Rye – one of the Cinque Ports – had been sacked
by the French only a few years earlier.

Dalyngrigge took his licence as one to start
building afresh, and built the castle a little way
from the site of his manor house. He raised a
castle with an inner quadrangle, and by diverting
some springs and the river into a rectangle of
marshy ground, he created an artificial lake
around it.

The approach to Bodiam today is by a bridge
from the north bank of the lake across a small
octagonal stone structure – perhaps the base of
another gatehouse. But originally entry was
along a causeway at right-angles to the gatehouse
wall, which left an enemy's right flank exposed
to fire from at least three towers.

Bodiam was one of the first castles designed to
minimise the danger of mutiny among retainers
who were, from the middle of the 14th century,
generally mercenaries and not the older feudal
levy men who could be trusted. There were no
connecting doors or passage-ways between the
owner's quarters and those for the retainers. On
the ground floor, for example, the retainers' hall
and kitchen were next to each other, but in no
way could a retainer get from either to any other
part of the castle except by venturing out into the
courtyard, where he would immediately come
under all-round surveillance from the gatehouse,
which was in the owner's control. The castle's
well was sunk in the south-west tower in the
owner's quarters.

Bodiam's defences were never severely tested.
The castle fell to a half-hearted attack in 1484 by
the Earl of Surrey, and again in the Civil War
when a Parliamentary army threatened to
bombard it with the latest type of cannon.

In 1917 a new owner, Lord Curzon, once
Viceroy of India, restored its outside walls to
their medieval appearance.
Location: 12 miles N of Hastings (A21, A229
then minor road).

Bolingbroke Castle *Lincs.*   *Map: 395 Db*
The castle was built in the 1220s by Ranulf, Earl
of Chester, who also built Beeston Castle.

During the 14th century, the castle became the
property of the powerful, land-grabbing John of
Gaunt, Duke of Lancaster, fourth son of Edward

III. Gaunt's son, Henry Bolingbroke – later
Henry IV – was born here in 1367.
Location: 4 miles W of Spilsby off A1115.

Bollington *Cheshire*   *Map: 393 Ff*
BOLLIN BANK The embankment, carrying the
Bridgewater Canal across the Bolling valley, was
built in 1767 by the engineer James Brindley. It
solved the problem of bridging a valley when it
was not possible to follow the natural contours of
the land. Embankments like this were used
extensively by later canal and railway engineers.
Location: 3 miles W of Altrincham on A56.

Bollington *Cheshire*   *Map: 394 Ac*
CLARENCE MILL The finest cotton mill in the
district is beside the Macclesfield Canal aqueduct.
The mill was built in 1824 by the Swindell
family, the leading Bollington cotton manufac-
turers of their day. It is not open to the public.
Location: 3 miles NE of Macclesfield (A523 then
B5090).

Bolsover Castle *Derbys.*   *Map: 394 Bc*
The Little Castle was built by Sir Charles
Cavendish between 1613 and 1646, on the site of
a former, ruined, medieval castle.

The new building was designed to resemble a
late-medieval tower house, with battlements and
corner turrets – but it is like a palace inside.

The castle was captured by Parliamentary
troops in 1644, when it was severely damaged.
Location: 6 miles E of Chesterfield on A632.

Bolton *Greater Manchester*   *Map: 391 Ea*
HALL-I'-TH'-WOOD Samuel Crompton – who in
1779 invented the spinning mule which improved the production of cotton thread – lived
here from 1759 to 1782. The 15th-century house
is now a museum with relics of the Crompton
family.
Location: 2 miles N of Bolton (A6 then A58).

Bolton Abbey *N. Yorks.*   *Map: 391 Fb*
The Augustinian priory, set in isolation near the
River Wharfe, was founded in 1150. With the
Dissolution of the Monasteries in 1536–40, the
Early English nave and the Decorated gatehouse
were spared; the nave for use as the parish
church, the gatehouse as a residence – now
Bolton Hall.

The inside walls of the church and tower bear
masons' marks – "signatures" of the men who
built them. The west-front wall has projecting
stones where new work was to be bonded to
the old.
Location: 5 miles NW of Ilkley off B6160.

Bolton Castle *N. Yorks.*   *Map: 391 Fc*
Lord Scrope, friend of Richard II, gave a
contract to John Lewyn, a leading English
military engineer, to build a quadrangular castle
with square towers on the corners. Building
started in 1378 and local legend had it that the
mortar was mixed with ox-blood to give it
durability.

Bolton Castle was designed to protect its
owner from internal mutiny as well as from
enemy assault, with the lord's quarters separated
from those of his retainers.

Mary, Queen of Scots stayed at Bolton for six
months in 1569, following her defeat at Langside

the year before by the Protestant Scottish lords.
Location: 14 miles SW of Richmond off A6108.

Bonawe *Strathclyde* Map: 388 Bf

This remote spot on the shores of Loch Etive is one of the most remarkable industrial sites in Britain. In 1752 an iron works was established here that remained in production until 1866. The site was selected because it had a good anchorage and a plentiful supply of timber – the furnace was one of the last to continue using charcoal as a fuel.

The ore was shipped round the coast from Cumbria, landed at Kelly's pier, and taken to the top of the hill, to store-houses near the road. Processing started there and continued downhill until the iron pigs, or castings, finished up back at the jetty ready for shipment.

The furnace, a square stone structure built into the slope of the hill, was in three sections: the charge house where material for the furnace was collected; a short bridge; and then the furnace itself, with a squat chimney. The ore was wheeled across the bridge and emptied directly into the top of the furnace. The molten metal was tapped off at the bottom.

The furnace could produce about 2 tons of pig-iron a day. It was expensive, because of high transport costs, but of such good quality that it remained in demand. One product was cannon balls, and it is said that shot from Bonawe was fired at Waterloo and Trafalgar.

Houses were built by the company for the work-force – an L-shaped block, being one of the earliest examples of its kind in this part of Scotland. The two-storeyed buildings, now empty, had an outside staircase to the upper storey.

The whole site is now preserved as a relic of Scottish industrial history.
Location: 12 miles E of Oban (A85 then B845).

Bontddu *Gwynedd* Map: 392 Cd

DOLGELLAU GOLD FIELD Bontddu is on the edge of an abandoned gold field, developed after gold was discovered in the area in 1843. By the mid-1850s there were 24 mines started near Dolgellau, reaching the peak of their activity between 1880 and the early decades of the 20th century.

On the banks of the Afon Cwm-llechan stands a stone bridge and the remains of the old ore-crushing mill. The bridge carried the tramway from the mill to St David's mine. Near the entrance there is a shaft, and close to the river a circle of wedge-shaped stones; this was a primitive crusher or arrastre.

Diligent searching among the spill heaps near by sometimes uncovers stone flecked with gold.
Location: 5 miles W of Dolgellau on A496.

Boot *Cumbria* Map: 390 Dc

ESKDALE WATERMILL This small stone mill dates from the Middle Ages. Although the present gearing and wheels were probably installed in the 18th century, the mill is significant for its unusual layout, having two water-wheels – each driving directly a pair of millstones.

Like many mills in this part of England, it has a drying kiln attached. Grain was spread over a floor of perforated iron plates, above a peat fire, and dried before grinding.

The mill opens regularly and can be seen working, although no grinding is done today.
Location: 13 miles W of Ambleside off Hardknott Pass.

Boscobel House *Salop* Map: 393 Fd

John Giffard, a staunch Catholic, built the house around 1600 as a hunting lodge, and a "place for concealment" – conscious of the growing anti-Catholic feeling in the country.

But it was a huge oak tree in the grounds that was to provide a more significant refuge. Charles II – dressed as a peasant – hid in it after his defeat at the Battle of Worcester in 1651. For two days the Roundheads scoured the locality, before the search moved on and the king was able to make his escape to France.

The descendant of the original oak tree still marks the spot – the inspiration for the "Royal Oak" inn signs throughout the country.
Location: 9 miles NW of Wolverhampton (A41 then minor roads).

Bosham *W. Sussex* Map: 398 Ca

CHURCH OF THE HOLY TRINITY King Harold worshipped in this church before his fateful meeting with William of Normandy at Hastings in 1066.

It is also said to be where King Canute's second daughter, who died in infancy, is buried.
Location: 4 miles W of Chichester off A27.

Bosherston *Dyfed* Map: 392Aa

ST GOVAN'S CHAPEL This tiny building is wedged into a narrow cleft of rock, nearly halfway down

CHAPEL ON THE CLIFFSIDE

There are between 60 and 70 steps leading down to this medieval chapel, dramatically sited on the cliffside at St Govan's Head. A legend says that if you count the steps when going down, the number never agrees when returning to the top.

the rugged cliffside of St Govan's Head.

The chapel, thought to be 13th century, has a single chamber – barely 20 ft by 10 ft wide, with an earth floor, stone altar and bench. There is a cell cut in the rock face – forming part of the wall to the north of the altar. According to a legend, St Cofen – recluse and wife of a 5th-century chief – lived in the cell, beside a well that had miraculous healing powers. The well has since run dry.

The chapel can be visited at all times, except when the firing range at Castlemain is in use. Inquire at Bosherston Post Office.

Location: Chapel is 1 mile S of Bosherston, which is 5 miles S of Pembroke off B4319.

Boston *Lincs.* *Map: 395 Db*
CHURCH OF ST BOTOLPH Crowned by an octagonal lantern, "The Boston Stump", St Botolph's magnificent Perpendicular tower is 272 ft high. The tower has been a landmark for the traveller for over six centuries.

The rest of the church is late-Decorated architecture. The Victorian font is by Augustus Pugin, who helped Charles Barry design the Houses of Parliament in 1863.

Location: Town centre, next to Market Place.
GUILDHALL A late-15th-century hall, built by the Guild of St Mary at the height of Boston's prosperity, when great quantities of wool were being shipped down the River Witham. The development of larger vessels and the silting of the estuary caused the town to decline.

The Guildhall is now the Borough Museum and includes the cells in which a number of the Pilgrim Fathers were imprisoned in James I's time, for the "crime" of wishing to emigrate to the more tolerant religious climates of Holland and America.

Location: South St, off Market Place.
OLD DOCKS A perfect example of an 18th-century port – virtually unchanged for 200 years.

Warehouses of the period line the waterfront, built of plain brick or weather-boarding. A few, such as the Customs House of 1725, have grander styling.

The docks fell into disuse as the River Witham began to silt up and the larger vessels were no longer able to reach the quays. New docks were built in 1880 as an enclosed basin, to replace the old docks, and the port now has a flourishing industry.

Location: South End (continuation of South St).

Bosworth Field *Leics.* *Map: 398 Bf*
The battlefield where Richard III lost his life and crown in 1485 can be explored by footpaths linked to car parks. The Battlefield Centre at Ambion Farm includes an exhibition, film theatre and model of the battlefield.

The crown was plucked from a bush and presented to Henry Tudor who was proclaimed king on Ambion Hill. Richard's mutilated body was strung across the back of a pack-horse and taken away for burial at Leicester.

Location: 5 miles N of Hinckley off A447.

Botallack Mine *Cornwall* *Map: 396 Aa*
The 19th-century mine at Botallack is one of the most spectacular of the Cornish mining sites, with the crumbling remains of its two engine-houses perched halfway down the edge of a steep cliff face. The site evidently was worth the effort involved, for profitable lodes stretched out under the sea bed. The shaft was sunk from a natural ledge on the cliffside. The upper house held the engine for winding men and material along the sloping shaft; the lower house had a pump to keep the mine dry.

Location: 1 mile N of St Just on B3306.

Bothwell Castle *Strathclyde* *Map: 388 Cd*
One of the most impressive buildings of medieval Scotland, and one of the most fought over. The castle, towering above the south bank of the Clyde, was probably started in the 1270s and largely finished by the 1290s.

It is a substantial stone enclosure with round towers on some corners and, at the extreme western end, the vast great tower. This was 90 ft tall, 60 ft in diameter and with walls 15 ft thick, surrounded by a moat.

In 1301 Edward I with an army of 7,000 men marched on the castle to recapture it – it had been an English stronghold during the Scottish Wars of Independence and fallen to the Scots in 1298, after a 14 month siege.

Among the king's troops were 40 engineers and masons, experts in siege work. With the aid of a huge belfry – a wooden tower on wheels, several storeys high – they attacked the castle. A drawbridge on the top of the belfry was lowered over the castle wall-walk, and a stream of armed men disgorged to start the attack. The siege lasted for nearly three weeks before the castle fell. The king then gave it to Aymer de Valence, Earl of Pembroke, whom he had appointed Warden of Scotland, as his headquarters.

In 1314 Bothwell was recaptured, when the Scots under Robert Bruce routed the English at Bannockburn. The castle was taken 20 years later by Edward III in his war against Bruce's son, David II, but in 1337 Sir Andrew de Moray recaptured it for Scotland.

Robert Bruce had urged Scotsmen to render useless all fortresses that could be of value to English marauders. One of Moray's acts of demolition was to split the great tower, or donjon, of Bothwell in two halves and throw the masonry of one half into the Clyde. The other half stands today as the most impressive remains of the old fortress.

Location: 8½ miles SE of Glasgow (A724 then N on B758).

Boughton House *Northants.* *Map: 398 Cf*
In 1530, Sir Edward Montagu, Henry VIII's Lord Chief Justice, built a manor house around a 15th-century monastic hall. Successive additions were made by his descendants, culminating in the magnificent north front, part of the 1st Duke of Montagu's attempt in the 1690s to create an "English Versailles" at Boughton.

The house has 7 courtyards, 52 chimney stacks and 365 windows. There are collections of paintings and furniture and a well-stocked armoury; with nature trails in the parkland.

Location: 4 miles NE of Kettering off A43.

Boughton Monchelsea *Kent* *Map: 399 Ec*
An Elizabethan house, built in 1567–75 by Robert Rudston, son of a wealthy London draper. The house has tapestries, furniture and a carriage display. A small deer park, with a herd of

fallow deer, still survives from Rudston's day.
Location: 5 miles S of Maidstone (A29, B2163
then minor road).

Bournville *W. Midlands*   *Map: 398 Af*
SELLY MANOR AND MINWORTH These two medi-
eval houses originally stood elsewhere – Selly
Manor 1 mile to the north, and Minworth
Greaves 3 miles north-east of Birmingham. The
houses were dismantled at the start of the century
and rebuilt on the Bournville Estate by George
Cadbury.

Both timber-framed houses have been
restored and are filled with furniture and domestic objects of the period.

When George and his brother Richard moved
their chocolate factory to the country in 1879,
George bought some land near by. He had been
appalled in his youth by the slum-dwellings of
Birmingham, and took the opportunity to build
housing near the factory. In 1900 a trust was
formed and there are now 7,500 dwellings,
complete with churches, shops and schools.
Location: 4 miles SW of Birmingham off A38.

Bourn Windmill *Cambs.*   *Map: 399 De*
This small post-mill is one of the country's oldest
surviving mills – a type common in the Middle
Ages – with a pitched roof, a small body and a
pair of millstones driven by two pairs of sails.

The mill, re-equipped in the 19th century, is
open to the public but not working.
Location: 10 miles SE of Huntingdon off A14.

Bow *Greater London*   *Map: 399 Dc*
TIDE MILLS A fragment of early industrial London
is preserved in the shadow of the new flyover,
with two mills at the end of Three Mill Lane
(there were once three). Goods and raw material
came by both road and river.

The House Mill, dated 1776, is derelict; the
Clock Mill beside it dates mainly from 1817.
The distinctive conical roofs and ventilators
indicate the position of the malting kilns.

Both had water-wheels driven by tidal water
flowing up Bow Creek from the River Lea.
Location: Near Bromley by Bow station off St
Leonards St, E3.

Bowes Castle *Durham*   *Map: 394 Af*
This is one of several huge rectangular towers
built in northern England during the late 12th
century, by Henry II, as a defence against the
Scots raiding the Border counties. However,
Bowes did not figure in any major conflict.
Location: 5 miles S of Barnard Castle on A66.

Bowes Railway see Springwell

Bowhill *Borders*   *Map: 389 Ec*
The Border home of the Duke of Buccleuch and
Queensberry – descendants of the 12th-century
Scotts of Buccleuch – is one of the great treasure
houses of Scotland. It contains a vast collection of
antiques and works of art.

According to legend, the origin of the name
Buccleuch stems from an incident that occurred
during the 12th century. A royal hunting party
was in a "cleuch" or deep ravine in the heart of
Ettrick Forest surrounding Bowhill – when a
buck turned on the hounds. A young member
of the Scott family seized it by the antlers and

threw it over his shoulders – hence Buck-cleuch.

A rare distinction is that for 30 generations
from the 11th century, the succession has passed
from father to son, with the one exception of
Anne, Countess of Buccleuch. In 1663 she
married James, Duke of Monmouth, natural son
of Charles II and Lucy Walter.

In order to suppress his son's growing
ambitions to succeed to the Crown, Charles was
forced to exile Monmouth to Holland. When the
king died, Monmouth returned to lead a
Protestant rebellion against the new king, James
II. Monmouth was defeated at the Battle of
Sedgemoor, in 1685, and beheaded on Tower
Hill, suffering hideously at the hands of a nervous
executioner. The shirt that he wore at his
execution, plus other relics such as his cradle,
teething ring, exquisite saddle and harness, are
displayed in the Monmouth Room.

The present mansion dates from 1812, with

A CHILDHOOD WEDDING

*A portrait of Charles I's eldest daughter, Mary Stuart,
aged 10, and William II, Prince of Orange, aged 15,
recording their wedding in May 1642. Such marriages
between children of the aristocracy were not uncommon
during the 17th century, arranged to strengthen
alliances – as in this instance – or to rescue a family
from financial difficulties. Sometimes, the newlyweds
would be returned to their parents after the ceremony to
continue their education until their late teens.*

*Both William and Mary died in their 20s of
smallpox, their son becoming King of England as
William III in 1689. The painting is in the Gallery
Hall at Bowhill.*

additions made in the 19th century. Sir Walter Scott (see Abbotsford), a kinsman and frequent visitor, took a keen interest in much of this development.

In the study is Sir Henry Raeburn's earliest portrait of Sir Walter Scott, dated 1808, and in a showcase, Scott's plaid, the manuscript of *The Lay of the Last Minstrel*, and proof editions of some of his works.

There is a nature trail in the grounds.
Location: 3 miles W of Selkirk off A708.

Bowmore *Isle of Islay, Strathclyde Map: 388 Aa*
KILLARROW PARISH CHURCH This round church – the only one of the period – was built in 1767, possibly from a plan drawn by John Adam (father of Robert).

It was a superstitious belief, common at the time, that corners could harbour evil spirits and

may account for the church having a round plan. Location: Ferry from Tarbet to Port Ellen, then 10 miles N on A846.

Boxford *Suffolk* *Map: 399 Fe*
CHURCH OF ST MARY The wooden porch, on the north side of this 14th-century church, is probably the oldest one in the country. It has a vaulted interior. The south porch, built a century later, is of Caen stone from Normandy.

There are two interesting monuments inside: a brass depicting a child who died in 1606; and another to four-times widowed Elizabeth Hyams, hastened to her end "by a fall, that brought on mortification . . . in her 113th year" Location: 14 miles W of Ipswich on A1071.

Boxgrove Priory *W. Sussex* *Map: 398 Ca*
The Benedictine Priory was originally a double

VICTORIAN MIDDLE-CLASS COMFORT

Moorside House, near Bradford's Industrial Museum, was built in 1875 – the home of John Moors, the man who built and owned the worsted spinning mills. The

interior has been refurnished throughout, with each room illustrating different periods in the life-style of Bradford's Victorian middle-class.

RETIRING ROOMS *The drawing-room (above) is furnished in the style of the 1870s – unusually restrained since Victorians associated quantity with wealth. The parlour (left), a room at the back of the house, was simply furnished and reserved strictly for the family's everyday use.*

DINING-ROOMS *Food was prepared in the kitchen (above) – characteristic of the 1890s – where the cook and the maids took their meals. The dining-room (left) is furnished in the style of the 1860s. Carving was done on a sideboard, which contained cutlery, table linen, condiments and wine.*

church: one half–the east end–used by the monks, the other half by the parishioners. After the Dissolution of the Monasteries in 1536–40, Thomas de la Warr, Lord of the Manor, bought the priory from Henry VIII. The parish used the more beautiful east end, and a screen was built between the two halves. As the west end fell into disrepair many of the stones were used by locals for building houses.

The chancel is a gem of Early English work.
Location: 4 miles NE of Chichester off A27.

Box Railway Tunnel *Wilts.*   *Map: 397 Ge*
The tunnel–3,212 yds long–was completed in 1841 as part of the Great Western Railway. At one time there were said to be 4,000 men working on the tunnel, and in the five years it took to build there were nearly 100 fatalities.
Location: 5 miles NE of Bath at Box on A4.

Boxted *Suffolk*   *Map: 399 Fe*
CHURCH OF THE HOLY TRINITY A flint-and-stone church, thought to have been built by an outlaw, Gilbert de Bek, as a penance exacted by the Abbot of Edmundsbury between 1199 and 1216.

The church has the private pew of the Poleys–a family associated with Boxted for over 600 years. Such pews were raised above the general floor level of the church for the practical purpose of keeping out draughts and dogs, as well as to emphasise the social superiority of their occupants. Pews were partitioned to separate the family from its low-born retainers.

Holy Trinity has a 17th-century effigy of Sir John Poley, who may have been immortalised in the celebrated nursery rhyme: "Frog who would a wooing go, with a roly poly, gammon and spinach." Rowley, Poley, Bacon and Greene are all families still living in Suffolk.

The church is in Boxted Hall park.
Location: 10 miles S of Bury St Edmunds off B1066.

Bradford *W. Yorks.*   *Map: 391 Fb*
BOLLING HALL During the Civil War, in 1642, Royalist artillery kept Bradford under siege. When the town was finally captured, the Duke of Newcastle used Bolling Hall as his headquarters.

The main part of the house is 17th century; additions include an 18th-century wing.

The house is now a local-history museum.
Location: 1 mile SE of Bradford off A650.
INDUSTRIAL MUSEUM A typical four-storey spinning mill of 1875 is now used as a museum. The mill-owner's house near by is also a museum, refurnished in its original Victorian style.

The woollen industry had existed in the region for centuries, but with the introduction of the steam-engine to textile manufacture, Bradford–near Yorkshire's extensive coalfields–became the major centre.

Some of the machinery and allied equipment used in the area can be seen in the museum.
Location: 2 miles NE of Bradford off A658.

Bradford-on-Avon *Wilts.*   *Map: 397 Ge*
AVONCLIFF AQUEDUCT The Kennet and Avon canal passes close to the south of Bradford-on-Avon, and one of its main features is the Avoncliff Aqueduct, a handsome three-arched structure designed by John Rennie in 1804. The canal is dry at this point.

Location: 1 mile W of town adjacent to Avoncliff Station.
CHURCH OF ST LAWRENCE A rare survival of Saxon architecture, said to have been founded by St Aldhelm–an 8th-century scholar and monk.

From the 12th century onwards it was used as a charnel house–where dead bodies or bones were kept–until by the 19th century it was "lost", hedged in by surrounding buildings. By this time the nave was used as a school and the chancel converted into a cottage. It was two sculpted angels, high up on the east wall of the nave, that led to the discovery of the church, and its subsequent restoration.
Location: 9 miles SE of Bath on A363.
TEXTILE TOWN During the 17th century, when Gloucester, Somerset and Wiltshire were the great sheep-farming counties of the west of England, Bradford-on-Avon developed as the centre of the wool trade. Workers wove cloth at home, until water-powered spinning mills were built in the 1790s.

There was a riot in 1791 when workers tried to stop the introduction of machines, but the age of domestic weaving was over. By the 19th century, there were more than 30 cloth factories in the town. They flourished for most of the century until, finally, the rubber industry was introduced in the 1890s.

Many of the old buildings in the town, including mills, weavers' cottages and merchants' houses from the earlier period of Bradford-on-Avon prosperity, are now part of a conservation area (see also pp. 62–63).

WHERE SAXONS WORSHIPPED

Small and atmospheric, the Church of St Lawrence at Bradford-on-Avon is one of the oldest buildings in Britain to have survived intact. It may have been built by an 8th-century monk, St Aldhelm.

Where wool was wealth

THREE CENTURIES OF BUILDINGS SURVIVE AT BRADFORD-ON-AVON IN WILTSHIRE AS MONUMENTS TO ITS HISTORY AS A CENTRE OF THE WOOL TRADE

In the 17th century Dutch and Flemish weavers were encouraged to settle in England, bringing their skills to the great sheep-farming counties of Gloucester, Somerset and Wiltshire.

By the 1630s, Bradford-on-Avon was a thriving centre of the woollen cloth trade, and in the early 1700s Daniel Defoe – author of *Robinson Crusoe* – observed: "Clothiers in the county were worth ten thousand to forty thousand pounds a man."

The merchants handed out wool to be spun and woven by workers in the town and outlying

---

BRADFORD-ON-AVON'S BUILDINGS

It was the wool trade of the 17th and 18th centuries that provided the prosperity reflected in the fine buildings of Bradford-on-Avon. But it was the town's nearness to Bath and Bristol, and the use of local stone that gave the architecture its character.

The map indicates some of the buildings that span the growth of the town. The mills are now used by the rubber industry; the houses are privately owned and not open to the public.

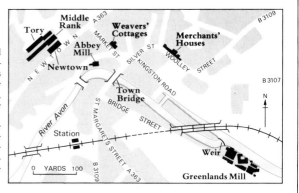

HILLSIDE HOUSING *Three long terraces range along the hillside overlooking the town. The Tory (above) has largely 18th-century houses – some of the kitchens dug out of the hillside; the Middle Rank and Newtown (right) are 17th-century weavers' cottages.*

WOOLLEY STREET *One of the grand Georgian houses that were built by cloth merchants, clearly reflecting their enormous wealth and power (left).*

They bought the wool from farmers and sold the cloth after it had been woven locally.

WEIR *This was built in the 1840s to regulate the water supply to the mills on the banks of the Avon (right). Water-power was used to drive the mill machinery.*

MARKET STREET *Typical weavers' cottages that were built about 1670.*

The ground-floor rooms with the large windows – only the wooden frames are modern – are thought to have held looms. Weavers worked at home until machines were introduced in 1791.

districts – spinners and weavers working in their own homes. In 1791 the workers rioted when machines were first introduced, but their action was in vain. Soon after 1800 there were 30 water-powered cloth factories in Bradford-on-Avon. In 1848 Stephen Moulton founded the rubber industry in the town, as the centre of the woollen trade began to shift to Yorkshire. By 1905 the last of Bradford-on-Avon's cloth mills had closed.

GREENLANDS MILL *A complex of five-storeyed buildings that was erected in the late 18th century, beside the River Avon. It was the largest cloth mill in the town and contained offices as well as long, well-lit workrooms.*

TOWN BRIDGE *The 14th-century bridge and its chapel were altered in the 17th century – the chapel converted into a lock-up. Since it was often occupied by drunks it became known locally as the Blind House.*

ABBEY MILL *A five-storeyed cloth factory that was built in the 1870s. It was the last cloth mill to be put up in the West Country.*

Brading *Isle of Wight*   *Map: 398 Ca*
A Roman villa that in its final form during the 4th century had three blocks surrounding a courtyard. Only the central one remains visible.

The best feature is its mosaic paving, which shows Orpheus charming animals with a lyre, and a unique and strange scene of a cock-headed man, a hut and two griffins – believed to be symbolic of a rite connected with the afterlife.

The best preserved floor has mythological panels surrounding a head of Medusa.
Location: 1½ miles SW of Brading off A3055.

Bradley Manor *Devon*   *Map: 397 Db*
An unaltered early-15th-century manor house with rough-cast and lime-washed walls. There is a great hall, buttery, solar and chapel.
Location: ½ mile SW of Newton Abbot off A381.

Bradwell-on-Sea *Essex*   *Map: 399 Fd*
CHURCH OF ST PETER'S-ON-THE-WALL The church was founded by the Christian missionary St Cedd in 654 – largely built of materials from the Roman fort of Othona, within which it stands.

The first known church built in Essex and one of the oldest in England, it has changed little from St Cedd's day.
Location: 21 miles E of Chelmsford (A414, B1010, then minor roads and track).

Braemar Castle *Grampian*   *Map: 387 Eb*
This 17th-century Scottish fortress was built by the Earl of Mar to counter the growing power of the Farquharson family in the neighbourhood, as well as to serve as a hunting seat.

The castle was burned by the Farquharsons in the Claverhouse revolt of 1689, bought by them in 1732, and restored in the 18th century.
Location: 57 miles W of Aberdeen on A93.

Bramber *W. Sussex*   *Map: 398 Db*
CASTLE Originally a motte and bailey, built about 1073, whose wooden palisade was later replaced by a stone wall. Further additions were made in the 13th and 14th centuries.

King John seized the castle in 1208 when he outlawed William de Braose, a former ally.
ST MARY'S In the Middle Ages the monks of Sele Priory at Beeding were wardens of the bridge across the River Adur. St Mary's is the wing of the 15th-century courtyard house in which they lived and gave shelter to travellers.
Location: 10 miles NW of Hove off A283.

Bramhall *Greater Manchester*   *Map: 393 Ff*
BRAMALL HALL Started in the 14th century and extended in the 1590s, Bramall Hall is one of the finest timber-framed houses in England.

There is a splendid spiral staircase leading to the Elizabethan drawing-room, and among the original furnishings are a 16 ft long high table held together by wooden pegs, a rare Flemish travelling bed and a Jacobean four-poster.

A tapestry in the master bedroom is the work of Dame Dorothy Davenport – one of the owners in the 1590s. It took her 36 years to complete. The house was restored in the 1880s.
Location: 3 miles S of Stockport off A5102.

Bramham Park *W. Yorks.*   *Map: 394 Bd*
Lord Bingley, Queen Anne's Chancellor of the Exchequer, built the house in the early 1700s and

is thought to have laid out the gardens. These are in the style of Le Notre's renowned gardens at Versailles, with broad walks.
Location: 4 miles S of Wetherby on A1.

Brampton *Cambs.*   *Map: 398 Df*
PEPYS' HOUSE Samuel Pepys, the celebrated diarist, lived here with his parents when attending Huntingdon Grammar School in 1644. Pepys owned the house from 1664 to 1680.
Location: 2 miles W of Huntingdon on A141.

Brandsby Hall *N. Yorks.*   *Map: 394 Be*
In the grounds of this mid-18th-century house is a well-preserved ice-house which, when in use, was almost as efficient for preserving meat as a deep freeze.
There are ceilings by Guiseppe Cortese, an Italian craftsman who lived in Yorkshire.
Location: 16 miles N of York off B1363.

Braunston Junction *Northants.*   *Map: 398 Be*
A small settlement at the meeting place of the Grand Union and Oxford Canals. It is one of the few places where working narrow-boats can be seen – especially in the winter months – carrying such cargoes as sand, gravel and coal.
Location: 7 miles S of Rugby (A426 then A45).

Breamore *Hants.*   *Map: 398 Ab*
BREAMORE HOUSE An Elizabethan manor house with tapestries, furniture and paintings. In the kitchen there is a display of copperware and a wheeled beer wagon, used in the servants' hall, from which staff filled their tankards.
Location: 8 miles S of Salisbury off A338.
COUNTRYSIDE AND CARRIAGE MUSEUMS Set in the grounds of Breamore House, the agricultural exhibits are arranged according to the seasonal activities of the farming year. The rural industries section has a blacksmith's and a wheelwright's shop, and a dairy and a brewery. There is also a reconstruction of a farm-worker's cottage before

the days when electricity was installed.
The Carriage Museum in the 17th-century stables includes the "Red Rover" – the last stage-coach to run between London and Southampton. It ran a regular service for over 40 years.

Brecon *Powys*   *Map: 392 Db*
CASTLE Started as a motte and bailey in the 1090s, Brecon Castle was enlarged during the 12th and 13th centuries.
It was fought over by the Welsh and English several times, and finally passed to Henry Bolingbroke – later Henry IV – through marriage.
Owain Glyndwr tried to take it by storm in 1404 but failed, and the constable of the castle was rewarded with an annuity for his stout defence.
Location: Castle Sq.
CATHEDRAL This was built as a priory church in the 13th century, administered by the monks of Battle Abbey, and made a cathedral in 1923.
Among the cathedral's contents are a medieval alms dish, a carved Norman font, and a cresset stone – the largest of its kind in Wales.
The stone has 30 cup-shaped hollows in it. Each contained oil and a floating wick to make a bright and effective night-light.
Charles I stayed at the cathedral towards the end of the Civil War in 1645.
Location: N of Priory Hill.

Brecon Y Gaer *Powys*   *Map: 392 Db*
The 2nd-century remains of a Roman fort that guarded the junction of at least five roads.
Three double-carriageway gates, and part of the defensive wall are still standing.
Location: 3 miles W of Brecon off minor road.

Bredon *Heref. & Worcs.*   *Map: 393 Fb*
CHURCH OF ST GILES Soaring 161 ft above the surrounding countryside, the spire symbolises the wealthy days of the 14th century, when additions in the Early English style were made

SURVIVOR FROM THE AGE OF STEAM
Bertha – *the first exhibit that started the Bressingham Steam-Engine Museum – was built in 1909. A 10 ton machine, with a 7 h.p. engine, it was largely used for farming work. It was linked by a belt to drive a threshing drum and straw elevator before the development of the combine harvester, which came into general use in the 1930s.*

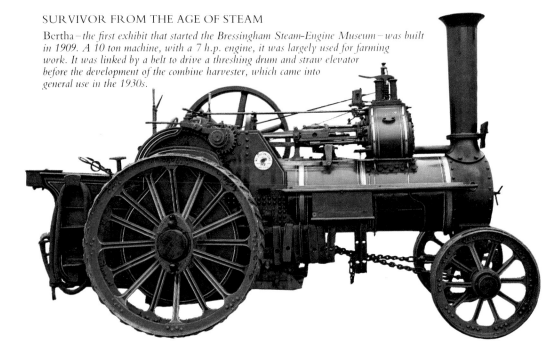

to the Norman church – founded about 1180.

St Giles's great treasure is an unusual set of 14th-century heraldic tiles – probably the finest in the county. There are 86 tiles in all, depicting 39 different coats of arms. An explanatory key is on the wall, beside the organ.

On the floor of the chancel there is a memorial brass to Bishop Prideaux. Deprived of his bishopric by Thomas Cromwell, for his loyalty to the Stuart kings, the bishop died in poverty at Bredon Rectory in 1650.

One of the arched tombs in the south wall contains a shield, depicting two hands holding a heart. The tomb is said to contain the heart of a Crusader from Bredon, who fell in the Holy Land during the wars with the Saracens.
Location: 3 miles NE of Tewkesbury off B4080.
TITHE BARN A 14th-century tithe barn built of local stone, to hold rents paid to the See of Worcester. In one of the porches there is an upper room with a fireplace, where the bailiff who managed the barn worked.
Location: Near the church.

Breedon on the Hill *Leics.*   *Map: 394 Ba*
CHURCH OF ST MARY AND ST HARDULPH Set within the ramparts of an Iron Age fort, the Norman and Early English church occupies the site of a Saxon monastery, sacked by the Danes in 873.

Surviving from the monastery are nearly 30 slabs of carving from a fragmented frieze – among the finest Saxon remains in England.
Location: 5 miles NE of Ashby de la Zouch off A453.

Bressingham *Norfolk*   *Map: 399 Ff*
STEAM MUSEUM The most comprehensive museum of steam power in Britain, with 14 traction and road engines, and rail loco-motives – including 18 standard gauge, main line and industrial locomotives.

Steam-hauled rides are given on miniature and narrow-gauge trains through 5 miles of the Bressingham Hall estates, which include steam-driven fairground roundabouts with organs, and 6 acres of informal gardens.
Location: 13 miles E of Thetford on A1066.

Bridge of Weir *Strathclyde*   *Map: 388 Cd*
QUARRIER'S HOMES Born at Greenock in 1829, William Quarrier worked in Glasgow before he was eight years old to help support his widowed mother and two sisters. He was often cold and hungry and vowed that if he ever had the means he would help destitute children.

By the age of 12 he was a shoemaker and by 35 owned three fine shops. An encounter with a starving match-seller reminded him of his childhood vow. To realise his dream of Cottage Homes, where groups of children under a house-father and mother could be brought up with a sense of security, he bought land at Bridge of Weir and in 1878 opened the first buildings.

When Quarrier died in 1903 there were already 64 buildings on the site, including the first tuberculosis sanatorium in Scotland. There are now nearly 90 buildings, with 450 children.
Location: 6 miles SE of Port Glasgow off A761.

Bridgnorth *Salop*   *Map: 393 Fd*
CASTLE The rectangular great tower leans at nearly 20 degrees from the vertical – caused by the cliff being mined during the Civil War.

The tower was built by Henry II in the 1150s on a motte and bailey guarding the River Severn between Shrewsbury and Worcester.
Location: East Castle St.
STATION The terminus of the Severn Valley Railway, opened in 1862. A regular passenger service is now run by a society of the same name, which owns more than 30 steam locomotives. These range from a side-tank engine, which started its working life on the Manchester Ship Canal Railway, to a splendid Great Western Railway locomotive – the last of the 2251 class.

Much of the rolling stock is GWR restored to its original livery.
Location: Town centre off Hollybush Rd.
TOWN HALL This was built in 1646, after most of Bridgnorth had been burned to the ground by the Parliamentarians during the Civil War. The half-timbered top storey was originally part of a farm-building in Much Wenlock.
Location: High St.

Brighton *E. Sussex*   *Map: 399 Da*
STATION Brighton Station, terminus of the London, Brighton and South Coast Railway, was designed by David Mocatta and opened in 1841.

The train shed (the covered section of the platform) with its slender colonnades was designed in 1881.
Location: North end of Queen's Rd.
THE ROYAL PAVILION In 1752 a certain Dr Russell published a treatise entitled *A Dissertation on the use of Sea Water in Diseases of the Glands*. It recommended not only sea-bathing, but also that sea water should be drunk – hot with a little milk or cream of tartar. The idea was disagreeable enough to catch on at once with fashionable society, always in search of health and relief from the consequences of over-indulgence, and within a few years a number of small south-coast fishing villages had been transformed into fashionable resorts.

Brighton was one of the first of these and its reputation as a centre of frivolity and fashion was well established by 1783 when the Prince of Wales – later George IV – made his first visit.

The prince, just 21 and escaping for the first time from the repressive influence of his father and the restrictions of court, was delighted with the place. He soon adopted the role of leader of a society which seemed to be permanently on holiday.

In 1785 he met and secretly married Mrs Fitzherbert – beautiful, ample and twice a widow at 25. In order to be near her (for she lived in her own villa in Brighton) the prince took a lease of a "superior farmhouse".

In 1787 the farmhouse was greatly enlarged and renamed the Marine Pavilion. It was given a central rotunda with a shallow dome, bow windows towards the sea and an overall surfacing of white stucco – or cement.

By 1823, and with the aid of his architect, John Nash, the prince's pavilion had been transformed into the most exotic and outrageous of all European palaces.

Queen Victoria found the pavilion too public and in the 1850s it was sold to the corporation of Brighton, who own it today. (See overleaf.)
Location: Centre of town on Old Steine.

"Prinny's" palace by the sea

A BLEND OF TALENTS AND THE PRINCE REGENT'S EXTRAVAGANCE HELPED TO
TRANSFORM A FARMHOUSE BY THE SEA INTO AN ORIENTAL PALACE

In 1815 John Nash was appointed by the Prince of Wales – later George IV – to finish the final stages in the transformation of the Royal Pavilion, at Brighton. Nearly 30 years earlier it had been a farmhouse; but a string of eminent architects – including Henry Holland – had slowly turned it into a palace.

Nash finished it with an Islamic fancy-dress exterior, adding domes and minarets, and pierced Gothic balconies. Tall windows with fanlights in the form of trumpet-shaped catalpa leaves completed the disguise.

As King George IV, "Prinny" made his last visit to the pavilion in 1827.

THE PAVILION SKYLINE *The domes and minarets were greeted in the 1820s with delight by many, and scorn by a few for their extravagant vulgarity.*

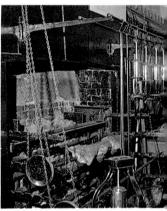

THE GREAT KITCHEN *Built in 1815 the vast kitchen (left) was where the celebrated Carême, the Prince Regent's chef, reigned. One of the banquets listed 116 dishes. The revolving spits (above) and many other fittings have survived.*

MUSIC ROOM *Guests retired to the Music Room (above) from the Banqueting Hall, where the Prince Regent – an ardent lover of music – often sang to them in his bass voice. His style was said to have been superior to that of a professional singer, despite the fact that he sang by ear. The magnificent scale of the room – 60 ft by 40 ft wide – made it ideal for use as a ballroom. The engraving (left) shows it in use in 1824.*

Bristol *Avon*   *Map: 397 Fe*

CATHEDRAL When Edward II was brutally murdered in Berkeley Castle in 1327, it had far-reaching consequences on the development of the abbey that was to become Bristol Cathedral.

Originally the Abbey Church of St Augustine's, it was established in 1148 by Robert Fitzhardinge, lord of nearby Berkeley Castle. When the king's body was brought to the abbey for burial, Abbot Knowle refused to accept it, out of respect for the Berkeleys. His loyalty proved to be expensive, for the body was taken to Gloucester Abbey, where public sympathy and pilgrimages transformed the king's tomb into a shrine, bringing wealth for the subsequent glorification of Gloucester's cathedral.

Meanwhile, St Augustine's fortunes declined. The Bishop of Worcester recorded at the time that it had: "*. . . fallen into such destitution that the canons, often at the hour of midday meal, have nothing on their board to eat or drink, having been compelled to send to the township of Bristol to obtain the bare necessities of living, either by loan or by gift.*"

In 1542, four years after the abbey was dissolved, it was raised to the status of cathedral, additions were made in successive centuries and the cathedral was sympathetically restored in the 19th century.

Although much of the abbey was destroyed at the Dissolution, what survived is of outstanding interest. Among the Norman remains are the Chapter House – where monks met to conduct their daily business – with a splendid vaulted interior. Against the south wall of the south transept there is a winding night stair. Every evening, the monks descended from the dormitory to the church for the midnight service – the longest one of the day. The worn stone steps clearly evoke these nightly journeys. Near the top of the stair, where a door leads to the treasury, a step unexpectedly changes direction – a trap for the unsuspecting thief.

Among the many monuments in the cathedral is one of Maurice, the 9th Earl of Berkeley who was ransomed for £2,000, following his capture by the French at Poitiers in 1356. There is also a gruesome effigy of Bishop Bush – the first Bishop of Bristol – portrayed like a corpse. It is the first Renaissance monument in the cathedral.

The cathedral has a rare 16th-century brass candelabra and – in the choir – a window said to have been donated by Nell Gwynne as a thanksgiving for her recovery from illness.
Location: College Green, near the Council House.

CHURCH OF ST MARK Also known as the Lord Mayor's Chapel, St Mark's is the only church in England owned by a corporation. It was formerly attached to a medieval hospital – now demolished – that was bought at the time of the Dissolution by the civic corporation. The church has been the mayor's official place of worship since 1721.

The church is renowned for its abundance of monuments, including mail-clad effigies of the Berkeley family – lords of the nearby castle.
Location: College Green.

CHURCH OF ST MARY REDCLIFFE St Mary's was visited by Elizabeth I in 1574, and described by her as the "fairest and goodliest" church in England. It remains the finest example of Gothic architecture in the county, with the character and

---

THE ENGLISH AT THE SEASIDE

Fashion at the seaside in the 1870s

In Scarborough in 1660, a Dr Wittie published a book recommending the use of sea water both for bathing and for drinking, claiming that it helped in "drying up superfluous humours, and preserving them from putrefaction; kills all manner of worms".

Scarborough already enjoyed popularity as a spa, where visitors took the "water cure" for ailments ranging from "windiness" to "leprosie". By the 1730s it was Britain's first seaside resort. In the early days, bathing was far from pleasurable, bathers taking early morning dips in the North Sea, often in winter, when – as physicians pointed out – "the pores were closed". It was other attractions that offered the real pleasures – Assembly Rooms for taking tea, playing cards, dancing or gossiping; the library, theatre and chapel for the less frivolous.

In 1750, Dr Russell moved from Lewes in Sussex to Brighthelmstone, a fishing village – that later became known as Brighton. His advocacy of bathing there made it a popular resort with Londoners. Dr Samuel Johnson was one of those who made a visit in 1782. He took a dip at six o'clock in the morning and found the experience "cold, but pleasant".

When George III was king, his son "the Prince of Pleasure" provided his unacknowledged wife, Mrs Fitzherbert, with a villa at Brighton, giving royal approval to the idea of a holiday by the sea. In 1789, the king himself, recovering from an illness, visited Weymouth and watched by crowds, swam to the sound of the town band playing *God Save the King*.

Both men and women were known to seek isolated spots to swim naked; but most undressed in bathing machines – wheeled huts – and emerged in the water to swim in sack-like clothing.

Not until the close of the century did bathing costumes become more practical and flattering, by which time a holiday by the sea – if only for a day – was considered desirable by all classes.

Bathing and beachwear in the 1870s

proportions of a cathedral.

The origins of St Mary's are uncertain but most of the present church was built between 1280 and 1380.

In the room above the two-storeyed north porch, the boy poet Thomas Chatterton – who committed suicide in 1750 when only 17 – wrote the "Thomas Rowley" verses, passing them off as the genuine works of a 15th-century monk.

THE PILGRIM'S DOORWAY

The north porch of St Mary Redcliffe was built about 1280. Inside is where the original shrine of Our Lady stood – complete with iron grilles – that was visited by pilgrims making their offerings at the church.

STATION OR CATHEDRAL?

Brunel's train shed at Temple Meads Station has a wooden mock hammer-beam roof that was built in 1840. The shed is now in use as a car park.

The roof of the nave has 1,200 bosses – carved knob-like projections on the ribs of the vaults. During restoration work in 1740, the women of Bristol gave their gold jewellery to be melted down and used to gild the bosses – a remarkable testament to their civic pride.

Location: SE of City Centre at junction of Redcliffe Way and Redcliffe Hill.

CLIFTON SUSPENSION BRIDGE The spectacular road bridge high across the Avon Gorge was the earliest and most treasured engineering venture of Isambard Kingdom Brunel. His design was the winner of a competition held in 1829–30, and the foundations for the west tower base were laid in 1831. But unrest at Bristol docks and shortage of funds continually held up work; in 1851 it was abandoned and the suspension chains sold. When Brunel died in 1859, only the west tower base was in position. The bridge was completed as a tribute to his memory, and opened in 1864. The chains used were from Brunel's Hungerford Bridge across the Thames, which had been replaced by Charing Cross railway bridge.

Location: The Portway through the Avon Gorge runs under the bridge.

SS GREAT BRITAIN The world's first iron-built, propeller-driven ship, *Great Britain* was launched from Wapping Dock, Bristol, on July 19, 1843. Designed by Isambard Kingdom Brunel, she was the world's largest ship, 322 ft long and 3,270 tons, and was not only a steamship but also a six-masted sailing ship. Rounding Cape Horn in 1886 she lost her topmasts, and struggled back to the Falkland Islands to become a storage hulk. In 1970 she was towed back to Bristol, and installed in Wapping Dock for restoration.

Location: The docks are SW of City Centre off Cumberland Rd.

TEMPLE MEADS STATION The terminus of Brunel's Great Western Railway – between Paddington and Bristol – was built in 1840. Its mock-Tudor frontage has since been altered.

Location: Temple Gate, SE of city centre.

Brixton Windmill *Gtr London*   *Map: 399 Dc*

Brixton Mill was built in 1816 to grind corn, and has a five-storeyed brick tower with a boat-shaped cap.

It was one of 12 mills in the borough of Lambeth, built to serve the rapid spread of housing in that area. It worked by wind until too many houses deprived it of wind in the 1880s, after which it continued to grind meal using a gas-engine.

Location: $\frac{3}{4}$ mile S of Brixton Station, in Blenheim Gardens SW2, off Brixton Hill (A23).

Brixworth *Northants.*   *Map: 398 Cf*

CHURCH OF ALL SAINTS This is the largest Anglo-Saxon church to have survived in Britain. It was probably built in the 7th century and was part of a monastery until 870. The spire and belfry are 14th-century work.

Location: 7 miles N of Northampton off A508.

Brodick *Arran, Strathclyde*   *Map: 388 Bc*

CASTLE AND GARDENS Brodick Castle was originally a Viking fort, converted in the 14th century into a stone L-shaped tower house.

There are two gardens: the formal walled garden dated 1710, with sub-tropical shrubs, and the 60 acre woodland or "wild" garden, regarded as one of the best rhododendron gardens in Europe.

Location: 11½ miles by ferry from Ardrossan to Isle of Arran, then 1½ miles N of Brodick.

ROSABURN HERITAGE CENTRE An old "smiddy" (blacksmith's workshop) where local smiths can be seen demonstrating their skills in ironwork, and shoeing ponies. Farm implements are on show at the smiddy, and a cottage opposite re-

creates a typical mid-19th-century Arran home.

Location: 1 mile N of Brodick.

Bromham Watermill Beds.   Map: 398 De
This 17th-century brick and half-timbered watermill occupies the site of earlier mills near a medieval bridge. There were originally two sets of corn-milling equipment in the mill, driven by two water-wheels. A late-19th-century water-

CLIFTON BRIDGE AS IT MIGHT HAVE BEEN

In 1753 a Bristol wine merchant, William Vick, left money to accumulate for building a bridge across the Avon Gorge in the Clifton district of Bristol. By 1829 the sum of £10,000 had accumulated, and a competition to find a suitable design was held in 1829–30.

TALL TOWERS *Thomas Telford, who designed the Menai Bridge, submitted an unadventurous plan.*

SUSPENDED CITY *This fantastic design had been put forward by William Bridges in 1765.*

AN ENGINEER'S WORK OF ART

Spanning 702 ft across the Avon Gorge, the Clifton Suspension Bridge was designed by Isambard Kingdom Brunel, who wanted it to harmonise with the grandeur of the scenery around it. His plan was daring – it called for a longer suspended span than any that had yet been built, and this at a breathtaking height of 245 ft above the river. Brunel did not live to see his vision take shape. The bridge was completed after his death in 1859, to a modified design drawn up by Sir John Hawkshaw and W. H. Barlow.

FIRST VOYAGE TO AUSTRALIA

The SS Great Britain dropping the pilot at Liverpool Bar at the start of the ship's first voyage to Australia in 1852. The voyage was controversial – taking 83 days rather than the anticipated 60.

wheel and gearing remain in the middle of the mill but the eastern wheel has gone.

The roof contains the typical galleried bin floor – where grain was stored before being ground – found in a large trading mill.
Location: 3 miles W of Bedford on A428.

Bromsgrove *Heref. & Worcs.*   *Map: 393 Fc*
AVONCROFT MUSEUM OF BUILDINGS An open-air museum, where buildings ranging from the 14th to the 19th centuries have been restored and re-erected. The agricultural buildings include a 16th-century barn from Herefordshire, and an 18th-century granary and wagon store from Worcestershire.

There is an 18th-century windmill, brought from Warwickshire. It has a pair of stones driven by two common sails and two spring-controlled shuttered sails. The mill is now operational, with occasional weekend demonstrations.
Location: 2½ miles SW of Bromsgrove (A38 then A4024).

CHURCH OF ST JOHN THE BAPTIST The churchyard has two stones, standing side by side, marking the graves of two railwaymen who died when their locomotive exploded in 1840. Both stones have carvings of engines; one has a poem that starts:

My engine now is cold and still.
No water does my boiler fill.
My coke affords its flame no more.
My days of usefulness are o'er.
Location: Town centre off A448.

PRESERVING THE PAST

The open-air museum at Bromsgrove consists of buildings that were in danger of demolition, brought from surrounding areas and re-erected on the site for permanent preservation and study.

CRUCK-FRAMED BARN *A 16th or early-17th-century cruck-framed barn that was originally on a farm near Herefordshire. The spaces between the oak framing are filled with a latticework of oak slats.*

18TH-CENTURY GRANARY *The elm-framed building was raised off the ground to keep the grain away from damp and vermin. Dogs lived beneath the steps in kennels to keep rats and thieves at bay.*

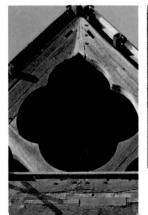

SKILFUL CARPENTRY *Parts of the Guesten Hall roof – guesten is the medieval plural of guest – illustrate jointing techniques in the oak framing.*

Adhesives and new wood have been used for repairs, but the original joints were pulled together and held by wooden pegs – without bolts or nails.

Bronllys Castle *Powys*   *Map: 393 Db*
A military fortress, built in the 1170s on the site of an earlier Norman motte and bailey. The cylindrical tower is one of the earliest built in Wales.
Location: ½ mile SE of Bronllys on A479.

Brontë Parsonage see Haworth

Brooke *Leics.*   *Map: 394 Ca*
CHURCH OF ST PETER A remote and fascinating medieval church that was reconstructed during the 16th century, and sympathetically restored during the 19th century. The Elizabethan interior has a stone-flagged floor, whitewashed walls, box pews, pulpit, reading desk and screen.

There is graffiti in the chancel stalls, thought to have been carved by bored parishioners in the 17th century.

In the north chapel there are the Rawlings' gravestones. Here, Henry Rawlings buried his first four wives in 1713, 1717, 1718 and 1722 respectively; his fifth wife buried him in 1742.
Location: 2 miles S of Oakham on minor road.

Brougham *Cumbria*   *Map: 391 Ed*
CASTLE The castle, built in the 1170s, came into the possession of Lady Ann Clifford during the 17th century. She used her wealth to restore several castles, including Brougham – where, in 1676, she died when nearly 90 years old.
Location: 2 miles E of Penrith off A66.
CHURCH OF ST NINIAN One of the few churches started in England during the Commonwealth periods, 1649–53. Despite 19th-century alterations, the interior and furnishings are still much as they were when completed in 1660.

There is a poor box dated 1666 – an obligatory piece of church equipment following the passing of Elizabeth's Poor Law in 1572.
Location: 3 miles E of Penrith N of A66.

Brough Castle *Cumbria*   *Map: 391 Ed*
"If this castle does not yield, no one shall be let out alive when it falls." Thus, William the Lion, King of Scotland, instructed his troops when they set siege to Brough Castle in 1174. It is not known if the king kept his word but the Scots devastated most of the castle.

In 1521 the castle was again attacked and burned by the Scots, and in 1659–62 restored by its owner, Lady Ann Clifford, who converted the great tower into a fine residence.
Location: 8 miles SE of Appleby-in-Westmorland off A66.

Broughton Castle *Oxon.*   *Map: 398 Be*
Just before and during the early part of the Civil War, Broughton Castle was the secret gathering place for opponents of Charles I. After the first major battle of the war at Edgehill, the Royalists besieged and captured the castle.
Location: 3 miles SW of Banbury on B4035.

Broxburn *Lothian*   *Map: 389 Dd*
ALMOND AQUEDUCT The Edinburgh and Glasgow Union Canal crosses the River Almond on a tall, five-arched aqueduct, built in the 1820s. The main structure is stone with an iron trough set into the masonry. The canal is no longer used.
Location: 2 miles SE of Broxburn (11 miles W of Edinburgh) on minor roads to Clifton Hall.

Bruton *Somerset*   *Map: 397 Fd*
CHURCH OF ST MARY Charles I and Charles II both worshipped at St Mary's while staying in Bruton; the Royal Arms of Charles II are above the north door. The church is largely 14th and 15th century, with 15th-century timber roofs.

There is a monument to Sir Maurice Berkeley and his two wives. Berkeley was Henry VIII's standard bearer and bought an adjacent abbey from the king when it was dissolved in 1539. The Berkeley family, who built the exquisite chancel in 1743, bought land in London – hence Berkeley Square.
Location: 7 miles SE of Shepton Mallet (A371 then B3081).

Brympton d'Evercy *Somerset*   *Map: 397 Fc*
PRIEST HOUSE The priest house and stables, in the grounds of the 15th-century house, are used as a museum relating to the rural life of the area. It has a collection of agricultural and craft hand-tools; a display of cider-making equipment; and a rare collection of unusual implements connected with cooperage – that is making barrels.
Location: 2 miles W of Yeovil off A3088.

Bryncelli-Ddu *Anglesey, Gwynedd Map: 392 Cf*
This large stone passage grave (a chambered tomb with an entrance passage) was built about 2000 BC, on the site of a former ritual henge – a monument of upright stones and ditches arranged in a circle. Cremated bones were found in the passage grave during excavations.

Outside the entrance, a stone-and-timber enclosure contained the bones of an ox, presumably sacrificed at the building or closing of the tomb.
Location: 3 miles SW of Menai Bridge off A4080.

Buckfastleigh *Devon*   *Map: 397 Db*
DART VALLEY RAILWAY The Great Western Railway opened a branch line from Ashburton to Totnes in 1872. The line was closed in 1962 and reopened in 1969: passengers are now carried on the 7 miles from Buckfastleigh and towards Totnes.

Visitors can travel in steam-hauled trains, the rolling stock of which has been restored to its original GWR livery. The return trip from Buckfastleigh takes an hour and a quarter.
Location: Buckfastleigh Station is at the junction of A38 and A384.

Buckland Abbey *Devon*   *Map: 396 Cb*
A Cistercian abbey of 1278 that was granted to Sir Richard Grenville in 1541. Secular owners, among them Sir Francis Drake, have lived in the abbey-church, and have adapted it for use as a house. Now a naval and Devon folk museum, it has relics of Grenville and Drake – including Sir Francis' celebrated drum. There is a medieval tithe barn in the garden.
Location: 11 miles N of Plymouth off A386.

Buckland Rectory *Glos.*   *Map: 393 Fb*
Probably the oldest rectory in England still used for its original purpose. It was built in the 15th century by William Grafton, priest at the nearby church of St Michael's. The rectory has a fine hammer-beam roof and staircase.
Location: 14 miles NE of Cheltenham off A46.

Bucklers Hard *Hants.*   *Map: 398 Ba*
MARITIME MUSEUM Bucklers Hard was once a major ship-building centre. During the 18th century the hard gravel bank where ships could be grounded and the sheltered estuary, with its proximity to Portsmouth, was an ideal site for building ships. The shipyard built, among many other vessels for the Royal Navy, the *Agamemnon*, commanded by Nelson in 1793.

The museum has many original documents, drawings, models and relics of Nelson.
Location: 2 miles SE of Beaulieu off B3054.

Bude Canal *Cornwall*   *Map: 396 Cc*
The canal, with its sea-lock and stone breakwater, was built between 1819 and 1823 to carry sand from Bude–it had a high lime content and was valued as a fertiliser–to inland farms.

Coal was brought from South Wales and local produce was exported.

The canal declined in the mid-19th century as railways developed, and closed in 1901. There remains only the section that runs inland to Helebridge where the old wharf is still visible.
Location: W of town centre on coast.

Builth Wells *Powys*   *Map: 392 Dc*
One of the ten castles built by Edward I in the 13th century–part of his conquest of Wales.

In 1282, Llywelyn the Last was a fugitive from King Edward, and tried to find shelter at the castle. Refused entry by the English garrison, he was making for Aberedw near by, when he was surprised by his enemies and killed.
Location: 20 miles N of Brecon on A470.

Bungay Castle *Suffolk*   *Map: 399 Gf*
Hugh Bigod, the powerful Earl of Norfolk, built Bungay Castle in 1165. Henry II, newly crowned and determined to end the anarchy of his predecessor's reign, forced Bigod to abandon the tower. The king ordered it to be mined, but work was halted when Bigod paid a cash ransom. The unfinished mine gallery can still be seen.
Location: 15 miles W of Lowestoft (A146, A1116).

Burford *Oxon.*   *Map: 398 Bd*
CHURCH OF ST JOHN THE BAPTIST In 1649, Oliver Cromwell held 340 mutinous soldiers captive in the church for three days and nights. The men had not received any pay for many months and were about to be sent to fight the Royalists in Ireland. Thwarted in their attempt to overthrow Cromwell, three of the leaders were "shot to death" in the churchyard. He reprimanded the rest from the pulpit then freed them.

The 14th-century font has a lead lining with the words "Anthony Sedley, 1649, Prisner" scratched on it.
Location: 18 miles W of Oxford off A40.

Burgh Castle *Norfolk*   *Map: 395 Ga*
This spectacular Roman fort was one of a chain built in the second half of the 3rd century to protect the coastline from Saxon pirate raids.

Three of the original walls still stand. The huge circular bastions were designed to support Roman ballistae–artillery machines capable of hurling stone balls and other missiles.
Location: 3 miles SW of Great Yarmouth off A12.

Burgh-le-Marsh *Lincs.*   *Map: 395 Eb*
WINDMILL This five-storeyed brick-tower windmill was built in 1833, with patent–shuttered and self-regulating–sails added about 1870.

The mill is still in working order and four of the floors can be inspected. There is also an exhibition relating to Lincolnshire mills and agriculture, including model windmills.
Location: 4 miles W of Skegness on A158.

Burghley House *Cambs.*   *Map: 394 Da*
England's largest Elizabethan house was begun in 1552 by William Cecil, who later became Lord Burghley, Elizabeth I's Secretary of State for 40 years. The house took 35 years to complete and survives much as Burghley conceived it, with State Apartments, the queen's bedroom, the celebrated Heaven Room–painted by Antonio Verrio–and carvings by Grinling Gibbons.

Burghley entertained scholars here, separate from his political life. On such occasions he would set aside his gown and staff, saying: "Lie thou there, Lord Treasurer."

The queen visited him at the house during his last illness. He died in 1598, aged 78.
Location: 1 mile SE of Stamford off B1081.

Burleigh Castle *Tayside*   *Map: 389 Ee*
One of the well-preserved early-16th-century tower houses in Scotland. The main roof has gone but the angle tower roof is intact. The tower entrance has gunloops in the walls.
Location: 2 miles NE of Kinross (A992 then A911).

Burnley *Lancs.*   *Map: 391 Eb*
CANAL To savour the 19th-century character of Burnley–one of the great cotton towns of the north–walk along the towpath of the Leeds and Liverpool Canal. It passes through the town centre on a high embankment, known (exaggeratedly) as "The Burnley Mile". Both sides are lined with 19th-century mills–most of them along the stretch that runs from the canal maintenance yard, near Finsley Gate Entrance.
Location: Finsley Gate Bridge, SE of town centre on Manchester road (A56).
TOWNELEY HALL A courtyard house that may have been founded in the 14th century. Later additions include a furnished Elizabethan long gallery and entrance hall, dated 1725.

BURNSWARK HORSE-BIT
An enamelled-bronze horse-bit, found on Burnswark Hill, may have been connected with the pre-Roman or Roman earthworks on the hill. It is thought to have been made in the north of Britain during the second half of the 1st century.

WARSHIP WITH CREW OF 600

More than 50 naval warships, as well as scores of merchant vessels, were built and launched from Bucklers Hard during the 18th and 19th centuries. The model of HMS Illustrious *(right and below) is one of many exhibits in the Maritime Museum – which illustrates local history when agriculture and shipbuilding were the main interests in the area. The model was made at the museum, with details taken from the original shipbuilder's drawings.*

HMS ILLUSTRIOUS *This model is of a 74-gun ship-of-the-line launched from Bucklers Hard in July 1789. She had a brief career – in 1794 she was dismasted during the war with the French Republic (1793–1801), and wrecked the following year off the coast of Genoa in a storm.*

The cut-away model suggests the scale of the original ship, which was 168 ft long, 46 ft wide and had a gross displacement of 1,603 tons. About 3,000 cartloads or tons of wood were used to make such a ship, involving the felling of about 60 acres of mature trees.

There were 600 in the crew when going into battle, slightly fewer at other times. A few livestock were carried in the manger – a compartment in the bows – to provide a limited amount of fresh meat and milk.

Beneath the manger was a larger compartment where the sails were repaired or stowed when not in use. The lowest deck of all was used for storing food and water, and powder and cannon shot.

Just in front of the ship's bell on the upper deck at the front of the ship was the galley stove, with the galley on the deck directly beneath it, where meals were prepared.

Beneath the poop deck – the highest deck of all at the rear – was the captain's quarters.

The model in the upper picture shows a platform near the hawse hole, through which the anchor cable passed. This precariously positioned platform or "seat of ease" was one of the seamen's lavatories – there was another on the other side of the bows.

There are two museums. One displays paintings and period furniture, the other a museum of local crafts and industries.
Location: 1 mile SE of Burnley on A6114.

Burns House see Dumfries

Burnswark *Dumfs. & Gall.*　　　*Map: 389 Eb*
Two Roman camps and a hill-fort are in an area used by the Roman army for training exercises.

The Iron Age hill-fort dates from the 7th century BC, when a defensive palisade was constructed. A rampart and ditch were built later, probably in the 2nd century BC.

The first Roman camp incorporates three spectacular large mounds: The Three Brethren. They protect the north rampart and supported catapult machines for bombarding the Iron Age fort on the top of the hill.

Excavations have revealed that Roman lead sling-bolts were fired after the hill-fort had been abandoned, suggesting the "attack" was a mock-up. The second camp was also used for exercises.
Location: 2 miles N of Ecclefechan off A74.

Burstow *Surrey*　　　*Map: 399 Db*
CHURCH OF ST BARTHOLOMEW Well-preserved medieval towers are rare in England – St Bartholomew's is thought to be the best of them. The massive timber frame-work is 15th century, and carries six bells – one weighing half a ton.

Early Norman in origin, the church has Perpendicular additions and Victorian furnishings.

John Flamsteed, the first Astronomer Royal, was rector of the church in 1684. Despite a lifelong struggle against crippling illness, he produced his celebrated *British Catalogue* of 2,935 stars for the benefit of marine navigators. He was buried in an unmarked grave in the chancel.
Location: 5½ miles NE of Crawley (A264, B2036, B2037, then minor road).

Burton Agnes Hall *Humberside*　*Map: 394 De*
A Jacobean mansion that was built between 1598 and 1610 by Sir Henry Griffith. It has splendid ceilings, a Great Hall with elaborate plasterwork, and collections of Post Impressionist and Impressionist paintings.

It was near this house that one of Sir Henry Griffith's daughters, Ann, was murdered by thieves. Before she died she begged that her head should be kept in the house she loved. Nevertheless, she was buried in the churchyard. A series of apparitions were then seen, until her skull was dug up and built into the house walls. The haunting then stopped.
Location: 6 miles SW of Bridlington off A166.

Burton Constable *Humberside*   *Map: 394 Dd*
An Elizabethan house built in 1570 and set in 200 acres of park landscaped by "Capability" Brown. Robert Adam was one of the architects who remodelled the inside during the 1750s.

The house has a doll's museum in what was, during the 19th century, a small theatre. A servants' passage, through which visitors walk, gives a hint of "life below stairs".
Location: 7½ miles NE of Hull (A165, then minor roads).

Burton Court *Heref. & Worcs.*   *Map: 393 Ec*
The house was started in the 14th century (the original hall still exists), finished in the 18th, and given a mock-Tudor frontage in 1912. This was done by Clough-Williams Ellis, the creator of Portmeirion Italianate village in Wales.
Location: 5 miles W of Leominster off A44.

Burton upon Trent *Staffs.*   *Map: 394 Ba*
BASS MUSEUM William Bass began brewing beer at Burton upon Trent in 1777, and this museum traces its development in the area.

Exhibits are in the brewery's joiners' shop, built in 1866. Outside the museum – since transport was vital to brewers – is a reconstructed railway siding. It has a Bass steam locomotive, a directors' coach, and an experimental brew house – all illustrating 19th-century brewery life.
Location: Horninglow St, ½ mile N of town centre on A50.

Bury *Greater Manchester*   *Map: 391 Ea*
TRANSPORT MUSEUM Rail exhibits include seven locomotives, which are regularly steamed. The oldest is a tank engine, the *Gothenburg*, built in 1903 for the Manchester Ship Canal Company.

Buses dominate the road section, and range in date from 1937 to 1957; many take to the road for rallies and other events.
Location: Castlecroft Rd, W of town off A58.

Bury St Edmunds *Suffolk*   *Map: 399 Fe*
ABBEY In 870, Edmund, the young King of East

Anglia, was captured by invading Danes. He was tortured and decapitated – his head flung into a nearby wood. Legend says that a mysterious voice calling "Here, here", helped searchers find the head, guarded by a wolf. When head and body were placed together for burial, they were allegedly reunited.

The king was canonised and his body was interred in the Saxon monastery of Beodericsworth, the present Bury St Edmunds Abbey. The royal relics made it wealthy and a place of international pilgrimage.

In 1214 King John's barons met at the abbey church, secretly swearing at the High Altar to compel the king to recognise the Magna Carta. It was sealed the following year at Runnymede.
Location: Abbey Gardens.
CHURCH OF ST MARY A Perpendicular church that reflects the prosperity brought to Bury by the cloth industry in the 15th century.

It has a magnificent hammer-beam roof in the nave and a wagon-shaped roof in the chancel. The east end of the chancel has the grave of Henry VIII's sister, Mary, who married Louis XII. The more socially important the deceased, the nearer the altar he or she was buried.
Location: Abbey Gardens.
MOYSES HALL MUSEUM The oldest surviving house in East Anglia, built in the 12th century, is now a museum of local history. It includes relics of a notorious murderer – the man who killed Maria Marten in the Red Barn.
Location: Buttermarket/
THEATRE ROYAL This restored Georgian playhouse, built in 1819 by William Wilkins, is still at regular intervals a working theatre.

The premiere of *Charley's Aunt* was staged there in 1829 – before an audience of 30 people.
Location: Westgate St, S of town centre.

Buscot Park *Oxon.*   *Map: 398 Bd*
A country house, built about 1780, with Victorian alterations and additions made by the 1st and 2nd Lord Faringdon.

The house contains 18th century and Regency furniture, and the celebrated cycle of paintings by Sir Edward Burne-Jones, known as *The Legend of the Briar Rose.*
Location: 3 miles NW of Faringdon on A417.

Byland Abbey *N. Yorks.*   *Map: 394 Be*
Byland was founded in the 12th century, and was one of the great Cistercian abbeys of the time. Dissolved in 1536, it is now in ruins.
Location: 9 miles SE of Thirsk off A170.

C

Cadzow Castle *Strathclyde* ·   *Map: 388 Dd*
The 16th-century tower house, now ruined, was built by the lords of Hamilton to replace an earlier castle.
Location: 2 miles SE of Hamilton off A72.

Caerlaverock Castle *Dumfs.*   *Map: 390 Ce*
The great triangular fortress on the Scottish shore

of the Solway Firth was fought over by English and Scots from the 14th to the 17th centuries.

Its last siege came in 1640, when the owner, Robert Maxwell, 1st Earl of Nithsdale, a staunch supporter of Charles I, held out for 13 weeks against an army of Covenanters (Scottish Protestants) before surrendering.
Location: 8 miles SE of Dumfries off B725.

Shield of the Solway Firth

CAERLAVEROCK CASTLE INSPIRED THE AWE OF A SCHOLAR-POET IN 1300, BUT IT FELL
TO EDWARD I OF ENGLAND'S MILITARY MACHINE

Caerlaverock Castle's outer defences of earth ramparts and moats are arranged concentrically, following the principles learned by 12th and 13th-century military architects during the Crusades. But the stone fortress in the middle does not carry that idea through. It is triangular, shaped like a medieval shield, with its vast gatehouse, enlarged in the 15th century, as the strongest point.

The origins of the castle are mysterious. It was built during the 1290s, but whether by the English or by the Scots is not known.

The Scots were in possession of it in 1300. Edward I of England led a siege force against them, and captured Caerlaverock after a short engagement which is remembered chiefly because a scholar from Exeter who took part in it

wrote an account, in French rhyme. He described the castle in tones of awe:

"It had but three sides round it, with a tower at each corner, but one of them was a double one, so high, so long and so wide that the gate was underneath it, well made and strong, with a drawbridge and a sufficiency of other defences. And it had good walls, and good ditches filled right up to the brim with water."

Today's ruins are not those of the castle the scholar saw. That was largely destroyed in about 1320 when the English-appointed keeper, Sir Eustace Maxwell, handed it to Robert Bruce in return for the remission of a debt of £32.

It was rebuilt a few years later, demolished by the Scots again in about 1357, and then rebuilt in the 15th century on the original plan.

BORDER STRONGHOLD

A modern reconstruction shows how Caerlaverock may have looked in the 15th century. Two earth ramparts, each with a moat behind it, guard the *daunting gatehouse. Hoardings on the flanking wall allowed defenders to drop missiles on any attacker who succeeded in crossing the inner moat.*

RENAISSANCE MANSION *The 1st Earl of Nithsdale built a classical three-storey house inside Caerlaverock in the 1630s. Its Renaissance style sits strangely among the medieval ruins.*

DUKE'S PRISON *Murdoch's Tower takes its name from Murdoch, Duke of Albany, reputedly imprisoned in it in 1425.*

ROMAN RECREATION GROUND

The Roman amphitheatre at Caerleon is the only one in Britain to have been fully excavated. Wooden seats which once ringed the arena could accommodate the entire garrison. The amphitheatre was used for training exercises, blood-sports and gladiatorial contests.

Caerleon *Gwent*   *Map: 393 Ea*
ROMAN FORTRESS Modern Caerleon occupies the site of Isca, a 50 acre Roman fortress which was the headquarters of the Second Augustan Legion from about AD 75 until the late 3rd century.

One wall of the fortress remains as an earth rampart with a ditch in front, and beside it are the foundations of a barrack block which held 80 men.

The oval amphitheatre outside the wall had seats for 6,000 people, the entire complement of the garrison. Its eight entrances can still be seen, and one of its two competitors' waiting-rooms has the original benches.

Items excavated in Caerleon are on show in a museum near the church.

Location: 3 miles NE of Newport on B4596.

Caernarfon *Gwynedd*   *Map: 392 Bf*
CASTLE When, in 1283, Edward I of England ordered work to begin on a castle beside the Menai Strait, he intended it to be not only a military stronghold, but also a symbol of his conquest of Wales.

Edward wanted to persuade the defeated Welsh that his sovereignty over their country continued a tradition established by the Romans centuries before. So he chose to administer North Wales from Caernarfon, just as the Romans did.

As an emblem of power and authority, Edward's castle had to be vast, majestic and derived in some way from Imperial Rome. The

---

THE ROMAN WAY: DEATH AS AN ENTERTAINMENT

The cruel traditions of the Roman arena, which required men and animals to fight, often to the death, for the entertainment of the onlookers, grew out of the religious rites of the Etruscans, Rome's near neighbours. But the religious aspect was swiftly forgotten, and the combats were cynically promoted, by Roman emperors and lesser magnates, as a diversion for the citizenry.

The capital of this grisly world was Rome's huge amphitheatre, the Colosseum, inaugurated in AD 80. There, during the opening ceremonies, 5,000 animals were slaughtered in one day, and a spearsman called Carpophorus took a prize of honour for slaying a bear, a lion and a leopard. An unnamed thief was crucified and mangled by a Scottish bear in a re-enactment of the death of the robber Laureolus. The total number of human victims was not recorded.

The Emperor Titus, who was described by his contemporaries as "good-natured", presided over the spectacle, and the poet Martial commemorated the occasion in a lengthy book of verse.

Britain's arenas could not rival the Colosseum for scale and variety of bloodthirsty amusement offered. Bears and bulls did duty for the lions and elephants which died in Rome. But even in Britain there were gladiators to ply their macabre trade, and their feats are celebrated on pots and mosaics which have survived. Before the combat, gladiators prayed to Nemesis, goddess of fate. A recess which may have contained a statue of her may be seen in one of the competitors' waiting-rooms at the amphitheatre at Caerleon.

The public execution of criminals would also have provided entertainment. And amphitheatres such as Caerleon served a secondary purpose – as a training ground for the legionaries stationed there.

The drawings below, based on Roman and medieval sources, show two popular Roman blood sports as they may have been practised in Britain.

BEAR–BAITING *Bears were still native to the British Isles in the 1st century AD. Some from Scotland were shipped to the Colosseum in Rome to appear in the opening ceremonies. Baiting, in which a tethered bear was confronted by an armed man, by dogs, or by a bull, was one use to which the animals were put.*

BOAR–SPEARING *The Romans regarded boar-spearing as a field sport rather than one to be staged in the arena, and boar hunts were a popular recreation among soldiers. In the absence of other, fiercer animals, captured boars could be released in an amphitheatre to reproduce a hunting scene for the onlookers.*

CAERPHILLY'S STOUT DEFENCES

Caerphilly Castle's broad moat was intended to keep besieging troops well away from its walls. The concentric design of the fortress meant that attackers *had to fight their way through a series of heavily defended sections, in any of which they could come under fire from behind and in front.*

resemblance of Caernarfon's walls and towers, with their bands of different kinds of stonework, to the monumental wall built at Constantinople by the Emperor Theodosius II in the 5th century is therefore no coincidence.

Edward had led an army on the Eighth Crusade and, as all crusading armies spent time at the former eastern capital of the Roman Empire, he had probably seen the wall. His great castle designer, Master James of St George, may have seen it, too.

The new castle, with its high walls, many-sided towers and well-fortified gatehouses, was laid out on an hour-glass plan around an earlier Norman motte which the Welsh had captured and held for a century before Edward drove them out. But the project must have been a great disappointment to the king. It was only half-finished by the time of his death in 1307, and was never completed.

Severe damage was done to Caernarfon in an attack by the Welsh under Madog ap Llywelyn in 1294–5. Edward had to use press-gang methods to get English craftsmen to come to the wilds of north-west Wales to build Caernarfon and his other castles, as he dared not trust the Welsh. By 1304, he had spent the equivalent of £1½ million on it, and half of the work was still to be done.

Despite this, the castle became the grandest of Edward's buildings in Wales. Its defences were formidable. Upper and lower shooting galleries were built below the battlemented parapet along the south side, and from these defenders could discharge a rain of missiles.

To get into the lower courtyard through the King's Gate, a fortress in itself, attackers would have had to cross a drawbridge, pass through five doors and under six portcullises and then cross a second drawbridge, while under fire all the way from defenders using arrow-slits and spyholes.

From the castle, a fortified wall with towers along it runs out to enclose the town.

According to tradition, Edward I's presentation of his son to the people of Wales as their new prince took place at Caernarfon in 1301. The castle was the setting for investitures of Princes of Wales in 1911 and 1969.

Location: Town centre.

ROMAN FORT The Romans built their fort of Segontium in about AD 79, and kept a garrison in the district until the late 4th century.

Segontium held 1,000 soldiers. The site has been extensively excavated, and coins, pots and other Roman items found in the area are on show in a museum at the entrance.

Location: ½ mile SE of town centre on A4085.

Caerphilly Castle *Mid Glam.* *Map: 393 Da*
Caerphilly's 13th-century castle, the largest in Wales, was the first fortress in Britain to be designed concentrically from the start. Its land and water defences were, in their day, among the most advanced in Europe, and despite sieges, periods of neglect and attempts at demolition after the Civil War, they remain a spectacular monument to English military power.

The Romans had a fort some 200 yds north-west of the present castle site. Soon after the Norman invasion, a motte and bailey was raised within the fort walls, but whether this was the work of the Normans or of the Welsh is not certain.

In 1266 Gilbert de Clare, Earl of Gloucester and one of the richest nobles in England, began a stone castle. Two years later, Llywelyn the Last, Prince of Wales, descended on the embryo fortress and destroyed it. De Clare tried again, and again Llywelyn savaged the structure. The third attempt at building was successful as the Welsh leader was by then occupied in the north of the country.

Work on the castle was carried out in several stages and spread over many years, though by 1316 it was strong enough to withstand a Welsh siege. The heart of the castle is an inner, four-sided enclosure with huge round towers at each corner and two twin-towered gatehouses. Around it is a second stone enclosure, also with twin-towered gates, and this is set in a broad artificial lake. Originally, there was a further line of defences. A great hornwork barred the approach from the west, curtain walls and turrets formed a screen to the east, and a second lake guarded the north.

In 1321 the castle was broken into by supporters of barons quarrelling with the owner,

DRESSING A KNIGHT FOR BATTLE

Armour worn by most knights about the time of the Battle of Agincourt in 1415 consisted of a complex series of garments made from iron plate and chain mail, which could together weigh 56 lb. or more.

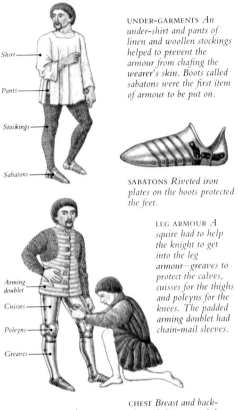

Shirt

Pants

Stockings

Sabatons

UNDER-GARMENTS *An under-shirt and pants of linen and woollen stockings helped to prevent the armour from chafing the wearer's skin. Boots called sabatons were the first item of armour to be put on.*

SABATONS *Riveted iron plates on the boots protected the feet.*

LEG ARMOUR *A squire had to help the knight to get into the leg armour—greaves to protect the calves, cuisses for the thighs and poleyns for the knees. The padded arming doublet had chain-mail sleeves.*

Arming doublet

Cuisses

Poleyns

Greaves

CHEST *Breast and back-plates (left) protected the upper body. Plates for the arms (below) went on next.*

Breast-plate

Besagues

Vambrace

Fauld

Back-plate

Rerebrace

Couter

HEAD *The helmet, called a bascinet, had a mail aventail below to guard the neck. Surcoat, sword-belt, spurs and gloves were put on last.*

Bascinet

Aventail

Surcoat

Dagger

Sword

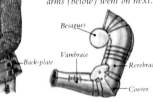

Spurs

VISOR *A detachable visor covered the wearer's face.*

GAUNTLETS *The knight's gloves had ringed metal plates over the fingers. Their spikes (gadlings) dealt a painful blow.*

Gadlings

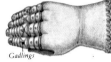

"FALSTAFF'S" CASTLE

Sir John Fastolf (1378–1459) lent his name to Shakespeare's Falstaff, but was far from being the cowardly buffoon the playwright portrayed. He won fame fighting the French, and used this experience to design Caister Castle.

Hugh le Despenser, favourite of Edward II. Edward himself, five years later, took refuge there while fleeing from his estranged queen, Isabella, and her paramour, Roger Mortimer.

The queen's army laid siege to the castle, from which Edward had escaped, leaving much of his treasure behind. When he was eventually captured, the garrison surrendered, and the castle was allowed to deteriorate.
Location: Town centre.

Caerwent *Gwent*   *Map: 393 Ea*
ROMAN CITY The village of Caerwent occupies part of the site of *Venta Silurum*—the name means "market of the Silures tribe"—founded by the Romans as a civilian settlement in the 2nd century AD.

The stone city walls, added at the beginning of the 3rd century, enclose an area of 44 acres, and in places are more than 15 ft high. Beside Pound Lane, there are the remains of two Roman houses and a temple. In the south-east corner are traces of an 11th-century motte-and-bailey castle.
Location: 5 miles SW of Chepstow off A48.

Cairnholy *Dumfs. & Gall.*   *Map: 388 Ca*
MEGALITHIC TOMBS Two Stone Age burial mounds dating from about 3000 BC lie within 200 yds of each other, and may be the graves of members of a single family. The tomb to the south is the better preserved. It has a façade of tall stones flanking the entrance to its first chamber, and a second, enclosed chamber beyond.
Location: 7 miles SW of Gatehouse of Fleet on minor road off A75.

Cairnpapple *Lothian*   *Map: 389 Dd*
HILLTOP GRAVES Prehistoric men chose the 1,000 ft summit of Cairnpapple Hill for a cemetery well before 2000 BC. They dug an arc of pits in which the cremated remains of 13 people have been found.

About 1600 BC, the Bronze Age Beaker people built a henge monument over the cemetery. An oval earth bank surrounds it, and there were originally 24 stone uprights.

Items excavated from the hilltop are displayed in a museum on the site.
Location: 2 miles N of Bathgate off B792.

Caister-on-Sea *Norfolk*   *Map: 395 Ga*
CAISTER CASTLE Sir John Fastolf built the castle from 1432 to 1435. Instead of the then-traditional stone, he used bricks baked in kilns on the site.

In Sir John's day, castles were changing from purely defensive structures to more elegant and comfortable ones. But although the 100 ft tower looks slender and frail, it was well fortified, with a parapet on top and a hexagonal turret on the side.
Location: 1½ miles W of Caister-on-Sea off A1064.
ROMAN TOWN The foundations of Caister's 3rd-century Roman defences and the remains of a courtyard building which may have been a seamen's hostel were excavated in the 1950s, revealing 150 Saxon burials.
Location: W of Caister-on-Sea on A1064.

Caistor St Edmund *Norfolk*   *Map: 395 Ga*
ROMAN TOWN After the Romans had crushed Boudicca's revolt in AD 61, they established the town, called *Venta Icenorum*, as the capital of her tribe, the Iceni. A mound marks the circuit of the town walls, and there are traces of their 3rd-century stone facings.
Location: 4 miles S of Norwich on minor roads off A140.

Calbourne *Isle of Wight*   *Map: 398 Ba*
WATERMILL A mill has existed on the site since before 1086. It produced flour until the end of the 19th century, when a second mill, using rollers to grind the grain, was built alongside. This operated commercially until 1955.

Old and new mills are preserved in working order. There is a museum of machinery and agricultural equipment in the millyard.
Location: ½ mile W of Calbourne on B3401.

Caldicot Castle *Gwent*   *Map: 393 Ea*
The original motte-and-bailey castle was founded by the Normans soon after 1100 to guard the road from Chepstow into South Wales. Later that century, members of the powerful de Bohun family, Earls of Hereford, added the curtain walls with four round towers.

The castle was restored in the 19th century.
Location: 5 miles SW of Chepstow on minor roads off A48.

Callanish *Lewis, Western Isles*   *Map: 386 Bd*
STANDING STONES The complex, started about 4,000 years ago, is the finest of three in this part of the island. A 270 ft avenue leads to the central circle.
Location: 16 miles W of Stornoway off A858.

Calstock *Cornwall*   *Map: 396 Cb*
RAILWAY VIADUCT The 1,000 ft, 12-arch viaduct, rising 117 ft above the surface of the River Tamar, was built at the beginning of this century.
Location: 6 miles SW of Tavistock (A390, then minor roads).

Calver Mill *Derbys.*   *Map: 394 Bc*
The first water-driven cotton mill beside the Derwent was built in the second half of the 18th century, but burned down during a snowstorm in 1802. It was replaced by the present building. Since 1920 the mill has been put to other uses. It is now a factory making kitchen equipment, and its two water-wheels have been removed.
Location: 5 miles N of Bakewell (A619 then B6001).

Calverton *Notts.*   *Map: 394 Cb*
KNITTERS' COTTAGES In the 16th century, the Rev. William Lee, a poor Nottinghamshire curate, invented a frame on which stockings could be knitted far faster than by hand. One story says he was inspired to do so because his girl-friend insisted on knitting while he tried to talk of his love for her. Lee died penniless, but his frame helped to transform a craft into an industry.

Frame-knitters worked in their own homes – cottages such as those in Windles Square. They are not open to the public, but the history of the knitting industry is depicted in a museum in Main Square.
Location: 7 miles NE of Nottingham off A614.

KNITTERS' HOMES

Large ground-floor windows which let light on to the knitting frames are typical of knitters' cottages. Those at Calverton were used for their original purpose well into this century. Frames knitted 15 times faster than by hand.

Camborne *Cornwall*   *Map: 396 Aa*
HOLMAN MUSEUM Camborne has been the centre of Cornish tin-mining for hundreds of years. The industry reached its peak in the 19th century, and the museum contains many exhibits from this period.

The South Crofty, at Pool, is still worked, but most of the mines around Camborne are now derelict. The surface buildings at the South Francis, near Troon, have survived largely intact since being abandoned.
Location: The Cross, town centre.

Cambridge *Cambs.*   *Map : 399 Ee*
CAMBRIDGE UNIVERSITY In 1209, a feud between townspeople and students in Oxford erupted into violence, and groups of scholars fled from the city, which was then just establishing itself as a home of learning.

Some, from the Midlands and East Anglia, settled in Cambridge, at that time the centre of England's most populated region outside London.

Others joined them, from Oxford and from Paris. Over the following century the forerunner of today's university evolved.

Many of the students came from poor families and the licence to teach, a Bachelor of Arts degree, was a passport to advancement.

The degree took four years to obtain. To become a Master of Arts required a further three years. And a doctorate demanded another ten years of study.

Instruction was dominated by the Church. The teachers were priests and monks, and the pupils took holy orders, even though they might eventually have little to do with Church affairs. But the first seven years of study were spent mainly on secular subjects – grammar, rhetoric and logic, with arithmetic, geometry, music and astronomy, taught according to the principles laid down by the Greek philosophers.

At first, the university had no buildings of its own and lectures, for which there was no formal enrolment, were given in private rooms and churches. Students lived in individual lodgings, or combined to rent houses.

Rents were high, one source of the tension between scholars and townspeople which flared up from time to time in fights and riots. However, the feud between town and gown was only one of several in medieval Cambridge. The students were divided into warring regional factions, and the masters quarrelled about whether their pupils should be prepared for a monastic life, or for a more relaxed type of priesthood.

The present college system grew out of attempts to resolve all these differences.

The earliest colleges at both Oxford and Cambridge were in fact halls of residence which provided living and working accommodation for selected masters, but still left the pupils, some only 14 years old, to fend for themselves. King's Hall, Cambridge, founded in 1336, was the first to admit students in their early teens. The idea was developed later in the 14th century at New College, Oxford.

The oldest of Cambridge's 31 colleges, Peterhouse in Trumpington Street, was founded by the Bishop of Ely in the 1280s. Its dining hall, built in 1286, has been enlarged and heavily restored.

Other halls of residence were established over the years. Pembroke (Trumpington Street), founded in 1347, has the first of Christopher Wren's architectural achievements – the chapel, completed in 1665.

Corpus Christi (Trumpington Street) was endowed by local merchants in 1352. Its Old Court is a medieval gem. Among its famous members was Christopher Marlowe (1564–93), who almost certainly wrote *Tamburlaine* there.

Henry VI founded King's (King's Parade) in 1440 for boys from the school he had established at Eton to continue their ecclesiastical studies.

Henry's queen, Margaret, endowed what is now Queens' (off Silver Street) in 1448 "to laud and honneur of sexe feminine", and Edward IV's wife, Elizabeth Woodville, gave a further endowment in 1465. The Dutch philosopher Erasmus worked in a turret-room above the Mill Pool between 1511 and 1516, grumbling "I am beset with thieves".

Jesus College (Jesus Lane) was founded in 1497 by Bishop Alcock of Ely, who closed the 12th-century St Radegund's Nunnery and turned its buildings over to the scholars.

In 1546, Henry VIII incorporated the 14th-century King's Hall and Michaelhouse into his new foundation, Trinity (Trinity Street). The college acquired its present dimensions in the 17th century, when the Master, Thomas Nevile, demolished several buildings to make way for the Great Court. Nevile added a second court, in the arcades of which Isaac Newton calculated the speed of sound in the 1660s. In Muttonhole Corner of Great Court, Lord Byron, who came up from Harrow School in 1805, kept a tame bear in protest against a college rule which forbade undergraduates to own dogs.

Emmanuel (St Andrew's Street) and Sidney Sussex (Sidney Street) were established, in 1584 and 1596 respectively, on the site of religious foundations dissolved during the Reformation. Both became strongholds of Puritanism. The members of Sidney Sussex, all candidates for ordination, lived as austerely as any monk. They were allowed into town only to attend approved sermons and lectures. Oliver Cromwell spent a year at the college in 1616–17. His mummified head was eventually buried in the chapel.

After Sidney Sussex, no new colleges were chartered until Downing (Regent Street) in 1800. But many of the existing ones were extended or rebuilt.

Clare (Senate House Passage), originally endowed as University Hall in 1326, was reconstructed in Renaissance style between 1638 and 1707. St Catharine's, founded in 1473, was entirely rebuilt between 1675 and 1775.

At Christ's (St Andrew's Street), chartered in 1448 by Henry VI, the three-storey Fellows' Building was added in 1640–3. The poet John Milton (1608–74), who spent seven years at the college, is said to have planted the mulberry tree in the Fellows' Garden.

Throughout most of its history, Cambridge University has been an exclusively male institution, and this did not begin to change until well into the 19th century. Girton College (Huntingdon Road, $2\frac{1}{2}$ miles NW) for women was founded in 1869 and Newnham (Sidgwick Avenue) followed two years later, but both remained inferior copies of their male counterparts for decades.

THE GLORY OF KING'S

The magnificent fan-vaulted roof of King's College Chapel, completed in 1515, crowns one of the major monuments of English medieval architecture. Henry VI specified the dimensions of the chapel, which he wanted to outshine any other in Cambridge. He urged the architects to avoid intricate decorations, but Henry VIII, under whom the building was completed, had no such inhibitions. The work done in his reign is ornate.

CAMBRIDGE CASTLE Only the original earth mound is left of the castle, founded in 1068 during William the Conqueror's reign. After 1400, references to it are scarce, and by the 16th century it was described as "utterly ruinated". Location: Corner of Castle St and Chesterton Lane.

Camelford *Cornwall*   *Map: 396 Cc*
NORTH CORNWALL MUSEUM The inside of a 19th-century Cornish cottage is reconstructed in the museum, which also displays farm equipment. Location: Town centre.

Camelot Hill see South Cadbury

Candleston Castle *Mid Glam.*   *Map: 392 Ca*
The Cantelupe family, several of whose members became royal stewards in the Middle Ages, built the square tower and polygonal curtain wall in the 14th century. The castle, now ruined, was lived in until Victorian times. Location: 3 miles SW of Bridgend off A48.

Cannon Hall *S. Yorks.*   *Map: 394 Bc*
John Carr of York remodelled the house in the mid-18th century. It stands in a landscaped park.
    As well as furniture and paintings, Cannon Hall has a large collection of glassware. Location: 5 miles W of Barnsley off A635.

VICTORIAN GLASS MODELS

Sailing ship of glass beads, *c.* 1860

The manufacture of novelty items and models in glass began as an exercise for apprentices. But the work became popular with the Victorians and developed into a profitable offshoot of the glass industry. These models are in the Cannon Hall, S. Yorkshire, collection.

Victorian villa in glass, *c.* 1865

Mead, *c.* 1730

Wine, with coin of 1758

Ale or wine, *c.* 1740

Ratafia (liqueur), *c.* 1760

Wine, *c.* 1745

Wine, *c.* 1780

FASHION IN GLASSWARE

Improved glass-making techniques and changing fashions transformed the appearance of drinking-glasses in the homes of the well-to-do during the 18th century. Plain, functional designs gradually gave way to rococo swirls and diamond facets. Bowl shapes became more complex. Sometimes a small silver coin was sealed into the hollow stem as an added decorative feature. The glass collection at Cannon Hall, S. Yorkshire, includes items from the 1st century AD to the present.

Canterbury *Kent*   *Map: 399 Fc*
CATHEDRAL When St Augustine landed in Kent in AD 597, he had come from Rome with a mission – to convert the heathen Saxons to Christianity. Before he died, seven years later, he had reintroduced the faith to much of southern England and founded at Canterbury what was to become the Mother Church of the Anglican Communion, seat of the archbishops who are Primates of All England.
    Fire destroyed the Saxon cathedral in 1067. It was rebuilt under the direction of Lanfranc, the first Norman archbishop, and enlarged by his successor, Anselm.
    In 1170, over-zealous knights acting on behalf of Henry II murdered Archbishop Thomas Becket near the steps leading to the cathedral's

high altar, a sacrilegious crime which shocked medieval Christendom. Becket's death gave the Crown supremacy over the Church, but it was a hollow victory for Henry. Within three years, Becket had been declared a saint, and thousands were flocking to his grave. As a gesture of penitence, Henry himself walked barefooted through Canterbury in 1174, and was whipped by monks.

Two months after Henry's visit, fire again gutted the cathedral. The vast Norman crypt, the largest of its kind in the world, survived undamaged, but the choir had to be rebuilt. William of Sens, a brilliant master-mason – the equivalent of today's architects – was given the task.

In 1178, the scaffolding on which William was working collapsed. Crippled by the fall, he went home to France, where he died two years later, leaving another William, called the Englishman, to finish the work.

The second William completed the choir, the presbytery and Trinity Chapel at the eastern end of the church. The golden shrine of St Thomas was installed in Trinity Chapel in 1220.

The tomb and effigy of the Black Prince were erected on the south side of the chapel in 1376. The prince, eldest son of Edward III, had won honour on the field at Crécy 30 years earlier, when he was only 16, by routing the French. His nickname may have come from the colour of his armour.

In the 350 years or so following Becket's death, the pilgrims brought great wealth to Canterbury, and the cathedral was continually enriched by such additions as the 14th-century Chapter House and Bell Harry Tower. The Chapter House has a barrel-vaulted timber roof surpassed in England only by Westminster Hall. Bell Harry, the great Gothic tower raised from the centre of the church in 1480, is among the finest of its period.

Henry VIII brought the cult of the martyred archbishop to an abrupt end in 1538, when, during the Dissolution of the Monasteries, he declared Becket to have been a traitor and a rebel. He ordered the shrine to be stripped of its treasures. Becket's bones were removed and probably burned.
Location: City centre.
ROMAN CITY Canterbury's medieval walls, still standing for half their circuit, were built on the same line as their Roman predecessors, which enclosed the city of *Durovernum Cantiacorum*, founded in the 1st century AD.

Excavations are continually revealing more details of Roman Canterbury. Remains of a town house with a mosaic floor and the foundations of a Roman theatre have been found. The Royal Museum, in the High Street, has a large collection of Roman material.
Location: City centre.
ST AUGUSTINE'S ABBEY Several kings of Saxon Kent and early archbishops of Canterbury are buried in the abbey, which was established about AD 600. Most of the abbey buildings are ruined, and many have disappeared entirely above ground level, but the foundations have been excavated.
Location: Monastery St, 200 yds E of Broad St.

STEPS TO THE SHRINE
The worn steps in Canterbury Cathedral were trodden by thousands of pilgrims to St Thomas Becket's shrine, which occupied the Trinity Chapel until 1538.

THE CANTERBURY PILGRIMS

Pewter badges depicting Thomas Becket were bought by pilgrims to Canterbury in the Middle Ages, as proof of their visit.

The Doctor of Physic
"Had a special love of gold"

The Cook
"Baked a tasty pie"

The Wife of Bath
"Liked to laugh and chat"

The Second Nun
"Soul in prison"

Geoffrey Chaucer (*c.* 1340–1400), who began writing the *Canterbury Tales* in the 1390s, never completed the work according to his original plan. Nevertheless, the stories told by the group of pilgrims who journey from London to Canterbury, and the commentary with which Chaucer links them, create a vivid picture of life and thought in the later Middle Ages. Chaucer combined a poet's skill with a shrewd knowledge of human foibles, acquired during his career as a courtier and diplomat.

Canvey Island *Essex*   *Map: 399 Ec*
DUTCH COTTAGE MUSEUM Items connected with
Thames shipping are displayed in a 17th-century
cottage built in a style brought to England by
Dutch engineers who reclaimed much of the
island from the water. The cottage is one of the
oldest surviving buildings on the island.
Location: 17 miles S of Chelmsford on A130.

Capesthorne *Cheshire*   *Map: 393 Ff*
Capesthorne is a Victorian architect's conversion
of a Georgian house into what he thought a
Jacobean mansion should look like. It was built
about 1720, remodelled in 17th-century style in
1837, and then rebuilt after a fire in 1861.

Inside, there are collections of Roman marble,
Greek pottery, Italian paintings and articles con-
nected with American history, brought by the
American wife of Walter Bromley-Davenport,
ancestor of the present owners.
Location: 7 miles S of Wilmslow on A34.

FOR HOUSEHOLD EMERGENCIES
*Bottles in a Victorian medicine chest at Capesthorne
Hall, Cheshire, contained popular 19th-century home
remedies. Bandages, plasters and other first-aid items
were kept in the lower drawers.*

Cardiff *S. Glam.*   *Map: 393 Da*
CASTLE The Normans founded the castle in a
corner of Cardiff's Roman fort in the 11th
century and added a shell keep in the 12th.

Henry I imprisoned his oldest brother, Robert,
Duke of Normandy, in the castle in 1106, after
several squabbles between them and a half-
hearted attempt by Robert to seize the English
throne. Robert spent 28 years in the castle until
he died in 1134 at the age of about 80, still in
captivity.
Location: City centre.
MELINGRIFFITH WATER PUMP The pump, now very
dilapidated, was built early in the 19th century to
supply water from the River Taff to the
Glamorganshire Canal.

Two rods suspended from wooden beams
drew the water into cylinders, and a water-wheel
supplied the power. A model of the pump is in
the National Museum in Cathays Park.
Location: Velindre Rd, NW of city off A4054.
ROMAN FORT Two complete outer walls and part
of a third have been restored to show how they

must have looked when they were built early in
the 4th century.
Location: At castle.
WELSH INDUSTRIAL AND MARITIME MUSEUM Eight
massive engines are displayed on the ground
floor of the museum, and many smaller ones on
the first floor. The larger exhibits include a triple-
expansion steam-engine, in which steam passed
through three cylinders before reaching the
condenser, and a beam engine from Cardiff
Waterworks.

The outdoor section has a collection of boats,
among them a pilot's cutter and canal craft,
locomotives and cranes.
Location: Bute St (A470), S of city centre.

Cardoness Castle *Dumfs. & Gall.* *Map: 388 Ca*
Cardoness is a well-preserved example of a 15th-
century tower house, with a basement and four
storeys massively built from local stone.
Location: 1 mile SW of Gatehouse of Fleet on
A75.

Carew *Dyfed*   *Map: 392 Ab*
CASTLE The original Norman castle on the site
was strengthened with four stout walls and
cylindrical corner towers in the 13th century.
But later owners were more interested in
comfort and display than in defence, and
weakened the castle's military effectiveness with
alterations during the 15th and 16th centuries.

Carew fell to Parliamentary troops in 1644,
and was left a partial ruin.
Location: 5 miles E of Pembroke on A4075.
TIDAL MILL A mill has existed on the site since
before 1558, and the present building, which was
in commercial use until 1937, was restored to
partial working order in 1972.

The waters of the River Carew, trapped in the
pool at high tide, supplied the power through
two water-wheels, one of which still turns.
Location: Town centre.

Carisbrooke *Isle of Wight*   *Map: 398 Ba*
CASTLE The Normans built a motte-and-bailey
castle at Carisbrooke in the 1070s, on the site of a
Roman fort. Stone defences were added during
the following century, and over the next 400
years the castle was expanded and strengthened.

Charles I was brought to Carisbrooke by his
supporters in 1647, after he had lost the Civil
War. The king still hoped to reach an accommodation with Parliament, but he failed, and was
moved as a prisoner to Hurst Castle on the
mainland the following year.
Location: 1 mile SW of Newport off B3401.
CHURCH OF ST MARY THE VIRGIN The church is of
Norman origin and was formerly part of a
priory. The south aisle dates from around 1200.
The tall west tower was added in the 15th
century.
Location: 1 mile W of Newport on B3323.
DONKEY WHEEL The wheel that works the 160 ft
well in the bailey of Carisbrooke Castle is still
turned by donkeys to show visitors how water
was raised for the garrison. The well itself was
sunk in 1150. The wellhouse and wheel were
installed in 1587 at a cost of just £16.

Carlisle *Cumbria*   *Map: 391 De*
CASTLE When William II of England marched
into Carlisle in 1092, the town, originally

founded by the Romans, was a derelict ruin. It lay in an area claimed by Scotland, but William ignored that, and put a wealthy Norman called Walter the Priest in charge of building a castle and a church.

In 1136 Stephen, who had been chosen by many barons as ruler of England in preference to Matilda, daughter of Henry I, gave three English earldoms to the Scots to bribe them not to support Matilda's claim to the throne. Carlisle changed hands as part of the agreement, and David I of Scotland moved there. He strengthened the defences and began building the castle's rectangular great tower.

But in 1157 Henry II of England demanded, and got, the three earldoms back. Carlisle became English once more, in an exchange without bloodshed. Over the next 600 years, competition between English and Scots for control of the city and castle was far more brutal.

In 1314 Robert Bruce, victor of Bannockburn, vowed he would take Carlisle. His long siege failed.

During the Civil War, Scots fighting for the Parliamentary cause were more successful, capturing city and castle in 1645. Exactly 100 years later, Carlisle fell to the Scots again. The English garrison surrendered to the followers of "Bonnie Prince Charlie" as they advanced into England, but when the prince withdrew once more to Scotland, the pursuing army of the Duke of Cumberland recaptured the castle with little difficulty. Cumberland executed the Scots he found there – among them the unknown author of *Loch Lomond*, who wrote the song while awaiting death.

Location: N of Bridge St (A595) and W of Eden Bridge (A7).

CATHEDRAL William II ordered a church to be built in his newly annexed stronghold of Carlisle at the end of the 11th century. Henry I raised it to the status of a cathedral, the most northerly in England, in 1133.

Disasters have struck the cathedral several times. The earliest, and most serious, came in 1292, when its newly enlarged Early English choir was badly damaged by fire.

Rebuilding started in 1300, and was carried out in the Decorated style. The presbytery and wooden vaulted ceiling date from this period, and so does the east window, richly moulded, with nine vertical divisions capped with tracery. The lower glass has since been replaced, but the panes in the uppermost section probably date from 1358–9.

In 1400 the central lantern was raised to its present height, and the choir stalls were added at about the same time. They include 46 carved wooden misericords – hinged seats on which tired monks could rest during long services. Behind the stalls are some 15th-century paintings done in oils on wood, depicting the apostles and the legends of St Augustine, St Anthony and St Cuthbert.

The cathedral's second major disaster occurred during the Civil War, when Parliamentary troops finally gained control of the city. They dismantled all but two of the eight bays on each side of the Norman nave and used the stones to repair Carlisle's defences. The cathedral's library disappeared, its plate was melted down for coinage, and the chapter house was destroyed.

VICTORIAN HOME MEDICINE

Until the end of the 19th century, most hospitals were places of dread, to which no sick person would be sent if there were any choice. From filthy, cramped wards disease and infection spread. Usually, the harassed nurses had received little training.

Conditions began to improve during the 1850s, when Joseph Lister pioneered the use of antiseptics and Florence Nightingale initiated her reforms of nursing and hospital organisation. But the process was slow, and throughout the Victorian era patients were treated, if possible, at home.

Victorian housewives were expected to know the basics of nursing, and a well-stocked medicine cabinet was an essential domestic item. It contained remedies for minor ailments and injuries which could be treated without a doctor's help, and also medicaments which were used, under a doctor's direction, for more serious complaints.

Books such as *The Family Doctor Complete Encyclopaedia of Domestic Medicine and Surgery*, published in 1859, listed the medicines a prudent housewife and mother should keep at home – sal volatile to treat fainting fits and hysteria, tincture of opium as a pain-killer, sweet spirit of nitre to cool fevers, tincture of parachloride of iron to stop bleeding after the application of leeches, and many more.

Some of the remedies that were popular with the Victorians were based on herbs whose healing properties had been known for hundreds of years. Nervous and digestive disorders, for example, were treated by drinking an infusion made by pouring boiling water on camomile flowers.

This was also the era of patent medicines. There were pills, drops, lozenges, cordials, liniments and elixirs by the dozen to cure all man's ills. Some are still available.

19TH-CENTURY MEDICAMENTS *Ipecacuanha, for asthma and whooping cough, tincture of arnica, for bruises, Goulard's extract of lead, for inflammations, and elixir of vitriol, a tonic and gargle, were common remedies in Victorian days.*

After the Jacobite uprising of 1745 had failed Carlisle settled into a more peaceful existence. With the peace came prosperity, reflected in the restoration work carried out in the cathedral during the Victorian era and later.

Mary, Queen of Scots worshipped in the cathedral in 1568, while a prisoner in the castle. The novelist Walter Scott married Charlotte Carpenter, daughter of a French refugee, there on Christmas Eve 1797.

Location: Off Castle St.

RAILWAY STATION Sir William Tite, architect of London's Royal Exchange, designed the Citadel Station, which was completed in 1847. He used a Tudor style throughout, with buttresses, mullioned windows, chimney stacks in groups of six and a clock tower like an octagonal lantern.

Location: City centre, off Court Sq.

Carlton Towers N. Yorks.　　Map: 394 Cd
Henry Stapleton, 9th Lord Beaumont, and the architect Edward Welby Pugin created the Gothic splendour of Carlton Towers in 1873–5.

The estate had been in the Stapleton family since the Norman Conquest. Underneath Pugin's trimmings are two earlier buildings, a three-storey Jacobean house of 1614 and a long wing, topped by a clock-tower, added in 1777. Location: 8 miles W of Goole (A614 then A1041).

ART IN THE FIREPLACE

The armorial bearings of the Stapleton family, Lords Beaumont, are the central feature of an ornate 19th-century fireplace in the Venetian Drawing-Room at Carlton Towers, N. Yorkshire. Pictorial panels below depict the seasons.

Carnasserie Castle Strathclyde　　Map: 388 Ae
The army of James II blew up the 16th-century castle in 1685, after capturing it from supporters of the rebel Duke of Argyll. The ruins are still imposing.
Location: 9 miles N of Lochgilphead on A816.

Carn Brea Cornwall　　Map: 396 Ab
HILL-FORT Men of the late Stone Age fortified part of the hilltop about 3000 BC. They built a rough stone wall around a cluster of huts. Finds of arrowheads and cleared patches of ground suggest they were both hunters and farmers.

During the Iron Age, 2,000 years later, the village defences were extended. Traces have been found of 15 circular huts from this period.
Location: 1 mile W of Redruth off A3047.

Carn Euny Cornwall　　Map: 396 Aa
IRON AGE VILLAGE The stone walls at Carn Euny are those of a village of the 1st century BC. There are traces of several houses in which storerooms and living-rooms open off a central courtyard.

The fogou, or underground chamber, dates from the 2nd century BC, when the villagers were still living in wooden huts. Its purpose is not known, but suggestions include storage, defence or ritual.
Location: 5 miles W of Penzance on minor roads off A30.

Carnforth Lancs.　　Map: 391 Eb
STEAMTOWN RAILWAY MUSEUM A large collection of steam locomotives, including the *Flying Scotsman*, which in 1928 made the first non-stop run from King's Cross to Edinburgh, is housed in the former engine-shed of Carnforth Station.
Location: Warton Rd, W of town centre.

Carn Gluze Cornwall　　Map: 396 Aa
STONE CAIRN The cairn is an archaeological oddity, not readily comparable with any other prehistoric monument in Britain.

At the centre is a T-shaped pit, possibly a late Stone Age grave. A double-walled dome, which still stands 12 ft high, was built over the pit, and the inside was filled with earth and stones. The whole construction was then enclosed in a second cairn.
Location: 1 mile W of St Just on minor roads.

Carreg Cennen Castle Dyfed　　Map: 392 Cb
The castle, perched on a limestone crag 300 ft above the River Cennen, was founded by the Welsh in the 13th century, though most of the present building is of later date. It changed hands several times during the campaigns of Edward I, finally becoming English in the 1280s.

In 1462, Yorkists captured the castle from the sons of the Lancastrian Gruffyd ap Nicholas. The Yorkists ordered its demolition, a job for which the workmen charged £28 5s 6d. But substantial ruins were left, and these were restored by the Earl of Cawdor in the 19th century.
Location: 3 miles SE of Llandeilo off A483.

Cartmel Cumbria　　Map: 391 Dc
PRIORY CHURCH OF ST MARY AND ST MICHAEL When William Marshall, Earl of Pembroke, founded a priory in his barony of Cartmel in about 1190, he insisted the priory church should also serve the parish.

This saved the church from destruction during the Reformation, when the priory was dissolved. The parishioners used the south aisle of the choir. The rest of the building was stripped of its wealth, including its roof, and left open to the weather for some 80 years, until it was restored in 1618.
Location: 2 miles NW of Grange-over-Sands off A590.

Castell Carndochan Gwynedd　　Map: 392 Ce
Little is now left of Carndochan Castle, which was built by the Welsh early in the 13th century. It originally had a tower shaped like a letter D.
Location: 13½ miles NE of Dolgellau off A494.

Castell Coch S. Glam.　　Map: 393 Da
The 3rd Marquess of Bute commissioned the

HOW THE BRITISH STAYED WARM

Norman castle-builders of the 11th and 12th centuries developed the fireplace – a wall recess linked at first to a hollow buttress with holes in it to let out smoke, and, by 1200, to a tall chimney. It gradually replaced the smoky, central floor hearth. Some medieval and 16th-century fireplaces were vast – one at Hampton Court Palace is 17 ft wide. But with changing architectural fashions, different fuels and better insulation the fireplace became smaller. The wealthy employed architects such as Robert Adam (1728–92) to make their fireplaces decorative features.

14TH CENTURY (left) Fires in the centre of the floor heated most halls in the early Middle Ages. A hole in the ceiling drew off smoke. The hearth at Penshurst, Kent, is of 1340.

18TH CENTURY (above) An ornate Adam fireplace at Kedleston Hall, Derbyshire, frames an iron basket to hold a fire of coal or small logs.

15TH CENTURY (left) By the mid-15th century fireplaces were replacing central hearths in even the largest halls. Some, as at Tattershall Castle, Lincolnshire, could burn huge logs.

20TH CENTURY (above) The use of coal-gas for heating brought a radical change in fires and fireplaces.

19TH CENTURY (above) The pre-Raphaelite ceramic artist William de Morgan designed tiles for the fireplace in the study at Carlton Towers, N. Yorkshire.

1890 (left) Although stoves are more efficient than open fires, their use was limited in Britain, as wood and coal were plentiful.

architect William Burges to restore Castell Coch in 1872. Burges had little to go on. The castle, put up in the 13th century, had been a total ruin for more than 300 years.

But with a combination of historical knowledge and artistic flair, the architect rebuilt it as it might have looked in the Middle Ages.
Location: 6 miles NW of Cardiff off A470.

Castell Dinas Bran *Clwyd*   *Map: 393 De*
Gruffydd ap Madog, a Welshman who earned the enmity of his countrymen by siding with the English against them on several occasions, established Dinas Bran as his stronghold in the 13th century. He put spyholes in the rooms and

passages to give himself added security. The Welsh drove him out of his lands in 1257, but he changed sides and regained them shortly afterwards.

Dinas Bran was being described as a ruin by 1578.
Location: 1 mile NE of Llangollen (minor road, then track).

Castell Dinas Emrys *Gwynedd*   *Map: 392 Ce*
A rectangular great tower, now ruined, formed the heart of the defences at Dinas Emrys, which was put up by the Welsh in the 13th century on the site of a late Romano-British fort.
Location: 1 mile NE of Beddgelert on A498.

Castell y Bere *Gwynedd*   *Map: 392 Cd*
When the Welsh built the castle in the 1220s, it equalled any the English had constructed until then.

Edward I's army took it in the 1280s, driving out Dafydd, brother of Prince Llywelyn the Last of Wales. Llywelyn was already dead, killed near Builth. Dafydd was hunted down and executed.

The Welsh recaptured Castell y Bere briefly, but by 1294 it was back in English hands. The English did not bother to repair it, and it is now only a heap of ivy-covered stones.
Location: 7 miles NE of Tywyn (A493 then minor road from Bryncrug).

Castle Acre *Norfolk*   *Map: 395 Fa*
CASTLE William de Warenne, cousin of William the Conqueror, raised a motte-and-bailey castle here soon after 1066. A polygonal shell keep was built on the motte in the 13th century, and inside its ruins archaeologists have recently discovered the remains of a rectangular great tower put up in the 12th century.
Location: 4 miles N of Swaffham off A1065.
PRIORY The impressive ruins of the priory, founded about 1190, include part of the church, the prior's house and the gatehouse.

Castle-an-Dinas *Cornwall*   *Map: 396 Bb*
IRON AGE HILL-FORT The earth fort, dating from the 2nd century BC, has two rings of defences, each consisting of two banks with a ditch between them. It was probably raised to give protection against raids by rival local communities.
Location: 3 miles E of St Columb Major on minor roads.

Castle Ashby *Northants.*   *Map: 398 Ce*
Castle Ashby, begun in 1574 by Henry, 1st Baron Compton, and continued by his son William Compton, 1st Earl of Northampton, stands in parkland landscaped by "Capability" Brown. The mansion takes the name "castle" from a fortified medieval manor house which once occupied the site.

The original E-shape of the building was altered by Inigo Jones in the 17th century.
Location: 8 miles E of Northampton off A428.

Castle Campbell *Central*   *Map: 389 De*
Colin Campbell, 1st Earl of Argyll, constructed the tall, oblong tower house in the 15th century. His descendants added the buildings round it over the next 200 years.
Location: 1 mile N of Dollar on minor road.

Castle Donington *Leics.*   *Map: 394 Ba*
DONINGTON COLLECTION Before the Second World War, Donington Park was a Grand Prix motor-racing circuit. Now it is the home of the Donington Collection of more than 70 single-seater racing cars.

The cars, some of them more than 60 years old, are in their original condition. The Leyland Historic Vehicles Collection, also at Donington, has more than 80 exhibits.
Location: 1½ miles SW of Castle Donington off A453.

Castle Dore *Cornwall*   *Map: 396 Cb*
The ramparts of this Iron Age hill-fort, raised early in the 2nd century BC, enclose a central compound and an annexe which probably sheltered cattle. Traces of 15 round huts have been found, suggesting that 50 or 60 people lived in the fort at any one time.

Arthurian legend links Castle Dore with King Mark of Cornwall, whose nephew Tristram is reputedly buried there with his lover Iseult.
Location: 2⅓ miles NW of Fowey on B3269.

Castle Drogo *Devon*   *Map: 397 Dc*
Julius Drewe (1856–1930), the son of a poor clergyman, founded the Home and Colonial Stores. By the age of 33 he had made his fortune, and he retired to live the life of a country gentleman.

Drewe was convinced he was descended from the Norman nobleman Drogo de Teigne. He bought a hilltop site near the village of Drewsteignton, named after the man he believed to be his ancestor, and in 1910 commissioned the architect Sir Edwin Lutyens to design him a castle there.
Location: 4½ miles NW of Moretonhampstead off A382.

Castle Fraser *Grampian*   *Map: 387 Fb*
The Z-plan castle of the Frasers was started in about 1575, when the square tower was built, and completed in 1617. The two low wings forming the courtyard were added later.
Location: 14 miles W of Aberdeen off A944.

Castle Hedingham *Essex*   *Map: 399 Ee*
CASTLE Hedingham, built in the 12th century, was once one of the strongest castles in England. Its tower, four storeys high including the basement, rises over 100 ft, and the four corner turrets, of which two remain, added a further 20 ft. The walls are from 10 to 12 ft thick, and are honeycombed with small rooms, or closets.

The entrance to the tower is at first-floor level. It was originally protected by a portcullis, and later a forebuilding was added. This has now disappeared, but the angle of its roof gable still shows in the masonry of the tower.

Hedingham Castle belonged to the de Vere family, Earls of Oxford. The 3rd Earl, Robert, was among the barons who forced King John to accept Magna Carta in 1215, but later that year John besieged Hedingham and eventually obtained its surrender through the sheer weight of his artillery power.

The 13th Earl, John de Vere, helped Henry Tudor to wrest the throne from Richard III at the Battle of Bosworth in 1485. After his victory, Henry was determined to show the nobles who was master, and he passed several laws intended to curb their powers.

One was the Statute of Livery and Maintenance, which restricted the giving or receiving of distinctive uniforms or badges. At dinner at Hedingham, the king noticed that de Vere's many servants were sporting the family insignia, a five-pointed star. Henry ate his meal, thanked his host and then added "I cannot have my laws broken in my sight. My attorney must speak with you." The surprised de Vere was charged and fined £10,000.
Location: 16 miles NW of Colchester off A604.
CHURCH OF ST NICHOLAS Although at first glance the red-brick tower and battlemented façade

suggest that the whole church dates from the 16th and early 17th centuries, parts of it are older.

The nave is a mixture of late-Norman and Early English styles, with Perpendicular windows and a hammer-beam roof. There are three Norman doorways.

The one on the south side has a "Dane skin door", on which, according to a tradition stemming from the raids of the Vikings, the skin of a would-be robber of the church was once nailed to discourage others from crime.

An ornate oak rood screen, carved in about 1400, separates the nave from the chancel, and there are several carved misericords—hinged seats—in the chancel itself.

The church has a fascinating register, written on vellum, which records the baptisms, marriages and deaths of parishioners from Elizabethan times. Some Puritans opposed the idea of infant baptism, as they felt that only an adult could possess the required faith. In 1653, during the Commonwealth of Oliver Cromwell, the church register was turned back to front and babies were entered simply as "born". Not until the Restoration in 1660 were they again entered as "baptised".
Location: Centre of village.

Castle Howard *N. Yorks.*   *Map: 394 Ce*
Sir John Vanbrugh (*c.* 1664–1726), author of *The Relapse* and other Restoration comedies, got to know many famous and influential people through his success as a playwright. He also had ambitions as an architect, and when Charles Howard, 3rd Earl of Carlisle, decided to replace the Howards' family home, which had burned down in 1693, the earl turned to Vanbrugh.

Though full of ideas, Vanbrugh had never designed a house before. But he was shrewd enough to employ Nicholas Hawksmoor, Christopher Wren's Clerk of Works, to help him.

Castle Howard is literally palatial, by far the biggest house in the county. Its approach drive is 5 miles long, and some of the state rooms are so vast that Lord Carlisle feared they would be too draughty to use. The earl was wrong. Vanbrugh later wrote: "He . . . finds that all his Rooms, with moderate fires, are Ovens."

The playwright-turned-architect went on to design Blenheim Palace and Seaton Delaval, but neither of those great houses enjoys a setting to equal Castle Howard.

Everything about the house is on the grandest scale. The marble entrance hall, lit by a huge many-windowed dome, the first in any private home in England, is an appropriate introduction to Vanbrugh's creation. There are tapestries by John Vanderbank depicting the Four Seasons near the main staircase, and on the walls are paintings by Rubens, Canaletto, Van Dyke and Holbein, whose picture of Henry VIII shows the

THE PEACOCK MALE

In the second half of the 18th century, male fashion reached a level of peacock elegance which it has not attained since. Coats and waistcoats worn at court balls, weddings and similar occasions were cut from expensive materials and lavishly decorated. The coat above, from the costume collection at Castle Howard, N. Yorkshire, is in figured velvet trimmed with embroidery and lace, and is worn over a matching satin waistcoat. Both were made about 1770. In The Tailor of Gloucester, *Beatrix Potter wrote of 18th-century tailoring: "The stitches were so small—they looked as if they had been made by little mice."*

WAISTCOAT *Intricate split-stitch embroidery has been used to decorate a waistcoat of ribbed ivory silk made about 1760.*

POCKET *Silver cord, tinsel and sequin trimmings decorate the pocket of a coat in russet-figured velvet. It dates from about 1765.*

much-married king as an embittered old man.

The stables at Castle Howard were designed by Carr of York with the same lavishness as the house itself. They now make a fine home for a collection of 3,000 costumes and 8,000 accessories spanning 300 years. Selected items from the collection are displayed on models set against backgrounds of the appropriate period.

In the grounds near the house is the Temple of the Four Winds, a decorative building intended to add interest to the landscape.

Sir John Vanbrugh died before Castle Howard was completed, and Sir Thomas Robinson added the west wing.
Location: 15 miles NE of York off A64.

Castle Kennedy *Dumfs. & Gall.*   *Map: 388 Ba*
Fire gutted the 15th-century tower house in 1716, and it was not rebuilt by its owner, the 2nd Earl of Stair. However, the formal gardens which the earl laid out, copying those at Versailles, have been restored.
Location: 3 miles E of Stranraer on A75.

Castle Rising *Norfolk*   *Map: 395 Ea*
William d'Albini, who married the widow of Henry I and became 1st Earl of Arundel, built Castle Rising's great tower in the 1130s, setting it inside a tall earth rampart.

For some 30 years the castle was the prison of Isabella, wife of Edward II, whom she deposed in 1327 and had murdered. Isabella's partner in the plot, her lover Roger Mortimer, was executed on the orders of her son, Edward III.
Location: 4 miles NE of King's Lynn off A148.

Castletown *Isle of Man*   *Map: 390 Ab*
CASTLE RUSHEN The castle's central tower was built in the 13th century and the outer defences were added 100 or so years later to create one of the finest medieval fortresses in western Europe. The inner plan is square, the outer one polygonal, and there is hardly a curved surface anywhere.
Location: Town centre.

Catcliffe *S. Yorks.*   *Map: 394 Bc*
GLASS CONE The cone, a brick structure in which glass blowers worked around a central furnace making bottles and similar items, is 68 ft high and 40 ft in diameter. It was built in 1740 and used until 1900. It is open to the public.
Location: 5 miles E of Sheffield (A630, A57 then B6066).

Cawdor *Highland*   *Map: 387 Dc*
CASTLE Despite what Shakespeare implies, Macbeth, Thane of Cawdor, never owned this castle. He lived in the 11th century, but Cawdor's central tower house was not put up until about 350 years later.
Location: 5 miles SW of Nairn on B9090.

Cawston *Norfolk*   *Map: 395 Fa*
CHURCH OF ST AGNES The church was built in the 14th and 15th centuries, when the wool trade flourished in East Anglia.

The fine hammer-beam roof has carved figures on its projecting beams. There is a 15th-century rood screen and an unusual poor box hollowed from a single block of wood.
Location: 11½ miles NW of Norwich (B1149 then B1145).

Cawthorne *N. Yorks.*   *Map: 394 Cf*
EARTHWORKS Roman soldiers dug the four sets of earthworks to enclose camps in about AD 100, probably as part of a training exercise.
Location: 5 miles NW of Pickering off A170.

Ceres *Fife*   *Map: 389 Ee*
FOLK MUSEUM A 17th-century weigh house and adjoining cottages have been skilfully restored to house the museum. Exhibits illustrate the domestic and rural history of Fife, and also include costumes and needlework.
Location: 8 miles SW of St Andrews on B939.

Cerne Abbas *Dorset*   *Map: 397 Fc*
CERNE ABBAS GIANT The naked, club-wielding figure of a man was probably cut into the chalk hillside near the village some 1,500 years ago, during the Roman occupation. Local legend links it with fertility.
Location: 10 miles S of Sherborne off A352.

Chacewater *Cornwall*   *Map: 396 Bb*
WHEAL BUSY COPPER MINE Although the mine, first recorded in 1718, has been abandoned, its buildings are in fairly good condition. They include a stone-built engine-house, a smithy and cottages.

The steam pioneer James Watt installed the first of his new pumping engines at Wheal Busy in 1777.
Location: 1 mile W of village off A390.

Chaldon *Surrey*   *Map: 399 Dc*
CHURCH OF ST PETER AND ST PAUL A rare mural of about AD 1200, rediscovered under layers of whitewash in 1870, covers one wall. It is painted in red and yellow ochre, measures 18 ft by 11 ft, and depicts Purgatory and the Ladder of Salvation. In the Middle Ages, such allegorical "doom paintings" were a favourite form of religious instruction.

The church itself dates mainly from the 11th–13th centuries, although there was an earlier building on the site.
Location: 3 miles W of Caterham off B2031.

Chalford *Glos.*   *Map: 393 Fb*
WOOLLEN MILLS The manufacture of woollen cloth, a Chalford industry since the Middle Ages, reached its peak there between 1790 and about 1830. New water-powered mills were built beside the River Frome, in some cases to replace older ones, and the mill-owners installed themselves in large houses.

The mills no longer work, but some of the buildings survive in private ownership, among them the four-storey St Mary's Mill, of about 1820, and Chalford Mill, which straddles the river.
Location: 4 miles SE of Stroud on A419.

Chappel *Essex*   *Map: 399 Fd*
CHAPPEL AND WAKES COLNE STEAM CENTRE The Stour Valley Railway Preservation Society owns a section of track on which it occasionally operates its trains.

Most of the locomotives on show are tank engines, among them the last one to be built for the Great Eastern Railway at its Stratford works, the ex-GER No. 999 of 1924.
Location: 7 miles W of Colchester on A604.

FROM GARDENER TO KNIGHT

Joseph Paxton (1803–65) spent 32 years as head gardener at Chatsworth, the Derbyshire home of the dukes of Devonshire (see p. 92). Paxton designed many of the present features of the garden, including the gravity-fed Emperor Fountain. His "conservative wall" (above) was part of a network of greenhouses in which he grew exotic plants gathered from all over the world. In 1838, the 6th Duke of Devonshire decided to move the whole village of Edensor because it spoiled the view from the house. Paxton helped to plan the new village. He, like the 6th duke, is buried in the churchyard at Edensor.

PALACE-BUILDER
Paxton used his skill in designing greenhouses to create the Crystal Palace for the Great Exhibition of 1851. It won him fame and a knighthood. The palace was later moved to Sydenham, Gtr London, where it stood until it burned down in a spectacular fire in 1936.

RARE BLOOMS *Paxton planted two* Camellia reticulata *in his "conservative wall" in about 1850. They still flourish, blooming in March and April.*

Charlecote *Warks.*　　　　*Map: 398 Be*
CHARLECOTE HOUSE AND PARK Sir Thomas Lucy, a member of a family associated with Charlecote since the 12th century, inherited the estate in 1551. He built the nucleus of the present house, later enlarged and redecorated in the 19th century, and added the stables and a brewhouse.

Deer roam the undulating park. Their ancestors are said to have tempted the young William Shakespeare, who was caught and punished for poaching by Sir Thomas, but took his revenge by satirising him as Justice Shallow in *The Merry Wives of Windsor* and *Henry IV Part 2*.
Location: 5 miles NE of Stratford upon Avon off B4086.

Charleston Manor *E. Sussex*　　*Map: 399 Ea*
Alured, cup-bearer to William the Conqueror, owned the manor during the last years of the 11th century. Part of the house is Norman, with 15th-century additions.

In the grounds, which are open to the public, there is a circular Norman dovecot and a large medieval barn, now used as an arts studio and theatre.

The portrait painter Sir Oswald Birley (1880–1952) lived in the house from 1931.
Location: 7 miles W of Eastbourne off A259.

Charlestown *Cornwall*　　　*Map: 396 Bb*
HARBOUR The industrialist Charles Rashleigh had the harbour built in the 1790s to ship china clay, a purpose it still fulfils.

Rashleigh's foundry near by produced pumping engines for the clay pits. It is still in use.

The Shipwreck Centre beside the harbour illustrates the causes of wrecks, the processes they undergo on the seabed, and how they provide information about the past.
Location: 2 miles SE of St Austell on A3061.

Chartwell *Kent*　　　　*Map: 399 Ec*
The plain red-brick house was the home of Sir Winston Churchill from 1924 until his death in 1965.

Churchill wrote most of his works of history in the study at Chartwell. Beneath a portrait of his father is the red dispatch box used by both father and son as Chancellor of the Exchequer.
Location: 2 miles S of Westerham off B2026.

another 17 years. After her death Chatsworth went to her second son, William Cavendish, later 1st Earl of Devonshire.

Apart from the moated Queen's Bower, in which the captive Mary passed her time, and the Hunting Tower, nothing is now left of Bess's house. The 4th Earl of Devonshire, raised to the dukedom by William III, began to improve it in

How chinaware got its whiteness

FOR 200 YEARS, CHEDDLETON'S WATER-DRIVEN MILLS GROUND THE FLINT USED FOR MAKING EARTHENWARE IN THE POTTERIES OF STAFFORDSHIRE

WEALTH IN WOOD

The heavily carved panelling and furniture in Chastleton House, Oxfordshire, are a monument to the taste and aspirations of a newly rich merchant at the beginning of the 17th century.

Chastleton House *Oxon.*   *Map: 398 Bd*
Walter Jones, who made himself rich in the wool trade, built the mansion in about 1603 and decorated it lavishly inside to reflect his success.

But he then used up the rest of his fortune supporting the Royalist cause and left little besides the house to his heirs. They could not afford to alter it, so Chastleton remains very much as it was in Walter's day.
Location: 5 miles NW of Chipping Norton off A44.

Chatsworth *Derbys.*   *Map: 394 Bc*
The "Palace of the Peak" owes its existence to a woman, the formidable Bess of Hardwick, and its grandeur to her descendants, the dukes of Devonshire.

Bess was born about 1527 at Hardwick Hall near Mansfield, to a family which, though it owned a manor house, had little money. By the age of 15, she had been married and widowed.

Bess's second marriage was to Sir William Cavendish, who made a fortune by grabbing up the estates of monasteries as Henry VIII dissolved them. Bess encouraged Cavendish to acquire lands at Chatsworth, where the couple started building a mansion in 1549.

Before the house was finished, Cavendish died and Bess remarried, only to be widowed for the third time shortly afterwards. In 1568, an extremely wealthy woman through her inheritances from three husbands, she married the 6th Earl of Shrewsbury.

The following year, Elizabeth I made Shrewsbury custodian of Mary, Queen of Scots, a duty which took up all his time, but left Bess free to indulge in extravagant building schemes, using his money, at Chatsworth and her other estates. Shrewsbury eventually realised how much Bess was spending, and started legal actions against her to try to get something back. He failed and died, worn out, in 1591. Bess lived

During the 17th century, Chinese porcelain began to appear in Europe in increasing quantities as trade with the Far East grew. Chinaware, as it came to be called, was admired not only for its delicacy, but also for its dazzling whiteness, which English potters were for years unable to copy satisfactorily.

In the 1720s, experiments showed that ground flint mixed with native clays whitens them, and it rapidly became an important ingredient in the making of earthenware.

Cheddleton North Mill, near Leek, was built between 1756 and 1765 to prepare flint for the potteries of Staffordshire, then emerging as a centre of the china industry in England because of its ready supply of coal to heat the kilns. The mill was linked to the canal system in 1777, so that flint pebbles from Sussex, Norfolk and Lincolnshire could be brought to it by boat, greatly reducing the cost of transporting them.

Three years later, the old corn mill near by, now Cheddleton South Mill, was converted to grind flint. Both North and South Mills supplied the Staffordshire potteries until 1963.

Flint pebbles were unloaded from narrowboats directly into kilns built into the canal bank, and calcined, or roasted, for 72 hours to make them crumbly. Then the flint was transferred in trucks to the grinding pan, where it was ground for 24 hours. The process took place under water so that flint dust, a form of silica, was not inhaled by the mill workers.

Ground flint and water formed a creamy liquid, which was diluted and thoroughly mixed in the wash tub. From there it went to the settling ark, in which the flint particles sank to the bottom as a sediment.

The surplus water was drawn off and the sediment, called slip, was dried in an open, heated bath, to emerge as a solid substance which could be easily cut into blocks for shipping to the potteries.

The Cheddleton mills are preserved in running order, with their water-wheels, and there is a display of millwright's tools.

On the restored canal, the narrow-boat *Vienna*, built in 1911, is typical of many of the barges which brought flint or coal for the kilns (see also p. 94).

1686, and over the following 20 years had it rebuilt completely, using gritstone from a quarry on the estate and marble from nearby Ashford.

The 4th Duke of Devonshire added the stables and bridge in the 1760s, and hired "Capability" Brown to landscape the park. The 6th duke built the north wing in 1820.

Chatsworth's spacious rooms, many with painted ceilings and ornately carved panelling, are a treasure-store of works of art, fine china and sculpture.

During the summer, an exhibition of live animals and models shows how food is produced from Chatsworth's farms (see also p. 91).
Location: 4 miles NE of Bakewell (A619 then B6012).

NARROW-BOAT *The Birmingham-built* Vienna *was one of the large fleet of horse-drawn cargo boats which plied Britain's canals in the early years of this century. She is 72 ft long, with a 7 ft beam, and could carry about 25 tons in her hold. Many narrow-boats were worked by "canal families", who made the tiny cabins their permanent homes and raised their children aboard. They vied with each other to decorate and furnish the boats lavishly.*

FLINT GRINDING *Flint pebbles were ground to particles under water in the pan at Cheddleton North Mill. The pan floor is chert – a hard stone. Boulders of chert were pushed by the arms to produce a grinding action.*

PREPARING COLOURS *The small granite grinding pans, or mullers, at Cheddleton South Mill date from about 1800 and were used in the Minton works at Stoke-on-Trent. Ores from which ceramic colours were derived were rough-ground, mixed and then roasted in ovens to break them down further. A second grinding, in the mullers, yielded an extremely fine powder. The box beside the mullers weighed out materials for glazing. It is made of wood, because metal might have contaminated the mix. Lead pieces on the outside ensured that all the boxes were the same weight.*

Chawton *Hants.*   *Map: 398 Cb*
JANE AUSTEN'S HOUSE The novelist lived in this red-brick house with her mother and sister from 1809 until just before her death in 1817. She wrote many of her books at Chawton, including *Emma* and *Mansfield Park*. The house is now a museum.
Location: 1 mile SW of Alton off A32.

Chearsley *Bucks.*   *Map: 398 Cd*
CHURCH OF ST NICHOLAS The church, recorded in the Domesday Book of 1086, was extensively rebuilt in the 14th century, and has the remains of a fresco painted then, depicting St Christopher and the Child Jesus.

In the 18th-century gallery there is a hinged seat designed for the musician who played the serpent, a wind instrument shaped like a writhing snake, and derived from the old wooden cornet.
Location: 7 miles SW of Aylesbury off A418.

Cheddleton *Staffs.*   *Map: 393 Fe*
CHURCH OF ST EDWARD THE CONFESSOR The church, founded about 1214, was restored in Elizabethan times, when the upper part of the tower and the porch were added. During a second, Victorian, restoration, windows in the chancel and north and south aisles were fitted with stained glass designed by the pre-Raphaelites William Morris, Ford Madox Brown, Dante Gabriel Rossetti and Edward Burne-Jones.

Outside the east gate there is a set of stocks.
Location: 3 miles S of Leek on A520.
FLINT MILLS There was a water-powered corn mill on the site from 1253 until the 18th century. A

Roman-style luxury for the rich

PROSPEROUS LAND-OWNERS REPLANNED THEIR VILLA AT CHEDWORTH IN THE COTSWOLDS TO HIGH STANDARDS OF COMFORT AND ELEGANCE

CHEDWORTH IN ITS HEYDAY

An artist's reconstruction shows Chedworth early in the 4th century AD. The villa's owners had linked existing buildings of the 2nd century with verandas and additional rooms, to create an inner garden and outer courtyard. Local limestone was used extensively in the villa.

Chedworth's 4th-century Romano-British owners did not stint themselves or their guests. When the extensions to the original 2nd-century villa were complete, it had two sets of baths, one equivalent to a modern Turkish bath and the other to a sauna. Elegant mosaic pavements had been installed, and white marble had been brought from the Mediterranean to face some inside walls. Part of the owners' wealth came from growing grain and, possibly, raising sheep. As recreation, they hunted in the nearby woods.

Some of the later occupants of the villa were Christians, who carved the Greek letters chi and rho, symbolising Christ, on to a cistern.

PAVEMENT *Craftsmen from Cirencester laid the mosaic floor of the dining-room. A hooded figure represents Winter, part of a depiction of the Four Seasons.*

TREASURES LEFT AS THE ROMANS FLED

By the end of the 4th century AD, the Roman Empire in Europe was under threat from barbarian tribes battering on its borders. Troops were pulled out of Britain to defend frontiers nearer to Rome, leaving the land vulnerable to attacks by Saxons, Picts and Scots. As the barbarian raids grew more frequent and more serious, Britain's villas were gradually abandoned.

During these troubled times, a wealthy family living at Mildenhall in Suffolk buried their silverware for safety. They never recovered it, and the hoard lay in the ground for nearly 1,600 years, until it was unearthed during ploughing in 1942.

The Mildenhall Treasure, now in the British Museum in London, is among the most important collections of Roman works of art yet found in Britain.

It consists of 34 highly ornamented items, including spoons, dishes, goblets and a large bowl with a lid, made from the finest-quality silver and almost perfectly preserved. Most of the pieces are from the 4th century, but a few may be up to 200 years older, suggesting family heirlooms assembled over several generations. The best items were made in the Mediterranean area, though some lesser ones may be Gaulish.

The Mildenhall Treasure is a superb memorial to Roman culture, which died in Britain as the empire crumbled.

BOWL *The silver bowl, which measures just over 6½ in. in diameter, is one of a matching pair in the Mildenhall Treasure. The rim, beaded and flattened to form a flange, is more elaborately decorated than that of the matching vessel, and includes leaves, flowers, grapes, birds and rabbits within the scrollwork. Inside, there is a rosette with 16 petals from which shallow, curved flutings radiate up the sides. Marks on the base probably denote the weight – 22 oz.*

LADLE WITH HANDLE *The ladle with its dolphin-shaped handle is one of four found complete at Mildenhall, though the solder joining the two sections has been eroded. The dolphin is a casting covered with silver gilt. Its eye sockets were inlaid, perhaps with semi-precious stones and its body is covered with dotted and incised details.*

GOBLET *A silver drinking goblet, 4½ in. high, has a shallow bowl and a broad base, decorated on the underside, so that it could have been turned upside-down to use as a platter.*

second watermill was built in 1756–65 to grind flint for the Staffordshire pottery industry, and in 1780 the original mill was converted to the same use.

Both are preserved. (See pp. 92–93.)

Chedworth Roman Villa *Glos. Map: 393 Fb*

The earliest part of the villa goes back to the 2nd century AD, but it was enlarged and made more comfortable in the 4th century. The original wings were linked by covered verandas to enclose a garden.

A museum on the site displays farm implements, and coins which imply by their dates that the villa was abandoned about the beginning of the 5th century. Stone figures of gods came from shrines in the villa's grounds (see left).
Location: 7 miles NE of Cirencester off A429.

Cheesewring Mines *Cornwall Map: 396 Cb*

Tin and copper were mined around the Cheesewring until the beginning of this century. There have since been several attempts to revive the workings, most recently during the Second

World War, but these did not lead to large-scale production.

The remains of the engine-house, boiler-house and ore-dressing building of the Phoenix United copper mine still stand near Caradon Hill.

The engine-house of the South Phoenix mine was converted into a house in 1914, and later abandoned.

Location: 7 miles N of Liskeard (B3254 then minor roads).

Cheltenham *Glos.*   *Map: 393 Fb*
PITTVILLE PUMP ROOM Joseph Pitt, who amassed a fortune as a banker, built the Pump Room in the 1820s to dispense spa water. He added an estate of fashionable houses, called Pittville, in which visitors could stay.

Forbes chose a classical style, based on the Greek temple of Ilissus, for the portico of the Pump Room.

Location: Pittville Park, 1 mile N of Cheltenham town centre off Evesham Rd (A435).

Chepstow Castle *Gwent*   *Map: 393 Ea*
William FitzOsbern, Earl of Hereford, built the first stone great tower in the British Isles at Chepstow shortly after the Norman Conquest. By 1071 it was ready for occupation.

The site he chose was a natural ridge, and over

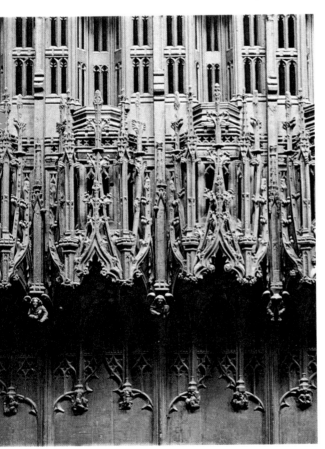

THE GLORY OF CHESTER'S CARVERS
The choir of Chester Cathedral is richly adorned with 14th-century carving. Above the stalls, there is an intricately worked canopy.

the centuries the castle spread along it as new defences and buildings were added. The height of the great tower was raised in the 13th century, showing that its role was still crucial then.

Chepstow fell to Parliamentary troops during the Civil War, but was not dismantled.

After the Restoration, Henry Marten, a signatory to the death warrant of Charles I, was imprisoned in the castle until he died in 1680.

Location: N of town centre.

Chester *Cheshire*   *Map: 393 Ef*
BISHOP LLOYD'S HOUSE The house, built early in the 17th century for George Lloyd, Bishop of Chester, is one of the finest examples of carved timber work in the city. The frontage is heavy with depictions of biblical scenes and animals.

Location: Watergate St.

CASTLE The square Agricola, or Caesar's Tower, in the south-west corner of Chester's well-preserved city walls, is the only substantial visible building left from the medieval castle.

In 1071, William I gave Chester to Hugh d'Avranches, who later led the northern thrust of the invasion of Wales and earned the nickname *Lupus*—"the wolf"—for his ferocity.

The original motte and bailey was strengthened in the 12th and 13th centuries, when inner and outer enclosures of stone were added.

Location: City centre, E of Grosvenor Rd.

CATHEDRAL The remains of St Werburga, a Saxon princess and abbess, who died about AD 700, were brought to Chester from Hanbury in the 9th century to protect them from Danish raids.

In 1093 Hugh d'Avranches, first Norman earl of Chester, founded a Benedictine abbey around St Werburga's church and shrine. The abbey was dissolved in 1540 and the church, rededicated to Christ and the Blessed Virgin, became a cathedral in the following year.

Part of St Werburga's shrine is at the west end of the Lady Chapel. It was severely damaged at the time of the Civil War. The remains of the monastery are extensive, and are among the best-preserved in England.

The cathedral is in a mixture of styles, from Early English to late Perpendicular, and the carvings of its choir stalls are unequalled elsewhere.

It is also the home of the Chester Mystery Plays, based on stories from the Bible, and believed to have been written by monks in the 14th century. The plays were performed until the end of the 16th century, and revived in 1951.

Location: City centre.

GROSVENOR BRIDGE The single arch that carries the Wrexham road across the River Dee is 200 ft long, the widest span of any stone bridge in Britain. It was designed by Thomas Harrison and completed in 1832.

Location: Grosvenor Rd, SW of city centre.

GAMUL HOUSE On September 24, 1645, Charles I watched from the walls of Chester as the remnants of his army were pursued by Parliamentary troops after the Battle of Rowton Moor. The king spent the night in the city, at the home of his friend Sir Francis Gamul, a former Lord Mayor of Chester.

Then Charles withdrew to Wales, asking the Chester garrison to hold out for ten more days. The city did not surrender until the following

February, when starvation had reduced the inhabitants to eating rats and dogs.

Gamul House, entered, like many in Chester's unique Rows, from the first floor, was recently extensively restored.
Location: Lower Bridge St.
ROMAN CHESTER The Romans founded a legionary fortress at the head of the Dee estuary in AD 76–78, to control the Welsh and Pennine tribes. They called it *Deva*, and from about AD 87 it was the base of the XXth Legion.

There are many fragments of the fortress visible on private property throughout the city. A more substantial relic is the north wall, preserved to its original parapet level, 15 ft high.
Location: City centre.
STANLEY PALACE The black-and-white half-timbered house, once the town residence of the Stanleys of Alderley, earls of Derby, was built about 1591.
Location: Watergate St.

Chesterfield *Derbys.*   *Map: 394 Bc*
CHURCH OF ST MARY AND ALL SAINTS The 228 ft steeple has been twisted for more than 500 years. Legend attributes the defect to a sneeze by the Devil, or to a gesture of respect made by the steeple to a virtuous maiden. In reality, the warping of the framing timbers, made worse by the effects of sun on the lead sheathing, is to blame.

The church is mainly Early English and Decorated in style. It has a Norman font, a 15th-century wooden screen and a Jacobean pulpit.
Location: Town centre.

Chesters *Northld.*   *Map: 389 Gb*
ROMAN FORT This was *Cilurnum*, a cavalry base on Hadrian's Wall (see p. 178). The well-preserved remains include parts of the gates and towers, the commandant's house, the headquarters building and, beside the River North Tyne, a bath-house.
Location: 5 miles N of Hexham (A6079 then B6318).

Cheswardine *Salop*   *Map: 393 Fe*
WOODSEAVES CUTTING The gorge which carries the Shropshire Union Canal to the west of Cheswardine is man-made, hewn with only picks and shovels in the 1820s, in many places through solid rock.

At the northern end of the cutting there is a wharf with a 19th-century warehouse.
Location: 4 miles SE of Market Drayton off A529.

Chew Green *Northld.*   *Map: 389 Fc*
ROMAN EARTHWORKS Three earthen camps, the earliest of about AD 80, and a small permanent fortlet were built near each other by Roman soldiers.
Location: 21 miles W of Rothbury (B6341 then minor roads via Harbottle and Alwinton).

Chichester *W. Sussex*   *Map: 398 Ca*
CATHEDRAL Chichester Cathedral has dominated the flat coastal plain of West Sussex since Norman times. Fires and storms have severely damaged it on several occasions, most recently in 1861, when the central tower, with its spire, came crashing down in a gale. Tower and spire were rebuilt on the original pattern.

The see of Chichester was founded in 1075 to replace a Saxon one at Selsey, a village 8 miles away on the coast. The move was part of William I's policy of siting cathedrals in important centres of population. In Chichester's case, the decision proved fortunate, because Selsey church eventually succumbed to erosion and disappeared beneath the sea.

The cathedral is essentially Norman, with Early English additions. Bishop de Luffa began building it in 1091, on the site of a Saxon church, and it was consecrated in 1184. Three years later fire destroyed the eastern end, a disaster which prepared the way for the cathedral's finest architectural feature. This is the retrochoir, the large area of the chancel behind the high altar, which was rebuilt in a transitional style.

As long ago as 1410, the structural weakness of the central tower was recognised. At that time it was judged to be too weak to support bells, so a separate bell tower or campanile was constructed to house them.

Shortly before the central tower finally gave way, the 15th-century stone screen which marks the division between choir and nave was dismantled and stored in the bell tower. It was put back in its original place in 1961.

Among Chichester's priceless treasures are two sculptured panels in the choir aisle, dating from 1125–50 and showing, in relief, Christ arriving at the house of Mary of Bethany and the raising of Lazarus. They were rediscovered in 1829 in a wall, where they had been used as building stones. The panels were originally coloured, and the deeply hollowed-out eyes may have held crystals or gems.

Near by is a unique 16th-century painting on board, by Lambert Barnard, which includes portraits of the kings of England from William the Conqueror – some irreparably damaged by Puritans.

The cathedral also has two modern works of art: a colourful tapestry behind the High Altar, designed by John Piper; and an oil painting on canvas by Graham Sutherland, depicting the appearance of Christ to St Mary Magdalene on the first Easter morning.
Location: West St.

Chingford *Greater London*   *Map: 399 Dd*
QUEEN ELIZABETH'S HUNTING LODGE The lodge was built by Henry VIII as a stand from which courtiers could watch deer-hunting in Epping Forest. It now houses the Forest Museum.
Location: Rangers Rd, ½ mile NE of town centre.

Chingle Hall *Lancs.*   *Map: 391 Eb*
This 13th-century moated manor house, built in the shape of a cross, is reputedly haunted.

There are four priests' hiding holes, for it was a place of Roman Catholic worship during the Civil War.
Location: Goosnargh, 5½ miles N of Preston (A6 then B5269).

Chippenham Castle Museum see Marshfield

Chipping Campden *Glos.*   *Map: 398 Ae*
CHURCH OF ST JAMES The church, originally Norman, was almost entirely rebuilt in the 15th century, when Campden was a prosperous centre of the wool trade. The nave is unusually high,

and is flanked with slender columns.

A pair of 15th-century embroidered altar hangings, the only complete set to have survived in England from that period, is displayed beneath the tower arch. Among the fine brasses is one in memory of William Grevel, who is described in Latin as "the flower of the wool merchants of all England". It measures 8 ft by 4 ft and is the largest in the county.
Location: 11 miles SW of Stratford upon Avon off A46.

WOOLSTAPLERS' HALL A 14th-century hall in which the wool that made Chipping Campden

MAN-TRAP
The 18th-century man-traps at Woolstaplers' Hall were used against poachers. A trap was covered with grass, and when a poacher trod on it the jaws snapped shut just below his knee. The injury often led to amputation of the leg.

rich was graded for sale. It now contains old kitchen utensils, farm tools – and man-traps.
Location: High St.

Chipping Norton *Oxon.*   *Map : 398 Bd*
BLISS TWEED MILL The town marks the eastern edge of the once busy west of England wool trade. One survivor is the tweed mill of W. Bliss and Son, established in the mid-18th century. The present ornate building replaced the original one in 1872. It was once steam-powered, and the chimney sprouts up from the middle of a central dome. Tweed is still made at the mill on modern machinery, and visitors can see the works if they obtain permission in advance.
Location: ½ mile W of town centre, off A44.

Chirk *Clwyd*   *Map : 393 De*
CASTLE This strong medieval fortress, built in the reigns of Edward I and II by the Mortimers, was turned into a residence in the 18th century.

In 1595 the castle was bought by Sir Thomas Myddleton, Lord Mayor of London in 1613, and it is still the family home. It was twice besieged in the Civil War, and on the second occasion it had

AN 18TH-CENTURY SERVANTS' HALL

The servants' hall at Chirk Castle has remained unaltered since the 18th century. The servants ate at an L-shaped table along two walls, with the chief steward seated at the head of the table by the warmth of the fire, on a slightly raised dais. The other servants were ranged in order of importance along the table, with the most junior servant, or a late arrival, sitting in the draughtiest place by the door. The leather buckets hanging from the beams in the hall were to be used for fighting fires.

BEER ON WHEELS
The servants' beer was passed along the table on a wheeled coaster. Rules for servants instructed them to sit at their proper place at table, drink in turn and not to waste food.

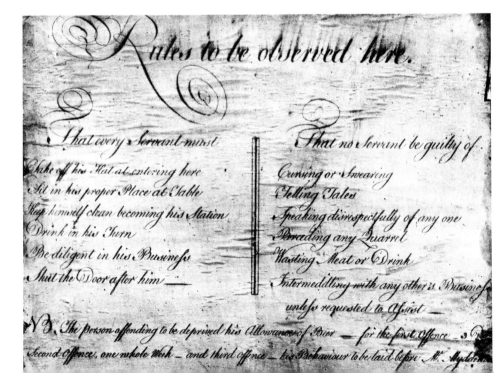

to surrender due to lack of water during an abnormally dry August.
Location: 1 mile W of Chirk on B4500.
CHIRK AQUEDUCT The aqueduct that carries the Llangollen branch of the Shropshire Union Canal across the Ceiriog Valley is a fine stone structure built by William Jessop in 1801.

Equally impressive in their way are the high embankment at the southern end and the tunnel and deep cutting at the northern. They were made by gangs of "navvies" using only gunpowder, picks, shovels and wheelbarrows.

Next to the aqueduct is the slightly larger railway viaduct built half a century later.
Location: The western edge of Chirk on B4500.

Chiswick House *Gtr London*   *Map: 398 Dc*
Completed in 1729 in the grounds of Lord Burlington's house to his own designs, Chiswick was a powerful influence on the architecture of the first half of the 18th century in England. It was based on a design by the 16th-century Italian architect Andrea Palladio. The garden was one of the first to depart from the strict geometry of the previous century. Temples, columns and rustic seats were placed to surprise the visitor and to make allusions to classical literature and Italian painting which were familiar to every educated gentleman of the early 18th century.
Location: Burlington Lane, W4.

Christchurch *Dorset*   *Map: 398 Aa*
CASTLE Christchurch Castle's first stone building was its great hall – domestic not military – erected in the 12th century. In the 13th century a medium-sized tower was put up on the site of a much earlier Norman motte.
Location: Church St, town centre.
PRIORY A belief that Christ in person helped to build this church gave the town, originally called Twynham, its name. The church, started in the 11th century, was to have been built at the top of St Catherine's Hill, but building materials were mysteriously removed each night. Taking this as a divine sign, workmen built the church where it now stands. As work progressed a carpenter arrived who would accept neither food nor drink. When a vital roof beam was cut short work was abandoned for the day, but next morning the beam was miraculously in place. It can still be seen above the ambulatory. The mysterious carpenter vanished, giving rise to the belief that he was Christ.

The church's reredos, or stone screen behind the high altar, is said to be one of the finest survivals of Decorated sculpture in England.
Location: Church St, town centre.

Church Stretton *Salop*   *Map: 393 Ed*
ACTON SCOTT WORKING FARM MUSEUM The farm demonstrates mixed-farming techniques of the 19th century, and is stocked with animals, such as Longhorn cattle, that were common at that time. Visitors may help with farm activities such as hay-making and harvesting, using 19th-century methods. Other farm work includes sheep-shearing, steam threshing and ploughing, bee-keeping and cider-making.
Location: 3 miles S of Church Stretton off A49.

Chysauster *Cornwall*   *Map: 396 Aa*
The best preserved of all the west Cornish Iron

A PLACE OF ENTERTAINMENT
Chiswick House was built not as a residence, but as a gallery for the Earl of Burlington's works of art, as a library and as a place to entertain his friends. A more comfortable Jacobean house, only 50 ft away, was for living in. The main family residence was about an hour's coach-ride away – Burlington House in Piccadilly, now the Royal Academy of Arts.

Age villages. Four pairs of houses front on to a village street. Each house had a central courtyard flanked by a living-room, small workshop and an open area covered by a lean-to roof. Some also had small storerooms. The orderly layout possibly reflects the influence of the Romans who controlled Cornwall at the time.
Location: 3 miles N of Penzance off B3311.

Cilgerran Castle *Dyfed*   *Map: 392 Bc*
Standing above the River Teifi, Cilgerran Castle was protected from attack on two sides by steep cliffs. But its position on the river was so important that it was captured at least five times between 1165 and 1405 in the wars between the Welsh and their English invaders.

The castle was built in the 12th century, and strengthened with two huge cylinder towers and a square gatehouse in the 13th century.
Location: 3 miles S of Cardigan off A478.

Cirencester *Glos.*   *Map: 393 Fb*
CHURCH OF ST JOHN THE BAPTIST St John's is the largest and grandest "wool" church in the county, dominating the town with its 162 ft tower. The Perpendicular tower was built with a gift made in gratitude by Henry IV. In 1399 the townspeople of Cirencester foiled an attempt by the earls of Kent and Salisbury to overthrow the king, and beheaded the conspirators in the market-place. Inside the church is a silver cup and cover owned by Anne Boleyn, second wife of Henry VIII.
Location: Town centre.
ROMAN CITY Cirencester (*Corinium*) was the second largest city, after London, in Roman Britain. Its wealth was based on corn and wool

A ROMAN KITCHEN

Cooking in a Roman villa was done in a kitchen like the one reconstructed at the Corinium Museum, Cirencester. The food was cooked over charcoal on a high stove made of masonry. Wood could be used if the food was to be smoked. The kitchen also contained a table, and water brought in from a well. Delicacies cooked there included snails fattened on milk, and dormice kept in earthenware jars and fattened on nuts. Pigeons were also fattened, and oysters were brought from breeding grounds around the British coast.

FRUIT AND VEGETABLES THE ROMANS BROUGHT

Food in a Roman villa included fruit and vegetables that the Romans introduced to Britain – peas, broad beans, radishes, celery, cherries, medlars (small apple-like fruit) and grapes. Honey was used for sweetening and there were many cheeses. The poor in Roman society lived mainly on bread and pea or bean broth.

Peas
(*Pisum sativum*)

Radish
(*Raphanus raphanistrum*)

Celery
(*Apium graveolens*)

Broad beans
(*Vicia faba*)

Cherry
(*Prunus cerasus*)

Medlar
(*Mespilus germanica*)

Grapes
(*Vitis vinifera*)

from villa estates, and is demonstrated by rich mosaics in the Corinium Museum, Park Street.

Few Roman monuments have been preserved on site, but the grassy mound of the amphitheatre and a stretch of stone defences still exist.

Locations: The amphitheatre is in Cotswold Ave, off Somerford Rd; the defences are north of London Rd, opposite the end of Beeches Rd and through the housing estate.

Cissbury *W. Sussex*   *Map: 398 Da*
Stone Age men dug flints from Cissbury Hill about 3000 BC. Circular depressions in the ground are the filled-in shafts. About 3,000 years later the hill became an Iron Age hill-fort, with two rings of banks, 20 ft high, enclosing 80 acres.
Location: 5 miles N of Worthing off A24 at Findon.

Clachnaharry *Highland*   *Map: 387 Dc*
CALEDONIAN CANAL The building of the sea-lock at the eastern end of the Caledonian Canal was one of the great engineering achievements of the canal age. Because the North Sea runs out a long way at low tide, the canal had to be extended 400 yds from high-water mark. Clay was dug from a nearby hill to build an embankment, and the sea-lock was built at the ocean end. The canal, which runs across Scotland, opened in 1822.
Location: 1 mile NW of Inverness on A9.

Clandon Park *Surrey*   *Map: 398 Dc*
Every servant employed between 1875 and 1888 is recorded in the Servants' Book at Clandon, one of the grandest Palladian houses in England. Wages included £55 a year for the butler, £40 for the housekeeper and £16 for a third footman.
   The owners, the Earls of Onslow, were generous employers. They paid for wedding breakfasts at Clandon for several female servants, and sent a sick house-maid to the seaside to recuperate.
Location: 3 miles E of Guildford off A426.

Clapham *Beds.*   *Map: 398 De*
CHURCH OF ST THOMAS BECKET The church tower was probably built just before the Norman Conquest of 1066, when Viking raiders periodically rowed their longboats up the River Ouse to pillage the countryside. The tower was used as a lookout, and when Viking ships were sighted

warning was given to nearby villages and farmsteads. Local people took refuge in the tower, entering through a door high above ground level, and pulling up the ladder once they were inside.

In the 12th century an extra storey was added to the tower, and nave and chancel were rebuilt.
Location: 2 miles NW of Bedford on A6.

Clare Castle *Suffolk*　　　*Map: 399 Ee*
The 100 ft high motte on which the castle stands is believed to be Saxon. The Normans built a wooden tower on it, and converted that to a stone shell-keep in the 12th century. It lies between two baileys, one of which was used as the station yard when the railway came to Clare. But the station has now, in its turn, been abandoned, and the site is a country park.
Location: 7 miles E of Haverhill (A604 and A1092).

Claremont *Surrey*　　　*Map: 398 Dc*
Clive of India's marble-lined bath survives in the basement of the great classical house built for him by "Capability" Brown in 1772.

In 1816 Claremont became the home of Princess Charlotte, only daughter of the Prince Regent; she died here in child-birth the following year. It later became a favourite holiday home of Queen Victoria.
Location: The house is $\frac{1}{2}$ mile SE of Esher on A244; the garden is $\frac{1}{2}$ mile S of Esher on A3.

Clava Cairns *Highland*　　　*Map: 387 Dc*
PASSAGE GRAVES The three stone cairns, each inside a stone circle, were built around 3000 BC. Two have passages leading to circular chambers in which human bones were found.
Location: 6 miles E of Inverness (A9 and B851).

Claverton *Avon*　　　*Map: 397 Ge*
CLAVERTON MANOR At the age of 23, Winston Churchill delivered his first political speech at a fête at Claverton Manor on July 26, 1897. He spoke in support of the Primrose League which had been formed by his father, Lord Randolph, to infuse new life into the Conservative Party.

Claverton, built in 1820, is now the American Museum, and contains reconstructions of American rooms from the 17th to 19th centuries.
Location: $3\frac{1}{2}$ miles SE of Bath off A36.
PUMPING STATION One problem facing John Rennie, engineer for the Kennet and Avon Canal, was supplying water to the canal. At Claverton in 1811, he converted an old mill, powered by the River Avon, to operate a beam pump. The pump lifts the water from the Avon 53 ft up the hillside to empty into the canal. So the power of the river itself is used to lift the river water. The pumping station has been fully restored.
Location: $3\frac{1}{2}$ miles SE of Bath off A36.

Claypotts Castle *Tayside*　　　*Map: 389 Ef*
Claypotts was built in the 1570s by John Strachan, lord of the land of Claypotts, who remembered the ravaging and looting of English armies in the 1540s. He may have feared that English invaders would come again in support of Mary, Queen of Scots, who had lost her throne in 1568.

The unusual fortress began as a rectangular stone tower house; then cylindrical towers were grafted diagonally on to two opposing corners, forming a Z-plan.

Gunloops in each of the towers cover two sides of the centre building which in turn covers both towers. In theory it should have been impossible to approach the castle from any angle without being in a direct line of fire.

This compact defensive structure is a fine example of more than 50 Z-plan castles built in Scotland in the 16th and 17th centuries.

The defences of Claypotts were never tested.
Location: $3\frac{1}{2}$ miles E of Dundee off A92.

Clayton Tunnel *W. Sussex*　　　*Map: 399 Db*
When the London-to-Brighton railway was being planned in the 1830s the surveyor, John Rennie Jnr, faced the problem of crossing the South Downs, north of Brighton. Many experts said a tunnel would be impossible, but Rennie went ahead. With the tramway engineer John Rastrick, he drove a tunnel more than $1\frac{1}{4}$ miles through the hills. The northern entrance was designed by the architect David Mocatta in the style of a Gothic castle, with turrets, arrow slits and battlements. Perched on top is the house where the tunnel's caretaker lived. For some years after the tunnel was opened in 1840 its interior was kept whitewashed and lit by gas, as were other tunnels on the line. The tunnel is still on the main line.
Location: 8 miles S of Haywards Heath by A273.

Clearwell Caves *Glos.*　　　*Map: 393 Eb*
The caves are part of two old iron-ore mines, called Old Ham and Clearwell. The area has been mined since prehistoric times, and the caves were heavily worked in the Middle Ages. They have been opened to visitors who can explore the complex chain of tunnels where the ore was extracted by candle light with pick and shovel. The 19th-century Pillar Chamber still has boreholes for explosives.
Location: 6 miles SE of Monmouth (A466 and B4231).

Cleeve Abbey *Somerset*　　　*Map: 397 Ed*
The dormitory used by the monks in the 13th century still survives at Cleeve Abbey. And the 15th-century refectory, or monks' dining-room, has one of the finest medieval roofs in Somerset.
Location: 6 miles SE of Minehead off A39.

Clevedon Court *Avon*　　　*Map: 397 Fe*
Clevedon is a fine example of a 14th-century manor house, with superb Gothic tracery in the chapel window. The Elton family have lived here since 1709, and among their visiting friends were the writers Samuel Taylor Coleridge, John Clare, Robert Southey and Charles Lamb.

Tennyson wrote *In Memoriam* after a visit to the tomb of his friend Arthur Hallam in Clevedon church in 1856.
Location: 10 miles W of Bristol (B3128 and B3130).

Clifton Campville *Staffs.*　　　*Map: 393 Gd*
CHURCH OF ST ANDREWS A Decorated church with a beautiful Early English chantry chapel.

In the 18th century, the rector of St Andrews recorded that there was a "Master who teaches, in a vestry room above the church, reading,

101

English, arithmetik, about thirty boys and girls".
Location: 6 miles NE of Tamworth off A453.

Clitheroe Castle *Lancs.*   *Map: 391 Eb*
The 35 ft square stone tower is probably the
smallest main tower of any castle in England. It
was built in the 11th century on the site of an
earlier wooden tower.
Location: Town centre.

Cliveden House *Bucks.*   *Map: 398 Cc*
Between 1739 and 1751 Frederick, Prince of
Wales, father of the future George III, lived at
Cliveden. In the grounds he heard the first
performance of Arne's *Rule Britannia*. The house
was burned down in 1795. It was rebuilt, but
destroyed again by fire in 1849. The existing
house was built in 1851 by Sir Charles Barry.
 In 1893 Cliveden was bought by the American
millionaire William Waldorf Astor who became
1st Viscount Astor. The 2nd Viscount's wife,
Nancy, was the first woman to sit as an MP. In
the 1930s she was the political hostess of the
"Cliveden Set", which included the Prime
Minister Neville Chamberlain, the Chancellor of
the Exchequer Sir John Simon and others who
favoured the "appeasement" of Hitler's
Germany.
Location: 4 miles N of Maidenhead off B476.

Clouds Hill *Dorset*   *Map: 397 Gc*
A brick cottage bought by T. E. Lawrence (of
Arabia) in 1925 when he rejoined the Air Force as
Aircraftsman Shaw. He was killed while
returning to Clouds Hill on his motor-cycle in
1935.
Location: 9 miles E of Dorchester (A35, B3390).

Clumber Park *Notts.*   *Map: 394 Cc*
Work on this great deer park began in 1707 for
the Duke of Newcastle, warden of neighbouring
Sherwood Forest. A house built in 1770 was
demolished in 1938, but the stables and 19th-
century chapel survive. There are walks between
ornamental trees and shrubs, and beside a lake
rich in waterfowl. Duke's Drive is a 3 mile
avenue of 3,000 lime trees in double rows.
Location: 3 miles SE of Worksop off B6005.

Clun Castle *Salop*   *Map: 393 Dd*
The great tower was built in the 12th century half
on and half off the earlier Norman motte,
because the motte would not carry its weight.
Location: 16 miles NW of Ludlow (A49, B4368).

Clynnog-fawr *Gwynedd*   *Map: 392 Be*
A chapel connected to the 16th-century church
by a passageway once contained the shrine of St
Beuno, a 7th-century missionary who died here.
Location: 9 miles S of Caernarfon on A499.

Coalbrookdale *Salop*   *Map: 393 Ed*
IRONWORKS The discovery by Abraham Darby
that iron-ore could be smelted with coke instead
of charcoal was a major factor in launching
Britain into the Industrial Revolution. Darby
acquired the Coalbrookdale ironworks in 1708 to
cast iron cooking pots, and later the works made
the first iron bridge and the boiler for the first
locomotive. (See opposite.)
Location: 9 miles N of Bridgnorth (B4373 then
A4169).

Birthplace of modern industry

AT COALBROOKDALE, COKE-SMELTING OF
IRON WAS DISCOVERED IN THE 18TH
CENTURY, LAUNCHING BRITAIN INTO
INDUSTRIAL GREATNESS

Coalbrookdale in Salop is often called The
Birthplace of the Industrial Revolution.
 Abraham Darby was a Bristol brass-caster
who devised a way of casting cheap cooking
pots, using iron. In 1708 he bought the ironwork at Coalbrookdale, and discovered how to

CLOCK-TOWER
*A visit to the
Coalbrookdale
ironworks begins at
the warehouse built
in 1838, with its
cast-iron clock-
tower added in
1843. Beyond is the
main site, built in a
valley so the
processes could
follow each other
downhill to the
River Severn,
easing transport
problems.*

OLD FURNACE *Part of the original ironworks that
Abraham Darby took over in 1708 is the old furnace.
Molten iron was tapped from a hearth at the bottom.*

THE HEARTH *The original lintel in the hearth has the
date 1638. The hearth was later enlarged, and a new
lintel reads "Abraham Darby (the third) 1777".*

EARLY RAILS *An
old railway
wagon stands on
rails cast at
Coalbrookdale.
The L-shaped
type of rail came
into use about
1790, and
railways carried
materials around
the works.*

use coke instead of charcoal as the fuel for his furnaces. Iron-making was at last removed from its dependence on Britain's dwindling stock of timber.

In the 1770s, parts were cast at Coalbrookdale for the world's first iron bridge, which still crosses the Severn Gorge at nearby Ironbridge. This was the first use of iron in architecture, and was the forerunner of the steel-framed buildings of today.

Richard Trevithick went to Coalbrookdale in 1796 to order a boiler for the world's first locomotive.

Iron is still cast at Coalbrookdale, but part of the original site is open to visitors. A small

museum tells the story of the works and shows examples of its products, including the humble cooking pots that began it all.

On the road to the River Severn, a group of cottages are being restored to illustrate the way of life of the Coalbrookdale workers. At the riverside is the wharf and warehouse where material was stored ready for shipment.

WORLD'S BIGGEST *In 1851 Coalbrookdale foundry was the world's biggest, producing 2,000 tons of finished iron a week.*

HOW IT STARTED *The first Abraham Darby discovered how to cast iron pots in sand, and launched his new business. The pots ranged up to 400 gallons.*

INKWELL *During the Victorian era Coalbrookdale was a major producer of ornamental castings, such as this inkwell and penstand. The inkwells are china.*

FLORAL HAT-STAND *Elaborate hat-stands were cast in iron at Coalbrookdale in the 19th century. This example is now at the museum.*

WROUGHT-IRON FLOWERS *Individual pieces, such as flowers or bosses, were made of wrought, or malleable, iron to be added to gates or large pieces of furniture.*

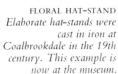

MINIATURE STOVE *This tiny stove (left) was a 19th-century hardware-salesman's sample.*

SEAT-BACK *The veins on nasturtium leaves show the precision with which iron was cast.*

ART IN IRON *Artists were commissioned by the Coalbrookdale works to design art castings such as this fruit plate.*

Coalport *Salop* *Map: 393 Fd*

CHINA WORKS Coalport pottery was set up in the 18th century by John Rose, and specialised in table-ware. William Billingsley (1758-1828), one of the finest English porcelain painters, worked there from 1819. By 1830, Coalport was one of the leading potteries of England.

In the mid-19th century, the works began producing porcelain in the style of Sèvres in France and Meissen in Germany, and in 1926 the company moved to Stoke-on-Trent. The old works is now a museum.

BRASS RECORDS OF MEDIEVAL LIFE

Under carpets in innumerable English churches are thousands of grave slabs inlaid with engraved plates known as brasses. Despite the great number that have been torn out for their metal, or by 19th-century collectors, more brasses remain in Britain than in the rest of Europe combined.

Brasses, especially the earlier ones, are magnificent examples of the engravers' art, and an excellent source of information on costume, armour, heraldry, ecclesiastical vestments and lettering. However there was almost no attempt to create portraits of the dead person until the 17th century.

Knights in armour
Most brasses are found in churches in the eastern counties, because the metal, an alloy of copper and zinc, was imported from the Continent.

The most celebrated brasses are those of knights in armour such as Sir John D'Abernon (1277) at Stoke

SIR JOHN D'ABERNON (1277) *A knight who saw service in Plantagenet England during the reign of Henry III now lies at Stoke d'Abernon church in Surrey.*

HIGHLIGHTS OF A POTTERY ERA

Coalport China Works stretched for a quarter of a mile along the Shropshire Canal in the 19th century. Two of the bottle-shaped kilns and the bottom section of a third have survived. The works are now part of the Ironbridge Gorge Museum.

TSAR'S PLATE *Coalport made a dessert service for the Tsar of Russia about 1850. One of three surviving pieces is at Coalport.*

GILDED VASE *Ornamental mantel vases were often made in sets of three.*

RACING TROPHY *A vase inscribed in gold was a trophy for Pains Lane races in 1844.*

The village is at the junction of the River Severn and the Shropshire Canal. The canal is interrupted by a hill and continues at a higher level. The two sections are joined by the Hay Incline, which carried tub boats up and down on wheeled undercarriages.
Location: 8 miles N of Bridgnorth off A442.

Cobham *Kent*   *Map: 399 Ec*
CHURCH OF ST MARY MAGDALENE The church contains the best collection of brasses in the country. Cobham takes its name from the Saxon name Cobba, and many of the brasses are memorials to the Cobham family, local land-owners who rebuilt the church in the 13th century.

The brasses escaped destruction or mutilation during the mid-16th and 17th centuries when Puritans considered brasses to be idolatrous or superstitious.
Location: 4½ miles W of Rochester off A2.
COBHAM HALL Glimpsed from a distance through the ancient trees of its park, the mellow red brick and the pepper-pot towers of Cobham Hall

---

d'Abernon, Surrey; Sir Roger de Trumpington (1289) at Trumpington, Cambridgeshire; Sir Robert de Bures (1302) at Acton, Suffolk, and Sir Robert de Setvans (1306) at Chartham, Kent.

The chancel of St Mary Magdalene's Church at Cobham, Kent, is covered with brasses, the most impressive series in the world.

Ladies, who frequently lie hand-in-hand with their husbands, provide a fascinating display of changing fashions and head-dress–"Sir J. Dyve" (1435) is shown with both his wife and mother, at Bromham church, Bedfordshire, and Sir Ralph and Lady Verney (1547) lie together at Albury church in Hertfordshire.

Medieval priests lie in their embroidered vestments in many churches. Examples are the brasses of T. de la Mare (*c.* 1370) in St Alban's Cathedral and L. de St Maur (1337) at Higham Ferrers, Northants.

Other church brasses show children, merchants, scholars, judges, figures draped in shrouds, and even skeletons. One of the most unusual brasses is in Salisbury Cathedral, and commemorates Bishop Wyvil who died in 1375. It shows him, with his mitre and crozier, gazing out of a fantasy castle, with a knight standing at its gate.

Taking rubbings from brasses
Among the most splendid of all is the enormous plate in St Margaret's Church at King's Lynn, Norfolk, showing Robert Braunche (1364) flanked by his two wives, all under canopies. The brass is engraved at the foot with a superb representation of the Peacock Feast given for Edward III in 1349.

For over a century, brass enthusiasts have been producing rubbings on paper, using cobblers' heel-ball. The hobby has become so popular that the conservation of the brasses is causing concern, and some churches no longer allow rubbings to be made without special permission and payment of a fee.

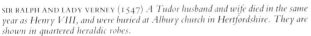

SIR RALPH AND LADY VERNEY (1547) *A Tudor husband and wife died in the same year as Henry VIII, and were buried at Albury church in Hertfordshire. They are shown in quartered heraldic robes.*

SAMUEL HARSNETT (1631) *A 17th-century Archbishop of York is shown in life-size effigy at Chigwell, Essex.*

symbolise the ideal English country house.

It was begun in 1584 for Lord Cobham, Lord Chamberlain to Elizabeth I, and was extensively altered in the following three centuries.

The Gilt Hall, with a moulded 17th-century ceiling and walls adorned with musical instruments of the 18th century, is not only a successful blend of two periods 100 years apart, but also one of the most beautiful rooms in England.

The house is now a girls' school, but is open on some days in April, July and August.

Location: 4 miles W of Rochester off A2.

Cockermouth *Cumbria*   *Map: 390 Dd*
WORDSWORTH HOUSE The poet William Wordsworth was born here in April 1770, and lived in the house until he was eight. The house and its garden figure in some of his poetry.

Externally it has not changed since the Wordsworth family took up residence, and three of the rooms are open to the public.

Location: Main St.

Cockley Cley *Norfolk*   *Map: 395 Ea*
A reconstruction of an Iceni village as it is thought to have been at the time of Queen Boudicca has been built near a 15th-century forge cottage, now a museum of local history.

Location: 3 miles SW of Swaffham on minor road.

Coggeshall *Essex*   *Map: 399 Fd*
PAYCOCKE'S HOUSE This early-16th-century half-timbered house was built by Thomas Paycocke, a farmer/butcher who also prospered from the East Anglian wool trade. Oak furniture of the 16th and 17th centuries is displayed in richly beamed and panelled rooms.

Location: 5½ miles E of Braintree on A120.

Coity Castle *Mid Glam.*   *Map: 392 Da*
The first castle at Coity was a wooden-palisaded earthwork. According to legend Morgan, a Welsh chieftain, was defending the castle during the Norman invasion of Glamorgan in the 11th century, when a French knight, Payn de Turbeville, threatened to storm it. But Morgan sent word that he would surrender only if de Turbeville would marry his daughter. De Turbeville agreed and the wedding took place.

In the following century the wooden castle was replaced by a stone enclosure with a tower on the western edge.

In the 13th century a second enclosure was built on the west of the first, making the castle a formidable stronghold that withstood a long siege by Owain Glyndwr, the Welsh rebel leader, in the early 1400s.

Location: 2 miles NE of Bridgend off A4061.

Colchester *Essex*   *Map: 399 Fd*
BOURNE MILL This charming two-storey water-mill with Dutch gables was built as a corn mill in 1591 from the remains of a nearby abbey. During the Cromwellian period it was used as a fulling mill for finishing cloth, and became a corn mill again in the mid-19th century.

Location: Bourne Rd, 1 mile S of town centre off Mersea Rd (B1025).

CASTLE Colchester has the most massive great tower in Britain – built by the Normans in the last years of the 11th century in similar shape to the White Tower of London but larger. Once four storeys high, with a ground area 151 ft by 110 ft, it was built largely of stone from the ruins of the old Roman town.

Colchester was an obvious site for a major Norman fortress. England still feared Viking raids on the east coast, and there was an excellent harbour that needed guarding.

In 1216 Colchester Castle was taken by the French force which aided the barons in rebellion against King John. The king recaptured it after a short but concentrated siege.

Thereafter the castle became a prison. In 1406 Matilda Haras, from a wealthy local family, was seized for reasons now unknown and tortured in the castle with a thumbscrew "till the blood oozed forth".

Between 1555 and 1558, 22 men and women of the town who opposed the Catholic policies of Mary I were burned at the stake, some in the castle bailey.

By the 1780s conditions in the prison became so revolting that they drew the attention of John Howard, the penal reformer. The castle was closed as a gaol in 1835.

Location: High St, town centre.

ROMAN CITY At the time of the Roman invasion of Britain in AD 43, Colchester was the centre of the most powerful tribal confederacy yet seen in the island. This Celtic stronghold was smashed by the invading Roman army, supervised in person by the Emperor Claudius.

A legionary fortress was built in the western part of the present town, but it was superseded six years later by the first civilian settlement. The town, inhabited largely by ex-soldiers, was for a time the capital of Roman Britain.

Claudius was worshipped in a vast classical temple, the foundations of which can be visited below the Castle Museum.

Colchester was the "citadel of everlasting dominion", wrote the historian Tacitus, and it was a target of Boudicca's revolt in AD 60. The British rebels sacked and burned the city killing hundreds of the inhabitants.

Later, possibly in the 2nd century, the city was surrounded by walls which survive for almost their entire length. The massive Balkerne Gate on the west side is particularly impressive.

BABY'S BOTTLE
A baby who died in the Roman town of Colchester about AD 180 was buried with this terracotta feeding bottle. In another baby's grave, terracotta toys in the shape of a boar, a bull and other animals were found. By Roman law only children could be buried within the walls of a city.

Combe Saw Mill *Oxon.*   *Map: 398 Bd*
The saw mill of Blenheim Palace, with its joiner's shop and smiths' forges, provided all the timber and ironwork for the estate. The steam beam engine, which is run on some weekends, was built in 1852 to drive the saw mill when the river

TUDOR GRANDEUR

The tall chimneys, mullioned windows and brick construction mark Compton Wynyates as one of the finest Tudor houses in England. Henry VIII,

Elizabeth I, James I and Charles I all stayed there, but in 1644 the house fell to the Roundheads. In the gardens, shrubs are pruned into fantastic shapes.

was too low. Equipment and tools used in the workshops are on display. The mill originally ground corn.
Location: 6 miles NE of Witney off A4095.

Compton *Surrey*   *Map: 398 Cb*
CHURCH OF ST NICHOLAS One of the ancient churches visited by the pilgrims on their way to Canterbury. The flint-and-stone tower was built by the Saxons 100 years before the Norman Conquest. The remainder of the church is largely Norman; the broach spire is 14th century.

A feature of the church is the two-storey chancel – a beautiful vaulted chamber with a tiny chapel above it, each with its own altar. The purpose of the upper chapel is unknown.

Inside the chancel, near floor level, is an aperture that was part of a Saxon anchorite cell, in which a religious hermit once lived, revered and fed by the villagers in return for his advice and solace.
Location: 3 miles SW of Guildford off A3.

Compton Castle *Devon*   *Map: 397 Db*
Compton Castle is a manor house that was fortified in the late 14th century as protection against the French raids that were frequently made along the south Devon coast.

In the 16th century it was owned by Sir Humphrey Gilbert, half-brother of Walter Raleigh and the founder of the English colony in Newfoundland.

The great hall and gatehouse have been restored.
Location: 3 miles NW of Paignton off A3022.

Compton Wynyates *Warks.*   *Map: 398 Be*
Compton Wynyates was one of the first of the great houses of England to be built for comfort rather than defence. It was built in the 1480s, as peace settled on Britain after the Wars of the Roses. Amid the prosperity of the Tudor years the house was enlarged in the 1520s by William Compton, a courtier to Henry VIII. Tall decorated chimneys rose from numerous fireplaces to give extra warmth; mullioned windows admitted more light, at the expense of security.

Henry VIII himself stayed here with the first of his six wives, Catherine of Aragon, and their emblems are painted on glass in the room where they slept.

Sir Henry Compton was a favourite of Queen Elizabeth, which demanded that he incur the enormous expense of entertaining the queen and her entire court at Compton Wynyates in 1572.

War came to Compton Wynyates in 1644 when it was attacked by Parliamentary troops. The house was protected by a moat and drawbridge, but after two days it was captured. The Parliamentarians filled in the moat so the house could never be defended again. But they never knew that the Countess of Northampton had been looking after wounded Royalist soldiers in the loft. Later, she and the servants helped them escape.
Location: 10 miles W of Banbury off B4035.

CHURCH OF ST MARY The church was built in 1665 after its predecessor was destroyed in the Civil War. Inside there is a magnificent set of heraldic hatchments, depicting the armorial bearings, crests and mottoes of the Compton family. Hatchments were hung outside a house following the death of a member of the family, and later hung in their church.
Location: In the grounds of Compton Wynyates.

Congleton *Cheshire*   *Map: 393 Ff*
LITTLE MORETON HALL Probably the most famous black-and-white (half-timbered) building in England.

Instead of the polished order and balance of most great houses, Little Moreton Hall is a cheerful jumble, extravagantly decorated, and leaning at disconcerting angles. The house is the product of three generations of the Moreton family, all with their own views of how a fashionable house should be designed. Fitting all their plans into the one cramped site proved all but impossible.

The original house was built by William Moreton the elder at the end of the 15th century, with a great hall flanked by living-rooms at one end and service rooms at the other. The house was set around a small courtyard and surrounded by a moat.

William Moreton the younger had loftier ideas. In the mid-16th century he built a large gatehouse, with an over-hanging upper storey on the only space available, next to the bridge across the moat. He also wanted to add the bay windows that were fashionable in Elizabethan country houses. There was no suitable position for them on the outside of the house, so two large bays were crammed into the tiny courtyard.

When William's son, John Moreton, took over the house, a long gallery had become the essential feature of a gentleman's house–a room for entertaining and displaying paintings, and the longer and loftier the better. But there was no room for a long gallery in the house. The only possible place left was on top of the gatehouse, and here the gallery was built. The triple-tiered gatehouse now completely dominated the house.

The gallery is a long bright room, lit by windows for almost its entire length, and looking giddily down to the hall and moat below. Panels at the ends are decorated with painted figures and mottoes, including a figure holding a celestial globe with the words: "The speare (sphere) of destinye whose rvler is knowledge." The work was probably carried out by craftsmen who could neither read nor write themselves.
Location: 4 miles SW of Congleton on A34.

Conisbrough Castle *S. Yorks*   *Map: 394 Bc*
This towering and gloomy fortress is one of the most impressive monuments of medieval England. The great tower, nearly 100 ft high, was built by Hamelin Plantagenet, half-brother of Henry II, in the 1180s on a mound overlooking the River Trent. It is circular, inside and out,

WHEN WOOD WAS CHEAP

Little Moreton Hall at Congleton was built in the Middle Ages when timber was so plentiful that it could be used as much for decoration as for the main framework of a house. The exterior walls of the house contain almost as much wood as plaster in between. Over the gatehouse, a long gallery (below) was added in the 16th century during the reign of Queen Elizabeth. It is 68 ft long, and was designed for formal entertaining in the contemporary fashion of the grandest Elizabethan houses.

TUDOR GLASS *In the 16th century, bays were added to the house. An inscription reads: "Richarde Dale Carpeder made thies windovs by the grace of God."*

WALL-PAINTING *A 16th-century painting of Susan and the Elders on the wall of the parlour.*

Conisbrough Castle: power in stone

TO ENTER THIS FORBIDDING FORTRESS A VISITOR HAD TO PASS A MOAT, AN OUTER
GATE, A BARBICAN, A PORTCULLIS AND A TWIN-TOWERED GATEHOUSE

Conisbrough Castle, built on a hill overlooking
the River Trent, was surrounded by a 35 ft high
stone wall, 7 ft thick. To get to the main gate a
visitor had first to gain admission at an outer gate
behind a drawbridge over a deep moat. Then he
entered a barbican, an open passage with high
battlemented walls on either side. This led him
along the main wall of the castle from which
defenders would be looking down. At the main
gatehouse with its twin towers, a portcullis had
to be raised before he could enter the inner bailey.

The outer wall splays outwards at the base so
that missiles dropped by defenders would ricochet
on to attackers below.

The royal family used the castle in the 14th
century, but probably lived in buildings inside
the wall, as the tower was so gloomy.

A MIGHTY RUIN *Conisbrough today has lost the conical
roof which crowned the tower during the castle's
heyday in the early 13th century.*

RESISTING INVADERS, STOREY BY STOREY

*Conisbrough Castle as it was in the early 13th
century. The entrance to the great tower is on the first
floor. Inside, stairs wind up within the wall. They
start on opposite sides on each storey so that attackers
would have to fight their way across each floor before
climbing up to the next.*

but with six wedge-shaped buttresses. The buttresses are solid except for one which contains a
chapel on the second floor.

The great tower has few windows, so life
inside would have been spent in perpetual twilight. The entrance chamber has no openings,
except for the door; it would have been permanently dark or lit by smoking torches.

Conisbrough was captured in 1317 during a
war between the owner John Warenne, Earl of
Surrey and Sussex, and the Earl of Lancaster.
Location: Town centre.

Conwy *Gwynedd*   *Map: 392 Cf*
ABERCONWY HOUSE Aberconwy is a Welsh word meaning the mouth of the River Conwy. It is also the name of the old timber-and-plaster house which has stood at the centre of the town since the late 13th century. It is one of the oldest houses in Wales, a survivor of the houses that were first built in the town in the Middle Ages.
Location: Junction of High St and Castle St.
BRIDGES Two old bridges stand, side by side, in the shadow of Conwy Castle. The older of the two is a suspension bridge built by Thomas Telford in 1826 to carry road traffic across the Conwy estuary. The supporting towers were crenellated in keeping with the site; even the little toll-house at the end of the bridge has battlements.

The railway bridge was designed 20 years later by Robert Stephenson, using an entirely new construction technique. It is built from huge hollow girders, inside which the track is laid. It was designed as a trial for the more ambitious Britannia Bridge across the Menai Strait, and completed in 1848, also in the medieval style.
Location: Across the Conwy estuary.
CASTLE Conwy Castle is one of ten castles built by Edward I in his campaign to conquer Wales in the late 13th century. When completed it was one of the most powerful castles in western Europe.

Conwy was designed by the king's castle engineer, Master James of St George, and mainly completed in four years, between 1283 and 1287. More than 1,500 men worked on it, and the cost came to £20,000.

The result was a military stronghold consisting of a high wall with eight huge flanking towers, the most compact assembly of turretry in the British Isles.

The towers are over 30 ft in diameter with walls up to 15 ft thick. Each is over 70 ft high with several storeys containing rooms and a staircase. One of them, known as the Prison Tower, has an extra storey – a concealed dungeon beneath a floor that appears to be the bottom of the tower. But below the floor is a deep circular pit with smooth walls. The only light or air that could get through to an occupant of the dungeon was through an 18 in. square shaft passing 12 ft through the wall.

This massive fortress, guarding the entrance to the River Conwy, represented all that Edward I stood for – strength, dominion, permanence and terror. And it was hated by the Welsh.

In 1294, seven years after it was completed, Prince Madog ap Llywelyn led a rebellion against English rule in North Wales. His forces descended upon Edward's castles, and caused great damage, particularly at Caernarfon. The king marched to North Wales and set up his base at Conwy. He was no sooner in the castle than the waters of the river rose, effectively trapping him and cutting off his supplies. Edward spent days waiting for the water to subside, living on a deteriorating diet of salted meat, suspect water and coarse bread. But after the river went down the king emerged to crush the rebellion and to order the building of Beaumaris Castle on Anglesey, strengthening his dominion over Wales.

A century later, a second king stayed at Conwy. Richard II was returning in disguise from Ireland to deal with his cousin Henry Bolingbroke, Duke of Lancaster, who was threatening his place on the throne. When he landed in Wales he hid at Conwy, and while there was duped by the Earl of Northumberland's offer of safe conduct to Chester to meet Henry. On the way the earl betrayed him to Bolingbroke who put Richard in Flint Castle where he was bullied into abdication.

The castle deteriorated in later years, and in 1609 it was described in an official report as "utterly decayed". In 1628 it was sold for £100 to Viscount Conway.

In the Civil War in the 17th century it was occupied by Royalist forces and besieged by Parliament and captured.
Location: S of the town centre.
PLAS MAWR The name is Welsh for Great Mansion, and this beautiful Elizabethan house dates from a less turbulent time than the town's castle and walls. By the 16th century Britain's growing trade had made farmers and merchants wealthy men. One such was Robert Wynne, an Elizabethan adventurer and local landowner. At the age of 59 he bought land inside the walls of Conwy and built his "great mansion".

Today Plas Mawr still maintains the air of a well-ordered, prosperous Elizabethan household. There is a bolting room (to "bolt" meant to sieve) for the sifting of flour for bread.

The great kitchen has a spit for the roasting of meat, with holes on either side of the vast fireplace to hold bread ovens. The small kitchen has a wooden breadsafe hanging from the ceiling, and a stone beside the fireplace where the cooks would sharpen their carving knives.
Location: High St, town centre.
"SMALLEST HOUSE IN GREAT BRITAIN" This tiny cottage which was occupied by a fisherman in the 19th century, is furnished as a typical Welsh cottage in Victorian times.
Location: On the quayside, facing the harbour.

Copford Green *Essex*   *Map: 399 Fd*
CHURCH OF ST MICHAEL AND ALL ANGELS A 12th-century church with the best medieval wall-paintings in Essex. Painted about 1140–50, they provided instruction in the scriptures for parishioners who could not read or write.

In the 16th century, the paintings were obliterated with whitewash by Puritans, who wanted to banish "superstitious imagery". The paintings were discovered during repairs in 1710, but were again whitewashed. They were fully revealed in 1871.

The church also has a 12th-century font, a 14th-century oak chest, and – framed on a wall – fragments of human skin that were originally fixed to the south, or Dane Skin, door. It was a practice in parts of Essex during the 9th and 10th centuries to punish sacrilegious Danes by flaying them alive, and nailing their skins to the south door as a warning to others.
Location: 5½ miles W of Colchester (B1022 then minor road).

Corbridge *Northld.*   *Map: 391 Fe*
OLD POTTERY Walker's Old Pottery, founded in the 19th century, was concerned with the humbler end of pot manufacture, turning out bricks, tiles and salt-glazed bottles. It has long been out

DEFENDING A MEDIEVAL TOWN

The town wall of Conwy was built by Edward I at the same time as the castle. It contains 21 flanking towers and three double-towered gateways, and is the finest example of a medieval town wall remaining in Britain.

It was intended to protect the new town of Conwy and also to serve as a defence for the castle against attack from the landward side. The wall towers are 50 yds apart and were designed as self-contained defensive units. If attackers climbed to the top of the wall, that particular section could be isolated by removing plank bridges on the walk-way near each tower. A force of 18 or 20 men armed with crossbows would have been needed to defend each section. The wall and towers contained a total of 480 arrow slits.

A drawing of 1600 (above) shows the town as it was in the days of Elizabeth I; right, the town today seen from the wall.

of use, but two of the old bottle kilns have survived. These are built of brick, 30 ft in diameter. Next to them are two Newcastle brick kilns, rectangular buildings in which bricks were fired. The bottle kilns are now leased by the Tyne and Wear Industrial Monuments Trust, but are not yet open to the public.
Location: Milkwell Lane, off B6321.

ROMAN TOWN In the 3rd and 4th centuries, the Roman town of Corstopitum was a flourishing supply depot for Hadrian's Wall, 3 miles to the north. On the north of the road are a pair of granaries, a fountain and an unfinished store building; to the south, a pair of military compounds containing houses, stores, workshops and clubs. A small museum contains some Roman

THE ART OF THE 18TH-CENTURY CHAIR-MAKERS

British furniture reached its golden age in the 18th century. In the 1720s mahogany from the West Indies replaced walnut for high-quality chairs and gave rise to ornate carved decoration. In the 1760s the architect Robert Adam promoted a fashion for the arts of ancient Rome, leading to lighter, less ornate styles.

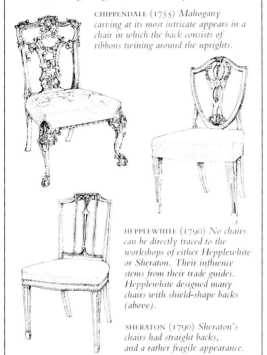

CHIPPENDALE (1755) *Mahogany carving at its most intricate appears in a chair in which the back consists of ribbons twining around the uprights.*

HEPPLEWHITE (1790) *No chairs can be directly traced to the workshops of either Hepplewhite or Sheraton. Their influence stems from their trade guides. Hepplewhite designed many chairs with shield-shape backs (above).*

SHERATON (1790) *Sheraton's chairs had straight backs, and a rather fragile appearance.*

sculptures, including a lion devouring a stag.
Location: ⅓ mile W of Corbridge off A69.
VICAR'S PELE One of the simpler border pele towers, built about 1300. Pele towers were small castles where a landowner and his tenants could shelter from raiding parties. "Pele" came from the Latin *palus*, a stake, as the towers first stood inside a wooden palisade.

The border country was so dangerous due to fighting between English and Scots that even parish priests were not safe. Vicar's Pele was built beside the church for the vicar's safety. It had three storeys, each a single room. The vicar's study was at the top, with windows protected by a battlemented parapet.
Location: Market Place (A68).

Corfe Castle *Dorset*   *Map: 397 Gc*
The castle began as a wooden Saxon tower on a natural mound, guarding a road through the Purbeck Hills. The stone-built great tower was probably built by Henry I in the 1130s, and added to by King John.

In 1202 King John was said to have sent 22 captured French knights to Corfe and starved them to death in the castle dungeons.

The castle supported the Royalist cause in the Civil War, and later was severely damaged.
Location: 4 miles SE of Wareham on A351.

Corgarff Castle *Grampian*   *Map: 387 Eb*
The castle, a fortified tower house, was attacked by marauders in 1571 and set on fire. The laird's wife, Margaret Forbes, with her children and servants – 25 in all – died in the fire.

A HOUSE FURNISHED BY CHIPPENDALE

Sir Paul Methuen, grandson of one of the richest of the 17th-century wool merchants of Bradford-on-Avon, collected Old Masters while he served the Royal Household early in the 18th century.

Corsham Court in Wiltshire was bought by his cousin in 1745 to house the paintings. To do them justice, "Capability" Brown enlarged the house and park and Thomas Chippendale furnished the rooms where the paintings still hang. The cost included 478½ yds of crimson silk damask, at 14 shillings a yard, to cover Chippendale's chairs.

CHEST AND TABLE *The Chippendale furniture includes a pair of mahogany chests-of-drawers (above) and a pair of tables with porphyry tops (below).*

ARMCHAIRS *The 30 Chippendale armchairs were covered with silk damask. The walls of the gallery were covered with 700 yds of similar material.*

The castle was rebuilt, and a wall with gunports was added in the 18th century.
Location: 14 miles NW of Ballater off A939.

Corsham Court *Wilts.*   Map: 398 Ac
Mr "Customer" Smythe, so called because of his office as Collector of the Customs of London, built Corsham in 1582.

In 1760 "Capability" Brown – an architect as well as a landscape gardener – was engaged to re-model the house to contain the collection of paintings and sculpture which the owner had inherited. Those rooms, with their Chippendale furniture, and the collection remain.

Brown also built a stone pavilion in the garden, called The Cold Bath House because of the uninviting little plunge-bath it contains.
Location: 4 miles W of Chippenham off A4.

Cosgrove *Northants.*   Map: 398 Ce
The Grand Union Canal passes through Cosgrove, and to the south of the town is the Great Ouse Aqueduct, which is reached by a short walk down the towpath. Originally, the river was crossed by a brick aqueduct but it collapsed in 1808. The canal was then brought down to river level and back up the other side by a flight of locks, but floods occurred and the scheme was abandoned. The present aqueduct, a plain iron trough on stone pillars, was built in 1811.
Location: 9 miles NE of Buckingham (A422, A508, then minor road).

Cotehele House *Cornwall*   Map: 396 Cb
By the middle of the 16th century it had become customary for the master of the house and his family to dine apart from the rest of the house-hold. At Cotehele the great table still stands in the hall where the multitude of retainers sat down to eat. In the family dining-room just off the hall is a smaller table with richly carved legs. It has probably been standing in this room ever since 1580.

In almost every room of this medieval-style house, walls are hung with tapestries to provide both decoration and insulation from the cold. In many instances they still hang over doors to exclude draughts. Bedrooms are dimly lit by small windows, and beds, still with their original hangings, are heavily curtained.

Most of Cotehele was complete by 1520; in 1553 the Edgcumbes, who owned it, began to build another house, Mount Edgcumbe, not far away on Plymouth Sound, and from the late 17th century the second house became their main home. Cotehele, remote in its woods, gradually fell asleep, used by the family only for occasional visits.

Next to the dining-room, and entered by raising a tapestry, is an intimate chamber known as the Punch Room. It is lined with tapestries illustrating wine-making, and a door gives access to a closet lined with 18th-century brick-built wine-bins.

A walk through woods takes the visitor to the mill, now turning and grinding corn again, and to the wheelwright's and the blacksmith's shops, all vital to the daily life of a remote country house up to three generations ago.
Location: 8 miles SW of Tavistock on minor roads off A390.

CLOCK WITHOUT PENDULUM, MIRROR WITHOUT GLASS

A clock made before the invention of the pendulum is still in its original place at Cotehele, Cornwall. It was installed in the chapel by the owner Sir Richard Edgcumbe in the 1480s. The clock has no face, but operated two bells, one to toll the hours, the other to toll for church services. It is driven by two iron weights. Most similar clocks were rebuilt when pendulums were invented in the 17th century. In one of the bedrooms at Cotehele is a steel speculum, or mirror, made about 1625 before glass mirrors were common.

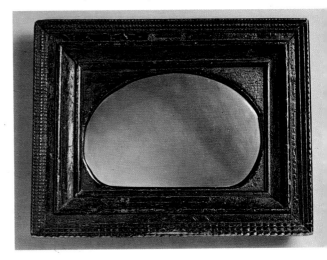

Cotswold Farm Park *Glos.*   Map: 393 Gb
Farm animals that were once widespread in Britain but now face extinction are being bred at Cotswold Farm Park. The farm has more than 20 rare breeds including the Cotswold sheep which created much of England's wealth in the Middle Ages, and Tamworth pigs which most resemble the animals that foraged in the oak forests of ancient Britain.

The science of breeding new types of animals was first developed in Britain in the late 18th century, when Robert Bakewell of Leicestershire established selective mating as a means of fatstock improvement. However, as new breeds developed, old ones were discarded and sometimes became extinct.

The animals at Cotswold Farm Park include Longhorn cattle, which are probably the nearest direct descendants of the wild cattle tamed by Stone Age farmers. The breed was improved by Bakewell, whose Longhorns were unrivalled in their ability to fatten, but it declined when smaller joints and therefore smaller animals became popular.

White Park cattle are believed to have been introduced by the Romans, possibly as sacrificial animals for a religious cult. When the Romans

ANIMALS FROM THE PAST

Farm animals threatened with extinction are being preserved at rare-breed farms so their genetic strains can be used by breeders of the future.

LONGHORNS *Only a few herds remain of these relatives of the wild cattle domesticated by Stone Age farmers. They are too big for modern joints of meat.*

WHITE PARKS *The breed was introduced by the Romans. Later the cattle took to the wild and were killed by hunters. A few survived on the great estates.*

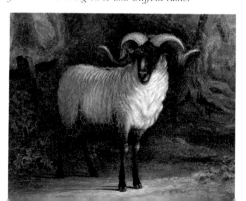

HORNED SHEEP *The ancient Jacob sheep (above) got its name from the story in Genesis in which Jacob chose spotted sheep as his wages. The last Norfolk ram (below) died in 1973, but a similar strain is being bred from the surviving ewes and Suffolk rams.*

left Britain, the cattle became forest animals.

Sheep at the farm include the Soay, the last survivor of Europe's prehistoric domestic sheep. They shed their wool, so farmers could pluck them instead of using shears.

In the Middle Ages, Norfolk Horn sheep foraged on the heathlands of East Anglia. But when the land was enclosed and farmed intensively, the Norfolk Horns were replaced by more-productive breeds. The last Norfolk Horn ram died in 1973, but by crossing surviving ewes with Suffolk sheep, which include a Norfolk strain, a "New Norfolk Horn" has been created to continue a breed close to the original.

Other sheep at the farm include the North Ronaldsay (or Orkney) sheep which grazes on seaweed in the Orkneys, and the St Kilda sheep, with a black fleece, yellow eyes and up to six goat-like horns, giving it an almost devilish look. The St Kilda is probably the last remnant of the Hebridean sheep which are thought to have been brought to the Hebrides by the Vikings.

Pigs at Cotswold Farm Park include the Gloucester Old Spot, which foraged on waste from cottages and small farms in the Vale of Berkeley.

A breeding experiment at the farm has produced a type of pig similar to those found on farms in the Iron Age by crossing a wild boar and a Tamworth sow.
Location: 7 miles W of Stow-on-the-Wold (B4077 then S on minor road). It is signposted from the B4077.

Coughton Court *Warks.*   *Map: 393 Fc*
The Throckmorton family, owners of Coughton Court, clung determinedly to the old Catholic faith after the Reformation in the 16th century. The sister of Thomas Throckmorton, master of Coughton, was married to Thomas Catesby, a ringleader in the Gunpowder Plot against James I.

On the night of November 5, 1605, a group of the plotters waited in the room over the main gate at Coughton for a message from Guido Fawkes, who had hidden barrels of gunpowder under the Houses of Parliament.

At last the message was brought by a manservant: the plot had failed and Fawkes had been arrested. The plotters scattered, but one by one they were tracked down and executed. But Thomas Throckmorton was not directly involved, and escaped suspicion.

Roman Catholic worship continued at Coughton for the next 200 years; part of the north wing was a secret chapel. Finally, after the Catholic Relief Acts, the family was able to worship openly again and in 1857 a Catholic church was built in the village.
Location: 12 miles N of Evesham off A435.

Coventry *W. Midlands*   *Map: 398 Bf*
CANAL Some of the industrial past that survived the Second World War bombs can be seen in a short walk along the towpath of the Coventry Canal. Start at the canal basin in St Nicholas Street, an attractive spot with its old cobbled yard and canopied warehouses. A small canal museum has been opened in the wharf office.

Walk past the old wharf and crane, and on your left is a Victorian building with rounded windows and a metal chimney. This is all that remains of Coventry Cotton Factory where, in 1896, Henry Lawson began the Daimler Motor Company. Coventry's car industry started here.

By the next bridge stands Cash's, where Joseph Cash built his weaving works in the 19th century. Houses are grouped on two sides of a courtyard, with the workshops above them. To get to their looms, the workers came up through trapdoors from their homes. These "top shops" are now used for storage, but garment labels are still woven in the courtyard workshops.
Location: St Nicholas St, north of Ringway.
FORD'S HOSPITAL These timber-framed buildings packed tightly around a narrow courtyard were almshouses founded in 1509 by a wealthy Coventry merchant, William Ford.
Location: Greyfriars Lane, city centre.
ST MARY'S GUILD HALL By the 14th century, increasing wealth from wool and cloth had made Coventry the fourth city of the kingdom after Bristol, York and London. A new middle class of prosperous merchants had banded into guilds for protection and trade, and St Mary's Guild Hall was begun in 1340 for a guild newly formed that year. It was extended in 1400.

The Mayoress's Parlour has a panelled ceiling showing the white-hart badge of Richard II which was not used after his death in 1399.
Location: Bayley Lane, city centre.

Cowfold *W. Sussex*   *Map: 398 Db*
Until the 19th century Cowfold was in the heart of Britain's iron industry. Many of the "hammer" or "furnace" ponds survive in the woods to the north. The ponds, or small dams, provided water to turn the water-wheels that powered bellows for the furnaces and hammers for the forges. They are triangular in shape, with the dam and sluices at the narrow end.

The nearest to Cowfold is just off A281. Go north 1½ miles to Crabtree, then take the minor road to the east. A small bridge crosses the mill-pond, and beside the bridge are the furnace foundations. The furnace closed about 1665.
Location: 7½ miles W of Haywards Heath on A272.

Coxwold *N. Yorks.*   *Map: 394 Be*
SHANDY HALL The parson-novelist Laurence Sterne lived in this idyllic country house from 1760 until his death in 1768. It contains first editions of his novels *Tristram Shandy* and *Sentimental Journey*.
Location: 8 miles SE of Thirsk off A19.

Craig Castle *Grampian*   *Map: 387 Eb*
Built in the 16th century, the castle has wide-mouthed gunports in the tower walls, and a large iron yett (portcullis) at the entrance.
Location: 14 miles SE of Dufftown (A941, B9002).

Craigellachie *Grampian*   *Map: 387 Ec*
OLD SPEY BRIDGE The A941 used to be carried over the River Spey by an iron bridge built in 1815 by Thomas Telford. The bridge has a single, gently curved span of 150 ft. A plate on one of the castellated towers that decorate each end tells the traveller that the parts were cast at the Plas Kynaston iron works at Ruabon in Denbighshire in 1814. The bridge has now been by-passed.
Location: 13 miles S of Elgin on A941.

SCOTTISH TOWER HOUSE
Craigievar Castle, like other Scottish tower houses, has overhanging turrets at the corners so that small arms could be used to give flanking fire along the walls. The conical roofs show French influence.

Craigievar Castle *Grampian*   *Map: 387 Fb*
An almost fairy-tale castle built of pink granite, with overhanging corner turrets. The castle, built in the 1620s, was formidably defended and could only be entered by one guarded doorway.
Location: 26 miles W of Aberdeen (A944 and A980).

Craignethan Castle *S'clyde*   *Map: 388 Dd*
Not long after it was built in the 16th century, Craignethan was attacked many times by the Protestant lords, because the owner supported Mary, Queen of Scots. In 1579 it was dismantled and not repaired for nearly a century.
Location: 5 miles NW of Lanark off A72.

Cranborne Manor *Dorset*   *Map: 397 Gc*
There is an air of romance and fantasy about this beautiful manor house, in the lonely landscape of Cranborne Chase, that sets it apart from all others in England. It was built between 1607 and 1611 as a hunting lodge by Robert Cecil, Earl of Salisbury. James I came here often.
Location: 10 miles N of Wimborne Minster on B3078.

Cranmore *Somerset*   *Map: 397 Fd*
EAST SOMERSET RAILWAY The railway is based at Cranmore Station. The eight steam-engines include three excellent examples of main-line locomotives – *Black Prince, Stowe* and *Green Knight*. Visitors can ride on the brake vans.
Location: 3 miles E of Shepton Mallet off A361.

Crathes Castle *Grampian*   *Map: 387 Fb*
The castle is a massive granite tower house with a side wing. It took nearly half a century, from 1550 to 1595, to build, and the top of the building was capped with turrets.
Location: 14 miles SW of Aberdeen on A93.

VILLAGE REMEDIES FOR ILLNESS

At Cregneish, as in other British villages, herbs were grown to treat illness. Vervain was used against nervous diseases; comfrey was made into a poultice for sprains and bruises; and feverfew was used for earache. Mugwort was worn to ward off evil spirits.

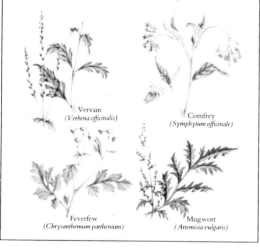

Vervain
(*Verbena officinalis*)

Comfrey
(*Symphytum officinale*)

Feverfew
(*Chrysanthemum parthenium*)

Mugwort
(*Artemisia vulgaris*)

A CROFTER'S KITCHEN

Harry Kelly's cottage at Cregneish is a typical crofter's cottage. It has two rooms, with a loft; the floor is hard-packed clay, and a peat fire burns on the hearth-stone, without any grate. A cooking pot and kettle hang from a chain in the chimney. The dresser displays chinaware from England, and wooden bowls and horn beakers made locally.

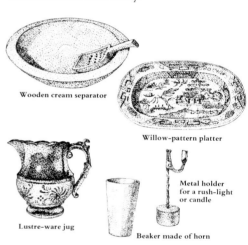

Wooden cream separator

Willow-pattern platter

Metal holder for a rush-light or candle

Lustre-ware jug

Beaker made of horn

Cregneish *Isle of Man*   *Map: 390 Ab*
MANX OPEN-AIR FOLK MUSEUM The windswept village of Cregneish is probably a survival of an ancient Celtic settlement. For centuries, a community of less than 50 people gained a living from the thin, acid soil that covers the rock of the Meayll peninsula. It was a self-contained community. Six families farmed 300 acres of arable and grazing land, while other families worked as labourers on the farms, or as fishermen. A blacksmith shoed the horses and repaired agricultural tools: a weaver made cloth from home-spun wool for the villagers to make their own clothes. Villagers spoke Manx Gaelic until the present century.

Five buildings of the old village have been restored – a farmstead, a cottage, a smithy, a weaver's shed and a turner's shop.

The cottage, owned by Harry Kelly who died in 1934, is a typical two-roomed crofter's cottage. The door opens into the large kitchen/living-room dominated by its fireplace. Off it is a smaller bedroom with a loft over half

the building, entered by a ladder, where children would sleep.

Heat was provided by a peat fire burning on the hearth-stone. The peat was cut from the nearby hill and stacked outside the house under a thatching of rushes.

The sheets and blankets in the cottage were hand-woven from home-spun thread; the quilt was made by a Cregneish weaver in 1860.

Harry Kelly made his living by keeping a few sheep and hens, catching fish from his boat and working for the farmers.

The native Manx sheep are the Loghtan, whose rams have from four to six horns. During the summer a small flock graze in the folk museum's fields.

Location: 5 miles W of Castletown (A7, A31).

Creswell Crags *Derbys.*   *Map: 394 Bc*
STONE AGE CAVES The gorge of Creswell Crags was formed by a stream which has cut its way for millions of years through the limestone ridge. The crags on each side of the gorge contain caves

and rock shelters, four of which were occupied by Early Stone Age hunters.

Neanderthal men, of the species which preceded modern man, seem to have used the gorge as a base for summer hunting during the warmer periods of the last Ice Age about 40,000 BC. The hunters left behind them some of the roughly chipped stone hand-axes and scrapers that they used to butcher their prey.

As the Ice Age drew to its end, conditions probably became more attractive. An ice-dammed lake may have formed near the caves and would have been a gathering place for animals. Stone Age families probably moved in more permanently after about 12,000 BC. By then the cave-dwellers had a wider range of tools and a more varied diet. Bone needles have been found, together with fine flint blades, awls and scrapers. Horse-meat seems to have been the main food, but smaller creatures such as hares and birds were also being caught.

After the Ice Age ended, about 10,000 BC, Middle Stone Age hunters used the caves, and people have lived there from time to time ever since – in Late Stone Age, Bronze Age, Roman, medieval and even later periods.
Location: 14 miles SE of Sheffield (A616 and B6042 at Creswell).

Criccieth Castle *Gwynedd*   *Map: 392 Be*
On a headland overlooking Cardigan Bay, Llywelyn the Great began building Criccieth Castle in the 1230s. His castle consisted of the outer of the two existing walls. It was flanked by two towers, one called the Engine Tower as stone-throwing machines were used on it.

In 1283 the castle was captured during Edward I's conquest of North Wales, and a second wall was built inside the first, making the castle almost concentric. The work cost £400.

Criccieth was burned by the Welsh patriot Owain Glyndwr in 1404 and left to deteriorate.
Location: 5 miles W of Porthmadog off A497.

THE TRAM AGE RE-LIVED

Double-decker trams, such as the Leicester 76, *are back in service at the Crich Tramway Museum. The* Leicester *tram was built in 1904 and ran until 1947.*

WHERE STONE AGE MEN HUNTED

Forty thousand years ago, Stone Age hunters watched from the caves of Creswell Crags for their prey, which included mammoths, rhinoceroses and wild horses. After killing them with spears, the hunters butchered the carcasses with flint axes and scrapers.

BONE ART *The best Early Stone Age art in Britain was found at Creswell Crags. The bone on the left appears to show a masked man, the other (top) is engraved with a horse's head.*

Crich *Derbys.*   *Map: 394 Bb*
TRAMWAY MUSEUM Over 40 trams, built between 1873 and 1953, are preserved in a limestone quarry. Electric trams run from a tram shelter that once stood in Birmingham. The track has been laid out on part of the bed of a mineral railway built by the railway pioneer George Stephenson in the early 19th century. There are also horse-drawn trams on display. Around the tramway an Edwardian town is taking shape.
Location: 5 miles N of Belper (A6 then B5035).

Crichton Castle *Lothian*   *Map: 389 Ed*
The castle began as a rectangular tower house in the 14th century, and was enclosed by a quadrangle of large apartments and walls in the 15th century. In the 16th century an inner face of the quadrangle was rebuilt, with a ground-floor arcade surmounted by a wall of faceted stonework. This was inspired by a palace in Italy which Crichton's owner, Francis Stewart, Earl of Bothwell, had been visiting.

Bothwell was even more vicious than his notorious uncle, the man who had Lord Darnley murdered, and married his widow, Mary, Queen of Scots. He lived a life of "continuous violence and uproar" in Scotland and abroad. He was

117

described as "a terror to the most desperate duellists of Europe and a subduer of the proudest champions, both Turks and Christians".
Location: 13 miles SE of Edinburgh (A68, B6367).

Crickhowell Castle *Powys*　　　*Map: 393 Db*
A castle of three periods: the 50 ft high motte (or mound) was put up by the Normans in the 11th century; a shell keep was built on it in the 13th century, probably by the Welsh who had captured the castle; and Edward I surrounded the keep with an outer wall after conquering Wales at the end of the 13th century.
Location: 5½ miles NW of Abergavenny on A40.

Crieff *Tayside*　　　　　　*Map: 388 Df*
INNERPEFFRAY LIBRARY The first public library in Scotland was founded in 1691 by Lord Madertie, the Laird of Innerpeffray Castle. It was housed in the adjacent St Mary's Chapel but was moved to the present building about 1750.

The collection of Bibles includes one of 1602 with a footnote by Lord Madertie that he was about to read it for the 13th time.

The Borrowers' Ledger, dating back to 1747, contains the names of tradesmen, craftsmen and students who used the library.
Location: 4 miles SE of Crieff off B8062.

Croft *N. Yorks.*　　　　　　*Map: 394 Bf*
CHURCH OF ST PETER The nave is dominated by a pew built about 1680 for the local Milbanke family. It is raised high above the surrounding pews and is reached by a grand staircase – a startling expression of 17th-century social pretentiousness.
Location: 3 miles S of Darlington on A167.

Croft Castle *Heref. & Worcs.*　　*Map: 393 Ec*
This 14th-century stone enclosure, with towers at the corners, was a rendezvous for Yorkist leaders in the Wars of the Roses (1455–85).
Location: 5 miles NW of Leominster (B4361, B4362).

Crofton *Wilts.*　　　　　　*Map: 398Bc*
PUMPING STATION The station was built in 1809 to pump water from a lake up to the summit level of the Kennet and Avon Canal, which linked

Where the factory age began

WHEN RICHARD ARKWRIGHT BUILT THE FIRST WATER-POWERED COTTON MILL AT CROMFORD IN DERBYSHIRE, HE LAUNCHED THE WORLD'S FACTORY SYSTEM

In 1771 Richard Arkwright built a mill at Cromford in the Derwent Valley, to spin cotton thread with his newly invented spinning-frame, which needed water to power it. Cromford had a plentiful supply of water but little labour, so Arkwright brought in workers, many of them pauper families. Most of the mill work was done

by women and children, who worked 13 hour shifts to keep the mill spinning day and night.

The main market for Arkwright's thread was the knitting industry of Derby, Nottingham and Leicester, but his spinning-frame could make cotton thread strong enough for the warp (the lengthwise threads) in cotton cloth. Previously, more expensive linen thread had to be used. He also patented and installed machinery for carding (straightening) the fibres.

Arkwright's Cromford factory was so successful that he built a number of others in Derbyshire and Lancashire, and by 1782 was employing 5,000 people. He was knighted in 1786, and when he died in 1792 had made a fortune.

Others copied and developed his system, and during the 1800s cotton manufacture became the main industry in the north of England. By the 1830s it employed about 450,000 people.

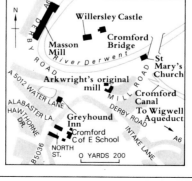

THE ORIGINAL MILL *Water was channelled across the road from Bonsall Brook and Cromford Sough. The water was warm, and kept the machinery going even when the weather was freezing.*

Two of the five storeys have been removed and new parts added. The mill is now in private use.

ARKWRIGHT'S TOWN

The town of Cromford was as much Arkwright's creation as were its mills. He built houses for his workers, the church, and the Greyhound Inn, and in 1790 obtained a market charter.

The mills employed few men. Some houses had top-floor workshops where they worked at home, knitting stockings on stocking frames.

Cromford's houses and mills are still in use, and are not open to the public.

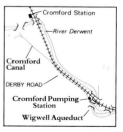

CROMFORD CANAL *Arkwright helped to build a canal near the mills to provide good transport for materials.*

London and Bristol. Two beam engines, including a Boulton and Watt engine of 1812, still work on special days. The 1812 steam-engine is the oldest in the world still doing its original job.
Location: Near Great Bedwyn, 6½ miles SW of Hungerford off A4.

Cromarty *Highland* *Map: 387 Dc*
HUGH MILLER'S COTTAGE This thatched cottage dating from 1650 was the birthplace in 1802 of Hugh Miller, a stonemason who became an eminent geologist, theologian and writer. The cottage contains letters to Miller from Charles Darwin and Thomas Carlyle.
Location: 19 miles NE of Inverness (B9161, A832).

Cromer *Norfolk* *Map: 395 Gb*
LIGHTHOUSE The 58 ft lighthouse was built in 1833 half a mile from the cliff edge, to avoid the fate of its predecessor. The original lighthouse was built near the cliff in 1719, but after numerous landslips it was declared unsafe, and in 1866 it was carried away by a cliff fall.
Location: Between Cromer and Overstrand.

THE WORLD'S OLDEST STEAM-ENGINE STILL AT WORK

This 1812 steam pumping engine, built by the firm of Boulton and Watt, pumped water into the Kennet and Avon Canal until 1958. It now works again.

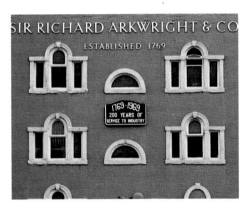

MASSON MILL *Arkwright built the six-storey mill in 1783, and its central block is little changed. It is now worked by the English Sewing Cotton Company.*

WILLERSLEY CASTLE *In 1788 William Thomas began to build Arkwright a baronial mansion. But Arkwright died in 1792, before the building was finished.*

NORTH STREET *Sturdy three-storey workers' houses are still standing. Water was drawn from street taps.*

CANAL *Near the first mill was the canal wharf. The canal was completed in 1793 by William Jessop. It ran about 15 miles southeast to join the Erewash Canal at Langley Mill, so linking local coal and lead mines and mills with the Midlands and south.*

WIGWELL AQUEDUCT *The 200 yd long aqueduct carried the Cromford Canal over the Derwent. At Cromford Pumping Station water was pumped from the river to the canal by an 1849 beam engine. The canal was abandoned in 1944, but the pumphouse and engine have been restored.*

Cromford *Derbys.*   *Map: 394 Bb*
TEXTILE TOWN An 18th-century Lancashire wig-maker, Richard Arkwright, invented a spinning machine that could be operated by a water-wheel. In 1771 he set up the world's first successful cotton-spinning mill at Cromford, and began the revolution that transformed the textile trade from a cottage craft into a world-monopoly industry. Arkwright chose Cromford partly because it was away from the old textile areas and the wrath of the hand spinners to whom his machines brought unemployment. (See pp. 118–19.)
Location: 2 miles S of Matlock on A6.

Crondall *Hants.*   *Map: 398 Cb*
CHURCH OF ALL SAINTS A Norman church built on the site of an earlier church mentioned 'in Domesday Book (1086). An entry in the churchwardens' accounts in 1543 reveals that the weight of the central tower was pushing out the chancel walls. In 1657–9 the tower was taken down and rebuilt on the north side for £428.
All Saints has an 18th-century pitch-pipe, a forerunner of the tuning fork.
Location: 3½ miles NW of Farnham off A287.

Crookston Castle *S'clyde*   *Map: 388 Cd*
The castle was built in the 1420s by Sir John Stewart, Constable of the Scottish Army in France. A descendant, Henry Stewart, Lord Darnley, married Mary, Queen of Scots in 1565, and they may have become engaged at the castle.
Location: 6 miles W of Glasgow (A737 then A754).

Crosskirk *Highland*   *Map: 387 Ee*
ST MARY'S CHAPEL The church, now a ruin, was once a medieval place of pilgrimage, possibly to St Nicholas of Myra (Santa Claus).
Location: 6 miles W of Thurso off A386.

Crossraguel Abbey *S'clyde*   *Map: 388 Bc*
Ruins of a Cluniac abbey founded in the 13th century. The original abbey was rebuilt after damage caused in the War of Independence in 1306.
Location: 11 miles S of Ayr on A77.

Crosthwaite *Cumbria*   *Map: 391 Dc*
CHURCH OF ST KENTIGERN The only church in England with a full set of 12 consecration crosses on the outside walls. The crosses which were carved on the walls in the 16th century, were anointed by the bishop during the church's consecration service.
A memorial to the poet Robert Southey, a regular worshipper, is in the south aisle, with an epitaph by Wordsworth. His grave is outside.
Location: 7 miles S of Windermere off A5074.

Crowland *Lincs.*   *Map: 395 Da*
TRINITY BRIDGE This 14th-century stone bridge in the centre of the village has three footways over the beds of three streams, now streets.
Location: 9 miles S of Spalding on A1073.

Culbone *Somerset*   *Map: 397 Dd*
CHURCH OF ST BEUNO England's smallest parish church still in regular use is 35 ft long and 13 ft wide. It was once at the heart of a community of charcoal burners, with a leper colony in the woods near by. Now it stands alone on an isolated stretch of coastline.
It dates mostly from the 12th century, but on the north side is a two-light Saxon window cut from a single slab of sandstone. Inside are a 14th-century rood screen, pre-Reformation benches and 17th-century family pew.
Location: 9 miles W of Minehead (A39, B3225 to Porlock Weir, then footpath).

Culloden *Highland*   *Map: 387 Dc*
On April 16, 1746, on "dark Drummossie Muir", ended the rising on behalf of James VIII of Scotland and III of England ("The Old Pretender") which had started with such fervour at Glenfinnan the year before.
Prince Charles Edward Stuart and his clansmen had penetrated as far south as Derby, when they retreated back to Inverness.
Meanwhile, the Hanoverian Duke of Cumberland, son of George II, had been appointed to crush the Jacobites, which he did with such zeal and cruelty that he earned the nickname "The Butcher". Cumberland reached Nairn, 15 miles from Inverness, on April 14, and the next day celebrated his 25th birthday. The 18 stone duke was four months younger than the athletic "Bonnie Prince Charlie".
For the battle, the prince chose open, flat ground on the Muir more suited to the duke's cavalry. On the afternoon of April 16 the battle began with the first shot from the Jacobite artillery killing two men standing near the duke. But Cumberland's artillery reply silenced the Jacobite guns, causing many casualties, and when the Highlanders charged, the duke's gunners switched to grapeshot with devastating results.
The battle lasted less than an hour. The Jacobites continued to fight individually long after it had been lost. Prince Charlie, not realising the battle was a disaster, left the field to replan his campaign.
Many Jacobite officers and men, rather than fall prisoner, made a final charge into the enemy ranks in the hope of taking one more Hanoverian with them when they died. Lord Strathallan, facing capture, charged into the midst of Hanoverian dragoons and was cut down. As he lay dying on the field, he was given his last Communion with oatcake and whisky.
The Hanoverian army went on to kill wounded Jacobites on the field, and women and children in the area. The "pacification of the Highlands" followed, with large areas being put to fire and sword.
Later, Cumberland had his Civil List pay raised from £15,000 a year to £40,000. Prince Charles Edward, never betrayed despite the £30,000 on his head, escaped to France on September 20.
The battlefield is now partly owned by the National Trust for Scotland, and a farmhouse which survived the battle is a museum, containing historical maps and relics.
Location: 5 miles E of Inverness (A9 then B9006).

Cullompton *Devon*   *Map: 397 Ec*
CHURCH OF ST ANDREW This fine parish church, rebuilt in 1430, has a superb wagon-roof running its entire length, and a rood screen stretching the width of the church.
The glory of St Andrew's is Lane's Aisle or

Chapel built in 1525 by John Lane, a successful wool merchant. It is 70 ft long, with a fan-vaulted roof. Lane is buried in the chapel, with his wife.
Location: 13 miles NE of Exeter off M5.

Culross *Fife*   *Map: 389 De*
CULROSS PALACE The house built between 1597 and 1611 by Sir George Bruce, member of a landed family who developed collieries and saltpans on the Forth estuary, is virtually unaltered as a fine example of a town mansion of the 17th century.
Location: 7 miles W of Dunfermline off A985.
OLD BURGH OF CULROSS The old houses of Culross have been preserved as a remarkable example of a small Scots harbour town of the 16th and 17th centuries. Culross was then a centre for coal and salt, and the manufacture of griddles.

Houses open to the public include the Town House, which contains the council room with a fine painted ceiling on the first floor.
Location: 7 miles W of Dunfermline off A985.

Culzean Castle *Strathclyde*   *Map: 388 Bc*
Culzean Castle (pronounced Kul-ane) is one of the greatest achievements in design and decoration by the Scottish architect Robert Adam.

The first building on this rocky cliff-top was a 16th-century tower house owned by the powerful Kennedy family.

In the 1770s David Kennedy, 10th Earl of Cassillis, commissioned Robert Adam to build "a dream castle" on the site. The work took ten years, and Adam started by building spacious salons where the old tower had been. Then he built a great kitchen, bake-house and brew-house. On the very edge of the cliff he built the round tower with its dramatic Round Drawing-Room overlooking the sea.

The stable block, the home farm, even the terraced gardens, are all Adam's work.

A later earl, faced with the threat of a Napoleonic invasion, defended the castle with 6 pound guns and raised a local regiment, the West Lowland Fencibles. Their weapons can still be seen in the armoury: 712 flintlock pistols, 111 hanger swords and 120 bayonet blades.

The grounds of Culzean are now a country park with an agricultural exhibition covering the years 1750–1850.
Location: 12 miles S of Ayr off A719.

Cupar *Fife*   *Map: 389 Ee*
SCOTSTARVIT TOWER The five-storey tower-house was built late in the 16th century, when Scotland's most turbulent days were over. It was the home

THE STUART CAUSE DIES ON CULLODEN'S BAYONETS

Less than 5,000 troops, supporting the House of Stuart, faced nearly 10,000 soldiers of the House of Hanover at Culloden in 1746. The Jacobites suffered heavily from the English guns; then their charge, which had been the terror of the English, was delayed. Finally, when the two armies met, the Jacobites fell to a new tactic: instead of attacking the man in front of him, each Redcoat bayoneted the exposed side of the

man to the right. The Hanoverian army lost 76 men to the Jacobites' 1,200. After the battle many more Jacobites died of wounds or were executed.

"WELL OF THE DEAD" *A stone slab marks the spring where the wounded leader of the Clan Chattan crawled away to die.*

GHOST OF A GIANT SLATE WORKS

In the remote Cwmystradllyn valley of North Wales, the ghostly shell of a deserted slate factory rears up beside the valley road. This remarkable building, which operated from the 1850s to 1870s, stands on a hillside littered with slate. The saws that cut the slate were powered by water, carried to the factory by aqueduct. The tramway track that brought slate from the Gorseddau quarries can still be seen.

of the poet Sir John Scott (1585–1670).
Location: 2½ miles SW of Cupar off A916.

Cwm Bychan *Gwynedd*   *Map: 392 Ce*
"ROMAN STEPS" The steps form part of an ancient track leading up to a mountain pass to the east of Harlech. It was a trade route used by the Celts long before the Romans came to Britain, and it was a pack-horse track right through the Middle Ages. So it is not possible, despite their name, to give a date to the stone steps built into the mountain side.

A walk up the steps to a cairn marking the mountain pass takes about 20 minutes, and goes through beautiful country inhabited by wild black-and-white goats.
Location: 5½ miles E of Harlech on minor road to Cwm Bychan (the steps are signposted from the car park by the lake).

Cwmystradllyn *Gwynedd*   *Map: 392 Ce*
SLATE FACTORY The ruins of the old slate factory, huge and impressive, look at first sight like a monastery or castle. To this building was brought slate from the nearby Gorseddau quarries to be cut and smoothed. Power for the factory came from a huge water-wheel; now only the millpond walls remain and the chasm of the wheel pit that slices through the centre of the derelict building.
Location: 4½ miles N of Porthmadog (turn off A487 along the Cwmystradllyn valley road to Tyddyn Mawr).

D

Dalemain *Cumbria*   *Map: 391 Dd*
A country house in a well-timbered park near Ullswater, Dalemain grew up round a 12th-century pele tower (a border tower protecting crops and livestock) – one of a line in the Eamont valley. It has a medieval banqueting hall, two Elizabethan wings and a Georgian façade.

Dalemain has been the home of the Hasell family since 1679. The pele tower now houses the museum of the Westmorland and Cumberland Yeomanry, which was raised by the Hasells.
Location: 3 miles SW of Penrith off A592.

Danebury *Hants.*   *Map: 398 Bb*
HILL-FORT Danebury may have been first occupied in the 4th century BC, when a timber-faced and backed rampart was built.

In the 2nd century BC there was an extensive settlement covering 13 acres, enclosed by a combined ditch and rampart 50 ft high. Neatly arranged rectangular buildings flanked the streets, and on the south-east there was an outer enclosure used as a cattle pound, with a drover's track through the surrounding arable fields.
Location: 7 miles SW of Andover off A343.

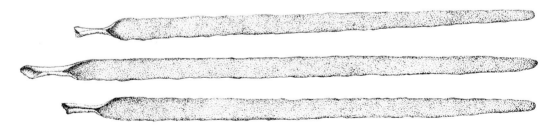

IRON AGE MONEY

Iron bars were used as currency by the ancient Britons during the 2nd and 1st centuries BC. They were mentioned by Julius Caesar in his writings describing Britain, and a hoard of 21 sword-shaped bars, like those pictured above, was found at Danebury hill-fort. Currency bars have been found mainly in southern and western England. Most are 31–35 in. long, the shape varying slightly in different areas.

Danny *W. Sussex*   *Map: 399 Db*
An E-shaped Tudor house with a fine great hall, built 1582–93 by Sir George Goring. It is one of a series of great houses built below the sheep-walks of the South Downs when the wool trade was one of England's main sources of wealth.
Location: 7½ miles N of Brighton (A23, A273).

Darite *Cornwall*   *Map: 396 Cb*
CARADON HILL MINES From about 1800 to 1840, Cornwall was the world's chief source of copper ore, and the slopes of Caradon Hill were a rich source of supply. The South Caradon mine, opened in 1836, was worked until 1885, after the main industry in the area had declined. Surface workers included bal-maidens – women who hammered the rock into suitable pieces, discarding worthless lumps, for storing, assaying and sale.
There are ruins of three engine-houses – used to pump up water from the workings and wind up ore – and you can still follow parts of the path of the Caradon-Liskeard railway. This took the ore to the canal for carriage to Looe then shipment to South Wales for smelting.
Location: 4 miles N of Liskeard off B3254.

Darley Abbey *Derbys.*   *Map: 394 Bb*
Now a suburb of Derby, Darley Abbey was once a separate village built by mill-owner Thomas Evans in the late 18th century to house workers for his cotton mill on the banks of the Derwent. An iron river bridge, still a toll bridge, linked the village and mill, which was first built in 1783 but rebuilt in 1789 after a fire.
The houses, unlike many in later cotton towns, are solidly built and have large gardens. The fine school was built by Walter Evans in 1826.
Location: 1 mile N of Derby centre off A6.

Darlington *Durham*   *Map: 391 Gd*
NORTH ROAD STATION The station is one of the oldest in the world. It was built in 1842 for the Stockton and Darlington railway, the world's first steam-powered public railway opened in 1825. The line was used mainly for transporting coal, but a few passengers were carried, and by 1842 the number had grown sufficiently for a station to be needed.
Now the station is the museum of the Stockton and Darlington and North Eastern Railways. Exhibits include a passenger coach of the 1840s and the locomotives *Locomotion* (1825) and *Derwent* (1845).
Location: Station Rd, off Northgate (A167).

Dartington Hall *Devon*   *Map: 397 Db*
A much-restored medieval courtyard house built 1388–1400 and one of the best of its date. The banqueting hall and gardens are open to visitors.
Location: 3 miles NW of Totnes off A384.

Dartmouth *Devon*   *Map: 397 Db*
CASTLE The first coastal fortress designed especially to carry guns, the castle stands on a rocky headland guarding the Dart estuary.
It was built in 1481 by the townsmen, who feared raids on the port from marauding French. They also wanted to guard against retaliation from foreign merchants whose ships they had robbed during the course of "trade".
Location: 1 mile SE of town off B3205.

NEWCOMEN ENGINE The atmospheric-pressure steam-engine invented by Thomas Newcomen (1663–1729) revolutionised the coal industry. It was the first practical steam-engine that could be used above ground for pumping up water from mine workings.
Newcomen, an ironmonger, lived in a house in Lower Street, Dartmouth, now demolished. One of his engines has been re-erected in the town in his memory. It is probably the oldest surviving atmospheric steam-engine that can still be seen in action.
Location: Royal Avenue Gardens, town centre.

Deal Castle *Kent*   *Map: 399 Gc*
Henry VIII built Deal Castle in 1539–40, along with Sandown and Walmer castles, to defend The Downs, a 4 mile stretch of water between the east Kent coast and the Goodwin Sands. The Downs was the safest anchorage for sailing ships on the south-east coast, and was strategically important in the defence of the Channel.
At the time the castles were built, Henry feared invasion from France and Spain on behalf of the Pope, who objected to Henry declaring himself supreme head of the English Church. Deal Castle was one of a chain of castles built to protect the south and east coasts (see p. 125).
One of the most up-to-date castles of its time, it took less than two years to build. Skilled masons and carpenters were paid 7d or 8d a day, labourers 6d – some only 5d. In June 1539 this led to a protest, the lower-paid men demanding 6d. The king's supervisor, Sir Edward Ryngley, persuaded them to return to work, and to discourage further stoppages he sent the nine ringleaders to gaol.

THE START OF THE STEAM AGE
Designed by George Stephenson, Locomotion pulled the first public train from Shildon to Stockton on September 27, 1825, with about 450 people aboard. The 20 mile journey took about 3 hours 7 minutes. Locomotion is now in the Darlington North Road Station Railway Museum.

Deal Castle: a fortress against invasion

FIVE TIERS OF GUNS BRISTLED FROM THE FORMIDABLE SIX-SIDED CASTLE BUILT BY
HENRY VIII TO PROTECT THE EAST KENT COAST AND ITS ANCHORAGE

The best fortified of Henry VIII's chain of coastal forts, Deal Castle has two rings of six semi-circular bastions with a central round tower, and is surrounded by a 56 ft wide dry moat.

Cannons with a range of about $1\frac{1}{2}$ miles were mounted on the bastions and tower top. Those on the seaward side could make the anchorage known as The Downs unsafe for enemy ships.

But if invading forces should reach the shore, the castle's defences were formidable. The only entrance was protected by a drawbridge and portcullis, a passage with "murder-holes" in the roof through which attackers could be peppered with missiles, and a cannon pointing at the heavy, iron-studded doors should they be forced open.

Every inch of the moat could be covered by small-arms fire from the 53 gun-ports round the outer bastions. Gun-ports on the inner bastions covered the outer bastions and courtyard.

ROUND SHOT *Four 32-pounder cannons of the 18th century now stand on Deal Castle's battlements. In Henry VIII's reign there were probably about 40.*

BUILT TO RESIST CANNON FIRE

Squat and sunk into the ground, Deal Castle is shown as it probably looked in 1540. Squared battlements replaced the rounded parapets – designed to deflect round shot – in 1732. The circular plan, with all rooms interconnected, allowed the 24-man garrison easy access to the ammunition supply.

Henry never needed Deal Castle – its very presence may have deterred invaders. The only time it was besieged was in 1648 after the Civil War, when The Downs fleet mutinied in support of the defeated king. Parliament sent an army to take the castle, whose defenders gave up without much fighting. (See also above.)
Location: Victoria Rd.

Deanston *Central*   *Map: 388 De*
One of the first villages in Scotland to be built round a cotton mill. The Buchanan family who founded it in 1785 were strict teetotallers, but the six-storey mill is now part of a distillery.
Location: 8 miles NW of Stirling (A84, B8032).

Deerhurst *Glos.*   *Map: 393 Fb*
CHURCH OF ST MARY Once part of a Saxon monastery, the church has a fine Saxon font. There are triangular-headed Saxon windows in the nave, and the lower part of the tower is also Saxon. Odda's Chapel near by was built in 1056.
Location: 4 miles S of Tewkesbury (A38, B4213).

Deganwy Castle *Gwynedd*   *Map: 392 Cf*
Maelgwn, Prince of Gwynedd, built a fort
overlooking the Conwy estuary in the 6th
century. A later castle was built by the Normans,
and the third, built 1211, was destroyed by
Llywelyn the Last, Prince of Wales, in 1263.
Location: 2 miles S of Llandudno off A496.

Denbigh *Clwyd*   *Map: 392 Df*
CASTLE Built in the time of Edward I (1272–1307),
the castle was a Royalist stronghold during the
Civil War (1642–7) and during the summer of
1646 withstood a siege lasting six months.

The Parliament attack was concentrated on
the Goblin Tower – in the town walls adjoining
the castle – which contained a well. There are still
traces of the earthworks dug to protect the
artillery that battered it.

The 500 Royalists finally surrendered because
there was little hope of relief, and the castle
became a prison for captured Royalists.
Location: To S of town. Entrance in Bull Lane.
CHURCH OF ST MARCELLA Known locally as
Whitchurch or *Yr Eglwys Wen* (The White
Church) – probably because it was whitewashed
in the 16th century – St Marcella's dates mainly
from the 15th century.

Its double-nave design is peculiar to the Vale of
Clwyd. Both naves have hammer-beam roofs,
and unusual carvings include a pair of shears,
representing the Guild of Tailors who had a
chantry chapel in the church in the 15th century.
Location: 1 mile SE of Denbigh off A525.

Deptford *London*   *Map: 399 Dc*
CHURCH OF ST PAUL One of London's most
splendid Baroque churches, designed by Thomas
Archer. Its western tower stands on a semi-
circular portico. St Paul's was built 1712–30,
when Deptford still had its great naval yard
founded by Henry VIII in the 16th century.
Location: Deptford High St, SE8.

Derby *Derbys.*   *Map: 394 Bb*
CATHEDRAL The 16th-century tower is the only
surviving part of the medieval collegiate church
(it became a cathedral in 1927). Most of the
remainder was demolished overnight in 1723, at
the direction of the vicar, the Rev. Michael
Hutchinson.

The church had become very dilapidated, and
the vicar was impatient of delays in arranging
rebuilding. The new classical-style church,
designed by James Gibbs, was completed in 1725.
An outstanding wrought-iron altar screen by
Robert Bakewell formed part of the design.

The many monuments include the grandiose
tomb of Elizabeth, Countess of Shrewsbury (Bess
of Hardwick). She had it erected before her death
in 1607.
Location: Town centre, Irongate.
INDUSTRIAL MUSEUM Thomas Lombe's silk mill,
opened on this site in 1721, was the first successful
textile mill in Britain to use water-powered
machinery. The present building was largely
rebuilt after a fire in 1910, but retains much of the
appearance of the original mill.
Location: Town centre, off Full St.

Devil's Arrows *N. Yorks.*   *Map: 391 Gb*
The three standing stones in a field at Boroughbridge may have been a sacred site during the

---

HENRY VIII's COASTAL FORTS

After his break with the Church of Rome, Henry VIII
feared invasion from France and Spain to re-establish
the authority of the Pope. So in 1538 he began a chain
of more than 20 coastal forts and blockhouses from
Kingston-upon-Hull on the north-east coast to Milford
Haven in south-west Wales.

The forts had the minimum of living quarters and
were designed to make the best use of the most modern
weapon – the gun. The cannons used were sakers (6 lb.
shot), culverins (8 lb. shot), basilisks (25 lb. shot), and
demi-cannons (32 lb. shot).

Most of the forts had a central tower protected by a
cluster of outer bastions. Much of the stone used was
taken from suppressed monasteries, and the bulk of the
building work was completed by 1543.

ST MAWES,
CORNWALL
*Three bastions
ring the tower
in a clover-leaf
plan. The walls
are curved to
deflect cannon
shot, and the
battlements
have wide gun
embrasures.*

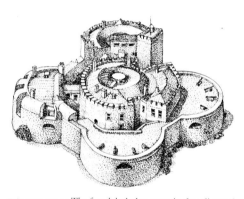

WALMER, KENT *The four-lobed plan gave the fort all-round
command against attack – from ships at sea or a landing party
that had set up gun positions.*

PORTLAND, DORSET *Fan-shaped in plan, the fort had three
tiers of guns guarding the bay. They ranged from cannons to
hand guns – 6 ft long arquebuses.*

---

earlier Bronze Age – 2000-1500 BC. According to
16th-century records they were part of a larger
group. Two of the stones are about 22 ft high and
the northern one about 18 ft high.

The stones stand in a straight line from north
to south, about 70 and 120 yds apart, and must
have been taken to the site on rollers from
the nearest source of millstone grit, near Knaresborough over 6 miles south-west.
Location: 6 miles SE of Ripon on B6265.

Devizes *Wilts.*   *Map: 398 Ac*
CAEN HILL LOCKS Almost in a straight line, the 29
locks at Caen Hill lift the Kennet and Avon
Canal, built by John Rennie, more than 130 ft.
Each lock has a side pond terraced into the hillside
to act as a reservoir.
Location: West of town beside A361.

Dewlish House *Dorset*   *Map: 397 Gc*
A long, low Queen Anne house with a hipped
roof (sloped-in at the ends). It was built in 1702
by a Thomas Skinner.
Location: 8 miles NE of Dorchester (A35, A354).

Didcot *Oxon.*   *Map: 398 Bc*
GREAT WESTERN SOCIETY MUSEUM Bristol merchants founded the Great Western Railway in
1833, to build a line between the port and
London. It was opened in 1840. The 118 mile
track, which was designed by Isambard
Kingdom Brunel, was originally 7 ft $0\frac{1}{4}$ in. wide
compared with the 4 ft $8\frac{1}{2}$ in. of other lines.
Brunel thought the wider track gave steadier,
more even running.
    About 20 GWR engines and over 50 coaches
and wagons are now housed beside the line in the
old GWR engine sheds at Didcot. Visitors can
take short train rides behind a steam-engine.
Location: 5 miles W of Wallingford off A4130.

Didsbury *Greater Manchester*   *Map: 393 Ff*
FLETCHER MOSS A late Georgian and early
Victorian parsonage built about 1800, now a
home for a collection of water-colour paintings.
Location: 5 miles S of Manchester off A34.

Dilton Marsh *Wilts.*   *Map: 397 Gd*
WEAVERS' VILLAGE For centuries England's
woollen cloth was made in the weaver's own
home, where from three to five spinsters fed yarn
to one loom. But spinning factories developed
with the invention of the spinning machine in the
18th century, and the weavers, still home-based,
would congregate in a factory area.
    More weavers flocked into the weaving
village of Dilton Marsh when spinning factories
were set up in centres such as Trowbridge near
by, and built a straggle of cottages along what is
now B3099. Many cottages still have outhouses
where looms were worked. After the 1870s,
power looms put most domestic weavers out of
business.
Location: 2 miles W of Westbury (A3098,
B3099).

Din Lligwy *Anglesey, Gwynedd*   *Map: 392 Bf*
ANCIENT VILLAGE Probably the home of a
Welshman of rank in late-Roman times, the 4th-
century village has some walls still standing to a
height of about 6 ft. There are two circular and
two rectangular buildings, surrounded by a wall.
Location: 9 miles N of Menai Bridge off A5025.
BURIAL CHAMBER A huge capstone weighing
about 25 tons covers this Stone Age grave (about
2500 BC). About 30 men, women and children
were buried there, probably over a long period.
Location: $\frac{1}{2}$ mile S of Din Lligwy village.

Dirleton Castle *Lothian*   *Map: 389 Fe*
An ancient Scottish stronghold built by the de
Vaux family in the 1230s, the castle was besieged
in 1298 by an English force led by the Bishop of

Durham for Edward I. His army almost starved
to death because the defenders had swept the
countryside of all provisions.
    By the time an English supply ship arrived in
the Firth of Forth, the attackers were reduced to
eating raw beans, but with supplies renewed
they forced the Scots to surrender. The castle
was held by the English until it was taken by
Robert Bruce in 1311.
Location: $2\frac{1}{2}$ miles SW of North Berwick on
A198.

Diserth *Powys*   *Map: 392 Dc*
CHURCH OF ST CEWYDD AND ST DAVID'S, HOWEY
The church has hardly changed since the 17th
century, having whitewashed walls, a three-
decker pulpit and many high box pews marked
with names and dates of the 17th–18th centuries.
Location: $3\frac{1}{2}$ miles S of Llandrindod Wells on
A483.

Dodington House *Avon*   *Map: 397 Ge*
This fine neo-Classical house in the Cotswolds
was built 1796–1817 by James Wyatt for wealthy
landowner Sir Christopher Codrington. The
Codrington family had grown rich from a West
Indian sugar plantation founded by an ancestor
who was governor of the Leeward Islands.
    Documents in the family museum include an
1811 inventory of slaves on the plantation in
Antigua: healthy slaves are valued at £160 each,
sick ones at £80 and the old and useless at 6d.
Location: 11 miles N of Bath off A46 (Exit 18
M4).
CARRIAGE MUSEUM Carriages and coaches
– vehicles with a suspended body to protect
passengers from the worst jolts – began to be
common in England during the 17th century.
    Many different types developed, such as the
open, four-wheeled phaeton and the closed,
two-wheeled hansom cab. More than 30 types
are on display at Dodington. They include the
family travelling chariot – equipped for long
journeys, like a modern caravan – also a hearse,
drawn by specially bred black geldings, and a
Black Maria. Horses and carriage harness can
also be seen, and carriage rides are available.
Location: Stables, Dodington House (see above).

Dogdyke *Lincs.*   *Map: 394 Db*
DRAINAGE PUMP The pump was built in 1796 to
drain water from the Fen peatlands into the
River Witham, and was originally powered by
a windmill. A 28 ft diameter scoop wheel,
powered by a steam-operated beam engine and
capable of moving 25 tons of water a minute,
was installed in 1855. It can be seen working on
open days.
Location: 10 miles S of Horncastle on A153.

Dolaucothi *Dyfed*   *Map: 392 Cb*
GOLD MINE The only Roman gold mine known
in Britain, where opencast workings and
underground galleries were used to extract the
gold-bearing ore. Water for breaking down the
soft beds and for washing the ore was brought in
along three channels, one of them 7 miles long.
    There are still shallow depressions visible that
were once reservoirs. Not all the galleries are of
Roman date – the mines were worked in the 19th
century and the 1930s.
Location: 9 miles SE of Lampeter off A482.

CARRIAGES AT DODINGTON

Horse-drawn carriages were in their heyday from about 1790 to 1890. The wealthy had their own vehicles driven by liveried coachmen. Others hired carriages or rode aboard the public stagecoach, which could be perilous. Two outside passengers on the Bath coach – similar to the one at Dodington (right) – froze to death in their seats in March 1812.

STAGECOACH *In the 1800s,* Comet *carried mail and passengers – about 14 people on top and 6 inside – from Charing Cross to Bristol, 116 miles in 12½ hours.*

PONY PHAETON *Queen Victoria herself used to drive the light, open carriage (above) round the Balmoral estate. It could be drawn by a single pony or a pair.*

GIG *Light, fast, two-wheeled vehicles, gigs (right) were usually driven by the owner rather than a coachman. They were much used by commercial travellers in the early 1800s.*

TRAVELLING CHARIOT *Sir Christopher and Lady Codrington made a Grand Tour of Europe in the family travelling chariot (right) in 1836–7.*

Dolbadarn Castle *Gwynedd*   *Map : 392 Cf*
A stronghold of the native Welsh princes, on a rock platform commanding the Llanberis Pass. It was probably built 1137–70.
  The castle's skilfully constructed defences were never besieged. Llywelyn the Last, Prince of Wales, who died in 1282, used it as a prison for his brother Owain Goch (Owen the Red) who had challenged his position as prince.
Location : 7½ miles SE of Caernarfon on A4086.

Dolforwyn Castle *Powys*   *Map : 393 Dd*
Little remains of this castle built by Llywelyn the Last, Prince of Wales, in the 1270s. But it was one of the best defended castles of its day.
Location : 4 miles NE of Newtown off B4568.

Dollar *Central*   *Map : 389 De*
DOLLAR ACADEMY A grand Palladian building houses the main part of this public school opened in 1818. John McNabb, a poor boy of Dollar

127

who became a sea captain and wealthy merchant, left a legacy for its foundation. The house is not open to the public.
Location: On Stirling road (A91).

Dolwyddelan Castle *Gwynedd*   Map: 392 Ce

The Welsh prince Llywelyn the Great was probably born in this castle on the lower slopes of the mountain Moel Siabod in 1173. He was the grandson of Owain Gwynedd, Prince of Wales from 1137 to 1170.

By the time of Owain's reign, the Welsh had realised the advantages of the stone castles introduced by the Normans, and had begun to build their own in the same style, although on a smaller scale.

Dolwyddelan was most probably built by Iorwerth, one of Owain's sons. It was surrounded by a stout wooden palisade that was later replaced by a 5 ft thick stone wall, and the great rectangular eastern tower on the rock edge was probably over 60 ft high.

Some time after Owain's death, Iorwerth was exiled by his half-brother Dafydd, who became the Lord of Gwynedd. At an early age Llywelyn began a campaign to regain the territory, and by 1202 was in control of most of North Wales. He married Joan, illegitimate daughter of King John of England, and Dolwyddelan was one of his residences.

Llywelyn began to extend his power into South Wales, and John sent an army against him in 1211. But Llywelyn intrigued with the barons who opposed John, and was influential in the drawing up of Magna Carta in 1215.

Through it he regained from John all lands and liberties unlawfully seized from Welshmen. By the time Henry III came to the English throne in 1216, Llywelyn was the prince of most of Wales. He died at Aberconwy in 1240.

Llywelyn's grandson, Llywelyn the Last, was Prince of Wales 1246–82. Dolwyddelan was one of his strongholds in his final struggle against Edward I of England. Llywelyn was killed in 1282 and Edward took the castle in 1283. Edward probably built the western tower. The castle was restored in the 19th century.
Location: 6 miles SW of Betws-y-coed on A470.

Donnington Castle *Berks.*   Map: 398 Bc

During the Civil War of 1642–7, 14th-century Donnington Castle – in a position commanding the London-Bath road – was held for the king by Colonel John Boys and about 225 men.

The colonel surrounded the castle with star-shaped earthwork defences, the lines of which can still be traced. From July 1644, these earthworks enabled the defenders to hold out for 20 months against almost constant siege and heavy bombardment from Parliament forces.

Colonel Boys surrendered in March 1646, when the Royalist cause was lost, and the defenders were allowed to march out with drums beating and colours flying. Most of the castle had been destroyed. Only the gatehouse was left.
Location: 1 mile N of Newbury on B4494.

STRONGHOLD OF WELSH PRINCES

Bleak and grey on a crag overlooking the valley of the River Lledr near Betws-y-coed, the castle of Dolwyddelan was once the stronghold of the native princes of Gwynedd, and is believed to have been the birthplace of Llywelyn the Great, who ruled most of Wales in the early 13th century.

In Llywelyn's time the castle probably looked down on the hendrefs (houses) of the tribal Welsh. But they spent much of their time following their flocks and herds and living in lightly built huts, or hafods. Under Welsh law, the men served the chieftain as soldiers for six weeks every year.

Dorchester *Dorset*   *Map: 397 Fc*
ROMAN TOWN Over 1,600 years ago, Maumbury Rings – earthworks near the railway bridge in Weymouth Avenue, Dorchester – was a Roman amphitheatre, and must have sometimes echoed to the roar of perhaps 13,000 voices during the excitement of gladiatorial and animal combats. The amphitheatre lay just outside the flourishing Roman town of *Durnovaria* (Dorchester), tribal capital of the Durotriges.

South Walks Road and West Walks mark the line of part of the Roman defensive walls – a fragment is visible in West Walks. There are remains of a 4th-century town house with hypocaust-heated rooms in Colliton Park behind County Hall.

Dorchester Abbey *Oxon.*   *Map: 398 Bd*
The village of Dorchester was, in Saxon days, the cathedral city of the kingdom of Wessex. The Normans moved the bishopric to Lincoln, and the cathedral, founded in 634, became an Augustinian abbey.

The abbey church was rebuilt 1120–70. When the monastery was dissolved (1536–8), a local benefactor, Richard Beauforest, bought the church and gave it to the parish.

In the fine Decorated sanctuary of about 1340 is one of the country's finest Jesse windows – showing Christ's descent from Jesse in the stone tracery.
Location: 9 miles S of Oxford (A423, B4015).

Dorney *Bucks.*   *Map: 398 Cc*
CHURCH OF ST JAMES In the north chapel, the alabaster tomb of Sir William Garrard (died 1607) is carved with small figures depicting his wife and 15 children. Such carving was common at the time. Some of the children hold a skull, indicating that they died before him.

First built in Norman days, the church has a brick Tudor tower. There is a 14th-century wall-painting on the north chapel arch.
Location: 3 miles W of Eton off B3206.

Doune *Central*   *Map: 388 De*
CASTLE The fine 14th-century castle was built by Robert Stewart, Duke of Albany, who was regent of Scotland 1406–20. The duke made no attempt to ransom his nephew, the young King James I, a prisoner in England for 18 years.

On his release in 1424, James executed the duke's son, Murdoch, who had taken over the regency after his father's death, and the castle became royal property.
Location: 9 miles NW of Stirling off A84.
DOUNE PARK GARDENS The Walled Garden is laid out in the traditional pattern of four quarters – a rose garden, a house garden with fruits, vegetables and flowers for cutting, a spring garden and an autumn garden. There is also a typical Scottish glen of 50 acres.
Location: 1½ miles W of castle on A84.

Dounreay nuclear power station see Thurso

Dover *Kent*   *Map: 399 Gb*
CASTLE The cliff-top castle guarding Dover harbour, the gateway to England, is one of the strongest and most impressive in Britain.

Its massive, cube-shaped great tower, almost 100 ft high, has walls 17–21 ft thick. Two rings of

NORMAN LEAD FONT

Dorchester Abbey's Norman font, which escaped destruction in the 16th-century Reformation, is one of the best preserved of the few remaining lead fonts in England. The relief moulding portrays the seated figures of the 12 apostles.

walls surround the great tower, the inner with 14 flanking towers and the outer with 20, including the huge Constable's Gate. In an inner courtyard tower, a well reaches 300 ft or more through the chalk cliff, and near the well-head are two lead pipes that were once connected to a cistern from which water could be pumped to various rooms in the castle.

In 1066, after defeating King Harold at Hastings, William the Conqueror headed direct for Dover, where he spent eight days improving the fortifications begun by Harold. But the existing stone castle was built mainly in the 1180s by Henry II, at the enormous cost of about £7,000. It was the first concentric castle in Britain – nearly 100 years ahead of any other.

King John extended the outer curtain wall and built a northern gatehouse (now the Norfolk Towers), but this gatehouse was attacked and damaged shortly after its completion by Prince Louis of France. In 1216 John's quarrel with his barons resulted in civil war, the barons inviting Prince Louis of France to the English throne. Louis besieged Dover Castle, held for John by Hubert de Burgh, and attacked the northern gate from high ground in front of it. He was able to undermine it, causing one of the towers to collapse.

The defenders held off the attackers by plugging the breach with timber. Then, with news of John's death and the succession of his baby son Henry III, Louis called off the attack.

After this the main gate was re-sited to the west, the Constable's Gate being built 1221–7. An outwork, or spur, was made towards the northern high ground, and a big round tower built in the ditch between. So that sallies could be made to the rear of an attacking force, an underground passage – high and wide enough to take a mounted armed knight – was cut through the chalk to link castle, tower and spur.

The underground passage was extended in the 18th and 19th centuries at the time of the Napoleonic wars. Other changes made at this time included cutting down the height of the outer-wall towers to make gun platforms.
Location: Enter by Canon's Gate Rd or Castle Hill.

CRABBLE MILL The six-story watermill beside the River Dour was built about 1812 to supply flour to the large Dover garrison during the Napoleonic wars. It ceased working about 1890 but was restored in 1973 and now includes a museum of milling.
Location: 1½ miles NW of Dover off A526.

ROMAN HOUSE In the 2nd century, Dover (Dubris) was the headquarters of the British fleet, gradually taking over from Richborough, near Sandown, as chief port. The Pharos lighthouse on the cliff top, in Dover Castle grounds, guided shipping round the coast.

No trace of the headquarters fort, Classis Britannica, is visible, but a Roman house from the civilian settlement around it was excavated in 1970. Its painted plaster walls are 9 ft high in places. The house was buried under a later Roman Fort of the Saxon Shore, of which part of the defences can also be seen.
Location: New St, near Market St.

Down House *Kent* *Map: 399 Ec*
Charles Darwin, the naturalist, lived at Down House for 40 years until his death in 1882, and many Darwin relics are now on display. He wrote *The Origin of Species* in the old study.
Location: 5½ miles S of Bromley off A233.

Drum Castle *Grampian* *Map: 387 Fb*
Drum, begun in the late 13th century, is one of Scotland's oldest tower houses. In the 1320s Robert Bruce gave the Forest of Drum to his armour-bearer, Irvine, and the castle's connection with the Irvine family continued until 1975.
Location: 10 miles SW of Aberdeen off A93.

Druminnor Castle *Grampian* *Map: 387 Eb*
The 15th-century stronghold of the Clan Forbes, the castle is still occupied by the family. It is now only a fraction of its original size. Restoration took place in 1966.
Location: 10 miles S of Huntly off A97.

THREE AGES OF DOVER

For centuries, Dover has been the guardian of the English Channel at its narrowest point. The British fleet was based there in Roman times, and a fort was built to defend the shore from Saxon raiders. The massive castle built by the Normans on top of the white cliffs was modernised in the early 1800s when Napoleon's army was massing on the French coast.

ROMAN DOVER *This wall plaster from a Roman house (left) is part of about 400 sq. ft of plaster still in position after about 1,800 years. The house stood near a 2nd-century fort.*

NORMAN DOVER *Henry II and his master mason, Maurice the Engineer, built the great tower of Dover Castle in the 1180s. The spiral stairways in the north-east and south-west corners of the tower rise sheer from the basement through two residential floors to the roof level, a height of almost 100 ft.*

NAPOLEONIC DOVER *Five boxed-in millstones at Crabble Mill were used to grind flour for Dover Castle garrison in the early 19th century.*

Drumlanrig Castle *Dumfs.*   *Map: 390 Cf*
One of the first great Renaissance buildings in Scotland, the castle was built in the 1680s by William Douglas, 1st Duke of Queensberry. The rich furnishings include a 16 branched silver chandelier of about 1680, weighing over 9 stone.
Location: 18 miles N of Dumfries off A76.

Dryslwyn Castle *Dyfed*   *Map: 392 Cb*
Rhys ap Maredudd, Lord of Dryslwyn, supported Edward I of England against the Welsh princes in 1282, but revolted in 1287 following a feud with the king's officers. Dryslwyn was taken and Rhys fled in 1289, but was captured and executed at York in 1291.
Location: 5 miles W of Llandeilo (A40, B4297).

Duart Castle *Isle of Mull, S'clyde*   *Map: 388 Af*
The stronghold of the Macleans, Duart Castle was built in the 13th century on a rocky mound overlooking the Sound of Mull. It was one of the earliest tower houses in Scotland.

The Macleans held Duart against the Scottish kings for centuries, harrying the coast of the mainland with raiding parties from their fleet of war galleys up to the early 17th century.
Location: 3 miles SE of Craignure off A849.

Dudley *W. Midlands*   *Map: 393 Fd*
BLACK COUNTRY MUSEUM A typical Black Country village of the early 19th century is being constructed at this open-air museum.
Location: Junction of A4037 and A4123.
CANAL TUNNEL Stretching for 3,000 yds under the streets of Dudley, the tunnel was built in the 1780s by Lord Dudley and Ward to link his limestone quarries with the Birmingham Canal Navigations network. It became an important Black Country trade route, but could only take one boat at a time. Netherton Tunnel was built to replace it in 1858.

Boatmen used to "leg" their boats through the tunnel by lying on their backs and pushing against the walls. Passengers on tunnel trips are given the chance to try this themselves.
Location: Birmingham New Rd or Pear Tree Lane.
CASTLE The hill-top castle overlooking the town dates mainly from about 1270 to 1300. Ralph de Somery began rebuilding it after Henry II had destroyed it in the 12th century during his son Henry's rebellion. Ralph's son John pillaged the area to raise money for its completion.

John Dudley, Duke of Northumberland and Protector of England 1551–3, obtained the deeds and spent lavishly on the castle. He issued his own coinage from a mint in the grounds.
Location: N of town centre on A459.

Duffield Castle *Derbys.*   *Map: 394 Bb*
A massive great tower with walls about 15 ft thick was built here in the 12th century by Henry de Ferrers. Only the foundations remain.
Location: 5 miles N of Derby on A6.

Duffus *Grampian*   *Map: 387 Ec*
CASTLE One of the few Norman motte-and-bailey castles in Scotland was built here in the 12th century by Freskin de Moravia, whose descendants changed their name to Moray.

When the castle was rebuilt in stone on the earth motte in the 14th century, one corner of a tower broke off and slid down the slope, coming to rest at an angle, but more or less intact.
Location: 4½ miles NW of Elgin off B9012.
CHURCH OF ST PETER The church was damaged by fire in 1298 during Edward I's campaigns. He gave 20 oaks towards its repair. Now a ruin, the church has a medieval porch and west tower base; the rest is 18th century.
Location: 5 miles NW of Elgin on B9012.

Duggleby Howe *N. Yorks.*   *Map: 394 Ce*
One of the biggest and earliest round barrows (burial mounds) in Britain, Duggleby Howe was built in the Stone Age, probably before 2500 BC. The barrow, 125 ft in diameter and originally over 30 ft high, covered a deep pit in which eight adults and two children were buried.

Personal belongings buried with them included a flint knife, arrow-heads and bone pins (now in Hull Museum). Over 40 cremations have been found in other parts of the barrow.
Location: 7 miles SE of Norton (B1248, B1253).

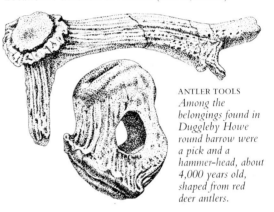

ANTLER TOOLS
Among the belongings found in Duggleby Howe round barrow were a pick and a hammer-head, about 4,000 years old, shaped from red deer antlers.

Dumbarton Castle *Strathclyde*   *Map: 388 Cd*
For over 1,500 years, the 250 ft high rock overlooking the Clyde has contained some kind of fortress. Dun Breatann, "fortress of the Britons", was probably the centre of the kingdom of Strathclyde from the 5th century to 1018.

In the 16th century the castle was one of the main strongholds of the supporters of Mary, Queen of Scots. It was taken in 1571 in a daring night raid led by Captain Thomas Crawford whose men scaled the highest part of the crag with rope ladders. Most of the existing fortifications are 17th–18th century.
Location: 1 mile SE of town centre off A814.

Dumfries *Dumfs. & Gall.*   *Map: 390 Ce*
BURNS HOUSE The poet Robert Burns rented this house in Mill Vennel (now Burns Street) in 1793, while working as a £95-a-year excise-man. He died here in 1796, and many of his personal possessions are now on display.
Location: Burns St, off St Michael's St.
PRINCE CHARLIE'S ROOM For three days in 1745, a room in what is now the County Hotel was the headquarters of Prince Charles Edward Stuart during his retreat towards Culloden.

He held the town to ransom, with a former provost (mayor) as hostage. The prince's stay cost the town £2,000 and 1,000 pairs of shoes for his army.
Location: High St, town centre.
RIVER BRIDGES The old bridge over the Nith from

Whitesands (once a horse fair) to Mill Road dates from the 15th century. In 1660 James Birkmyre, a barrel-maker, lived in the old bridge house at the Mill Street end.

He was allowed to hold the house for an annual payment (feu) on condition that he stopped heavy loads of timber from crossing the bridge until the town council had been notified. The new bridge (Galloway Street) was opened in 1794 and widened in 1893.

Dunbar *Lothian*   *Map: 389 Fd*
CASTLE In 1339 the castle was besieged for six weeks by the English forces of Edward III, and was successfully defended by "Black Agnes", the Countess of March and Dunbar. She is said to have jeered at the besiegers from the battlements and to have sent maids to wipe away the marks made by stones and lead balls.

Mary, Queen of Scots, fled to the castle with the Earl of Bothwell in 1567. After she had been deposed, the castle was destroyed by the Regent, the Earl of Moray, in 1568.
Location: N of town overlooking harbour.
TOWN HOUSE AND TOLBOOTH The Renaissance building of 1620 was the meeting place of the town council for 355 years until 1975. The curfew was sounded from the belfry each night to empty the taverns.
Location: High St (A1087).

Dunbeath *Highland*   *Map: 387 Ed*
LAIDHAY CROFT A thatched Caithness longhouse, sheltering family and livestock. Furnishings include a box bed with doors and ceiling.
Location: 20 miles SW of Wick on A9.

THE BEGINNINGS OF GOLF

No one is certain where golf originated, but it was a popular game in Scotland by 1457, for in that year the king forbade it because it interfered with archery practice. In England, the game did not become popular until the late 1800s.

Wooden balls and clubs were used at first, but by the early 1600s, leather balls stuffed with feathers had been introduced (one is on show at the Spalding Golf Collection at Dundee). They could probably be driven about 200 yds, but soon became sodden in damp weather, and were expensive.

Golfing became cheaper with the invention of the gutta-percha (solidified resin) ball in 1850. This led to the development of iron clubs, previously used mainly for getting balls out of ruts. Rubber-core balls were introduced in 1902.

With the formation of golf clubs and societies – the first in Edinburgh in 1744 – "uniforms" became popular. The usual dress was a red coat, with the colour of the collar varying for different clubs.

Playing golf in 16th-century Scotland

Dunblane Cathedral *Central*   *Map: 388 De*
The only remains of a Norman cathedral on the site are the lower storeys of the tower. The present cathedral was begun in 1237 and dates mainly from the 13th to 15th centuries.

Towards the end of the 16th century the roof of the nave fell in, the nave remaining roofless for 300 years until 1889–93. In the meantime, the congregation used the choir.

Margaret Drummond, who was secretly married to James IV of Scotland, is buried in the choir together with her two sisters. All three were mysteriously poisoned in 1501.
Location: From High St to Cathedral Sq.

Dun Carloway *Lewis, Western Is.* *Map: 386 Bd*
BROCH The Pictish tower dwelling of about the 1st century BC is still 20 ft high, and is one of the best preserved in the Western Isles.
Location: 18 miles W of Stornoway off A858.

Duncombe Park *N. Yorks.*   *Map: 391 Gc*
GARDENS One of the earliest English landscaped gardens, laid out in the 18th century, possibly by Sir John Vanbrugh. The house is not open.
Location: 1 mile SW of Helmsley off B1257.

Dundee *Tayside*   *Map: 389 Ef*
FRIGATE UNICORN The 46 gun, 152 ft long wooden sailing frigate is the oldest British-built warship afloat. She was launched in 1824 for the Royal Navy, and carried a crew of 300 men.

The *Unicorn* was retired in 1968 after 144 years of peaceful service, chiefly as a drill ship for the Royal Naval Volunteer Reserve. She is now being fully restored.
Location: Victoria Dock, Camperdown St.
JUTE MILLS In the 19th century, Dundee was one of the chief centres of the jute textile industry. Jute, used to make coarse cloth for such things as sails and tents, was at first spun and woven in workers' homes, but there was a rush of mill building from 1830 to 1870.

Many old mills survive, the finest being the Camperdown Works in Methven St, Lochee.
Location: 2 miles NW of city centre off A923.
TAY RAIL BRIDGE Britain's longest railway bridge (2 miles long), the Tay bridge was opened in 1887. Eight years earlier the first rail bridge over the Tay had collapsed in a high wind, plunging a train into the river with the loss of 78 lives.
Location: Riverside Drive (A85).
THE SPALDING GOLF COLLECTION Golf clubs and other relics covering 300 years of golf are contained in the collection, which is on display at Camperdown House. Exhibits include a top hat used to measure the quantity of boiled feathers needed to tightly fill the leather case of a "featherie" golf ball.

A neo-Classical mansion of 1824–8, the house was designed by William Burn for the 2nd Viscount Camperdown (created an earl in 1831). He was the son of Admiral Adam Duncan, made a viscount after defeating the Dutch at the Battle of Camperdown in 1797.
Location: 3 miles NW of city on A928.

Dundrennan Abbey *Dumfs.*   *Map: 390 Cd*
A Cistercian abbey founded in 1142. From the 17th century the ruins were quarried for stone, although part was used as a church until 1742.
Location: 6 miles SE of Kirkcudbright on A711.

Dunfermline Palace *Fife*   *Map: 389 De*
One of the favourite royal palaces of the Scottish
kings, Dunfermline was originally the guest-
house of a vast 12th-century Benedictine
monastery, rebuilt about 1315 after destruction
by Edward I. Only a wall, tower and archway
remain.

Charles I was born in the palace in 1600, and
Charles II stayed there in 1650 while trying to
rouse Scottish support against Cromwell.
Location: Pittencrieff Park off Monastery St.

Dunkeld Cathedral *Tayside*   *Map: 387 Ea*
In 1689 the 14th-century cathedral was the scene
of a bloody battle between 5,000 Highlanders
supporting the deposed James II, and 1,200
Cameronians of William III's army.

The Cameronians occupied the cathedral,
already partly ruined. They used the solid oak
pews to set fire to houses occupied by the
Highlanders, and stripped lead from the roof to
make gunshot. When the Highlanders withdrew, all but three houses and the cathedral had
been burned down. The restored choir of the
cathedral is now used as the parish church.
Location: Cathedral St.

Dunnottar Castle *Grampian*   *Map: 387 Fb*
At the time of the Commonwealth, the Scottish
crown and sceptre were kept in this lonely 14th-
century castle on the cliff edge. Cromwell's
troops besieged it in 1652, but the regalia was
smuggled out, some of it by a minister's wife
who disguised the sceptre as a distaff.

During the Duke of Argyll's rebellion against
James II in 1685, 200 of his followers were
imprisoned in the castle, and made to pay for
their food and water. Many died of privation,
and some who tried to escape were tortured by
having pieces of lighted tow placed between
their fingers.
Location: 2 miles S of Stonehaven on A92.

Dunrobin Castle *Highland*   *Map: 387 Dd*
One of Scotland's oldest inhabited castles, for
over 500 years the home of the Earls and Dukes
of Sutherland.
Location: 12 miles N of Dornoch on A9.

Dunrossness *Shetland*   *Map: 387 Gd*
SHETLAND CROFT Built about 1850, the croft is
furnished in the traditional manner. A barn and
corn-drying kiln stand next to the house.
Location: 21 miles S of Lerwick on A970.

Dunstable Priory *Beds.*   *Map: 398 Dd*
The Augustinian priory was founded about 1131
by Henry I, and dissolved in 1540. The Norman
nave is now the parish church of St Peter.

In 1533 Archbishop Cranmer held a court in
the Lady Chapel to judge Henry VIII's divorce
case against Catherine of Aragon. When
Catherine failed to appear – she was at Ampthill
near by – the marriage was declared null and void
and the divorce notice was pinned on the church
door. This was the beginning of the Protestant
Reformation in England.
Location: Near the A5 and A505 junction.

Dunstaffnage Castle *Strathclyde*   *Map: 388 Af*
The 13th-century castle built on a rock beside
Loch Etive has walls about 10 ft thick. Once a

ROYALIST AND ROUNDHEAD

*Thomas Luttrell of Dunster
Castle supported Parliament
in the Civil War and twice
repulsed Royalist attacks,
although he eventually surrendered the castle. His clothing in the portrait (right) is
typical of the simple style
favoured by Parliament supporters. Royalists were often
extravagantly dressed and had
long flowing hair, as in the
Portrait of a Young Cavalier
by Edward Bower (above) at
Dunster. Royalists were often
called Cavaliers because of
their swashbuckling manner,
and Parliamentarians were
dubbed Roundheads because
a few cropped their hair, but
most wore it shoulder-length.*

royal castle, it was given to the Campbells in the
15th century.

Flora Macdonald was imprisoned there for a
few days in 1746, after helping in the escape of
Prince Charles Edward Stuart. She was later
taken to the Tower of London, but freed in 1747.
Location: 3 miles NE of Oban off A85.

Dunstanburgh Castle *Northld.*   *Map: 389 Gc*
Little now remains of the 14th-century clifftop
castle. It was one of the largest of the Border
castles, its walls enclosing 9 acres.

The castle was badly damaged during the
Wars of the Roses. In 1462 it was besieged by
10,000 Yorkists led by the Earl of Warwick. Sir
Ralph Percy, the constable, surrendered and
swore allegiance to Edward IV, but a year later he
handed the castle back to the Lancastrians.
Warwick returned and took it in 1464.
Location: 9 miles NE of Alnwick off B1340.

Dunster Castle *Somerset*   *Map: 397 Ed*
The oldest-surviving part of the castle is the
13th-century gatehouse flanked by semi-circular
towers. Each tower has a prison with a lock
operated by eight keys. The castle was built by

133

the Mohun family, but they sold it to the Luttrell family in 1376.

Thomas Luttrell surrendered the castle to Royalists in 1643, and in 1645 it was besieged by Parliamentarians for six months before the commander, Colonel Wyndham, surrendered.
Location: 3 miles SE of Minehead (A39, A396).

Dun Telve *Highland* *Map: 386 Cb*
BROCHS Dun Telve, built 100 BC–AD 100, is one of the best-preserved Pictish tower dwellings on the mainland. Parts of its double walls still reach a height of 33 ft, and the tower can be climbed to the level of the first gallery. Another broch, Dun Troddan, is 200 yds east.
Location: 10 miles W of Shiel Bridge.

Dunvegan Castle *Skye, Highland* *Map: 386 Bc*
The 13th-century loch-side castle has been the stronghold of the Macleods for more than 700 years. Within the 14th-century tower house, its walls 9 ft thick, is a trap-door dungeon or "oubliette", 16 ft deep. Here, shackled prisoners were lowered to die of cold or starvation. The weights and chains date from the 15th century.
Location: 22 miles W of Portree on A850.

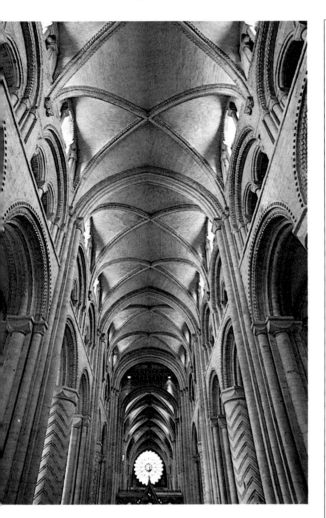

VAULTING AT DURHAM CATHEDRAL

Durham's Norman cathedral was the most up-to-date building of its age. For the first time in England, and probably in Europe, ribs were used to strengthen the vaulted roofs of the nave, transepts and choir. Ribs did not become common in England until after 1150.

Norman arches are usually round, but some transverse ribs of the cathedral vaulting were slightly pointed, foreshadowing the transition from Norman architecture to the pointed arch of the Gothic style that prevailed in England from about 1190 to 1550.

Part of the Norman vaulting of the choir cracked and was replaced with Gothic in 1242, when the Chapel of the Nine Altars was built at the east end of the cathedral.

THE CHURCH AS A PLACE OF SANCTUARY

In medieval England, a fugitive could seek temporary refuge from the law or an angry mob by claiming the right of sanctuary in a church–although this right was denied to heretics, witches and those who committed a crime in church.

The custom, which lasted from the 7th century to 1623, was recognised by the highest and humblest in the land, and few dared to violate it. The penalty might be excommunication or death. Granting sanctuary was the Church's way of alleviating the violence and cruelty of the times, when laws were often illogical and punishment severe.

To gain sanctuary, a fugitive had to reach a churchyard or pass a cross marking the boundary of consecrated ground. Many churches, for example, Durham Cathedral, have so-called sanctuary knockers on their doors, but it was not necessary, despite popular legend, for the fugitive to grasp the knocker.

Anyone who sought refuge was expected to enter the church unarmed, confess his sins, promise to repay any debts and be humble and obedient. He could then stay for a period of grace lasting 30–40 days.

During this time, the case was discussed with the bishop or priest, and at the end the fugitive could decide to leave and stand trial. Alternatively he could plead guilty and abjure the realm–a medieval form of deportation. If he neither submitted nor confessed, he could be starved into submission.

An abjurer's life was spared, but he often had to travel to a port at the other end of the realm, dressed in sackcloth, bareheaded and barefooted, and carrying a cross. He was safe only if he kept to the main road–if he strayed he could be executed on the spot.

FUGITIVE *Hubert de Burgh, chief officer of state, was accused of many crimes by Henry III in 1232. He was seized from sanctuary at Brentwood, but the Bishop of London ordered his return. Later he was starved out.*

Durham *Durham*   *Map: 391 Fd*
CASTLE The stronghold of the prince-bishops of Durham, the castle is close to the great Norman cathedral. It began as a Norman motte-and-bailey structure, but was built in stone in the 12th century.

In the Middle Ages, the powerful prince-bishop, appointed by the king, maintained an army for defence against the Scots or for incursions over the border. The last prince-bishop gave the castle to Durham University in the 1830s.
Location: Saddler St.
CATHEDRAL The finest example of Norman architecture in Europe, Durham Cathedral was begun in 1093 and the greater part of it finished 40 years later. Particularly interesting are the massive cylindrical columns that flank the nave. They are 22 ft round and some are incised with zigzag ornament.

The cathedral crowns a high rock cliff that is almost surrounded by a horseshoe curve of the River Wear. This site was chosen in Saxon times by the monks of Lindisfarne, who had been driven from their island sanctuary by Danish raiders. With them they brought the body – still remarkably preserved – of St Cuthbert, Bishop of Lindisfarne, who died in 687.

The monks had wandered with their sacred burden for many years before settling in Durham in 995 and founding a Benedictine monastery on the cathedral site. The Normans rebuilt the monastery, and the Saxon church built to shelter the body of St Cuthbert was demolished to make way for the cathedral. But the saint's shrine was replaced in its original position behind the altar.

A Lady Chapel – dedicated to the Virgin Mary and traditionally always at the east end of a cathedral – was started, but had to be abandoned after a series of structural failures. This was taken to be a sign of St Cuthbert's disapproval, since he was thought to have been a man who disliked women. So in 1175 a Galilee Chapel was built at the west end of the cathedral instead.

In medieval times, no woman – queen or commoner – was allowed to approach St Cuthbert's shrine. In fact, very little of the cathedral was open to women – a black marble slab in the nave slightly east of the font marks the point beyond which they were not allowed to pass.

On the south side of the choir is the Bishop's Throne, said to be the highest in Christendom. It was built by Bishop Hatfield (Bishop of Durham 1318–33) as part of his own memorial – his altar tomb is in the lower part.

The Galilee Chapel contains the tomb of the Venerable Bede, who died in 735. His remains were stolen from Jarrow by a monk named Aelfred and brought to Durham in 1022.

In 1650 the cathedral was a prison for about 4,000 Scots captured by Cromwell at the Battle of Dunbar. Starving and exhausted, they smashed up most things that would burn – including the original choir stalls – to make fires. The clock was spared, perhaps because carvings on it included a Scottish thistle. The existing choir stalls, part of a 17th-century restoration, are the work of an unknown carver.

The monastic buildings have been extensively restored, and the monks' dormitory of 1398–1404 is now a museum. Treasures in the under-croft include the remains of St Cuthbert's carved wooden coffin, and the unique embroidered Anglo-Saxon stole that came from it, its delicate silks still glowing with colour.

Dutton Viaduct *Cheshire*   *Map: 393 Ef*
WEAVER VIADUCT The sandstone viaduct of 20 arches, built by Joseph Locke in 1837, once carried the Grand Junction Railway over the River Weaver between Dutton and Acton Bridge.
Location: 7 miles W of Northwich off B5153.

Duxford Airfield *Cambs.*   *Map: 399 Ee*
A Battle of Britain airfield in the 1939–45 war, Duxford has hangars dating from the 1914–18 war, and now houses more than 60 historic aircraft. They range from an RE8 – a British reconnaissance aeroplane introduced on the western front in 1916 – to the prototype of Concorde. There is also a collection of military vehicles, including tanks.
Location: 7½ miles E of Royston off A505.

Dyffryn Ardudwy *Gwynedd*   *Map: 392 Ce*
LONG CAIRN Built with large stones and drystone walling, the cairn contains two Stone Age burial chambers. The earliest is the western chamber, which has a porched doorway formed by side slabs projecting beyond the entrance. It was enclosed in the long cairn in about 2000 BC, when the eastern chamber was built. Articles discovered in the tombs include two fine stone plaques that may have been worn as amulets.
Location: 5 miles S of Harlech on A496.

Dynevor Castle *Dyfed*   *Map: 392 Cb*
Rhodri Mawr, King of North Wales, is said to have built a fort on this site in the 870s. The 12th-century stone castle, now in ruins, was the seat of the Lord Rhys, Prince of South Wales, who died in 1197. His descendants surrendered the castle to Edward I in 1283.
Location: 1 mile W of Llandeilo off A40.

Dyrham Park *Avon*   *Map: 397 Ge*
The estate probably takes its name from the Saxon *deor-hamm* – deer enclosure – and is recorded in the Domesday Book. The long, low many-windowed house that now overlooks the deer park was built 1692–1704 by William Blathwayt, Secretary at War to William III.

Blathwayt served as a diplomat at The Hague, and many of the furnishings are Dutch. In the Great Hall there is a pair of oak book presses – the earliest type of bookcase known in England, replacing the lidded chest. They are similar to a pair made for the diarist Samuel Pepys 1666–1705.
Location: 8 miles N of Bath off A46.

Dyserth mines *Clwyd*   *Map: 392 Df*
In the 19th century the area around Dyserth was a flourishing iron and lead-mining centre. To the south of the town there are extensive remains of an old iron-ore mine at Cwm, and near Rhualt there is a large engine-house, part of the Pennant lead mine. Just north of the town, the remains of an engine-house of 1860 of the Talargoch lead mine stand beside A547.
Location: 3 miles S of Prestatyn (A547, B5119). The sites are derelict, so go carefully.

E

Earls Barton *Northants.*   *Map: 398 Ce*
CHURCH OF ALL SAINTS Built for refuge as well as
worship, the 60 ft high Saxon tower is the finest
in Britain. When an attack was expected from
Danish raiders, the villagers blocked the main
door and climbed into the first-floor door by a
ladder which they hauled up after them.

Originally the tower formed the body of the
church, with a small chancel attached, but the
chancel was replaced in the 11th century by a
Norman nave. A rare feature of the tower is the
strip-like stonework simulating an earlier
timber-built church.
Location: 7 miles NE of Northampton (A45 and
B573).

Earlston *Borders*   *Map: 389 Fc*
RHYMER'S TOWER An ivy-covered relic of the
home of Sir Thomas Learmount, the 13th-cen-
tury poet, known as Thomas the Rhymer.
Location: 5 miles N of St Boswells on A68.

East Grinstead *W. Sussex*   *Map: 399 Db*
SACKVILLE COLLEGE This stone building of 1619,
providing 20 homes for poor citizens of East
Grinstead, is arranged around a courtyard, with
chapel, hall and Common Room.
Location: S of town centre on A22.

East Harling *Norfolk*   *Map: 399 Ff*
CHURCH OF ST PETER AND ST PAUL The glass in the

A 500-YEAR-OLD PORTRAIT IN GLASS

*Sir Robert Wingfield, who gave the stained glass for
the east window of East Harling church in 1480, is
portrayed in one of the window's 20 panels. Another
panel shows Sir Robert's wife's first husband.*

east window was made in 1480. It was removed
in the 17th century to save it from Cromwell's
image-smashers and not found until 1736, in an
attic at East Harling Manor House.
Location: 10 miles E of Thetford (A11, B1111).

East Linton *Lothian*   *Map: 389 Fd*
PHANTASSIE DOOCOT This dovecot near Preston
Mill is a massive structure with nests for 500 birds.
It was probably built in the 16th century.
PRESTON MILL The watermill, in fine preservation,
was built in 1660 as the local estate mill,
preparing oatmeal, wholemeal flour and animal
feeds. At the north end, linked by a bridge at first-
floor level, is the circular drying kiln. This was
where the grain, particularly oats, was dried on a
perforated floor over a peat or anthracite fire
before it was ground.

The mill is two-storeyed with the drive from
the water-wheel occupying the ground floor and
the two pairs of millstones on the upper floor.
Location: 6 miles W of Dunbar (A1 then B1407).

Easton Farm Park *Suffolk*   *Map: 399 Ge*
The farm is centred on the Model Dairy Farm
built by the Duke of Hamilton in 1870. The
ornate dairy with its floral tiles and central
fountain is still standing, and the farm buildings
house displays of agricultural equipment.

There is a large collection of early breeds of
livestock, including longhorn cattle and Jacob,
Soay and St Kilda sheep.

Early horse-drawn farm equipment and steam
machines are regularly demonstrated and a
blacksmith is at work at weekends.
Location: 9 miles NE of Woodbridge (A12,
B1116 and minor road to Easton).

East Riddlesden *W. Yorks.*   *Map: 391 Fb*
The Murgatroyds, clothing manufacturers who
built much of the house in the 17th century, were
so tyrannical and debauched that "the River Aire
changed course in protest at their doings".

The last of the Murgatroyds ended up in chains
in the dungeon of York Castle for debt and
attempted gaol-breaking.

The stone-flagged kitchen of the house
contains a collection of 18th and 19th-century
pewter. The Timbered Barn is one of the finest in
the north of England.
Location: 1 mile NE of Keighley on A650.

Eastwood *Notts.*   *Map: 394 Bb*
D. H. LAWRENCE MUSEUM The poet and novelist
was born in 1885 at 8a Victoria Street, a miner's
cottage now a museum of his early life. His father
worked in nearby Brinsley pit.
Location: 8 miles NW of Nottingham off A610.

Ecclefechan *Dumfs. & Gall.*   *Map: 389 Eb*
CARLYLE'S BIRTHPLACE Thomas Carlyle, the
Scottish historian and political writer, was born
here in 1795. The house was built by his father
and uncle, both master masons, in two wings
over an archway giving access to stables and
outhouses behind. The room where Carlyle was
born is furnished as his study. Personal relics

include his correspondence with the German writer Goethe.

Carlyle is buried in the nearby churchyard.
Location: 9 miles NW of Gretna Green off A74.

Edinburgh *Lothian*   *Map: 389 Ed*
BRIDGES Two of Edinburgh's finest road bridges are Thomas Telford's early 19th-century Dean Bridge across the Water of Leith and the cast-iron North Bridge of the 1890s at the east end of Princes Street.

At Craiglockhart, the Union Canal and the Caledonian Railway cross the river and A70 (Slateford Rd) side by side. The aqueduct and viaduct look very similar, but the aqueduct can be identified by the guardrail along the towpath.
CANONGATE TOLBOOTH The Canongate was the "gait" or road along which the canons of Holyrood Abbey once walked to Edinburgh City. It was a separate burgh and had its own court house and gaol in the Tolbooth (town hall). The building, which dates from 1591, is now a museum. Among the exhibits is the 1820 tartan pattern book by William Watson of Bannockburn.
Location: The Royal Mile.
CRAIGMILLAR CASTLE The castle **was** built in the 1370s as a tower house, and was later fortified with walls and towers.

Mary, Queen of Scots moved here in 1566 to recover from her grief after the murder of her secretary David Rizzio in Holyrood Palace. A clique of Scottish nobles met at Craigmillar while the queen was there and planned to murder her husband Lord Darnley who had been responsible for Rizzio's death. Among them was James Hepburn, Earl of Bothwell, who may by then have become Mary's lover.

When Darnley was killed in 1567 most Scots believed that Mary was implicated. Less than two years later she was a refugee in England.
Location: 3 miles SE of city centre off A68.
EDINBURGH CASTLE In the 11th century, Malcolm III, King of Scotland, erected a wooden fort on the huge rock mass that dominates the city. Later kings built a stone citadel, consisting of several buildings inside a surrounding wall.

During the Scottish War of Independence, the castle was attacked by Edward I in 1296 "with engines which cast stones over the walls, sore beating and bruising the buildings within". It fell within a week. However, the Scots recaptured it

STAIRCASE TO 16TH-CENTURY FLATS

Gladstone's Land, a 16th-century Edinburgh tenement, was originally divided into five one-storey flats, entered by a staircase on the left of the building.

in 1313 when 30 men climbed the rock and took the defenders by surprise.

In 1566 Mary, Queen of Scots gave birth to the future James VI and I in the royal apartments.
GLADSTONE'S LAND A fine example of a Scottish tenement dating back to the 16th century. Thomas Gledstanes (or Gladstone) bought the property in 1617 and virtually rebuilt it to make five apartments on different floors. Gladstone, a merchant, and his wife probably lived on the third floor. The other four flats were occupied by a minister, a merchant, a knight and a guild officer.

Over the next 300 years the building was subdivided many times and gradually decayed. It was saved from demolition as a slum in 1935.
Location: Lawnmarket, in Royal Mile.
HUNTLY HOUSE This 16th-century town house, close to the Palace of Holyroodhouse, is now a museum of local history. Among the exhibits is a cut-glass epergne (dinner-table ornament) made by the Holyrood Glass Works for the accession of Queen Victoria in 1837. It is 39 in. high, contains 40 separate pieces and took two years to make.
Location: Canongate (Royal Mile).
JOHN KNOX'S HOUSE The house was built in 1490,

THE RISE AND FALL OF THE TENEMENT

Tenements, which in Victorian Britain came to mean slum buildings, started in Edinburgh as the first British blocks of flats.

The word "tenement" originally referred to narrow plots of land owned by burgesses in Scottish cities in the 16th century. The owners built their houses and shops facing on to the street, and the parts covered by the buildings were called "lands". Each burgess was required to cultivate the tenement, or holding, behind the house to provide food in time of siege.

Alleyways to the "back lands"
In 1558 the population of Edinburgh was about 7,500, but by 1694 it had grown to 21,000. So intense was the demand for housing that the tenements themselves were built on – hence the changed meaning of the word. These "back lands"

were reached by alleys that were shut off at night.

Some of the buildings reached great heights – up to 13 storeys – and the tenants had no option but to walk up the stairs. But each apartment had ample family accommodation. One of the remaining tenement buildings in Edinburgh, Gladstone's Land, consisted of five apartments, each with a living-room, up to four other rooms, and kitchen.

Descent into slums
However, by the 18th century, wealthier tenants began to move out of the city. The tenement buildings were subdivided to hold more families and began to decay. When the New Town of Edinburgh was built late in the century the process accelerated and the "lands" became slums. A descendant of the tenements was the notorious 20th-century Glasgow slum area, the Gorbals.

and is probably the oldest in Edinburgh. It was severely damaged by fire when English troops burned the city in 1544, but the interior was rebuilt and rented to John Knox, the Scottish Protestant leader, from about 1561 until his death in 1572.

On the second floor is a tiny room built for Knox as a study, and on the same floor is the bedroom in which he probably died.

Water supply for the house came from a well which still exists outside.

Location: High St (Royal Mile).

LADY STAIR'S HOUSE The house takes its name from the 1st Countess of Stair who owned it in the early 18th century, but it was built in 1622. It is now a museum of relics of Sir Walter Scott, Robert Burns and Robert Louis Stevenson. Scott's relics include his desk and the printing press on which the Waverley novels were printed.

Burns is represented by portraits, letters – and a piece of oatcake baked by his wife Jean.

Location: Lawnmarket (Royal Mile).

LAURISTON CASTLE The castle is a 16th-century tower house with an early-19th-century mansion built on. The first owner was Sir Archibald Napier, the father of the Scottish mathematician

Sun Insurance, founded 1770

Scottish Union, founded 1824

Friendly Society of Edinburgh, founded 1720

Caledonian Insurance, founded 1805

MARKS FOR FIRE-FIGHTERS

When fire insurance was created in the 17th century insurance companies formed their own fire brigades. Firemen would attempt to save a house only if it was insured with their company, so metal fire marks were fixed to the front wall for quick recognition. Huntly House, Edinburgh, has a collection of them.

John Napier (1550–1617) who invented logarithms.

Location: Cramond Rd South, off Queensferry Rd.

OUTLOOK TOWER AND CAMERA OBSCURA Outlook Tower was the town house of the 17th-century Laird of Cockpen, but in 1853 the Camera Obscura was added by an Edinburgh optician named Short and opened to the public as "Short's Popular Observatory". It operates like a periscope, projecting a panorama of Edinburgh on to a table.

Location: Castlehill (Royal Mile).

PALACE OF HOLYROODHOUSE When King David I of Scotland founded the Augustinian Abbey of Holyrood in 1128, a guest-house was included which was used as lodgings by Scottish kings. It became the basis of a Royal residence. About 1498 James IV made Edinburgh the capital of Scotland, and a palace was built. In 1676 Charles II reconstructed the Palace of Holyroodhouse as it is now.

When Mary, Queen of Scots spent the few tempestuous years of her reign at Holyrood in the 1560s, her apartments were on the second floor of the James V Tower. Below them were the rooms of her husband Lord Darnley.

On the evening of March 9, 1566, Darnley and a group of conspirators climbed the stairs joining the floors and burst into the queen's rooms, where she was having supper with guests, including her Italian secretary and adviser David Rizzio. In front of the queen, who was seven months pregnant, Rizzio was stabbed and dragged outside to his death – the result of Darnley's jealousy. Within a year Darnley himself was murdered by a group of nobles led by the Earl of Bothwell, Mary's favourite. In 1568 Mary fled into exile, and eventual execution, in England.

The queen's apartments at Holyrood were altered during the 17th-century reconstruction, but the original oak ceilings and some murals remain.

The Picture Gallery contains portraits of 111 Scottish kings. They were all produced by the Dutch painter Jacob de Wet under contract to Charles II at a fee of £120 a year. As they go back to Fergus, claimed to be the founder of the Scottish monarchy in AD 330, de Wet must have used considerable imagination.

Prince Charles Edward Stuart ("Bonnie Prince Charlie") held a grand ball at Holyrood in 1745 – on the crest of the Jacobite wave that was so quickly to recede. (See Culloden.)

Location: East end of Royal Mile.

PARLIAMENT HOUSE The Scottish parliament sat here from 1639 until the Act of Union with England in 1707. The Great Hall, famed for its hammer-beam roof, is 120 ft long, 49 ft wide and 60 ft high. Around its walls are portraits and statues of jurists, including Sir Walter Scott whose fame as a writer overshadowed his career as an Advocate, Sheriff and Principal Clerk of Session. The building now houses the Supreme Court, Court of Session and High Court.

Location: Parliament Square, off the Royal Mile.

ST GILES' CATHEDRAL John Knox, the Scottish Protestant leader, was the first minister of St Giles after the Reformation in the 16th century. When he died in 1572, he was buried in the churchyard, and a statue to him stands near by.

CAT AND MOUSE – BY THE CAPTIVE QUEEN OF SCOTS

In Queen Mary's bedroom at the Palace of Holyrood-house are two embroidered panels worked by Mary, Queen of Scots, while she was a prisoner in England. One of the panels depicts a ginger cat, which may represent Queen Elizabeth, and a mouse, perhaps Mary herself, under the cat's gaze. To the right of the cat the queen has worked the monogram MA, a common contraction of Mary.

At the south-east of the church is the Thistle Chapel, containing the stalls of the Knights of the Thistle, Scotland's oldest Order of Chivalry.

In the Moray Aisle chapel is a memorial to Robert Louis Stevenson, author of *Treasure Island*, and the window at the west end is by William Morris and Sir Edward Burne-Jones. Location: High St (Royal Mile).

THE GEORGIAN HOUSE The north side of Charlotte Square, in the New Town of Edinburgh, was designed by Robert Adam in 1791 to look from the outside like an Italian Renaissance palace. Behind the façade it was divided into a row of terraced houses, occupied by wealthy upper-class and professional families.

Three storeys of No. 7 have now been redecorated and furnished as they would have been when first occupied in 1796.

In the basement, the kitchen is painted blue, a colour believed to repel flies. All roasting was done on an open coal fire in an iron range, with an oven for bread. A hot plate was fired separately.

On the ground floor, the dining-room has dumb-waiters from which the family could serve themselves after dismissing the servants, so gossip would not be overheard.

The first floor has the drawing-room running the full width of the house, a formal room used only for important occasions. Location: 7 Charlotte Sq.

PLENTIFUL SERVANTS, SCARCE GLASS

At the Georgian House, Charlotte Square, servants were plentiful in the 18th century, and dining tables were laid for one course at a time. Between courses, the servants would replace the plate and cutlery with a fresh set. Glasses, however, were scarce and only one was used by each diner during the meal. Between different wines, the glass was placed in a water-filled cooler beside it.

Edington *Wilts.*   *Map: 397 Gd*
CHURCH OF ST MARY, KATHARINE AND ALL SAINTS
This imposing church, with tower, battlements
and pinnacles, dates from the mid-14th century,
when William of Edington, Bishop of
Winchester and first Prelate of the Order of the
Garter, rebuilt it as a monastic church.

A hundred years later, in 1450, the Bishop of
Salisbury took refuge in the church during the
Jack Cade rebellion when citizens of Kent
rebelled against the corrupt government of
Henry VI. The church was stormed by a mob,
and the bishop was dragged out and murdered.
Location: 3½ miles E of Westbury off B3098.

Edzell Castle *Tayside*   *Map: 387 Fa*
The oldest part of the castle is a tower house built
in the early 16th century. Later in the century a
quadrangle of buildings with an inner courtyard
was added. But the castle is best known for the
walled garden, or "Pleasaunce" added at the
beginning of the 17th century.

The inner walls of the Pleasaunce are
intricately decorated, and the garden is maintained in the original manner, with shrubs
trained to spell out mottos such as "Dum spiro
spero"–"While I breathe I hope". The money
spent on the garden by the owner Lord
Edzell–together with various failed business
enterprises–left his family impoverished when
he died in 1610.
Location: 6½ miles N of Brechin off B966.

Egilsay Island *Orkney*   *Map: 387 Ef*
CHURCH OF ST MAGNUS An impressive ruin of one
of the oldest churches in Orkney, built in the 12th
century. The western round tower is 48 ft high
and rises over the roofless nave and chancel like a
great chimney.
Location: W side of island.

Eildon Hill North *Borders*   *Map: 389 Fc*
This is the largest Iron Age hill-fort in Scotland,
with 39 acres of land enclosed by its double banks
and ditches. Up to 1,000 people of the powerful
Selgovae tribe lived here at the time of the
Roman invasion of Britain in AD 43. However,
the Romans captured the fort in AD 79 and built
a wooden signal station inside a circular enclosure
on top of the hill.
Location: 1 mile S of Melrose off A6091.

Eilean Donan Castle *Highland*   *Map: 386 Cb*
A huge tower house was built on this tiny rocky
island by Alexander II in the 13th century to
combat Viking raiders. Fresh water was obtained
from a well sunk in the rock to a depth of 32 ft, an
enormous engineering feat for the time.

After the first Jacobite rebellion collapsed in
1716, the castle was occupied by Spanish
mercenaries on the Jacobite side. This led to a
severe bombardment of the castle by the English
warship *Worcester*. The castle has been restored.
Location: 8½ miles E of Kyle of Lochalsh on A87.

Elcho Castle *Tayside*   *Map: 389 Ef*
An earlier fortress on this site is said to have been
used as a hiding place by Sir William Wallace, the
leader of Scottish resistance to Edward I, when
fleeing from English search parties.

The present castle is a tower house built in the
16th century. It was attacked by an angry mob in

the 1770s because the owner was thought to be
using it to hoard grain during a crop failure.
Location: 5 miles SE of Perth (A90 and minor
road).

Elgin *Grampian*   *Map: 387 Ec*
CATHEDRAL Spectacular ruins of the cathedral
church, rebuilt in 1270. After the bishopric of
Moray was suppressed in 1560 the church
declined, and in 1711 the great central tower fell.
Location: King St, off South College St.

Elham *Kent*   *Map: 399 Fb*
CHURCH OF ST MARY THE VIRGIN An Early English
church, later enlarged. In the chancel is a small
window with a 15th-century stained-glass figure
of Thomas Becket. Another window was
designed, painted and made by a brother of the
vicar at the end of the 19th century. Although it
shows David playing the harp for Saul, the faces
are those of well-known people–Thomas
Carlyle, Gladstone, Disraeli, the Marquess of
Salisbury (then Prime Minister), and three
daughters of Queen Victoria.
Location: 7 miles N of Hythe on B2065.

Eliseg's Pillar *Clwyd*   *Map: 393 De*
This 9th-century memorial stone carried a
eulogy of Eliseg, chief of the house of Powys,
by his great-grandson Cyngen, who died in 854.
The stone was battered during the Civil War and
is now illegible. The mound it stands on is the
burial place of a chieftain who died in the 5th or
6th century.
Location: 1½ miles N of Llangollen on A542.

Ellesmere Port *Cheshire*   *Map: 393 Ef*
BOAT MUSEUM The museum is in the basin of the
Shropshire Union Canal, where it once met the
Mersey but now joins the Manchester Ship
Canal. The boats in the collection range from the
earliest type of canal craft to the broad Mersey
flat boat *Mossdale*, built in the 1870s.
Location: 6½ miles N of Chester (M531, exit 5).

Elmore Court *Glos.*   *Map: 393 Fb*
The house, in a loop of the River Severn, was
begun in 1564 by the Lord of the Manor John
Guise as a home for his bride Jane Pauncefoote.
The work took 24 years, and was finished in the
year of the Spanish Armada. The interior is still as
it was in the days of John and Jane Guise.
Location: 4½ miles SW of Gloucester (A430, A38
and minor roads).

Eltham Palace *Greater London*   *Map: 399 Ec*
Tucked away behind the ribbon development of
a south London suburb stand the noble remnants
of the favourite palace of the kings of England
from Edward II to Henry VII. The great hall with
its splendid timber roof dates from 1482.

Edward III received the captive John II of
France at Eltham in 1363. In the French king's
train was the chronicler Froissart, who described
it as "a very magnificent palace". In 1820 it was
serving as a barn, but was later restored.
Location: Court Yd, off Eltham High St.

Ely *Cambs.*   *Map: 399 Ef*
CASTLE Cherry Hill is the mound of a motte-and-
bailey castle put up soon after the Norman
Conquest in 1066. The castle was strengthened

HOW A MEDIEVAL CATHEDRAL WAS BUILT

When William of Normandy conquered England in 1066 he brought with him the beginnings of an architectural miracle. Throughout Europe men were learning how to build on a scale not known since the decline of Rome 600 years before. And they were putting their new skills to building stone churches and cathedrals as monuments to the glory of God.

The Norman invaders brought this knowledge from Europe and used it to impose their rule over the English people. William created scores of new dioceses throughout the realm and appointed bishops from among his own countrymen.

During the next 400 years vast cathedrals were to rise in breathtaking grandeur over the hovel towns of medieval England. The combination of Norman political skill and popular religious fervour led to buildings of a size and beauty that have rarely been equalled.

Arrival of the Gothic arch

At first, churches and cathedrals were built with semi-circular (or Norman) arches, and mostly with wooden roofs. But fire took a great toll. The answer lay in stone ceilings, or vaulting, but to build vaulting with round arches presented great problems where nave and transept crossed. From this dilemma grew the pointed (Gothic) arch which could span almost any height and width.

The pointed arch introduced the great age of cathedral building. Between 1150 and 1550 nearly 30 cathedrals were built with stone vaults soaring as much as 100 ft above the worshippers' heads. As well as reducing the fire risk, vaulting became a symbol of man's heavenly aspirations and his belief in the glory of God, culminating in the lace-like beauty of fan-vaulting in the 16th century (see p. 322).

A cathedral took between 40 and 100 years to build, giving decades of work to armies of masons, carpenters, sculptors and labourers.

Long before the first spadeful of turf was lifted, a score or more men set to work in a quarry. With only picks, axes, chisels and wedges, they cut and prised thousands of tons of stone from the living rock. Sometimes stone was brought from Normandy.

The building was designed and supervised by the master mason, who was the highest-paid man on the site, with a sable robe and gloves as symbols of his status. He was hired by the year – or perhaps for life – with a generous pension when he was too old.

The master mason had a thatched hut on the site where he and his freemasons prepared drawings and discussed problems. Freemasons were skilled men who worked freestone – a fine-grained stone particularly suitable for face-work and intricate carving. Plans of the cathedral were drawn by the master mason and his assistants on sheets of parchment, with full-size details of carpentry joints, carvings and furnishings.

Masons and other skilled craftsmen were hired by the week, unskilled labourers by the day. In the 13th century, craftsmen were paid four pence a day, and a master mason three or four times as much. Most skilled workers had 30–40 days off, with pay, during the season.

Work started at sunrise and finished at sunset – an average working day of 14 hours – with a half-hour for breakfast, an hour-and-a-half for a midday meal, and a half-hour break in the late afternoon. Saturday afternoons and Sundays were free.

From October onwards, the main work force – 200 or more – were laid off, and the top of any unfinished stone-work was covered with thatch, or straw and dung, to protect it from frost.

As the walls rose, so did the scaffolding – poles lashed together with rope and supporting platforms of woven twigs. Scaffolding was cantilevered from the top of the walls, like brackets, to save the forest of timber that would have been needed to cover the great height. These platforms were reached by permanent spiral stone staircases, built at the same time as the walls.

Roof timbers were assembled on the ground – then taken apart, hoisted into position and reassembled. Plumbers followed, covering the timber roofs with boarding and lead sheeting.

Accidents were frequent: men fell to their deaths from scaffolding hundreds of feet high, or were crushed by falling masonry. While supervising the construction of the choir vaulting of Canterbury Cathedral, William of Sens – the master mason – fell 50 ft to the paved floor of the nave. He survived, but remained crippled for life, "by the vengeance of God or the spite of the Devil".

Disaster as spires collapse

A cathedral's towers and spires were often added long after the first master mason had died or left the job. Existing foundations were sometimes inadequate and towers collapsed, sometimes into the body of the cathedral. This happened at Ely and Hereford, and at Lincoln where three monks were killed and several others injured.

As a cathedral neared completion and some of its original creators were in the twilight of their lives, it was the turn of the metalsmiths and enamellers. Between them they enriched shrines and tombs, screens and candelabra, and made priceless sacramental vessels.

It was often nuns who made the final contribution, with richly embroidered wall hangings, tapestries and vestments for the clergy.

Then, as now, a medieval cathedral was a structural miracle, a skilful balance of thrust and counterthrust – a monument to man as well as a gift to God.

A CATHEDRAL GROWS *A medieval manuscript shows a master mason taking instructions from the king to build a cathedral. Alongside, the cathedral takes shape, with stone being hauled by windlass to masons who place it in position at the top of the wall.*

THE GENIUS OF MEDIEVAL CRAFTSMANSHIP

The glorious Lantern lets a glow of light into the very heart of Ely Cathedral, where the nave and the transepts meet. The Lantern was a miracle of medieval engineering. Eight massive oak beams, 63 ft long and *3 ft thick, had to be lifted 94 ft above the floor of the cathedral and held in an upright position while 16 struts were attached to secure the whole structure to the body of the building.*

by the Bishop of Ely in the 1130s, during the anarchy of Stephen's reign. The upper part is not open to the public.
Location: City centre.
CATHEDRAL Ely Cathedral marks a fenland island where a Saxon queen became a saint, and a Saxon nobleman made a stand against the military force of William the Conqueror.

In 673 Queen Ethelreda, wife of King Egfrid, created a monastery for both nuns and monks, and became the abbess. In 679 she died and was buried in the graveyard. Sixteen years later, when her body was moved into the church it was found to be "free of corruption". Miracles were attributed to her and she was canonised.

In 870 the Danes invaded Ely, massacred the monks and nuns, sacked the monastery and burned the church. But St Ethelreda's relics were saved and a Benedictine monastery was later established.

In 1071 Hereward the Wake, a Lincolnshire thegn (lord), attempted to resist the Norman invasion, using some of the monastic buildings in the still undrained fens as a "Camp of Refuge". It fell in a few weeks when William the Conqueror himself led an attack, and Hereward disappeared into the mists of legend.

William appointed a Norman abbot who started rebuilding the church in 1083, working from the east end. In 1109 the east end was complete and Ely church became a bishop's seat and consequently a cathedral.

In 1322 the central tower of the cathedral collapsed, leading to the building of Ely's crowning glory–the Octagon and Lantern, said to be the only Gothic dome in existence.

Two brilliantly inventive men were responsible: Alan of Walsingham and William Hurley–sacrist (church official) and master-carpenter. At the junction of the nave and the transepts, they built the Octagon, consisting of eight large piers, soaring up to form four 72 ft high arches. From the piers sprout ribs of vaulting that form the octagonal-shaped opening on which the Lantern sits.

The Lantern has a framework of eight massive oak uprights, each nearly 3 ft thick and 63 ft long. Alan of Walsingham scoured the country for them, strengthening the roads and bridges around Ely for their transportation. The uprights, together with the glass and lead that complete the Lantern, impose a load of 400 tons on the Octagon. The work was completed in 30 years and today, 600 years later, it is still an unrivalled testament to medieval craftsmanship.

The final triumph at Ely was the completion of the Lady Chapel, linked to the south transept, between 1320 and 1349. It has the widest medieval vault in England, 46 ft wide and rising only 13 in. higher at the centre than the sides–a vault too delicate to support a man's weight.
Location: City centre.

Eochar *Western Isles*   *Map: 386 Ac*
BLACKHOUSE MUSEUM Prince Charles Edward Stuart spent weeks hiding in a South Uist blackhouse, such as the one at Eochar, after the collapse of the Jacobite Rebellion of 1745. Blackhouses have no chimney and only a small window. A contemporary report says "his shirt, hands and face were all patched with soot-drops".
Location: By the South Uist–Benbecula bridge.

Epworth *Humberside*   *Map: 394 Cc*
RECTORY John Wesley, who founded Methodism, was born at Epworth Rectory in 1703. The present house replaced the one which was burned down in 1709 by parishioners who objected to his father's political views.
Location: 18 miles S of Goole off A161.

Erddig *Clwyd*   *Map: 393 Ee*
A 17th-century country house, occupied until 1973, and now restored as a living example of a country estate (see overleaf).
Location: 1 mile S of Wrexham off A483.

Escomb *Durham*   *Map: 391 Fd*
CHURCH OF ST JOHN A rare example of a well-preserved Saxon church, built in the 7th or early 8th century. The proportions of the interior – long, narrow and tall – are typical of the small church of the period.

Much of it was built with stones from the Roman camp at Binchester.
Location: 2 miles W of Bishop Auckland off B6282.

Eskdale Moor *Cumbria*   *Map: 390 Dc*
STONE CIRCLES Five stone circles stand on Eskdale Moor, all built about 1500 BC and containing one or more stone cairns. Eskdale Circle has five cairns, each of which covered the cremated remains of a Bronze Age Briton.
Location: 13 miles W of Ambleside via Hard Knott Pass, then bridlepath N from Boot.

Eton College *Berks.*   *Map: 398 Cc*
"The King's College of Our Lady at Eton beside Windsor" was founded for poor scholars in 1440 by the pious Henry VI. For more than 500 years it has been the principal place of education for the sons of the British ruling class. The tuition given to the 70 poor scholars of the foundation was soon shared by sons of the aristocracy, who boarded in the town. In time the Oppidans, as these boys came to be called, outnumbered the scholars and official accommodation was provided in boarding houses presided over by masters. This arrangement has become standard at every British public school. Eton now has 1,200 boys.
Location: 1½ miles N of Windsor on B3022.

Everton *Merseyside*   *Map: 393 Ef*
CHURCH OF ST GEORGE St George's is said to have been the world's first church to have cast-iron used in its construction. The conventional stone carcase has a prefabricated cast-iron interior – unexpectedly bright and delicate.
Location: Heyworth St (continuation of Everton Rd), 1½ miles NE of centre of Liverpool.

Evesham Abbey *Heref. & Worcs.* *Map: 393 Fc*
The abbey was founded early in the 8th century. Very little now remains except the detached bell-tower, 110 ft high, built in the 1530s. Many large churches had detached towers but almost all have now disappeared.
Location: The centre of Evesham.

Ewelme *Oxon.*   *Map: 398 Cd*
CHURCH OF ST MARY THE VIRGIN A beautiful group of 15th-century church, almshouse and school were all built to the order of Geoffrey Chaucer's grand-daughter Elizabeth, and her husband William de la Pole, Duke of Suffolk.

The church's showpiece is the monument to the duchess. She lies at prayer carved in alabaster. Around her are little stone angels in feather trousers, while below, if you lie on the floor with a torch, you will see, once again in alabaster, the decaying corpse of the duchess.
Location: 10 miles NW of Henley (A423 then minor roads).

Ewloe Castle *Clwyd*   *Map: 393 Df*
This was a Welsh castle built by Llywelyn the Great early in the 13th century. Its main feature

DOVECOT AT ERDDIG
Dovecots were once a source of food, particularly in winter. The one at Erddig still has a revolving ladder, used to collect eggs and squabs (baby birds).

GRAFFITI AT ETON
A desk panel at Eton's Upper School carries the names of Walpole and Pitt (the Elder) among those of other lesser-known Old Etonians. Upper School is the largest classroom, with space for 200 boys.

was a D-shaped great tower, inside an irregular-shaped enclosure.
Location: 8½ miles W of Chester on A55.

Ewyas Harold Castle *Heref.*   *Map: 393 Eb*
The 53 ft high motte may have been raised in the 1050s by Osbern Pentecost, a Norman knight and friend of Edward the Confessor. This would make it one of the few motte-and-bailey castles built before 1066. Only the mound is left.
Location: 12 miles SW of Hereford (A465 and B4347).

A portrait gallery from below stairs

PICTURES IN THE SERVANTS' HALL—COACHBOY AND CARPENTER, HOUSEMAID AND
GARDENER—BRING AN OLD COUNTRY ESTATE VIVIDLY BACK TO LIFE

ERDDIG FROM THE EAST *The 18th-century wrought-iron screen now at the end of the garden canal was made by a local craftsman. It was brought to Erddig in 1908 and repaired by the estate blacksmith, Joseph Wright.*

A brick-built mansion in a 150 acre park, Erddig is a complete picture of a self-supporting estate. It stands a mile south of Wrexham in Clwyd.

About 15 house servants and 30 outside staff were needed to run the 1,900 acre estate, which included farmhouses and cottages. Generations of them are commemorated by portraits hung in the servants' hall and passage, some enlivened with verses penned by the master of the house.

Erddig was built between 1684 and 1687, and John Meller, a London lawyer, bought and enlarged the house in 1716. He left it to his nephew, Simon Yorke, whose descendants lived there for 240 years until 1973. Many original furnishings remain, and there are fruit trees of early 18th century types, such as Spanish Musk Pare and Orange Apricock.

WHERE THE SERVANTS WORKED

The servants' hall was in the basement. Here they ate their meals and received their free quota of beer, served from leather black jacks.

Laundry, bakehouse and scullery were grouped round a yard between the house and stables. Joiners, blacksmiths and other outdoor staff were based in the estate yard some distance to the south of the house.

NEW KITCHEN *Feeding the Erddig household was a full-time job, not made easier by the fact that many of the Yorkes were vegetarians. About three kitchen maids helped the cook with food preparation. Most of the food came from the estate, including eggs and squabs (unfledged birds) from the dovecot. The new kitchen built in 1772–3 was detached from the house because of Philip Yorke's fear of fire, but was linked during the 19th century.*

JOINERS' SHOP
Carpentry work on the estate—such as mending furniture and fences, wagons and roofs—employed probably two joiners and an apprentice in the joiners' shop (left). Each man had his own tools and a stamp by which his work could be identified. Timber was felled on the estate and seasoned in lean-tos round the estate yard. It was sawn into planks in a two-man saw pit.

LAUNDRY *Clothes were boiled in fire-heated copper cauldrons in the wet laundry. In the dry laundry (below), they were wrung on rollers passed beneath a wheel-turned box mangle weighted with stones. A laundry stove warmed drying racks and heated flat irons for smoothing and goffering irons for crimping.*

THE MASTERS' VERSES

Service at Erddig was often a family affair. Jane Ebbrell, a housemaid, married the coachman and, in the words of Squire Yorke, "brought us forth a second whip." Both the daughters of Thomas Rogers, carpenter, worked in the household. One, Harriet, became cook and housekeeper, and her niece Ellena was a lady's maid.

Squire Philip Yorke I wrote verses to go with the staff portraits of the 1790s. Simon Yorke II followed suit in the 1830s, and Philip Yorke II kept up the tradition in 1887 and 1912.

BLACKSMITH *William William's job included repairing farm tools and making hinges and latches. He is pictured aged 70 in 1793.*
"Our Erthig Smith, who fifty year
Was Surgeon-general to the gear . . .
High callings which his father bore
And eke his Grandfather before."

GARDENER *Thomas Pritchard was 67 when his portrait was painted in 1880, after years of tending Erddig's lawns and orchards.*
"Our Gardener, old and run to seed,
Was once a tall and slender reed . . ./He shone more bright in Marriage state/And reared young plants from teeming Mate."

COACHBOY *This is the earliest of the staff portraits. The verse was written 50 years after the 18th-century painting.*
"Of the Conditions of this Negro
Our information is but megre.
However, here he was a dweller
And blew the horn for Master Meller."

SPIDER-BRUSHER *John Meller brought housemaid Jane Ebbrell with him from London. She was 87 when pictured here in 1793.*
"To dignifie our Servants' hall
Here comes the Mother of us all./For seventy years, or near, have passed her Since Spider-brusher to the Master."

CARPENTER *Thomas Rogers was nearly carried off by a naval press-gang in 1815, when 33, but Squire Yorke paid for his release.*
"Another Chip from Nature's Block/Is added to the Parent Stock./Apprentice first unto a Wheelwright,/This Here might have been a Keelwright."

KITCHEN MAN *About to enjoy a pinch of snuff, bachelor Jack Nicholas, 71, is pictured in 1791 as he set off on an errand.*
"Reflected here as in a glass
We recognise Jack Nicholas. . . .
Then in the Kitchen corner stuck/He pluck'd the fowl and drew the duck."

GAMEKEEPER *Jack Henshaw kept Squire Yorke's game preserves free of poachers. He was 59 when pictured in 1791.*
"Near forty years through bush and bryr/He beated for the elder Squire, Who now, together with his gun, Has made him over to his son."

WOODMAN *A part-time trooper in the Yorkes' Denbighshire Militia, Edward Barnes, 68, is pictured with his sabre in 1830.*
"The last not least at Master's Call
Here stands the Cerberus of our Hall.
United to his loving Mate
He guarded well the Erthig Gate."

Exeter *Devon*   *Map: 397 Ec*
CATHEDRAL Exeter has the only old cathedral in
England without a central tower. The roof runs
uninterrupted from end to end of the building,
giving the longest stretch of Gothic vaulting in
the world.

Two massive towers stand on the north and
south sides of the cathedral and are the only

BOATS USED BY PREHISTORIC
BRITONS

*Fishermen in British rivers were catching fish from
coracles even before the Romans arrived. The little
boats were made of flexible twigs, such as willow, then
covered with animal hides and sewn with leather
thongs. They were light enough for the fisherman to
carry to a river and around any unnavigable stretch of
water, and were easily manoeuvred with a paddle. As
they had no keel they could be taken into very shallow
water. The construction of the coracle was so simple
that fishermen could make their own repairs. Coracles
are still used for fishing in Wales, but are now made of
canvas covered with several coats of tar.*

SEVERN CORACLE *Fishermen caught salmon using a
pair of coracles. They drifted down on the fish, trailing
a net between them. The method was so effective it has
now been banned on the Severn.*

TEIFI CORACLE *An oblong boat, built at Newcastle
Emlyn in Dyfed, and used on the River Teifi, is 4 ft
10 in. by 3 ft.*

TYWI CORACLE *The boat was built at Carmarthen on
the River Tywi and is 6 ft 6 in. long and 3 ft 3 in. wide.*

major remains of an earlier Norman building.
The cathedral was rebuilt in the 14th century and
is almost entirely Decorated Gothic, with the
exception of the towers and the Perpendicular
west front.

The pulpitum, or stone screen separating nave
from choir, was made between 1318 and 1325 in
Purbeck marble, and has 17th-century paintings
in the arcading along the top.

Behind the screen, in the choir, is the 60 ft high
bishop's throne, carved in Devon oak between
1313 and 1317. It is among the finest examples of
medieval woodwork in the country.
Location: City centre.
MARITIME MUSEUM This large collection of boats
is housed partly in the basin of the Exeter Canal.
The canal, built in 1566 to by-pass a weir on the
River Exe, was the first in England to have
pound locks – the now familiar standard canal
locks.

The museum's boats come from a great
variety of periods and countries. Among the
most interesting British boats is the steam-
dredger *Bertha*, designed by Isambard Kingdom
Brunel and built in 1844. It is still in working
order and was in use until 1964, making it the
oldest working steam-boat in the world.
Location: Haven Rd, off Alphington St (A3085),
and The Quay off Inner By-Pass.
ROMAN TOWN Exeter, like many of the towns of
Roman Britain, started as an army garrison post,
in this case from the mid-50s to the mid-70s AD.
Then it became a tribal capital. A circuit of walls,
enclosing about 100 acres, was built around the
town, probably in the 3rd century to strengthen
the earlier earthwork defences.

These walls were much repaired in medieval
times and later, but the neat rows of Roman
masonry are still conspicuous near Eastgate
House, High Street, and especially near South
Street, where part of the guard chamber of the
south gate has been laid out.

Eyam *Derbys.*   *Map: 394 Bc*
In 1665 the plague broke out in Eyam and the
villagers isolated themselves to prevent it spreading to other villages. Before the epidemic ended
13 months later, 262 of the 350 inhabitants were
dead (see overleaf).
Location: 12½ miles NW of Chesterfield (A619,
A623, then B6521).

Eye Castle *Suffolk*   *Map: 399 Ff*
The Norman motte-and-bailey castle was leased
by Henry II to Thomas Becket, Archbishop of
Canterbury. In 1164 Becket had to pay £300 to
Henry in arrears on the property.
Location: 4 miles S of Diss off B1077.

Eynsford Castle *Kent*   *Map: 399 Ec*
A very early example of a stone enclosure with
no great tower inside. The curtain wall was built
about 1100 with a 36 ft square watch tower. In
the 12th century a large hall and solar (a room for
the lord's family) were put up.
Location: 6 miles S of Dartford off A225.

Eynsham *Oxon.*   *Map: 398 Bd*
FLASH LOCK The attractive stone toll bridge which
crosses the Thames south of Eynsham was part of
the 18th-century turnpike system under which
roads and bridges were built and the cost was

recouped by imposing tolls on the travellers.

Downstream from the bridge, below a lock, a small stream joins the Thames on the north side. Originally this too was navigable and boats used to pass through a flash lock. A flash lock had only one set of gates. The water built up behind it and when a boat wanted to pass downstream the gate was opened and the boat rode through on the "flash" of water. Remains of the flash lock can be seen by the little bridge near the stream's junction with the Thames.

Location: ½ mile SE of Eynsham on B4044.

HIGHLIGHTS OF EXETER CATHEDRAL

The vaulting of Exeter Cathedral resembles a 300 ft avenue of palm trees, frozen in stone. The cathedral was mostly built in the 14th century and is a good example of Decorated Gothic architecture, abounding in chapels, tombs and commemorative tablets. Captain Robert Falcon Scott's sledge flag from his 1900 Antarctic expedition hangs in the nave.

ANGEL MUSICIANS *The 14th-century minstrels' gallery has carvings of 12 angels playing medieval musical instruments, including a bagpipe.*

ANCIENT CLOCK *The dial of this 15th-century clock consists of concentric rings representing earth, moon and sun. Time is indicated by their positions in relation to each other. The works are modern.*

VAULTING *The 69 ft high vaulting over the nave is supported by piers each made up of 16 shafts of Purbeck marble, clustered like tree-trunks.*

LACE CARVED IN ALABASTER *The effigy of Lady Dodderidge, who died in 1614, shows her in an Elizabethan ruff with the lace on her bodice delicately carved in the alabaster. Her husband Sir John Dodderidge was a judge and Solicitor-General to James I in 1604.*

The village that defied the plague

WHEN THE BUBONIC PLAGUE BROKE OUT IN EYAM IN 1665 THE 350 VILLAGERS ISOLATED
THEMSELVES TO PREVENT IT SPREADING; BEFORE IT ENDED 262 OF THEM HAD DIED

In 1665 the Great Plague which was raging in London broke out in the remote Derbyshire village of Eyam. The dreadful epidemic started when a tailor, George Viccars, received a bundle of damp cloth from London and hung it round his fire to dry. Next morning he was delirious and in a few days he was dead, his body marked with the purple blotches that gave the flea-borne plague its medieval name of Black Death.

Before Viccars was buried the disease had spread to other households, heralded by a strange sweet scent, detectable only by the victim.

The rector of Eyam, William Mompesson, realised that if the people fled they might spread the epidemic through the county. He persuaded them to isolate themselves and face the sacrifice that would almost certainly follow. For 13 months the plague gripped Eyam, and when it subsided 262 of the 350 villagers were dead.

To make the isolation of his village possible, William Mompesson set boundaries round Eyam and arranged places where people from other villages could leave food, clothing and medicine, and collect money in payment without meeting the infected people of Eyam.

Attempting to reduce the spread of the disease in the village Mompesson closed his church and led prayers in the open air at Cucklet Delph, south-west of the village.

Cucklet Delph was also the secret meeting place of Emmott Sydall, an Eyam girl who had lost most of her family, and Rowland Torre, her sweetheart from the neighbouring village of Stoney Middleton. All through the winter of 1665–6 they came to the spot to call to each other across the rocks. One day in the spring Rowland waited in vain. He thought Emmott had been prevented from coming. In the autumn, when the plague was over, Rowland was one of the first to enter Eyam, to find that Emmott had died in April and that her mother had gone mad with grief.

One of the last to die was Mompesson's wife Katharine, after spending nearly a year caring for plague victims whose relatives had died before them. One August evening she and her husband were walking in the fields when she commented on the sweet smell of the air. Mompesson recognised the tragic omen and in a few days his wife was dead.

SERVICE OF REMEMBRANCE

The bubonic plague, which almost wiped out the population of Eyam village, began gradually. In September 1665 it took its first victim, George Viccars, the tailor, and then five others. In October, 23 villagers died from the disease, and in August 1666, 78 died including the wife of the Rector, William Mompesson. A commemorative service still takes place on the last Sunday in August every year, and Eyam is given the honour of being the last village in the Derbyshire well-dressing ceremonies that take place each summer.

VILLAGE LEADER
Eyam's rector, William Mompesson (left), persuaded his congregation to isolate themselves to prevent the plague spreading. Mompesson worked closely with the nonconformist minister Thomas Stanley.

MOMPESSON'S CHAIR
A chair which was in the rectory during the plague now stands in Eyam church.

DEATH TOLL *The church register lies open at the entries for August 1666, when 78 people died.*

NO TIME FOR FUNERALS

A few richer people fled from Eyam when the plague started, including the Bradshaws of Bradshaw Hall, the ruins of which stand by the Methodist church. For the great majority there could not even be proper funerals. They were buried by relatives or friends in graves scattered through the village.

PLAGUE COTTAGES *The epidemic broke out in September 1665 in one of three cottages near the church, now called Plague Cottages (on the right in the picture). A tailor, George Viccars, died first.*

KATHARINE'S TOMB *The rector's wife was buried in Eyam churchyard. Mompesson himself left Eyam in 1670 to become rector of Eakring in Nottinghamshire, and lived for another 40 years.*

TRADING POINTS *People from nearby villages brought food to Eyam and left it at points around the village. One place was Mompesson's well (far left), on the Grindleford road. Money left in payment was washed in spring water and vinegar. On a path to Stoney Middleton, holes in a stone were filled with vinegar and coins dropped in.*

TRAGIC LOVERS *Emmott Sydall lost her father, brother and three sisters within a month. For the next year she secretly met her sweetheart from a neighbouring village at Cucklet Delph, near the cavern where church services were held (right). In 1666, Emmott herself died.*

FAMILY GRAVES *During one week in August 1666, an Eyam woman saw her husband, John Hancock, and her six children die in the epidemic. They were buried by a path running to the east of the village (right). Mrs Hancock later fled from Eyam to her surviving son in Sheffield.*

F

Fairbourne Railway *Gwynedd* *Map: 392 Cd*
The railway was built in the 1890s as a horse-drawn freight tramway, carrying building materials from a brickyard near Fairbourne Station to Penrhyn Point. Passenger-carrying trams were introduced in 1916. Later that year, the line was converted to the present 15 in. gauge when steam traction was introduced. The line now carries passengers between Fairbourne and Barmouth Ferry for the 12-seater boats to the quay.
Location: 10 miles N of Tywyn on A493.

Fairford *Glos.* *Map: 398 Ad*
CHURCH OF ST MARY THE BLESSED VIRGIN A church renowned for its 15th-century stained glass – among the best to have survived in England. The 28 windows may have been made for St Mary's when it was rebuilt, about 1500, by a rich wool merchant, John Tame. The glass may have come from the school of Henry VII's Master Glass Painter, Barnard Flower – who glazed part of Westminster Abbey.
The chancel stalls have carved misericords – hinged bracket-seats – depicting grotesques and people in scenes from contemporary life.
Location: 8 miles E of Cirencester on A417.

Fair Maid's House see Perth

Falkirk *Central* *Map: 388 De*
CARRON IRONWORKS The ironworks, founded in 1759, made the carronades – large-bore cannons – used by the Royal Navy. Specimen carronades made for the Napoleonic Wars stand inside the gates of the factory which is still in use, and is not open to visitors.
Location: 2 miles N of town centre.

Falkland *Fife* *Map: 389 Ee*
PALACE Although Falkland Palace belongs to the sovereign, no reigning monarch has lived in it since Charles II, and for 300 years it has been in the custody of Hereditary Keepers. The palace was a favourite hunting lodge of the Stuart kings, and is still occupied by a descendant of the Stuarts.
In 1502 James IV renovated the great hall or Lyon Chamber on the site of an existing 13th-century stronghold, and from it grew the palace itself. Since Falkland was to be a place for hunting and recreation, the palace was built around a large court with no provision for defence.
James V added considerably to the palace, in 1541, bringing over French craftsmen to work with Scottish masons. The king himself sometimes engaged masons and on at least one occasion sacked one; but the accounts reveal that he and the queen often rewarded good work with "drinksilver" – a tip.
The Chapel Royal is still in use, and has the only original interior surviving at the palace. The King's Bedchamber – which has the splendid Golden Bed of Brahan – is where James V died, possibly of jaundice, in 1542. On being told that the queen had given birth to a daughter (the future Mary, Queen of Scots), he uttered his celebrated prophecy about the Scottish throne: "It cam' wi' a lass (referring to Robert Bruce's daughter) and will gang wi' a lass."
Mary spent some of her happiest childhood days at the palace, and visited Falkland annually from 1561 to 1565, riding out over the Lomond Hills or, on wet days, playing backgammon or embroidering with her maids of honour – "the Queen's Maries".
Unique in Scotland is the Royal Tennis Court built by James V in 1539 and still used by exponents of this difficult game. Royal – or real – tennis, the forerunner of lawn tennis, was originally played with the hand; the racket was introduced later. The game slightly resembles squash rackets in that the court has four sides – two of which are known as "penthouses", their angled roofs used in serving. The racket, ball and scoring procedures are different from those used in lawn tennis.
Location: 11 miles N of Kirkcaldy (A92, A912).
THE OLD BURGH The former Royal Burgh, which grew up beside the royal palace from the early 17th century, has been preserved within a conservation area that embraces the palace buildings and orchard.
The burgh includes some of the finest domestic Scottish architecture of the period, with weavers' cottages and the houses of those who were attached to the royal household (all are private houses). Brunton House bears the carved arms of the Simsons of Brunton, Hereditary Falconers, under the crest of a flying falcon.
These old Falkland houses are notable for their "marriage lintels" – carved stones above the doorways bearing the initials of the young couple and the date they moved in – sometimes with added inscriptions.
Location: 11 miles N of Kirkcaldy (A92, A912).

Farleigh Hungerford *Somerset* *Map: 397 Gd*
CASTLE The castle was built in 1383 by Sir Thomas Hungerford, Speaker of the House of Commons. Apparently he fortified the building without a licence, for there is a record of his being pardoned for the offence.
The castle changed hands during the Wars of the Roses, and was also the scene of action during the Civil War when a Hungerford, who was a Royalist, lost the castle to his brother, a Parliamentarian.
Location: 3 miles W of Trowbridge on A366.

Farnborough Hall *Warks.* *Map: 398 Be*
When William Holbech inherited this 17th-century manor in 1751, his brother Hugh lived at Mollington, about half a mile away. So close was the friendship of the brothers that William laid out a terrace walk so he could stroll to the edge of his property each morning, to meet Hugh.
The interior of Farnborough Hall, with paintings by Canaletto and elaborate plaster ceilings, reflects the Grand Tour made by William.
Location: 6 miles N of Banbury off A423.

WHERE KINGS AND THEIR COURTIERS PLAYED

The tennis court at Falkland Palace was built by James V in 1539. Royal tennis – centuries older than lawn tennis – is still played here, and the court is the only one in Scotland to have survived from the Stuart period. The covered space – "penthouse" – is one of two that are primarily used in serving.

Farnham *Surrey*   *Map: 398 Cb*

CASTLE This 12th-century castle was used as a residence by the bishops of Winchester throughout the Middle Ages.

During the Civil War, the castle was held by Parliament until November 1642, when it was evacuated after threats from a Royalist army. A month later, the Royalists who had taken it were besieged by Sir William Waller, who blew up the gate with a grenade. The Royalists yielded and the castle remained in Parliamentary hands until 1645 when, in a lightning raid which caught the garrison unaware, it was recaptured by the Royalists.

The original tower has gone but the motte, an irregular shell keep and a deep well survive in an impressive ruin.
Location: N of town centre on A287.

THE OLD KILN MUSEUM An open-air collection of horse and tractor-operated farm implements from all parts of England. The museum includes rare wooden ploughs and a display of farm wagons.

A covered area has a smithy, a wheelwright's shop and a hop press, showing some of the local brewing processes.
Location: 3½ miles S of Farnham (A287 then minor road).

Faversham *Kent*   *Map: 399 Fc*

CHART GUNPOWDER MILLS These water-powered mills are the oldest of their kind in the world – dating from about 1760. Until 1934, Faversham was the centre of Britain's explosives industry, with a mile-long factory stretching from Ospringe to Faversham Creek.

Since gunpowder mills were prone to accidental explosions, they were flimsily built, sited well apart and had trees planted between them – all to minimise possible damage.

One of the mills is restored. It was used for mixing (rather than grinding) gunpowder ingredients: charcoal, salt-petre and sulphur.
Location: Ospringe Rd (A251) continuation of South Rd (B2040), off A2.

AN ANCESTOR OF LAWN TENNIS

The origins of tennis are obscure, but the game is believed to have originated in medieval France – where it was a popular pastime among the French aristocracy before reaching England during the 14th century. Tennis was one of the first ball games to be formalised with rules, and is thought to have influenced the growth of several other court games, such as fives.

Games in the cloisters

Real or royal tennis is thought to have been played in monastery cloisters, and later in castle courtyards. The sloping roof of the cloisters and cow-shed roofs in the courtyards were part of the game, used for rolling the ball along. Later, when courts were built specially for the game, the same shape and characteristics were retained – enclosures along two sides for spectators, with their sloping roofs used for serving. Other features, such as a buttress, were also included.

A cord was strung between facing walls, with a fringed-tassel to reveal whether or not the ball had passed over the "net". There were no rackets at first – the game was known as *jeu de paume* (game of the palm) – and the balls were made of tightly rolled and stitched pieces of cloth. Later a glove was worn or the hand was bound with strips of leather. Finally – probably during the 14th century – a crude form of short-handled bat was used.

By the end of the 16th century, royal tennis was extremely popular, played with stringed rackets and white leather balls stuffed with dogs' hairs, feathers or wool.

Lawn tennis

About the time royal tennis was being played by the aristocracy, the populace were developing a game that may have been another forerunner of lawn tennis. It was played in the open air, on large flat and grassy spaces, without any boundaries, and with groups of opposing players on each side of a dividing line. The game flourished for a while, and was briefly popular among the gentry; but it never really caught on. Not until the 1840s did lawn tennis achieve wide popularity.

Playing tennis in Charles I's time

LOVERS' LINTELS

Some of the houses in the old burgh of Falkland have carved stones – "marriage lintels" – above the front doors, bearing the initials of the newly weds and the date they moved in. The upper of the two lintels was the home of Nicol Moncreif, a personal bodyguard to James VI and I.

Fishbourne: A Briton's Roman palace

AN ARMY OF CRAFTSMEN WAS BROUGHT FROM THE CONTINENT ABOUT AD 75 TO BUILD ONE OF THE MOST SPLENDID ROMAN PALACES IN NORTHERN EUROPE.

In the 1st century AD, Fishbourne on the Sussex coast near Chichester was the site of a splendid palace covering 10 acres. Walls were inlaid with marble from Greece and Turkey, or covered with painted plaster and moulded stucco friezes, and floors were paved with mosaics of intricate design. In AD 75 no Briton would have been capable of such workmanship – craftsmen must have been brought from the Continent.

The owner of this magnificent and expensive palace was most likely to have been a Briton: Cogidubnus, king of the Atrebates tribe, who was a client-king under the guidance of Rome. Chichester was his capital, and it would have been a slight to have had an official Roman residence so near. Cogidubnus had been an ally of Rome since the invasion of Britain in AD 43, and the Roman historian Tacitus tells of his unswerving loyalty.

Fishbourne palace was probably the home of Cogidubnus in his later years. Only after his death was his kingdom formally annexed to the Roman province. By the middle of the 2nd century, the palace had been split into a series of independent units, and at the end of the 3rd century it was destroyed by fire.

ENTRANCE HALL *Beyond the six tall columns of the porch was a huge arched waiting-room where light slanted in from semicircular windows, and visitors looked across a pool to the distant audience chamber.*

CONCOURSE *This hallway, floored with a black and white mosaic pavement, gave access to a suite of administrative rooms north of the audience chamber in the west wing. Here people may have waited, perhaps gathered round a brazier on winter days, to conduct business with Cogidubnus or his officials.*

The south door of the hallway led to a colonnaded veranda overlooking the formal gardens, which were designed for viewing from the west wing. The north door led to a 17 ft wide corridor where guests could stroll or play games. Both corridor and veranda stretched the length of the west wing, which was on a level 5 ft higher than the rest of the palace.

BEDROOM *The private guest suites in the north wing were arranged round small colonnaded gardens. Floors were black and white mosaics laid in strong geometric patterns, still to be seen after 1,900 years.*

WHO LIVED WHERE IN THE PALACE

It was in the vaulted audience chamber in the west wing that Cogidubnus received official visitors. Most entered through the entrance hall and approached the audience chamber through the formal gardens along an avenue 40 ft wide lined by box hedges. Important guests stayed in private suites in the comfortably equipped north wing, and low-ranking visitors in simpler suites in the east wing. Cogidubnus had his private apartments in the south wing, with a natural garden and landing stage on the south side. The heated bath suite was close by in the south of the east wing. Servants' quarters, not yet discovered, were most likely to the west of the palace.

These drawings show the palace as it would have looked about AD 100. Today the north wing remains are displayed under cover, with a museum near by.

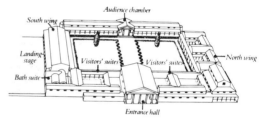

PLANTS THAT CAME WITH THE ROMANS

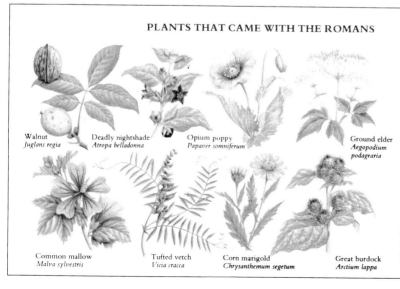

Walnut
Juglans regia

Deadly nightshade
Atropa belladonna

Opium poppy
Papaver somniferum

Ground elder
Aegopodium podagraria

Common mallow
Malva sylvestris

Tufted vetch
Vicia cracca

Corn marigold
Chrysanthemum segetum

Great burdock
Arctium lappa

Many plants first appeared in Britain in Roman times, some by accident – perhaps on clothing or among seeds or packaging. Troop movements, roadworks and forest felling would have assisted their spread. Plants brought in for cultivation included the walnut, the mulberry and the medlar, ground elder (used as a pot-herb), and the drug plants opium poppy and deadly nightshade (belladonna).

Fazeley Junction *Staffs.*   *Map: 393 Gd*
Beside the Birmingham and Fazeley Canal, near the point where it meets the Coventry Canal, stands the cotton mill built in 1795 by Robert Peel, whose son became prime minister.

The three-storeyed mill was originally water-powered. On the opposite side of the canal, there is a five-storeyed mill of 1883, with a tall chimney, indicating that it was steam-powered. Both mills are still in use but no longer for cotton spinning – neither is open to the public.
Location: 1½ miles S of Tamworth on A4091.

Felbrigg Hall *Norfolk*   *Map: 395 Fb*
The Hall was built about 1620, added to in 1680, and substantially altered during the 1750s by James Paine. The library, in the Gothic Revival style, has books that belonged to Dr Johnson.

There is a walled garden – which in the 17th and 18th centuries provided fruit, flowers, herbs and vegetables for the household.
Location: 2 miles SW of Cromer (A148, B1436).

Felin Geri *Dyfed*   *Map: 392 Bc*
The flour mill was built in 1604 and is in full operation. There are two water-wheels, one for the flour mill and one for the 19th-century saw-mill.
Location: 1½ miles NW of Newcastle Emlyn (on track running NE off B4333).

Filkins *Oxon.*   *Map: 398 Bd*
THE COTSWOLD MUSEUM A 16th-century cottage, with a small collection of farm hand-tools, and 19th-century kitchen implements.

Next to the museum is a village lock-up, large enough to hold one man overnight. It is a narrow stone building with a sleeping platform at one end. A prisoner's friends could pass drinks through a narrow grating in the door to help him through the night.
Location: 3 miles N of Lechlade off A361. Museum is in the village centre.

Finchale Priory *Durham*   *Map: 391 Gd*
The priory was founded in 1196 – on the site of St Godric's hermitage – and is now a picturesque ruin on the banks of the River Wear. Godric died at Finchale in 1170, aged 105.
Location: 5 miles NE of Durham (A167 then minor road).

Finchcocks *Kent*   *Map: 399 Eb*
Although Finchcocks is not a huge house it was built in the grand baroque manner in 1725. It is the best house of the period in Kent – a superb example of the bricklayer's craft.

Finchcocks has a collection of early keyboard instruments, some of which are played for visitors during the summer months when the house is open.
Location: 1½ miles SW of Goudhurst off A262.

Finchingfield *Essex*   *Map: 399 Ee*
CHURCH OF ST JOHN THE BAPTIST The church, set in a picturesque village, complete with green and duck pond, dates from the Norman period. Dividing the nave and chancel is a fine carved wooden screen – one of the best in Essex.

In the Kempe Chapel there is a monument to William Kempe (died in 1628) who, having wrongly accused his wife of unfaithfulness, vowed not to speak for seven years. He kept the vow.

The entrance to the churchyard is through the timber-framed 15th-century guildhall.
Location: 8 miles NW of Braintree on B1053.

Finlarig Castle *Central*   *Map: 388 Cf*
The first owners of this 17th-century castle – who were a branch of the Campbells – were remarkably violent people. In the grounds there is a stone tank which they built, ostensibly as a reservoir for water, but which local legend states was used for executions. Victims were thrown into the tank and their heads were pushed into the drain outlet, and then chopped off.
Location: 22 miles SW of Aberfeldy on A827.

Firle Place *E. Sussex*   *Map: 399 Ea*
The 18th-century elevations of Firle Place conceal a Tudor courtyard-house.

The Gages, who have lived in Firle Place for 500 years, remained true to the Catholic faith until early in the 18th century. During the 16th and 17th centuries the family suffered much from the fines imposed on families who refused to submit to the Protestant faith.
Location: 4 miles SE of Lewes off A27.

Fishbourne *W. Sussex*   *Map: 398 Ca*
Remains of a 1st century Roman palace, discovered in 1960, are on display, with parts of the formal garden restored to its original Roman plan. (See pp. 152–3.)
Location: 1¼ miles W of Chichester on A27.

Flamborough *Humberside*   *Map: 395 De*
LIGHTHOUSE There is a tall structure on the point at Flamborough Head – a sea-mark erected in 1669. The present lighthouse was built by the architect Samuel Wyatt in 1806. It is an 87 ft high stone tower, with its light 214 ft above sea-level. The present optical system was installed in 1974: the light is 3,500,000 candela (candle power) with a range of 29 miles.
Location: 6 miles NE of Bridlington (B1255, B1259).

Fleet Air Arm see Yeovilton

Flete *Devon*   *Map: 396 Db*
An Elizabethan house that was substantially enlarged in 1878 by Norman Shaw for an Australian magnate. Shaw – who designed New Scotland Yard – used a picturesque neo-Elizabethan style.
Location: 10 miles E of Plymouth off A379.

Flint Castle *Clwyd*   *Map: 393 Df*
Flint was one of the first of the Edwardian castles built in Wales during the first campaign against Llywelyn the Last in 1277. In 1282 the Welsh leader and his brother Dafydd rose again and both Flint and Rhuddlan were besieged. But the war ended effectively when Llywelyn was killed at Builth and Dafydd was caught and executed.
Location: N of town off A548.

Floors Castle *Borders*   *Map: 389 Fc*
The castle was built from 1721 for the 1st Duke of Roxburghe by William Adam – father of Robert – and extended 100 years later.

Floors is said to be the largest inhabited house

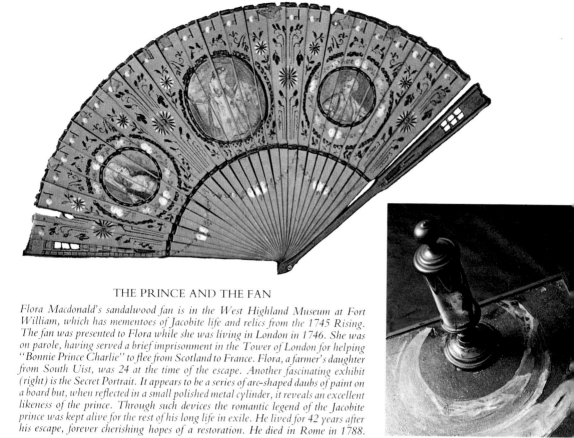

THE PRINCE AND THE FAN

Flora Macdonald's sandalwood fan is in the West Highland Museum at Fort William, which has mementoes of Jacobite life and relics from the 1745 Rising. The fan was presented to Flora while she was living in London in 1746. She was on parole, having served a brief imprisonment in the Tower of London for helping "Bonnie Prince Charlie" to flee from Scotland to France. Flora, a farmer's daughter from South Uist, was 24 at the time of the escape. Another fascinating exhibit (right) is the Secret Portrait. It appears to be a series of arc-shaped daubs of paint on a board but, when reflected in a small polished metal cylinder, it reveals an excellent likeness of the prince. Through such devices the romantic legend of the Jacobite prince was kept alive for the rest of his long life in exile. He lived for 42 years after his escape, forever cherishing hopes of a restoration. He died in Rome in 1788.

in Scotland, and is notable for its exquisite tapestries, and paintings by Reynolds, Raeburn and Lely.
Location: 1 mile NW of Kelso off A6089.

Forde Abbey *Dorset*   *Map: 397 Fc*
Before the Reformation, Forde had been a Cistercian monastery for 400 years. It was dissolved in 1539, but its last abbot, a learned and cultivated man named Thomas Charde, made additions that demonstrate some of the finest Tudor stone-work in England.
In the 1650s it was altered as a private house.
Today, the abbey is in an 18th-century setting of lawns, ponds and fine trees.
Location: 4 miles SE of Chard (B3162).

Ford Green Hall *Staffs.*   *Map: 393 Fe*
A 16th-century timber-framed manor house that is probably the oldest dwelling to survive in the Potteries.
The timber-framed house is now a museum of domestic equipment and furnishings.
Location: Ford Green Rd, Smallthorne, 4 miles N of Stoke-on-Trent (B5049 then B5051).

Foreland Point *Devon*   *Map: 397 Dd*
LYNMOUTH FORELAND LIGHTHOUSE This was built in 1900 – a circular tower, 50 ft high and 300 ft below the crest of the headland. Visiting the lighthouse involves taking a 2 mile walk along a rather precarious cliffside.
Location: 15 miles W of Minehead off A39.

Foremark *Derbys.*   *Map: 394 Ba*
CHURCH OF ST SAVIOUR A Gothic-looking church built in 1662. Inside, most of the 17th-century furnishings have survived intact. There are box

pews, a three-decker pulpit and 18th-century wrought-iron communion rails.
Location: 6½ miles NE of Burton upon Trent (B5008 to Repton, then minor road).

Forfar *Tayside*   *Map: 389 Ef*
MEFFAN INSTITUTE MUSEUM The town museum has a witches' bridle, used in the 17th century when nine women were burned near by for practising witchcraft. The bridle has an iron collar, hinged to fit the neck and with a metal prong or gag in front to stifle screams. A chain secured the victim to the stake.
Location: High St.

Fort William *Highland*   *Map: 386 Cb*
WEST HIGHLAND MUSEUM The 18th-century building houses historic exhibits, including personal belongings of Prince Charles Edward Stuart ("Bonnie Prince Charlie").
Location: Cameron Sq.

Fotheringhay *Northants.*   *Map: 398 Df*
CHURCH OF ST MARY AND ALL SAINTS This is a church with many royal associations, founded by Edmund Langley, son of Edward II. He began the chancel in about 1370, and his son, Edward, founded a college in the church in 1411.
After the Dissolution of the Monasteries (1536–40), Edward VI gave the college to the Duke of Northumberland who demolished both the chancel and disbanded the college.
Fotheringhay Castle – once on a nearby mound – was where Mary, Queen of Scots, was held prisoner from 1586 until 1587 and then beheaded by command of Elizabeth I.
Location: 4 miles N of Oundle (A605 then minor road).

The riches of Fountains Abbey

WEALTHY, POWERFUL AND SEEMINGLY INDESTRUCTIBLE, FOUNTAINS WAS ONE OF THE MANY MONASTERIES TO BE SWEPT AWAY BY HENRY VIII

In 1132 St Mary's at York was a well-established abbey, whose inmates had settled into an easy-going routine. But 13 of the monks favoured a return to austerity and left to start their own foundation. They chose an isolated site in Yorkshire, on the banks of the River Skell – where there was an abundance of fresh water – and called it Fountains Abbey.

In the early years the monks suffered extreme hardship, but the tide turned in 1135, when Hugh, the retiring dean of York, settled at Fountains, bringing to it a considerable fortune and a library. Building started and, as other benefactions flowed in, the abbey grew.

Prosperity increased throughout the 13th century, with as many as 500–600 lay-brothers

1 CHURCH *Monastic life was centred on prayer and meditation in the abbey church.*

2 CHAPTER-HOUSE *Where the business of the monastery was conducted, presided over by the abbot.*

3 CLOISTERS *Covered passages around a courtyard. Monks taught or studied in the cloisters.*

4 ABBOT'S HOUSE *The abbot lived on the first floor.*

5 DORMITORY/UNDERCROFT *Monks' sleeping quarters were on the first floor; the undercroft below was probably used as a workroom.*

6 REFECTORY *The room where monks took their meals.*

7 KITCHEN *This served the monks' refectory, and the lay-brothers' refectory.*

8 LAY-BROTHERS' REFECTORY *Unlettered monks had their own dining hall.*

9 CELLARIUM *The abbey storehouse.*

10 INFIRMARY *Where sick and aged lived.*

11 LAY-BROTHERS' INFIRMARY

12 HOSPICE *Guest house.*

farming the vast estates the abbey had acquired. By the end of the century, it was the richest Cistercian house in England, with an annual count of 15,000 sheep. Fish were also farmed, with 20 acres of ponds on the abbey lands.

When Henry VIII broke with Rome and became head of the Church of England in 1535, Fountains and other monasteries were surrendered to the Crown, providing the king with an impressive treasure-trove of wealth.

THE ABBEY IN THE 16TH CENTURY

Few ruins in England offer a clearer picture of life in a medieval monastery. The reconstruction (below) shows Fountains Abbey as it was about 1530.

THE MONASTIC WAY OF LIFE

At a time "when sleep was sweetest" – 2 a.m. or thereabouts – a bell tolled softly, stirring monks or nuns from their straw mattress beds to the first of many periods of worship. It was the start of a monastic day that did not cease until sunset.

As the sleep-drugged inmates shuffled down the night stairs to the abbey church, their heads hooded and their feet clad in soft leather "night shoes", a lantern-bearer led the way. If, during the service, he saw a monk dozing, he held the light in front of his drowsy colleague's eyes, shook him awake and gave him the lantern. It was then the new lantern-bearer's turn to ensure his colleagues stayed awake.

In winter the abbey church – like the rest of the buildings – was often damp and foggy, and at times unbearably cold. Yet, despite the hardship, the average age of a monk was 55 – higher than that of the general population of medieval Britain.

Sacrifice and self-control
All inmates observed the rules of obedience, poverty and chastity. They were allowed few possessions: a knife for meals, a pen, a handkerchief, and simple garments and footwear. Inmates washed their feet on Saturdays, had their heads shaved every three weeks, and took a bath every three months.

Discipline was strict, and sins – which were expected to be confessed – were punishable by flogging, the sinner stripped to the waist. This was considered to be an excellent method of helping the weak to improve their self-control. Serious crimes, such as violence, could mean imprisonment in a cell attached to the infirmary.

Monastic food was excellent, though bad eating habits tended to cause indigestion. On most days inmates had two meals: a two-course dinner – the first full meal of the day – and a light meal in the evening. There was invariably a choice of fish, vegetables, pastry, fruit and cheeses, with wine, beer, milk or water to wash them down. On feast or festival days there would be pork pies, capons, fig tarts and a pittance – an extra dish of fruit, nuts and cheeses.

Inmates ate in the refectory, where conversation was forbidden, each person anticipating the needs of his neighbours, while readings were given from the Bible.

The sick or the infirm stayed in the infirmary, treated with periodic blood lettings, hot or cold baths, and drugs – made chiefly from herbs grown in the garden.

Working at an anvil

Work and study
In some communities lay-brethren did the manual work; in others, inmates did it themselves – scrubbing floors, caring for the sick and infirm, or tending the land. They also spent time teaching novices or local inhabitants; writing and illuminating manuscripts; or reading the Classics.

Monks in the stocks

The Orders
The Benedictine Order was the one upon which all others were founded, initially imposing a life of extreme austerity on its inmates. Among other Orders were the Cistercians – who lived as self-contained communities and were accomplished farmers; Augustinians, who played a great part in parochial matters; and the Franciscans – noted for their religious teaching.

If a monastery or nunnery had the status of an abbey it was ruled over by an abbot or an abbess – the father or mother of the community.

Monk drawing a bee

WHERE MEDIEVAL MONKS WORSHIPPED

The long floodlit nave of the abbey church, like the rest of Fountains Abbey, has fallen into ruin since it was abandoned in 1540. The Cistercian Order was a strict and self-contained community of farmers, and use of the church was reserved solely for resident monks and lay-brothers.

Fountains Abbey *N. Yorks.*   Map: 394 Be
The eloquent ruins of Fountains Abbey, on the banks of the River Skell, have traces of all the great Cistercian abbey's buildings, from its foundation in 1132 to its decline after the Reformation. (See pp. 156–7.)
Location: 4 miles SW of Ripon off B6265.

Foxfield Colliery *Staffs.*   Map: 393 Fe
FOXFIELD LIGHT RAILWAY The railway is a former colliery standard-gauge branch line, linking Foxfield Colliery with the main line at Blythe Bridge. The line is now run by the Foxfield Light Railway Society Ltd, and visitors can see more than a dozen locomotives and take a ride to Blythe Bridge and back. Although it was an industrial line, the 4 mile run passes through a pleasant rural landscape.
Location: Foxfield Colliery is just N of Dilhorne which is 3 miles W of Cheadle off A521.

Foxton *Leics.*   Map: 398 Cf
FOXTON STAIRCASE The Leicester arm of the Grand Union Canal passes to the west of the village, and climbs 75 ft up the hillside by the Foxton staircase. This consists of two groups of five locks, in which each lock opens directly into the next. There is a short stretch of water between the two sets to allow boats to pass, but even so on a busy summer day Foxton can become a canal bottleneck. To overcome this, the canal company built an inclined plane in 1900 to by-pass the locks. Boats were floated into huge wheeled tubs or "caissons" which were hauled up rails by a steam winch. The plane closed in 1911, but its track remains to the east of the locks.
Location: 3 miles NW of Market Harborough off A6. Follow towpath W from Foxton for ½ mile.

Framlingham *Suffolk*   Map: 399 Ge
CASTLE Framlingham was the castle to which Mary Tudor, elder daughter of Henry VIII, fled in 1553 during an attempt by the Duke of Northumberland to make his daughter-in-law, Lady Jane Grey, the new sovereign. Northumberland's bid for power followed the death of Mary's brother, the boy King Edward VI.

But even while the duke was marching against Framlingham his scheme collapsed, and thousands of Mary's supporters camped outside the walls of the castle to herald her as queen. It was from Framlingham that Mary began her triumphant procession to London as Mary I.

Framlingham was first built about 1100, as a wooden house fortified by a palisade and ditch. It was the home of the Bigods who were immensely powerful in East Anglia. In 1173 Hugh Bigod, 1st Earl of Norfolk, used it and his other castles to challenge the supremacy of Henry II. Eventually Bigod surrendered and the first castle was dismantled.

His son Roger Bigod began to rebuild the castle in stone around 1190. The result, which can be seen today, is a remarkable enclosure of high walls with 13 flanking towers, some 60 ft high, on the outskirts of the town above the River Ore. The castle was once also protected by a second enclosure of ditch and rampart, and partly by a moat.

In 1213 Earl Roger entertained King John inside the new structure, but within two years he was supporting the barons who had compelled John to agree to Magna Carta. In the war that followed, foreign mercenaries besieged Framlingham and took it on behalf of the king.

The castle was turned into a home for paupers in the 17th century, and the existing Poor House building was put up in the 17th and 18th centuries.
Location: 11 miles N of Woodbridge (A12 then B1116).

CHURCH OF ST MICHAEL This Perpendicular church, mainly of the 15th century, has one of the most splendid wooden roofs in Suffolk.

The font, of about 1380, is carved with lions and wild men, and has a font-cover which was left discarded during the Commonwealth.

On the north wall of the nave are the remains of a medieval wall-painting of the Trinity.

But the fame of St Michael's comes from a superb series of early renaissance monuments to Henry, Duke of Richmond (an illegitimate son of Henry VIII) and the 3rd and 4th Dukes of Norfolk. Another monument commemorates Sir Robert Hitcham who bought Framlingham

Castle in 1635 and bequeathed it to Pembroke College, Cambridge.
Location: Beside the castle.

Froghall *Staffs.*   *Map: 394 Ab*
FROGHALL BASIN The basin is the terminus of the now restored Caldon Canal, which was used to carry limestone from the Caldon quarries to Stoke-on-Trent.

The stone was brought from the quarry, 4 miles to the north-east, by horse-drawn tramways. Three tramway lines were built; the one of 1802 incorporated three inclined planes up which the trucks were hauled by a stationary steam-engine. The 900 ft Great Froghall Plane can be seen beside A52.
Location: 10 miles E of Stoke-on-Trent on A52, at junction with B5053.

Froncysyllte *Clwyd*   *Map: 393 De*
PONTCYSYLLTE AQUEDUCT The Ellesmere Canal, now popularly known as the Llangollen Canal, is carried across the River Dee on the Pontcysyllte Aqueduct, one of the finest structures in the whole British canal system.

Originally the aqueduct was planned as a conventional masonry structure. However, Thomas Telford persuaded the canal's chief engineer, William Jessop, to adopt his plan to use the revolutionary technique of carrying the water in a cast-iron trough.

The towpath is cantilevered over the water, reducing the width available for boats to 7 ft 2 in. The aqueduct can be seen from the A5, but if you want to walk across, join the towpath at Froncysyllte.
Location: 3½ miles E of Llangollen off A5.

Furnace *Dyfed*   *Map: 392 Cd*
BLAST FURNACE The furnace was built in 1755 by the Staffordshire iron-master Jonathan Kendall. It was a charcoal-fuelled, iron-smelting furnace, and is one of the best preserved of its type in Wales. The site was chosen because of the abundant timber for charcoal, water for the water-wheels – and cheap Welsh labour.

The hearth is marked by a Gothic arch, and behind the furnace is the pit where the water-wheel that powered the bellows once turned. Parts of a later water-wheel remain.
Location: 6½ miles SW of Machynlleth on A487, beside the Einion river.

Furness Abbey *Cumbria*   *Map: 390 Dc*
The abbey, which was built here in the 12th century, was once very rich – one of the principal monastic establishments in England, often attacked during Scottish raids. The extensive ruins include the church's western tower, choir and transepts.
Location: 2 miles N of Barrow-in-Furness off A590.

Furze Farm Park *Devon*   *Map: 396 Cc*
A rare-breeds farm stocking Longhorn cattle, various breeds of sheep, and Tamworth and Old Spot pigs.

A display of farm equipment illustrates the evolution of agricultural techniques. Visitors can watch sheep-dipping, see corn threshed with steam, take wagon rides and sample cider made on the farm.
Location: 6 miles SE of Bude (A3072, south on B3254, then minor road to Bridgerule from where the farm is signposted).

BRITAIN'S FINEST AQUEDUCT

The iron trough carrying the Ellesmere Canal across the Dee valley at Froncysyllte is 1,007 ft long, and at its highest point is 121 ft above the Dee. The base of the trough is a series of 19 cast-iron arches, each 53 ft wide, supported on stone pillars. They are constructed of solid masonry up to a height of 70 ft, then left hollow. The Pontcysyllte Aqueduct was designed by Thomas Telford and completed in 1805.

G

Gaddesby *Leics.*   *Map: 394 Ca*
CHURCH OF ST LUKE One of the largest village churches in Leicestershire, mainly of the 13th and 14th centuries. The external decoration is thought to have been halted abruptly by plague. The oak pews are original. The near life-size marble horse and rider in the chancel is of Colonel Cheney, who had four horses killed under him at Waterloo.
Location: 10 miles NE of Leicester (A607 then B674).

Gainsborough Old Hall *Lincs.*   *Map: 394 Cc*
This medieval manor house of timber, plaster, brick and stone was rebuilt in the 15th and 16th centuries after extensive damage during the Wars of the Roses. Richard III visited in 1484, and it was here that Henry VIII met Catherine Parr,
who became his sixth wife – and his widow.
The Hall was a meeting house of the Pilgrim Fathers in the early 17th century. It still has its great hall and medieval kitchen with two open fireplaces, each big enough to roast an ox.
Location: Gainsborough town centre.

Gatehouse of Fleet *Dumfs.*   *Map: 390 Be*
COTTON MILLS This was one of the first centres for the establishment of cotton mills in Scotland. The English firm of Birtwhistle came to Gatehouse in the 1790s, attracted by the cheap labour, and built two mills. They employed 300 workers, 200 of them children. The wages bill was £50 a week, an average of 3s 4d.
The mills, now in ruins, stand beside the bridge across the river.
Location: 8 miles NW of Kirkcudbright (A755, A75).

Gawsworth Hall *Cheshire*   *Map: 393 Ff*
This black-and-white Tudor hall was the home of the Fitton family. Mary Fitton, born at the hall in 1578, is believed by some authorities to be the "dark lady" of Shakespeare's sonnets. She was the grand-daughter of Sir Edward Fitton, Vice-Treasurer of Ireland, and in 1595 Mary became a maid-of-honour to Elizabeth I.
Another possible contender for the "dark lady" title was her sister Anne, who was a friend of Will Kemp, the actor and friend of Shakespeare.
Location: 3 miles SW of Macclesfield off A536.

HOW AN ELIZABETHAN GIRL DRESSED

In the Elizabethan Age children dressed in the same style as adults. An upper-class girl would start wearing corsets at the age of about six to compress her rib-cage to the fashionable 18 in. waist.

CHEMISE *First she would put on a linen chemise, or smock, which reached below the knees, and might be embroidered. Her stockings were made of linen or knitted wool, or silk if she was from a rich family. They were held up by garters.*

CORSET *Next came a linen corset, long and pointed in front, and stiffened with whalebone to restrict the waist.*

HOOP *A French farthingale, or hoop of wood or cane, was tied into holes on the corset.*

BODICE *A petticoat, embroidered at the front, went over the farthingale. The bodice had sleeves matching the front of the petticoat. A basque round the waist was worn to hide the join between bodice and skirt.*

SKIRT *The little girl's gown was completed by putting on the skirt, often made of velvet to match the bodice and basque. The skirt was always left open at the front to display the embroidery work on the petticoat.*

RUFF *A pleated ruff of white linen went round the neck, and an embroidered cap on the head.*

TUDOR BLACK-AND-WHITE

Gawsworth Hall is a 15th-century half-timbered house with roofs on five different levels. The roof slates alone weigh more than 350 tons.

THE NEEDLE-WOMAN'S CRAFT

In the days when girls spent long hours training in needlework, accessories were popular gifts for birthdays and weddings. Elaborate tools, made of carved ivory or wood or engraved silver, were expensive and might be kept for a lifetime. Needlework tools of the 18th and 19th centuries, such as those in the Kay-Shuttleworth Collections at Gawthorpe Hall, Lancashire, are now collectors' items.

FOLD-OUT BOX *A Victorian needle-case and thread box folds into a double box – one inside the other.*

CLAMPS *Embroidery clamps were screwed to a table to hold fabric for hemming, or to wind thread.*

IVORY *Carved ivory and bone were used for hooks, shuttles, pin-cushions, scissor cases and thread winders.*

BOBBINS *Lace bobbins made of ivory, bone and wood are decorated with pewter and brass.*

PIN-CUSHIONS *Decorative cushions were made in the shape of baskets or as balls that could be hung from the waist.*

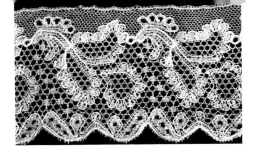

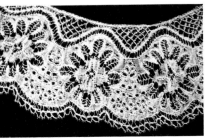

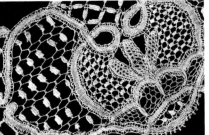

THE AGE OF LACE
In the 17th and 18th centuries huge flounces of lace were worn by both men and women, particularly on cuffs and collars. Most lace was made with linen thread attached to bobbins. The work was rested on a pillow, and was known as bobbin or pillow lace. The lace collection at Gawthorpe Hall, Lancashire, contains English types, including Buckinghamshire (above), Bedfordshire (top left) and Honiton (bottom left).

Gawthorpe Hall *Lancs.*   *Map: 391 Eb*
Gawthorpe was built in the 17th century by the Shuttleworth family who had made a fortune in law practice during Elizabeth's reign.

The foundations were laid in August 1600; the stonemason was paid 2s 4d a day, and the labourers 4d. In the old basement kitchens, above an original fireplace, is the motto "Waste Not, Want Not".
Location: 2½ miles W of Burnley off A671.

Geddington *Northants.*   *Map: 398 Cf*
ELEANOR CROSS When Queen Eleanor died in 1290 at Harby, Nottinghamshire, her grieving husband Edward I came to accompany the corpse of "the Jewel which he most esteemed" back to Westminster.

Wherever the bier rested for a night, Edward built a cross – 12 in all, of which three remain; the others are at Hardingstone and Waltham Cross. At Geddington, the tall cenotaph bears three statues of a veiled Eleanor against a background of cottages.
Location: 3½ miles N of Kettering on A43.

Gibside Chapel *Tyne & Wear*   *Map: 391 Fe*
An outstanding example of Georgian architecture, Gibside Chapel was designed by James Paine in 1760, though work on it was not

SAMPLES OF A GIRL'S SKILL

Embroidery samplers were first made as records of patterns, in days before any books existed to reproduce designs in print. A needlewoman would embroider patterns she had learned and invented on a narrow piece of linen and add to it over the years. Eventually the sampler would be passed on to her daughter. When pattern books became available (the first was printed in 1523) samplers became a method of teaching children needlework techniques, and usually carried the date. They are now widely collected.

MORAL VIRTUES
Samplers of the 18th and early 19th centuries often consisted of a border, some floral designs and a piece of verse. Moral virtues and obedience to parents were learned together with sewing techniques. This sampler, worked by nine-year-old Jane Sewell in 1833, contains the advice: "Let prudence regulate your choice/Take caution for your guide." *The design was worked in silk thread on linen backing. In the 18th and 19th centuries, samplers were part of a girl's school work. Orphanage girls, who mostly became servants, were taught various styles of lettering so that they could embroider names on household linen and underwear. Needlework was also used to teach geography, with samplers consisting of maps.*

completed until the 19th century. It stands within the grounds of the now-ruined Gibside Hall, once the home of the powerful local Whig politician Sir George Bowes.
Location: 6 miles SW of Gateshead (A692 to Burnopfield, then B6314 for 1 mile).

Giggleswick *N. Yorks.* Map: 391 Eb
CHURCH OF ST ALKELDA The church was built on the site of an earlier building probably destroyed in 1319 during a Scottish raid. Inside the main door is a stout beam which, when drawn across and fitted into a socket, gave extra protection to sheltering villagers in times of danger. The pulpit and poor box are from the 1680s.
Location: 17 miles NW of Skipton off A65.

Gilling Castle *N. Yorks.* Map: 394 Ce
The mid-14th-century basement of a square tower and the Elizabethan Great Chamber remain untouched at Gilling.
Location: 18 miles N of York on B1363.

Gisburn *Lancs.* Map: 391 Eb
TODBER MUSEUM OF STEAM Traction engines and steam-wagons are regularly steamed at this museum which is devoted to the use of steam on the road.
There are two magnificent showmen's engines, which were used both for haulage and for powering fairground rides. Other engines include six rare steam-wagons, two of which were brought back from Australia, and a fairground organ.
Location: 1½ miles S of Gisburn on A682.

Glamis *Tayside* Map: 389 Ef
ANGUS FOLK MUSEUM Six cottages and a farming section illustrate how country people lived in Angus until early this century. (See right.)
Location: 5 miles SW of Forfar off A94.
CASTLE Glamis Castle was a hunting lodge of the kings of Scotland from the 11th to the 14th centuries. One of the oldest parts, the original Main Hall, has a trapdoor into a vaulted dungeon. The even older Duncan's Hall may have been a guard-room to the Main Hall.
An early thane of Glamis, Macbeth, became King of Scotland after killing King Duncan in 1040. He in turn was killed by Duncan's son.
In 1372 the Lyon family, later earls of Strathmore, became thanes of Glamis. Relics of the family's Jacobite allegiance include the coat, breeches, sword and watch of James VIII and III (the Old Pretender) who came to Scotland from France for six weeks for the abortive Jacobite rebellion in 1715.
According to legend, a monstrous child was born into the Strathmore family 200 years ago and was incarcerated in the castle walls. As each heir to the earldom reached 21 he was shown the rightful earl – an immensely strong creature with a huge hairy body. It is said that he lived until the 1920s.
Location: 1 mile N of Glamis off A928.

Glasgow *Strathclyde* Map: 388 Cd
CATHEDRAL The best-preserved example in Scotland of a pre-Reformation Gothic church.
It was established as a Celtic monastery in 543 by St Kentigern – known by his nickname of St Mungo – the traditional founder of Glasgow.

THE SCOTTISH RURAL PAST

The Angus Folk Museum at Glamis commemorates a country existence that has long since gone. The reconstructed 19th-century kitchen (above) contained not only a cooking range and dresser but also a spinning-wheel and two box beds. The cord on the cradle enabled the mother to rock it while working.

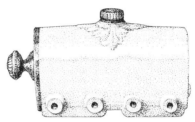

PIGS' FEEDING BOTTLE *When a sow was unable to suckle her young, they fed from a "teated" stone bottle filled with cow's milk.*

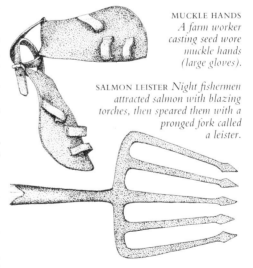

MUCKLE HANDS *A farm worker casting seed wore muckle hands (large gloves).*

SALMON LEISTER *Night fishermen attracted salmon with blazing torches, then speared them with a pronged fork called a leister.*

HORSES' BOOTS *Horses were fitted with boots before drawing lawn-cutting machines, to prevent hoof marks.*

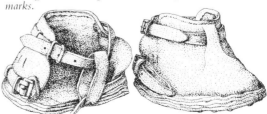

A new church was started about 1200, and by the middle of the 13th century the choir and the crypt beneath it were complete.

The nave was built at the beginning of the 14th century, and the central tower during the next century.

The crossing space beneath the tower has the best fan-vaulted roof in Scotland and contains the shrine of St Mungo.

In 1650 Oliver Cromwell attended Divine Service, and the sermon was given by Bishop Zachary Boyd, who strongly disapproved of Cromwell's politics. From the pulpit, Boyd "railed at him to his face". Cromwell's secretary wanted the bishop punished, but the Protector preferred a more effective response. He invited Boyd to dinner and terminated the meal with prayers that lasted for three hours.
Location: Cathedral Sq. off Castle St.

POLLOK HOUSE This splendid mansion in 350 acres of parkland was designed as a country house by William Adam, father of the architect Adam brothers, for Sir John Maxwell of Pollok. It was completed in 1752 in Palladian style.

It now contains one of the best collections of Spanish paintings outside Spain, with works by El Greco, Goya and Murillo.
Location: Pollokshaws Rd (A736), $3\frac{1}{2}$ miles SW of city centre.

PROVAN HALL The Hall was built in the late 15th century as a country seat for the Prebendaries (officials) of Glasgow Cathedral. Despite its clerical occupants, it was intended to be defended – with portholes for guns in the staircase turret, and very small windows.

James IV, in remorse for his part in his father's death in the Civil War of 1488, became a Prebendary, and may have lived here.
Location: Auchinlea Rd, Glasgow E4.

PROVAND'S LORDSHIP The house, the oldest in Glasgow, was built about 1471 for the priest-in-charge of St Nicholas Hospital.

In January 1567 Mary, Queen of Scots probably stayed here when she came to Glasgow to visit her husband Lord Darnley, ill with "a great fever of the pox" at a nearby house.

Mary, who was already having an intrigue with the Earl of Bothwell, had Darnley removed to a house at Kirk o' Fields, Edinburgh. On February 10 the house was blown up and Darnley was murdered. Mary married Bothwell in May, and was quickly accused of playing a part in Darnley's murder.

While in Provand's Lordship Mary may have written the Casket Letters to Bothwell which later revealed her affair with him.
Location: 3 Castle St, near the cathedral.

ST ENOCH'S STATION Glasgow's underground railway was opened in 1896, 12 years after London's Inner Circle Line. The Glasgow underground, also a circle, was drawn by a cable powered by a stationary engine. Passengers could travel any distance for a penny. The cable system was replaced by electrical power, but some of the original stations remain. The most impressively ornate is St Enoch's.
Location: St Enoch's Sq., off Argyle St.

SINGER FACTORY The biggest survivor of Strathclyde's 19th-century engineering works is the still-functioning Singer factory in Clydebank. Isaac Singer, an American shop-keeper, designed and built his first sewing machine in 1851. The Singer concern grew and expanded into Europe. The Clydebank factory, built in the fashionable Renaissance style, was completed in 1884. Soon it was employing 3,500 workers and turning out 8,000 sewing machines a week.
Location: Kilbowie Rd, Clydebank – 7 miles W of Glasgow centre off Dumbarton Rd (A814).

TEMPLETON FACTORY One survivor of Glasgow's 19th-century industry is probably the most

---

THE HOUSEWIFE'S FRIEND

Sewing machines were the first complex machines to be used in the home, after the clock. They increased the speed of sewing by up to 30 times, freeing women from the chore of making family clothes by hand. Sewing machines were used in factories in the late 19th century, launching the ready-made clothing industry.

HIRE PURCHASE *Efficient and reliable sewing machines were invented in America in the mid-19th century and made in large numbers. To help sell the $100 machines the Singer Company devised the first system of hire purchase in the 1860s. This small model was made by James Weir of London in 1872.*

MASS PRODUCTION *The Singer New Family machine was made in 1865, and 4 million were produced in the next 20 years. The price in Britain ranged from £4 4s to £20, depending on the cabinet. Machines "richly ornamented in pearl" cost 10s extra.*

RUST-PROOF *In 1869 William Jones of Guide Bridge, Lancashire, began a sewing-machine business which continues today. The machine above was built for the tropics, and metal-plated against rust.*

ARABIAN NIGHTS FACTORY

The Templeton Carpet Factory in Glasgow is an astonishing example of 19th-century industrial architecture. The façade is a mixture of Romanesque, Gothic and Arabian Nights fantasy, with arches, pinnacles and turrets. Materials used include coloured bricks, tiles and mosaic work.

exotic factory in Britain – the Templeton Carpet Factory. The façade of the building, which is still in use, is covered in elaborate decoration.
Location: Glasgow Green, off Saltmarket.

Glastonbury *Somerset*   *Map: 397 Fd*
ABBEY Here among the impressive ruins is said to be the cradle of British Christianity. According to legend, Christ's follower Joseph of Arimathea came to England in the 1st century and built a wattle chapel. He brought with him the Holy Grail – the wooden chalice used by Christ at the Last Supper, for which King Arthur and his Knights later searched unsuccessfully. And here, King Arthur and Queen Guinevere are said to have been buried.

The present abbey was built in the 12th and 13th centuries to replace one founded in 940.

With the Dissolution of the Monasteries, the abbey came to an end in 1539. The last abbot refused to surrender his office and was dragged to the top of Tor Hill and hanged and quartered.
Location: Town centre.
LAKE-VILLAGE A series of mounds are the sites of dozens of circular timber huts built on marshy ground in the 1st century BC. They were preceded, in the 3rd century BC, by rectangular huts of superior construction occupied by people with advanced skills in carpentry.
Location: E of the road from Glastonbury to Godney.
SOMERSET RURAL LIFE MUSEUM The museum is housed in the 600-year-old tithe barn of Glastonbury Abbey and the adjacent abbey farmhouse and outbuildings. Tools and equipment relating to cider-making, peat-digging and the withy industry are on display, and there are demonstrations of rural crafts.
Location: SE of town centre off A361.

Glemham Hall *Suffolk*   *Map: 399 Ge*
This Elizabethan mansion was the home of the "famous and valiant Edward Glemham", a privateer as bold and unscrupulous as Drake.

In the early 18th century the estate passed to Dudley North, whose wife was a daughter of Elihu Yale, founder of the American university.
Location: 9 miles NE of Woodbridge on A12.

A BARN FOR GOD'S PRODUCE

The medieval tithe barn of Glastonbury Abbey held farm produce given each year by farmers to support the monks. It now contains a rural life museum.

Glenbuchat Castle *Grampian* *Map: 387 Eb*
Glenbuchat was built in the late 16th century.
One of its owners, John Gordon, was a hero of
both Jacobite rebellions. Such was his devotion
to the Pretender's cause that George II was said to
be haunted by Gordon in his dreams.
Location: 21 miles S of Huntly on A97.

Glen Coe *Highland* *Map: 388 Bf*
The massacre in Glen Coe on February 13, 1692
is considered by many Scots to be the most
shameful episode in their turbulent history.
William III had decreed that all Highlanders
who had taken arms in support of the deposed
James II of England (VII of Scotland) would be
pardoned if they took an oath of allegiance to
himself by January 1, 1692. Because of a snowstorm and his advancing age, MacIan, chief of the
MacDonalds of Glen Coe, failed to do so until
January 6. These MacDonalds had recently plundered the lands of the Campbells of Glen Lyon,
forcing the impoverished laird, Robert Campbell, to take a commission in the regiment raised
for William by the Earl of Argyll, head of the
Clan Campbell. The authorities in London
ignored MacIan's late submission and the order
was given for "rooting out that damnable sept".
Captain Robert Campbell of Glen Lyon was
given the task.

On February 1, with 120 men, mostly Campbells, he moved into the glen on the pretext that
they were to be quartered there. For 12 days
they accepted hospitality, played cards and drank
with their hosts. On the morning of February
13, reputedly when a fire was lit on Signal Rock
(near Clachaig Inn), they fell on the MacDonalds,
shooting and butchering men, women and children. MacIan was shot dead, but his wife was
spared and his two sons escaped with their
families. Forty men and an unknown number of
women and children were slain and of those who
escaped many died in the snow.

The name Campbell was held in contempt in
Scotland for many generations, for they had
committed the most heinous of all crimes,
"murder under trust".
Location: 18 miles S of Fort William on A82.

Glenfinnan *Highland* *Map: 386 Cb*
The Glenfinnan monument marks the spot
where on August 19, 1745, Prince Charles
Edward Stuart raised the Jacobite standard,
launching his ill-fated rising against the
Hanoverian monarch, George II.

Charles, son of James VIII of Scotland and III
of England in Jacobite eyes (the Old Pretender
to the Hanoverians), had landed on the island of
Eriskay on July 23 from a French frigate. He
brought with him 1,800 broadswords, a few
small pieces of artillery (soon lost in a bog), and
4,000 louis-d'or gold coins.

He was greeted by a party of MacDonald
chiefs who vainly tried to persuade him to return
to France until he could come again with
substantial forces. But his charm, his unshakeable
determination and his sense of destiny prevailed,
and the MacDonalds agreed to join the uprising.
Cameron of Lochiel, one of the most powerful
chieftains, was persuaded and the die was cast.

Glenfinnan, a magnificent site at the entrance
to three glens, was chosen for the gathering
of the clans. The Camerons and MacDonalds

ORDER FOR A MASSACRE

*The order for the Glen Coe massacre was issued by
Major Robert Duncanson of the Earl of Argyll's
regiment: "You are hereby ordered to fall upon the
rebels, the MacDonalds of Glen Coe, and put all to
the sword under seventy. You are to have a special
care that the old fox and his sons do upon no account
escape your hands. You are to secure all the avenues
that no man escape. This you are to put in execution
at five of the clock precisely and by that time, or very*
*shortly after it, I'll strive to be at you with a stronger
party. If I do not come to you at five, you are not to
tarry for me, but to fall on."*

OFFICER IN CHARGE
*Captain Robert Campbell
was later rebuked for
allowing some of the
MacDonalds to escape.*

were there, some Stewarts and Rob Roy's MacGregors, but others were held up and some chose to join the march en route. Altogether fewer than 1,500 were present.

After the standard had been displayed to the clansmen, James was proclaimed as King of Great Britain and Ireland. James had stayed at home in Rome suffering from melancholia, but his commission was read appointing "our dearest son, Charles Prince of Wales, to be our sole regent in our kingdoms".

The prince and his clansmen left Glenfinnan on August 21 on the long march which, after much glory, much mismanagement and success almost in sight when they reached Derby, was to end in disaster at Culloden eight months later.

A visitor centre illustrates the campaign.
Location: 16½ miles W of Fort William on A830.

Glossop *Derbys.*   *Map: 393 Ff*
DINTING RAILWAY CENTRE At the old Great Central Railway depot, steam locomotives of the London Midland and Scottish Railway have been restored to their crimson livery. Among them are examples of the Jubilee and Royal Scots classes. Locomotives are regularly steamed, and visitors can ride in the brake vans.
Location: 1 mile NW of town centre off A57.

Gloucester *Glos.*   *Map: 393 Fb*
BISHOP HOOPER'S LODGING John Hooper, second Bishop of Gloucester, was one of 300 victims of Mary Tudor's persecution of Protestant leaders. When she began her five year reign in 1553, all the officers of the Church were called upon to reject their Protestant faith, which had been introduced by Mary's father Henry VIII.

Hooper refused, and he was burned at the stake in St Mary's Square in 1554. He spent the night before his execution in this solid timber-framed house—now a folk museum.
Location: Westgate St, city centre.
CANAL DOCKS The Gloucester and Sharpness Canal was completed in 1827, enabling large ships to bypass the shoals and mudbanks of the Severn and bring their cargoes to Gloucester.

The docks developed as a major inland port, and have scarcely changed in the last century. The tall warehouses range around the basins, and behind them is the little sailors' church.
Location: Commercial Rd–Severn Rd junction.
CATHEDRAL At Christmas in 1085, William the Conqueror is reputed to have held a meeting in the earlier Chapter House at Gloucester Cathedral—then a Benedictine abbey. Here he "had very deep speech with his Council about the land of England, how it was held, and with what sort of men". The result the following year was Domesday Book, a survey of property in England, listing the amount each was assessed for taxation.

Founded in 681, the abbey became a Benedictine foundation in 1042, but by the time of the Norman Conquest had seriously declined. William, aware of Gloucester's strategic importance on the River Severn, revived the monastery by installing Serlo, his chaplain, as abbot in 1072. Serlo demolished the remains of the Saxon building and began the Norman abbey in 1089. His crypt is the oldest part of the building remaining.

In 1327 Edward II was murdered in Berkeley

WHERE THE CLANS GATHERED

The Glenfinnan monument stands at the head of Loch Shiel, dedicated to the men who joined "Bonnie Prince Charlie" in his ill-fated uprising of 1745.

WEAPONS OF THE HIGHLANDS

For centuries, the Highlands of Scotland were a warlike region, where gun and dirk were used between feuding clans and in the Jacobite uprisings.

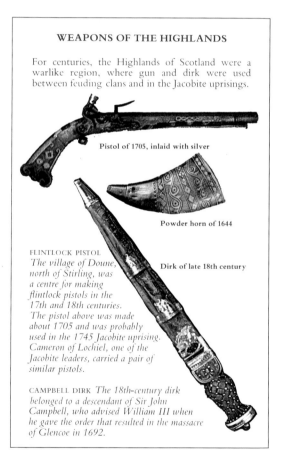

Pistol of 1705, inlaid with silver

Powder horn of 1644

Dirk of late 18th century

FLINTLOCK PISTOL *The village of Doune, north of Stirling, was a centre for making flintlock pistols in the 17th and 18th centuries. The pistol above was made about 1705 and was probably used in the 1745 Jacobite uprising. Cameron of Lochiel, one of the Jacobite leaders, carried a pair of similar pistols.*

CAMPBELL DIRK *The 18th-century dirk belonged to a descendant of Sir John Campbell, who advised William III when he gave the order that resulted in the massacre of Glencoe in 1692.*

Castle, and his body was brought to Gloucester. The king's shrine became a place of pilgrimage and brought wealth to the monastery. A massive reconstruction of the abbey was started, transforming most of the Norman church—with the exception of the nave—into a building that appears to be Perpendicular.

The work started in the south transept but reached its zenith in the old choir. Here the east end and the roof were removed and a delicate cage of stonework was erected on the inside of the Norman arcade. The cage rises to a 92 ft high lierne-vaulted roof (see p. 322).

The window at the east end was built between 1337 and 1350 and is the largest window in the country containing medieval glass.

Gloucester Cathedral is a rich storehouse of tombs and treasures. Before the High Altar there is a wooden effigy of Robert Curthose, William I's eldest son. Smashed by Puritans during the Civil War it was restored soon after.

The murdered Edward II's tomb is near by, on the north side of the choir. The alabaster effigy is contained within a Purbeck stone shrine. His aesthetic features are thought to have been modelled from his death mask.
Location: College St, off Westgate St.

NEW INN After the murder of Edward II in 1327, pilgrims flocked to his tomb at Gloucester Abbey (now the Cathedral). Pressure on accommodation at the abbey became so great that in the middle of the 15th century a new guesthouse was built outside the abbey. It is a timber-framed house around a courtyard, with open galleries around the upper floor.

After the Reformation, it became the New Inn, an important stop on the stagecoach route from London to South Wales. It is still an inn today.
Location: Northgate St, city centre.

Glynde Place *E. Sussex*   *Map: 399 Ea*
This mellow Elizabethan house of flint and brick has an incomparable parkland setting beneath the Downs, with a stable block and church built

WHERE THE MONKS WASHED

In the Great Cloister at Gloucester Cathedral is the Lavatorium where, from 1400, the monks washed their hands before meals. Water from a stream on which the monastery was built was probably kept in a lead tank on the long shelf. The ceiling has some of the earliest fan vaulting in Britain.

by an 18th-century owner, Richard Trevor, Bishop of Durham.
Location: 3½ miles SE of Lewes off A27.

Gnosall *Staffs.*   *Map: 393 Fe*
CHURCH OF ST LAWRENCE This imposing church, with its pinnacled central tower, contains some of the best Norman work in the county. Under the tower are great decorated Norman arches, and in the south transept a spiral staircase leads to the upper gallery.
Location: 6½ miles W of Stafford off A518.

Godinton Park *Kent*   *Map: 399 Fb*
Godinton is an early 17th-century brick house with gables. The drawing-room contains a frieze showing the drill movements and exercises of the militia at the time the house was built.
Location: 2 miles W of Ashford off A20.

Godolphin House *Cornwall*   *Map: 396 Aa*
All British bloodstock descends from three little Arab stallions imported into England in the 18th century. One, Godolphin Arabian, was taken to this house by the 2nd Earl of Godolphin whose chief interest was horse racing.

The 1st Earl, Sidney Godolphin, was Queen Anne's First Minister from 1702 to 1710, and a close friend of the Duke of Marlborough.
Location: 6 miles NW of Helston (A394, then B3302 and minor roads).

Godshill *Isle of Wight*   *Map: 398 Ba*
CHURCH OF ALL SAINTS A legend recalls that when the first church was being built a few miles away in Saxon times, the stones were miraculously transferred on three successive nights to the present site. After that the builders accepted the divine message.

A medieval wall-painting shows Christ crucified on a triple-branched lily.
Location: 5½ miles S of Newport on A3020.

Golcar *W. Yorks.*   *Map: 391 Fa*
COLNE VALLEY MUSEUM Golcar is an old Yorkshire weaving and spinning village that retains many of its original workers' cottages. A group of three built against the hillside in the centre of Golcar now houses the Colne Valley Museum. This recreates the working life of hand-weavers, clogmakers and cobblers of the last century, and also shows the living conditions of a typical weaving family.
Location: 3½ miles W of Huddersfield (A62, then minor roads).

Goodrich Castle *Heref. & Worcs.* *Map: 393 Eb*
Goodrich Castle was a border fortress guarding a strategic crossing of the Wye between England and Wales. Perched on a high natural crag, the castle has two sides rising up from the river bank, while the other two were protected by a deep moat cut into the rock.

The oldest part, a 12th-century great tower, was surrounded by a stone enclosure in the 13th century, and in the 14th century an outer curtain wall was added.

Despite the impressive defences, Goodrich was besieged and taken twice – once in 1326 and again in the Civil War.
Location: 5 miles SW of Ross-on-Wye off B4428.

COTTAGE INDUSTRIES IN YORKSHIRE

The weaving looms in the stone-walled workshop, the homely clutter of the workers' living-room, the gas-lit clogmaker's and cobbler's benches covered with equipment – all give the visitor to the Colne Valley Museum, Golcar, a vivid picture of what life was like for those who worked in the traditional cottage industries of the village.

CLOGMAKER'S SHOP *Tools and half-finished boots and clogs cover benches. Shavings from soles lie on the floor.*

CLOGS
*Adults'
clogs and
children's (above)
had clasps of brass
or black-painted steel.*

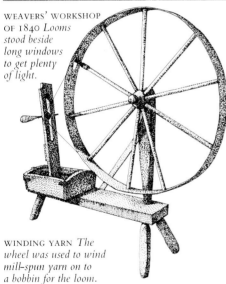

WEAVERS' WORKSHOP OF 1840 *Looms stood beside long windows to get plenty of light.*

WINDING YARN *The wheel was used to wind mill-spun yarn on to a bobbin for the loom.*

WEAVERS' LIVING-ROOM *One room about 20 ft square served the family as kitchen, dining-room and somewhere to relax after the long working day.*

Goodwood House *W. Sussex*   Map: 398 Ca
Goodwood was bought in 1697 by the 1st Duke of Richmond to enable him to hunt with the Charlton Hunt (the first to pursue foxes in preference to deer). His grandson built the great stable block in the 1750s, and it remains more imposing than the house itself. The hounds were housed in a classical building designed by James Wyatt in 1787, now Goodwood Golf Club.

The 2nd duke, like some other 18th-century noblemen, established a menagerie in a wood behind the house. He kept a lion, a tiger, bears, eagles and ostriches. When the lion died, a life-size effigy in stone was erected over its grave.
Location: 3½ miles NE of Chichester off A285.

Goole *Humberside*   Map: 394 Cd
GOOLE DOCKS Goole owes its existence to the construction of the Aire and Calder Navigation in 1703 to provide Leeds with access to the sea. In the 1820s the canal company developed the port from a hamlet beside the River Ouse.

Coal is still brought to Goole from the South Yorkshire coalfield in vessels known as "Tom Puddings", basically an iron tub or pan, carrying 35 tons of coal.

The tubs are linked together and pulled by a tug, arriving every day at Goole docks. Here they are raised on a hydraulic hoist, turned upside-down and emptied into a waiting coaster.
Location: S of town centre.

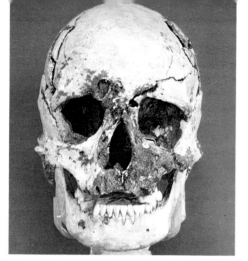

Gough's Cave *Somerset*   *Map : 397 Fd*
Stone Age families lived in Gough's Cave as the
last Ice Age was ending about 12,000 to 8000 BC.
They left behind stone tools and other items,
including fox teeth from a necklace, engraved
pebbles and two decorated bone "batons". One
of the batons was probably buried with a male
skeleton, 90 ft back from the entrance, about

LAST OLD STONE AGE HUNTER?

*"Cheddar Man," whose skeleton was found in
Gough's Cave, died about 8000 BC – the end of the
Old Stone Age, when all men lived by hunting.*

LIFE IN A STONE AGE CAVE

The first human beings to live in Britain walked
over from the Continent on dry land about 300,000
BC. They ventured no further than the river
valleys of southern England where they hunted
animals with crudely made flint hand-axes. Most
of the rest of the country, north of the River
Thames, lay under a sheet of ice.

It was not until about 40,000 BC that Stone Age
men began to explore the hill country to the north
and west. By then the ice sheet had retreated to the
Vale of York, and the hunters penetrated north
into the Pennines and west into Wales, the Mendip
Hills of Somerset and the Cornish peninsula. In the
south-east they had sheltered in flimsy windbreaks
made of branches, but in the hills they found caves,
which were welcome shelters from the cold and the
wet of the higher altitudes.

Caves as family homes
For the remainder of the Ice Age – from 40,000 to
10,000 BC – caves in the highlands of England and
Wales were occupied by Stone Age families.

In winter the caves were warm and dry, and the
families slept on thick piles of ferns. If a cave was
chosen carefully it was safe from the heaviest storms,
the strongest winds and the most severe floods. In
summer it was cool to live in and was an excellent
storage place for meat.

Life in the Stone Age was mostly spent catching
and butchering animals, and gathering wild fruit
and roots to make the diet more varied.

The most common animals – horses, deer and
reindeer – were probably hunted with spears or
arrows tipped with sharp flint points. When an
animal had been brought down the hunters used
heavy sticks and stones to kill it.

Larger animals, such as woolly rhinoceroses and
large hairy elephants with curved tusks called

mammoths, were also occasionally hunted and
caught. They were probably driven over precipices
or into deep gullies, and then beaten to death. Birds
and small animals such as hares were also caught,
probably with simple spring-and-noose traps.

Although the biggest animals were partly butchered where they fell, most of the carcasses were
dragged back to the cave, and the work of skinning
the beast and hacking up its flesh was done in and
around the cave-mouth. Skins were carefully
removed from the animals, scraped clean and made
into clothing. Bone needles were sometimes used
to sew garments together, with thongs or sinews
as the thread. The meat was cooked on the fires
that were kept burning near the mouth of the cave.

Caves were used for another purpose apart from
shelter for the hunters and their families. They
were also burial grounds. There is no evidence that
bodies were buried in caves while they were
occupied as homes, but caves such as Gough's Cave
and Aveline's Hole in Somerset were used for
burials, as well as being occupied at various times.

During the last Ice Age, man was beginning to
believe in the supernatural, and some burials took
place with ritual ceremonies. At Gough's Cave,
"Cheddar Man" was probably buried with a
decorated bone "baton" after the flesh had been
removed from the skeleton, mainly by leaving the
body exposed to the weather.

Shelters of branches and skins
When the Ice Age ended after 10,000 BC and the
temperature rose, caves were occupied less frequently, and the hunters began making their
shelters from posts and branches, covered with
bracken or skins. But some caves continued to be
used occasionally as homes right through the
prehistoric period and even by medieval farmers.

PREHISTORIC COMFORT *A well-chosen cave, such as one of those in the Cheddar Gorge, Somerset, was warm in
winter and gave cool storage space for food in summer. Meat was cooked on a fire near the cave mouth.*

8000 BC. Animals killed for food included horses, bears and wolves.
Location: 8 miles NW of Wells (A371 and B3135). The cave is S of the road through Cheddar Gorge.

Grantham *Lincs.* *Map: 394 Cb*
CHURCH OF ST WULFRAM This splendid Early English church has a spire 282 ft high. A chained library, given to the church in 1598, is kept in the south porch.
Location: Church St, off Castlegate.
GRANTHAM HOUSE This stone house beside the River Witham retains a hall from the 14th-century home of a family of wool merchants.
Location: Castlegate.

Grasmere *Cumbria* *Map: 390 Dc*
CHURCH OF ST OSWALD St Oswald was King of Northumbria in the 7th century, and although there was probably a Saxon church at Grasmere, the present building dates from the 13th century.

William Wordsworth and his wife Mary are buried in the churchyard. Near by lie two of their children, Catherine and Thomas, who died aged four and six. Eight of the yew trees in the churchyard were planted by Wordsworth.
Location: Centre of village.
DOVE COTTAGE William Wordsworth moved into Dove Cottage in 1799 with his sister Dorothy, and in the next eight years produced some of his greatest work. As well as tending the garden, cutting firewood and keeping the well clear, Wordsworth wrote his autobiographical poem *The Prelude*, and many other poems including *To the Cuckoo, The Leech-Gatherer* and *The Ode to Immortality*.

Three years after moving in, he married Mary Hutchinson, and their first three children were born at the cottage. By 1808 the spartan little cottage was overcrowded, and the family – including Dorothy – moved to a larger house.
Location: S end of the village.

Great Brington *Northants.* *Map: 398 Ce*
CHURCH OF ST MARY THE VIRGIN The church is the Valhalla of the Spencer family of the nearby great house, Althorp. The Spencer chapel contains a stunning series of monuments. The earliest is to Sir John Spencer, who died in 1522. He lies, carved in alabaster, with his wife.

The strangest monument is to Sir Edward Spencer by John Stone, showing him emerging from a funerary urn. There are also sculptures by Joseph Nollekens, John Flaxman and Sir Francis Chantrey. In the chancel is the tombstone of Laurence Washington (died 1616), great-great-great-grandfather of George Washington, first President of the United States.
Location: 6½ miles NW of Northampton (A428 then minor road).

Great Chalfield Manor *Wilts.* *Map: 397 Ge*
In this late-15th-century manor house the first hint of symmetry can be seen, a trend that was to lead to the familiar E-plan houses of the 16th and early 17th centuries.

The house was built by Thomas Tropnell, a Member of Parliament. On the dining-room wall is a portrait, which for centuries was covered with whitewash. It is probably of Tropnell and as such is the earliest portrait of an MP.

Through the eyes of three grotesque carved masks, the ladies could keep watch from the solar on what went on in the hall below.
Location: 2½ miles NE of Bradford-on-Avon (B3109 then minor road).

Great Coxwell *Oxon.* *Map: 398 Bd*
THE GREAT BARN The barn is one of the great architectural glories of England. Why the 13th-century monks of Beaulieu Abbey, who owned the nearby manor, should have chosen to house farm produce so splendidly is not known. It is 152 ft long and 48 ft high, and William Morris thought it "as noble as a cathedral". It is still in use and its nobility is unimpaired by the geese that parade through its great arched doorways.
Location: 10½ miles NE of Swindon off A420.

Great Dixter *E. Sussex* *Map: 399 Fb*
In 1909 Nathaniel Lloyd, owner of this fine 15th-century timber-framed house, decided to restore it. With his friend, the architect Sir Edwin Lutyens, he toured the Weald to seek ideas for the restoration. At Benenden they found a Tudor house encased in corrugated iron and serving as a barn. They bought it for a few pounds and moved it to Great Dixter, which is therefore two houses, ingeniously linked together by Lutyens, who also designed the garden.
Location: 12 miles N of Hastings off A28.

Great Durnford *Wilts.* *Map: 398 Ab*
CHURCH OF ST ANDREW A Norman church with an Early English tower at the west end. Inside is a Norman font, a 13th-century holy-water stoup and remains of medieval wall-paintings.
Location: 5½ miles N of Salisbury off A345.

Great Malvern *Heref. & Worcs.* *Map: 393 Fc*
GREAT MALVERN PRIORY CHURCH The priory was founded during the reign of William the

IMMORTALISED IN ALABASTER

Sir John and Lady Spencer who bought nearby Althorp House in 1508 are shown in life-like alabaster at St Mary's Church, Great Brington. The church also has an effigy of their great-great grandson Robert who owned 19,000 sheep and was said to have more ready money than anyone else in the kingdom.

Conqueror, and much of the first church survives.

Great Malvern is famous for its medieval stained glass. Among the many pictures are portraits of Henry VII, and his elder son, Arthur, Prince of Wales, in the north transept window.

The carved seats of the choir stalls illustrate seasonal occupations, such as sowing, haymaking, weeding and gathering grapes.
Location: Church St, town centre.

Great Maytham Hall *Kent* *Map: 399 Fb*
A huge red-brick neo-Georgian house designed in 1909 by Sir Edwin Lutyens. Buried within is a house of 1721 which was the childhood home of Frances Hodgson Burnett, author of *Little Lord Fauntleroy* (1886) and *The Secret Garden* (1911).
Location: 4 miles SW of Tenterden on A28.

Great Paxton *Cambs.* *Map: 398 De*
CHURCH OF THE HOLY TRINITY This Saxon church, built in about 1000, was enlarged during the Gothic period. Some medieval woodwork and fragments of stained glass remain.
Location: 6 miles S of Huntingdon on B1043.

Great Sampford *Essex* *Map: 399 Ee*
CHURCH OF ST MICHAEL THE ARCHANGEL Built mainly in the 14th century, the church has a fine chancel with a window almost filling the wall.
Location: 11 miles NW of Braintree on B1053.

Great Witley *Heref. & Worcs.* *Map: 393 Fc*
CHURCH OF ST MICHAEL AND ALL ANGELS The 18th-century church is joined to the gaunt ruins of Witley Court, partly destroyed by fire in 1937. It is renowned for the Baroque splendour of its gilt and white interior. In the early 18th century, the princely Duke of Chandos built himself a palace, Canons, near Edgware, Middlesex. In 1747, to pay debts, the house was demolished and its contents sold. Lord Foley of Witley Court bought ceiling paintings by Antonio Bellucci and stained glass by Joshua Price and inserted them into his mother's new church.
Location: 10 miles NW of Worcester off A443.

Great Yarmouth *Norfolk* *Map: 395 Ga*
ELIZABETHAN HOUSE MUSEUM Behind a 19th-century façade are remains of a medieval merchant's home with 16th-century panelled rooms, adapted as a museum of domestic life.
Location: South Quay.
MARITIME MUSEUM FOR EAST ANGLIA The building was opened in 1861 as a home for shipwrecked sailors rescued along the east coast. One room is now devoted to lifeboats and life-saving devices.

Other rooms exhibit sailmakers' tools, a model of a 19th-century Norfolk shipyard, models of local black-sailed wherries, and mementoes of Norfolk's hero Nelson.
Location: Marine Parade.
TOLHOUSE MUSEUM In the Middle Ages the Tolhouse was the town's courthouse and gaol. The prison cells in the dungeons can now be visited.
Location: Tolhouse St.

Greenknowe Tower *Borders* *Map: 389 Fd*
A tower house built in 1581, when border battles still continued, Greenknowe Tower still has its yett, or portcullis. It has two spiral staircases, one leading to the main hall on the first floor, the other to higher storeys.
Location: 9 miles NW of Kelso (A6089 then A6105 towards Earlston).

Greenock *Strathclyde* *Map: 388 Bd*
WATT LIBRARY James Watt, the steam-engine pioneer, was born in Greenock in 1736. The Watt Library, built by his son in 1837, contains letters and scientific books left by Watt.
Location: Union St, West End.

Greensted *Essex* *Map: 399 Ed*
CHURCH OF ST ANDREW The oldest timber building in Europe. The nave is made of tree trunks split in half and stood on end, and the age of the wood has dated the building to AD 850.

The 19th-century Tolpuddle martyrs, who were transported to Australia for forming an agricultural trade union, were resettled in Greensted after being pardoned. One, James Brine, married in 1839, an event recorded in the parish register.
Location: 12½ miles W of Chelmsford (A122, then A113 and minor road).

Greenwich *Greater London* *Map: 399 Dc*
CHARLTON HOUSE The house was built in 1612 by Sir Adam Newton, tutor to Henry, Prince of Wales, eldest son of James I.
Location: Corner of Charlton Rd and The Village, SE7.
CHURCH OF ST LUKE CHARLTON The red-brick church, built about 1630, contains Sir Francis Chantrey's bust of Spencer Perceval, the only British prime minister to be assassinated. Perceval was shot dead in the lobby of the House of Commons by the deranged John Bellingham in May 1812. He was buried in the family vault at Charlton church.
Location: Charlton Church Lane.

THE GRANDEST BARGE ON THE THAMES

In Georgian times the Thames was a highway crowded with small boats. It was the main route for traffic between Westminster, the City and Greenwich, and anyone crossing from bank to bank would probably hire a boat rather than walk to London Bridge. Boatmen in wherries (carrying eight passengers) or small skiffs plied for the river trade. The grandest boats on the river were the state barges of city dignitaries and noblemen. And the most regal of all belonged to Prince Frederick, eldest son of George II. His barge, now at the National Maritime Museum, Greenwich, was designed by William Kent, a coach-painter's apprentice who became a lion of the Hanoverian Court. The 63 ft boat is festooned with gilded carving and cost £1,002. It is likely that Handel's Water Music *was played during the barge's first outing in 1732.*

CUTTY SARK The *Cutty Sark*, one of the last of the clipper ships, is berthed at Greenwich pier. She was built in 1869 for the China tea trade, but was launched at the end of an era; the Suez Canal was opened the same year, enabling steamers to take a short cut to the Far East. She found fame on the Australian wool run.

Location: King William Walk, SE10.

QUEEN'S HOUSE Britain's first classical architect, Inigo Jones, designed the Queen's House in 1618 for the wife of James I. It was the first building in this country to be built on the principles of proportion practised in Ancient Rome. The Queen's House began a revolution in British architecture known as the Palladian style, which after a lull reached its climax with the work of Lord Burlington a century later. It is now part of the National Maritime Museum.

Location: Romney Rd, SE10.

ROYAL NAVAL COLLEGE The medieval palace of Placentia (or Plaisance), birthplace and favourite home of Henry VIII, was demolished by Charles II and eventually replaced by a hospital for naval pensioners. The two great domed blocks that dominate the river were designed by Christopher Wren and Nicholas Hawksmoor. The Painted Hall has a magnificent Baroque ceiling painted by Sir James Thornhill at £3 per sq. yd. The Hall and the chapel are open to visitors.

Location: Romney Rd, SE10.

THE OLD ROYAL OBSERVATORY The Observatory was built in 1675 by Christopher Wren at the command of Charles II "for perfecting navigation and astronomy".

The Rev. John Flamsteed was the first Astronomer Royal and his observations led to the acceptance of Greenwich as longitude zero in 1884. The Octagon Room, from which the early observations were made, has been arranged as it looked in Flamsteed's day.

Location: Blackheath Av. in Greenwich Park.

CLIPPER Cutty Sark
was built in 1869 to carry cargoes of tea. Her sail area of 32,000 sq. ft drove her at up to 17 knots, the equivalent in power of a 3,000 hp engine. She achieved fame carrying wool from Australia in the 1880s.

Gressenhall *Norfolk*   *Map : 395 Fa*
NORFOLK RURAL LIFE MUSEUM Beech House, an
old workhouse–which was known for years as
the Union–has been turned into a museum that
illustrates Norfolk agriculture and country life of
the past. (See below.)
Location : Beech House is 3 miles N of East
Dereham (B1110 then B1146).

Gretna Green *Dumfs. & Gall.*   *Map : 389 Eb*
In the 18th century, secret marriages conducted
by clergymen gaoled for debt in London's Fleet
Prison had reached scandalous proportions. The
marriages, although not approved by the Church,
could be recognised by courts. Fleet marriages
were used by young couples whose parents
opposed the match, but they were also used to
force women into marriage and to trick wealthy
young men into marriage for their money.
    In 1754 Parliament ruled that a marriage was
illegal unless it was conducted in church after
banns had been published in the normal way. But
in Scotland a couple could marry simply by
making a declaration in front of two witnesses.
    The Act brought a boom to Gretna Green, the
first stop over the border. Young English couples
fleeing from disapproving parents could be
married by local tradesmen for a fee ranging
from two guineas to a dram of whisky.
    From about 1826 the Old Smithy at Gretna
Green became the most popular place for these
marriages "over the anvil", and one blacksmith
"priest" claimed to have married 7,744 people
between 1811 and 1847.

In 1939 the presence of a minister or registrar
became compulsory. But in Scotland the
marriageable age was 16, not 21 as in England,
and in 1966 there were still more than 500
marriages at Gretna registrar's office.
    The minimum age is now 16 in both countries,
but couples may still go through the anvil
ceremony at the Old Smithy, just for fun.
Location : 10 miles NW of Carlisle off A74.

Grey Mare *Dorset*   *Map : 397 Fc*
Long barrows with stone chambers are rare on
the chalk lands, because of the shortage of stone.
The Grey Mare is an exception, containing a
single Stone Age burial chamber built of sarsens,
or sandstone boulders. The barrow has a shallow
forecourt for burial rituals.
Location : 8½ miles NW of Weymouth (B3157
then minor roads from Portesham).

Grey's Court *Oxon.*   *Map : 398 Cc*
DONKEY WHEEL For generations, the water supply
at Grey's Court came from the 200 ft deep 13th-
century well, buckets being lifted by a vertical
wheel 19 ft in diameter. It was turned by a donkey
which trod the boards on the inner rim of the
wheel. The buckets emptied into a lead tank from
which the water was pumped to the house. The
well was in use until 1914.
Location : 3 miles W of Henley-on-Thames on
minor road to Rotherfield Peppard.

Grime's Graves *Norfolk*   *Map : 399 Ff*
Grime's Graves is the largest prehistoric flint

WORKING ON A NORFOLK FARM

*Farm tools and machinery and demonstrations of old
farming methods bring Victorian agriculture vividly
to life at the Norfolk Rural Life Museum, Gressenhall. Other displays include craft workshops and a
reconstructed schoolroom and labourer's cottage.*

STEAM-ENGINE *Compact, easily
transportable steam-engines were a
boon to the Victorian farmer. He
could take them from barn to barn,
where, by means of a belt drive,
they could, for example, cut chaff.
Such engines were versatile : they
were also used to provide power at
fairgrounds.*

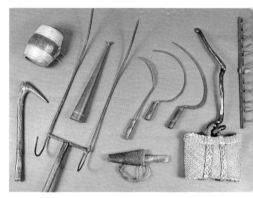

HARVESTING TOOLS *The harvester needed considerable equipment for the job. Equally vital were his frail
basket, containing his lunch, and his costrel, a small
barrel of beer, cider or tea.*

BARN TOOLS *The basket was known as a winnowing
fan. Corn was tossed up in it and the chaff was blown
away. The broad-bladed knife was used for cutting
hay from the stack to give to livestock.*

WHAT IT REALLY MEANT TO BE A FARMER'S BOY

The Victorian farm worker was a bitterly discontented man. Hodge, as he was familiarly and patronisingly known, was one of the lowest paid male workers in the country. In the early 1870s six long days of 6ften back-breaking work earned him a mere 10s 6d to 15s a week.

Among the most discontented were the men of East Anglia. This "granary of England" had long been progressive in its farming techniques, but labourers had little share in the prosperity. Their cottages were damp and dismal places. The floors sometimes consisted merely of bricks, or even earth, and roofs leaked because landlords refused to renew their long-outworn thatch. Furnishings were bare and relieved only by the occasional treasured heirloom – a wooden cradle, a framed print, a family Bible.

Water was fetched from a well or nearby stream. It was heated on an open fireplace or a kitchen range. Coal, which cost 1s a hundredweight, was supplemented as fuel by fallen branches and gorse. The home was lit by rushlights (dried rushes dipped in mutton fat), candles or oil lamps.

The luxury of meat
One specialised trade of East Anglian farmers was fattening sheep and cattle for market, but labourers could rarely afford to buy any of this meat. "Fresh meat would come like Christmas, once a year," wrote Joseph Arch, who formed the National Agricultural Labourers' Union in 1872.

Farm workers and their families lived mainly on bread. Even that made a large hole in their wages. Like farm workers in many other parts of the country, the East Anglian often breakfasted on nothing more than "kettle broth" – hunks of bread, sprinkled with salt for flavour and saturated in hot water to make them more digestible. This meagre diet was supplemented by small quantities of cheese, treacle, sugar and tea; vegetables and herbs from the garden; and by an occasional piece of bacon.

By the 1870s some of the most strenuous work had been taken out of agricultural labour. For example, the steam-threshing machine had replaced the flail on many farms, and horse-drawn reapers cut some of the corn. But mechanisation was a mixed blessing, for it enabled farmers to cut down their work force. They could thus also keep down wages, for the labourer in work became thankful that he had a job at all.

The harvest, which usually lasted three or four weeks, was the labourers' most prosperous time of the year. After farmers and men had bargained for weeks to fix a price, the men could each receive a lump sum of as much as £10 for the whole operation.

Child labour
This capital sum for the harvest work enabled the farm worker to pay off any debts and to buy a few essentials, such as boots, for the coming year, and perhaps a few luxuries. Even so his budget was so tight that his children would invariably have to start work at the age of eight or nine, acting as crow-scarers for 3d a day. Some wives – and some children – worked for more than 12 hours a day in agricultural gangs which were hired out by contractors to the highest bidder. Two of the main tasks of such gangs were weeding and picking up stones from the fields. A law of 1867 banned children under eight from such work, but the law was evaded for 20 years.

Suddenly, in the 1870s, to the surprise of farmers and townspeople, Hodge turned against his master. In the 1870s strikes occurred in many parts of the country. The struggle was prolonged, but most farm workers emerged from it with 1s to 3s a week extra.

Shortly afterwards, however, cheap imports – vast quantities of wheat from the United States and Canada, and frozen meat from Australia – brought an abrupt end to the prosperity of many British farmers and led to mass unemployment among their labourers. Many were forced to seek work in the towns, and in spite of the higher wages they could earn, some could not adapt themselves to urban life. Soon they were embarking on ships bound for destinations thousands of miles away. They were leaving Britain for good, to seek a new life on the farms of the New World.

THRESHING MACHINES
From the 1840s steam-powered machines took the hard work out of removing grain from the chaff. The engine powered a revolving drum with flails.

---

mine in Europe, with 350 known shafts. The vertical shafts, 20–40 ft deep, have passages radiating outwards from their base. The Stone Age and Bronze Age miners took flint from the walls of the shaft and from the seams of flint that the passages followed. The flint was probably roughly shaped near by and then traded over most of southern England to be used to make axes. Grime's Graves were in use between 2600–1600 BC.
Location: 7 miles NW of Thetford (A134 then minor road and track).

Grimsby *Humberside*　　　　*Map: 395 Dd*
DOCKS A 309 ft tower beside the entrance at Grimsby docks is an accumulator for the dock's hydraulic system. It was built in 1852 to ensure a good pressure of water to power the hydraulic lock-gates, cranes and other machines. It is now a television relay station.
Location: Cleethorpe Rd, N of town centre.

Grimspound *Devon*　　　　*Map: 397 Dc*
Over 3,000 years ago, sheep and a few cattle grazed within the encircling wall of this Bronze

Age village on Dartmoor, covering about 4 acres. The people lived in closely grouped round huts built of granite blocks, probably with thatched roofs; the remains of 20 or 30 huts can still be seen today, and also traces of plots where crops, perhaps barley, were grown. Although the weather was milder then, and slopes protected the village on all but the west side, at an altitude of 1,500 ft it was still fairly exposed: some huts have projecting walls to protect their doorways from the strong winds.
Location: 6 miles SW of Moretonhampstead (B3212 then minor road).

Groombridge *E. Sussex*   *Map: 399 Eb*
CHURCH OF ST JOHN THE EVANGELIST In 1625 John Packer, owner of Groombridge Place, built this warm red brick chapel because Charles I, then Prince of Wales, had not made a Spanish princess his wife. Near the altar is a 1697 monument to Packer probably by John Bushnell.
Location: 4 miles W of Tunbridge Wells (A264 then B2110).

A TOWER OF REFUGE

Little is known of the ancient people who built Gurness broch – one of many in the far north of Scotland – on the Orkney sea-shore in the 1st century BC. But the defences show that they lived in fear of attack. The high, open, round tower, 60 ft across, could be entered only by a narrow doorway flanked by guard cells. A hearth stood in the ground-floor court, and there was an underground well-chamber with a natural spring. Encircling the tower was an outer wall and three defensive ditches cut from the rock. The broch was probably replaced as a dwelling in the 1st century AD by nine or ten slab-built houses which surround it.

Grosmont Castle *Gwent*   *Map: 377 Fb*
A formidable, moated, Welsh border castle, Grosmont was one of the 13th-century castles of Hubert de Burgh, Henry III's chief minister. In 1233 Henry was surprised here by the combined forces of the Welsh prince Llywelyn the Great and Richard, Earl of Pembroke, but escaped.
Location: 13½ miles SW of Hereford (A465 then SE on B4347).

Guildford Castle *Surrey*   *Map: 382 Dc*
Early in the 14th century, Guildford Castle was the chief gaol for Surrey and Sussex. But the 200-year-old castle was in such bad repair that the gaoler, Henry de Saye, complained that he could not guarantee the security of prisoners. Repairs were carried out about 50 years later, but records show that in 1391 several prisoners escaped. The 12th-century great tower had been built on the side of the original Norman motte because the engineers did not trust the summit to support its weight: later it was surrounded by a polygonal shell keep.
Location: Castle St, near High St.

Guisborough *Cleveland*   *Map: 391 Id*
CHURCH OF ST NICHOLAS This late Gothic church was built about 1500, to the north of the priory church of which only the ruins remain. Some medieval stained glass in the west window of the south aisle include a figure of the Virgin and Child. Near by is a splendid memorial to the family of Robert the Bruce, known as the Brus Cenotaph. It was given to the priory church by Henry VII's daughter Margaret Tudor and was carved in 1521, probably in Scotland.
Location: 9 miles SE of Middlesbrough on A171.

Gurness broch *Mainland, Orkney Map: 371 Hg*
Built about 2,000 years ago of unmortared stone, the circular broch still remains to a height of about 40 ft. Within the double walls, the outer one without windows, a stone stairway leads to an upper gallery, and there are traces of a ledge that supported an upper floor. With the narrow doorway blocked, people in the tower were well out of reach of attackers. The harshness of the times is evident from discoveries on the site – two severed, be-ringed hands.
Location: 16 miles NW of Kirkwall (A965 then A966 and minor road).

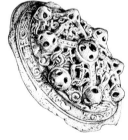

A VIKING RELIC
The broch of Gurness was centuries old when the Vikings came to settle in its shadow.
This tortoise-shaped, bronze, 10th-century brooch about 3 in. long was discovered in a Viking grave.

Gwydir Castle *Gwynedd*   *Map: 377 Ff*
A Tudor mansion built in 1555, Gwydir Castle, now much restored, was once the home of the Wynn family who were direct descendants of Owain Gwynedd, an early prince of North Wales. It incorporates some stonework of an earlier castle on the same site.
Location: ½ mile S of Llanrwst off B5106.

H

Haddington *Lothian*   *Map: 389 Fd*
HADDINGTON HOUSE The house is the oldest
surviving dwelling in the town, built soon after
1650 by Alexander Maitland. He and his wife had
nine children – all long-lived, with combined
ages totalling 738 years. In the 18th year of their
marriage they had triplets whose united ages
were to reach 256 years.
Location: Sidegate off High St.
LADY KITTY'S GARDEN AND DOOCOT Originally
used for archery and bowling, the garden was
restored by Lady Catherine Charteris in 1771.
The cylindrical doocot (dovecot), with 568
nesting-boxes, was built on top of a square
pavilion. In the 19th century the pavilion is said
to have been the home of an old man, Adam
Elder, and his wife, who used to look after the
shinty sticks (similar to hockey sticks) for
schoolboys who played on a field close by. Now
it houses an exhibition of town history.
Location: Ball Alley near Nungate Bridge.

Haddo House *Grampian*   *Map: 387 Fc*
This splendid mansion was built around 1731 by
William Adam – father of Robert – for the 2nd
Earl of Aberdeen, and the family still live there.
There are fine public rooms on the first floor and
among the many portraits is a Van Dyck of
Charles II, who rewarded the family for their
loyalty on his restoration.
Location: 22 miles NW of Aberdeen (A92 then
B9005 from Ellon).

Haddon Hall *Derbys.*   *Map: 394 Bb*
The estate was part of the territory given by
William I to his illegitimate son, Peveril. It was
acquired in 1155 by William de Vernon and has
since been owned by only two families.
    The medieval manor house, overlooking an
Elizabethan rose garden, has a galleried-
banqueting hall dating from 1370. Close by there
are the medieval kitchen, buttery and bakehouse.
Location: 2 miles SE of Bakewell, off A6.

Hadleigh Castle *Essex*   *Map: 399 Fc*
Hadleigh Castle was an enclosure with towers
and a deep ditch around the outside, built in the
1230s and overlooking the Thames estuary. The
castle was reconstructed in the 1360s by Edward
III, to guard the estuary against possible
retaliation following his military successes in
France. He also wanted to use Hadleigh Castle as
a royal residence.
Location: 5 miles from Southend-on-Sea off
A13.

Hadrian's Wall *Cumbria-Northld.* *Map: 391 Fe*
A 73 mile long wall, built from the Tyne to the
Solway by order of Emperor Hadrian (between
122–30) as a defence against attack by northern
barbarians. (See overleaf, also Chesters,
Corbridge, Housesteads, South Shields and
Vindolanda.)

Hadstock *Essex*   *Map: 399 Ee*
CHURCH OF ST BOTOLPH After defeating Edmund
Ironside in 1016, King Canute built a large

church as a memorial to the dead of both sides.
Much of St Botolph's dates from this time and
may be Canute's minster.
    The north door is Saxon and once had a piece
of human skin (now in Saffron Walden Museum)
nailed to it. The skin is reputed to have belonged
to a thief who was flayed alive.
Location: 4½ miles N of Saffron Walden on
B1052.

Hailes Abbey *Glos.*   *Map: 393 Fb*
The Cistercian abbey was founded in 1246 by
Richard, Earl of Cornwall – Henry III's younger
brother. Henry and Queen Eleanor attended the
dedication ceremony in 1251.
    Most of the monks and lay-brothers at Hailes
Abbey died when the second wave of the Black
Death (1361–2) swept through England.
    The abbey fell into ruin after the Dissolution
of the Monasteries in 1539, but the site has since
been excavated. There is also a museum on the
site containing relics from the abbey.
    The nearby church has stained-glass windows
from the abbey's church, as well as wall-
paintings, a 15th-century rood screen and 17th-
century choir stalls, box pew and pulpit.
Location: 8½ miles NE of Cheltenham off A46.

LAUNDRY TALLY AT HADDON HALL

*Household washing in large houses in Stuart times
was a huge affair, done every two or three months. To
help laundrymaids – some of whom were unable to
read – tally boards were used. At Haddon Hall in
Derbyshire, this was a piece of wood, faced with a
sheet of transparent horn and edged with brass. Lists of
clothing and household linen had revolving discs
beneath them which were turned to record the number
of items in the wash.*

Hadrian's Wall: an emperor's vision

THE TROOPS WHO MANNED THE ROMAN WALL FOR NEARLY 300 YEARS WERE THE
GUARDIANS OF ROME'S CONSTANTLY MENACED NORTH–WEST FRONTIER

FRONTIER DEFENCE *The stretch of Hadrian's Wall to the west of Housesteads fort illustrates the Roman builders' skilful use of the terrain, forcing attackers to adopt a defensive role.*

The most staggering of all the legacies the Romans left in Britain is Hadrian's Wall, a 73 mile long fortification stretching across the neck of England, from the mouth of the River Tyne in the east, to the Solway Firth in the west.

Between AD 121 and 125, the Emperor Hadrian toured the frontiers of his empire to consolidate his predecessors' conquests. His visit to Britain in AD 122 came shortly after there had been attacks by tribesmen from the north. To strengthen his grip on the province, Hadrian ordered a wall to be built that would "separate the Romans from the barbarians".

The scale of the undertaking was enormous, needing vast resources of money and manpower, and administrative skills of the highest order – both to build the Wall and to garrison it. Work started in AD 122 and the Wall was finished in just over seven years. It was a spectacular achievement – no ordinary wall but an immensely complicated operation, which was constantly being modified.

The work was done by detachments of legionaries – soldiers who were also skilled engineers, craftsmen and masons – working in groups of 80 men. The western section was initially built of turf, where limestone was difficult to obtain – and later replaced with stone 15 ft high, with a timber sentry-walk along the top. The rest of the Wall to the east was built of stone – about 15 ft high and 8 and 10 ft wide, with a 6 ft parapet on top. There was a flat area of ground on the north side of the Wall, about 20 ft wide, and then a defensive V-shaped ditch, about 27 ft wide and 9 ft deep. Except where cliffs made it unnecessary, the ditch accompanied the whole of the Wall.

Milecastles and forts

Attached to the Wall at intervals of one Roman mile (1,620 yds) were fortlets or posts, known as milecastles, with gates in the north and south walls. Each milecastle was manned by about 30 men – frontier police. Between the milecastles were pairs of turrets – small signalling towers,

about 14 ft square internally – which acted as observation posts.

About two years after building had started there was a dramatic change of plan, probably as a result of the hostility of the tribesmen, no longer able to make contact with others beyond the new frontier. Firstly, the main body of fighting men, hitherto stationed in existing forts some miles to the south of the Wall, were brought to serve on the Wall itself. They were housed in newly constructed forts – 16 forts were eventually built – that either straddled the Wall, were built on to the back of it, or were detached. The forts were manned to ensure that any frontier trouble could be dealt with swiftly.

The second change was even more remarkable. A continuous earthwork, known as the vallum, was dug a short distance to the south of the Wall, and parallel to it, for its entire length, and the Wall extended eastwards to Wallsend.

The vallum was a flat-bottomed ditch, some 20 ft wide at the top and 8 ft at the bottom, flanked by 30 ft strips of flat ground, and turf mounds 20 ft wide and 6 ft high. The vallum was less formidable than the V-shaped ditch to the north of the Wall, but was clearly designed as a major obstacle not to be crossed, except at special points, such as frontier posts or customs-barriers opposite each fort. The vallum served the dual purpose of strengthening the frontier, and preventing Britons inside the province from straying too close to the Wall.

Manning the Wall

It is thought that about 11,000–12,000 men were needed to man all forts and milecastles.

About 20 years after the Wall was finished, another – Antonine's Wall (see pp. 28–29) – was built about 100 miles to the north, by Hadrian's successor, Antoninus Pius. This second wall pushed the Roman frontier north, and was the cause of Hadrian's Wall being temporarily abandoned in AD 139–41.

Throughout the following centuries, Hadrian's Wall was successively damaged and patched up until, by AD 400, it was finally abandoned to the elements. Despite its battered state it remains a powerful monument to military might and pride.

A visit to the Wall – of which many fine stretches still survive – is best preceded by a visit to the Museum of Antiquities in Newcastle University, which has an outstanding collection of Roman stones and inscriptions from the Wall.

The first remains on the Wall are 2 miles west of Newcastle at Benwell. The fort itself is now under a reservoir and a housing estate, but the temple to Antenociticus, a native god, and the only surviving example of a vallum crossing-gate are preserved: both signposted from A69.

Continuing to travel from east to west, on A69 then B6528, there is a turret at Brunton, 19 miles from Benwell – where the Wall thickness was reduced – containing part of a corn mill.

A mile to the west is the first surviving fort at Chesters (see pp. 96–97), with visible remains of a bath house, including an undressing-room, as well as – outside the fort – a museum containing carved and inscribed stones taken from the Wall.

A short distance from Chesters is Limestone Corner, where the ditch is unfinished – abandoned when the rock proved to be too hard for the ditch-diggers. Half-cut blocks of stone are lying about, testifying to the laborious nature of the work, done without the aid of explosives.

Two miles to the west is Carrawburgh fort, now a grassy mound, but near by are remains of the little Temple of Mithras.

Housesteads fort

Five miles on is Housesteads fort (see p. 196), the most impressive of all the forts, with extensive remains including a barrack block, commandant's building, granaries and a latrine. A walk along the Wall from Housesteads offers splendid views across a tract of the Northumberland fells. Other sections, less well known but equally well preserved, are at Peel Crag and Walltown Crags, 3 and 9 miles respectively to the west of Housesteads.

At Willowford, 4 miles past Walltown Crags, you can follow the Wall down to the bridge abutment which carried it over the River Irthing, which has since changed course.

A mile to the west, off B6318 at Birdoswald, is a well-preserved wall-fort, where the entire line of its defences, complete with gateways and interval-turrets, can be seen.

AN ENGINEERING MIRACLE

It took just over seven years to build the 73 mile long Hadrian's Wall across the neck of England, with Roman soldiers, who were also engineers and craftsmen, quarrying 27,000,000 cu. ft of stone. At Walltown Crag (above), remains of the Wall – once about 15 ft high – illustrate its solid construction; the aerial view (right) shows the magnitude of the work involved. The Wall can be seen cresting the ridge alongside Crag Lough, Northumberland.

Hailes Castle *Lothian*   *Map: 393 Fb*
A 13th-century castle that was besieged in 1402 by Hotspur Percy, the great Northumbrian warrior who rebelled against Henry IV. The attack failed. During the Civil War, Oliver Cromwell's cannon partly reduced the castle to the ruin it is today.
Location: 1½ miles SW of East Linton on minor road S of River Tyne.

Halifax *W. Yorks.*   *Map: 394 Ad*
PIECE HALL In 1775, the merchants of Halifax joined together to build a new trading centre–Piece Hall–where pieces of cloth were bought and sold. The elegant three-storeyed building has 315 merchants' rooms, ranged around an open courtyard, with entry through a wide gateway, topped by a cupola and weather-vane in the form of a fleece.
Today, Piece Hall contains an industrial textile museum, craft shops and exhibitions.
Location: Westgate, off Market St.

Hall Green *W. Midlands*   *Map: 398 Af*
SAREHOLE WATERMILL A late 18th-century mill, which has two water-wheels that between them drove five pairs of millstones. In 1850 a steam-engine was installed to increase the mill's capacity. The south wheel is still used for grinding tool blades.
Location: 4 miles SE of Birmingham City Centre at junction of Wake Green Rd and B4146.

Hallsands *Devon*   *Map: 397 Da*
Here are the remains of a fishing village which, in the 19th century, consisted of 20 cottages, an inn, and a street parallel with the sea.

The village was damaged in 1917 as a result of shingle being dredged off the shore for building work in Devonport. In places the beach was lowered by as much as 15 ft and a rock stack–known as Wilson's Rock–was left standing alone.
A gale in 1917 completed the destruction of the village–only a few cottages survive. The inn has been restored.
Location: 7½ miles SE of Kingsbridge (A379 then minor roads from Chillington).

Haltwhistle *Northld.*   *Map: 391 Ee*
CHURCH OF THE HOLY CROSS A simple and well-preserved Early English church.
At the west end there is a Holy Water stoup, not many of which have survived the Reformation. Tradition says that this one was used by St Paulinus in the 7th century when converting local inhabitants to Christianity.
In the chancel there are the recumbent effigy of a cross-legged knight in armour and three 14th-century stone coffin lids.
Location: 17½ miles W of Hexham off A69. The church is in Market Place, town centre.

Hambledon Hill *Dorset*   *Map: 397 Gc*
This is one of the most impressive of Iron Age hill-forts, its triple defences festooning the hillside in spectacular fashion. By the time it had grown to its present size of 25 acres, it was probably packed with small circular huts, indicated by depressions in the ground. In the early decades of the 1st century AD its population would have run into many hundreds of people.
Location: 5 miles NW of Blandford Forum (A350 then minor roads to Iwerne Courtney).

A HOUSE "FURNISHED LIKE A GREATE PRINCE'S"

In 1678 John Evelyn wrote in his diary: "After dinner, I walked to Ham, to see the house and garden of the Duke of Lauderdale, which is indeede inferior to few of the best villas in Italy itselfe; the house furnished like a greate Prince's." Much of the furniture Evelyn saw then can be seen in the house today. A contemporary painting in the White Closet shows the south front and the gardens as they were in Evelyn's time.

SLEEPING CHAIR *A rare late-17th-century armchair, uphol-stered in damask, in the Queen's Closet. It was referred to in a contemporary inventory as a "sleeping chair" – probably because the back can be adjusted to different angles.*
Charles II possessed several similar chairs.

DUTCH DESIGN *An ebonised table with gilded legs and silver ornamentation, made about 1670. Dutch craftsmen worked at Ham House during this time and table legs, modelled as caryatids – female figures – are characteristic of Dutch design. The table is in the Green Closet.*

17TH-CENTURY SECRETAIRE *A writing cabinet from the Duke's Closet. The front folds down to form a writing surface. There are drawers at the back.*

Ham House *Greater London   Map: 398 Dc*
A country house and its furnishings that illustrate
the elegant style of life enjoyed by the Duke and
Duchess of Lauderdale during the 1670s.

The family rooms are on the ground floor,
with the dining-room in the centre, the duke's
suite to the right – the duchess's to the left. The
State Rooms on the floor above include the
queen's bed-chamber, prepared for a visit by
Charles II's queen, Catharine of Braganza.
Location: Ham St off Petersham Rd, 3 miles S
of Richmond.

Hampton Court *Greater London   Map: 398 Dc*
The original palace was begun in 1514 by
Thomas Wolsey, the most powerful man in the
realm after the king himself, as a retreat from
London. Hampton Court had 1,000 rooms, and
3 miles of lead plumbing, and took 2,500 men
five years to build. It was a palace to rival any in
the kingdom, expressing the status of a man who
had risen from being the son of an Ipswich
butcher to become a cardinal and Lord Chancellor of England.

In 1525 Wolsey presented the palace to Henry
VIII in a desperate attempt to regain royal
favour. The king enlarged the palace by adding
the Great Hall, the Tilt Yard for jousting, the
Royal Tennis Courts and the vast kitchens.
During the 18th century, these had to cater for
500 people, and iron spits on which whole beasts
were roasted can still be seen. One of the
fireplaces is 17 ft wide.

Henry brought three of his wives on honey-
moon to Hampton Court, and the lodgings
designed for Anne Boleyn were completed for
Jane Seymour; her son, Edward VI, was born in
them.

Both Mary and Elizabeth held court at Hampton, and in 1604 James I presided there over the
conference out of which emerged the Authorised
Version of the Bible in 1611.

Charles I honeymooned at Hampton Court
in 1625. On later occasions he came to it as a
refugee from the London mob and, finally, as a
prisoner in 1647. The palace was pillaged during
the Civil War, but since Cromwell was to use it
as his country home, the buildings escaped
serious damage.

During the reign of William (1689–1702), Sir
Christopher Wren was commissioned to pull
down one-third of the palace and build, around
what is now Fountain Court, two sumptuous
suites of State Rooms. One was for the king –
linked by a gallery to another for the queen.

In the King's Guard Room 3,000 weapons are
arranged on the walls where they were placed
by William III's gunsmith.

George II and Queen Caroline spent a lot of
time at Hampton Court and on occasions dined
in the Public Dining-Room. George III had no
use for the palace and granted many of its rooms
as "grace and favour" apartments to private
individuals, among whom was "Beau" Brum-
mell, the celebrated English dandy.

Queen Victoria opened the palace to the public
in 1838 to mark her accession.

Hampton Court remains a place of public
recreation and partly the home of retired people
who have given notable service to the country.
Location: Hampton Court Rd (A308) on N
bank of Thames.

METALWORK BEAUTY AND THE STONE BEASTS

*One of 12 wrought-iron
panels at Hampton Court,
made by the celebrated iron-
smith Jean Tijou in 1690.
Tijou was an artist-crafts-
man from France, employed
in England between 1689
and 1712 by Sir Christo-
pher Wren, both at Hamp-
ton Court and at St Paul's.*

*The heraldic beasts
(right), known as the King's
Beasts, were erected in 1910
(replaced with the present
carvings in 1950), and flank
the bridge leading to the
Great Gatehouse. The lion
is a supporter of the royal
arms.*

Hamsterley *Durham   Map: 391 Fe*
FURNACE A derelict 18th-century furnace used
for making "blister steel" – a primitive form of
steel. Iron and charcoal were placed together in
sealed earthenware containers and heated for
several days. Eventually, some of the carbon was
absorbed by the iron, converting it to steel.

The furnace is a tall cone, built of rough-stone
blocks, with a hearth each side of the flue
through which the containers were placed.
Location: 5½ miles NE of Consett (A694) then 1
mile E of Hamsterley. Furnace is beside a
woodland track leading off to N of A694.

5,400 YEARS OF TIME-KEEPING

About 3500 BC, the shadow cast by a vertical stick in the ground was used as a means of gauging time. Sundials followed in Egypt during the 8th century, with water-clocks and sand-glasses developed as indoor timekeepers. Mechanical alarms – primitive clocks – may have been invented and used in monasteries to regulate the monastic life; the oldest to have survived in England, dating from 1386, is in Salisbury Cathedral. Thereafter, clocks rapidly developed as time played a more dominant role in dictating the life of the community.

SAND–GLASS *Late 16th and early-17th-century sand-glasses consisted of two flasks, sealed together with a waxed cord. A metal plate between the flasks, with a pin-hole in it, allowed dry sand to flow from one flask to another for a predetermined time – usually 15, 30, 45 or 60 minutes. The sand-glass illustrated is a 15 minute timer. Sand-glasses were often used in churches to time sermons, and were invaluable to mariners, since the flow of sand was unaffected by a ship's motion.*

TABLET SUNDIAL *A pocket-size sundial that was made in Germany in 1597. The top opened until the twine was taut – designed to correspond with the angle of the earth's axis. The dial was then orientated with the built-in compass – the twine's shadow indicating time on the figured-ring.*

NOCTURNAL *The night-time equivalent of the sundial was used to find the time from the position of the stars. First, the date was set on the outer scale. The nocturnal was then held by the handle and the North Star sighted through a pin-hole in the centre plate. The pointer was turned until it lined up with the Great or Little Bear, according to the date. Once set, the time could be read indoors.*

LANTERN CLOCKS *The lantern clock was so-named because the mechanism was enclosed in a lantern-shaped case. The clocks illustrated were made during the 1650s, driven by weights controlled by escapement gear; clocks from the second half of the century were controlled by pendulums. The single hand showed the hours; the small inner dial set an alarm-bell.*

Hanley *Staffs.*   Map: 393 Fe
ETRURIA The site where Josiah Wedgwood opened his pottery in 1769. He planned to rival the ancient Etruscans and the first fruits of the Etruria works were his six First Days vases, which bore the inscription: "*Artes Etruria Renascuntur*" – "the Arts of Etruria are reborn". All that now remains of the works is the derelict Round House, once used for pottery moulding.

Wedgwood's home, Etruria Hall – now used as offices – is on the opposite side of the Trent and Mersey Canal.
Location: ½ mile W of Hanley on A53.

Hanwell *Greater London*   Map: 398 Dc
THREE BRIDGES Three forms of transport intersect here. The Grand Union Canal crosses over the Great Western Railway line, and Windmill Lane passes over the canal.
Location: Windmill Lane, near junction of Tentelow Lane, Ealing.

Hardingstone *Northants.*   Map: 398 Ce
QUEEN ELEANOR'S CROSS One of the 12 memorials erected by Edward I in 1291–4, to mark the spot where his queen's body lay for a night on its funeral journey to Westminster Abbey. (See also Geddington.)
Location: 1½ miles S of Northampton on A508.

Hardknott Roman Fort *Cumbria*   Map: 390 Dc
Little imagination is needed to visualise the original appearance of this Roman fort – one of the impressive sites of Roman Britain. The shell of the external bath-house, the complete circuit of the fort wall and its gates, and the granaries, headquarters building and commandant's house

17TH-CENTURY SUN CLOCK

The ring sundial at Hardwick Hall was made in London about 1600–25. It was originally fixed in the gardens, the central rod positioned according to the latitude of the area. The shadow cast by the rod on the figured ring indicated the time.

TREASURE HOUSE OF TALENTS

At Harewood House in the 1770s it was the genius of Robert Adam, architect and decorator, that inspired Thomas Chippendale, the celebrated cabinet-maker, to produce some of his finest work. Much of the furniture came from Chippendale's workshop, designed by Adam who drew his inspiration from studies of ancient Roman architecture.

CLASSICAL FAÇADE *The north front of Harewood House was built by John Carr in the 1760s. The south front was altered by Charles Barry in the 1840s.*

CHIPPENDALE CHAIR *One of eight similar chairs in the entrance hall at Harewood House, made by Thomas Chippendale in 1767.*

ADAM CEILING *Part of the richly decorated ceiling in the entrance hall at Harewood House, designed by Robert Adam.*

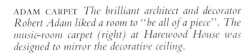

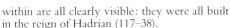

ADAM–CHIPPENDALE TABLE *Combined talents produced this inlaid table in the music room.*

ADAM CARPET *The brilliant architect and decorator Robert Adam liked a room to "be all of a piece". The music-room carpet (right) at Harewood House was designed to mirror the decorative ceiling.*

within are all clearly visible: they were all built in the reign of Hadrian (117–38).

Outside the fort there is a superb example of an artificially levelled Roman parade ground.
Location: 10 miles W of Ambleside on Hard-knott Pass.

Hardwick Hall *Derbys.*   *Map: 394 Bb*
In 1591, Bess of Hardwick – over 60 and four-times married – started building Hardwick Hall with the help of the Elizabethan architect Robert Smythson. Its leaded windows are so large that an old rhyme speaks of "Hardwick Hall, more glass than wall". The fretted stone-work on the parapets repeats the ES monogram of Bess as Countess of Shrewsbury.

The Presence Chamber, on the third floor, has been described as the most beautiful room in Europe. The long gallery displays more than 100 Tudor and Elizabethan portraits, and has superb collections of tapestry and needlework.
Location: 6½ miles NW of Mansfield off A617.

Hardy's Cottage see Higher Bockhampton

Harewood House *W. Yorks.*   *Map: 391 Gb*
Some of the greatest talents of the mid-18th century combined to create Harewood House. It was Edwin Lascelles, heir to the estate, who conceived plans for a great park; John Carr of York who designed the house; Robert Adam who added flourishes to Carr's more conserva-tive plans (as Adam's brother said, "he tickled it up so as to dazzle the eyes of the squire"), and "Capability" Brown who designed the grounds.

The house was occupied in 1772, and began to be filled with the treasures for which it has always been known.

Robert Adam, still a young man and just back from a study-tour in Italy, was invited to work on the house. He wanted each room to be an entity, and his designs formed the basis for work by the greatest artists and craftsmen of the day.

There is a celebrated collection of Sèvres and Chinese porcelain, and a fine collection of Old Masters, including El Greco's *A Man, A Woman and a Monkey.*
Location: 8 miles N of Leeds at junction of A61 and A659.

Harlech Castle *Gwynedd* Map: 392 Ce

The second phase of Edward I's monumental fortress-construction programme in his newly won dominion of Wales embraced four of the biggest castles in Britain – Beaumaris (p. 47), Caernarfon (pp. 76–77), Conwy (pp.110–11) and Harlech. Beaumaris and Harlech are concentric, and while Beaumaris took over 35 years to build, Harlech was largely completed inside seven years – from 1283 to 1290.

Harlech was designed and probably personally supervised at the building stage by Master James of St George. It was one of his most splendid creations, and from 1290 to 1293 he was its constable, a well-paid job that gave him status as well as the time to superintend the other works.

The design was relatively simple and yet immensely formidable (see pp. 410–11). A high inner wall, with huge round towers on the corners and buildings ranged round the inside, is surrounded by an outer low battlemented wall with small turrets. The east and south sides were further protected by a deep moat and the north side by a mass of rock obstacles. The west side was a sheer rock face sloping down to the sea of Tremadoc Bay.

Harlech was additionally defended by its huge gatehouse tower set in the east wall behind the moat. This massive oblong structure, 80 ft by 54 ft, three-storeyed and double-towered, with walls 9 ft to 12 ft thick, was a fortress-residence in itself, with a complex of portcullises, doors, arrow slits and murder holes along the entry passage. Upstairs above the first storey, which was a fighting platform, were the living quarters.

Harlech's seeming impregnability was tested in 1294, when an attack by Welsh patriots led by Prince Madog ap Llywelyn was successfully resisted.

In 1404 Owain Glyndwr surrounded the castle to besiege it. The structure proved too strong to take by storm; so the great Welshman starved the garrison into surrender.

Owain moved in with his family and set up his headquarters. He held a second Parliament of Welshmen here (the first had been at Machynlleth), and for four years he managed his remarkable campaign to free Wales from English rule. Then, in 1409, the English king Henry IV sent a strong force under Gilbert Talbot against Harlech and a siege forced the Welsh to yield. Among those taken were Owain's wife and four children, but the elusive leader slipped away. The fall of Harlech marked the end of his career and he disappeared from history.
Location: N of town centre on A496.

Harlington *Greater London* Map: 398 Dc

CHURCH OF ST PETER AND ST PAUL The church has a 12th-century nave, a 14th-century chancel and a 15th-century tower, topped with an 18th-century cupola. The churchyard has a yew tree thought to be more than 1,000 years old.

A custom maintained by the bell-ringers since 1605 is to hold the Leg of Pork Supper on November 5, to celebrate the escape of king and parliament from the Gunpowder Plot. A condition of the anonymous donor's endowment is that on that day the bells are rung at sunrise and sunset.
Location: St Peter's Way, off Harlington High St (A437), Hayes.

Harringworth *Northants.* Map: 398 Cf

WELLAND VIADUCT The $\frac{3}{4}$ mile-long viaduct spans the Welland Valley with 82 brick arches. It was built between 1878–80 by the Midland Railway.
Location: 7 miles N of Corby on minor roads.

AN ELIZABETHAN GARDEN PARTY

The painting (left), by Joris Hoefnagel at Hatfield House, depicts a fête held in 1592 on the banks of the Thames at Bermondsey, near London Bridge. The Tower of London is in the background. The lady guest of honour, accompanied by two aristocrats, is at the head of a procession emerging from the church on the right, preceded by two fiddlers, and four servants carrying cakes. Leaning against the tree in the foreground is the painter Hoefnagel. Kitchen staff are still preparing food and the long table in the open-ended barn is laid ready for the guests. On the left of the picture there is a maypole.

ELIZABETH'S STOCKINGS *Hatfield House has many of the Virgin Queen's belongings, including her garden hat, a pair of gloves and a pair of yellow silk stockings (left). The gloves are made of kid with pieces of jet sewn on to the lace cuffs with gold thread.*
The silk stockings are thought to have been the first pair to have been brought into England.

Harrogate *N. Yorks.*   *Map: 394 Be*
CRIMPLE VIADUCT The ⅓ mile-long viaduct was built by the York and Midland Railway and opened in 1847. It crosses Crimple Beck and the route of the old main line from Leeds to Thirsk.
Location: Best seen from A61, 1 mile S of town.

Hartland Point *Devon*   *Map: 396 Cd*
LIGHTHOUSE The 59 ft high lighthouse was built in 1874. The sea caused serious erosion to the cliffs and in 1925 a high sea-wall was built to protect the lighthouse.
Location: 17 miles W of Bideford (A39, B3248 and on minor road).

Hartlebury Castle *Heref.*   *Map: 393 Fc*
THE COUNTY MUSEUM The north wing of the castle has an exhibition of bygone local industries, and a display of toys and costumes. In the grounds there are gypsy caravans, farm wagons and a cider press dating from the 1700s.
Location: 3½ miles S of Kidderminster (A449 then B4193).

Hartshill *Warks.*   *Map: 393 Gd*
The maintenance yard beside the Coventry Canal is still in use–a fine example of late-18th-century canal architecture.
Location: 2½ miles NW of Nuneaton (A47, B411).

Harvington Hall *Heref. & Worcs.* *Map: 393 Fc*
This late-medieval timber-framed house passed in 1630 to the Throckmortons–a Roman Catholic family who had been implicated in the Gunpowder Plot (see Coughton Court). Since they lived under constant threat of arrest and persecution they built an extraordinary variety of hiding places for themselves, for fellow-

Catholics evading arrest, and for the priests, who led lives of deadly danger, moving from one house to another to hold secret services.
Location: 3½ miles SE of Kidderminster (off A448).

Hastings *E. Sussex*   *Map: 399 Fa*
CASTLE The 12th-century castle was built near the site of the first motte-and-bailey castle raised in England by William the Conqueror in 1066. It is now in ruins.
Location: Castle Hill Rd off Castle St (A21).

Haswell *Durham*   *Map: 391 Gd*
COLLIERY ENGINE-HOUSE Built around 1800, the engine-house has been preserved as a reminder of the part the steam-engine once played in the development of the north-eastern coalfield. The house, notable for its massive construction with walls up to 8 ft thick, may have contained a vertical engine or–more likely–a Cornish beam-engine, used for pumping water from the pit.
Location: 5½ miles E of Durham (A181, B1283 then B1280).

Hatfield House *Herts.*   *Map: 399 Dd*
The Bishop of Ely's Hatfield property was acquired by Henry VIII in 1533, as a country retreat for his children. Princess Elizabeth was then three months old. At one stage she was waited on by her older half-sister Mary as a punishment for Mary's refusal to acknowledge the legality of their father's marriage to Anne Boleyn. Later, Elizabeth shared lessons there with her brother Edward, and rode through the neighbouring countryside.
During the dangerous spell of Mary's reign, Elizabeth lived a secluded life. After a period in the Tower, fearing execution at any moment, she

was allowed to return to Hatfield. It was beneath an oak tree – the gnarled remains of it still survive in the grounds – that Elizabeth heard of her succession in 1558. She held her first Council of State in the great hall.

Robert Cecil, James I's Secretary of State, was responsible for the present appearance of the house. After being created Earl of Salisbury in 1605 he pulled down three wings of the old Tudor palace and set up a superb Jacobean mansion. It has remained in the Cecil family ever since.

Among Hatfield's many historic mementoes, are letters exchanged between Mary, Queen of Scots, and Queen Elizabeth. Other relics include Mary's death warrant and Charles I's cradle. The armoury has armour that was worn by men of the Spanish Armada. In the Marble Hall there are the celebrated tapestries of the Four Seasons, woven in 1611 by the Sheldon factory in Warwickshire.

The 3rd Marquess, who died in 1903, was three times prime minister between 1885–1902. He had a private waiting-room at the station that was used by VIPs.
Location: Off A1000 in Old Hatfield near railway station.

Hatton Locks *Warks.*　　　*Map: 393 Gc*
The Grand Union Canal at Hatton climbs the hill towards Birmingham through the 21 broad locks of the Hatton flight – known as "The Golden Steps to Heaven". Rebuilt in the 1930s they lift the canal almost 150 ft.
Location: 1 mile NW of Warwick off A41.

Haughley Park *Suffolk*　　　*Map: 399 Fe*
The original red-brick house was built in 1620 by Sir John Sulyard. His grandfather had been one of the first to support Mary Tudor when she stayed in Framlingham Castle in 1553, before entering London to claim the throne.

In 1961, after nine months of restoration, the interior was gutted by fire; but the owners have meticulously re-created it. The parkland and a sequence of contrasted gardens include clumps of woodland and a walled garden.
Location: 4 miles NW of Stowmarket on A45.

Haughmond Abbey *Salop*　　　*Map: 393 Ed*
Impressive ruins can be seen here of an Augustinian abbey founded in 1135 and later rebuilt. Among the Norman remains there are the abbot's lodging, the kitchen – unmistakable with its huge chimney breasts – and the infirmary.
Location: 4½ miles NE of Shrewsbury off B5062.

Havant *Hants.*　　　*Map: 398 Ca*
LEIGH PARK GARDENS Sir George Staunton, a keen botanist, laid out these gardens in the early part of the 19th century. He introduced many garden plants from China and some of the species are on display.

Farm animals were a common part of 18th and 19th-century parklands and breeds of livestock surviving from this period can be seen grazing here. Among them are such rare breeds as Gloucester and White Park cattle; Jacob, Soay, St Kilda and Portland sheep; and Berkshire and Gloucester Old Spot pigs.
Location: 1½ miles N of Havant on B2149, in Petersfield Rd.

Havenstreet *Isle of Wight*　　　*Map: 398 Ba*
STEAM RAILWAY As well as being a working museum, the railway offers passengers rides on the 1½ mile run to Wootton. Two of the four steam locomotives were used locally and have been restored to their original livery.

Most of the rolling stock came from the London, Brighton and South Coast Railway and the South Eastern and Chatham Railway.
Location: 3½ miles SW of Ryde (A3054 then minor roads). The station is ½ mile S of village.

Haverfordwest Castle *Dyfed*　　　*Map: 392 Ab*
The Norman stronghold, crowning an 80 ft hill above the town, was strengthened and probably enlarged in the 13th century. During the early 1400s a French force of about 3,000 men – supporters of Owain Glyndwr's rebellion – failed to penetrate the castle's defences.
Location: Town centre.

Haverthwaite *Cumbria*　　　*Map: 391 Dc*
LAKESIDE AND HAVERTHWAITE RAILWAY A standard-gauge line operating steam-powered passenger services from Haverthwaite Station to Lakeside at the southern tip of Lake Windermere, where it connects with steamer services.

There are former passenger and industrial locomotives, the oldest (industrial type) dating from 1919. When not in use they are displayed at Haverthwaite Station.
Location: 6 miles NE of Ulverstone on A590.

Hawarden Old Castle *Clwyd*　　　*Map: 393 Ef*
The ruins of a stone castle that was built in Edward I's time. It was captured by Dafydd, brother of Llywelyn the Last, in his desperate bid to continue the struggle against England. Dafydd was caught and executed in 1283 and the castle was re-taken by the English.

William Gladstone, the great 19th-century prime minister, lived in the nearby 18th-century house for about 50 years.
Location: 6 miles W of Chester off A55.

Hawick *Borders*　　　*Map: 389 Fc*
CASTLE The motte-and-bailey castle was put up by a Norman adventurer called Lovell, who settled at Hawick at the end of the 11th century.

The motte – about 28 ft tall and 40 ft in diameter – once held a large wooden tower.
Location: Loan Howgate, S of High St.
WILTON LODGE The Langlands, powerful lairds for 500 years, are known to have had a home on the site from about 1290. The house has been altered over the centuries, and it is now used as a museum of local life and crafts. One of the rooms concentrates on Hawick's knitwear industry, with exhibits ranging from a stockingmaker's frame – introduced in 1771 by Bailie John Hardie to found the hosiery trade – to modern machinery.
Location: Wilton Park Rd, SW of town centre.

Hawkesbury Junction *Warks.*　　　*Map: 398 Bf*
The junction between the Oxford and Coventry canals – also known as Sutton Stop – is spanned by an elegant cast-iron bridge, and was formed in 1836. Previously, the canal companies had failed to agree and the canals ran parallel.

On the canal-side there is an old engine-house

that once housed a Newcomen engine to pump water from a well into the canal. It was installed in 1821 but formerly worked at the Griff colliery. The engine has now gone.
Location: 5 miles NE of Coventry (A444 then follow Hurst Rd from Longford).

Hawkshead Courthouse *Cumbria Map: 391 Dc*
The abbots of Furness Abbey were lords of the manor of Hawkshead, administering their territory at the Hall and drawing revenues from sheep farms, coppice woods and forges. All that remains of the medieval Hall is the single-chambered gatehouse that was used as a setting for manorial courts.
   Today the courthouse is a folk museum, with farm implements and other exhibits relating to the Lakeland fells from medieval days to the recent past. There is also a nursery with a piano that belonged to Beatrix Potter.
Location: ⅓ mile N of Hawkshead at junction of B5285 and B5286.

Haworth *W. Yorks.*   *Map: 394 Ad*
BRONTË PARSONAGE MUSEUM In 1820 Patrick Brontë brought his wife, Maria, and their six children to live at the parsonage, a severe Georgian house in the village of Haworth.
   Brontë was a man with a fierce temper and an uncompromising faith. Born in an Irish hovel in 1777, his talents took him to Cambridge University and finally led to him becoming the parson at Haworth, where he wrote and published some sermons.
   In 1821, a year after the move to Haworth,

700-YEAR-OLD FIREPLACE
A 13th-century sandstone fireplace, decorated with dog-tooth mouldings characteristic of the period. The fireplace is in Hawkshead Courthouse and may date the building; alternatively the fireplace may have been brought to it from elsewhere in the 15th century. The adjustable pot-hangers – rattencrooks – hang from an adjustable iron fire-crane over the peat fire.

Maria Brontë died of cancer. Her dying words, "Oh God, my poor children", expressed prophetic apprehensions about the grim environment of their new home. Four years later her two oldest children died of tuberculosis.
   For some years Charlotte, Anne and Emily were taught at home by their aunt; Branwell by

WHERE THE BRONTË SISTERS WROTE

For 25 years, behind the bleak frontage of Haworth Parsonage in W. Yorkshire, the Brontë sisters wrote the celebrated novels that earned them an unrivalled place in English literature.

THE PARSONAGE *The house where the Brontës lived (above), and the family dining-room (below). Patrick Brontë dined, alone, in his study, and his children were forbidden to enter without permission.*

ANNE BRONTË'S SAMPLER *Among the many relics of the Brontë sisters at Haworth Parsonage is this sampler by Anne, finished in 1828 when she was eight years old. She was 28 when she wrote her masterpiece* The Tenant of Wildfell Hall, *only to die the following year in 1849.*

187

his father. The girls began to write fantasies in miniature books – the smallest only $1\frac{1}{2}$ in. long.

After a series of personal disappointments – hopeless love affairs and a plan for a school in the parsonage that came to nothing – the gauche, unworldly girls began to write novels.

In 1847 Charlotte, Emily and Anne published their first novels: *Jane Eyre*, *Wuthering Heights* and *Agnus Grey*. The frustrations of the three young women were beginning to find an outlet. Branwell, who had originally shown more promise than his sisters, turned to alcohol and opium – frustrated by ambitions that outstripped his talent.

In 1848, while Charlotte was writing *Shirley*, tragedy struck – first Branwell died in September, then Emily in the December. The following May, Anne died – all victims of tuberculosis.

For the next five years, Charlotte and her father lived alone, until she married Arthur Nicholls, the curate at Haworth. Nine months later, she caught a chill and died, aged 38. Patrick Brontë remained at the house until 1861, when he died at the age of 84.

Valley of the weavers

FROM MEDIEVAL TIMES TO THE TURN OF THE CENTURY, HEBDEN BRIDGE IN WEST YORKSHIRE WAS A THRIVING CLOTH-MAKERS' COMMUNITY

The stone-built village of Heptonstall marks the original area from which Hebden Bridge developed. The village was the centre of a weaving community that settled there in medieval times. Men and women spun yarn and wove cloth in their homes, using wool brought to the village on pack-horses that had crossed the moors.

When water-powered spinning machines were introduced in the 1770s, the factory age was born. Mills were built beside the fast-flowing Hebden Water and workers moved down the valley to establish the town of Hebden Bridge. The first machines were suitable for spinning cotton – rather than wool – and so cotton became the dominant industry of the area. Gibson Mill, built about 1800, still survives. It employed 21 workers – most of whom were under 21 and who worked a 72 hour week.

The introduction of steam-engines gave mill owners another source of power and the freedom to build nearer major transport routes. Steam power came to Hebden Bridge in 1860. The new mills with their tall chimneys, and single-storeyed sheds for powered looms, were built beside the Rochdale Canal, close to the turnpike road and railway.

WEAVERS' COTTAGES *These stone-built houses in Heptonstall, from the mid-18th century, were owned by men and women who worked at home.*

OLD PACK-HORSE BRIDGE *The bridge crosses Hebden Water and dates from about 1510. In 1643 it was the scene of a battle during the Civil War.*

WESLEYAN CHAPEL *The Methodist chapel was built in 1764 – the oldest continually used chapel to survive.*

BUTTRESS PATH *Pack-horse tracks were one of the vital links in the commercial traffic of pre-industrial Britain. Buttress Path leads to Hebden Bridge.*

The house has been preserved as near as possible as it was when the Brontës were alive, with many of their furnishings and relics.
Location: 4 miles S of Keighley (A629, A6033 then minor road).

KEIGHLEY AND WORTH VALLEY RAILWAY Haworth Station is the main centre of this line which runs for 5 miles from Keighley to Oxenhope. The route passes through beautiful Pennine scenery and the trains have to climb 330 ft. There are some fine stations, including Oakworth – restored to look much as it did at the start of the century – and the setting used for the film *The Railway Children*.

Diesel and steam locomotives are in regular use, and rolling stock can be seen at the shed in Oxenhope and at the Haworth workshop.
Location: 3½ miles S of Keighley (A629, A6033 then minor road).

Haxted *Surrey*   *Map: 399 Eb*
WATERMILL MUSEUM The present watermill, dating from about 1680 – on 14th-century foundations – and with a weather-boarded struc-

---

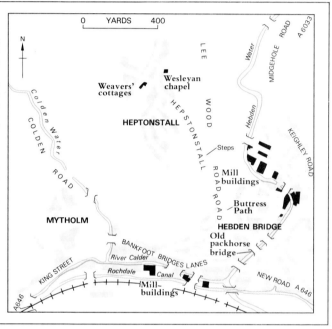

TOURING HEBDEN

To tour Hebden Bridge and its immediate surroundings is to see the history of the textile industry.

Start at the stone-built village of Heptonstall, on the hill overlooking the town. See the Wesleyan chapel, go down Buttress Path – the old pack-horse route – and cross the bridge. This is at the centre of Hebden Bridge.

Round to the south, by Rochdale Canal, are some Victorian mills, built when steam-engines replaced waterwheels as the source of power.

Workers' houses were clustered around the mills on the hillside – the only space available in the vicinity of the mills. The rows of terraced houses were "stepped" to fit the slopes of the ground – hence they have four storeys on one side and two on the other.

HEBDEN BRIDGE *At the heart of the town are the mills, hemmed in by the millworkers' houses, that rise in terraces up the hillside. In the foreground are the partly glass-roofed power-loom sheds.*

RELICS OF A REVOLUTION *Across the River Calder, from the south-east side of Hebden Bridge, stand the tall chimneys of Victorian mills – stark reminders of the Industrial Revolution.*

ture, has a water-wheel driving two pairs of millstones.

It is now used as a museum, with working machinery models, and exhibits illustrating the story of water-wheels in south-east England.
Location: 13½ miles NW of Tunbridge Wells (A264, B2026 to Edenbridge; minor road to Lingfield).

Hayle Dock *Cornwall*   *Map: 396 Aa*
The port developed in the 18th century because the copper miners of Cornwall needed to send their ore across the Bristol Channel to South Wales for smelting. The Copperhouse smelting works was established in the 1870s but failed to compete with the Welsh.

Hayle was also the home of the Harveys, the most celebrated of all Cornish beam-engine builders. Remains of their works face the harbour at Carnsew in the centre of the town.

Haytor Vale *Devon*   *Map: 397 Db*
GRANITE TRAMWAY Stone from Haytor's quarries at Dartmoor was used in buildings like the British Museum and the National Gallery.

In the 1790s James Templar built the Stover Canal to transport china clay. In 1820 his son, George, linked the granite quarries at Haytor to the canal by the unique tramway – constructed entirely from granite, including the rails. Teams of 18 horses pulled trucks along the line, much of which remains. In spite of the efforts to improve transport the quarries closed in 1865, unable to compete with more accessible sites.
Location: 7 miles N of Ashburton (A38 then minor roads). Tramway is NW, off road to Manaton.

Heatherslaw Mill *Northld.*   *Map: 389 Gc*
The three-storeyed building, dating from 1805, stands on the west bank of the River Till and has two complete water-driven corn mills, each driving three pairs of millstones.

The water-wheels also drive a pearl-barley machine. Grains of barley were husked and polished inside a perforated iron cylinder, in which a millstone rotated vertically. About 15 tons of barley were treated each week.
Location: 11 miles SW of Berwick-upon-Tweed on B6354 S of Etal.

Hebden Bridge *W. Yorks.*   *Map: 394 Ad*
CLOTH TOWN The area is rich in relics of the textile industry. It was a weaving community in the Middle Ages and a cotton-spinning centre during the 18th century. (See p. 188.)
Location: 7 miles W of Halifax off A646.
GIBSON WATERMILL A three-storey cotton mill, built about 1800, that employed 21 workers. Their cottages are beside it – a convenience with this kind of isolated mill, built some distance out of the town. The mill is not open to the public.
Location: 2½ miles NW of town centre, on minor road (no cars on last mile) to Hebden Water.

Heckington *Lincs.*   *Map: 394 Db*
CHURCH OF ST ANDREW The church is one of the finest buildings in Lincolnshire – built entirely in the Decorated style by the abbey of nearby Bardney in 1345.

Inside, St Andrew's has a wealth of fine carving, including an Easter sepulchre. Every Good Friday in the Middle Ages, the Host and the altar crucifix were placed on the sepulchre – a tomb in a recess in the chancel – and watched over day and night by celebrants until Easter morning, when Host and crucifix were placed on the High Altar. The ritual symbolised the burial and resurrection of Christ.
Location: 12 miles W of Boston (A1121 and A17).
WINDMILL The only surviving windmill in the British Isles with eight sails, was built in 1830. The replacement cap, sails and eight-armed cross were bought from a mill at Boston in 1890.
Location: S of village on B1394.

Helensburgh *Strathclyde*   *Map: 388 Ce*
HILL HOUSE Only two houses by Charles Rennie Mackintosh, the great Scottish architect, have survived – Hill House and another in Kilmacolm. Hill House was built in 1902 and has the furniture Mackintosh designed for it, including his celebrated "ladder-back" chairs, and furniture with the characteristic square motif.

The L-shaped guest bedroom has built-in furniture – a feature of the house – with bench-type seating, wardrobes and the bed itself.
Location: 1 mile N of town off B832.

Helmingham Hall *Suffolk*   *Map: 399 Fe*
Only the park and gardens, surrounded by a moat, are open to the public, but they give all-round views of the quadrangular moated house. Its Tudor half-timbering is largely overlaid with Georgian and Victorian alterations and crowned with Nash battlements. The two drawbridges are still raised every night.

The park has about 700 red and fallow deer and ornamental waterfowl. Visitors can travel round the grounds in specially fitted farm trailers.
Location: 8 miles N of Ipswich on B1077.

Helmsley Castle *N. Yorks.*   *Map: 394 Ce*
The castle may have been started by Walter L'Espec, who founded nearby Rievaulx Abbey and died in 1154. But the earlier stonework dates more accurately from about 1200.

The castle had an uneventful history, except during the Civil War when it was held for Charles I for three months against Sir Thomas Fairfax. The governor surrendered in 1644 and Parliament destroyed the castle, splitting the D-ended great tower in half, as can be seen today.
Location: 13 miles W of Pickering on A180.

Helston *Cornwall*   *Map: 396 Aa*
CHURCH OF ST MICHAEL The best example of a Georgian church in Cornwall. St Michael's was built by the Earl of Godolphin – godson of John Evelyn, the diarist – in 1763, to replace an earlier building which had been struck by lightning. A brass survives from this earlier church.

The memorial to Henry Trengrouse (1772–1854), inventor of the rocket life-saving apparatus, can be seen outside the south porch.
Location: Church St near town centre.

Hemel Hempstead *Herts.*   *Map: 398 Dd*
CHURCH OF ST MARY A Norman church with a central tower, and a 14th-century spire. The earliest part of the building is the rib-vaulted chancel, about 1150.

In the chancel there is a memorial to Sir Astley

Paston Cooper, who was rewarded with a baronetcy in 1820, after removing a wen from George IV's head.

Location: The old Hemel Hempstead High St.

PICCOTTS END Medieval pilgrims and wandering friars broke their journeys at inns, hostels and chapels. The hall-house at Piccotts End was probably a former pilgrims' hostel, its walls decorated with devout 14th-century paintings to inspire the wayfarer.

Location: 1½ miles N of town in Piccotts End Rd, beyond High St.

Hemingbrough *N. Yorks.* Map: 394 Cd

CHURCH OF ST MARY A 12th-century church with a 14th-century tower, and a 15th-century spire that is 120 ft high and unusually slender.

The one surviving misericord – a carved bracket on a hinged seat – is in the choir stalls; it is probably the oldest misericord in England, dating from about 1200.

In the north chapel there is a 16th-century stone monument representing a skeleton in a shroud – a reminder that all men must die.

Location: 4½ miles E of Selby off A63.

Hendon *Greater London* Map: 399 Dd

ROYAL AIR FORCE MUSEUM Britain's national museum of aviation is based on the old RAF station at Hendon. The aircraft hall has a selection of aircraft showing the main lines of development over the past 70 years, from various First World War aeroplanes to the P1127 – the prototype vertical take-off aircraft.

The galleries tell the story of aviation from 1870 – each gallery dealing with a different topic, such as the control cabin of a rigid airship and a Royal Flying Corps workshop.

Films are shown daily.

Location: Colindale Av, off Edgware Rd, NW9.

Hengistbury Head *Dorset* Map: 398 Aa

IRON AGE PORT The promontory of Hengistbury Head, overlooking and controlling Christchurch harbour, was an important settlement and port in the later Iron Age. Behind the double dykes which cut off and defended the promontory from attack by land, craftsmen plied their trades and produced pottery and silver coinage for the tribal chieftain. Imported coins and pottery from Brittany and Normandy, and wine jars from Italy, are evidence of the site's significance as a focus for overseas trade.

Location: 2 miles SE of Christchurch (A35, B3059 and minor road to foot of dykes).

Heptonstall *W. Yorks.* Map: 394 Ad

CHURCH OF ST THOMAS THE APOSTLE Two churches share a churchyard high in the Pennines – one old and one new church, side by side.

The old, now a roofless ruin, was abandoned after storm damage in 1847. By the porch, there is the grave of David Hartley, who was hanged in 1770 for clipping gold coins.

The new church was consecrated in 1854.

Location: 7 miles W of Halifax off A646.

SCHOOL A wealthy clergyman, Charles Greenwood, endowed Heptonstall Grammar School in his will of 1642. The endowment provided free tuition for the pupils, and the school continued until 1889, when it became a bank.

In 1824 the average attendance was 50 to 60

pupils, who were taught English, reading, writing and arithmetic – 17 scholars were also given instruction in Latin. The school is now a museum with several pieces of original school furniture.

Location: 1 mile NW of Hebden Bridge on minor road off A646.

Hereford *Heref. & Worcs.* Map: 393 Ec

CATHEDRAL Within the pink sandstone walls of the cathedral are some of the country's finest possessions – many of them unique. It has the best collection of brasses in any cathedral; the Chained Library – the largest of its kind in Britain, with nearly 1,500 books; and the Mappi Mundi, a map of the world drawn on vellum and depicting the world as it was known in 1290.

Near the High Altar there is a 12th-century chair, said to have been used by King Stephen in 1138.

Hereford possessed a bishopric as far back as 676, and is the burial place of Ethelbert, the Christian King of East Anglia, who was beheaded in 792 by Offa, King of Mercia. Miracles attributed to the martyred king made the Saxon cathedral a place of pilgrimage and it was rebuilt in the middle of the 11th century. It was plundered soon after by a force of Welsh and Irish and lay in ruins until after the Norman

WHERE STUART CHILDREN STUDIED

A reconstruction of the mid-17th-century grammar school at Heptonstall includes original desks and benches used by pupils. The bookcase contains late 18th and 19th-century Greek and Latin text-books.

Conquest, when Robert de Losinga was installed as the first Norman bishop in 1079.

The reconstruction work which he started was finished by his successors by about 1200. It includes the beautiful Lady Chapel in the Early English style. In the 14th century, the central and west towers were added.

Disaster occurred on Easter Monday in 1786, when the western tower collapsed, bringing down the west front and a bay of the nave. Signs of cracking long beforehand had given warning and no one was killed.

The man called in to restore the stricken building was James Wyatt, a brilliant architect who was nevertheless nicknamed "The Destroyer" because of his ruthless and sometimes insensitive approach to restoration work. He swept the ruined portions of the cathedral aside and built a new west front.

HEREFORD'S CHAINED LIBRARY

One of Hereford Cathedral's treasures is the Chained Library in the upper chamber of the north transept. There are nearly 1,500 books with 227 in manuscript form. Among the larger printed volumes, 52 are incunabula – that is, printed before 1500. Two of them are by William Caxton. The earliest manuscript is the Anglo-Saxon Gospels. The Hereford Breviary of 1270 is the only known manuscript with music.

He also shortened the nave by a bay, tore down the Norman clerestory and vaulting in the nave and replaced them with his own versions.

His west front was subsequently replaced with a "Decorated" design in 1904 to commemorate the Diamond Jubilee of Queen Victoria.
Location: Near the River Wye in town centre.
ST JOHN AND CONINGSBY HOSPITAL AND MUSEUM A Dominican priory dating from 1322 that was converted by Sir John Coningsby into a private mansion in 1614. The old preaching cross in the friars' cemetery is the only example in England to have survived. Sir John also built almshouses in 1614 using the old hall and chapel of the Knights of St John of Jerusalem. The almshouses have a museum of armour, models and objects connected with the Order of St John and with the history of the Coningsby Hospital.
Location: Widemarsh St, N of city centre.
WATERWORKS MUSEUM When the Victorian waterworks opened in 1856, pumping was done by two beam-engines. These were replaced in 1895 by a triple-expansion steam-engine – in which steam passes through three cylinders at ever-decreasing pressures. The oldest of its kind in Britain, it is still regularly steamed.
Location: Broomy Hill, W of town centre.

Hereford Beacon *Heref. & Worcs. Map: 393 Fb*
IRON AGE HILL-FORT The summit of the Beacon was first fortified about 200 BC, but shortly before the Roman invasion the defences were extended to enclose over 30 acres.
Location: 4 miles S of Great Malvern off A449.

Hermitage Castle *Borders Map: 389 Eb*
A massive 14th-century tower house, with 15th-century improvements, including a gun-platform.

In 1566 when the castle was owned by the Hepburns, earls of Bothwell, James Hepburn was carried there after being wounded in a border skirmish. His lover, Mary, Queen of Scots, alarmed at the news, rode 25 miles from Jedburgh to be by his side, despite the fact that her husband, Darnley, was still alive.
Location: 15 miles S of Hawick (B6399 then minor road ½ mile S of Hermitage).

Hertford Castle *Herts. Map: 399 Dd*
A Norman motte-and-bailey castle, reinforced with stonework, that fell in the war between King John and his barons in 1216, and remained a royal castle for several centuries. John, King of France, was imprisoned here in 1356.
Location: Castle St, off Gascoyne Way (A414).

Hetty Pegler's Tump *Glos. Map: 397 Ge*
This long barrow – or burial mound – is over 100 ft long, contained within a drystone wall. The burial area is concentrated at the east end in a group of chambers which open off a central passage or gallery. Entrance to the gallery is through a deeply recessed forecourt area, probably used for funerary rituals. At least 23 bodies were buried here about 3000 BC.
Location: 5½ miles SW of Stroud on B4066.

Heveningham Hall *Suffolk Map: 399 Gf*
The best Georgian mansion in the county, and one of the first to show the stamp of James Wyatt, who designed the attractive interiors and

THE WORLD OF "THE WHINING SCHOOLBOY"

Until modern times poor boys had little chance (and girls almost no chance) of receiving a good education. In the Middle Ages, a few poor boys learned music, Greek and Latin at cathedral and abbey schools; and a few obtained a place at public schools such as Eton and Winchester, which had been set up for the benefit of poor children. But most were sent out to work at an early age, like their parents before them. In the 16th and 17th centuries, grammar schools, like the one at Heptonstall (see p. 191), were founded for the education of local boys (though primarily middle-class ones).

Many of them were established by rich merchants who wanted to give boys the classical education which they themselves often lacked. The merchants paid for the maintenance of the school and the master's salary.

Bleak rooms and long hours
Classrooms were barely furnished: a few crude desks and benches for the pupils, the master's desk and chair, a small collection of books, and perhaps one or two wall charts. The school day was much longer than it is today. Lessons started at 6.00 or 7.00 in the morning and went on until 5.00 in the evening. There were usually three breaks – for breakfast, lunch and afternoon play.

Pupils usually entered grammar school at the age of eight, having already learned the rudiments of reading and writing at a dame school, which charged a few pence a week, or from the local curate, who sometimes gave instruction free.

In these elementary schools, where printed books were still a rarity, each child had a hornbook. This was a sheet of paper or parchment, attached to a flat bat-shaped piece of wood, with a simple alphabet, a set of numerals, and the Lord's Prayer printed on it. The sheet was protected with a thin layer of transparent horn.

Unrelieved Latin and Greek
Some boys left grammar school at the age of 14 to be apprenticed to a public notary (a man who drew up contracts) or an apothecary (a chemist). Others stayed on, sometimes until the age of 18, with the intention of going to university to become doctors, lawyers or clergymen. For these a good knowledge of Latin was essential. The hard-pressed boys had to decline Latin nouns and conjugate Latin verbs for hours on end, and later to learn by heart long extracts from Latin poets and historians such as Ovid and Caesar.

Eventually, if a boy was bright enough, he would be asked to compose his own verses and orations in Latin. Sometimes the boys also studied Greek, but there was usually no other variety in the lessons.

At some grammar schools, music was the exception, and for those pupils whose parents could pay the fees there was private tuition in singing and playing musical instruments.

Most schoolmasters – probably three-quarters or more – were also clergymen, but that did not prevent them from using the birch on backward or reluctant pupils. Boys were faced with a harsh alternative: they either learned their lessons or were punished for not knowing them. Shakespeare wrote with pity of "the whining schoolboy . . . creeping like snail unwillingly to school".

Examinations in scholastic proficiency, included written papers and oral disputations.

A wider curriculum
During Elizabethan times education had been divided into two main branches – the *trivium* (Latin, logic and rhetoric) and the *quadrivium* (arithmetic, geometry, astronomy and music). This rigid curriculum, and the equally rigid methods of teaching it, persisted until the 18th century. To supplement their income, many schoolmasters (whose salary had often been unalterably fixed when the school was founded) started to offer, for a fee, a broader and more modern education. In addition to the classical languages, they taught English, geography, history and French. These were far more useful than the "dead" languages to boys who wanted to go into business or the services.

As optional extras, there were classes in writing, drawing and even dancing. Some schoolmasters also provided board and lodgings for pupils who lived at a distance.

Through the excellence of the education they provided, the original public schools, set up for poor boys, had drawn an increasing proportion of aristocrats' and wealthy men's sons, and by the 18th century they were also charging fees. Thus the term "public school" took on its modern meaning.

It was not until the Education Act of 1880 that it was made compulsory for children, from the age of five up to the age of ten, to attend school. If by that age they had not registered sufficient attendances, they were compelled to continue their education until they were 13.

An act in 1889 empowered local authorities to levy a penny rate for technical education.

Dame school: rudimentary reading and writing.

Grammar school: backwardness was punished.

Dancing class: an option at some schools.

Public school: fee-paying replaced free tuition.

part of the furniture to go with them.

The Hall was built in 1780 for Sir Gerard Vanneck, MP, on an estate bought by his father.

"Capability" Brown's ambitious plan for the "Alterations and Continuation of the Water" in the park had to be curbed, because neighbouring landowners were worried about their river-bank rights in the stream feeding the estate.
Location: 4 miles SW of Halesworth on B1117.

Hever Castle *Kent* *Map: 399 Eb*
Henry VIII confiscated the 13th-century castle, owned for generations by the Boleyn family, after he had his second wife, Anne Boleyn, executed in 1536. The king gave the castle to Anne of Cleves, his fourth wife, as a sop for a quick divorce after marrying her in 1540.
Location: 2½ miles E of Edenbridge.

Hexham Abbey *Northld.* *Map: 391 Fe*
The earliest church was built in 674 by St Wilfrid, and parts of it–including earlier Roman work–have survived. The stone throne of St Wilfrid is in the choir, and there are carved Roman stones in the Saxon crypt.

The south transept has the tombstone of 25-year-old Flavinus, a Roman standard-bearer, and the Night Stair–its steps worn by monks descending from their dormitories for services.
Location: Off Market Place, town centre.

Heysham *Lancs.* *Map: 391 Db*
CHURCH OF ST PETER A church with many reminders of its Saxon origins, including rare carvings and a churchyard cross. There is also a 13th-century stone coffin lid.
Location: Off Main St (A589), on the coast.

THRONE OF JUDGMENT

The throne in Hexham Abbey is said to date from the 7th century. It was St Wilfrid's bishop's throne and may have been used for the coronation of some of the kings of Northumbria. Later, it became known as a frith stool, used as a seat of sanctuary. Fugitives seeking sanctuary in the church (see also p. 134) had their case considered by the bishop, occupying the chair. It stands in the middle of the choir.

Higher Bockhampton *Dorset* *Map: 397 Gc*
HARDY'S COTTAGE
It faces west, and round the back and sides
High beeches, bending, hang a veil of boughs,
And sweep against the roof.
This was Thomas Hardy's own description of the modest cottage in which he was born in 1840. There he grew up and wrote *Under the Greenwood Tree* (1872) and *Far from the Madding Crowd* (1874).
Location: 3 miles NE of Dorchester off A35.

Highland Folk Museum see Kingussie

Highland Wildlife Park *H'land* *Map: 387 Db*
The park has a collection of animals and birds of Scotland, including rare breeds of sheep and poultry, among them Soay and St Kilda sheep, and Scots Grey chickens.

There are also animals that once ran wild in Scotland, such as wild boars, brown bears and the first wolves to raise cubs in the Highlands since the last wild wolf was killed in 1743.
Location: 7 miles S of Aviemore off A9.

High Rochester *Northld.* *Map: 391 Ef*
ROMAN FORT The hamlet lies within Bremenium, the most northerly occupied fort of the Roman Empire after the final withdrawal from Scotland about AD 275.

Substantial remains can be seen.
Location: 5½ miles NW of Otterburn off A68 at Rochester.

Hill Top *Cumbria* *Map: 391 Dc*
Beatrix Potter (1866–1943), the artist and children's writer who created Peter Rabbit, Jemima Puddleduck and Pigling Bland, lived at Hill Top for about 17 years–the greater part of her creative life.

The cottage is as she left it–its interior characteristic of her book illustrations.
Location: Village of Near Sawrey, 2 miles S of Hawkshead on B5285.

Hinckley *Leics.* *Map: 398 Bf*
Knitting started in Hinckley in 1640 and it has continued as the centre of the hosiery industry ever since. A 17th-century knitter's house is preserved as a town museum.

During the early 19th century, pay was reduced to starvation level throughout the Midlands and the knitters–mainly men–began the organised destruction of factory machines; at least 1,000 knitting frames were smashed. They called themselves Luddites, after Ned Ludd, the idiot boy who destroyed some stocking frames in Leicestershire about 1782.
Location: Museum is in Lower Bond St (A47).

Hirwaun Ironworks *Mid Glam.* *Map: 392 Db*
The ruined late-19th-century ironworks form a prominent landmark. There are the shells of four blast furnaces built against the hillside, and the extensive remains of the tramway that linked the ironworks to the quarries at Penderyn, 3 miles to the north.

The causeway and stone bridge across the River Cynon have stone sleeper blocks intact.
Location: 4 miles NW of Aberdare on A4059. The ironworks are off Station Rd, centre of village.

Hod Hill *Dorset* *Map: 397 Gc*
The Iron Age hill-fort, with its single massive
rampart and ditch, was one of the places captured
by the Roman Second Legion during its assault
on the west of England in AD 43. The Romans
built a garrison fort in one corner, using the
existing defences for two sides, but constructed
their own chalk rampart and ditches on the south
and east. The post-manned for less than a
decade-is well preserved.
Location: 3 miles NW of Blandford Forum off
A350.

Holker Hall *Cumbria* *Map: 391 Dc*
The Hall, built in the early 17th century but
largely rebuilt in 1871 after a fire, has been in the
hands of the Cavendish family since 1756. The
library has 3,500 volumes, some by Henry
Cavendish, who discovered the properties of
hydrogen in 1760.
Elsewhere in the house are a screen embroidered by Mary, Queen of Scots, and a cartoon
by Van Dyke.
The monkey puzzle tree in the garden is said
to be the oldest in England, planted in 1851.
Location: 4 miles W of Grange-over-Sands
(B5277 and B5278).

Holkham Hall *Norfolk* *Map: 395 Fb*
In 1734, Thomas Coke, 1st Earl of Leicester,
commenced building Holkham Hall, for which
William Kent had prepared drawings. In 1776
the estate descended to a great-nephew, Thomas
William Coke, later known as "Coke of Norfolk". He enlarged the park, and his name
became legendary as a hero of the "Agricultural
Revolution".
Coke continued the work of tree planting,
improving the soil by marling, and introduced
new methods of crop rotation and sheep breeding.
Location: 2 miles W of Wells-next-the-Sea off
A149.

Holme on Spalding Moor *Hum.* *Map: 394 Cd*
CHURCH OF ALL SAINTS The church's pinnacled
Gothic tower is a magnificent landmark, perched
on a hill top high above the village.
All Saints has a Jacobean pulpit, an 18th-
century gallery and a barrel organ. In the early
19th century, barrel organs were commonplace
in churches, being used to play hymns. Few of
the instruments have survived-they were
replaced as churches acquired bellows organs.
Location: 13 miles W of Beverley (A1079 then
A163). The church is E of village.

Holm of Papa Westray *Orkney* *Map: 387 Ff*
A spectacular megalithic tomb on an islet that
appears never to have been inhabited in historic
times. A pair of houses near by of roughly
contemporary date were probably the homes of
the family buried in the tomb. The chamber is
over 75 ft long, and has 14 beehive chambers
opening off it, each thought to have been used
as a tomb.
Location: The islet is reached by steamer from
Kirkwall.

Holt Castle *Clwyd* *Map: 393 Ee*
One of the four castles put up in North Wales
by Edward I's barons during his war with the

Welsh in the 1280s. The castle commanded a
vital crossing of the Dee-its moat fed at two
points by the river.
Location: 5 miles NE of Wrexham on A534.

Holyhead (Caerygybi) *Gwynedd* *Map: 392 Bf*
ROMAN WALLS Late in the 4th century, the
Romans put up three walls, which now enclose
the churchyard of St Cybi, to protect their
harbour below. A fourth wall may have existed
as well. The defences have been restored and
altered over the years, but the bastion at the
north-west corner is substantially Roman.
St Cybi, to whom the 15th-16th-century
church is dedicated, founded a monastery within
the walls in about AD 550.
Location: Victoria Rd in town centre.

Holywell *Clwyd* *Map: 393 Df*
BEAUFORT CHAPEL A legend says that a local lady,
Winifred, was coveted by a 7th-century chieftain, Caradoc. She fled to her uncle, St Beuno,
but was caught by Caradoc who sliced off her
head for resisting his advances. St Beuno restored
Winifred's head to her body and the earth opened
up and engulfed Caradoc. A spring bubbled up
on the spot where the head had fallen and the site
became a place of pilgrimage.
Henry VII's mother, Lady Margaret Beaufort,
built the well and the chapel over it at the end of
the 15th century. The chapel survived the Reformation and was visited in 1686 by James II. It is
still a place of pilgrimage.
Location: Greenfield St (New Rd)-B5121.

Hopetoun House *Lothian* *Map: 389 Dd*
The magnificent house was started in 1699 by
Sir William Bruce for the 1st Earl of Hopetoun,
and substantially enlarged by his pupil, William
Adam. Adam's sons, John and Robert, com-
pleted the work in 1760.
There are fine Adam ceilings; paintings by
Titian and Canaletto; and a massive carved
chimney piece by the celebrated sculptor, Rys-
brack, of Antwerp. The house also has most of
its original furniture.
In the grounds there are herds of Red and
Fallow deer and the rare black four-horned St
Kilda sheep.
Location: 10 miles NW of Edinburgh (A90,
A904).

Horkstow *Humberside* *Map: 394 Cd*
CHURCH OF ST MAURICE An Early English Knights
Templar church, dedicated to St Maurice-a
Roman soldier martyred for his belief in Chris-
tianity.
The chancel is higher than the nave, possibly
raised to accommodate a vault for the Shirley
family-once landowners in the area.
George Stubbs, the celebrated 18th-century
painter of horses, lived in the village while
preparing his picture *Anatomy of a Horse*.
Location: 4½ miles SW of Barton-upon-Humber
(A1077 and B1204).

Horsey Windmill *Norfolk* *Map: 395 Ga*
The 200-year-old windmill was rebuilt in 1912
by Dan England-a millwright renowned for his
work on the pumping mills of Norfolk.
Location: 8½ miles NW of Caister-on-Sea (A149
then B1159).

195

Horton Court *Avon*   *Map: 393 Fa*
In 1521, William Knight – chief clerk at the supreme church court at the time of Henry VIII – extended the 12th-century house. Six years later, Knight was sent to Rome to help in negotiating the king's attempted divorce from Catherine of Aragon.

In 1708 John Paston owned the house at a time when Catholicism was still suspect, following the expulsion of James II and the threats of Jacobite rebellions in Scotland. Paston built a floor across the old hall to form an upper room, using it as a secret chapel. It was used as a school from 1849 until 1884, when the hall was restored.
Location: 3 miles NE of Chipping Sodbury in Horton village.

Houghton Conquest *Beds.*   *Map: 398 De*
CHURCH OF ALL SAINTS The church is mainly Decorated and Perpendicular. A contract of 1393 exists for building the west tower and prices the foundations at ten shillings a foot, and the walls at thirteen shillings a foot – to be finished in three years.
Location: 6 miles S of Bedford off A418.
HOUGHTON HOUSE Sir Philip Sidney's sister built the house in 1615. In 1675 it was the inspiration for the House Beautiful in John Bunyan's *Pilgrim's Progress*.
Location: 7½ miles S of Bedford off A418.

Hound Tor *Devon*   *Map: 397 Dc*
The remains of a medieval village that was deserted during the 13th or 14th century. The first houses were of turf, replaced in the 12th century by stone-walled buildings, the remains of which can be seen today.

There are traces of massive corn-drying kilns, set in pairs – each in the form of a circular oven with a long flue leading to a stoke hole – suggesting that in the Middle Ages the climate was warmer, suitable for extensive arable farming.
Location: 5 miles S of Moretonhampstead.

Housesteads *Northld.*   *Map: 391 Ee*
The most celebrated of all Roman forts on Hadrian's Wall is Housesteads, strategically positioned on a craggy precipice. Its ramparts and gateways are all well preserved, and excavations have uncovered many of the buildings, including the best preserved latrine from Roman Britain.

There is a museum near the fort, containing maps, models, pottery, coins and other objects found at the site. (See also p. 178.)
Location: 7 miles NE of Haltwhistle, N of B6318.

Howden *Humberside*   *Map: 394 Cd*
ST PETER'S MINSTER This was once a great 14th-century collegiate church with a 15th-century tower. The chancel fell into ruin after the Reformation, when the parish could only afford to maintain the nave and the 135 ft high tower.
Location: 3½ miles N of Goole off A614.

Hubberholme *N. Yorks.*   *Map: 394 Ae*
CHURCH OF ST MICHAEL AND ALL ANGELS A Norman church with later additions, including a 15th-century font. An unusual survival is the Rood Loft, thought to have been brought from Coverham Abbey after the Dissolution of the Monasteries (1536–40).
Location: 9 miles SW of Aysgarth off B6160.

Huddersfield *W. Yorks.*   *Map: 391 Fa*
One of the great 19th-century centres of the Yorkshire woollen industry, that illustrates Victorian industrial development. Much of the town centre has been redeveloped, but there are 19th-century mills – some still in use – lining the River Colne and the adjoining canal. There are tall spinning mills beside low weaving sheds, and terraces of workers' houses in the valley.

Hughenden Manor *Bucks.*   *Map: 398 Cd*
In 1848 Benjamin Disraeli, later Earl of Beaconsfield and twice prime minister during Victoria's reign, bought the estate with money from his wife and political supporters. He wrote novels there, including his last, *Endymion*, in 1880.

The Jacobean house was re-faced in 1862, and the interiors transformed into Victorian Gothic.
Location: 2 miles N of High Wycombe off A4128.

Hunterston Castle *Strathclyde*   *Map: 388 Bd*
The 15th-century castle – with 17th-century additions – and the motte-and-bailey structure there before it, were owned by the Hunter family for 800 years, possibly longer. One of the family is believed to have come to England with William the Conqueror.
Location: 5½ miles S of Largs off A78.

Huntingdon *Cambs.*   *Map: 399 Df*
CROMWELL MUSEUM The museum was once part of a 12th-century hospital that was converted into a grammar school in 1565. Oliver Cromwell was born in the town in 1599, and attended the school. Samuel Pepys was also a pupil in 1640.

Cromwell served as MP for Huntingdon, and in the Civil War was instrumental in rallying most of East Anglia to the Parliamentary cause. The campaign is symbolised in the museum by his sword, water-bottle and a copy of *The Soldier's Catechism* of 1644.
Location: Market Sq., town centre.

Huntingtower Castle *Tayside*   *Map: 389 Df*
Two 16th-century tower houses that are joined together with a third tower of later date. The castle is also known as Ruthven Castle, because it belonged to the Ruthven family.
Location: 2½ miles NW of Perth on A85.

Huntly *Grampian*   *Map: 387 Fc*
CASTLE Huntly is one of the finest baronial castles in Scotland, a 15th-century tower house next to a 17th-century palace building.

In 1562, Mary, Queen of Scots had the castle sacked after defeating Lord Huntly.
Location: N of town centre on bank of River Deveron.

Hurlers *Cornwall*   *Map: 396 Cb*
These three stone circles arranged in line are believed, in local lore, to represent the petrified remains of three rings of men who were turned to stone when they were caught hurling a ball on the Sabbath. In fact, the stones were erected during the Bronze Age.
Location: 5½ miles N of Liskeard off B3254.

Hurst Castle *Hants.*   *Map: 398 Ba*
One of the coastal fortresses built during the period of the 1538–40 French invasion scare, to

guard the approach to Southampton Water. The castle was never needed for defensive purposes and was allowed to deteriorate.

Charles I was confined there for a few weeks in 1648, before going to London for his trial and execution, two months later.
Location: 4 miles S of Lymington (A337, B3058 and minor roads), then 1½ mile walk on shingle. Or ferry from Lymington (during season).

Hutton-in-the-Forest *Cumbria Map: 391 Dd*
Hutton is largely a 17th-century house – incorporating a 14th-century pele tower – with Victorian additions.

The house has a collection of furnishings, paintings and tapestries acquired by the family during the past 450 years.
Location: 6 miles NW of Penrith (A6 then B5305).

Hutton-le-Hole *N. Yorks.   Map: 394 Cf*
RYEDALE FOLK MUSEUM A collection of agricultural implements and tools relating to rural crafts are housed in early-18th-century farm buildings. The grounds contain reconstructions of buildings from the area which would otherwise have been demolished. These include an Elizabethan glass-furnace, manor house, medieval long-house, cruck-built cottages, a smithy and craft shops.
Location: 8¼ miles NW of Pickering off A170.

Hylton Castle *Tyne & Wear   Map: 391 Ge*
A five-storeyed gatehouse tower that was built in the 15th century by William de Hylton. It was designed to be defended against unreliable retainers inside the castle, as well as from outside attackers.
Location: 3 miles NW of centre of Sunderland on A1290.

LONELY OUTPOST OF ROMAN BRITAIN

It is at Housesteads fort (below), more than anywhere else on Hadrian's Wall, that the flavour of life on the Roman frontier can be experienced. It is a dramatic site – its Roman name was Vercovicium, meaning "hilly spot" – clinging to the edge of a rugged precipice in a lonely part of Northumberland.

Excavations have so far revealed the commandant's house, headquarters buildings, a workshop, a pair of granaries, several barrack blocks, a hospital, and a latrine.

The latrine, the best preserved in Roman Britain, has deep sewers that originally had wooden seats above them, and channels in the stonework filled with running water for rinsing sponges – the Roman equivalent of toilet paper. Not until the 20th century were Roman standards of hygiene equalled.

Sewage was carried through pipes to emerge on the hillsides, 100 yds away from the fort, and is thought to have been used on the land as a fertiliser.

The fort's water supply system is unknown, but gutters exist that conveyed rainwater to stone storage tanks – the water periodically used to flush the latrines.

Outside the fort there was a civilian settlement with houses clustered together on a series of artificial terraces. Much of the settlement has yet to be excavated, but one house uncovered in 1932 is known as the "Murder House". Skeletons of a man and a woman – with part of a sword in the man's ribs – were found buried beneath a shop floor. Since burial within a settlement was forbidden by Roman law, the bodies are assumed to be those of victims of a crime.

STONEWORK AT HOUSESTEADS *Part of the latrines (above) at the Roman fort, and carved hooded figures (below), thought to depict local deities.*

I J

Icknield Way *Oxon.* *Map: 398 Cd*
This prehistoric hill track once stretched some 190 miles from Hunstanton on the Wash almost to Stonehenge. Parts of it still remain. It may have been used as early as 3000 BC, but it was probably the flint trade from the East Anglian mines 1,000 years later which made it important. Overlooking its course are ancient monuments – causewayed camps, long and round barrows and hillforts. A pleasant walk runs between Watlington Hill and Beacon Hill, south of Aston Rowant.
Location: Aston Rowant is 10 miles W of High Wycombe off A40.

Ickworth House *Suffolk* *Map: 399 Fe*
Frederick Augustus Hervey, 4th Earl of Bristol, began his mansion in 1794. It was designed as a round house with curved corridors to one wing for paintings and a second wing for sculpture. He was an avid collector and spent so lavishly abroad that many European hotels are called *Hotel Bristol* after him. Many of his treasures were seized by Napoleon before they could reach Ickworth and it was left to the Hervey family to complete the

THE LUXURY OF SUGAR
These silver-gilt sugar bowls at Ickworth House were made in 1758 by the Huguenot silversmith Frederick Kandler, for the 2nd Earl of Bristol to take to Spain when he became Ambassador. At around 1s 6d a lb., sugar was a luxury, although it had been available in small amounts since the 16th century. Annual consumption ran at only 8 lb. a head in the 1750s compared with about 114 lb. today.

But the end of the Seven Years War with France in 1763 meant that Britain acquired vast plantations of tea, coffee and sugar in the West Indies. Tea became a popular drink and the consumption of sugar rose. It was also used in sweets and sugared puddings.

house and collection after the earl's death in 1803.
Location: 4 miles SW of Bury St Edmunds off A143.

Iffley *Oxon.* *Map: 398 Bd*
CHURCH OF ST MARY THE VIRGIN This delightful building is one of the best Norman churches in the country. Impressive now, it must have been astounding to the 12th-century villagers who saw it rise among their crude little houses. There is a wealth of zigzag and beak-head decoration. Carvings on the west doorway show 16 medallions with the symbols of the Evangelists and the Signs of the Zodiac. The south doorway is even more ornate and the font is also Norman. Some of the windows contain 15th-century stained glass.
Location: 2 miles SE of Oxford off A4158.

Ightham *Kent* *Map: 399 Ec*
CHURCH OF ST PETER On the fringe of a still-picturesque village, the 15th-century church, with traces of Norman work, has a number of interesting monuments. The earliest is a 14th-century effigy, with a lion at its feet, of Sir Thomas Cawne, who lived at Ightham Mote near by. Another, by Nicholas Stone's pupil Edward Marshall, is to Dorothy Selby, who died in 1641 and is reputed to have played a part in discovering the Gunpowder Plot.
Location: 5 miles E of Sevenoaks on A25.

Ightham Mote *Kent* *Map: 399 Ec*
This is the most complete small medieval manor house in Kent. It was built in 1340 around a courtyard in the traditional style. It is approached by a stone bridge across its moat and entered by a castellated gatehouse. Attractive though it is, it must have been a gloomy house in which to spend a winter. Its peace was disturbed only once when in 1585, its owner, Sir Christopher Allen, put a cook in the stocks as punishment for theft. In revenge, the cook accused him of keeping "a vyle and papisticall house". Sir Christopher was cleared of the charge, but he died soon after.
Location: 5 miles N of Tonbridge off A227.

Ilkley *W. Yorks.* *Map: 394 Ad*
MANOR HOUSE Part of this Tudor house, now a museum of Ilkley's history with relics of Roman times, was built from remains of Roman buildings.
Location: In Castle Yard, W end of town.

Ilminster *Somerset* *Map: 397 Fc*
CHURCH OF THE BLESSED VIRGIN MARY The beauty of this 15th-century Perpendicular cruciform church owes much to the golden Ham Hill stone used for the tower, chancel and transepts.

The north transept was built to house the monument, with two brasses, to Sir William Wadham, sheriff of Devonshire, who died in 1452. But the more famous monuments are to his great-great grandson, Nicholas Wadham (d. 1618) and his wife, Dorothy, who founded Wadham College, Oxford.
Location: Off Barton Court, S of High St.

Inchcolm Abbey *Fife*   *Map: 389 Ee*
The abbey was founded by King Alexander I in 1123, after he was driven on to Inchcolm Island in a gale and fed for several days by a hermit living there. It is now a well-preserved ruin.
Location: On Inchcolm Island, Firth of Forth.

Inchmahome Priory *Central*   *Map: 388 Ce*
The priory was founded in 1238 on an island in the Lake of Menteith, and is now an attractive ruin. After the Battle of Pinkie in 1547, the five-year-old Mary, Queen of Scots took refuge there to prevent the victorious English from arranging a marriage between her and Edward VI.
Location: 4 miles E of Aberfoyle on A81, then boat from Port of Menteith.

Inchtuthil *Tayside*   *Map: 387 Ea*
ROMAN FORTRESS Excavations, now reburied, revealed the outline of a timber fortress begun by the Roman general Agricola around AD 83 and abandoned four years later when Agricola was recalled to Rome. The most dramatic find was a hoard of 1 million unused Roman nails, buried so Scottish tribesmen could not use them.
Location: 7 miles E of Dunkeld (A984, then track from junction with B947).

Ingatestone *Essex*   *Map: 399 Ed*
CHURCH OF ST EDMUND AND ST MARY Originally Norman but with many additions, the church has a splendid 15th-century red brick tower. The south chapel was added in 1556 by the Petre family who still live at Ingatestone Hall, which was acquired by Sir William Petre in 1539. He was Privy Counsellor to Henry VIII, Edward VI, Mary I and Elizabeth I. He is buried in the church beneath an alabaster monument.
Location: 6 miles SW of Chelmsford off A12.

Ingestre *Staffs.*   *Map: 393 Fe*
CHURCH OF ST MARY THE VIRGIN With its fine plaster ceiling and good woodwork, the design of the church is attributed to Sir Christopher Wren. He was certainly a friend of the local squire, Walter Chetwynd, who in the late 17th century was given permission by the Archbishop of Canterbury to pay for a new church.
Location: 4 miles E of Stafford (A518 then minor roads).

Innerleithen *Borders*   *Map: 389 Ec*
TRAQUAIR HOUSE The oldest inhabited and most romantic house in Scotland, Traquair dates from the 10th century. It has a unique 18th-century brewhouse still producing ale. Mary, Queen of Scots was one of 27 monarchs who stayed there, and the king's bed which she used can be seen with her crucifix, rosary and the cradle for her infant son, who became James VI of Scotland and I of England.
Location: 1 mile S of Innerleithen off B709.

Inveraray Castle *Strathclyde*   *Map: 388 Be*
The present castle was built in the late 18th century and is the seat of the Dukes of Argyll and headquarters of the Clan Campbell. Designed by Roger Morris and Robert Mylne in the style of a French chateau, the turreted castle has a splendid collection of Beauvais tapestries, fine furniture and plate, and family portraits. In the Armoury Hall is a vast collection of early Scottish arms including the dirk handle and sporran of Rob Roy.
Location: ½ mile N of Inveraray on A83.

Invergarry *Highland*   *Map: 386 Db*
WELL OF THE SEVEN HEADS After the death of Keppoch of the Clan MacDonnell in the 17th century, his seven brothers took over his estate and murdered his two sons. The family bard had the murderers killed and their heads washed in the well before presenting them to the Mac-Donnell chief at Glangarry Castle.
Location: 7 miles SW of Fort Augustus on A82.

Inverness *Highland*   *Map: 387 Dc*
ABERTARFF HOUSE Built in the 16th century, the house is a solid rectangular block with crow-stepped gables and protruded stair-tower. It was once occupied by the Frasers of Lovat, prominent in the 1745 Jacobite Rising, and is now the headquarters of An Comunn Gaidhealach, the Gaelic cultural organisation.
Location: Church St.

Iona Abbey *Strathclyde*   *Map: 386 Ba*
The present abbey was founded by the Benedictines around 1203. But the religious history of the tiny island of Iona goes back to the landing of the Irish missionary St Columba in AD 563.

No trace remains of the monastery he built, but the excavated St Columba's Cell and slab of stone are traditionally thought to be where he slept. Iona remained his headquarters for 34 years while he converted a large part of Scotland to Christianity. So sacred did the island become that nearly all the Scottish kings up to the 11th century were buried in the graveyard, including Duncan, slain by Macbeth in 1040. About 40 kings are buried there, some of them Norwegian. Part of the "Street of the Dead", which brought them from the shore, has been preserved. Near by are three mighty Celtic crosses.
Location: By ferry from Fionnphort, Mull.

Ipsden *Oxon.*   *Map: 398 Cc*
THE KING WILLIAM This pub and its garden have a display of horse gear and farm equipment from the 19th and early 20th centuries.
Location: At Hailey, 4 miles SE of Wallingford off A423.

Ipswich *Suffolk*   *Map: 399 Fe*
CHRISTCHURCH MANSION The house was built in the mid-16th century on the site of an Augustinian priory and reconstructed after a fire in the 17th century.

At the end of the last century it was endowed as a town museum by F. T. Cobbold, a local banker. One of the Cobbold family was the clergyman-novelist Richard Cobbold. His book *Margaret Catchpole* is based on the true story of one of the Cobbold's 18th-century girl servants, who became involved with a local smuggler and was transported to Australia.

In 1931 a picture gallery was added to the house to commemorate Cardinal Wolsey, the Ipswich butcher's son who became Henry VIII's principal minister. The last trace of Wolsey's unfinished college in the town is a Tudor gateway in College Street bearing Henry VIII's arms.
Location: Christchurch Park.

Legacy of Abraham Darby, ironmaster

OUT OF THE POTENT MIXTURE OF COAL AND IRON-ORE IN THE IRONBRIDGE AREA OF SHROPSHIRE GREW ONE OF THE MOST INFLUENTIAL CENTRES OF INDUSTRY IN BRITAIN

The first bridge in the world to be made of iron is the centre-point of the Ironbridge Gorge Museum.

Early in the 18th century, well before the railways had been invented or good roads developed, the area had become a centre of industry. Iron-ore, coal and clay had been discovered and ironworks and potteries were set up, powered by water-wheels in the tributaries of the River Severn. The Severn itself carried the finished goods to the markets.

The Ironbridge story begins in 1708 when Abraham Darby took over an old ironworks (see Coalbrookdale). He built a successful business, making iron cooking pots, and generations of the Darby family helped develop the region. One of their major concerns was the improve-

TOLL-KEEPER'S HOUSE

The engineer Thomas Telford was County Surveyor of Shropshire from 1787 to 1834. A toll-house which was built by Telford on his Holyhead road in the late 1820s has been reconstructed at Blists Hill.

PARLOUR *The toll-house was built at Shelton, west of Shrewsbury, for a toll-keeper who collected money from all traffic using the new road.*

ment of local roads, including building a bridge across the Severn Gorge. Drawings for a bridge were prepared by a local architect, Thomas Pritchard, who planned to use iron for the construction, something that no one had attempted before. But Pritchard died in 1777 and the work fell to the head of the Darby works, Abraham Darby III. The result revolutionised bridge building, and was the forerunner of the steel-framed buildings of today. The bridge has a single soaring arch with a 100 ft span, rising 45 ft above the water.

Much of the industrial activity of the Ironbridge region was at Blists Hill to the east, now the main museum site. Between the bridge and Blists Hill stand a pair of blast furnaces known as the Bedlam furnaces. These were run by William Reynolds, a relative of Darby, and were part of the Madeley Wood works. Visitors in the 18th century were often overawed by the sight of the ironworks. The poetess Anne Seward wrote of "pond'rous engines", "red and countless fires" and "thick, sulpherous smoke". It all seemed like a madman's dream, so it was given the name Bedlam.

The Blists Hill Museum itself concentrates on four main industries: iron, coal, pottery and transport. Many of the exhibits remain on the site from the 18th and 19th centuries; others have been brought to Blists Hill and re-erected.

Different types of coal mines have been reconstructed along Miner's Walk. The simple drift mine was made by driving a tunnel horizontally into the hill and propping it up with timber. Iron rails have been laid for the coal-filled trucks which were pushed in the 18th century by women and children.

In the 1780s a tunnel, 1,000 yds long, was driven under Blists Hill to bring out coal from the pits. It struck a deposit of natural bitumen which still exudes from the walls. A business was set up to collect and sell the "tar", and an Italian who visited the tunnel reported that the workmen looked "like the imps described by Dante in his *Inferno* as gathering with a hook the souls of the damned in a sea of pitch, so horribly disfigured and begrimed are they".

PRINT SHOP *Industries that flourished in Shropshire in the 18th and 19th centuries are being reconstructed at Blists Hill. They include a 19th-century print shop with all its equipment. During the Industrial Revolution printing was the only way of spreading information.*

KITCHEN *The wood-fired range is the focal point of the kitchen. Outside is a sample of a Telford road, made of graded stones and chippings.*

LEARNING TO BUILD WITH IRON

When the first iron bridge was planned in the 1770s, the builders had no idea of the structural properties of cast iron. So they built it with wide safety margins. No bolts were used in the bridge – sections were treated like wood, and fitted together with dovetail and shoulder joints. Finally the bridge was coated with pitch to protect it from rust.

BEDLAM *Because of the flames and heat these blast furnaces were nicknamed Bedlam.*

BOAT TRACK *The Hay Inclined Plane lowered canal boats from Blists Hill to the Severn. A pair of 6 ton boats could be lowered in 3½ minutes, compared to about two hours by the conventional lock system.*

THE BLAST *Huge blowing engines produced the blast of air for the furnaces.*

CLAY MINE *Red Clay Mine is 600 ft deep, with layers of clay, coal and ironstone.*

TAR TUNNEL *A deposit of natural bitumen was tapped in a tunnel running 1,000 yds under Blists Hill from Coalport.*

"Wheel-houses" of the Iron Age

WHILE THE ROMANS RULED ENGLAND, IRON AGE PEOPLE WERE LIVING ON A REMOTE
ATLANTIC SHORE IN THE SHETLANDS IN ROUND HOUSES MADE OF STONES

WHEEL-HOUSES *The wheel-houses built beside the broch in the 2nd century AD were roofed with slabs of stone and were about 10 ft high. They were entered along a low stone passage which had a loft above it. A wooden door closed off the passage at its outer end.*

CENTRAL FIREPLACE *The wheel-houses are up to 40 ft across and get their name from the partition walls which divide each house into several compartments. Each of these "rooms", with its paved floor, faces into a central area where a peat fire burned on a hearth.*

In the 1st century BC, Iron Age immigrants from the Continent built a massive stone tower, or broch, at Jarlshof in Shetland. They were among several waves of people who lived at Jarlshof over 2,000 years, and their broch was one of hundreds built on the coast of northern Scotland and the nearby islands. Brochs were homesteads fortified against sea-raiders, with a central area open to the sky.

The families who lived in the broch kept cattle, sheep and pigs; they fished and caught seals and birds; and they grew barley, which they ground on saddle-shaped grindstones.

Two hundred years later, stones were used from the broch to build circular "wheel-houses" alongside it.

These houses were probably still occupied when Viking raiders arrived at Jarlshof in the early 9th century, at the same time as other Vikings were sacking the coast of Scotland and northern England.

The Vikings settled at Jarlshof, and the village remained occupied until the 16th century.

SETTLERS MAKE NEW HOUSES FROM OLD

An artist's reconstruction of Jarlshof as it would have appeared in the 2nd century AD. The people of the village had built their "wheel-houses" in the courtyard of the old broch, using stones from the broch itself. Eventually the broch was also turned into a wheel-house.

Ironbridge *Salop*   *Map: 393 Ed*
The whole area around Ironbridge, which takes its name from the first iron bridge ever built, is an industrial museum. (See pp. 200–1.)
Location: 8 miles N of Bridgnorth on B4373.

Isleornsay *Skye, Highland*   *Map: 386 Cb*
CROTAL MILL This was originally a school, built in 1876 under the Act of Parliament which made education in English compulsory. The mill, set up in 1969, makes "Skye Crotal" knitwear.
Location: 8½ miles SE of Broadford off A851.
OLD SHOP Built in 1812 in Isleornsay village on the Isle of Skye when fishing was the main industry, the shop became the largest between Glasgow and the Hebrides. Edward VII once

went here with Lily Langtry and spent the large sum of £80. It is now the headquarters of Fearann Eilean Iarmain, the local estate enterprise.
Location: 8½ miles SE of Broadford off A851.

Ivinghoe *Bucks.*   *Map: 398 Cd*
FORD END WATERMILL Although it has an iron wheel, the 18th-century mill is typical of the period before the Industrial Revolution.
Location: 4 miles NE of Tring on B488.

Izaak Walton's Cottage see Shallowford

Jarlshof *Shetland*   *Map: 387 Gd*
ANCIENT VILLAGE The earliest remains are four Bronze Age houses built in the 8th century BC, some with saddle-shaped grinding stones by the door. Close by are stone huts of the 5th and 4th centuries BC. In the 1st century BC a broch tower was built, and replaced 200 years later with stone "wheel-houses". The village also has the remains of a Viking settlement and medieval farm. (See opposite.)
Location: Just S of Sumburgh Airport off A970.

Jarrow *Tyne & Wear*   *Map: 391 Ge*
CHURCH OF ST PAUL Parts of the Saxon church dating from before AD 684 remain, including the inscribed dedication stone. The tower was prob-ably built around 1075. Near by are the ruins of the monastery where the great Saxon historian, the Venerable Bede (673–735), lived and worked.
Location: 3½ miles E of South Shields on A185.
JARROW HALL On a hill above the town, the Hall is 18th century and has finds from excavations of the monastic site of St Paul's.
Location: In Church Bank, E of Tyne Tunnel.

Jedburgh *Borders*   *Map: 391 Ef*
CASTLE Built in 1823 on the site of a medieval castle, the Georgian prison, now empty, still looks very castle-like with its battlemented cur-tain wall, gatehouse, vaulted ceilings and turret holding the alarm bell. The separate, heated cells and open exercise yards were designed to meet the newly accepted humanitarian principles laid down by the Howard Reform League.
Location: Top of Castlegate, overlooking town.
QUEEN MARY'S HOUSE Mary, Queen of Scots is supposed to have occupied this house in 1566 while she presided over the Circuit Court at Jedburgh. The house has been completely restored and is now a museum filled with relics associated with the queen. They include part of the garment she wore at her execution, her death mask, her seal and a letter dated September 25, 1566, signed Marie R.
Location: In Queen St through Smith's Wynd from High St.

K

Kedleston Hall *Derbys.*   *Map: 393 Ge*
Sir Nathaniel Curzon (1726–1804), who became the 1st Lord Scarsdale, was an avid collector of antiques and works of art. He inherited Kedleston in 1758, and immediately set about demolishing the existing Queen Anne house, to replace it with a grander mansion in which his treasures could be properly displayed.
   Three architects in succession worked on the project. The last was Robert Adam (1728–92), who revised the earlier plans and built the centre block.
   The interior of the main house is mostly Adam's work, too, and much of the furniture he carefully chose to complement his designs is still on show.
Location: 4½ miles NW of Derby on minor roads, near Quarndon.

Kegworth *Leics.*   *Map: 394 Ba*
FRAME KNITTERS' WORKSHOP In the 18th and early 19th centuries most hosiery knitting was done in the workers' own homes, but this practice gradually declined as workshops were estab-lished. The workshop building at Kegworth, of about 1840, is well preserved, though it is no longer used.
Location: 10½ miles SE of Derby on A6.

Keighley *W. Yorks.*   *Map: 391 Fb*
CLIFF CASTLE MUSEUM The museum is in a large 19th-century house which was once the home of the Butterfields, local cloth merchants.

The exhibits include three reconstructed craftsmen's workshops, among them one of a clog-maker.
Location: Spring Gardens Lane, NW of town centre.

Kellie Castle *Fife*   *Map: 389 Fe*
Kellie Castle is huge, with three towers joined to a central building to form the shape of a T. It was started in the 14th century, enlarged over the following 300 years and renovated in the second half of the 19th century.
   There are several fine 17th-century plaster ceilings, and the drawing room is decorated with landscapes painted on to the wooden panelling.
Location: 3 miles NW of Pittenweem (minor road, then W on A921).

Kellie Castle *Tayside*   *Map: 387 Fa*
The substantial tower house which looms above Elliot Water was laid out in the shape of an L in the 17th century, on the site of a fortress established some 500 years earlier.
Location: 2 miles W of Arbroath off B9127.

Kempsford *Glos.*   *Map: 398 Ad*
CHURCH OF ST MARY John of Gaunt, Duke of Lancaster and father of Henry IV, added the tower to the Norman church between 1385 and 1399. He had inherited the dukedom, and lands at Kempsford, through his wife Blanche.
Location: 11 miles SE of Cirencester (A419 then minor road).

Lake-fortress of Elizabeth I's suitor

KENILWORTH CASTLE, ONCE A STRONGHOLD OF KING JOHN, WAS GIVEN BY QUEEN ELIZABETH I TO HER "SWEET ROBIN" — ROBERT DUDLEY, EARL OF LEICESTER

RUINED SPLENDOUR *Parliamentary troops who occupied Kenilworth in the Civil War partly dismantled it and drained the lake. Its ruins remain impressive.*

When the barons forced King John to accept Magna Carta in 1215, they required him to hand over Kenilworth as part of the agreement. Their demand was understandable, for John had developed the castle into a formidable fortress.

A vast artificial lake protected Kenilworth on three sides and rendered it virtually impregnable, as followers of the rebel baron Simon de Montfort showed in 1266. They held the castle for nine months against the army of Henry III, and surrendered only through lack of food.

After 1361, when Kenilworth passed to John of Gaunt, the castle's owners concentrated more on equipping it for comfort than on defence. From 1563 Elizabeth's favourite, the Earl of Leicester, turned Kenilworth into a palace designed to impress the queen. (See also p. 206.)

QUEEN'S FAVOURITE
*Robert Dudley (c.1532–88)
was expected to marry Elizabeth I.
She gave him Kenilworth,
but not her hand.*

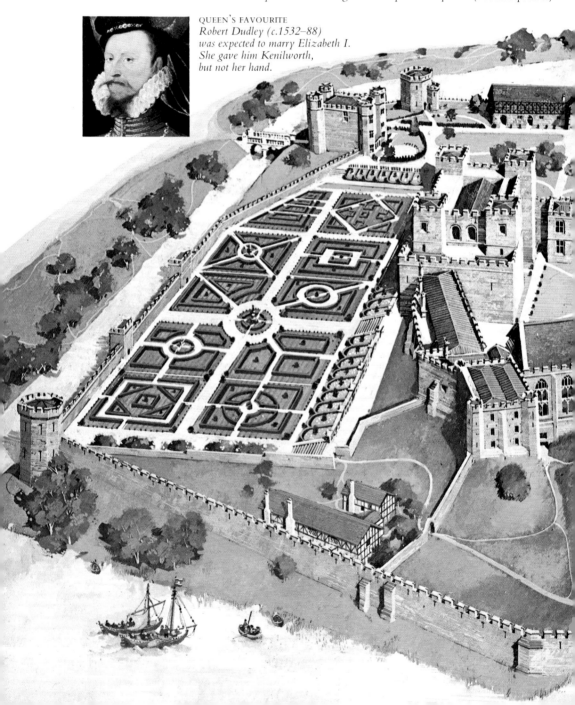

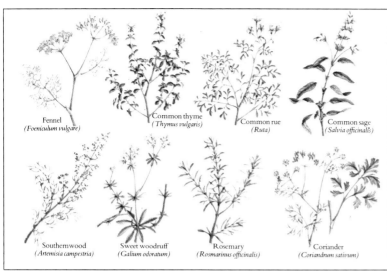

HERBS OF A TUDOR GARDEN

The English love of gardens as places of relaxation developed during the peace and prosperity of Elizabeth I's reign. Leicester's Garden at Kenilworth is typical of many of the period. Its beds, called knots, were laid out in geometrical patterns which followed Tudor fashions in house decoration. Plants were chosen for fragrance as well as for beauty, and included sweet-smelling herbs also valued as medicine and flavouring.

Fennel
(Foeniculum vulgare)

Common thyme
(Thymus vulgaris)

Common rue
(Ruta)

Common sage
(Salvia officinalis)

Southernwood
(Artemisia campestria)

Sweet woodruff
(Galium odoratum)

Rosemary
(Rosmarinus officinalis)

Coriander
(Coriandrum sativum)

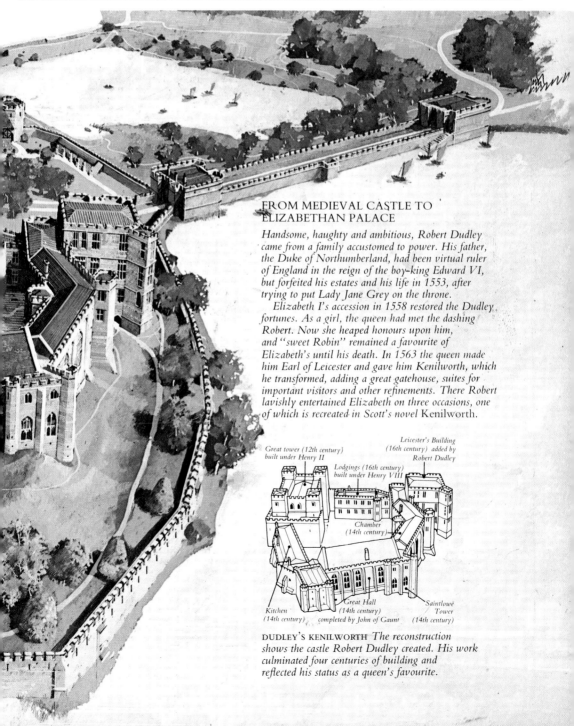

FROM MEDIEVAL CASTLE TO ELIZABETHAN PALACE

Handsome, haughty and ambitious, Robert Dudley came from a family accustomed to power. His father, the Duke of Northumberland, had been virtual ruler of England in the reign of the boy-king Edward VI, but forfeited his estates and his life in 1553, after trying to put Lady Jane Grey on the throne.

Elizabeth I's accession in 1558 restored the Dudley fortunes. As a girl, the queen had met the dashing Robert. Now she heaped honours upon him, and "sweet Robin" remained a favourite of Elizabeth's until his death. In 1563 the queen made him Earl of Leicester and gave him Kenilworth, which he transformed, adding a great gatehouse, suites for important visitors and other refinements. There Robert lavishly entertained Elizabeth on three occasions, one of which is recreated in Scott's novel Kenilworth.

Great tower (12th century) built under Henry II

Leicester's Building (16th century) added by Robert Dudley

Lodgings (16th century) built under Henry VIII

Chamber (14th century)

Kitchen (14th century)

Great Hall (14th century) completed by John of Gaunt

Saintlowe Tower (14th century)

DUDLEY'S KENILWORTH *The reconstruction shows the castle Robert Dudley created. His work culminated four centuries of building and reflected his status as a queen's favourite.*

VICTORIAN SEWING CORNER

An embroidery frame and treadle sewing-machine make up the sewing corner of a reconstructed Victorian/Edwardian farmhouse bedroom at Abbot Hall in Kendal. The dressing-table and chair show how slowly country tastes changed. They were made in the 19th century, but, apart from the flourishes on the mirror frame, they are in a style which first appeared 200 years earlier.

Kendal *Cumbria*   *Map: 391 Ec*
ABBOT HALL The stable block of the elegant house, built in 1759, contains a museum of Lakeland life and industry. A pre-1914 farmhouse has been re-created. Its rooms are decorated and furnished in styles of different periods. There are also sections devoted to printing, weaving and other local crafts.
Location: Town centre, next to parish church.

Kenfig Castle *Mid Glam.*   *Map: 392 Ca*
Little is now left of the castle, founded by the Normans in the 12th century. It was captured by Welsh rebels in 1295 and again in 1321, but there are no authentic records of its later history.
Location: 5 miles SE of Port Talbot (A48, B4283, then minor road).

Kenilworth Castle *Warks.*   *Map: 398 Bf*
Kenilworth's great tower was built on an earlier Norman motte in the 1160s and 1170s. King John added the curtain wall in the 13th century, and surrounded the castle with a broad artificial lake, drained after the Civil War. (See p. 204.)
Location: 5 miles N of Warwick (A429 and B4103).

Kennett Avenue *Wilts.*   *Map: 398 Ac*
Two lines of stones which make up the avenue run 1½ miles from the great henge at Avebury to the much smaller monument known as the Sanctuary at East Kennett. The stones were put up about 2000 BC, and there were originally some 100 pairs. (See p. 35.)
Location: Beside B4003 SE of Avebury.

Kensal Green *Greater London*   *Map: 399 Dc*
CEMETERY By the 1830s, the graveyards of most London churches were full to overflowing and a danger to public health. Commercial companies were formed to promote alternative places of burial – newly designed cemeteries in outer suburbs. Kensal Green, opened in 1833 and covering 56 acres, was one of the first.

The trend was bitterly attacked. Vicars, who faced the loss of burial fees, objected to the secular and pagan imagery used in many cemetery buildings and monuments. Others opposed the blatant commercialism of the promoters.

But many rich and famous people chose to be buried in cemeteries – among them the Duke of Sussex, who was interred at Kensal in 1843. And in 1850 Parliament passed a law creating public cemeteries. It also granted the monarch the power to order the closure of graveyards.

Those buried at Kensal Green after the 1850 law include the novelist Anthony Trollope (1882) and the engineer Isambard Kingdom Brunel (1859).
Location: Harrow Road (A404). Opposite Kensal Green Station, NW10.

Kent and East Sussex Railway see Tenterden

Ketton *Leics.*   *Map: 398 Cf*
CHURCH OF ST MARY St Mary's was built in the 13th and 14th centuries, and restored by the Victorian architect Sir Gilbert Scott. The Norman west doorway is a fine transitional work, done as the Gothic style was emerging.
Location: 3 miles SW of Stamford on A6121.

Kew *Greater London*   *Map: 398 Dc*
CHURCH OF ST ANNE Queen Anne gave land and £100 to build the yellow brick church in 1710–14. George III enlarged it in 1770 and again in 1805, when the gallery at the west end was added to accommodate his many relatives.
Location: Kew Green, off Kew Rd (A205).
KEW GARDENS Examples of more than 25,000 species and varieties of plants and trees grow in the 300 acre botanic gardens. Kew's link with botany dates from 1759, when Princess Augusta, mother of George III, set aside a section of the original Kew Palace grounds for experiments in cultivation. Other royal lands were merged into the gardens over the years.
Location: The main entrance is by Kew Green.
KEW PALACE The small brick mansion, built in 1631 for a merchant of Dutch descent and known for years as the Dutch House, became Kew Palace by default.

The original palace of 1730–5, which stood a few yards away, was a favourite retreat of George III. But he decided it was not grand enough and commissioned a new castle-like structure, also close at hand. While work on this was under way, he moved into the Dutch House.

After George's death in 1820, the original palace was pulled down. The half-finished new palace was demolished in 1827, leaving only the Dutch House.
Location: N corner of Kew Gardens.
PUMPING STATION Kew's pumping station supplied West London with drinking water from

STEAM GIANT

The 100 in. beam engine at Kew Pumping Station, installed in 1869, pumped 10 million gallons of water a day from the Thames.

1838 until 1944, and is now preserved, together with its five engines. The oldest is a Boulton and Watt of 1820, which is, with others, still steamed each weekend for visitors. (See p. 207.)

The 1869 beam engine, built by Harvey's of Hayle, has a cylinder with a diameter of 100 in., and is the largest of its kind in Britain.
Location: Kew Bridge Rd, N of Kew Bridge.

Kidsgrove *Staffs.*   *Map: 393 Fe*
HARECASTLE TUNNELS The engineer James Brindley started to cut the earliest of the three tunnels through Harecastle Hill in 1766, to carry the Trent and Mersey Canal. It was the first major canal tunnel to be attempted, and work on it took 11 years. It eventually collapsed early this century.

Thomas Telford built the second canal tunnel, which is still open, in 1824–7.

The Harecastle railway tunnel, which carried the line from Stoke, was closed in the 1960s after a century of use.
Location: 5½ miles NW of Hanley on A50. The tunnels begin 300 yds S of the railway station.

Kidwelly *Dyfed*   *Map: 392 Bb*
CASTLE Kidwelly is one of the two major concentric castles in South Wales, and was completed later than the other, Caerphilly. The inner quadrangle was built in the 1270s on a site first fortified by the Normans in the early 12th century.

In 1298 ownership of the castle passed by marriage to the House of Lancaster, and the outer walls were added shortly afterwards. They were so high that, to protect the soldiers manning them, the inner towers had to be raised by one storey.

Kidwelly's only serious engagement in warfare came in 1403, when a mixed force of Welsh, French and Bretons under Owain Glyndwr attacked it, setting fire to the gatehouse and causing damage which cost nearly £600 to repair.
Location: 9 miles NW of Llanelli off A484.

Kiessimul Castle *Western Isles*   *Map: 386 Ab*
Kiessimul, one of the earliest medieval stone castles in Scotland, stands on a rocky offshore island. For centuries it was the stronghold of the piratical Clan MacNeil of Barra, and was restored from 1938 by one of their American descendants.
Location: Ferry from Oban or Lochboisdale to Castlebay, Barra, then ferry to castle.

Kilbarchan *Strathclyde*   *Map: 388 Cd*
WEAVER'S COTTAGE The cottage, rebuilt in 1723, was used for weaving until 1940 and is now a museum. One of the original looms is in working order.

Household items and tools associated with weaving are displayed, with examples of the cloths, including tartans, which were made there.
Location: 12 miles W of Glasgow (A737 then A761 and minor roads).

Kildalton *Islay, Strathclyde*   *Map: 388 Aa*
CELTIC CROSS Biblical scenes carved on to the free-standing cross are still very clear after more than 1,000 years' exposure to wind and weather. One shows Abraham preparing to sacrifice Isaac. The cross was put up in the 8th century.

Location: 7½ miles NE of Port Ellen (A846 then minor roads).

Kildrummy Castle *Grampian*   *Map: 387 Eb*
Kildrummy, now ruined, is a rare Scottish example of an enclosure with towers in all the angles of the walls and a huge twin-towered gatehouse. It was built towards the end of the 13th century, and has features in common with English castles constructed in Wales in the same period.

In 1306 Nigel, brother of Robert Bruce, held Kildrummy against the English for weeks. He was betrayed by his blacksmith, Osborne, who started a fire which forced the garrison to yield, in return for as much gold as he could carry. The English duly paid – by pouring the molten metal down his throat.
Location: 18½ miles SW of Huntly on A97.

Kildwick *W. Yorks.*   *Map: 391 Fb*
CHURCH OF ST ANDREW The "Lang Kirk", so called because it is 145 ft long, dates mainly from the 14th and 15th centuries.

An earlier church once stood on the site, and the base of a pier in the south aisle is an inverted Norman capital from it. There are fragments of Saxon crosses in the south aisle.

The church owns the Kildwick Cope, a vestment made from an embroidered bridal skirt smuggled out of the Imperial Palace in Peking in 1947.

The village stocks, outside the church, were last used in 1858.
Location: 5 miles NW of Keighley on A629.

Kilpeck *Heref. & Worcs.*   *Map: 393 Eb*
CHURCH OF ST MARY AND ST DAVID Part of the nave wall is Saxon, but the rest of the church is mainly 12th-century Norman.

The stonework is richly carved, inside and out. Under the eaves, it is decorated with more than 70 grotesque heads, and depictions of animals and birds. The south doorway bears dragons, animals and soldiers.
Location: 8½ miles SW of Hereford off A465.

Kindrochit Castle *Grampian*   *Map: 387 Eb*
Robert I of Scotland had a residence at Kindrochit in the 14th century. Sir Malcolm Drummond fortified it about 1390, turning it into one of the biggest tower houses in Scotland.

By 1618, the castle was a total ruin. How it became so is a mystery. Local legend says the inhabitants contracted plague and were walled in by the people of nearby Braemar, who then bombarded Kindrochit with cannons. But excavations have failed to produce evidence to support the tale.
Location: S of Braemar off A93.

King's Lynn *Norfolk*   *Map: 395 Ea*
GUILDHALLS Two types of guild flourished in medieval England. Merchant guilds, which were formed to help their members in times of need, recruited people from many occupations. The specialised craft guilds drew people from only one trade or occupation, and existed to protect their commercial interests.

Holy Trinity was the most important of the merchant guilds in King's Lynn. The mayor was elected from its members, and it took responsibility for the town defences. Its 15th-century hall is now part of the Town Hall.

The merchant Guild of St George was founded in 1406. Its hall, with warehouses behind and a crypt below, was restored in the 1940s and re-opened in 1951 as a theatre, a function that the building has performed more than once during the past.

After the suppression of the guilds in the 16th century, the hall was used for dramas presented by travelling companies of players. In 1766 a proper playhouse was built within the hall. It closed in 1814.
Location: St George's Guildhall, Queen St. Holy Trinity Guildhall, King St. Both town centre.

King's Sutton *Northants.* *Map: 398 Be*
CHURCH OF ST PETER AND ST PAUL The 14th-century spire, 198 ft high, is one of the finest in the county. Inside, the church has a plain stone Norman font fashioned from an earlier Saxon one. The plaster monument to Thomas Freke (died 1769) shows Christ in triumph above a skeleton, symbolising resurrection.
Location: 4½ miles SE of Banbury off A41.

Kingston upon Hull *Humberside* *Map: 394 Dd*
TOWN DOCKS MUSEUM In the 17th and 18th centuries, Hull fishermen sailed the northern waters around Greenland and Spitsbergen in search of whales, a valuable source of oil for use in lamps and as a lubricant.

The tools of the whale fisherman's dangerous trade are displayed in one section of the museum. Another is devoted to the history and techniques of trawling.

The museum is housed in the former Docks Office, a 19th-century domed building which was once the hub of the town docks complex, begun in the 1770s and closed in 1969.
Location: Queen Victoria Sq. in town centre.
WILBERFORCE HOUSE The 17th-century home of the Wilberforce family, Hull merchants, has been linked to two adjoining Georgian houses to form a museum commemorating William Wilberforce (1759–1833), whose efforts led to the abolition of the slave trade.

Relics connected with slavery are on show in one room, and other rooms are furnished in period style.
Location: High St, E of city centre.

King's Weston *Avon* *Map: 393 Ea*
ROMAN VILLA The remains of the villa, built between AD 270 and 300, consist of two wings linked by a corridor. One room has a hypocaust, an under-floor-heating system, and there are two mosaics and a small bath suite.
Location: King's Weston Av., 1 mile SW of Avonmouth off B4054.

Kingswood *Warks.* *Map: 398 Af*
KINGSWOOD JUNCTION A 220 yd branch canal, opened in 1802, links the Stratford-on-Avon Canal to the Grand Union. The junction comes half-way up the Lapworth flight of locks on a section of the Stratford Canal which was restored by volunteers in 1964, the first such restoration in England.

A lock gives access to the branch. Beside it, there is a small barrel-vaulted lock-keeper's cottage of a type found only on the Stratford

Canal. The bridge across the tail of the lock is split into two sections, an arrangement which allowed the tow rope to pass through in the days when canal boats were pulled by horses.
Location: 7½ miles NW of Warwick (A41 then B4439).

Kingussie *Highland* *Map: 387 Db*
HIGHLAND FOLK MUSEUM Tools, clothes, furniture and other items which illustrate the life of the inhabitants of Scotland's highlands and islands until well into this century are preserved in the museum.

Its buildings include a Georgian shooting lodge, a water-driven mill and a reconstructed Lewis blackhouse – a long, low thick-walled cottage which was the home of a farmer in the Western Isles. The earliest blackhouses were made from turf, which contrasted with "white houses" of stone.
Location: 12 miles SW of Aviemore on A9.

Kinlet *Salop* *Map: 393 Fd*
CHURCH OF ST JOHN THE BAPTIST A Norman church on the site was rebuilt and enlarged in the 12th and 13th centuries.

St John's has several monuments with alabaster effigies. One of them, to Sir George and Lady Blount, members of a prominent local family, echoes a medieval tradition, though it was not raised until 1584. It shows two figures kneeling under a canopy while below them, visible through arches, is the replica of a corpse.
Location: 9 miles S of Bridgnorth on B4363.

Kinnairds Head *Grampian* *Map: 387 Fc*
LIGHTHOUSE The lighthouse, built in the tower of a 16th-century castle in 1787, was the first to be set up in Scotland by the Commissioners of Northern Lights.
Location: N of Fraserburgh town centre.

Kinneil House *Central* *Map: 389 De*
Dr John Roebuck, founder of the Carron Ironworks, famed for its cannons, called carronades, lived at Kinneil from about 1760. The steam pioneer James Watt (1736–1819) obtained a patent for his pumping-engine with Roebuck's assistance, and started to build the first full-scale model of it in an outhouse on the estate in 1769.

The outhouse is preserved as a memorial to Watt's efforts, and has a cylinder from one of his engines.
Location: 1 mile W of Bo'ness on A904.

Kirby Hall *Northants.* *Map: 398 Cf*
Inigo Jones modernised the original Elizabethan house in 1638–40 for Christopher, 1st Baron Hatton of Kirby, a high official in the court of Charles I. Hatton's descendants allowed it to fall into decay during the 19th century, and it is now only a shell, set in fine rose gardens.
Location: 11 miles NE of Kettering off A43.

Kirby Muxloe Castle *Leics.* *Map: 398 Bf*
The brick-built, rectangular fortified manor house was begun in 1480 by William, Lord Hastings, a favourite of Edward IV. But Edward's successor, Richard III, suspected Hastings of plotting against him, and had the nobleman seized and executed in 1483.

Kirby Muxloe was never completed. Its building records have, however, been preserved. One item shows that the master mason in charge of the work was paid 8 pence a day.
Location: 4 miles W of Leicester (A47, B5418).

Kirkcaldy *Fife*   *Map: 389 Ee*
MCDOUALL STUART MUSEUM John McDouall Stuart (1815–66) explored vast regions of Australia in six expeditions. He was the first explorer to reach the centre of the continent, and the first to cross it from north to south and back again. His birthplace is now a memorial to his achievements.
Location: Rectory Lane, Dysart, 1½ miles NE of Kirkcaldy.

Kirkcudbright *Dumfs. & Gall.*   *Map: 390 Be*
BROUGHTON HOUSE The impressionist painter E. A. Hornel (1864–1933) left the 17th–18th-century mansion in trust as a public art gallery and library. The works on show include 40 by Hornel himself.
Location: 12 High St, W of town centre.
MACLELLAN'S CASTLE The town provost, Sir Thomas Maclellan, built the fortified mansion in the 1570s, using stones from a derelict convent.
Location: Town centre.

Kirkdale *N. Yorks.*   *Map: 394 Ce*
MINSTER CHURCH OF ST GREGORY A Saxon called Orm, the son of Gamal, rebuilt the church in 1060 from the ruins of a 7th-century monastery, according to a sundial above the south door. The tower was added in 1827, over a Saxon arch which is only 2 ft 6 in. wide.
Location: 8¼ miles W of Pickering off A170.

Kirk Hammerton *N. Yorks.*   *Map: 391 Gb*
CHURCH OF ST JOHN THE BAPTIST The Saxon tower, nave and chancel were built in the 1060s. The church was enlarged in 1891.
Location: 10 miles NW of York off A59.

Kirkoswald *Cumbria*   *Map: 391 Ed*
CHURCH OF ST OSWALD King Oswald of Northumbria converted the villagers to Christianity in the 7th century. The church named after him has traces of Norman work. The bell-tower stands away from the main building, on top of a hill.
Location: 9½ miles NE of Penrith (A6 then B6413).

Kirkoswald *Strathclyde*   *Map: 390 Af*
SOUTER JOHNNIE'S COTTAGE In 1775, the 17-year-old Robert Burns was sent to Kirkoswald to improve his mathematics. There he met the village shoemaker, John Davidson, whom he later immortalised as "Souter Johnnie" in his poem *Tam o' Shanter*.
Davidson's thatched cottage is preserved as a museum. Inside are cobblers' tools, family relics and a bill showing that, in Burns's day, the cost of soling and heeling a pair of boots was 1s 9d.
Location: 4½ miles SW of Maybole on A77.

Kirkwall *Mainland, Orkney*   *Map: 387 Ee*
BISHOP'S PALACE AND EARL PATRICK'S PALACE The 12th-century Bishop's Palace, extensively rebuilt by Bishop Robert Reid about 1545, was acquired by Robert Stewart, Earl of Orkney, in 1568.

His son, Patrick, added a magnificent Renaissance palace near by, and then linked the two in a vast fortified complex.
From there, he ruled despotically over Orkney, imposing harsh taxes to finance his taste for high living.
After complaints from the oppressed citizens, Patrick was brought to trial in Edinburgh in 1609. His properties were confiscated. In 1614 he was implicated in a plot to recapture them, and was executed after a few days' delay to allow him to learn the Lord's Prayer.
Location: City centre.
ST MAGNUS CATHEDRAL Magnus Erlendsson, to whom the red and yellow sandstone cathedral is dedicated, shared the Earldom of Orkney in the early 12th century with his cousin Haakon. Ill-feeling developed between the two, and Haakon had Magnus murdered on the island of Egilsay about 1117.
The dead earl was canonised by popular acclaim. His nephew and eventual successor, Earl Rognvald, raised the cathedral in Magnus's honour from 1137.
Location: Broad St, city centre.
TANKERNESS HOUSE A 16th-century merchant's mansion, built round a courtyard, the house is now a museum depicting Orkney life over the past 4,000 years.
Location: Broad St, city centre.

Kirkwhelpington *Northld.*   *Map: 391 Fe*
CHURCH OF ST BARTHOLOMEW The parish church, mainly 13th century, was once much larger, with transepts and aisles, but these have disappeared.
On the north side of the churchyard is the grave of Sir Charles Parsons (1854–1931), pioneer of the steam-turbine.
Location: 21 miles NW of Newcastle upon Tyne off A696.

Kirriemuir *Tayside*   *Map: 387 Ea*
BARRIE'S BIRTHPLACE James Barrie (1860–1937), the novelist and playwright who created Peter Pan, spent the first eight years of his life in the two-storey weaver's cottage, now restored to look as it did when he was a child.
Barrie's earliest efforts at drama were acted out in the wash-house behind the cottage. The price of admission was pins, a marble or a top.
Location: 9 Brechin Rd, off B957, NE of town centre.

Kit's Coty House *Kent*   *Map: 399 Ec*
Kit's Coty House, a New Stone Age tomb, has been virtually destroyed by treasure-seekers and by ploughing over the centuries. Nothing is left of its covering barrow and only three of the stones which formed the chamber remain.
A second tomb, Little Kit's Coty, 400 yds to the south, has been reduced to a jumbled heap of about 20 stones.
Location: 3½ miles N of Maidstone off A229.

Knapton *Norfolk*   *Map: 395 Gb*
CHURCH OF ST PETER AND ST PAUL The mainly 14th-century church has a massive double hammer-beam roof, added in 1503–4, and decorated with 160 carved angels and other figures. The roof is 73 ft long and about 30 ft wide.
Location: 8½ miles SE of Cromer (B1159 and B1145).

Knaresborough *N. Yorks.*   *Map: 391 Gb*
CASTLE Knaresborough's 12th-century great tower, set between two baileys, was demolished in about 1310 by Edward II, who replaced it with a larger one at a cost of more than £2,000.

Parliamentary troops reduced the castle to a ruin after the Civil War.
Location: Castlegate, SW of town centre.
CHURCH OF ST JOHN THE BAPTIST Work of all medieval periods from the 12th century appears in the church. The north chapel contains monuments to the Slingsby family, including one for the Cavalier Sir William Slingsby (died 1634), which shows him standing cross-legged holding a shield emblazoned with the family arms and resting his elbow on the hilt of his sword.
Location: Junction of Church Lane and Vicarage Lane SW of town centre.

Knebworth House *Herts.*   *Map: 398 Dd*
Edward Bulwer-Lytton (1803–73), the writer and politician, inherited the house from his mother, whose family had lived there since 1492. He transformed it into a Gothic mansion, adding battlements, heraldic symbols and gargoyles.

Bulwer-Lytton entertained many of his fellow-writers, including Charles Dickens and the novelist Wilkie Collins, at Knebworth. Letters from Dickens are displayed in the study.
Location: 6 miles S of Hitchin off B656.

Knightshayes Court *Devon*   *Map: 397 Ec*
The red sandstone mansion, set in beautiful gardens, was built in 1869–71 for John Heathcoat-Amory, Liberal MP for Tiverton. It was designed by William Burges, the architect who restored Cardiff Castle, but he was sacked for extravagance before he could carry out his lavish plans for the interior.

Heathcoat-Amory's grandfather, John Heathcoat, patented a bobbin net machine for making lace in 1808. His factory in Loughborough was wrecked in 1816 by the Luddites, who felt that the machines threatened their jobs, and Heathcoat moved the business to nearby Tiverton.
Location: 2 miles NE of Tiverton on minor roads.

Knole *Kent*   *Map: 399 Ec*
Thomas Bourchier, Archbishop of Canterbury, bought Knole in 1456 from William Fiennes, whose great-grandfather, Lord de Say, had acquired the estate in the previous century.

The archbishop paid £266 13s 4d for a jumble of medieval buildings which he set about converting into a palace worthy of his position.

FABRICS FIT FOR A STUART KING

The 17th-century furnishing fabrics in the state rooms at Knole, Kent, are rare surviving examples of their period. Many were woven on the looms of Italy, France and Flanders for the Stuart kings, and the materials used – velvet, silk, silver thread – are worthy of a monarch.

The most luxurious fabric of all is the gold and silver cloth which adorns the King's Bed, constructed in 1670–80 for the future James II, then Duke of York, at a total cost of £7,000. The material was probably woven in Lyons, and no other examples of it have survived.

CUSHION *Appliqué of kid covered with silver thread decorates a velvet cushion on a chair of state.*

CHAIR SEAT *The development of upholstery during the 17th century added beauty and comfort to chairs and stools in the homes of the wealthy. Sumptuous velvets from the workshops of Genoa were in wide demand throughout Europe as chair-covering material, and they were often decorated in the elaborate curlicued patterns of the Baroque style. The blue-green Genoa velvet seat covering above is on a chair in the Cartoon Gallery, Knole. It has a matching silk trim.*

CARPET *The thick weave and velvet-like finish of the carpet are typical of Turkey work, a style which originated in the East but was extensively copied in 17th-century England.*

211

So splendid was Bourchier's creation that in 1538, when a later archbishop, Thomas Cranmer, was in residence, it attracted the greedy eyes of Henry VIII.

The king forced the reluctant Cranmer to hand Knole over, and spent lavishly on improvements. But Henry is only known to have stayed there once afterwards.

After Henry's death, Elizabeth I granted Knole to Robert Dudley, Earl of Leicester, who became embroiled in disputes over sub-letting. He eventually returned the property to the queen, and in 1566 she gave it to her wealthy cousin, Thomas Sackville, Lord Treasurer of England. However, there was a tenant in the palace and Thomas did not manage to get him out until 1603. The Sackville family has lived in Knole since then.

Thomas Sackville embellished the outside of Bourchier's palace with curved gables surmounted by his family emblem, a leopard, and remodelled the inside in the grandest manner.

The layout of Knole's many rooms illustrates the way in which the house of an important man in the 15th and 16th centuries was both a home and a symbol of power and wealth.

The lord and his family lived, as they still do at Knole, in low-ceilinged, simply furnished apartments on the ground floor. The suite of state rooms on the first floor, approached by the Great Hall and the Painted Staircase, was designed to impress visitors as they made their way through galleries hung with rich tapestries, past liveried retainers, to the presence of their host.

Charles Sackville, 6th Earl of Dorset, was Lord Chamberlain to William and Mary in the 17th century. His position entitled him to the state furniture of the previous monarch, and that is why there are at Knole two state beds of James II and royal chairs and footstools in the galleries. The hangings and coverings of velvet, damask and silver embroidery are original.

Knole, with its seemingly random mixture of courtyards and towers, is often said to be more like a village than a house, and like a village it was, in its heyday, self-supporting. A document preserved in the house lists the names and duties of 119 servants and craftsmen who sat down daily to dinner there in 1613.

They included Henry Keble, Yeoman of the Pantry, who dined at the Clerks' Table; and John Marockoe, a blackamoor, who ate with Diggory Dyer and Marfidy Snipt at the Kitchen and Scullery Table.
Location: Off S end of Sevenoaks High St (A225).

Knowlton Circles *Dorset*   *Map: 398 Ab*
Ancient man laid out the three circular henge monuments, religious sites surrounded by earth banks and ditches, in a line some 4,000 years ago.

Only the central one is well preserved. Within it are the ruins of a Norman church.
Location: 3 miles SW of Cranborne on B3078.

OLD AND NEW RELIGIONS

During the 12th century, the Normans built a church now ruined, within one of three 4,000-year-old henge "temples" at Knowlton, Dorset – perhaps to show the ascendancy of Christianity over the old religion. The ivy-clad tower and bush-choked, roofless nave stand on a spot occupied during the Bronze Age by a circle of timber posts or standing stones, in which human victims may have been sacrificed.

L

Lacock Abbey *Wilts.*　　　　*Map: 398 Ac*
An oriel window in the south gallery at Lacock
was the subject in August 1835 of the world's
oldest surviving photographic negative, now on
display in the house. It was made by a former
owner, William Henry Fox Talbot, whose
experiments laid the foundations of modern
photography.

The large country house was converted in
1539 from an Augustinian nunnery of 1232, and
has fine 13th–14th-century cloisters. The Great
Hall of 1754–5 is one of the earliest examples of
Gothic Revival architecture.
Location: 4 miles S of Chippenham off A350.

Laggan *Highland*　　　　*Map: 386 Cb*
CALEDONIAN CANAL The highest part of the canal
– the 1½ miles linking Loch Lochy and Loch Oich
– was excavated about 1810. The Laggan cutting,
over 50 ft deep, was dug partly by steam dredgers
but mostly by men with spades and pickaxes.
Location: 9 miles SW of Fort Augustus (A82).

Lambourn *Berks.*　　　　*Map: 398 Bc*
SEVEN BARROWS The Bronze Age (1800–650 BC)
cemetery has the remains of over 40 barrows, or
burial mounds. The biggest concentration is in
two parallel rows, each with six barrows.

The cemetery was looted by early anti-
quarians, who left little record of their discoveries. The remains of cremations have been
found in two barrows.
Location: 2½ miles N of Lambourn off B4001.

Lanark *Strathclyde*　　　　*Map: 388 Dd*
CLYDE BRIDGES The Cartland Bridge built by
Thomas Telford in 1822 carries the A73 across
Mouse Water. The three-arched Clydesholm
Bridge of 1699, which once carried the A72 over
the Clyde, was replaced by a single-arch span in
1958. Hyndford Bridge, another three-arched
bridge 2 miles south-east of Lanark, built in 1773,
now carries the A73 across the Clyde.

Lancaster *Lancs.*　　　　*Map: 391 Eb*
CASTLE The great tower of the castle was one of
the earliest in England, built probably in the 1100s
on the hilltop site of a Roman camp. It was
strongly fortified by King John, and was held for
him in his war with the barons in 1215.

The castle, much altered since medieval days,
has been used as a prison for centuries. The 19
Lancashire witches, accused, among other crimes,
of plotting to blow up the castle by magic, were
imprisoned and tried there in 1612; ten were
hanged.
Location: Castle Hill.
LUNE AQUEDUCT The stone-built aqueduct that
carries the Lancaster Canal 62 ft above the River
Lune is one of the finest in the country. Built by
John Rennie, it is 600 ft long and was completed
in 1797.
Location: 2 miles N of city centre on A683.
ST GEORGE'S QUAY From about 1750 until 1800,
when the Lune silted up, Lancaster was the chief
port for trade with the West Indies. Many old
stone warehouses line the quay, and the Customs

TUDOR BREW-HOUSE

*Brewing was a routine job in Tudor country houses,
for ale and beer were everyday drinks. There were
many varieties, such as cherry ale, spruce beer and
cock ale (sack and ale in which a cock had been
steeped). Children drank small beer – from a second
brewing after the strong beer had been drawn off.
Lacock Abbey has a well-preserved country-house
brewery, in use from the 16th to the 18th century.*

House of 1765 was built by Richard Gillow,
founder of the Lancaster furniture industry.
Location: S bank of river, near Carlisle Bridge.

Lanchester *Durham*　　　　*Map: 391 Db*
ROMAN ALTAR The fort of *Longovicium* was built
about AD 140. In the 3rd century the garrison
was a unit of Suebians, originally a Germanic
tribe, who built an altar to their goddess
Garmangabis. It is now in the porch of the
Church of All Saints.
Location: 7 miles NW of Durham on A691.

Lanercost Priory *Cumbria*　　　　*Map: 391 Ee*
The Augustinian priory, founded in 1169, was
built largely of stone taken from the nearby
Hadrian's Wall. The extensive remains include
the guest-house used by Edward I and King
Robert Bruce in the 14th century.
Location: 3 miles NE of Brampton off A69.

Langton-by-Spilsby *Lincs.*　　　　*Map: 395 Dc*
CHURCH OF ST PETER AND ST PAUL The small red-
brick church of 1725, with inward-facing pews
and a three-decker pulpit, still looks much the

VICTORIAN COUNTRY-HOUSE DAIRY

The Victorian kitchen quarters at Lanhydrock House, Cornwall, were designed to make sure that food was kept cool and fresh. The tiled, north-facing dairy (above right) had a marble slab in the middle of the room, with water from a spring on the hillside brought in and channelled to flow round the edge.

Utensils were cleaned and scalded in the dairy scullery (above left), where milk was delivered from the farm in large cans. Milk for making butter was first cooled in pans left to stand in slate troughs. The cream was then skimmed off and worked into butter by being rocked in the barrel churn.

same as it did when Dr Johnson attended there in the 18th century, when visiting a friend who lived near by.

The roof was stripped of lead in 1792, possibly to make bullets for the Napoleonic Wars.
Location: 9 miles E of Horncastle off A158.

Lanhydrock House *Cornwall*   *Map: 396 Bb*
The Jacobean house completed in 1642 for Lord Robartes was gutted by fire in 1881, only the gate-house and long gallery surviving. When rebuilding was completed in 1884, the interior had been remodelled in Victorian style.

The house still retains an elaborate complex of Victorian service rooms – still-room (for storing preserves), bakehouse, meat, fish and game larders – complete with their original fittings. To keep food hot, an iron hot-cupboard in the serving-room adjoining the dining-room was heated by hot-water pipes.
Location: 2½ miles SE of Bodmin off B3268.

Lanyon Quoit *Cornwall*   *Map: 396 Aa*
The 90 ft long barrow (burial mound) is the best preserved in Cornwall, where they are uncommon. It was originally built about 2500 BC, but the stone burial chamber at the northern end – a huge granite slab on three upright stones – was completely rebuilt in 1824.
Location: 3 miles NW of Penzance off B3312.

Lastingham *N. Yorks.*   *Map: 394 Cf*
CHURCH OF ST MARY Monks from Lindisfarne founded a monastery at Lastingham in 654. A later Saxon church was destroyed by Danish raiders in the 8th and 9th centuries. The Normans partly rebuilt it in 1078, but abandoned it ten years later, and it became the parish church. There are several fragments of Saxon carving in the crypt.
Location: 6 miles NW of Pickering off A170.

Launceston *Cornwall*   *Map: 396 Cc*
CASTLE Robert of Mortain, the brother of William the Conqueror, was given the earldom of Cornwall after the conquest of 1066, and built himself a motte-and-bailey castle at Launceston. The stone round tower and shell keep were built in the 12th–13th centuries.

George Fox, the founder of the Society of Friends (Quakers), was arrested for distributing religious tracts, and imprisoned in the castle in 1656.
Location: Town centre.
CHURCH OF ST MARY MAGDALENE The large church built of Cornish granite in 1511–24 is profusely decorated with carvings. It is attached to the tower of a 14th-century church.

The carvings include a group of minstrels with musical instruments such as the rebec and lute (on the east wall). They are said to represent the St Mary Minstrels of about 1440, who were noted in the district.
Location: Church St, town centre.

Lavenham *Suffolk*   *Map: 399 Fe*
CHURCH OF ST PETER AND ST PAUL One of the most splendid churches in Suffolk, built mainly about 1480–1530 by the wealthy clothiers of the town.

A tiny brass monument of 1631 in front of the altar rails shows an infant in a "chrisom" robe, signifying that he died before his mother could be churched – that is, attend thanksgiving after childbirth.
Location: Church St.
GUILDHALL When the half-timbered Tudor Guildhall was built in 1529, Lavenham had been a prosperous centre of the wool trade for more than 100 years. Many timber-framed buildings, once the homes of clothiers and weavers, still cluster around it.

The Guildhall was built as a business and social centre by the Guild of Corpus Christi, which controlled wages, prices and work standards in the local cloth trade. Members ranged from merchants and employers to wage-earning craftsmen and apprentices, although the employers controlled most of the policy. Guilds helped their members in sickness and old age, and also regulated their religious lives.

Lavenham's blue cloth was famous in its day. It was stamped with a fleur-de-lys trademark – this attested that the cloth had been passed by a tax official as conforming to the standard length and breadth. The fleur-de-lys trademark, like many other features of the trade, was introduced by Flemish weavers who had been invited to settle in England by Edward III. They taught Englishmen the secrets of their craft.

The wool trade in the area had already begun to decline when the Guildhall was built, partly because of the rise of the worsted wool industry in Norfolk, partly because of the restrictive practices of the guilds, which failed to adapt to new ideas. It was also hastened by the development of fulling machines.

Fulling was a process by which the cloth was soaked and pounded into a felted broadcloth. At first pounding had been done by foot, but fulling machines pounded the cloth with hammers powered by water-wheels. So the trade drifted to rural areas, particularly the West Country with its fast-running streams.

The Guildhall became a town hall and then a gaol, so poorly maintained that prisoners could sometimes kick their way out through the crumbling walls. In 1555 Dr Rowland Taylor, rector of Hadleigh and Archbishop Cranmer's chaplain, was imprisoned there for two days before being burned at the stake, one of the many Protestant clergy executed by Mary I.

Today the Guildhall contains weaving exhibitions, including examples of horsehair weaving carried out during the 1914–18 war, when workers had looms in their own cottages in the same way as their medieval predecessors. The cellars that once housed the guild's wine butts now have an exhibition of the tools and techniques of the cooper's trade.
Location: Market Place, town centre.
LITTLE HALL A 15th-century clothier's house with a high, open-timbered hall, now the headquarters of the Suffolk Preservation Society.
Location: Market Place.

THE FIGHT AGAINST FIRE

In the days of timber and thatch houses, with open fires and rush lights, fire was a constant risk. One of the earliest fire precautions was the curfew – from the French *couvre feu* (cover fire) – ordered by William the Conqueror. The evening curfew bell was the signal for fires to be doused. Edward I (1272–1307) ordered town watchmen to be on duty at night in case of fire.

For centuries there was no means of quenching flames other than with buckets of water. Ladders, buckets and grappling hooks for pulling down burning thatch were kept in the church for parish use. If necessary, houses on the perimeter of a fire were pulled down to prevent it spreading.

Even at the time of the Great Fire of London in 1666, which raged for three days, destroyed more than 13,200 houses and left perhaps 80,000 people homeless, the chief fire-fighting machine was a three-man metal syringe about 3 ft long that had to be filled from a bucket, then squirted at the flames.

Fire-engines were in use in the 17th century, mainly on the Continent, but were not very successful. But in the 1720s, Richard Newsham of London invented a hand-operated fire-engine commonly used in Britain for the next 200 years. It carried flexible leather hoses – a Dutch invention introduced by William III (1688). Such an engine is on show at Lavenham (below). To add to the pumping power, men could also stand aboard the larger engines and work foot treadles.

The first fire brigades were raised by the fire-insurance companies that came into being after the Great Fire. By the start of the 1800s most brigades had large, horse-drawn engines, and steam-powered pumps, still horse-drawn, became general in the 1860s.

FIREFIGHTERS OF 1805
Uniformed fire brigades run by fire-insurance companies fought fires on property they had insured – identified by a wall plaque. Bystanders helped with the pumping.

LAVENHAM'S 18TH-CENTURY FIRE-ENGINE

When the old fire station in Lady Street, Lavenham, was demolished in 1954, the fire-engine of 1725 was put on display in the Guildhall. It was of a type invented by Richard Newsham of London. Two pumps were immersed in a wooden trough filled by buckets or hose, and operated by levers at each side.

Laxey *Isle of Man*　　　　*Map: 390 Bc*
GIANT WATER-WHEEL In 1854 lead-mining was one of the Isle of Man's chief industries, and pumping water from the Laxey mine was becoming difficult as the depth of shafts increased. There was no coal near by to fuel steam pumps, so it was decided to use water power instead.

A 72 ft diameter water-wheel was built, the biggest in Europe at that time. It was capable of lifting 240 gallons of water a minute from a depth of 1,200 ft, and was in operation until 1929. It still turns for visitors, but does not pump.
Location: 9 miles NE of Douglas off A2.

Laxton *Notts.*　　　　*Map: 394 Cb*
OPEN-FIELD VILLAGE For about 1,200 years, the fields of Laxton have been farmed in scattered strips by individual farmers–a system once common in England but which gradually disappeared as land was enclosed under private ownership.

The farmhouses are closely grouped along the main street, and many of the buildings date back to the mid-18th century. In early medieval times, each farmer probably farmed about 30 acres–perhaps in as many as 100 strips that were equally divided between about three fields.

The ancient strip system ensured that each farmer had a fair share of good and poor land, and was convenient for using the communally owned ploughs and draft oxen or horses.

In the 17th century, the average size of strips at

WHERE MEDIEVAL FARMS SURVIVE
Laxton is the only village in England where open fields are still worked in strips. Today there are three fields – West Field, South Field and Mill Field – totalling about 480 acres and divided into 167 strips. In 1625 there were about 1,300 acres in more than 2,000 strips. Some of the land was withdrawn from the system as freeholders exchanged strips to create small fields which they enclosed and owned privately. The map of Laxton above was prepared for the lord of the manor in 1635.

Laxton was half an acre–generally long and narrow, but length and breadth varied, depending on the lie of the land. By the end of the 19th century, strips had increased to about three-quarters of an acre–perhaps as the result of more efficient ploughs and the increasing use of horses, which could plough a bigger area each day than oxen. There was usually a three-year crop rotation system–winter-sown crops such as wheat, spring-sown crops such as barley, peas and beans, and a fallow area, used for grazing.

Each farmer also had strips in the common meadows for haymaking. The meadows were enclosed in the 18th century, but there are still grassed areas called sykes among the open fields. Until 1780 it was common to find animals tethered there to graze, but since then it has been the practice to leave the sykes ungrazed and to sell the grass by public auction.

Until the 1930s animals that strayed from the grazing areas were collected by an official known as the pinder and impounded in the village pinfold. Today, the pinder informs the owner of a stray animal and charges for its keep on his own land until it is collected.

The village land was owned mainly by the lord of the manor with the farmers as tenants. Strips, held by the same person year after year, were allocated by the lord of the manor and the Court Leet of village elders. Today the Ministry of Agriculture owns the manor and the Court Leet still administers the holdings, a jury of tenant farmers controlling the cropping and grazing. Display boards in the church and on the pinfold show the layout of the village.
Location: 4 miles E of Ollerton off A6075.

Layer Marney *Essex*　　　　*Map: 399 Fd*
CHURCH OF ST MARY THE VIRGIN The church was built early in the 16th century by Sir Henry Marney, at the same time as his house–Layer Marney Tower. It is a fine example of Tudor brickwork, and there is a Tudor fireplace in the Marney chapel containing the Marney tombs.
Location: 7 miles SW of Colchester off B1022.
LAYER MARNEY TOWER The massive brick and terracotta Tudor gatehouse is 80 ft high, the highest of its time. It was built about 1510 by Sir Henry Marney, privy councillor to both Henry VII and Henry VIII, and was intended as the entrance to a mansion. But the mansion was never completed, for Sir Henry died in 1523 and his only son died without an heir in 1525.
Location: 7 miles SW of Colchester off B1022.

Leadhills *Strathclyde*　　　　*Map: 390 Cf*
ALLAN RAMSAY LIBRARY Local lead miners who had formed a reading society set up the library in 1741. The oldest subscription circulating library in Britain, it was named after Allan Ramsay, poet and author of *The Gentle Shepherd*, who was born in the village in 1686. He ran a lending library from his bookshop in Edinburgh, and provided the idea for the Leadhills library and some of its first books.
Location: 6 miles SW of Abington on B797.
LEAD MINES The villages of Leadhills and Wanlockhead in the Lowther Hills were the centre of the Scottish lead-mining industry from about the 13th century to the early 20th century.

Remains of mining–such as spoil heaps and disused shafts, some dangerous to explore–can

TRADESMEN'S SHOPS OF OLD LEEDS

Cottages, workshops and shops dating from the late 18th and 19th centuries can be seen in three streets typical of old Leeds that have been reconstructed at the Abbey House Museum, Leeds. Most of the buildings are taken from the Leeds area, and have been rebuilt exactly as they were found.

The shops and workshops include a typical barber's shop of 1900 – John Mason, Gentlemen's Hair Cutter of Commercial Street – pictured above. Perfumes, wigs and tobacco were also sold there.

Abbey Fold is an example of one of the enclosed cobbled yards, or folds, surrounded by houses and workshops that developed during the Industrial Revolution. In Stephen Harding Gate and Harewood Square, the buildings have interiors typical of the 1880s. Stephen Harding Gate has a tollboard from the tollgate that once stood at the junction of York and Selby roads, Leeds. Tolls were paid according to the width of the wagon-wheel rim and the weight of goods carried.

TIN-TACK MAKER *Peter Gartside of Ashton-under-Lyne made tin tacks by hand in his workshop (left). They were for home use and for straightening fibres (carding) in cotton mills.*

CLAY-PIPE MAKER *Sampson Strong of Cottage Street made clay pipes in this workshop until 1953. Clay-pipe smoking was common from about 1600 until about 1850 when wooden pipes came into use.*

---

be seen all round the village. The track of the railway to Wanlockhead, abandoned in 1938, can be followed from the village centre. It had the highest summit level of any main-line rail track in Britain – 1,498 ft.
Location: 6 miles SW of Abington on B797.

Leeds *W. Yorks.*   *Map: 391 Gb*
ABBEY HOUSE MUSEUM Part of the building was once the gatehouse of the Cistercian Kirkstall Abbey, founded in 1152. After the abbey was dissolved in 1539, the last abbot, John Ripley, lived there until his death in 1568, and it remained a dwelling house until 1925.

Now the Abbey House is a museum of the life and work of the people of the region from the 12th century. It includes a costume collection and reconstructions of some streets of old Leeds.
Location: 2 miles NW of city centre off A65.

MIDDLETON COLLIERY RAILWAY A wooden-railed wagonway, authorised in 1758, took coal 3½

miles from the colliery to the growing population of Leeds. Later, iron rails were laid on stone sleepers, and the route included inclines where stationary steam-engines hauled up wagons.

John Blenkinsop, the colliery agent, introduced steam locomotives and a rack-and-pinion rail system. The locomotive *Salamanca*, designed by Matthew Murray in 1812, was the first commercially successful steam locomotive to run on rails. Later, standard-gauge rails were introduced, and today there is a seasonal weekend steam passenger service along the track.
Location: Tunstall Rd and Moor Rd junction, Hunslet.

Leeds Castle *Kent*   *Map: 399 Fc*
The castle takes its name from Ledian, or Leed, the chief minister of Ethelbert IV, King of Kent, who lived on the riverside site in the middle of the 9th century.

A stone castle was built there by the Normans,

and in 1278 it passed to royal ownership for 300 years. It was bought by Edward I's wife, Eleanor of Castile, and it was the favourite home of many other English queens. Most of the present building dates from the 13th century and later.
Location: 4 miles E of Maidstone off A20.

Leek *Staffs.* *Map: 393 Fe*
ALBION MILL In the 17th and 18th centuries, Leek was a centre of the silk thread industry. Albion Mill in Albion Street (off Compton Road, A520), built in 1815, is the best preserved of the mills where the silk was twisted. (It is still a working mill and not open to the public.)

The mills gradually replaced silk twisting by hand in workers' cottages. Such cottages in King Street (all private dwellings) can be recognised by the long windows of the upper floor, where workrooms were connected so that a good length of continuous thread could be worked.
BRINDLEY MILL James Brindley, a Leek millwright, was the engineer who built Britain's first canal for the Duke of Bridgewater in the 1760s. The stone-built watermill, now a Brindley Museum, was probably built by Brindley. It has a stone inscribed "TI 1752 JB". The mill was used for grinding grain until the 1940s, and was restored to working order in 1974.
Location: Mill St (A523).

Leicester *Leics.* *Map: 394 Ba*
ABBEY PUMPING STATION Until the second half of the 19th century, Britain's sewage was discharged directly into cesspools or rivers, often contaminating the water supply. A system of carrying sewage to special areas for treatment was developed in Victorian times, and pumping stations were built to maintain the flow.

The elaborate Victorian Abbey Pumping Station, with four massive beam-engines of 1891, is now the Leicestershire Museum of Technology. The engines can be seen working on "steaming" days.
Location: Corporation Rd, off Abbey Lane.
BELGRAVE HALL An early-18th-century house in a walled garden with herbaceous borders, the Hall is now a museum showing the main styles of English furniture in the 18th and 19th centuries. The stables house a museum of agriculture and a coach collection.
Location: 2 miles N of city centre on A6.
CASTLE John of Gaunt, Duke of Lancaster, who died in 1399, entertained lavishly in the 12th-century stone castle, built on the site of an earlier motte-and-bailey structure.

Little of the castle now remains. Parts of the Great Hall are incorporated in the Assize Courts, and Castle Yard was once the inner bailey. In the 17th century the castle was described to Charles I as ruinous, but the Parliamentarians managed to patch it up and use it as a fortress in the Civil War.
Location: Castle St, city centre.
GEORGIAN MILL Much of Leicester's prosperity in the 18th century was based on the textile industry, especially hosiery. The fine Georgian mill, now the Donisthorpe factory, was one of a number of cotton mills built to spin yarn for the stocking makers.

The mill backs on to the Grand Union Canal, and is best viewed from the open space beside Tudor Road on the opposite bank of the canal.
Location: Bath Lane, off Welles St.

ROMAN BATHS The Jewry Wall—no one knows the origin of the name—is a fine piece of Roman masonry 30 ft high. It formed part of a 2nd-century exercise hall for the town's public baths. Only the foundations of the rest of the baths remain.

Leicester was the Roman *Ratae*, the administrative centre of the Coritani tribe. Raw Dykes, an earthwork in Aylestone Road (A426), was possibly part of a Roman aqueduct system.
Location: St Nicholas's churchyard.

Leighton Buzzard *Beds.* *Map: 398 Cd*
CHURCH OF ALL SAINTS Medieval graffiti on the walls and pillars of the 13th-15th-century church include a picture of a man and woman, dressed in the style of about 1400, arguing. No one knows its origin, but it is believed to illustrate an old story of how the simnel cake got its name—Simon and Nell arguing then compromising over its preparation.

The church has a 191 ft high spire, and many stained-glass windows by C. E. Kempe, a noted 19th-century stained-glass artist.
Location: Church Sq.
LIGHT RAILWAY The 3½ mile industrial line, with a 2 ft gauge, was built in 1919 to carry sand, but work ceased in 1967. Now passengers are carried along the line, which has a number of short, steep gradients. There is also a collection of industrial steam and diesel locomotives, including *Chaloner*, built in 1877.
Location: Pages Park Station, ½ mile SE of Leighton Buzzard on A4146.

Leighton Hall *Lancs.* *Map: 391 Ec*
In the 19th century, the Hall was for a time the home of the Gillow family, well-known furniture manufacturers, and many pieces of their furniture are on show. The Georgian house was given a Gothic façade in the early 1800s.
Location: 3 miles N of Carnforth off A6.

Leith Hall *Grampian* *Map: 387 Fb*
The mid-17th-century house, built round a courtyard, was for nearly 300 years the home of the Leith family. Many of the Leiths had Jacobite sympathies, and there are a number of mementoes of Prince Charles Edward Stuart.
Location: 7 miles S of Huntly (A97, B9002).

Leominster Priory *Heref.* *Map: 393 Ec*
The three-naved parish church of St Peter and St Paul was part of a 12th-century Benedictine priory until the priory was dissolved in 1539. The church was badly damaged by fire in 1699, when sparks from a workmen's brazier set light to dried pea-haulm used as a packing under the lead of the south nave roof.

A ducking stool—once used to punish scolding women or dishonest tradesmen—is preserved in the church. It was last used in 1809 to duck a woman named Jenny Pipes in the river.
Location: The Priory, off Church St.

Lerwick *Mainland, Shetland* *Map: 387 Gd*
The Norse (or Viking) invaders of the 8th and 9th centuries ruled the Shetland Islands until the 15th century, and Lerwick—the most northerly town in Britain—takes its name from the Norse *Leir-vik*, which means clay creek.

The town grew up in the 17th century

through barter with Dutch fishing fleets. The houses in the older part have their foundations in the sea, with lodberries (from the old Norse *hlad-berg*, loading-rock) that enabled merchants to move cargoes directly from boat to warehouse.

On the last Tuesday in January is held the annual Up-Helly-Aa festival, when a 30 ft Norse longship is paraded through the streets by torch-light. It is then ceremonially burned – an ancient rite welcoming the return of the sun – and the whole night is spent in revelry.

Location: 25 miles N of Sumburgh on A970.

Levens Hall *Cumbria*   *Map: 391 Dc*
The park and gardens at Levens Hall, an Elizabethan mansion incorporating an earlier hall and pele tower, are still laid out to the original plan of 1690, and include massive topiary (shaped trees and shrubs).

The gardens were designed by Guillame Beaumont, a Frenchman trained by Le Nôtre at Versailles, who settled in England and died at Levens in 1727. In the former brewhouse there is a collection showing steam-power development.

Location: 5½ miles SW of Kendal off A6.

Lewes Castle *E. Sussex*   *Map: 399 Eb*
Much of the castle was pulled down in 1382 during local riots – their cause is unknown. It had originally been built in early Norman times and had two mounds with a bailey between. A shell keep was built in the 12th century, and the fine gatehouse in the 14th century.

Location: Off High St.

Lexden Tumulus *Essex*   *Map: 399 Fd*
The low mound was once thought to be the burial ground of Cunobelinus, king of the Belgae from about AD 5 to 40, and remembered as "Old King Cole" of the nursery rhyme. Colchester (Camulodunum) was his capital.

Recent research suggests, however, that it was one of his predecessors, Addedomarus, who was buried there in AD 1.

Location: Lexden Park, at S end of Fitzwalter Rd on W side of Colchester.

Lichfield *Staffs.*   *Map: 393 Gd*
CATHEDRAL The first wooden church on the site was founded in 700 to enshrine the body of St Chad, bishop of the Anglo-Saxon kingdom of Mercia from 669 to 672. A stone Norman cathedral was built to replace it between 1135 and 1140, but it was too small to accommodate the many pilgrims who came to visit St Chad's shrine. In 1195 it was taken down, piece by piece, as the present cathedral was begun.

The red sandstone cathedral is the only one in England with three spires – they are known as "the Ladies of the Vale". It was completed about 1340 and is mainly Early English and Decorated in architectural style.

St Chad's head, which at some period became detached from his body, was kept as a separate relic in the specially built Chapel of St Chad's Head begun in 1225. In the 14th century his shrine was moved to a central position in the newly built Lady Chapel, so that it could be more easily approached by pilgrims. A gallery was added to the Chapel of St Chad's Head so that the casket containing the saint's head could be held aloft for pilgrims to see.

St Chad's shrine was destroyed by Protestant extremists in 1541 during the Reformation. All that remains is a slab behind the High Altar.

Lichfield's Royalist supporters used the cathedral as a fortress in 1643 and 1646, during the Civil War. By coincidence, a siege by Parliamentarians was begun on St Chad's Day, March 2, and bombardment by a heavy cannon brought down the central tower and spire and smashed part of the roof. The Royalists capitu-lated and Parliamentary troops despoiled the building, which was more badly damaged than any other cathedral in England.

The cathedral was restored during the reign of Charles II and further restoration took place in the 18th and 19th centuries. The 16th-century stained glass in the Lady Chapel came from the dissolved Herckenrode Abbey in Belgium.

Location: Westgate, off Bird St.

LICHFIELD'S PRICELESS GOSPELS

The 8th-century illuminated Book of Gospels, handwritten in Latin, was acquired by the cathedral about 935, and has since been known as St Chad's Gospels. The page that is pictured above is the beginning of St Matthew's Gospel, and reads: Christus autem generatio sic erat cum esset – "Now the birth of Jesus Christ was on this wise: When . . ."

During the Civil War, St Chad's Gospels were saved from destruction by the cathedral precentor, Canon Walter Higgins, who smuggled them out of his house when he was expelled by Parliamentarians in 1646. The Gospels are now in the cathedral library; facsimiles can be seen on application to the Dean.

FINGERS WERE USED BEFORE FORKS

Until about 300 years ago, people in Britain ate mostly with their fingers, using spoons to eat soups and stews. Men and women usually carried their own knives for cutting meat from the joint.

Forks were used for serving, but they were not used for eating until introduced into fashionable circles from Italy in the early 1600s. They were not in common use until about 100 years later. Early forks had two long, sharp prongs and were probably used only to hold food while cutting.

By the late 1700s, most wealthier households had sets of cutlery for guests, and blunter, three-pronged forks were used. But well into the 1800s, many people carried a knife and fork in a case when travelling.

EATING KNIFE *The wooden-handled knife with a pointed steel blade dates from the early 1500s.*

Such knives were used for cutting meat.

WEDDING KNIVES *Until about the end of the 1600s, a woman usually carried knives in a sheath fixed to her girdle, and it was the custom for a bridegroom to present his bride with a pair.*

One of the pair shown is inscribed: "Anna Micklethwait Anno 1638". They have amber handles backed with cut foil and inlaid with ivory. The linen sheath is embroidered with silver-gilt thread.

KNIFE AND FORK *After forks had been introduced in the 1600s, matching pairs of knives and forks were manufactured. The pair shown, dated 1698, has ivory handles inlaid with silver wire.*

Tapering cylindrical handles became increasingly popular after 1650.

SCIMITAR BLADE *The shape of the knife blade changed during the 1600s. The point became rounded, and a scimitar shape developed, as in the travelling knife and fork of the late 1600s shown. During the 1700s the curve at the tip of the scimitar blade was often more pronounced.*

PISTOL-BUTT HANDLE *From 1700 until about 1800, pistol-shaped handles were popular. In good-quality cutlery, handles were often of porcelain, as in the pair shown – made between 1750 and 1775. Forks became three-pronged in the late 1700s.*

DR JOHNSON'S HOUSE The tall Queen Anne house, now a Johnson museum, was the birthplace in 1709 of Dr Samuel Johnson, writer, wit and compiler of a *Dictionary of the English Language*. His father kept a bookshop on the ground floor of the house.

Dr Johnson spent most of his first 28 years in the house before moving to London in 1737 to eke out a living as a writer. Money was always a problem, and he wrote *Rasselas* in one week in 1759 to pay for his mother's funeral.
Location: Breadmarket St, town centre.

FORKLESS INNS

In the 17th and 18th centuries travellers carried their own table cutlery because inns did not usually provide it. This matching set of a knife and two-pronged fork dates from about 1740 and was the travelling cutlery of Dr Johnson's wife Elizabeth, who was 20 years his senior. She died in 1752.

Limehouse *Greater London*   *Map: 399 Dc*
CHURCH OF ST ANNE The church's spectacular stone tower overlooks Limehouse Reach on the River Thames, and is a landmark of London's East End.

The church was built in 1714–30 by Nicholas Hawksmoor, Sir Christopher Wren's assistant, and was one of 50 churches ordered by the government to serve the capital's spreading suburbs. The interior was restored in 1851 after being gutted by fire.
Location: Junction of Commercial Rd and Newell St, E14. Key from 5 Newell St.

Lincoln *Lincs.*   *Map: 394 Cc*
CASTLE In 1068 William the Conqueror demolished 166 houses in Lincoln to make way for the castle. Two mottes were raised, and the shell keep was later built on one of them.

The 13th-century tower known as Cobb Hall was the site of a gallows from 1778 until 1859. The walls bear inscriptions scratched by prisoners confined in the tower.
Location: Castle Hill, near cathedral.
CATHEDRAL One of Britain's rare earthquakes rippled through Lincoln in 1185, and the tremors were sufficient to bring down most of the Norman cathedral that dominated the heart of the city. It had been established in 1072 on the site of a Saxon minster.

Hugh of Avalon, a French Carthusian monk, was appointed bishop by Henry II shortly after the cathedral collapsed. The Norman west front and two west towers were incorporated into the new cathedral that Hugh set about rebuilding in 1192. When he died in 1200 the choir and transepts were well advanced. Hugh was canonised in 1220, and the choir is now known as St Hugh's Choir. After Salisbury and Wells it is the earliest and finest example of Early English architecture in a cathedral.

The Dean's Eye, the great circular window at the north end of the Great Transept, dates from about 1220 and still has most of its original stained glass. It overlooks the gardens of the old deanery.

The polygonal (many-sided) Chapter House built 1220–35 by Bishop Robert Grosseteste was the first of this shape in Britain, and, with a diameter of 62 ft, the largest. Its flying buttresses were added in the 14th century. Edward I held several parliaments there, including the one in 1301 at which he created his 17-year-old son, Edward, Prince of Wales.

The central tower of the cathedral collapsed in 1237, killing some of the congregation.

According to Matthew Paris, a chronicler of the period, the fall occurred while a canon was delivering a bitter attack on Bishop Grosseteste – an unpopular though vigorous reformer – and had just exclaimed: "If we were to be silent, the very stones would cry out!"

By the time of his death in 1253, Bishop Grosseteste had rebuilt most of the tower. In the 14th century, all three towers were given spires. The central one, which soared to 524 ft, was blown down in 1548, the other two were removed in 1807.

The architectural glory of Lincoln Cathedral is the Angel Choir, built to house the shrine of St Hugh and accommodate the many pilgrims who visited it. The east end of St Hugh's Choir was pulled down to make way for the Angel Choir, which was consecrated in 1280.
Location: Eastgate, off Pottergate (A46).
HIGH BRIDGE The 12th-century bridge carries the High Street over the River Witham. On its west side there is a timber-framed 16th-century house standing over the water.
NEWPORT ARCH The only Roman archway still in use in Britain, the arch at the north end of Bailgate was the 3rd-century north gate of Roman Lindum (Lincoln). The road below it then was 8 ft lower than today.

Lindum was founded about AD 60 as a military fortress for the 9th Legion, and was succeeded by a town about 18 years later. Many stretches of the stone defences survive.
ST MARK'S STATION Built by the Midland Railway in 1846, the station has a classical façade with a portico of Ionic columns. Near by there is an unusual octagonal signal box.
Location: Off High St (A15).

Lindisfarne *Holy Island, Northld. Map: 389 Gd*
CASTLE The Tudor fortress on Beblowe Crag was built about 1550 to guard the harbour, where troops were landed on their way to deal with Border forays by the Scots. It was left to deteriorate after the union of the English and Scottish crowns in 1603, but restored in 1903 by Sir Edwin Lutyens.

Location: 10 miles SE of Berwick-on-Tweed off A1.

PRIORY Only a few inscribed stones remain of the monastery founded by St Aidan in 634, from where travelling monks spread Christianity to most parts of England. The monks left in 875 after the island had become vulnerable to Danish raiders, and finally settled at Durham.

The existing ruins are of a priory founded from Durham in 1093. It was dissolved in 1537, and then used for a time as a military storehouse.
Location: SW tip of island.

Lingfield *Surrey*   *Map: 399 Db*
CHURCH OF ST PETER AND ST PAUL The church was rebuilt in the 15th century by the 3rd Baron Cobham of Sterborough Castle, 2 miles away. The effigies or brasses on the tombs of the 1st baron (died 1361), the 2nd baron (died 1403) and the 3rd baron (died 1446) show the changes in the development of a knight's armour.
Location: 3½ miles N of East Grinstead.

Linlithgow *Lothian*   *Map: 389 Dd*
AQUEDUCT The stone aqueduct carrying the Union Canal over the River Avon was opened in 1822. It is 80 ft high and 800 ft long, and the water is held in an iron trough embedded in the stone.
Location: View from A706 bridge, 1½ miles SW of town centre.
PALACE The heavily fortified loch-side palace was begun by James I of Scotland in the 1420s, on the site of an earlier mansion. It was the birthplace of Mary, Queen of Scots in 1542, six days before the death of her father, James V. The palace was gutted by fire in 1746 while in use as a barracks.
Location: On S bank of loch, off A803.

Litcham *Norfolk*   *Map: 395 Fa*
CHURCH OF ALL SAINTS There is a fine rood screen of 1436, with panel paintings of 22 saints. They include a boy, William of Norwich, who was supposed to have been martyred by the Jews in the 12th century.
Location: 9 miles NE of Swaffham (A1065, B1145).

Little Billing *Northants.*   *Map: 398 Ce*
WATERMILL In medieval times, millers often paid their rent in cash and eels, so many mills had an eel trap. Billing Mill, built in the late 18th century, is now a museum of corn milling, and has an eel trap with a sluice gate operated from the water-wheel.
Location: 3 miles E of Northampton off A45.

Littlecote House *Wilts.*   *Map: 398 Bc*
The Tudor manor house of 1490–1520 became the home of Sir John Popham, later Lord Chief Justice, in 1589. In the Great Hall are the finger stocks he was said to have used to make sure prisoners stood still in the dock.

His grandson, Colonel Alexander Popham, was a supporter of Cromwell, and raised his own force, known as Littlecote Garrison. The helmets, cuirasses and buff buckskin jerkins they wore now hang in the Great Hall.
Location: 2½ miles NW of Hungerford off A419.

Little Gidding *Cambs.*   *Map: 398 Df*
CHURCH OF ST JOHN THE EVANGELIST When Nicholas Ferrar moved into Little Gidding

Manor (now demolished) in 1625, the small church had been used as a barn. He restored it, and with his mother, brother and sister and their families, set up an independent religious community.

They lived a life of prayer, work and charity, setting up a school and caring for the poor and sick of the neighbourhood. Their visitors included Charles I, twice as king and in 1646 as a fugitive who was given shelter for the night.
Location: 11 miles NW of Huntingdon off A1.

Little Longstone *Derbys.*   *Map: 393 Gf*
MONSAL VIADUCT Built in 1863, the viaduct carried the Midland Railway over the River Wye in Monsal Dale. When it was built there was an outcry from Victorian conservationists who objected that the railway spoilt the valley.
Location: 3 miles NW of Bakewell (A6, B6465).

Little Maplestead *Essex*   *Map: 399 Fe*
CHURCH OF ST JOHN THE BAPTIST The circular church was built in 1335 by the Knights Hospitallers, a military religious order founded in the 11th century during the Crusades.
Location: 2 miles NE of Halstead off A131.

Little Moreton Hall see Congleton

Little Salkeld *Cumbria*   *Map: 391 Ed*
WATERMILL A small north-country watermill built about 200 years ago to grind oatmeal. It still has one wheel grinding wholemeal flour.
Location: 6½ miles NE of Penrith off A686.

Liverpool Docks *Merseyside*   *Map: 393 Ef*
Liverpool first flourished as a port during the 18th-century "triangular" slave trade, when Merseyside goods were exchanged for slaves in Africa, who were in turn traded for cash and various plantation crops, such as sugar and tobacco, in the West Indies.

So important was this trade, and so little was its morality questioned, that the bells of St Nicholas's Church (overlooking Pierhead) were rung whenever a slaver returned safely to harbour. The first dock was opened in 1715; Steers House, an office block in Canning Place, now occupies the site.

During the first half of the 18th century, the city's population more than trebled, but the port's greatest growth was in the 19th century with the development of the Lancashire cotton industry. Raw cotton was imported from America and cotton yarn and cotton goods were sent all over the world through Liverpool, which became the second largest port in Britain, surpassed only by London.

St George's Dock, built in 1771 but later filled in, is now the site of Pierhead, the hub of the port. The disused 19th-century docks (not open to the public) lie southwards, and the modern docks stretch 5 miles northwards. At the north end of Pierhead is the Royal Liver Building of 1911, with twin towers nearly 300 ft high each surmounted by a Liver bird–modelled from the cormorants on the city coat of arms.

Lizard Lighthouse *Cornwall*   *Map: 396 Aa*
The lighthouse was built in 1752 on the southernmost tip of the British mainland, and first had a coal-fire beacon. Later, oil lamps were

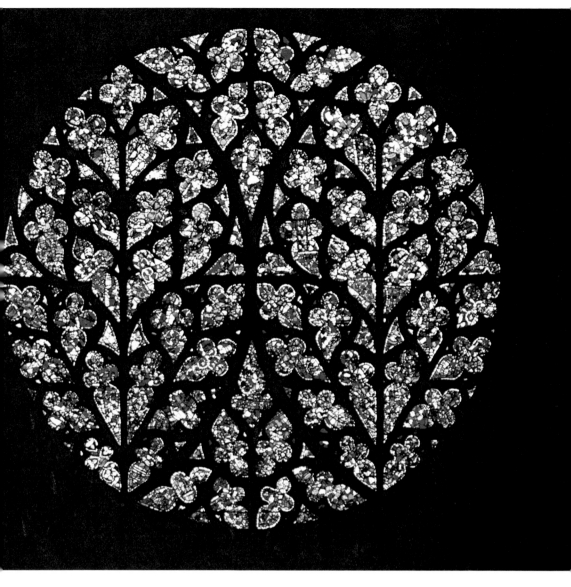

THE BISHOP'S EYE

The circular window in the south transept at Lincoln Cathedral is known as the Bishop's Eye because it overlooks the ancient Bishop's Palace. It dates from about 1325, but the glass in its flowing stone tracery was assembled about 1788 from fragments that had survived destruction in the Civil War.

installed, and finally electricity in 1950. Inside is a small lighthouse museum.
Location: 9½ miles S of Helston on A3083.

Llanberis *Gwynedd*   *Map: 392 Cf*
LAKE RAILWAY The Padarn Railway was built in the mid-19th century to carry slate and quarrymen the 9 miles between the Dinorwic Quarries on Elidir mountain and Port Dinorwic.

The railway closed in 1961, but in 1970 part of the Padarn line was re-laid and reopened using some of the surviving steam locomotives. It is now a narrow-gauge passenger service running 4 miles along the eastern shore of Lake Padarn.
Location: Gilfachddu, ¾ mile E of town.
NORTH WALES QUARRYING MUSEUM The huge Dinorwic slate quarries rise in row upon row of

terraces from the southern end of Lake Padarn to a height of 2,000 ft. They were at their peak in the late 19th and early 20th centuries.

The quarries closed in 1969, and the old slate workshops at the quarry foot–built in 1870, 60 years after quarrying began–now house the museum. They remain much as they were in their working days, when power from a 50 ft diameter water-wheel was transmitted by shafts to different departments.
Location: Gilfachddu, ¾ mile E of town.
SNOWDON MOUNTAIN RAILWAY The mountain railway was opened in 1896 to carry passengers about 5 miles to the summit of Snowdon (3,650 ft). It is the only surviving rack-and-pinion steam railway in Britain, and has 2 ft 7½ in. gauge track.
Location: Base station in town centre.

Llanblethian *S. Glam.*   *Map: 392 Da*
ST QUINTIN'S CASTLE The 14th-century stone enclosure, with a huge gatehouse, was built by the de Clare family which also built Caerphilly Castle. It was a prison in the later Middle Ages.
Location: 7 miles SE of Bridgend (A48, B4270).

Llandaff Cathedral *S. Glam.*   *Map: 393 Da*
Begun in 1120, the cathedral is on a site reputed to be the burial place of St Teilo, a Welsh bishop who died about 580. His shrine was a place of pilgrimage up to the religious Reformation of the 16th century.
After the Reformation, the cathedral fell into ruins, and during the Civil War (1642–7) Parliamentary troops are said to have used it as an alehouse. The south-west tower fell in 1723. Much of the 19th-century restoration work was destroyed in 1941 by a landmine. The cathedral was restored again in the 1950s.
Location: 2 miles NW of Cardiff off A4119.

Llanddewi Brefi *Dyfed*   *Map: 392 Cc*
CHURCH OF ST DAVID The patron saint of Wales, St David, attended a synod here in the 6th century. According to legend, the earth rose to form a mound while the saint was speaking, and the church is said to be built on that mound.
Built into the church wall are a few fragments of a 7th-century gravestone to Bishop Idnert. The inscription reads: "Here lies Idnert son of Jacobus who was slain because of the plunder of the Sanctuary of David." This is the earliest-known written reference to St David.
Location: 8 miles NE of Lampeter on B4343.

Llandogo *Gwent*   *Map: 393 Eb*
COED ITHEL FURNACE In the woods near Tintern are the blackened brick walls of a 17th-century furnace built for smelting iron ore for Tintern's wire-makers. The fuel used was charcoal, and the woodland site ensured a plentiful supply.
Behind the furnace there are remains of a pit that housed a water-wheel, used to power the

blast bellows for the furnace.
Location: 1 mile N of Tintern off A466. See map at Tourist Information Centre in Tintern Abbey car park.

Llandovery Castle *Dyfed*   *Map: 392 Cb*
Part of an enclosing wall built by the Normans was pulled down by Welsh raiders in 1116 almost before the mortar had dried. But not until 50 years later did the Welsh capture the castle, which they held, on and off, for the next century. Only a few remains survive today.
Location: S of town centre off A40.

Llanegryn *Gwynedd*   *Map: 392 Cd*
CHURCH OF ST MARY AND ST EGRYN The finely carved rood loft and screen is believed to have come from Cymer Abbey some 12 miles away.
When the abbey was dissolved in 1536, the monks are said to have carried the loft and screen overnight (perhaps mainly by sea) to isolated Llanegryn church for safety. The loft is about 21 ft long and 6 ft wide.
Location: 4 miles N of Tywyn off A493.

Llanengan *Gwynedd*   *Map: 392 Be*
CHURCH OF ST ENGAN A *llan* was originally a tribal enclosure, but later came to mean a church and the buildings within its enclosure.
St Engan's Church developed from a 5th–6th-century monastery on land given by Engan (or Einion), a 5th-century Celtic princeling, and in the Middle Ages was a place of pilgrimage. The present building dates mainly from the 15th and 16th centuries.
Location: 7½ miles SW of Pwllheli off A499.

Llanfair *Gwynedd*   *Map: 392 Ce*
SLATE QUARRY The disused late-19th-century slate quarry, now open to visitors, has many large, ma-made caves joined by tunnels and slopes along which the slate was moved on railed tracks.
Location: 1 mile S of Harlech off A496.

Llanfair Caereinion *Powys*   *Map: 393 Dd*
WELSHPOOL AND LLANFAIR LIGHT RAILWAY When it was opened in 1903, the 2 ft 6 in. gauge steam-railway linked Llanfair with the main line at Welshpool 9 miles away. After 1931 only goods were carried and in 1956 the line closed down. Now part has been reopened, and two of the original steam locomotives are in use.
Location: 8 miles W of Welshpool on A458.

Llanfoist *Gwent*   *Map: 393 Db*
BRECON AND ABERGAVENNY CANAL Transport was a major problem for the many ironworks in this hilly region, so work began on the canal in 1793. It was linked with the Monmouthshire Canal, reaching the sea at Newport, in 1812.
Horse tramways were built from the iron-works to the canal. Part of the tramway from Garnddyrys Ironworks to the canal wharf at Llanfoist can still be seen.
Location: 1 mile SW of Abergavenny. The wharf is on the road uphill past the church.

Llanfrynach *Powys*   *Map: 393 Db*
BRYNICH AQUEDUCT The Brecon and Abergavenny and Monmouthshire canals were amalgamated in 1865 and are now known as the Monmouthshire and Brecon Canal. The four-

HORSE-WAGON TRAMWAY AT LLANFOIST

In the 19th century, horse wagons carrying iron plied along this tramway between the Garnddyrys Ironworks and the canal. The iron rails, about 4 ft apart, rested on stone sleeper blocks. Trucks were winched up and down the last slope to the wharf.

arched stone aqueduct carries the canal over the River Usk.
Location: 2 miles SE of Brecon (A40, B4558).

Llangollen *Clwyd*   *Map: 393 De*
CANAL MUSEUM A small museum on the wharf at Llangollen illustrates the part played by the 18th–19th-century canal system in the country's development. It includes a life-size model of a section of a 19th-century coal-mine.

The Llangollen Canal was begun in the late 1700s to feed water from the Horseshoe Falls on the Dee to the Ellesmere Canal at Ruabon. There are now regular horse-drawn boat trips.
Location: Wharf Hill, N of town off A539.
PLAS NEWYDD Lady Eleanor Butler and the Honourable Sarah Ponsonby left Ireland in 1776 to set up house together. For over 50 years they lived in the black-and-white house, Plas Newydd, that they transformed from a country cottage, and many distinguished people came there to visit the "Ladies of Llangollen".
Location: Butler Hill, E of town off A5.

Llanrwst *Gwynedd*   *Map: 392 Cf*
CHURCH OF ST GRWST In the Gwydir Chapel, the mausoleum of the Wynne family, is a stone coffin said to be that of the Welsh prince Llywelyn the Great (died 1240). It is supposed to have been brought there by the monks of Aberconwy Abbey when it was dissolved (1536–8). The rood screen and loft may also have come from the abbey.
Location: 14 miles S of Colwyn Bay (A55, A470).

Llanstephan Castle *Dyfed*   *Map: 392 Bb*
Its position on a headland overlooking the River Tywi made the castle strategically important during the English campaigns in Wales in the 12th and 13th centuries. It was developed from a Norman castle built in the 1140s.
Location: 8 miles SW of Carmarthen on B4312.

Llawhaden Castle *Dyfed*   *Map: 392 Ab*
The bishops of the see of St David's were the lords of Llawhaden, which dates mainly from the 13th century. Bishop Barlow, who held it from 1536 to 1547, stripped the lead from the roof and sold it to provide a dowry for his daughter.
Location: 8½ miles E of Haverfordwest off A40.

Llwyngwern Quarry *Powys*   *Map: 392 Cd*
The disused 19th-century slate quarry is now a Centre for Alternative Technology, and houses displays showing how energy and food can be provided from sun, wind and water.
Location: 3 miles N of Machynlleth off A487.

Llywernog *Dyfed*   *Map: 392 Cd*
SILVER-LEAD MINE Prospecting began in the 1740s and the mines were worked until the 1880s. Today a permanent exhibition covers the 7 acre site, which has been restored to capture the atmosphere of the 1870s mining boom.
Location: 10½ miles E of Aberystwyth on A44.

Loch Doon Castle *S'clyde*   *Map: 390 Bf*
The 14th-century castle with a shell keep was originally built on an islet in the loch. But earlier this century the loch was enlarged as part of a hydro-electric scheme, so the castle, with walls

7–9 ft thick, was re-erected on the loch shore.
Location: 23½ miles SE of Ayr off A713

Lochgilphead *Strathclyde*   *Map: 388 Ae*
CRINAN CANAL Built in 1793, the 9 mile ship canal links the Sound of Jura and Loch Fyne, and provides fishing boats with a short cut to the Atlantic, avoiding the long haul round the Mull of Kintyre. Each of the movable bridges has a bridgekeeper's house, often built against the canal bank and with the lower part used for storage and stabling.
Location: NW from town beside A816, B841.

Loch Leven Castle *Tayside*   *Map: 389 Ee*
Mary, Queen of Scots was imprisoned here in 1567 after being defeated by the Scottish Protestant lords led by her half-brother, the Earl of Moray, who became regent. Escape seemed impossible, for the castle is on an islet in the loch, and the five-storey tower house was entered by a ladder to the second floor.

But Mary charmed the younger brother of her gaoler, who helped her to escape in May 1568.
Location: Ferry from Kinross.

Lochty *Fife*   *Map: 389 Fe*
LOCHTY PRIVATE RAILWAY Once a branch line of the East Fife Central Railway, the Lochty railway now runs along a 2 mile track from Lochty Farm (Sundays only). Rolling stock includes a London Northern and Eastern Railway observation car built in 1937 for *Coronation Scot*.
Location: 10½ miles SE of Cupar on B490.

TOOLS THAT DUG THE CANALS

Thousands of men, working mainly with pick, shovel and wheelbarrow, dug out nearly 3,000 miles of Britain's canals from about 1760 to 1830 (see the Canal Museum at Llangollen, above). The men who dug them were known as navvies – short for navigators – and they moved across the country with the job.

In good conditions, an experienced navvy could move about 13 tons of earth a day. Canal beds were made watertight with puddle clay, tramped in by navvies' feet.

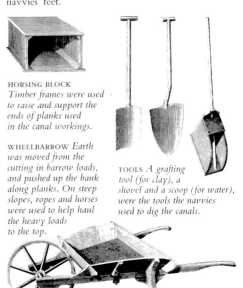

HORSING BLOCK *Timber frames were used to raise and support the ends of planks used in the canal workings.*

WHEELBARROW *Earth was moved from the cutting in barrow loads, and pushed up the bank along planks. On steep slopes, ropes and horses were used to help haul the heavy loads to the top.*

TOOLS *A grafting tool (for clay), a shovel and a scoop (for water), were the tools the navvies used to dig the canals.*

London

APSLEY HOUSE (WELLINGTON MUSEUM) Apsley was the London house of the Duke of Wellington, victor of Waterloo. The Waterloo Gallery was added in 1828 as a setting for the banquet held on each anniversary of the battle.

In the vestibule is a gigantic white marble statue of a nude Napoleon by Canova; it stood in the Louvre in Paris and was bought for Wellington in 1816 by the British government.

Many of the pictures in the house were captured in the baggage train of the fleeing Joseph Bonaparte, King of Spain, after the Battle of Vitoria in 1813. Wellington's offer to return them to the legitimate king was rejected, and they remained his personal prize.
Location: Hyde Park Corner.   *Map: 400 Ba*

BANQUETING HOUSE In Stuart times, the Banqueting House was the ceremonial centre of the king's court – part of the rambling Whitehall Palace beside the River Thames. The Banqueting House stood by the main palace gate, where Horse Guards Avenue now enters Whitehall.

A Tudor banqueting house, probably on the same site, was demolished in 1606 by order of

The palace where a king was beheaded

BUILT FOR JAMES I, THE BANQUETING HOUSE SAW THE GLORIES AND TRIUMPHS OF THE STUART KINGS, AND ALSO THEIR DARKEST HOUR – THE EXECUTION OF CHARLES I

REMNANT OF A PALACE *In 1529 Henry VIII took over York Place, Cardinal Wolsey's Thames-side town-house, and it was then known as Whitehall Palace. It became the main royal residence in London until the 1680s. The only substantial part remaining is the magnificent Banqueting House in Whitehall.*

DOORWAY TO DEATH *It was probably from a first-floor staircase window in the now demolished northern entrance to the Banqueting House that Charles I stepped to the scaffold in 1649. The window is shown in the picture with the letters C. R. and crown above.*

Inigo Jones built the Banqueting House for James I in 1619–23, at a cost of more than £15,000. It provided an up-to-date setting for state functions held at the antiquated Whitehall Palace, and in particular for the court masques of which James and his queen were so fond.

These masques were colourful plays and pageants, for many of which Ben Jonson wrote the words and Inigo Jones designed the settings. Masked members of the court took part in the pageant, but professional actors usually played the spoken parts. During the show, the masked courtiers would leave the pageant and dance with members of the audience.

The first masque was held at the Banqueting House on Twelfth Night, 1622, before the building was completely finished. The last was staged in 1635. The masques ceased to be held there because of the installation in that year of the magnificent Rubens paintings ordered by Charles I to fill the panels of the vast, carved ceiling. He feared that smoke from the masque torches would damage them.

Divine Right and death

The main theme of the Rubens paintings was the glorification of James I and the benefits of his government. They demonstrated Charles's own beliefs about the Divine Right of Kings – beliefs that within the next 20 years were to bring about Civil War and his death.

On a bitterly cold day in January 1649, the Banqueting House was the setting for a national drama, the gaiety of the court masques long forgotten. On January 30, Charles I was beheaded outside the walls of his own palace.

After he had been condemned to death by a court at Westminster Hall on Saturday, January 27, a scaffold was erected at the northern end of the Banqueting House. The following Tuesday morning, a party of halberdiers escorted the king from St James's Palace across St James's Park to Whitehall.

The king waited for several hours in his private apartments at Whitehall Palace while Parliament hastily passed a bill making the proclamation of a new king illegal. Then, at about 2 o'clock, he emerged on to the black-draped scaffold through a first-floor window. He was invisible to the crowds below, although windows and roof-tops of neighbouring build-

James I, and a new one built. But this was burned down in January 1619, and six months later the present two-storey building was begun.

It was the masterpiece of Inigo Jones – the first building in the Classical style to be completed in England – and was strikingly different from the rest of the medieval and Tudor palace.

After 1689 Whitehall Palace declined in importance because William III preferred Kensington Palace and Hampton Court. In 1698 it was destroyed by fire, and of the principal apartments, only the Banqueting House survived.

George I employed Sir Christopher Wren to convert the Banqueting House into the Chapel Royal, a function it fulfilled for about 200 years. It was restored and refaced with Portland stone in 1829, and in 1890 Queen Victoria gave it to the Royal United Service Institution as a museum. Not until 1964 was it restored as a banqueting house. (See below.)
Location: E side of Whitehall.   *Map: 400 Ca*

BUCKINGHAM PALACE The palace has been the principal residence of the kings and queens of England for 150 years. It was originally Buckingham House, the 17th-century country

ings were packed with onlookers. They were too far away to hear his last speech, and as the execution block was only 10 in. high, many saw only the raised axe before it fell.

Eleven years later the monarchy was restored, and on May 29, 1660, Charles II marched in triumph to the Banqueting House to receive vows of loyalty from Parliament. Once more the building became a ceremonial centre.

Touching for the King's Evil
Charles II also carried out there, as had his grandfather James I, the ceremony of Touching for the King's Evil – the name by which the

disease of scrofula was known. It was believed that the touch of royal hands would cure the disease, so sufferers were brought before the king for him to stroke their cheeks.

It was at the Banqueting House that the struggle between Parliament and the Stuarts finally ended. On February 13, 1689, the Lords and Commons were ceremoniously received there by William of Orange and his wife, Mary Stuart, and William and Mary were jointly offered the crown in place of her father, James II. They accepted on the terms laid down by Parliament, providing the foundation for Britain's constitutional monarchy.

THE EXECUTION OF CHARLES I

No one knows for sure who beheaded the king, for the executioner and his assistant were heavily disguised. Richard Brandon, the public executioner, was said to have refused the job, and his assistants could not be found. There were even rumours that Thomas Lord Fairfax or Oliver Cromwell had done the deed.

The painting of The Execution of Charles I by John Weesop in 1649 shows a portrait that could be Lord Fairfax (inset top right) holding the axe. The king's portrait is also inset (top left), and insets at the bottom show (left) the king being escorted from St James's Palace and (right) people gathering souvenirs after the execution. The painting is in the Scottish National Portrait Gallery, Edinburgh.

Eyewitnesses said that the king met his end with courage and dignity. His last words, to Bishop Juxon, were: "I go from a corruptible to an uncorruptible Crown, where no disturbance can be, no disturbance in the world."

ROYAL SHIRT *Charles I wore two shirts at his execution, to keep him from shivering on the bitterly cold day. He did not want to appear afraid. One of the shirts can be seen at the London Museum.*

4 TONS OF REGAL SPLENDOUR

The Gold State Coach which carries kings and queens to their coronations is the only royal coach that cannot travel at a trot. It weighs 4 tons and is pulled by eight *horses. The coach, which is kept at the Royal Mews, Buckingham Palace, has panels painted in 1762 by Giovanni Battista Cipriani.*

house of the Duke of Buckingham, bought in 1762 by George III for his queen. In 1825 John Nash was asked by George IV to make a palace of it.

The palace itself is not open to visitors, but the Queen's Gallery, converted out of the bombed-out chapel, contains exhibitions of pictures, furniture and works of art from the royal collections.

The Royal Mews can also be visited. To mew means to moult, and a mews once meant coops in which hawks were confined during the moult. The Royal Mews stand on the site of the former mews of the king's hawks. They contain the carved and gilded 18th-century Coronation Coach.
Location: Buckingham Gate, SW1. *Map: 400 Ba*

CARLYLE'S HOUSE In this small terrace house Thomas and Jane Carlyle lived from 1834 until their deaths in 1866 and 1881. It has changed little in 100 years. The sound-proof attic study in which Carlyle laboured for 12 years at *The History of Frederick the Great* remains with his desk, books and chair.
Location: 24 Cheyne Row, SW3. *Map: 400 Aa*

CHURCH OF ALL HALLOWS The church was built on part of London's Roman Wall, and the vestry stands on the site of a Roman bastion. When All Hallows was a parish church, a preacher leaving the choir stalls to go to the pulpit had to climb a staircase in the vestry and briefly left his parish.

George Dance the Younger, the architect who later designed Newgate Prison, was only 24 when he built All Hallows in 1765.
Location: London Wall, EC2. *Map: 400 Db*

CHURCH OF ALL HALLOWS BY THE TOWER All Hallows was probably built in the 7th century, but has been considerably altered since.

Bomb damage in the Second World War revealed a Saxon arch, dated about 680, now probably the oldest arch in the City.

The church contains a superb 17th-century wooden font cover, carved with cherubs, a dove, fruit and corn, possibly by the great woodcarver Grinling Gibbons.
Location: Byward St, EC3. *Map: 400 Db*

CHURCH OF ALL SOULS This unusual church – with a portico like a round temple – was designed by John Nash, George IV's favourite architect. It was a terminal point to Regent Street – part of a royal route that was to lead from Carlton House in the Mall, via Waterloo Place, to a pleasure pavilion in Regent's Park. The pavilion was never built.
Location: Langham Place, W1. *Map: 400 Bb*

CHURCH OF ST BARTHOLOMEW THE GREAT The church is a portion of the Priory Church, founded in 1123 by Rahere, a member of Henry I's court and Canon of St Paul's. After the Dissolution, all the monastic buildings were demolished. What remains is the choir and transepts of the impressive Norman church, with Rahere's monument to the north of the altar.

Across Smithfield is St Bartholomew's hospital, also founded by Rahere.
Location: West Smithfield, EC1. *Map: 400 Cb*

CHURCH OF ST BENET PAUL'S WHARF The church was rebuilt by Sir Christopher Wren after the medieval church had been destroyed in 1666 by the Great Fire.
Location: S of Queen Victoria St, EC4, 200 yds E of Mermaid Theatre. *Map: 400 Cb*

CHURCH OF ST BOTOLPH, ALDERSGATE The church-yard houses the Memorial Cloister to Heroic Self-Sacrifice, that was founded in 1899 to

THE HORSE AND CARRIAGE IN 19TH-CENTURY LONDON

Today the Royal Mews, with its coaches, coachmen and stables, seems part of a long-vanished age. Yet there are many people still living who have clear memories of horse-drawn transport and its own unique atmosphere, for it remained the chief means of conveyance in London and other cities well after the introduction of the motor car and right up to the outbreak of the First World War.

In the late 19th century the streets of London were even more congested than they are today, for there were about 300,000 horses in the capital. Huge carts stood parked two or three deep for hours at a time. Every shower of rain produced a crop of accidents, with horses falling on the slippery roads. Slow, heavy traffic hugged the uncambered centre of the roads, where there was less chance of the horses falling, and impatient private coachmen and cabbies would try to cut in and pass. It was not until more policemen were used to regulate traffic in the late 19th century that driving on the left became customary.

Noise and droppings

The clattering and grinding of hooves and carriage wheels on the roads of those days was so great that some hospitals strewed the surrounding streets with straw, as did private householders if one of the family were ill. And there were horse droppings everywhere; it was estimated in the 1890s that 400–500 tons of manure had to be removed from London's streets every day.

Most vehicles on the streets were for hire. Running one's own carriage, such as the sedate and popular four-wheeled brougham, was an expensive business. The carriage, harness and horse called for an initial outlay of about 250 guineas. It cost another £100 a year to maintain a coachman, £40 to feed the horse and to stable it. In addition, if the carriage were to be used at night, a cheaper horse would be needed, as a good carriage horse was too valuable to risk leaving it

out in the chill night air. For night work, too, an assistant would be needed for the coachman.

The private mews of London, in which these men worked, constituted a world of their own. Work there sometimes did not end until 2 or 3 a.m. in the morning, when the last carriage returned from a ball or party, and it started again three hours later, when the coachman and groom came out to feed and groom the horses. So many hours were spent in these tasks and in exercising the animals, polishing their harnesses and cleaning the carriages, that there was rarely an opportunity for the owner to use his carriage more than once a day.

Coaches and drivers for hire

For the rich man who required a private carriage, it was often cheaper and less risky to hire vehicle, horses and coachmen by the month, season or year. The men who provided this service were called jobmasters, and there were about 140 of them in London. As more and more rich families turned to hiring carriages, several of these jobmasters prospered. Two of the largest concerns were Joshua East's, which had about 1,000 carriage horses at Willesden, and Tilling's which stabled about 2,500 horses of all kinds at Peckham. A brougham, horse and coachman could be hired for £200 a year.

At the dawn of the 20th century, the first primitive motor cars began their challenge to the horse-drawn carriage and to create their own problems of noise, pollution and, later, congestion. But these were scarcely greater than those which beset the horse-and-carriage era at its height.

LONDON TRANSPORT – 1890S STYLE *The horse omnibus, which provided cheap transport for the masses, was introduced in 1829. The hansom cab, a two-wheeler for the man-about-town, was invented in 1834; and the brougham, a sedate four-wheeled cab for the respectable and elderly, in 1838.*

honour Londoners who died while saving others. Location: St Martin's le Grand.   *Map: 400 Cb*

CHURCH OF ST GEORGE, HANOVER SQ. St George's was designed by John James in 1721, and over the altar is a painting of the Last Supper attributed to William Kent, the 18th-century architect. Location: St George St, W1.   *Map: 400 Bb*

CHURCH OF ST GILES CRIPPLEGATE St Giles, a medieval church, survived the Great Fire of 1666, but was burned out by bombs in 1940. It has been restored and stands in a newly created piazza beside the wall of the City of London.

Oliver Cromwell married at St Giles in 1620, and John Milton was buried there in 1674. Location: Fore St, EC2.   *Map: 400 Cb*

CHURCH OF ST HELEN Once the church of a 13th-century Benedictine nunnery, St Helen's has its nave divided into two, one part for the nuns, the other for parishioners. It contains many fine monuments.
Location: Bishopsgate, EC3.   *Map: 400 Db*

CHURCH OF ST JAMES The church was built by Sir Christopher Wren between 1676 and 1684 to serve the new residential area around St James's Square. It was severely damaged by bombing in 1940, but was restored by 1954. The font is one of the few marble sculptures by the master-carver Grinling Gibbons, portraying the Tree of Life with Adam and Eve beside it. Gibbons also carved the wooden reredos and organ-case.
James Gillray, the savage caricaturist of the reign of George III, was buried at St James's.
Location: Piccadilly, W1.   *Map: 400 Bb*

CHURCH OF ST JOHN, HAMPSTEAD An 18th-century church, with a battlemented tower and a spire. In the graveyard lie John Constable, the painter, Richard Norman Shaw, the architect, and Sir Herbert Tree, the actor-manager.
Location: Church Row, NW3.   *Map: 400 Ad*

CHURCH OF ST MAGNUS THE MARTYR Only a stone's throw from Pudding Lane, where the Great Fire of 1666 began, the medieval church was one of the first to be destroyed.
St Magnus stands at the approach to the old London Bridge, the footway actually going through the tower. It was rebuilt by Sir Christopher Wren between 1671 and 1685, and most of his furnishings survive.
Location: Lower Thames St, EC3. *Map: 400 Db*

CHURCH OF ST MARGARET, WESTMINSTER The 16th-century Perpendicular parish church nestles beside the great abbey church of Westminster. Beautiful stained glass in the east window commemorates the engagement of Catherine of Aragon to Prince Arthur, Henry VII's son. He died in 1502, aged 16, only five months after the wedding. Catherine then married Henry VIII.
Location: Parliament Sq., SW1.   *Map: 400 Ca*

CHURCH OF ST MARTIN-IN-THE-FIELDS The porticoed Renaissance church was built in 1722–6 by James Gibbs. The plans appeared in his *Book of Architecture* and the church was widely copied in Britain and America. The total cost was £34,000, of which Gibbs received £632 4s 6d.
The Renaissance church replaced a decayed 16th-century church that was pulled down. When the foundations were dug, the skeleton of an 8 ft giant was uncovered, possibly one of the many giants who used to be on view at exhibitions at nearby Charing Cross.
Location: Trafalgar Sq., WC2.   *Map: 400 Cb*

CHURCH OF ST MARY-LE-BOW The medieval building was destroyed during the Great Fire in 1666, and was rebuilt by Sir Christopher Wren as an almost exact square.
Connected to the north-west by a lobby is one of Wren's finest towers and spires. In the tower are the famous Bow Bells. The range of their sound is said to define the area in which Cockneys are born.
A small garden at the west end contains a statue of Captain John Smith, one of the founders of the state of Virginia.
Location: Cheapside, EC2.   *Map: 400 Cb*

CHURCH OF ST MARY-LE-STRAND Isolated in the middle of the Strand, sandwiched between Somerset House and Bush House, is the little baroque masterpiece of James Gibbs, who later designed St Martin-in-the-Fields in Trafalgar Square. St Mary's was built from 1714 to 1717.
Location: Strand, WC2.   *Map: 400 Cb*

CHURCH OF ST OLAVE, HART STREET The church was one of the few in the City of London to escape damage during the Great Fire of 1666. It was damaged in the Second World War, but has been restored.
It is an attractive Gothic building with a crypt, tucked away near Fenchurch Street Station.
Samuel Pepys, the diarist, worshipped and is buried at the church. High on the wall by the chancel is a monument he erected to his wife, who died in 1669.
Location: Seething Lane, EC3.   *Map: 400 Db*

CHURCH OF ST PANCRAS The church is the earliest in England in a strict Grecian style, and was designed by William and Henry Inwood, father and son, in 1822.
The tower is modelled on the octagonal Temple of the Winds at Athens. The Ionic portico, and the two eastern porches are all copied from the Erechtheum, a temple on the Acropolis at Athens. The porches have caryatids (female figures) instead of columns.
The magnificent pulpit is said to have been made from wood from the giant, 1,000-year-old Fairlop Oak, of Hainault Forest in Essex, which blew down in 1820.
Location: Upper Woburn Pl., WC1 *Map: 400 Cb*

CHURCH OF ST PAUL, COVENT GARDEN Covent Garden once belonged to the abbey at Westminster, but after the Dissolution it was acquired by the Russell family.
The 4th Earl of Bedford planned a grand piazza on the site in the 17th century, and asked the architect Inigo Jones to design him a church, but said the expenses were to be kept as low as possible. Jones said the earl would have the "handsomest barn in England".
Consecrated in 1638, it is the first church built in London following the Reformation. Its style was revolutionary at the time – a simple hall with a Tuscan portico facing the piazza. Among those buried there are Sir Peter Lely, the Stuart painter, Grinling Gibbons, the famous carver, and Ellen Terry, the actress.
Location: Bedford St, WC2.   *Map: 400 Cb*

CHURCH OF ST PETER UPON CORNHILL The medieval church was destroyed in the Great Fire, and the present one was built by Sir Christopher Wren. The 17th-century woodwork includes the 1681 organ which was played by Mendelssohn in 1840. His autograph is kept in the vestry.
Location: Cornhill, EC3.   *Map: 400 Db*

CHURCH OF ST STEPHEN WALBROOK One of Sir Christopher Wren's masterpieces, built after the Great Fire of 1666. Many of the furnishings remain from Wren's day – the reredos, font cover

THE MOST FASHIONABLE CHURCH IN LONDON

When St Martin-in-the-Fields opened in 1726 it was the most fashionable church in London. The king himself was a church warden, and his composer Handel played the Voluntary on the organ on Sundays. Pews were rented for up to £10 a year, and a London paper commented that St Martin's could "produce as handsome a show of white hands, diamond rings, pretty snuff-boxes and gilt prayer books as any cathedral". High up in the west end of the church a box was built for charity children. St Martin's was as fashionable for burial as for worship, and by the end of the 19th century the crypt was packed with 3,000 bodies in their coffins. They were removed to Camden Town cemetery.

and canopied pulpit. There is a monument to Nathaniel Hodges, reputed to be the only doctor to remain nursing his patients during London's Great Plague in 1665.
Location: Walbrook, EC4.   *Map: 400 Db*

CHURCH OF THE HOLY SEPULCHRE This medieval church was gutted during the Great Fire of 1666. It now retains its Gothic walls, but has a 17th-century interior.
    Sir Henry Wood, founder of the Promenade Concerts, was organist at the church when he was 14, and is buried in the chapel on the north aisle.
    Across the road, where the Old Bailey now is, was the notorious Newgate Prison until 1902. A tunnel from the church led to the prison so that a hand bell, still kept in the church, could be rung outside the condemned cell at midnight.
Location: Holborn Viaduct, EC1. *Map: 400 Cb*

COOPER'S ROW ROMAN WALL A fine stretch of Roman wall stands in the courtyard behind Midland House. The wall is 35 ft high but the section above 13 ft is medieval. (See p. 242.)
Location: Cooper's Row, EC3.   *Map: 400 Db*

CROSBY HALL Formerly part of a City mansion of 1466, Crosby Hall was rebuilt in Chelsea in 1910. In 1483, Richard, Duke of Gloucester – soon to be Richard III – held court in the hall. Sir Thomas More owned it for six months in 1523.
Location: Cheyne Walk, SW3.   *Map: 400 Aa*

DICKENS' HOUSE In this late-18th-century terrace house Charles Dickens lived with his wife and growing family from 1837 to 1839. He completed *Pickwick Papers* there, and wrote *Oliver Twist* and *Nicholas Nickleby*.
Location: 48 Doughty St, WC1.   *Map: 400 Cb*

DR JOHNSON'S HOUSE Dr Samuel Johnson, essayist and critic, lived in this early-18th-century house from 1748 to 1759, compiling his *Dictionary of the English Language*. The garret room was "fitted up like a counting house" with a long desk at which six clerks could write standing.
Location: Gough Sq., EC4.   *Map: 400 Cb*

FENTON HOUSE This red brick house built in 1693 contains a collection of early keyboard instruments including Handel's harpsichord. There is a fine walled garden.
Location: Hampstead Gr., NW3.   *Map: 400 Ad*

GEFFRYE MUSEUM A range of early-18th-century almshouses was converted into a museum in 1914 to exhibit English furniture of various eras, concluding with a 1930s "lounge".
Location: Kingsland Rd, E2.   *Map: 400 Dc*

PEASANT MUSIC THAT ROSE IN THE SOCIAL SCALE
A hurdy-gurdy was a European medieval peasant instrument. It was played by turning a wheel with one hand and operating keys to "stop" strings with the other. The hurdy-gurdy was introduced into the drawing-rooms of 18th-century London during a rustic vogue, when fashionable men and women dressed as shepherds and shepherdesses. This one is in the collection of keyboard instruments at Fenton House, Hampstead.

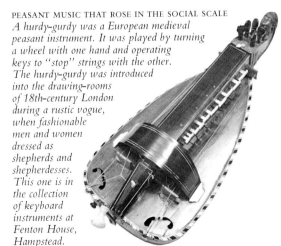

GEORGE INN The best-preserved coaching inn in London. The George was built in the 17th century, and the Dover coaches came into the courtyard through an arched entrance to load and unload passengers.
Location: 77 Borough High St.   *Map: 400 Da*

GUILDHALL The site of the present hall has been the centre of the government of the City of London for more than 1,000 years. The first mayor was installed there in 1192 and it is still the setting of the annual Lord Mayor's banquet. The building mostly dates from 1411. Beneath a window are the standard imperial measurements – 1 ft, 2 ft and 1 yd. On the floor, brass plates measure 66 ft (a chain) and 100 ft.
Location: Gresham St, EC2.   *Map: 400 Db*

HIGHGATE CEMETERY The cemetery was consecrated in 1839 to help relieve the hopelessly overcrowded churchyards of central London. Most churchyards were finally closed by law in 1855.
    The Old Cemetery, now closed to the public, contains the Catacombs, a circular building with family vaults in which coffins were placed in niches.
    The New Cemetery, opened in 1856, has the tombs of Karl Marx, founder of Communism, Dante Gabriel Rossetti, founder of the Pre-Raphaelite Brotherhood of painters, and the parents, wife and ninth child of Charles Dickens. (Dickens himself is buried at Westminster Abbey.)
Location: Swain's Lane, N6.   *Map: 400 Bd*

HMS BELFAST This Second World War cruiser, launched in 1938, served as an escort for Russian convoys, fired the first shots in the Battle of North Cape and led the bombardment before the Normandy landings. She took part in the Korean War before being withdrawn from service in 1964.
Location: Off Tooley St, SE1.   *Map: 400 Db*

HMS DISCOVERY The *Discovery* was the first British ship built for scientific exploration. She was launched in 1901, one of the last large vessels to be built of wood. But her bows were reinforced for use in polar waters.
    Captain Robert Scott used her for his first Antarctic expedition of 1901–4. Scott's quarters in the *Discovery* and those of his officers and scientists have been preserved, together with relics of the expedition.
Location: Victoria Embankment, near Temple Station.   *Map: 400 Cb*

KEATS HOUSE In this little white Regency house John Keats lived from 1818 to 1820. Here he wrote the famous *Odes*, developed a desperate passion for 18-year-old Fanny Brawne and first showed symptoms of the consumption which killed him at the age of 25.
Location: Keats Grove, NW3.   *Map: 400 Ad*

KENSINGTON PALACE In 1689 William III bought Nottingham House, Kensington, as a country house where his chronic asthma would be free from aggravation by London smoke. Wren was the architect of the conversion.
    Queen Victoria was born in the apartments occupied by her mother, the Duchess of Kent, and they shared a room until the day in 1837 on which the 17-year-old princess awoke to the news that she was queen.
Location: Kensington Gardens.   *Map: 400 Aa*

KENWOOD HOUSE This elegant 18th-century house in a fine park adjacent to Hampstead Heath is famous for its association with two eminent Scotsmen: the lawyer Lord Mansfield (1705–93), who owned it for nearly 40 years, and the architect Robert Adam, of whose mature style the library is a notable example.
    Lord Mansfield's judgments in 32 years as Lord Chief Justice contributed largely to the development of English law and of court procedure. In one famous judgment he pronounced in favour of a Negro slave who, brought to England by his master, claimed his freedom under the law of England.
    Kenwood contains old Dutch master paintings and 18th-century English furniture.
Location: Hampstead Lane, N6.   *Map: 400 Ad*

KING'S CROSS STATION The plainest of London's great stations, built in 1852. The vast double-arched train shed was designed by the engineer William Cubitt. It is a perfect example of "engineer's architecture"; all its design comes from the needs of the railway, none from decoration for its own sake.
Location: Euston Rd, N1.   *Map: 400 Cc*

LANCASTER HOUSE "I come from my house to your palace," Queen Victoria is said to have remarked to the Duchess of Sutherland on one of her visits. This grandest of all London houses played a great part in the social and political life of early-Victorian London. Successive dukes and duchesses of Sutherland were supporters of liberal causes. Lord Shaftesbury advocated the cause of factory children there; Garibaldi, the Italian independence leader, stayed there in 1864.
Location: Stable Yard, SW1.   *Map: 400 Ba*

LEIGHTON HOUSE At the age of 25 Frederic Leighton exhibited a picture at the Royal Academy which was bought by Queen Victoria for the large sum of £600. He rose steadily in the artistic firmament of late-Victorian England and died in 1896 a peer and for 18 years President of the Royal Academy.
    Behind the red-brick façade of his house is one of the most exotic and surprising of London interiors. The domed Arab Hall, with a marble pool and fountain, is a miniature pastiche of the Alhambra Palace in Granada.
    The house contains an exhibition of High Victorian art, including paintings by Leighton and his contemporaries, and a collection of de Morgan pottery.
Location: Holland Park Rd.   *Map: 400 Aa*

MIDDLE TEMPLE HALL Members of Middle Temple, one of the three Inns of Court, have dined in the hall since 1570.
    When law books were few and legal training was by discourse and disputation, a Reader expounded the law to his student barristers for subsequent debate. Until 1830 the hall was warmed by an open central hearth.
Location: Off Fleet St, EC4.   *Map: 400 Cb*

MONUMENT Christopher Wren's 202 ft high memorial to the Great Fire stands near the site of the bakers' shop in Pudding Lane where the fire began on September 2, 1666. Visitors can climb to the top.
Location: Monument St, EC3.   *Map: 400 Db*

NOBLE STREET A large Roman fort was built in the north-west of the city of London early in the 2nd century. When the city wall was built later in the century the north and west walls of the fort became part of it. A long stretch is still visible. (See p. 242.)
Location: Noble St, EC2.   *Map: 400 Cb*

OLD ST THOMAS'S OPERATING THEATRE In this room, operations – mainly amputations – were carried out on women patients for 25 years before anaesthetics came into use.

The theatre was opened at Old St Thomas's Hospital in Southwark in 1822, and has now been restored to its original appearance. It is the only surviving operating theatre of the early 19th century in England, and probably in the world. Throughout its working life surgery was conducted without any thought to antiseptic methods. The revolutionary lessons of cleanliness taught by Joseph Lister in 1860 were not applied in London hospitals until the 1870s.

The room has no plumbing and no ventilation. A bowl of water was provided for the surgeons to wash their hands, which they did more often after the operation than before.

The operating table, made of deal with a wooden headrest, stands in the centre of the room, with tiers for spectators rising in a semi-circle around it. During operations, the room was crowded with students, frequently calling "Heads, heads" to those around the table whose heads obstructed their view. The operating area itself contained the surgeon, his assistants, visiting surgeons and distinguished guests.

The surgeon probably dressed in an old frock coat stiff with pus and blood from previous operations. Beneath the table was a box of sawdust which he could kick to any place where blood was running off the table.

Into the crowded, noisy room the patient was led, blindfolded so she could not see the instruments laid out in readiness. She had probably been partially sedated with opium or alcohol in preparation for the ordeal to come. In the case of an amputation she was held down by the surgeon's assistants so that the operation could be completed as quickly as possible – three to five minutes was usual.

In an account of an operation in 1824, the *Lancet* reported: "Mr Green amputated a leg above the knee, in consequence of a diseased knee joint. Immediately after the operation . . .

OPERATIONS WITHOUT ANAESTHETIC

The operating theatre at Old St Thomas's Hospital, where operations were carried out before the arrival of anaesthetics, was lit by two gaslights over the wooden table. Routine operations were done in natural light from a large skylight. The gaslight was used for emergencies and on foggy days. Even ten years after this theatre closed, 20 per cent of hospital patients died after surgery.

Mr Green did not examine the joint, as there were scarcely any students present; that gentleman, however, expressed his intention of doing so at another appointment."

The first mention of anaesthesia at St Thomas's is in 1849 when an inquest was held on a patient who died from the effects of chloroform given before the extraction of an ingrowing toenail.

The Old Operating Theatre was closed in 1862 when St Thomas's Hospital moved from Southwark to Lambeth.
Location: St Thomas St. SE1.   *Map: 400 Da*

AMPUTATION KNIVES *Surgeons at the Old Operating Theatre, St Thomas's Hospital, used knives such as these to amputate limbs in the early 19th century.*

RULES FOR NURSES

"No person shall be received into the house who is visited, or suspected to be visited, with the Plague, Itch [scabies], Scald-Head [ringworm of the scalp], or other Infectious diseases, and if any such be taken in, then to be discharged as soon as discovered."

❖❖❖❖❖❖

"Patients shall not Swear, nor take God's Name in vain, nor revile, nor miscall one another, nor strike or beat another, nor steal Meat, or Drink, Apparel, or other thing, one from the other."

❖❖❖❖❖❖

"No Patient with the Foul disease [syphilis] shall go out of his Ward, nor come into the House to fetch anything, nor within the Chapel, nor sit upon the seats in the Courtyards, upon pain of Expulsion."

❖❖❖❖❖❖

"Every tenth bed is to be left empty to air and not more than one patient is to be put into each bed."

❖❖❖❖❖❖

"Old sheets shall be washed and given the Surgeons for Dressings."

❖❖❖❖❖❖

"No surgeon shall suffer his servant to perform any operation . . . except the Master of such Servant be present . . ."

❖❖❖❖❖❖

"The Sexton shall keep the Chapel and yards clean and make graves six feet deep, six feet long and three feet wide at eighteen pence each."

From *Standing Orders of St Thomas's Hospital, 1699–1752*

ROMAN ARMY SURGERY

When the armies of Rome invaded Britain in AD 43, they brought their own doctors, who could heal wounds and treat illness with blood-letting. They also amputated limbs and cauterised tumours. Anaesthetics were limited to mild narcotics from herbs. Roman instruments, now in the British Museum, include a bleeding cup, speculum for dilating cavities of the body, drug box, scalpel, spatula for pressing down the tongue, probe for removing arrows, spoon for eye-drops, forceps, ointment pot and probes.

PADDINGTON STATION The Great Western Railway's inventive genius, Isambard Kingdom Brunel, created the enormous glass roof with its cathedral-like transepts. It opened in 1854.
Location: Eastbourne Ter., W2.   *Map: 400 Ab*

PALACE OF WESTMINSTER Westminster was the king's principal palace from the reign of Edward the Confessor in the 11th century until the reign of Henry VIII in the 16th. Since the 13th century it has also been the meeting place of Parliament. In 1834 a spectacular fire destroyed all the Palace except Westminster Hall and the Jewel Tower, and the present Houses of Parliament were built.
Location: Parliament Sq., SW1.   *Map: 400 Ca*

THE KING'S COURTS *When it was built by William II as part of the royal palace, Westminster Hall was probably the largest Hall in Europe. Its length was 240 ft and width 67 ft, and it was the ceremonial centre of England. For 500 years – from the 14th century to the 19th – Westminster Hall also contained the Law Courts. The Court of Chancery, the King's Bench and the Common Pleas sat against different walls, and lawyers competed to be heard above the noise of tradesmen selling goods to the public from stalls along the remaining walls.*

In 1649 Charles I was brought to the Hall to be tried and sentenced to death for treason. A small plate marks the spot where he sat.

When the rest of the Palace of Westminster was destroyed by fire in 1834, the present Houses of Parliament were built, dwarfing and almost enveloping the historic building. The Law Courts moved to the Strand and the silent old Hall, still with the finest hammer-beam roof in Britain, has since served for the lying-in-state of monarchs.

THE WESTMINSTER SKYLINE IN TUDOR LONDON

In 1547, when the Thames was still London's principal highway, the west bank at Westminster was dominated by three buildings – St Stephen's Chapel where the Commons sat, Westminster Hall – the home of the Law Courts – and Westminster Abbey. After trials in the Hall, condemned traitors, such as Sir Thomas More in 1535 and Anne Boleyn in 1536, were taken down-river to execution at the Tower of London. In 1834 fire destroyed St Stephen's Chapel and the rest of the Palace with the exception of Westminster Hall. The new Houses of Parliament were designed by Sir Charles Barry and A. W. N. Pugin in the Gothic style. They stretch along the river front, obscuring the Hall, and the Westminster skyline is now dominated by the soaring pinnacles of Victoria Tower and Big Ben.

JEWEL TOWER *A fragment of the medieval palace – where royal treasures were kept – stands almost unnoticed opposite the Houses of Parliament.*

LIVERPOOL STREET STATION *Iron and glass form a delicate pattern in the high roof of the station built on the site of the old Bethlehem hospital for the insane, which had moved almost 100 years earlier. The station, opened in 1874, has a massive clock tower and was built by the Great Eastern Railway. The architect was Edward Wilson. The station's Great Eastern Hotel, in a French Renaissance style, is still open. Liverpool Street has no connection with the city of Liverpool: it was named after Lord Liverpool, who died in 1828 after ending a 15 year term as prime minister.*

CATHEDRALS OF THE RAILWAY AGE

In the rush to link London and provincial centres during the "railway mania" of the 19th century, competing companies built majestic stations and hotels in the capital.

The most famous surviving example of railway buildings in the grand style is the St Pancras Station Hotel, with its extravagant array of Gothic pinnacles and turrets. The hotel, designed by Sir Gilbert Scott, was built in the late 1860s. In its heyday, it was the last word in luxury. There were beds for 400 guests and every first-class sitting room had its own piano. Now, however, the hotel is used as offices.

St Pancras Station, adjoining the hotel, at the east end of Euston Road, is just as impressive, in its own way. The design, by W. H. Barlow, features a ridged roof 690 ft long and 243 ft wide. Station and hotel were built by the Midland Railway.

Engineer's architecture

Next door to St Pancras is the more modest King's Cross Station, built in 1852. It is largely a replica of the Czar's Riding School in Moscow, and a perfect example of "engineer's architecture". The great double-arched train shed was designed by Lewis Cubitt to suit the needs of the railway, rather than to be merely decorative. Although a modern forecourt building has been added, most of the original façade can still be seen. Between the two arches, overlooking the street, is a large clock which was bought at the Great Exhibition of 1851. The station was built for the Great Northern Railway, whose trains came from York.

Paddington Station, opened in 1854 at Praed Street, off the Edgware Road, was the work of the engineer Isambard Kingdom Brunel and the architect Digby Wyatt. A great glass-paned roof is supported on iron columns which form an intricate series of curves, as in a cathedral: there are also double transepts. Wyatt contributed interesting detail such as the oriel windows above the platforms, with their Roman and Gothic-style arches. The station was built for the Great Western Railway, whose trains ran from Bristol.

Vanished arch

Little is left of the first major London station, built at Euston by Philip Hardwick in the late 1830s. A magnificent Doric arch through which passengers approached the station was demolished in 1962. One important survival is the Round House engine shed (now a concert hall and theatre) at nearby Camden Town. At the Round House, in Chalk Farm Road, locomotives which could not manage the incline from Euston were turned on a turntable (which also survives), while coaches were run up or down the slope by cable.

Marylebone Station – built in Park Road, off Marylebone Road, in 1899, without the aid of an architect – is a charming structure, with a porch supported by delicate iron pillars. In front of it, in Marylebone Road, is the much larger Hotel Great Central, now British Rail's offices.

In the City of London, Liverpool Street Station and its Great Eastern Hotel were built between 1874 and 1884. The station's lofty roof is of wrought and cast iron and glass.

ROUND HOUSE *A 19th-century locomotive waits in the engine shed at Camden Town to be turned round on the turntable at the centre. Coaches were hauled by cable on the gradient between Camden Town and Euston Station. The Round House is now an arts centre.*

REGENT'S CANAL The canal linking the Grand Union Canal with the Thames at Limehouse was planned in 1812. The towpath provides an attractive walk from Lisson Grove to Camden Town, going through Regent's Park past the zoo. *Map: 400 Bc*

ROUND HOUSE Designed by Robert Stephenson in 1846, the Round House had 23 berths for locomotives with a central turntable 36 ft wide. It is now an arts centre. (See left.)
Location: Chalk Farm Rd, NW1. *Map: 400 Bc*

ST ALPHAGE'S CHURCHYARD (ROMAN WALL) The double thickness of the Roman wall was created when the wall of the early fort was strengthened to become part of the city wall. Look down on it from the stairway in the garden to see the join. (See p. 242.)
Location: Off Wood St, EC2. *Map: 400 Db*

ST PANCRAS STATION The former hotel at the front of the station is one of the most exotic flowerings of Victorian architecture, a vast Gothic château, with spires and turrets. It was built by Sir Gilbert Scott in 1868 but is now offices. The station is more workmanlike but no less remarkable – a glass-roofed structure 690 ft long and 243 ft wide. (See left.)
Location: Euston Rd, NW1. *Map: 400 Cc*

ST PAUL'S CATHEDRAL The first man to be buried in one of the world's greatest baroque cathedrals was its creator, Sir Christopher Wren. His grave is in the crypt, marked by a simple black slab of marble, with a Latin inscription on the wall above it declaring: *Lector si monumentum requiris circumspice* (Reader, if you seek a monument, look around you).

The earliest religious building on the site of St Paul's was a Saxon church built in the 7th century. Like its four successors it was destroyed by fire. The last one, Old St Paul's, was a victim of the Great Fire in 1666.

As Surveyor-General, Christopher Wren persuaded Charles II and his royal commissioners, to pull it down and start afresh. During the next five years Wren prepared three different designs for a new cathedral. The first two, produced in 1670 and 1673, were rejected as not being traditional enough. The second design was built as a superb oak model – 20 ft long and costing £600 to make – which may still be seen in the trophy room. Wren despaired at its rejection but went on to prepare a third design in 1675 which was finally approved.

It had a Gothic plan – a cruciform arrangement – as the commissioners demanded, but Wren was given permission to make slight "variations, rather ornamental than essential". Shrewdly and skilfully, he modified the design as work proceeded, until the end result was notably different from the accepted version.

When Wren was planning the site he is said to have asked a workman for a stone to mark the centre of the dome on the ground. The piece Wren was given came from a gravestone and had the inscription: *Resurgam* (I shall rise again). This so impressed Wren that he had the word cut in the pediment above the south door.

St Paul's took 35 years to complete, and Wren lived to see his son lay the final stone in 1710. St

Paul's was the first cathedral in England to be built from start to finish under the control of its original creator.

The glory of the cathedral is the magnificent dome, 102 ft in diameter, which sits on a colossal stone drum, supported by the columns at the central crossing. The dome, however, is not what it appears to be, for it consists of three domes in all: the inner one, which can be seen from the inside of the cathedral; a middle cone-shaped one, which is made of brick and supports the stone lantern above; and the outer dome—made of timber and clad with lead for protection. This ensures that the dome appears proportionally correct, from inside and out. The weight of all three domes is 68,000 tons.

The top of the cross surmounting the dome is 365 ft above ground level—a foot for every day of the year.

One architectural curiosity is the Whispering Gallery, 100 ft above floor level, and so-called because of its acoustic qualities that allow a whisper on one side of the gallery to be heard with absolute clarity on the other, a distance of 107 ft.

Among his artists and craftsmen, Wren chose Grinling Gibbons to carve the choir stalls and the organ cases, and the Frenchman Jean Tijou to make the wrought-iron gates at the entrance to the aisle and sanctuary screens.

The interior of the cathedral is a mausoleum of monuments for national heroes. Lord Nelson and the Duke of Wellington were both buried in the crypt—Nelson in a marble sarcophagus originally made for Cardinal Wolsey. Both the crypt and the whispering gallery are closed to the public during services.
Location: Ludgate Hill, EC4.　*Map: 400 Cb*

SIR JOHN SOANE'S MUSEUM Sir John Soane (1753–1837), one of the most imaginative and original of all architects to work in the Classical tradition, lived here for the last 24 years of his life. He designed the house partly to live in and partly as a setting for his large collection of works of art and architectural drawings.

The house remains much as he left it, a fascinating illustration of the taste and way of life of a cultivated and somewhat eccentric 18th-century English professional gentleman.
Location: 13 Lincoln's Inn Fields.　*Map: 400 Cb*

SOMERSET HOUSE Until Tudor times London consisted only of the walled City and, 2 miles to the west, the seat of government at Westminster.

The first buildings to be erected in between were the great riverside palaces of the nobility. Some are commemorated by street names: Arundel, Buckingham, Savoy, York. Only Somerset House survives to give an idea of the great area each covered. Its builder, the Lord Protector Somerset, was beheaded in 1552 and his house passed to the Crown.

It served as the London palace of the queen consort until George III bought Buckingham House for his queen, and in 1775 it was rebuilt to the splendid designs of the king's favourite architect, Sir William Chambers. In the Strand side of the great quadrangle are The Fine Rooms, a series of beautiful neo-Classical rooms, which are open to the public during exhibitions.
Location: The Strand, WC2.　*Map: 400 Cb*

SOUTHWARK CATHEDRAL The oldest Gothic building in London, in the parish where Shakespeare is said to have lived and worked, stands on the site of a former Roman settlement.

In 1106 an Augustinian Priory was founded. The church was destroyed by fire in 1207 and rebuilt by Peter des Roches in Early English design. The retrochoir (the space behind the High Altar, also known as the Lady Chapel) is among the finest architectural gems of this period.

The retrochoir was, and still is, used as a Consistory Court where the bishop sits to try ecclesiastical cases. Here, during the persecution of Protestants in 1554—when Queen Mary attempted to reintroduce Roman Catholicism—seven martyrs were tried. Two of them, the Bishops Latimer and Ridley, were burned at the stake at Oxford, chained back to back.

When the priory was dissolved in 1540, the priory church, now called St Saviour's, was leased to the parish. In 1905 the Diocese of Southwark was created and St Saviour's became the cathedral.

The Harvard Chapel was furnished by "the sons of Harvard University in memory of their founder, John Harvard", who was born in Southwark High Street, the son of a butcher. He was baptised in St Saviour's in 1607, went to Emmanuel College, Cambridge and graduated in 1635. Two years later—having inherited property from his step-father—he emigrated to America, where he died of consumption in 1638. He left his library and half his money to the newly founded college in Massachusetts, which was renamed in his honour.

The cathedral contains many other memorials, one of which is William Shakespeare's, in the south aisle. His younger brother, Edmund, and John Fletcher and Philip Massinger—all fellow players at the Globe Theatre—were buried in the crypt. Three stones in the floor of the choir mark the fact. The Globe Theatre originally stood on a site 250 yds to the west.

In the south aisle, beside the High Altar, there is the canopied tomb of Bishop Lancelot Andrewes, who died in 1636. Andrewes translated part of the Authorised Version of the Bible. In this aisle is the cathedral's only brass, to Susannah Banford who died in 1672 aged 10. It carries the poignant inscription: "The Nonsuch (paragon) of the world for pieties in soe tender yeares."
Location: Borough High St, SE1.　*Map: 400 Db*

SPANIARDS INN In the 18th century, the Turnpike Trusts began to build roads to a standard which Britain had not known since the Romans left more than 1,000 years before. Costs were recovered by charging tolls to travellers.

One of the turnpike roads is now Spaniards Road, Hampstead. At Spaniards End, the road narrows, and here the toll bar was lowered to bar the way while the tolls were collected from those using the road.

Opposite is Spaniards Inn, a stopping-place for north-bound coaches. The poet Keats, who lived in Hampstead, came with his friends, and the highwayman Dick Turpin drank in the upstairs room where he could look out for likely victims setting off across Hampstead Heath.
Location: Spaniards End, NW3.　*Map: 400 Ad*

INSIDE THE WHISPERING GALLERY

Below the great dome of St Paul's Cathedral runs the Whispering Gallery (right), 100 ft above floor level. It is an architectural curiosity with acoustic qualities that allow a whisper uttered on one side of the gallery to be heard with absolute clarity on the other side, a distance of 107 ft away.

JOHN DONNE'S SHROUD
The present cathedral, built by Sir Christopher Wren, replaced a Gothic cathedral badly damaged in the Great Fire of 1666. The only survival from the old building is a macabre effigy of John Donne, the metaphysical poet who was Dean of St Paul's from 1621 to his death in 1631. In his last years Donne became obsessed with death and posed for a painting wrapped in a shroud. The sculptor Nicholas Stone carved the monument from the painting.

TEMPLE CHURCH Tucked away south of Fleet Street is London's only circular church, one of the few remaining in England. It was built by the Knights Templar, guardians of the Church of the Holy Sepulchre in Jerusalem, and consecrated in 1185 by Heraclius, Patriarch of Jerusalem. The elegant choir was added to the church in the 13th century.

A group of Purbeck-marble effigies of Knights Templar on the floor include William Marshal, Earl of Pembroke, who was Regent of England at the end of King John's reign, and Geoffrey, Earl of Essex. Geoffrey had been excommunicated for avaricious and rough behaviour, and the Templars could not bury him when he died. So they soldered him up in lead, and hung him from a tree by the Thames until the pope absolved him.

Location: Inner Temple, EC4.   *Map: 400 Cb*

TEMPLE OF MITHRAS When London was a Roman city this temple was a centre of Mithraism, an eastern religion popular with merchants and soldiers. (See p. 242.)

Location: 11 Queen Victoria St.   *Map: 400 Db*

THAMES MARITIME MUSEUM An exhibition of historic ships includes the last Nore lightship, once stationed by The Nore sandbank in the Thames estuary.

The museum also contains the last steam tug to operate on the Thames, the topsail schooner *Kathleen & May*, the steam herring drifter *Lydia Eve* and the coaster *Robin*. The ships are on show at St Katharine's Yacht Haven, formerly St Katharine's Dock.

Location: St Katharine's Way, E1. *Map: 400 Db*

TOWER OF LONDON The most famous castle in the world began as a simple earthwork thrown up by the Normans in 1066. It was built in England's biggest city by William the Conqueror to establish himself as undisputed ruler.

The work was begun in the south-east corner of the old Roman city. About 1080 William began the White Tower, one of the first and largest great towers in Britain, 107 ft by 118 ft at the base and over 90 ft tall.

This great stone structure was finished by the Conqueror's son William Rufus, probably towards the end of the 1090s, and in 1100 it was to have its first prisoner, Ranulf Flambard, Bishop of Durham. Ranulf had been William Rufus's chief minister and had ruled by fear and greed. Henry I threw him in the Tower but he escaped in 1101 by having a coil of rope smuggled to him in a jar of wine and letting himself down from a window.

For the next three centuries, the White Tower (first known by that name in the reign of Henry III who had its walls whitewashed) accommodated a galaxy of famous prisoners. Among them were Richard II who signed his abdication there in 1399, and the Duke of Orleans, captured at Agincourt. Apart from its use as a palace, castle and prison, the Tower has housed the Royal Mint, the Royal Menagerie, the public records and even the Royal Observatory. It has held the Crown Jewels for centuries.

Inside the castle grounds is Tower Green where, on a private scaffold, a sad roll of victims lost their heads. Among them were Anne Boleyn and Katherine Howard, second and fifth wives of Henry VIII, Margaret Countess of Salisbury, last of the Plantagenets, and Lady Jane Grey, the "Nine Days Queen".

The Bloody Tower was given its name in the 16th century. It was said to be the scene of the murder of the Princes in the Tower (Edward V and Richard of York, sons of Edward IV). They were alleged by Tudor historians to have been killed at the orders of their uncle Richard III, who usurped the throne in 1483, but ever since the 17th century the charge has been hotly contested.

Location: Tower Hill, EC3.   *Map: 400 Db*

TOWER HILL: PLACE OF PUBLIC EXECUTION

Beside the Tower of London, a permanent scaffold once stood. Among the eminent people beheaded there were Sir Thomas More (for refusing to accept Henry VIII as supreme head of the English church), Thomas Cromwell (Henry's chief administrator), and two 1745 Jacobite leaders (above).

PRINCES *These stairs lead to the room in the Bloody Tower where Edward V and his brother Richard of York are said to have been murdered.*

GUY FAWKES *In this room in Queen's House, Guy Fawkes was questioned after being tortured. He admitted trying to blow up Parliament.*

TRAITORS' GATE *Important prisoners were brought by boat to the Tower, and were often taken to Westminster for trial through the same gate.*

THE GREATEST FORTRESS

The oldest building in the Tower of London is the White Tower started by William the Conqueror about 1080. In the 13th century Henry III and his son Edward I enclosed it with two rings of walls and towers, making it the greatest fortress in England, with the one possible exception of Dover Castle.

HELMET *In the 1570s this helmet was made for William Somerset, 3rd Earl of Worcester. It is now at the Tower.*

SCOLD'S BRIDLE *The iron mask was part of a scold's bridle, used in the 17th and 18th centuries to punish abusive women. Bridles were fixed to a woman's head, with an iron gag in her mouth, and she was paraded in public.*

LONDON'S OLDEST CHAPEL ROYAL *St John's Chapel, part of the White Tower, was built before 1100. It is one of the great examples of Norman architecture.*

THE ROMAN FORT THAT GREW TO BE THE CITY OF LONDON

London, one of the greatest cities in the world, was created by the Romans. When the troops of Emperor Claudius invaded Britain in AD 43 – nearly 100 years after Julius Caesar's British expeditions – they set up a fort on the north bank of the Thames, at the lowest firm bridging point.

The fort swiftly grew into the town of Londinium, a thriving commercial centre rivalling the capital city of the time, Colchester (Camulodunum). Then, in AD 60–61, the rebel Queen Boudicca's Iceni hordes destroyed London.

By this time, however, London was so well established that it quickly rose from the ashes. By the end of the 1st century, it was the commercial and political centre of Britain.

Visible defences
In the early 2nd century a new fort had been built in the north-west corner (now the Barbican area). The fort's west gate can still be seen, on the north side of the road called London Wall. A long stretch of the western defences is visible from Noble Street, near by.

Later in the 2nd century, all except the river side of London was enclosed by a wall which ran for 2 miles and incorporated the fort. Double masonry, showing where the fort wall was thickened to match the town wall, can be seen from Noble Street, and also from a stairway in St Alphage's churchyard (off Wood Street). Other fine stretches of the town wall are visible in the grounds of the Tower of London, as well as on Tower Hill and behind Midland House, Cooper's Row. In the 4th century the wall was completed along the river, and a section has been preserved in the Tower of London.

At one time, a vast forum and basilica (market place and courthouse) stood on what is now Cornhill, but no trace is visible today.

In 1954, the 2nd-century Temple of Mithras was found north of Cannon Street. The worship of the god Mithras was at one time a serious rival to Christianity. It was a secret religion and, like freemasonry, had different grades of members.

Followers of Mithras were persecuted by the Christians, whose religion became the official faith of the

FORTIFICATION *Outside the walls of London, homes burn after an attack by Saxon invaders. In this artist's impression of a snow-covered Roman London about AD 400, seen from the south-east, the rectangular Roman fort is in the far corner of the city (centre top). The great forum and basilica (or courthouse) are in the city centre. Between fort and forum,* *the Walbrook flows into the Thames, just up-river from the early London Bridge. The Temple of Mithras stood beside this stream, which now flows underground. In the immediate foreground corner, the Tower of London was eventually built: parts of the Roman wall can still be seen there and on Tower Hill near by.*

THE ANCIENT ROADS

Some of today's main routes in central London still follow the general line of ancient Roman roads which struck out across the whole of Britain. Perhaps the most striking example of a surviving route is the old Silchester Road, followed by present-day Oxford Street, Bayswater Road, Notting Hill and onwards through Chiswick to the west. The northern section of Watling Street, which crossed London from south-east to north-west, is still followed by the Edgware Road. It took Roman traffic to Verulamium.

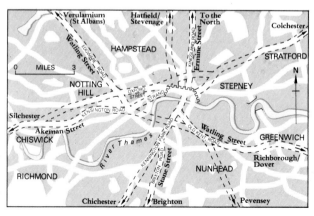

Roman state in the 4th century. Because of the persecution, Mithras worshippers often had to hide their religious objects. This may account for the discovery of statues under the London temple.

The temple was built on the east bank of the Walbrook stream – a tributary of the Thames which ran through Roman London and is now underground. The remains of the temple have been moved from the original site and now stand 60 yds to the west, in front of Bucklersbury House, Victoria Street.

Elegant town house

Another Roman London discovery is a town house, with private bath-suite, in Lower Thames Street.

Part of the bath-suite was first found more than 130 years ago, during excavations for the old Coal Exchange building. More recently, the Exchange was demolished to make way for a new office block, and still more of the Roman house was discovered.

The remains have been preserved in a special basement under the new block, and there are plans to open it to the public.

WORSHIP *The Temple of Mithras was built in the 2nd century by followers of Mithraism, a religion that ran a close rival to Christianity. It stood on the east bank of the Walbrook stream, and is shown above as it would have looked when the Romans worshipped there.*

TRAVEL *One of the three western exits from fortified London was on the site of medieval Newgate. The road had a gatehouse with square towers: the whole structure was about 100 ft wide. From Newgate, a main road ran to the present Marble Arch area before dividing in two – the westward road to Silchester and Watling Street north-west to Verulamium (St Albans). Other gates in the city wall were at Aldersgate to the north of Newgate and Ludgate to the south. Aldersgate is believed to have had towers similar to those at Newgate. Roman London also had at least three other gateways: at Cripplegate and Bishopsgate in the north and Aldgate in the north-east.*

EVERYDAY THINGS FROM ROMAN LONDON

Numerous finds from Roman London are on display at the Museum of London. The amber necklace (left), still on its original flax string, was found at the Walbrook stream. The fir-wood writing tablets and iron-tipped bronze stylus (above) are from the same area. The Roman dice and box (above, right) were assembled from various parts of ancient London. The Museum of London, in Aldersgate Street, Barbican, also displays part of the medieval London town wall, in its original position. Many other discoveries from Roman London can be seen in the British Museum, Bloomsbury.

WESLEY'S CHAPEL AND HOUSE A bronze statue of John Wesley, founder of Methodism, stands by the chapel of which he laid the foundation stone in 1777. When he died he lay in state while thousands of his followers filed past his coffin. Afterwards he was buried in the little graveyard behind.

The house alongside the chapel, where Wesley lived for the last 12 years of his life, has been opened as a museum to Methodism. The rooms have been restored so that they are again much as Wesley knew them.
Location: 49 City Rd, EC1.   *Map: 400 Db*

WEST GATE The gate on the west side of London's Roman fort is within a locked enclosure – open at lunch-times – reached by steps on the north side of London Wall. The gate was built early in the 2nd century. (See p. 242.)
Location: London Wall, EC2.   *Map: 400 Db*

WESTMINSTER ABBEY It was Edward the Confessor, a pious and gentle man, and the last but one of the Saxon kings, who founded the abbey church at Westminster about 1050. He selected a site that is

TWIN TOWERS – 200 YEARS LATE

The bottom section of the twin towers of Westminster Abbey was built between 1376 and 1506. They were left incomplete until the 18th century, when the upper portions were partly designed by Christopher Wren and completed by Nicholas Hawksmoor.

thought to have been used for religious buildings since the time of the Romans, and while the abbey was being built, lived in the nearby Palace of Westminster. But he was never to enter the great abbey alive. He died a few days after its consecration in 1065 and was buried near the High Altar.

On Christmas Day in 1066, the new King of England, William of Normandy, held his coronation in the abbey. He did so to reinforce his right to the throne, for being crowned within yards of the Confessor's tomb lent sanctity to the ceremony. William started a coronation ritual that has continued to the present day. With only two exceptions – Edward V who was murdered in the Tower, and Edward VIII who abdicated – all the monarchs of England have been crowned in Westminster Abbey.

In 1163 Edward the Confessor was canonised and multitudes of pilgrims began to visit his tomb. In 1245 Henry III – a devoted follower of St Edward – decided to build a new abbey to provide a more fitting shrine for the saint, and to have a larger and more beautiful space for the coronation of sovereigns.

The Confessor's abbey was replaced by one of the country's most outstanding examples of Early English architecture, with a nave 102 ft high – the loftiest Gothic nave in England.

Many additions have been made to the abbey over the centuries, but its great architectural triumph is the Chapel of Henry VII, with its superb fan-vaulting, built between 1503 and 1512. The tomb of Henry VII and his queen, Elizabeth of York, is one of the finest Renaissance monuments in Europe, the work of the Italian sculptor Pietro Torrigiani.

The remains of Mary, Queen of Scots were brought to the abbey in 1612, from Peterborough Cathedral, by her son James I, so that she might have "like honour" to the queen who ordered her beheading.

George II was the last of the English sovereigns to be buried in the abbey. Since then, the traditional burial place of monarchs has been at Windsor Castle.

St Edward's Chapel contains the Coronation Chair. It was made in 1300 to enclose the Stone of Scone which Edward I captured from the Scots in 1296. The stone had been part of the Scottish coronation ceremony, and was said to have been brought by the Scots from their original homeland, Ireland, in the 6th century. During coronation ceremonies, the Chair is moved into the Sanctuary.

During the Dissolution of the Monasteries the abbey was dissolved, and is now called an abbey only by tradition. Its official title is the Collegiate Church of St Peter in Westminster. One unbroken link with its monastic past, however, remains in the College Garden. Here herbs were grown for the treatment of sick and aged monks in the Infirmary, and the garden has been under continuous cultivation for nine centuries.

Below the cloisters, in the undercroft – originally the monks' common-room – is the Abbey Museum. There are many exhibits connected with the abbey's history, notably wax funeral effigies, such as Lord Nelson and Charles II. The king's face is thought to be a death mask, in painted wax.
Location: Parliament Sq., SW1.   *Map: 400 Ca*

CHAPEL OF HENRY VII

As the nave of Westminster Abbey was being completed in the 15th century, Henry VII pulled down the Lady Chapel and built a new east end of the abbey, now called the Henry VII Chapel. Beneath the elaborate fan-vaulting, stands the tomb of Henry and his queen, Elizabeth of York. It has been the chapel of the Knights of the Bath since 1725, and the banners of the senior Knights Grand Cross of the order hang in the chapel. When each knight dies his banner is taken down and given to his next of kin. The aisles each side of the chapel contain the tombs of Elizabeth I and the queen who was executed at her orders, Mary, Queen of Scots.

"ROYAL ROSEBUD" Princess Sophia, daughter of James I, died the day after she was born at Greenwich in 1606. She is buried at the abbey, and her monument is inscribed "Sophia, a royal rosebud, untimely plucked by death". Her sister Mary who died at the age of two the following year is buried close by.

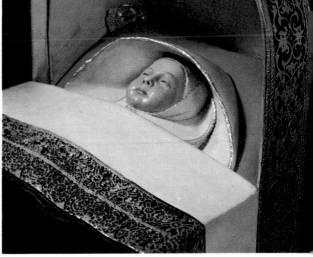

Longdon upon Tern *Salop*   *Map: 393 Ed*
AQUEDUCT The disused Shrewsbury Canal passes
through Longdon and although most traces have
vanished the aqueduct across the Tern remains,
and can easily be seen from across the road.

Designed in cast iron by Thomas Telford
about 1795, it is rather ungainly, but was the
first of its kind and the forerunner of Telford's
superb Pontcysyllte Aqueduct.
Location: 9 miles E of Shrewsbury (B5062,
B5063).

Longleat *Wilts.*   *Map: 397 Gd*
The earliest true Renaissance house in Britain.
Its completion in 1580 after 12 years of building
marked the dawn of the great age of Elizabethan
architecture. The flat roof scattered with massed
chimney-stacks, the correct use of classical proportions, the tiers of huge windows and the
symmetry are all features without precedent in
the 16th century.

The park, of exceptional beauty, was the 18th-
century creation of "Capability" Brown.
Location: 4 miles SW of Warminster off A362.

Long Melford *Suffolk*   *Map: 399 Fe*
CHURCH OF THE HOLY TRINITY Suffolk's finest
"wool" church is a 15th-century testament to the
piety and prosperity of the county's wool
merchants. Built in the Perpendicular style, it has
the magnificence of a small cathedral.

The Lady Chapel has its own cloister, or
covered way, around three sides. A multipli-
cation table scratched on the east wall is an
evocative reminder of the 17th century when the
chapel was used as a "Publicke School for
Melford".
Location: 3½ miles N of Sudbury on A134
MELFORD HALL Until the Reformation the estate
belonged to the abbots of Bury St Edmunds, but
then passed to William Cordell, who was
cunning enough to please both Henry VIII and
Queen Mary, and provide "sumptuous feas-
tinges" for Queen Elizabeth on her Suffolk
progress in 1578.

The red bricks for the Tudor house were made
beside the village pond, still called Claypits.
Location: N end of village.

Longthorpe Tower *Cambs.*   *Map: 398 Df*
The tower belonged to a 13th and 14th-century
fortified house. It was reached by a passage from
the house next door, and was built as protection
from invasion by French raiders up the River
Nene. Medieval wall-paintings were discovered
recently under centuries of whitewash.
Location: 2 miles W of Peterborough on A47.

Longton *Staffs.*   *Map: 393 Fe*
GLADSTONE POTTERY A working museum of the
pottery industry, at which craftsmen can be seen
using traditional techniques (see p. 248).
Location: Uttoxeter Rd, town centre.

Loose Howe *N. Yorks.*   *Map: 395 Cf*
This burial mound of about 1600 BC covered an
oak tree-trunk coffin containing a Bronze Age
body dressed in linen and wearing leather shoes.
A dagger lay alongside the body, and next to the
coffin was a 9 ft long dug-out canoe. A later
burial in the same mound was accompanied by
a stone battle-axe and a bronze dagger.
Location: 3½ miles NW of Rosedale Abbey.

Loseley House *Surrey*   *Map: 398 Cb*
In the hall of this Elizabethan house is a
remarkable series of canvas panels painted in
1543–7. They probably once lined Henry VIII's
tent during the medieval-style tournaments in
tented encampments that he enjoyed so much.
Location: 3 miles SW of Guildford (A3100 then
B3000).

Lotherton Hall *W. Yorks.*   *Map: 391 Gb*
This Victorian and Edwardian House, set in
pleasant gardens, contains works of art and
costumes from 1700 to the present day.
Location: 3 miles NE of Garsforth (A642 and
B1217).

Loughborough *Leics.*   *Map: 394 Ba*
MAIN LINE STEAM TRUST Loughborough Station
stands on the last major railway to be built in
Britain, the Great Central. The Main Line Steam
Trust now runs a regular passenger service
between Loughborough and Rothley. The
locomotives include the powerful *Duke of
Gloucester* (1954), last steam express locomotive
to be built for British Railways.
Location: Great Central Rd, off A60.

Loughor Castle *W. Glam.*   *Map: 392 Ca*
A 13th-century stone tower was built on a
Norman motte which had been raised in the
corner of an old Roman fort.
Location: 6 miles NW of Swansea on A4070.

AN ESTATE FOR £53

*Longleat House was built by Sir John Thynne who
bought the estate for £53 in 1540. Longleat began as
a priory built by Augustinian Canons in the 13th
century by a stream known as the Long Leat. The
priory was dissolved in the 1530s following Henry
VIII's break with the Church of Rome. John Thynne,
a land-owner who acquired a fortune by marriage and
in the service of the Duke of Somerset, built the
present house. It cost him £8,016 13s 8¼d. The
Thynne family still own it, having in the meantime
become marquesses of Bath.*

DESSERT, TUDOR STYLE

Six children of a 16th-century family eat dessert – in company with the family pets, a parrot and a marmoset. Dessert in noble households usually consisted of locally grown fruit – apples, pears, grapes, *cherries – and cheese. The portrait, which hangs at Longleat House, shows Lord and Lady Cobham with their six children and Lady Cobham's sister. The Cobhams were friends of the owners of Longleat.*

THE ELIZABETHAN HOUSEWIFE: A WOMAN FOR ALL SEASONS

Every Elizabethan girl was taught that her adult life would be spent running a house, whether it were a large country estate or a simple cottage. Most girls received no formal schooling, unless they came from noble families. They spent their childhood learning all the skills of a housewife, from making soap to keeping accounts.

In the reign of Queen Elizabeth, household work had hardly changed from medieval times. There were no labour-saving devices, and everything had to be done by hand. Heating came from wood fires which had to be set and cleared every day. All hot water had to be heated over an open fire in the kitchen. Lighting came from candles or rush-lights which were made at home. Clothes were made by hand, possibly from material spun and woven in the house. All cooking was done over an open fire or in an oven. Even in most towns, many households kept a few animals themselves, such as pigs or poultry, and meat from slaughtered animals had to be preserved for the winter.

Preserving meat for winter

Autumn was the busiest time of year for the Elizabethan housewife. She had to ensure that she had enough food to feed the whole family throughout the winter, with enough left over for guests and for poor travellers who might call at the door.

Meat from animals slaughtered in autumn was preserved in wine vinegar or by salting – either by packing in granular salt or by soaking in a strong solution of salt and water. Fruit and vegetables were stored for use fresh, or were made into pickles. Fruits were also made into syrups and jellies. Herbs were cut and dried, to help make the salt meat more appetising.

As winter wore on, the housewife or her servants had to sort through the stored apples and vegetables and throw out any that had gone rotten, or else the rot might spread through the whole batch.

Wealthier houses would relieve their diet of salt meat through the winter by using game caught on their own land and baby pigeons bred in dovecots.

Home-made wines and cordials

When summer arrived the country housewife would make wines from black and red currants, elder flowers and cowslips. Large households made their own beer at least once a month, and in country houses bread, butter and cheese were made every day.

Tea, coffee and chocolate had not yet arrived in Britain, and the water supply was often impure because of poor sewerage. So home-made wines and fruit cordials were an important part of an Elizabethan meal.

The country housewife made her own soap by mixing left-over fat and wood ashes, scenting it with herbs. But every town had a soap works alongside the slaughterhouse, the soap-makers getting their fat from the scraped hides of the slaughtered animals.

Clothes were washed with soap or with a liquid called lye, which could be made from wood ashes or hen dung, soaked in water and strained. After washing, the clothes – made of wool or linen – were rinsed in running water and the linen was spread out in the sun to bleach.

In a wealthy household, where silk was worn, potato water was made for sponging the material clean. Raw potato was grated into cold water, allowed to soak and then strained.

By the 1550s well-to-do households ate only two meals a day, but the work in the kitchen was not reduced. A man's table was a sign of his success, and elaborate meals were served, lasting two or three hours.

Louth *Lincs.*   *Map: 395 Dc*
CHURCH OF ST JAMES This late-Gothic church has a superb spire rising nearly 300 ft. The spire was built early in the 16th century at a cost of £305 8s 5d; the list of subscribers still exists in the churchwarden's accounts.

The church has a fine chest, the Sudbury Hutch, given before 1504, and carved with the heads of a king and queen, said to be Henry VII and Elizabeth of York. In the north chapel are two medieval wooden angels.
Location: Westgate, town centre.

Lower Brockhampton *Heref.*   *Map: 393 Ec*
This is a fine example of the type of manor house in which a squire and his family lived in 14th-century England.

The country was under strong government when the house was built. Unlike houses in the wilder north, Lower Brockhampton was not fortified with towers and battlements – just a moat, three sides of which remain.

It is a spacious half-timbered hall-house. The 15th-century gatehouse stands apart.
Location: 11 miles W of Worcester off A44.

A Victorian pottery that still lives

CRAFTSMEN DEMONSTRATE TRADITIONAL SKILLS AT THE 19TH-CENTURY GLADSTONE POTTERY, WHOSE BOTTLE OVENS FORM A RARE LANDMARK

The Gladstone Pottery at Longton, Staffordshire, was built in the 1850s and it is the only potbank in Britain where visitors can see demonstrations of various stages in pottery making as it was carried on in Victorian times. The pottery closed as a commercial concern in the mid-1960s but was then taken over by a charitable trust and kept alive as a working museum of the potter's craft.

The ovens, workshops, store rooms, exhibition galleries and offices are grouped around a cobbled courtyard. The only access to the yard is through a tunnel under the manager's office. This enabled him to observe every coming and going.

How the clay was treated
The first step in the traditional process of pottery making was that clay and other raw materials

SYMBOLS OF STAFFORDSHIRE

Bottle ovens (above) and the potter's wheel (below) are two symbols of an industry that has flourished in the north Staffordshire towns for 300 years. Most of the bottle-shaped kilns have disappeared, supplanted by gas and electric ovens. Gone, too, is the potter's wheel, which was hand-turned by a boy to revolve a turntable for a man throwing pots. A woman kept him supplied with balls of clay.

WEDGING CLAY *After clay had been weathered, it was cut into blocks. A worker sliced each block in half and repeatedly slammed one half hard on the other until the clay was air-free.*

PRESSING *In the early 19th century ware was mass-produced by "pressing". In the case of simple objects, like washbasins, a sheet of clay of even thickness was simply pressed on to a plaster mould and allowed to dry.*

DECORATING *Some of the pottery's ware was hand-painted and gilded – a delicate task calling for steady hands and good, even light. The job was usually done by women in a large room on the top floor with skylights.*

Ludgershall Castle *Wilts.* *Map: 398 Bc*
Matilda, daughter of Henry I, spent most of
King Stephen's reign trying to take the throne
from him. On one occasion in the 1140s she took
refuge in Ludgershall's earthwork castle. Stone
buildings were added later.
Location: 6½ miles NW of Andover on A342.

Ludlow *Salop* *Map: 393 Ec*
CASTLE In 1139 King Stephen was besieging
Ludlow Castle, which was held for his cousin
Matilda in her fight to take his throne. One
morning, the king and Prince Henry of Scotland
were walking near the gatehouse when a grappling iron was let down on a rope. Its hook
caught in the prince's cloak and gradually he was
lifted off the ground. Stephen grabbed him and
slashed the rope with a knife. The prince was
saved, but the castle was not taken. Soon afterwards the gatehouse was heightened to make it
into a great tower.
  In 1483 the 12-year-old Edward V was staying
at Ludlow when he heard that his father Edward
IV had died and that he was king. He left Ludlow

were brought into the yard by cart and dumped.
There they were left to weather for several years.
  When they were fully weathered the materials
were taken to the mixing house, and stirred in a
large vat by a propeller driven by a small steam-
engine in the next building. The mixed clay was
then wedged – cut into pieces which were
slammed together to expel any pockets of air.
This work was often done by small boys who
worked 70 or more hours a week, for a wage of
two shillings.
  A proportion of the mixed, wedged clay was
partly dried for use by craftsmen in the workshops. Some of these threw (shaped on a potter's
wheel) symmetrical objects such as bowls. Others
cast non-symmetrical articles, such as teapots, in
plaster of Paris moulds.
  Once shaped, the pottery was ready for firing,
or baking in the oven. It was placed in saggers,
or fireproof containers, which were then taken
to a bottle oven and stacked inside the oven's
central coal-stoked furnace.
  The fired ware, known as biscuit ware, was
then decorated. Some was hand-painted on the
upper floors, where roof lights provide good,
even illumination. The rest was printed with
transfers.
  The final process was glazing. The decorated
article was dipped in glaze, a solution of chemi-
cals which, when heated, sets in a hard transparent layer. This makes the article impervious to
liquids, protects the design and provides a glossy
finish. (In the 19th century, lead was a major
constituent of many glazes, and as a result many
workers suffered from lead poisoning.) The
article was then fired again, this time in what is
known as a glost oven.

Fame never came to Gladstone
The finished articles were stored in the warehouse, after some samples had been set aside for
display in the showrooms beside the office.
  The Gladstone Pottery was never well known
like the potteries that produce Wedgwood,
Royal Doulton or Spode. Its interest lies in its
survival as a typical 19th-century pottery of the
smaller kind.
  The exhibition galleries at Gladstone display
not only its own wares but also those made at
other Staffordshire potteries.

PRODUCTS OF THE POTTERIES

*Apart from being a working museum, the Gladstone
Pottery has galleries which illustrate ceramic tiles,
sanitary ware and the history of pottery through the
products of other British and foreign potteries. The
historical gallery traces the development of the decoration of pottery and the progress of sanitation, and
displays ceramics used for exterior decoration in the
18th and 19th centuries.*

CHIMNEY POTS *Ornately shaped
terracotta chimney pots have long
been part of the Staffordshire landscape.*

WASHBASIN *The floral decoration
of this late-19th-century washbasin
typifies Victorian design in sanitary
ware.*

CERAMIC TILES *One of the tiles
commemorates William Gladstone,
the prime minister after whom the
pottery was named.*

with his young brother Richard, but on the way they were intercepted by their uncle, Richard, Duke of Gloucester who took them on to London. The boys were later murdered in the Tower and Gloucester became Richard III.
Location: Castle Sq., town centre.
FEATHERS HOTEL The hotel, built in 1603, is a half-timbered building elaborately decorated with carving on the timbers. Inside, the plaster ceilings are moulded with vines, roses and thistles.
Location: Corve St, town centre.
READER'S HOUSE The house was built of stone in the 13th century and used by the local school-master. In the 17th century it was taken over by the Reader, the assistant priest of the parish, and a half-timbered extension was added.
Location: East end of St Lawrence's Church.

Lullingstone *Kent*   *Map: 399 Ec*
ROMAN VILLA The remains of a Roman country house stand in Lullingstone Park. The villa contains one of the earliest known Christian chapels in Britain. (See below.)
Location: 6 miles N of Sevenoaks off A225.

Lullingstone: a Roman country house

SPLENDID MOSAICS AND MURALS DECORATED A VILLA IN KENT THAT IS ONE OF
THE EARLIEST KNOWN PLACES OF CHRISTIAN WORSHIP IN BRITAIN

The original house at Lullingstone was a simple flint and mortar dwelling built about AD 80 by a native farmer. In the 2nd century a Roman of wealth and taste added to and enriched the original building, by building baths at the west end, kitchens, and a cult room in honour of three water nymphs. A decayed fresco of the nymphs survives. For some reason, about AD 200, the Roman owner had to leave in a hurry, and for most of the 3rd century the villa was derelict.

About AD 280 a Romano-British farming family reoccupied and restored the property, and it was continuously occupied until it was mys-teriously destroyed by fire in the early 5th century. They built a temple-mausoleum, and in the house a dining and a reception room with superb mosaic floors. One mosaic shows Zeus, in the form of a bull, abducting Europa.

In the late 4th century one room was con-verted into a Christian chapel, and the villa became one of the earliest known places of Christian worship in Britain.

SACRED MONOGRAM *Religious murals decorated the Christian chapel. Among them was a Chi Rho monogram, from the first two Greek letters of Christ's name.*

HOW LULLINGSTONE VILLA PROBABLY LOOKED IN AD 360

An artist's reconstruction shows the house as it might have appeared when it was owned by a Romano-British farming family. By the mid-4th century they were not yet Christians, and the temple-mausoleum in the left background was for pagan worship. A young man and woman were buried in the mausoleum, and a ritual was periodically performed in the domed temple built above it.

SILVER OFFERINGS TO A ROMAN CHRISTIAN CHURCH

At some time during the reigns of the Roman emperors Valentinian I and Valens (AD 364–78), the Romano-British farmer and his family who owned Lullingstone Villa were converted to Christianity. The Christian religion had become accepted in the Roman Empire in AD 313, and three British bishops had attended the Council of Arles in France in AD 314.

Two rooms at Lullingstone were transformed into a chapel and an ante-chamber, and these may have been used as a place of worship for Christians from the neighbouring villas as well.

To this sanctuary new converts would have brought offerings. Sometimes these would have been precious objects, vessels of gold or silver, as in the pagan religions they had recently relinquished. Throughout antiquity, sacred vessels bore no outward difference to everyday ones. Only inscriptions and Christian symbols on some identify them as having belonged to the Church.

Finds at Lullingstone Villa, excavated from 1949 to 1960, included marble portrait busts, tin and copper coins, bronze, bone and iron ornaments, glass bottles and bowls, semi-precious stones, bronze vessels and much pottery.

However, no gold or silver ware, either religious or secular, was unearthed. This is not unusual. Such vessels have usually been found in hoards some distance away from villas – probably buried at a time of danger, to prevent them from falling into the hands of barbarian attackers. Such hoards have been uncovered at Water Newton in Huntingdonshire, Mildenhall in Suffolk, and other sites throughout Europe.

SACRED SILVER *The silver used in Christian ceremonies at Lullingstone would probably have been not unlike the hoard of 4th-century Christian silver found in 1975 at* Water Newton, near Peterborough. The triangular plaques, which were offerings, bear the Christian Chi Rho monogram.

Luton Hoo *Beds.*   *Map: 398 Dd*
The 3rd Earl of Bute, who dominated George III in the early years of his reign, bought Luton Hoo in 1762 when he was briefly and unsuccessfully prime minister. He resigned the following year and engaged Robert Adam to reshape the house and "Capability" Brown to landscape the grounds.

The house now contains a collection of tapestries, pictures, china and jewellery, including Russian Fabergé jewellery.
Location: 1 mile S of Luton off A6129.

Lydford Castle *Devon*   *Map: 396 Dc*
A Norman tower was built at the end of the 12th century as a prison. Then a huge ditch was dug around the tower and the earth thrown up against it, submerging it to first-floor level.

Lydford's role as a prison lasted for centuries. Its rough justice became well known. A 17th-century poet described how he had often heard of "Lydford law, how in the morn they hang and draw, and sit in judgment after".
Location: 7½ miles SW of Okehampton (A30, A386 and minor road).

Lydiard Park *Wilts.* *Map: 398 Ac*
A medieval house can be detected behind the smooth pedimented façade of about 1740, and vestiges of three great avenues of trees give a clue to the character of the formal garden that was swept away in the 18th century in favour of the present park. A walled garden, where all flowers, fruit and vegetables would have been grown, also survives.

Lydiard Park was the home of the St John family, whose magnificent monuments fill the adjacent church.
Location: 4 miles W of Swindon (A420 and minor roads).

Lyme Hall *Cheshire* *Map: 393 Ff*
The dramatic Palladian façade of the house, designed in 1725, conceals a Tudor mansion with a long gallery and Tudor drawing-room.

In the Stag Parlour, a group of Cheshire landowners with Jacobite sympathies held secret meetings in the 1690s.

Half a century later Thomas Chippendale made four chairs for the Parlour, upholstering them in cloth from the cloak worn by Charles I at his execution in 1649. The chairs are still there today.
Location: 6½ miles SE of Stockport off A6.

Lympne *Kent* *Map: 399 Fb*
LYMPNE CASTLE This small stone castle was built mainly in the 14th century, probably as protection against raids from French naval forces.
Location: S of Lympne, 3 miles W of Hythe.
STUTFALL CASTLE The forlorn walls of a late 3rd-century Roman fort, tossed around by landslides, belonged to the chain of forts designed to protect south-east Britain from Saxon pirate raids.
Location: S of Lympne, 3 miles W of Hythe.

Lytes Cary *Somerset* *Map: 397 Fd*
This medieval manor house is typical of many others in the West Country: long ownership by one family, decline in the 18th and 19th centuries, and resurrection in the 20th. From the 13th to the 18th century it was the home of the Lyte family, whose most distinguished son, Henry Lyte, was a pioneering botanist and translator of *Lyte's Herbal* (1578).
Location: 8 miles NE of Yeovil off A37.

Lyveden New Bield *Northants.* *Map: 398 Cf*
The 16th-century architect Sir Thomas Tresham designed a house on the plan of a cross, but work stopped when he died in 1605. It is now a picturesque ruin.
Location: 4 miles SW of Oundle off A427.

M

Macclesfield *Cheshire* *Map: 393 Ff*
CHURCH OF ST MICHAEL AND ALL ANGELS Begun in the late 13th century, the church has been extensively altered since.

The Savage Chapel was built in 1504 by Thomas Savage, Archbishop of York, and monuments range from 15th-century alabaster effigies to the reclining figure of Earl Rivers (1696) by the London sculptor-mason William Stanton.

On the west wall of the chapel is a brass to Roger Legh who died in 1506. The inscription records that the pardon for saying five Paternosters, five Aves and one Creed is 26,000 years and 26 days (a probable reference to a period of remission from Purgatory).
Location: Market Place, town centre.
SILK INDUSTRY Macclesfield was a major centre of the British silk industry in the 18th century, and many old mills and silk weavers' cottages survive. Silk manufacture was brought to England by Huguenot refugees who settled in London in the late 17th century. It spread to the Midlands about 50 years later.

In Park Green there is a mill built about 1785 by William Frost and Sons, and now used by small firms. In nearby Parsonage Street are the workers' houses.

A CHIEF'S TOMB THAT WAS RAIDED BY VIKINGS

Maes Howe prehistoric tomb is covered by a mound of clay and stones 24 ft high, and is entered through a low stone passage 26 ft long. The stone roof is held on corbels (overlapping courses of stone). In the corners of the room upright stone slabs act as buttresses. When Viking raiders first visited the tomb many centuries ago it was probably already more than 3,000 years old. They left runic inscriptions on the walls (below), one recording that they had found treasure.

DEATH AT MAIDEN CASTLE

The Iron Age fortress of Maiden Castle is half a mile long and encloses an area of 47 acres. When the Romans invaded Britain in the 1st century AD it would have contained a sizeable township.

DEFENCES *At the entrance, platforms were built for slingers, and an arsenal of 54,000 beach pebbles was found.*

SHOT IN THE SPINE *One of the Britons who defended Maiden Castle against the Romans died when an iron bolt from a Roman ballista drove through his spine.*

Maenclochog *Dyfed*   *Map: 392 Ab*
PENRHÔS COTTAGE A rare "clom" and stone cottage. For the poorest families in 19th-century Pembrokeshire, often the only way to get a house was to build a "one-night house" that would establish squatters' rights on a piece of land. If a shack, built largely of turf, was finished by the morning, with the roof on and a fire burning in the hearth, it could later be replaced by a permanent cottage with "clom" walls – clay mixed with straw and twigs.
Location: 10 miles SE of Fishguard off B4313.

Maes Howe Tomb *Orkney*   *Map: 389 Ee*
The finest example of prehistoric architecture in Britain, Maes Howe was probably built about 2500 BC. Beneath a great mound is a vaulted stone chamber 14 ft square, and behind three of the chamber walls are small burial places. The entrances are raised about 18 in. above floor level, and were blocked by closely fitting stone blocks, now resting on the floor. The tomb was the burial place of a powerful chieftain, but it was ransacked centuries ago by Viking raiders.
Location: 5 miles NE of Stromness on A965.

Maesllyn *Dyfed*   *Map: 392 Bc*
WOOLLEN MILL A working museum shows how a fleece is transformed into woven cloth. The

mill was built in 1881 and was originally water-powered. Its two water-wheels are still in working order. One is a Pelton wheel, forerunner of the turbine. It is an enclosed wheel into which water is injected through a nozzle.
Location: 11 miles S of New Quay (A486 and minor road).

Maes-y-Cwymmer *Mid Glam.*   *Map: 393 Da*
VIADUCT A curved viaduct on 16 arches was built in 1858 to carry the Great Western Railway over the River Rhymney. It is no longer in use.
Location: 5 miles N of Caerphilly (A469, A472).

Maiden Castle *Dorset*   *Map: 397 Fc*
The sweeping ramparts of the great Iron Age hill-fort of Maiden Castle dominate the landscape for miles around. They evoke the militant spirit and uneasy tribal relationships that existed in the last century before the Roman invasion. And they indicate the power wielded by the tribal leader who ordered their construction.
A fortified settlement was first built on the site about 300 BC. It was defended by an earth rampart surmounted by a timber wall. Inside the rampart were clusters of circular huts and rectangular buildings approached by narrow streets or lanes. Corn was grown in fields around the fort, and stored in deep circular pits. Wool

from the community's flocks of sheep was spun and woven.

About the beginning of the 1st century BC, the defences were completely remodelled and triple ramparts and ditches greatly extended the size of the fort. The defences were huge–60 ft from the bottom of the ditch to the top of the rampart.

The sling, a major new weapon of siege warfare introduced about this time, was used to defend the stronghold. At strategic points platforms were built for the slingers, and on the platforms great heaps of slingstones (beach pebbles) were placed. One heap contained over 20,000 stones.

The approaches were also remodelled, forcing attackers to follow a tortuous and no doubt hazardous route to the wooden gates themselves, first through a series of overlapping out-works, then up a defended and overlooked approach passage. These defences would have been enough to deter any local enemies but the Roman army was not so impressed.

In AD 43 the 2nd Augustan Legion, under the future Emperor Vespasian, attacked Maiden Castle. The attack was begun by a barrage of iron bolts shot from ballistae (catapults) which would have cleared the ramparts of defenders and given the legionaries some cover as they attacked the weaker of the two gateways, at the east end. The attackers set fire to some huts inside the out-works. Under cover of the smoke they attacked the gateway, very possibly using the "tortoise", in which groups of legionaries locked their shields above their heads to make themselves invulnerable to projectiles hurled by the defenders.

Once inside, the legionaries slaughtered the defenders, mostly men between the ages of 20 and 25, but including some women and older men.

The remains of the British defenders were found in hastily dug graves by the east gate, the skeletons still bearing the ugly wounds made by the short swords of the incensed Roman soldiers.

Maiden Castle was abandoned after the Roman assault. Three and a half centuries later a pagan temple, with an inner shrine and surrounding ambulatory, was built inside the rampart to some unknown deity.
Location: 2 miles SW of Dorchester off A354.

Maidenhead *Berks.*   *Map: 398 Cc*
THAMES VIADUCT The railway crosses the Thames on a brick viaduct designed by Isambard Kingdom Brunel and completed in 1838. It has remarkably flat, wide arches.
Location: By A4 on eastern edge of town.

Maidstone *Kent*   *Map: 399 Ec*
TYRWHITT-DRAKE MUSEUM OF CARRIAGES The collection is in the magnificent Archbishop's Stables, built in the 15th century to accommodate the animals of the Archbishop of Canterbury's train of carts and wagons as he moved between Canterbury and London. The stables are 150 ft long and have an external staircase and a crown post roof.

There are more than 60 carriages in the collection. Among them are a number of royal carriages, including the Russian droshky presented to Queen Victoria in 1850 by Tsar

Nicholas and the tiny pony carriage used by Victoria's children.

The collection also contains other vehicles such as an Edwardian bier, a traditional gipsy caravan, sledges, a penny-farthing and other early cycles.
Location: Mill St.

Mallwyd *Gwynedd*   *Map: 392 Cd*
CHURCH OF ST TYDECHO The church is said to have been founded in the 6th century. The present building dates from the 14th century.
Location: 11 miles E of Dolgellau on A470.

Malmesbury *Wilts.*   *Map: 398 Ac*
AVON MILL The old woollen mill on the Avon, now an antiques showroom, was built in 1790 by a cloth merchant, Francis Hill. Hill moved to Malmesbury from Bradford-on-Avon to set up his mill because he feared the Bradford cottage spinners might wreck his new machines. The move was a wise precaution–the Bradford mills were wrecked in 1791.

The mill was originally water-powered and the old sluice gates that controlled the flow are still by the road bridge.
Location: By the main road bridge across the Avon.
MALMESBURY ABBEY A noble and impressive portion of the Norman nave is all that survives of a once great church. There is some splendid Norman carving in the south porch, and over the porch is a room with four volumes of an illuminated 15th-century Bible.

In the 11th century, a monk at the abbey, called Elmer, attached wings to his hands and feet and projected himself from the top of the church tower. William of Malmesbury, the historian, recorded that he glided for a furlong before landing and breaking his legs.
Location: Town centre.

Mam Tor *Derbys.*   *Map: 393 Gf*
PREHISTORIC VILLAGE The exposed and windy crest of Mam Tor, 1,700 ft above sea-level, must have been an unpleasant place to live, but it offered security from attack to a prehistoric village community. The inhabitants enclosed 16 acres of the summit with a ditch and rampart, and built huts inside.

Pottery from the huts and a fragment of a Late Bronze Age axe suggests that Mam Tor may be one of the earliest hill-forts in the country built about 1200 BC.
Location: 8 miles E of Whaley Bridge (A6, A625 and minor road to Edale).

Manchester   *Map: 391 Ea*
BARTON ARCADE Probably the most attractive shopping precinct in the north of England was built in 1871. It has a glass and iron roof and balconies with delicate iron tracery.
Location: Deansgate, city centre.
BRIDGEWATER CANAL One of the first true canals in Britain was built in 1761 to join the Duke of Bridgewater's mines at Worsley to Manchester, 10 miles away. The canal ended at Castlefield basin, off Castle Street. Most of the old buildings have been destroyed, but one, the Merchants' Warehouse, still stands in Castle Street by the junction of the Bridgewater and Rochdale Canals. It is not open to the public.

CATHEDRAL Amid the rebuilding of modern Manchester stands the medieval collegiate church which became its cathedral in 1847. The building dates from the 15th century and is Perpendicular Gothic, with much alteration during the 19th century. The great treasures of the cathedral are the canopied choir stalls, with a superb set of misericords (tip-up seats). Marvellous carving portrays unicorns, lions, monsters, bear-baiting and a pig playing bagpipes.
Location: Junction of Deansgate and Chapel St.
CHURCH OF ST ANN This Wren-style church is the only remaining 18th-century building in the city centre. There is some good 18th-century woodwork including the pulpit.
Location: St Ann's Sq., M2.
LIVERPOOL ROAD STATION The world's first passenger railway station was built in Manchester in 1830 for the Liverpool and Manchester Railway. The railway, which opened the same year, was the first to be built specifically to carry both goods and passengers in steam-hauled trains. The station was later converted to goods traffic.
Location: Liverpool Rd, off Deansgate, M2.
ROCHDALE CANAL The canal, completed in 1804, runs up through the city from the Bridgewater Canal, on a flight of nine locks, to Ducie Street junction and then on to Rochdale. The old canal wharf is now a car park in Ducie Street, but the original Canal Company offices still stand. One of the locks is actually right under the foundations of a modern tower block in Piccadilly beside the car park. The canal can be seen in various parts of the city, including Canal Street.

In the other direction, from Ducie Street you can follow the towpath of the Ashton Canal, completed in 1797, which gives a view of Victorian Manchester, with the old cotton mills and warehouses beside the locks.
ROYAL EXCHANGE During the 19th century, Manchester earned the nickname "Cotton-

opolis". One of the few survivors of those days is the Royal Exchange where the cotton merchants traded. A fine example of exuberant Victorian architecture, it now houses a theatre.
Location: Cross St, M1.
SHIP CANAL The development of Manchester as a major port came with the opening of the Ship Canal in 1894. This brought sea-going vessels to the heart of the city. One ship, the steamer *Westward Ho*, is permanently berthed as a floating pub at Pomona Docks, at the end of Hulme Hall Road.

Manorbier Castle *Dyfed*   Map: 392 Aa
Manorbier was the home of Gerald of Wales, the 12th-century Welsh-speaking Norman

BEFORE THE MOTOR CAR
At the Tyrwhitt-Drake Museum, Maidstone, Kent, carriages of all kinds illustrate the development of private transport from the 17th century until the carriage was superseded by the motor car.

LANDAU *Four passengers could travel in the landau (above), which was designed in Germany in the mid-18th century. It was normally drawn by two horses and was open-topped or had a withdrawable cover.*

SEDAN CHAIR *Two bearers, one in front, one at the rear, carried the sedan chair, which originated in Sedan, France. It was introduced into England in 1634, and could be hired in the street as well as being privately owned.*

historian. He was born in 1146 in the castle and described the pleasures of life there, with fine fishpond and beautiful orchards.

The castle was attacked about 1330 in a local riot in which the insurgents took away most of the contents and murdered some of the servants. The castle is still well preserved.
Location: 5 miles SW of Tenby (A4139 and B4585).

Mapledurham *Oxon.*   *Map: 398 Cc*
MAPLEDURHAM HOUSE This beautiful Elizabethan house beside the Thames carries evidence of the 200 year struggle of the Catholic families of England against prejudice, official ostracism and penal legislation.

The Blounts were such a family, and their portraits tell part of this story. Among the men there are no soldiers or sailors, for Catholics were disbarred; the family was never ennobled, nor, after the Protestant succession was assured in 1688, were they even knighted.

The nearby church is split in two. The nave is for the Protestant parish, the aisle, walled-off, was the burial place of Catholic squires.
Location: 4 miles NW of Reading (A4074 and minor road).
WATERMILL Mapledurham Mill on the Thames dates from Tudor times. At the end of the 19th century the mill had two external water-wheels each of which drove two pairs of millstones. In 1924 one wheel was replaced by a large water-driven turbine which supplied water from the Thames to the Mapledurham estate.
Location: Near Mapledurham church.

CANAL HORSE-POWER

Until recent years, horses towed the boats on Britain's canals. Where a tow-path changed from one side of a canal to the other, a "snake-bridge" (above) might be built so the horse could be taken across without untying its tow-rope. When the canal went under a main road, the horse had to be unhitched and led through a horse-shaped tunnel beneath the road (left). At Marple, near Manchester, there are examples of both types of bridge.

Marble Hill *Greater London*   *Map: 398 Dc*
The Countess of Suffolk, for whom Marble Hill was built in 1724–9, was the mistress of the Prince of Wales (later George II) and Woman of the Bedchamber to his wife. Her house was a villa, which in the usage of the day meant a small house, intended as a place of retreat from the formality of life at Court.

In Lady Suffolk's chamber the bed is placed in a recess, a formal arrangement derived from the Continent, where the rising and retiring of kings and queens and their grandest subjects were occasions of public spectacle.
Location: Richmond Rd, Twickenham.

March *Cambs.*   *Map: 399 Ef*
CHURCH OF ST WENDREDA The glory of the church is the double hammer-beam roof built about 1500, with its two tiers of angels with out-stretched wings. St Wendreda, to whom the church is dedicated, was a Saxon lady who founded a small religious community at March. The church was built in the 14th century, probably on the site of an earlier one.
Location: Church St, south end of the town.

Margate *Kent*   *Map: 399 Gc*
DRAPER'S MILL This smock windmill was built in the 1840s by the famous Kentish millwrights, Holmans of Canterbury. The four-storeyed mill is surmounted by a cap with a fantail and four shuttered sails. Bins of grain on the third floor were fed to three pairs of millstones. The mill was worked by wind until 1916, and by a gas engine up to 1939.
Location: St Peter's Footpath, College Rd.

Marisco Castle *Lundy Island*   *Map: 396 Cd*
Lundy Island was a haven for the pirate William Marisco in the 1230s. When royal forces captured him they took over the island as Crown property, and built a small castle from local stone. It was largely paid for by selling fur from rabbits that infested the island.

Markenfield Hall *N. Yorks.*   *Map: 391 Gb*
A "licence to crenellate", or build a fortified house, was granted to a local landowner John de Markenfield in 1310. The moat still exists, but a bridge has replaced the old drawbridge.

Beside the kitchen, which lies beneath the Great Hall, are vaulted cellars.

In 1569 Thomas Markenfield took part in a North Country rising against the Crown, and the house was forfeit. It eventually became a farmhouse.
Location: 3 miles S of Ripon off A61.

Market Harborough *Leics.*   *Map: 398 Cf*
CHURCH OF ST DIONYSIUS The 14th-century spire, which is a dominant landmark, is not quite so high as it was. A storm in January 1735 carried away the top.
Location: The Square, town centre.

Marple *Greater Manchester*   *Map: 393 Ff*
The Peak Forest Canal and the Macclesfield Canal meet in Marple, and to the south of the junction is a "snake" or roving bridge. This type of bridge is found only on the canals as it was built where the towpath changed from one side of the canal to the other. It enabled the boatman

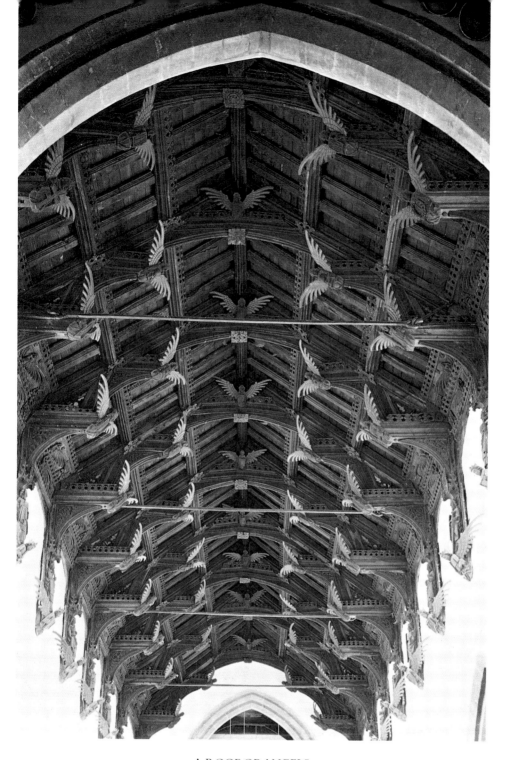

A ROOF OF ANGELS

The glorious double hammer-beam roof at March church in Cambridgeshire has angels carved in wood at the ends of the hammer-beams. Some of the angels hold medieval musical instruments including the shawm (a *type of oboe), clarion, lute, pipe, organ and fiddle. The roof, built about 1500, has 120 angels, including the 12 Apostles. The devil has also been included, possibly by a mischievous craftsman.*

to walk his horse across the canal without unhitching the tow-rope.

North of the junction is a set of lime kilns built by the Peak Forest Canal's chief promoter, Samuel Oldknow. Oldknow was a cotton magnate who built the canal to improve transport to his works, including one at Marple.

A flight of locks takes the canal on towards Manchester over the magnificent aqueduct across the River Goyt valley that was opened in 1800.
Location: The canal junction is by B6101, near its junction with A626.

Marsden *Tyne & Wear* *Map: 391 Ge*
SOUTER POINT LIGHTHOUSE The lighthouse was built in 1871 with a 76 ft high circular tower. It was one of the first to have electric light.
Location: 5 miles N of Sunderland on A183.

Marsden *W. Yorks.* *Map: 391 Fa*
CHURCH OF ST BARTHOLOMEW In the graveyard is the tomb of Enoch Taylor, a machine-maker at the time of the Luddite riots in the early 19th century. The Luddites, who rioted against the use of machinery in mills, gave his name to the hammers they used to smash machines: "Enoch did make them and Enoch shall smash them."

In the graveyard also are the village stocks. The old church was replaced by the present one at the end of the 19th century.
Location: 7 miles SW of Huddersfield on A62.
STANDEDGE TUNNEL The Huddersfield Narrow Canal, completed in 1811, passes under Standedge Fell through Britain's longest canal tunnel – 3 miles, 176 yds long. At the Marsden end of the tunnel are the tunnel-keeper's cottage and the canal maintenance yard.

The adjoining railway tunnel, built in 1849, follows a parallel course and is linked to the canal tunnel for ventilation. When a train came through, canal boatmen found themselves enveloped in smoke.
Location: By A62 at the W end of Marsden.

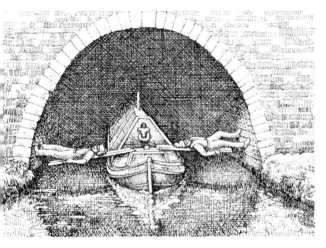

"LEGGING" THROUGH A TUNNEL

Standedge canal tunnel at Marsden, Britain's longest, had no towpath, so boats had to be "legged" through for more than 3 miles. Hired teams of "leggers" lay on their backs and pushed the boat along with their feet against the tunnel walls.

Marshfield *Avon* *Map: 393 Fa*
CASTLE FARM FOLK MUSEUM A medieval thatched longhouse, in which a farming family lived with their animals, has become the centrepiece of a museum of farming and rural life. It is attached to a working farm. The longhouse was built on crucks (curved timbers) at each end and still retains part of the original thatch fastened with wild clematis (old man's beard). There are also an 18th-century stable and a stone shepherd's hut furnished with shepherds' equipment.
Location: The museum is signposted from Marshfield, off A420, 8 miles W of Chippenham.

Martham *Norfolk* *Map: 395 Ga*
CHURCH FARM A working agricultural museum re-creates village life in the second half of the 19th century. Craftsmen such as a blacksmith

and a wheelwright work on the farm, and during the summer heavy horses can be seen working in the fields. Visitors are invited to help with the work.
Location: 9 miles N of Great Yarmouth (A149 to Rollesby, then turn right).

Mary Arden's House see Wilmcote

Mary Tavy *Devon* *Map: 396 Db*
METAL MINES The area of Dartmoor around Mary Tavy has been mined for tin, copper, lead – and arsenic, which was used for dyes and pesticides. The Wheal Friendship mine was begun in the late 18th century. At first it was a tin mine with workings extending right under the main village street. In the 1880s, it was reopened by the Devon Arsenic Company, and the ruins of the arsenic extraction plant – including the condensers and the 300 ft long condensing flue – still remain on the hillside above the village.

Just over a mile to the north, visible from the main road, is the ruined engine-house of Wheal Betsy. The mine was worked in the 19th century for both lead and silver until the deposits ran out. It was abandoned in the 1870s. The engine has gone, but the building is preserved.
Location: 4 miles NE of Tavistock on A386.

Mauchline *Strathclyde* *Map: 388 Cc*
BALLOCHMYLE VIADUCT The railway viaduct was built of sandstone by John Miller in 1848 with a central span 181 ft wide and 163 ft high. For many years it was the biggest span in Europe.
Location: The viaduct can be seen W of A76, a mile S of Mauchline.

Meare *Somerset* *Map: 397 Fd*
ABBOT'S FISH HOUSE The medieval stone building was built in the 14th century close to the former summer palace of the abbots of Glastonbury. The Fish House was used for salting and storing fish caught in the nearby lake. It has five rooms and had an outside staircase to the first floor.
Location: 3½ miles NW of Glastonbury on B3151.

Meikleour *Tayside* *Map: 387 Ea*
BEECH HEDGE The giant hedge of beech trees is believed to have been hastily planted by estate foresters at Meikleour House before they joined the Jacobite Rebellion of 1745. It is 100 ft high and forms the eastern border of the Marquis of Lansdowne's Meikleour estate.
Location: 4 miles S of Blairgowrie on A93.

Melbourne Hall *Derbys.* *Map: 393 Ge*
When the ancient manor of the bishops of Carlisle was bought by the Coke family in the 17th century, they incorporated in their rebuilding stonework from ruined Melbourne Castle. Thomas Coke, Vice-Chamberlain to Queen Anne and George I, engaged the royal gardeners to lay out his grounds.

The property passed to the Lambs, one of whom became 1st Lord Melbourne. His son was Queen Victoria's first and favourite Prime Minister, and gave his name to the Australian city.

Melbourne's study includes his writing table and other relics of himself and Palmerston.
Location: 8 miles S of Derby on B587.

Mellerstain House *Borders* *Map: 389 Fc*
The house is one of Scotland's most perfect Adam creations. William Adam built the two wings about 1725; his son Robert added the central block 40 years later and designed the interior.

The library, with its decorated ceiling, is one of his greatest masterpieces. Several other rooms contain Adam chimneypieces and furniture.
Location: 8 miles NW of Kelso off A6089.

Melrose Abbey *Borders* *Map: 389 Fc*
An imposing ruin of the Cistercian Abbey founded by David I of Scotland in 1136.

The heart of Robert Bruce is buried there. Before his death from leprosy in 1329, Bruce ordered his friend Sir James Douglas to carry his heart to Jerusalem for burial. On the way, Douglas became involved in a hopeless battle with a Moorish army. He hurled the silver casket containing the heart into the thick of the enemy and charged after it to his death. The heart was eventually returned to Melrose, although Bruce's body is buried at Dunfermline.
Location: 4 miles SE of Galashiels (A7, A6091).

Melverley *Salop* *Map: 393 Ed*
CHURCH OF ST PETER A delightful timber-and-plaster church beside the River Vyrnwy. The interior has fine timber framing, and it is said that not one nail was used.

An entry in the register for December 17, 1776, reads: "This morning I have put a tye, No man could put it faster, 'Tween Matthew Dodd, the Man of God, And modest Nellie Foster."
Location: 11 miles W of Shrewsbury (A458, B4393 and minor road).

Menai Bridge *Gwynedd* *Map: 392 Cf*
Two bridges join the mainland to Anglesey. The older bridge was designed by Thomas Telford as part of his Holyhead road and was opened in 1826. It is a suspension bridge, crossing the channel 100 ft above the water with a single span of 579 ft.

The railway is carried by Robert Stephenson's Britannia Bridge, opened in 1849. It used a novel construction technique, with the rails being laid inside huge hollow girders. There are two main spans, 460 ft long and 70 ft above the water. It was damaged by fire in 1970, and the sides of the tubes have been removed.
Location: 1 mile W of Bangor on A5.

Menstrie Castle *Central* *Map: 388 De*
The castle is a fortified tower house of the 16th century. It was the birthplace of Sir William Alexander, 1st Earl of Stirling, who was appointed lieutenant for the settlement of Nova Scotia in the 1620s. The castle is now council flats, with one room as a museum.
Location: 7 miles W of Dollar on A9.

Mere *Wilts.* *Map: 397 Gd*
CHURCH OF ST MICHAEL THE ARCHANGEL A large Decorated church with a 124 ft west tower. The 15th-century parclose screen survives, and misericords (tip-up seats) in the chancel have medieval carvings, one showing a man poking out his tongue.

The south chapel contains two brasses of medieval knights and four 14th-century stained-glass figures in one of the windows.

One of the memorials in the churchyard is to a man who died in 1737 after experimenting on himself with smallpox vaccine.
Location: 10 miles S of Warminster (A350, B3095).

Mersea Island *Essex* *Map: 399 Fd*
TUMULUS Wealthy families of the early Roman period in south-east Britain buried the cremated remains of their dead beneath vast conical mounds of earth (tumuli). The tumulus on Mersea Island is the only one in Britain where you can actually enter the burial cavity. The

A PAIR OF WAR HORSES IN HARNESS

A pair of Suffolk Punch horses harrow a barley field for spring sowing at Church Farm, Martham, in Norfolk. Suffolk Punches were first known in England in 1506. They were used as war horses and also for farm work, renowned for their ability to keep a steady pace throughout a working day.

HOUSES
Cyfarthfa Castle (right) was built in 1825 when Merthyr Tydfil was in its heyday as a centre of the world's iron industry.
The workers lived beside the works. Their terraced houses (left) are still occupied.

EPITAPH *Robert Crawshay presided over Merthyr's decline as an iron town from 1860–80, as the iron ore ran out – a period marked by riots and strikes. His headstone at Vaynor reads: "God forgive me."*

IRON-MASTERS OF MERTHYR TYDFIL
William Crawshay, one of the iron-kings of Merthyr Tydfil, built a mock-Gothic castle from the vast wealth he acquired from iron. He named it Cyfarthfa after the first of two ironworks he had established beside the River Taff. His son Robert was an early photography enthusiast and would summon his daughters to pose for him with a blast of a whistle. Many of his photographs are on show at the castle.

cremation urn is in Colchester Museum.
Location: Turn left off B1025 immediately after crossing the causeway to the island.

Merthyr Tydfil *Mid Glam.* *Map: 392 Db*
IRON TOWN Early in the Industrial Revolution Merthyr Tydfil became the greatest producer of iron in the world.

The iron industry had started at Merthyr in the 16th century when iron was smelted with charcoal. When charcoal smelting gave way to coke smelting, English iron-masters moved into South Wales where iron ore and coal existed together.

The Guest family arrived from Shropshire about 1765 and helped to establish the biggest of the Merthyr ironworks, the vast Dowlais com-pany. The site, beside A4102, is still in use.

A second iron dynasty was founded by the Crawshay family who established the Cyfarthfa works on the west bank of the River Taff, followed by the Ynysfach works near by.

The Guests and the Crawshays were tyrannical employers. If the workers complained about wages or conditions they were not only sacked but could also be taken before the magistrates and gaoled for "causing unrest".

Surviving documents include many letters like one from a Dowlais workman who wrote to his employer from a cell in 1799: "I ham sorry that I abueses your Honor in taking so much Upon me to Speek for Others."

William Crawshay built himself the mock-Gothic Cyfarthfa Castle in 1825, and his son

WORLD'S FIRST STEAM RAILWAY
The first steam train in history ran along a 9 mile track south of Merthyr Tydfil on February 15, 1804. Many critics would not believe the iron wheels would grip the iron track, but the train carried 70 passengers at 5 mph. The rails have now vanished but the route can be followed along the Taff valley where the stone sleepers protrude through the soil. One stretch of sleepers is 2 miles south of Merthyr Vale. At Fiddler's Elbow, near Quaker's Yard Station, a small road leads to the track which can be followed either north or south.

Robert turned it into a centre of Victorian society. It is now a museum containing tools and artefacts used by iron and steel workers, together with details of local ironworks.
Location: Cyfarthfa Castle is in Cyfarthfa Park, off A470, north-west of the town.
PENYDARREN TRAMWAY Merthyr Tydfil was the site of the world's first steam railway line. In 1804 Richard Trevithick, a Cornish engineer, built a steam locomotive at the Penydarren ironworks in the north of Merthyr. Three local works had built an iron tramway on which horses pulled trucks between Merthyr and the Glamorgan Canal, 9 miles to the south. On February 15, 1804, Trevithick connected his locomotive to five open wagons loaded with 10 tons of iron and 70 passengers and made the journey at a speed of 5 mph.

After a few runs the track was damaged and the locomotive was abandoned, but Richard Trevithick became known as the "Father of the Steam Locomotive."

Michelham Priory *E. Sussex*   *Map: 399 Ea*
The priory was founded in 1229 for 13 canons of the Augustinian order. The 13th-century refectory and the prior's 16th-century house have been furnished in the style of the period, and the watermill has been restored.
Location: 3 miles N of Polegate off A22.

Middleham Castle *N. Yorks.*   *Map: 391 Fc*
The castle, first built in the 12th century, was the favourite home of Richard, Duke of Gloucester, who became Richard III in 1483. His son, Edward, is said to have been born there. Richard spent a lot of time in the north of England, administering the area for his brother, Edward IV, and was well liked by the people.

In Richard's time, the massive, oblong great tower stood in a quadrangular enclosure of high walls. Today the buildings are in ruins.
Location: 16 miles NW of Ripon on A6108.

Middlesbrough *Cleveland*   *Map: 391 Gd*
NEWHAM GRANGE LEISURE FARM An agricultural museum has been set up on an 18th-century farm. A farm trail runs through the fields which are stocked with modern types of cattle, and some rare breeds of pigs, sheep and poultry. There is also a 19th-century veterinary surgery and an agricultural merchant's shop.
Location: Newham Way, 4½ miles S of town centre (A172, A174, B1365).
TRANSPORTER BRIDGE This is one of only two transporter bridges in Britain and is the more impressive. It was built across the Tees in 1911 to replace a ferry service. It has a span of 570 ft, and from the deck an electrically powered carriage is suspended which can take 600 passengers and up to ten vehicles across the river to the Hartlepool road – 160 ft above the water.
Location: Durham St (A178).

Middleton *Derbys.*   *Map: 393 Ge*
CROMFORD AND HIGH PEAK RAILWAY In the early 19th century railway trucks were hauled up the Middleton Incline by a stationary steam-engine at the top of the hill. The engine, with two 25 in. cylinders, was built at the Butterley Ironworks at nearby Ripley. It is now preserved in its engine-house.

The Cromford and High Peak Railway was built to join the Cromford Canal near Cromford to the Peak Forest Canal at Whaley Bridge. The trucks were hauled by horses, but stationary engines were used on steep inclines.
Location: Rise End, S edge of town on B5023.

Middleton *Greater Manchester*   *Map: 391 Db*
CHURCH OF ST LEONARD After the English army defeated the Scots at Flodden, Northumberland, in 1513, Sir Richard Assheton rebuilt St Leonard's as a thanksgiving. In a window in the chancel is probably Britain's oldest war memorial, commemorating Sir Richard and 17 Middleton archers who fought at Flodden.
Location: 6 miles N of Manchester in New Lane, off Long St.

Midford Brook Viaduct *Avon*   *Map: 397 Ge*
The A36 is carried over Midford Brook on a long, high stone viaduct built in the early 1800s. The designer is reputed to be Thomas Telford.
Location: 4 miles SE of Bath on A36.

Midhowe *Rousay, Orkney*   *Map: 387 Ef*
TOMB AND BROCH The tomb, set in a long cairn, is divided into 12 compartments by slabs projecting from each wall. The central passage runs through each of the compartments, and most of the recesses on the east side contain a low bench on which the human remains were placed. Twenty-three people, including eight children, were buried in the tomb about 2000 BC.

Near by is the broch of Midhowe, built more than 1,000 years later by Iron Age people.
Location: Ferry from Tingwall.

Mildenhall *Suffolk*   *Map: 399 Ef*
CHURCH OF ST MARY Over the large north porch of St Mary's is the Parvis Chamber, which was also used as a schoolroom in the Middle Ages. The roofs of the aisles and nave are splendid examples of Gothic timbering, with elaborate decoration. The angels on the hammer-beams in the north aisle are without wings – they were sawn off by Puritans in the 17th century.
Location: 11 miles NW of Bury St Edmunds on A1101.

Mildenhall *Wilts.*   *Map: 398 Bc*
CHURCH OF ST JOHN THE BAPTIST St John's is mostly a Norman church with Saxon windows in the tower. In the early 19th century it was furnished in the neo-Gothic fashion of the time, and has not been tampered with since. The box pews, west gallery, canopied pulpit, font, panelling and pews in the chancel, create an atmospheric reminder of what many churches were like nearly 200 years ago.
Location: 1 mile E of Marlborough on minor road.

Milford Haven *Dyfed*   *Map: 392 Ab*
CHURCH OF ST KATHARINE Sir William Hamilton, British Envoy in Naples, acquired property in Pembrokeshire on the death of his first wife Catherine in 1782. He appointed as his agent his nephew, Charles Greville, who obtained an Act of Parliament in 1790 creating the town of Milford Haven to develop the harbour. St Katharine's was built as part of the scheme.

In 1800 a national scandal broke out over the

affair between Hamilton's second wife Emma and Lord Nelson, the naval hero. Tradition, probably wrongly, has always maintained that the foundation stone of St Katharine's was laid by Lord Nelson the following year.
Location: Great North Rd.

Mill of Tore *Highland*   *Map: 386 Dc*
This small watermill at Balnain was grinding oats from the crofts and farms of the glen until the 1950s. It has now been restored.
Location: 4½ miles W of Drumnadrochit on A831.

Millom *Cumbria*   *Map: 390 Dc*
IRON MINES Beside the sea are the remains of the largest iron mines in Britain. Hodbarrow Mines were busy throughout the 19th century, reaching a peak in the 1880s with 11 shafts. They continued in use until 1968. A hundred years of mining caused the land to subside and sea walls were built to keep the water out, two of which remain. The mine buildings have been demolished and the area landscaped, but a full-scale reconstruction of a mine has been built at Millom Folk Museum, St Georges Rd.
Location: 1 mile S of Millom on minor road.

Milton Abbas *Dorset*   *Map: 397 Gc*
MILTON ABBEY The great 14th-century abbey church stands today on the lawn of a large country house by Sir William Chambers (1770). The hall of the Benedictine abbey, dissolved in 1539, is incorporated in the house.
A little market town grew around the abbey, but it was swept away in 1770 by the owner, Lord Milton, and the inhabitants were rehoused in a neat model village of identical pairs of thatched cottages with a new church and almshouses, placed conveniently out of sight of Lord Milton's new house.
Such drastic measures to improve the landscape were not uncommon in the 18th century, but Horace Walpole's opinion of Lord Milton, "the most arrogant and proud of men", is no surprise.
The buildings, in a setting of romantic solitude created by "Capability" Brown, are now a boys' public school.
The abbey church itself was begun in 1331 after the earlier building had been struck by lightning. The monastery was founded in 938 and became an abbey in 964.
The ruins consist of the choir, crossing and transepts only – the nave has disappeared. In the north transept is the monument to Lady Milton (died 1775), designed by Robert Adam. She lies beside the widower.
Location: 7 miles SW of Blandford Forum (A354 and minor road).
MUSEUM OF BREWING Like many other Dorset villages, Milton Abbas had its own brewery. It continued making beer until 1950, and is now a museum of brewing and agriculture.
Location: Main street of the village.

Milton Manor House *Oxon.*   *Map: 398 Bd*
This charming 17th-century manor house was bought in 1764 by Bryant Barrett, a London lacemaker and embroiderer, whose descendants still own it. Barrett added two wings, in one of which is a library in the fanciful "pastry cook's"

Gothic of the 18th century. It is one of the best rooms of its kind.
Milton Manor is a Catholic house and its most treasured possessions are the 18th-century vestments of Bishop Challoner, the leader of English Roman Catholics in the 18th century. Challoner lay buried in the church until his remains were removed to Westminster Cathedral in 1946.
Location: 4 miles S of Abingdon off A34.

Minstead *Hants.*   *Map: 398 Bb*
CHURCH OF ALL SAINTS All Saints is a Norman church altered in later periods. In the 18th century a private pew, like a sitting-room, was built on to the north side of the chancel. It was for the owners of nearby Castle Malwood and has a fireplace for their comfort during winter services. It was entered from the outside rather than through the body of the church. To fit the pew in, the chancel roof had to be raised by 2 ft.
The south transept was later enlarged to accommodate the Compton family of Minstead Manor and their tenants.
Sir Arthur Conan Doyle, creator of Sherlock Holmes, is buried in the churchyard.
Location: 3 miles N of Lyndhurst (A337 and minor road).

Mobberley *Cheshire*   *Map: 393 Ff*
CHURCH OF ST WILFRED The 13th-century church has medieval paintings on the north wall and a fine rood screen of 1500.
Two stained-glass windows commemorate George Leigh-Mallory, who died in 1924 while climbing Mt Everest, and his brother Air Chief Marshal Sir Trafford Leigh-Mallory, Head of Fighter Command. They were sons of a former rector.
Outside are the village stocks and whipping post.
Location: 4 miles W of Wilmslow on B5085.

Moccas Court *Heref. & Worcs.*   *Map: 393 Ec*
Moccas Court is an 18th-century red brick house in a beautiful "Capability" Brown park overlooking the River Wye. The house itself was designed by Robert Adam, and the interior has all the Georgian elegance for which Adam is famous. A circular room in the bow-front overlooks the river, and its decoration is in Adam's "Etruscan" style, actually based on work he had seen at Pompeii.
Location: 12 miles W of Hereford (A465 and B4352).

Moira *Leics.*   *Map: 393 Gd*
IRONWORKS This small village was once the site of a large ironworks. The remains of a great stone blast furnace, built about 1805, still stands 50 ft high at the southern edge of the village. The foundry buildings next to it were converted into private houses.
Location: 3 miles S of Swadlincote off B586.

Mompesson House see Salisbury

Moniaive *Dumfs. & Gall.*   *Map: 390 Cf*
MAXWELTON HOUSE Maxwelton is renowned as the birthplace in 1682 of Anna Laurie, subject of the love song *Annie Laurie*.
Anna was the daughter of Sir Robert Laurie, a Royalist. Her romance with William Douglas, a

hot-blooded Jacobite, resulted in a duel between William and Sir Robert. Anna intervened to stop it and continued to meet Douglas secretly on the Bonny Braes (hillsides) near Maxwelton. Douglas wrote the words of the song.

Anna later married his kinsman Alexander Fergusson of Craigdarroch and became known as the Lady Bountiful of Nithsdale and a noted matchmaker. She died in 1764, aged 82.
Location: Maxwelton is 3 miles S of Moniaive off B729.

Monkton Combe *Avon*   *Map: 397 Ge*
DUNDAS AQUEDUCT One of John Rennie's fine aqueducts, built in the classical style in 1804, carries the Kennet and Avon Canal over the Avon in a single arch.
Location: 2 miles SE of Bath on A36.

Monmouth *Gwent*   *Map: 393 Eb*
BRIDGE In medieval times Monmouth was fortified and entry was through four gates. One of these, the Western or Monnow gate, still stands on the bridge across the River Monnow. The bridge house once had a portcullis.
Location: Monnow St.
CASTLE In 1387 Henry, Prince of Wales, grandson of John of Gaunt and later to be Henry V, was born, probably in the great tower of Monmouth castle which was even then about 250 years old.

Before Henry reached maturity Monmouth was attacked by the forces of Owain Glyndwr, the Welsh rebel leader, but the garrison held firm.

In 1645, during the Civil War, the Royalist garrison yielded to a Parliamentary force of more than 3,000 men.
Location: Between Agincourt Sq., and the River Monnow.

Montacute House *Somerset*   *Map: 397 Fc*
Great Elizabethan houses were built to be conspicuous, to dominate and to impress. Montacute, completed in 1601, does all three. The family of Phelips who built it were, like many landed families, so impoverished by the agricultural depression of 1870–1914 that they were forced to sell. From 1915 to 1917, Lord Curzon, a member of the War Cabinet, lived at Montacute with Elinor Glyn, the novelist. His bath in a mock Jacobean cupboard in the corner of his dressing-room remains.
Location: 3½ miles W of Yeovil on A3088.

Montgomery Castle *Powys*   *Map: 393 Dd*
When Llywelyn the Great was uniting the Welsh to drive out the English in the 13th century, Henry III built Montgomery Castle, partly of wood. In 1228, the half-finished castle was besieged by Llywelyn who withdrew when he heard the king was marching to the rescue.

More stonework was added to the castle later.
Location: On the north edge of the town.

Monymusk *Grampian*   *Map: 387 Fb*
CHURCH OF ST MARY The locality was probably converted by Christian missionaries during the 6th century. A priory was founded during the 12th century, but all that remains are the tower and church. It is one of the oldest churches in Scotland. A door was added in 1660 so the minister could enter the pulpit without having to

brave the dogs in the church. In country areas, dogs accompanied their owners to services and when fights broke out they often had to be ejected, sometimes with long iron tongs with which to grip them by the neck.
Location: 18 miles W of Aberdeen (A96, B994 and B993).

Moreton Corbet Castle *Salop*   *Map: 393 Ee*
Moreton Corbet was an early-13th-century enclosure with a tower. In Elizabeth I's reign a Tudor mansion was built on the south flank. In the Civil War it was captured and burned in a night attack by Parliamentary troops.
Location: 5 miles SE of Wem on B5063.

Morlais Castle *Mid Glam.*   *Map: 392 Db*
Morlais was built by a powerful family of the Welsh Marches, the de Clares, in the late 13th century. It is now a ruin with two towers.
Location: 2 miles N of Merthyr Tydfil off A465.

TUDOR COLOUR

Elizabethan houses glowed with colour from rich fabrics. In 1638, Montacute House had 27 carpets and more than 30 wall hangings. The wool-and-silk tapestry above was probably made in Belgium in the 1480s. During the day, rooms were filled with sunlight coloured by stained-glass windows.

Morwellham *Devon*　　　　*Map: 396 Cb*
MORWELLHAM QUAY OPEN-AIR MUSEUM During
the 19th century, Morwellham was a major port
on the River Tamar but the water has now
retreated, leaving quays and bollards exposed
among the fields. The port was built to take
copper and manganese ore from the nearby
mines down the Tamar for processing.

Ore was brought to Morwellham by a canal
which connected the port with Tavistock. But
the canal ended high above the quay and was
joined to it by an inclined-plane railway.

Arsenic from the Dartmoor mines was also
shipped from Morwellham, much of it to
America where it was used to combat boll weevil
in the cotton plantations. Arsenic was also used in
Britain for dyes, paints and sheep dips.

The open-air museum includes lime-kilns, and
an ancient copper mine. A 32 ft water-wheel was
brought from Dartmoor and rebuilt in the
wheel-pit of the original one.
Location: 5 miles SW of Tavistock (A390 then
south on the road to Calstock).

Morwenstow *Cornwall*　　　　*Map: 396 Cc*
CHURCH OF ST JOHN BAPTIST The church has a
Norman arcade and south doorway. The rest is
Early English. The original medieval roofs sur-
vive in the nave and south aisle.
Location: 10 miles N of Bude (A39 and minor
road).

Moseley Old Hall *Staffs.*　　　　*Map: 393 Fd*
The brickwork facing of Moseley Old Hall is a
Victorian coating over a much older timber-
framed building. On the evening of September
7, 1651, four days after the Battle of Worcester,
Charles II arrived at the house as a fugitive,
heavily disguised with his hair cropped and his
face stained with walnut juice. When search
parties called at the house, he hid in a secret
chamber near his room.

Charles escaped to Bristol by accompanying
a party of supporters as a servant.
Location: 4 miles NE of Wolverhampton off
A460.

Mottisfont Abbey *Hants.*　　　　*Map: 398 Bb*
William, Lord Sandys, was a trusted servant of
Henry VIII and acquired Mottisfont Abbey at
the Dissolution of the Monasteries in 1536. He
converted it and its church into a house, which
in the 18th century was given a red brick
exterior.
Location: 4½ miles NW of Romsey off A3057.

Mount Grace Priory *N. Yorks.*　　*Map: 391 Gc*
The priory was founded for Carthusian monks
in 1398. The monks lived separately in small
houses around the cloister, each with a living-
room, study and bedroom.
Location: 11 miles N of Thirsk off A19.

Mousa broch *Shetland*　　　　*Map: 387 Gd*
The best-preserved broch (stone tower) in Britain was built in the 1st century BC, and still
stands nearly 44 ft high. At ground level there
are three rooms, each with its own cubby-hole
for food and valuables, built into the 12 ft thick
wall. Above were two more floors made of
wood supported on ledges that still exist.

Access to the first floor was by ladder. Even
if the narrow, outer entrance was battered down
by attackers, such as the marauding people of

KEEPING THE ABBEY RECORDS

*The cellarium, or store room, is the best preserved
medieval part of Mottisfont Abbey, founded in the
12th or early 13th centuries. The man in charge of
the cellarium, the cellarer, not only looked after the
abbey's provisions but also its lands. The records kept
by one cellarer, Walter de Blount, from 1340 to 1345,
survive in an illuminated Rental Book. The title page
(left) lists the gardens, fields, orchard and other
possessions of the abbey. Shortly after the book was
written, the Black Death of 1348–9 killed two of the
priors. The monastery was dissolved by Henry VIII
in 1536 and given to William Lord Sandys, the Lord
Chamberlain, in return for the two villages of Chelsea
and Paddington.*

the Western Isles, the occupants could still be safe above. From the first floor, stairs led up to galleries built within the wall.
Location: A boat can be hired in Sandwick, 15 miles S of Lerwick, to visit Mousa island.

Muchelney *Somerset*   *Map: 397 Fd*
ABBEY The Benedictine abbey, founded in the 10th century, housed about 20 monks. The ruins include refectory, common room and kitchen.
Location: 13 miles SE of Bridgwater (A372 and minor road).
THE PRIEST'S HOUSE One of very few pre-Reformation priests' houses to survive in England. The internal arrangement is identical to that of much more substantial houses of the 14th and 15th century, with a hall that once was open to the thatched roof.
Location: In Muchelney village.

Much Hoole *Lancs.*   *Map: 391 Ea*
CHURCH OF ST MICHAEL A small brick building mainly of 1628, but enlarged in 1722 when the stone-faced tower was added. Many of the interior fittings are contemporary.
Location: 6 miles SW of Preston on A59.

Much Marcle *Heref. & Worcs.*   *Map: 393 Eb*
HELLEN'S This old house has been standing for almost 700 years. Begun in 1292, it has had many additions over the centuries—part is Jacobean, and the brick dovecot was built in 1641.
Location: 12 miles SW of Great Malvern on A449.

Much Wenlock *Salop*   *Map: 393 Ed*
GUILDHALL The Guildhall was built in 1577 over the stone medieval lock-up which still survives at one end of the building. It was a council chamber and court room. The Butter Market, for the sale of perishable produce, was held beneath the building. On one of the oak arches are iron rings enabling it to be used as a whipping post. A set of wheeled stocks that were once kept in the Guildhall are now in the museum across the road. They could be used to fetter three prisoners anywhere in the town.
Location: 8 miles NW of Bridgnorth on A458.
WENLOCK PRIORY King Merewald of Mercia founded a nunnery about 680 for his daughter Milburge who became the abbess. Nearly 200

years later marauding Danes destroyed it. A second community was created in the mid-11th century by Leofric, Earl of Mercia, and gradually became the great Cluniac abbey, of which only the beautiful ruins now remain.
Location: On NE side of Much Wenlock, off B4378.

Mull of Galloway *Dumfs.*   *Map: 390 Ad*
LIGHTHOUSE At the end of the peninsula, the most southerly point in Scotland, stands the 85 ft stone lighthouse built in 1830.
Location: 5 miles S of Drummore off B7041.

Mull of Kintyre *Strathclyde*   *Map: 388 Ac*
LIGHTHOUSE In 1788 a lighthouse was built at the end of the peninsula, one of the most dangerous points on the Scottish coast. It is only 13 miles from the coast of Donegal in Ireland.
Location: 20 miles SW of Campbelltown (B842 and minor roads).

Muncaster Castle *Cumbria*   *Map: 390 Dc*
The castle, which dates back to the 13th century, overlooks the once busy harbour of Ravenglass. During the Wars of the Roses, Henry VI found refuge in the castle after the Battle of Hexham in 1464.
Location: 15 miles S of Whitehaven on A595.

Muness Castle *Shetlands*   *Map: 387 Ge*
Muness, the most northerly castle in Britain, was built in the late 16th century. In 1627 it was attacked and burned by raiders from Holland. In the following century, the top storey of the tower was taken down and the stone used to build an enclosing wall.
Location: 3 miles E of Uyeasound, Unst.

Munslow Aston *Salop*   *Map: 393 Ed*
THE WHITE HOUSE This 14th-century house contains an agricultural museum with a dairy and farm kitchen complete with bacon-curing equipment. Pigs were for centuries the chief source of meat for ordinary people.
In the farm buildings there is horsedrawn equipment and hand tools. The grounds also contain a cider house with a horse-operated cider press, and a 13th-century dovecot.
Location: 10 miles SW of Much Wenlock on B4368.

N

Nairn Viaduct *Highland*   *Map: 387 Dc*
The 600 yd long viaduct is one of the most spectacular features on the Highland Railway. It was opened in 1898 and completed a direct line between Aviemore and Inverness through the Nairn Valley by Culloden Moor.
The viaduct, said to be the most graceful in Britain, has 28 arches with a span of 50 ft, and an arch over the river of 100 ft. At its greatest height it is 130 ft above the ground.
Location: 6 miles E of Inverness on B9006 (¼ mile E of B851 junction).

Nanteos *Dyfed*   *Map: 392 Cc*
This Georgian mansion was built in 1739 by the Powell family, whose wealth came from local lead mines and the ownership of a large part of Aberystwyth. The entrance hall has the largest fireplace in the house, capable of burning a ton of logs in a day.
The kitchen has its original dresser and long table. A battery of bells on the wall was once connected to rooms throughout the house to summon the servants.
Location: 3 miles SE of Aberystwyth off A4120.

Nantwich *Cheshire*　　　*Map: 393 Ee*
CHURCHE'S MANSION The gabled house, built in
1577 for Rychard Churche, a local merchant, is
a rare example of a Tudor town mansion. A
carving on the front confirms that "Thomas
Clease made this worke" in the 19th year of the
reign of our "noble Queen Elisabeth".
In Victorian times the mansion was used first
as a corn store then as a school.
Location: In Hospital St, off the square.
CHURCH OF ST MARY The cruciform church with
an octagonal tower and splendidly canopied
choir stalls is mainly of the 14th century. Carvings decorate the misericords, or tip-up seats.
Some of the bells date from 1713.
Location: Town centre.

Narberth *Dyfed*　　　*Map: 392 Bb*
CASTLE Only fragments remain of the stronghold
built in the 1240s on the site of an earlier castle
and dismantled after the Civil War.
Location: 9½ miles N of Tenby on A478.

Naseby *Northants.*　　　*Map: 398 Cf*
BATTLE AND FARM MUSEUM Model layouts and
many relics illustrate the major victory won at
Naseby by Oliver Cromwell's army over
Charles I in 1645. The battlefield 1 mile north of
the village is marked by two stone obelisks, one
said to pinpoint the site from which Cromwell
himself led the final cavalry charge.
Location: Phornby Rd, village centre.

Nash Point *S. Glam.*　　　*Map: 393 Da*
LIGHTHOUSES The two lighthouses were built in
1832, placed high on the cliffs to mark the
position of the Nash sands after the passenger
steamer *Frolic* went aground with a heavy loss of
life. The eastern lighthouse, 122 ft high, was
modernised in the 1900s and the western one, 73
ft high, abandoned.
Location: Road past the church in Marcross,
then the footpath at the end of the road for 1 mile.

Needham Market *Suffolk*　　　*Map: 399 Fe*
CHURCH OF ST JOHN THE BAPTIST The roof of this
15th-century church has been called by one
historian, "the culminating achievement of the
English carpenter". It is as high as the walls on
which it rests, and if removed whole and placed
on the ground would make a substantial building
of its own. It is of hammer-beam construction
with carved angels, some with their wings
outspread, others upswept. The angels were
added in the 19th century. The clerestory is also
incorporated into the roof. The chancel and
sanctuary are spacious and the exterior of the
church is unusual.
Location: 7 miles NW of Ipswich off A45.

Nenthead *Cumbria*　　　*Map: 391 Ed*
VILLAGE This mining village was built by the
London Lead Company in the early 19th century. You can still see the original houses, the
Miners' Reading Room and the Miners' Arms.
All around the village are the derelict remains of
mining, including the blacksmith's shop and the
old smelt mill just south of the main road
through the village. The whole area is riddled
with shafts and mine entrances, some of which
are dangerous.
Location: 4½ miles SE of Alston on A689.

Nether Stowey *Somerset*　　　*Map: 397 Ed*
COLERIDGE'S COTTAGE The poet Samuel Taylor
Coleridge moved to Nether Stowey in 1796
with his wife and baby son, and stayed for three
years. His poem *The Ancient Mariner*, conceived
on a walk with Wordsworth, then a neighbour,
includes references to places in the area.
Location: 8½ miles W of Bridgwater off A39.

Nevern *Dyfed*　　　*Map: 392 Ac*
CHURCH OF ST BRYNACH The cruciform church is
built on what has been a Christian site since the
6th century. It is mainly Perpendicular with a
Norman west tower. Its greatest treasure is a
3 ft high Celtic Cross, probably of the 10th or
11th centuries.
A mounting block, one of only two left in
Wales, outside the churchyard, is a reminder of
the times when people came to church on
horseback.
Further up the hill to the west is a cross cut in
the rock, probably a wayside shrine for pilgrims.
Location: 8 miles SW of Cardigan (A487 then
B4582).

Newark-on-Trent *Notts.*　　　*Map: 394 Cb*
NEWARK CASTLE This was an ecclesiastical castle
built by and for the bishops of Lincoln. The
earliest work was started in the 12th century and
the castle rose to become a magnificent structure
on the bank of the Trent. King John died there
in 1216. And in 1603, James VI of Scotland
stopped at the castle on his way to London to
succeed Elizabeth as James I of England. He was
so appalled by the condition of prisoners at
Newark that he released them. Much of the
castle was destroyed during the Civil War but
the west wall has survived as well as the fine
gatehouse. (Only the grounds are open.)
Location: Off Castle Gate, W of town centre.

Newbold on Avon *Warks.*　　　*Map: 398 Bf*
OXFORD CANAL The canal passes to the north of
the town but it is a later version built on a
straighter line as part of a 19th-century improvement scheme. The original 18th-century canal
followed a winding course passing through a
tunnel, the entrance of which can be seen in the
field next to the church. The old line, with
wharves and bridges but no water, can be
followed away from the tunnel entrance.
Location: 2½ miles NW of Rugby on B4112.

Newburgh Priory *N. Yorks.*　　　*Map: 391 Gc*
This part-Elizabethan, part-Georgian country
mansion in the village of Coxwold was the home
of Sir George Orby Wombwell, who was the last
surviving officer to have been at the Charge of
the Light Brigade in 1854. He died in 1913 aged
81. Remains of the 12th-century priory which
once occupied the site can be seen in the house.
Location: 9 miles SE of Thirsk off A19.

Newby Hall *N. Yorks.*　　　*Map: 391 Gb*
The original house was built for Sir Edward
Blackett in the style of Wren around 1695.
William Weddell inherited Newby in 1748 and
commissioned Robert Adam to redesign the
interior to house his collection of furniture and
rare Gobelin tapestries. The 25 acres of gardens
lead down to the River Ure.
Location: 4 miles SE of Ripon off B6265.

FOUR BRIDGES ACROSS THE TYNE

Four bridges of totally different styles cross the Tyne at Newcastle within 900 yds of each other. They are, from the top: the New Tyne Bridge, built in the 1920s; Robert Stephenson's High Level Bridge *opened in 1849, its upper deck carrying the railway, its lower one the road; the King Edward Railway Bridge, erected in 1906; and the 1876 Swing Bridge, which is now electrically operated.*

Newcastle Emlyn *Dyfed*   *Map: 392 Bc*
CASTLE The mid-13th-century castle was built by the Welsh within an S-bend of the River Teifi which made a natural moat for it. The English captured it in 1287 after heavy bombardment from siege engines. It was rebuilt in 1485 but almost totally destroyed by the Parliamentarians during the Civil War.
Location: North side of the River Teifi, off A475.

Newcastle upon Tyne *Tyne*   *Map: 391 Fe*
BRIDGES The oldest of the four bridges which cross the Tyne within a river span of some 900 yds is the High Level Bridge, designed by Robert Stephenson and the architect John Dobson and opened in 1849. There are two decks supported on five stone piers. The upper level carries the railway, the lower one the road. Next to it is the

Swing Bridge, built in 1876, which replaced the Roman and medieval bridges that spanned the same part of the river. The present bridge was originally moved by steam-powered, hydraulic pumps supplied by William Armstrong, who designed the hydraulics for Tower Bridge in London. The hydraulic pumps are still in use, but now electrically powered. The New Tyne Bridge, built in the 1920s, has a steel arch rising 193 ft above high water, and a span of 531 ft. The King Edward Railway Bridge, erected in 1906, is a few hundred yards down river.
CATHEDRAL St Nicholas's was the parish church of Newcastle for more than seven centuries before it became the cathedral church of the newly created diocese in 1882. Its most splendid feature is the daring and delicate spire balancing on two intersecting diagonal arches. The spire was built in the 15th century.

Beneath the north transept is a vaulted 14th-century crypt, once used as a charnel house. Charnel houses, or bone-holes, were common in medieval churches, and were used to store bones dug up from overcrowded churchyards to make room for new burials.

In the south ambulatory is a magnificent brass of 1441, one of the largest in the country. It commemorates Roger Thornton, his wife and their many children.
Location: Mosley St, city centre.

THE BAGPIPE MUSEUM In the 800-year-old gatehouse, built as part of the castle's western defences, there are bagpipes from India, Bulgaria, France and Greece, as well as Scotland.
Location: Black Gate, St Nicholas St.

New Lanark *Strathclyde*   *Map: 388 Dd*
The small village of New Lanark is famous as the place where Robert Owen began a social experiment in the late 18th century, and it has scarcely changed since Owen's day.

The New Lanark story starts with Richard Arkwright, inventor of the first successful machines for spinning cotton in a factory. He went into partnership with a Glasgow merchant, David Dale, to equip a mill at New Lanark, which began production in 1785.

In 1800, Robert Owen arrived from Lancashire to manage the mill. At the age of 27, he had a reputation as a successful mill manager, but he was determined to try a different system from the slave-like conditions he had found in Lancashire mills. He was convinced that over-long hours only resulted in slow work, badly done. He was also appalled at the treatment given to young children.

When Owen arrived at New Lanark, he found a community in which, in his own words, "theft and the receipt of stolen goods was their trade, idleness and drunkenness their habit". Much of the work of the mill fell to children, some only six years old, who worked 13 hours a day.

Owen set to work with a reforming zeal. Instead of punishing offenders, he set about changing the conditions that bred them. He closed down the evil pot-houses and insisted on decent standards of cleanliness in all the houses of the village. He banned work by children under ten, sending them to school instead, and reduced the working hours of the remainder. In the mills each worker had a "silent monitor" by his work-place. It was a block of wood with different colours on each side. The colour at the front indicated the worker's conduct the previous day – black for bad, blue for indifferent, yellow for good and white for excellent. Thousands came to New Lanark to see how these revolutionary social ideas worked in practice.

The starting point of any visit to New Lanark is the group of mill buildings beside the Clyde. They were the source of all employment in the community. Originally the mills were water-powered, and the "lade" (or channel) which brought water from the river is still there.

The village is ranged up the hillside. One of the buildings is the New Institution, where both adults and children were educated. Visitors in Owen's day were always taken there and the children danced for them. Not all the visitors appreciated the entertainment. The poet Robert Southey thought their "puppet-like" motions

could have belonged to one of the mill machines.

New Lanark had few imitators, but when Owen left in 1825 to try new experiments in co-operative working the mills were more profitable than when he had arrived.
Location: 1 mile S of Lanark off A73.

Newland *Glos.*   *Map: 393 Eb*
CHURCH OF ALL SAINTS This spacious church has aisles almost as wide as the nave, giving it the local name of the Cathedral of the Forest.

It contains a strange and unique brass showing a helmet with a miner as a crest. He carries a pick, and has a candle in his mouth. Sir John Greyndour, Sheriff of Gloucester, went to France with Henry V in the early 15th century. There, with a company of Forest of Dean Miners, he helped to capture Harfleur, and became its governor. He was granted the miner's crest by the king to commemorate the exploit.

The church also has a monument, with a recumbent effigy of a bowman, dating probably from the early 17th century.
Location: 4 miles SE of Monmouth (A466 and B4231).

Newport *Gwent*   *Map: 393 Ea*
CASTLE The castle was begun by the Normans in the 12th century. Additions in the 1440s included a watergate where boats could moor in a lake created by the high tide.
Location: W side of Newport Bridge over the Usk.

CATHEDRAL Tradition relates that a man named Gwynllyw took his bride, the daughter of the Lord of Brecon, by force. When converted to Christianity, he was told in a vision that as a penance he should build a church on a hill top, where he would find a white ox with a black spot on its head.

Eventually the Normans built their church in the same place. St Gwynllyw's Church (gradually corrupted to St Woolos) was created a cathedral in 1949. The splendid Norman nave has some typically massive columns.
Location: Stow Hill.

Newport *Isle of Wight*   *Map: 398 Ba*
ROMAN VILLA The small villa is an excellent example of a modest Roman house in which a series of rooms open off a connecting corridor. It was probably built in the 3rd century.
Location: Avondale Rd, off the Sandown road.

New Romney *Kent*   *Map: 399 Fb*
CHURCH OF ST NICHOLAS A sturdy Norman church, enlarged eastwards in the 13th and 14th centuries. New Romney was a flourishing port in the Middle Ages, and the sea came up to its churchyard wall. However, storms and floods in 1287 changed the course of the River Rother, and eventually New Romney found itself a long way from the sea. The church used to be the meeting place for the town council. It has box pews and screens, and two late brasses of 1510 and 1610.
Location: 8 miles SW of Hythe on A259.

Newstead Abbey *Notts.*   *Map: 394 Bb*
According to tradition, a great Augustinian priory was founded about 1170 by Henry II, to atone for the murder of Thomas Becket.

ROBERT OWEN'S MODEL VILLAGE

At the end of the 18th century, when the poor of Scotland lived and worked in misery, Robert Owen began to create a model mill village at New Lanark, on the River Clyde south of Glasgow.

The mill, for spinning cotton into yarn, was built beside the river so that its machines could be driven by 11 water-wheels. Owen housed his 1,800 workers in tenement blocks, built up the steep hillside (above). Because of the slope they have more storeys on the lower level than on the upper. They are built of solid sandstone with slate roofs and are still sound after nearly 200 years.

Newstead was bought in 1540 by Sir John Byron, who paid Henry VIII £810 for it. Lord Byron, the poet, inherited Newstead in 1798, and it contains many of his relics.
Location: 11½ miles N of Nottingham off A60.

Newton-le-Willows *Lancs.* Map: 393 Ef
SANKEY BROOK VIADUCT The St Helens Canal was opened in 1759 to make the Sankey Brook navigable. In 1830 the Liverpool and Manchester Railway was opened, crossing the canal and the river on a nine-arched viaduct. It was the first major viaduct built to carry a railway, and is now preserved as a monument of national importance.
Location: 1 mile SW of town off A572.

Newtown *Isle of Wight* Map: 398 Ba
OLD TOWN HALL Before the Reform Bill of 1832, Newtown was a notorious rotten borough, enjoying the right to return two members of Parliament when there were almost no voters left. The town hall was the building in which the ceremony of election took place. John Churchill (later the 1st Duke of Marlborough) and George Canning (who became prime minister) both represented Newtown, though it is unlikely that either visited his constituency.
Location: 6 miles W of Newport (A3054 and minor road).

Nine Stones *Dorset* Map: 397 Fc
This diminutive stone circle, only 25 ft across, was probably the shrine of a Bronze Age family rather than of a whole community.
Location: S of the A35, ½ mile W of Winterbourne Abbas.

Noltland Castle *Westray, Orkney Map: 387 Ef*
Noltland was built in the 1570s with tiers of gun loops in nearly all the outer walls. It was a hideout for Gilbert Balfour, Master of the Household to Mary, Queen of Scots. He was one of the plotters in the murder of Mary's husband, Lord Darnley, in 1567. Long after Mary had been deposed, Balfour was still fighting on her behalf. Finally he was driven out of Scotland and fled to Sweden.
Location: ½ mile W of Pierowall.

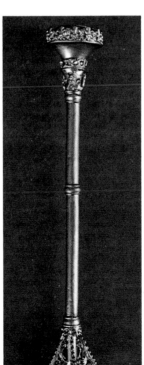

MACE OF PEACE

The Newtown mace, probably made in the 15th century, was carried by the mayor at elections. The borough of Newtown, on the Isle of Wight, returned two MPs for 250 years when the only voters were two landed families (they appointed one MP each). The mace illustrates the evolution of the battle mace into the mayoral civic mace. In the Middle Ages a battle mace was carried upside-down in processions, to show peaceful intentions. The knob on the handle was gradually enlarged to form an elaborate ceremonial head.

Norham Castle *Northld.*   *Map: 389 Gd*
Norham Castle, a stronghold owned by the
bishops of Durham, was the target of many
sieges in the wars between the Scots and the
English.
  As a wooden motte and bailey it was taken
twice by David I of Scotland in the 1130s. As a
stone fortress it was captured by Alexander II in
the 13th century, and in 1318 it was besieged by
Robert Bruce, using the latest types of siege
engine. Bruce invested the castle for a year but
the great tower held out. He tried again in 1319
and again in 1322, but failed both times.
  In 1513 James IV of Scotland besieged Norham, battering its walls with heavy cannon. The
garrison ran out of ammunition after a week and
surrendered.
Location: 8 miles SW of Berwick (A698 and
B6470).

Normanby Hall *Humberside*   *Map: 394 Cd*
Life-size figures in period dress occupy several
rooms in this Regency house. There is an original
Edwardian bathroom, a 19th-century nursery
and a late Victorian sitting-room laid for after-
noon tea.
  The house was built in 1830 by the architect
Robert Smirke, who also designed the British
Museum.
Location: 4 miles N of Scunthorpe off B1430.

Normanton Down *Wilts.*   *Map: 398 Ab*
About two dozen earth barrows make up a
Bronze Age cemetery, most of them neatly
arranged in a line running roughly east–west.
  One of the smallest, Bush Barrow, contained
the skeleton of a chieftain, together with three
daggers, an axe, a gold scabbard hook, gold
breastplate and a mace. It is the richest Bronze
Age burial yet found in Britain.
Location: 8 miles N of Salisbury (A360, then E
on A303 and minor road S).

Norris Castle *Isle of Wight*   *Map: 398 Ba*
A "Norman" fortress theatrically placed on the
headland overlooking Cowes Roads. It was built
in 1799 by James Wyatt, as part of the burgeon-
ing interest in the Middle Ages.
Location: 1 mile NE of East Cowes.

Northampton *Northants.*   *Map: 398 Ce*
ABINGTON PARK Shakespeare's only surviving
grandchild, Elizabeth, inherited his estate,
including his books and manuscripts. After 20
years in the Tudor house at Abington with her
second husband, Sir John Barnard, she died
childless. What became of the priceless manuscripts is not known, but they may have been
sold off by the widower.
  The house has become a museum, the grounds
a public park. The hall has a 16th-century
hammer-beam roof.
Location: Off Wellingborough Rd (A45), NE
of city centre.
CHURCH OF THE HOLY SEPULCHRE One of the few
remaining circular churches, founded in 1110 by
Simon, Earl of Northampton.
Location: Sheep St, city centre.
SHOE-MAKING TOWN Northampton was for centuries the centre of the boot and shoe industry.
The grandest of all the Victorian shoe factories
is the Renaissance style Mansfield factory in

Campbell Square, built in 1857. It is not open to
visitors.

North Elmham *Norfolk*   *Map: 395 Fa*
SAXON CATHEDRAL An early-11th-century cathedral converted into a 14th-century manor
house. For the Saxon period, the cathedral was
built on a grand scale. It is 123 ft long, with an
aisle-less nave and transept. There were twin
towers, but the remains are now only 10 ft high.
Location: 5 miles N of East Dereham on B1110.

North Foreland *Kent*   *Map: 399 Gc*
LIGHTHOUSE There has been a light at North
Foreland since the beginning of the 16th century.
The first light was no more than a simple candle
lantern. In 1634 a coal-fire beacon was installed;
it was later enclosed in a lantern to protect it
from the weather. It proved unsatisfactory and
the present tower was built in 1790. The light
stands 188 ft above sea-level and is visible to
shipping for 20 miles.
Location: 3 miles E of Margate on B2052.

North Leigh *Oxon.*   *Map: 398 Bd*
ROMAN VILLA The villa gives a clear idea of the
layout of a large Roman farming estate-centre
at the summit of its prosperity during the 4th
century. The rooms are arranged round three
sides of a large courtyard, closed on the fourth
by a wall and entrance gate. The servants' range
is on the west side and the main living quarters
for the owner is on the north, including a heated
dining-room with a mosaic floor laid by workmen from Cirencester. Other structures, perhaps
the farm buildings, stood further to the west,
but the size of the estate is unknown.
Location: 3 miles NE of Witney off A4095.

North Leverton Windmill *Notts.*   *Map: 394 Cc*
The tower mill was built in 1813 and is kept at
work grinding corn by a company of farmers
who own it. The three-storeyed mill is built of
tarred brick and is surmounted by a cap with four
shuttered, self-regulating sails.
  There are three sets of millstones; two for
animal feeds and one for flour.
Location: 5 miles E of East Retford, on the minor
road to North Leverton.

North Petherton *Somerset*   *Map: 397 Ed*
CHURCH OF ST MARY THE VIRGIN Somerset is
renowed for the splendour of its church towers,
and St Mary's is one of the best – 109 ft high. This
is reflected inside the church by the immense
tower arch. The pulpit is 15th century, and there
are two carved bench ends dated 1526 and 1629.
Location: 2 miles S of Bridgwater on A38.

Northwich *Cheshire*   *Map: 393 Ef*
SALT INDUSTRY The "wich" towns of Cheshire
– Northwich, Nantwich and Middlewich – form
the centres of the salt industry. From Saxon
times brine from springs was boiled to make
salt. In the 17th century, deposits of rock salt
were discovered and were mined throughout
the 19th century. One Northwich mine reached
a peak of 100,000 tons a year in the 1880s. In
modern times, mining was replaced by brine
pumping. There is a permanent exhibition on
the salt industry in the Weaver Hall Museum in
London Road.

Norton Conyers *N. Yorks.* Map: 391 Gc
This Jacobean house is said to have been the
original for Thornfield Hall in Charlotte
Brontë's novel *Jane Eyre*. It has been owned by
the same family since 1624.
Location: 3½ miles N of Ripon (A61 and minor
road to Wath).

Norwich *Norfolk* Map: 395 Ga
CASTLE Even at the time of the Norman Conquest, Norwich was one of the largest towns in
England, and William the Conqueror had a
motte-and-bailey castle built on a ridge of rising
ground near the River Wensum. It involved
pulling down about 100 houses.

During the reign of Henry I (1100–35), a great
tower was built on the mound, nearly 100 ft
square and 70 ft high. It has decorative tiers of
arcading on its outer walls (refaced in the 1830s),
suggesting it may have been built by the same
engineers who later worked at Castle Rising
near King's Lynn.
Location: City centre.
CATHEDRAL Norwich is one of England's great
Norman cathedrals, almost unaltered by later
centuries. This can be seen at once inside – the
powerful nave, the tower arches, and particularly
the marvellous Norman apse.

The later additions, such as the Perpendicular

A MEDIEVAL HEROD'S FEAST

*The cloisters at Norwich Cathedral took over 130
years to rebuild, between 1297 and 1430. The
vaulting has dozens of roof bosses carved in stone by
medieval masons. They illustrate Bible stories, including Herod's Feast, with the characters dressed in the
clothing of the Middle Ages.*

Gothic clerestory and vaulting at the east end,
only enhance the earlier work.

Behind the altar is the Bishop's Throne, a
stone chair thought to date from the 8th century.
The stalls in the choir were made in the 15th
century, and each retains its misericord (tip-up

VICTORIAN SITTING-ROOM

*A reconstruction of a Victorian sitting-room in the
Stranger's Hall Museum at Norwich is furnished
mainly in the style of 1851, the year of the Great
Exhibition when Britain was at the peak of her
industrial power. In a middle-class home, the walls
were covered with rich wallpapers and the furniture
with embroidered fabrics. The white marble fireplace
is decorated with ormolu, or gilded bronze. Ornaments
in the room include stuffed birds, shellwork and wax
fruit. Paraffin lamps provide the lighting.*

seat), carved underneath. Among the scenes illustrated are a man riding a pig, a knight, an old woman chasing a fox, and a monk smacking the bottom of a schoolboy.

In the cathedral are several painted panels from medieval altar-pieces.
Location: Wensum St.

STRANGERS HALL This medieval mansion probably gets its name from Dutch and French religious refugees who fled to Norwich in the 16th and 18th centuries.

The oldest part of the building is the undercroft of about 1320. The Great Hall above was added in 1450. Extensive improvements were made in the 16th century by a rich Norwich grocer who became mayor of the city.

The house is now a museum of local domestic life with toys of several centuries, fabrics, and period furniture in settings such as a Georgian dining-room and Regency music room.
Location: Charing Cross.

DINING BY CANDLE LIGHT

Candle light reflects from a cut-glass chandelier in the elegant Georgian dining-room at Strangers Hall, Norwich. The "urn" shape of the central shaft is characteristic of Robert Adam's designs. The chandelier, which was probably made between 1765 and 1780, includes pieces of purple glass.

THE BATTLE AGAINST DARKNESS

In prehistoric times the chief source of artificial light was the fire, with lamps made from a hollowed-out stone, filled with animal fat or oil, and a wick of plant fibres.

The Romans brought to Britain lamps fashioned of bronze and pottery. They also invented candles, but these were expensive and rarely used.

From biblical times, the cheapest and most common form of lighting was made from rushes. Easy to gather and needing only the addition of waste cooking fats to turn them into efficient tapers, they were still used in Britain until the 1850s.

How rushlights were made
The rushes were cut in the summer, as long as possible, stripped of their outer rind and dried in the sun. The pithy core was then dipped into melted fat or grease. An average rush, about 2 ft long and roughly ¼ in. thick, would burn for about an hour, giving off a level of light comparable to that of a modern night-light candle.

Various types of rush holders were made, either to stand on a table top or hang on a wall. Some designs included a candle holder, for use in more prosperous households.

Rushlights were often used as an alternative to candles in servants' quarters, sick rooms or children's rooms.

In the 17th century, housewives often made tallow candles. Twists of cotton or dried rush were alternately dipped and dried several times in waste lard or mutton fat, until the candle was about 1 in. in diameter.

The best-quality candles were made solely of beeswax. For those who could afford it, candles could be bought by the pound-weight from chandlers, or from itinerant candle-makers.

Candle holders ranged from candlesticks, candelabra and wall fittings to elaborate chandeliers that were suspended from ceilings and often had as many as 16 candles. Materials ranged from wrought iron and brass to pewter and silver.

Oil lamps existed in the homes of the better off throughout the 16th and 17th centuries, burning vegetable oil and, in some coastal regions, whale oil. But the lamps were never popular, as they were smoky and needed constant attention.

In America, in the late 1850s, petroleum was developed as a by-product of oil, and paraffin became widely available as a cheap form of lighting fuel. It was the first stage in a sequence of discoveries – including cheap and plentiful paraffin wax candles – that was to revolutionise domestic lighting.

Lamps were manufactured in tens of thousands, designs passing from the functional simplicity of the early hurricane lamps to a range of elegant styles at the turn of the century.

The gas and electricity revolution
Early experiments in coal-gas lighting were made by William Murdoch, a Scottish engineer, who lit his own home in Cornwall with gas lighting in 1792. Progress was slow and for the next 30 years gas was confined to street lighting. But by 1840, before the paraffin boom, those who could afford it had gas lighting in their homes; and by 1870 it was widespread. The first gas lights were crude, but the invention of the gas mantle – a material that could be heated to incandescence – provided a power and purity of light that was to be bettered only by the electric lamp.

Electric lighting was based upon the principle of heating a thin filament of wire to incandescence in a vacuum within a sealed glass globe. Sir Joseph Swan was credited as the inventor of electric light lamps in England.

It took 20 years to perfect the tungsten-filament lamp, but its permanence was assured; by the early 1920s, gas lighting had been replaced by electricity throughout most of the country.

But both fuels had played a vital role in an even greater social revolution, as street lighting made travel by night easier and safer; and domestic lighting encouraged book-reading and helped to spread the growth of literacy.

STONE AGE LAMP *A primitive lamp made of hollowed-out sandstone, filled with animal fat or oil, and with a floating wick made from a twist of plant fibres (above).*

ROMAN LAMP *A typical 4th-century AD bronze lamp, used in Roman villas, burning vegetable oil or animal fat (right). A wick projected from the "spout".*

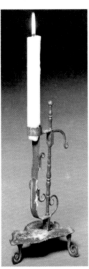

RUSH HOLDER *An iron holder (left) used for centuries in poor households. The rush was gripped by jaws at the top – opened by lifting the hook.*

IRON CANDLESTICK *An early-17th-century candlestick and combined grease pan (right). Wrought-iron holders of this period, with florid designs, were rare.*

BRASS CHANDELIER *A late-17th-century brass chandelier of English or Dutch design. Also made of silver and pewter, these elaborate fittings were suspended from the centre of ceilings on chains.*

ARGAND OIL LAMP *During the early 1780s a Swiss, Pierre Aimé Argand, invented an improved oil lamp that introduced a revolutionary principle, providing a light that burned ten times brighter than any other oil lamp that preceded it. The burner consisted of two concentric metal tubes, with a ring-shaped wick between them. When the wick was alight, air was sucked up the central tube to make the flame burn more brightly. A glass chimney directed the flow of air around the wick, adding to the flame's brightness. Various designs were made using the Argand burner. The fitting (upper left) is a swivelled wall bracket made of brass.*

GAS LIGHTING *In 1840, gas started to be used as a replacement for oil lighting in the homes of the wealthy. At first gas lights were used chiefly in the hall, kitchen and main sitting-rooms; the rest of the house was lit by oil lamps or candles. By 1870 gas lighting was in use throughout the whole of a house. The brass wall fitting (left) dates from the 1850s. A fish-tail jet of flame was protected by an acid-etched glass globe.*

GEORGIAN CANDLESTICK *A three-branched wall fitting, made of gilded wood and gesso – moulded plasterwork – dating from the mid-18th century. Large houses had a number of wall fittings in conjunction with a large centrally positioned chandelier in each of the principal sitting-rooms.*

Nostell Priory *W. Yorks.* *Map: 391 Ga*
Nostell is famous for its Chippendale furniture, and the accounts Chippendale sent for his work survive. There is one of £54 10s for "a Dome bedstead with Rich Carv'd Cornices, feet, Posts And Sundry other ornaments".

The exterior of the house has not changed since 1785, when the 5th baronet, Sir Rowland Winn, died.
Location: 6 miles SE of Wakefield on A638.

Nottingham *Notts.* *Map: 394 Bb*
CASTLE The original castle was the headquarters of Prince John when in 1192–3 he tried to usurp the throne of his brother Richard I, absent on the Third Crusade. It was destroyed after the Civil War and the Duke of Newcastle put up a new building. In 1831 it was burned by a mob

COLLIERY HORSE GIN

The horse gin at Wollaton Hall, Nottingham, was used until the 1950s to raise and lower men at Pixton Green colliery, near Nottingham. A horse walked in a circle, turning the central drum which wound and unwound the rope attached to the pit cage.

angered by a later duke's opposition to the Great Reform Bill. It was later renovated by the city.
Location: Castle Boulevard.
WOLLATON HALL INDUSTRIAL MUSEUM The stables of Wollaton Hall contain machinery connected with lace-making, hosiery, tobacco and mining. In the courtyard is a colliery horse gin which was used for about 150 years, until the 1950s, to wind men and coal up and down a mine.
Location: Off Wollaton Rd, W of city centre.

Nuneham Courtenay *Oxon.* *Map: 398 Bd*
MODEL VILLAGE This village of identical double cottages along a main street was constructed in 1761, when Nuneham House was built for the powerful Harcourt family.

The Harcourts demolished the earlier farming village so that it would not spoil their view. However, they took a pride in rehousing their workers in the new, model village.
Location: 5 miles SE of Oxford on A423.

Nunney Castle *Somerset* *Map: 397 Gd*
The small but compact castle consists of a central rectangular great tower with four round towers at its corners. It looks something like the old Bastille in Paris which fell in 1789 and heralded the French Revolution.

Nunney was built under licence in 1373 and was surrounded by a moat. In 1645, a Parliamentary force attacked it with cannon. The first shots smashed huge holes in the masonry round the entrance, and the garrison surrendered.
Location: 4 miles SW of Frome off A361

Nunwell House *Isle of Wight* *Map: 398 Ba*
The Oglanders came to England with William the Conqueror and have lived at Nunwell since 1522. Charles I came to dinner while a prisoner at Carisbrooke Castle, before his execution in 1649.
Location: ½ mile S of Brading on A3055.

Nympsfield Long Barrow *Glos. Map: 393 Fb*
Between 20 and 30 people were buried in the three chambers of the barrow between 3000 and 2000 BC. Funeral rituals involving fires were probably held in the forecourt.
Location: 4 miles SW of Stroud, just W of the B4066, close to the junction with the minor road from Nympsfield.

O

Oakes Park *S. Yorks.* *Map: 393 Gf*
The original Elizabethan house was remodelled in 1673 and again early in the 19th century, when the gardens were laid out, possibly by John Nash.

The iron gates at the front of the park were made by local craftsmen in the 18th century from ore mined on the estate.

For some 200 years, Oakes Park has been a home of the Bagshawes, a Derbyshire family whose ancestor William (1628–1702) earned the nickname "The Apostle of the Peak" for his nonconformist preaching and writing.

Location: 4½ miles S of Sheffield (A616 then A6102).

Oakwell Hall *W. Yorks.* *Map: 391 Fa*
John Batt, a local landowner, built the house in 1583. It has been altered little since then.

Charlotte Brontë visited Oakwell in the 1830s, while a relative of her schoolfriend Ellen Nussey was living there, and later used it as the model for "Fieldhead" in her novel *Shirley*, published in 1849.

The house has a large collection of oak furniture, domestic implements and utensils

which date from the 16th and 17th centuries.
Location: 5½ miles SE of Bradford (A650, A651,
A652 then minor roads).

Oare *Somerset* *Map: 397 Dd*
CHURCH OF ST MARY R. D. Blackmore (1825–
1900), whose grandfather was rector of Oare,
described the church in his best-known novel,
Lorna Doone. There, Lorna married John Ridd,
and was shot immediately afterwards by Carver
Doone.

The church still has much of its 18th-century
furniture – pulpit, lectern, box pews and a painting of Moses which may once have formed part
of an altar-piece.
Location: 12½ miles W of Minehead off A39.

Ockham *Surrey* *Map: 398 Dc*
CHURCH OF ALL SAINTS A church existed at
Ockham at the time of the Domesday Book of
1085, but the present building is mainly 13th
century. Its chief glory is its east window, which
has seven lancets – high-pointed arches – decorated inside with marble shafts which have
finely carved capitals.

The window dates from about 1260, and may
have been brought from nearby Newark Abbey
when it was dissolved.

A marble memorial to Peter, 1st Lord King
(died 1734), depicts him in his lord chancellor's
robes.
Location: 6½ miles NE of Guildford (A3 then
B2039 via Ripley).

Odiham Castle *Hants.* *Map: 398 Cc*
King John built the castle in 1207–12. During his
wars with the barons a garrison of only 13 men
successfully resisted a two-week siege. It is now
a ruin.
Location: 9 miles N of Alton off A32.

Offa's Dyke *Map: 393 Dc*
Offa, King of Saxon Mercia, ordered the dyke,
a ditch and earth rampart, to be dug in the late
8th century, to define and defend the boundary
between his territory and Wales. It runs for
nearly 170 miles from the River Severn to the
Dee, with some gaps where there was originally
thick forest. A footpath follows most of its
course.
Location: A well-preserved 7 mile stretch of the
dyke starts at Knighton, 16 miles W of Ludlow
on A4113. There is an information centre in the
village.

Ogmore Castle *Mid Glam.* *Map: 392 Ca*
A rectangular great tower was raised on an
earlier Norman mound in the 12th century and
a curtain wall was added in the 13th century.

Ogmore was built as part of a chain of
fortresses to hold down the Welsh in the Vale of
Glamorgan. It was not attacked until followers
of Owain Glyndwr sacked it in 1404.

Beside the castle, ancient stepping stones cross
a ford in the River Ewenny.
Location: 3 miles SW of Bridgend (B4265 then
B4524).

Okehampton Castle *Devon* *Map: 396 Dc*
The castle ruins, which mostly date from the
14th century, spread over a ridge which leads to
a steep mound.

Okehampton belonged to the Courtenay family, earls of Devon. In 1538, Henry Courtenay,
1st Marquis of Exeter, was convicted of plotting
against Henry VIII. He was executed for treason
and the castle was ordered to be dismantled.
Location: ½ mile S of town on A30.

Old Beaupre Castle *S. Glam.* *Map: 392 Da*
The remains of a 16th-century fortified mansion
stand on those of a 14th-century castle. Both
belonged to the Bassets, a family that came over
with the early Norman settlers.

The main defensive feature is the outer gatehouse on the north wall, which has towers on
both sides of a covered passage. It was built in
the 1580s, at the time of the threatened Spanish

SAXON FRONTIER WITH WALES

*The 8th-century earthwork of Offa's Dyke is in
places 12 ft high with a ditch of equal depth. Each
Saxon village along its 170 mile route was probably
given responsibility for digging and maintaining a
stretch. The rampart may have been topped in places
with wooden palisades.*

invasion. The inner porch was added about 1600.
Location: 9½ miles SE of Bridgend (A48 then minor roads).

Oldham *Lancs.*   *Map: 391 Fa*
At the end of the 19th century, Oldham had about 250 cotton mills, one-fifth of the total in Lancashire. Many are now disused or adapted for other purposes, but they still stand, plain red-brick buildings surrounded by long rows of terraced houses in which the cotton-workers – men, women and children – lived.

Some mill-owners tried to relieve the monotony of the townscape. Glen Mills has a water tower in French chateau style and Summerville Mills is very ornate.
Locations: Glen Mills is in Greenacres, off Huddersfield Rd (A62). Summerville Mills is in Fletcher St, off Manchester Rd (A62).

Old Radnor *Powys*   *Map: 393 Dc*
CHURCH OF ST STEPHEN THE MARTYR There was probably already a church on the site in the 1060s when King Harold of England dominated much of Wales from a base at Radnor. The present building is mainly 15th and 16th century.

The font, which is said to have been made from a pagan altar, was hollowed out by Celtic priests some 1,400 years ago.
Location: 9 miles S of Knighton (B4357 then minor road).

Old Sarum *Wilts.*   *Map: 398 Ab*
Old Sarum had been, successively, an Iron Age fort and a Saxon settlement of some size when the Normans fortified it. Their earth and timber castle was given stone defences in the 12th century, and a cathedral was built near by. This was dismantled in the 13th century, when it was replaced by the present Salisbury Cathedral.
Location: 2 miles N of Salisbury off A345.

Old Shoreham *W. Sussex*   *Map: 398 Da*
CHURCH OF ST NICOLAS The Saxon church was enlarged into a cruciform building with a central tower by the Normans, and extended again during the 13th century. A crude sundial has been scratched on a buttress of the south transept.
Location: St Nicolas Lane N of town centre.

Old Soar Manor *Kent*   *Map: 399 Ec*
The entire solar, or owner's private quarters, and the chapel survive from the 13th-century house. The site of the hall, the main living-room in the Middle Ages, is now occupied by a 17th-century red brick farmhouse.
Location: 6 miles NE of Tonbridge (A227 then minor roads).

Ongar Castle *Essex*   *Map: 399 Ed*
A substantial mound and ditch are all that is left of Ongar Castle, founded in the 11th century by Eustace, Count of Boulogne.
Location: 7 miles NW of Brentwood off A128.

Orchardton Tower *Dumfs.*   *Map: 390 Ce*
The only medieval cylindrical tower house in Scotland – others of the period are rectangular – was put up by John Caryns, Provost of Lincluden, in the mid-15th century. It is very small and is unlikely to have been occupied for long, except under siege. Other buildings which once stood around it probably contained more comfortable living quarters.
Location: 5½ miles SE of Castle Douglas (B736 then minor road).

Orford Castle *Suffolk*   *Map: 399 Ge*
Henry II constructed Orford Castle in the 12th century, near what was to become a flourishing port, as part of his plan to break the power of the barons.

The king knew that to control the country he had first to control its castles, but in East Anglia he had none. He put this right by confiscating several, including four from Hugh Bigod, Earl of Norfolk.

In 1165 Bigod got two of his fortresses back, on payment of a £1,000 fine. The same year, Henry started work at Orford. The great tower was rapidly completed, and a bailey wall with towers was added round it.

The castle was finished in 1173, just in time to provide a base from which Henry's men could counter a revolt in East Anglia led, among others, by Bigod, who by then was 80 years old.

The garrison stocked up with provisions – bacon, cheese, salt, iron, ropes, tallow and handmills for grinding corn – and waited for the attack. But it never came.

Instead, the king's supporters used the castle as a springboard from which to launch an assault against Bigod's strongholds, which the aged earl lost for the second time.

Orford remained a key fortress in East Anglia for 200 years. It changed hands several times during Henry III's struggles with the barons, but never faced a serious siege, and was more or less in its original condition until the 1600s.

Since then, the walls have disappeared, leaving only the 90 ft great tower, which is like no other in Britain. The outer surface is many sided, with three rectangular buttress-turrets built into it. The inside is cylindrical.

Two of the turrets contain rooms all the way up from the ground floor, including kitchens to serve the lower and upper halls. The third turret houses the spiral staircase.
Location: 12 miles E of Woodbridge (A1152 then B1084).

Orleans House Gallery *G. London Map: 398 Dc*
James Johnston, Joint Secretary of State for Scotland, built the Twickenham villa now known as Orleans House in 1710. In 1720, when Caroline, wife of the future George II, was due to visit him, Johnston commissioned James Gibbs, the architect of St Martin in the Fields, to design the Octagon, an annexe of brick and stone decorated inside in Baroque style by the Italian stuccoists Artari and Bagutti.

The house takes its present name from Louis-Philippe, later Duke of Orleans, who lived there from 1815 to 1817. Louis-Philippe became king of the French in 1830, but was forced to abdicate in 1848. He fled to England, travelling under the name "Mr Smith" and died in 1850.

About two years later, his widow bought the villa back.

Most of the house was demolished in 1926–7. The Octagon and two remaining wings have been adapted as an art gallery.
Location: On the River Thames at Twickenham, approached by Richmond Rd (A305).

Ormesby Hall *Cleveland*   *Map: 391 Gd*
The Pennyman family, one of whom was made a baronet for services to the Royalist cause during the Civil War, owned Ormesby from 1600. The original Jacobean house was converted into a small Georgian mansion by Dorothy Pennyman about 1750.

Her nephew, Sir James Pennyman, the 6th baronet, spent £47,500 on redecoration and the addition of the stables. But he over-reached himself and his creditors' bailiffs seized the estate to offset his debts.

A painting of Sir James, commissioned from Joshua Reynolds for £20, hangs above the dining-room fireplace.
Location : 3½ miles SE of Middlesbrough off A171.

Osborne House *Isle of Wight*   *Map: 398 Ba*
When Queen Victoria married Prince Albert of Saxe-Coburg-Gotha in 1840, the young royal couple had three residences – Buckingham Palace, Windsor Castle and Brighton Pavilion. All were better suited to court ceremonial than to family life.

Victoria bought Osborne and its surrounding estate in 1845 as, in her words, "a place of one's own, quiet and retired" where "we can walk anywhere without being followed and mobbed". It was her favourite home for the rest of her life.

Albert himself designed a new house, with the help of the builder Thomas Cubitt, and planned the grounds. He modelled Osborne on an Italian villa, in a style which came to be widely copied.

The Pavilion Wing was the first section of the building to be completed. The main room on the ground floor, in the shape of a letter U, was divided by columns to form the drawing-room, dining-room and billiard room – an early example of open planning which had a practical benefit for the Gentlemen of the Household who attended the queen. In the billiard room, they were within earshot, but out of Victoria's sight, so they could sit down or play billiards while technically still in her presence.

Upstairs in the Pavilion Wing are the private apartments of the queen and her consort – two dressing-rooms, two bathrooms, a sitting-room and a bedroom. The windows look out, through trees which Albert planted, to the Solent and the mainland beyond.

When Albert died in 1861, the grief-stricken Victoria retired to Osborne to mourn, and decreed that his dressing-room should remain as he left it.

Since her death at Osborne in 1901, the queen's bedroom, with its huge canopied bed, and the other rooms have changed little. They are crowded with furniture and bric-à-brac and hung with prints, photographs and water colours, many painted by Albert. Nothing in them dates from a century other than the 19th.

Osborne gave Victoria the chance of sea-bathing, which she took for the first time on July 30, 1847, recording in her diary "I thought it delightful till I put my head under the water". The queen, attended by her maids, used a bathing machine which was lowered down a sloping pier.
Location : 1 mile SE of East Cowes off A3021.

SIDE BY SIDE

Portraits of family and friends cover the writing tables of Prince Albert (right) and Queen Victoria (below), placed next to each other in the private sitting-room at Osborne. The prince, whose advice on affairs of state the queen increasingly valued, sat on his wife's left, preparing documents for her inspection while she wrote letters or studied government dispatches. A bell-push on the queen's desk summoned servants or aides.

HAND IN HAND
Hands of queen and consort clasp symbolically under a crown on an inlaid table in their bedroom at Osborne House.

COLOURED RICHNESS OF AN ADAM CEILING

Ostrich feathers radiate from a golden sunflower at the centre of the rich stucco ceiling in the drawing-room of Osterley Park, Greater London. The architect *Robert Adam, who remodelled Osterley from 1761, prided himself on his use of colour in ceilings "to take off the glare of white, so common . . . till of late".*

Osterley Park *Greater London*   *Map: 398 Dc*
Robert Adam completely remodelled the original Tudor house on the site for members of the Child family, wealthy bankers. He started at Osterley in 1761, and continued work there on and off for 20 years.

Adam supervised every detail of the furnishings and decorations to create a mansion which the writer Horace Walpole called "the palace of palaces" after a visit in 1773. Osterley has been little altered since the 18th century.
Location: Jersey Rd, Osterley.

Otley *W. Yorks.*   *Map: 391 Fb*
CHURCH OF ALL SAINTS There was a Saxon church on the site, and there are fragments of stone crosses from it in the tower and baptistry.

The present chancel is Norman. The nave, transepts and towers were added about 1240, and the aisles and south porch in 1485–1500.

In the south transept, a monument with recumbent effigies commemorates Lord Fairfax (died 1640) and his wife, grandparents of the Parliamentary general.
Location: 10½ miles NW of Leeds on A660.

Otterburn *Northld.*   *Map: 391 Ef*
MILL A watermill has stood on the site since the 13th century. The present one has belonged to the same family since 1821, and it still produces woollen cloth. The wool is spun on machines called mules, wound on to the looms and then woven.

Originally, the cloth was pounded by large wooden hammers, driven by the water-wheel, to thicken and shrink it. The equipment has been left in place, but is not used.
Location: 30 miles NW of Newcastle upon Tyne on A696.

Ottery St Mary *Devon*   *Map: 397 Ec*
CHURCH OF ST MARY Bishop Grandisson of Exeter rebuilt and enlarged St Mary's from 1337, making it one of the finest parish churches in the south-west, very similar in its architecture to Exeter Cathedral.
Location: 12 miles E of Exeter (A30 then B3174).

Outwood Windmill *Surrey*   *Map: 399 Db*
Grain has been ground in the mill since 1665, and visitors still can buy freshly ground flour.

Outwood is a post mill, a type in which the whole section of the mill containing the millstones and machinery is turned to direct the sails into the wind. The canvas shutters on the sails are sprung to adjust themselves to wind pressure.
Location: 5½ miles SE of Redhill (A23 and minor roads).

Over Haddon *Derbys.*   *Map: 393 Gf*
MANDALE MINE Mandale claims to be the oldest mine in an area known for its lead since Roman times, though no one is certain when it was first worked.

The buildings on the site, which is preserved, date from around 1800. They include the engine-house, which contained a beam-engine used to pump water from the workings, and a wheel pit. This held a 50 ft water-wheel, which powered the stamps that crushed the lead ore.
Location: 2¼ miles SW of Bakewell off B5055. The mine is 1 mile W of the village.

Ovingham *Northld.*   *Map: 391 Fe*
CHURCH OF ST MARY At the west end of the mainly 13th-century cruciform church is a tall Saxon tower, built about 1050. Some of its stones may have been brought from Hadrian's Wall.

Fragments of Saxon crosses, found in the 1940s, are displayed inside the church, and there is a monument in the chancel to Thomas Bewick, the wood-engraver, who died in 1828.
Location: 13 miles W of Newcastle upon Tyne off A695.

Oxborough *Norfolk*   *Map: 399 Ef*
CHURCH OF ST JOHN THE EVANGELIST The church dates from the 14th century and until 1948 had one of only two medieval stone spires in the county. It collapsed in April of that year, destroying part of the building.

The chantry chapel on the south side was not damaged. It contains two lavish 16th-century monuments to members of the Bedingfeld family, made in terracotta. A memorial of 1583 commemorates Sir Henry Bedingfeld, a governor of the Tower of London.

Location: 7 miles SW of Swaffham on minor road.

OXBURGH HALL A moat surrounds the red-brick manor house, built in 1482 by the Bedingfeld family, who still live there. The Bedingfelds remained staunch Roman Catholics through 300 years of persecution, and there is a hiding-place for their priest near the main bedroom.

Henry VII visited the house towards the end of the 15th century, and slept in a chamber in the 80 ft gateway tower.

Oxford *Oxon.* *Map: 398 Bd*

CATHEDRAL In the 1520s, the powerful Cardinal Wolsey decided to found an Oxford college which would outstrip all others in its magnificence. He started to clear land for it, and among the buildings which he planned to pull down was the priory of St Frideswide, established in Saxon times.

Demolition began, but in 1529 Wolsey fell from favour with Henry VIII, and the work stopped. Part of the priory's Norman church survived, to become a cathedral in 1546, and the chapter house and refectory were also spared.

The cathedral is the smallest in England and is the chapel of Christ Church, the college which Wolsey started.

The church's chief glory is its vaulted choir, with stone pendants dating from the second half of the 15th century. In the north choir aisle is the reconstructed shrine of St Frideswide, founder of the priory, who died about AD 735.

Sir Gilbert Scott restored the east end of the cathedral in the 19th century.

Location: St Aldate's St, city centre.

CHURCH OF ST MICHAEL The Saxon west tower is the oldest building in Oxford, and the Gothic east window has the city's oldest stained glass, from about 1290. Its four panels depict the Virgin and Child, St Michael, St Nicholas and St Edmund.

Beside the 14th-century font, William Shakespeare stood in 1606 as godfather to William D'Avenant, whose parents kept the Crown Tavern where the playwright stayed on his journeys between London and Stratford.

Location: Cornmarket St, city centre.

GAMES A VICTORIAN CHILD PLAYED

Many of the games loved by Victorian children are still popular today, and are easily recognisable in this compendium of about 1840, preserved at Oxburgh Hall, Norfolk. Dominoes and the equipment for housey-housey, a type of bingo, have changed little. Victorian tiddlywinks (front right) were made of slate. For more vigorous play, most 19th-century children owned a top with a whip to spin it (left of box). The diabolo, a piece of wood shaped like a dumb-bell which was made to spin and jump on a string attached to two sticks, and the cup and ball game (both right of box) were other favourites. On the box lid is a board for a game resembling solitaire. It was played with the pieces lined up (front left).

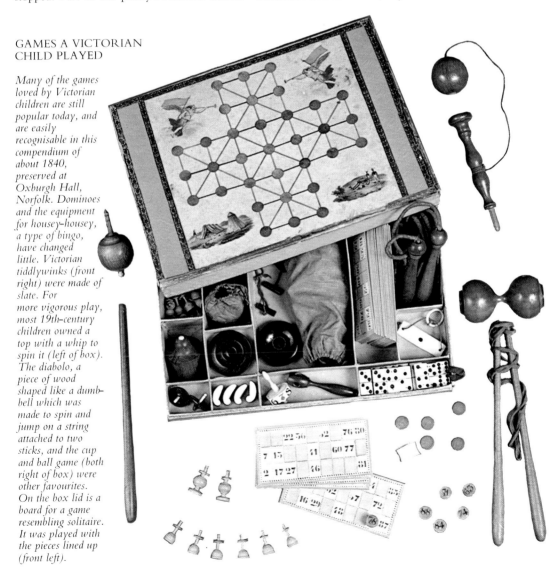

OXFORD UNIVERSITY At the time of the Norman Conquest, Oxford had three monasteries, to which the town governor appointed by William I added a college of secular canons. The four religious foundations acquired a reputation for learning, and by the early 12th century they boasted teachers like Theobald of Etampes, who called himself a Master of Oxford and impressed the cultivated Henry I with his wisdom.

In 1167 there was a mass influx of English students from Paris, then the leading European centre of knowledge outside Italy. Whether they were recalled by Henry II or expelled by the French is uncertain, but from that date Oxford was to vie with Paris as a university.

The scholars' presence irked the Oxford citizens. To protect themselves against high rents and violence, students banded together in comfortless halls and inns, bought or rented by their joint efforts. At night, they slept and fed in the halls. By day, they went out to seek enlightenment from the monks and friars.

The students, some of whom were only 14 years old, sat no formal entrance examinations. They studied Latin grammar, rhetoric and logic, together with geometry, arithmetic, astronomy and music. To become a Bachelor of Arts took four years, and to sit for a Mastership took a further three, followed by two more years of study known as "Necessary Regency".

In 1249, the budding university received its first major benefaction – the sum of 310 marks left by a priest called William of Durham to buy premises in which 12 Masters of Arts could study theology. William's foundation eventually became University College (High Street).

Others followed his example: John of Balliol, who had insulted the Bishop of Durham, endowed what is now Balliol College (Broad Street) as a penance for his misdeed about 1265; the King's Chancellor, William de Merton, founded Merton (Merton Street) in 1274.

Of the three earliest colleges, Merton is the only one which still has its original buildings. Its ground plan is haphazard, in contrast to the systematic arrangement developed later, and its library of 1371 is the oldest in England.

The first colleges at Oxford were for graduates only. Undergraduates continued to lodge in halls of residence, of which one survives, St Edmund's (Queen Street). It gained college status in 1957. A row of small medieval "mansiones" which made up another hall now forms part of Worcester College (Worcester Street).

Further colleges – Exeter (Turl Street), Oriel (Oriel Square) and Queen's (High Street) – were added in the early 14th century. Then, in 1379, William of Wykeham, Bishop of Winchester, established his New College (New College Lane). It was the first to admit undergraduates, and it set the pattern for future college development.

William's foundation was massively endowed and its buildings were laid out in a systematic pattern. The basic elements in the design were: a gatehouse in which the Warden had his rooms (at New College he still does) so he could see the comings and goings of the students; a great quadrangle with chapel and hall on the north side so that they would not cast a shadow across it; and little groups of rooms reached by individual staircases.

In 1437, Henry Chichele, Archbishop of Canterbury, endowed All Souls (High Street). In its statutes and its buildings it closely followed the model of New College, but it had never admitted undergraduates, except for four Bible students, until 1926. In the 18th century, the old cloister and burial ground was replaced by a great new quadrangle by Nicholas Hawksmoor.

Magdalen (pronounced Maudlin), in the High Street, was founded in 1458. Its graceful Gothic tower, from which an anthem is sung by the choir at dawn every May Day morning, stands sentinel at the eastern approach to the city centre.

The 16th century was another period of rapid expansion for the university. Colleges added then were Brasenose (Radcliffe Square), Corpus Christi (Merton Street), Jesus (Turl Street) and St John's (St Giles), which had originally been established as St Bernard's by Archbishop Chichele.

But none of these can equal Christ Church (St Aldate's), founded in 1525, for size, beauty and wealth, nor for the achievements of its graduates, who have included 13 prime ministers and 11 governors-general of India. The grandeur of Christ Church reflects the personalities of Cardinal Wolsey, who began it, and Henry VIII, who finished it.

Oxford's colleges had grown extremely wealthy by the 17th century, and Charles I drew heavily on their resources during his struggles with Parliament. In 1642, he moved his court to Oxford, installing himself in Christ Church. New College became his arsenal and New Inn Hall, on the site now occupied by St Peter's, was his mint, where ancient college plate was melted down to pay his army.

After the Restoration of 1660, the university sank into a period of intellectual lethargy which lasted for more than 150 years, until it was swept away by the zeal of the new middle classes, and reforms which ensured that money was spent for the benefit of the university as a whole, rather than for individual colleges.

Keble (Parks Road), built in 1868–82 in two-coloured stone layers, was the first new college for 120 years. It was followed by the earliest women's halls, Lady Margaret (Norham Gardens) and Somerville (Woodstock Road), finally recognised as colleges in 1960.

The history of Oxford as a university is largely linked to its colleges, but it has other fine buildings as well – among them the 15th-century Divinity School (Broad Street), in the same complex as the Bodleian Library, re-established by Sir Thomas Bodley in 1598.

Christopher Wren designed the Sheldonian Theatre (Broad Street) in 1669, and Nicholas Hawksmoor created the nearby Clarendon Building in 1713. The Ashmolean Museum (Beaumont Street) was founded in 1678.

TREASURES OF OXFORD

Every Oxford college has its library, its dining hall and its chapel. Merton College library (above right) was built in the last quarter of the 14th century and is among the oldest in England. Some of its volumes are still chained to the shelves, a precaution against theft adopted in the Middle Ages, when books were rare and expensive. The splendid 16th-century hall of Christ Church (below right) is 115 ft long and 50 ft high.

UNIVERSITY BOTANIC GARDEN The oldest botanical garden in Britain was laid out in 1621 by Henry Danvers, Earl of Danby, for the study of medicinal herbs. It occupies the site of a medieval Jewish cemetery, and cost Danby £5,000 to create.
Location: High St, near Magdalen Bridge.

Oxwich Castle *W. Glam.* *Map: 392 Ba*
Sir Rhys Mansell, a tough Welshman who enjoyed brawling, incorporated the ruins of a 12th-century Norman castle in the mansion he built himself in the 1540s. A few years later, during a quarrel between Sir Rhys and his neighbours over the cargo of a wrecked ship, his daughter Anne was killed in the doorway by a stone.
Location: 13 miles SW of Swansea off A4118.

Oystermouth Castle *W. Glam.* *Map: 392 Ca*
Rhys, Prince of Deheubarth, burned down the Norman-built wooden fortress of Oystermouth in 1189. The English replaced it with a castle of stone, which the Welsh sacked in 1287. It was then rebuilt in its present form.
Location: 4½ miles SW of Swansea on A4067.

P Q

Packwood House *Warks.* *Map: 398 Af*
Lawyer John Fetherston, whose ancestors had built the nucleus of Packwood in the 1550s, could not decide which side to join in the Civil War.

He compromised by staying at home and planning the house's yew garden, in which carefully shaped trees represent the Sermon on the Mount. John also collected sundials. There are several in the grounds.
Location: 8½ miles NW of Warwick (A41, B4439 and minor roads).

Painscastle *Powys* *Map: 393 Dc*
The original 12th-century motte-and-bailey castle, with its massive earthworks, was replaced by a stone fortress in the mid-13th century. It belonged to the de Braoses, a powerful Anglo-Norman family.

During Henry III's war with the barons in 1264–5, Painscastle was attacked and severely damaged by the Welsh. It is now a ruin.
Location: 5½ miles NW of Hay-on-Wye (B4351 then minor roads).

Painswick *Glos.* *Map: 393 Fb*
COURT HOUSE Thomas Gardner, a local clothier, built the main part of the house in Cotswold stone about 1605. On the first floor of a three-storey block added a few years later is the panelled chamber once used by the Consistory Court, which tried ecclesiastical offences.
Location: 3 miles NE of Stroud on A46.

Pamber Priory *Hants.* *Map: 398 Cc*
Baron Henry de Port, son of a knight who came to England with William the Conqueror, founded the priory about 1110. Only the church tower and choir remain of the original buildings.

There is a fine 14th-century effigy of a knight, over 6 ft tall and carved from a single block of oak. The warrior is depicted in armour and surcoat, with crossed legs resting on a lion. His identity is not known.

Several carved Purbeck marble slabs were probably the coffin lids of 12th and 13th-century priors.
Location: 4½ miles N of Basingstoke off A340. The priory is 1 mile S of Pamber Green.

Papplewick *Notts.* *Map: 394 Bb*
CHURCH OF ST JAMES The medieval church was entirely rebuilt at the end of the 18th century, apart from its tower. Inside, it has a gallery and most of its Georgian fittings remain.

Grave slabs in the church floor are decorated with the tools of the trades of the men who lie beneath – the bow and horn of a Sherwood forester and the bellows of a blacksmith among them.
Location: 7 miles N of Nottingham on B683.
PUMPING STATION Two 19th-century beam-engines which once pumped drinking water for Nottingham from a natural reservoir 210 ft underground are steamed occasionally for visitors. The engines were among the last manufactured by the Birmingham company of James Watt and Co.

The station, opened in 1884, is lavishly decorated inside, using themes related to water life.
Location: 2½ miles E of village (B6011, N on A60 and E on first minor road).

Parham *W. Sussex* *Map: 398 Db*
Sir Thomas Palmer, a fabric merchant, built the house around an earlier and smaller one in the 1570s. His grandson, who as a child of two, had laid the foundation stone according to an Elizabethan custom which was thought to bring luck, sold it in 1601 to the Bysshopp family, later Barons Zouche, for £4,500.

Portraits in the panelled great hall include one of Elizabeth I, god-mother to Thomas Palmer's daughter-in-law Eleanor.
Location: 9 miles SE of Petworth on A283.

Parracombe *Devon* *Map: 396 Dd*
CHURCH OF ST PETROCK Petrock, or Pedrog, was a 6th-century Welsh monk who founded several churches in Cornwall and Devon. The present building, preserved but no longer used, dates from the late 11th century.
Location: 12 miles NE of Barnstaple off A39.

Parys Mountain *Gwynedd* *Map: 392 Bf*
The mountain was stripped of vegetation and soil to obtain copper ore in the 18th and 19th centuries. In its heyday, it was the biggest copper-mining site in Europe, employing 1,500 men and yielding 3,000 tons of ore each year.

When the ore ran out, Parys was abandoned, leaving the bare mountainside dotted with the remains of the workings – shafts and tunnels, the

INDUSTRIAL ART FOR THE FEW

Papplewick pumping station, Nottinghamshire, cost nearly £40,000 to build and decorate in 1884. Part of the money went on the ornate interior, which only a handful of workmen were expected to see.

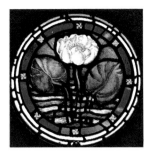

STAINED GLASS *Each stained-glass window at Papplewick depicts an aquatic plant, such as the water lily, in a romantic expression of the station's purpose. The theme is developed in the rest of the decor.*

SHINING BRASS *The cylinder heads of Papplewick's two 19th-century beam-engines, each 46 in. in diameter, are kept burnished to a sheen.*

WROUGHT IRON *Iron columns in Classical style at Papplewick have trimmings of brightwork. The capitals of the columns are encased in water-lily leaves, also made of iron. By contrast to the elaborately decorated interior, the wheels of the two pumping engines appear stark and functional.*

tower of a windmill, a ruined engine-house and the precipitation pits in which dissolved copper salts were treated to remove the metal.

The site is dangerous, and is most safely viewed from the road.
Location: On Anglesey, 15 miles NW of Menai Bridge off A5025.

Pass of Killiecrankie *Tayside   Map: 387 Ea*
In 1688, the obstinacy of James II of England (VII of Scotland) in trying to re-establish the dominance of the Roman Catholic Church helped to spark the revolution which ended his three year reign. James slipped away to France, where he was welcomed by Louis XIV. The following year Parliament in London offered the English throne jointly to James's nephew and son-in-law, the Protestant Dutch prince William of Orange and his wife Mary. The Scots assembly declared William and Mary their king and queen shortly afterwards.

But James was not without supporters in

Scotland, foremost among them John Graham of Claverhouse, Viscount Dundee. Dundee recruited a Highland army and moved to Blair Castle in Atholl, which had been held for James. He had about 2,500 men.

To counter "Bonnie" Dundee's threat, Major-General Hugh Mackay, William's commander in Scotland, marched a 4,000-strong force to Dunkeld and prepared an assault on Blair Castle. His advance party secured the Pass of Killiecrankie.

There, the first shot in the Jacobite cause was fired, on July 27, 1689, by one of Dundee's scouts, Iain Ban Beag Mac-rath. He killed a cavalry officer beside the gully called Trooper's Den.

Mackay's force got through to the north end of the pass, where they found Dundee awaiting them on the high ridge near Urrard House. The battle lasted only two or three minutes. In the face of a Highland charge, Mackay's soldiers broke and fled. Some 2,000 were killed or taken prisoner. The rest escaped, among them Donald MacBean, who jumped the River Garry at a spot known as Soldier's Leap. The Jacobites lost 600 men.

Dundee died in the fighting, and without his leadership the first Jacobite rising collapsed. After a fierce battle with government troops at Dunkeld on August 21, the Highlanders drifted away to their homes.

The information centre at Killiecrankie provides an audio-visual account of the battle.
Location: 2½ miles NW of Pitlochry on A9.

Pateley Bridge *N. Yorks.* Map: 391 Fb
FOSTER BECK MILL When it was built in 1864, the mill was used for the spinning of flax. The stem of this blue-flowered plant is used in the manufacture of linen, a cloth that takes its name from the flax seed, linseed. The mill has now been converted into a hotel and public house, but it retains many of its original features, including a huge water-wheel, 35 ft across.
Location: 1 mile N of town on Low Wath Rd, off B6265.

Patrington *Humberside* Map: 395 Dd
CHURCH OF ST PATRICK For more than six centuries the spire of St Patrick's, soaring nearly 190 ft high, has been an impressive landmark for travellers on the flat expanses of Holderness. The fertile soil of the region brought prosperity to Patrington in the Middle Ages, and this reflected in the church, which is built on the scale of a small cathedral. It is known locally as the "Queen of Holderness", and its tower spire is one of the glories of English Gothic architecture. The reredos, the screen behind the altar, is a memorial to King George V.
Location: 15 miles E of Hull on A1033.

Peel Castle *Isle of Man* Map: 390 Ac
Britain's only castle that contains a cathedral. The cathedral, St Germans, came first. It was started in the 1230s and took over a century to complete. It was frequently attacked by Vikings and Scots, and in the 1390s the king of the island, William le Scrope, built a stone castle around it for protection.

In 1651 the castle walls were damaged during an unsuccessful rising against the Stanleys, kings of Man.
Location: NW of Peel harbour.

Pembridge *Heref. & Worcs.* Map: 393 Ec
CASTLE This 13th-century castle belonged to the de Pembridge family. It was dismantled by Parliament after the Civil War, but was repaired later in the 17th century.
Location: 7 miles W of Leominster on A44.
CHURCH OF ST MARY The church, basically Norman, has no tower, but the bells are housed in a separate, massive 14th-century structure. The font is 13th century.
Location: In market place.

Pembroke Castle *Dyfed* Map: 392 Ab
Henry Tudor, the man who put an end to the horrors of the Wars of the Roses when he broke the Yorkist forces of Richard III at Bosworth Field, was born at Pembroke Castle in 1457. His birth chamber was probably the room above the portcullis in Pembroke's huge gatehouse.

Pembroke was begun during the Norman invasion of Wales in the 1070s. Arnulf, son of Roger de Montgomery, who led the invasion's central thrust, threw up a palisaded earthwork on a rocky headland jutting into the River Pembroke. A century later it had become a triangular enclosure, surrounded for the most part by the waters of the estuary. Richard de Clare, Earl of Pembroke (known as Strongbow), used the castle as a base to launch his invasion of Ireland in 1166. It was Strongbow's son-in-law, William the Marshal, who erected the massive great tower, at the beginning of the 13th century.

This impressive edifice, nearly 80 ft high, was built with walls as much as 15 ft thick at the base, and carried a stone dome with a second fighting deck on its top.

The gatehouse and other defences were strengthened in the mid-13th century, but the castle did not see action until the early 1400s, when it was besieged, unsuccessfully, by Owain Glyndwr.

In the Civil War the castle was held by Parliament, but in 1648 the governor, General Laugharne, changed his allegiance and thus brought down upon the castle the full fury of Oliver Cromwell, who besieged it in person. A lengthy assault with cannon reduced much of the outer enclosure. The great tower held firm, but the garrison had to yield after a traitor showed the Parliamentarians how to cut off the castle's water supply. The defenders exacted a poetic revenge upon their betrayer – he was killed and his corpse stuffed into the well pit.
Location: By river, NW of town, off B4320.

Pencarrow House *Cornwall* Map: 396 Bb
This cream-yellow Palladian building, in a setting of lawns and hanging woods, symbolises the 18th century at its most civilised. The house, completed in 1775, belongs to the Molesworth-St Aubyn family, and the garden was created by the politician Sir William Molesworth, to compensate himself after being rejected by his constituents in 1836 for his radical views.

The portraits are the treasure of the house, and include 11 members of the Molesworth family by Sir Joshua Reynolds.
Location: 4 miles NW of Bodmin off A389.

Pendeen *Cornwall* Map: 396 Aa
GEEVOR TIN MINES Geevor, which is still being worked, includes the old Levant Mine, scene of

an accident in which 31 miners died in 1919.
Levant had a "man engine", a pump with platforms attached to its rod on which miners could travel up and down the shaft. Its linkage snapped, plunging the men to their deaths.

A museum at the entrance to the mine has many items from Levant, including the broken linkage.
Location: 7 miles NW of Penzance (A3071 and B3318).

Pendennis Castle *Cornwall*   *Map: 396 Ba*
The squat, cylindrical castle was built between 1539 and 1543 as part of Henry VIII's coastal defences. It was not put to the test until 1595, when four Spanish galleons raided the south Cornwall coast and sacked Penzance and other towns. After the raid, the old castle was enclosed within a large star-shaped stone-and-earth fort, raised by some 400 men over two years.

Pendennis was besieged by Parliamentary forces during the Civil War, and the garrison held out for five months, until their supplies ran out. In recognition of their bravery they were allowed to march out with colours flying.
Location: ½ mile SE of Falmouth town centre.

Penhow Castle *Gwent*   *Map: 393 Ea*
A small Norman castle, built for Sir Roger St Maur – a name that in later generations was altered to Seymour. The square tower was constructed in the 12th century. The high curtain wall was a 13th-century addition.
Location: 7½ miles E of Newport off A48.

Penn *Bucks.*   *Map: 398 Cd*
CHURCH OF THE HOLY TRINITY During restoration work in the 1930s workmen discovered what turned out to be a 15th-century painting of the Last Judgment. It had been plastered over during the Reformation. The church, built in the 11th century, contains many monuments to the local Penn family, whose most famous son, William, was the founder of Pennsylvania in America.

There are also monuments to the Curzon family, and the 18th-century pulpit was brought from the Curzon Chapel in London's Mayfair.
Location: 3 miles NW of Beaconsfield on B474.

Pennard Castle *W. Glam.*   *Map: 392 Ca*
Pennard was one of the fortresses built by the Normans to hold the newly won Gower peninsula.
Location: 8 miles SW of Swansea off A4118.

Penrhyn Castle *Gwynedd*   *Map: 392 Cf*
Lord Penrhyn's fortunes were made by his vast slate quarries in North Wales. In 1827, he commissioned Thomas Hopper to build him a house in the fashionable Gothic style. It was modelled on the Norman fortress at Castle Hedingham in Essex. The house stands in 40 acres of parkland, in which there is a museum of old industrial locomotives.
Location: 1 mile E of Bangor off A5.

Penrith Castle *Cumbria*   *Map: 391 Ed*
The bishops of Carlisle built the castle in the early 14th century to protect Penrith against Scottish raiders. It was captured by Parliamentary troops in the Civil War and dismantled.
Location: Near Penrith town centre.

Penshurst Place *Kent*   *Map: 399 Eb*
The finest 14th-century manor house in England. Penshurst was the birthplace of Sir Philip Sidney, the soldier poet who became a byword for gallantry when, as he lay mortally wounded on a Dutch battlefield in 1586, he passed his flask of water to a common soldier with the words: "Thy necessity is greater than mine."

The prosperity of England in the Middle Ages derived from wool, and it is no coincidence that the builder of Penshurst was a draper, the vastly rich Sir John de Pulteney, four times Lord Mayor of London between 1331 and 1337.
Location: 5 miles SW of Tonbridge (A26 then B2176).

Penzance *Cornwall*   *Map: 396 Aa*
THE EGYPTIAN HOUSE The Egyptian-style facade was copied in the 1820s from an exhibition hall in Piccadilly, London. The building, originally a museum, has been restored, and is now an information centre for the National Trust.
Location: Chapel St, town centre.

Pershore Abbey *Heref. & Worcs.*   *Map: 393 Fc*
Pershore Abbey was founded in 689, though the oldest part remaining is 11th-century work in the south transept. The early-14th-century lantern tower is comparable to that at Salisbury Cathedral.

INSIDE THE GREAT HALL

Penshurst's 14th-century hall survives miraculously almost without alteration. Only the louvre in the roof, which allowed smoke to escape from the central hearth, has gone. The house is still in the ownership of the Sidney family.

THE REMARKABLE SHRINKING HALL

In medieval England most houses contained a large room, the hall, with a fire burning in the middle to keep it warm. All the occupants, from the owner to his most humble retainers, ate and lived in this one room without any privacy. In the following three centuries extra rooms were added at either end of the hall where the owner and his family could sleep and entertain in private, and where food could be kept and cooked. As more rooms were added the hall declined in importance. In peasant houses it remained the kitchen or main living-room, but in the architect-designed houses of the aristocracy it became a reception and staircase area, finally leading to the small and dark vestibule which today retains its old title "the hall."

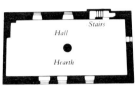

NORMAN *Houses were of two storeys, with the hall on top. Entry was by a stairway that could be defended. Beneath was a cellar for storing food.*

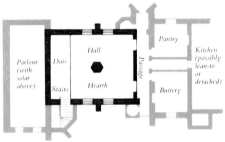

MEDIEVAL *A 14th-century manor house had a dais at one end of the hall where the lord's family ate. Behind the dais was their parlour and above it their solar, or bedroom. At the other end were a pantry for bread and buttery for ale.*

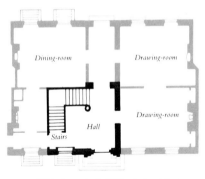

GEORGIAN *With the arrival of Classical architecture and its emphasis on symmetry, the hall became an entrance area. Doors led to reception rooms on each side, and a fine staircase rose up to the first floor.*

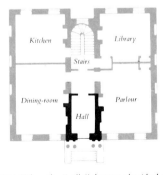

VICTORIAN *When the "villa" became the ideal suburban house of the 19th century, the hall was reduced to no more than a narrow vestibule inside the front door.*

The abbey's nave and Lady Chapel were pulled down in 1540 during the Dissolution of the Monasteries. The townspeople bought the monks' choir to use as a church, and Gilbert Scott restored the building in 1862–4. The font is Norman.

Location: 9 miles SE of Worcester on A44.

Perth *Tayside*   *Map: 389 Ef*
CITY MILLS The remains of two watermills stand beside a lade, or watercourse, dug in the 15th century. Both ground grain.

The upper mill, which dates from the 18th century, is now a hotel. Its wheel is 15 ft in diameter.

The lower mill, of about 1800, has a slightly larger wheel. It is in a state of disrepair and is not open to visitors.

Location: West Mill St, city centre.
FAIR MAID OF PERTH'S HOUSE Catherine Glover, the legendary beauty whom Sir Walter Scott made the heroine of his historical novel *The Fair Maid of Perth*, published in 1828, reputedly lived in Curfew Row at the end of the 14th century.

The present house is partly 16th century. It was used as the hall of the glove-makers' guild from 1629 until 1786, was restored in 1894 and now contains a crafts and antiques centre.

Location: North Port, off Atholl St, city centre.
PERTH BRIDGE John Smeaton, architect of the first stone lighthouse on the Eddystone Rocks, designed the graceful road bridge across the Tay. It was completed in 1771.

Location: NE of city centre.

Peterborough *Cambs.*   *Map: 398 Df*
CATHEDRAL Peada, King of Saxon Mercia, founded a monastery at Peterborough, then called Medeshamstede, in AD 654. It was sacked by the Danes in 870 and left in ruins for about 100 years, until Ethelwold, Bishop of Winchester, re-established it.

After the Norman invasion of 1066, East Anglia became a stronghold of Saxon resistance. The Saxons' leader, Hereward the Wake, allied himself with the Danes and plundered the monastery about 1070, removing holy relics.

The monastery church survived Hereward's raid only to be burned down in strange circumstances in 1116. Legend says that a monk, frustrated over a bakehouse oven which would not light, cursed it, howling: "Devil light the fire!" The fire flared up, got out of control, and destroyed all the monastic buildings.

Work on a new church, the present cathedral, started in 1118. The nave, one of the best examples of Norman architecture in England, took 80 years to complete. Its richly painted wooden ceiling – including figures of saints and monsters – dates from about 1220.

The Early English style of building that evolved from the end of the 12th century was used for Peterborough's west front, which has three cavernous arches, each 81 ft high.

In 1536 Catherine of Aragon, the divorced first wife of Henry VIII, died at Kimbolton, Cambridgeshire, and was buried near Peterborough's High Altar. The presence of her grave helped to save the church from destruction, for Henry spared it when he dissolved the monastery in 1539.

Catherine's tomb was prepared by Robert

Scarlett, a gravedigger. His portrait hangs on the west wall of the nave. Robert also buried Mary, Queen of Scots, whose body was brought to Peterborough in 1587, after her execution at Fotheringhay Castle. Mary's son James I of England (VI of Scotland) had the remains moved to Westminster Abbey 25 years later.

During the Civil War, the area around Peterborough strongly supported the Parliamentary cause. Parliamentary soldiers broke into the cathedral in 1643, destroying tombs and monuments, stained-glass windows and priceless documents.
Location: Cathedral Gateway, Market Place.

Petersfield *Hants.* *Map: 398 Cb*
BUTSER ANCIENT FARM Prehistoric farmers ploughed the downland slopes of Butser Hill

HOW IRON AGE MEN FARMED

Butser Ancient Farm, near Petersfield in Hampshire, is a working reconstruction of an Iron Age settlement, built and operated according to the techniques used by Celtic farmers in England about 2,300 years ago.

HAND MILL *In some Iron Age querns, or hand mills, the upper grinding stone moved about a wooden peg in the lower one. Grain poured into the hole in the top emerged at the edges as flour.*

PREHISTORIC FARMYARD *The fenced living compound contains hay ricks, a goat pen and a round house like those in which Iron Age families ate and slept.*

LOOM *Wool from Iron Age sheep was spun into yarn on a spindle and then woven into cloth on a simple loom. Some looms were upright wooden frames on which the warps (vertical threads) were kept straight by means of pear-shaped clay weights hung on their lower ends. The thread may have been dyed, using plants such as woad, and woven in tartan-style patterns.*

OAK AND HAZEL *A ring beam strengthens the round house roof. The rafters are ash poles with hazel rods between them, making a sturdy basket-work frame.*

LIVING-ROOM *Iron Age families cooked in beehive-shaped ovens or on an open hearth, and both also provided warmth. Smoke filtered out through the thatch of the roof, helping to tan goat and deer hides as it went.*

long before the Romans arrived, and traces of their field boundaries can still be seen. Since 1972, a spur on the northern side of the hill has been the centre of the most intensive research ever undertaken into the way prehistoric farmers lived.

The research area is not open to the public, but the results are shown in a working reconstruction of an Iron Age settlement, where crops and animals are raised according to what is known of Iron Age methods.

The farm's main building is a thatched roundhouse, 42 ft in diameter and 36 ft high, made from oak stakes with hazel rods woven between them and daubed with clay and other materials. It is based upon the remains of an Iron Age house found at Pimperne Down, Dorset.

A stockaded bank and ditch, intended to keep out animals, surrounds the living compound. Its ground plan has been copied from the East Castle earthworks in Wiltshire.

Two fields are planted with crops commonly grown during the Iron Age, of which the most important were spelt and emmer, primitive varieties of wheat developed from the accidental crossing of wild grasses. Animals raised on the farm include Exmoor ponies, Dexter cattle and Soay sheep, the nearest surviving equivalents to prehistoric breeds.

There are working replicas of Iron Age kilns in which pottery was fired, and a reconstruction of an upright loom used in weaving the yarn from Iron Age sheep.
Location: Queen Elizabeth Country Park (see below).

QUEEN ELIZABETH COUNTRY PARK The park covers 1,400 acres of downland and forest. Its Sheep Management Area includes a 19th-century shepherd's hut, and in the Forest Craft Demonstration Area pegs, brooms, hurdle fences and wooden wheels are made by methods used for centuries until the era of mass production.
Location: 4 miles S of Petersfield on A3.

Petersham *Surrey*   *Map: 398 Dc*
CHURCH OF ST PETER The church was founded in the 13th century and extensively altered from the 17th century onwards. Inside are Georgian box pews, galleries and a two-deck pulpit.
Location: 1 mile S of Richmond Station on Petersham Rd (A307).

Petworth House *W. Sussex*   *Map: 398 Cb*
For more than 500 years from 1150 the manor of Petworth belonged to the powerful and warlike Percy family, Earls of Northumberland and owners of vast tracts of land in northern England. Joscelyn Percy, the 11th earl, died in 1670. With his death, the male line of the Percy family ended.

The family estates, including Petworth, passed to Joscelyn's daughter, who was married three times before she reached the age of 16. It was her third husband, Charles Seymour, Duke of Somerset, nicknamed the Proud Duke for his haughty manner and obsession with his ancestry, who began the present baroque palace in 1688.

In the fashion of the 18th century, the state rooms at Petworth lead into each other without corridors. They were built and decorated at a time when trade was developing with the Far East, and much of the furniture shows that the Duchess of Somerset had an expensive liking for the artistic products of China. There are vast blue and white vases, each 4 ft high, lacquered cabinets and heavily decorated Chinese screens.

Petworth's principal treasures, however, are its paintings and sculptures. The Proud Duke's grandson, who became the 2nd Earl of Egremont, added 17th-century Dutch and Italian pictures to the noble series of portraits by Van Dyck, Lely and others he had inherited from his ancestors.

Agents working for the earl in Italy assembled a collection of ancient sculpture which was still unpacked on his death in 1763. His son built a gallery to contain it and there it remains, a unique expression of the taste of a rich and cultivated 18th-century nobleman. Among the treasures in the collection is a head of the goddess Aphrodite, attributed to Praxiteles, the Athenian sculptor of the 4th century BC.

The 2nd Earl of Egremont also gave Petworth its landscaped park, one of the first designed by "Capability" Brown. Its 738 acres were a major source of inspiration to the painter J. M. W. Turner in the 1830s.

The 3rd Earl of Egremont was both friend and patron to Turner, and gave him his own studio at Petworth. The painter was noted for his shyness and clumsy manner. At breakfast in the house one morning, he upset a jug of cream over a young lady's dress. By luncheon, he had produced a little watercolour depicting the incident to make amends. It is one of 22 Turner paintings in the house.

The 3rd earl was a pioneer of agricultural reform and made efforts to improve the lot of the small farmer. The poor of the neighbourhood were entertained annually to a great feast at Petworth. In 1835 it was held in the park, and a picture in the house shows several thousand people eating at a huge horseshoe of tables set up for the occasion.
Location: In Petworth at A272/A283 junction.

Pevensey Castle *E. Sussex*   *Map: 399 Ea*
The Romans built a massive fort at Pevensey in the 4th century AD. Within its walls, which still stand 30 ft high for about three-quarters of their circuit, Count Robert of Mortain, half-brother of William the Conqueror, put up a great tower early in the 12th century. Further defences were added in the 13th century.

Pevensey was equipped against attack as recently as 1940, when machine-gun emplacements were installed in preparation for a German invasion.
Location: 5 miles NE of Eastbourne off A259.

FACE PROTECTION
The visor from the helmet of a 14th-century knight was found in a drain at Pevensey.

Peveril Castle *Derbys.*   *Map: 393 Gf*
William de Peverel, a powerful Norman baron,
began the stone castle in the 1090s, and his son,
also called William, enlarged it. The younger
William was accused of poisoning Ranulf, Earl
of Chester in 1155. Henry II confiscated Peveril
from him and used the castle for short stays
when travelling to the north-west. He put up a
square great tower.
Location: 15 miles SW of Sheffield on A625, S
of Castleton village.

Pickering *N. Yorks.*   *Map: 394 Ce*
CASTLE Although there was a motte-and-bailey
castle at Pickering from the time of William the
Conqueror's reign, its stone fortifications were
not added until a century later, about 1180.

In 1322 the Scots under Robert Bruce were
pillaging Yorkshire. They burned Ripon and
threatened Pickering, but the castle was saved
from damage when the townspeople bought off
Bruce with money and hostages. Edward II
stayed in the castle the following year, and
greatly strengthened the defences.

By 1652 the castle was a ruin. It was sold for
breaking up for £200, but the work was never
carried out.
Location: Castlegate, N of town centre.
CHURCH OF ST PETER AND ST PAUL Pickering's
original early-Norman church was enlarged and
altered several times during the Middle Ages. It
has one of the most complete series of medieval

THE WORLD OF WALTER RALEIGH

*A globe map of the world bearing the date 1592, at
Petworth House, West Sussex, is the work of the
first man in England to make such globes, Emery
Molyneux, and is believed to have been given by Sir
Walter Raleigh to the 9th Earl of Northumberland.
They shared an interest in science, and both spent
years as prisoners in the Tower of London on charges
of treason. When the globe was drawn, the shape of
the American continent was roughly understood, but
the South Pacific – the "Southern Ocean" – remained
uncharted, and the North-West Passage across the top
of North America had yet to be found.*

LANGUAGE OF THE FAN

The prehistoric hunter who first waved a leaf in front of his face to cool himself or to drive away flies invented the fan, and the history of fan-making in the countries of the Mediterranean, Africa and the East stretches back thousands of years.

Early fans were rigid, made from woven straw, cloth or feathers, but in the 16th century Portuguese sailors returned from Japan with folding fans, which were easier to carry and use. They became a fashion accessory in the hot, sticky cities of southern Europe, spreading from there to Paris and then to England. Folding fans were of vellum, cloth or, later, paper. Some had jewelled ivory handles and leaves which were painted or patterned and trimmed with lace.

Fan languages–there were several–probably evolved in Spain in the 17th and 18th centuries, as a way round the social rule which prevented unmarried women from talking to men. The idea was widely copied elsewhere, partly as a method of flirtation and partly as a way of drawing attention to the beauty of the fan-holder's hands, and it lasted into the 20th century in England.

In 1711 Joseph Addison wrote in *The Spectator*: "Women are armed with fans as men with swords." More than 100 years later, the statesman Benjamin Disraeli added his comment to Addison's: ". . . and sometimes do more executions with them." Towards the end of the 18th century, an academy was set up in London to teach young ladies "the exercise of the Fan". The enterprising instructress ran separate classes for men, so they could interpret the fan signals.

I WISH TO SPEAK TO YOU *A Victorian lady signals that she is ready to open conversation.*

DO NOT BE IMPUDENT *A gentleman could be reprimanded by the wave of a fan.*

I LOVE YOU *The open fan held to the left of the head was an outright declaration of love.*

NO! *A half-opened fan held by the left cheek denoted "no" in fan language.*

FOLLOW ME *An open fan held in front of the face in the right hand signalled "follow" to a Victorian.*

KISS ME *The closed fan with handle held to the lips was an open invitation, despite the demure look.*

wall-paintings in England. They date from the mid-15th century and show the Seven Acts of Mercy, Christ's Passion, episodes from the lives of the saints and other religious themes. The paintings were an important source of religious instruction in the days when few could read.
Location: E of Market Place, town centre.

NORTH YORKSHIRE MOORS RAILWAY The line from Whitby to Pickering was opened in 1836 by the engineer George Stephenson and closed in 1965. An 18 mile section from Pickering to Grosmont Junction, passing through the North York Moors National Park, has since been reopened. Diesel engines are generally used between Pickering and Goathland. From Goathland to Grosmont the trains are steam-hauled, and other steam locomotives are on show at Grosmont.
Location: Pickering Station, off Market Place, town centre.

Piercebridge *Durham*   *Map: 391 Fd*
ROMAN FORT Piercebridge village lies on the site of a large Roman fort built early in the 4th century AD. It is still being excavated.

Part of the fort wall is visible–reached from a path just north of the church. Remains of the Roman bridge across the River Tees, uncovered in 1972, have been preserved.
Location: 5½ miles W of Darlington on A67.

Pitcaple Castle *Grampian*   *Map: 387 Fb*
A 19th-century mansion has been built on to a Z-plan tower house of 1457, for more than 500 years the home of the Leslie and Lumsden families, descendants of a favourite of King Malcolm Canmore.

James IV and Charles II both stayed at Pitcaple, and Mary, Queen of Scots dined there.
Location: 4 miles NW of Inverurie on A96.

Pitmedden Garden *Grampian*   *Map: 387 Fb*
Sir Alexander Seton of Pitmedden started to lay out formal gardens in front of his mansion about 1675, using ideas brought back from the Continent by Charles II and his followers at the Restoration.

The lower, or Great, garden, has a sundial with some 24 faces, and several fountains. The gardens were restored to their 17th-century grandeur in the 1950s.
Location: 14½ miles N of Aberdeen (A92 and B999).

Pitstone Windmill *Bucks.*   *Map: 398 Cd*
The mill was built in 1627 to grind grain, and was refitted in the 19th century. It is no longer used, but its two sets of millstones are in place.

Pitstone is a post mill, in which the entire body containing the machinery could be turned on a central king post to enable the sails to face the wind.
Location: 3¼ miles NE of Tring off B488.

Plas Newydd *Gwynedd*   *Map: 392 Cf*
When French cannon shot away the leg of the 2nd Earl of Uxbridge at the Battle of Waterloo in 1815, the earl's reaction earned him a place in history. "By God, sir," said the stricken Uxbridge to his commander, the Duke of Wellington, "I've lost my leg." The Iron Duke took his eye off the French for a second to reply: "By God, so you have, sir."

A leg from the earl's trousers, still spattered with Waterloo mud, and his artificial limb are among the relics preserved at Plas Newydd, one of his two country mansions. The house, originally 16th century, was extensively altered in the 18th century.
Location: On Anglesey, 3 miles SW of Menai Bridge (A5 then A4080).

Platt Hall *Greater Manchester*   Map: 393 Ff
One of the most comprehensive costume collections in the country is displayed at Platt Hall, a Georgian house built in the 1760s. The collection includes more than 2,000 dresses from the 1700s onward and many accessories.
Location: Wilmslow Rd (A6010), off A34, 2 miles SE of Manchester.

FASHION REVOLUTION

From the Middle Ages until the First World War, women's dresses encased the wearer to the ankles, concealing the legs and hampering movement. In the 1850s, women's rights campaigners, led by the American Amelia Bloomer, tried to promote a more rational form of dress, in which a skirt coming to just below the knee was worn over baggy, harem-style trousers, the original "bloomers". The idea did not catch on, and it was not until about 1915, as the result of wartime shortages and emancipation, that women of fashion began to wear skirts which showed their calves.

At the same time, mass production made fashions both more practical and more democratic, a theme illustrated in the collection of costumes at Platt Hall, Greater Manchester.

CAP *This richly embroidered man's cap, made in the first quarter of the 17th century, was worn indoors during the evenings. It is of white linen decorated with silver thread.*

FOR THE BRIDE *By the mid-19th century, white was firmly established as the most fashionable colour for wedding dresses. A hand-coloured fashion plate of 1848 from the collection at Platt Hall shows a bridal gown in white silk trimmed with lace. Its bodice is boned, and the dress would have been worn over a tight, boned corset and layers of heavy petticoats stiffened with horse hair. The bridesmaid has a mauve silk dress and the typically demure bonnet worn by women of the Victorian period.*

FOLDING FAN *Elaborately painted scenes decorate the paper leaf of an 18th-century fan in the Platt Hall collection. The fan was made in England and belonged to Lady Anne Pennefeather, a noted beauty of Bath. During the 18th and 19th centuries such fans were indispensable fashion accessories for women. Some men used them, too – a custom of which Queen Victoria disapproved.*

Pleshey Castle *Essex*   *Map: 399 Ed*
The earthworks of the motte-and-bailey castle look much as they did when they were raised in the 12th century, but the later stone defences have been removed.
Location: 7½ miles NW of Chelmsford (A130 then minor road).

Plymouth *Devon*   *Map: 396 Cb*
DEVONPORT DOCKYARDS William III founded the Royal Naval Dockyard in 1689. It has been enlarged many times since then, and covers more than 330 acres.
The older buildings are mainly from the 18th century. They include an elegant gabled stores of 1760 and a shipbuilding slip of 1763.
In South Yard there is a ropery, or rope-walk, in which men walking slowly backwards and forwards wove hemp strands into rope. The technique was the only method of making rope until the mid-19th century.
Location: 2½ miles W of city centre (A374 then A3042).
NO. 33 ST ANDREW'S ST A four-storey Elizabethan town house, once owned by a wealthy privateer, William Parker, has been restored to its original structure. (See p. 427.)
SMEATON'S TOWER Two earlier wooden light-houses on the Eddystone Rocks, 14 miles off Plymouth, had been destroyed when the York-shire engineer John Smeaton built a masonry one there in 1759. He dovetailed blocks of Portland stone to produce a structure which could resist the worst storms, and which revolutionised lighthouse design
Smeaton's Eddystone lighthouse was replaced in 1879–82, because its foundations were being eroded. The top section was brought back to Plymouth and reassembled.
Location: The Hoe, S of city centre.

Polegate Windmill *E. Sussex*   *Map: 399 Ea*
The four-storey brick tower mill was built in 1817 to grind grain, and is still in working order. A fantail automatically turns the cap – the top section – and its four shuttered sails to face the wind.
Location: 4 miles N of Eastbourne off A22.

Polesden Lacey *Surrey*   *Map: 398 Dc*
R. B. Sheridan, author of *The Rivals*, bought the Polesden Lacey estate in 1797. He planned to rebuild its dilapidated 17th-century manor house, but lacked the money.
After Sheridan's death in 1816 the house was pulled down and the property sold. The architect Thomas Cubitt built a Regency villa there in 1821–3. It was altered and enlarged by a succession of owners, and in 1906 was bought by the Hon. Ronald Greville and his wife Margaret, daughter of a Scots brewing millionaire.
Mrs Greville was a celebrated hostess. For nearly 40 years she entertained the rich, the powerful and the famous at Polesden Lacey. Their signatures appear in the Visitors' Book, headed by that of Edward VII.
Location: 1½ miles SW of Great Bookham off A246.

Pontefract Castle *W. Yorks.*   *Map: 391 Ga*
After Richard II had lost the throne to his cousin Henry Bolingbroke in 1399, the former king was imprisoned in Pontefract Castle, where he died a year or so later. Henry's supporters claimed Richard deliberately starved himself to death. Others maintained he was murdered, though an examination of Richard's remains in the 1870s revealed no signs of violence.
The castle, founded in the 11th century near the site of a Saxon palace, now lost, was largely dismantled during the Civil War, but part of its 13th–14th-century great tower and some of the walls remain.
Location: Castle Garth, town centre.

Pont Scethin *Gwynedd*   *Map: 392 Ce*
BRIDGE The medieval stone bridge of Pont Scethin carried the road from Dolgellau to Harlech across the River Ysgethin until the late 18th century, when the present coastal route was opened.
The line of the old road which was used by the London to Harlech stagecoaches is still clear, though few stretches remain paved.
Location: 7 miles NE of Barmouth (A496, minor road N of river at Tal-y-Bont, track to Cors-y-Gedol, then footpath. Care should be taken in wet weather, as the ground is marshy).

Pontypool *Gwent*   *Map: 393 Db*
GLYN PIT Two derelict 19th-century engine-houses contain the crumbling remains of their engines. One was used to pump water from the coal mine. The other wound men and materials up and down the pitshaft.
Location: 1 mile W of town (A472 then narrow lane. Follow sign for College of Education)

Pontypridd *Mid Glam.*   *Map: 393 Da*
GLAMORGANSHIRE CANAL The coal and iron industries transformed Pontypridd from a small village during the late 18th and early 19th centuries. North Country ironmasters moved into the district to exploit the ample resources of ore from 1750, and the first colliery opened about 1790. Coal-mines, active and disused, still dominate the town.
In 1794 the Glamorganshire Canal was completed. It carried iron from the foundries around Merthyr Tydfil to the docks at Cardiff. The canal is no longer used, but a section in the centre of Pontypridd has been cleared, and the 18th-century lock-keeper's cottage, with a stable for the barge-horses, has been rebuilt and opened to the public.
A spur of the canal leads off, under a cast-iron bridge of 1856, to the Brown Lennox chain works, founded in 1816 and still in operation. The works are private property.
Location: Town centre.
TAFF BRIDGE In 1750, when Pontypridd was emerging as a centre of the iron industry, a self-taught local mason called William Edwards agreed to build a stone road bridge across the River Taff. His first structure was swept away by a flood. Edwards built a second bridge, but this collapsed because of a fault in the design.
Once again the mason tried to span the river, and in 1756 he hit upon a novel idea to reduce the weight of the stone without weakening the structure. He left large holes in the spandrils, the area above the base of the bridge on either bank.
Edwards' third bridge still stands as a monument to his tenacity. Its single span is 140 ft, the

RELICS OF CORNWALL'S COPPER INDUSTRY

The former engine-house of the United Hills copper mine at Porthtowan, Cornwall, is perched castle-like above a moorland valley. Below, on the valley floor, *the chimney-stack of a second engine-house has been decorated to resemble a turret. The mines flourished in the 18th and 19th centuries, but are now derelict.*

longest in Britain until London Bridge opened in 1831.
Location: N end of Taff St.

Portchester Castle *Hants.* Map: 398 Ca
The Romans built a fortress at Portchester nearly 1,700 years ago as one of a chain to guard the Saxon Shore, the area of the south coast which was most vulnerable to pirate raids from the Continent. Large sections of its defences are intact.

After the Romans left, Saxons occupied the fort. Then, in the 12th century, Henry I added a great tower and enclosed it with extra stone walls.

Edward III sailed from Portchester in 1346 to begin the French campaign which was to bring him victory at Crécy. In 1415 Henry V embarked from there for France and another great victory, at Agincourt.

During the Napoleonic Wars, the castle housed French prisoners.

Inside, there is an exhibition devoted to the Forts of the Saxon Shore.
Location: 3 miles E of Fareham off A27.

Port Erin *Isle of Man* Map: 390 Ab
RAILWAY MUSEUM Steam trains still run on the $15\frac{1}{4}$ mile, 3 ft gauge single-track line from Douglas to Port Erin, which was opened in 1873. The oldest locomotive was built in 1874.

The coaches, of 1926 and earlier, were the first in Britain to be fitted with electric lights. A museum in Port Erin Station traces the history of the line.
Location: Town centre.

Porthmadog *Gwynedd* Map: 392 Ce
FESTINIOG RAILWAY The line, constructed in the 1860s to carry slate from the mines and quarries of Blaenau Ffestiniog to the coast, is being restored to take passengers. It is worked from Porthmadog by eight narrow-gauge locomotives, including two double-ended Fairlie engines.

There are fine views from the trains of the lakes and mountains of Snowdonia, and of

Harlech Castle. The first locomotive used on the line, *Princess*, is on display at Blaenau Ffestiniog.
Location: Harbour, SE of town centre on A487.

Porthtowan *Cornwall* Map: 396 Ab
COPPER MINES Throughout the 18th and 19th centuries, the deep valley which runs inland from the sea at Porthtowan was mined for its copper ore. The remains of several mines lie in a wild moorland setting.

At the top of the hill, the large engine-house of the United Hills mine gives fine views. Lower down is a second, smaller engine-house which belonged to the same concern. It is now ruined. Both buildings contained beam-engines which pumped water from the workings.

A third engine-house, on the valley floor, has a chimney-stack which is crenellated like a castle turret, an unusual decorative touch.
Location: 12 miles NE of Hayle (A30 then minor roads and footpath).

Portland *Dorset* Map: 397 Fb
LIGHTHOUSES Treacherous cross-currents which seethe off the tip of the Portland peninsula are a constant hazard to ships using the harbour in its lee. A 136 ft lighthouse, built in 1906, warns navigators of the dangers.

It replaced an earlier structure of 1789, which is now used as a bird observatory.
Location: Portland Bill, off A354.
PORTLAND CASTLE Henry VIII ordered the castle to be built to protect Weymouth harbour in 1538–40, when it was feared that an alliance of European nations might invade England to uphold the authority of the pope.

The castle was manned again later in the 16th century, at the time of the Spanish Armada. It was occupied by Royalist forces during the Civil War, and fell to Parliamentary troops in 1646.

The design is based on a segment of a circle, with inner and outer fortifications and a moat. The officers of the garrison had their living quarters in the tower and wings. The men lived in barracks in the courtyard, which was originally roofed.
Location: $4\frac{1}{2}$ miles S of Weymouth off A354.

Portsmouth *Hants.*   *Map: 398 Ca*
HMS VICTORY Nelson's flagship, now preserved in the Royal Dockyards, is a superb example of the men-of-war that fought in the Napoleonic Wars of 1793–1815. She was launched in 1765 but did not see action until 1778, during the War of American Independence. From then until 1812 she was involved in many major battles, of which the most decisive was that fought off Cape Trafalgar, Spain, in 1805. There she led the British fleet that overwhelmed the combined fleets of France and Spain. The British commander-in-chief, Lord Nelson, met his death on board her during the final phase of victory. Since 1928 the ship has been restored to the condition she was in at Trafalgar.

Opposite the *Victory* is the Royal Naval Museum, which displays personal belongings of Nelson and his associates, and relics of naval history since Trafalgar, including a vast panoramic picture of the battle by W. L. Wyllie.
Location: Entrance is at junction of Queen St (A3019) and The Hard, W of city centre.

Poulton-le-Fylde *Lancs.*   *Map: 391 Db*
CHURCH OF ST CHAD The tower is 17th century and the vault of the Fleetwood-Heskett family dates from 1699, but the rest of the church was rebuilt in the 1750s.

There are Georgian wooden galleries on three sides of the interior, and in the sanctuary is a brass candelabrum of 1710.
Location: 3½ miles NE of Blackpool (A586 and A588).

ON BOARD THE *VICTORY*

Men took second place to guns in the use of the restricted space on board a man-of-war. On each gun deck of the Victory *there were 28 or 30 guns, 10 ft apart, and seamen had to eat and sleep as best they could between them. Officers were not privileged in this respect. They lived in the cramped quarters of the orlop, or lowest, deck, below the water line – and also had to contend with the stink of rancid butter from the adjoining hold.*

MEALS AMID THE CANNON *Suspended between each pair of guns on the lower gun deck was a mess table, at which the crew ate their meals.*

SEAMAN'S HAMMOCK *Hammocks were slung from the deck-head. Only alternate spaces were occupied at any given time, as one watch was on deck.*

DISCIPLINE *Offenders on board ship were punished by a flogging on the bare back with a cat-o'-nine-tails (left), a rope of nine unplaited strands. The crew was assembled on deck to watch this savage punishment administered. Regulations restricted the number of lashes to a dozen, but some captains ordered four times this amount. A detachment of armed marines stood on the deck above the crew, ready to quell any rebellious reactions. The "persuader" (right) was a solid rope which petty officers used to hustle the crew along in their daily tasks.*

NELSON'S COT *Like most naval officers of the period, Lord Nelson often slept in a suspended cot. The drapes are replicas of those made for the cot by Lady Hamilton, Nelson's mistress.*

LIFE IN NELSON'S NAVY

The life of a seaman on the *Victory* or one of the other British warships of Nelson's time was hard, ill-paid and dangerous. Its only rewards were the satisfaction of defeating the enemy and an occasional small amount of prize money.

The men were adequately fed, but the food was of poor quality. Each man was issued with a daily ration of 1 lb. of hard tack (ship's biscuit) or bread, 1 gallon of beer and a measure of grog (watered rum). He also received a weekly ration of salt pork or beef (fresh meat if it was obtainable), oatmeal, dried peas, butter, cheese, sugar and cocoa. But often the hard tack was so tough that it broke the men's teeth, the cheese was equally hard and the butter rancid.

Scurvy, the killer disease
By far the worst aspect of the seaman's diet was its shortage of fresh fruit or vegetables – particularly in wartime, when it was more difficult to put into port for provisions. This lack of vitamin C often caused scurvy, a disease that rotted the gums, caused internal bleeding and could kill. It was not until 1795, when the Admiralty ordered a daily issue of lemon juice, that scurvy was virtually stamped out.

Other diseases remained rampant, however, particularly typhus, dysentery, tuberculosis and tropical illnesses. The work itself caused many deaths, too – especially during storms and high seas. For every one seaman who was killed by enemy action during the Napoleonic Wars of 1793–1815, about 13 died from disease, accident or shipwreck.

Low pay, harsh discipline
Pay was poor, even by the standards of the time. When the seamen of the Channel Fleet mutinied at Spithead in 1797, they had not had a pay rise for nearly a century and a half. Within a month of the mutiny they had secured a small increase, and after the Battle of Trafalgar in 1805, they received another. This brought the wages of an ordinary seaman up to 25s 6d a month (which was still less than the pay of a merchant seaman or soldier) and those of an able seaman up to 33s 6d. Out of these wages, the seaman had to provide his own clothes. He either bought them ready-made from the purser or made his own.

Discipline was harsh. For drunkenness, laziness, or sometimes simply laughing in the presence of an officer, some captains would order three or four dozen lashes with the cat-o'-nine-tails.

Until 1853, when long-term engagements for seamen were introduced, the Navy relied for its crew on volunteers and the victims of press gangs – bands of tough sailors who roamed the ports and boarded merchant ships to seize any able-bodied seaman they came across.

By law, only seamen born in Britain and aged between 18 and 55 could be taken into service in this way. But during the Napoleonic Wars, civilians, foreigners, boys and old men were illegally seized. On occasions, the victims were even local notables such as aldermen and ship-owners, and at one time 48 of the 628 crew serving on the *Victory* were foreigners.

There were usually a few women on board ship, too – stowaways who later helped to care for the wounded and to carry powder to the guns.

The fury of battle
Once a warship sailed into action, the hardships of everyday life were forgotten in the intense activity of preparation and in the fury of battle itself.

On the upper deck, gun crews took up their stations by the lightest guns, the 12-pounders (which fired the *Victory's* first shots in the Battle of Trafalgar).

The middle deck, normally used for patching sails and cooking, had been cleared for action, the gun ports opened and the 24-pounders run out. And on the lower deck – the broadest and strongest, to support the ship's main guns, the 32-pounders – the gun crews stood stripped to the waist and with kerchiefs tied around their ears to muffle the explosions.

As the ships engaged the enemy, each crew cheered at the top of its voice to hearten the others and to terrify the enemy. The guns roared, the ship's timbers trembled with the repeated explosions, and a pall of acrid smoke would sometimes blot out light from the battle area.

Most of the gunners on the lower deck usually saw nothing of the action until it was all over. Then a horrifying scene would often meet their eyes. John Nicol, a gunner who served under Nelson during the Battle of the Nile in 1798, has left a vivid account of his experiences. When he left the powder magazine after the battle and went up on deck he saw that "the whole bay was covered with dead bodies, mangled, wounded and scorched . . ."

Only when final victory was won were the men free to go home to their own pursuits – an incentive which ensured that they fought hard.

The press gang: enlistment by force.

Flogging: a savage punishment.

Manning the guns: heat and din.

Meals: eaten amid the guns.

Powderham Castle *Devon*   *Map: 397 Ec*
Home of the Courtenay family, earls of Devon, for the past 600 years, the 14th–15th-century castle was in the 18th and 19th centuries converted into one of the finest mansions in the country.
Location: 7 miles S of Exeter off A379.

Powis Castle *Powys*   *Map: 393 Dd*
Gruffydd ap Gwenwynwyn, a Welsh prince who supported Edward I of England, built the first castle on the site in the 13th century. The Welsh sacked it in the 1270s, but it was reconstructed.
    The Herbert family, ancestors of the earls of Powis, bought the castle in 1587, and over the centuries transformed it into a stately house.
Location: 1 mile SW of Welshpool off A483.

Prestatyn Castle *Clwyd*   *Map: 393 Df*
Only the central mound remains of the castle, which was raised in the 12th century. It was held in the 1160s by Owain Cyfeiliog, a prince of Powys.
Location: Town centre, corner of Prestatyn Rd and Bodnant Av.

Prestonpans *Lothian*   *Map: 389 Ed*
PRESTONGRANGE MUSEUM Displays in the converted power house of the former Prestongrange Colliery trace the history of Scottish coal-mining. An 1874 beam engine which pumped water from the mines has been restored to working order.
Location: 7½ miles E of Edinburgh (A1 then B1348).

Preston Tower *Northld.*   *Map: 389 Gc*
Robert Harbottle, governor of Dunstanburgh Castle, constructed the tower in the early 1400s to provide local families with a refuge for themselves and their livestock during the constant border skirmishes between English and Scots.
Location: 8½ miles N of Alnwick (A1, B6347 and minor roads).

Preston-under-Scar *N. Yorks.*   *Map: 391 Fc*
LEAD SMELTERS During the 19th century, the Pennines were a centre of the lead industry, and remains of the buildings associated with lead production dot the landscape.
    Locally mined ore was heated in hearths, or smelters, such as the one at Keld Heads Mill near Preston, to release the metal. But in the process, much of the lead escaped as a vapour.
    To reduce pollution, and help to increase the amount of metal recovered, smelters were fitted with long horizontal flues in which the vapour cooled and deposited lead particles.
    The sandstone flue from Keld Heads Mill runs nearly 2 miles to its tall chimney, still a prominent landmark.
Location: 12½ miles SW of Richmond (A6108 then minor road). The flue starts N of village.

Preston Watermill see East Linton

Prestwich *Greater Manchester*   *Map: 391 Ea*
HEATON HALL Sir Thomas Egerton, father of the 1st Earl of Wilton, built a square brick house at Heaton in 1750. The architect James Wyatt remodelled it in 1772, his first country house commission.
Location: 4 miles N of Manchester city centre in Middleton Rd (A576).

Priddy *Somerset*   *Map: 397 Fd*
LEAD SMELT MILLS Lead was mined in the Mendip Hills around Priddy from Roman times until the end of the 17th century. In the 19th century, improved production techniques made it possible to extract the metal from ore left in the abandoned spoil heaps.
    There are several ruined smelting hearths, in which the ore was heated, from this period. The flues, where lead vapour was condensed, are partially intact.
Location: 4½ miles N of Wells on minor roads.

Prudhoe Castle *Northld.*   *Map: 391 Fe*
William the Lion of Scotland besieged the newly completed castle in 1174 during his invasion of Northumberland. Prudhoe's English owner, Odinel d'Umfraville, went to seek help, while the garrison resisted gallantly. After three days, William abandoned the siege and marched to Alnwick, where a party of English, including d'Umfraville, captured him. William was eventually released after accepting a peace treaty.
    Prudhoe passed in 1381 to the earls of Northumberland.
Location: 10½ miles W of Newcastle upon Tyne on A695.

Purse Caundle Manor *Dorset*   *Map: 397 Fc*
During the 13th century, the owners of Purse Caundle held the manor directly from King John. As rent, they had to "keep and lodge the King's sick or injured hounds . . . when the Lord King hunts game in Blakemore (Blackmore Vale)". The present building dates from the 15th century.
Location: 4½ miles E of Sherborne off A30.

Quainton *Bucks.*   *Map: 398 Cd*
CHURCH OF ST MARY AND HOLY CROSS St Mary's, built in the 14th century and restored in the 19th, contains many brasses and some of the finest monumental sculptures in the country.
    The black and white marble effigies of Richard Winwood and his wife date from 1689 and the massive memorial to Mr Justice Dormer from about 1730.
Location: 6 miles NW of Aylesbury (A41 then minor road).
QUAINTON RAILWAY CENTRE *King Edward I,* built for the Great Western Railway in 1930, is among the locomotives being restored. There is a large collection of rolling stock. Steam-train rides take place on open days.
Location: Quainton Railway Station.

Queensferry *Lothian*   *Map: 389 Ed*
FORTH RAILWAY BRIDGE The Forth bridge was one of the great engineering triumphs of the Railway Age. When it opened in 1890 it was the longest in the world, and it earned Benjamin Baker, who designed the main section, a knighthood.
    The two spans are each 1,700 ft long, and they rise 150 ft above the water. The bridge is painted continuously to protect it from rust.
Location: 8 miles NW of Edinburgh by A90.

MEMORIAL TO A SOLDIER

The mason-sculptor Thomas Stayner carved the marble memorial to Richard Winwood at Quainton, Buckinghamshire, in 1689. Winwood, in full armour and a wig, is shown after death, but the effigy has none of the rigid and formal pose which was traditional until the Reformation. His wife reclines beside him.

CHURCH MONUMENTS: A "NATIONAL GALLERY" OF SCULPTURE

Sculptured monuments in Britain's churches span seven centuries of the carver's art and are a treasure-store of information about the tastes, beliefs and fashions of our forbears. The earliest, in stone, marble or, occasionally, wood, date from the 13th century and invariably show the subject laid out after death.

From the 16th century, monuments became grander, reflecting the wealth or importance of the subject. And in the early 1600s, the master-mason Nicholas Stone set a new fashion. His figures no longer lay or knelt, but sat, stood or reclined, though the pose was melancholy. By the late 18th century, sculptors were using themes from ancient Greece and Rome.

17TH CENTURY Sir Giles Mompesson (died 1633) holds a book and his wife a skull in a carved monument at the Church of St Mary the Virgin, Lydiard Tregoze, Wiltshire. Seated or standing figures began to appear in funerary sculpture from the early 1600s.

13TH CENTURY Early sculptured effigies are natural-looking and piously posed, showing the subject laid out after death. Purbeck marble was widely used, as in King John's monument in Worcester Cathedral. It was carved about 1230 and was originally painted.

18TH CENTURY The reclining figure in Classical style on the tomb of Mary Russell (died 1786) at Powick, Hereford & Worcester, makes no concession to pious imagery. The sculptor was Thomas Scheemakers (1740–1808).

15TH CENTURY By the 15th century, easily worked alabaster was preferred to marble. But the style of sculpture had changed little. The effigies of Sir Ralph Fitzherbert (died 1483) and his wife are at Norbury, Derbyshire.

16TH CENTURY The tradition of showing the subject in death was less strictly observed after the Reformation. The alabaster memorial to Sir Thomas Sonds (died 1592) and his wife at Throwley, Kent, depicts them kneeling either side of a prayer desk.

18TH CENTURY Joseph Nollekens (1737–1823), the most fashionable sculptor of his day, created the memorial to Sir Robert Cunliffe (died 1778) at Bruera, Cheshire. The putto, or cherub, is seated beside an urn on which is a portrait medallion of the dead man.

R

Last stronghold of the Cavaliers

AFTER A TEN WEEK SIEGE, RAGLAN CASTLE – LAST OF THE ROYALIST FORTRESSES – FELL TO THE ROUNDHEADS, HERALDING THE END OF THE CIVIL WAR

PITCHED STONE COURT *The pitching – or cobbling – that gave one of the two courtyards its name at Raglan Castle.*

Raglan Castle was started in 1432 by Sir William ap Thomas, and completed by his successors towards the end of the 16th century. It has hexagonal towers and turrets, with outer walls enclosing two courtyards, separated by a buttery, chapel and hall. A first-floor bridge led to the Great Tower, set within a moat.

In 1646, during the Civil War, the castle was owned by the Marquis of Worcester. With a garrison of 800 men he held out against the Parliamentary forces, commanded by Sir Thomas Fairfax. At one time, 3,500 men were besieging the citadel, with daily bombardments of cannon balls against the Great Tower.

Worcester finally yielded when there seemed little hope of relief, marking the end of the Civil War. The castle was partly demolished by the Parliamentarians – the Great Tower rendered defenceless by mining.

WHERE CHARLES I WAS A GUEST

A reconstruction of Raglan Castle, Gwent, as it might have appeared in 1645. The owner, the Marquis of Worcester – said to have been the richest man in England – entertained Charles I at the castle on several occasions. To garrison the castle during the Civil War cost the marquis £40,000 of his own money.

THEATRICAL MAGNIFICENCE

The breath-taking interior of the Great Hall in Ragley Hall, Warwickshire, designed and decorated by James Gibbs, dates from 1750. The focal point of the entire house, it is 70 ft long, 40 ft wide and 40 ft high, with its ceiling at roof level. In the Great Hall, parties of visitors would be entertained for weeks on end with music, dancing, games or long sessions of political, literary or philosophical discussions, or by marathon bouts of gambling with cards or dice.

The furniture was made specifically for the room in 1756, painted with the family crest. The two marble busts are of the prince regent by Joseph Nollekens.

GILDED GRANDEUR
This ornate overmantel is in the small dining-room at Ragley Hall. Made in 1756 by Thomas H. Kendall of Warwick, the carved plasterwork is in the rococo style – a flamboyant phase of Renaissance architecture fashionable between 1720 and 1760.

Ragley Hall *Warks.*   Map: 393 Fc
It was the scientist and mathematician Robert Hooke, Curator of the Royal Society, who designed the hall for the Earl of Conway in 1680. The land had been given by the Saxon King of Mercia to the Abbey of Evesham, and the Conway family bought it in 1591.

At the end of the 17th century the Conway heiress' married one of the Seymours – a family which rose to prominence during Henry VIII's reign (1509–47).

It was Francis Seymour Conway, the 1st Marquess of Hertford, who brought the house to its full brilliance in the second half of the 18th century, using the finest architectural talent that money could buy. James Wyatt added the portico to the front of the house in 1783.

James Gibbs designed the Great Hall in 1750, its vast scale and beautiful plasterwork making it one of the great rooms of Europe.

Life in a house like Ragley was luxurious. In the 18th century the old English reliance on huge quantities of meat, poultry and fish of the finest quality as the staple diet – which caused amazement to generations of European visitors at the time – was being augmented by more and more vegetables. Meat dishes were accompanied by salads, potatoes, cabbages, carrots, sprouts and cucumbers, and this accounts for the kitchen garden, with its gardener's house, playing a prominent part in the plans of the estate. Puddings, too, were more elaborate than before,

with ice cream being especially popular. The mound near the stables contains an ice house – a chamber where ice, cut in the winter, could be stored underground without melting, to be used for cooling desserts and drinks during the summer.

The house has stayed in the hands of the Seymour family to the present day, and the neglect of earlier generations has been repaired, so that there are now direct links with the carelessly opulent past – such as the dining-room, laid out for a State banquet with exquisite Sèvres porcelain, and the bedroom in which the Prince Regent slept during visits in the 1800s.
Location: 8 miles W of Stratford-upon-Avon (A422 then A435).

Ranger's House *Greater London* Map: 399 Dc
The 18th-century country home of Lord Chesterfield, in whose celebrated letters to his son it is referred to as "Petite Chartreuse" – his monastic retreat from London society.

The house has a fine collection of Jacobean and later portraits.
Location: Chesterfield Walk, off Shooters Hill Rd (A2).

Ranworth *Norfolk*   Map: 395 Ga
CHURCH OF ST HELEN'S A mainly Perpendicular building that occupies the site of a Saxon church. The 15th-century screen is rare – built across the full width of the church and with original

paintings on it, that were recently restored.

A unique survivor of the Reformation (1538–88) is the Cantor's Desk, similar to a lectern but used by the singers for their music. Another rarity is the Antiphoner, a medieval Latin service book on sheepskin pages, decorated with 19 miniatures. It was written and painted by the monks of Langley Abbey in 1478.
Location: 9 miles NE of Norwich (B1140 then minor road from Panxworth).

Ravenglass *Cumbria*   *Map: 390 Dc*
ROMAN BATH HOUSE The walls of a bath house, attached to a nearby fort, stand 12½ ft high – making it the best-preserved Roman structure in the north of England.
Location: 17 miles S of Whitehaven off A595.
THE RAVENGLASS AND ESKDALE RAILWAY This line was built in 1875 to a 3 ft gauge, reduced to its present 15 in. in 1916. Four steam locomotives provide a regular passenger service over the 7 mile run through Lakeland scenery.
Location: British Rail Station.

Ravenscraig Castle *Fife*   *Map: 389 Ee*
Ravenscraig was probably the first castle in Britain to be designed for defence with firearms. It was commissioned in 1460 by James II, King of Scotland (1437–60), who loved guns and considered himself an expert in artillery. He died that same year trying to take Roxburgh Castle by means of cannons – when one of them exploded in his face.

David Boys had been appointed master of works at Ravenscraig and, after the king's death, continued with the building for the king's widow, Mary of Gueldres. By about the middle of 1461, the castle was advanced enough for some of the queen dowager's servants to stay there.

Nine years later, in 1470, James III gave the castle to William Sinclair, Earl of Orkney, as a token of compensation for having insisted on Orkney giving up the earldom which the king wanted for himself.

Ravenscraig Castle was raised upon an imposing site jutting out into Kirkcaldy Bay. The cliff rises sheer on its western side to about 80 ft above the sands and falls to the eastern shore in a series of steep terraces. The castle was planned to straddle this awkwardly shaped cliff. Its western tower house, with a basement and four storeys, has walls in places that are 14 ft thick. The eastern tower was similarly designed but with one less storey. Between the towers there was a block of apartments, built around an entrance, in front of which there was a ditch.

Ravenscraig was defended by means of key-hole-shaped shot-holes for guns on either side of the entrance, in the walls of the tower houses and the lower part of the courtyard wall. Embrasures for small guns were built in the wall over the entrance and along the front of the block. Gun platforms for movable cannons were laid out at lower levels on the tower houses.

Like many fortresses erected in good strategic positions and built to play both defensive and offensive roles, Ravenscraig Castle does not appear ever to have had to resort to using its armament in battle.
Location: Junction of Nether St (A92) and St Clair St (A955), NE town centre.

Rayleigh Mount *Essex*   *Map: 399 Fd*
A motte and bailey was built on the Mount by Sweyn, the son of a Norman lord who came to England in the reign of Edward the Confessor and won favour with William the Conqueror after Hastings. His grandson, Henry, strengthened it with flint and rubble, but in 1157 he was disgraced for cowardice in battle. The castle and other lands were confiscated. For the next two centuries Rayleigh was a royal castle and buildings were added. But it was never used for military purposes.
Location: 6 miles NW of Southend-on-Sea off A127.

Reculver *Kent*   *Map: 399 Gc*
The twin-towered Saxon and medieval church, now in ruins, was once a prominent landmark for navigators. It stands within the battered walls of a 3rd-century Roman fort, almost half of which has been washed away by the sea.
Location: 3½ miles E of Herne Bay off A299.

Redcar *Cleveland*   *Map: 391 Gd*
ZETLAND MUSEUM The museum is in a former lifeboat house, built in 1877. It contains the Zetland, the oldest lifeboat in the world – built in 1800 – that saved over 500 lives. There are displays illustrating the history of fishing communities in the north-east of Yorkshire.
Location: King St, off High St.

Redruth *Cornwall*   *Map: 396 Ab*
EAST POOL ENGINE-HOUSE A prominent engine-house beside the road with a beam winding-engine, built in 1887. It has a 30 in. diameter cylinder, and was used to wind men and material up a 1,300 ft shaft in a copper and tin mine.

Across the road, at Taylor's Shaft, there is another engine – a 90 in. diameter cylinder with a 52 ton beam. Built locally in 1892 it was used for pumping water.
Location: 1½ miles W of Redruth off A3047.

Repton *Derbys.*   *Map: 393 Ge*
CHURCH OF ST WYSTAN The remains of a Saxon church, built about 975, include a small, almost square crypt, with its groined vault supported by four crude spiral columns.
Location: 7½ miles SE of Derby (A38, B5008).

Restormel Castle *Cornwall*   *Map: 396 Cb*
Restormel is one of the best surviving examples of a medieval shell-keep castle in Britain. Although it is roofless and centuries of neglect have left their mark on the stonework, the internal walls, the gateway, staircases and the battlemented parapet, give a realistic idea of what the castle was like in the days of the Black Prince (1330–76). The prince, who was also Duke of Cornwall, owned and occasionally stayed at the castle.

At Restormel, the outer ring of stone wall, built on an earthwork at the end of the 12th century, is over 8 ft thick and 25 ft high. Its circumference is broken on the west side by a square gate tower which is older, and which was inserted in an otherwise wooden palisade. Inside is an inner ring of stone, and between these two rings was a continuous range of apartments – mostly two-storeyed.

Exchequer records of 1337 draw attention to

THE BLACK PRINCE'S CASTLE

The 13th-century stone-built shell keep at Restormel, Cornwall, was owned by the Black Prince – Edward III's son. Various buildings were ranged around the inner courtyard. The lower floor contained storehouse,

stables and armouries; the upper floor – reached by steps either side of the gatehouse – were guest rooms, garderobe (lavatory), bedrooms, small chapels, solar, great hall, larder, kitchen and a second garderobe.

the state of the castle, indicating that the stables for 20 horses on either side of the gateway had become ruinous. The same record mentions the water supply brought in from outside by means of a lead conduit to every room. Inside the shell-keep, a well was sunk to provide a reserve – a precaution against interference to the supply in time of a siege.

In 1644 the castle was swiftly refurbished for the Civil War on the orders of Parliament, but it was recaptured after a short siege by Richard Grenville on behalf of the king. It was never used again and escaped dismantling by Parliament after the war.
Location: 1 mile N of Lostwithiel.

Rey Cross *Durham*   *Map: 391 Fd*
At the summit of the Stainmore Pass are the earthworks of a Roman marching camp – an overnight entrenchment built by an army on the march.

The camp at Rey Cross is the best preserved example to survive in Britain.
Location: 9½ miles SW of Barnard Castle (A67 then A66).

Rhuddlan Castle *Clwyd*   *Map: 392 Df*
A great concentric castle that was designed by Master James of St George for Edward I between 1277 and 1283. Three sides are moated and the fourth is protected by the River Clwyd. The castle was planned so that the garrison could, in an emergency, be supplied from the sea.

Hundreds of men diverted the river by digging a deep channel, over 2 miles long.
Location: 2½ miles SW of Rhyl (A525 then A547). The castle is on E bank of river.

Ribchester *Lancs.*   *Map: 391 Eb*
ROMAN FORT The village is on the site of the Roman fort of Bremetannacum. Much of the fort has been washed away but parts of two granaries can be seen in the museum garden. The museum is next to the church, and contains a variety of inscribed stones from the fort, and a replica of a cavalry parade-helmet found on the site during the 18th century (the original is in the British Museum).
Location: 10 miles NE of Preston (B6243 then B6245).

ROMAN HELMET *A bronze and silvered cavalry helmet of the late 1st or early 2nd century AD, found during excavations at Ribchester fort in 1796, and now in the British Museum. A replica is on display in the fort museum. The decorated helmet and mask were worn only on ceremonial occasions.*

301

Riber Castle *Derbys.* *Map: 393 Ge*
CASTLE FAUNA RESERVE AND WILD LIFE PARK A
park with a large collection of British and
European animals and birds, having rare breeds
of cattle, pigs, poultry and goats, and European
lynxes.
There are also farm carts, and life-size models
of prehistoric animals.
Location: 2½ miles SE of Matlock (A615 then
minor road from Tansley).

Richards Castle *Heref. & Worcs.* *Map: 393 Ec*
Richards Castle was one of the few motte and
baileys raised in England before the Norman
Conquest. It was built by friends of Edward the
Confessor.
The wooden tower and palisade were replaced
with stonework in the 12th century.
Location: 4 miles SW of Ludlow (A49, B4361).

Richborough *Kent* *Map: 399 Gc*
In AD 43, about two months after the Romans
had landed at Richborough, the Emperor
Claudius arrived. His visit was brief – about 16
days – but it finalised another stage in the expansion of his empire. For the remainder of the
century, Richborough was the chief port of
Roman Britain. The site now represents three
centuries of Roman rule.
First, it was the beachhead camp of the
invading army – traces of the ditches remain.
Next, it was a stores depot, its timber buildings
now outlined in concrete.
About AD 85 a triumphal arch was built – a
massive rectangular structure, nearly 90 ft high,
with bronze and marble statuary.
In the 3rd century, the existing triple ditches
surrounding the arch were dug, and the monument stripped of its ornament and used as a

SILENT SENTINELS FROM 2000 BC

*The stones of Brodgar henge appear to have been
specifically selected – all of them tall, thin and pointed.
The number of stones in such circles varied, and what
special significance the numbers had, if any, is not
known.*
*Two of the stones have inscriptions on them from
a later period: one with Ogham script, the other with
Runic. Ogham, named after the Celtic god of writing,
is the earliest form of script known in Ireland and was
probably used first about AD 300. Runes, also from
about AD 300, stem from Denmark, or possibly from
the Mediterranean.*

signal tower. Later that century stone defences
were built when the province was under threat
from Saxon pirates.
Location: 1½ miles NW of Sandwich off A257.

Richmond Castle *N. Yorks.* *Map: 391 Fc*
One of the earliest stone fortresses in England,
that was begun in the reign of William the
Conqueror and completed by the 1150s. Dominating the Swale valley, the castle is an impressive
example of military architecture, yet few arrows
or gunshots were fired at it or from it in anger.
William the Lion, King of Scotland, was temporarily imprisoned there in 1174.
Location: S of River Swale off A6136.
THE GEORGIAN THEATRE A playhouse that was
built in 1788 by the actor-manager Samuel
Butler. It is the best-preserved 18th-century
theatre in the country.
Location: Friar's Wynd, off Market Place, town
centre.

Ridgeway *Oxon.* *Map: 398 Bc*
A routeway along which prehistoric man, and
his animals, travelled for 3,000 years or more.
The Ridgeway runs for about 40 miles from the
Thames, near Streatley, to the Vale of Pewsey.
Apart from dozens of Neolithic and Bronze Age
barrows, which mark its route, it passes within
a mile of many major monuments, such as
Avebury and Silbury Hill.
A pleasant walk along the Ridgeway is from
Uffington Hill-fort for a little more than a mile,
to Waylands Smithy to the west.
Location: Uffington Hill-fort is 6 miles W of
Wantage off B4507.

Rievaulx Abbey *N. Yorks.* *Map: 391 Gc*
Magnificent ruins of the Cistercian abbey,
founded in 1131 and suppressed in 1539, can be
seen on the banks of the River Rye.
Location: 15½ miles W of Pickering (A170 then
B1257 from Helmsley).

Ring of Brodgar *Orkney* *Map: 387 Ef*
A double-entranced henge (see p. 372) that was
built about 2000–1800 BC. Remains of 40 stones
survive – two of them with much later inscriptions: one in the Viking, Runic script and the
other in the Celtic, Ogham script.
Location: On Mainland, 11 miles W of Kirkwall
(A965 then B9055).

Ring of Stenness *Orkney* *Map: 387 Ef*
Whether there ever was a complete ring of
stones at Stenness is uncertain; only four survive,
the tallest of them 18 ft high, dating from about
2000–1000 BC.
Location: On Mainland, 10 miles W of Kirkwall
(A965 then B9055).

Ripley Castle *N. Yorks.* *Map: 394 Be*
Little remains of the castle except for the 15th-
century gatehouse. Cromwell was an uninvited
guest at the castle following his victory at
Marston Moor in July 1644. Lady Ingleby, the
owner's wife, allowed him to stay overnight but
insisted that he sit up all night on a sofa in the
library while she kept him covered with two
pistols.
Location: 3½ miles N of Harrogate off A61. The
castle is W of village.

CASTLE AND CATHEDRAL

During the 1080s, the motte-and-bailey castle at Rochester was converted to stone and alterations were made to the cathedral. Work on both buildings was *supervised by the Bishop of Rochester, Gundulf, who was also in charge of building works at the Tower of London.*

Ripon N. Yorks.   Map: 391 Gb
CATHEDRAL Ripon is the only English cathedral to include a 7th-century Saxon crypt. The Saxon church was attached to a Benedictine monastery, built in 672 by St Wilfrid. He built the crypt to display relics of saints brought from Rome, which were viewed from above through a slanting window-shaft piercing the east wall of the crypt.

Near the nave choir stalls is a small medieval staircase leading down to a narrow passage beside the crypt. During the Middle Ages, it is said that a superstition arose that if a woman accused of adultery was able to crawl into the crypt through a hole, 18 in. high, 13 in. wide – known as St Wilfrid's Needle – it would prove her chastity.

This alarming trial by ordeal – commonplace at the time – may have been linked with the right of sanctuary, granted to Ripon in 934 by King Athelstan. The right of sanctuary was extended to a fugitive who was within a mile of the church. The only one of the four boundary crosses to have survived – marking the limits of the sanctuary area – is at Sharow, a mile to the east of the cathedral.

The rest of St Wilfrid's monastery and church was destroyed by Danes during a raid in 950. Soon after the Conquest, the Normans destroyed a second church on the site, and built a bigger one in its place. This church was rebuilt to provide most of the structure that exists today: a mixture of late-Norman and Perpendicular.

Ripon suffered badly during the Civil War when windows and monuments – including St Wilfrid's shrine – were destroyed by Puritans.

Ironically, it was in 1660 – the year of the restoration of the monarchy – that the spire collapsed, smashing part of the roof and damaging the choir. Four years later, both spires of the west tower were removed.

Extensive restorations were made during the 19th century and in 1836 Ripon was granted cathedral status.

In the choir stalls are 34 superb misericords – hinged seats – carved by local craftsmen in 1487–94. In the south aisle, there is part of a large

14th-century brass, made in a Flemish workshop, depicting a lion, and a man kneeling in a grove of trees. The brass is said to have been used by merchants when counting out money during business deals.

The library, above the south transept, has books dating from before 1500. Among them is a 12th-century manuscript copy of the Bible, and an Old Testament tract from Fountains Abbey.
Location: The cathedral dominates the city.

Rochester *Kent*   Map: 399 Ec
CASTLE One of William the Conqueror's early motte-and-bailey castles overlooks the river Medway and the main London to Dover road. It may have been converted into a stone castle before his death in 1087. This work was supervised by Gundulf, Bishop of Rochester. The castle's great tower was built in the 12th century.

The castle was successfully besieged by King John in 1215 (see pp. 304–5).
Location: The Esplanade, E of River Medway.
CATHEDRAL The Norman cathedral is on the site of a Saxon church built for Justus, the first Bishop of Rochester, in 604.

After the Norman Conquest, Bishop Gundulph began to rebuild the cathedral in about 1080. Against the north wall between the transepts is the lower part of Gundulph's Tower – probably built for defence. The impressive west front is restored Norman work, as is the nave. To the east, the choir and presbytery are of the earlier Gothic period. Off the south transept is a beautiful Decorated doorway leading to the Chapter Room.

On the wall of the choir is a painting of a 13th-century Wheel of Fortune. Fortune turns a large wheel – two people struggle up with it – while on top a king is about to fall off. In the crypt are displayed some leather jerkins left behind by Cromwell's soldiers. It was in the crypt that people sheltered from the Zeppelin raids during the First World War.
Location: Boley Hill, Northgate, off A2. E of River Medway.

A MEDIEVAL CASTLE UNDER SIEGE

The history of warfare in the 12th and 13th centuries is largely the story of sieges. Castle design had to keep pace with – and overtake if it could – developments in siege techniques and equipment.

The attackers had a formidable battery of weapons. Several machines were operated by twisted-rope mechanisms to hurl a variety of missiles over the walls. Chief among these "siege engines" were the ballista, the mangonel, and the trebuchet. Missiles ranged from large stones and pieces of iron to putrefying animal carcases, and the deadly "Greek Fire" – an incendiary mixture, the composition of which was kept – and remains – a secret.

Breaching the walls

Attempts to breach the walls or to batter down the gates were made with a ram or a bore. To protect the assault party – who were exposed to fire from the battlements – a penthouse – nicknamed the "cat" or "sow" – was assembled. This was a portable timber tunnel, roofed with hides or iron plates, that was wheeled up to the walls of the castle.

Another portable structure was a belfry – a tower on wheels from the top of which assailants could rake the castle parapets with arrows or stones. A flap could be lowered to allow attackers to storm the parapets.

To repel assaults, defenders could surround the top of a castle tower with a hoarding – a projecting wooden gallery with a slatted floor through which missiles were dropped. Defenders could also ward off scaling ladders with Y-shaped forks of timber, and reduce the effect of battering rams by lowering a pad of sacking down the outer face of the walls.

Mining was sometimes used as a last resort by attackers. The siege of Rochester Castle in 1215 illustrates how effective it could be. During the civil war which followed the confrontation between King John and his barons at Runnymede, some of the barons' supporters seized Rochester Castle. The constable took up defensive

MANGONEL *A siege engine for catapulting stones weighing up to 50 or 60 lb. each. The engine had a wooden arm, pivoted in the middle of a frame, with a rope-torsioned mechanism at one end as the power source.*

TREBUCHET *Invented by the French in the 12th century especially for siege work. When the counterweight at one end of the beam was released, the other end was flung up, hurling missiles weighing up to half a ton.*

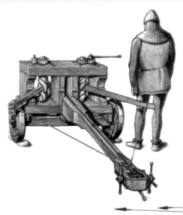

BALLISTA *A siege engine which, like the mangonel, was invented by the ancient Greeks. It operated like a giant crossbow to launch smaller stones, heavy arrows and iron bolts. Tensile power was created by twisting ropes with windlasses.*

BORE *A beam with a sharp metal spike was rammed into the mortar between stonework to loosen areas of the wall for the ram.*

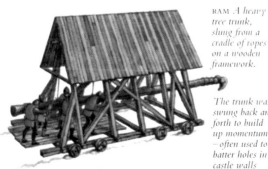

RAM *A heavy tree trunk, slung from a cradle of ropes on a wooden framework.*

The trunk was swung back and forth to build up momentum – often used to batter holes in castle walls and gateways.

MANTLET *A mobile shield for archers to hide behind when attacking a castle.*

positions with several hundred troops, ready to resist the king's inevitable assault. Within days, John had broken into the city, positioned siege engines on and around the old motte, and had begun a preliminary barrage of fire against the bailey wall in the south. Before attacking the great tower, he decided to undermine it, ordering "as many picks as you are able" from the sheriffs at Canterbury.

The mine shaft was dug and a tunnel driven towards the tower's south-west corner. A few weeks later – during which siege engines were pounding the tower walls – the sappers arrived beneath the corner foundations. Beams and props were set up as temporary supports and the tunnel crammed with the corpses of "forty of the fattest pigs", which were then set alight. The bodies burned for some hours, until the supports gave way, and the south-west corner of the great tower collapsed, leaving a huge, gaping hole into the basement.

The king's men rushed in, chased the defenders behind the crosswall, and there fought their way through, floor by floor, until the occupants finally surrendered. The siege of Rochester had lasted nearly two months.

Wide moats and round towers

The taking of Rochester Castle emphasised the essential weakness of the rectangular great tower – its right-angled corners. When the south-west corner was rebuilt the new corner turret was cylindrical. Rounded towers were harder to undermine and missiles were more likely to glance off them.

In response to the powerful trebuchet and the threat of undermining during the 13th century, castles were built with wide moats, high curtain walls and numerous, rounded flanking towers. Eventually, a second curtain wall was added to produce the concentric castle – the high point of military fortification in medieval Britain. (See p. 410.)

BELFRY *A mobile siege tower that was assembled out of range of the castle archers and then wheeled up against the walls. It was built at least as high as the wall under attack so the attackers could shoot arrows and stones at the defenders on the castle parapet. They would try to storm the castle from the top, over a flap that was lowered like a drawbridge. Wet hides were sometimes used to prevent the belfry being set alight by flaming arrows.*

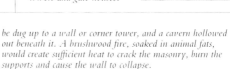

HOARDINGS *Covered platforms supported on beams projecting from the tops of castle walls. The floor was slatted so that defenders could pour boiling liquids or drop missiles on attackers underneath.*
Hoardings were vulnerable to fire and missiles, unlike the stone equivalent, machicolations, which were built on to wall-towers and gate houses.

MINING *Provided a castle was not surrounded by a deep moat or built on rock, mining was often the only way of breaching the defences. But it was a last resort, for the work was dangerous and – more important – slow. A tunnel would* *be dug up to a wall or corner tower, and a cavern hollowed out beneath it. A brushwood fire, soaked in animal fats, would create sufficient heat to crack the masonry, burn the supports and cause the wall to collapse.*

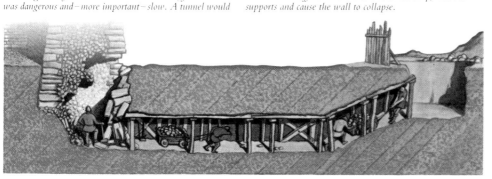

Rockbourne *Hants.*   *Map: 398 Ab*
ROMAN VILLA The remains of the villa – three
wings ranged around a courtyard – are over-
grown but a museum on the site is crammed
with relics from the original building.
Location: 10 miles S of Salisbury off the A354.

Rockingham Castle *Northants.* *Map: 398 Cf*
For nearly 500 years, Rockingham Castle was a
royal fortress – from the time of William the
Conqueror to the reign of Henry VIII. Its
strategic position was relatively unimportant,
but being near Rockingham Forest it provided
the kings with a fine hunting lodge and administrative centre.
  In 1095 Rockingham was the scene of a
meeting of the council of William II (Rufus),
which banished Anselm, Archbishop of Canterbury, who disagreed with the king usurping the
pope's authority and appointing bishops.
Location: 2½ miles NE of Corby off A6003.

Rollright Stones *Oxon.*   *Map: 398 Bd*
Three megalithic – large stone – monuments at
Rollright are linked by folklore. They consist of
a circle of about 70 stones, an upright monolith
a few yards to the east of the circle, and, 300 yds
further on, five megaliths in a group. The
monolith is said to be the king, the five megaliths
his knights, and the stone circle the men-at-
arms – all of whom were turned to stone by a
local witch. It is also said that "the man shall
never live who shall count the stones three times
and find the number the same".
  The real reason for the stones is unknown.
Location: 4 miles N of Chipping Norton off
A34.

Romaldkirk *Durham*   *Map: 391 Fd*
CHURCH OF ST ROMALD The present building, on
the site of a Saxon church, dates from the 12th
century, but has later additions. The north aisle
has a fine effigy of Sir Hugh Fitzhenry – who
died in 1305 from wounds received fighting the
Scots with Edward I. The effigy is dressed in
armour of the chain-mail period.
  The north door is blocked up. This was often
done to churches during the late-medieval
period, to keep out the devil, who was thought
to lurk outside the north door.
Location: 5½ miles NW of Barnard Castle off
B6277.

Romsey Abbey *Hants.*   *Map: 398 Bb*
The church was founded in 907 by Edward the
Elder, son of Alfred the Great. The present
building was begun in 1120, and is thought to
have been a memorial to Henry I's wife, Matilda,
who died in 1118. After the Dissolution of the
Monasteries in 1536-40, the townspeople saved
the church from becoming a ruin by buying it
for £100.
  On the outside west wall of the south transept,
beside a fine Norman door, is a celebrated
carving of Christ crucified, nearly 7 ft high. It is
thought to date from the first half of the 11th
century.
  There is also a rare painted reredos – a carved
screen behind one of the altars – dating from
about 1525.
Location: 10½ miles SW of Winchester (A3090,
A31). The abbey is in the town centre.

Rosedale Abbey *N. Yorks.*   *Map: 394 Cf*
IRON-ORE MINES One mile south-west of Rosedale Abbey, at the top of Rosedale Bank Road,
is a derelict set of calcining kilns built in 1860.
They were used to heat the iron-ore from the
nearby West Mines to drive off water and gases.
This reduced the weight of the ironstone and
saved transportation costs, and royalty payments
(sixpence per ton) to the landowner. A further
two sets of kilns (East Mines) can be seen on the
opposite side of the valley.
Location: 11 miles NW of Pickering (A170 then
minor road from Wrelton).

Roslin *Lothian*   *Map: 389 Ed*
ROSSLYN CHAPEL One of the most remarkable
churches in Scotland, with a riot of exuberant
carving, that dates from the 15th century. The
choir was built before the death of the founder,
Sir William St Clair, in 1484. At the south-east,
near the entrance to the crypt, is the renowned
"Apprentice Pillar". It is said that the master-
mason would not start work on it until he had
been to Rome for inspiration. While he was
away the carving was done by an apprentice.
When the master-mason returned he was so
jealous of the result that he killed the boy.
Although the story may be legendary, it is
known that the chapel was reconsecrated after
the incident was said to have happened.
Location: 7 miles S of Edinburgh (A701 then
B7006).

Rossdhu *Strathclyde*   *Map: 388 Ce*
Rossdhu in Gaelic means "the Black Headland"
and on it, jutting out into the waters of Loch
Lomond, stands the stately Georgian home of
the chiefs of the Clan Colquhoun. The
Colquhouns have held and tended lands there
for 1,000 years.
  The house was probably built by John Baxter
in 1773, to replace a 14th-century castle. Among
its many fine rooms, there is the Boxing
Room – with a fine collection of prints and china
figures of celebrated prize fighters.
Location: 9½ miles N of Dumbarton off A82.

Rotherfield Greys *Oxon.*   *Map: 398 Cc*
CHURCH OF ST NICHOLAS A Norman church in
origin that was enlarged in the 13th century.
  The North Chapel was built in 1605 by Sir
Francis and Lady Knollys's son, William, to
house the glorious monument to his parents,
with reclining and kneeling effigies, cherubs,
heraldry, urns, colouring and gilding. Effigies of
William and his wife can be seen kneeling on the
canopy, their children around the base. The
whole is a superb example of Jacobean monumental art.
Location: 2½ miles W of Henley-on-Thames.

Rotherhithe *Greater London*   *Map: 399 Dc*
MAYFLOWER INN In the early part of the 16th
century, this inn was known as The Ship. For
several years the *Mayflower* was moored alongside the wharf outside, before its historic voyage
to America in 1620 with the Pilgrim Fathers.
The captain, Christopher Jones, lived locally,
and a copy of his passenger list is displayed in the
inn.
  The building was damaged during the Second
World War but it has been carefully restored,

ROUSHAM PARK - A GARDEN OF EDEN

Townsend's Temple – an elegant little Doric temple in Rousham Park – was designed in 1738 by William Townsend, an Oxford architect. He sited the sandstone temple beneath a now towering cedar of Lebanon in a small clearing of conifers, achieving a picturesque composition that was in harmony with the celebrated gardens designed by his mentor, William Kent, between 1720 and 1725.

KENT'S ARCADE *Part of the woodland walk through Rousham Park includes this sheltered resting place, designed by William Kent in 1722.*

VENUS'S VALE *Two of a series of pools – there were once four – in Rousham Park, designed as part of a cascade, using the natural slope of the ground.*

and many of its original features have been retained.

Location: 117 Rotherhithe St, SE16.

Rothesay Castle *Strathclyde*   *Map: 388 Bd*
The castle probably began as a low-level motte surrounded by a wide ditch, erected in the 12th century. Some time during the 13th century the motte was crowned with a stone-wall enclosure, 150 ft in diameter, making it an enormous shell keep – the only one known in Scotland. It was battlemented round the top, but filled in later, when the wall was heightened. The line of this original parapet can still be seen. The merlons – the solid vertical projections – had loopholes for archers to watch through while they reloaded their weapons before darting in front of the embrasures to fire a rapid shot and then step back again.

In the 13th century four stout cylindrical towers were added to the outside of the shell keep, at equal distances around the circumference, and between the west and east towers a simple square-plan gateway was inserted. This was considerably altered and enlarged by James IV in the early 1500s.

In 1230 Rothesay was besieged by Vikings from the Western Islands and Scandinavia under a chief called Uspak. His men broke through the wall under the protection of a penthouse (see pp. 304–5) by hacking at the stonework with axes, for both the stone and the mortar were relatively soft. The castle fell again to the Vikings, this time under their king, Haakon of Norway, in 1263. But a few weeks later Haakon and his forces were decisively defeated by Alexander III at the Battle of Largs.

When the Stuarts became kings of Scotland in

the 14th century Rothesay passed into royal hands. James IV altered the gateway and expanded it into a great gatehouse tower, known as "le dungeoun".

In the 17th century, Rothesay Castle was held for the Royalists in the Civil War, but the Parliamentarians drove them out and took it over as a military fortress for controlling the district. In 1659, soon after Richard Cromwell had resigned the Lord Protectorship so unwillingly taken on by him when his illustrious father, Oliver, had died, the Parliamentarian garrison withdrew, pulling down much of the stonework as they left. In the 1870s it became the property of the 2nd Marquess of Bute who began to restore the castle to its present shape.
Location: Ferry from Wemyss Bay to Rothesay, on island of Bute. The castle is in town centre.

Roughting Linn *Northld.*　　　*Map: 389 Gc*
A small Iron Age hill-fort that is the site of a great rock covered with some of the best prehistoric rock art in Britain, carved at the start of the Bronze Age.
Location: 7 miles NW of Wooler (B6525 then minor road).

Rousham House *Oxon.*　　　*Map: 398 Bd*
The gardens of the house comprise one of the earliest surviving English landscape designs in the natural manner and remain almost as William Kent (*c.* 1685–1748) modelled them in 1738 on the basis of earlier plans. At the same time Kent reconstructed the 17th-century house, adding neo-classical pavilions.

A walk through the wooded grounds reveals at unexpected intervals small classical buildings, statues, glades, pools and views of the surrounding countryside. The aim was to imitate the landscapes of classical antiquity as imagined in the paintings of Claude and Poussin.
Location: 12 miles N of Oxford off A423.

Rudbaxton *Dyfed*　　　*Map: 392 Ab*
CHURCH OF ST MICHAEL A Norman church with a fine 17th-century memorial to the Howard family, consisting of five almost life-size figures.
Location: Great Rudbaxton village, 3½ miles N of Haverfordwest off A40.

Ruddington *Notts.*　　　*Map: 394 Bb*
FRAMEWORK KNITTERS MUSEUM The Reverend William Lee of Calverton, Nottinghamshire, invented the first knitting machine in 1589. A frame operated by levers and treadles looped threads together, as in hand knitting.

Framework knitting flourished in the East Midlands from the early 18th century. In Chapel Street, Ruddington, special frameshops and cottages were built for the workers in 1829. The complex, which contains 11 hand frames, is the only known surviving example of the transition from domestic to factory working.
Location: 5 miles S of Nottingham on A60.

Rudston *Humberside*　　　*Map: 394 De*
STANDING STONE The tallest standing stone in Britain, more than 25 ft high, is in the village churchyard. It was probably hauled to Rudston in the Stone Age as part of a now-buried complex of ritual monuments.
Location: 5½ miles W of Bridlington on B1253.

Rufford Old Hall *Lancs.*　　　*Map: 391 Da*
The medieval timber-framed house, built about 1480 for the Hesketh family, is an outstanding example of an English house of this period. It has a carved hammer-beam roof and screen. The Jacobean brick east wing was built in 1662.

A folk museum depicts agricultural and domestic life of the past.
Location: 5½ miles NE of Ormskirk off A59.

Runnymede *Surrey*　　　*Map: 398 Cc*
A memorial erected by the American Bar Association recalls that this broad meadow by the Thames was where King John sealed the draft of Magna Carta, or the Great Charter, in 1215. The document promised redress for the grievances of the barons who presented it to the king, but it also set out general human rights that were to form the basis of English liberty as we know it today.
Location: 3 miles SE of Windsor on A308.

Rushton *Northants.*　　　*Map: 398 Cf*
TRIANGULAR LODGE Sir Thomas Tresham (1545–1605), a defiant Roman Catholic twice imprisoned for his beliefs, built the lodge in 1593–5 in the grounds of Rushton Hall, the family home. The lodge is full of religious symbols. It has three sides, three floors, a three-sided chimney stack, trefoil windows and three 33 ft long friezes – prayers that each contain 33 letters. All this symbolises the Holy Trinity – and is also an elaborate play on Tresham's own name and the three trefoils of his coat of arms.
Location: 4½ miles NW of Kettering off A6003.

Ruthwell Cross *Dumfs. & Gall.*　　*Map: 390 De*
The 18 ft high Northumbrian cross stands in an apse of Ruthwell village church. It dates from AD 650–75 and is covered with biblical scenes, texts from the Vulgate, or Latin, Bible, and the longest British inscription in Runic characters – an alphabet common in northern Europe from the 3rd century AD. The cross probably celebrates the triumph of the Roman Catholic Church.
Location: 6½ miles W of Annan off B724.

Rydal Mount *Cumbria*　　　*Map: 391 Dc*
William Wordsworth lived in the house with his family from 1813 until his death in 1850. There he was visited by the eminent people of his day and entertained as many as 500 chance visitors a year.

The house provides glorious views of Rydal Water and surrounding lakes and fells. It was originally a 16th-century yeoman's cottage but was extended into a family house in the mid-18th century. The poet himself laid out the 4½ acres of gardens. The house contains Wordsworth's furniture, some first editions of his works and family portraits.
Location: 1½ miles NW of Ambleside off A591.

Rye *E. Sussex*　　　*Map: 399 Fb*
CHURCH OF ST MARY THE VIRGIN A French raid of 1377 damaged the largely Norman structure, and some of the cannon balls are on display. Figures strike each quarter hour on a mid-16th-century turret clock that is probably the oldest still working in the country.
Location: Church Sq.

LAMB HOUSE The American-born novelist Henry James lived in this early-18th-century house from 1898 until 1914.

It was at Lamb House that he dictated some of his most celebrated novels, such as *The Ambassadors* and *The Wings of the Dove*.

He died in Chelsea in 1916. The panelled Henry James Room and parlour contain photographs and relics of the writer.
Location: West St, off High St.

Ryhope *Tyne & Wear*   *Map: 391 Ge*
PUMPING STATION A chimney soaring above the rooftops of Ryhope pinpoints one of the finest industrial relics in the north-east. It is a pumping station built in 1868 to supply water to the Sunderland district. Two steam-powered beam-engines, each with a 33 ft long beam, pumped water from a deep well. The equipment has been restored to working order.
Location: 3½ miles S of Sunderland off A19.

S

Saffron Walden *Essex*   *Map: 399 Ee*
CASTLE The castle at Saffron Walden was dismantled by Henry II in 1157, in his campaign to destroy castles used by barons during the turbulence of the previous reign. Some of the ruins remain.
Location: Castle St.
CHURCH OF ST MARY THE VIRGIN The church, the largest in Essex, was built between 1450 and 1525. The nave, illuminated by a clerestory, is a superb example of Perpendicular building. Simon Clerk and John Wastell, master masons at King's College Chapel, Cambridge, worked at Walden.
Location: Town centre.

St Agnes *Cornwall*   *Map: 396 Bb*
St Agnes was one of the major copper and tin-mining centres of Cornwall in the 19th century. Old engine-houses surround the town. The most romantic ruins are the engine-houses on the cliff top at St Agnes Head.

To the east of the town, just north of the B3285, Wheal Kitty still has its old count house. It was here that teams of miners came to bid for work on different sections. The group putting in the lowest bid got the job.

The Miners and Mechanics Institute, in the centre of St Agnes, has many old photographs of the town in its busy working days.

The mines have long been abandoned and should be explored with care.
Location: 4 miles SW of Perranporth.

St Albans *Herts.*   *Map: 398 Dd*
ABBEY About the year 304 Alban, a pagan Roman soldier stationed at Verulamium, gave shelter to a Christian and was converted by him. For helping the Christian to escape, Alban was beheaded on a nearby hill top, and became the first English martyr.

A church was later built on the site of his martyrdom, and in the 8th century King Offa II of Mercia founded an abbey, rebuilt the church and placed St Alban's bones in a special tomb.

Three hundred years later, after the Norman Conquest, the present building was begun. The Roman city had become a ruin, so the Normans used its bricks for their church. They can still be seen, especially in the tower. Columns from the Saxon church were used in the triforium (upper arcade) of the south transept. On the nave piers are some fine medieval wall-paintings depicting the Virgin Mary, St Christopher and St Thomas of Canterbury.

Behind the high altar is the shrine of St Alban. It was broken up after the Reformation, but more than 2,000 fragments were discovered a century ago, and the shrine was reconstructed.

The abbey also contains the 17th-century Bread Boxes, from which loaves are still distributed on Sundays to poor women of the town.
Location: Entry from Romeland.
KINGSBURY WATERMILL The three-storey watermill dates from the 16th century but was altered in Georgian times. The three pairs of millstones are driven by an early-18th-century waterwheel. It is a musem of milling with good exhibits of mill machinery.
Location: W end of Fishpool St.
ROMAN CITY St Albans grew up around the shrine of St Alban, on the hill where he was martyred for his Christian sympathies (see Abbey). This has left nearly the whole of the Roman town where he lived, Verulamium, in open fields on the western outskirts of St Albans.

The most complete Roman structure is the open-air theatre. The seats are arranged on earth banks surrounding the stage, where pantomime and cock-fighting were probably more commonly shown than classical drama.

Near by is the outline (in concrete) of the earliest shops of Verulamium, burned down by Boudicca in her uprising of AD 61. There is also a long stretch of the city walls, with the foundations of the London Gate. The splendid Verulamium Museum in St Michael's Street helps bring to life the Roman city and its inhabitants.

St Andrews *Fife*   *Map: 389 Fe*
CASTLE The castle began as a fortress built for the Archbishop of Scotland in the 12th century. During the Reformation it was captured by Protestants. A siege was launched by Catholic troops who – incredibly – dug a mine through solid rock up to the tower where defenders were sinking a countermine to meet it. The castle surrendered before the two tunnels were completed, and they can still be seen.
Location: N end of Castle St.
CHURCH OF ST REGULUS The church, probably built before the Norman Conquest, was the first church of the Augustinian priory and was succeeded by the great cathedral near by, of which little now remains.
Location: Pends Rd.

The white gold of Cornwall

ABOUT 200 YEARS AGO, ST AUSTELL GAINED A NEW, PROSPEROUS INDUSTRY. WITH IT CAME A STRANGE LANDSCAPE OF CONICAL WHITE WASTE HEAPS – THE "CORNISH ALPS"

In the middle of the 18th century, a Plymouth chemist, William Cookworthy, discovered that local clay could be used to make porcelain. His discovery began a new era for the Cornish town of St Austell, where tin-mining was on the decline, for near by were some of the world's biggest and most easily developed high-quality deposits of china clay, or kaolin, formed from decomposed granite.

Wheal Martyn, a clay works near St Austell, is now a museum showing how the clay was recovered, processed and transported. It no longer produces clay, but at the end of the 19th century about 20 people worked there, producing 150 tons a week. About 12 men worked in the pit, where after removal of the topsoil, the clay was washed down from the open sides. Originally this was done by diverting streams, and the clay had to be broken up with dubbers, tools similar to pick axes, but after 1880 pressure hoses were introduced.

The clay-laden water, or slurry, was pumped from the pit for refining, and coarse material left behind was loaded into trucks and built up into a waste heap. There are about 8 tons of waste for each ton of clay.

THE CORNISH CHINA CLAY MUSEUM

One of the best preserved 19th-century clay works, Wheal Martyn, was established in 1820 by a St Austell draper, Elias Martyn, and worked until 1968. Now it shows how clay was produced in the 1880s.

SETTLING PIT *After refining, the clay was left in a settling pit for two to three days, surface water being removed from time to time. Then it passed to a settling tank.*

INTO THE KILN *Clay stood in the settling tank for two to three months until it reached a consistency similar to that of Cornish clotted cream. It was then taken by wagon into the kiln for drying.*

WATER-WHEEL *The main slurry pumps at Wheal Martyn were operated by a system of rods stretching half a mile from a 35 ft diameter water-wheel.*

St Ann's Head Lighthouse *Dyfed Map: 392 Ab*
Two lighthouses were built on St Ann's Head in 1714, to guide ships safely into Milford Haven harbour. The lights were placed one behind the other. If a ship's captain aligned the two he knew he would avoid the dangerous Crow Rock.

In the 1840s the front light was in danger from cliff erosion and a new tower was built 30 ft from the cliff edge. It is still in use, but the rear light was closed in 1910 and is now used as a coastguard station.
Location: 14 miles SW of Haverfordwest.

St Asaph Cathedral *Clwyd*   *Map: 392 Df*
St Asaph is the smallest ancient cathedral in the British Isles. A religious community is thought to have been founded about 560 by Kentigern, a Scottish bishop. During the invasion by Edward I in the late 13th century the Norman church was ruined. The cathedral was rebuilt during the 14th century, only to be set on fire by Owain Glyndwr, the Welsh rebel, in 1402. Restoration work was completed by 1482.

During the Civil War, local Puritans housed horses and oxen in the cathedral, and the innkeeper – who had taken over the Bishop's Palace – used the font as a horse-trough.
Location: 13 miles E of Colwyn Bay off A55.

St Austell *Cornwall*   *Map: 396 Bb*
WHEAL MARTYN MUSEUM The museum tells the story of the china clay industry, starting at one of the original pits dug in the 1820s. (See above.)
Location: 2 miles N of St Austell on B3374.

About eight people worked in the processing plant. The slurry passed through a series of drags and channels to remove sand and mica, and after two days in settling pits was left two to three months in a settling tank before drying. Until about 1850 clay was air-dried, being cut into blocks about 1 ft square while still soft. When hard enough blocks were stacked in open-sided sheds to dry in the wind for about six months.

Drying by heat in a coal-fired kiln was introduced about 1850 and by 1900 had superseded air-drying. It took one to two days. The soft clay was marked into blocks with a rake-like tool, and after further heating the blocks shrank and cracked across the rake marks. Dried blocks each weighing about 15 lb. were stacked in a store known as a linhay.

CLEANING CLAY BLOCKS *Air-dried blocks still had some mica adhering to the outside, and they also became moss-covered during drying. Women workers – bal-maidens – scraped them clean.*

PACKING THE CLAY *High quality clay was usually packed in casks – bags were introduced in the early 1900s. But some of the clay was sent in rough blocks straight from the kiln.*

TRANSPORTING THE CLAY

William Cookworthy used china clay for making porcelain near Plymouth. After his patent lapsed in 1782, clay was sold mainly to the Staffordshire Potteries. It was shipped from Par, Fowey, Charlestown and Pentewan round the west coast to Runcorn, then by the Trent and Mersey Canal.

STEAM-ENGINES *Now on show at Wheal Martyn, the 1899 engine (left) belonged to the Lee Moor tramway on Dartmoor, near Plymouth, where there were also clay workings. The 1937 engine (right) was used for loading on the dockside at the port of Par.*

HORSE WAGON *Clay was taken to the ports for shipment in horse-drawn wagons each carrying a load of about 3 tons. They were pulled by teams of three horses. Lorries began to be used in 1916.*

St Bees Priory *Cumbria*   *Map: 390 Cd*
The priory was founded about 1120 as a small community of Benedictine monks. Only the church survives, still with its magnificent Norman west door dating from 1160.

The chancel was rebuilt in the Early English style about 1190, and some of this work still survives. From 1817 it was part of a north-country theological college, founded by the Bishop of Chester, which closed in 1894. Today it is known as Old College Hall and is part of St Bees School.

After the Dissolution of the Monasteries in the 16th century, the nave, walled off from the old chancel, became the village's parish church. It was much restored in 1855–68.
Location: 4 miles S of Whitehaven on B5345.

St Catherine's Castle *Cornwall*   *Map: 396 Cb*
This small fort was built in the 1520s to guard Fowey harbour. It was attacked by Dutch raiders early in the 17th century and was manned during the Napoleonic wars.
Location: ½ mile S of Fowey on the coast.

St Catherine's Lighthouse *IOW Map: 398 Ba*
The lighthouse stands at the southernmost point of the Isle of Wight. The first light was established in 1323 and the present octagonal tower was built in 1840.

Originally, the tower was 127 ft high, but the top was sometimes lost in the mist so it was reduced by 43 ft in 1875. A small adjoining tower holds the foghorn.
Location: 4½ miles W of Ventnor off A3055.

The folk life of Wales

RE-ERECTED FARMHOUSES, COTTAGES AND WORKSHOPS IN THE GROUNDS OF A
16TH-CENTURY CASTLE ILLUSTRATE LIFE AND WORK IN OLD WALES

At 16th-century St Fagans Castle in South Glamorgan, old buildings from all over Wales, exhibition galleries and the castle itself constitute a museum whose aim is to illustrate the everyday life, crafts and culture of Wales as they have developed over the last several centuries.

The outstanding feature of the museum is the old buildings, some dating back to medieval times. After being dismantled on their original site, they were painstakingly rebuilt in the grounds of the castle and furnished in the style of the period when they were built. They include Welsh farmhouses, cottages, mills, workshops, a tollgate house, a chapel and a cock-fighting pit.

The visitor can look around all the buildings, and a keeper will answer questions about the history, ownership and furnishings of the houses – which on cold days are heated by wood and peat fires lit in open hearths. The gardens are laid out in period style and planted with kitchen herbs.

The workshops include an 18th-century tannery, which converted hides into leather and tanned it with oak bark, and a smithy of the same period. The smithy is unusual in having two hearths for heating iron.

A museum-block houses several specialist galleries. An early potato-peeling machine, a huge box-mangle, an Eisteddfod ceremonial sword, primitive tooth extractors and a Welsh hornpipe are just a few of the intriguing exhibits on display in the Gallery of Material Culture. The Gallery of Agriculture illustrates the development of soil drainage.

The castle is an Elizabethan mansion that incorporates the remains of a medieval house. It contains a wide range of period furniture and a

WHERE ORDINARY WELSH PEOPLE LIVED AND WORKED

The open-air section of the museum consists of farms, cottages, barns, workshops and other buildings from all over Wales that present a varied picture of the national folk life. The buildings were re-erected at St Fagans in exact reproduction of the originals. The dwellings have been fitted out with period furnishings, and the workshops have been equipped with traditional craftsmen's tools.

LLAINFADYN *Boulders were used to construct this moorland cottage of 1762.*

ABERNODWYDD *Straw provided the roof, and beaten earth the floor, for many 16th-century timber-framed farmhouses.*

KENNIXTON *Mortar floors in this 17th-century farmhouse are typical of Glamorgan.*

GIPSY CARAVAN *The colourful gipsy families who were once common in South Wales lived in gaily painted caravans.*

OPEN HEARTH *The oldest house at the museum, 15th-century Hendre'r-ywydd Uchaf farmhouse, has an open hearth in the hall. Smoke escaped through doors and windows.*

WOOLLEN FACTORY *The loom room at Esgair Moel Woollen Factory, built about 1760, still produces textiles. Water powers the mill. A millwheel turns a cogwheel and then a belt drum.*

kitchen with spits, one of which was turned by a dog. In a coach house in the castle yard are several aristocrats' semi-state coaches and the coach of the Plymouth family, who owned the castle from 1730 to 1947.

Near by are two craft workshops. In one, a wood turner produces traditional bowls, spoons and ladles for sale; and in the other, one of the last practising coopers in Wales makes casks for brewers and dairy farmers.

LOVE SPOONS *A large collection of wooden spoons carved by young men for their sweethearts is displayed in the folklore section of the Gallery of Material Culture. The spoons, and their racks, were not functional but tokens of love and proof of artistic skill, often carved with only a penknife. The earliest spoon in the collection dates back to 1667.*

FROM ORGANS TO FARM WAGONS

One gallery at the museum illustrates furnishings, cooking, medicine, music and other aspects of Welsh domestic, social and cultural life; and other galleries are devoted to costume and agriculture.

KITCHEN FURNITURE *A collection of dressers from different areas of Wales is among the displays in the Gallery of Material Culture.*

BARREL ORGAN *In the 19th century, barrel organs provided church as well as street music. This one from Pennard Church, Gower, incorporates 17th-century woodwork.*

CRAFTSMEN'S WAGONS *The farm wagons each represent a local tradition of craftsmanship.*

St David's Cathedral *Dyfed*   Map: 392 Ab
The site is one of the most venerable in Wales. According to tradition, the cathedral is built where St David, the patron saint of Wales, was born, and where he established a religious community in the 6th century.

Behind the cathedral's High Altar, in the Holy Trinity Chapel, is a casket of iron and oak, containing bones believed to be those of St David and his confessor, St Justinian.

The present building was started about 1180 and work continued for 300 years. The nave is in the late Norman style, with rounded arches, and above is a superb 15th-century wooden roof. In the choir, beyond a massive stone screen, are 15th-century oak choir stalls, carved in tracery patterns. One of the stalls is reserved for the reigning sovereign.
Location: 15 miles SW of Fishguard on A487.

St Day *Cornwall*   Map: 396 Bb
This little village was once known as "the mining capital of Cornwall". The village itself consists of miners' houses in granite terraces, mostly built in the 19th century. On United Downs to the east, engine-houses mark the entrances to the old mines. A particularly large group near Twelve-heads belonged to Consolidated Mines. They were abandoned in 1857, and now stand derelict. Care should be taken when exploring the area; do not enter open mines.
Location: 3 miles E of Redruth on minor roads.

St Endellion *Cornwall*   Map: 396 Bb
CHURCH OF ST ENDELIENTA A college of priests was attached to this small parish church in the Middle Ages. Three 15th-century houses remain, and one is now the rectory.

Endelienta was a local virgin saint of the 6th century who lived solely on cow's milk.
Location: 6 miles N of Wadebridge on B3314.

St Fagans *S. Glam.*   Map: 393 Da
CASTLE The stone enclosure was built in the 13th century and a mansion added in the 16th century. One of the last battles of the Civil War took place at St Fagans in 1647. The Parliamentary troops won, and now only some of the old walling survives.
Location: 5 miles W of Cardiff (end of St Fagans Rd, off Western Av.).
WELSH FOLK MUSEUM This museum of rural life contains farmhouses, some dating back to the Middle Ages, which have been furnished as they would have been when first built. (See left.)
Location: In the grounds of St Fagans Castle.

St Germans *Cornwall*   Map: 396 Cb
CHURCH OF ST GERMANUS In Saxon times there was a cathedral at St Germans, but the present church is basically Norman with two west towers. The east window contains 19th-century stained glass by Sir Edward Burne-Jones.
Location: 9 miles SE of Liskeard (A38, then B3249).

St Mary's Island *Tyne & Wear*   Map: 391 Ge
LIGHTHOUSE The island is linked to the mainland by a causeway which can be crossed at low tide. The lighthouse was built in 1898 on the burial ground of Tynemouth Priory.
Location: 2½ miles N of Whitley Bay off A193.

St Mawes Castle *Cornwall*   *Map: 396 Ba*
St Mawes is one of the coastal fortresses built by
Henry VIII to combat any invasion from the
Continent after his break with the Church of
Rome (see p. 125). Built in trefoil plan round a
cylindrical tower, it stands on the east coast of
Falmouth Bay opposite Pendennis Castle.
Location: 17 miles SW of St Austell (A390,
B3287 and A3078).

St Michael's Mount *Cornwall*   *Map: 396 Aa*
About the year 710 a vision of St Michael is said
to have appeared on the summit of this off-shore
outcrop, and for the following 800 years it was
occupied by monks, eventually becoming a fully
fledged monastery. After the Dissolution of the
Monasteries it belonged to the Crown, and in
the 1660s was acquired by the old Cornish family
of St Aubyn who added more buildings in the
18th and 19th centuries. It is approached by a
causeway, which is flooded at high tide.
Location: $\frac{1}{4}$ mile from the shore at Marazion.

St Neot *Cornwall*   *Map: 396 Cb*
CHURCH OF ST NEOT This 15th-century church has
a remarkable collection of stained glass from the
15th and 16th centuries in a dozen windows.
Some contain figures of saints and heraldry of
local families. One illustrates the story of Noah,
the Creation, the Temptation, the Expulsion of
Adam and Eve, and Cain murdering Abel.
In the churchyard is a portion of the finest
Celtic cross in the county.
Location: $4\frac{1}{2}$ miles NW of Liskeard (A38 and
minor road).

St Neot's *Cambs.*   *Map: 398 De*
CHURCH OF ST MARY THE VIRGIN There has been a
church on the site since the 12th century, though it
was largely rebuilt in the 15th century. The tower,
which was completed in 1535, dominates the
church and is 128 ft high. Because of its size the
church was sometimes called "The Cathedral of
Huntingdonshire".
Location: 17 miles W of Cambridge on A45.

WORKING-CLASS LIFE IN THE NORTH

*One of the reconstructed buildings at Lark Hill Place,
Salford's open-air museum, is a two-roomed cottage
typical of the dwellings built in the industrial North
during the mid-19th century. The inhabitants of such
cottages had no drainage or refuse disposal (rubbish
was thrown into the street to rot), obtained their water
from a communal pump, and shared a bucket-type
privy with at least 12 other households. The upstairs
room of the cottage served as a bedroom for the entire
family. The downstairs room (above) was used for
cooking, eating and washing. The pottery dogs on the
mantelpiece are typical ornaments of the time. An
onion hanging from the ceiling was believed to ward
off disease.*

HEATING WATER
*The trivet was
wedged on to the
front of the range
to absorb the heat
of the fire. Kettles
of water were
boiled on it.*

CATCHING FLIES
*The fly was
attracted to a sweet
substance through
a hole in the bottom
of the jar and was
then trapped inside.*

THE CATHEDRAL OF "NEW SARUM"

The needle-like spire of Salisbury Cathedral soars 404 ft above the river meadowland where the cathedral was built in the 13th century. It was created at Salisbury after the bishop and clergy abandoned the city of Old Sarum, about a mile to the north. The old building, whose foundations can still be seen, stood on a wind-blown hill and was short of drinking water. It stood close to a castle, the remains of which have been uncovered, and constant friction occurred between soldiers and clergy. When a storm damaged the cathedral in 1218, Bishop Richard de Poore moved his see to the present site. The trading town of "New Sarum" (later Salisbury) grew up around his superb new cathedral, built in the Early English Style.

500 MILLION TICKS The oldest clock in England struck the hours at Salisbury Cathedral for 498 years until the 19th century. In that time it ticked more than 500 million times. The clock was made about 1386 of hand-wrought iron. It had no dial and struck the hours only. It was replaced in 1884, but was restored to working order in 1956 and now stands in the nave.

A HOME FOR THE WORKING MAN

The two-roomed cottage at Lark Hill Place, Salford, is typical of the cramped, unhealthy conditions in which most factory workers lived during the Industrial Revolution. But for some there was a way of eventual escape from such dwellings. The better-paid workers, and the more thrifty and determined of the lower paid, could save regularly with one of the early building societies (which had first emerged in the 1770s) in the knowledge that one day they would own a home of their own.

Whether that day came sooner or later depended on chance. For the first building societies were simply clubs that pooled the savings of their members in order first to buy a plot of land and then to build houses for the members one by one – and allotment was determined by ballot. In 1800 houses cost less than £100 each and members saved about ten shillings a month.

The early societies had a restricted membership and wound up their affairs after every member had been housed.

Greater home-buying opportunities came with the introduction in the 1840s of permanent building societies with their modern-style mortgages. These offered membership to all, and their greater funds enabled them to offer the borrower a large enough advance for the immediate purchase of a house.

Salford *Greater Manchester*   *Map: 391 Ea*
LARK HILL PLACE A reconstructed street of old buildings, ranging in style from the 17th to the 19th century and each furnished according to the period, vividly recreates life in Salford during the past. Among the buildings is a chemist and druggist's shop of the 1860s, whose contents include a tongue-scraper, pocket hot-water bottle, face-ache pills and apparatus for making powders and lozenges. It stands opposite a late-Victorian pub.
Location: Peel Park

Salisbury *Wilts.*   *Map: 398 Ab*
CATHEDRAL Salisbury Cathedral is the finest example of Early English architecture in the country. It is the only medieval cathedral to have remained as it was planned, without the usual piecemeal additions being made over successive centuries.

Its spire – immortalised on canvas by John Constable in the 1820s – rises 404 ft, and is the highest in England. And the colonnaded cloisters are the largest of any cathedral, enclosing a 140 ft square.

The cathedral was founded in 1220 and – but for the spire – was finished by 1258. In 1331 the spire was begun and took 21 years to build. Its grace and elegance belie its enormous weight of nearly 6,000 tons. The stonework is so thin that the original workmen's scaffolding was left inside, as additional support, and remains there today. There is also a wooden winch that was used to hoist materials aloft during progress. According to folklore a fragment of the Virgin Mary's robe was placed inside a lead casket in the tip of the spire.

The weight of the spire, as so often happened with cathedrals, caused problems in later years as the foundations settled, and the piers at the crossing between the nave and the transepts had to be strengthened in the 15th century. In 1668 they were again reinforced, this time by Sir Christopher Wren who used bands of iron made by anchor-makers in Portsmouth Dockyard.

Inside the cathedral is a monument to Lord Stouton, who murdered two people in a family quarrel and was hanged with a silken cord in the market-place in 1556. Edward Seymour's monument includes a statue of his wife Catherine, who was Lady Jane Grey's sister. Their marriage angered Elizabeth I and Edward was imprisoned for nine years and fined £15,000.

In the cathedral library there is one of the four surviving copies of the Magna Carta – a beautifully inscribed parchment – sealed at Runnymede in 1215 by King John.

The cathedral also contains a mechanical treasure – the oldest clock in the country. Dating from 1386 and carefully restored, it is still in perfect working order.

MOMPESSON HOUSE Buildings of all periods form The Close at Salisbury, a worthy setting for one of the great monuments of Christendom. Mompesson House, built in 1701, has a stone front and hipped roof, with good plasterwork inside of about 1740.

Location: North side of The Close.

Sall *Norfolk* *Map: 395 Fa*
CHURCH OF ST PETER AND ST PAUL Almost cathedral-like in its scale, Sall church was built in the Perpendicular style during the beginning of the 15th century when the wool trade had brought prosperity to East Anglia.

There is a memorial brass to Geoffrey Boleyn, a local farmer, whose grand-daughter Ann married Henry VIII and gave birth to Queen Elizabeth I.

The church font has a magnificent counter-weighted cover, with splendid carving. Font covers were introduced early in the 13th century to prevent holy water being stolen for black magic rites.

Location: 12 miles NW of Norwich (A140, B1149, B1145 and minor road).

Saltaire *W. Yorks.* *Map: 394 Ad*
This small town, now in the west of Shipley, was the creation of a manufacturer of alpaca cloth, Sir Titus Salt. As mayor of Bradford in 1849 he became disgusted by the squalor of the manufacturing districts, and built his own model factory and community.

The mill itself is a large Italianate building straddling the Leeds and Liverpool Canal. It is still in use. Beyond the canal is the River Aire, with a riverside park set out by Salt.

Back up the hill, past the attractive church, are the rows of houses built by Salt for his workers. They are much larger than the average terraced houses of Bradford and have the same ornate styling as the mill.

Along the main street are shops, school, hospital, library and almshouses for the old – everything except a pub, for Salt was a strict teetotaller and banned the sale of alcohol.
Location: 3 miles NW of Bradford on A6037.

Saltash *Cornwall* *Map: 396 Cb*
ROYAL ALBERT RAILWAY BRIDGE The last major work of the engineer Isambard Kingdom Brunel. The bridge crosses the River Tamar, and the Admiralty insisted that it be high, with wide arches to keep the river free for navigation.

There are two major spans, each 465 ft long. Brunel suspended the main rail deck by chains from huge curved iron tubes. Work ended in 1859, by which time Brunel was seriously ill. He was taken across the bridge on an invalid couch on a flat truck. A few weeks later he died.
Location: Beside A38 road bridge.

CLEANLINESS THROUGH THE AGES

The earliest known bath was found in the Minoan palace of Knossos, built in 1700 BC. It is elegant, and its water supply and drainage system are far more advanced than any that existed in England in the 18th century. Rome in the 4th century AD had 11 public baths, each built to take 1,600 bathers at a time. Roman London also had public baths which fell into disuse after the Romans left.

Medieval people were cleaner than is popularly supposed. Monks regularly washed their hands before meals, while elsewhere finger bowls were used at table; and sometimes families and guests took communal baths in large round wooden tubs of warm water.

The 16th and 17th centuries saw a decline in personal cleanliness – perhaps as the result of the Dissolution of the Monasteries in 1536–40, for the monks had set the standard for hygiene. In the early 18th century bathing was scarcely more common. Poor people washed at a street pump. However, others took part in public bathing at medicinal spas and, from the mid-18th century, at seaside resorts.

In France, metal baths were introduced in the 18th century, but they were rare in England, where even in the early 1800s it was still thought eccentric to take a bath. But in Victorian times bathing gradually came to be recognised as hygienic, and a wide variety of baths was produced. When a regular supply of hot water was made possible by the kitchen boiler and, after 1868, by the gas geyser, people began to take baths as much for pleasure as for cleanliness.

From 1916 mass production of the cheap cast-iron porcelain-enamelled bath made it a standard fixture in most homes.

MEDIEVAL LAVABO *In the Middle Ages, before the days of piped running water for washing, water was poured from a jug into a fixed stone basin, known as a lavabo, lavatoria or laver. The 12th–14th-century undercroft, or vaulted basement, of Wells Cathedral, Somerset, contains a lavabo (left) with a carving of a dog chewing a bone.*

Saltram *Devon*   *Map: 396 Db*

In 1789 Saltram was lent to the Royal Family during an official visit to the West Country. Fanny Burney, who accompanied the queen, wrote: "The house is one of the most magnificent in the kingdom; its view is noble."

Today the magnificent kitchen is on show with all its equipment, including the cockroach-catchers – glass traps baited with stale beer.

Sir Joshua Reynolds was a friend of the owner, and many of his works hang in the house. Location: 3½ miles E of Plymouth off A38.

TAKING A BATH – BEFORE PLUMBING

Before plumbing arrived in the 19th century, people bathed in front of the fire. At Saltram the equipment consists of an enamelled hip-bath and foot-bowl, together with cans for carrying water from the kitchen 50 yds away. A screen protected the bather against draughts.

SLIPPER BATH *All but the bather's head and shoulders were concealed from view in the slipper bath – also known, from its shape, as the boot bath. The example at Wallington Hall, Northumberland (above), dates from the mid-18th century.*

SITZ BATH *The bather could only sit in a Sitz bath. Water came up to the waist, and some advertisers suggested that there was no need to undress the top half of the body. This type of bath was popular in the mid-19th century.*

MAHOGANY AND MARBLE *When the 3rd Marquess of Bute and architect William Burges renovated medieval Cardiff Castle in the 1860s and 1870s, they designed a bathroom of mahogany inset with polished marble.*

VICTORIAN EXTRAVAGANZA *Lady Bute's bedroom of 1881 at Castell Coch, S. Glamorgan, had a washstand with castellated water tanks.*

"EUREKA" BATH *At Kinloch Castle on the Isle of Rum is a patent bath of the 1890s that offered an extraordinarily wide range of bathing methods. The six taps provided a Douche, a stream of water that poured down on to the head; a Wave, a horizontal gush of water at shoulder level, from the rear of the canopy; a Shower, from overhead; a Spray, jets of water from more than 100 tiny holes in the canopy; a Plunge, a normal bathful of water, from an opening in the tub; and a Sitz, a fountain-like spray from the base of the tub. The cost of the bath was £16.*

SALTWOOD

Saltwood Castle *Kent*   Map: 399 Fb
Some kind of fort stood at Saltwood at the time of the Norman Conquest. The Normans built a great tower, and in the civil war of the 1130s and 1140s between King Stephen and his cousin Matilda it was one of the strongest castles in southern England.

Henry II, who succeeded Stephen, gave it to one of his knights, Sir Ranulf de Broc, who was believed to have given shelter there to the four knights who murdered Thomas Becket at Canterbury in 1170.

In the 14th century, the great tower was made into a gatehouse with two huge towers.
Location: 4 miles W of Folkestone off A20.

Samlesbury Hall *Lancs.*   Map: 391 Ea
The house, begun in 1325, is half-timbered, but has medieval brickwork on the south-west side to protect it from the weather. An archery field, still in use, is said to date from the period of Agincourt (1415).
Location: 4 miles E of Preston on A677.

Sandringham House *Norfolk*   Map: 395 Ea
In 1862 Queen Victoria bought the house as a shooting lodge for the Prince of Wales, later to become Edward VII. By 1870 it had been replaced by a Jacobean-style building. When the prince married Princess Alexandra of Denmark the local gentry presented them with the elaborate cast-iron gates, which had been made by Norwich craftsmen.

It became his favourite residence; and his son George V declared it "the place I love better than anywhere else in the world". George VI established a royal tradition of spending Christmas there. Now it is usually spent at Windsor, with the family visiting Sandringham for the New Year.

Both George V and George VI died there.
Location: 7 miles NE of King's Lynn off A149.

Sapperton Tunnel *Glos.*   Map: 393 Fb
The tunnel on the Thames and Severn Canal is 2 miles, 297 yds long, the second longest canal tunnel in Britain. It was completed in 1789 with an entrance in the Classical style – the Coates Portal. Like most early canal tunnels it had no tow-path. Boats had to be "legged" through by men lying on their backs and pushing against the tunnel wall with their feet. At Sapperton professional leggers offered their services for five shillings a boat. The canal closed in 1927.
Location: 4 miles W of Cirencester (A419 and minor road to Coates). The tunnel entrance is by the Tunnel House Inn, W of village.

Saxted Green *Suffolk*   Map: 399 Ge
THE POST MILL The windmill, which dates back to the 18th century, is a large post mill on a brick round-house. The ladder up to the moving body carries a fantail which keeps the mill turned to the wind. The present gearing and windshaft were inserted in 1854 and show the high point which had been reached in mill construction.
Location: 14 miles E of Stowmarket on A1120.

Scalloway Castle *Shetland*   Map: 387 Gd
According to legend the four-storey tower house was built by Patrick Stewart, "wicked" Earl of Orkney, about 1600, using forced labour, and mortar mixed with the blood of the workmen.
Location: 6 miles W of Lerwick on A970.

Scarborough *N. Yorks.*   Map: 394 Df
CASTLE Before the Norman Conquest, a Viking chief called Skarthi (the Harelip) set up a stronghold where the castle now stands, 300 ft above the North Sea.

In the 1170s, Henry II built a great tower which was later surrounded by stone walling with towers, barbican and gatehouse.

In 1312 Thomas, Earl of Lancaster, uncle of Edward II, and a group of allies, declared war on the king to force him to dismiss his homosexual favourite, Gaveston. Gaveston was charged by the king to defend Scarborough, and he did so with great courage, refusing to surrender. When food ran out, Gaveston had to yield, and was promised safe conduct. When he emerged he was seized and beheaded.
Location: Castle Rd.
CHURCH OF ST MARY Founded in the 12th century, the church was used in 1645 by Cromwell's troops as a gun site for shooting at Royalists in the castle. As a result, the choir was shot away.

Anne Brontë died in the town in 1849 and her grave is in the churchyard.
Location: Castle Rd.
ROMAN SIGNAL STATION In an unavailing attempt to repel invaders, the Romans erected a chain of signal stations along the Yorkshire coast from Redcar to Flamborough Head about AD 370. This was one of them. None lasted more than 30 years and some met a violent end. The days of Roman rule were numbered.
Location: On the cliff-edge, E of the castle.

Scone Palace *Tayside*   Map: 389 Ef
The palace (pronounced Skoon) stands on possibly the most historic site in Scotland.

Scone was the capital of the ancient Pictish kingdom until AD 843 when Kenneth Mac-Alpine, King of Scots, subdued the Picts and united the rival nations. To Scone, MacAlpine brought the Stone of Destiny, possibly from Iona, and Scottish kings were crowned on it for the following 400 years. According to legend, Jacob had used the stone as a pillow when he dreamed that God prophesied his descendants "shall be like the dust of the earth". The stone was eventually removed by Edward I of England in 1296 in his vain efforts to curb the Scots, and placed under the Coronation Chair in Westminster Abbey.

Scottish kings continued to be crowned at Scone, including Robert Bruce in 1306. The last coronation was that of Charles II in 1651, after his defeat in the Battle of Worcester.

A monastery was established at Scone by Alexander I in 1120 and the first dwelling on the site of the present palace was the Bishop's Palace. Abbey and palace were sacked and burned by Protestant reformers in 1559.

The lands later passed to Sir David Murray, who accompanied James VI to London in 1603 when he became also James I of England. The Murray family became earls of Mansfield, and still live at the palace.

In 1802–8 the architect William Atkinson enlarged the palace, restyling it in Gothic, probably to recall the royal abbey. Remains of the older buildings are encased in the present palace.

318

In front of the palace is an artificial mound known as the Moot (or Boot) Hill. According to tradition it was created centuries ago with earth brought from all parts of Scotland. When the early kings were crowned they should have toured the kingdom to receive the homage of their chiefs, but travelling was dangerous and it was decreed that the chiefs should come to Scone. By filling their boots with their own earth they were able to pay homage "standing on their own land", and the boots were then ceremoniously emptied of their soil on to the Moot Hill.

The palace now contains French furniture, china and ivories, 16th-century needlework, and French and English clocks.
Location: 2 miles N of Perth off A93.

Scotlandwell *Tayside*　　　　*Map: 389 Ee*
A hospice, or home for the sick, was established by the Bishop of St Andrews in the early 13th century around the "health-giving waters" of the village spring. The patients included Robert Bruce, King of Scotland, who suffered from leprosy, and Charles II took the waters while staying at Dunfermline Palace. The waters now bubble up in a 19th-century cistern.
Location: 6 miles W of Glenrothes on A911.

Scotney Castle Garden *Kent*　　*Map: 399 Eb*
The ruins of the 14th-century castle, together with the "new" 19th-century castle on the hill above, and the landscape that includes them both comprise one of the most successful examples of early-19th-century Picturesque design.
Location: 10 miles SE of Tonbridge on A21.

Seaham *Durham*　　　　*Map: 391 Gd*
CHURCH OF ST MARY This little church, tucked away behind the coastal cliffs, has an 11th-century nave containing re-used Roman stones.

An entry in the register shows that on January 2, 1815, Anne Isabella Milbanke, daughter of Sir Ralph Milbanke, of Seaham Hall, was married (with her parents' consent) to Lord Byron.
Location: 7 miles S of Sunderland (A1018 then B1287).
HARBOUR The harbour was built in the early 19th century by the Londonderry family to handle coal from their own collieries. The coal was brought to the harbour on four-wheeled railway wagons drawn by horses and unloaded into ships down tall coal-chutes.

The harbour is still in use and coal trucks are carried above the harbour on modern staithes, to be unloaded into the holds of waiting ships.

North Dock is open at all times. Permission to visit South (Commercial) Dock can be obtained during working hours from the Dock Office.

Seahouses *Northld.*　　　　*Map: 389 Gc*
LIME KILNS Large lime kilns were built at the harbour in the late 18th century to heat limestone for making cement or fertiliser. The kilns are now used as stores by fishermen.
Location: 3 miles SE of Bamburgh on B1340.

Seaton Delaval *Northld.*　　*Map: 391 Ge*
CHURCH OF OUR LADY The Norman church was built by the Delavals whose descendants in the 18th century built the great house.

A SCOTTISH KING ENTHRONED

Alexander III was only eight years old when he was made King of Scotland at Scone in 1249. The seal of Scone Abbey, at Scone Palace, is thought to picture the event. The king was invested by the Bishop of St Andrews and the Abbot of Scone, and enthroned by the earls of Fife and Strathearn, whose shields are shown at the king's feet on each side of his own.

The stone effigies of a cross-legged knight and a lady whose feet rest on a dog, are probably of members of the family.
Location: 4 miles N of Tynemouth on A192.
SEATON DELAVAL HALL This vast classical house, near the North Sea coast, was built in the early 18th century for Admiral George Delaval, a member of a powerful Border family. The architect was Sir John Vanbrugh, the playwright-turned-architect, and it is believed by some experts to be his masterpiece. Both architect and owner died before it was finished in 1728.
Location: 2 miles NE of Seaton Delaval on A190.

Sedgefield *Durham*　　　　*Map: 391 Gd*
CHURCH OF ST EDMUND The building is almost entirely 13th century, with an imposing west tower added in the late 15th century.

Sumptuous 17th-century woodwork inside the church includes screen, panelling and choir stalls. The pulpit, given in 1859, was made from oak from the monks' dormitory at Durham Cathedral.
Location: 7 miles NW of Stockton on A177.

Selborne *Hants.*　　　　*Map: 398 Cb*
CHURCH OF ST MARY This Norman church was built on land given by Edward the Confessor in 1049. The 12th-century south door is noted for its impressive ironwork. The grave of Gilbert White, the 18th-century naturalist, is near the vestry door on the north-east side of the church. In the south aisle is the Gilbert White memorial window showing St Francis preaching to the birds.
Location: 4 miles SE of Alton on B3006.
THE WAKES Two remarkable men are commemorated in this village house: Gilbert White (1720–93) and Lawrence Oates (1880–1912).

White, the father of British naturalists, lived all his life at Selborne, observing and recording the behaviour of birds, insects and animals. *The Natural History and Antiquities of Selborne*, based on his journals, was published in 1789. Both the wall of the parlour and the front of White's desk are boldly carved with his initials and the date.

Captain Oates's sledge can be seen upstairs – a moving memento of his heroic death on the return from the South Pole with Captain Scott in 1912.

Selby Abbey *N. Yorks.* *Map: 391 Ga*
A spectacular church which has survived a series of catastrophes since the 12th century. At the east end of the Norman nave are some extremely distorted arches, the result of the tower foundations sinking during construction.

In 1690 the tower collapsed and demolished the south transept. It was rebuilt, but in 1906 the entire roof was burned off, the tower was burned out, and its bells crashed into the church. Everything was repaired by 1909.
Location: The Crescent, town centre.

Seton *Lothian* *Map: 389 Ed*
CHURCH OF ST MARY AND THE HOLY CROSS (Seton Collegiate Church). The church was built from the early 15th century – cruciform with central tower.
Location: 3 miles E of Prestonpans on A198.

Shackerstone *Leics.* *Map: 393 Gd*
SHACKERSTONE RAILWAY SOCIETY The society has its home in the old Shackerstone Station. There are 13 locomotives, 11 of which are steam powered, and a working steam crane. Trains are regularly run. The station also houses a museum, which includes a complete block signalling system. This system was introduced in the 1850s to improve rail safety. The line was divided into sections or blocks, and once a train had entered a block no new train could be allowed on to the line until it cleared the signal box at the far end. Visitors can work the system for themselves.
Location: 11 miles N of Nuneaton (A444 and minor road).

Shallowford *Staffs.* *Map: 393 Fe*
IZAAK WALTON COTTAGE Izaak Walton, famous for his book *The Compleat Angler, the Contemplative Man's Recreation,* was born in Stafford in 1593, and went to London as a draper's apprentice. In London he became a friend of the poet John Donne, and later wrote his biography.

Walton spent much of the Civil War years in Staffordshire and bought Halfhead Farm at Shallowford. He was 60 when he wrote his great book, and was to live another 30 years. He did much of his fishing with a friend in the River Dove on the border of Derbyshire.

When Walton died he directed that the income from the farm should be used each year to apprentice two poor boys of Stafford to a trade, to provide a dowry so a servant girl could marry, and to provide coal "for some poor people . . . in the last week in January or in every first week in February . . . the hardest and most pincing times".

The farm cottage is now furnished as a typical late-17th-century house, such as Walton would have known.
Location: 5 miles NW of Stafford (A5013 and minor road from Great Bridgeford).

Shandy Hall see Coxwold

Shardlow *Derbys.* *Map: 394 Bb*
The Trent and Mersey Canal was opened in 1777, and joined the River Trent where Shardlow now stands. A small port was developed around warehouses to store goods awaiting transhipment between narrow canal craft and the larger river boats. Shardlow soon grew up around the port.

Some of the original buildings, including warehouses, canal pubs and houses, remain. The outstanding building is the Trent Corn Mill, built in 1780, by the road bridge. It is built over a wide arch under which boats could be floated for loading. It has been restored as a boat centre and museum.
Location: 6½ miles SE of Derby on A6.

Sharpness *Glos.* *Map: 393 Eb*
DOCKS Sharpness is the southern terminus of the Gloucester and Sharpness Ship Canal, completed in 1827 to allow sea-going vessels to reach the heart of Gloucester. By the 1870s the lock joining the canal to the River Severn had proved too small. A new ship lock was completed in 1871 and new warehouses were built along the canal. The port and the canal are still in use.
Location: 2½ miles N of Berkeley on B4066.

Shaw *Greater Manchester* *Map: 391 Fa*
DEE MILL ENGINE Steam-engines had become very complex machines by the beginning of the 20th century. The Lancashire textile mills were growing ever larger and demanding more and more power. In 1907, Dee Mill installed a twin tandem compound engine to drive the textile machines. It consists of two matched engines, set side by side. Each has a high-pressure and low-pressure cylinder arranged one behind the other on a single piston. Between the two engines is the common flywheel, which weighs 84 tons. The engine is preserved.
Location: Eastern edge of the town, just south of the B6197.

Shawbost *Lewis, Western Isles* *Map: 386 Bd*
SHAWBOST MUSEUM Old methods of fishing, crofting and weaving are illustrated in a disused church. A Norse-type watermill, built in the 19th century, has also been restored.
Location: 18 miles NW of Stornoway (A857 and A858).

Shawford Mill *Somerset* *Map: 397 Gd*
The mill on the River Frome is one of the many woollen mills that once lined the whole length of the river, taking their power from water wheels. It was built early in the 19th century, and was a fulling mill, used for finishing cloth. First the cloth was thickened and shrunk. Then the nap was raised and trimmed.

The interior is only occasionally open to visitors, when it is being used as a theatre.
Location: 7½ miles NE of Warminster on A36, beside bridge over River Frome.

Sheffield *S. Yorks.* *Map: 393 Gf*
BISHOPS' HOUSE This half-timbered and stone house is a good example of a prosperous house of the 16th century, and is believed to have been the home of two bishops. Two rooms are

furnished according to the period, and the garden is laid out in 17th-century style.
Location: Norton Lees Lane, Meersbrook, 2½ miles S of Sheffield off A61.
SHEPHERD WHEEL Beside the River Porter is one of the few remaining examples of the water-powered grinding works which were common throughout Sheffield in the 19th century. In works such as these, men sharpened knives and put points on forks.

There are two workshops, each containing grindstones driven by the one water-wheel, which is still in good condition. The metal dust attacked the lungs of the workers, and a Sheffield doctor produced statistics in the 1840s to show that half the fork grinders of the region died before the age of 30. The site has now been restored.
Location: Whiteley Wood, SW of town centre (A625 to Hunters Bar roundabout and turn right into Rustlings Rd and Hangingwater Rd).

Sheffield Park E. Sussex   Map: 399 Eb
BLUEBELL RAILWAY This steam railway runs between Sheffield Park Station and Horsted Keynes, 5 miles to the north. It has 20 vintage

WOODLAND STEAM TRAIN

The 20 locomotives of the Bluebell Railway were mostly built before the First World War, the oldest in 1872. The line took the name from its woodland route which in spring is carpeted in bluebells. British Rail closed the line, part of the old Southern Railway, in 1958, but a preservation society based at Sheffield Park Station, E. Sussex, re-opened it two years later, and now passengers once again can travel by steam train through the Sussex woods. The Bluebell Railway and the other steam railways that still operate in Britain are reminders of a very recent past. In the 1950s steam trains were still a major part of the nation's transport. The last one was finally retired by British Rail in 1968.

UNION CERTIFICATE *Archibald Hawkes became a member of the Southall Branch of the Associated Society of Engineers and Firemen on April 11, 1898. His certificate is now in the Bluebell Museum.*

RESCUED

Blackmore Vale, *a West Country Class locomotive that once ran on Southern Railways, was saved from being scrapped in 1970, and now runs on the Bluebell Railway in Sussex.*

SIGNAL BOX *Trains on the Bluebell line near Sheffield Park are controlled from this signal box. The box was built in the 1930s and can now be visited when it is not in use.*

locomotives, mostly from the old Southern Railway. The rolling stock includes vintage carriages and goods vehicles.

Sheffield Park Station was built in 1882 and is being restored to its original condition, down to the oil-lit platform lamps.
Location: 10 miles N of Lewes on A275.
GARDEN The splendid woodland garden of Sheffield Park House covers more than 100 acres, with five lakes. It is based on a landscape designed by "Capability" Brown in 1775.
Location: 10 miles N of Lewes on A275.

Sheldon *Derbys.* *Map: 393 Gf*
MAGPIE MINE One of the best preserved lead mines in Britain lies in open country ½ mile south of the village.

Mining in the area began in the Middle Ages, but most of the surface remains date from the early 19th century. Magpie Mine ceased work in

THE GLORY OF FAN-VAULTING

One of the great glories of Sherborne Abbey, which took nearly 100 years to build in the 15th century, is the fan-vaulting over the nave and choir.

the 1950s. There are two engine-houses. One housed the pumping engine for removing water from the mine, the other held the winding engine for raising and lowering men and materials in the mine shaft. At the entrance to the site are the remains of the smithy, and the mine manager's house.
Location: 3 miles W of Bakewell (A6 and minor road).

Shelmore Bank *Salop* *Map: 393 Fe*
The road that links Gnosall Heath to Norbury runs beside a mile-long embankment that carries the Shropshire Union Canal. This huge earthwork took 5½ years to build, employing 400 men and 70 horses. There were frequent landslips before it was finished in 1835.
Location: Gnosall Heath is 7 miles W of Stafford on A518.

Shelsley Walsh *Heref. & Worcs.* *Map: 393 Fc*
CHURCH OF ST ANDREW A simple little church, with a Norman nave and a later chancel. The north doorway and the font are Norman and across the nave is a 15th-century screen enclosing a small chantry chapel. The floor of the chancel contains many 15th-century tiles.
Location: 10 miles NW of Worcester (A443, B4204 and minor road).

Shepton Mallet *Somerset* *Map: 397 Fd*
CHURCH OF ST PETER AND ST PAUL The church has possibly the best timber wagon roof in the country. Wagon roofs, which are most common in the west of England, are lined with boarding, giving the impression of the inside of a covered wagon. The 15th-century roof at Shepton Mallet has about 350 separate panels, each with a carved boss. The panels are also carved, and not one design is repeated.
Location: Church Lane, off the Market Place.

Sherborne *Dorset* *Map: 397 Fc*
ABBEY There was a cathedral at Sherborne before the Norman Conquest, and according to tradition King Alfred was educated there. The Normans rebuilt the Saxon church, and this was replaced by the present Perpendicular building during the 15th century. The last abbot surrendered the monastery to the king in 1539, and the parish of Sherborne bought the abbey church for 100 marks (£66 13s 4d), plus another £260 for the lead on the roof and the bells.
Location: Cheap St.
CASTLE Built for the bishops of Salisbury in the 12th century, the castle was never an important military fortress. At the end of the 16th century it was owned by Sir Walter Raleigh.
Location: Castleton Rd.

Sheringham *Norfolk* *Map: 395 Fb*
NORTH NORFOLK RAILWAY The railway is based at Sheringham Station in the town centre. It operates a regular steam-train service between Sheringham and Weybourne along 3 miles of the old Midland and Great Northern Railway track.

Sheringham Station has retained many of the features from the time the line opened in 1887, including an original signal box which is usually open to visitors.
Location: 25 miles N of Norwich (A140, A149).

VAULTING: A MEDIEVAL ART

The Normans brought Roman vaulting to England as a means of roofing cathedrals and churches with a durable fire-proof material, achieving breathtaking effects with carved stonework. Roofs were built above the vaults to protect the stonework from frost.

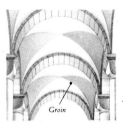

GROINED VAULT *Early medieval vaults were round-arched tunnels. When two vaults intersect at right-angles to each other, the meeting lines, formed by the curved planes are called groins.*

RIBBED VAULT *By bridging the diagonal corners with narrow arches—or ribs—a lighter vault could be built. The spaces between the ribs were filled with thin stonework.*

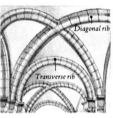

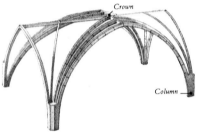

POINTED-ARCH VAULT *It was discovered during the 13th century that by using pointed—instead of round—arches, intersecting vaults having different spans could be built to meet at the same height.*

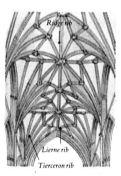

TIERCERON AND LIERNE VAULTING *Extra ribs were used in the Early English and Decorated periods. Ridge-ribs and tierceron (intermediate) ribs gave extra support, and panels became smaller. Lierne (tie) ribs between any ribs springing from the supports were purely decorative.*

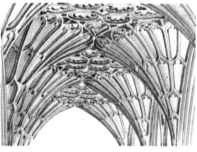

FAN VAULTS *A development of the Perpendicular period. Clusters of arched ribs spread fan-like from corner columns to the centre of each bay of the vault. The ribs and panels in between were decorative—carved from stones forming the roof.*

Shibden Hall *W. Yorks.*　　　*Map: 394 Ad*
The Oates family were the first to live at Shibden—in 1425. Remains of their original house survive in the 12–18 in. floorboards held with wooden pegs. Shibden Hall, now the West Yorkshire Folk Museum, has rooms illustrating life in the 17th and 18th centuries, and adjoining workshops demonstrating pre-industrial crafts in the Pennines.
Location: ½ mile E of Halifax on A58.

Shildon *Durham*　　　*Map: 391 Fd*
STOCKTON AND DARLINGTON RAILWAY Shildon was one of the major junctions on the Stockton and Darlington Railway, which launched the railway age when the world's first regular steam-hauled service was introduced in 1825.

At Shildon's Soho Engineering Works, Timothy Hackworth designed and built locomotives such as *Royal George* in 1827 and *Sans Pareil* in 1829.

Next to the remains of the works in Soho

THE SADDLER: KEY CRAFTSMAN IN RURAL BRITAIN

West Yorkshire Folk Museum at Shibden Hall, near Halifax, has a series of workshops with equipment used by craftsmen—cloggers, coopers, blacksmiths, farriers. Until the 20th century the saddler was a key craftsman. He made the harness for horses which had been the main form of transport and farm power for centuries. The leather was held in a wooden clamp while he worked on it.

Street are railway workers' cottages and Hackworth's own house, which has been refurnished and contains exhibits of his life and work.

Opposite Hackworth's house, part of the Stockton and Darlington Railway works has been restored and contains a full-size replica of the *Sans Pareil* made in 1978.

Walks have been laid out along the original line, including the Brusselton Incline and Adamson's Coach House, Shildon, reputed to be the world's first railway station.
Location: 9 miles N of Darlington (A68, A6072).

Shipton Hall *Salop*　　　　*Map: 393 Ed*
An Elizabethan manor house, built of stone in 1587 to replace an earlier timber house. The interior combines Georgian furnishings with the Tudor woodwork.
Location: 6 miles SW of Much Wenlock on B4378.

Shobdon *Heref. & Worcs.*　　　*Map: 393 Ec*
CHURCH OF ST JOHN THE EVANGELIST In 1756 Viscount Bateman, Treasurer of the Household of George II, pulled down the old Norman church and erected the chancel arch and two doorways as a remantic "eye-catcher" in the park of Shobdon Court. He then rebuilt the present church in fanciful Gothic style, with everything painted blue and white. The south transept was for the family (it has a fireplace), the north transept for the servants (no fireplace).
Location: 12 miles SW of Ludlow (A49, B4361 and B4362).

Shottery *Warks.*　　　　　*Map: 393 Gc*
ANNE HATHAWAY'S COTTAGE Shottery was the home of the Hathaway family from 1470 down to 1892, and in this cottage lived Anne Hathaway, who married William Shakespeare in 1582, when he was 18 and she 26. The house itself has changed little, and contains furniture which belonged to the Hathaway family, including a Tudor bed with hand-embroidered cover.
Location: 1 mile W of Stratford-upon-Avon on A422.

Shottesbrooke Park *Berks.*　　*Map: 398 Cc*
CHURCH OF ST JOHN THE BAPTIST An almost completely Decorated Gothic church, built in the 14th century with a central tower and spire.
Location: 3 miles E of Twyford off B3024.

Shovel Down *Devon*　　　　*Map: 396 Dc*
This seems to be one of several places on Dartmoor which were viewed with reverence between 2000 and 1000 BC. Three avenues of standing stones lead to cairns, one of which has four concentric rings of upright stones.
Location: 3½ miles W of Chagford through Teigncombe.

Shrewsbury *Salop*　　　　*Map: 393 Ed*
CASTLE Fifty-one houses were demolished to make room for the motte-and-bailey castle which was put up by the Normans in William the Conqueror's reign. In the 13th century Dafydd, brother of Llywelyn the Last, was put to death in the castle yard after attempting to continue the war against the English. The buildings today are mostly of a later date.
Location: Castle Gates.

CHURCH OF ST CHAD An unusual classical church of the late 18th century. The circular nave has cast-iron columns supporting the ceiling.
Location: St Chad's Terrace.
LION HOTEL A Georgian coaching inn, partly built on a 15th-century timber-framed house. Charles Dickens stayed there, and Benjamin Disraeli harangued the crowds from the hotel's balcony during an election campaign.

Joined to the inn at one end is another 15th-century building called Henry Tudor House. Here Henry, Earl of Richmond, stayed after landing in South Wales on his way to the Battle of Bosworth Field and, eventually, his coronation as Henry VII.
Location: Wyle Cop.

Shugborough *Staffs.*　　　　*Map: 393 Fe*
SHUGBOROUGH HALL The house was built on the site of a palace of the bishops of Lichfield in the 17th and 18th centuries.

Admiral Lord Anson was born there in 1697. In 1740 he sailed on a voyage round the world, lost most of his ships in rounding Cape Horn and most of his crew from scurvy, but survived to reach the Pacific, where he captured a Spanish treasure galleon and became a millionaire.

His brother Thomas was a founder of the Society of Dilettanti who studied the antiquities of Greece and Rome. As a result, the grounds of Shugborough contain replicas of Classical monuments, including the Lanthorn of Demosthenes, Temple of the Winds, a Roman triumphal arch honouring Admiral Anson's voyage, and a 20 ft high monument to one of the Ansons' pet cats.

The estate brewhouse, coachhouses and laundry are also open to visitors.
Location: 5 miles E of Stafford off A513.
SHUGBOROUGH PARK FARM Farming techniques of the region from the late 18th century are illustrated at the farm. It is also a breeding centre for some of the animals that were common in the county 200 years ago: Longhorn cattle, Tamworth pigs, and Shropshire sheep. The main farm buildings date from the early 19th century, and contain a watermill.
Location: As above, or signposted from Great Haywood, 4 miles NW of Rugeley off A51.
THE RAILWAY BRIDGE The Trent Valley Railway, opened in 1847, crosses Shugborough Park on an ornamental bridge. The company agreed with the Earl of Lichfield to build a bridge in Classical style to fit the setting.

Shute Barton *Devon*　　　　*Map: 397 Ec*
A picturesque group of buildings consisting of remains of a 14th-century manor house and a magnificent Elizabethan gatehouse.
Location: 4 miles W of Axminster (A35 and B3161).

Shuttleworth Collection see Biggleswade

Silbury Hill *Wilts.*　　　　*Map: 398 Ac*
Folklore says that the enormous mound of Silbury Hill is the work of the devil and that it hides the burial of a mounted warrior in gold armour. Excavations have failed to find evidence in support of either claim.

Silbury is the largest artificial hill in Europe, and was built between 3000 and 2500 BC, towards the end of the Stone Age. The hill is 130

PLANE FOR A ROMAN CARPENTER

This jack plane, similar in shape to a modern one, was made for a carpenter at Silchester, when it was one of the towns of Roman Britain. The wooden body of the plane has rotted away, leaving only the iron framework with the original blade in position. The blade is set at 65 degrees, rather steeper than a modern plane. The tool was one of many that possibly were all made by the same blacksmith. They included new and unfinished tools for carpenters, shoemakers, farmers and smiths. The carpenters' tools included axes, chisels, hammers, drills and part of a folding rule made of bronze.

ft high, covers $5\frac{1}{2}$ acres and contains over 12 million cu. ft of soil. The work would have occupied 700 men for ten years.

Archaeologists still do not know who built it or why. It can only be assumed that the man who organised the building of the mound – or who was buried in it – was a very powerful figure indeed.

Location: $5\frac{1}{2}$ miles W of Marlborough by A4.

Silchester *Hants.* Map: 398 Cc
CHURCH OF ST MARY THE VIRGIN The little church, with its western bell-turret, stands just inside the Roman town. It was built about 1125. The north aisle was added about 1180 and the south aisle about 1220. Wall-paintings in the church date from 1230.
Location: 8 miles N of Basingstoke (A340 and minor road).
ROMAN TOWN Unlike most of the towns of Roman Britain, Silchester was abandoned after the Romans left, and its foundations now lie beneath a blanket of soil. Calleva Atrebatum, as the Romans called it, is the best known of Romano-British towns, for the whole area has been excavated – market place and town hall in the centre, baths, an inn, temples and even a tiny Christian church. None of this is now visible, but the entire circuit of city walls, in parts very well preserved, can be followed. The rich haul of finds from Silchester are on display in Reading Museum. There is also a site museum. The amphitheatre near Manor Farm, outside the walls, is a conspicuous earthwork with a pond-filled arena.
Location: The Roman town is 1 mile E of Silchester.

Singleton *W. Sussex* Map: 398 Cb
WEALD AND DOWNLAND MUSEUM Ancient buildings threatened with demolition have been moved to this 35 acre open-air museum. Among them is a large barn, aisled like a church, farmhouses from the 15th and 16th centuries, an 18th-century granary, an early-16th-century market hall, a smithy, a watermill and a tollhouse. Visitors can enter the buildings.
Location: 6 miles N of Chichester off A286.

CHARCOAL-BURNERS' CAMP

A 19th-century charcoal-burners' camp has been reconstructed at the Weald and Downland Museum at Singleton. In camps like this for centuries men turned forest timber into charcoal for industry.

Sissinghurst Castle *Kent*   *Map: 399 Eb*
Queen Elizabeth was entertained for three days at Sissinghurst in 1573. The most conspicuous feature surviving from the mansion of that time is the brick tower crowned by twin cupolas, which today dominates the enchanting garden created among the ruins by the writer Vita Sackville-West and her husband Sir Harold Nicolson in the 1930s. The garden is a series of open-air rooms, each planted with flowers of one colour or for effect at one season of the year.
Location: 16 miles W of Ashford (A28 and A262).

Sittingbourne *Kent*   *Map: 399 Fc*
SITTINGBOURNE AND KEMSLEY LIGHT RAILWAY The narrow-gauge line was part of a system built in 1906 to serve local paper mills. It now carries a passenger service along the 2 mile line.
Location: Milton Rd, near British Rail station.

Village life 4,500 years ago

ABANDONED IN THE FACE OF A STORM 4,500 YEARS AGO, THE STONE AGE VILLAGE OF SKARA BRAE IN THE ORKNEYS IS STILL MUCH AS THE INHABITANTS LEFT IT

When the sandstorm that engulfed it struck the village of Skara Brae about 2500 BC, the people left in haste, leaving behind many of their possessions and treasures. One woman broke her beads as she squeezed through a doorway, leaving a trail of them along an alley.

Thousands of years later, when the village was dug out of the sand, the huts and their furnishings were found intact, giving a more vivid picture of life in Britain 4,500 years ago than any other site in Britain. The site had been inhabited for about 600 years.

There were seven or eight huts in the village, linked by narrow, roofed lanes. The walls, still 8 ft high, were built mainly of flagstone blocks, exposed outer sides being thickly plastered with

STONE AGE LIVING-ROOM *A pestle and mortar stand beside the stone sideboard (right). The cubby hole above the bed was for storing personal belongings.*

INSIDE THE HUTS

Each of the huts was roughly square with rounded corners, and had a main room 14–20 ft square. The entrance was about 4 ft high and probably had a wooden door that could be barred from inside. The square hearth in the centre of the hut may have been open to the sky. Against the wall on either side were beds – oblong stone boxes with upright slabs at the front corners to support a canopy. Bedding was probably heather covered with skins.

Dry food may have been stored in the sideboard, built of stone slabs, against the rear wall. Limpets and other shell fish were kept fresh in small square boxes built into the floor and waterproofed with clay. There were small, beehive-shaped chambers in the 3 ft thick walls. Some seem to have been stores, others toilets, for there was a system of drains. The stench from the toilets must have mingled with that of the food debris littered on the floor of the hut, as well as that stacked up around the outside

SEA-SHORE SETTLEMENT *The cluster of huts was on a sloping plain beside a bay, about 20 ft above sea level.*

Sizergh Castle *Cumbria*   *Map: 391 Dc*
Sizergh, a 14th-century pele tower, has belonged to the Strickland family for 740 years. Sir Walter Strickland committed himself to service of an almost feudal nature to the Earl of Salisbury in 1448, undertaking to provide a small army for the earl's use in war – anywhere.

One of the agreement documents survives at Sizergh Castle, and indicates the sort of dangers that faced kings in the Middle Ages, with powerful landowners able to call up military forces at short notice.
Location: 3½ miles S of Kendal on A6.

Skara Brae *Mainland, Orkney*   *Map: 387 Ef*
A 4,500-year-old village has been preserved by sand, as it was when the villagers fled, probably during a severe storm. (See below.)
Location: On Bay of Skaill, 7 miles N of Stromness (A967 then B9056).

---

clay. Slate-like shale was used as paving slabs, and roofs were probably covered with skins or turf laid across timber or whalebone rafters. Tons of food debris – especially shell fish – and peat ash had been piled up round the huts, probably to provide insulation and protection from wind and rain.

About 30 people probably lived at Skara Brae. They ate sea food and some venison, and kept cattle and sheep. They also grew small amounts of wheat and barley which they ground into flour to make bread. Clothing was probably made from animal skins, and the villagers may have painted their bodies, because small stone cups containing red, yellow and blue pigments were found there.

Some of the refugees returned to Skara Brae when the sand had partially buried their homes – remains of fires were found beside the walls. But the village was never re-occupied.

FIRST-AID DRESSING *The cotton-like inner tissues of pieces of puff-ball fungus found in the village were probably used to staunch bleeding. Puff-balls are found in summer and autumn.*

VILLAGE TOOLS AND TREASURES

Finely carved stone balls and miniature implements, and a wide range of bone pins, awls, pendants and blades, show that the people of Skara Brae were skilled craftsmen. Pottery remains were also found.

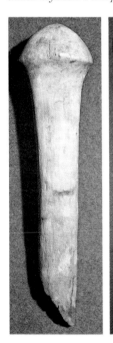

WOOD AND BONE
Quite a lot of wood was found in the village, including some driftwood. Some pieces of driftwood were spruce from North America. A few objects had been shaped from the wood, including part of a handle (far left), perhaps belonging to an axe. The 10 in. long bone pin (left) is shaped from walrus ivory. Both are in the National Museum of Antiquities in Edinburgh.

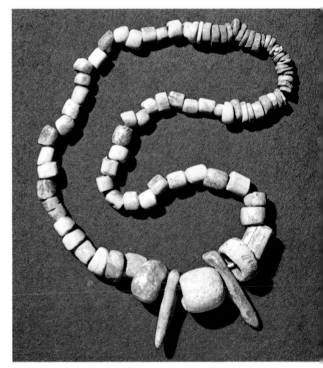

TOOTH NECKLACE *Villagers adorned themselves with animal-tooth beads such as the string above, now in the National Museum of Antiquities, Edinburgh.*

CARVING *The design on the stone tool (left) was probably religious.*

ROPE FRAGMENT *Rope made from twisted heather was probably used to tether animals. Two different thicknesses were found.*

Skegness *Lincs.*   *Map: 395 Eb*
CHURCH FARM MUSEUM The farm contains agricultural tools that were used on small Lincolnshire farms at the turn of the century. The
farmhouse is furnished in the same period.
Location: Church Rd South, off A52.

Skelton *N. Yorks.*   *Map: 394 Be*
CHURCH OF ST GILES A superb example of that
rarity among parish churches–one built in a
uniform style throughout, without subsequent
additions. Erected about 1250, under the patronage of the treasurers of York Minster, it is a gem
of Early English architecture.
It is a small church, only 44 ft long and 32 ft
wide, austere outside, but with a wealth of
delicate mouldings inside.
Location: 4 miles NW of York off A19.

Skenfrith Castle *Gwent*   *Map: 393 Eb*
Skenfrith is a stone enclosure with four round
corner towers, built by Hubert de Burgh, chief
counsellor to Henry III, in the 1230s. Inside the
enclosure is the shell of a three-storeyed great
tower. The castle began as a Norman structure
and was one of a group of fortresses built to
command the east–west routes from England
into south Wales.
Location: 7 miles NW of Monmouth (A466,
then W on B4521).

Skipsea Castle *Humberside*   *Map 394 De*
This is an early motte-and-bailey castle where
the motte (or mound) was erected several
hundred feet away from the bailey (or castle
yard). In between lay soggy marshland where
tidal sea-water flowed in and created a mere. A
causeway on wooden piles ran across it.
Location: 5 miles N of Hornsea on B1242.

Skipton Castle *N. Yorks.*   *Map: 391 Fb*
From Norman beginnings, Skipton developed
into a substantial stronghold in the 14th century.
Its principal feature was the gatehouse flanked
by huge towers. It was owned until the 17th
century by the powerful Yorkshire family of
Clifford, who built Clifford's Tower in York. It
retains much of its medieval atmosphere.
Location: Head of Skipton High St.

Sledmere House *Humberside*   *Map: 394 Ce*
There had been a manor house at Sledmere for
hundreds of years before the estate was inherited
by the Sykes family in 1748. A new Georgian
house was built and "Capability" Brown was
commissioned to landscape the park.
Sledmere was renowned for its stud farm for
racehorses, founded in 1803 and still in operation.
Location: 7 miles NW of Great Driffield (A166
then B1252).

Smallythe Place *Kent*   *Map: 399 Fb*
One evening in the 1890s the actress Ellen Terry
was travelling by dog-cart from Rye to Tenterden. On the way her eye was caught by this
little medieval yeoman's house, then forlorn and
uninhabited, by the side of the road. She asked
a passer-by to let her know if ever it were for
sale. It is easy to imagine the man gaping after
the vanishing dog-cart with a card in his hand
on which was written one of the most famous
names in the world. He did as he had been asked,

and in 1899 Ellen Terry bought Smallythe and
spent the rest of her life filling its little rooms
with mementoes of her long stage career.
Location: 2 miles S of Tenterden on B2082.

Smedmore *Dorset*   *Map: 398 Aa*
Since the 14th century, Smedmore House has
never been sold. It has passed from one owner to
the next by inheritance.
The present house, dating from the early 17th
century, is a few hundred yards from the sea. It
was built to enable the owner, Sir William
Clavell, to exploit the alum from Kimmeridge
Bay. Alum is a chemical used in making paper
and leather. It was shipped from a little quay,
the remains of which can still be seen.
Location: 7½ miles S of Wareham (A351, B3069
then minor road).

Smethwick *W. Midlands*   *Map: 393 Fd*
BIRMINGHAM CANAL The main line of the canal
passes through Smethwick, for much of the way
in a deep cutting. Galton Bridge was designed
by Thomas Telford in the 1820s to carry Roebuck Lane across the canal. Between Brasshouse
Lane bridge and Bridge Street, Telford built the
Engine Arm aqueduct to carry a feeder branch
of the old Birmingham canal over his new one.

Snailbeach *Salop*   *Map: 393 Ed*
LEAD MINE The tiny village is surrounded by the
remains of a lead mine, once the richest in
England. It was owned by the Marquis of Bath
and exploration began in the 1780s. Production
reached a peak in the mid-19th century, when
3,500 tons of ore a year were raised. By the early
1900s the ore was exhausted. Mountains of spoil
were left behind and derelict surface buildings
still stand. There is an engine house, built in 1856
to hold a big Cornish pumping engine. The
engine shed and track of a narrow-gauge railway,
built in 1877 to join the mine to the main line
at Minsterley, also remain.
Explore with care, as there are a number of
open shafts.
Location: 11 miles SW of Shrewsbury off A488.

Snarford *Lincs.*   *Map: 394 Dc*
CHURCH OF ST LAWRENCE Three splendid monuments in the church commemorate members of
the St Pol family who died during the reigns of
Elizabeth I and James I. The most elaborate is
the earliest, to Sir Thomas who died in 1582. It
is an alabaster six-poster bed, with two recumbent effigies, and children kneeling on the top.
Location: 8½ miles NE of Lincoln off A46.

Snowdon Mountain Railway see Llanberis

Soar Chapel *Dyfed*   *Map: 392 Cc*
The most remote chapel in Wales once served
isolated farms from Tregaron in the west to
Abergwesyn in the east. The farmers and their
families rode on horseback to the Sabbath service, which was often the only occasion on
which they met their neighbours. The bodies in
the little graveyard were brought miles across
mountain tracks to their final resting place.
Location: 20 miles NE of Lampeter (A485 to
Tregaron, then turn east over river on to minor
road to Abergwesyn. After 5½ miles turn S at
telephone box for 3 miles).

WHERE CAMELOT MAY ONCE HAVE STOOD

The remains of 5th-century Cadbury Castle crown an isolated 500 ft hill ringed by prehistoric ramparts and ditches. The location of the castle, its size and *evidence of a great feasting hall suggest that, if King Arthur's fabled court of Camelot did exist, this hill at South Cadbury may well have been its site.*

Somerleyton Hall *Suffolk*   *Map: 399 Gf*
Railway entrepreneur Sir Samuel Morton Peto bought the Elizabethan manor house in 1844 and largely rebuilt it as a Victorian mansion. The writer George Borrow (1803–81), who lived locally, denounced the Hall in his travel book *Romany Rye* (1857) as "pandemonium in red brick". But Borrow had a grudge against Peto, who had built a railway line across the writer's land.
In fact the Hall is a fascinating blend of architectural styles and contains luxuriously appointed rooms and fine wood carving.
Location: 5 miles NW of Lowestoft off B1074.

Sompting *W. Sussex*   *Map: 398 Da*
CHURCH OF ST MARY THE VIRGIN The Saxon tower, all that survives of the original church, is the only one in England that preserves its original spire. This, known as a "Rhenish helm", consists of four shingle-clad, diamond-shaped faces tapering to a point. The rest of the church was rebuilt in the 12th century by the Knights Templar, who attached to the south side a chapel with its own sanctuary. The parishioners were later granted the use of this chapel.
Location: 2½ miles NE of Worthing off A27.

Sotterley *Suffolk*   *Map: 399 Gf*
AGRICULTURAL MUSEUM Tractors dating from the First World War, and Suffolk-made ploughs, drills, threshing machines, reapers and binders form the bulk of the collection, which is housed at Alexander Wood Farm.
Location: 5 miles SE of Beccles (A145 and minor road).

Southampton *Hants.*   *Map: 398 Bb*
MEDIEVAL TOWN More than half the medieval town wall survives, and 13 of its towers and five gates still stand – a greater proportion than in any other town in Britain. Fragments of Henry II's 11th–12th-century royal fortress can also be seen.
Location: Castle remains in Castle Way, SW of city centre.

South Cadbury *Somerset*   *Map: 397 Fd*
CADBURY CASTLE According to tradition, this ancient hill-fort was Camelot, the legendary seat of King Arthur, British scourge of the Saxons. The site was first occupied in the 3rd–1st centuries BC by Iron Age people, who built an 18 acre enclosure on top of the hill. Excavations have revealed that this contained wattle-and-daub circular huts, two shrines and a metal-workers' quarter: furnaces, smiths' tools and finished weapons have been found.
The Britons of the area refortified the site as a defence against Saxon invaders during the late 5th and early 6th centuries – the period when Arthur is believed to have ruled. Inside the British stone defences an impressive timber hall suitable for feasting and ceremony has been discovered.
Location: 5½ miles SW of Wincanton off A303, ¼ mile S of South Cadbury village.

South Creake *Norfolk*   *Map: 395 Fb*
CHURCH OF ST MARY St Mary's is a large church and one of the finest in East Anglia. The impressive hammer-beam roof is decorated with two rows of angels holding shields. The 15th-century rood screen is another fine piece of woodwork, but the painted saints in the lower panels were mutilated by Puritans. The eight panels of the font, dating from the same period, are also damaged. They represent the Crucifixion and the seven sacraments – baptism, the Eucharist, confirmation, taking holy orders, matrimony, penance and extreme unction.
Location: 5½ miles NW of Fakenham on B1355.

Southsea *Hants.*   *Map: 398 Ca*
CASTLE The coastal fort guarding the approach to Portsmouth was built in 1544 as part of a defensive chain around the south coast. It now houses a military museum. (See p. 125.)
Location: Castle Esplanade, S of town centre.

South Shields *Tyne & Wear*   *Map: 391 Ge*
ROMAN REMAINS AND MUSEUM The ruins form part of the Roman fort of *Arbeia*, built in the 2nd century AD to guard the east flank of Hadrian's Wall and the mouth of the River Tyne. In the early 3rd century the fort was remodelled as a store base for the Scottish campaigns of 208–11 of the emperor, Severus. More than 20 granaries have been located, but

parts of only ten are visible. The museum contains items from the fort, including tombstones, surveying instruments, gaming counters, and a splendid sword inlaid with representations of the Roman eagle and the war god Mars.
Location: Fort St, N of town centre.

South Stack *Gwynedd*   *Map: 392 Bf*
LIGHTHOUSE The lighthouse rises from a rock called South Stack off the westernmost tip of Holy Island. Its light flashes 200 ft above sea level, at the top of a 91 ft high white tower, built in 1809 to warn shipping in the Irish Sea to keep away from this dangerous coast.
Location: 3 miles W of Holyhead on minor roads.

Southwell *Notts.*   *Map: 394 Cb*
MINSTER In 1884 the minster was raised to the status of cathedral. Because Southwell is a small town, the building is often called the village cathedral.
The architecture of the minster spans the 12th-14th centuries. The fine twin-towered west front, the nave and the transepts are Norman, the choir is Early English, and the chapter house and the carved stone screen separating nave and choir are Decorated. Caricatures of more than 200 human figures ornament the choir screen. The late 13th-century stone carvings of foliage in the chapter house are magnificent.
Location: 7½ miles W of Newark-on-Trent, town centre.

Southwold *Suffolk*   *Map: 399 Gf*
CHURCH OF ST EDMUND, KING AND MARTYR A magnificent Perpendicular church dedicated to the king of East Anglia who was murdered by the Danes in 870 for refusing to renounce Christianity. The present church was built after a fire of about 1430 destroyed the 12th-century original. The 15th-century screen, which retains its original painted panels and gilding, is one of the most splendid in England. Southwold Jack, a 15th-century wooden soldier, begins each service by striking a bell with his sword.
Location: 4½ miles NE of Blythburgh on A1095.

Sowerby Bridge *W. Yorks.*   *Map: 391 Fa*
CANAL BASIN An intriguing group of late-18th-century warehouses stands where the Calder and Hebble Navigation meets the Rochdale Canal. They are the largest surviving canal warehouses with "shipping holes" – water-level arches through which barges were floated to be loaded under cover. The basin is now used for pleasure craft.
Location: 2 miles SW of Halifax on A58.

Spean Bridge *Highland*   *Map: 386 Cb*
The village is named after the bridge which the celebrated engineer Thomas Telford (1757–1834) built across the River Spean in 1819. The three-arched bridge is one of the most impressive of the many bridges Telford built in the Scottish Highlands.
Location: 10 miles NE of Fort William on A82.

Speke Hall *Merseyside*   *Map: 393 Ef*
One of the finest and best preserved half-timbered houses in Britain. The richly decorated black-and-white Hall, built between 1490 and 1612,

looks almost exactly as it did in Tudor times. The great parlour, built for the Norris family about 1524–35, has a superb stucco ceiling with mouldings of fruit and flowers. There are two yew trees more than 400 years old in the garden. A late Elizabethan stone bridge leads visitors to the cobbled courtyard.
Location: ¾ mile SE of Liverpool Airport off A561.

Spofforth Castle *N. Yorks.*   *Map: 391 Gb*
The powerful Percy family of Northumberland began building the castle in the early 1300s. It was more of a fortified house than a military stronghold. In 1461 it was badly damaged by the Lancastrians in the Wars of the Roses.
Location: 5½ miles SE of Harrogate off A661, W of Spofforth village.

Springwell *Tyne & Wear*   *Map: 391 Ge*
BOWES RAILWAY The railway pioneer George Stephenson laid out the first section of this railway. It opened in 1826 to carry coal from Mount Moor Colliery and Springwell to Jarrow, on the River Tyne, for shipment by coasters. It served 13 collieries, but since 1974 the National Coal Board has operated only the Monkton–Jarrow section. The County Council now owns the 1¼ mile section from Black Fell Bank Head to Springwell Bank Head, which includes two inclines, over 40 wagons and workshops. Tyne and Wear Industrial Monuments Trust is restoring these, and it demonstrates the rope-worked trains on advertised days.
Location: 6 miles SE of Gateshead (A1, N on B1288). Crosses the B1288 road in the village.

Staindrop *Durham*   *Map: 391 Fd*
CHURCH OF ST MARY Some blocked-up windows survive from the nave of the original 8th-century Saxon church. The Normans added a west tower, and the church was gradually enlarged during the Gothic period. The stalls and font are Perpendicular. Among the impressive monuments are a splendid alabaster group of Ralph, Earl of Westmorland (d. 1425) and his two wives, and the late 18th and 19th-century tombs of the earls of Darlington and dukes of Cleveland and their wives.
Location: 11 miles NW of Darlington on B6279.

Stamford *Lincs.*   *Map: 394 Da*
BREWERY When All Saints Brewery, built in the last century, closed in 1974 it was converted into a museum which displays much of the original equipment, including a 1910 steam-engine.
Location: All Saints St, town centre.

Standen *W. Sussex*   *Map: 399 Db*
The interior of Standen, a house built in 1894 by the architect Philip Webb (1831–1915), is remarkable for its contrast with the sombreness of the conventional Victorian interior. White-painted panelling, William Morris wallpapers, blue-and-white china and gilt-framed water-colours form part of a decor that heralds the 1920s revolution in domestic architecture.
Location: 2 miles S of East Grinstead, signposted from B2110.

Stanford on Avon *Northants.*   *Map: 398 Bf*
CHURCH OF ST NICHOLAS A fine 13th-century

church which contains monuments of the Cave family and has medieval stained glass in some windows. The organ (of which only the restored case remains) once belonged to Charles I and was used at Whitehall Palace.

Location: 6½ miles NE of Rugby off B5414.

STANFORD HALL The house, which stands beside the River Avon, dates from the late 17th century, but the Cave family has lived on the site since 1430. The contents of the Hall include Elizabethan costumes, Stuart relics and old kitchen utensils. In the impressive stable block is a museum of antique cars and old motor-cycles and a replica of the flying machine constructed in 1898 by the pioneer aviator Percy Pilcher, a friend of the Cave family. A monument to Pilcher stands in an adjoining field where he crashed fatally the following year, aged only 33.

Stanley *Tayside*   *Map: 389 Ef*

The former cotton mills which rise from this Tayside village were among the first established in Scotland. The first mill was built in the late 1780s and is a tall, narrow building six storeys high. Two more mills were added in the following century. Power was provided by water carried from the Tay through 200 yd long tunnels. Many houses survive from the original village built by the mill owners. They include the brick terraces of Mill Street and Store Street.

Textiles are still made at the mill on a small scale.

Location: 6½ miles N of Perth (A9, B9099).

Stanmore, Little *Gtr. London   Map: 398 Dd*

CHURCH OF ST LAWRENCE This unexceptional-looking 18th-century church with its medieval tower contains one of the finest baroque church interiors in the country. It is decorated with wood carvings by Grinling Gibbons (1648–1721) and wall-paintings by various minor masters of the period. The painted Chandos Mausoleum contains a large tomb and monument, covering one wall, to the Duke of Chandos, for whom the church was rebuilt; the monument was designed by Gibbons.

Location: Whitchurch Lane, Edgware.

Stanstead Abbots *Herts.   Map: 399 Dd*

CHURCH OF ST JAMES The finely preserved interior of this mainly 13th-century church has a plastered roof with exposed tie-beams, box-pews and a three-decker pulpit. The fine timber south porch dates from the 15th century. The monuments include one to Sir Felix Booth (1775–1850), who in 1829 set out in the *Endeavour* to find the North-West Passage but discovered instead the magnetic north pole. The church is now administered by the Redundant Churches Fund.

Location: 3 miles NE of Hoddesdon on A414.

THE LONELY LIGHT OF SOUTH STACK

The sea swirls around the rocky island of South Stack (right), crowned by a lighthouse that has flashed warnings to shipping for 170 years. To reach the tower, keepers and visitors descend 400 steps carved in the cliff face of the mainland, then cross a suspension bridge over a 90 ft wide gorge. Before the bridge was built in 1828, keepers crossed in a basket suspended from a cable.

PRECISION MACHINERY *Apparatus installed in 1909 rotates the six-sided lighthouse lens once a minute, so that it flashes a light every ten seconds.*

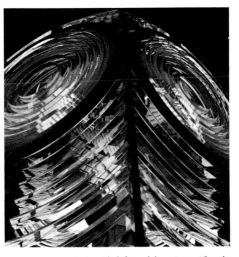

MIGHTY LENS *A six-sided fresnel lens intensifies the light of an electric bulb in the tower to 2½ million candlepower. The lens, installed in 1909, is 9 ft high and casts a beam for 20 miles.*

Stanton Drew *Avon*   *Map: 397 Fe*
STONE CIRCLES The three circles date from the early Bronze Age (*c.* 2000–1600 BC). The largest has 27 of its original stones and is about 360 ft across. South-west of it is a circle of 12 stones, and north lies a circle of eight stones. The central and northern circles each have an avenue leading to the river. Near by is a "cove", a three-sided enclosure similar to one at Avebury, Wiltshire.

Local legend claims that the monuments represent a wedding party who were turned to stone for continuing their revelry into Sunday morning. The "cove" represents the parson, the bride and the groom.
Location: 7½ miles S of Bristol (A37, and then B3130).

Stanton Moor *Derbys.*   *Map: 394 Bb*
NINE LADIES STONE CIRCLE In about 1600 BC Bronze Age man raised a large number of stone monuments over 150 acres of the moor. They include more than 70 round burial cairns. Those excavated have revealed cremation urns and miniature cups, knives and daggers for use in the after life. There are also stone circles and isolated standing stones. The main concentration of monuments is west of the road between Stanton Lees and Stanton in Peak.
Location: 4½ miles NW of Matlock (A6, B5057, then minor roads).

Stanwick *N. Yorks.*   *Map: 391 Fc*
FORTIFICATIONS The defences were built by the Brigantes tribe between about AD 50 and 70. The original enclosure of 17 acres protected by a bank and ditch was eventually extended to 750 acres by the addition of another, stone-faced bank and a 15 ft deep ditch. But the fortifications were incomplete when they were successfully stormed by the Romans about AD 70.
Location: 7 miles N of Richmond on B6274. The fort lies east and west of the road.

Stapleford Park *Leics.*   *Map: 394 Ca*
A Tudor mansion of 1500, restored in 1633, when biblical, historical and mythical sculptures were added to the exterior. The building was extended later in the century and in Victorian times. It contains paintings, tapestries and a fine collection of Victorian Staffordshire pottery portrait figures.

In 1846 Lord Harborough, the owner, succeeded in having the Midland Railway diverted from the estate. Ironically, the present owner, Lord Gretton, is a railway enthusiast who has built a 10¼ in. gauge passenger-carrying miniature railway through the grounds
Location: 5 miles E of Melton Mowbray off B676.

Start Point Lighthouse *Devon*   *Map: 397 Da*
The 92 ft high granite tower, built in 1836, stands at the tip of Start Point headland. The light is 200 ft above sea level and can be seen for 25 miles in clear weather.
Location: 9½ miles SE of Kingsbridge (A379 to Chillington, then minor roads).

Stawley *Somerset*   *Map: 397 Ed*
CHURCH OF ST MICHAEL A Norman church, enlarged during the Gothic period. The south door, with its original iron hinges, has been in use since the 13th century. Most of the furnishings were replaced in the 18th century, and the interior, with its box-pews and high pulpit with dome-like canopy, gives a good idea of what many parish churches were like until they were restored by the Victorians.

Over the west door is an early-16th-century inscription inviting prayer for the souls of a former parishioner and his wife.
Location: 5 miles S of Wiveliscombe (A361 then minor roads).

Steeple Ashton *Wilts.*   *Map: 398 Ac*
CHURCH OF ST MARY THE VIRGIN The impressive west tower of this mainly 15th-century church was crowned by a 93 ft spire until 1670, when lightning struck it. Stone lierne vaults (vaults with short ribs connecting the main ribs) roof the north and south aisles–a rare feature in a parish church. The vicar's library, in a room above the south porch, includes a 15th-century Latin Book of Hours, an illustrated book of prayers for fixed times of the day.
Location: 4½ miles S of Melksham (A350 then minor road)

Stevington *Beds.*   *Map: 398 Ce*
WINDMILL The four sails of the mill, which was built in 1770 and restored in 1951, turned two pairs of millstones on the upper floor. These ground grain into meal, which was stored in bins on the lower floor. The miller ground the villagers' own grain, retaining a proportion as a charge.
Location: 7 miles NW of Bedford (A428 then minor roads).

Stewkley *Bucks.*   *Map: 398 Cd*
CHURCH OF ST MICHAEL AND ALL ANGELS Few Norman churches in England have survived with so little alteration to their original appearance. The long, high, narrow interior of the 12th-century church consists of a nave, central space and chancel, and is an example of the final stage in church development before aisles were added to accommodate more worshippers.

The arches of the central space are enriched with bird-beak and zigzag mouldings that are among the finest examples of late Norman carving in the country. There is similar work around the door and windows of the west front.
Location: 12½ miles SE of Buckingham (A413 then B4032).

Steyning *W. Sussex*   *Map: 398 Db*
CHURCH OF ST ANDREW The fine 12th-century Norman nave gives some indication of the splendour of the original, much larger church. The carved marble font also dates from this period. The chancel, transepts and tower were replaced in the late 16th century.

The father of King Alfred was buried in an earlier church on the site in 857.
Location: 5 miles NW of Shoreham on A283.

Sticklepath *Devon*   *Map: 396 Dc*
FINCH FOUNDRY An early-19th-century foundry in which iron was forged into steel to make agricultural and mining tools for the surrounding district. It remains in working order. (See opposite.)
Location: 3½ miles E of Okehampton on A30.

Forging tools for Devon's farmers

FOR 150 YEARS, THE FINCH FOUNDRY AT STICKLEPATH HARNESSED THE WATERS OF
THE RIVER TAW TO MAKE HAND TOOLS FOR MINING AND AGRICULTURE

In 1814 an iron founder called William Finch took over the lease of a water-powered cloth mill at Sticklepath in Devon, converting it into a workshop to make farm and mining tools. The venture was successful, and in 1835 Finch rented a second local watermill. This he turned into a grinding house, where cutting tools such as scythes and hooks were given their edge.

The business flourished for nearly 150 years, and William Finch's descendants were connected with it throughout that time. It employed about 20 craftsmen, who between them could turn out 400 hoes a day together with other tools.

In 1960 the business closed and now the site is preserved as an industrial museum.

An overshot water-wheel, 12 ft in diameter and driven by water channelled from the River Taw, supplied power to the forge, where the main part of the manufacturing process took place. The wheel worked the heavy shears, on which bar steel was cut, and the trip hammers,

which beat the metal into the approximate shape required before they were hand-finished by a smith.

A second water-wheel powered the grindstone in the grinding house, and a third pumped air to the hearths in the tool smithy.

Wood for tool handles was cut in a sawmill, now gone, and then hand-shaped with spokeshaves and planes in the joiner's shop before being attached to the steel blade.

SHARPENING
Workmen sharpened hooks and scythes while lying on a narrow platform above the grindstone. They had little protection against dangerous flying fragments.

HAMMERS DRIVEN BY WATER

Three water-wheels supplied the power to work the machinery in the Finch Foundry. The largest (above left) is 12 ft in diameter and has 48 elm buckets fixed between its iron rims. A channel called a leat brings water to the wheels. Two trip hammers (above right), linked to a water-wheel, beat heated steel into tools. *The hammer heads, and the anvil tops beneath, were moulded to the shape required, and could be changed to suit the type of tool which was being made at any time.*

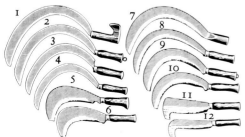

THE PRODUCTS *The Finch Foundry made or distributed dozens of different tools and implements, from axes to mole traps. It offered an astonishing number of varieties of each tool, such as 12 kinds of hook.*

1. *Reap hook*
2. *Rib trimming hook*
3. *Crank grass hook*
4. *Straight grass hook*
5. *Half turn hook, knob handle*
6. *Half turn hook, plain handle*
7. *Staff hook*
8. *Bramble hook*
9. *Browse hook*
10. *Straight browse hook*
11. *Bill hook*
12. *Spear hook*

Stirling *Central*   *Map: 388 De*
CASTLE In the 13th and 14th centuries the fortress–on a great crag overlooking Stirling
–symbolised Scottish military resistance to
England. During the wars between the two
countries it changed hands several times until in
1314, after the Battle of Bannockburn, Robert
Bruce won and kept it for Scotland.

The present structure dates from the 15th to
the 18th centuries. Its military importance never
diminished, even after the Union of the Scottish
and English crowns in 1603. Cromwell successfully besieged it in 1651 during his Scottish
campaign, and Bonnie Prince Charlie's Highlanders tried in vain to take it in 1746 from a
garrison commanded by General Blakeney.
Location: Upper Castle Hill, NW of town centre.

SKILLS OF THE BOAT PEOPLE

*The Waterways Museum at Stoke Bruerne brings
back the life led by those who worked Britain's canals
and rivers in their heyday. The exhibits include the
cabin of a canal narrow boat and the costumes worn by
boatmen and their wives.*

HORSE'S BONNET *The
horses that pulled canal
boats wore crocheted
bonnets to keep flies out of
their eyes.*

BOAT WOMAN'S
BONNET *Crocheted
bonnets, trimmed with
lace, were also worn by
boatmen's wives–as part
of their traditional costume,
and as protection from the sun.*

CHURCH OF THE HOLY RUDE In this fine medieval
church the infant James VI (later James I of
England) was crowned King of Scotland in 1567.
Location: St John St, town centre.
GUILDHALL (COWANE'S HOSPITAL) On his death-
bed John Cowane (1570–1633), Dean of Stirling's Merchant Guildry, bequeathed his money
to the guild for the building of a hospice for
members in need. By 1700, however, conditions
for a place in Cowane's Hospital, as it was called,
became so restrictive that it ceased to be used as
a hospice. It became, and remains, a guildhall–a
meeting place for merchant guilds.
Location: Off St John St, town centre.

Stockton-on-Tees *Cleveland*   *Map: 391 Gd*
CHURCH OF ST THOMAS Sir Christopher Wren,
architect of St Paul's Cathedral, may have been
the designer of the church, which was completed
in 1712. It has a fine Georgian pulpit.
Location: High St, town centre.

Stogursey *Somerset*   *Map: 397 Ed*
CHURCH OF ST ANDREW The parish church and a
neighbouring dovecot are all that survive of a
Benedictine priory founded about 1100. The
church, enlarged in succeeding centuries, pos-
sesses a Norman font, 16th-century bench-ends
and several monuments, including one of the
14th century.
Location: 8 miles NW of Bridgwater (A39, then
minor road).

Stoke Bruerne *Northants.*   *Map: 398 Ce*
WATERWAYS MUSEUM Boatmen's equipment,
photographs and other exhibits tell the story of
Britain's inland waterways in a museum that
stands beside the main line of the Grand Union
Canal. The warehouse containing the museum is
part of a village that developed and prospered
after the canal was completed in 1805.
Location: 7 miles S of Northampton (A508 then
minor road).

Stoke Charity *Hants.*   *Map: 398 Bb*
CHURCH OF ST MARY AND ST MICHAEL The lonely,
attractive small church stands in the middle of a
field. Part of the north aisle was probably the
original Saxon church. The Normans built on to
the south of this. The interior contains medieval
items–a font, brasses, stained glass and a fine
carving of the Mass of St Gregory.
Location: 6½ miles N of Winchester (A33 then
minor road).

Stoke d'Abernon *Surrey*   *Map: 398 Dc*
CHURCH OF ST MARY The south wall of the
original 7th-century church survives. It incorporates Roman brickwork and includes a doorway that is the earliest known trace of a Saxon
lord's gallery. St Mary's also contains the oldest
brass in England–to Sir John D'Abernon who
died in 1277.

There is much fine medieval stained glass, a
13th-century mural and a 15th-century Flemish
altar painting. The 17th-century pulpit of English walnut still has its sounding board and tester,
and on the wall beside it is a wrought-iron hour
glass used to time the lengthy sermons of early
post-Reformation days.
Location: 3 miles NW of Leatherhead (A245
then Manor House Drive).

Stoke-on-Trent *Staffs.* *Map: 393 Fe*
STOKE STATION The station, designed in 1848 for the North Staffordshire Railway Company, is an imposing example of the neo-Jacobean style the Victorians sometimes used for public buildings. It stands in a square, and the former railway hotel opposite, and other buildings, were built in the same style as the station, to harmonise with it. Outside the hotel stands a statue to the celebrated Staffordshire potter Josiah Wedgwood (1730–95).
Location: Winton Sq., E of town centre.

Stoke Poges *Bucks.* *Map: 398 Cc*
CHURCH OF ST GILES In the north wall of the mainly 13th-century church there is a private entrance from the nearby Manor House.
A monument erected in 1799 to the poet Thomas Gray (1716–71) stands in the meadow next to the churchyard where in 1750 he finished writing his celebrated *Elegy Written in a Country Churchyard*. He is believed to have been inspired to write the poem as he sat beneath the yew tree by the south-west door of the church. Gray is buried in the same tomb as his mother and aunt

outside the east window of the south chapel.
Location: 3 miles N of Slough off B416.

Stokesay Castle *Salop* *Map: 393 Ed*
The best preserved as well as one of the oldest fortified manor houses in England. Stoke is derived from an Anglo-Saxon word meaning place, secondary settlement or farm, and de Say was the name of the Norman family who built the original domestic buildings in the 13th century, around an existing Saxon hall.
A rich wool merchant, Lawrence of Ludlow, bought the property about 1281 and it was held by his descendants for more than 300 years. The banqueting hall of about 1285 still has some original beams, blackened by smoke from the central hearth. Lawrence fortified the manor between 1291 and 1305 by adding the south tower and an outer wall, which has almost disappeared, and surrounding it with a moat.
Parliament laid siege to the castle during the Civil War, but the owner, Lord Craven, anxious to preserve the house, surrendered, and it survived almost intact.
Location: 7 miles NW of Ludlow off A49.

LAWRENCE'S "CASTLE"

Stokesay Castle is actually a medieval manor house fortified by a wool merchant, Lawrence of Ludlow, between 1291 and 1305.

GATEHOUSE *The timber of the Elizabethan building is decorated with carvings of religious subjects.*

OVERMANTEL *The elaborately carved Flemish oak frieze surmounts a stone fireplace in the solar (a private room in a medieval house). It was sent to Stokesay in 1648 by Lord Craven, who then owned the castle.*

GREAT HALL *Arching roof timbers look down from a height of 34 ft on the 13th-century hall where the entire household ate and the servants slept.*

Stone *Kent*   *Map: 399 Ec*
CHURCH OF ST MARY The interior of the 13th-century Gothic church makes it one of the architectural splendours of Kent. The capitals of the clustered columns in the nave are decorated with superbly carved foliage, and the spandrels (the triangular spaces between arches) in the large chancel are also richly carved. The similarity of the work to that of the same period at Westminster Abbey has led to the theory that the same masons were responsible for both.
Location: 2½ miles E of Dartford on A226.

Stonehaven *Grampian*   *Map: 387 Fb*
TOLBOOTH MUSEUM The 16th-century tolbooth is the oldest building now standing in Stonehaven. It was built as a storehouse for nearby Dunnottar Castle and later became a court and prison. Since 1963 it has housed a museum of Stonehaven's fishing industry and local history.
Location: 15 miles S of Aberdeen on A92.

Stonehenge *Wilts.*   *Map: 398 Ab*
The original purpose of Britain's most celebrated prehistoric monument, a complex of vast stones erected on Salisbury Plain between about 2750 and 1300 BC, remains a mystery. One suggestion, that it was a huge open-air observatory, is based on the alignment of stones with the midsummer sunrise and midwinter moonrise and of other stones with lunar sightings.
The first stage of building, about 2750–2000 BC, was the work of Late Stone Age men. They dug a circular ditch and raised a bank behind it. These still enclose the site. Just inside the bank they dug a ring of 56 pits (known as the Aubrey Holes after their 17th-century discoverer John Aubrey). Outside the entry to the enclosure they erected a leaning stone called the Heel Stone.
The second phase, about 2000–1700 BC, was probably carried out by copper-working Beaker People, who had colonised Britain from the Continent. They built a 2 mile long avenue to link the circle with the River Avon and erected

a double ring of 80 bluestones in the centre of the enclosure. These blue-coloured rocks were brought to the avenue entrance on the Avon from the Prescelly Mountains of south-west Wales (a journey of 240 miles), probably on rafts and boats.
The third phase began about 1700 BC. Early Bronze Age men replaced the bluestones with 80 sarsens – blocks of sandstone dragged from Avebury, 20 miles away. With these they constructed a circle of upright stones topped by lintels. Inside this they erected trilithons – pairs of 50 ton uprights, each pair capped by a lintel – arranged in a horseshoe pattern.
These great sarsens were probably raised with wooden levers and rollers and thong ropes, and the lintels raised on a timber platform that was gradually heightened. Mortise-and-tenon joints cut in the stone ensured that the lintels were firmly joined to the uprights. During this period, some bluestones were returned to the centre of the circle.
Finally, about 1300 BC, a circle of bluestones was erected between the sarsen ring and horseshoe. (Also see p. 372.)
Location: 8½ miles N of Salisbury (A360 then E on A303).

Stony Littleton *Avon*   *Map: 397 Gd*
LONG BARROW This Stone Age burial mound is one of the best preserved in Britain. A passage into it leads into a gallery, off which open six side chambers and an end chamber. The barrow was pillaged in about 1760 and excavated as early as 1816. Its contents disappeared, but it is known that some of the bones in it were charred. This hints at the possibility of cremation – not known elsewhere in the south-west at this period.
Location: 5½ miles S of Bath (A367, then minor roads via Wellow).

Stourhead *Wilts.*   *Map: 397 Gd*
The sumptuous interior of this Palladian house was completed in 1722 for the banker Henry Hoare. His son Henry created the lakeside gardens later in the century; they are among the most celebrated in Europe. Their vistas of water, classical temples, trees and statues were inspired by the second Henry's travels in Italy and admiration for the French painters Poussin and Claude. Rhododendrons and rare shrubs and trees planted in the 19th century enhance the beauty of the gardens.
Location: 3 miles NW of Mere off B3092.

Stourport-on-Severn *Heref.*   *Map: 393 Fc*
CANAL BASIN Stourport is the only town in Britain that was built specifically to serve a canal. It was begun when the Staffordshire and Worcestershire Canal was built, between 1766 and 1772, and it lies at the point where the waterway joins the River Severn. The canal basin is still busy with craft. Two sets of locks connect it with the river; the narrower ones were built for canal barges, the wider for the broad river boats known as Severn Trows. Trows may date back to Anglo-Saxon times and may have been based on wrecked Viking ships left in the Severn after an attack on Worcester in AD 890. Their name is a corruption of the Anglo-Saxon *trog*.
Location: The basin is ½ mile S of the town centre.

ELEGANT CANAL SIDE

Graceful Georgian buildings rise beyond one of the barge locks at Stourport canal basin. They were built at the same time as the canal, in the late 18th century. The long red brick Tontine Hotel accommodated visiting traders. The customs warehouse to the far left is topped by an attractive clock tower.

PREHISTORIC ASTRONOMY

Dawn lights up the most impressive megalithic monument in Europe, the great circles of stones on Salisbury Plain known as Stonehenge.

The monument was built in three distinct phases from 2750 BC onwards, the first two phases including astronomical alignments. The Heel Stone, erected during the first phase, stands on the axis of sunrise at the summer solstice, the longest day of the year. Erected beyond the Heel Stone at the same time were 40 posts coinciding with the axis of moonrise at winter solstice, the shortest day of the year. The moon's position on this day changes from year to year over a cycle of 18.61 years, and the posts marked all the positions. The four Station Stones on the outer circle of the enclosure stand at the intersections of lunar sight-lines.

A double circle of bluestones was started on during the second phase, which began about 2000 BC. Eight stones in this circle and two stones in the centre of the avenue marked the line of sunrise at summer solstice more clearly. The final phase of building, started a century later, was monumental and symbolic and apparently had no astronomical function.

STONEHENGE I *Stones and posts marked the rising and setting of sun and moon at summer and winter solstices.*

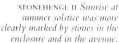

STONEHENGE II *Sunrise at summer solstice was more clearly marked by stones in the enclosure and in the avenue.*

STONEHENGE IIIA AND IIIB *The central bluestones were removed and replaced by trilithons—two uprights topped by a lintel—surrounded by sarsen stones.*

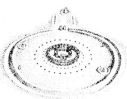

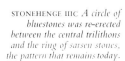

STONEHENGE IIIC *A circle of bluestones was re-erected between the central trilithons and the ring of sarsen stones, the pattern that remains today.*

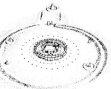

Stow *Lincs.* *Map: 394 Cc*
CHURCH OF ST MARY The Norman bishop Remigius of Lincoln began rebuilding the original Saxon church in the late 11th century after it had fallen into ruins. However, its outstanding feature remains the massive Saxon crossing arches, which are 30 ft high. In the north transept are the remains of a 13th-century wall painting of St Thomas Becket.
Location: 7½ miles SE of Gainsborough (A156, B1241).

Stow Bardolph *Norfolk* *Map: 395 Ea*
CHURCH OF THE HOLY TRINITY A 17th-century chapel containing monuments to the local Hare family is the chief interest of this Norman church, which has been successively enlarged. The monuments include one in alabaster to Sir Ralph Hare (*d.* 1623) and an unusual one in wax to Sarah Hare (*d.* 1744).
Location: 2 miles N of Downham Market on A10.

Stowe Nine Churches *Northants.* *Map: 398 Ce*
CHURCH OF ST MICHAEL Two monuments make St Michael's well worth a visit. One, to Lady Carey, was carved during her lifetime, in the early 17th century, and is a masterly portrait by the sculptor Nicholas Stone. The other is an 18th-century monument to Dr Thomas Turner, President of Corpus Christi College, Oxford, whose life-size effigy stands on two globes. The church retains its original Saxon west tower.
Location: Church Stowe, 7 miles NW of Towcester off A5.

Stowmarket *Suffolk* *Map: 399 Fe*
MUSEUM OF EAST ANGLIAN LIFE Saddle-making, barrel-making, old methods of cultivation and other activities at this open-air museum vividly recreate rural life of the past in East Anglia, an area that has been called the Granary of England.
The museum stands on land attached to Abbot's Hall, the medieval manor house of Stowmarket, and the hub of the museum is the Hall's tithe barn dating from the 13th century. A storm of 1968 brought down 60 ft of the barn's original 160 ft, but it is still an impressive structure. It now houses old carts, ploughs and other large pieces of agricultural equipment.
The Wagon Room contains a collection of large horse-drawn wagons and a reconstructed 19th-century wheelwright's shop. Exhibits in nearby buildings include a rare set of harness-maker's tools, agricultural hand implements dating back through the centuries, and mussel-fishing tackle used along the East Anglian coast.
Among the open-air exhibits are two farm-workers' cottages. They were originally built as one dwelling, at the beginning of the 18th century, but were later converted. The interior of one has been left exactly as it was during the occupancy of the last tenant from 1935 to 1975. The other cottage has been furnished as it would have been in the last century.
The cottages stand on their original site, but the other buildings on show come from surrounding villages and have been re-erected at the museum. Alton Mill is an 18th-century water-mill transferred from a site near Ipswich, together with the miller's house and his cart lodge, where he also stored his flour. A mill-pond is being

constructed, and the mill will again grind corn.
Edgar's Farmhouse is a 14th-century aisled hall from Combs, south of Stowmarket. It was probably the home of the Adgors, a Combs family of yeoman farmers. One of its bays is now equipped as a classroom of the 1920s. There is also an 18th-century smithy from Grundisburgh, north-east of Ipswich.
All these exhibits stand in 76 acres of farmland. A tenant farmer works some of the land, and ploughs, sows and harvests 1 acre by traditional methods. These activities take place on Saturdays, for the benefit of visitors.
The saddle-making and barrel-making are demonstrated during summer weekends, along with butter and cheese-making, bee-keeping, weaving, spinning, wheel-making and shoeing horses.
Location: 12¼ miles NW of Ipswich on A45.

Stratfield Saye *Hants.* *Map: 398 Cc*
Parliament bought 17th-century Stratfield Saye House for the Duke of Wellington in 1817, on behalf of the nation. The embroidered tricolour banners that hang in the hall were given to the victor of Waterloo after his entry into Paris in 1815. Roman mosaic pavements are set into the floor of the hall. They were excavated by the second duke in 1866 at nearby Silchester.
Two unusual features of the house are central heating dating back to the 1840s and still partly in use, and prints stuck directly to the wallpaper and almost covering the walls of several rooms. Both were introduced by the first duke himself.
A case in the library contains a lock of hair from the mane of the duke's favourite charger, Copenhagen, which he rode all day at the Battle of Waterloo. A headstone marks the horse's grave in the grounds. An exhibition in the stable block tells the story of Wellington's life.
Location: 9 miles S of Reading (A33, then minor roads).

Stratford-upon-Avon *Warks.* *Map: 398 Ae*
CHURCH OF THE HOLY TRINITY In the chancel are the graves of William Shakespeare, his wife Anne Hathaway and other members of his family. There is also a monument to the playwright, a photostat of the register recording his baptism in 1564 and his burial in 1616, and a font in which he was probably baptised.
Location: Old Town, river bank.
HALL'S CROFT A fine Tudor house that from 1607 to 1616 was the home of Shakespeare's daughter Susanna and her doctor-husband John Hall. Among the items on display is a patient's note to the doctor.
Location: Old Town, S of town centre.
HARVARD HOUSE This tall, gabled Tudor house with its richly carved frontage was the birthplace of John Harvard (1607–38), after whom America's oldest university was named. Harvard, who became a Puritan minister in America, bequeathed half his estate to the university, which was founded two years before his death. An American bought the house in 1909 and gave it to Harvard University, which still owns it.
Location: High St, town centre.
NEW PLACE Only the foundations survive of the house where Shakespeare lived from 1610, when he retired from London, until his death in 1616. The adjoining Knot Garden is a reconstruction of

COUNTRY LIFE IN EAST ANGLIA

The open-air Museum of East Anglian Life at Stowmarket, Suffolk, recaptures a rural working life that has long since vanished. Visitors can, for example, watch a blacksmith shoeing horses with the equipment of an 18th-century smithy (above), transferred from Grundisburgh village, 20 miles away.

FARM WAGON *Each district of England had its own traditional size, shape and colour for farm wagons. The East Anglian wagon was built to carry heavy loads of wheat and had a large, high body that curved up fore and aft. The bodywork was generally painted blue and the underframe red.*

MUSSEL-FISHING BOAT *Some East Anglian fishermen still cultivate mussels in the creeks of north Norfolk by traditional methods. They sow beds with seed mussels and harvest them in nets.*

SHEEP-DIP CART *After dipping immersion in a trough of disinfectant as a protection against skin disease – the sheep ran up into the cart to dry, and disinfectant drained into the trough.*

the kind of garden New Place would have possessed, and near by grows a descendant of a mulberry tree beneath which Shakespeare sat. Location: Chapel St, town centre.
SHAKESPEARE'S BIRTHPLACE In Shakespeare's time the early-16th-century, half-timbered house was two buildings. John Shakespeare, William's father, bought the property in 1556 and used one building for his glove-making and wool-dealing business and the other as the family home. Visitors can see the bedroom where the dramatist was born in 1564 and the desk at which he was probably given his first lessons.
Location: Henley St, town centre.

Stretham *Cambs.*   *Map: 399 Ef*
BEAM PUMPING ENGINE The engine was built in 1831 for fen drainage and is the only surviving example of its kind. Steam power drove its great steel beam up and down and this turned a shaft,

which in turn rotated a 37 ft wide scoop wheel. At each revolution the wheel lifted about 30 tons of water into a dike 12 ft above. It was replaced by a diesel engine in 1925.
Location: 3½ miles SW of Ely off A10.

Stretton *Staffs.* Map: 393 Fd
AQUEDUCT This short cast-iron structure was built in 1832 to carry the Shropshire Union Canal across the Holyhead Road (now the A5). A plaque in the centre commemorates the fact that Thomas Telford (1757–1834) built both canal and road.
Location: 10 miles SW of Stafford (A449, then A5).

Strumble Head *Dyfed* Map: 392 Ac
LIGHTHOUSE The tower occupies a lonely position on one of several small rocky islands just off the cliffs of Strumble Head. It was built in 1908 to protect ships entering Fishguard harbour. A footbridge connects the island to the mainland.
Location: 6 miles NW of Fishguard (A40, then minor roads, then footpath).

Studland *Dorset* Map: 397 Gc
CHURCH OF ST NICHOLAS The fabric of the church is almost completely Norman. Outstanding are the massive arches beneath the unfinished tower. Below the eaves of the nave are carvings of grotesque human and animal heads.
Location: 3 miles N of Swanage (minor road, then E on B3351).

Styal *Cheshire* Map: 393 Ff
QUARRY BANK MILL Samuel Greg, the son of a Belfast shipowner, opened Quarry Bank cotton-spinning mill on the banks of the River Bollin at Styal in 1784. He had inherited a textile business from his mother's family, the Hydes of Manchester, and decided to launch out into the rapidly developing cotton trade.
Styal was a rural area with a small population, so he had to bring in his workers. The community he built for them, and watched over with a fatherly eye, is today one of the best-surviving examples of a rural factory colony of the early days of the cotton industry. Greg supplied everything – homes, shop, chapel, school, a farm with fresh dairy produce for sale, and a village pub where no one was allowed to drink more than two glasses of beer.
Life was hard for the mill workers, and wages low. In 1790 a doffer who changed the bobbins on the machines earned about 1s 6d a week, an overlooker in the carding room about 15s. But many of the families had come from the Poor Houses of southern England, where increasing enclosure of land was leaving many people without a livelihood. In Styal, a village in lovely surroundings, they had sturdy homes, gardens, credit for small amounts in the local shop, and community life. So most chose conditions at Styal rather than the higher wages and slums of nearby Manchester.
By the 1790s about 260 people worked at the mill, about 80 of them apprentices – children of nine years and over who lived under the care of a master and mistress in the Apprentice House in Holt's Lane (now a private house).
Some apprentices came from Poor Houses and worked in return for housing, food and clothing. Others were engaged under a contract made with their parents and were housed and fed and given a small weekly wage.
The apprentices slept two to a bed and had clean sheets once a month. Their working day began at 6 a.m. and ended at 7 p.m., with a ten-minute break for breakfast, brought to them at the mill, and usually half-an-hour for lunch. Sometimes they worked overtime, for which they were paid about one penny an hour. On Sundays they went to chapel in the morning and school in the afternoon, the teachers including Samuel Greg's own children.
Breakfast and supper were mainly porridge or milk and bread, and the midday meal usually stew or bacon and potatoes, sometimes pork, with fresh vegetables in season. A number of apprentices ran away and were prosecuted, but, from their statements, the reason was not usually the conditions but because they were homesick for their mothers. About 2,000 children were apprentices at Quarry Bank in the 60 years or so that the system lasted. It was ended in 1847.
Samuel Greg's cotton business became one of the largest in the land. Quarry Bank Mill, one of four he built, went over to power-loom weaving in 1834, and continued in production until the 1920s, run by Greg's descendants and many of those of his original workers at Styal. Today it is a textile machinery museum.
Location: 1 mile N of Wilmslow (A34, B5166).

Sudbury *Suffolk* Map: 399 Fe
GAINSBOROUGH'S HOUSE Thomas Gainsborough (1727–88) ranks among the finest of England's portrait and landscape painters. The house in which he was born in 1727 was Tudor, but in 1723 his cloth-merchant father had added an elegant Georgian façade. The house contains many of Gainsborough's pictures, some of his belongings, contemporary prints and furnishings and a gallery for temporary art exhibitions.
Location: Gainsborough St, town centre.

Sudbury Hall *Derbys.* Map: 393 Ge
The Hall is the most richly decorated of Stuart country houses. It remained the property of the Vernon family, for whom it was built in the mid-17th century, until 1967. An outstanding feature of the house is the Great Staircase, with its ornate plasterwork, and ceiling paintings.
Location: 9½ miles NW of Burton upon Trent off A50.

Sudeley Castle *Glos.* Map: 393 Fb
Sir Thomas Seymour (1508–49), Lord Seymour of Sudeley, was the most celebrated owner of the castle, begun in the 15th century. Seymour was the lover of Catherine Parr (1512–48), sixth wife of Henry VIII, and in 1547 married her after the king's death. Two years later he was executed for treason. Catherine is buried in the castle chapel.
Location: 8 miles NE of Cheltenham off A46.

Sueno's Stone *Grampian* Map: 387 Ec
The original purpose of this 9th or 10th-century stone is unknown, but the carvings on its four 20 ft high faces may commemorate a military victory; they show scenes of combat and a procession.
Location: 1 mile NE of Forres off A96.

DRIVING FORCE AT STYAL

In 1818 driving wheels and shafts at Quarry Bank Mill were turned by a 32 ft water-wheel. Samuel Greg and his workers dug a ¾ mile tunnel to channel extra water. Turbines replaced the wheel in 1903.

QUARRY BANK MILL *The red-brick mill is topped by a bell-cote – the factory bell was the workers' only timepiece, for few could afford a clock or watch. Originally the mill had four storeys. Later a fifth storey was added.*

MANAGER'S OFFICE *The day-to-day running of Quarry Bank Mill took place from this office. At least two managers began at the mill as apprentices.*

341

Treasures of a ship-burial

TO COMMEMORATE A 7TH-CENTURY EAST ANGLIAN KING, AN 89 FT SHIP WAS
BURIED IN THE SANDS AT SUTTON HOO, LADEN WITH PRICELESS GOODS

At Sutton Hoo, in Suffolk, there are ten or so barrows—earth mounds—marking the site of a Saxon burial ground. The contents of one, excavated in 1939, constitute the most spectacular archaeological find made in the British Isles. It contained the outline of a large vessel for 40 oarsmen, together with priceless utensils, weapons and other "grave goods".

The burial may have been made in honour of King Anna, who died in AD 654. Coin evidence suggests an even earlier date—in AD 630 when King Raedwald died. It certainly commemorates some member of the Wuffings royal family who settled in East Anglia from Sweden in the late 5th century. Most of the finds are now in the British Museum—a few in Ipswich Museum.

THE SHIP'S SKELETON—1,300 YEARS AFTER IT WAS BURIED

The magnificent ship at Sutton Hoo was 89 ft long and 14 ft wide, with a depth amidships of 4 ft 6 in. The construction can still be seen: a clinker-built hull, stiffened with 26 ribs and secured with wooden pegs and iron bolts.

The central portion had a burial chamber 14 ft long, in which 41 gold objects were found, including a belt buckle, two shoulder clasps, sword mounts and a purse lid: all made by a Scandinavian goldsmith in East Anglia. There were also a sword, shield and a helmet, thought to have been Scandinavian heirlooms brought by the new settlers.

Chemical analysis of the burial remains suggests that a body may have been included as well, but this cannot be proved.

THE SHIP UNDER SAIL *The ship is believed to have used sail when there were following winds. At other times it was driven by 40 oarsmen, with a large steering oar, or rudder, over the starboard side, near the stern. The steersman is thought to have stood on a platform, where part of the ship's side appears to have been reinforced. The ship is one of the most important finds from Anglo-Saxon Britain.*

Sunderland *Tyne & Wear*   *Map: 391 Ge*
MONKWEARMOUTH STATION MUSEUM The railway station itself is the main exhibit of the museum, which traces the development of land transport in north-east England. The station, opened in 1848 as part of the York, Newcastle and Berwick Railway and closed in 1967, is an outstanding example of the style known as Victorian neo-classicism. The booking office has been restored to its Edwardian appearance, complete with models of passengers at the ticket windows. Galleries display cycles dating back to Victorian times, and photographs and models of old trams and buses.
Location: North Bridge St (A19), N of town.

CHURCH OF ST PETER A monastery was founded on the bank of the Wear in 675 and, together with neighbouring Jarrow, became a centre of art and learning by the 8th century. Part of the early church survives.
Location: St Peter's Way, Sunderland.

Sutton Hoo *Suffolk*   *Map: 399 Ge*
The largest of a group of 7th-century barrows—or burial mounds—was excavated at Sutton Hoo in 1939, revealing one of the richest archaeological finds in Britain—an 89 ft long burial ship, with priceless contents. It commemorates a king of the Swedish Wuffings dynasty which settled in East Anglia in the late 5th century. (See above.)

THE LAST VOYAGE

Money, weapons, utensils and priceless personal ornaments were buried with the Sutton Hoo ship, symbolising the journey to the next world of the dead person – in this case an East Anglian king.

WOODEN BUCKET
A reconstruction of an iron-bound wooden tub found at Sutton Hoo. There were three buckets on the ship. The one shown is about 14 in. high and 14 in. wide. It was thought to have been used to hold wine or ale, from which drinking vessels could be filled. Alternatively, it contained food.

GILDED-BRONZE HELMET *A replica of the Sutton Hoo helmet, based upon fragments found in the ship. The helmet was probably worn by a warrior king.*

GERMAN "ROUND LYRE"
A reconstruction (right) of the Sutton Hoo lyre. Fragments of the six-stringed instrument, made of maplewood with pegs of poplar or willow, relate to contemporary lyres found in German graves at Württemberg and Cologne.

TRIPOD LAMP *A rusted iron lamp found at Sutton Hoo. The inside has traces of beeswax that was originally used as fuel.*

DRINKING VESSELS
Reconstructed horns (above) have traces of original silver-gilt mouthpieces found at Sutton Hoo. The original horns came from the auroch – an extinct bull-like animal.
A bottle (left) was similarly decorated. The maplewood sphere is a reconstruction.

Location: 9 miles NE of Ipswich (A12, A1152, B1083). The site is reached by a track off the right-hand side of the B1083.

Sutton Park *N. Yorks.*   *Map: 391 Gb*
An outstanding early Georgian house built in 1730. The three-storey central section overlooks fine terraced gardens. Inside there is furniture by Chippendale and Sheraton.
Location: 8 miles N of York on B1363.

Swansea Castle *W. Glam.*   *Map: 392 Ca*
The outer wall and a round tower are all that remain of the 14th-century manor house built for Bishop Henry Gower. The wall has an arcaded parapet – unusual for a military building.
Location: Castle St, E of city centre.

Swanton Mill *Kent*   *Map: 399 Fb*
The machinery of this largely 17th and 18th-century watermill has been restored, and visitors can sometimes watch it grinding wheat.
Location: 3 miles SE of Ashford (A20, then minor road through Mersham to South Stour).

Sween Castle *Strathclyde*   *Map: 388 Ad*
The ruined castle, on a rocky promontory overlooking Loch Sween, is probably the oldest medieval stone fortress in Scotland. It was built in the late 11th century, or the early 12th,

THE DAYS OF STEAM

At the GWR Museum, Swindon, the railway lover can browse among locomotives like the North Star of 1837 and 19th-century track equipment.

INSTRUMENTS *The horn was used by track lookouts, the truncheon by railway police.*

TOKEN *Engine-drivers needed a token to enter single track.*

probably by Normans. It was destroyed during the Civil War by the Royalists.
Location: 8 miles SW of Lochgilphead (A816 NW, B841, B8025 S then minor road beside loch).

Sweetheart Abbey *Dumfs.* Map: 390 Ce
The ruined abbey church was founded in 1273 by the wife of John Balliol of Barnard Castle. On his death, she kept his heart in an ivory casket, and when she herself died in 1289 the heart was buried with her in the church.
Location: 6½ miles S of Dumfries off A710.

Swindon *Wilts.* Map: 398 Ac
GREAT WESTERN RAILWAY MUSEUM In 1843 the Great Western Railway established engine works outside Swindon, and built a settlement for the railway workers. Among the accommodation was a model lodging house, which had more than 100 bedrooms and its own bakery. It was later converted into a Wesleyan chapel, and since 1962 has been the GWR Museum. The Brunel Room is devoted to the 19th-century railway engineer Isambard Kingdom Brunel.
Location: Emlyn Sq.

Syon House *Greater London* Map: 398 Dc
In 1415 Henry V founded a nunnery at Syon as penance for his father Henry IV's connivance at the murder of Richard II.
The Duke of Somerset, Lord Protector during the reign of Edward VI (1547–53), built a house on the site, incorporating parts of the nunnery. During the 1760s, Robert Adam (1728–92) reconstructed and refurnished the interior for the Earl, later Duke, of Northumberland. The gardens were landscaped by "Capability" Brown.
Location: Park Rd, Isleworth.

T

Tain *Highland* Map: 387 Dc
TOLBOOTH Every evening at 8 p.m., the town bell, cast in 1630, rings the curfew from the tolbooth tower, restored in 1733 after being damaged in a gale. Tain, the birthplace of St Duthac, was once a place of pilgrimage. The ruins of his sanctuary are behind the tolbooth.
Location: High St (A9), town centre.

Talley Abbey *Dyfed* Map: 392 Cb
There are only a few remains of the lake-side abbey. It was founded for the Premonstratensian Order (known as White Canons) by Lord Rhys, Prince of South Wales, in the late 12th century.
Location: 7½ miles N of Llandeilo (A40, B4302).

Tamworth Castle *Staffs.* Map: 393 Gd
The Norman castle built by the Marmion family probably stands on the site of an earlier Saxon stronghold built in 913 by Ethelfleda, daughter of Alfred the Great. Tamworth was once the capital of the Saxon kingdom of Mercia, and Offa – one of the most powerful Mercian kings (756–95) – held court there.

Much of the interior dates from Jacobean times, but there is some early-Norman herringbone masonry (slanting courses of stone leaning alternately left and right) on the wall running down the motte from the shell keep.
Location: Holloway St (A453), town centre.

Tanfield *Durham* Map: 391 Fe
CAUSEY ARCH In the 18th century, wooden-railed horse-wagon tramways linked Tanfield's collieries with Teams on the River Tyne, from where coal was taken by sea to London.
A local mason, Ralph Wood, built Causey Arch – 80 ft high and spanning 105 ft – to carry a tramway across the gorge of Houghwell Burn. Completed in 1727, it is the world's oldest railway bridge. It ceased to be used about 1787 and fell into decay, but is now being restored.
Location: 7 miles SW of Newcastle upon Tyne (A692, A6076). W off A6076 at Causey.

Tantallon Castle *Lothian* Map: 389 Fe
Cliffs protect the castle on three sides, for it stands on a promontory jutting into the North

Sea and Firth of Forth. In the 14th and 15th centuries it was the stronghold of the fierce and powerful Douglas family, who had a vast private army that on occasions numbered 2,000 men. They repeatedly defied the Scottish kings, and the castle was twice unsuccessfully besieged – by James IV in 1491 and James V in 1528.
Location: 3 miles E of N. Berwick off A198.

Tarbolton *Strathclyde*   *Map: 388 Cc*
BACHELORS' CLUB In 1780, 21-year-old Robert Burns, the Scottish poet, with his brother Gilbert and five other young men, formed what was probably the first debating society in rural Scotland, the Bachelors' Club.

Burns himself drew up the membership rules. The last one was: "Every man proper for a member . . . must have a frank, open heart; above everything dirty or mean; and must be a professed lover of one or more of the female sex . . ."

The club met in the 17th-century thatched house where Burns became a Freemason in 1781, and it is now preserved as a museum.
Location: 7½ miles NE of Ayr (A758, B744). Key from 7 Croft St, Tarbolton.

Tardebigge *Heref. & Worcs.*   *Map: 393 Fc*
TARDEBIGGE LOCKS Fifty-eight locks lift the 30 mile long Worcester and Birmingham Canal about 430 ft from the River Severn to the Birmingham plateau. They include the longest flight in Britain – the 30 Tardebigge locks, opened in 1815, that stretch for about 2 miles.

The 14 ft deep top lock at Tardebigge is one of the deepest narrow-boat locks in the country. It replaced a 64 ton vertical lift, wound by two men, that was in use from 1808 to 1815.
Location: 3 miles NW of Redditch on A448.

Tattershall Castle *Lincs.*   *Map: 394 Db*
The great tower of Tattershall Castle stands 100 ft high to the battlemented tops of the four corner turrets, and dominates the country for miles around.

It is all that remains of the 15th-century moated castle built by Ralph, Lord Cromwell, on the site of an earlier fortified manor house. The castle was built with red bricks, nearly a million of them, made from local clay. In the 15th century, red bricks used with a plaster facing became increasingly popular for building.

Lord Cromwell was Treasurer of England, one of the highest positions in the land, from 1433 to 1443, and the castle provided him with a dwelling suitable to his high office. It was both a fortress and a comfortable home, the tower being five storeys high and housing about 100 servants and hangers on.

The tower's basement walls were nearly 20 ft thick, and although the large windows and unguarded doorways at ground level on the east wall appear vulnerable, the row of machicolations 80 ft above were by no means just decorative. The openings could be used to drop missiles or boiling liquid on attackers below.

Tattershall passed to the crown after Lord Cromwell died without an heir, and later was owned by the earls of Lincoln until 1693. In 1911 the castle was derelict, and Lord Curzon bought and restored it after intervening to prevent parts of it being shipped abroad. The incident led to the Ancient Monuments Act of 1913, the foundation of the present official arrangements for preserving ancient buildings.
Location: 9 miles SW of Horncastle on A153.

Tatton Park *Cheshire*   *Map: 393 Ff*
A Classical mansion in a park of more than 1,000 acres, Tatton was begun in the 1790s by the architect Samuel Wyatt for William Egerton, who wanted a more modern house on the estate that had belonged to his family since 1598. It was completed in 1813 by Samuel's nephew Lewis for William's heir, Wilbraham.

Before piped water was available, maids wheeled a bath on castors to dressing rooms as required. Water was warmed by a charcoal fire in a box at one end of the bath, and it had a smoke flue that could be stuck up the chimney. The bath can be seen in the Silk Dressing Room.

With its fine paintings and furnishings, hunting trophies, rare shrubs and luxuriant gardens, Tatton gives a good picture of the pursuits of wealthy landowners. The Japanese garden, laid out in 1910, includes a specially imported Shinto temple. The Tenants' Hall museum includes the family state coach and some early motor cars.
Location: 3½ miles N of Knutsford (A50, A5034).

Taunton Castle *Somerset*   *Map: 397 Ed*
Built in the 12th century, the castle was a stronghold of the bishops of Winchester, and had an 80 ft high great tower, one of the biggest in the West Country. In 1685 Judge Jeffreys held the Bloody Assize – the trial of followers of the Duke of Monmouth's uprising – in the surviving 13th-century Great Hall. The castle houses the Somerset County Museum.
Location: Castle Bow, off North St.

Taversöe Tuick *Rousay, Orkney*   *Map: 387 Ef*
A two-storeyed tomb built of large stones, dating from about 2000 BC. The upper chamber is entered from the north at ground level, the lower from the south through a sunken passage. Several skeletons, pottery and a granite hammerhead were found in the lower chamber.
Location: ¾ mile W of Brinyan, N off B9064.

Tellisford *Somerset*   *Map: 397 Gd*
PACKHORSE ROUTE From the 14th to the 19th centuries, the River Frome provided power for the woollen industry, at first for fulling mills where cloth was pounded under hammers, and later also for spinning mills.

Wool and cloth were carried between farmers, weavers, mills and traders by trains of pack animals – horses or mules. The old cobbled pathway from the eastern end of Tellisford down to the river and across the narrow bridge was a packhorse route.
Location: 4 miles SW of Trowbridge (A366, B3109).

Temple Newsam *W. Yorks.*   *Map: 394 Bd*
The Tudor and Jacobean house was the birthplace of Henry Stewart, Lord Darnley, in 1545. He married Mary, Queen of Scots in 1565, and was the father of James I (James VI of Scotland). Darnley was murdered in 1567 on the order of Mary's lover, the Earl of Bothwell. The house is now a museum and art gallery.
Location: 4 miles SE of Leeds off A63.

Tenby *Dyfed*   *Map: 392 Bb*
CASTLE AND TOWN WALLS Little remains of the
12th-century Norman castle, whose walls were
breached in 1648 when Oliver Cromwell took
it from rebellious Parliamentary troops after a
short siege. The 13th-century town walls are
complete except for a 50 yd stretch, but only the
West Gate (Five Arches) remains.
Location: Castle on Castle Hill, by harbour.
TUDOR MERCHANT'S HOUSE In Tudor times Tenby
was a flourishing port exporting food, clothes
and hides and bringing in spices, wine and other
luxuries. The gabled merchant's house was built
of local stone in the early 15th century.
Location: Quay Hill, off Tudor Sq.

Tenterden *Kent*   *Map: 399 Fb*
CHURCH OF ST MILDRED The west tower built
1450-96 is one of the finest in Kent. There is a
15th-century alabaster relief carving of the Resurrection in the north chapel. Before the 16th-
century Reformation, most churches had such
carvings as altarpieces, but now they survive
mostly in museums.
Location: 12 miles SW of Ashford on A28.
KENT AND EAST SUSSEX RAILWAY The line was the
first to be constructed under the 1896 Light
Railways Act, which allowed local lines to be
built without a special Act of Parliament. It was
opened in stages 1900-5, and ran 21 miles from
Headcorn to Robertsbridge, where it linked
with the main Tonbridge-Hastings line.
  The line closed in 1961, but volunteers are
restoring a 10 mile stretch between Tenterden
and Bodiam. The first section was opened for
weekend steam passenger services in 1974.
Location: Station Rd, to N of High St.

Tetbury *Glos.*   *Map: 397 Ge*
CHURCH OF ST MARY The church was rebuilt in
1777-81 in Gothic Revival style by a Warwick
architect, Francis Hiorn. An unusual feature is the
passage surrounding most of the building. The
clock chimes four times a day to the tune of the
hymn "O Faith of England taught of old".
Location: 10½ miles SW of Cirencester on A433.

Tewkesbury *Glos.*   *Map: 393 Fb*
ABBEY Begun in 1092 and consecrated in 1121,
the abbey church is one of the finest Norman
buildings in England. The church, with a gateway and part of the Abbey House, is all that
remains of the once extensive Benedictine monastery dissolved in 1539. The townspeople saved
the church by paying Henry VIII £453 for it,
the estimated value of the bells and roof lead.
  In May 1471, a fierce battle of the Wars of the
Roses took place at Tewkesbury. The defeated
Lancastrians fled to the abbey church but were
pursued and slain in the aisles by the Yorkists,
led by Edward IV. Among those killed was
Edward, Prince of Wales, son of Henry VI.
Location: Church St (A38), town centre.
LITTLE MUSEUM A medieval shop of about 1450
has been restored, with furniture of the period.
The shutters were originally pivoted to form a
counter by day. (See plan.)
Location: Church St (A38).
MYTHE BRIDGE Thomas Telford built the cast-
iron bridge across the River Severn in 1828. It
has a single span of 170 ft.
Location: ½ mile N of town centre on A438.

Shopping in the Middle Ages

15TH-CENTURY SHOPPERS OFTEN
BOUGHT GOODS AT THE PLACE WHERE
THEY WERE MADE, IN SHOPS LIKE THIS
ONE AT TEWKESBURY

In early medieval times, weekly markets and less-
frequent fairs were the main trading places.
Gradually, permanent shops began to take the
place of some market stalls, although markets
continued to be held. One of these shops, at
Tewkesbury in Gloucestershire, has been restored
and opened as a museum.

Essential tradesmen - such as shoemakers, iron-
mongers and coopers - were found in every
town, and in larger towns there were also less
essential shops such as haberdashers. Large towns
more often had food shops, because people had
little opportunity to grow and store food. In
London, customers at cookshops could buy meat
pies or take their own meat to be cooked.

Shops selling goods of the same kind were
grouped together, and sometimes streets came to
be called after the trade, such as Butcher Row at
Shrewsbury. Shops kept by tanners and fishmon-
gers (because of the smell) and potters (because of
the fire risk) were usually restricted to outlying
areas.

Prices, wages and the quality of goods were
strictly controlled by trade guilds, and a retailer
could not trade unless he was a member. Dishonest traders were put in the stocks or pillory, or
the punishment might be fitted to the crime. A
seller of bad ale, for example, might be made to
drink all he could hold, then have the rest poured
over him.

SHOP FRONTS *There were no glazed shop windows.
The shop front was open, with a shutter to close it at
night. The shutter was built on a pivot, and during
the day could be lowered to serve as a counter. Some
wares were probably displayed on it, or hung across
the opening. Shops sometimes had signs by which
they could be recognised, such as the barber's pole and
the baker's wheatsheaf.*

WHERE TRADESMEN LIVED AND WORKED

About 1450, a row of timber-framed shops was built beside Tewkesbury Abbey, perhaps to sell the abbey produce. Some have now been restored, and one, pictured above as it might have looked in medieval times, has been opened as a museum. The hall of the museum has been furnished with oak-built copies of medieval furniture.

The shop is small, like most medieval shops, with a frontage of about 11 ft 6 in. and a depth of 7 ft 4 in. A side door and narrow passage lead to the main living area at the rear, which had a central fireplace with smoke drifting up to the roof and a staircase leading to sleeping quarters above the shop. Lean-to

extensions at the rear of the building were probably extra workshops and storehouses.

Because of the difficulties of travel, medieval trade was localised. Articles were often made to order, perhaps from material supplied by the customer. Goods were mostly made in the shop, and buyers could see the craftsmen at work. If goods were below standard, a trader could be fined by the trade guild.

Apprentices learning the trade lived in as part of the family. After a period of four to ten years – usually seven – an apprentice qualified as a journeyman, who worked for wages. In time he might save enough to set himself up as an independent craftsman.

The Binns *Lothian*   *Map: 389 Dd*
Since 1612, The Binns has been the home of the
Dalyells (pronounced Dee-ell), the most famous
of whom was General Tam Dalyell, a staunch
Royalist who routed the Covenanters (Presby-
terians) for Charles II at Rullion Green in 1666.
In 1681 he raised the British cavalry regiment,
the Royal Scots Greys, at The Binns. They took
their name from the grey uniform he chose as
camouflage.
Location: 15 miles W of Edinburgh (A90, A904).

The Bratch *Staffs.*   *Map:393 Fd*
BRATCH LOCKS So close together are the three
locks that boats can pass from one to the other
only if two locks have their gates open. The
locks are at the east end of the village, on the 46
mile Staffordshire and Worcestershire Canal
begun by James Brindley in the 1760s.
   There is an octagonal toll-house by the road
bridge, and at the bottom of the locks is the
ornate Bilston Waterworks, built in 1895.
Location: 5 miles SW of Wolverhampton
(A449).

The Breidden Hill-fort *Powys*   *Map:393 Ed*
The volcanic ridge of Breidden Hill, towering
1,000 ft above the Severn valley, was thought to
have been the site of the last stand of the British
King Caratacus against the Romans in AD 51.
But recent opinion favours a site further west,
near Caersws.
   The Breidden was a place of refuge probably
as early as the 8th century BC, and about the 1st
century BC there was a settlement of circular
wattle-and-daub huts with their doorways sheltered by small porches.
Location: 12 miles W of Shrewsbury (A458,
B4393).

The Rumps *Cornwall*   *Map: 396 Bc*
PROMONTORY FORT Cut off from the mainland
by three ramparts, the fort covered about 6 acres
and was built in the 1st century BC by a
community who lived mainly by sheep-herding.
Fragments of wine vessels from the Mediterranean show that they obtained expensive imports.
Location: 12½ miles W of Camelford (A39,
B3267, B3314, then path from Pentire Farm).

The Sanctuary *Wilts.*   *Map: 398 Ac*
Originally, The Sanctuary was a circular timber
building about 65 ft across with six rings of
posts. It was built 2500–2200 BC in connection
with the Avebury Stone Circle (see p. 35).
   Soon after 2000 BC the timber structure was
pulled down and replaced by two stone circles,
the outer one about 130 ft in diameter. The
dedication ceremony appears to have included
the burial of a 14 year old, with a Beaker drinking
vessel, at the foot of one of the stones.
Location: Overton Hill, 1½ miles S of Avebury
(B4003 then on S side of A4).

Thetford *Norfolk*   *Map: 399 Ff*
CASTLE Thetford's huge 11th-century motte,
over 80 ft high and 1,000 ft round at the base,
was one of the biggest of the Norman motte-
and-bailey castles. Only the mound and part of
the bailey earthworks remain. A stone castle
may have been built in the 1100s and dismantled
in 1174 by Henry II when his son Henry rebelled.

The castle was owned by Hugh Bigod, Earl of
Norfolk, the king's most dangerous adversary.
Location: Castle St, SE of town centre.
THE ANCIENT HOUSE A rich burgher probably
built the black-and-white house soon after 1500.
It was originally detached with a side carriage
entrance, but was later split into two cottages
and plastered over, until restoration in 1867.
Some of the original timberwork remains. It is
now a Thetford and Breckland Museum.
Location: White Hart St, off A11, town centre.
WARREN LODGE In late medieval times, rabbit
flesh was considered a greater delicacy than
chicken, and the 15th-century flint-built lodge
was used by warreners who made a living snaring
rabbits in the surrounding sandhills. In later ages,
rabbit pelts were used to make top-hats, and in
the 19th century this and flint-knapping were
the main industries in Brandon near by.
   The house is not open to the public, but

THE SERVANTS WHO CARED FOR "A PERFECT GENTLEMAN"

A century ago some of the wealthiest aristocrats
employed literally hundreds of servants in their enormous country homes. In the 1890s the Duke of
Portland had about 300 servants at Welbeck Abbey,
while the Duke of Westminster employed a similar
number at his home in Eaton Hall in Cheshire. Few
lords were rich enough to employ so many servants
and most had to make do with 30–40 – the average for
a large Victorian country house, such as Thoresby Hall
in Nottinghamshire.
   As Henry James, the American expatriate author,
wrote: "It takes a great many people to keep a perfect
gentleman going."

Rigid divisions of rank
Life below stairs was organised with a regimental
discipline and with rigid divisions of rank. The chief
male servant was the house steward who kept the
accounts and was generally responsible for the smooth
running of the household. Below him was the groom
of the chambers, whose duties were of a more delicate
nature – such as filling inkwells, or lighting candles.
The valet, or gentleman's gentleman, performed a
more intimate service, looking after his master's
clothes, helping him to dress, and accompanying him
on his travels. Ladies' maids performed a similar duty
for the mistress of the house and her older daughters.
   The butler – in white tie and tails – supervised the
serving of meals; guarded the valuable gold and silver
plate; and kept an eye on the contents of the cellar – a
duty which he sometimes performed so enthusiasti-
cally, that he ended up with gout!

BELOW-STAIRS ELITE *The type of uniform worn in a
wealthy Victorian household by male upper servants – the
house steward, groom of the chambers, valet and butler.*

visitors can go into the enclosure and look inside through the window-gratings.
Location: 1½ miles W of Thetford off B1107.

The Trundle *W. Sussex*　　　*Map: 398 Cb*
HILL-FORT Built about 300–100 BC by Iron Age men, the fort is surrounded by a bank and ditch and covers more than 12 acres. The two entrances were designed so that attackers could not enter without being exposed to fire from above.
Location: 4 miles N of Chichester off A285.

The Vyne *Hants.*　　　*Map: 398 Cc*
Sir William Sandys, who became Lord Chamberlain to Henry VIII, built The Vyne about 1500–20. The king three times visited him there. Sir William's great-grandson, who was also Lord Chamberlain, entertained Queen Elizabeth at The Vyne in 1569.
　The Vyne is thought to take its name from

the Roman *Vindomis* (House of Wine), which was sited thereabouts in the 2nd century AD.
Location: 4½ miles N of Basingstoke off A340.

The Wrekin *Salop*　　　*Map: 393 Ed*
HILL-FORT Before the Romans came in the 1st century, the fort was probably the tribal capital of the Cornovii. Its last defender may have been called Virico, for his name was given to the Roman capital that replaced it – Viroconium, or Wroxeter, 4 miles west.
Location: 10 miles SE of Shrewsbury off A5.

Thoresby Hall *Notts.*　　　*Map: 394 Cc*
Lady Mary Wortley Montagu, an 18th-century writer and traveller, was brought up in the original hall, burned down in 1745. She introduced inoculation against smallpox to England from Turkey about 1720, and it was used until Edward Jenner discovered vaccination in 1796.

　Employers preferred to have tall men as servants as they looked more dignified, especially footmen who went out with the carriages. Footmen were usually well over 6 ft tall and as carefully matched in height as were the carriage horses. Outdoors, the footmen wore a gorgeous livery, with a cocked – or top – hat and white stockings, sometimes padded out to make their legs look more shapely. Indoors, when waiting at the table, they wore a less flamboyant livery.

　The chief female servant was the housekeeper, a formidable figure in her long, plain black dress and white frilly cap, who could strike fear into the heart of a lazy, careless or flighty maid. The cook – usually a woman in all but the wealthiest houses – could also be a tyrant, terrorising her kitchen staff. There were numerous other maids, including housemaids, who started work at 6 a.m. and had to clean the whole house by midday with nothing but brooms, buckets, feather dusters and "elbow grease". The afternoon was spent mending linen.

　There was just as great a consciousness of rank and status downstairs as there was upstairs in the drawing-rooms. All servants usually ate the first course of their dinner together in the servants' hall, with the upper servants – the house steward, the groom of the chambers, the valet, the butler, housekeeper, cook, chief ladies' maid and head nurse – retiring to the house steward's room to eat their second course. Free wine was provided in the steward's room and beer in the servants' hall.

　There was an equivalent consciousness of status during working hours. Valets thought it beneath their dignity to wait at the table, and no self-respecting butler soiled his hands with work outside the house. Women did all the heavy work, such as carrying coals

and huge jugs of boiling water upstairs; a footman might deign to carry up a pair of shoes or a letter.

　When big country houses like Thoresby Hall were built in mid-Victorian times, they were designed to accommodate this great number of servants, which helps to explain why it has no fewer than 78 bedrooms. The lower female staff usually slept in small attics, while their male counterparts often slept in partitioned dormitories. But upper servants had their own bedrooms, and equivalent accommodation had to be provided for servants of house guests, such as valets and ladies' maids.

　Both the house steward and the housekeeper also had their own sitting-room.

Commission for unscrupulous stewards
By the standards of the times, aristocrats' servants were well paid. A house steward received about £100 a year – as much as any skilled craftsman – plus board and accommodation. Unscrupulous upper servants, such as the cook or the butler, could often supplement their income by demanding commissions from tradesmen; while others, such as the valet – who earned about £60 a year – had recognised perquisites in the form of his master's cast-off clothing. Even the housemaids in a Victorian household, on £26 a year, earned more than some farm labourers.

　Servants also expected to receive, and often got, tips from house guests – an ancient custom which many employers tried to stop without success.

　The expense of maintaining such huge staffs cost some aristocrats as much as 40% of their income. Many of them also gave pensions to retired servants or provided accommodation for them in almshouses on their estates.

WOMEN OF AUTHORITY *Distinctive uniforms were worn by the housekeeper, ladies' maid, head nurse and cook in a large Victorian house.*

LOWER SERVANTS' DRESS *Uniforms as worn by footmen, housemaids, kitchen maids and tweenies – girls who helped housemaids in the morning and the cook in the afternoon.*

The present hall, built 1864-71, is Victorian neo-Tudor, designed by Anthony Salvin. The estate was enclosed from Sherwood Forest in 1683, and there is a statue of Robin Hood, the legendary 12th-century outlaw, in the forecourt. About 2 miles away is the Major Oak, where Robin is said to have hidden supplies.

Location: 4 miles N of Ollerton off A614.

VICTORIAN MANSION

Thoresby Hall in Nottinghamshire, built in the 1860s for the 3rd Earl and Countess Manvers, shows Victorian wealth and luxury at its height. The Blue Drawing-Room (above) has walls hung with blue silk damask, and the Library beyond the maple and walnut doors glows with red brocade and contains about 5,000 books.

Thornborough *N. Yorks.* Map: 394 Be
HENGE MONUMENTS The three earth circles that stand in a line from north-east to south-west were centres of ritual worship about 2000 BC, and probably for centuries afterwards. The northern circle is the best preserved.

Location: 6½ miles N of Ripon off A6108, to N and S of West Tanfield-Thornborough road.

Thornbury *Devon* Map: 396 Ca
DEVON MUSEUM OF MECHANICAL MUSIC At the beginning of this century, public bars often had a coin-operated piano standing in the corner - the forerunner of the modern juke box. A barrel piano of 1901 is among the many mechanical musical instruments on show at the museum, all regularly played.

Another exhibit is the German-designed Polyphon of 1880, a musical box that played from separate metal discs, foreshadowing the record-player of today.

Location: 4½ miles NE of Holsworthy off A388.

Thornton *Leics.* Map: 394 Ba
CHURCH OF ST PETER By the south door of the 14th-15th-century church stands a great yew tree planted in 1723, its trunk about 10 ft round. Inside the church the fine bench ends were all carved by one man, Robert Baken, between 1500 and 1560.

The nave columns lean noticeably towards the north, probably due to disturbance of the foundations when burial vaults were made. But there is a story that during a violent storm in 1813, the roofing lead rolled to the north, causing the whole church to lean that way.

Location: 9½ miles NW of Leicester off A50.

Thornton Abbey *Humberside* Map: 394 Dd
Much of the Augustinian abbey founded in 1139 is now a ruin, but a fine brick gatehouse of 1382 - probably built as the abbot's house - still remains. After the abbey was dissolved in 1539, some of the stone was used for local buildings.

Location: 3 miles SE of Barrow upon Humber on minor road.

Threave Castle *Dumfs. & Gall.* Map: 390 Ce
Archibald the Grim, 3rd Earl of Douglas, built the 14th-century castle on an island in the Dee. The four-storey great tower is 70 ft high.

In 1455, during the Douglas rebellion, James II of Scotland besieged the castle and blew holes in the stonework with the great cannon Mons Meg (now at Edinburgh Castle). When properly charged, the cannon - 13 ft long and with a 20 in. bore - had a range of 1,400 yds. James Douglas yielded under this bombardment.

Location: 4 miles W of Castle Douglas off A75.

Thursford *Norfolk* Map: 395 Fb
THE THURSFORD COLLECTION Between the 1850s and 1930s, people walked miles for the fun and spectacle of the travelling fairground, brought to them by the huge showman's steam-engine.

Steam traction engines such as *Victory* of 1920, on display at Thursford, provided haulage and supplied power for the roundabouts, ornate mechanical organs - often with mechanical figures - and electric lights.

For many people, the bright fairground lights were their first experience of electric lighting. It was the fairground also that introduced the bioscope, the earliest cinema, between 1896 and 1914. Thursford's *Edward VII*, built 1905, was used with a bioscope show.

Many steam-engines, including ploughing engines, are on display, and mechanical and keyboard organs for fairs, cinemas and dance halls can be seen and heard. They include the Mighty Wurlitzer, the fourth largest cinema organ in Europe, built for the Paramount Cinema at Leeds.

Location: 6½ miles NE of Fakenham off A148.

Thurso *Highland* Map: 387 Ee
DOUNREAY EXHIBITION AND OBSERVATION ROOM In 1954 the United Kingdom Atomic Energy Authority took over a disused Royal Naval Air Station to build Britain's first experimental fast breeder reactor at a cost of about £30 million. Contained in a 135 ft diameter steel sphere, it was the first of its kind to generate electricity for public use. The exhibition and observation room are housed in the old control tower.

Location: 10 miles W of Thurso on A836.

Tilbury Fort *Essex* Map: 399 Ec
Originally the fort was a blockhouse built by Henry VIII in 1539 as part of his coastal fortifi-

THE MIGHTY FAIRGROUND ORGAN

Giant mechanical organs with elaborately decorated fronts were a feature of the fairgrounds of the early 1900s. The 101-key Belgian showman's organ above, *built in 1900, can be seen at the Thursford Collection, Thursford, Norfolk. Fairground organs were driven by steam traction engines.*

cations (see p. 125). It was strengthened in Elizabeth I's reign when Spain threatened invasion, and it was at Tilbury that the queen made the stirring call to her forces in August 1588, to resist the Spaniards.

The blockhouse was submerged in a larger, star-shaped fort in 1670–83, when Charles II reorganised the national defences.
Location: Fort Rd, ¼ mile E of Riverside Station.

Tingwall *Mainland, Shetland*   *Map: 387 Gd*
AGRICULTURAL MUSEUM An old granary, stable and bothy (workmen's lodgings) of 1750 house the museum, a collection of farm tools and domestic equipment of a Shetland croft.
Location: 5 miles NW of Lerwick (A970, A971 then S on minor road to Gott. The museum is at 2 Veensgarth, Gott).

Tinkinswood *S. Glam.*   *Map: 393 Da*
LONG CAIRN At the eastern end of the 140 ft long cairn, large stones and dry-stone panels form the walls of the burial chamber and support a huge capstone weighing about 40 tons.

This stone is almost as heavy as the largest at Stonehenge, but it was manhandled into position perhaps 1,000 years earlier – about 2500 BC. About 70 people were buried in the chamber during the course of many centuries, each laid to rest beside a few possessions.
Location: 6½ miles SW of Cardiff off A48.

Tintagel *Cornwall*   *Map: 396 Bc*
CASTLE For centuries, Tintagel Castle has been associated with the story of King Arthur and his Knights of the Round Table – a legend first publicised by Geoffrey of Monmouth in the 1140s, when the existing castle was being built. But Arthur was a Romano-British cavalry leader of the 5th century – long before the days of medieval chivalry – and there is no evidence to connect him with Tintagel.

The castle was built on the site of a 6th–9th-century Celtic monastery by Reginald, Earl of Cornwall, an illegitimate son of Henry I.

VICTORIAN ORGANETTE

On Sunday evenings, hymn tunes could be wound out by the fireside on the small reed organ, about 100 years old, now in the Devon Museum of Mechanical Music, Thornbury. Tunes were fed in on paper strips.

Although it is in a splendid defensive position on a sea-girt headland, it has had about 800 years of peaceful history.

Over the centuries the narrow neck of land between the headland and the mainland was washed away, and 13th-century extensions to the castle were joined to the older parts by a bridge. By the 16th century the bridge had fallen and the castle was derelict. Today the older part of the castle can be reached only by steep steps up the cliff.
Location: ½ mile NW of Tintagel.
CHURCH OF ST MATERIANA The isolated cliff-top parish church dates mainly from Norman times. There is a stone bench round the walls of the south transept – a reminder of the days when churches had no pews. Such a bench was some-

times built for the old or infirm who could not stand; thus "the weakest went to the wall".
Location: On cliffs to W of Tintagel.

OLD POST OFFICE The stone-built 14th-century house roofed with thick, uneven slates became a letter-receiving office in 1844, after the introduction of the penny post had increased the amount of post to be handled. It remained a post office until 1892.
Location: Village centre.

Tintern Parva *Gwent*   *Map: 393 Eb*
TINTERN ABBEY The abbey was founded in 1131 by Cistercian monks, an order that farmed on a large scale with lay brothers doing the manual labour. The picturesque ruins beside the Wye date mainly from the 13th century. The abbey was dissolved in 1536.

Remains of the warming house, with its central fireplace, lie to the north of the cloister. It was the only room, apart from the kitchen and infirmary, allowed a fire.
Location: 5 miles N of Chepstow on A466.

WIRE-DRAWING MILL In Elizabethan times, Tintern became Britain's main centre for making brass and iron wire, drawn out from metal rods.

Charcoal for smelting was made in the surrounding woods, and the Wye tributaries supplied water power for the wheels that operated the furnace bellows and forge hammers. The industry was active until the late 1800s, when charcoal finally gave way to coke for smelting.

The old wire-drawing mill, now disused, is one of many industrial sites in the area to which footpaths have been cleared. A map can be obtained at the Tintern Tourist Information Centre in the abbey car park.
Location: ¼ mile W of abbey, W off A466.

Tintinhull *Somerset*   *Map: 397 Fc*
CHURCH OF ST MARGARET OF ANTIOCH On the outside walls there are old scratch dials used by medieval priests to time the Mass. A stick was placed in the central hole, and the time calculated by its shadow. Inside, there are three pews with servants' seats attached to the bench ends.

OLDEST MAN-MADE OBJECT?

Among the tools found in Kent's Cavern, near Torquay, was this crude flint hand-axe made by Old Stone Age men about 300,000 years before the birth of Christ. One of the earliest man-made tools ever found in Britain, the hand-axe was probably used to kill and skin small animals hunted for food.

Remains of the village stocks stand by the gate.
Location: 4 miles NW of Yeovil off A37.

TINTINHULL HOUSE In about 1720, an unknown provincial builder added the fine west front of golden stone to this gabled 17th-century farmhouse. Stretching before it are the fine formal gardens planned about 1900 by the owner, Dr S. J. M. Price, a distinguished botanist. They were extended by later owners in 1933.
Location: Farm St, E from The Green.

Titchfield *Hants.*   *Map: 398 Ba*
CHURCH OF ST PETER The west wall of the nave and the lower two-thirds of the tower are Saxon work. The south chapel contains fine tombs of the Wriothesley family. Sir Thomas Wriothesley, later Earl of Southampton, was granted the nearby 13th-century Titchfield Abbey in 1537 after its dissolution, and converted it into a family mansion.
Location: 2 miles W of Fareham off A27.

Tiverton Castle *Devon*   *Map: 397 Ec*
Begun about 1106, the castle was the stronghold of Richard de Redvers, Earl of Devon. It has a fine 14th-century gatehouse.
Location: N of town off Park Hill (A396).

Todmorden *W. Yorks.*   *Map: 391 Fa*
STEANOR BOTTOM TOLL-HOUSE Toll-gates were set up mainly in the 17th and 18th centuries to collect fees from travellers for the upkeep of turnpike roads. Payment was made at the toll-house, where fees were displayed on a board.

Steanor Bottom toll-house was built about 1821 on one of the main routes across the Pennines. Charges varied from 7d for a gentleman's carriage to ¼d a head for sheep and pigs.
Location: 3 miles S of Todmorden on A6033.

Tolgus Tin Mill *Cornwall*   *Map: 396 Ab*
Nearly 200 years ago, a water-wheel was installed at Tolgus Tin Mill to power the heavy stamps used to crush the ore so that tin could be separated from the waste. The wheel and stamps are still in use as part of the Tolgus Tin streaming mill, and visitors can see them in action.

Streaming – washing deposits from the stream bed to recover the ore – is the oldest method of extracting ore. It is still in use at Tolgus – machinery is used to sift and wash deposits.
Location: 1½ miles N of Redruth on B3300.

Tomen-y-mur *Gwynedd*   *Map: 392 Cc*
ROMAN FORT Soldiers stationed at the 1st–2nd-century fort in remote Snowdonia had their own small amphitheatre for off-duty entertainment. Its remains can be seen beside the road, at the cattle grid. Near by is the parade ground.
Location: 14 miles N of Dolgellau, E off A470.

Tonbridge Castle *Kent*   *Map: 399 Eb*
William Rufus burned down the original motte-and-bailey castle, and most of the nearby houses, in 1088 when its owner, Richard Fitz-Gilbert, rebelled against him.

A stone shell keep was built on the motte in the 12th century, and a massive gatehouse added in the 13th century. A survey made for the Crown in the 1520s described the castle "as strong a fortress as few there be in England".
Location: Off High St, town centre.

THE BEST BEDROOM, IN A LAKELAND FARMHOUSE

Visitors usually slept in the canopied oak bed of 1670 in the best bedroom at Townend, Troutbeck, the home of wealthy yeomen farmers. The bed is carved with the initials of the owners, George and Ellinor Browne, as is the oak cradle at its foot. There are fine 18th-century glasses in the corner cupboard.

Tong *W. Yorks.* Map: 394 Bd
CHURCH OF ST JAMES Although a Norman arch survives in the tower, the church was largely rebuilt about 1727. The interior still has most of its 18th-century furnishings, including a three-decker pulpit and the large squire's pew complete with fireplace.
Location: 5 miles SE of Bradford in Tong Lane, off Wakefield Rd (A650).

Tongland Bridge *Dumfs. & Gall.* Map: 390 Be
Thomas Telford designed the battlemented and turreted bridge over the River Dee. It was completed in 1808.
Location: 1¾ miles N of Kirkcudbright off A711.

Torquay *Devon* Map: 397 Eb
KENT'S CAVERN Old Stone Age hunters took refuge in the cave 250,000–300,000 years ago. They left behind crude flint hand-axes, some of the earliest man-made implements found in Britain. The cave was occupied intermittently throughout the Ice Ages, which ended about 8500 BC. Remains of the prehistoric cave-dwellers and the animals they hunted – including the cave bear and sabre-tooth tiger – are displayed at the entrance and in the Torquay Museum, Babbacombe Road.
Location: Ilsham Rd, 1 mile NE of harbour.

Totnes Castle *Devon* Map: 397 Db
In a commanding position overlooking the Dart valley, the castle has a 14th-century shell keep with well-preserved battlements. A manorial court was held there in the Middle Ages, and the manor tenants kept the castle in repair as part of their feudal dues.
Location: Castle St, off High St, town centre.

Townend *Cumbria* Map: 391 Dc
A typical Lakeland farmhouse of the 17th century, Townend at Troutbeck has stone-built walls, a slate roof and massive round chimneys. The lower floor is divided in two by the hallan – a narrow passage from front to rear. On one side is the "down house" (kitchen) and on the other the "fire house" (living quarters).

A prosperous family of yeomen farmers, the Brownes, lived at Townend from 1623 to 1943. The furnishings include carved oak furniture made by the family during the winter.
Location: 3 miles N of Windermere off A592.

Traprain Law *Lothian* Map: 389 Fd
HILL-FORT During the first 500 years AD, the stronghold on the 500 ft high hill was the capital of the Votadini tribe, its earthwork fortifications enclosing up to 40 acres.
Relations with the Romans seem to have been cordial, and alongside the iron weapons and implements found on the site was much imported Roman ware, including a fine hoard of silver vessels now in the National Museum of Antiquities in Edinburgh.
Location: 2 miles S of East Linton (minor rd).

Tredegar *Gwent* Map: 393 Db
SIRHOWY IRONWORKS One of the first ironworks in Monmouthshire to use coke for smelting, Sirhowy Ironworks began production in 1778. By the 1840s its four blast furnaces were producing 7,000 tons of iron a year. The works closed in 1882 when local iron-ore deposits became exhausted. It was recently excavated from under a slag heap.
Location: 1 mile NE of town off A4048.
TREDEGAR PATCH In the late 1700s and early 1800s, iron-ore and coal for the local ironworks were dug out from the hillsides, each miner being allotted a measured patch in which to work. Tredegar Patch, on the hillside ½ mile west of town, was such an area of workings. Coal (to make coke for smelting) and ore were brought down by horse-wagon tramway.

Tredegar House *Gwent* Map: 393 Da
Rare breeds of domestic animals can be seen in the grounds of the fine 17th-century Tredegar House, which also has extensive early-18th-century walled gardens. The rare breeds include pigs similar to those kept by Iron Age farmers – obtained by crossing a wild boar with a Tamworth sow – or a Gloucester Old Spot.
Location: 3 miles SW of Newport (A48, B4329).

HOW PLACE NAMES REVEAL THE PAST

In the language of the original settlers, place names had meanings describing the character of the settlement. The oldest place names that can be recognised date back to the Celtic people who spread across Britain from about 500 BC.

Many rivers and mountains have Celtic names. Sometimes they vary in form according to the local dialect – Axe, Exe and Usk all mean water, from *isca*, the Latin form of the British word. Some names have been assimilated by later settlers and translated by sound into words with a different meaning. Brown Willy on Bodmin Moor, Cornwall, was originally Bryn Huel, Celtic for Hill of the Tin Mines.

Because the Celtic Britons were pushed back into the western fringes of the island, Celtic names are most numerous in Wales and Cornwall, where the Brythonic form of Celtic was spoken, and in Scotland, where the Gaelic form developed – mainly after settlement by Goidelic Celts from Ireland. The Romans who ruled Britain for about 400 years from AD 43 introduced few new place names, but latinised many Celtic ones, including Londinium.

Anglo-Saxon heritage

Names of Anglo-Saxon origin are by far the most common in England. The Angles and Saxons from north-west Europe settled in the south-east in the 5th century, and gradually spread across England. They adapted some Romano-British words, such as *castra*, fort, which appears in Old English (Anglo-Saxon) as the suffix -chester or -caster; for example Lancaster, meaning Roman fort on the River Lune. *Strata*, Roman street, is often found in place names along the line of the old Roman roads, such as Stratford and Stretton.

North and east of an imaginary line from London to Chester, the Viking, or Norse, invasion and settlement of the 9th century left a crop of Scandinavian names, such as Lowestoft (Hlodver's *toft* or homestead).

The Norman conquerors of 1066 brought a few new names, but more often they changed the form of existing ones. Because they could not pronounce ch, -chester tended to become -cester, and their habit of dropping an initial S caused, for example, Snotingaham (village of Snot's people) to become Nottingham. Many double-barrelled names such as Stoke Poges result from the name of a Norman overlord being added to a place name. Stoke is Old English for place, here probably a holy place, and Poges is from Norman French meaning "of the le Pugeis family".

Common suffixes and prefixes that indicate the origin and meaning of names are given below.

Suffix or prefix	Modern place name
aber (Celtic) river mouth, confluence	Aberdeen (Grampian) Mouth of River Dee
beck (Scandinavian) stream, brook	Troutbeck (Cumbria) Trout stream
by (Scandinavian) town	Whitby (N. Yorks.) White town
combe (Anglo-Saxon) narrow valley	Ilfracombe (Devon) Valley of Alfred's people
dun (Celtic) fortified hill	Dundee (Tayside) Hill of God
ham (Anglo-Saxon) village, manor, estate	Feltham (Gtr London) Village in a field
ing (Anglo-Saxon) people of	Reading (Berks.) People of Reada (Reada is the name of the leader)
ley (Anglo-Saxon) glade, clearing, meadow	Fazeley (Staffs.) Bull's glade
thwaite (Scandinavian) clearing	Bassenthwaite (Cumbria) Bastun's clearing
ton (Anglo-Saxon) town	Wilton (N. Yorks.) Town among the willows
tre (Celtic) hamlet	Treneglos (Cornwall) Hamlet of the church

Trefignath *Anglesey, Gwynedd* Map: 392 Bf
PREHISTORIC TOMB Originally the large stones of the tomb, built 2500–2000 BC, were covered by an earth mound. They form a long gallery divided by cross slabs into three or four chambers, each of which may have contained a single burial. In the 18th century some of the stones were removed to make gateposts.
Location: 1 mile S of Holyhead off B4545.

Tregaseal *Cornwall* Map: 396 Aa
STONE CIRCLES Only one of the two Stone Age moorland circles – ancient temples dating from 2500–2000 BC – is recognisable, with 16 of its 20 stones still in place. The stones are 6–7 ft tall and conical or rectangular in outline.
Location: 1 mile NE of St Just off B3306.

Trent *Dorset* Map: 397 Fc
CHURCH OF ST ANDREW It is said that the church pews, with carved bench ends of about 1500, were hidden by parishioners or the lord of the manor during the 16th-century Reformation, so escaping destruction by Puritans.
Lord Fisher of Lambeth, the 99th Archbishop of Canterbury who died in 1972, is buried in the churchyard.
Location: 3 miles NE of Yeovil off A30.

Tre'r Ceiri *Gwynedd* Map: 392 Bc
HILL-FORT During the first 400 years AD, the bleak hill-top was a bustling settlement – "Town of the Giants" – surrounded by a drystone defensive wall still 13 ft high in parts. There are remains of about 150 stone huts; many are too small to be houses and were probably stores and workshops. Some huts are grouped round enclosed yards, and look like small farmsteads built within the safety of the defences.
Location: 7½ miles N of Pwllheli (A499, B4417).

Trerice *Cornwall* Map: 396 Bb
An E-shaped Elizabethan manor house completed in 1573 by Sir John Arundell. It has unusual curved gables – Sir John may have got the idea for them while soldiering in the Low Countries.
Location: 3 miles SE of Newquay (A392, A3058).

Tresco Abbey *Isles of Scilly* Map: 396 Ad
In 1834 Augustus Smith, descendant of a family of wealthy London bankers, leased the Scilly Isles from the Duchy of Cornwall. He styled himself Lord Proprietor and devoted his life and wealth to developing the islands.
He built his house on Tresco, the second-largest island, near the remains of an 11th century priory, and transformed the tree-less, windswept waste into one of the finest sub-tropical gardens in Europe. The Valhalla Museum, a collection of figureheads from ships wrecked on the islands' shores, was founded about 1840.
Location: 1 mile S of New Grimsby harbour.

Trethevy Quoit *Cornwall* Map: 396 Cb
BURIAL CHAMBER Built 2500–2000 BC, the massive chamber has four upright stones nearly 15 ft high surmounted by an 11 ft long capstone. The only entrance is a small hole just large enough for a body to be passed through. The

A WEST COUNTRY WOOL TOWN

From medieval times, Trowbridge, Wiltshire, was one of England's foremost cloth-making towns, at its most prosperous in the 18th and 19th centuries. A few clothiers' houses, weavers' cottages, and cloth mills remain to show how the industry developed.

CLOTHIER'S HOUSE *This wealthy clothier's house, built about 1730, is one of a row on The Parade. Clothiers supplied wool for home wearing.*

WEAVERS' COTTAGES *Until as late as the 1870s, some weavers worked at home, usually on a top floor with long windows to light the loom. Cottages (left) in Yerbury Street are among the few remaining.*

STUDLEY MILLS *Teasels, used to raise a nap on the cloth, were stored in the handle house. Its walls were perforated to let in air to dry the plants.*

chamber was originally covered with an earth mound.
Location: 3 miles N of Liskeard off B3254.

Tretower Castle *Powys*   *Map: 393 Db*
Roger Picard, an Anglo-Norman lord, built the large shell keep in the 12th century. When the Welsh prince Llywelyn the Last captured the castle in the 1260s, it may have been badly damaged, for after the Picards recovered the castle, they moved out and built the nearby 14th-century Tretower Court.
Location: 9 miles NW of Abergavenny (A40, A479).

Trevelgue Head *Cornwall*   *Map: 396 Bb*
PROMONTORY FORT The fort overlooks a harbour that may have been used for transporting tin in the late Bronze Age – about 800–700 BC. But huts found inside the fort are of a later date, and an Iron Age chariot lynch pin, probably about 2,000 years old, was found there. It is now in Truro Museum.
Location: 1 mile NE of Newquay, W off B3276.

Trevose Head *Cornwall*   *Map: 396 Bb*
LIGHTHOUSE Completed in 1847, the lighthouse is 87 ft high and stands on 200 ft high cliffs overlooking the Bristol Channel. The area is prone to fog, and from 1896 to 1919 a 36 ft long fog horn was successfully tested there.
Location: 4 miles W of Padstow off B3276.

Tring *Herts.*   *Map: 398 Cd*
ZOOLOGICAL MUSEUM First opened in 1892, the museum began as two small cottages built in 1887 to house the zoological collection of Lionel Walter, 2nd Baron Rothschild.
An eminent naturalist, Lord Rothschild began collecting insects at the age of 7, and when he died in 1937 had amassed the largest natural history collection ever made by one man. His museum is now an annexe of the British Museum (Natural History).
Location: Akeman St, off High St.

Trotton *W. Sussex*   *Map: 398 Cb*
CHURCH OF ST GEORGE Built about 1300, the church has two fine brasses. One is to Margaret De Camoys (died 1310), the other to Thomas, Lord Camoys (died 1419) and his wife.
Location: 3½ miles W of Midhurst on A272.

Trowbridge *Wilts.*   *Map: 397 Gd*
CLOTH-MAKING TOWN Trowbridge became a centre of the cloth industry in the 14th century, and for 400 years wool was spun and woven in workers' homes. At the end of the 18th century the system began to move from the home to the mill, and there was unrest and rioting. But mills flourished, and by 1830 there were 19 in the town. Some still survive, but at the end of the 19th century trade declined in the face of competition from Yorkshire, where lower-grade cloth was able to capture the new mass markets.

Trumpington *Cambs.*   *Map: 399 Ee*
CHURCH OF ST MARY AND ST MICHAEL The brass monument to Sir Roger de Trumpington, who died in 1289, is the second oldest in England.
Location: 2 miles S of Cambridge off A10.

Tullibardine Chapel *Tayside*   *Map: 389 De*
Sir David Murray of Dumbarton founded the collegiate church in 1446, and it has remained almost unaltered since its completion.
Location: 2½ miles W of Auchterarder (A824, A823 then minor road).

Tummel Bridge *Tayside*   *Map: 387 Da*
Built in the 1730s as part of General George Wade's programme of military road construction, the stone bridge across the River Tummel is over 200 ft long and has two arches.
Location: 13 miles NW of Aberfeldy on B846.

Tunbridge Wells *Kent*   *Map: 399 Eb*
CHURCH OF KING CHARLES THE MARTYR Tunbridge Wells became a fashionable spa in the 1600s, and one of the earliest visitors was Henrietta, wife of Charles I. The red brick church, opened in 1678, was dedicated to Charles I, executed in 1649.
Location: London Rd and Nevile St junction.

Turnberry *Strathclyde*   *Map: 388 Bc*
LIGHTHOUSE The 80 ft high lighthouse overlooking the Firth of Clyde was established in 1873, following many shipwrecks on nearby Bristo Rock. It stands among the ruins of Turnberry Castle, where in 1307 Robert Bruce began the war for Scottish independence.
Location: 6 miles N of Girvan off A77.

Tutbury Castle *Staffs.*   *Map: 393 Ge*
Tutbury has been a stronghold since Saxon days, but most of the surviving buildings date from the 15th century. Mary, Queen of Scots was imprisoned there for periods between 1568 – when she sought asylum in England after defeat by the Scottish Protestant lords – and 1586.
Location: 4 miles NW of Burton upon Trent on A50.

Twycross *Leics.*   *Map: 393 Gd*
CHURCH OF ST JAMES THE GREAT French stained glass dating back to 1145 can be seen in the east window of the 13th-century church. It was originally in the royal church of St Denis near Paris and was probably bought in Paris after the French Revolution in 1789. It was presented to the church in 1840.
Location: 8½ miles N of Nuneaton on A444.

Tynemouth Castle *Tyne & Wear*   *Map: 391 Ge*
On a prominent headland on the north shore of the Tyne mouth, the castle grew up in medieval times round a monastery that had been established in the 7th century. The monks could probably have done without military protection, for the castle was a strategic border fortress, and they had to help finance the garrison during the frequent border warfare.
Location: Front St, off The Promenade (A193).

Tywyn *Gwynedd*   *Map: 392 Cd*
TALYLLYN RAILWAY The narrow-gauge (2 ft 3 in.) railway was opened in 1866 to carry slate from the Bryn Eglwys quarries above Abergynolwyn 7¼ miles to Tywyn for transfer to the main-line railway. From 1867 it also served as a passenger service for local people and quarrymen.
    The quarry closed in 1947, and in 1951 the railway became the first to be taken over by a preservation society. Two of the original engines, *Talyllyn* and *Dolgoch*, are still in use.
Location: Wharf Stn, Neptune Rd, off A493.

U V

A 2,000-YEAR-OLD HORSE
The White Horse of Uffington, cut into a chalk hillside, is the oldest of many white horses in England. Above it is an Iron Age hill-fort.

Uffington *Oxon.*   *Map: 398 Bc*
CHURCH OF ST MARY The church is mainly mid-13th century, with the original south door that retains its decorative wrought-iron hinges. A medieval stone coffin lid is kept in the porch.
    A brass plate commemorates a local boy, Thomas Hughes, who was baptised in the church in 1822 when his grandfather was vicar. He later became famous as the author of *Tom Brown's Schooldays*.
Location: 7½ miles W of Wantage (B4507 and N on minor road).
WHITE HORSE Legend claims that the small flat-topped hill which is overlooked by the White Horse is where St George slew the dragon. The huge horse itself – over 350 ft long and 130 ft high – was probably cut into the chalk downs in the 1st century BC, although some archaeologists believe it is Anglo-Saxon.
    It is similar to galloping horses on late Iron Age coins, and was probably the emblem of the Atrebates who controlled the area.
Location: 6 miles W of Wantage off B4507.

Ufford *Suffolk* *Map: 399 Ge*
CHURCH OF ST MARY The 15th-century font cover
is a masterpiece of woodwork in the form of a
prodigious spire rising in a mass of fine pinnacles,
with a pelican at the top.
Location: 3½ miles NE of Woodbridge, off
B1438.

Uley Bury *Glos.* *Map: 397 Ge*
HILL-FORT Placed in a superb defensive position,
the Iron Age hill-fort has comparatively unim-
pressive man-made defences around its 32 acres.
But its interior has recently produced evidence
of a wealthy population in the 1st century BC.

Excavators have found jewellery of bronze, glass
and shale, iron currency bars and a gold coin of
the Dobunni – the tribe within whose territory
the fort is situated.
Location: 6½ miles SW of Stroud off B4066.

Upleadon *Glos.* *Map: 393 Fb*
CHURCH OF ST MARY THE VIRGIN A Norman
church with a 16th-century timber-framed
tower.

A tombstone to James Broadstock, the local
blacksmith who died in 1768, proclaims: *My
sledge and hammer he's reclined/ My bellows too has
lost its wind/ My fire extinct my forge decayed/ And*

18TH-CENTURY LIFE IN MINIATURE

*A dolls' house at Uppark in W. Sussex contains
perfect replicas in miniature of the contents of an
early-18th-century English house. It was made for the
young Sarah Lethieullier of Belmont in Middlesex
who married Matthew Fetherstonhaugh in 1746, and
so became mistress of Uppark. When she moved to
her new home, the dolls' house went with her. The
dolls' furniture is all made in the style of the Queen
Anne period (1702–14).*

ITALIAN FAÇADE *The house is
an Italian-style
building with
an arcaded
bottom storey.
The Lethieullier
family coat-of-
arms is painted
on the pediment.
The front of
the house
opens out to
reveal nine
furnished rooms.*

BEDROOM *Twin babies lie in a cot at the foot of their
mother's bed, under the eye of a nurse. The miniature
bed-warmer is made of copper.*

KITCHEN *The precisely made pots, frying pans and
plates are made of the correct metal – pewter, copper or
brass. A chinaware coffee-pot stands on the table. The*
*house even has a complete tea-set made of hall-marked
silver. The dolls are perfectly dressed, down to the
right number of petticoats.*

in the dust my vice is laid/ My coal is burnt My iron's gone/ My nails is drove My work is done.
Location: 8 miles NW of Gloucester (A40, B4215 and minor road).

Up Marden *W. Sussex*   *Map: 398 Cb*
CHURCH OF ST MICHAEL Apart from a farm, there is only this delightful 13th-century church at Up Marden, remote and high on the Downs and almost untouched by unsuitable restoration.
Location: 9 miles SE of Petersfield (B2146, B2141 and minor roads from North Marden).

Upminster *Greater London*   *Map: 399 Ec*
TITHE BARN MUSEUM An exhibition of old agricultural implements, farm and craft tools and domestic bygones is housed in a 15th-century thatched timber barn.
Location: Hall Lane, beside golf course.

Upnor Castle *Kent*   *Map: 399 Ec*
Upnor is a Tudor fortress built on the edge of the River Medway to protect shipping at anchorage off Chatham. It was improved in the 17th century and later converted to a gunpowder magazine.
When the Dutch navy sailed up the Medway in 1667, it was bombarded by guns at Upnor. Suddenly the firing stopped, and the Dutch sailed on up river and burned a large number of ships. The failure of the Upnor guns was not for want of courage: supplies had run out.
Location: 1½ miles NE of Rochester along Frindsbury Rd (A228) then Frindsbury Hill.

Uppark *W. Sussex*   *Map: 398 Cb*
In 1816 the Duke of Wellington considered acquiring Uppark as part of his gift from a grateful nation, but he turned it down because the steep approach would be too expensive in horses. The elevated situation of this beautiful house, high on the crest of the Downs, is exceptional for a 17th-century house, and was only made possible by the invention by the builder's grandfather of a pump to raise water from a spring a mile away.
Uppark has a romantic history. In 1746 a young Northumberland man named Matthew Fetherstonhaugh was left a fortune of £400,000 by a remote kinsman, on condition that he bought a baronetcy and an estate in the south of

SANDAL FOR A ROMAN LADY
This Roman lady's sandal is stamped with the name of the maker – Lucius Aibutius Thales, whose high-quality footwear was sent all over the Roman Empire. It was found at the Roman fort of Vindolanda, Northumberland, and probably belonged to the wife or daughter of the commander about AD 100.

England. The condition was soon fulfilled and in addition Sir Matthew married a pretty and talented wife. In 1747 the couple set about reconstructing the interior of their new house at Uppark in the up-to-date style of the day. They put masons, carpenters and plasterers to work, and set off on a Grand Tour that lasted for three years, returning with great quantities of European pictures. In London they bought giltwood rococo looking-glasses, "Red Anchor" Chelsea porcelain, splendid lacquer commodes, mahogany furniture, services of silver and silver-gilt, and Axminster carpets specially woven for the house. Most of their purchases remain at Uppark today and are outstanding examples of the most advanced taste of the period.
The Fetherstonhaughs had one child, Harry, who was only 20 when his father died. He inherited Sir Matthew's fortune and cultivated tastes without his strength of character, and soon fell in with the high-living set that revolved around the Prince of Wales. For a while "Prinny" was a frequent visitor to Uppark and the bed in which he always slept can still be seen.
Two scrawled letters are mementoes of the year that Emma Hart spent at Uppark under Sir Harry's protection. It was there no doubt that she met Charles Greville who was in turn to pass her on to his uncle, Sir William Hamilton, through whom she met Horatio Nelson.
In about 1810, Sir Harry and the prince fell out. The old friend was no longer welcome in "Prinny's" London circle and he retired, querulous and gout-ridden, to Uppark, to devote himself to its improvement with the help of the equally old and crotchety landscape designer Humphrey Repton.
At the age of 71 he fell in love with his dairymaid, sent her to be educated in France and married her in the Saloon in 1825. This incongruous match brought the old man contentment, and when he died in 1846 at the great age of 92, he left Uppark to his widow, Mary Ann, and thereafter to her sister, Frances. For the rest of the 19th century these two ladies, who had been born in a cottage in the village at the foot of the hill, kept Uppark "just as Sir 'Arry 'ad it" and in consequence the Victorian age passed it by.
It was this sense of the pulse of a past age still softly beating that communicated itself to H. G. Wells who, as the son of the housekeeper, spent some of his childhood at Uppark during the old age of the dairy-maid's sister and her companion. In his autobiography he compares the "shrunken routines" of the two old ladies in the parlour above with the zest of life below stairs.
Both parlour and housekeeper's room survive unchanged today. Sir Harry's wheel-chair is there, and from his youth the tortoise-shell cane with, appropriately, Eros inset in the handle. The little columned dairy also survives as it was when the dairy-maid's fortunes so suddenly changed.
Location: 5 miles SE of Petersfield off B2146.

Urquhart Castle *Highland*   *Map: 386 Db*
Jutting out into Loch Ness are the ruins of a castle which was a focal point of Highland warfare. The Normans erected a motte with two baileys on the site of an Iron Age fort, and between the 14th and 16th centuries it was converted into a stone castle.

Urquhart controlled the passes out of the western Highlands along which the Macdonalds, Lords of the Isles, would travel in search of enemies to fight and farms to burn in the north-eastern plains. Ownership of the castle changed hands continually.
Location: 16½ miles SW of Inverness off A82.

Valle Crucis Abbey *Clwyd*　　*Map: 393 De*
Imposing ruins survive of a Cistercian abbey founded in 1201 and left to decay after its dissolution in the 16th century.
Location: 1½ miles N of Llangollen off A542.

Vindolanda *Northld.*　　*Map: 391 Ee*
ROMAN FORT Discoveries at this fort behind Hadrian's Wall include a series of wooden writing tablets, still legible, which give details about life on the frontier of Roman Britain in the late first century – such as the soldiers' diet (mostly corn and meat) and a request for under-pants.
Many of the finds are in the museum near by. The visible remains on the site belong to a 3rd and 4th-century fort and its civilian settlement.
Location: At Chesterholme, 6 miles NE of Haltwhistle (A69 then minor roads).

W

Waddesdon Manor *Bucks.*　　*Map: 398 Cd*
This French-Renaissance-style chateau, com-pleted in 1889, was built by Baron Ferdinand de Rothschild. Many art treasures can be seen.
Location: 5½ miles NW of Aylesbury, off A41.

Walkerburn *Borders*　　*Map: 389 Ec*
SCOTTISH MUSEUM OF WOOL TEXTILES The museum is housed in a mill built in 1854 by the Ballantyne family. They were strict employers: workers were not allowed to talk or have meal breaks, although the mill rules did not specify punishments. The Ballantynes built the village around the mill, which still produces yarn.
Location: 2 miles E of Innerleithen on A72.

Wall *Staffs.*　　*Map: 393 Gd*
ROMAN BATH-HOUSE The bath-house is a survival from a settlement on Watling Street, where a traveller in Roman times could find a room for the night and a stable for his horses.
Location: 2½ miles S of Lichfield (A5127 then minor road).

Wallace Monument *Central*　　*Map: 388 De*
A 220 ft monument on Abbey Craig, near Stirling, commemorates the 13th-century Scots hero Sir William Wallace. His sword is in the museum there.
Location: 2 miles NE of Stirling (A9 then A91 and footpath).

THE BEAUTY OF BUTTONS

Old buttons today can be collectors' items, and at Waddesdon Manor there is a superb collection from the 18th and 19th centuries. The buttons are of various materials, including silver, mother-of-pearl, enamel, porcelain and verre églomisé – glass decorated at the back by painting or gilding. Many of the buttons were designed to decorate men's coats or women's riding habits. There are sets of identical buttons, and other sets with varying designs on particular themes. The collection also includes 18th-century "habitat" buttons, on which insects or grasses are fixed to painted wax backgrounds.

Left: gilt-set ceramic, 18th-19th century.

Above (left and right): late-18th-century enamel.

Above and left: 19th-century porcelain with bird designs.

Verre églomisé, about 1800.

Painted design set in gilt, probably 19th century.

Wallington Hall *Northld.*   *Map: 391 Fe*
The original hall was built in 1688 by a businessman, Sir William Blackett, on the site of a pele tower and house previously owned by the Fenwick family. In 1777 Wallington passed into the hands of the Trevelyans: 20th-century historian G. M. Trevelyan, who died in 1962, lived there as a child. Costly interior decoration by Italian and English craftsmen can be seen. There are also displays of porcelain, needlework, dolls' houses and toys.
Location: 11½ miles W of Morpeth (B6343, then S from Cambo on B6342).

Walmer Castle *Kent*   *Map: 399 Gc*
The castle was built by Henry VIII in 1538–40 as part of a major fortification plan to defend the coast against French invasion. During the Civil War, in 1648, it was besieged by Parliamentary forces. The Royalist garrison surrendered after three weeks. In the early 18th century the castle became the official residence of the Lord Warden of the Cinque Ports. Holders of that office have included the Duke of Wellington and Sir Winston Churchill.
Location: Kingsdown Rd, Walmer.

Walpole St Peter *Norfolk*   *Map: 395 Ea*
CHURCH OF ST PETER AND ST MARY This is so magnificent that it is known as "the Cathedral of the Fens". There has been a church on the site since at least the year 1021. The oldest part of the present building, the tower, dates from about 1300. The altar is raised nine steps above the chancel because it is built over a passage known as the Bolt Hole. In the passage are rings to which horses used to be tethered during services.
Location: 5 miles NE of Wisbech (A47 and minor road).

Walsingham Abbey *Norfolk*   *Map: 395 Fb*
Only ruins survive from the priory (now known as the abbey) established in 1153. It was the site of the shrine of Our Lady of Walsingham, built about 1061 by the lady of the manor who is said to have seen the Virgin Mary in a vision. The shrine was a famous medieval place of pilgrimage, and Walsingham became a place of pilgrimage once again in 1922.
Location: 4 miles N of Fakenham on B1105.

Waltham Abbey *Essex*   *Map: 399 Dd*
The abbey church, consecrated in 1060, became the burial place of King Harold, killed in the Battle of Hastings six years later. Most of the original abbey was demolished in Henry VIII's time. The magnificent Norman nave is the parish church.
Location: 6 miles SW of Epping (A11, A121).

Waltham Cross *Herts.*   *Map: 399 Dd*
ELEANOR CROSS About 50 ft tall and much rebuilt, this is one of three crosses surviving of 12 built by Edward I to mark his wife's funeral route from Lincoln to her burial in London in 1290.
Location: 3 miles NE of Enfield on A10.

Walthamstow *Greater London*   *Map: 399 Dd*
VESTRY HOUSE This was built as a workhouse in 1730 and remained one until 1870. After various other uses it became a local-history museum in 1930. Over the door is inscribed this warning:

"If any would not work, neither Should he eat." Inmates wore uniforms labelled WP (for Walthamstow Poor) and were fed on porridge, soup, bread and beer. Men did market gardening and dug gravel, women sewed clothes and picked oakum (unravelling old hemp rope for re-use) and the children knitted garments.
Location: Vestry Rd, E17.

Wanlockhead *Dumfs. & Gall.*   *Map: 390 Cf*
LEAD-MINING MUSEUM The village was built to house workers for lead and gold mines in the region. The Museum of the Scottish Lead Mining Industry – in Goldscaur Row, the site of early gold washings – has many relics of the industry dating from the last century. There is also an open-air display, including mine-head installations, a beam-engine, smelting mills and tramways, which can be reached by a visitors' walkway.
Location: 6 miles E of Sanquhar (A76, B797).

Wansford *Northants.*   *Map: 398 Df*
NENE VALLEY RAILWAY The railway runs for 6 miles through the Nene Valley from Wansford to Orton Mere, along the route of the old Northampton and Peterborough line. Twenty historic steam locomotives are housed at Wansford and most are used on the regular passenger service. The collection includes Thomas the Tank Engine, which inspired the children's book of that name by the Reverend Wilbert Awdry in 1946.
Location: 5 miles SE of Stamford on A1.

Wanstead *Greater London*   *Map: 399 Dc*
CHURCH OF ST MARY This replacement for the medieval parish church was built in 1790, at a cost of £9,000. Many Georgian fittings survive, including box pews, galleries and an elegant pulpit with a sounding-board canopy supported on palm-tree columns. A relic transferred from the medieval building is an elaborate monument to the banker Sir Josiah Child, who died in 1699. He is shown in an unlikely combination of Roman dress and full-bottomed wig.
Location: Overton Drive, E11.

Warblington *Hants.*   *Map: 398 Ca*
ST THOMAS A BECKET CHURCH The building is partly Saxon, with a nave added in the 13th century. In the churchyard are two huts built in the early 19th century for guards who watched for body-snatchers. Some gravestones are carved with representations of the ways in which those buried met their deaths. Near by is a ruined turret, the only remnant of Warblington Castle, which was destroyed by Cromwell's troops in 1643.
Location: 1¼ miles W of Emsworth on A27.

Warburton *Greater Manchester*   *Map: 393 Ff*
ST WERBURGH OLD CHURCH The old church, parts of which are believed to date from the 12th century, was superseded in 1885 by a bigger building near by. The old building is partly of timber construction. A square brick tower was added in 1711. In an oak door below the tower is a spyhole once used in watching for body-snatchers.
Location: 2 miles NE of Lymm (A6144 then minor road N).

NOAH AND ALL HIS FAMILY

Among the many exhibits at Wallington Hall, in Northumberland, is a 19th-century Noah's Ark, a toy based on the Bible story of the Flood from which Noah escaped with two animals of every kind. The

Ark – with Noah, his wife and family and 60 animals, in pairs – is carved in wood. It was a gift to Wallington House, and on the back of the ark itself is the inscription "Ethel Shipman from her father: 1895".

Wardle *Greater Manchester*   *Map: 393 Ee*
The village grew up with the textile industry early in the 19th century. In Ramsden Road, in the southern part of the village, is a well-preserved group of former weavers' cottages – private homes – their second-storey workshops identified by long windows which allowed light for the looms. Wardle Mill, where the wool yarn was spun, is near the church: the owner's house and more workers' cottages – also private homes – are next to the mill. Higher up the hill is the old mill pond.
Location: 3 miles NE of Rochdale (A58 and minor road).

Warfield *Berks.*   *Map: 398 Cc*
CHURCH OF ST MICHAEL An interesting Early English and Decorated church mainly dating from the 14th century. In the east window there is a good flowing tracery design. A rare survival is the 15th-century Rood Loft. A monument to John Walsh, who died in 1797, is an example of fashionable sculpture of the period: a life-sized figure of a woman mourning beside an urn.
Location: 3 miles N of Bracknell (A3095 then minor road).

Warham Camp *Norfolk*   *Map: 395 Fb*
Iceni tribesmen built a fort on this 3½ acre site, probably in the first half of the 1st century AD. The outlines of the double ditch and embankment fortifications can be seen. All are perfectly circular, a design sometimes also used by the Danes.
Location: 2 miles SE of Wells-next-the-Sea (A149 then B1105, minor road and footpath).

Warwick *Warks.*   *Map: 398 Be*
WARWICK CASTLE As early as the 10th century there was a fort on the rising ground beside the Avon, where Warwick Castle now stands. A Norman castle on the site was sacked by Simon de Montfort in the Barons' War of 1264.

In the 13th century, the earldom of Warwick passed to the Beauchamp family, who were responsible for most of the structure which has

survived. The east end of the castle was made almost impregnable, with a huge gatehouse tower and two other towers on either side of it. One of these, the 12-sided Guy's Tower, is 128 ft high and has walls 10 ft thick. The other, Caesar's Tower, is 132 ft tall and has a double array of battlements.

The castle's most noted owner was Richard Nevill (1428–71), who married Anne Beauchamp, only daughter of the Earl of Warwick, and became earl at the age of 21. His successful intrigues against Henry VI and then his own cousin, Edward IV, earned him the nickname "King Maker". Nevill was killed in 1471 by Edward's forces, in the Battle of Barnet.

An English poet, Sir Fulke Greville, 1st Baron Brooke, was given the castle in 1604. The earldom of Warwick was granted to the Greville family in 1759.

There are fine collections of art and armour.
Location: Castle Lane, Warwick.
CHURCH OF ST MARY A great fire destroyed much of the 14th-century building, as well as more than 200 houses, in 1694: the heat was so fierce that it melted the church bells. The superb 15th-century Beauchamp Chapel survives, with monuments to earls of Warwick (15th century) and Leicester (16th century). The nave and the 174 ft tower date from 1704.
Location: Church St.
THE COURT HOUSE One of the finest buildings in Warwick is the Court House, built in the 1720s by Francis Smith, a bricklayer's son who became a master builder and twice mayor of the town. It has a second-storey ballroom.
Location: Corner of Jury St and Castle St.
LORD LEYCESTER HOSPITAL These lovely timber-framed houses were built in the late 14th century as a merchant guild's headquarters. In 1571 Robert Dudley, 1st Earl of Leicester (or Leycester) took them over – and the adjoining St James Chapel, perched on the town's West Gate – as a "hospital" or home of rest for retired soldiers. The hospital still houses ex-servicemen and their wives.
Location: High St.

OKEN'S HOUSE The timber-framed house that is now the Warwick Doll Museum was the 16th-century home of Thomas Oken, a wealthy local dealer in silks and other fabrics. Oken, who was born poor and attained his success through shrewdness and industry, never forgot his humble beginnings and left his fortune for the founding of almshouses. The doll museum was founded in 1955 by Joy Robinson, who inherited and enlarged a collection of old dolls. The display contains more than 1,000 antique dolls – including clockwork and musical dolls from all over Europe.

Location: Castle St, town centre.

DOLLS THROUGH THE AGES

The collection of old dolls at Oken House in Warwick is a fascinating illustration of how these toys developed from the early 18th century onwards. But the history of dolls may stretch back into antiquity – for some authorities believe that tiny Egyptian religious figures of painted wood, dating back to 2000 BC, and similar ceremonial figures unearthed in Africa, South America, Greece and elsewhere, were later handed on to children as playthings.

The earliest surviving European dolls are 13th-century clay ones found in Germany, but wood and fabric were the most widely used early materials. Mass-produced, simple wooden Dutch dolls – from Germany as well as Holland – became popular in England from the 17th century. At the same time, finery was introduced into dolls' dress, in imitation of the model mannequins which had long been used by French fashion houses to advertise their clothes.

During the 19th century, wax and porcelain took over from wood as the most popular materials, and in their turn these have been largely replaced this century by rubber and plastic.

WOODEN DOLLS *Not all wooden dolls were simple figures mass-manufactured for poor children. The late-17th-century Lord and Lady Clapham (left), part of a valuable collection of dolls in London's Victoria and Albert Museum, are carved with considerable skill. The most celebrated wooden dolls, now on display at Kensington Palace, are the 132 which Queen Victoria owned as a girl. She and her governess dressed these as stage characters and contemporary ladies of the court.*

BISQUE DOLLS *In the 19th century porcelain dolls became increasingly popular because the material not only lent itself to lifelike reproduction of the human face but, unlike wax, was also durable. Bisque, or unglazed porcelain, was especially suitable for heads because the lack of glaze resulted in more precisely defined features. The legs and arms of such dolls (below) were also of bisque, but bodies were wood or linen.*

WAX DOLLS *Apart from its fragility, wax is the perfect material for modelling the faces of dolls. English doll-makers began using wax in the early 1800s and by the middle of the century they were producing fine dolls like the one of 1862 above.*

Washington *Tyne & Wear*   *Map: 391 Ge*
RESTORED COLLIERY Washington "F" Pit, which
was closed in 1968 after nearly two centuries of
coal-mining, now houses an industrial museum
in the restored winder house. Other colliery
buildings have been removed. Among the exhibits is the 200 ft high winding engine which was
installed at "F" pit in 1888 and wound men and
materials up and down the shaft, in cages, for 80
years. The wheels and steam-valves are now
worked by electricity, for display purposes.
Location: Albany Way, Washington New
Town.
WASHINGTON OLD HALL Direct ancestors of America's first president, George Washington, lived
on this site between 1183 and 1613. In 1183,
William de Hartburn acquired Wessyngton
(Washington) village from the Bishop of Durham, in exchange for Hartburn, 20 miles further
north. Following custom, he became de Wessyngton. The present house, built in the early
17th century, is now a museum.
Location: In Washington village, 6 miles W of
Sunderland, off A1231.

Watford *Herts.*   *Map: 398 Dd*
CHURCH OF ST MARY The flint-built church is
basically of 13th-century construction, with
major additions from the 15th and 16th centuries
and woodwork from the 19th. Its west tower
has a stair turret capped by a small spirelet – a
typical Hertfordshire feature. Two brasses commemorate a judge named Hugh de Holes, who
died in 1415, and his wife, who died the following year.
    In the north chapel are monuments by Nicho-
las Stone, England's leading sculptor in the first
half of the 17th century.
Location: Watford town centre, off High St.

Watford *Northants.*   *Map: 398 Cf*
WATFORD STAIRCASE Seven locks on the Grand
Union Canal's Leicester section, completed in
1814 and still in use, climb north towards
Watford, forming the Watford Staircase. It raises
the canal level by 52 ft 6 in. between the B4036
and M1 road bridges. Each lock opens directly
into the next, the top gates of one lock forming
the bottom gates of the next one up.
Location: 4 miles NE of Daventry on B4036
before M1 crossing.

Wath *N. Yorks.*   *Map: 394 Be*
CHURCH OF ST MARY The original church, probably Saxon, was altered and enlarged over the
centuries, although it is still not big – there is no
aisle in the nave. The sanctuary contains a
splendidly decorated 14th-century Flemish oak
chest. A monument to a former vicar, the
Reverend Thomas Brand, who died in 1814, is
by John Flaxman, the Yorkshire-born sculptor
and artist who became the leading exponent of
the neo-classical style in England.
Location: 4 miles N of Ripon on minor road.

Wavertree *Merseyside*   *Map: 393 Ef*
CHURCH OF THE HOLY TRINITY A landmark in its
neighbourhood, the church was originally built
in 1794. The present east end, designed by Sir
Charles Reilly, was added in 1911. Alterations at
that time also included the removal of the
galleries on the north and south sides, although

THE PERILS OF MINING

"PENITENT" *In the early days of mining, a man draped in
water-soaked sacking would explode a pocket of gas with a
long torch. From his garb, he was known as a "Penitent".*

Flooding, roof falls, collapsing shafts, suffocating
gases – all these made the life of the early miner a highly
dangerous as well as a hard one. But one of the greatest
hazards was firedamp, a combustible mixture of
methane and air. Before the days of electricity, a naked
flame was the only form of working light available to
miners, and, as a result, horrifying explosions occurred.
One of them, at Fatfield near Sunderland in 1708,
hurled mine workers high into the air from the bottom
of a 340 ft deep shaft. In the early 18th century a steel
mill was invented to produce light from sparks. But it
still ignited the gas.
    It was not until 1816, as the result of an explosion on
the Durham coalfield that killed 92 miners, that the
invention of a safety lamp by Sir Humphry Davy, a
Cornish chemist, gave every miner who used it
protection against firedamp.

THE MINERS' BOON
*The invention of
Sir Humphry Davy's
safety lamp drastically
reduced explosions in
mines. The wire mesh
which enclosed the oil
lamp absorbed its heat
and prevented the
ignition of gas. It was
also a warning lamp,
as its flame changed
colour in the presence
of firedamp.*

the west gallery remains. On the opposite side of
the road are mounting-steps once used by worshippers who went to church on horseback.
Location: Church Rd, $3\frac{1}{4}$ miles E of Liverpool
city centre, off Wavertree High St (B5178).

Wayland's Smithy *Oxon.*   *Map: 398 Bc*
According to folk-lore, this ancient tomb was the
home of an invisible blacksmith named Wayland,
who would shoe a traveller's horse if a penny was
placed on a great flat slab which forms the roof of
one chamber.
    The part of the megalithic monument which
can still be seen, was built about 3500 BC. The
broad southern end of the tomb was fronted by
six great stones: four of these still stand like

sentries guarding the entrance to the burial chambers. A small ante-chamber leads into a 22 ft long passage, with two chambers on each side forming a cross-shaped burial area. At least eight people were buried there. This imposing burial place lies above a smaller monument usually known as an earthen long barrow.

It appears that the visible tomb was deliberately built over the earlier barrow. This may have been a means of maintaining continuity in a family or dynastic cemetery at a time when the style of burial was changing. The earlier monument would have consisted of an oblong timber mortuary house, covered by a barrow. In such a barrow, a succession of dead would be buried, as a final act after they had been originally buried or laid out elsewhere.

When the mortuary house was full – with perhaps 14 bodies lying there – it would be carefully covered with boulders and then sealed off with an oval mound of chalk. The funerals, and the eventual closing of the mortuary house, are likely to have been accompanied by rituals of which there is no trace at this site, although there are hints of them at other sites. Rituals appear to have included funeral feasting, simple offerings to the dead, and sometimes a sorting out of skeletal remains to recover particular bones which were probably used in magical rites.
Location: 7½ miles W of Wantage off B4507.

STONE AGE TOMB

The entrance to Wayland's Smithy, a Stone Age burial-place believed to date from about 3500 BC, is guarded by great stones, two of which can be seen on the left and right of the picture. In the background is an ante-chamber with a flat stone roof: according to legend, if a traveller placed a penny on the stone an invisible blacksmith named Wayland would shoe his horse for him.

Weald and Downland Museum see Singleton

Weardale Forest *Durham*   *Map: 391 Ed*
KILLHOPE LEAD MINE A huge water-wheel, almost 34 ft across, is the landmark for this disused lead mine and processing plant, built in the 1860s, which ended production in 1917. The wheel is all that remains of the mine's machinery. It was used to drive crushing rollers; the water which powered the wheel was collected by a system of races 11 miles long. Near by, close to the mine entrance (which is now sealed off), is a building which once housed a smithy, manager's office and miners' lodgings. Although this is designated a picnic area, visitors should take care when looking around the old buildings.
Location: 8 miles SE of Alston off A689.

Weeting Castle *Norfolk*   *Map: 399 Ef*
The ruins of a 12th-century fortified manor house, probably founded by William de Warenne, a friend of William the Conqueror, stand in a moated rectangular enclosure. The castle was at one time owned by the Howard family (who were to become the dukes of Norfolk). Little is known about the manner of its destruction.
Location: 8 miles NW of Thetford (B1107, B1106 and minor road).

Wellow *Notts.*   *Map: 394 Cb*
CHURCH OF ST SWITHIN The Gothic church, partly 12th and 13th century, has a Norman font and a fine 300-year-old wooden-case clock, with a face made locally to commemorate the coronation of Elizabeth II in 1953. The village, on the fringe of Sherwood Forest, still has its ducking-stool and remains of punishment stocks.
Location: 11½ miles NW of Newark-on-Trent off A616.

Wells *Somerset*   *Map: 397 Fd*
WELLS CATHEDRAL The serene and beautiful cathedral at Wells, begun in 1180, is one of the best loved in the country. It was the first cathedral in England to be built wholly in the Gothic style – with pointed arches throughout. Unique scissor-like double arches – an inverted arch standing on the point of an upright one – were built after alarming cracks appeared in 1340 in the wall supporting the central tower.

The celebrated west façade of the cathedral, completed in 1282, was designed as a magnificent open-air gallery to display nearly 400 painted statues of saints, bishops, prophets and kings. In the 17th century some statues were destroyed or mutilated by Puritans. However, most have survived, although they are eroded.

Inside the cathedral are superb figure carvings (at the top of columns in the transepts). In the north transept is a 14th-century astronomical clock. A worn and winding stone Prior's Staircase leads to the Chapter House – also 14th century – which is one of the cathedral's architectural triumphs. This is a great eight-sided chamber, with huge, intricate-patterned windows and a soaring vaulted roof: the 32 ribs of the vault spring from a central marble pillar.

The glory of Wells is completed by a group of buildings which include the moated Bishop's Palace, the vast cloister and Vicar's Close – the only complete medieval street left in Britain.
Location: St Andrews St.

Welwyn *Herts.* *Map: 399 Dd*
ROMAN BATH-HOUSE A small Roman bath-house, discovered just in time to be saved from obliteration by road-building, is now preserved in a vault beneath the A1(M). The bath-house was built in the middle of the 3rd century for a Roman villa. Also in the vault is a display of pre-historic and Roman material.
Location: 2½ miles N of Welwyn Garden City off A1000. The entrance is on a slip road connecting B197 and B1000.

Wensley *N. Yorks.* *Map: 391 Fc*
CHURCH OF THE HOLY TRINITY The chancel dates from 1245, when an older Saxon church on this site was replaced. Most of the rest of the present building is from the 14th to 17th centuries. A fine, almost life-size, brass on the floor of the sanctuary commemorates Sir Simon de Wenslawe, a priest of the parish who died in 1394. There are remnants of a 14th-century wall-painting
Location: 1½ miles SW of Leyburn off A684.

Weobley Castle *W. Glam.* *Map: 392 Ba*
The castle was started in the 13th century and buildings were added to it up to the 15th. Early in the 15th century, the Welsh rebel Owain Glyndwr attacked the castle and badly damaged it. The damage was repaired and the castle later passed to Rhys ap Thomas, a supporter of Henry VII. After Thomas's death, his heir, Rhys ap Gruffydd, was executed by Henry VIII for treason, and the castle was eventually sold to the Earl of Pembroke. He rented part of it to a farmer, and the rest fell into disrepair. What remains, including the 13th-century hall, has been well preserved.
Location: 13½ miles W of Swansea (A4118, B4271 and minor roads).

West Bromwich *W. Midlands* *Map: 393 Fd*
OAK HOUSE The black-and-white gabled mansion, built in the 16th century, is surmounted by an unusual "lantern turret"—a tall tower with large windows which allow extra light into the centre of the house. About 1635 the back of the mansion was faced with brick. The house is now a museum, furnished as it might have been in Jacobean times.
Location: Oak Rd, off High St (5 miles NW of Birmingham city centre off A41).

Westbury-on-Severn *Glos.* *Map: 393 Fb*
WESTBURY COURT GARDEN Although Westbury Court itself has gone, the garden survives—a rare example of the water-garden fashion introduced to England in the 17th century by supporters of William of Orange. This garden, first laid out in about 1700, has the original pavilions, as well as the canals filled with water lilies and edged with closely clipped yew trees.
Location: 9 miles SW of Gloucester off A48.

Westerham *Kent* *Map: 399 Ec*
QUEBEC HOUSE General James Wolfe, who was killed at the age of 32 while taking Quebec from the French in 1759, spent his early childhood in this charming 16th-century red brick house, which was then called Spiers. The mementoes of Wolfe which are on display include the only known portrait of him from life—a pencil profile drawn by one of his military staff during the Quebec campaign.
Location: E end of town at the junction of A25 and B2026.
SQUERRYES COURT The Warde family, friends of General Wolfe, owned this handsome William and Mary house in his time and still do so. The house still contains its 18th-century furniture and tapestries, as well as a fine collection of pictures, including works by Van Dyck and Reubens.
Location: W end of town off A25.

HOW THE ROMANS BUILT A ROAD

The highways built by the Romans during their occupation of Britain are among their most distinctive memorials. These roads, linking military and civilian centres, were as straight as possible, except where hilly terrain made a winding or zigzag course inevitable. In many places, the road was built on a raised embankment (an "agger") to help drainage. The agger could be as much as 5 ft high and up to 50 ft wide. Sometimes it was a simple earth mound; where necessary, it was carefully built up in layers of gravel or stone. Sometimes, just below the surface was a foundation of large stones, although smaller stones or layers of rammed gravel were usually thought sufficient.

The road surface itself was gravel. Paving slabs do not appear to have been commonly used. As a result, the original surface has usually been washed away – as in the Roman road on Wheeldale Moor, N. Yorkshire, shown in the picture.

How our Saxon ancestors lived

A VILLAGE OF WOODEN HUTS THAT FLOURISHED MORE THAN 1,000 YEARS AGO IS BEING RECONSTRUCTED AT WEST STOW, SUFFOLK

Traces of about 80 buildings from a village which flourished between AD 400 and 650 were found during excavations at West Stow, Suffolk. These remains, with other relics such as clay loam weights, bone weaving pins, bone combs, pot sherds and the bones of sheep, cattle, birds, fish, deer, horses, pigs and dogs, have enabled archaeologists to build up a detailed picture of life in this typical East Anglian Saxon village.

The excavations showed that the Anglo-Saxons lived in substantial huts with wooden floors built over central pits.

The huts were clustered around larger buildings, used as communal halls or meeting-places. Several buildings are being reconstructed from archaeological evidence, with a view to developing the site as a living experiment with typical 7th-century crops, animals and handicrafts.

The reconstruction, using scientific evidence from the charred remains of burned-out buildings, is being done by ancient methods. Only iron tools such as those the Anglo-Saxons would have had (axe, adze, spoon auger, chisel and knife, but no nails) have been used.

HOMES OF OAK AND THATCH

Three reconstructions of Saxon houses at West Stow: on the right, a traditional interpretation — sunken house with bivouac roof. On the left, the newer interpretation – a substantial walled house built over a pit. The third building is a communal hall. Walls and floors are of oak, the rafters of ash. The thatched roof is supported by hazel hurdling. Each hall is believed to have been a focal point for a large family group. The houses were stores and workshops as well as living quarters.

HUT ROOF *Ash rafters and hazel hurdling support the thatch on the roofs of the huts.*

HALL BEAMS *In the communal hall, roof beams have been jointed, using Saxon-style tools.*

WALL JOINT *Clay was used to seal joints in the hut walls as a modern timber-saving economy.*

West Kennet *Wilts.*　　　　*Map: 398 Ac*
LONG BARROW Behind a row of huge stones lies a 330 ft long mound containing five burial chambers. These could possibly date from as long ago as 3250 BC. Remains of at least 46 people, including a dozen children, were found during excavations in the 1950s. Many may have

been related to each other. Some had also suffered from arthritis, probably because of their poor living conditions.
Location: 5½ miles W of Marlborough off A4.

Weston Park *Staffs.*　　　　*Map: 393 Fd*
The great Weston Park mansion was built in

BRONZE BROOCH *One of the Anglo-Saxon relics found in the cemetery at West Stow: the elaborately fashioned brooch, about 6 in. long, dates from around AD 550.*

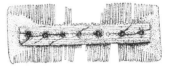

BONE COMB *Another Anglo-Saxon relic discovered at West Stow is a 6 in. long bone comb dated between AD 400 and 625.*

DRESS-FASTENER *The "hook and eye" system was used in this Saxon bronze dress-fastener, about 3½ in. long.*

BEAUTY AIDS *Bronze tweezers, made to be suspended from a woman's belt, are among the beauty aids used by Saxons. Other instruments included ear picks and nail cleaners.*

GAME COUNTER *This bone counter, well-worn but still clearly showing its decorative carving, was probably used in some form of draughts.*

SAXON FIRESIDE *Inside one of the reconstructed Anglo-Saxon family huts at West Stow, a prominent feature is the round clay hearth for the fire. Beyond the hearth is a foot-operated wood lathe. To the left of the lathe is the door, standing open. The interior view of the typical Saxon home clearly shows the method of construction used by the original builders, over 1,000 years ago. These huts were traditionally built with a wooden floor covering a pit. At one time, it was believed that the inhabitants lived in the pit, actually below ground level. But more recent research has suggested that the pit provided a "damp course", and that the floor of the hut was supported over it to keep the floorboards well away from the damp ground.*

1671 for Sir Thomas and Lady Wilbraham and designed by Lady Wilbraham herself. She produced one of the finest Restoration houses in Britain. The front overlooks a park laid out 100 years later by "Capability" Brown.
Location: On A5 at Weston under Lizard, 6 miles W of junction 12 on M6.

West Stow *Suffolk* Map: 399 Ff
ANGLO-SAXON VILLAGE On the most completely explored Anglo-Saxon settlement of its kind in Britain, a village which flourished in AD 400–650 is being rebuilt. (See above.)
Location: 7½ miles NW of Bury St Edmunds (A1101 and minor road).

367

West Wales Farm Park *Dyfed*   *Map: 392 Bc*
A large collection of rare horses, cattle, sheep, pigs, goats, rabbits and poultry – many breeds first imported to Britain more than a century ago – are kept on the farm.
Location: 12 miles NE of Cardigan (A487 then S on minor road at Plwmp).

Westwood Manor *Wilts.*   *Map: 397 Gd*
The manor is a small stone house of great charm, founded in about 1400. It was enlarged in about 1480 and again after 1515, when wealthy clothier Thomas Horton bought the house. Westwood Manor has a number of inside porches of panelled oak – decorative draught-excluding devices.
Location: 2 miles SW of Bradford-on-Avon off B3109.

West Wycombe Park *Bucks.*   *Map: 398 Cd*
In the 18th century, the great house at West Wycombe became notorious as the focal point of a "Hellfire Club" led by Sir Francis Dashwood. Sir Francis, who refashioned the previous brick house into a Palladian-style mansion, was in turn a dilettante traveller, MP, Chancellor of the Exchequer and Postmaster General. Orgies and black-magic rites were a feature of the gatherings of Dashwood and his rakes.
Location: 2½ miles NW of High Wycombe off A40.

Whaley Bridge *Derbys.*   *Map: 393 Ff*
CANAL-RAILWAY INTERCHANGE A railway was opened in 1831 to link the Peak Forest Canal at Whaley Bridge with the Cromford Canal, 33 miles south-east, on the far side of the Peak hills. The railway met the canal in a covered terminus: rails emerged from one end and the canal from the other. The building, in the town centre, is now an art gallery.
Location: 7 miles NW of Buxton on A6.

Wharram Percy *N. Yorks.*   *Map: 394 Ce*
From Roman times until the Middle Ages, a village flourished on this site. Around 1500, it became one of thousands inexplicably deserted. Excavations have disclosed remains of houses from the 12th to 16th centuries.
Location: 7½ miles SE of Malton (B1248 and SW on minor road at Wharram le Street).

Wheeldale Moor *N. Yorks.*   *Map: 394 Cf*
WADE'S CAUSEWAY The most impressive piece of original Roman highway to be seen in Britain is a 1¼ mile stretch of the road which once ran 21 miles north from Malton to Whitby. The gravel top surface has long vanished, but the foundation slabs, with some drainage culverts and kerbstones, remain. According to legend, the road was built by a giant named Wade.
Location: 11 miles SW of Whitby (A169 then minor road via Goathland).

Whitby *N. Yorks.*   *Map: 394 Cf*
ABBEY The original abbey, founded on a cliff-top in 657, was one of 12 set up by St Oswy, King of Northumbria, in thanks for his victory over the King of Mercia two years earlier. The abbey was destroyed by the Danes in 867 and refounded about 1078. The second abbey is now a spectacular ruin.
Location: Abbey Lane, on E bank of R. Esk.

CHURCH OF ST MARY The church, near the abbey ruins, was begun in 1100 and underwent alterations up to the 19th century. It has a mass of 18th-century galleries and box-pews, and a three-deck pulpit dating from about 1778.
Location: E. Cliff, E bank of R. Esk.

WHITBY HIGH LIGHTHOUSE An eight-sided stone tower, 44 ft high and built in 1858, carries a warning light 240 ft above sea level.
Location: Off Hawsker Lane, High Whitby.

Whitchurch *Hants.*   *Map: 398 Bb*
SILK MILL The original water-wheel of this 18th-century mill survives, although it is not used. Visitors can still see silk being woven.
Location: Winchester St (A34), SW of town centre.

White Castle *Gwent*   *Map: 393 Eb*
The castle, begun in the 12th century and strengthened by Edward I in the 13th, got its name because at one time the walls were plastered white.
Location: 7 miles NE of Abergavenny (B4521 and minor road).

Whitehaven *Cumbria*   *Map: 390 Cd*
DUKE PIT The ruins of a coalmine first sunk in 1747 and modernised in the 1840s resemble at first sight a derelict castle. In the modernisation, massive stone walls, in medieval Gothic style, were built around the mine shaft.
Location: South Beach recreation area.

OLD QUAY Some of the oldest coaling wharves in Britain are to be found in Whitehaven harbour – built in the 17th century so that coal from local pits could be shipped to towns in the south. The Old Quay is the earliest part of the harbour. Work on it began in 1634.
Location: Harbour.

WELLINGTON PIT At this mine, opened near to Duke Pit in 1840, the Gothic style was even more elaborately used. The owner, the first Earl of Lonsdale, employed the architect Sydney Smirke, who made the surface buildings resemble the battlements of some great fortification.
Location: South Beach recreation area.

White Horse see Uffington

White House see Munslow Aston

Whitley Castle *Northld.*   *Map: 391 Ed*
ROMAN FORT A remarkable system of ditches is an impressive reminder of this fort, even though no stonework is now visible. The fort was built in the 2nd century and rebuilt in the 3rd; its Roman name is unknown. Ask at Whitlow Farm for permission to visit.
Location: 2½ miles NW of Alston (A689 to just beyond bridge over stream, then track on left).

Whittington Castle *Salop*   *Map: 393 Ee*
The stout gatehouse and walls survive from the castle rebuilt by the warlike baron Fulke Fitzwarine after it was damaged in an attack by Llywelyn the Great in the 1220s.
Location: 16½ miles NW of Shrewsbury on A5.

Whittlesey *Cambs.*   *Map: 399 Df*
CHURCH OF ST MARY A magnificent vaulted spire was added in the mid-15th century to the church

which had been largely rebuilt after fire damage in the 13th. There is a monument to General Sir Harry Smith, a former Governor of the Cape of Good Hope, who died in 1860 and is buried in the town cemetery. The South African town of Ladysmith, which was to become famous because of its siege in 1899, was named after his wife, who is buried in the same cemetery.
Location: Market St (B1093) off Market Pl.

Wicken Fen *Cambs.*   *Map: 399 Ef*
NATURE RESERVE Almost all that is left of the ancient Great Fen of East Anglia, which once covered 2,500 sq. miles, is now the Wicken Fen nature reserve, little more than 1 sq. mile in area. A wide variety of water birds visit the fen and there are at least 300 kinds of flowering plants and 5,000 species of insects.
Location: 8½ miles S of Ely (A10 then E on A1123).
WICKEN FEN MILL In the 18th century as many as 700 windmills, equipped with water scoops, were being used to drain the fens. Eventually they were replaced with diesel or electric pumps. This windmill was built in 1908 and stood on Adventurers' Fen, part of the nature reserve. In 1956 it was moved to Wicken Sedge Fen and is now used to help to keep up the water level so that the peat bed will not dry out.
Location: At E end of Wicken Sedge Fen.

Wickham *Berks.*   *Map: 398 Bc*
CHURCH OF ST SWITHIN Many effigies of angels (and eight papier-mâché elephant heads, brought from the Paris exhibition of 1862) decorate the ceiling of this church, most of which was rebuilt in the mid-19th century. The tower dates from the 11th century and includes some Roman balusters of an earlier period, re-used. It once served the purpose of watchtower and beacon. A high doorway, now blocked, was reached by a ladder which could be drawn up.
Location: 5½ miles NW of Newbury on B4000.

Wigan *Lancs.*   *Map: 391 Ea*
LEEDS AND LIVERPOOL CANAL A mound at the edge of the wharf in the canal basin is all that remains to show where the jetty that became famous as Wigan Pier once stood. The section of canal joining Wigan and Liverpool was opened in 1772, and passenger boats used to leave the pier daily at 7 a.m., taking eight hours for the 35 mile journey. The canal is still in use.
Location: ½ mile S of town centre, crossed by A49.

Willoughby on Wolds *Notts.*   *Map: 394 Ca*
CHURCH OF ST MARY AND ALL SAINTS This picturesque church has an interesting group of monuments, in stone and alabaster, to medieval members of the Willoughby family. There are figures of Sir Richard de Willoughby – a judge under Edward II – and his son, also Sir Richard, who replaced him on the bench in 1324.
Location: 14½ miles NE of Leicester (A46 and minor roads).

Wilmcote *Warks.*   *Map: 398 Ae*
MARY ARDEN'S HOUSE William Shakespeare's mother, Mary Arden – the daughter of a wealthy farmer – lived in this half-timbered Tudor house before she married John Shakespeare, a glove-

maker. Eventually the house was bequeathed to her. After the marriage, probably in 1557, the couple moved to Stratford-upon-Avon. The house and farm buildings are now a Shakespeare countryside museum.
Location: 3½ miles NW of Stratford-upon-Avon (A34 and minor road W).

Wilmington *E. Sussex*   *Map: 399 Ea*
LONG MAN A 240 ft high outline cut into the chalk of the Sussex Downs appears as restored in 1874, although it may date from Roman times or even earlier. Today the Long Man holds two plain staffs, but he may originally have carried a rake and scythe or (representing the pagan god Woden) two spears.
Location: 8 miles NW of Eastbourne (A22, A27 then S on minor road).

Wilton *Wilts.*   *Map: 398 Ab*
CARPET FACTORY Carpets have been made at Wilton for centuries. The present Wilton Royal Carpet factory premises were built in the late 18th century. Visitors can see Wilton and Axminster carpets at all stages of manufacture, but it is advisable to book in advance.
Location: King St, town centre.
WILTON HOUSE The long, perfectly proportioned south front, set off by wide lawns, ancient cedars, the River Nadder and an exquisite Palladian bridge, make this one of the most beautiful of English houses. Wilton was built in the 16th century by the 1st Earl of Pembroke, but has been greatly changed since then. The bridge was built by the 9th earl in 1737.
When the 2nd earl lived at Wilton with his wife, Mary – sister of the statesman-poet Sir Philip Sidney – the house was visited by many leading literary figures, including Ben Jonson, Edmund Spenser and Christopher Marlowe.
Location: 3 miles W of Salisbury off A36.

Wimborne Minster *Dorset*   *Map: 398 Aa*
The minster was founded as a nunnery about 713. The brother of Alfred the Great was buried there in 871. An astronomical clock is said to date from 1320 and there is a chained library of 240 books, founded for the public in 1686.
Location: King St (A31), town centre.

Winchcombe *Glos.*   *Map: 398 Ad*
CHURCH OF ST PETER Grotesque carved heads beneath the battlements are a striking feature of the church, built during the 15th century, when Winchcombe grew prosperous from the wool trade. Inside, an altar cloth made from priests' copes of the 14th century is displayed. In a border which has been added can be seen an embroidered pomegranate, the heraldic badge of Catherine of Aragon – first wife of Henry VIII. She is said to have done some of the embroidery while staying at nearby Sudeley Castle. A magnificent weathercock was added to the church in the 19th century: it came from the church of St Mary Redcliffe, Bristol.
Location: 6½ miles NE of Cheltenham on A46.

Winchester *Hants*   *Map: 398 Bb*
CASTLE A Norman motte-and-bailey castle was a royal residence by the end of William the Conqueror's reign, and Domesday Book was kept there. King John's son, later Henry III, was

CARING FOR THE POOR AND THE OLD

Poor people–especially the old and ill–have been helped by their fellow citizens down the years in many ways, some more charitable than others. In the Middle Ages, the task was tackled by trade guilds, wealthy people with a social conscience, and the Church (as with the Hospital of St Cross at Winchester).

Some of the guilds built almshouses for their retired workers: the London brewers' guild did so in 1423, to help "poor Britheren, Soosteren of ye craffte and Fraternite".

The Church helped in various ways. Monasteries traditionally gave food, drink and shelter to beggars as well as travellers. Relief for the poor and sick was organised parish by parish. Most churches (and many inns) had collecting boxes. Sometimes, churchwardens held a "church ale" – the medieval equivalent of today's charity bazaar. Such events were often held in the church itself, and this led to opposition from bishops who objected to "semi-pagan" merrymaking on the premises. The practice died out in the 16th century.

However, the problem of destitution did not die out: it continued to grow. This was partly because of the Dissolution of the Monasteries and the decay of the guilds.

Under Elizabeth I, the Poor Law Acts of 1598 and 1601 established a national system to provide for the "necessary relief of the lame, impotent, old and blind". In each parish, custodians were appointed to collect a special rate from householders and distribute the income in cash or in kind.

Under the new laws, the able-bodied poor were sent to a workhouse or "house of correction", where they spun wool or picked oakum – the harsh, tedious task of unravelling old hemp rope, to be re-used in caulking ships' timbers. A pauper found begging in any parish but his own could be whipped or put in the stocks.

Parishes were authorised to build almshouses or old people's homes out of the rates, but few did so. It was more usual to rely on the generosity of the local lord or squire. In the 17th and 18th centuries, wealthy people all over Britain set up almshouses.

In the 19th century the Industrial Revolution swamped the system with a great wave of local unemployment and poverty. In 1834 a new law forced parishes to combine into groups, or "unions", and build huge workhouses for the poor.

To discourage any "idle poor" (those thought not to wish to work), conditions in the workhouse were made deliberately harsh. Families were separated. Able-bodied men were given hard labour, such as breaking stones. Food was kept to the barest minimum.

In 1908 the introduction of an old-age pension (25p a week) helped many old people to retain some independence. But the Poor Law and the workhouse were not finally abolished until 1948.

REGIMENT OF THE DESTITUTE *Obedient inmates were photographed at the Marylebone workhouse, in 1903, by George R. Sims, author of the poem* Christmas Day in the Workhouse. *The institution, in Marylebone Road, London, housed up to 2,000 men, women and children.*

born at Winchester Castle, and built its Great Hall – perhaps the finest medieval hall in England after Westminster. A round table, made in the Middle Ages to commemorate King Arthur and his knights, hangs in the hall.
Location: Castle Hill, off Westgate.

WINCHESTER CATHEDRAL Because Winchester, formerly the capital of England, was still very important after the Conquest, William I and some of his successors were crowned at the cathedral, as well as at Westminster Abbey. This cathedral is the longest in Europe–556 ft–and during the Middle Ages Winchester was the richest see in England.

In 1079, William appointed Bishop Walkelyn to replace the original Saxon cathedral with one worthy of the Conquest. The bishop was granted the right to as much timber as he could get with the aid of carpenters in four days and nights. He angered the king by recruiting an army of workmen who felled an entire forest within the time allowed. Part of Walkelyn's cathedral can be seen today.

The tower at the central crossing collapsed in 1170, and piecemeal reconstruction continued into the 15th century.

Remains of many Saxon kings lie in the cathedral. King Canute and his queen, Emma, are buried there. So is William Rufus, the "Huntsman King" – killed by an arrow in 1100.

The most valuable treasure is the illuminated 12th-century Winchester Bible. The wedding stool on which Mary Tudor knelt for her marriage to Philip of Spain at the cathedral in 1554 can also be seen.
Location: The Close, off Market St.

WINCHESTER COLLEGE William of Wykeham, Bishop of Winchester, was the first educator to devise a system of tuition which carried a pupil from boyhood to young manhood. He opened Winchester College in 1394, to ensure a supply of suitable students for New College, Oxford, which he had founded earlier. Parts of the original building which survive include the outer court and gatehouse, chamber court and gatehouse, with chapel and hall, and the cloister.
Location: College St, SE of town centre.

HOSPITAL OF ST CROSS For nearly 900 years, this hospital has sheltered the poor. It was founded in 1136 by Bishop Henry of Blois, a grandson of William the Conqueror. The present buildings date from about 1445, although the original chapel can still be seen.
Location: 1½ miles SW of town off A333.

Windermere *Cumbria*   *Map: 391 Dc*
STEAMBOAT MUSEUM The 41 ft steam yacht *Dolly*, built about 1850 and claimed to be the world's oldest powered boat in working order, is among a collection of historic pleasure boats of the type once popular on the lake at Windermere.
Location: Rayrigg Rd (A592).

Windmill Hill *Wilts.*   *Map: 398 Ac*
Three rings of causewayed ditches mark an example of what was probably the earliest type of communal ritual monument built in Britain. It is believed that about 3000 BC, people of a wide surrounding region met once or twice a year for ceremonies including ritual slaughter of animals, and feasting.
Location: 1½ miles NW of Avebury off A361.

Windsor *Berks.*   *Map: 398 Cc*
CASTLE William the Conqueror built a fortress on this site in the late 11th century and a succession of kings extended it. In the 12th century, Henry II built a vast stone shell keep, 100 ft across and 35 ft high. Edward III added a great tower. In the 1820s, under George IV, a 33 ft high "hollow crown" was added to the tower, making it 230 ft high – the tallest castle building in Britain. For centuries, Windsor Castle has been a royal residence. It has also been used in part as a prison. Charles I was buried in the precincts, in St George's Chapel, after his execution in 1649.

The castle houses many works by famous artists, including Leonardo da Vinci and Rubens, as well as armour and a spectacular dolls' house made for George V's queen, Mary, in 1922.

ST GEORGE'S CHAPEL The sumptuous chapel, inside the castle boundaries, was begun by Edward IV in 1477, for the Order of the Garter. Kings and queens are buried in the chapel: Charles I, Henry VIII and his favourite wife, Jane Seymour; Edward IV, Edward VII and Queen Alexandra, and George VI.

Wingfield *Suffolk*   *Map: 399 Gf*
CHURCH OF ST ANDREW An impressive 14th and 15th-century church with a clerestory (a row of windows beneath the roof) in both nave and chancel. Monuments to the de la Pole family date back to the 14th century. They include one to John de la Pole (*d.* 1491), Duke of Suffolk and husband of Edward IV's sister Elizabeth. Location: 7½ miles SE of Diss (B1118, then minor roads).

GOLDEN AGE OF STEAMBOATS

Steamboats came into fashion as pleasure craft in the 19th century and Windermere was a steamboat cruising centre for half a century. A unique collection of boats, in working order, can be seen at the Windermere Steamboat Museum. The collection includes the steam launch Dolly, built about 1850; the steam yacht Esperance, which is more than 100 years old; the steam launch Branksome, built in 1896; and a sailing yacht which is about 200 years old. The museum also has a small rowing boat once used by the children's author Beatrix Potter, who lived in the Lake District at Sawrey, near Hawkshead, and whose stories include The Tale of Peter Rabbit.

When the internal combustion engine arrived, steamboats gradually fell into disuse: some of the craft on display were salvaged from lake beds.

DOLLY (ABOUT 1850) *The 41 ft long steam launch Dolly was used on Windermere and then on Ullswater as a private craft for almost 50 years, until she sank in 1895. The boat lay forgotten on the lake bed until 1960, when she was salvaged.*

ESPERANCE (1869) *Barrow industrialist H. W. Schneider built Esperance to ferry him between Bowness and the special train which carried him to work from Lakeside.*

BRANKSOME (1896) *The teak-hulled Branksome, built for private use, is a superb example of Victorian elegance. Her cabin has walnut panelling, upholstery of leather and embossed velvet, and a solid white marble wash-hand basin. The Branksome has a copper tea urn, common in Windermere boats of its period, which is worked by boiler steam passing through coiled pipes. It can boil a gallon of water in ten seconds. The boat is 50 ft long with a 9 ft beam, and travels at 14 mph.*

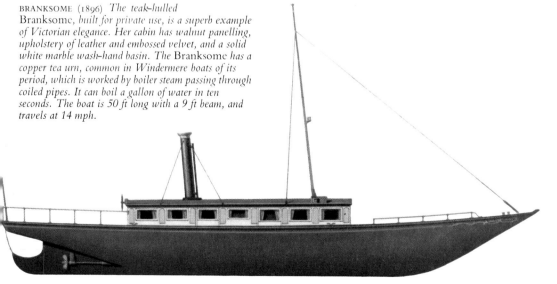

Winslow Hall *Bucks.*   *Map: 398 Cd*
One of the few scarcely altered houses outside
London designed by Sir Christopher Wren
(1632–1723). It houses a collection of early-18th-
century English furniture and Chinese Tang art.
Location: 6½ miles SE of Buckingham on A413.

Winterborne Tomson *Dorset*   *Map: 397 Gc*
CHURCH OF ST ANDREW A 12th-century church
with a Norman apse and 18th-century furnishings, including box-pews and a two-decker
pulpit. It was restored in 1931 after it had fallen
into neglect.
Location: 9 miles SW of Wimborne Minster off
A31.

Winterbourne Stoke *Wilts.*   *Map: 398 Ab*
BARROW CEMETERY About 20 barrows, or earthen
burial mounds, lie less than a mile west of
Stonehenge. Apart from a single Stone Age long
barrow built about 3000 BC, they are round
barrows made by the Beaker people who came
to Britain from the Continent about 2000 BC.
Location: 8¼ miles NW of Salisbury. Cemetery
is 2 miles E of village (A303, N on A360).

Wirksworth *Derbys.*   *Map: 393 Ge*
Lead-mining made Wirksworth a busy town
from Roman times until the end of the last
century, when overseas competition made the
industry collapse. Along the High Peak Trail,
engine houses and spoil heaps remain as a record
of the mining past. In the town itself a museum
tells the story of local lead mining, and the Moot
Hall, the old law courts, preserves a 15th-century
dish used to measure the miners' output.
Location: 4 miles S of Matlock (A6 and B5023).

Wisbech *Cambs.*   *Map: 395 Ea*
PECKOVER HOUSE North Brink is a row of elegant
Georgian houses beside the River Nene, and
Peckover House is the finest of them. Tuscan
columns and a portico frame the front door of
its well-proportioned red and yellow-brick exterior, built in 1722. Inside, ornately carved
wood and plaster work reflects the wealth of its
19th-century banker owners, the Peckovers.
Location: North Brink, W of town centre.

Witney *Oxon.*   *Map: 398 Bd*
MANOR FARM The farmhouse, a tithe barn and
church are all that remain of the medieval village
of Cogges. The farm is now a museum that tells
the story of Oxfordshire farming. Demonstrations are given of flail and steam threshing, sheep
shearing and hurdle making.
Location: Church Lane, 1 mile SE of town
centre off B4022.

Woburn Abbey *Beds.*   *Map: 398 Ce*
Henry VIII bequeathed the abbey, then a ruined
monastery, to the 1st Earl of Bedford in 1547.
The mansion that now stands in its place was built
in the 17th and 18th centuries and was embellished
by the 4th, 5th and 6th dukes of Bedford. Much
of the furniture, porcelain, silver, sculpture,
books, paintings and other rare and beautiful
items they acquired is on display in the abbey.
The fine park that surrounds the mansion was
landscaped by Humphry Repton (1752–1818).
Location: 9 miles NW of Dunstable (A5, A5130
then minor road).

Woden Law *Borders*   *Map: 389 Fc*
FORT AND SIEGE WORKS Roman siege banks and
ditches encircle a small Iron Age fort on a hill.
The siege lines were probably built for peacetime
practice and not used in an actual assault.
Location: 10 miles SE of Jedburgh (minor roads).

Wollaton Hall *Notts.*   *Map: 394 Bb*
This Tudor and Gothic mansion built for Sir
Francis Willoughby in 1580–88 is fantastically
ornamented with towers, turrets, pinnacles,
pilasters and mouldings. It also has a window for
each day of the year. Its cost left Sir Francis in
debt at his death. The building now houses the
Natural History Museum of Nottingham.
Location: 2½ miles W of Nottingham off A609.

PAGAN TEMPLES OF PREHISTORIC BRITAIN

The best known sacred site of the ancient Britons,
Stonehenge, is only one of more than 80 henges in the
country. Its great stone circles were later additions, and
the original henge was like all the others, including
nearby Woodhenge.

These temples of prehistoric Britain were built by
late Stone Age men around 2000 BC. They consisted
of a bank and ditch enclosing a circular or oval area,
entered through one, two or four gaps in the bank.

Britain's largest henge, at Durrington Walls alongside Woodhenge, has been almost completely
destroyed above ground, but it was over 1,600 ft in
diameter, surrounded by a bank 100 ft wide, and a
ditch 50 ft wide and 20 ft deep.

Recent research suggests that henges were gathering
places for communities spread over large areas, who
took part in a well-developed prehistoric religion. The
henges would have been important social centres as
well as temples.

Woodhenge had a large, circular timber hall in
which religious ceremonies took place, and evidence
of even larger halls has been found in other henges,
including Durrington Walls. The halls may also have
been meeting places for the senior members of the
tribe – the council of elders.

Libations of blood, beer or water?
Three rituals seem to have taken place at most henges.
First, small pits were dug, and appear to have been
filled in again with soil soon afterwards. Libations
(liquid offerings) were probably poured into the pits,
perhaps to spirits of the dead. Whether the liquid was
blood, beer or water is not known.

Cremation burials took place at a number of henges,
and at Stonehenge many of the pits (known as Aubrey
Holes, after their discoverer) contained cremations
placed in them after the pits had been filled in. Henges
may have been a favoured spot to be buried, or the
cremations may have followed human sacrifices.

Burials of bodies are much rarer than cremations
inside the henges. When they do occur, they are
often found near the centre. At Woodhenge a three-
year-old child with a cleft skull was buried, strongly
suggesting a sacrificial burial. Burials at the base of
four of the stones in the Avenue leading up to the
Avebury henge included some which were put there
when the stones were placed in position: in other
words they were foundation burials, almost certainly
of people who were sacrificially killed to commemorate the erection of the Avenue and henge.

"Priests" probably officiated at the henges, forerun-
ners, perhaps, of the Druids of the Iron Age.

The burial places of Stone Age farmers who worshipped in the henges still stand out on the skyline of
Britain. Sometimes the stone chamber alone survives,
stripped of its earthen mound by nearly 4,000 years of
wind and rain. But at Hetty Pegler's Tump in
Gloucestershire and Wayland's Smithy in Berkshire
20th-century man can still step into the cold darkness
of a Stone Age tomb.

0

Wolverton *Hants.*   *Map: 398 Bc*
CHURCH OF ST CATHERINE A graceful red brick
neo-classical church built early in the reign of
George I (1714–27). It retains its original furnishings – the reredos, pulpit, reading desk, box-pews
and wrought-iron communion rails.
Location: 7 miles NW of Basingstoke off A339.

Woodbridge *Suffolk*   *Map: 399 Ge*
TIDE MILL River tides powered this grain mill
built about 1793. High tide on the River Deben
filled a 7½ acre pond beside the mill. When the
water was released at low tide, it turned a water-
wheel, which rotated four pairs of millstones.
The grain was stored in an upper storey and later
loaded on to sailing vessels that tied up at the

adjacent pier. The mill pond is now a boat
marina, but the mill has been restored to working
order.
Location: Quayside, E of railway station.
WAGON-WEIGHING MACHINE In the 1740s an Act
of Parliament levied extra tolls on wagons loaded
beyond a certain limit, and wagon-weighing
machines were built. The one mounted on the
wall of Ye Olde Bell and Steelyard Inn is one of
the few left in England. From the wall projects
a 20 ft long steelyard whose pivotal point is only
2½ in. from one end. The wagon was suspended
from the end of the steelyard nearest the pivot
and weights were attached to the other end until
the wagon was raised level with them.
Location: New St, town centre.

HALLS FOR STONE AGE WORSHIP *Two circular halls, made of timber, were built inside the huge henge at Durrington Walls, Wiltshire, about 2500 BC. The buildings were surrounded by a circular earthen bank, 100 ft wide and 1,600 ft in diameter. Inside the bank was a ditch 50 ft wide and 20 ft deep. It has been calculated that 900,000 man-hours were needed to dig the ditch and bank, and that 10 acres of woodland would have been felled to construct the larger building alone. The halls are shown as they may have looked when they were first built.*

ROTUNDAS *The two buildings were the work of skilled Stone Age carpenters. The larger rotunda was about 130 ft across with an open courtyard. The smaller may have had a roof over the centre.*

LONG BARROW *Stone Age men of around 3000 BC buried their dead in long barrows such as Fussell's Lodge in Wiltshire. The barrow is believed to have been the burial place of a local chieftain and his family. It is shown as it probably looked when built.*

ROUND BARROW *Bronze Age farmers and chiefs around 2000 BC were buried in round barrows such as Bush Barrow at Normanton Down, Wiltshire. Bush Barrow is about 50 ft in diameter and 11 ft high.*

Woodhenge *Wilts.*   *Map: 398 Ab*
The remains at Woodhenge are those of a great ceremonial hall that dates back to before 2000 BC and is even older than the stone temple of Stonehenge, 2 miles to the south-west. Inside an elliptical bank and ditch, excavations of 1925 revealed six concentric rings of holes that once contained upright wooden posts. These supported the roof of a hall 140 ft across, with an open area at the centre. Short concrete pillars now mark the positions of the wooden posts.
Location: 1 mile N of Amesbury off A345.

A SITE OLDER THAN STONEHENGE

In 1925 an aerial photograph revealed six concentric rings of holes 2 miles from Stonehenge. Excavations showed that they once contained wooden posts – roof supports of a hall older than the stone temple of Stonehenge. Concrete pillars now mark the holes.

Wookey Hole *Somerset*   *Map: 397 Fd*
PAPER MILL Beside the access path to the vast Wookey Hole Caves stands an old paper mill that still produces paper as it was made in the early 17th century. Cotton fibre is pulped, tossed like a pancake, squeezed between two pieces of flannel in a press, dried, dipped in soap, alum and water, and finally polished by being rolled between zinc sheets.
The result is best-quality paper used by watercolour artists and by printers who produce high-class books.
Location: 2 miles NW of Wells (A371 then minor road N).

Woolpit *Suffolk*   *Map: 399 Fe*
CHURCH OF ST MARY The interior of this Perpendicular church is enriched with a double hammer-beam roof carved with angels, a screen painted with saints, a 16th-century brass eagle lectern and bench ends decorated with figures and animals.
Location: 8 miles E of Bury St Edmunds off A45.

Woolsthorpe Manor *Lincs.*   *Map: 394 Ca*
In this small limestone house a scientist of genius was born on Christmas Day 1642. He was Isaac Newton, and it was in this house that he formulated the three principles that revolutionised physics and astronomy: the laws of motion, the composition of white light and the law of universal gravitation. He formulated these in a mere 18 months, from 1665–7, when the plague had closed Cambridge University.
Newton is popularly supposed to have discovered the law of gravitation after watching an apple fall in the garden of the house. Some of the diagrams and drawings scratched in the plaster and stone of the house are believed to have been done by Newton when he was a boy.
Location: 8 miles S of Grantham off A1 near Colsterworth.

Wootton Wawen *Warks.*   *Map: 398 Ae*
CHURCH OF ST PETER Villagers have worshipped in this church for 900 years. Four splendid arches support the Saxon tower, the core of the church. There is 13th-century glass in the east window and a 15th-century monument to a knight.
Location: 6 miles NW of Stratford-upon-Avon off A34.

Worcester *Heref. & Worcs.*   *Map: 393 Fc*
CATHEDRAL At its core, this splendid Gothic building on the banks of the Severn is Norman. After the Conquest, Wulstan, the bishop of the Saxon monastery church which stood on the site, began rebuilding it in Norman style. He started in 1084 with a stately crypt which is almost a church in itself. The chapter house – the earliest circular one in the country – was built early the next century.
In 1203 fire damaged the cathedral, and the tower collapsed. After the canonisation of Wulstan in the same year and the burial of King John in the cathedral in 1216, pilgrims flocked to it and donated money for its reconstruction. Over the centuries this rebuilding embodied each successive stage of Gothic architecture.
The most outstanding of the many fine monuments in the cathedral is that in Purbeck marble to King John – the oldest royal effigy in England. Fascinating carvings decorate the 14th-century tip-up hinged seats. They include a naked woman riding on a goat, a butcher killing an ox, and knights tilting.
Location: Off College St, city centre.
CHURCH OF ST SWITHIN The fine 18th-century interior of the church is no longer used for worship. It has been taken over by the Redundant Churches Fund, and now the mock-Gothic vaulted nave provides a splendid setting for concerts and meetings.
Location: Church St, city centre.
PORCELAIN WORKS The Worcester Royal Porcelain Company, established in 1751, is the oldest surviving porcelain works in England. Worcester was one of the first potteries to use transfer-printing, which was much cheaper than hand painting and brought decorated wares within the means of a wider market.
The Dyson Perrins Museum traces the story of the firm from its earliest days, and tours of the factory can be arranged.
Location: Severn St, S of city centre.
THE COMMANDERY In 1085 St Wulstan, Bishop of

Worcester, founded a hospital just outside the city walls. It became known as the Commandery because the masters of the hospital called themselves commanders. The present timber-framed building dates from the late 15th century. It has a beautifully carved staircase and on the first floor are religious wall-paintings, probably of the 16th century. In 1651 the closing stages of the Battle of Worcester (which ended in the rout of Charles II's troops) were fought in the grounds.
Location: Sidbury, S of city centre.

TUDOR HOUSE AND GREYFRIARS Tudor House is a mid-16th-century timber-framed inn that is now a museum of local domestic life. Its collections range from carts to drinking mugs. On the opposite side of the street is Greyfriars, the former guest house of a 15th-century Franciscan friary, with a long curving façade.
Location: Friar St, city centre.

Worksop *Notts.* Map: 394 Bc
PRIORY CHURCH The former priory of Radford was founded in 1103. Its twin-towered church,

---

THE VARIETY OF ENGLISH PORCELAIN

Porcelain, a translucent earthenware, was first made in China about the 8th century AD, but the secret of its manufacture was not discovered in Europe until 1,000 years later. The first English porcelain factory was established at Chelsea in 1745. It was soon followed by others, at Bow, Derby, Worcester and other towns, each works producing its own distinctive ware, often based on Chinese or Japanese designs.

WORCESTER *The exotic bird on this dessert dish made at the Worcester factory in about 1765 is a common motif on English porcelain, and was copied not from nature but from other, European designs. The dish is one of a pair that simulate baskets.*

CHELSEA *Leaf-shaped dishes, like this one of about 1755, were popular early products of the Chelsea works. They were often decorated with paintings of plants taken from the illustrations in* The Gardener's Dictionary.

BOW *Copies of Chinese paintings of prunus blossom (almond, cherry, plum), as on this mug of about 1755, were popular at the short-lived Bow works (1744–76). The style was known as Famille Rose. Bow porcelain was heavier and less transparent than that produced by other factories.*

DERBY *One of a pair of dessert plates from the large Trotter service, designed for a Hertfordshire man of that name, at the Derby factory about 1815. The plates were painted by Moses Webster (1792–1870), one of the works' several specialist artists, at a time when Derby porcelain had passed the artistic peak reached in the late 18th century. Derby porcelain is distinct from Royal Crown Derby, whose factory did not begin production until 1890.*

SWANSEA *A pair of ink-stands made at Swansea about 1820. The decoration is by William Pollard (1803–54). The factory, which operated for only nine years, produced two distinctive types of porcelain, one known as "duck egg" because of its greenish hue, and the other possessing a pitted surface like pigskin.*

WHEN BABIES GOT THEIR OWN CARRIAGES

Probably because of the poor state of the roads, wheeled conveyances for children were not used until about the 1800s. The earliest were designed for toddlers rather than babies, who were thought best kept indoors. An upright wooden perambulator with *a handle for pushing was invented about 1840, and became a status symbol for the wealthy. Others continued to use its forerunner, a hand-pulled miniature cart. Not until 1880 did prams become widely available for babies.*

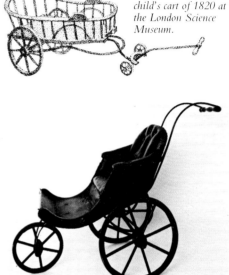

STICK WAGON *A child's cart of 1820 at the London Science Museum.*

THREE-WHEELER *A pram of about 1840 on show at Tudor House, Worcester, one of the first designed to be pushed. Children could easily fall out.*

BASSINETTE *After 1880 all prams had four wheels, like this model at Tudor House, Worcester. The first four-wheeler in 1876 was classed as a road vehicle and could not be pushed on the pavement.*

built about the same time, embodies architectural styles down through the centuries – from the magnificent nave of about 1170 to the modern eastern extension of 1973. The 14th-century priory gatehouse retains its original oak beams.
Location: Priorswell Rd, town centre.

Wormleighton *Warks.*   *Map: 398 Be*
OXFORD CANAL The late-18th-century waterway is an outstanding example of contour cutting, the favourite technique of its engineer James Brindley (1716–72). Brindley allowed his canals to follow the natural curves of the landscape. This is particularly noticeable on the long, lock-free section between Napton and Fenny Compton. To appreciate its graceful twists and turns, the visitor can take a boat, walk along the towpath or climb to the top of Wormleighton Hill.
Location: 9 miles N of Banbury (A423 and minor road, which crosses the canal).

Worsbrough Mill *S. Yorks.*   *Map: 394 Bc*
The water-driven part of the mill, called Old Mill, probably dates from about 1625. In 1843 this mill, which drove three pairs of millstones, was augmented by the steam-powered New Mill, which drove two pairs. In 1972 the New Mill steam-engine was replaced by an old oil engine. The mill still occasionally produces flour.
Location: 2½ miles S of Barnsley off A61, by canal reservoir.

Worsley *Greater Manchester*   *Map: 391 Ea*
BRIDGEWATER CANAL Britain's entire canal system sprang from this spot, for Worsley was where engineer James Brindley (1716–72) started constructing the first canal in the country. It was built for the Duke of Bridgewater, who needed transport to carry the coal from his mines at Worsley Delph (now just east of the M62 junction) to Manchester. The waterway, completed in 1761, halved the price of coal in Manchester. It is still in use.
Location: 6¼ miles W of Manchester off A572.

Worstead *Norfolk*   *Map: 395 Ga*
CHURCH OF ST MARY An impressive flint church of the late 14th century, with a 109 ft tower. The nave has a hammer-beam roof, and the chancel screen is delicately carved and decorated with painted saints. All this was paid for by the rich medieval wool merchants of Worstead — which gave its name to worsted cloth.
Location: 4 miles SE of North Walsham off A149.

Wortley *S. Yorks.* *Map: 394 Bc*
TOP FORGE The thud of a hammer pounding red-hot metal was a familiar sound on the site from 1640, when the water-powered forge was founded. Cast iron from local furnaces was reheated, refined and hammered into malleable wrought iron. The forge, an early-18th-century reconstruction of the original buildings, continued to operate, making chains and railway axles, until 1912. It is now being restored by the Sheffield Trades Historical Society.
Location: 11 miles NW of Sheffield (A629, B6088 and minor road to Thurgoland).

Wotton-under-Edge *Glos.* *Map: 393 Fa*
NEW MILLS This imposing gabled woollen mill, with its clock tower and its great pond, has remained in use since it was built about 1800. At that time its employees included six-year-old children. Today it is a narrow-fabrics and elastic factory, but its old buildings can be visited by appointment. Among them is a wool stove (now a stationery store), and a circular kiln in which washed wool was dried.
Location: 9½ miles SW of Nailsworth off B4058.

Wrest Park *Beds.* *Map: 398 De*
The French-château style of Wrest House, built in 1834, and the formality of its spacious gardens, give the estate the appearance of a miniature Versailles. "Capability" Brown (1715–83) worked on the gardens, which include a canal, a Chinese bridge and an orangery. The house, now used by the National Institute of Agricultural Engineering, is not open to the public.
Location: 9½ miles N of Luton off A6.

Wrexham *Clwyd* *Map: 393 Ee*
CHURCH OF ST GILES One of the most magnificent towers in Britain crowns the 15th–16th-century church. The tower is 136 ft high, pinnacled, and decorated with carved figures of saints and royalty standing in niches. In the north aisle is a monument by the outstanding French sculptor Louis Roubillac (1695–1762). The wrought-iron church gates were built in 1720 by two local smiths, the brothers Robert and John Davies.

The chapel tower of Yale University, in America, is a replica of St Giles' tower. One of the founders of the university, Elihu Yale (1649–1721), came from a Wrexham family and was buried in St Giles' churchyard.
Location: Church St, town centre.

Wroxeter *Salop* *Map: 393 Ed*
ROMAN TOWN Wroxeter is the site of what was the fourth largest town in Roman Britain, Viroconium. The town was founded on the site of a legionary fortress of about AD 58–75 whose garrison was later removed to Chester.
The most impressive remains are The Old Work, standing masonry that was part of a covered exercise hall for bathers. The masonry has survived centuries of weathering and medieval pillaging of its stonework and is remarkably well preserved. Most of the baths can be seen.
Location: 5½ miles SE of Shrewsbury (A5 then B4380).

Wymondham *Norfolk* *Map: 399 Ff*
CHURCH OF ST MARY AND ST THOMAS OF CANTERBURY A curious series of events gave this fine Norman church its two towers. A priory was founded in Wymondham in 1107, and its large church was used by both monks and the local people. Sharing the church led to perpetual disputes, and in about 1400 the monks built an octagonal east tower for themselves and sealed off the High Altar with a wall. In retaliation, the parishioners built their own larger west tower, completed about 1448.
Location: 10 miles SW of Norwich off A11. The church is in Vicar St, off B1135.

Wythenshawe Hall *G. Manchester Map: 393 Ff*
A half-timbered manor house built in the early 16th century with Georgian brickwork extensions. Since 1926 it has been owned by the City of Manchester. It contains 17th-century furniture, arms and armour and oil paintings, and 20th-century ceramics, including a fine collection of Royal Lancastrian pottery.
Location: Wythenshawe Rd, 5½ miles S of Manchester (A5103 then B5167).

Y Z

Yafford Mill *Isle of Wight* *Map: 398 Ba*
The 18th-century water-powered grain mill is still in working order. There are displays of old farm tools, and the grounds are stocked with now-rare breeds of farm animals.
Location: 6 miles SW of Newport off B3323.

Yardley *W. Midlands* *Map: 393 Gd*
BLAKESLEY HALL A massive porch adorns the hall, a timber-framed farmhouse of about 1575. Inside, there are displays of traditional local crafts and 17th-century furniture.
Location: 5 miles E of Birmingham off A45.

Yarmouth Castle *Isle of Wight* *Map: 398 Ba*
In 1545 a French raiding party sailed into the

Solent and landed on the Isle of Wight, where it was eventually repulsed by local militia. The castle was built as part of a programme to tighten the island's defences. It was in service by 1547 and was garrisoned until 1885. In the late 17th century, artillery positions were moved so that all the guns pointed out to sea.
Location: 9 miles W of Newport on A3054.

Yarm Viaduct *Cleveland* *Map: 394 Bf*
Some 7 million bricks went into the 43-arch viaduct, built to carry the North-Eastern Railway over the River Tees. It was opened in 1852 and is still in use.
Location: 5 miles S of Stockton-on-Tees off A135.

Yarnbury Castle *Wilts.*   *Map: 398 Ab*
In the 1st century BC, Iron Age men enlarged a small, 200-year-old enclosure, defended by a single bank and ditch, to create a hill-fort covering more than 28 acres.

The entrances through the double earth ramparts and ditches are guarded by complex outworks.
Location: 8 miles W of Amesbury off A303.

Yate *Avon*   *Map: 397 Ge*
CHURCH OF ST MARY The church, originally Norman, has a fine 15th-century tower and some medieval glass in the North Chapel. A brass depicts Alexander Staples (*d.* 1590) with his two wives, six sons and five daughters.
Location: 1½ miles W of Chipping Sodbury on A432.

Yaxley *Suffolk*   *Map: 399 Ff*
CHURCH OF ST MARY Over the south door of the 700-year-old church hangs a Sexton's Wheel, one of two which survive in England. It consists of a pair of iron wheels on one axle, and was used in the Middle Ages to choose the days of Lady Fasts, periods of abstinence. When both wheels were spun, strings attached to the outer one eventually caught on the inner, braking both to denote the fast day.
Location: 1½ miles W of Eye on minor roads.

Yeavering *Northld.*   *Map: 389 Gc*
IRON AGE FORT A great stone wall surrounds the 13 acre Iron Age stronghold of Yeavering Bell. Inside there are the remains of about 150 stone huts, dating from the 1st century BC.
Location: 5 miles W of Wooler (A697, B6351).

250 years of old Yorkshire

GEORGIAN AND VICTORIAN STREETS AND OLD SHOPS BRING YORKSHIRE'S PAST TO LIFE AT THE CASTLE MUSEUM, YORK – HOUSED IN TWO 18TH-CENTURY PRISONS

The far-sightedness of one man brought York's Castle Museum into existence. He was John Kirk, a country doctor with a practice in the North Riding of Yorkshire. On his rounds he became fascinated by everyday objects of the past and started collecting them. He began with horse brasses and ended by acquiring fire-engines and shop fronts.

In 1935 he presented his collection to the City of York. Over the next three years he installed it in the former Women's Prison, a classical building of 1780 designed by York's finest architect, John Carr. The result was one of the world's outstanding folk-history museums.

Since 1952 the museum has expanded into another elegant building, the adjoining Debtors' Prison, built in 1705 by Sir John Vanbrugh, the playwright and architect of Blenheim Palace.

The museum's greatest attraction is a series of reconstructed streets under cover. These bear realistic names like Kirkgate, in honour of the museum's founder, and Alderman's Walk, after Alderman Morrell, an early benefactor. All the shop fronts, street lamps and even roadways are genuine.

In Kirkgate, stands a hansom cab, invented by Joseph Hansom, a York architect, and the Sheriff of York's elegant state coach emblazoned with the city's arms. Kirkgate also contains an apothecary's shop with Georgian double bow-fronted windows, a coach office and saddler's, and a fire station with hand-pumped engines.

In Princess Mary Court is a sweetshop once owned by Joseph Terry, the 20th-century York

HALF MOON COURT *An Edwardian street has been created in the former exercise yard of the Debtors' Prison. The gas-lit King William IV hotel of 1840 retains its original atmosphere, and outside stand a Victorian pillar box and a barrel organ.*

MOORLAND COTTAGE KITCHEN *A spinning wheel reflects the occupation of the inhabitants of this mid-19th-century rustic cottage. Glass walking sticks won at a local fair stand by the hearth. The rug, cushions and bedspread on the four-poster are home-made.*

Yeovil *Somerset* *Map: 397 Fc*
CHURCH OF ST JOHN BAPTIST During the Middle Ages, Yeovil's rector was also lord of part of the manor, and collected its revenues on behalf of the church. The arrangement angered the citizens. In 1349 they rioted and besieged St John's for a day, trapping the Bishop of Bath and Wells inside.

The riot was eventually quelled and the ringleader, Roger Warmwell, was sentenced to public floggings in four Somerset towns, fined £20 and made to go on a pilgrimage to Canterbury Cathedral.

About 1380 the church was entirely rebuilt in the early Perpendicular style, using money amassed from the manor. Beneath the chancel is a vaulted crypt.
Location: Town centre.

Yeovilton *Somerset* *Map: 397 Fd*
FLEET AIR ARM MUSEUM More than 40 historic aircraft form part of the display, which depicts the development of naval flying from 1903 to the present.

There is also a large display of aero-engines, armaments, models and uniforms. The museum is on the Royal Navy Air Station.
Location: 6 miles N of Yeovil (A37, B3151).

York *N. Yorks.* *Map: 394 Ce*
CASTLE MUSEUM Two former prisons, both built in the 18th century, have been adapted to house a museum of York life. Reconstructed streets, houses and shops show the city as it was in Georgian, Victorian and Edwardian times (see below).
Location: Tower St, city centre.

chocolate manufacturer. It contains sugar pigs, spice mice and other Victorian favourites.

There are five period rooms: a solid and sombre hall of the 1690s, an elegant Georgian room of 1790, a moorland cottage kitchen of 1850, a cluttered Victorian parlour of 1870, and a farmhouse kitchen of 1910.

The Chapel Gallery (the original chapel of the Women's Prison) illustrates the farming year in Yorkshire. The Music Gallery displays instruments ranging from 17th-century virginals to barrel organs, the Green Gallery contains bizarre Victoriana, and there is also an Agricultural Gallery and a Hearth Gallery of kitchen equipment.

Specialist collections are devoted to military uniforms and relics, arms and armour, costumes through the ages, and old toys. In addition, there are many craftsmen's workshops.

The condemned cell of the Debtors' Prison is preserved intact, as it was when occupied by Dick Turpin the highwayman, hanged at York in 1739.

WHEELWRIGHT'S SHOP *Exactly fashioned elm hubs, oak spokes, ash rims and metal tyres commemorate the craftsmanship of the village wheelwright, an essential tradesman in the days of carts and wagons.*

CRAFTSMEN'S SHOPS IN PRISON CELLS

Several cells in the old Debtors' Prison were converted in 1952 into reconstructed workshops, to display the skills of traditional Yorkshire craftsmen, among them the blacksmith, cutler, printer and cooper. One workshop is devoted to the metal engraving of Henry Wells, of Castlegate, York, who, using hand gravers, scrapers and burnishers, produced many beautiful designs and inscriptions.

Steam and the iron road

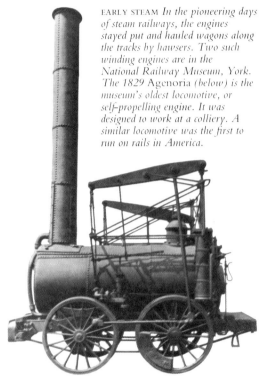

EARLY STEAM *In the pioneering days of steam railways, the engines stayed put and hauled wagons along the tracks by hawsers. Two such winding engines are in the National Railway Museum, York. The 1829* Agenoria *(below) is the museum's oldest locomotive, or self-propelling engine. It was designed to work at a colliery. A similar locomotive was the first to run on rails in America.*

During the Victorian age, two railway companies carried passengers from London to Scotland, and in the 1890s their rivalry resulted in the "Races to the North". The London and North Western Railway left Euston Station daily on the west coast route via Crewe; Great Northern trains took the east route from King's Cross.

The grand finale came in a race from London to Aberdeen on August 22, 1895. The trains stopped only three times, changing locomotives on each occasion. The LNWR section from Crewe to Carlisle was taken by the locomotive *Hardwicke* at an average speed of 67.2 mph, helping the company to win the race. Their train completed the 540 miles in 512 minutes, just six minutes faster than the Great Northern.

Hardwicke is now one of nearly 30 historic locomotives displayed at the National Railway Museum in York on two great turntables in a former engine-shed. Among the others are *Mallard*, which in 1938 reached a speed of 126 mph while hauling seven carriages to set a world record for steam that still stands, and *Ellerman Lines*, a 1949 steam locomotive from which one side has been removed to show the interior.

Some exhibits pre-date the age of railway steam. A horse-drawn wagon of 1797 carried limestone from quarries in the Derbyshire Peak District to the canal basin at Buxworth. Another horse-drawn wagon, a Dandy cart, had room aboard to carry the horse on downhill sections.

ROYAL SALOON *Queen Victoria's coach of 1869 was used on journeys to Balmoral. The upholstery is royal blue silk. The saloon was the queen's favourite railway vehicle. Originally, the carriage was in two halves linked by a gangway, but Victoria disliked walking from one to the other while the train was moving, and the two were joined to make one large car. The oldest royal coach in the York museum was built in 1842 for Queen Adelaide, widow of William IV. A forerunner of the sleeping-car, it can have a bed made up in it from poles and webbing.*

CLIFFORD'S TOWER William the Conqueror put up two motte-and-bailey castles at York in 1068–9, one on either bank of the River Ouse. Both were sacked in 1069, when the citizens allied themselves with a Viking raiding party against the Normans.

The castle on the west bank was not rebuilt, but its earthworks remain around Baile Hill.

Clifford's Tower stands on the mound of the original Norman castle on the east bank of the Ouse. It was constructed in the mid-13th century to replace a wooden fortress destroyed during

STIRLING SINGLE *The sleek Stirling Single of 1870 was one of the first locomotives to incorporate sanding gear. Sand dropped on the rails gave a firmer grip when starting.*

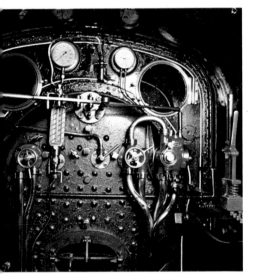

ON THE FOOTPLATE *Controls and firebox of the Stirling Single are sheltered in a shallow cab which gave the crew little protection in bad weather.*

GUARD'S EQUIPMENT *Red and green flags, lamp and cap were part of a 19th-century guard's equipment. The dog's ticket is of the same period.*

CHECKING THE SPEED *The speed and horsepower of a locomotive could be measured by a dynamometer car joined to the train. A paper roll unwound 2 ft for every mile, tracing graphs as it moved. This 1906 coach was used on Mallard's record run in 1938.*

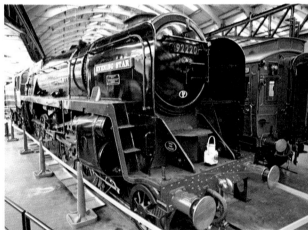

EVENING STAR *Built in 1960, Evening Star was the last steam locomotive to enter service with British Railways. It could reach speeds of 90 mph and more.*

---

anti-Jewish riots in 1190. The town's Jewish population had been given shelter in the castle, but when they refused to let the sheriff in, the castle was set on fire and 150 Jews died.

The tower, laid out on a quatrefoil plan, a design based on four overlapping circles, is named after the de Cliffords, powerful barons during the Middle Ages. Roger, 2nd Lord de Clifford, rebelled against Edward II and was hanged in chains from the top of the tower in 1322.

Location: Tower St, city centre.

MERCHANT ADVENTURERS' HALL During the Middle Ages, the Merchant Adventurers were York's wealthiest and most influential guild. Their Hall dates from the 14th and 15th centuries.
Location: Between Piccadilly and Fossgate, city centre.

YORK'S GLORIOUS GLASS

More medieval stained glass survives in York Minster than anywhere else in England. The minster's magnificent Great East Window, of 1405–8, was the work of John Thornton of Coventry. It includes scenes from the first book of the Bible, Genesis, through to the last, Revelation, under a depiction of God as Alpha and Omega. Above, the fifth day of the world – the creation of birds and fishes.

MINSTER The archbishops of York rank second only to those of Canterbury in the hierarchy of the Church of England. The minster – a word which in early Saxon times denoted a mission centre – is their seat and technically, therefore, a cathedral.

York Minster can trace its origins back to AD 627, when Edwin, King of Northumberland, was baptised in a small wooden church near the site. No archaeological evidence of that building has been found, but tradition has named a dried-up well in the minster crypt after the king.

A second Saxon church, of stone, replaced the wooden one. It, too, has completely disappeared, destroyed when York defied the Normans in 1069. Thomas of Bayeux, bishop and chaplain to William the Conqueror, constructed a third church in 1070–1100. It was severely damaged by fire in 1137 and only part of the foundations remain, in the crypt.

Roger of Pont l'Eveque, Archbishop of York from 1154 to 1181, rebuilt the choir. The massive

The Vikings' capital

SEA-RAIDERS WHO SETTLED IN YORK CREATED A PROSPEROUS CENTRE OF COMMERCE AND CULTURE WHICH BELIED THEIR WAR-LIKE IMAGE

On June 8, AD 793, sleek warships with dragon's head prows and stubby square sails raced on to the beach at Lindisfarne, the Holy Island off the coast of Saxon Northumbria. From the boats spilled tall, fair warriors armed with swords and fearsome battleaxes, in search of plunder. The prize was rich – Lindisfarne monastery, with its church and shrine of St Cuthbert.

Swiftly the sea-raiders looted, slaying many of the monks and dragging others off as slaves to their Scandinavian homeland.

From America to Russia

The raid on Lindisfarne began 250 years of Viking expansion, during which the men from the north pushed back the frontiers of the known world, sailing rivers and oceans in their keeled longships, the finest vessels of their day, from North America in the west to Russia in the east.

The ferocity of their sudden attacks and their cruelty earned the Vikings an awesome reputation. For centuries, Christians in England and throughout Europe prayed: "From the fury of the Northmen deliver us, O Lord!" But behind the marauders came merchants, craftsmen and farmers, bearers of a developed civilisation and a language which gave English the word "law"

In 865, Vikings from Denmark launched their biggest attack on England, an invasion intended to secure, not just booty, but territory. They carved out an area north of a line from the Thames to the Mersey, the "Danelaw" conceded to them by King Alfred in 886.

An orderly city

York became the Vikings' English capital, and grew, under the rule of Eric Bloodaxe, into a city of 10,000 people, the equal of any in the Viking empire. Houses of planks and thatch were built end-on to streets laid out in an orderly fashion not seen since Roman times. In the workshops, smiths, potters, carpenters and masons created not only everyday objects, but also jewellery and intricate carvings in wood and stone. Merchants brought amber and furs from the Baltic and silks and spices from the East.

Viking York prospered for nearly 90 years, until the Saxons recaptured it. The rich legacy the Norsemen left is preserved in York's "gates", from the Viking word for street, and in the archaeological treasures now being uncovered.

VIKING HOMES
Viking houses, like their ships, were well built of sturdy oak planks. The remains of three have been found in York, with timbers preserved to a height of 6 ft by the wet ground. The drawing shows how the houses may have looked when first built.

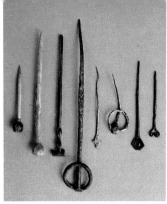

PINS *Viking-era pins found at York were used to fasten dresses or cloaks. The three on the left are bone, the others bronze and iron.*

SCALES *A merchant's folding scales are flanked by coins of King Ethelred, minted at York about 980.*

GRAVE *This carved corner from a 10th-century Viking grave cover is in local limestone.*

SHEATHS *Knives, the most common weapon and tool, were carried in leather sheaths.*

COMBS *Decorated combs were made from the antlers of deer in a "factory" in Viking York. The one at the top still has its case, also of antler, which was worked with a metal file. Like most of the other objects on this page, it was found at the Viking site in Coppergate, York, where timber buildings have been found.*

ICE SKATES *The Vikings developed bone skates to carry them across frozen rivers and lakes. Leather thongs bound the skates to the wearer's boots.*

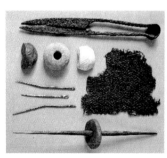

TEXTILES *Viking textile tools included iron shears (top), needles, and spindles with whorls of bone or stone.*

PENDANTS *Amber used in these 10th-century beads and pendants probably came from the Baltic.*

JEWELLERY *Glass beads found at York include two coated with gold (centre). The rings are pewter.*

FASTENINGS *The belt clasp (top) is bronze. Pewter was used for the badge (right) and the two brooches.*

BOWLS *Ash and yew bowls were worked with iron tools. They date from the 10th century.*

LOCKS *Four iron keys and two padlocks of the same metal come from Viking-age levels at York.*

south transept, begun about 1220 by Archbishop Walter de Gray, set the scale for the building work carried out over the next 200 years, which made the minster the largest medieval church in England.

Among York Minster's glories is its eight-sided Chapter House, built in the Decorated style between 1260 and about 1300. It is 58 ft in diameter and its soaring roof has no central support.

The three minster towers were completed by about 1480. The central, lantern tower was begun by William of Colchester, Henry IV's master mason. Statues of kings of England, from William the Conqueror to Henry VI, adorn the choir screen, built from 1475 to 1500.

York Minster is celebrated for its collection of medieval stained glass, the finest and largest in England. There are more than 100 splendid windows, with glass of every century from the 12th to the 20th.

During the Civil War, York fared better than most cathedrals, largely due to the protection of the Parliamentary General Fairfax, whose family came from Yorkshire. But it suffered serious damage in two 19th-century fires.

There are many monuments in the minster, some carved by Grinling Gibbons. Its other treasures include the ivory drinking-horn of Ulfus, donated to the church in the 11th century, and the *Gospel Book*, written about AD 1000.
Location: Off Deangate, city centre.

NATIONAL RAILWAY MUSEUM Historic locomotives, rolling stock and railway items are displayed in a former engine shed (see pp. 380–1).
Location: Leeman Rd, city centre.

RAINDALE WATERMILL The 18th-century corn mill, brought from its original site on the Yorkshire Moors, is still in running order.
Location: Grounds of Castle Museum, city centre.

ROMAN YORK Eburacum, as the Romans called

York, was founded as a legionary fortress in the AD 70s. It became the military capital of the north, attracted a large civilian settlement and, from AD 197, was the administrative centre of Britannia Inferior, the northern half of Roman Britain.

Long stretches of the Roman fortress walls remain. The massive part-Roman, part-medieval Multangular Tower, in Museum Gardens, was still playing a role in the city defences during the Civil War in the 17th century. There is a Roman steam bath, with its underfloor heating system, in St Sampson's Square.
Location: City centre.

TREASURER'S HOUSE A treasurer looked after York Minster's plate and other valuables until the Dissolution of the Monasteries in the 16th century, when the minster was stripped and the office abolished.

Little remains of the original Treasurer's House, but the present building, an elegant 18th-century mansion, preserves the name. It contains fine furniture, china and glass.
Location: Chapter House St, city centre.

VIKING YORK Vikings from Denmark and Norway over-ran Anglo-Saxon York in AD 867 and settled there, turning the town, which they called Jorvik, into their main base in England. The Vikings were driven out by King Edmund of the Saxons in 954, but York's links with Scandinavia continued until after 1066.

Three well-preserved timber buildings dating from the Viking occupation have so far been found in York, and continuing excavations may reveal others. The oak plank walls are 6 ft high in some places. (See pp. 382–3.)
Location: Coppergate, city centre.

Y Pigwn *Dyfed*   Map: 392 Cb
ROMAN CAMPS When Roman marching battalions pitched their tents for the night, they usually surrounded the site with a ditch and stockaded earth rampart.

At Y Pigwn, a Roman marching-camp was built inside a larger, earlier one. Both date from the 1st century AD. Traces of their ramparts remain.
Location: 3½ miles SE of Llandovery (A40 then minor road).

Ystalyfera *W. Glam.*   Map: 392 Cb
GURNOS TINPLATE WORKS Although the works, opened in 1876, are now derelict, the buildings are well preserved. Two rows of chimneys mark the tinning bays, in which thin sheets of iron were dipped into molten tin. The plate then went to factories in the Swansea Valley to be made into cans.
Location: 9 miles N of Neath (A474, A4067).

Zennor *Cornwall*   Map: 396 Aa
WAYSIDE MUSEUM A collection of industrial and farm tools and domestic implements illustrating life in south-west Cornwall over the centuries is housed in a former watermill, founded about 1500.
Location: 4½ miles W of St Ives on B3306.

ZENNOR QUOIT Five stone slabs completely enclose the main chamber of the quoit – a New Stone Age tomb. The capstone which formed the roof has slipped from its original position.
Location: 1½ miles SE of Zennor off B3306.

CORNISH COUNTRY KITCHEN

A vast fireplace built about 1700 dominates the kitchen of the former mill house at Zennor, Cornwall, which is now a museum. The fire was used for cooking, as well as to provide warmth. Beside it stand a wooden cradle and a settle, or seat, both in styles which remained unchanged in country houses for several centuries.

PART THREE

Maps to pin-point the Past

SYMBOLS ON THE FOLLOWING PAGES INDICATE PLACES
WHERE YOU CAN DISCOVER BRITAIN'S PAST.
DETAILED DESCRIPTIONS OF THESE PLACES ARE GIVEN IN
PART TWO, IN ALPHABETICAL ORDER. IN MANY OF THE
LARGE TOWNS THERE IS MORE THAN ONE PLACE TO VISIT

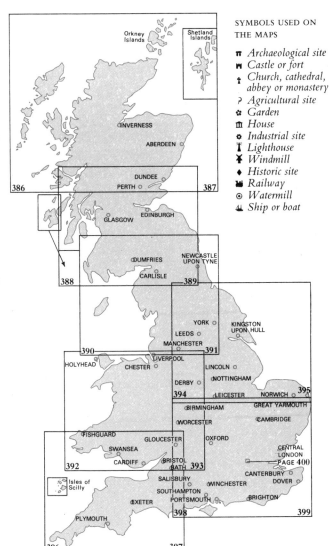

SYMBOLS USED ON
THE MAPS

ᛏ *Archaeological site*
ᛗ *Castle or fort*
✝ *Church, cathedral, abbey or monastery*
ᛈ *Agricultural site*
❀ *Garden*
🏛 *House*
✿ *Industrial site*
ᛁ *Lighthouse*
✖ *Windmill*
◆ *Historic site*
ᛞ *Railway*
⊙ *Watermill*
⚓ *Ship or boat*

MILES
0   10   20   30   40

C   **D**

f

e

A 857

Shawbost 🏛   🏛 Arnol
🏛 Dun Carloway   *e w i s*
🏛 Callanish   Stornoway
A 866
A 858

Lochinver

Hebrides

Isle   A 859

Tarbert   Ullapool
A 837
A 835

d

Outer

A 865   Lochmaddy
A 861   Gairloch
A 832
North Uist
A 832
Benbecula
Qingwa
A 850   A 896   A 833
🏛 Eochar
A 890
Beauly
Island
A 863   Portree
of   Carbost   A 890
A 865   Kyle of Lochalsh   Mill of Tore
South Uist   A 850   Urquhart Castl
Lochboisdale   *Skye*   🏰 Eilean Donan Castle
A 861   A 850   A 887
A 851   🏛 Dun Telve   A 87
🏛 Isleornsay   Fort Augustus
Barra   A 87
🏰 Kiessimul Castle   *Sound of Sleat*   ◆ Invergarry
A 388
Rhum   Mallaig   ✿ Laggan
Hebrides
Eigg
A 830   ✿ Spean Bridge
Glenfinnan ◆ A 830   ✿ Banavie
🏛 Fort William

A 861
Coll   A 884   Glen Coe ◆
Tobermory   A 828   A 82
Island   A 848
Tiree   *of*
Inner   *Mull*   Dunstaffnage Castle
Duart Castle 🏰   Finlarig Cas
A 85
Oban   A 85 ◆ Bonawe
Iona Abbey ✝   A 849   A 816   Crianlarich   A 85
Firth of Lorn   A 819   A 82
S T R A T H   *C L Y D E*

c

b

a

Orkney Islands

Papa Westray
⛩ Holm of Papa Westray
🏰 Noltland Castle
Westray
Eday
Sanday
Rousay
Midhowe ⛩ ⛩ ✝ Egilsay
Gurness ⛩ ⛩
⛩ Taversöe Tuick
Mainland
Skara Brae ⛩
Ring of Brodgar ⛩ 🏰 Maes Howe Tomb
Ring of Stenness ⛩ ⛩ 🏰✝ Kirkwall
Stronsay
Shapinsay
Orkney Islands
Hoy
South Ronaldsay

Pentland Firth

Shetland Islands

Yell
Unst
🏰 Muness Castle
Fetlar
Tingwall ⬦ Lerwick
Scalloway Castle 🏰
Shetland Islands
⛩ Mousa broch
✝ Dunrossness
🏰 Jarlshof

Crosskirk ✝
⛩🏰 Thurso

Wick

✝ Dunbeath

A 897

🏰 Dunrobin Castle

Dornoch
🏛 Tain

Moray Firth

🏛 Cromarty
Forres
Sueno's Stone
Keith
🏛 Banff
Kinnairds Head
Fraserburgh
⛩✝ Duffus
✝ Elgin
Peterhead
Haddo House
🏛 Cawdor
Culloden
Nairn Viaduct
Clava Cairns
Craigellachie
Balvenie Castle
Ballindalloch
🏰 Huntly
Pitmedden Garden
Craig Castle 🏰 Druminnor Castle
🏰 Pitcaple Castle
Leith Hall
Kildrummy Castle
Glenbuchat Castle
Monymusk ✝ Castle Fraser
Boat of Garten
Corgarff Castle
🏰 Craigievar Castle
Aberdeen
Highland Wildlife Park
Crathes Castle 🏰 Drum Castle
Kingussie
Aviemore
Braemar Castle
Kindrochit Castle 🏰
🏛 Stonehaven
🏰 Dunnottar Castle
A 94

Edzell Castle 🏰
Blair Atholl 🏰
◆ Pass of Killiecrankie
Tummel Bridge
🏛 Aberlemno
Kirriemuir 🏛
🏛 Forfar
Aberfeldy
Glamis
✝ Dunkeld Cathedral
Kellie Castle 🏰 ✝ Arbroath Abbey
Inchtuthil 🏰 Meikleour
Kinclaven Castle
Huntingtower Castle 🏛
Stanley
🏰 Claypotts Castle
Dundee
Scone Palace 🏛
Elcho Castle
Crieff 🏛
Perth
Cupar 🏛 🏰 St Andrews
Ceres

389

387

C   386   D

Tummel Bridge

Aberfel

T

A

Glen Coe

A 828

A 848

A 82

f

Island

Duart Castle ☗

☗ Dunstaffnage Castle

A 849

Bonawe

Finlarig Castle ☗

of Mull

A 85

A 85

Crie

A 816

A 819

CENTRAL

Ardoch Fort

☗ Inveraray Castle

A 821

Callander

Auchindrain

A 83

Dunb

Cathe

e

☗ Carnasserie Castle

A 83

A 84

Doune ☗☗

Deanston

A 81

Inchmahome Priory ✝

Menstrie Castle

M9

A 811

Wallace Monument ☗☗

Lochgilphead

A 888

A 83

Stirling ☗

Bannockburn

M80

A 814

☗ Rossdhu

M

☗ Helensburgh

Falki

Antonine Wall

Sween Castle ☗

A 888

☗ Greenock

A 80

A 73

Dumbarton Castle ☗

A 803

d

Port Glasgow

A 8

Bridge of Weir

M73

Glasgow ☗☗

Rothesay Castle ☗

☗

Isle

Kilbarchan ☗

☗ Crookston Castle

of Bute

Largs

A 8

Bothwell Castle ☗

A 760

A 736

Blantyre

Craignethan Castle ☗

Hunterston Castle ☗

Cadzow Castle ☗

A 726

A 83

A 77

A 735

Lanar

New Lanar

Ardrossan

A 78

STRATHCLYD

Isle

Tarbolton ☗

☗ Mauchline

A 70

of

Brodick ☗☗

Arran

A 841

Auchinleck ✝

c

Campbeltown

Ayr

A 70

Leadhi

A 719

Alloway ☗

A 713

A 76

Wanlockhea

✝ Mull of Kintyre

A 77

Culzean Castle ☗

Drumlanrig Castle ☗

Kirkoswald ☗

✝ Crossraguel Abbey

✝ Turnberry

☗ Loch Doon Castle

DUMFRI

Moniaive ☗

b

Colonsay

A 714

New Galloway

Jura

A 712

A 713

A 762

Threave C ☗

A 718

Castle Kennedy ☗

A 75

Newton Stewart

Gatehouse of Fleet

A 886

Stranraer

Cardoness Castle ☗

Tongland

Orchard

Islay

Cairnholy ☗

Bridge

☗ To

A 747

A 714

A 746

Kirkcudbright ☗

A 846

A 842

✝ Bowmore

A 716

Luce Bay

✝ Dundren

Abbey

a

Kildalton ☗

Port Ellen

✝ Mull of Galloway

388   A   B   C   390   D

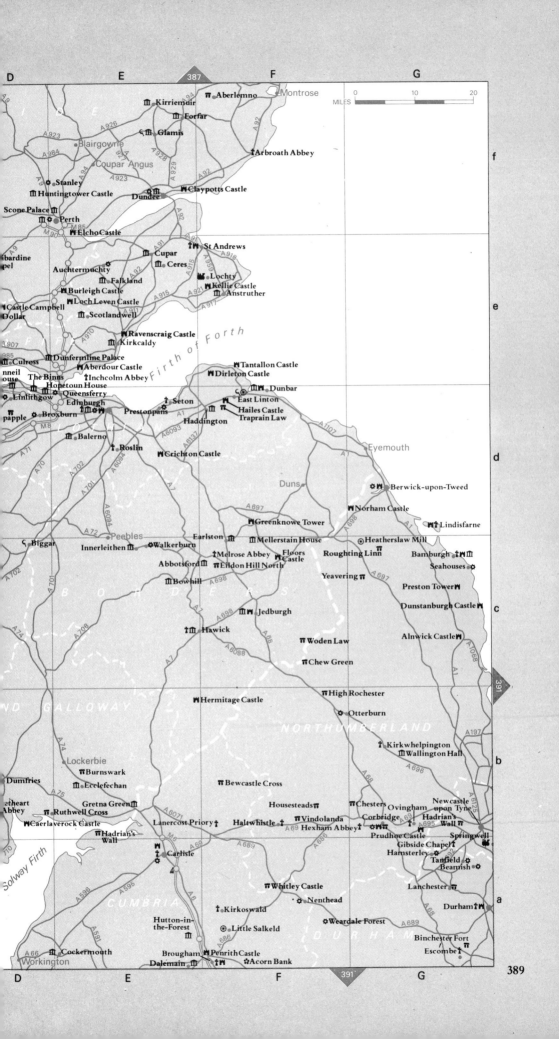

North-West England

388

f
- †•Auchinleck
- Ayr A70
- A76
- ⌂ •Alloway
- A719
- A77
- A713
- Leadhills ✿☷•
- Wanlockhead •✿
- A74
- A708
- A702
- Culzean Castle ⌂ ⌂☷
- Kirkoswald ☷ †Crossraguel Abbey
- ⌂ Turnberry
- Drumlanrig Castle ⋈
- A77
- Loch Doon Castle ⋈
- DUMFRIES AND GALLOWAY
- Moniaive ☷
- A714
- A102
- A76
- A74
- Lockerbie •
- ⋈Burnsw
- ☷•Ecclefec
- A712
- New Galloway
- A75
- A713
- ⋈ Dumfries
- Sweetheart †Abbey
- Gretna G
- ⋈ ⋈•Ruthwell Cross
- ☷Caerlaverock Castle
- ⋈Had Wall
- A762
- A711
- A75
- A718
- ⋈ •Castle Kennedy
- Newton Stewart
- ⋈Threave Castle
- Stranraer
- A75
- Gatehouse of Fleet
- A710
- Cardoness Castle⋈
- Cairnholy⋈
- Tongland Orchardtown
- ☷•Bridge
- ⋈Tower
- Kirkcudbright ☷
- Solway Firth
- A747
- A714
- A746
- A711
- †Dundrennan Abbey

e

d
- Luce Bay
- A716
- ⌂Mull of Galloway
- A596
- A66 ☷ •Cockermouth
- Workington
- A5086
- ✿ •Whitehaven
- †St Bees Priory
- Grasme
- A595
- Eskdale Moor⋈
- Boot • ✿ ⋈Hard Roma
- Ravenglass⋈☷ 丗
- ☷Muncaster Castle
- A593

c
- A10
- A10
- ⌂•Ballaugh Ramsey
- Isle of Man
- A3
- A14
- A2
- Peel Castle ⋈
- A18
- ✿Laxey
- A36
- A4
- •Millom
- A590
- Douglas
- A25
- Furness Abbey†
- Port Erin ⋈
- Cregneish ⌂
- ⋈•Castletown

b
- Morec Ba

- Blackpo

a
- South

0   10   20
MILES

A   B   392   C   D

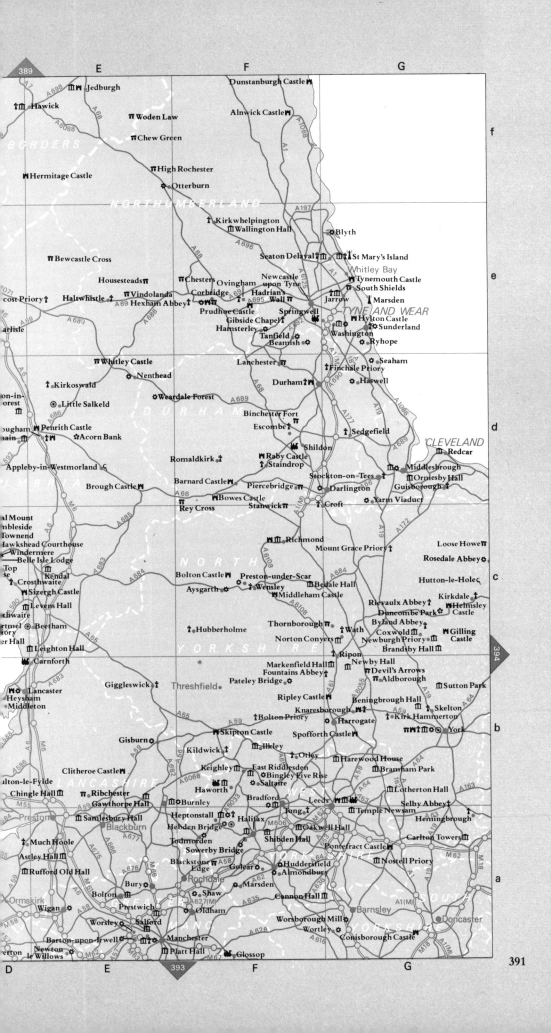

E   F   G

Jedburgh

Hawick

Woden Law

Chew Green

Dunstanburgh Castle

Alnwick Castle

f

BORDERS

High Rochester

Hermitage Castle

Otterburn

NORTHUMBERLAND

Blyth

Kirkwhelpington

Wallington Hall

Bewcastle Cross

Seaton Delaval

St Mary's Island

Whitley Bay

e

Housesteads

Chesters

Ovingham

Newcastle upon Tyne

Tynemouth Castle

South Shields

cost Priory

Haltwhistle

Vindolanda

Hexham Abbey

Corbridge

Hadrian's Wall

Jarrow

Marsden

Prudhoe Castle

Gibside Chapel

Springwell

TYNE AND WEAR

Hylton Castle

arlisle

Hamsterley

Tanfield

Washington

Sunderland

Beamish

Ryhope

Whitley Castle

Lanchester

Finchale Priory

Seaham

on-in-
Forest

Kirkoswald

Nenthead

Durham

Haswell

Little Salkeld

Weardale Forest

ougham

Penrith Castle

Binchester Fort

Escombe

Sedgefield

ain

Acorn Bank

Shildon

CLEVELAND

Redcar

Romaldkirk

Raby Castle

Staindrop

DURHAM

Appleby-in-Westmorland

Stockton-on-Tees

Middlesbrough

Barnard Castle

Piercebridge

Darlington

Orplesby Hall

Brough Castle

Guisborough

Bowes Castle

Rey Cross

Stanwick

Croft

Yarm Viaduct

l Mount
mbleside
Townend
Hawkshead Courthouse
Windermere
Belle Isle Lodge
se
Top
Kendal

Richmond

Mount Grace Priory

Loose Howe

NORTH

Rosedale Abbey

Crosthwaite

Bolton Castle

Preston-under-Scar

Hutton-le-Hole

Sizergh Castle

Aysgarth

Wensley

Bedale Hall

Kirkdale

Levens Hall

Middleham Castle

Rievaulx Abbey

Helmsley
Castle

thwaite

Duncombe Park

rtmel Beetham
iory
r Hall

Hubberholme

Thornborough

Wath

Byland Abbey

Coxwold

Gilling
Castle

Norton Conyers

Newburgh Priory

Leighton Hall

Brandsby Hall

YORKSHIRE

Ripon

Carnforth

Newby Hall

Markenfield Hall

394

Giggleswick

Fountains Abbey

Devil's Arrows

Threshfield

Pateley Bridge

Aldborough

Sutton Park

Lancaster
Heysham
Middleton

Ripley Castle

Beningbrough Hall

Knaresborough

Skelton

Gisburn

Skipton Castle

Spofforth Castle

Harrogate

Kirk Hammerton

York

b

Kildwick

Ilkley

Otley

LANCASHIRE

Clitheroe Castle

Keighley

East Riddlesden

Harewood House

lton-le-Fylde

Ribchester

Haworth

Bingley Five Rise

Bramham Park

Chingle Hall

Gawthorpe Hall

Burnley

Saltaire

Bradford

Leeds

Lotherton Hall

Preston

Samlesbury Hall

Heptonstall

Halifax

Tong

Temple Newsam

Heningbrough

WEST

Selby Abbey

Blackburn

Hebden Bridge

Oakwell Hall

Carlton Towers

Much Hoole

Todmorden

Shibden Hall

Astley Hall

Sowerby Bridge

Pontefract Castle

Rufford Old Hall

Blackstone
Edge

Golcar

Huddersfield

Nostell Priory

Bury

Rochdale

Marsden

Almondbury

Ormskirk

Bolton

Shaw

Cannon Hall

YORKSHIRE

Wigan

Prestwich

Oldham

Barnsley

A1(M)

SOUTH

Worsley

Salford

Worsborough Mill

Doncaster

Barton-upon-Irwell

Manchester

Wortley

Conisborough Castle

Newton
le Willows

Platt Hall

Glossop

D   E   393   F   G

Wales

Parys Mountain
Din Lligwy
Anglesey

South Stack · **Holyhead**
Trefgnath
Holy Island

Deganwy Castle · **Conwy**
Dyserth
Rhuddlan Cast

Beaumaris
St Asaph Cathe

Menai Bridge
Barclodiad y Gawres · **Bryncelli-Ddu** · **Penrhyn Castle**
De

Plas Newydd

Bethesda

CAERNARFON
Caernarfon
Dolbadarn Castle · **Llanrwst**
Llanberis
Gwydir Castle
Betws-y-coed

BAY
Dolwyddelan Castle

Clynnog-fawr
Castell Dinas Emrys
GWYNEDD

Blaenau Ffestiniog

Tre'r Ceiri
Cwmystradllyn
Ffestiniog

Criccieth Castle · **Porthmadog**
Tomen-y-mur
Bala

Harlech Castle
Cwm Bychan
Castell Carnd
Llanfair

Llanengan
Dyffryn Ardudwy
Pont Scethin
Bontddu

Barmouth Viaduct
Fairbourne Railway
Mallwyd

Castell y Bere

Llanegryn
Llwyngwern
Tywyn
Machynlleth

CARDIGAN
Furnace

BAY

Llanidloes

Aberystwyth
Llwernog

Nanteos
A4120

Llandrindod-W

c
Llanddew Brefi
Diser

Soar Chapel
West Wales Farm Park
Builth We

Cardigan
Maesllyn
Lampeter

Gilgerran Castle
Strumble Head
Nevern · **Newcastle Emlyn**
Felin Geri
Dolaucothi

Fishguard
DYFED

Talley Abbey
Llandovery Castle
Y Pigwn
Brecon Y Gae

Maenclochog
Llandeilo
B

St David's Cathedral
Carmarthen
Dryslwyn
Dynevor Castle

b
Rudbaxton
Castle
Carreg Cennen Castle

ST BRIDES
Haverfordwest Castle
Llawhaden Castle
Morlais

BAY
Blackpool Mill
Narberth
Ystalyfera
Merthyr Tydfil

Milford Haven
Llanstephan Castle
Kidwelly
Hirwaun Ironworks

St Ann's
Carew
Llanelli
Aberdare

Head
Pembroke Castle
Tenby
Carmarthen
Loughor Castle
Neath

Lighthouse
Manorbier Castle
Bay

Bosherston
Weobley Castle
Swansea Castle
WEST
M4

Pennard Castle
Oystermouth
GLAMORGAN

Oxwich Castle
Castle
MID

a
Coity Castle

Kenfig Castle
Bridgend

Candlestone Castle
Ogmore C

Llanblethian Castle
Old Beaupre Castle

Nash Point

Bristol Channel

0   10   20
MILES

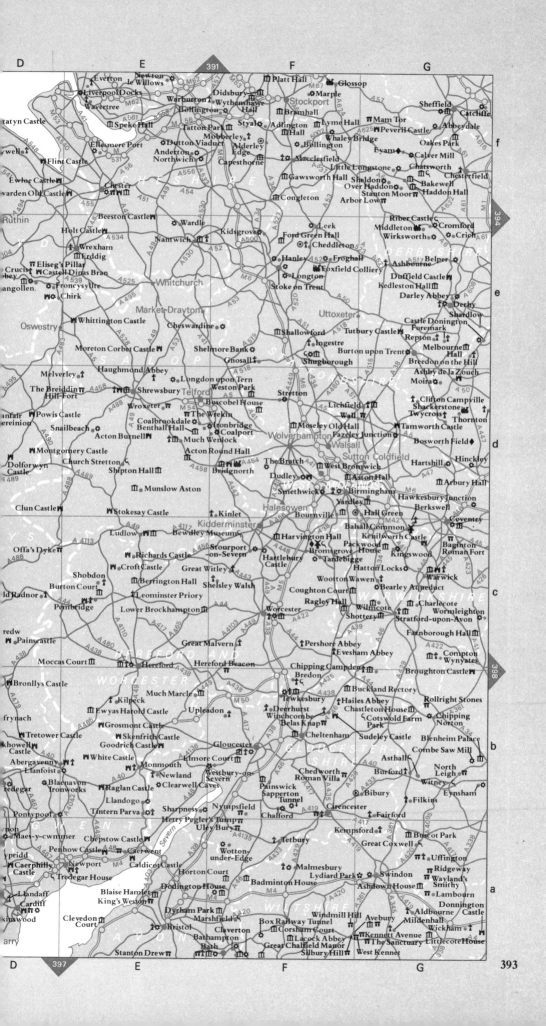

North-East England

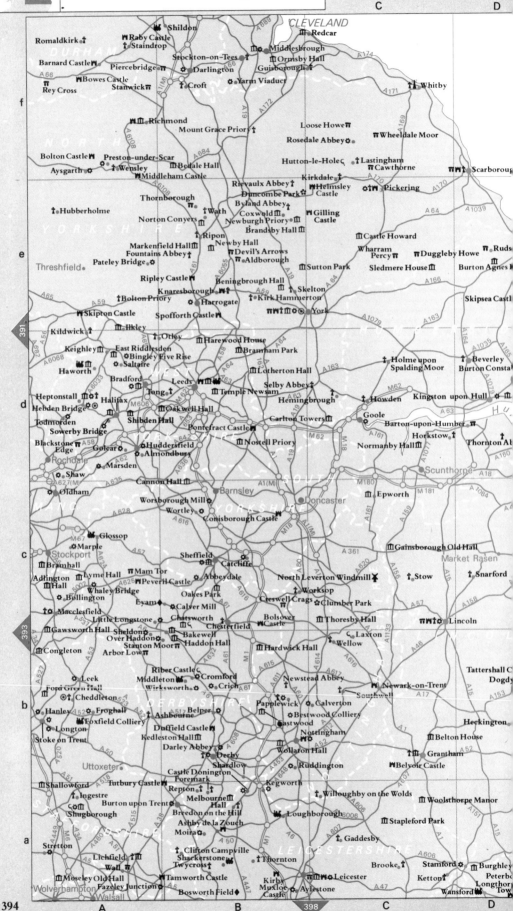

MILES 0   10   20

D   E   F   G

f

e

d

nborough Head

✝ Patrington

Grimsby

c

✝ Louth

✗ Alford Windmill

✝ Langton-by-Spilsby

Burgh-le-Marsh
ngbroke Castle   ✗ ⌒ Skegness

b

Sheringham
THE WASH   Holkham Hall ⌂   ✝ Cromer
    Warham Camp ⚲   ✝ Binham Priory
    Walsingham Abbey ✝   Baconsthorpe   ⌂ Felbrigg Hall
    South Creake ✝   Castle   ✝ Knapton
       Thursford ✿
✝ Boston   Fakenham
    ⌂ Sandringham House   Blickling Hall ⌂
    ⋔ Castle Rising   Sall ✝   ✝ Worstead
ding   ✝ Cawston   Horsey Windmill ✗
  ⌂ King's Lynn   ⚲ North Elmham
  ✝ Walpole St Peter   ✝ Litcham   ⌒ Martham
land   ⋔ ✝ Castle Acre ⌒ Gressenhall   Ranworth ✝   Caister-
   ⌂ Wisbech   East Dereham   on-Sea
     ✗ Acle ✝
  Stow Bardolph ✝   Swaffham   ⌂ ✝ Norwich   Great Yarmouth ⌂
       Burgh Castle ⚲
   Oxborough ✝⌂ ⚲ Cockley Cley   Wymondham ✝   ⚲ Caistor St Edmund

a

D   E   F   G

South-West England

Talley Abbey

Maenclochog

St David's

Rudbaxton

Dynevor Castle

Carmarthen · Llane

St Brides Bay

Haverfordwest Castle

Llawhaden Castle

Narbeth Castle

Dryslwyn Castle

Carreg Cennen

Llanstephan Castle

Blackpool Mill

Milford Haven

St Ann's Head

Carew

Kidwelly

Pembroke Castle

Tenby

Carmarthen Bay

Manorbier Castle

Bosherston

Llanelli

Loughor Castle

Weobley Castle

Swansea Ca

Oystermou

Castle

Oxwich Castle

Pennard Castle

Marisco Castle

Ilfracombe

Parraco

Arlington Court

Tresco Abbey

Tresco

Bryher

Barnstaple or Bideford Bay

Barns

Hartland Point

Isles of Scilly

St Martins

St Marys

St Agnes

Bideford

Atherington

Morwenstow

Ashley Hou

Bude Canal

Thornbury

Holsworthy

Furze Farm Park

Okehampton Castle

Sticklep

Tintagel

Camelford

Lydford Castle

Launceston

Sho Do

The Rumps

St Endellion

Mary Tavy

Trevose Head

Cheesewring Mines

Cotehele House

Calstock

Padstow

Blisland

Hurlers

Pencarrow House

St Neots

Darite

Buckland A

Trethevy Quoit

Bodmin

Lanhydrock House

Morwellham

Trevelgue Head

Castle-an-Dinas

Restormel Castle

Liskeard

Newquay

Lostwithiel

St Germans

Saltash

Saltra

Trerice

Castle Dore

Antony House

Plymouth

St Austell

St Catherine's Castle

Flete

St Agnes

Charlestown

Porthtowan

Chacewater

Carn Brea

St Day

Truro

Tolgus Tin Mill

Redruth

Camborne

Pendeen

Zennor

Hayle Dock

Carn Gluze

Lanyon Quoit

Chysauster

Botallack Mine

Falmouth

Godolphin House

St Mawes Castle

St Just

Penzance

Pendennis Castle

Carn Euny

St Michael's Mount

Helston

Tregaseal

Mounts Bay

Lizard Lighthouse

Llandovery Castle
Bronllys Castle
Brecon Y Gaer
Brecon
Sennybridge
Llanfrynach
Kilpeck
Ewyas Harold Castle
Much Marcle
Tewkesbury
Hailes Abbey
Winchcombe
Sudeley Castle
Belas Knap
Deerhurst
Upleadon
Grosmont Castle
Ross-on-Wye
Tretower Castle
Crickhowell Castle
Skenfrith Castle
Cheltenham
POWYS
Llanfoist
White Castle
Goodrich Castle
Gloucester
Morlais Castle
Abergavenny
Monmouth
Elmore Court
Blaenavon Iron Works
Newland
Westbury-on-Severn
Tredegar
Ebbw
Clearwell
Painswick
Ystalyfera
Hirwaun Ironworks
Vale
Caves
Raglan Castle
Aberdare
Pontypool
Llandogo
Sharpness
Stroud
Sapperton
Tunnel
Neath
Tintern Parva
Hetty
Chalford
Cirencester
Abercynon
Maes-Y-cwmmer
Berkeley Castle
Pegler's
Uleybury
Nympsfield
A419
Maesteg
Tump
Chepstow Castle
Caerwent
Wotton-under-Edge
Tetbury
Pontypridd
Penhow Castle
Caerphilly Castle
Newport
Caldicot Castle
Malmesbury
Coity Castle
Tredegar House
Horton Court
Badminton House
M4
Castell Coch
Yate
Dodington House
Ogmore
St Fagans
Llandaff
King's Weston
Chippenham
Castle
Cardiff
Blaise Hamlet
Dyrham Park
Llanblethian Castle
Tinkinswood
Clevedon Court
Marshfield
Corsham Court
Old Beaupre Castle
Portishead
Bristol
Box Railway Tunnel
Nash Point
Barry
Bathampton
Claverton
Great Chalfield
Weston-super-Mare
Bath
Manor
Bristol Channel
Stanton Drew
Bradford-on-Avon
Midford Brook Viaduct
Devizes
Foreland Point
Aveline's
Monkton Combe
Westwood Manor
Lighthouse
Hole
Stoney Littleton
Steeple Ashton
Farleigh Hungerford
Trowbridge
Culbone
Gough's Cave
Tellisford
Minehead
Priddy
Shawford Mill
Edington
Wookey Hole Paper Mill
Dilton Marsh
Dunster Castle
Stogursey
Wells
Nunney Castle
Cleeve Abbey
Nether Stowey
Shepton Mallet
Longleat
Meare
Cranmore
Warminster
Bridgwater
Glastonbury
North Petherton
Bruton
Stourhead
Stawley
Taunton Castle
Lytes Cary
Mere
South Cadbury
Muchelney
Shaftesbury
Knightshayes Court
Yeovilton
Tintinhull
Trent
Tiverton
Montacute House
Purse Caundle Manor
Castle
Ilminster
Brympton
Sherborne
Hambledon Hill
Bickleigh Castle
d'Evercy
Yeovil
Hod Hill
Cranborne
Cullompton
Chard
Manor
Honiton
Blandford
Forum
Knightshayes Forde Abbey
Cerne
Milton Abbas
Exeter
Ottery St Mary
Shute Barton
Abbas
Winterborne
Beaminster
Dewlish House
Tomson
Castle Drogo
Athelhampton
Bere Regis
Lyme
Wolfeton House
Clouds Hill
Ashton
Powderham
Regis
Dorchester
Higher Bockhampton
ound
Castle
Bicton Gardens
Nine Stones
Maiden Castle
ound Tor
A la Ronde
Exmouth
Lyme Bay
Grey Mare
Studland
Corfe Castle
Bradley Manor
Weymouth
ckfastleigh
n Castle
Torquay
Berry Pomeroy Castle
otnes
Paignton
Portland
astle
mouth
Hallsands
be Start Point Lighthouse

MILES 0 10 20

South-East England

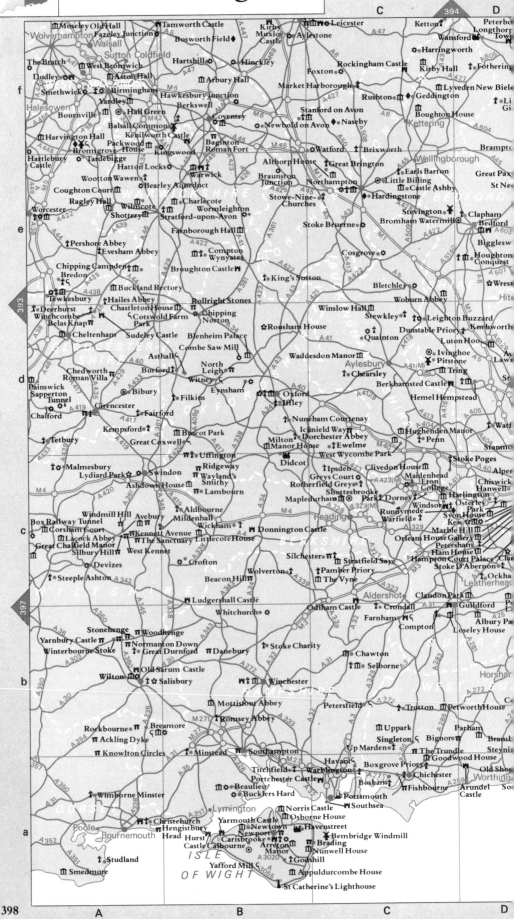

D   E   F   G

March

Oxborough   Cockley Cley   Wymondham   Caistor St Edmund

Somerleyton Hall

Weeting Castle   Grime's Graves   Bungay Castle   Lowestoft

East Harling   Sotterly   **f**

Ely   Thetford   Bressingham

Wingfield   Southwold

Stretham   Mildenhall   Yaxley   Eye Castle   Blythburgh

Wicken Fen   West Stow   Heveningham Hall

Bury St Edmunds   Woolpit   Saxtead Green   Framlingham

Cambridge   Ickworth House   Haughley Park

Trumpington   Stowmarket   Easton Farm Park   Glemham Hall

Helmingham Hall

Boxted   Needham Market

Duxford Airfield   Lavenham   Ufford   **e**

Hadstock   Clare Castle   Long Melford   Woodbridge   Sutton Hoo   Orford Castle

Sudbury   Boxford   Ipswich

Saffron Walden

Audley End

Great Sampford   Castle Hedingham

Anstey   Finchingfield   Little Maplestead

Chappel

Lexden Tumulus   Colchester

Coggeshall

Copford Green

Bishop's Stortford   Layer Marney   Clacton-on-Sea

Mersea Island   **d**

Stanstead Abbots   Pleshey Castle

...eld House   Bradwell-on-Sea

Ongar Castle   Chelmsford

Greensted

Waltham Abbey   Blackmore

...am   Ingatestone

...ross

...ingford   Brentwood

Walthamstow   Rayleigh Mount

Alexandra Place   Wanstead   Upminster

Bow   Hadleigh Castle   Southend-on-Sea

Limehouse   Canvey Island

...the   Greenwich   Thames

...rd   Rangers House   Stone   Tilbury Fort

Brixton

Windmill   Eltham Palace   Isle of Sheppey

Beddington   Rochester   Upnor Castle

Cobham   Whitstable   Reculver   Margate   **c**

Lullingstone   Sittingbourne   North Foreland

Eynsford Castle   Ramsgate

Down House   Kits Coty House   Aylesford   Faversham   Richborough

Westerham   Ightham   Allington Castle   Canterbury

Chartwell   Maidstone   Deal Castle

Ightham Mote   Old Soar Manor   Leeds Castle   Barfreston   Walmer Castle

Haxted   Hever Castle   Boughton Monchelsea

Lingfield   Tonbridge Castle   Dover

East Grinstead   Penshurst Place   Godinton Park   Ashford   Elham

...den   Bayham Abbey   Tunbridge Wells

Groombridge   Sissinghurst Castle   Swanton Mill

...stow   Finchcocks   Lympne   Folkestone

Balcombe Viaduct   Scotney Castle Garden   Tenterden   Saltwood Castle   **b**

Great Maytham Hall   Smallhythe Place

Sheffield Park   Bodiam Castle   Great Dixter

Bateman's   New Romney

Haywards Heath   Rye

Clayton Tunnel

Lewes Castle   Michelham Priory   Hastings

Glynde Place   Battle

Firle Place   Pevensey Castle   Bexhill-on-Sea

Wilmington

Alfriston   Polegate Windmill

Charleston Manor

Eastbourne

a

NORFOLK   SUFFOLK   ESSEX   KENT   SUSSEX   Newmarket

0   10   20
MILES

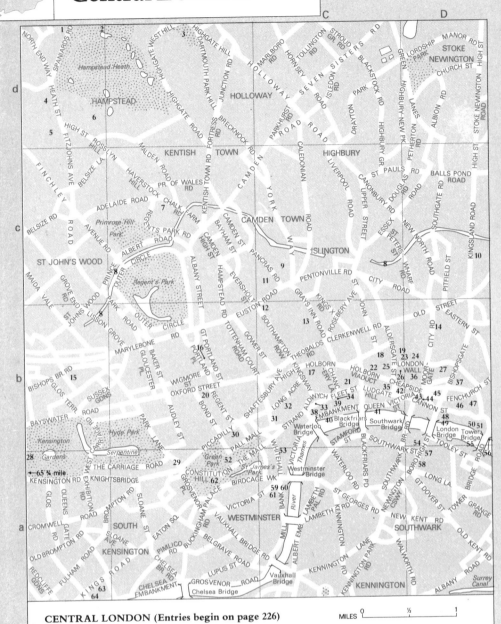

CENTRAL LONDON (Entries begin on page 226)

MILES 0   ½   1

PART FOUR

Legacy of the Centuries

THE STORY OF THE PAST IS TOLD IN THE BUILDINGS
WHERE OUR ANCESTORS LIVED, WORSHIPPED AND FOUGHT,
AND IN THE MONUMENTS OF THE INDUSTRIAL REVOLUTION

Hill-forts for Iron Age warriors

HILL-TOP VILLAGES PROTECTED BY MASSIVE BANKS WERE THE MAIN FORTRESSES IN
BRITAIN FROM THE 7TH CENTURY BC UNTIL THE ROMAN INVASION

IRON AGE WEAPONS

The arrival of iron technology in Britain introduced metal into
the lives of many people for the first time. Bronze, which had
been used previously, was always in short supply because the
tin needed to make it was found only in Cornwall. It was also
too soft to use for really effective tools. Iron ore was more
plentiful and the metal was better for working objects such as
ploughshares, nails and saws. Iron weapons became available to
many who had never owned a metal weapon before. Bronze
continued to be used for decorative work and scabbards, and in
some cases for armour.

About the 7th century BC the knowledge of
how to smelt iron was brought to Britain by
Celtic craftsmen from Europe. Before long,
iron ore was discovered and iron weapons
began to be made in primitive forges.

The spread of these weapons intensified
conflict between small groups of people who
banded together for self-defence. They built
fortified encampments on hill tops with huge
ditches and ramparts, and turned them into
tribal capitals. Hill-forts occupied huge areas.
Maiden Castle in Dorset covered 45 acres, and
the Breidden in Powys 65 acres.

DAGGERS *Iron daggers
with decorated bronze
scabbards were made
in the south-east in
the 5th and 4th
centuries BC,
probably for
aristocratic clients.*

SWORD HANDLE *This continental
sword was probably brought
to the London area
by a trader in the 6th
or 5th century BC. The hilt,
like an insect's antennae,
is typical of
European swords of the time.*

BRITISH SWORDS *The three
swords with bronze and enamel
decoration were made in the 1st
century AD by the Brigantian
tribe of northern England.*

SHIELD *A masterpiece of British
Celtic art, the bronze shield boss
is decorated with an elegant
pattern hammered in from the
reverse side*

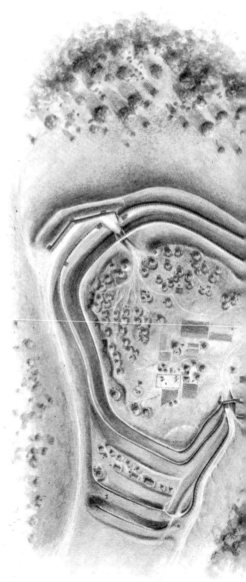

Hundreds of men laboured to make a hill-fort. They were equipped with only simple hand tools, possibly picks and shovels made of wood or iron. First the top of the hill was flattened. Around the perimeter of the village, a ditch was dug and the earth heaped up to form a rampart. Finally, a timber palisade was built on top of the rampart. The distance from the bottom of one of the ditches to the top of its rampart at Maiden Castle is 60 ft.

Early hill-forts of the Iron Age generally had one or, occasionally, two rings of ditch-and-rampart. Later generations built extra rings lower down the slope of the hill. These extra lines (Maiden Castle had three) are thought to have been the result of a developing form of warfare, stone-slinging.

Expert slingers could score hits with stones at 100 yds or more. Several lines of defence, therefore, would better protect the inhabitants at the centre of a hill-fort. The village's best slingers would stand on firing platforms near the fort entrances and return the fire. Their missiles were heaped in piles beside them. One heap, containing 22,000 round beach stones, was found in the excavations at Maiden Castle.

ENTRANCE MAZE
The entrance gate to a hill-fort was a maze of paths winding between towering walls. Defenders standing on the walls would hurl missiles at confused attackers.

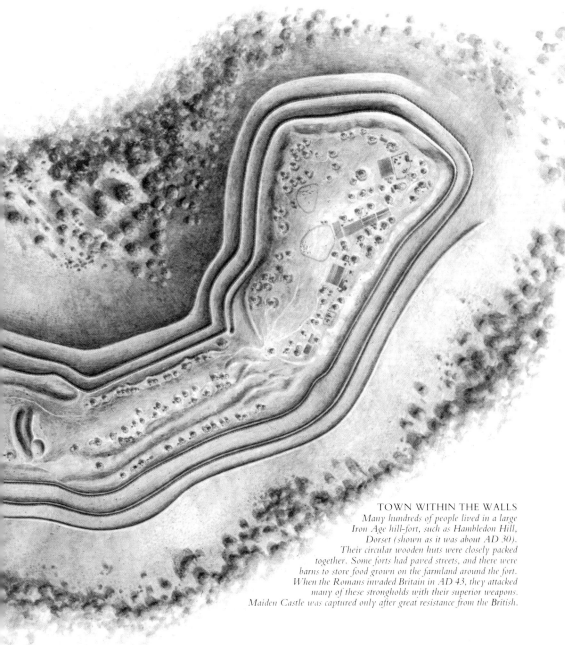

TOWN WITHIN THE WALLS
Many hundreds of people lived in a large Iron Age hill-fort, such as Hambledon Hill, Dorset (shown as it was about AD 30). Their circular wooden huts were closely packed together. Some forts had paved streets, and there were barns to store food grown on the farmland around the fort. When the Romans invaded Britain in AD 43, they attacked many of these strongholds with their superior weapons. Maiden Castle was captured only after great resistance from the British.

Strongholds of Imperial Rome

IN ITS 400 YEARS IN BRITAIN, THE ROMAN ARMY DOTTED THE COUNTRY WITH
MILITARY BASES, FROM HADRIAN'S WALL TO THE SHORE FORTS OF THE SOUTH–EAST

For the Romans, Britain was the western frontier of empire, beyond which stretched a limitless sea. In this cold land at the end of their supply lines, they had first to conquer native tribes and then keep other, undefeated, peoples at bay.

Julius Caesar stayed too briefly to build anything permanent when he raided Britain in 55 and 54 BC. But 97 years later Aulus Plautius, a well-seasoned commander, brought an army of 40,000 infantry and cavalry across the Channel and landed at Richborough in Kent.

The Roman conquest of southern Britain was swift and complete. Within five years Roman legions controlled the countryside south of a line from Lincoln to Devon.

The rebellion of Queen Boudicca

North of the Thames, however, some of the eastern British led by Boudicca, queen of the Iceni tribe, rebelled in AD 60. While the main Roman forces were campaigning in Wales, Boudicca and her army descended on the Roman settlements at Colchester, London and St Albans which had not been fortified. All three were burned and 70,000 inhabitants – soldiers, civil servants and Britons working for the Romans – were massacred.

Later that year, however, Boudicca was defeated, probably not far from Leicester. She took her own life and the revolt ended.

The Romans re-fortified their settlements and in addition built three major fortresses to control the country – at Caerleon in South Wales, at Chester and at York. These huge legionary fortresses covered between 50 and 60 acres. Each contained barracks for about 6,000 troops, with granaries, bath houses, a hospital and workshops. They were protected by an earth rampart, sometimes with a skin of stone, and a ditch beyond it. Later the ramparts were replaced with stone walls.

Smaller forts were built for detachments of troops near major roads or in dangerous areas.

An uneasy truce existed between the Romans and the Scottish tribes until 118 when rebellion broke out. The new emperor, Hadrian, decided to build a wall across the country from the Tyne to the Solway Firth. It consisted of 73 miles of stone wall, 8–10 ft thick, with a 6 ft high parapet. Small forts were built along it every Roman mile (1,620 yds) with two turrets in between each fort. Hadrian's Wall remained the northern frontier of Roman Britain for the next two centuries.

In the middle of the 3rd century, Saxon pirates began to raid the east coast of Britain in search of spoils. To repel them, a chain of forts was built around the coast from the Wash to the Solent, now called the Roman Forts of the Saxon Shore.

By the 5th century, however, the Western Roman Empire was being pressed on all sides by barbarians and the Roman legions were recalled. The abandoned British, after a determined resistance, had either to accept Anglo-Saxon dominion or flee to the fastnesses of Wales, Cornwall or the north-west.

BALLISTA *One of the main Roman artillery weapons was the ballista, a giant crossbow that could throw a 10 ft javelin or a whole bunch of arrows. Giant catapults were also used to throw rocks or showers of stones. Some were big enough to throw a dead horse into an enemy fort.*

THE ROMAN TROOPS WHO CONTROLLED BRITAIN

The Roman army consisted of legionaries and auxiliaries who fought under separate leadership and lived in separate forts. The auxiliaries, who were recruited from provinces of the empire, were stationed at frontier posts. Legionaries, who were citizens of Rome, were held in reserve in huge fortresses to be used in emergencies.

CENTURION *A centurion (below) was the commander of 80 men, and was a tough professional soldier who provided most of the leadership in battle.*

ARCHER *Auxiliary troops often carried the weapons of their homeland. Syrians (below) might be armed with bows and arrows, a sword and a dagger. The bows were made of wood and sinew.*

CAVALRYMAN *These elite frontier troops were armed with long swords and a lance. Their armour might be of iron or bronze scales.*

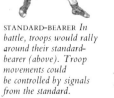

STANDARD-BEARER *In battle, troops would rally around their standard-bearer (above). Troop movements could be controlled by signals from the standard.*

INFANTRYMAN *A spear and short sword were the main weapons of the ordinary soldier (above). He wore armour made of iron strips, and a bronze helmet with cheek plates.*

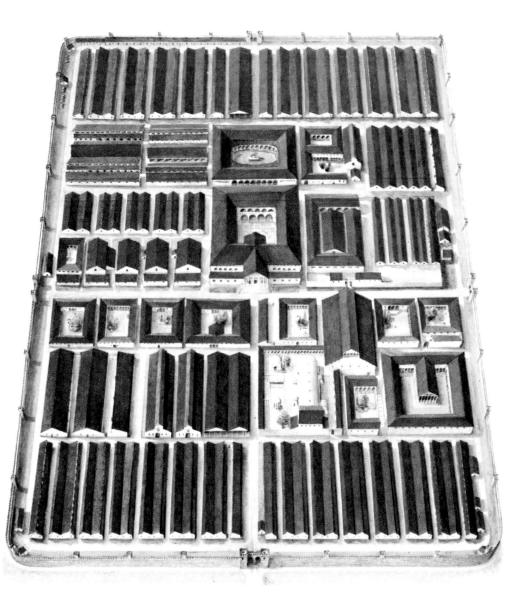

LIFE IN A LEGIONARY FORTRESS

The Roman legions were based in huge fortresses covering 50 or 60 acres, such as Caerleon, South Wales (shown as it was about AD 100). The legionaries, the crack troops of the Roman army, lived in long barracks, each containing a centuria of 80 men. Groups of eight soldiers ate and slept in cubicles, with adjoining cubicles for their equipment. Their commander, a centurion, lived in larger quarters at one end of the barracks. At the centre of the fort was an administrative building, and beside it was the house of the commandant, or legate, who was a Roman senator. Fortresses had latrines flushed with running water, and a hospital for treating ill or-wounded soldiers. Outside the walls was a bath house. Civilian settlements also stood outside the walls; women were not allowed inside a Roman fort.

SAXON SHORE FORTS
To repel invasions from Saxon raiders, the Romans built forts along the coast of south-east England, including Portchester in Hampshire (shown as it was about AD 300).
They had stone walls up to 30 ft high, with bastions mounted with ballistae.

Symbols of the Conqueror's might

MOTTE–AND–BAILEY CASTLES – MOUNDS OF EARTH SUPPORTING WOODEN TOWERS –
IMPOSED THE POWER OF WILLIAM THE CONQUEROR ON ANGLO–SAXON ENGLAND

Iron Age forts had been built for the defence of the community. But the castle was a private fortress for a powerful lord or military commander, built to overawe and subdue a conquered people. It was a symbol of a new social and political order, feudalism. And it was brought to Anglo-Saxon England by the supreme exponents of the feudal system, the Normans.

Even before he had routed the army of Harold of England on Senlac Hill in 1066, Duke William of Normandy built a wooden tower on a mound near by at Hastings. He pressed local Anglo-Saxons into doing the work and it was a sign of things to come.

Nothing stood in their way

Though his army numbered little more than 6,000 men, William the Conqueror meant to impose his will upon a nation of over a million people, and the castle, in association with armoured horsemen, was his principal weapon.

Castles began to spring up almost overnight at strategic points. They were to dominate towns (as at Norwich, York and Oxford), river crossings (Rochester, Exeter and Lewes), and harbours (Dover and Bristol). Nothing was allowed to stand in the way; 98 houses in Norwich and 166 in Lincoln were knocked down to make room for them. Sixty acres of farm land were buried beneath Windsor Castle.

The commonest type of castle was the motte and bailey. It consisted of two parts–a mound (or motte) with a wooden tower on top, and a yard (the bailey) surrounded by a huge ditch. The bailey contained wooden buildings such as stables, barns, storehouses, quarters for the lord's servants and retainers, and in some cases a chapel. In time of siege, if the bailey buildings were taken, the occupants could seek refuge in the tower and carry on the fight.

The fortifications were extremely difficult to breach. Troops of mail-clad knights could not hope to get over the ditches and palisades unless they dismounted, when they immediately

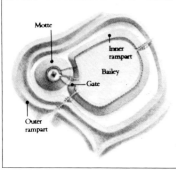

CASTLE LAY-OUT
The motte was a mound on which a wooden tower was built, creating the castle's main stronghold. The bailey was an enclosed yard where the lord's retainers and animals lived, with storehouses for food.

Motte
Inner rampart
Bailey
Gate
Outer rampart

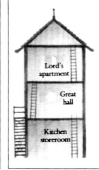

THE TOWER *The lord and his family lived in the tower. Kitchen and storeroom were on the ground floor, the great hall in the middle and the lord's apartment at the top. During a siege, all the defenders might move to the tower.*

Lord's apartment
Great hall
Kitchen storeroom

became vulnerable to defenders' arrows. If they did succeed in capturing the bailey, the motte would prove a much greater obstacle. Unless they could seize the stepway, they would have to crawl up the sides yard by yard, hammering stakes into the earth and pulling themselves up with ropes, which left them exposed to whatever missiles or liquids the defenders threw down.

Attackers might try to burn the castle with flaming arrows. The defenders could counter by hanging wet hides over the walls.

A time of lawlessness and wicked men

The construction of these castles spread into Wales where Norman lords created domains for themselves in the Welsh Marches.

When England was governed by strong rulers like the Conqueror and his sons William II and Henry I, the number of castles was controlled. But after Henry's death in 1135, the country fell into confusion and lawlessness, and scores of new castles were built all over the land.

In 1137 the Anglo-Saxon Chronicle complained that the barons "sorely burdened the unhappy people of the country with forced labour on the castles; and when the castles were built they filled them with devils and wicked men . . . they seized those whom they believed to have any wealth . . . and in order to get their gold and silver they put them in prison and tortured them with unspeakable tortures . . ."

BUILDING THE MOTTE *The Bayeux Tapestry, which illustrates the Norman Conquest, shows the construction of a motte-and-bailey castle. Anglo-Saxon villagers were rounded up and ordered to dig a circular ditch, several hundred feet in circumference. The earth was thrown into the middle in layers and rammed down. When it was 30 or 40 ft high a deep well was sunk and a wooden tower was built.*

STRONGHOLDS AGAINST ATTACK *Palisades of sharpened stakes on the outer rampart were effective defences against enemy knights. If they breached the palisade they might try to burn the central tower with flaming arrows. If this failed they had to dismount and attempt to climb the steep embankments, exposed to heavy bombardment from arrows and stones.*

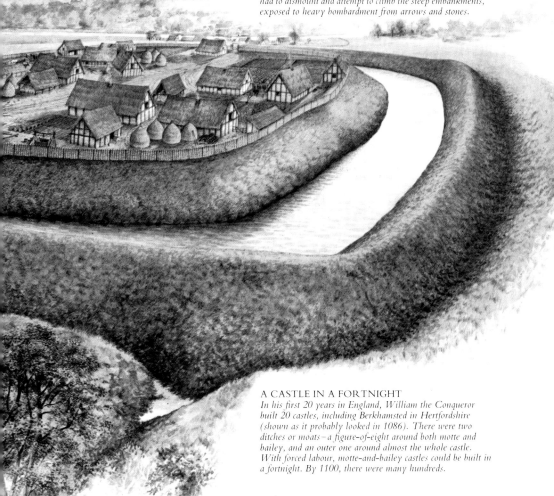

A CASTLE IN A FORTNIGHT
In his first 20 years in England, William the Conqueror built 20 castles, including Berkhamsted in Hertfordshire (shown as it probably looked in 1086). There were two ditches or moats – a figure-of-eight around both motte and bailey, and an outer one around almost the whole castle. With forced labour, motte-and-bailey castles could be built in a fortnight. By 1100, there were many hundreds.

Fortresses of stone

THE NORMAN CONQUERORS TIGHTENED THEIR CONTROL OVER THEIR ENGLISH
SUBJECTS WITH TOWERING CASTLES THAT STILL STAND AFTER NINE CENTURIES

THE PEOPLE WHO LIVED THERE

THE LORD'S FAMILY *The owner of a castle was the powerful ruler of a large area, with responsibility to help the king in time of war. In his absence his wife would run the castle for him.*

THE ADMINISTRATORS *Castles were centres of administration. The reeve was chief magistrate of the area. The clerk controlled the estate. The steward ran the household. The priest held religious services.*

THE DEFENDERS *Under the feudal system land-owning knights were obliged to spend 40 days a year serving the lord on castle duty. In wartime, infantry and archers would also live in the castle.*

THE HOUSEHOLD STAFF *At mealtimes meat was served on spits by the cooks, a ewer provided water for hand washing, and wine was served by the botiler (butler). The women spun thread for clothes.*

THE ENTERTAINERS *Music was a vital part of every meal, and a nobleman would keep musicians in his household. Visiting bands of jugglers, acrobats and jesters performed when the meal was over.*

William the Conqueror imposed his rule over the English with the motte-and-bailey castle, but permanent dominion required impregnable fortresses of stone. Within 20 years of the Norman Conquest, construction had begun on the first stone castles. And the predominant type became known, and feared, in medieval Britain as the "great tower" or "donjon".

By the end of the 1070s the Conqueror had laid the foundations of the White Tower of London and Colchester great tower, the biggest great towers ever built. The White Tower, now the central building in the Tower of London, is 118 ft by 107 ft and rises 90 ft.

Some great towers replaced an earlier wooden tower on a motte, but others – because of their weight – were built on natural ground.

The walls were very thick (up to 20 ft at Dover Castle) and often contained rooms.

The tower had only one entrance, usually at first-floor level. It was reached by a stairway, usually inside a battlemented forebuilding.

Dark basement for prisoners

The interior of a great tower was planned with care, as it was to be the residence of a powerful lord as well as a fortress. And in time of siege the number of people inside might be swelled by additional defenders.

With the main entrance one storey up from ground level, the ground floor became the basement, accessible only from above. Hardly any light entered it, and it was generally used only for storage – and occasionally for keeping prisoners. The castle's well might have its access point here, but in some castles the well-head was raised to the floor above.

The upper floors consisted of large halls with rooms off each side, acting as small bedrooms, larders and armouries. There might also be garderobes, or medieval latrines, with shafts running down inside the walls and out at the base into a ditch or moat. The central hall might be partitioned with a curtain to provide self-contained quarters for the owner and his family, or for senior officials. They would sleep in comfort, on beds with sheets and rugs. But for the rest of the household there was no privacy and little comfort. They slept around the fire in the hall on coarse mattresses or rushes. And the castle dogs shared the space.

During the day the hall was used for eating, when left-over bones were thrown on the floor for the dogs. If there was no fireplace, a fire would burn in the centre of the room. The interior of a castle was smoky, draughty and smelly – and life was lived in perpetual twilight.

To build a great tower took years. The annual building rate was at the most 10 ft of elevation. They were usually built by gangs of men recruited or pressed into service from the surrounding area. If the castle was to be put on a rock base, the rock was first flattened by hundreds of men chipping it away with iron chisels. If the base was earth, deep foundations of rammed-down hardcore were laid. A stone plinth was then set down, and the first feet of wall built on top. At an early stage scaffolding

WINDOW *Without glass, windows were small but splayed to let in light.*

FIREPLACE *Smoke from the fire escaped through a primitive flue in the wall.*

A LORD'S RESIDENCE
In some castles, including Castle Hedingham in Essex, the third and fourth storeys sometimes had no floor between them, creating a huge galleried hall. The illustration shows the castle in 1200.

was erected, consisting of poles held together with rope. The walls were made of rubble bound together with a mortar of sand and lime. Cut stone, or ashlar, was used for the outer skin. When the walls were completed, the tower was topped with a gabled roof.

Two other types of castle were also being built in the 12th century – the shell keep and the stone enclosure.

The shell keep was simply a stone wall around the top of a motte, in place of the original wooden palisade. Buildings were put up around the inside of the wall, and a small courtyard was usually left in the middle.

Stone enclosures consisted of a high stone wall with turrets along it, enclosing a number of buildings. The wall is often called the curtain as it appears to hang between the towers.

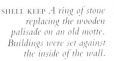

GREAT TOWER *A huge stone building in which the whole household lived under one roof. An internal well provided water.*

SHELL KEEP *A ring of stone replacing the wooden palisade on an old motte. Buildings were set against the inside of the wall.*

STONE ENCLOSURE *High walls with turrets enclosed large areas. The gatehouse was heavily fortified.*

The ultimate weapon of medieval war

THE FIERY WELSH WERE FINALLY TAMED BY THE MOST POWERFUL STRONGHOLDS TO BE
CONCEIVED BY MEDIEVAL BUILDING SCIENCE – CONCENTRIC CASTLES

British medieval castles reached their zenith in the wonders of Edward I's concentric castles in Wales.

The turbulent principality had maintained its independence for 200 years after the Norman conquest of England. But when the Welsh leader Llywelyn the Last refused to pay homage to Edward I in 1277, English forces were sent on a final campaign of subjugation. Five years later Llywelyn was dead and Wales was annexed. Determined that English rule would never again be challenged, Edward built a mighty chain of castles in Wales.

Edward had been a crusader in the Holy Land and had studied the fortifications of the Byzantines and the Saracens. The concept of protecting one stone-walled enclosure with a larger ring around it had been established there for many years. And the idea had already been introduced to Britain when Henry II began the outer wall at Dover Castle in the 1180s.

The first complete concentric castle to be built in Britain – and one of the finest – was Caerphilly in South Wales, where Gilbert de Clare, Earl of Gloucester, was trying to hold the area against Llywelyn the Last in the 1270s.

Colossal cost in men and materials
When Edward began his campaign of castle-building a few years later he used the same principle. Four of the ten monuments to his dominion over the Welsh were completely concentric – Rhuddlan, Aberystwyth, Harlech and Beaumaris castles.

Edward's scheme was colossal, and involved men, materials and money on an unprecedented scale. Some 3,000 workmen were recruited from England, offered bonuses for good work, but docked wages for absenteeism.

By no means all workers recruited from England came willingly. Three sergeants were paid seven-pence ha'penny a day to guard a contingent of workmen on the way from Yorkshire, in case the men should abscond.

Edward gave the job of superintending the whole programme to Master James of St George, one of the leading military designers in Europe, at a salary of three shillings a day.

The innermost stronghold of the concentric castle was a quadrangle of high stone walls with flanking towers at the four corners. Encircling this fortress was another wall, lower in height but with towers along it.

The main gatehouse of the castle was a vast, elaborate structure, with one, two or even several portcullises and gates. At Denbigh Castle, also in Wales, the gatehouse consisted of three towers arranged in a triangle. A visitor entered through a passage between two towers and expected to find himself inside the castle. Instead he was confronted by the third tower whose face formed, with those of the first two, a chamber from which he could only get out through one passage, and under surveillance through concealed spy-holes.

Edward I's castle-building was not limited to Wales. A number of English castles, including the Tower of London, were made concentric.

To the English, castles brought work
By the time of Edward's reign, the reaction of ordinary people in England to castles had changed. England was no longer a land crushed under the heel of an alien conqueror, and castles brought employment to the district. While workmen might resent being forced to work in a distant land, it was another matter to build a local castle as defences against invasion, or take a job as a resident craftsman. Castles were no longer used to frighten ordinary people, and there was little to fear from them.

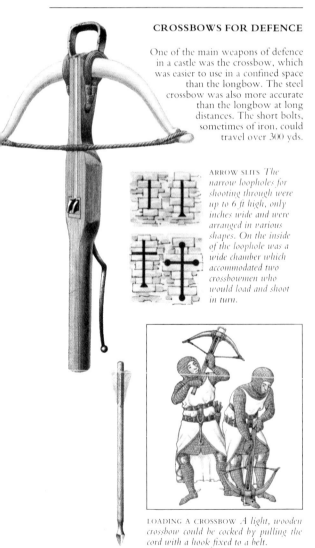

CROSSBOWS FOR DEFENCE

One of the main weapons of defence in a castle was the crossbow, which was easier to use in a confined space than the longbow. The steel crossbow was also more accurate than the longbow at long distances. The short bolts, sometimes of iron, could travel over 300 yds.

ARROW SLITS *The narrow loopholes for shooting through were up to 6 ft high, only inches wide and were arranged in various shapes. On the inside of the loophole was a wide chamber which accommodated two crossbowmen who would load and shoot in turn.*

LOADING A CROSSBOW *A light, wooden crossbow could be cocked by pulling the cord with a hook fixed to a belt.*

BATTLEMENTS *Archers shot arrows through the open sections in the walls (embrasures), and hid behind the solid sections (merlons). Slits in the merlon allowed them to see out.*

DRAWBRIDGE
A castle entrance was protected by a drawbridge. In this type, a weighted beam, joined to the bridge by a chain, would raise or lower it.

MISSILE HOLES
Stone platforms (machicolations) jutted out from the top of the castle wall. Missiles or quicklime could be dropped on attackers through apertures in the floor.

SHUTTERS *Extra protection was given to defenders by shutters on the embrasures. They opened outwards, allowing an archer to shoot down at attackers.*

PORTCULLIS
Castle gates were defended by a portcullis made of iron-plated oak. It was lifted up grooves in the walls by ropes and pulleys.

FIRE DEFENCES
Machicolations above a gateway enabled the defenders to pour water on fires set against the wooden gate by the attackers.

STRONGHOLD OF THE MEN OF HARLECH

Concentric castles, such as Edward I's fortress at Harlech in North Wales (shown as it was in 1290), consisted of a high inner wall with towers at each corner surrounded by a second wall, lower in height. The distance between the two walls was only a matter of yards. This allowed defenders on the battlements of the inner wall to shoot over the heads of the soldiers on the outer. Groups of defenders could sally forth from the castle and attack a besieging army, confident of their advance or retreat being covered from the inner defences. A huge gateway defended the main entrance, and in some castles such as Harlech the gatehouse became the most powerful part of the castle. In addition, Harlech Castle was protected on two sides by a deep moat, on the third by a sheer cliff and on the fourth by a mass of rock obstacles.

Other castles, including Beaumaris, also had a barbican, or open passageway between high walls leading to the entrance. Defenders could bombard attackers in the barbican from the top of the walls.

411

Cradles of Christianity

TRAVELLING MONKS SPREAD CHRISTIANITY THROUGH SAXON BRITAIN, AND THE EARLY
CHURCHES WERE PARTLY SACRED SHRINE, PARTLY VILLAGE FORUM

Wayside crosses were the first Christian places of worship in most of Britain. Here people gathered to hear the missionary monks who travelled the land in the 6th and 7th centuries.

Christianity was established in the Kingdom of Kent by St Augustine and his monks, sent from Rome by Pope Gregory in 597. But much of Britain was converted by Celtic monks from Iona and Lindisfarne.

The first churches were rough wooden shelters put up as a protection against bad weather. They had a small chamber (the chancel) for the priest and the altar on which the bread and wine of the Mass were consecrated, and a larger chamber (the nave) for the people. The altar was always placed at the east end, a custom that probably arose from pagan worship of the sunrise.

Most churches were built by lords of the manor for their families and retainers. The lords appointed resident priests, who were usually freemen and were often married, although church laws required celibacy. Priests were paid with tithes, one-tenth of the parish produce, which was used for church expenses and the upkeep of the chancel.

The people looked after the upkeep of the nave, which was their village hall and court of justice. Trial by ordeal was often held there.

About ten stone-built Saxon churches have survived more or less unaltered.

OPENINGS *Most Saxon doors and windows were round arched, often with the arch hewn from a single stone. Some were triangular, with two flat stones slanted together, as at Deerhurst, Gloucestershire (left). Windows were filled with hole-pierced horn, wood or thin stone.*

TOWERS *Not all Saxon churches had towers, but those that did usually had them at the west end. They were tall and narrow, and were built to house the church bells that called people to worship.*

Walls were decorated with pilasters – narrow vertical strips of stone. Sometimes pilasters were linked by struts or arches – known as carpentering work because of its resemblance to timbering.

Roofs were sometimes pyramidal, as at Sompting, W. Sussex (left), but original Saxon roofs are rare.

COPED TOMB *Many Saxon church monuments were destroyed or were dismembered and re-used by the Normans. This sloping coffin lid of sculptured stone at Bakewell, Derbyshire (left), is 3 ft 4 in. long. It dates from about the 9th century and was discovered during rebuilding in 1841.*

SAXON ARCHITECTURE
One of the best-preserved Saxon churches is at Escomb, Durham, shown below as it probably looked when first built in the 7th century. A western annexe was built in later Saxon times.

Saxon churches (600-1066)

1 CHANCEL *This housed the wooden altar, known as Christ's Board, that symbolised the table at the Last Supper.*

2 CHANCEL ARCH *A division between chancel and nave, to evoke a reverent atmosphere.*

3 NAVE *People stood or knelt on a floor strewn with straw or rushes. There was no heating.*

4 SOUTH DOOR *The usual entrance. Superstition grew up round the north door – the Devil's door.*

5 WALLS *The stones used were often taken from Roman ruins.*

6 LONG AND SHORT WORK *Corners were made with stones laid alternately upright and flat.*

SAXON CROSSES *Carved crosses erected in churchyards marked them as holy ground. Most remaining Saxon crosses are in the north – some may be the crosses where the monks preached in early Saxon times. One of the finest is the elaborately carved cross at Eyam, Derbyshire (left), probably dating from the 8th century.*

The coming of the Normans

After the conquest of 1066, the Normans built hundreds of new churches and rebuilt many Saxon churches. They needed larger churches for the increasing population and also for the more elaborate ritual they brought from the Continent.

Many new monasteries were founded, and often were granted most of the revenues of a parish church, leaving the priest in poverty.

CHURCHMEN

A priest's black cassock was lined with sheepskin, and over the top he wore a loose white surplice. A gravedigger wore a tunic and hose.

COLUMNS *Most Norman columns were round with a cushion-shaped capital (head stone) topped by a square slab, as in the crypt of St Mary-le-Bow, London (left). Scalloped capitals – grooved like a scallop shell – became common in later work.*

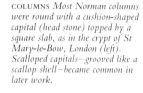

ORNAMENT *Zigzags or chevrons were common Norman decoration, also animal heads with long beaks, as at the Church of St Peter-in-the-East, Oxford (left). Early ornament was shaped with an axe and never deeply cut, but as the chisel began to be used, carvings became deeper and more abundant.*

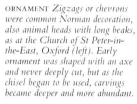

FONT *Used for baptism, the font was near the main door and had a lockable wooden cover to prevent the theft of holy water, believed to have magical powers. Some Norman fonts were made of lead, as at Ashover, Derbyshire (left).*

Norman churches (1066–1190)

1 ALTAR *Made of stone, and in richer churches probably lit by beeswax candles for early morning Mass.*

2 WINDOWS *Small, with a steep inside slope to let in as much light as possible. Mostly filled with shutters.*

3 NAVE *Inside walls were coloured with paintings.*

4 DOORWAY *Deeply recessed, with rich carvings on arches and columns.*

5 TYMPANUM *A carved stone slab between a square door and its arch.*

6 WALL *Very thick; two skins of stone with rubble between.*

7 BUTTRESS *A broad, flat wall reinforcement to resist outward thrust from an arch or roof.*

8 ARCH *Round and built of small stones. Arches were stepped to fill the wall.*

9 ARCADING *Blind arches flanking doors, windows.*

10 STRING COURSE *A band of stone round the wall.*

NORMAN ARCHITECTURE

Stewkley church in Buckinghamshire is a typical Norman church of the 12th century, massive and solid with a low-built central tower and round-arched doors and windows. It is shown above as it probably looked when first built. Pinnacles and a parapet were added to the tower in the late 14th or early 15th century.

Centres of village life

MEDIEVAL COMMUNITIES REVOLVED ROUND THE CHURCH. MEN POURED IN THEIR
WEALTH AND SKILL TO MAKE IT AS BEAUTIFUL AS POSSIBLE FOR THE GLORY OF GOD

Few people in medieval Britain could read or
write. They learned morality and the scriptures
mainly from the wall paintings and stained-
glass windows in their churches, which
illustrated such themes as the Tree of Jesse
(Christ's family descent). On rare occasions the
priest would give a sermon in English on
Christian doctrine.

The church was the hub of village life.
People called in on their way to work or home
to listen to the daily Mass, meet friends, or do
business. The bells that were rung to announce
the prayers said by the priest at certain times of
the day were the local clock.

Occasionally there was revelry and feasting
in the nave – at the seasonal church ales, when
everyone drank ale brewed in the church
vessels. Churchwardens, men or women elected
each year, organised the ales and looked after
the affairs of the nave. They also prosecuted
those who did not attend Mass regularly.

Ordinary people took little part in services,
which were in Latin. A rood screen across the
chancel arch obscured the altar from their
view, and set them apart from the priest. They
took Communion two or three times a year.

*COLUMN A typical Early English
column, taller and narrower than
in Norman times, had a central
shaft with four detached outer
shafts. The capital (head stone)
was deeply chiselled with stiff-
leaved foliage and topped by a
round slab, as at West Walton,
Norfolk (left).*

*PISCINA AND SEDILIA A stone
drain in the south wall of the
chancel, the piscina was used to
clean the chalice after Mass. It
often adjoined the sedilia – stone
seats for the priests – as at
Rushden, Northants (left).*

*BROACH SPIRE Many an Early
English bell tower was capped
with a tall, imposing broach
spire – "a finger pointing
heavenwards" – that served as a
local landmark.
Early English spires were
octagonal, and a broach, a half
pyramid of masonry, was used at
each corner of the square tower to
shape the spire, as at Frampton in
Lincolnshire (left). Two or three
tiers of dormer windows or
ventilators relieved the large
expanse of the spire brickwork.*

Early English churches (1190–1300)

1 ROOD *A painted,
life-size figure of
the Crucifixion,
with St John and
the Virgin Mary.*

2 ROOD SCREEN
*Carved from wood
or stone to seclude
the chancel.*

3 PARCLOSE SCREEN
*To enclose a side
chapel.*

4 AUMBRY
*A cupboard for
storing the sacred
vessels.*

5 AISLE *A side
extension to the
nave. Existing
churches had aisles
added by piercing a
wall with arches.*

6 BUTTRESS
*Narrower and
deeper than in
Norman times to
strengthen thinner
walls with larger
windows.*

7 LANCET
WINDOWS *Tall and
narrow and
sometimes grouped
under one arch.*

8 DOG-TOOTH
ORNAMENT *Carved
in arch mouldings.*

9 HOOD-MOULD
*Above a window or
door to throw off
rainwater.*

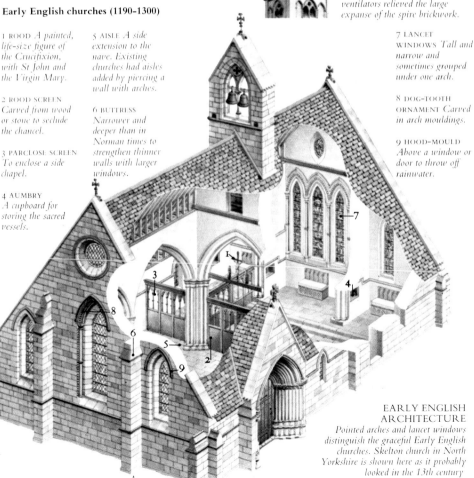

EARLY ENGLISH
ARCHITECTURE
*Pointed arches and lancet windows
distinguish the graceful Early English
churches. Skelton church in North
Yorkshire is shown here as it probably
looked in the 13th century*

Exuberant decoration

The lavish ornamentation of early 14th-century churches reflected the pomp and ostentation of the age of chivalry. Chancels were made longer as ritual became more elaborate and complex.

Transepts – small arms of the nave to the north and south – sometimes housed chantry chapels, endowed by wealthy parishioners. Here a priest prayed at a separate altar for the souls of the benefactor and his family.

Decorated churches (1300-50)

1 ALTAR CLOTH *The altar was usually covered.*

2 ROOD LOFT *A gallery behind the rood, often used by musicians.*

3 FONT *Six-sided and richly carved.*

4 PORCH *A shelter for the main door. Weddings, the preliminaries of baptisms, and penances took place there.*

5 BUTTRESS *Deeper than Early English types to strengthen walls with even larger windows.*

6 PINNACLE *Used to top a buttress. It was carved with crockets – clumps of foliage.*

7 NICHE *A wall recess to hold a saint's figure.*

8 WINDOW TRACERY *In the flowing style.*

9 SOUTH TRANSEPT *A transverse arm of the nave.*

WINDOWS AND ORNAMENT *Upright bars (mullions) divided windows into two or more sections. The upper parts of the bars were twisted into patterns (tracery) that were at first geometrical but in later work became flowing, as at Leominster, Hereford and Worcester (left). A ball-flower ornament was often used to decorate mouldings.*

COLUMNS *Octagonal columns and columns of clustered shafts separated by small hollows were common. Capitals (head stones) were carved with naturalistic foliage and topped by a round or octagonal slab, as at Patrington, Humberside (left).*

BRASSES *At the end of the 13th century, monument slabs with a formalised portrait of the dead person engraved on a metal plate began to be used. This memorial to Lady Joan Cobham at Cobham, Kent, is dated 1320. Most brasses are dated, and clearly show the costume of the period. The metal used was called latten, and was an alloy of copper and zinc hammered into a thin rectangular sheet.*

DECORATED ARCHITECTURE *Heckington church in Lincolnshire shows the elaborate, flowing ornamentation of the Decorated period, which faded as the devastation of the Black Death brought in a more sober spirit. The church is pictured as it probably looked in the 14th century.*

Pinnacles of pride

CHURCHES BECAME MORE MAGNIFICENT AS WEALTH INCREASED, AND WERE AT THE HEIGHT OF THEIR SPLENDOUR BY THE START OF THE 16TH-CENTURY REFORMATION

Men took pride in the status of the church round which their lives revolved, and as the country's wealth increased from trade, so the parish churches increased in spendour.

More and more chantry chapels were endowed by guilds – religious or trade fraternities – and chantry priests were employed to say masses every day. At other times they acted as parish schoolmasters.

Separate church halls began to be built for social gatherings, but markets were held in the churchyard on feast days and Sundays, despite attempts by the bishops to prevent them.

Because of its emphasis on vertical lines, the 14th–16th century architectural style is called Perpendicular. This style was the culmination of medieval church building. Few churches were built during the 16th-century religious strife that destroyed church unity.

PRIESTS' VESTMENTS

When celebrating Mass, the priest wore a cloak, called a chasuble, over a long white garment (an alb) and a long embroidered stole. His deacon wore a cloak known as a dalmatic. Both had a long, maniple over the left wrist.

COLUMNS *In Perpendicular churches, columns were tall and slender, often octagonal or formed by four small shafts attached to a larger central shaft. Columns often merged into arches without a capital (head stone). Shallow capitals were sometimes carved with foliage or figures, as at Stoke-in-Teignhead, Devon (left).*

ORNAMENT *Heraldic emblems such as the portcullis and fleur-de-lis were popular. An emblem known as the Tudor flower was often used as a crest on screens, as at East Markham, Nottinghamshire (left).*

GARGOYLE *Common in the 15th century, gargoyles – carved rainwater spouts – were also believed to protect the church from the devil. They were often grotesque human or animal figures, as at Thaxted, Essex (left).*

MISERICORD *A tip-up wooden seat with a ledge underneath gave a priest support while standing. Misericords were often carved, as at Ludlow, Salop (left).*

HOW TIMBER ROOFS DEVELOPED

Most churches had timber roofs, although stone vaulting was sometimes used in chancels and porches. Construction methods varied from district to district. After about 1350 most timber roofs were rebuilt when naves were heightened by adding a clerestory. This gave extra light to reveal the magnificence of the carving.

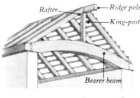

BEARER-BEAM ROOF *Saxon roofs probably had rafters resting on wall-to-wall bearer beams and a ridge pole supported by king-posts from the beams. Roofs were heavy, and only narrow spans were possible.*

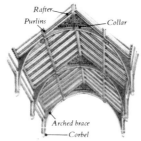

WALL-TOP SUPPORT *(below) Rafters reached to the outer edge of the wall, and uprights were positioned at the inside edge. This triangle was the forerunner of the hammer-beam.*

TRUSSED-RAFTER ROOF *A construction used up to about 1400. Rafters were supported by wall-top uprights and collars and braces near the roof apex.*

ARCH-BRACED ROOF *From about 1300, horizontal beams, or purlins, were used to support rafters at mid-span. Purlins rested on principal rafters supported by arched braces rising from a wall block, or corbel.*

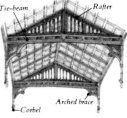

ARCHED-BRACE TIE-BEAM ROOF *In the 14th and 15th centuries, lower-pitched roofs were built by using a tie-beam with arched-brace supports to tie pairs of principal rafters.*

HAMMER-BEAM *(below) A braced strut projecting from the wall. An upright from the hammer-beam supported the rafter.*

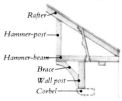

HAMMER-BEAM ROOF *Common in the south-east during the 15th century, this method used a hammer-beam construction at intervals to support purlins.*

BENCH-END *Fixed seats began to be used in the 14th century. They were wooden benches with solid ends often shaped and carved with a figurehead, as at Cley-next-the-Sea, Norfolk (left). The figurehead, or poupée, became known as a poppy head. The name pew originally applied to a reserved seat.*

SEVEN-SACRAMENT FONT *Most Perpendicular fonts were octagonal with carved panels. In East Anglia particularly, seven panels often depicted the seven sacraments – baptism, confirmation, eucharist, holy orders, penance, matrimony, extreme unction – as at East Dereham, Norfolk (left). The eighth had the Crucifixion.*

TOMB *Mourning figures, or weepers, were often carved on the sides of tombs, as at Youlgreave, Derbyshire (left). The wealthy or well-born had tombs in church, others were buried in the churchyard.*

LECTERN *Every chancel had a book-desk, or lectern, to hold a Bible from which readings were made during the mass. Early lecterns were usually wooden and were sometimes double-sided, as at Hawkshead, Suffolk (left). Eagle shapes, made of wood or brass, were popular, because the eagle soared near to Heaven.*

Perpendicular Churches (1350-1550)

1 BATTLEMENTS *Common on parapets.*

2 REREDOS *A carved screen backing the altar.*

3 TOWER LIGHTS *Belfry sound holes.*

4 PORCH *North and south doors often had porches.*

5 TRANSOM WINDOW *This had horizontal bars (transoms) and uprights (mullions).*

6 QUATREFOIL BAND *Carved ornament of four-lobed flowers.*

7 FRIEZE *A band of sculptured shields.*

8 SQUARE HOOD MOULD *Common over doors, with carvings between hood and arch.*

9 FONT COVER *Spire-shaped and raised on a pulley.*

10 SEVEN-SACRAMENT FONT *(see left).*

11 PORCH CHAMBER *Used for storage, meetings or as a schoolroom.*

12 PILLAR BASE *High and only slightly projecting.*

13 PEWS *Men and women were segregated. Seat rents swelled church income. The cost varied from about 4d to 20d yearly.*

14 PULPIT *Sermons in English were more common and pulpits became general. They were carved and painted.*

15 BUTTRESS *Very deep to strengthen wide-windowed walls.*

16 ROOD SCREEN *Arched or square-framed and finely carved.*

17 STAINED GLASS *Rich hues of yellow, green, blue and red in the large windows bathed the church in colour.*

18 CLERESTORY *Windowed top storey of nave.*

19 ARCH *Pointed, but flatter than in previous styles.*

20 ROOF *Low-pitched, with elaborate open timberwork.*

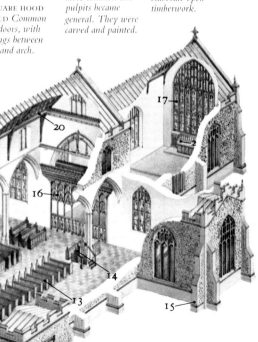

PERPENDICULAR ARCHITECTURE
Churches had tall, majestic towers, often without spires. They were light and spacious, and the large windows had rigid rather than flowing tracery. Sall church in Norfolk, shown as it probably looked in the 15th century, is a fine example.

Temples for God's word

CENTURIES OF TRADITION AND RITUAL WERE SWEPT AWAY BY THE REFORMATION, AND CHURCH BUILDERS LOOKED TO ANCIENT ROME FOR INSPIRATION

After Henry VIII's break with the Church of Rome in 1534 and the rise of Puritanism, the medieval splendour of the parish church was lost for ever.

The Protestant reformers believed in a personal relationship with God through the scriptures rather than through an intermediary priest, and considered preaching and Bible study more important than symbolic rites. Extremist reformers–Puritans–wanted to purge the church of anything suggestive of superstition or image worship.

Chantries were suppressed, stone altars flung out, wall paintings whitewashed over, the rood torn down, and statues and stained glass destroyed. Church life was transformed. Priests came out from the seclusion of the chancel to hold services in the nave–in English instead of Latin–and the sermon became more important than the Mass, now called Communion.

A royal coat of arms replaced the rood over the chancel arch, and the Lord's Prayer and Ten Commandments were inscribed on the whitewashed walls. Windows were reglazed with plain glass and family pews filled the chantry chapels. Those who could not conform to the new church worship were penalised–for example, they could be fined for not attending church and were forbidden to hold their own religious meetings.

Renaissance churches
The new churches built after the Reformation were designed so that everyone could hear the sermon. They often had one large, undivided chamber, usually with galleries on three sides.

Medieval churches had been built by groups of craftsmen under master masons. Post-Reformation churches were designed by professional architects, many of whom considered medieval architecture to be barbaric, or "Gothic".

Architects turned for their inspiration to the temples of ancient Rome, with their pillars and porticos. The most influential church builders were Inigo Jones (1573–1652) who built St Paul's in Covent Garden, Sir Christopher Wren (1632–1723), who rebuilt 52 London churches after the Great Fire of 1666, and James Gibbs (1682–1754) who built London's St Martin-in-the-Fields.

REFORMED DRESS

After the Reformation, priests abandoned the rich vestments used for the Mass. Many wore a black gown over a cassock and a white, cravat-like collar. The parish clerk and choristers usually wore black coats.

THREE-DECKER PULPIT *In Georgian times the sermon, which might last two hours and was timed with a sand-glass, was delivered from the top stage of a three-decker pulpit surmounted by a sounding board, as at Whitby, North Yorkshire. The bottom stage was for the clerk who read parish notices and led responses, the second for the curate to read prayers and lessons.*

FONT *Smaller than in medieval times, fonts were usually on slim pedestals. Sometimes covers were elaborately carved, as at All Hallows, Barking-by-the-Tower, London, attributed to Grinling Gibbons. Carved ornament often included cherubs, fruit and flowers. Sometimes the font was placed in a separate room or transept, with a christening pew beside it.*

TOMB *Effigies on 17th-century tombs were often standing, kneeling or resting on one elbow. Memorial tablets were commonly a cartouche–a marble slab resembling a scroll, as at Uffington, Oxfordshire. In the 18th century, symbols such as urns became more usual.*

Ionic   Corinthian

COLUMNS *Two kinds of Roman column often used by Renaissance architects were Ionic and Corinthian, distinguishable by their capitals (head stones).*

WINDOW *Renaissance windows were usually round-arched with small panes of clear glass, and were undivided by bars of stone or wood. Both window and door surrounds were often rusticated–made slightly prominent and roughened to give an impression of strength, as at St Martin-in-the-Fields, London.*

PORTICO *Four Tuscan columns support a triangular roof, or pediment, to form the portico–colonnaded porch–of St Paul's, Covent Garden, London (1631–8), the first Renaissance parish church to be built in Britain.*

DOORWAY *Elaborate ornament and twisted columns characterise the Baroque porch designed by Nicholas Stone in 1637 for St Mary's, Oxford. The Baroque phase of Renaissance architecture did not develop strongly in Britain.*

Renaissance churches (1630–1830)

1 PORTICO *Colonnaded porch built of stone.*

2 PEDIMENT *Low-pitched gable front of porch roof.*

3 CORINTHIAN COLUMN *The capital (head stone) is decorated with carved acanthus leaves.*

4 ROYAL ARMS *Displayed on churches after the Reformation.*

5 DOOR *With pediment and rusticated (see left) surround.*

6 WINDOW *Round-arched with rusticated surround.*

7 CORINTHIAN PILASTER *A flat column projecting from the wall.*

8 SEATING *High box pews, which were rented, were usual. St Martin's had no centre pews until 1758 because Gibbs felt they clogged the interior.*

9 WALLS *Made of brick, with stone at corners.*

10 ALTAR RAILS *Communion was taken at the rails, which became common after 1660.*

11 TEXTS *Panels inscribed with the Ten Commandments and the Lord's Prayer replaced the medieval reredos.*

12 COMMUNION TABLE (OR ALTAR) *Although first used in the nave during the Reformation, it was eventually returned to its eastern position.*

13 PRIVATE BOX *The squire usually had a private pew or compartment, often furnished. The north box at St Martin's was used by the royal family.*

14 CHANCEL *The area between two side boxes often formed a small chancel.*

15 CEILING *Panelled and gilded plaster ceilings took the place of medieval open-timbered roofs.*

16 GALLERY *Filled with high box pews, often used by servants and children.*

17 TOWER AND STEEPLE *Designed to house the bells, and often Baroque in style.*

18 ORNAMENTAL URN *Typical Baroque decoration.*

The Methodist movement, which began in the 18th century through the preaching of John Wesley (1703–91), gradually broke away from the Church of England, which at the beginning of the 19th century was at a low ebb. A few privileged clergy had rich livings while others were poor. Many country churches were poorly attended while the swelling industrial areas were without churches.

New urban churches began to be built. There was a brief revival of classical Greek architecture in the early part of the century, but in the later part church architecture turned full circle to the Victorian Gothic Revival.

Along with the Gothic Revival went administrative reform and spiritual revival, as well as a return to some of the ritual and vestments of former times. The lengthy sermon and three-tier pulpit were cast aside, and the altar, raised on two steps, restored as the focus of worship. Contention between High Church (ritualist) and Low Church (puritanical) factions continued into the 20th century, but eventually both forms of worship were accepted within the Anglican Church.

NEO-GREEK CHURCH *St Pancras Church, London, built 1819–21, is modelled on a 5th-century BC temple, the Erechtheum of Athens. The belfry is modelled on the Athenian Tower of the Winds.*

RENAISSANCE ARCHITECTURE
St Martin-in-the-Fields, London, built 1721–6 by James Gibbs, is typical of the period. It is shown here as it probably looked when first built.

419

Palaces of Faith

THE LARGEST AND MOST SPLENDID BUILDINGS IN THE LAND, CATHEDRALS WERE
REGIONAL CENTRES OF CHURCH AUTHORITY AND SUPREME SYMBOLS OF CIVIC PRIDE

A cathedral is the principal church of a diocese, the district governed by a bishop. To match its station, it is larger and grander than a parish church, and the finest craftsmen were employed in its construction. Roofs were usually vaulted (see p. 322), and the chancel was nearly as long as the nave to accommodate the many priests and choristers, and in medieval times often monks.

From Norman times until the Dissolution of the Monasteries (1536–40), many bishops were also abbots of monasteries, so the cathedral adjoined the abbey and was used for worship by the monks. The administrative body is known as the chapter. In monastic cathedrals it consisted of a number of monks; in others, a number of priests headed by a dean.

In medieval times, the nave was used for town meetings and as a law court. Ordinary people were restricted to the nave and aisles, except for pilgrims visiting the shrine of a saint. People met in a cathedral to conduct business, talk to friends, or for private prayer. Weary pilgrims often slept in the aisles, and lovers liked to linger behind the vast pillars.

BISHOP'S THRONE *The name cathedral is derived from the word cathedra (from the Greek for chair), or bishop's throne. The throne is positioned to one side of the chancel, and in medieval times was hidden from the congregation by the rood screen and pulpitum. The ornate, finely carved throne at Exeter, Devon (left), dates from 1313–17. It is square with a canopy supported by carved arches and surmounted by an ornamented pinnacle.*

BOSS *Carved keystones at rib intersections in vaulting were known as bosses, and were often painted. They were carved with flowers, leaves or angels' heads, or depicted religious events. A boss in the south transept at Worcester (left) probably shows St Wulstan's canonisation. Bosses were also used at beam intersections in timber roofs.*

British cathedrals

1 WEST DOOR *The main door, used for processions. Some cathedrals have a western porch known as a Galilee Porch; it was used during processions to symbolise Christ entering Galilee after the Resurrection.*

2 NAVE *In monastic days, the nave had many chapels where monks and priests said daily Masses for various saints. Altars, which could be used for only one Mass a day, were placed against the west sides of pillars.*

3 TRIFORIUM *Arcaded wall above the nave arches and below the clerestory. There is usually a passage behind the arcading, sometimes used to house the library.*

4 TOWER *Most cathedrals have a central tower over the crossing, formed by the transepts, that separates the nave from the chancel. Some also have western towers.*

5 LADY CHAPEL *A chapel dedicated to the Blessed Virgin Mary, usually sited at the extreme east end of the cathedral. Veneration of the Virgin became popular in the 13th–14th centuries.*

6 PRESBYTERY *The sanctuary round the High Altar, where only officiating priests were allowed. In some cathedrals, the space behind the High Altar is known as the retro-choir. It often contained a feretory chapel (with the shrine of a saint) and an ambulatory (walking way) for pilgrims and processions.*

7 CHOIR *The area reserved for the priests and choir, and monks in medieval days.*

8 PARLOUR *A room where the monks could converse. The chamber above was often the treasury, where valuable vessels were kept.*

9 CHAPTER HOUSE *Where the chapter held meetings.*

10 REFECTORY *The monks' dining hall, or Frater.*

11 CLOISTERS *Covered walks between the cathedral and the abbey, often used by the monks as a study.*

12 GARTH *The area that the cloisters surrounded.*

13 FLYING BUTTRESS *An arched prop to counteract the thrust of vaulting.*

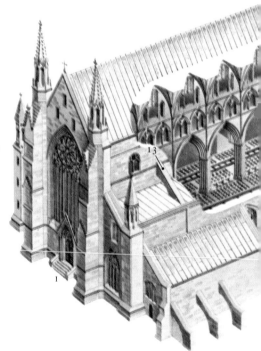

WORCESTER CATHEDRAL
Like many English cathedrals, Worcester was begun in Norman times on the site of a Saxon building. Altered and restored through the ages, it has a succession of architectural styles from Norman to Perpendicular. It was much restored in Victorian times.

SHRINE *Before the Reformation most cathedrals had the shrine of a saint or martyr, such as the shrine of St Alban (left) at St Alban's, Hertfordshire. Pilgrims visited shrines in the hope of curing an illness or as an act of penance. Their offerings swelled the cathedral revenue.*

PULPITUM *The monks' choir was shut off from the public by a stone screen with a central opening, such as at Southwell Minster, Nottinghamshire (left).*

CLOCK JACK *Mechanical clocks have been used in cathedrals and churches since the 1100s. Before the 1300s they had no dials but set off an alarm to warn watchmen it was time to ring the bell. Mechanical figures were often used to strike bells. The figure known as Jack Blandifer (left) by the clock of about 1390 at Wells, Somerset, strikes the quarters.*

Life in a medieval yeoman's "hall"

IN THE MIDDLE AGES, HOME LIFE REVOLVED AROUND THE HALL WITH ITS OPEN FIRE ON
THE CENTRAL HEARTH AND THE TABLE WHERE THE FAMILY ATE

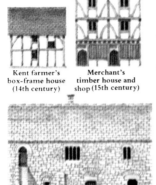

Kent farmer's box-frame house (14th century)

Merchant's timber house and shop (15th century)

HOUSES BUILT OF STONE *The Norman conquerors who invaded England in 1066 built castles and churches throughout the country using stone. But the cost of building a stone house made it unthinkable for most English farmers or merchants. So most houses in medieval England were made of wood – and they were frequently burned down by the open fires that heated them. By the 15th century, when prosperity had spread from the wool trade, stone houses were being built in upland areas such as the Cotswolds and Yorkshire, where sheep and stone were found together.*

Norman manor house (c. 1200)

Cotswold merchant's house (late 14th century)

Early in the Middle Ages, most people in Britain lived in flimsy huts which they built rather as a bird builds its nest. They collected branches, interlaced them into panels, and plastered them with a mixture of mud, straw and dung. They made a roof from thatch or turf.

These were the peasants who worked on the land of the local lord.

In the 14th century conditions of peasant life began to change. In 1349 the Black Death, or bubonic plague, swept through Britain, killing more than one-third of the population. The feudal landlords were left short of labour, and the peasants began to assert themselves. Many more were able to rent land, creating a new class of yeoman farmers many of whom reared sheep for the textile trade.

Increased prosperity brought a better style of house for small farmers during the late 14th and 15th centuries. The houses were built around a frame of jointed timbers – in the south and east of England it was usually a rectangular "box-frame", elsewhere it was a cruck frame shaped like an "A".

Rectangular wall frames were assembled on the ground, then erected and joined together. The spaces between the timbers were filled with wattle and daub (panels of woven branches and clay), then painted with a mixture of lime and water for protection. Windows had no glass; wooden shutters gave protection from wind and rain when necessary.

THE PEOPLE WHO LIVED THERE

THE SELF-SUFFICIENT YEOMAN FAMILY *Yeoman farmers were the tenants or freeholders who worked small farms of about 30 acres. The yeoman and his family were self-sufficient, cultivating their land themselves, and keeping sheep, cattle, hens, pigs and bees. In time of war the yeoman could be called on to fight for his lord, and he was compelled by law to own a bow and arrows. Many yeoman families became wealthy and rose high in medieval society.*

Framework based on crucks
"Crucks" were pairs of curved timbers which supported the framework for the roof and walls. In parts of the Midlands and the north of England crucks were used for houses as late as the 16th century, and for cottages and barns even later.

All medieval houses, from cottages to mansions, contained a hall open to the roof. In a peasant house, everybody in the family, which probably included three generations, shared the hall for eating, sleeping and relaxing. With greater prosperity, a room for sleeping may have been introduced at first-floor level at one end of the hall. In some houses food was cooked over the hall fire, in others the kitchen was in a separate building because of the risk of fire.

In much of England, rural houses were usually grouped together as a village around a green, which contained the village well and the church.

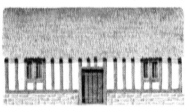

WHERE A 14TH-CENTURY FAMILY ATE AND SLEPT
The main part of a medieval house was the hall, with its fire burning in the centre, and smoke drifting into the rafters. Meals were cooked either over the fire or in a detached kitchen. In a simple yeoman's house, the family probably slept in a first-floor room or solar. Sometimes a parlour was divided off beneath the solar, and store-rooms for food were often attached at the other end of the hall. The drawing shows Minworth Greaves, Warwickshire, as it may have looked in the 14th century.

The animals drank at the pond and grazed on common land.

In the towns of Britain, the new wealth from the textile trade in the 15th century also began to be spent on better buildings.

At first, many of the town houses were halls with two-storey sections at one or both ends, like the house of a yeoman farmer. But as populations grew, and demand for ground space increased, town houses began to be built three storeys high, and halls were built behind rather than on the valuable street frontage.

Craftsmen and small merchants used the ground floor as a shop. Customers could either enter the shop or buy goods through the window. The wooden shutters which served instead of glass might be lowered and used as a counter. (See p. 346.)

The family lived in the hall behind the shop and on the first floor. The top floor was usually for storage. Because of the pressure on space, medieval town houses were usually joined together, sometimes with stone party walls between them.

The chimney revolution

BRICKS BECAME WIDELY AVAILABLE IN THE 16TH CENTURY, ALLOWING EVERY
HOUSE TO HAVE A CHIMNEY, AND GRADUALLY ELIMINATING THE OLD OPEN HALLS

PROSPERITY *Under the
stability of the Tudor
monarchs, landowners
built mansions of brick
or timber; and farm
labourers began to live
in well-built cottages.*

Cottage at Branscombe, Devon

Mapledurham, Oxon.

During the reign of the Tudor monarchs,
Britain expanded into a great maritime power.
Woollen goods were being exported as far as
Persia, and adventurers such as Francis Drake
and John Hawkins brought back gold and furs
from the newly discovered continents of North
and South America.

The new prosperity introduced a "Great
Rebuilding", when brick houses began to
appear alongside the traditional wooden
buildings.

Timber had become scarce and expensive
because of over-use, and builders had begun
looking for new materials. Bricks, which
previously had been used only for the most
expensive houses, started to compete in price
with timber.

Chimneys were easier to build with the new bricks. This meant that fires need no longer burn in the centre of the main room, but could be moved to a fireplace in one wall. With the smoke escaping up the chimney rather than through the rafters, a ceiling could be built across the main room, and other rooms built above. The two-storey house now became widespread.

Glass was now being widely used, so houses of all classes, even labourers' cottages, were lighter, warmer and more comfortable.

Farmhouses with "wings"

Many houses built by yeoman farmers had one large chimney across the middle of the house with fireplaces on both sides. One fireplace heated the kitchen, and the other the family living-room.

In a large farmhouse some of the work, such as making butter, carding wool, or drying seeds, would be done in a wing or outbuildings at one end of the house. Other buildings needed for the daily work of the farm – barns, stables and cowhouses – might be placed around the other sides of the farmyard.

Outside the village there often stood a large mansion occupied by the major landowner. In the Elizabethan age it would generally be built of red brick or golden stone, with high chimneys. The new period of peace following the Wars of the Roses meant that large houses no longer needed to be defended. So large windows were introduced, with vertical stone mullions dividing the glass.

Classical style of ancient Rome

Nearly 100 years later, in the mid-17th century, mansions were built in the neat classical style, based on the architecture of ancient Rome, and introduced to Britain by architects such as Inigo

Jones who designed the Queen's House at Greenwich. Gradually the influence of the new style spread until it was to become the dominant form of architecture of the 18th century, the Georgian Age.

THE PEOPLE WHO LIVED THERE

LAKELAND FAMILY *A yeoman family in the early 17th century dressed in the simple, Puritan style that was being taken to America by the Pilgrim Fathers.*

HOUSE OF A PROSPEROUS LAKELAND FARMER
The "Great Rebuilding" that started in lowland England about 1570 reached the Lake District 50 years later. The old timber-framed farmhouses were rebuilt in stone, with one or more chimney stacks. The yeoman farmer added buildings at right-angles to his house where the work of the farm was done. One might be a dairy and the other a barn. The household work – the brewing, baking and cooking – were all done in the kitchen, or "down house". Joints of cured and smoked meat were hung in a meat loft above the fireplace. Oatmeal was kept in chests in the kitchen, and peat and wood were stored there for the fire.

Cities of Shakespeare's England

IN THE 16TH AND 17TH CENTURIES BRITAIN'S CITIES WERE CROWDED, DIRTY,
DISEASE-RIDDEN AND FIRE-PRONE, BUT THEY HAD NEVER BEEN RICHER

STONE TOWN HOUSES *The Tribunal House in Glastonbury, Somerset (left),
was built in the 16th century, with typical Tudor mullion windows. Lord Burghley's almshouses
at Stamford, Lincolnshire, were built in the early 17th century.*

Tribunal House

Lord Burghley's Hospital (almshouses)

The prosperous trading towns of the
Elizabethan Age became a magnet for the
adventurous and the ambitious seeking their
fortunes.

Populations grew rapidly and by 1600
London was one of the greatest trading cities of
Europe with a population of 200,000. One of
its residents was William Shakespeare, part-
owner of the Globe Theatre in Southwark.

The other major cities – Bristol, Norwich and
York – each had about 20,000 people. All the
commercial centres, particularly the ports, were
becoming enormously rich, and in the
buccaneering atmosphere of the time class
divisions were far less rigid than in the rural
villages. Housing reflected this, with less
extremes between the homes of rich and poor.

Living space strained to the limits

As the numbers in the cities swelled, the living
space within the medieval boundaries became
strained to the limits. Vacant lots were filled;
earlier houses extended or completely rebuilt.
Small houses were squeezed in along the alleys
that joined street to street.

THE PEOPLE WHO LIVED THERE

MERCHANT ADVENTURER AND HIS FAMILY *A lord mayor of
Plymouth, William Parker, lived in No. 33 St Andrew's Street,
Plymouth (see opposite), early in the 17th century. He was an
Elizabethan sea captain who prospered as a privateer against the
Spanish and became a wealthy merchant. Parker probably modernised
the woodwork of the house and would have decorated it with booty
from his pirate raids.*

To make greater use of ground space, extra
storeys were added to the narrow houses.

The town houses of the time had a
characteristic "jettied" appearance – each storey
protruding further out over the street than the
one below. This served two purposes: jetties
were symbols of wealth, and they could
increase the floor space on each storey by 10-
20%.

As the houses in the expanding towns grew
higher, each storey leaned further out until they
almost touched across the narrow streets.

All these crowded houses, built of timber,
were heated by fires, and in an age before the
fire brigade was known the result could be
disastrous. Devastating fires sometimes
destroyed whole districts, as happened in
London in 1666 and Northampton in 1675.
The opportunity to rebuild London opened the
way for a new breed of man, the speculative
builder and property developer.

Early in the 17th century, James I banned the
building of jettied houses and enforced the use
of brick or stone as the main building material
in towns. If a town had to be rebuilt after a
fire, the city fathers specified the widths of
roads and the height of houses.

The result was the terrace – similar houses
joined together along the full length of a street,
with uniform interiors.

The terraces were the houses of shopkeepers,
tradesmen and small merchants who had
become a large proportion of a town's
population in the 17th century. They provided
services and goods to the rich, and gave
employment to unskilled labourers. They were
the linch-pin of a town's prosperity.

Outbreaks of disease

Despite the material progress of the time,
hygiene had hardly improved since the Middle
Ages. Household waste was still tipped into the
streets, and drinking water came from
unreliable wells. There were constant outbreaks
of disease, culminating in the Great Plague of
1665 during which 70,000 people died in
London alone. In the latter half of the 17th
century improvements to the drains and sewers
of the City helped to put an end to the
outbreaks of plague, and in 1707 London was
described as "the most healthy city in the
world".

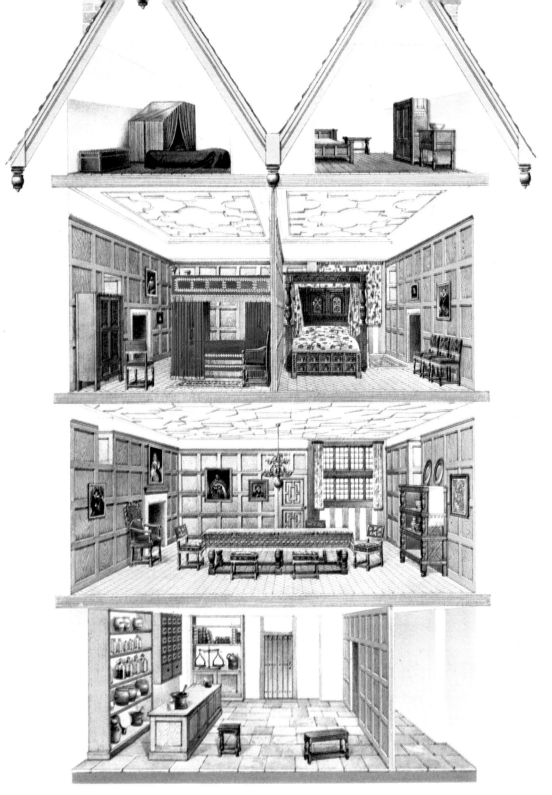

GREATER COMFORT, BUT NO PLUMBING

City life in 16th and 17th-century England was becoming more comfortable, and house interiors more attractive. Curtains were hung over the windows, reducing draughts, and late in the 17th century walls began to be covered with wallpaper. Floors were covered with rugs or rush matting instead of a layer of loose rushes. After dark, however, life was spent in perpetual gloom. People bought candles of wax or tallow if they could afford them; the poor made their own from kitchen fat, which smelled badly when burning. There was to be no plumbing for another 200 years or more, so people rarely took baths. When they did, it was in a wooden tub before the bedroom fire with water brought from the kitchen. Toothbrushes were not introduced until about 1650, but people regularly used toothpicks. The house illustrated above and left, based on No. 33 St Andrew's Street, Plymouth, is shown as it could have been in the early 17th century.

Sculptors of the landscape

CLASSICAL MANSIONS IN 18TH-CENTURY ESTATES DEMANDED NOBLE RURAL
SETTINGS, AND IF A VILLAGE SPOILED THE VIEW IT MIGHT BE MOVED OUT OF SIGHT

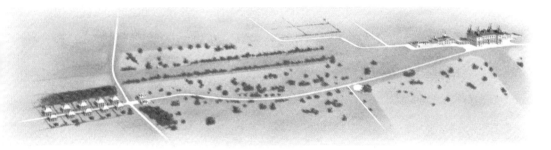

NEW HOUSE, NEW VILLAGE *Sir Robert Walpole, Britain's first prime minister, was born at Houghton Hall in Norfolk. After making a profit of 1,000% on his stock in the South Sea Bubble, he rebuilt the house in the 1720s as a masterpiece of the current Palladian fashion, based on the work of the 16th-century Italian architect Andrea Palladio. The village of Houghton was moved out of sight of the house, and rebuilt with model cottages for the estate workers.*

The English countryside broke from the old medieval pattern in the 18th century, and began to take on the appearance it retains today.

At the beginning of the century much of the countryside still consisted of large open fields in which each farmer worked a number of strips. But new and profitable methods of crop rotation encouraged landowners to enclose the open fields by Acts of Parliament, which redistributed the land into self-contained fields and ended the common rights of grazing on arable land. The enclosure movement resulted in many small farmers losing their land and becoming tenant farmers or labourers on the large estates which, in turn, grew even bigger.

To display their new wealth the landowners called in architects to build grand houses in the classical Italian manner – architects such as the Adam brothers who would design an entire house, right down to the furniture.

And to put the new mansions into surroundings worthy of their cost, they summoned the new-style landscape architects, such as William Kent and Lancelot "Capability" Brown, so called because of his frequent comment, "I see great capability of improvement here". An elaborately contrived parkland would be built around the house, often by creating artificial lakes, moving whole hills and planting groves of trees. The aim was to form the perfect "natural" landscape. Sweeping lawns would be dotted with grazing sheep or deer within view of the house. The new park might be decorated with pseudo-classical temples, grottos with running water, sham castles and even sham ruins of castles.

But sometimes a village might spoil the plans of the landscape designer by being in sight of the house. And then it would be moved. This happened at Houghton Hall in Norfolk when it was rebuilt in the 1720s by Sir Robert Walpole, Britain's first prime minister. And at Milton Abbas in Dorset the market town disappeared under the waters of an artificial lake, and reappeared in a nearby valley.

Moving from hovels to new cottages

Some villagers benefited from the move. Enlightened landowners employed their architects to design the new villages to a much higher standard than the overcrowded hovels that many farm workers still lived in. The new cottages might have two bedrooms, a parlour, and a kitchen with an oven.

The 18th century also saw the development of the canal system and the first good road network in Britain since the Romans had left 1,300 years before.

Building materials could now be transported long distances, and regions that had previously used only stone or timber or brick could use a variety of materials, provided the owner could afford the transport costs. By the mid-18th century regional differences in building were

---

THE PEOPLE WHO LIVED THERE

A GROOM AND HIS FAMILY *Outdoor servants at an 18th-century country house often lived in cottages on the estate. A groom might have a whole two-storey cottage, but humbler servants, such as an undergardener, would probably have only two rooms on one floor for himself and his family. The groom cared for the horses, and might also ride beside his master's carriage.*

MODEL COTTAGES FOR FARM WORKERS

The little market town of Milton Abbas disappeared beneath an artificial lake in 1770 to create an imposing park for Lord Milton. The inhabitants were rehoused in model cottages, each divided into two dwellings with a central door. The cottages, shown as they were in 1770, each had two bedrooms, a parlour and a kitchen. They were a great improvement on the traditional hovels of the rural poor. Each living-room had a large fireplace with a brick oven for baking bread. The oak beams which supported the chimneys came from Milton Abbey's tythe barn which was pulled down when the town was moved. Behind each cottage, a lean-to shed probably contained a copper for boiling water – and often a $4\frac{1}{2}$ gallon barrel of beer from the local brewery.

becoming less, and the distinction between houses was based more on the social position of the family who lived in them.

In between the houses of the squire and the labourer there were houses of the middle classes – vicars, doctors, small tradesmen and independent craftsmen.

Accommodation for servants took up a large part of the house. Even a curate would employ one or two servants, and a middle-class household would have two or three servants living in the attics as well as extra staff coming

in each day. Each house had its kitchen, larders, pantries and cellars.

The hill country of Wales and the west of England was not so prosperous and was not so affected by the changes. Local traditions and building materials continued to be used.

In the Scottish countryside two-storey cottages were beginning to appear for the first time, as improving landlords rebuilt villages, many of which had been destroyed in the terrible revenge carried out by government forces after the Jacobite uprising of 1745.

The Georgian terrace

IN THE 18TH CENTURY, BRITAIN'S TOWNS WERE TRANSFORMED BY A NEW STYLE OF
ARCHITECTURE THAT TURNED HOUSE-BUILDING INTO STREET-BUILDING

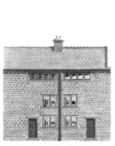

Cromford, Derbyshire

Dickens' house, London

Charlotte Square, Edinburgh

TERRACES FOR ALL CLASSES *The terraced house could be adapted by builders to match the social level of the potential occupant. Rows of terraces were built for workers in the booming textile industry, for middle-class city dwellers, and for the rich who lived around stately squares and crescents. The finest terraces were designed to resemble Italian palaces of the Renaissance, with each house occupying a part of the total frontage.*

After the Great Fire of 1666, large areas of the City of London had to be rebuilt, and the terraced houses put up by the developers became the standard type of town housing in Britain for the next 150 years.

The old wooden houses, which had each been a little different from its neighbour, were replaced by rows of identical brick terraces.

The terrace style was ideal for the new breed of builders and developers. No ground space was wasted, and the style was infinitely adaptable for all social levels. According to the wealth of the potential resident the builder could expand or contract the width of the house, add extra storeys, provide more or less space between one row of houses and the next.

At the top of the scale came grandiose terraces in the shapes of squares, crescents or circuses, such as Charlotte Square in Edinburgh, Royal Crescent in Bath and the fine squares of Mayfair. Whole terraces were designed to resemble Italian Renaissance palaces, and behind each house there were mews to keep horses, carriages and the staff to run them. Houses such as these were designed by architects, a new professional group which included the Adam brothers in London and Edinburgh, and John Carr in Yorkshire.

At the bottom end of the scale the houses opened directly on to narrow streets. They had two or three storeys with perhaps a cellar. The space between one row and the next left only room for a yard with an outdoor toilet, and an alley with an open drain.

Throughout most of the 18th century, industry was based in the countryside, along the streams that powered the mills. The workers' terraces in the towns were mostly for outworkers, who made textiles and leather goods at home. The family lived in the first two storeys, and worked on the third.

Entire towns were built in the Georgian terrace style. It was the age when bathing became fashionable, at spas such as Bath and Harrogate, and at the new seaside resorts such as Brighton. New commercial towns were founded like the Cumbrian port of Whitehaven or the canal town of Stourport-on-Severn.

These were neatly planned places, in which the size of the houses, the materials, the good-size gardens and open spaces were all laid down by the landowner.

The arrival of the factories

But at the end of the century, as the steam-engine brought factories into the towns, these regulations were forgotten.

Where the residents were wealthy – in the centres of the great cities and in the elegant resorts – the open squares and parks were preserved. But in the expanding industrial centres the achievements of the Georgian builders were soon engulfed in the slums and the suburbs of the 19th century.

THE PEOPLE WHO LIVED THERE

FAMILIES IN "SOCIETY" *The leaders of society in late-18th-century Britain were the 500–600 families with incomes of more than £2,500 a year, mostly landowners, merchants and bankers. The richest of the landowners, such as the Duke of Newcastle, were worth more than £120,000 a year, but £2,500 was sufficient to provide a fine town house staffed with several servants. At the same time, a university teacher was earning £60 a year, and 2 million people had incomes of £55.*

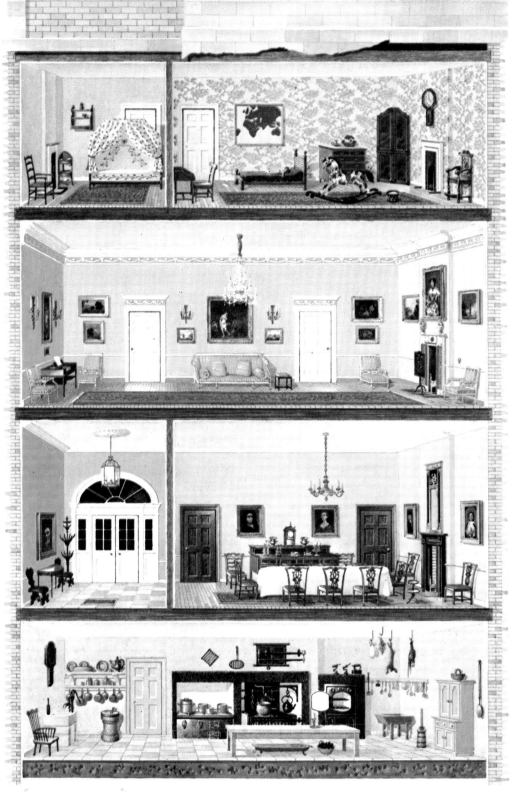

UPSTAIRS AND DOWNSTAIRS IN THE 18TH CENTURY

*The power-house of an 18th-century city mansion was the basement. It was a servants'
world where food was cooked on an open range, metal implements were polished daily, and
the clothes of the whole household were washed and ironed. The basement was connected to
the rest of the house by a network of bells by which servants could be summoned to make up
fires, carry coal, fetch hot water for baths, and remove chamber pots. On the floor above was
the entrance hall and dining-room, with possibly a bedroom behind. The first floor contained
the showplace of the house – the drawing-room where all formal entertaining took place.
Like the rest of the house, it was lit only by candles, and on a winter's evening the light
would be bad, despite the chandelier and the wall brackets. Behind the drawing-room was
a smaller, more intimate, parlour where the family usually lived. The top floor would
contain the nursery, and dormitories for some of the servants.*

431

The age of the suburbs

IN THE 19TH CENTURY, FAMILIES WHO COULD AFFORD TO ESCAPE FROM THE GRIMY
CITY CENTRES MOVED TO "VILLAS" IN THE RAPIDLY GROWING SUBURBS

SLUMS AND GRANDEUR *The worst excesses of slum building took place in the 19th century. "Back-to-back" houses, sometimes three or four storeys high with one room on each floor, shared their back and side walls with neighbouring houses. At the other end of the scale, grand Classical buildings were going up in city centres, either as private houses or gentlemen's clubs.*

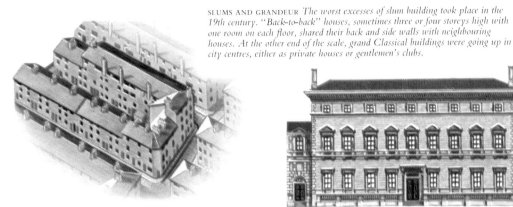

Sussex Square, Nottingham

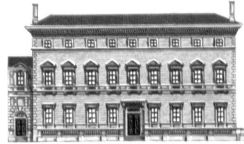

The Reform Club, Pall Mall, London

In the opening years of the 19th century, factories – now driven by steam-engines instead of water-wheels – could be built in the towns rather than along river valleys. The influx of country people to the cities in search of work coincided with a rapid increase in population as medicine improved.

The towns of industrial Britain became filled with barrack-like factories surrounded by monotonous lines of workers' "two-up, two-down" houses.

The housing consisted of parallel rows of terraces with tiny back yards and a shed, backing on to an alley with a central drain. The alley and the narrow road at the front were often the only open spaces for recreation.

High cost of land in the towns and profiteering by "jerrybuilders" led to houses being built from cheap materials that decayed rapidly. Workers' houses were built in Birmingham in the 1820s for £60 each.

The families of industrial workers had little time to notice their miserable conditions. All of them, even the children, worked punishing hours. In 1874 one of the reforming Factory Acts reduced working hours in factories to 57 a week and raised the minimum age to ten.

"Model" workers' housing

By the middle of the century, reformers began to improve living conditions with "model" workers' housing, and improved tenement blocks were built by charitable trusts.

The arrival of railways allowed middle-class Victorian families to move out of the smoke-filled towns to the new suburban areas growing around them.

The suburban house or "villa" could be detached, semi-detached or terraced, with space for at least one living-in servant as well as working space for others. Mr Pooter, the City clerk from *Diary of a Nobody*, lived in a "nice six-roomed residence, not counting basement, with front breakfast-parlour" in Holloway, London. He had a front and back garden. He depended on the train or a horse-drawn cab for his transport, and kept a cook who lived in, as well as employing a charwoman.

New mansions for the new rich

In the country, huge houses were being built by families who had made their money in industry and were moving into the land-owning, and titled, classes. The houses were used for entertaining on a vast scale, and whole regions were set aside to accommodate staff, including the servants of weekend guests.

Houses such as this expressed the confidence of the Victorian Age, and nothing like them was ever to be built again. Now many of them are used as institutions or lie empty – utterly impractical in the 20th century.

THE PEOPLE WHO LIVED THERE

A SERVANT FOR EVERY MIDDLE-CLASS FAMILY *During the 19th century the number of people living in towns rose from a quarter to two-thirds of the population. The spread of industry caused a great broadening of the middle range of society. The "middle class" extended from rich industrialists to the thousands of clerks who worked in banks and offices, recording every transaction by hand. However low a man stood in the middle class, he could still afford at least one servant – at a wage of about five shillings a week.*

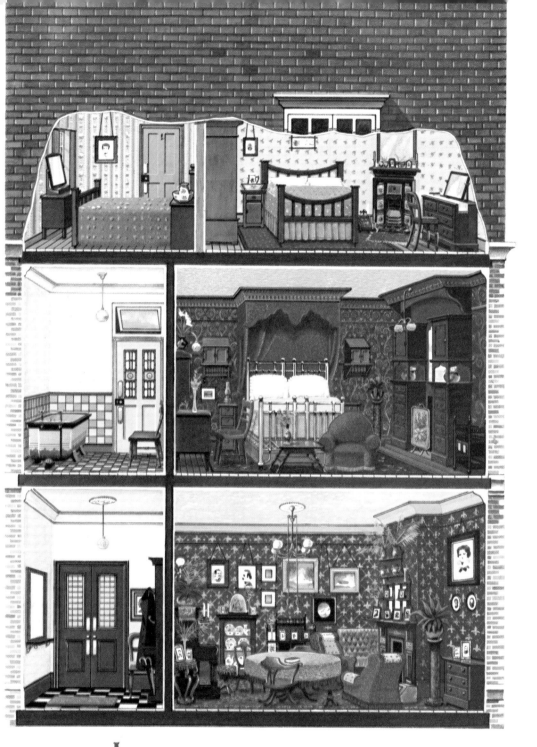

VICTORIAN COMFORT FROM PLUMBING AND GAS-LIGHTS

Plumbing arrived in well-to-do British homes between 1875 and 1900. Once water pipes had been built into the house, hot and cold running water could be supplied wherever it was needed. A room could be set aside as a bathroom, with a fixed bath that emptied direct into the drains rather than having to be emptied manually. A flushing lavatory was installed in a room of its own. Running water to the kitchen sink was heated in a boiler built into the cooking range or in a back-boiler behind a fireplace. All cooking and heating was done with coal fires, and each room had its own fireplace which had to be cleaned and re-set daily. Gas cookers and gas fires were not widely used until after 1900. Most homes were lit by a mixture of gas-lights, oil lamps and candles. The drawing-room of a Victorian house was crowded with furniture and ornaments, and was kept in perpetual gloom behind drawn curtains, as wallpapers faded if exposed to sunlight. A middle-class house, such as this one in Bedford Park, West London, built in 1878, would have had carpets on the floors of the main rooms, but they had to be swept with a stiff broom – the vacuum cleaner was not invented until 1901. Linoleum, patented in the United States in 1860, might be used to cover the floors of other rooms.

The wheels of medieval industry

THROUGHOUT THE MIDDLE AGES, MILLS DRIVEN BY WATER OR WIND WERE THE ONLY
LARGE-SCALE MACHINES – GRINDING CORN, PUMPING WATER, "FULLING" CLOTH

THE HAZARDOUS LIFE OF THE MILLER

Before the Industrial Revolution, Britain had 10,000 windmills. The wind which turned the mill could also be its greatest enemy. There was a temptation for a miller to keep his sails turning when a gale threatened, to make use of the power. But as the wind grew, the brake-power needed to stop the sails became so great that the friction could set the mill on fire. Many mills were burned down during gales. Mills could also be blown over by high winds.

POST MILL *The earliest windmills were suspended on a huge central post made from a tree trunk. To keep the sails facing into the wind, the miller had to turn the whole building by pushing on a "tail pole" protruding from the rear.*

TOWER MILL *The weakness of post mills was the difficulty in keeping them balanced, with the grindstones perfectly level. From the 16th century, sails began to be attached to a rotating cap on top of a brick tower. Eventually, a wind-wheel, consisting of several vanes, was fitted to the cap to turn the sails into the wind automatically.*

SMOCK MILL *The wooden version of the tower mill was named after the countryman's smock, a loose, shirt-like garment. Windmill sails were originally like ship's sails – canvas on a wooden frame. Later, they were replaced by spring-operated shutters.*

The driving power that launched the Industrial Revolution in the 18th century was provided by water-wheels. Watermills and windmills had been the only machines of any size in Britain throughout the Middle Ages, so it was inevitable that Britain's first factory – a spinning mill in Derbyshire – should be driven by water.

The water-wheel was brought to Britain by the Romans, and was used mainly for grinding corn for bread. After the Romans left, watermills continued in use, and the Domesday Book records 5,624 mills in 1086. In the Middle Ages, windmills were introduced to the lowlands of eastern England.

Mills were owned by the lord of the manor, and all grain grown in the manor had to be ground on his mill. He took a toll of one-sixteenth of the grain.

The principle of harnessing grindstones to a source of power, could be adapted to the geography of each village. If a good stream was available, a watermill would be built. On the coast, a village might have a tide mill, which trapped the rising tide water and then released it to turn the wheel. In exposed areas, windmills were more common.

Because bread was the staple diet for most people, the miller was a key man in the village. The supply of flour depended on his competence and the deduction of a fair toll depended on his honesty. The dishonest miller is a common figure in medieval literature.

The water-wheel also had uses in industry before the Industrial Revolution.

Cloth made in Britain up to the 18th century was mostly of wool, and had to be "fulled", or pounded, under wooden hammers to shrink and thicken it. This was done in fulling mills, powered by water-wheels.

A major problem in mines was flooding, and until the steam-engine was invented most mine pumps were powered by water-wheels.

The windmill could also pump water and was used to drain the Fens in the 17th century.

DRESSING THE STONES *Millstones weigh up to a ton each, and a pair consists of a fixed lower stone and a rotating upper one. They were often made of millstone grit from the Peak District. Dressing the grinding surfaces is a skilled craft, involving the cutting of intricate patterns of grooves.*

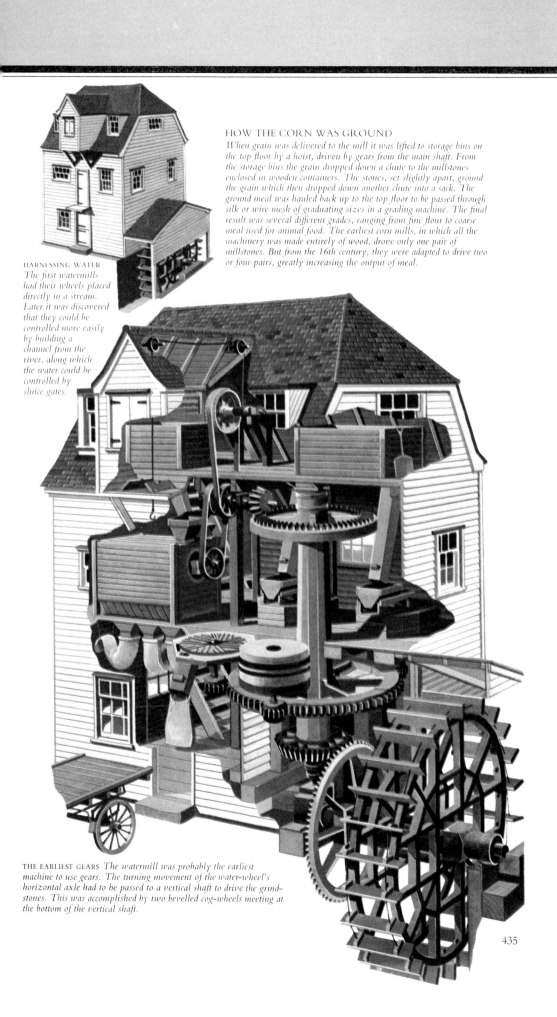

HOW THE CORN WAS GROUND

When grain was delivered to the mill it was lifted to storage bins on the top floor by a hoist, driven by gears from the main shaft. From the storage bins the grain dropped down a chute to the millstones enclosed in wooden containers. The stones, set slightly apart, ground the grain which then dropped down another chute into a sack. The ground meal was hauled back up to the top floor to be passed through silk or wire mesh of graduating sizes in a grading machine. The final result was several different grades, ranging from fine flour to coarse meal used for animal food. The earliest corn mills, in which all the machinery was made entirely of wood, drove only one pair of millstones. But from the 16th century, they were adapted to drive two or four pairs, greatly increasing the output of meal.

HARNESSING WATER The first watermills had their wheels placed directly in a stream. Later it was discovered that they could be controlled more easily by building a channel from the river, along which the water could be controlled by sluice gates.

THE EARLIEST GEARS The watermill was probably the earliest machine to use gears. The turning movement of the water-wheel's horizontal axle had to be passed to a vertical shaft to drive the grindstones. This was accomplished by two bevelled cog-wheels meeting at the bottom of the vertical shaft.

When cotton was king

THE TEXTILE CRAFTS ERUPTED IN THE 18TH CENTURY INTO BRITAIN'S BIGGEST
INDUSTRY, WITH RIOTS, SLAVE CONDITIONS FOR CHILDREN AND RICHES FOR A FEW

The meteoric development of the textile industry is possibly the most dramatic story of the Industrial Revolution. In a few decades, the textile mills became the biggest employer of labour in Britain. They drove the country-craft workers out of business, resulting in near-starvation and riots. And they led to some of the worst excesses of child labour.

Until the 18th century most of Britain's cloth was made from wool, and the industry was in areas where there were both sheep and ample water for the various processes, such as the West Country, Yorkshire and Lancashire. It was a cottage industry with much of the work carried out in the workers' homes.

The system had lasted for centuries, but in the 18th century a change began. It started gradually with the invention of the "flying shuttle", which halved the number of men needed to weave broadcloth. About the same time cotton goods began to be imported from India and were immensely popular. Britain's overseas empire also provided a market for light cotton cloths, suited to warmer climates. British manufacturers began to import raw cotton from Egypt and America, and the cotton industry was formed.

The great breakthrough came in the 1770s when Richard Arkwright devised spinning machines which greatly increased output and could be powered by water-wheels in mills. When he set up the first cotton mill at Cromford in Derbyshire it was the beginning of a revolution that was to affect the whole textile industry.

Huge demand for child labour

As more mills were built there was a huge demand for cheap child labour. The youngest children – only six years old – performed the simplest tasks, such as crawling under the machines to repair broken threads. Living-in apprentices received little more than food and lodging, plus perhaps a penny a week; children living at home got sixpence a week.

Lancashire, with its west-coast port of Liverpool, rapidly became the centre of the cotton industry, eventually consuming almost the entire American cotton crop. Arkwright and other successful mill-owners became rich.

In 1788 steam was used for the first time to drive spinning machines, and the mills could be moved away from the rivers to the towns.

The revolution was complete

When a power loom was invented to weave the cloth the textile revolution was complete: every process could be carried out in factories.

The changes in the cotton industry were remarkable. Production of yarn rose from less than £1 million a year in the 1780s to more than £40 millions in the 1830s, while the price fell from nearly £2 a pound to three shillings.

Similar changes occurred in the woollen industry, with growth of the major textile centres such as Bradford and Huddersfield.

Britain began with a virtual world monopoly in textiles but gradually other countries whittled away the lead, and in the 1930s Depression many firms collapsed.

COTTAGE SPINNING *Up to the 18th century most of Britain's cloth was made from woollen thread, spun on a simple wheel by women working at home.*
The wool was first "carded", or straightened, by children, sometimes no older than five.

COTTAGE WEAVING *The thread was woven into fabric by weavers, usually men. For broadcloth, two men were needed to throw the shuttle back and forth. The cloth was then pounded under hammers in a fulling mill, brushed with teazles and trimmed with shears.*

1733 – "flying shuttle" replaces weavers

The world-wide revolution in the textile industry began in 1733, when John Kay of Bury near Manchester invented his "flying shuttle". The invention replaced one of the two-man team necessary to weave broadcloth.

ONE-MAN BROADLOOM *A simple mechanical "picker" threw the shuttle back and forth across the loom, freeing one weaver to operate a second machine. If only the spinners could supply greater amounts of yarn, the production of cloth could be doubled.*

WOOL OR SILK *Before the cotton industry began in Britain most clothes were made of wool or silk.*

1770 – Arkwright's great breakthrough

Richard Arkwright, a Lancashire wigmaker, made a revolutionary spinning machine and set up the first textile mill at Cromford, Derbyshire. He brought in workers from the poor houses, and craft spinners rioted at this threat to their livelihood. In Chorley, Lancashire, 2,000 spinners burned a new mill.

NEW CLOTH *Cotton, introduced from India, began to be used for fashionable women's clothing.*

WATER-POWERED MILLS *As the spinning frame was operated by a water-wheel, factories were built in river valleys. Arkwright chose places such as Derbyshire, to be away from the traditional textile areas, and the wrath of the spinners.*

1779 – fine thread from Crompton's mule

Samuel Crompton, a Lancashire weaver, invented the spinning mule which produced a fine yarn, for light, cleanable cloth.

CHILDREN'S FASHIONS *Middle-class boys wore woollen suits ; girls cotton or silk dresses.*

THE CHILD LABOURERS *The new mills ran on cheap child labour. From the age of six they worked 12 hours a day, for as little as a penny a week plus board. There might be 500 children in a mill, with day shift replacing night.*

1788 – steam power comes to spinning

At Papplewick, north of Nottingham, a steam-engine was used for the first time to drive the spinning machines, and the pattern of the textile industry was changed. The mills were no longer tied to fast streams; they could be moved to the towns near the supply of labour, transport and coal.

SPORTS *Outdoors, sportsmen wore woollen coats and leather breeches. Women wore a woollen top coat and wool or silk skirt.*

THE NEW MILL TOWNS *A new type of industrial town grew up in the north of England, with the factories surrounded by terraces of back-to-back houses. Often the houses were verminous slums, as on the River Irwell in Manchester.*

1800 – power weaving arrives

Edmund Cartwright, a Leicestershire clergyman, invented a power loom following a visit to Arkwright's spinning mills in 1784. His invention eventually placed the entire textile industry on the factory system.

COTTON FOR BOYS *Muslin, made of cotton, was widely worn by women, and boys had cotton trousers.*

THE WEAVERS RIOT *Loom sheds were built beside the spinning mills, and the hand weavers were reduced to near-starvation. Rioting workers, known as Luddites, smashed machinery in the north and Midlands. But the power looms had come to stay.*

Coal: driving force of the steam age

WHEN THE STEAM-ENGINE WAS INVENTED IN THE 18TH CENTURY IT REVOLUTIONISED
LIFE IN BRITAIN AND CREATED AN UNPRECEDENTED DEMAND FOR COAL

The heat that powered the Industrial Revolution during the peak years between 1750 and 1850 came from coal. It was coal that heated the boilers of the new steam-engines and the furnaces of the iron industry. And it was coal that heated the houses of the new towns.

In the Middle Ages, coal had been extracted from shallow mines following seams close to the surface. But as the accessible deposits were used up mines had to go deeper, and often were flooded by water.

The solution came in 1712 when Thomas Newcomen built a steam pumping engine at a colliery near Dudley Castle in Staffordshire. It was based on the discovery that steam, when cooled, creates a partial vacuum which could suck a piston into a cylinder. The engine consisted of a massive beam, pivoting at the centre. One end was linked to a piston, the other to a pump. It was highly successful and opened the way to a new age of deep mining.

The deep mines, however, brought the new problem of how to lift the coal to the surface. In 18th-century Scotland the work fell to women, carrying the coal in baskets on their backs. Other collieries used a horse gin for winding men and materials up and down the shaft. A horse turned a drum, which wound up the haulage rope.

Help in shifting coal underground came with the introduction in 1776 of underground railways on which the coal could be moved on trucks. The job of hauling the trucks, however, often fell to young children, both girls and boys, who were harnessed to the wagons, sometimes being forced to crawl on their hands

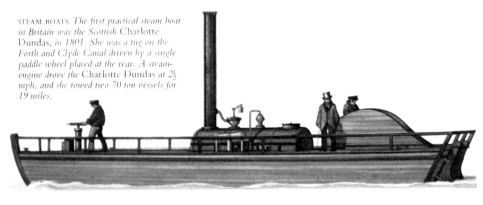

STEAM BOATS *The first practical steam boat in Britain was the Scottish* Charlotte Dundas, *in 1801. She was a tug on the Forth and Clyde Canal driven by a single paddle wheel placed at the rear. A steam-engine drove the* Charlotte Dundas *at $2\frac{1}{3}$ mph, and she towed two 70 ton vessels for 19 miles.*

FIGHTING FIRE WITH STEAM *In the first half of the 19th century, London's main fire brigade, financed by a group of insurance companies, was equipped only with hand-pumps. The first steam-driven pumps in London were introduced by volunteer groups of fire-fighters in the 1850s and were drawn by horses. The steam fire-engine* Sutherland *became known as "the most famous fire-engine in the world".*

and knees. In one mine near Chesterfield in Derbyshire, boys less than ten years old pulled trucks weighing up to a ton for 60 yds along a roadway only 2 ft high. They worked as long as 14 hours a day for a few pence.

Real improvement in haulage and winding came with developments in the steam-engine. In the late 18th century James Watt developed an engine that could operate the winding engine as well as the pumping engine, for it could cause machinery to rotate. Its use in other industries developed rapidly.

The new technology, however, did little to help the man underground. Until well into the present century, coal was still removed by men using pick axes and shovels. Seams could be as narrow as 18 in., and the men were forced to hack at the coal while lying on their sides.

The miners were paid mostly by results. A man who was set to work in a bad seam could work twice as hard as another miner for half the return. The coal itself was the property of the men who owned the land above it, who also often had the capital to set up coal-mining companies.

CORNISH PUMPING ENGINES *The tin and copper mines of Cornwall needed more efficient pumping engines than the Newcomen type used in the coalfields. Fuel was plentiful in the collieries, but had to be carried at great expense to Cornwall. The need was filled by James Watt in 1765 who built an engine with a separate condenser, giving a great saving in fuel. Cornish engine houses became prominent landmarks.*

WOMEN OF BURDEN *In 18th-century Scotland, coal was lifted to ground level by women. An observer told of one woman carrying 170 lb. of coal in a basket 150 yds along a tunnel and up 117 ft of ladders. She made 24 trips in a ten-hour shift for a wage of eight pence a day.*

STEAM ON THE FARM *Steam-engines were used to drive ploughs and threshing machines on British farms from 1850 to after the First World War. Ploughs were pulled by a wire cable fixed at each side of the field. A traction engine at one end provided the power. The plough was balanced in the middle like a see-saw, and when the ploughman sat on one end his weight brought one set of plough shares to the ground. At the end of the furrow he changed seats and ploughed the reverse furrow.*

STEAM-DRIVEN MERRY-GO-ROUNDS *Steam arrived at British fun-fairs in the 1860s with the first steam-powered merry-go-rounds. Swing-boats followed, and switch-back railways driven by steam were introduced in the 1880s.*

STEAM TRANSPORT *After the repeal of the "Red Flag Act" in 1896 allowing motor vehicles to travel faster than walking pace, a few steam buses ran in London. In 1902 a double-decker ran between Hammersmith and Oxford Circus. But in 1905 the first motor buses arrived and the steam bus was doomed. Steam cars, mostly built in America and France, were driven in Britain from the late 19th century until the 1930s. The Stanley Gentleman's Speedy Roadster could do 60 mph, and in 1906 a Stanley clocked 127.66 mph on a Florida beach.*

The metal that built a new age

WHEN COKE WAS FIRST USED TO SMELT IRON IN 18TH-CENTURY SHROPSHIRE, AN
ANCIENT INDUSTRY BECAME THE FRAMEWORK OF THE NATION'S MIGHT

Without iron the dynamic process which turned Britain into the greatest industrial power on earth could never have started in motion. Industrial Britain of the 18th and 19th centuries needed iron aqueducts and rails to move its raw materials, iron parts for its machines, and iron for the steam-engines to drive the machines.

Iron occurs naturally as an ore which is turned into metal by heating to a high temperature in a blast furnace. In 16th and 17th-century Britain, a blast of air was supplied to the furnace by bellows worked by a water-wheel, and the fuel was charcoal. The industry was established in wooded river valleys, such as those of the Sussex Weald, and trees were felled in great numbers to make the charcoal.

Large amounts of iron were being used to make nails, horseshoes, tools, cannon and shot, and at the beginning of the 18th century there were fears that the supply of timber would run out. Coal could not be used as it introduced too many impurities, but in 1709 Abraham Darby of Coalbrookdale in Shropshire succeeded in smelting iron with coke. Now the iron-makers had unlimited supplies of fuel.

The iron from the Darby process had a high carbon content and could only be used for casting, or pouring into moulds. But malleable wrought iron, which is virtually the pure metal, was needed for many processes: it was used by blacksmiths for nails and horseshoes and for household implements.

Making wrought iron by "puddling"

In 1784 Henry Cort, who owned an ironworks near Fareham in Hampshire, devised a process known as "puddling", which could be fuelled with coke. The molten metal had to be stirred with iron bars, which at first was done by hand. The heat was so intense that the men had to wrap wet sacking around their arms and legs.

As the iron-making process became independent of charcoal, the newly developed steam-engine replaced the water-wheel as the supplier of the blast. And the industry underwent a dramatic geographical shift. It left its old river valleys, and the Weald and the Wye valley slid back into rural peace. The new industry moved to the areas where coal and ore were found together – to Staffordshire, Scotland, Yorkshire and South Wales.

The owners of the ironworks had been known since the Middle Ages as iron masters, and stern masters they now proved to be. In some areas, including South Wales, they were the sole employers, and any disagreement by a worker was treated as breach of contract.

The development of steel

In the 19th century a third form of iron – steel – became increasingly important. Steel contains more carbon than wrought iron but far less than cast iron. Its property of holding a cutting edge had long been known, but its value as a framework for buildings was only discovered in the 19th century. So one of the great industrial developments remained largely hidden behind the stone or brick facing of the new buildings of the Victorian Age.

CASTING IRON POTS *Cast iron from 18th-century furnaces was poured straight into sand moulds to make anything from cooking pots to parts of giant steam-engines. Limitless numbers of castings could be run off by pressing the same pattern into the sand.*

IRON FOR SHAPING *Wrought iron was produced as bars or rods. It might then go to a large forge where tilt hammers, powered by a water-wheel, would shape it under heat to make agricultural tools. Or a blacksmith might turn it into horseshoes.*

Iron decoration for Victorian houses

Cast iron was an ideal material for 19th-century houses, as it could be moulded into the elaborate patterns loved by the Victorians. Balconies made of cast iron were widely used in expanding towns, such as Brighton and Cheltenham.

DOOR KNOCKER *Knockers began to be mass-produced in cast iron late in the 18th century. After 1840, when the penny post was introduced, some had letter plates.*

DOOR KNOB *Iron door knobs became popular in the second half of the 19th century.*

DOOR PORTERS *Iron door stops prevented doors slamming. The names of the men who designed the patterns are no longer known.*

By the living-room fire . . .

Until the 18th century, most living-room fires were burning logs resting on iron fire-dogs. Free-standing grates arrived with coal fires in the 18th century, followed by complete iron fire-places built into the wall.

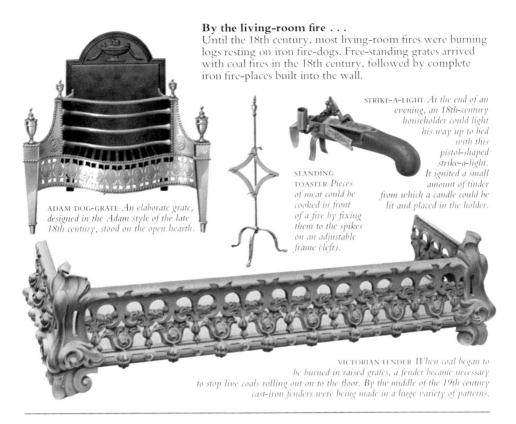

ADAM DOG-GRATE *An elaborate grate, designed in the Adam style of the late 18th century, stood on the open hearth.*

STANDING TOASTER *Pieces of meat could be cooked in front of a fire by fixing them to the spikes on an adjustable frame (left).*

STRIKE-A-LIGHT *At the end of an evening, an 18th-century householder could light his way up to bed with this pistol-shaped strike-a-light. It ignited a small amount of tinder from which a candle could be lit and placed in the holder.*

VICTORIAN FENDER *When coal began to be burned in raised grates, a fender became necessary to stop live coals rolling out on to the floor. By the middle of the 19th century cast-iron fenders were being made in a huge variety of patterns.*

Iron implements for "below stairs"

Kitchens of the 18th and 19th centuries had numerous iron implements – spits, cauldrons, toasters, girdle plates, saucepans, and ironing equipment for the elaborate clothes of the time.

GRID-IRON *To grill steak in the 18th century, a grid-iron (right) was rested over the open kitchen fire. The forked legs fitted on the top bar at the front of the grate and the rear legs rested on the fireback.*

BOX IRON *A 19th-century box iron (below) had several iron "billets" which were heated in the fire, then inserted in the hollow body of the iron to provide a steady heat. A cool billet was replaced with a hot one.*

GOFFERING IRON *Linen frills were pressed into rounded shapes on a goffering iron (right), which was heated with a hot poker.*

SUGAR CUTTER *Sugar was sold in large lumps in the 19th century and had to be broken up into usable pieces with a sugar-cutter (below).*

TRIVET *A trivet (right) was placed in front of a fire to keep food or drink hot, or to warm plates. A kettle of water could be boiled if the trivet was close to the fire, or coffee kept warm if it was moved back.*

FIRE-BAR TOASTER *The toaster (right) was hooked over the grate, and meat was roasted on the fork. Juices dripped into a dish held in the circular frame.*

Perils of the road

MEDIEVAL ROADS WERE JUST MUDDY TRACKS, BUT INCREASING INDUSTRIALISATION
BROUGHT BETTER ROADS AND BRIDGES – AND THE GREAT AGE OF THE STAGECOACH

In the Middle Ages, the ordinary traveller in Britain moved from place to place on foot. If he set out on a pilgrimage to the shrine of a saint, he walked in company with others as protection against the thieves who infested the way. The route he followed had probably existed since prehistory or might be the neglected remains of a Roman road – deeply rutted, and muddy in wet weather.

On the way he would be overtaken from time to time by wealthier travellers riding on horseback. He might encounter herds of farm animals or flocks of geese being driven to the city markets. The herds could be half a mile long, moving slowly across the countryside with a noise that carried for miles.

Slow coach for a shilling a day
By the 16th century a cheap form of transport arrived – the stage wagon. Twenty or thirty people could ride sheltered from the weather under a cloth cover. The fare was a shilling a day, but a day's journey covered only 10 to 15 miles. By the 1750s journeys were advertised between London and Manchester in the "incredible" time of 4½ days – 42 miles a day. However the wagon from Edinburgh to London continued to average only 28 miles a day, making it a tedious fortnight's journey.

Throughout the Middle Ages each parish had been responsible for maintaining its own roads by using local labour. The result was a network of often impassable roads. But in the 17th century increased industrialisation brought a demand for better roads to move goods around the country, and a new system of toll roads began. They were called "turnpikes", and were run by private trusts set up by Act of Parliament. With the improved conditions the stagecoach arrived.

Stagecoaches could cover 100 miles in 24 hours, but they charged high fares (a shilling for every 5 miles on some routes).

The stagecoaches, which changed their four or six horses every 10 miles, carried up to ten passengers inside and several more on top, clinging perilously to low handrails. Stagecoach

travel involved a variety of dangers. Passengers could be killed or injured if a coach overturned, and in winter the cold was bitter. In 1812 two outside passengers froze to death on the London–Bath coach.

Coaches were also prey to highwaymen, particularly within a 20 mile radius of London. In 12 years, between 1759 and 1771, 250 highwaymen were publicly hanged at Tyburn. Experienced travellers often carried a second purse to hand over if they were robbed. British highwaymen were renowned in Europe for their courtesy, particularly towards women, but anyone who defied them might be shot.

CLAPPER BRIDGE *Britain's oldest bridges consist of rock slabs laid on piles of stones. They were intended only for pack animals and people on foot. Clapper bridges, such as Postbridge over the East Dart River on Dartmoor (left), are as much as 2,000 years old.*

PACK–HORSE BRIDGE *Stone bridges supported by a round arch were introduced to Britain by the Romans, and continued to be built throughout the Middle Ages. Pack-horse bridges, such as the one at Stow, Borders (left), were used by pack-animals.*

STAGE WAGONS *Slow, uncomfortable but cheap, stage wagons were the first type of long-distance public transport. The 20 or 30 passengers would spend a fortnight getting from London to Edinburgh. Service at inns was poor as landlords knew they had little money.*

Medieval wagon tracks
In the Middle Ages, Britain's roads were mostly dirt tracks – muddy and full of holes. The parishes, which were responsible for their upkeep, usually neglected them, and in Staffordshire pot-makers often dug their clay from the middle of the roads.

ARCHED BRIDGE *Medieval wagons usually crossed rivers at a shallow spot, but stone bridges such as the Bridge of Dye in Tayside were sometimes built to carry major roads. The bridges were supported on semi-circular stone arches, with spans up to 90 ft.*

BONE-SHAKERS *Before the Elizabethan Age even royalty rode in unsprung wagons.*

The turnpike system

In the late 17th century, Parliament allowed businessmen to build roads for the extra traffic caused by Britain's developing industries. Gates, or turnpikes, were set up for toll collection.

FLATTER ARCHES *A segmented arch, consisting of only a segment of a circle, gave a flat curve, as at Llanrwst Bridge, Gwynedd (left). Rivers could be crossed with fewer pillars, reducing the pressure of water.*

LEATHER-STRAP SUSPENSION *Coach bodies suspended by leather straps from four posts became widespread in the 17th century. Passengers found that they swayed alarmingly.*

Fast travel by stagecoach

By the middle of the 18th century, stagecoaches were travelling the 200 miles between York and London in only four days. Mail began to be carried by coach in 1784, and Royal Mail coaches carried a guard armed with a blunderbuss and a pair of pistols.

PIERCED BRIDGE *In the 1750s, a Welsh builder, William Edwards, designed bridges pierced by large holes to reduce weight. The technique gave unprecedented spans of 140 ft. John Smeaton used the method on Coldstream Bridge, Borders (left).*

THE ARRIVAL OF STEEL SPRINGS *Steel springs which flexed as the coach passed over potholes gave 18th-century passengers a smoother ride. A rear basket carried luggage and lower-class passengers.*

Travelling post-chaise

In the 18th and 19th centuries, rich families travelled to fashionable resorts or to the Continent in their own coaches with their own drivers. The less rich could hire a post-chaise at posting-inns. The horses and driver would be changed at each inn.

THE FIRST IRON BRIDGE *A revolution in bridge-building came in 1779 when the world's first iron bridge was built over the Severn at Ironbridge, Salop. Iron was lighter and stronger than stone, making wider spans possible. It was also cheaper.*

POSTILION INSTEAD OF DRIVER *A post-chaise was driven by a postilion who rode on one of the two or four horses, instead of on the coach. Post-chaises usually travelled more slowly than stagecoaches.*

Driving for sport

By 1800 road surfaces of compacted small stones had been introduced by engineers such as Thomas Telford and John McAdam. Light carriages could be used, pulled by faster horses. Driving became a sport for wealthy young bloods, and the coaching era reached its climax.

SUSPENSION BRIDGE *There is a limit to the span of an arch, and the suspension bridge was developed for bridging deep water. The oldest in Britain is the Union Bridge at Berwick, built in 1820. It is 350 ft long and the roadway is held up by chains anchored to pylons.*

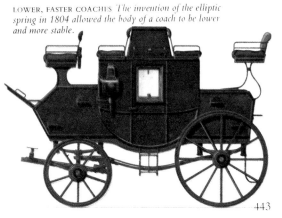

LOWER, FASTER COACHES *The invention of the elliptic spring in 1804 allowed the body of a coach to be lower and more stable.*

The canals: arteries of a revolution

FOR 80 YEARS – FROM THE 1760S UNTIL THE COMING OF THE RAILWAYS – THE
CANAL NETWORK SUPPLIED THE LIFE-BLOOD OF INDUSTRIAL BRITAIN

The canals of Britain, with pencil-slim boats that plied along them at walking pace, provided the main transport network of the Industrial Revolution.

They carried coal to drive the factories in the new industrial towns of the Midlands and the north of England. And they carried much of the raw material, such as china clay, iron ore, and raw cotton, to make the new products.

In the 18th century, engineers calculated that a pack-horse could carry one-eighth of a ton on its back, but the same horse could pull 50 tons loaded on the still waters of a canal.

The 3rd Duke of Bridgewater seized on the principle to reduce the cost of moving coal from his mines at Worsley in Lancashire to the growing city of Manchester. He decided to build the first major canal in Britain, and entrusted the work largely to a millwright, James Brindley. The Bridgewater Canal was opened in 1761, and Brindley became Britain's leading canal engineer.

He was put in charge of the most ambitious scheme of the canal age – "The Grand Cross". It was to link the four great estuaries of England – the Thames, Severn, Humber and Mersey, meeting near Birmingham.

Brindley laid out his canals by "contour cutting", following the contours of the land, and avoiding the need for tunnels and locks. On one section of the Oxford Canal, boatmen said they could travel all day and still hear the same church clock strike the hours.

But locks were sometimes needed, and at

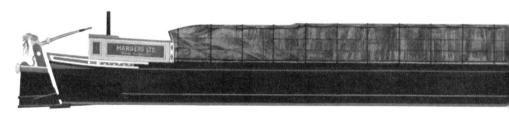

first Brindley built them 15 ft wide, but they used too much water so he halved the width. The size of a lock determines the size of boat that can use the canal, so a new type of craft came to be built – the narrow-boat.

For more than a century the bulk of canal traffic consisted of narrow-boats, pulled along by a horse or mule at 4 mph.

Prodigious workers and drinkers

A new class of workmen grew up with the canals. They were known as "navigators" from their work on the "navigations", and this became abbreviated to "navvy". At first they were recruited locally, but they soon developed into a specialist workforce, moving from digging to digging, many of them from the depressed areas of Ireland and Scotland. They did prodigious work – a good navvy could shift over 12 cubic yds of earth in a day – about 13 tons. But they also had a reputation for drinking, fighting and rioting; the riots could last for days.

After Brindley's death in 1772, a second generation of canal engineers used new techniques to build straighter canals. They dug deep cuttings through hills, and built high banks across valleys. They built longer tunnels and magnificent aqueducts.

The coming of the railways in the 1830s brought an end to canal building. The canal boatmen tried to compete by improving their service, with "fly" boats running virtually non-stop. But today, the working narrow-boat has almost disappeared, and the canals have found a new use as routes for pleasure craft.

CLOTHES OF THE CANALS *Crochet was a popular craft among canal women, as it could be kept in a pocket while they worked the boat. Crochet lace decorated their bonnets, shawls and blouses, and the clothes of the babies. Even the men often wore embroidered belts and braces – and the horses had crocheted bonnets.*

ONE-HORSEPOWER BOATS
Most narrow-boats were towed by a horse and travelled no faster than walking pace. Horses had to be shod every fortnight, and blacksmiths' shops were set up at regular intervals along the canals. Stabling and feed were provided by canal-side inns. Some narrow-boats were powered by steam-engines in the last four decades of the 19th century, but the engines and boilers took up valuable cargo space and they were replaced by semi-diesel engines in the early 20th century.

LIFE AFLOAT *The tiny cabin of a narrow-boat, only 9 ft by 7 ft, was never intended as living quarters. In the prosperous days of the canals in the late 18th century, a boat-owner employed a crew of two to help him operate the boat on daily or weekly trips while his family lived ashore. But with the arrival of the railways in the 1840s, work became more scarce and owners had to cut their rates. Many were forced to dismiss the crew and move their families on to the boat to operate it. With them, they took their household crockery, curtains, patchwork quilts, and often birds in cages. Meals were cooked on a coal-burning stove. At night a double bed was folded down from one end of the cabin and a seat at the other end became a single bed. A curtain could be drawn between the two. The boat-people developed as a separate community. They often inter-married, and the pubs alongside the canals became their meeting places.*

ROSES AND ROPES

Canal narrow-boats, particularly those owned by the families who ran them, were highly decorated with paint and ropework. The sides of a boat and its equipment, such as poles, water cans, lamps and buckets, were painted with roses, scenes of castles and geometric patterns. Fenders for protecting the boat as it entered locks were made from woven rope. The techniques of ropework came from naval traditions, although few canal-boat owners had ever been to sea. The canal families had little contact with land-based people, so their crafts developed separately as hallmarks of the canal era.

LAMP *An oil lamp on the bow showed up a boat in a tunnel or after dark. In winter, boats travelled for hours in darkness.*

WATER CAN *Drinking water came from taps beside the canal and was carried in cans. Other water was taken from the canal.*

RAM'S HEAD *The rudder (or "ram's-head") was decorated with ropework, often in a "turk's-head" pattern, together with a beribboned horse's tail. A rope fender was also fixed to the rear of the rudder.*

The Railway Age

THE RAILWAY STORY IS THE STORY OF THE STEPHENSONS, FATHER AND SON, WHO
CREATED THE EARLY LINES AND THE TRAINS THAT RAN ON THEM

The Railway Age, which was to revolutionise world transport, began more than a century before the first steam locomotive was built.

Through the 18th century the coal mines on Tyneside had been linked to the ports by tramways. These were wooden or iron tracks, on which wagons were pulled by horses or cables powered by stationary steam-engines.

At last, in 1804 the first self-propelling steam-engine was run on rails in a South Wales ironworks. It was not a great success (the weight broke the rails), but it opened a new era. Only 25 years later the first passenger railway was opened between Liverpool and Manchester. One of its locomotives, the *Rocket*, had been built by George Stephenson and his son Robert whose names were to resound through the Railway Age. George Stephenson was a colliery engineer who set up business to build both railway lines and locomotives. Britain then entered the years of The Railway Mania, as investors poured money into railway schemes. Fortunes were made and lost in a mad-cap, steam-powered gold rush.

The 5 mph beginning

A Cornish engineer named Richard Trevithick built a locomotive for the Penydarren ironworks near Merthyr Tydfil in 1804. It pulled 70 passengers and a 10 ton load along the Penydarren tramway at a speed of 5 mph – the world's first journey by a steam train; but the cast-iron rails broke under the weight.

On Tyneside, George Stephenson built his first locomotive in 1814 to haul coal at Killingworth Colliery, near Newcastle.

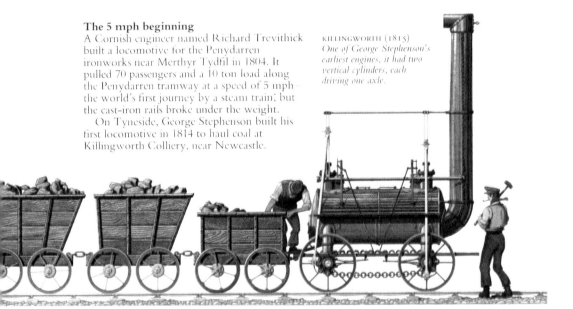

KILLINGWORTH (1815)
One of George Stephenson's earliest engines, it had two vertical cylinders, each driving one axle.

The railways come of age

In 1823 Stephenson was asked to survey a route for a tramway to carry coal from pits at Darlington to the wharves at Stockton-on-Tees. He became engineer to the line at a salary of £300 a year for working one week in each month. He and his son Robert also made the locomotive to run on the line, *Locomotion*, and in 1825 the line was opened, carrying both goods and passengers.

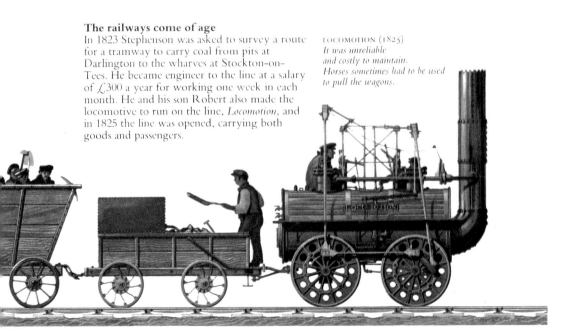

LOCOMOTION (1825)
It was unreliable and costly to maintain. Horses sometimes had to be used to pull the wagons.

"Rocket" launches the railway boom

Stephenson's next commission was the Liverpool and Manchester Railway, the first railway in the world to carry a high proportion of passenger traffic. In 1829 trials to find the best locomotive for the line were won by Stephenson's *Rocket* at 30 mph.

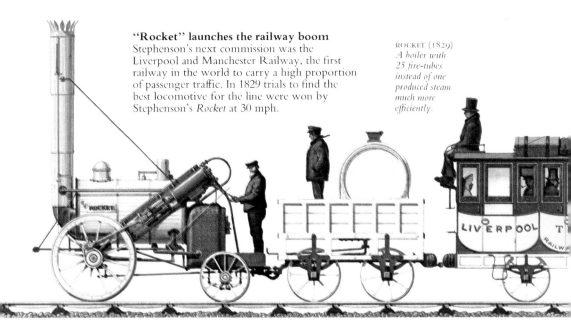

ROCKET (1829)
A boiler with 25 fire-tubes instead of one produced steam much more efficiently.

The battle of the gauges

The engineer Isambard Kingdom Brunel built the Great Western Railway from London to Bristol with rails 7 ft apart instead of the usual 4 ft $8\frac{1}{2}$ in. He commissioned the Stephensons to build the first locomotive, *North Star*, in 1837. The wide gauge gave a better ride, but after 50 years standard 4 ft $8\frac{1}{2}$ in. gauge was accepted as the system of the future.

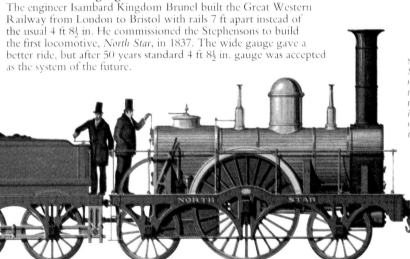

NORTH STAR (1837)
Six wheels had now been adopted to distribute the locomotive's increased weight more evenly over the rails.

The boom and bust of The Railway Mania

Between 1840 and 1850, 4,600 miles of lines were built. In the speculative scramble, routes were duplicated and small towns found themselves with two or even three stations. Many routes lost money, and small lines amalgamated into big groups to force out rivals.

A-TYPE (1847)
Robert Stephenson increased the length of the boiler in relation to the wheel base, so that more steam could be built up. The driver had a choice of more power or a saving in fuel.

Riding on the first passenger trains

The opening of the first passenger railway, the Liverpool and Manchester, in 1830 was a grand affair that ended in tragedy. The Duke of Wellington was there, with Sir Robert Peel and the MP for Liverpool, William Huskisson. During a watering stop on the inaugural trip, Mr Huskisson fell in front of a train, which crushed one of his legs. He died that evening, victim of the world's first railway accident.

Passengers on the Liverpool and Manchester Railway had a choice of three classes of travel. The first-class carriages were similar to stage-coaches, whereas third-class passengers rode, standing up, in roofless trucks. It was also possible to take your personal riding-carriage on an open wagon – a precursor of Motorail.

In 1844 Parliament decreed that each line should run at least one train a day, at a minimum speed of 12 mph, and that third-class passengers should be carried under cover at a penny a mile. For the first time, fast long-distance travel became available to large numbers of people. Workers in the over-crowded industrial towns could escape by train into the countryside and to the seaside, whose delights had only recently been discovered.

In 1841 the first chartered excursion train was run between Loughborough and Leicester for a temperance meeting. The return fare was a shilling and 570 people went on the 24 mile journey. For the 33-year-old printer who organised the trip it was the beginning of a new career. His name was Thomas Cook.

THE NAVVIES *Railway lines were laid by armies of navvies, fresh from building the canals. They dug tunnels and cuttings, often through solid rock. Thousands lived in crude shanties, terrorising the area with their drinking and brawling.*

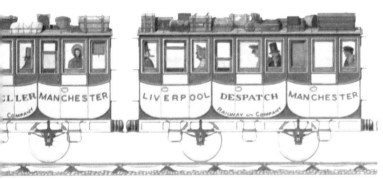

"THE QUALITY" *First-class carriages of the 1830s were "a series of stage-coach insides tacked on to one another". Passengers sat three abreast. Royal Mail coaches were more luxurious with passengers two abreast. Or travellers could sit in their own road carriage, isolated from strangers but dangerously exposed to weather.*

THE LESSER CLASSES *Second-class carriages were open, with an awning to protect passengers from rain and cinders. Third-class travellers stood in open boxes. The Great Western carried cheap passengers on wagons with no sides. On Christmas Eve 1841, some fell off and were killed.*

PART FIVE

The builders of Britain

ARCHITECTS, STONE-MASONS, LANDSCAPE GARDENERS,
CRAFTSMEN AND INDUSTRIALISTS ALL LEFT BEHIND
VISIBLE LANDMARKS ON OUR JOURNEY TO THE PRESENT

Robert Adam *(1728–92)*
When Robert Adam was a young man, British architecture was in the grip of rigid principles laid down nearly two centuries earlier, by the Italian Andrea Palladio. Buildings in the strict Palladian style were restrained, balanced, severe and lacking in decoration. It was the great contribution of Robert Adam and his brothers, James, John and William, to enliven this style and make it more human. They used ornament and decoration, but at the same time retained the Palladian virtues of balance and proportion.

The new style was immensely successful, and Adam became one of the busiest architects in the country. His designs ranged from Syon House (1760–9), Osterley Park (1761–80) and Kenwood House (1767–9) in London to Culzean Castle (1777–9) in Ayrshire.

But Adam failed to earn the fortune that his popularity should have ensured. His most ambitious housing project, the Adelphi (1768–72), a group of private houses in central London, brought him to the brink of bankruptcy.

Adam's interior designs were as splendid and

meticulously carried out as his exterior buildings. He is particularly noted for his elegant fireplaces and furniture.

Thomas Archer *(1668–1743)*
The Baroque architecture of southern Europe – its ornate, theatrical buildings of the 17th and early 18th centuries – never really took root in England. Its sole successful practitioner was Thomas Archer. In 1689 he embarked on the then fashionable Grand Tour of Europe, and was fascinated by the works of Italian Baroque architects like Francesco Borromini (1599–1667).

After setting up practice in England as an architect, he designed the north front of Chatsworth House (1702–5) in Derbyshire. His best-known churches are the Cathedral of St Philip (1709–25) in Birmingham and, in London, the church of St Paul (1712–30) at Deptford and the magnificent St John's, Smith Square (1714–28).

Sir Richard Arkwright *(1732–92)*
The man who was to become one of the Founding Fathers of the Industrial Revolution began his career as a barber's apprentice. He set up his own

barber's shop in Bolton, just as the fashion for wigs declined.

By 1767 he had turned to inventing, and within two years had improved the existing spinning frame. Eventually, Arkwright's frame virtually replaced the craftsman spinner and revolutionised the spinning of yarn for the weaving industry. The secret of the machine was to produce threads suitable for both warp and weft.

By his fifties Arkwright was prosperous enough to spend time giving himself the education he had missed as a boy. He was knighted in 1786, for his services to industry. By then he was the owner of numerous spinning-mills, insisting on order, cleanliness and firm standards of quality.

He had boundless energy, habitually working a 16 hour day even when his business was soundly established.

Sir Charles Barry *(1795–1860)*
Barry, who designed the Houses of Parliament, was one of the foremost architects of the 19th century.

His early works included several neo-Gothic churches in the north of England, notably All Saints in Prestwich, St Matthew in Greater Manchester, and Holy Trinity in Oldham.

His graceful adaptation of Greek and Italian classical ideas brought him commissions for houses and public buildings from patrons weary of the extravagances of the Gothic revivalists. He built Eynsham Hall near Witney, Oxfordshire, and rebuilt Cliveden House in Buckinghamshire.

In London his work varied from clubs like the Reform and the Travellers in Pall Mall to Pentonville Prison and the fountains in Trafalgar Square.

In 1836, after the Houses of Parliament had been destroyed by fire, he won a competition for designing the new Houses. The competition rules specified a Gothic or Elizabethan style, but the finished scheme owed a great deal to Barry's classical tastes. The building was opened by Queen Victoria in 1852, but was not completed until after Barry's death eight years later. His design was embellished by A. W. Pugin.

REVOLUTIONARY MACHINE *Richard Arkwright's water-powered spinning frame of 1769 greatly increased the output of weaving thread, made the hand frame obsolete and ushered in the factory system.*

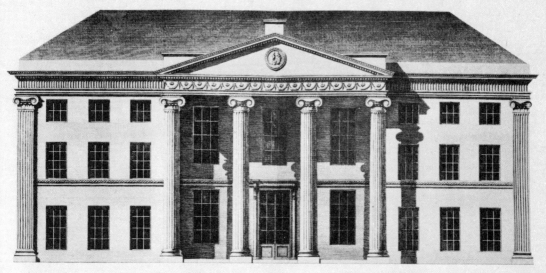

CLASSICAL YET ORNAMENTAL *The north front of Kenwood House, Hampstead, illustrated in a contemporary volume on Robert and James Adam's architecture, displays the more decorative form of Palladianism, or neoclassicism, that the brothers introduced in the late 18th century.*

Edward Blore *(1787–1879)*

Blore was a prominent architect of the Victorian Gothic Revival, a reintroduction of highly decorative medieval building. He began as a book-illustrator specialising in architectural drawings. Then in 1816 he met Sir Walter Scott who was looking for an architect to rebuild his house, Abbotsford, Borders, in the fashionable Gothic style. Blore produced a set of sketches and was hired to do the work. It was the start of a brilliantly successful career.

He was appointed special architect to both King William IV and Queen Victoria, and finished Buckingham Palace after the downfall of Nash.

James Brindley *(1716–72)*

The pioneer of Britain's canal network was apprenticed at 17 to a millwright near Macclesfield, where his skill with machinery soon showed. Brindley later set up business at Leek as a repairer of machines. Among his customers were the Wedgwoods, the pottery family, who commissioned him to build mills for grinding glazing powders.

At the age of 43, Brindley was commissioned by the Duke of Bridgewater to build a canal linking the duke's coalmines at Worsley to Manchester. It was a major undertaking, and included an aqueduct to carry the canal over the River Irwell. Brindley's reputation as a canal engineer was made, and he went on to build more than 365 miles of canals. Most were contour canals which detoured for miles to avoid the need for locks and changes of level. They created a valuable transport network for carrying both raw materials and finished products.

Brindley remained unable to spell, but his brilliant powers of observation made up for the handicap. He carried out all his engineering calculations in his head, and when faced with a particularly difficult problem, he would retire to bed to think it over.

Lancelot "Capability" Brown *(1716–83)*

The pre-eminent figure of British 18th-century landscape gardening was born in the Northumberland village of Kirkharle, and first worked as a gardener for a local landowner. By 1740 he was gardener to Lord Cobham at Stowe in Buckinghamshire, where he met William Kent, a supporter of the new informal style of garden layout.

Between them, they transformed the then-traditional formality of Stowe's park into an informal–though carefully contrived–vista which became famous. Country gentlemen

PIONEERING WORK *To carry the Duke of Bridgewater's canal (1759–61) across the River Irwell at Barton, canal engineer James Brindley built the first major aqueduct in Britain. It has since been demolished.*

from all over England came to seek Brown's advice in the replanning of their own parks, and when Lord Cobham died in 1749, Brown left Stowe to become a consultant landscape designer.

He gained his nickname from his habitual comment when he first examined a garden or park: "I see great capability of improvement here."

Brown helped to change the face of England. The grounds of many great houses were landscaped in his style, with its apparently random but carefully planned arrangements of trees grouped in clumps, often around an irregularly shaped lake. Such a park was designed to set off the architecture of the house like a landscape painting.

Brown even tried his hand at architecture, in the Palladian style, with Corsham Court in Wiltshire and other country houses.

In 1764 he was appointed Surveyor to His Majesty George III's Gardens and Waters, and redesigned Kew Gardens.

Among his finest parks that have survived are those at Blenheim Palace, Oxfordshire (1765), Castle Dodington Park, Avon (1764) and Nuneham Courtenay, Oxfordshire (1778).

BRUNEL'S MIGHTY VESSEL *The design of Isambard Kingdom Brunel's ships was even bolder than that of his bridges and railways. His last vessel, the 12,000 ton* Great Eastern, *was the largest ever built at that time. Because of the ship's bulk, it took three months to launch her.*

Isambard Kingdom Brunel
(1806–59)

A Victorian engineer on the heroic scale, Brunel was the son of a French naval officer and engineer, Marc Isambard Brunel, who fled to England after the French Revolution. Isambard gained his first commission in 1829, when he was only 23, to build a suspension bridge across the Avon Gorge at Clifton, near Bristol. Although work was delayed by the Bristol Riots (when Brunel served as a special constable) and by lack of money, Brunel's design was radical enough to make him famous.

When he was asked to build the Great Western Railway from London to Bristol, he rejected the 4 ft 8½ in. gauge chosen by Stephenson and other railwaymen in favour of a 7 ft gauge track.

This allowed him to build engines and coaches that were set between their wheels rather than above them, so that they were lower, wider and more stable than trains on other lines. Not only would Brunel's trains run faster, but when accidents did happen, the coaches often stayed on the rails.

But it was marine engineering which saw Brunel's boldest ideas. He built his first ship, the *Great Western,* in 1838 to make regular fast trips from Bristol to New York, at a time when only one steamship had crossed the Atlantic. He built her with propellers and paddles, driven by marine steam-engines twice the size of any made before. At 2,300 tons, she was the biggest steamship afloat and on her maiden voyage she crossed the Atlantic in a record time of 15 days.

Brunel's next ship, the *Great Britain,* was the first ocean-going ship to have an iron hull, and to rely on propellers alone for propulsion. She weighed more than 3,000 tons, was more than 300 ft long and her engines delivered 1,500 horsepower. She is now on display at Bristol.

The *Great Eastern,* Brunel's last ship, was his biggest – twice the length of the *Great Britain.* She went on to lay the first trans-Atlantic telegraph cable, but she was to be Brunel's last great work. Overwork and anxiety, the two occupational diseases of the Victorian engineer, had sapped his strength and he died in 1859 aged 53, soon after completing Saltash Bridge, Cornwall.

William Burges *(1827–81)*
A key figure in Victorian Gothic Revival architecture. Early in his career, Burges developed a keen interest in medieval architecture, and toured the Continent to study different styles. In 1856, at the age of 29, he won a competition to design Lille Cathedral in France. Six years later he began building Cork Cathedral (1862–76) in Ireland. He was also responsible for the restoration and rebuilding of Cardiff Castle in medieval style (1865), and for the remodelling of Castle Coch near Cardiff (1875).

Lord Burlington
(1694–1753)
Burlington became devoted to the cool, elegant, neo-classical style of the Italian Renaissance architect Andrea Palladio, just as Inigo Jones had 100 years before. After the death of Jones in 1652, the style had given way to the more theatrically ornate Baroque. But Burlington resolved to change that.

He first retained the architect Colen Campbell to redesign the frontage of his Piccadilly town house (now the Royal Academy of Arts) in Palladian style. But Burlington soon became confident enough to carry out his own designs. By 1724 he had built his first public building, the Dormitory of Westminster School. He later went on to

INFLUENTIAL BOOK *A design from Thomas Chippendale's* Gentleman and Cabinet Maker's Director *(1754).*

triumphs like the Assembly Rooms in York and his own house at Chiswick.

But his greatest achievement lay in placing fellow-devotees of Palladianism in positions of architectural influence.

John Carr *(1723–1807)*
The son of a Yorkshire quarry-owner, Carr designed a grandstand for the Knavesmire Racecourse in York in 1754, and soon became the most successful architect in the north of England. He had an original style, but also followed Palladian architects such as Burlington, Kent and the Adam brothers.

He worked on Harewood House, the Assize Courts in York and the Castle Museum.

Sir William Chambers
(1723–96)
In 1755, Chambers set up practice as an architect and had the extraordinary luck to be offered the post of architectural tutor to the Prince of Wales. The post secured him the basis of a prosperous career.

He designed many public buildings in London, including Somerset House (1776–86), and his reputation brought him commissions for country houses such as Cobham Hall, Kent.

He built the Queen's Lodge at Windsor, an observatory in Richmond's Old Deer Park for George III, and the Pagoda at Kew Gardens.

Thomas Chippendale
(1718–79)
The fame of this furniture-maker began after the publication of his book the *Gentleman and Cabinet Maker's Director* in the 1750s. It was the most comprehensive collection of furniture designs published in England, and brought a steady stream of upper-class patrons to Chippendale's home and workshop in St Martin's Lane, London.

Later research showed that Chippendale had not been the original designer suggested by the book. He had collected other people's ideas together under the umbrella of the English Rococo style–marked by elaborate scrollwork and other ornate decorations–and this style had become totally identified with him.

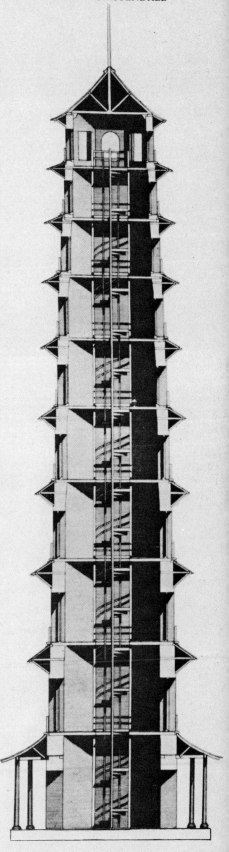

KEW LANDMARK *Sir William Chambers' Pagoda (1757–61), in London's Kew Gardens.*

453

Henry Cort *(1740–1800)*
Cort was a contractor for the Royal Navy at a time when British wrought iron was so poor that only imported iron could be used on warships. He began experimenting, and discovered the two techniques of puddling and rolling iron, which made it tougher and more workable.

Samuel Crompton
(1753–1827)
Crompton was the third of the inventors who transformed the spinning of yarn into a modern industry.

Like James Hargreaves and Richard Arkwright, he was born into a poor family. His father died when he was only five, and he had to help support his family by spinning yarn on a spinning jenny. The thread was coarse and weak so Crompton set to work to improve the machine.

The result was the spinning mule, so named because it was a hybrid, between Hargreaves' jenny and Arkwright's spinning frame. The yarn it produced was fine, smooth and strong.

Crompton lacked Arkwright's business ability and spent the money voted him by Parliament on failing enterprises. He died a poor, embittered man.

Abraham Darby I
(1678–1717)
The founder of a dynasty which helped to revolutionise the iron-making industry.

Abraham Darby taught himself industrial iron casting at the ironworks he bought at Coalbrookdale in Shropshire. He experimented with firing his furnaces with coal instead of charcoal, but found that coal did not work because of its sulphur content. Then he borrowed the method used by brewers for drying malt – he first turned the coal into coke by heating it to a high temperature in an airless vessel.

Coke succeeded brilliantly where coal had failed. Furnaces fired by this fast-burning, fierce-burning fuel liquefied the iron to a greater degree and allowed lighter and more detailed castings to be made.

When Darby died in 1717 at the age of 39, he had established a prosperous business.

Abraham Darby III
(1750–91)
The grandson of Abraham Darby I, Abraham III took over the Coalbrookdale ironworks in 1768 when he was 18.

He designed and built the world's first cast-iron bridge over the Severn at Ironbridge, near Coalbrookdale in 1779. Parts were fastened together using woodwork techniques such as dovetail joints, rather than bolts or rivets. Later, kits of parts for assembling similar bridges were sold to customers abroad.

The Darbys were good employers. They ploughed most of their profits back into improving the works and the conditions of the employees.

Charles Fowler *(1791–1867)*
Fowler was a specialist in handling the new Victorian building materials – plate glass and cast iron.

He achieved fame with his designs for the Covent Garden and Hungerford food markets in London and also for the conservatory at Syon House, Isleworth.

Grinling Gibbons
(1648–1720)
The most prodigiously gifted woodcarver to work in Britain, Grinling Gibbons could cut a leaf in wood with such delicacy and sureness of touch that it almost seemed to tremble. Gibbons worked in softwoods, such as lime and pear, producing life-size and lifelike festoons of flowers, fruits, birds, fish, shells and other objects.

As his model he took the still-life and flower paintings of Holland, his native land.

In 1671 his work drew the notice of John Evelyn, the diarist. Evelyn introduced him to Charles II, who engaged him to decorate Hampton Court. Some of Gibbons' finest work is in St Paul's Cathedral, London.

James Gibbs *(1682–1754)*
One of the most prosperous and successful architects of the early 18th century. His design for St-Mary-le-Strand church in London (1714–17) established his reputation, but his masterpiece was St Martin-in-the-Fields, Trafalgar Square (1722–6). He also built the Senate House in Cambridge (1722–30) and the magnificent domed Radcliffe Library at Oxford (1737–49). His *Book of Architecture* (1728) spread his influence to the United States, and the White House in Washington DC was based on one of its illustrations, "Design for a Gentleman's House"

Nicholas Hawksmoor
(1661–1736)
Hawksmoor was one of the most original architects of the English Baroque movement, which spread from Italy in the 17th century. It was characterised by complex design and decoration.

At the age of 18, Hawksmoor, a farmer's son, took a job as clerk in the office of Sir Christopher Wren. Five years later, he was working as Wren's supervisor at the Palace of Winchester.

Hawksmoor collaborated with Sir John Vanbrugh at Castle Howard in Yorkshire (1700–26) and at Blenheim Palace in Oxfordshire (1705–22). When Vanbrugh broke with Sarah, Duchess of Marlborough, during the building of Blenheim, Hawksmoor took over.

He was later responsible for building new churches for the City of London, including St Anne's, Limehouse (1712–24), and Christ Church, Spitalfields (1713–29), which were perhaps his greatest works.

George Hepplewhite
(?–1786)
Hepplewhite was a major figure in the development of a style of furniture that matched the graceful, carefully decorated neo-classical buildings of the Adam brothers in the late 18th century. He was apprenticed to Robert Gillow, a Lancaster cabinet-maker, before he opened his own business in London.

His reputation was made by *The Cabinet-Maker's and Upholsterer's Guide* (1788), published two years after his death. It contained almost 300 of his designs, which featured inlaid satinwood and neo-classical decoration.

Robert Hooke *(1635–1703)*
Hooke, a brilliant scientist, was appointed one of six City surveyors to decide on a plan

SIMPLICITY AND ELEGANCE *This drawing of the north face of the Queen's House, Greenwich (1616–35), shows the neo-classical simplicity, proportion and lack of ornamentation that the architect, Inigo Jones, had learned from his study of the Italian Renaissance architect Andrea Palladio.*

for rebuilding London after the Great Fire of 1666.

Another of the surveyors was Christopher Wren. Together Hooke and Wren worked on the Monument (1671–7) and, between 1670 and 1686, on many of London's finest churches.

James of St George *(?–1309)*
Master-mason and brilliant military architect, James came from the village of St Georges d'Esperanche in Savoy. By 1278 he was in Britain, working on the series of castles which Edward I was building to hold down his conquests in Wales. In 1283 he was appointed King's Serjeant.

James' castles included Conwy (1283–7), Denbigh (1282–1322), Caernarfon (1283–1330) and Harlech (1283–90). They are marked by their formidable strength, and several are concentric.

Inigo Jones *(1573–1652)*
The first man to bring classical Palladian architecture to England, introducing a restrained, balanced style which was to last for most of the following century.

Jones was the son of a clothmaker in Smithfield, London. He became a landscape painter, and attracted the notice of William Herbert, Earl of Pembroke. Lord Pembroke sent Jones "over Italy and the politer parts of Europe" to buy works of art for him, and Jones came into contact with the architecture

MASTER WOODCARVER *Grinling Gibbons' decorations in the Carved Room at Petworth House, W. Sussex, show how he could imitate in wood the texture of almost any substance.*

of ancient Rome.

In England he first became famous as a stage designer, arranging masques by Ben Jonson, though later the two men became bitter enemies. Jonson said that if he wanted words to express the greatest villain in the world, he would call him an Inigo.

Back in Italy in 1613, Jones came into contact with the designs of Andrea Palladio. On his return to England he took up architecture in the Palladian

style and was appointed Surveyor-General of the King's Works. The Queen's House at Greenwich (1616–35) and the Banqueting House at Whitehall (1619–22) are two of his best-known works.

He also built London's first square, Covent Garden (1631), including St Paul's Church.

William Kent *(1684–1748)*
A barely literate coach-painter who rose to design some of the most fashionable houses in 18th-century England.

Kent was born in Bridlington, Yorkshire. Apprenticed to a coach-painter at 13, he left for London at 18. His talent for art brought him enough commissions to travel to Italy to buy works of art for wealthy collectors.

While in Rome he met his most powerful patron, the Earl of Burlington, who brought him back to England in 1719 to decorate the interior of Burlington House in Piccadilly. Commissions under Burlington's patronage included the Royal Mews (1732) – since demolished – the Treasury, Whitehall (1734–6), and the Horse Guards (1750–8), built to his designs after his death.

Kent was also one of the first to revolt against the formal 17th-century garden, preferring a carefully planned landscape to set off the buildings. In the 1740s, with the help of "Capability" Brown, he designed the park at Stowe in Buckinghamshire.

Sir Edwin Lutyens
(1869–1944)
The architect who designed the Cenotaph in Whitehall.

Lutyens, born in London, was chosen in 1912 to lay out the capital of India, New Delhi.

After the First World War, as architect to the Imperial War Graves Commission, he designed many memorials, including the Cenotaph (1922).

He also planned Hampstead Garden Suburb, in North London.

John McAdam *(1756–1836)*
One of the few engineers to add his name to the language.

John McAdam, born at Ayr, helped to provide Britain with reliable road surfaces. On the existing soil, rammed hard, he laid stone chips in layers to a depth of 10 in. Traffic pounded this into a solid mass.

"Macadam" roads soon spread over all the major routes of Britain, and McAdam's methods formed the basis of modern road-building. Tar macadam ("tarmac"), a 20th-century improvement, binds the stone chips with tar.

Charles Rennie Mackintosh
(1868–1928)
One of the leaders of the art nouveau movement in British architecture.

Mackintosh, born in Glasgow, was apprenticed to a local architect and went to evening art classes. In his twenties, he designed furniture, posters and other works.

MACKINTOSH CHAIR *A strikingly designed high-backed chair is an example of the work of Charles Rennie Mackintosh – architect and pioneer of art nouveau in Britain – which is on display at one of the houses which he also designed: Hill House, in Helensburgh, Strathclyde.*

Later, he designed buildings for the Glasgow School of Art – the first significant art nouveau architecture in Britain. But Mackintosh's first love was art, and by the outbreak of the First World War he had given up designing buildings, to concentrate on watercolour painting.

John Metcalfe *(1717–1810)*
The blind man who became one of the most celebrated road builders of the Industrial Revolution.

"Blind Jack of Knaresborough", who lost his sight through smallpox at six, at first earned a living as a wandering violinist in his native Yorkshire. Later he worked as a carrier.

When a turnpike road was planned between Boroughbridge and Harrogate in 1765, he put in a successful bid to build 3 miles of it. So Blind Jack began a road-building career which resulted in 200 miles of roads and bridges over some of the wildest country in northern England.

He surveyed routes on foot, assessing surfaces with a long staff.

William Morris *(1834–96)*
A designer who reacted vigorously against Victorian industrialism and championed traditional crafts.

Morris was a versatile man. After earning a reputation as a poet at Oxford, he became apprenticed to an architect, then turned to painting.

In 1859, with the help of his

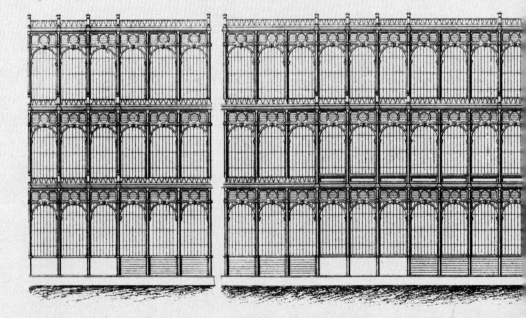

architect friend Philip Webb (1830–1915), he designed his own country house – The Red House, at Upton, Kent.

In this house he taught himself to design wallpaper, fabrics, furniture, tapestries and stained glass. He joined friends to manufacture these, and in 1862 founded the Arts and Crafts Movement. In 1890 he founded the Kelmscott Press and produced beautiful books.

Morris believed passionately in protecting individual craftsmanship from being swamped by the machine age. His own fabrics, furnishings and hand-printed books are still sought after.

John Nash *(1752–1835)*
A Regency architect and town planner whose reputation was made by London's Regent Street and wrecked by a scandal over work on Buckingham Palace.

Nash was the son of a Lambeth millwright, and began work as a draughtsman. At 25, he set up as a builder and gained a reputation with his country houses.

In 1811 Nash was engaged to lay out Regent's Park and join it to the West End by a completely new road, Regent Street. The elegantly curved park terraces brought Nash into royal favour.

In 1813 the Prince Regent ordered Nash to rebuild his palace at Brighton in the fashionable Oriental style, and then to convert Buckingham House in London into his main royal palace.

Nash began work on Buckingham Palace in the 1820s. When the job was half finished, he was accused of profiteering and in 1830 he was dismissed. The palace was finished by Edward Blore.

The triumphal arch which Nash intended as the main entrance was placed at Hyde Park and became known as Marble Arch.

Thomas Newcomen *(1663–1729)*
A Dartmouth ironmonger who invented the first commercially successful steam-engine.

Newcomen's engine worked a pump to remove water from the coal mines of Britain, and consisted of a balanced wooden beam with a pump at one end and a piston and cylinder at the other.

The engine produced power for mines for more than 60 years and was the foundation on which James Watt designed the steam-engines that drove the factories of the Industrial Revolution.

James Paine *(1716–89)*
One of the most successful architects in the north of England in Georgian times.

At 19 he was commissioned to work on Nostell Priory in Yorkshire. He also designed Heath House, Wakefield, and offices and stables at Chatsworth House, Derbyshire.

In the London area, Paine's work includes the Thames bridges at Walton, Kew and Chertsey.

Sir Joseph Paxton *(1801–65)*
An expert in handling the two new building materials produced by Victorian technology: iron and glass.

Paxton began his career as a gardener for the Duke of Devonshire, and was 39 before he tried his first building project – a conservatory at Chatsworth House in Derbyshire. He used sheets of glass supported on a framework of iron columns.

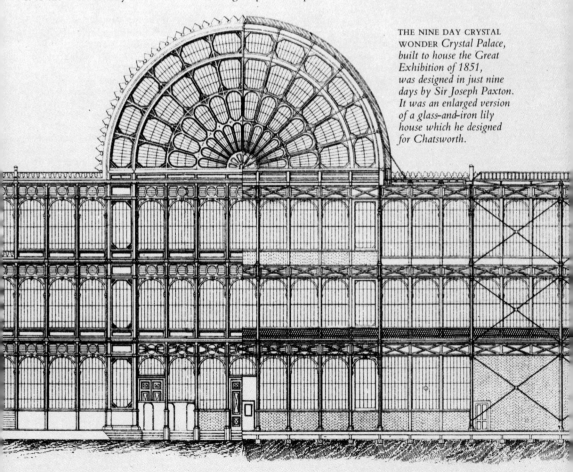

THE NINE DAY CRYSTAL WONDER *Crystal Palace, built to house the Great Exhibition of 1851, was designed in just nine days by Sir Joseph Paxton. It was an enlarged version of a glass-and-iron lily house which he designed for Chatsworth.*

The conservatory project set him on a totally new career, designing many of the monuments of the new industrial age, such as waterworks and gasworks. Paxton's best-known work was the Crystal Palace, built to house the Great Exhibition of 1851. All earlier designs had been rejected, and Paxton had just nine days to produce his own. His design was an enlarged version of the conservatory he had built at Chatsworth. It took 2,000 workmen eight months to erect, enclosed 33 million cu. ft and covered four times the area of St Peter's in Rome.

Augustus Welby Pugin
(1812–52)
The "high priest" of the Victorian Gothic Revival, which reintroduced into architecture pointed arches, buttresses, tracery windows and other Gothic elements.

Pugin, born in London, had a passion for medieval churches. Among his own best churches are Nottingham Cathedral and St Augustine's, Ramsgate, Kent. He was also responsible for the decorative detail of the Houses of Parliament.

Pugin was plagued by illness and died at 40.

Humphry Repton
(1752–1818)
Successor to "Capability" Brown as landscape artist to the rich.

Repton, a tax-collector's son born at Bury St Edmunds, Suffolk, began catering for a new fashion in landscapes – more picturesque than classic – in 1791, eight years after Brown's death.

He would sometimes recommend altering a house to produce a better blend with the landscape, and reached an agreement with the architect John Nash, by which Nash did the recommended architectural work and paid Repton a commission.

Repton's most outstanding work was Regent's Park, in London – completed in 1820. He had previously laid out the gardens of Russell Square and Bloomsbury Square, in 1800.

Anthony Salvin (1799–1881)
An expert on medieval architecture and a vital figure in the Victorian Gothic Revival.

Salvin, son of a general, was born at Worthing, W. Sussex, and learned his architecture in the office of John Nash. He built or restored many country houses, but his real skill went into his restoration of castles, including Windsor, Alnwick, Carisbrooke, Caernarfon, Dunster, Durham and Warwick.

Sir George Gilbert Scott
(1811–78)
A highly successful architect of the Gothic Revival.

Scott, evangelistic son of a clergyman, became head of a large firm of architects, restoring and building great numbers of churches throughout the country. These included St Giles, Camberwell, and St Mary Abbots, Kensington, both in London, and the chapels of Exeter College, Oxford and St John's, Cambridge.

He also designed the Albert Memorial in London (1864) and the extravagantly pinnacled St Pancras Station Hotel (1865).

Richard Norman Shaw
(1831–1912)
One of the most influential domestic architects of the late Victorian era.

Shaw, born in Edinburgh, at first designed buildings – including a number of churches – in the neo-Gothic style fashionable at the time. Later he turned to the Queen Anne style.

His best-known buildings include Swan House, Chelsea Embankment; Lowther Lodge, Kensington (now the home of the Royal Geographical Society); and the Piccadilly Hotel, in London's West End.

Shaw was responsible for the first garden suburb – Bedford Park, built in the 1880s in West London.

Thomas Sheraton
(1751–1806)
A cabinet-maker who was largely responsible for the style of British furniture of the later 18th century.

Sheraton was born at Stockton-on-Tees, and as a youth was apprenticed to a furniture maker. However, he was an enthusiastic artist, and when he set up in business in London's Soho (at the age of 39) it was as a teacher of perspective and architectural ornament.

His *Cabinet-Maker and Upholsterer's Drawing Book* (published in four parts, from 1791) made his reputation, mainly on the strength of his impeccable draughtsmanship. Sheraton's designs relied on the natural beauty of the wood, avoiding the heaviness and elaborate decoration favoured by his predecessors.

Although Sheraton produced very little finished work himself, his style was widely copied, and it dominated furniture-making at the turn of the century.

John Smeaton (1724–92)
A London instrument-maker who turned to building lighthouses, canals and harbours.

One of Smeaton's greatest works was the Forth-Clyde canal, which cut across the waist of Lowland Scotland with a 38 mile waterway – including 39 locks.

He also built bridges, at Perth and Banff, which still stand. But his best-known monument was Eddystone Lighthouse, completed in 1759 on treacherous rocks outside Plymouth.

Smeaton made a 70 ft tall tower of extraordinary strength, using dovetailed blocks of stone. The lighthouse stood in place until 1877. Even then it was replaced only because the reef beneath had been undermined by the sea. The upper part of Smeaton's lighthouse was dismantled and moved to Plymouth Hoe, where it still stands.

Robert Smirke (1781–1867)
The designer of the British Museum, and one of the most successful architects of the early 19th century.

Smirke, a Londoner, was commissioned by the Earl of Lonsdale, while still in his twenties, to build Lowther Castle, in Cumbria.

His Greek Revival style was dignified and reliable, and he became in demand for public buildings such as the Shire Halls at Hereford, Gloucester, Maidstone and Shrewsbury. He also designed the Carlton Club House in Pall Mall and the Royal Mint at Tower Hill.

Robert Smythson
(1536–1614)

The only major Elizabethan architect whose reputation has survived.

In an age when the new breed of merchants were building huge country houses as symbols of their success, Smythson's gift for the romantic and spectacular made him rich and famous.

Smythson was first heard of when he became principal freemason at Longleat House, in Wiltshire. Five years later, in 1551, he began his masterpiece – Wollaton Hall, in Nottinghamshire.

George Stephenson
(1781–1848)

An uneducated colliery worker who created the Railway Age.

Stephenson was the son of a steam-engine fireman employed at a colliery near Newcastle upon Tyne. The family were too poor to send the boy to school, so he watched cows for a farmer, for twopence a day. Later he began colliery work, earning sixpence a day picking stones out of coal.

When Stephenson was 14, he started working on mine engines, and three years later was made engineman, even though he still could not read or write.

Later he was appointed mine engineer (at a salary of £100 a year), and became responsible for the hauling of coal trucks along 160 miles of underground track.

This work led him to think of a steam locomotive – he had seen one of Richard Trevithick's engines working at another pit.

In 1814 Stephenson built his first crude, but workable, locomotive. His great opportunity came seven years later, when he was asked to survey a route for a tramway to carry coal from the pits around Darlington to the river wharves at Stockton-on-Tees. Stephenson planned the route and took a part-time job as engineer to the line, at a salary of £600 a year.

The railway was begun in May 1822, and was ready for opening in September 1825. Stephenson also made the locomotives, including *Locomotion*, which hauled the first train of 30 wagons, laden with spectators.

Stephenson's next commission was the world's first passenger railway, the Liverpool and Manchester Line. He met enormous problems with it. The Liverpool end of the line had to begin with a deep tunnel under the city streets, followed by a rock cutting through Olive Mount. There were rivers and canals to be crossed and finally the treacherous Chat Moss bog, outside Manchester: Stephenson bridged this with brushwood rafts carrying an earth embankment.

By this time, Stephenson was in demand to build railways all over England. He was rich enough to retire, but worked until he was 63. He died in 1848, aged 67.

Robert Stephenson
(1803–59)

The son of George Stephenson, who helped his father to lay the foundations of railway engine design for the whole of the steam age.

Robert Stephenson's

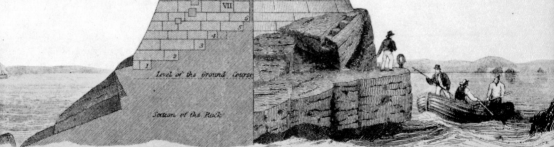

THE LIGHTHOUSE MODELLED ON A TREE *Architect John Smeaton took an oak trunk as the model for his Eddystone lighthouse, and built it with granite and Portland stone.*

locomotives introduced features that were to become standard throughout the country, including multi-tube boilers and connecting rods to drive the rear wheels.

In 1829, when the Liverpool and Manchester Line was planned, the directors held trials at Rainhill, near Liverpool, to decide which type of locomotive to use. The Stephensons' powerful and reliable Rocket won the day, with a top speed of 35 mph.

Robert Stephenson supervised the building of the London to Birmingham Railway (completed in 1838), which was the first of the great main lines that were to change the face of Britain.

His engineering projects became more and more ambitious: Kilsby Tunnel, near Rugby, was a mile and a half long and took four years, 1,250 navvies, 200 horses and 13 steam pumping engines to build.

Stephenson went on building lines and bridges all over the world, but overwork took its toll. He died in 1859, eleven years after his father, at the age of 56.

Thomas Telford *(1757–1834)*
A Scottish shepherd's son who became one of the greatest civil engineers of all time.

Telford was first a stonemason: he worked on Edinburgh New Town and on Somerset House, in London.

When he was 30, he was made Surveyor of Public Works for Shropshire. In six years, he built 40 bridges, of varying sizes. Six years later, in 1793, Telford was appointed chief engineer of the Ellesmere Canal, which linked the Mersey, the Dee and the Severn. At Pontcysyllte, North Wales, the canal had to be carried for more than half a mile at a height of 127 ft above rapids.

Telford dealt with this problem by containing the canal in a cast-iron trough supported on graceful stone piers. The aqueduct took ten years to build, partly because of Telford's extreme care for the safety of his workmen. Only one life was lost, in an age when such a major project usually meant a heavy cost in death and injury.

In Scotland, Telford built the Caledonian Canal (1803–47), which saved ships from having to make the dangerous passage round the northern tip of Britain.

His last great public assignment was to survey a new route across the mountains of North Wales, to Holyhead, to make it easier for Irish MPs to travel between London and Dublin.

Telford spent 18 months just choosing the best route. Then he bridged the Menai Strait with his graceful suspension bridge (1817–26), which was high enough for sailing ships to pass beneath. The route was opened nine years after work had started.

Richard Trevithick *(1771–1833)*
The first man to put the steam-engine on wheels.

Trevithick, a Cornishman, began by building stationary steam-engines that could take higher pressures than those of his predecessor, James Watt.

His first moving engines were used on roads, but were hampered by the bad surfaces. Trevithick decided it was more sensible to run them on the railed tramways which were then common in collieries. In 1804 he built an engine to haul trucks at the Penydarren ironworks in South Wales. The engine moved at only 4 mph, and then the cast-iron rails broke, but the experiment showed the way for those who followed – such as George Stephenson.

Sir John Vanbrugh *(1664–1726)*
The playwright, soldier and part-time architect who designed Blenheim Palace.

Vanbrugh, born in London, was the grandson of a Flemish Protestant merchant who had fled from Ghent to escape Catholic persecution. His play, *The Provok'd Wife*, was one of the last of the risque Restoration comedies.

Suddenly, in his thirties, Vanbrugh turned to architecture – with apparently no training and little experience, but fanatical enthusiasm.

In 1699 he was commissioned by the Earl of Carlisle to design Castle Howard.

Vanbrugh's ornamental, theatrical style was perfectly suited to large-scale work such as Seaton Delaval, Northumberland (1720–8), which many consider his finest. But his best-known design was Blenheim Palace, the gift of a grateful nation to the Duke of Marlborough for his military victories.

However, the duchess accused Vanbrugh of mismanagement and in 1716 he resigned.

THE WEDGWOOD GENIUS *A page from Josiah Wedgwood's first design pattern book is an example of the genius which transformed him from a small-time potter into the master of an enormously successful business.*

Sir Cornelius Vermuyden
(1595?–1633)
A Dutch engineer famed for draining the English fens.

Vermuyden came to Britain in 1621 to repair the embankments of the River Thames in Essex. Later he was involved in schemes to drain the fens of eastern England and change them into productive

farmland. After eight years, Vermuyden pronounced the task finished, but the land was dry only in mid-summer – and unusable for farming.

George Wade *(1673–1748)*
A soldier who built roads to beat the rebel Scots.

Wade had two careers. As a professional soldier, he

campaigned in Britain and Europe, rising to the rank of Field-Marshal. As an engineer, he brought the Scottish Highlands closer to the rest of Britain by building a network of roads and bridges so that troops could be rushed to Jacobite trouble spots. His bridge across the Tay was finished in 1733.

ENGINES OF THE REVOLUTION *The improved steam pumping engine designed by James Watt in the 1760s set him on the path to fortune: his later invention, an engine which could drive a rotating shaft, was to become the driving force behind Britain's Industrial Revolution at the turn of the century.*

James Watt *(1736–1819)*
The Scottish builder's son whose brilliance as an inventor created the driving force of the Industrial Revolution.

Watt was the sole, frail survivor of five children; he was plagued by migraine headaches for most of his life. Yet his love of books, and skill with his hands, made him one of the great figures of the new industrial age.

He began working for Glasgow University as an instrument maker. In 1763 he was asked to repair a

demonstration model of a Newcomen steam-engine. In fact, he built a model of a new engine which was much more efficient.

However, no one had yet produced cylinders sufficiently accurate to enable a full-size version of the engine to work properly. It was not until Watt met Matthew Boulton, owner of the Soho engineering works in Birmingham, that his ideas were put into practice, and a Watt steam pumping engine was put on the market.

The Cornish tin mines were

eager customers; so were coalmines, ironworks and waterworks.

Watt went on to produce a steam-engine which could drive a rotating shaft, and work machinery other than pumps. The potential market for this was almost limitless.

By 1800, this Watt engine was a mainstay of industry.

Josiah Wedgwood *(1730–95)*
The boy potter who transformed his trade from small-time craft to full-scale industry.

461

Wedgwood was the 13th and youngest son of a family who lived at Burslem, Staffordshire. From the age of nine he earned his living by pottery.

At 21, he was a partner in a small pottery at Stoke. His brilliantly inventive mind evolved new types of pottery, including the enormously popular Queen's Creamware, in which Cornish china clay was used, instead of coarse local clay.

As Wedgwood grew rich (he became the Queen's Potter) he financed a model village called Etruria, to house some of his workers near Burslem. He also paid for roads and canals to improve his trade communications.

William of Ramsey
(? – 1349)
A London mason who pioneered the Perpendicular Gothic style in British churches.

In 1325 William of Ramsey was earning sixpence a day working on the cloisters of St Stephen's Chapel in the Palace of Westminster. Eleven years later, he was made Chief Surveyor of the King's Works, at a salary of one shilling a day for life – and a new robe every year.

His other public commissions included advising on a new presbytery for Lichfield Cathedral.

Between public and private practices, William of Ramsey grew wealthy. In 1348 he bought a country property at Enfield, north of London. However, he died in the following year, probably a victim of the Black Death.

William of Sens *(? – 1180)*
A French mason who remodelled part of Canterbury Cathedral.

William, a master mason, was summoned from Sens, France, in 1174, to supervise building work at Canterbury Cathedral.

He remodelled the choir in three years. Then he fell from scaffolding in the cathedral and returned to France a cripple. He died three years later.

John Wood *(1704–54)*
The Yorkshire architect who made the city of Bath an outstanding example of Georgian town planning.

Early in the 18th century, Bath became the most fashionable resort in England, under the leadership of the dandy Richard ("Beau") Nash. The city needed a new appearance, to suit its new role.

John Wood produced a grand design for redeveloping it. However, this proved too ambitious for the city corporation, so Wood sent sections of his plan to individual landowners. Commissions flooded in, and Wood rebuilt parts of the city in golden Bath stone.

Wood died in 1754, before the work was done. His greatest project, the Circus, was completed by his son, John Wood the Younger.

Christopher Wren
(1632–1723)
The scientist who became a master-architect of the English church, and builder of St Paul's Cathedral.

Wren, son of a Dean of Windsor, studied anatomy at Oxford and carried out experiments on the circulation of the blood. Then he switched to astronomy: at 25 he became Professor of Astronomy at Gresham College, London.

Next, his mind turned to architecture and he designed a new chapel for Pembroke College, Cambridge – as well as the Sheldonian Theatre in Oxford.

In 1663 Wren was appointed to a commission which was to repair the old St Paul's Cathedral. He went to Paris and studied architecture, and in the year he returned, 1666, the Great Fire destroyed large areas of London – including St Paul's.

Wren, still only 34, and with little experience of architecture, produced a plan for rebuilding the ruined City, but this was rejected because of landownership complications.

However, he was made one of the commissioners responsible for rebuilding London, and became the surveyor in charge of rebuilding the City's churches.

He designed 51 churches and his masterpiece, the new St Paul's.

The style he chose for the churches was a less elaborate version of the highly decorated Baroque architecture being used in Europe.

Inigo Jones had introduced the classical architecture of ancient Rome earlier in the century, with such buildings as St Paul's Church, Covent Garden, but it was Wren who used the style for the first time to build churches in large numbers.

Wren's City churches were built between 1670 and 1686; at one time, 30 were being built simultaneously. Some of the best known are St Stephen Walbrook, St Clement Danes, in the Strand, and St James's, Piccadilly. Wren's inventive mind produced a wide variety of ideas for towers and spires.

His design for the new St Paul's included a dome which is one of the most majestic in the

WYATVILLE'S WINDSOR *Jeffry Wyatville's design for Windsor Castle included new state apartments.*

world, and he lived to see the building finished.

When Wren died, aged 91, he became the first person to be buried in his own St Paul's Cathedral.

James Wyatt *(1746–1813)*
One of the most popular architects of the late 18th century.

Wyatt, son of a Staffordshire builder, was brilliantly successful, mainly because he was flexible enough to give his customers what they wanted. Many of them wanted their buildings designed in the style of Robert Adam: Wyatt did this so well that he was accused of simply stealing ideas.

After studying in Italy for some years, Wyatt returned to England and worked on country houses including Heaton, in Lancashire and Heveningham Hall, in Suffolk.

He also built Belvoir Castle, in Leicestershire, using the medieval Gothic Revival style.

Wyatt's excursions into the restoration of great buildings, including several cathedrals, Westminster Abbey and Windsor Castle, earned him the derogatory nickname "the Destroyer".

Sir Jeffry Wyatville
(1766–1840)
The man who rebuilt Windsor Castle for George IV.

Sir Jeffry was a nephew of James Wyatt: he changed his surname to avoid confusion between his alterations at Windsor, which earned him his knighthood, and those by his uncle.

His own work at Windsor included raising the Round Tower and creating a whole range of new State apartments.

WREN'S HERITAGE *18th-century view from Somerset House, London, showing St Paul's and Wren spires.*

PICTORIAL ACKNOWLEDGMENTS

The publishers wish to thank the following for their help in obtaining photographs and preparing artwork

Abbot Hall Art Gallery and Museum of Lakeland Life and Industry: Aerofilms Limited: Mrs A. V. Alexander, the 'Fan Circle': John A. Ashworth, BArch, RIBA, MRTPI: Jeremy Benson, AADipl, FRIBA: Stephen J. Best, Nottinghamshire County Council Local Studies Library: Bethnal Green Museum of Childhood: Bournville Village Trust: British Architectural Library/RIBA: A. C. Cass: Castle Museum, York: City Museum and Art Gallery, Plymouth: Department of the Environment: Dickens House: Dorset County Museum: Gallery of English Costume, City of Manchester Art Galleries: Martin Gostelow: Peter Hammond, Education Officer, HM Tower of London: Richard Harris, MA: Ironbridge Gorge Museum Trust: D. M. Keith-Lucas, MA, PhD: National Maritime Museum: National Monuments Record: National Railway Museum: The National Trust: The National Trust for Scotland: Gordon J. Offord, Coachbuilder to HM The Queen: Dr and Mrs D. E. Olliff: C. H. P. Pearn, Dipl Arch (L'pool), RIBA: Dr. Derek Renn: George Robb, RIBA: Royal Commission on Ancient Monuments, Scotland: Science Museum: Society for the Protection of Ancient Buildings: Society of Archer-Antiquaries: University of Reading, Museum of English Rural Life: Victoria and Albert Museum: Waterways Museum, British Waterways Board: Christopher Wilson, Leverhulme Fellow in Medieval Architecture, University of York: Windermere Steamboat Museum: Woolstaplers Hall Museum: York Archaeological Trust.

Photographs and artwork in THE PAST ALL AROUND US came from the following people

Except where stated, credits read from left to right down the page. Work commissioned by the Reader's Digest is shown in *italics*. Drawings are credited after the photographs in Parts One and Two.

PART ONE: THE MAN-MADE LANDSCAPE

10 *Patrick Thurston*: 11 James Hancock: 12 Cambridge University Collection, copyright reserved: 13 Cambridge University Collection, copyright reserved: 14 Aerofilms: 15 James Hancock: 16 Aerofilms: 17 Aerofilms: 18 Cambridge University Collection, copyright reserved: 19 Aerofilms: 20 Clive Coote: 21 Aerofilms: 22 *Patrick Thurston. All drawings by Robert Micklewright.*

PART TWO: DISCOVERING THE PAST

24 Clive Coote: Clive Coote: *Clive Coote*: 25 *Clive Coote*: artist *Robert Micklewright*: 27 Georg Gerster, John Hillelson Agency: 29 *Tom Scott*: 30 *Tom Scott*: 31 Michael Holford, Victoria & Albert Museum: Crown copyright, Victoria & Albert Museum: by permission of Mr F. H. M. FitzRoy Newdegate, Arbury Hall: 32 Crown copyright reserved: artist *Robert Micklewright*: 33 artist *Richard Bonson*: 35 *Malcolm Aird*: Stukeley, 'A Temple of the British Druids', 1743: artist *Robert Micklewright*: 36 artist *Barbara Brown*: 37 artist *Brian Delf*: 38 artist *Robert Micklewright*: 39 by permission of the Masters and Fellows of Corpus Christi College, Cambridge: 41 Michael Holford: *Penny Tweedie*: Michael Holford: 42 Michael Holford: artist *Robert Micklewright*: 43 Lucinda Lambton: *Michael Freeman*: *Michael Freeman*: by permission of Mrs Alan Sorrell: Michael Holford: 44 British Tourist Authority: *Clive Coote*: North of England Open Air Museum, Beamish: 45 *Clive Coote*: 46 Daily Telegraph Colour Library: Lucinda Lambton: 47 *Colin Molyneux*: artist *Robert Micklewright*: 50 *John Perkins*: artist *Robert Micklewright*: 51 *Philip Dowell*: 53 Clive Coote: 55 A. F. Kersting: Mansell Collection: 57 Colin Molyneux: 59 *Tom Scott*: 60 *Patrick Thurston*: 61 Michael Holford: 62 Clive Coote: Clive Coote: *Patrick Thurston*: 63 *Patrick Thurston*: *Malcolm Aird*: Clive Coote: 64 Michael Holford: 66 Erich Hartmann, Magnum: *John Freeman*, British Museum: Ronald Sheridan: Picturepoint, London: John Bethell: 67 artist *Barbara Brown*: 68 Bernard Cox: Clive Coote: 69 Ian Yeomans, Susan Griggs Agency: engravings, Bristol Museum & Art Gallery: 'Great Britain', National Maritime Museum, London: 70 *Colin Molyneux*: 72 National Museum of Antiquities of Scotland: 73 *Michael Freeman*: 75 Crown copyright reserved: Christina Gascoine, Robert Harding Associates: K. M. Andrew: 76 Malcolm Aird: artist *Robert Micklewright*: 77 Colin Molyneux: 78 Aspect Picture Library: artist *Barbara Brown*: 79 Clive Coote: 81 Erich Hartmann, Magnum: 82 *Patrick Thurston*: 83 *Mike Wells*: Museum of London: 84 *Patrick Thurston*: 85 *Patrick Thurston*: 86 *Patrick Thurston*: 87 Jeremy Whittaker: John Bethell: John Bethell: *Patrick Thurston*: Jo Reid, from 'Stove Book', 1977: Michael Holford: 89 *Patrick Thurston*: 91 *Philip Dowell*: Mansell Collection: Michael Holford: 92 Adam Woolfitt, Susan Griggs Agency: 93 Lucinda Lambton: 94 Patrick Thurston: reconstruction, National Trust, artist *Ivan Lapper*: 95 by permission of the Trustees of the British Museum: 96 Michael Holford: 98 Jarrold Colour Publications: Jeremy Whittaker: artist *Robert Micklewright*: 99 Erich Hartmann, Magnum: 100 *Patrick Thurston*: artist *Richard Bonson*: 102 *Philip Evans*: Clive Coote: *Philip Evans*: Clive Coote: 103 Clive Coote: *Patrick Thurston*: *Patrick Thurston*: *Patrick Thurston*: *Philip Evans*: *Patrick Thurston*: *Philip Evans*: *Patrick Thurston*: 104 *Patrick Thurston*: knight, Crown copyright, Victoria & Albert Museum: 105 Crown copyright, Victoria & Albert Museum: 106 *Michael Freeman*: 107 *Mike Taylor*: 108 Lucinda Lambton: Brian Seed, John Hillelson Agency: The National Trust: 109 Brian Seed, John Hillelson Agency: 111 by courtesy of the Marquess of Salisbury: *Colin Molyneux*: 112 *Patrick Thurston*: artist *Robert Micklewright*: 113 The National Trust: *Patrick Thurston*: 114 Institute of Agricultural Economics, Oxford, *Eileen Tweedy*: Rothamstead Experimental Station, *Eileen Tweedy*: the Earl of Mansfield, Scone Palace, *Tom Scott*: Norfolk Museums Service (Norwich Castle Museum): 115 *Julian Plowright*: 116 Patrick Thurston: artists *Richard Bonson* and *Robert Micklewright*: 117 bones, by permission of the Trustees of the British Museum: Spectrum Colour Library: Patrick Thurston: 118 *Patrick Thurston*: 119 Clive Coote: aqueduct, *Malcolm Aird*: others, *Patrick Thurston*: 121 copyright reserved: *John Bulmer*: 122 Clive Coote: artist *Robert Micklewright*: 123 Patrick Thurston: 124 *Ian Yeomans*: Crown copyright, by permission of HMSO: 125 artist *Robert Micklewright*: 127 *Patrick Thurston*: 128 Colin Molyneux: 129 Archbold, Robert Harding Associates: 130 *Malcolm Aird*: Kent Archaeological Rescue Unit: *Malcolm Aird*: 131 artist *Robert Micklewright*: 132 artist *Barbara Brown*: 133 The National Trust: 134 Patrick Thurston: John Topham Picture Library: 136 Bernard Cox: 137 The National Trust for Scotland: 138 *Tom Scott*: 139 Reproduced by gracious permission of Her Majesty The Queen: *Tom Scott*: 141 by permission of the Board of the British Library, Ms Cott Nero Dc f23v: 142 Michael Holford: 143 *Colin Molyneux*: *Peter Keen*: 144 *Colin Molyneux*: 145 The National Trust: 146 *Patrick Thurston*: 147 *Patrick Thurston*: 148 by permission of Sheffield City Art Galleries: *Keith Morris* 149 *Patrick Thurston*: others, Patrick Thurston: 151 The National Trust for Scotland: artist *Barbara Brown*: 152 artist *Ivan Lapper*: 153 artist *Richard Bonson*: 155 *Patrick Thurston*: *John Bulmer*: 156 artist *Brian Delf*: 157 by permission of the Board of the British Library, Ms Roy EIV f250, f248 & f222v: 158 *Patrick Thurston*: 159 Clive Coote: 160 Lucinda Lambton: artist *Barbara Brown*: 161 *Patrick Thurston*: 162 *Patrick Thurston*: bottom, Turners (Photography) Ltd, Newcastle: 163 Martin Johnston Ltd, Edinburgh: artist *Robert Micklewright*: 164 Science Museum photo, Crown copyright: 165 Lucinda Lambton: Somerset Rural Life Museum: 166 National Library of Scotland, Adv Ms 23–6–24: Picturepoint, London: 167 *Malcolm Aird*: *Patrick Thurston*: 168 Lucinda Lambton: 169 *Patrick Thurston*: artist *Robert Micklewright*: 170 *Patrick Thurston*: *Colin Molyneux*: 171 *Eric Meacher*: 173 by permission of the 'Cutty Sark' Society: John Watney: National Maritime Museum, London: 174 *Patrick Thurston*: Norfolk Museums Service (Norfolk Rural Life Museum, Gressenhall): 175 artist *Robert Micklewright*: 176 Georg Gerster, John Hillelson Agency: artist *Robert Micklewright*: 177 David Mather: 178 Ian Berry, Magnum: 179 *Patrick Thurston*: Aerofilms: 180 The National Trust: 181 Malcolm Aird: 182 time keepers, Michael Holford: ring sundial, The National Trust: 183 Patrick Thurston: *Malcolm Aird*: 184 by courtesy of the Marquess of Salisbury: 185 *John Bulmer*: 187 Brian Seed, John Hillelson Agency: artist *Robert Micklewright*: 188 cottages, *Penny Tweedie*: others, Clive Coote: 189 Clive Coote: 191 *Malcolm Aird*: 192 *Penny Tweedie*: 193 artist *Robert Micklewright*: 194 Patrick Thurston: 197 Brian Brake, John Hillelson Agency: Patrick Thurston: Norman McCord, University of Newcastle: 198 *Mike Busselle*: 200 *Patrick Thurston*: *Patrick Thurston*: *Philip Evans*: 201 Clive Coote: Clive Coote: *Patrick Thurston*: *Philip Evans*: Spectrum Colour Library: Spectrum Colour Library: *Philip Evans*: 202 Scottish Tourist Board: Scottish Tourist Board: Crown copyright reserved: 204 Patrick Thurston: National Portrait Gallery, London: artist, *Ivan Lapper*: 205 artist *Richard Bonson*: 206 Malcolm Aird: 207 Clive Coote: 211 The National Trust: 212 Georg Gerster, John Hillelson Agency: 213 The National Trust: 214 The National Trust: 215 Museum of London: The National Trust: 216 The Bodleian Library, Oxford: 217 *Malcolm Aird*: 219 by permission of the Dean and Chapter of Lichfield Cathedral: 220 Michael Holford, Victoria & Albert Museum: 221 Reader's Digest: 223 Sonia Halliday: 224 Clive Coote: 225 Rees, 'Cyclopaedia': 226 *Patrick Thurston*: Crown copyright, by permission of HMSO: 227 by permission of Lord Primrose, Scottish National Portrait Gallery: Museum of London: 228 Godfrey Argent: 229 artist *Robert Micklewright*: 231 John Bethell: The National Trust: 233 Michael Holford: 234 John Watney: Michael Holford: 235 photo, Howard C. Moore, Woodmansterne Ltd: Mary Evans Picture Library: Brian Seed, John Hillelson Agency: 236 Lucinda Lambton: 237 Illustrated London News: 239 Pitkin Pictorials: *John Blomfield*: Ian Bradshaw, Susan Griggs Agency: 240 Museum of London: 241 top four, Anthony Howarth, Susan Griggs Agency: helmet and mask, Crown copyright, by permission of HMSO: chapel, Erich Hartmann, Magnum: 242 Museum of London: 243 temple, Illustrated London News: Newgate, Museum of London: Michael Freeman: 244 Patrick Thurston, © Time-Life International (Nederland) BV from the Great Cities series: 245 Fred Mayer, John Hillelson Agency: photo, Nick Servian, FIIP, Woodmansterne Ltd: 246 Penny Tweedie: 247 by permission of the Marquess of Bath: 248 Patrick Thurston: *Malcolm Aird*: artist *Robert Micklewright*: 249 *Malcom Aird*: 250 by permission of the Trustees of the British Museum: Crown copyright, by permission of HMSO: 251 Observer Magazine/Transworld: 252 Adam Woolfitt, Susan Griggs Agency: 253 by permission of the Society of Antiquaries of London: aerial, Georg Gerster, John Hillelson Agency: 255 *Patrick Thurston*: 256 Philip Lloyd: 257 Michael Holford: 258 artist *Robert Micklewright*: 259 *Patrick Thurston*: 260 *Colin Molyneux*: sleeper block, Brian Bracegirdle: 263 Penny Tweedie: 264 Hampshire County Records Office: The National Trust: 267 Patrick Thurston: 269 British Tourist Authority: British Tourist Authority: *Patrick Thurston*: 271 Bernard Cox: 272 Patrick Thurston: 273 Science Museum photo, Crown copyright: Michael Holford: Cotehele House, The National Trust: Turners (Photography) Ltd, Newcastle: Turners (Photography) Ltd, Newcastle: Turners (Photography) Ltd, Newcastle: Science Museum photo, Crown copyright: Turners (Photography) Ltd, Newcastle: 274 Clive Coote: 275 Colin Molyneux: 277 Ian Yeomans, Susan Griggs Agency: 278 Lucinda Lambton: 279 *Patrick Thurston*: 281 *Lucinda Lambton*: 283 Clive Coote: 285 Daily Telegraph Colour Library: 287 *Patrick Thurston*: 288 Crown copyright, by permission of HMSO: 289 *Patrick Thurston*: 290 artist *Barbara Brown*: 291 *Malcolm Aird*: The Gallery of English Costume, City of Manchester Art Galleries: *Malcolm Aird*: 293 Clive Coote: 294 John Watney, by permission of the Commanding Officer, HMS 'Victory': 295 artist *Robert Micklewright*: 297 *Lucinda Lambton*: artist *Robert Micklewright*: 298 *Malcolm Aird*: Crown copyright, by permission of HMSO: 299 John Bethell: 301 David Cockroft: by permission of the Trustees of the British Museum: 302 Georg Gerster, John Hillelson Agency: 303 Adam Woolfitt, Susan Griggs Agency: 304 artist *Stanley Paine*: 307 Lucinda Lambton: Erich Hartmann, Magnum: Lucinda Lambton: 310 *Colin Molyneux*: 311 *Colin Molyneux*: artist *Robert Micklewright*: 312 top three, Colin Molyneux: others, Philip Evans: 313 Welsh Folk Museum, St Fagans: *Philip Evans*: *Philip Evans*: Colin Molyneux: 314 *Malcolm Aird*: 315 Georg Gerster, John Hillelson Agency: *Malcolm Aird*: 316 Lucinda Lambton: 317 Lucinda Lambton, 'Temples of Convenience', published by Gordon Frazer: 319 artist *Robert Micklewright*: 321 *Patrick Thurston*: 322 Michael Holford: 323 *Penny Tweedie*: 325 *Patrick Thurston*: Picturepoint, London: 326 C. M. Dixon: Bill Vaughan: 327 The National Museum of Antiquities of Scotland: artist *Robert Micklewright*: 329 *Gordon Moore*: 331 exterior, *Adam Woolfitt*: interiors, John Watney: 333 top two, *Colin Molyneux*: Sticklepath Museum of Rural Industry: artist *Robert Micklewright*: 334 artist *Marjorie Gayner*: 335 Patrick Thurston: 336 Clive Coote: 337 David Cockroft: artist *Robert Micklewright*: 339 Patrick Thurston: 341 *Lucinda Lambton*: 342 Mercie Lack: artist *Stanley Paine*: 343 by permission of the Trustees of the British Museum: 344 *Lucinda Lambton*: 346 artist *Ivan Lapper*: 349 artist *Barbara Brown*: 350 Adam Woolfitt, Susan Griggs Agency: 351 Cushing's Steam Engine and Organ Museum, Thursford: *Colin Molyneux*: 352 *Peter Cooper*: 353 The National Trust: 355 *Colin Molyneux*: 356 Georg Gerster, John Hillelson Agency: 357 The National Trust: 358 Sunday Times: 359 The National Trust, Waddesdon Manor, Aylesbury, Bucks: 361 Turners (Photography) Ltd, Newcastle: 362 Crown copyright, Victoria & Albert Museum: Michael Holford, Victoria & Albert Museum: Michael Holford, by permission of Mrs S. A. Khan: 363 North of England Open Air Museum, Beamish: artist *Robert Micklewright*: 364 *Patrick Thurston*: 365 *Patrick Thurston*: 366 *Patrick Thurston*: 367 *Patrick Thurston*: artist *Robert Micklewright*: 370 Mary Evans Picture Library: 371 artist *Stanley Paine*: 373 artist *Ivan Lapper*: 374 *Patrick Thurston*: 375 Turners (Photography) Ltd, Newcastle: 376 *Lucinda Lambton*: stick wagon, artist *Robert Micklewright*, after a drawing by Stanley Lewis from Arnold Haskell 'Infantilia' published by Dennis Dobson: 378 *Patrick Thurston*: 379 *Patrick Thurston*: 380 Jarrold Colour Publications: 381 *Patrick Thurston*: 382 photo, Nick Servian, FIIP, Woodmansterne Ltd: 383 *Patrick Thurston*: 384 *R. Marshall*.

PART FOUR: A HISTORY SPOTTER'S GUIDE

402 *Richard Bonson*: 403 *Richard Bonson*: 404 *Richard Bonson*: *Barbara Brown*: 405 *Richard Bonson*: 406 *Richard Bonson*: 407 photo, Michael Holford: Michael Holford: 408 *Barbara Brown*: 409 *Brian Delf*: 410 *Brian Delf*: *Barbara Brown*: 411 *Brian Delf*: 412 *Brian Delf*: 413 *Barbara Brown*: *Brian Delf*: 414 *Brian Delf*: 415 *Brian Delf*: 416 *Barbara Brown*: *Brian Delf*: 417 *Brian Delf*: 418 *Barbara Brown*: *Brian Delf*: 419 *Brian Delf*: 420 *Brian Delf*: 421 *Brian Delf*: 422 *Charles Pickard*: 423 *Charles Pickard*: 424 *Charles Pickard*: 425 *Charles Pickard*: 426 *Brian Delf*: *Barbara Brown*: 427 *Brian Delf*: 428 *Les Smith*: *Barbara Brown*: 429 *Les Smith*: 430 *Charles Pickard*: 431 *Charles Pickard*: 432 *Roy Castle*: *Barbara Brown*: 433 *Roy Castle*: 434 *Brian Delf*: *Barbara Brown*: 435 *Roy Castle*: 436 *Charles Pickard*: 437 *Charles Pickard*: 438 *Stanley Paine*: 439 *Stanley Paine*: 440 *Les Smith*: 441 *Les Smith*: 442 *Stanley Paine*: 443 *Stanley Paine*: 444 *Marjorie Saynor*: 445 *Marjorie Saynor*: 446 *Stanley Paine*: 447 *Stanley Paine*: 448 *Stanley Paine*.

PART FIVE: BUILDERS OF BRITAIN

450 Ronan Picture Library: 451 GLC, Iveagh Bequest, Kenwood: Mansell Collection: 452 Giraudon: 453 Mary Evans Picture Library: Sir John Soames Museum: 455 Campbell, 'Vitruvius Britannicus', 1717: The National Trust: 456 Keith Gibson: 457 Mary Evans Picture Library: 459 Mary Evans Picture Library: 460 by courtesy of Josiah Wedgwood & Sons Ltd: 461 Ronan Picture Library: 463 copyright reserved: Mansell Collection:

1350	The Perpendicular Gothic style begins to dominate architecture.
1382	John Wycliffe produces the first complete English translation of the Bible. He and his followers, the Lollards, attack abuses in the Church, and the power of the pope and prelates.

HOUSE OF LANCASTER (1399–1461)

1404	Welsh rebel Owain Glyndwr, with French help, takes Carmarthen and Harlech.
1408	Recapture of Harlech marks restoration of English rule in Wales.
1455	Yorkist victory at St Albans opens Wars of the Roses.

HOUSE OF YORK (1461–1485)

1461	Yorkist victory at Mortimer's Cross brings Edward IV to throne.
1476	William Caxton, the first English printer, sets up printing press at Westminster. For the first time, books gradually become available to ordinary Englishmen.

HOUSE OF TUDOR (1485–1603)

1485	Henry Tudor, Earl of Richmond, defeats Richard III at Bosworth Field, and ends the Wars of the Roses.
1501–3	James IV of Scotland agrees to marry daughter of Henry VII and signs treaty of perpetual peace with England.
1513	Scots invade England and suffer a bloody defeat at Flodden.
1533	Henry VIII divorces his first wife Catherine of Aragon in defiance of the Roman Catholic Church, and marries his mistress Anne Boleyn.
1534	Henry declares himself head of the Church of England. In 1536 he begins the Dissolution of the Monasteries, which adds wealth to the English Crown. Many of his subjects profit; some no longer needing castles, build great brick mansions.
1536	Act of Union annexes Wales to England.
1538	Fearing a continental invasion on behalf of the pope, Henry begins a string of coastal forts, including Walmer, Deal and St Mawes. They are the last coastal forts, if not castles, built for military purposes.
1553	Queen Mary attempts to restore Roman Catholicism.
1556	Archbishop Cranmer burned as a heretic, one of the many Protestant martyrs executed during Mary's reign.
1558	Elizabeth I succeeds to the English throne.
1559	In Scotland John Knox incites Protestants to attack churches.
1567	Lord Darnley, husband of Mary, Queen of Scots, murdered.
1568	Mary escapes to England, where Queen Elizabeth imprisons her.
1577	Francis Drake begins his voyage around the world.
1587	Mary, Queen of Scots, executed. Drake raids Spanish coast.
1588	Spanish Armada, sent by Philip II to launch a Catholic invasion of England, defeated by English fleet.
1600	Foundation of East India Company. The opening up of the New World and the East brings new wealth to England. London becomes a major financial centre. With 200,000 people, it is the largest city in Europe. William Shakespeare begins to write his great tragic plays, *Hamlet, Othello, Macbeth* and *King Lear*.

HOUSE OF STUART (1603–1714)

1603	Union of Scotland and England under James VI of Scotland and I of England.
1605	Gunpowder Plot, to blow up Houses of Parliament, fails.
1611	English, Scots colonise Ulster. Authorised Version of Bible published.
1620	Pilgrim Fathers settle in America.
1642	Civil War breaks out between Parliament and Charles I, who insists on preserving the Divine Right of Kings.
1649	After defeat in battle and trial for treason, Charles I is beheaded. England governed as Commonwealth.
1651	Victory over Charles II at Battle of Worcester makes Oliver Cromwell master of Britain.
1653	Cromwell dissolves the Rump Parliament and declares himself Lord Protector, governing the Commonwealth with a Council of State.
1660	Charles II invited home by Parliament to restore the monarchy.
1665	Great Plague strikes England, killing 20,000 in London.
1666	Great Fire of London destroys 13,200 houses and 89 churches.
1673	Test Act forbids Catholics and Non-Conformists from holding public office.
1675	Christopher Wren begins work on new St Paul's Cathedral.

CONTINUED FROM INSIDE FRONT COVER

Alexa - Happy Valentines
Day 2/08

I saw this Book, and al
thought to myself- this is
my Sissy - il love you
dearly - and no matter what I
love mom -

ANDRE DE DIENES

MARILYN

ANDRE DE DIENES

MARILYN

Edited by Steve Crist and Shirley T. Ellis de Dienes

TASCHEN

HONG KONG KÖLN LONDON LOS ANGELES MADRID PARIS TOKYO

Contents

(Re)Discovering André   When a young photographer on assignment for
Vogue left New York for Los Angeles in the early 1940s, he could have hardly
imagined the future that awaited him. Ultimately, he would end up relocating
to California and spending the next four decades of his life photographing
beautiful women — famous and those aspiring to fame alike — while living an
impassioned and sometimes tormented existence in the hills above Hollywood.
Of the many beautiful women that would ultimately cross his path, one woman
would come to have special significance in his life: Marilyn Monroe.

    This book is the first substantial view of André de Dienes's work since
his death in 1985, as well as the definitive collection of his images and
writings pertaining to the young Norma Jeane — the future Marilyn Monroe.
André became Marilyn's confidant and lover, but she would also become
a source of frustration — driving him to near obsession at various times
throughout his life. From a simple chance meeting in November of 1945, André
de Dienes would forever be changed by his personal and private moments with
a Hollywood star that perhaps has no comparison in today's celebrity-
filled society.

    Images of Marilyn Monroe as a Hollywood icon are so prolific that they
almost blend together in our collective memory of her. The entire world seems
to know Marilyn, and the many photographs of her are hard to distinguish from
one another, revealing little of the artistry or identity of the individual

photographers that created them. Despite this, André's vision of Marilyn is
unique. He captured a young Norma Jeane and a newly-named Marilyn's innocence,
naïveté and natural beauty long before her transformation into the epitome of
Hollywood glamour. Photographs of Marilyn later in life show an experienced
model and actress who knew how to work the camera and her adoring audience. It
was before André's camera that Marilyn first attempted her craft. Decades
later, André's images of her are significant and refreshing, in that they
suggest a naturalness and sincerity, and even in some instances reveal
a darker, more hidden side of who Marilyn truly was.

Interestingly, André often refrained from photographing Marilyn
throughout their relationship. He felt that many exploited her to their own
advantage, and his diaries unveil his desire to maintain a special friendship
with her that was based on more than simple image making to further enhance
either of their careers. He never solicited her for work and he protectively
kept their affairs private. His feelings for her were genuine and his
photographs of her lovingly reflect that. Despite all of this, André did
become consumed with Marilyn. In the final analysis, it can be said that
André seemed to both love her personally, and adore her with a passion
similar to that of any fervent fan.

In the last few years before his death from cancer, André began typing
his memoirs, a good portion of which comprise this volume. Knowing full well

that he was dying, André wrote in a loose, passionate style that was true
to his real life personality. Most of his life, André was considered a
colorful character. He had a temper and hated injustice. His life and writing
contained many exclamation points. It should be mentioned that it's unlikely
that André, unlike numerous others that have written about their relationships
with Marilyn, embellished much on what really occurred. He loved his privacy,
but realized the importance of the special experiences he had with her.
Knowing André, it's also probable that he purposely left some stories out.
To the end, he remained a gentleman. Perhaps to some, events in his memoirs
may seem at times almost unbelievable — but the reality of Andre's life was
almost as remarkable as Marilyn's.

  Andor Ikafalvi de Dienes was born in 1913 in the Transylvanian village
of Turia, a former possession of Hungary. When André was eleven, with the
Hungarian currency devalued and his family in crisis, Andre's mother
committed suicide by throwing herself down a well on the family property.
Devastated by the loss and the breakup of his family, André struck out on
his own at age fourteen. He found his way to Budapest and tried to rejoin
his estranged father. Unable to make a lasting connection, he was alone at
a very young age. He took a job in a fabric store and spent the formative
years of his youth surrounded by wealthy women and expensive fabrics.
At night, he would work as a stagehand in order to see the operas and

musicals he loved in the Budapest theater. These years in Budapest nurtured his interest in the arts, culture, and women.

Eager to see the world and bored with the routine of fabric sales — he left Budapest to travel through Europe and Africa at age eighteen. Joining a group of traveling artists, he learned to paint and made his first photographs on that journey. While photographing statues in a park in Paris in 1934, he was stopped by a British clothing designer, Captain Edward Molyneux, and was asked to become his exclusive fashion photographer. Opting for a more French sounding name, he remade himself as André de Dienes. His photographs from that time period were primarily fashion assignments for Molyneux, but from 1935 to 1938 he created thousands of portraits and street images in Paris and all over France. It was Andre's first venture into photographing people from all walks of life, something he continued to do throughout his photographic career. Very few of André's fashion images have survived from his days in France (he destroyed many and later wrote that he regretted it) — but happily almost two thousand images of France remain in his archive.

After meeting Arnold Gingrich, the editor of Esquire magazine on holiday in Paris, André accepted his offer to relocate to New York and pursue assignments with Esquire's sponsorship. His decision to move to New York ushered in a new chapter of his life and put him on a course that would

ultimately define his career. Arriving in New York in 1938, André began shooting for Vogue, Bazaar, and Town and Country. He was quite comfortable with the powerful editors who ran and influenced the magazines in New York and quickly established himself in the city.

As time progressed however, André felt increasingly stifled by the confinements of fashion photography. Although he had become quite successful as a fashion photographer, he always made time for personal image making. He began to use every opportunity to photograph subjects that he felt drawn to in his newly adopted country. His adventurous spirit led him to explore many diverse subjects, including female nudes. As a European in America, he did not subscribe to the common prejudices of the day. He took many opportunities to photograph African Americans in Harlem, as well as the Southern states, and Native American tribes across the entire United States. Back in New York, André was dumbfounded by the lack of interest photo editors had for these images. He was shocked at the injustice of it all, yet continued to photograph all people he felt a connection to. It was a theme that would continue, and his lack of interest in assignment photography led him to seek out a direction that was more soulful and artistic.

In Harlem, André found a prosperous and successful community of African Americans that captured his attention. He walked the streets and made hundreds of unposed and spontaneous portraits, giving much attention to

the children playing on the streets. On the reverse side of some Harlem prints, he would sometimes write about the people he met and photographed. He was moved by the dignity, poise and beauty of this rarely photographed American community. When he proudly showed these images to a major publication of the day, he was devastated that they were totally uninterested in publishing them.

When his travels took him to the southern states of Louisiana, Mississippi and Georgia, he encountered African American workers in the fields. He relished the opportunity to photograph the workers and made many return trips to the area to continue the effort. His images of the workers showed a proud and dignified people rarely recorded on film during that time period.

Native American tribes became another great source of inspiration in his life. The majority of tribes were certainly not the subject of much serious photography. André fell in love with many different tribes, and proceeded to document thousands of images over many decades. Frequently, he would find himself at the end of a road, walking with his cameras and introducing himself to a secluded group of Native Americans unused to visitors or interest from mainstream America. Presenting himself to tribal leaders, he was often invited to stay as a guest, allowed to embrace tribal life and photograph rituals like few outsiders had.

André was an excited, wide-eyed student of life that loved the promise of the vast, open countryside. The West beckoned to him, and he dove into all it had to offer. Like his earlier travels throughout the eastern parts of America, André loved the western states and especially their indigenous peoples. He also loved the open skies and the outdoor lifestyle agreed with his free spirit. He envisioned a career for himself photographing women with the western landscape as the backdrop. This desire led him to move to the famed Garden of Allah Hotel in Hollywood in 1945. Many well-known artists, writers and actors had called the hotel home at one time or another. It was on that fateful first day that he met the future Marilyn Monroe. His life would never be the same.

The Norma Jeane of 1945 was married and all of nineteen years old. In a strained relationship while her husband was shipped out to the events of World War II, she was a story waiting to happen. Norma Jeane stepped through André's hotel door, and in typical André style, he fell head over heels for the young brunette. She was a simple girl from a troubled background and was just gaining confidence in her aspiration to become a model. Even by today's standards, it's hard to imagine how quickly events unfolded in her life. Less than six months after he first photographed her, André's stature as a photographer landed Norma Jeane her first magazine cover. André's photograph of her debuted on the cover of Family Circle,

April 26, 1946 — despite the fact she was an unknown model at the time.
In short time, many more André covers followed.

Traveling extensively during this time period, André happened to be in
New York when news broke out of the end of World War II. He rushed to Times
Square and made an indelible set of images from the street celebrations of
the day. In typical André style, he would file these photographs away and
they would stay there for the rest of his life, with no explanation as to why
they were overlooked.

Wine, good food, and opera were all part of Andre's daily requirements
for life. His love of books, physical exercise, and time in the outdoors
became his mantra. Women would come and go, and Marilyn left for the stardom
and marriages she was destined for. There were frequent relationships in his
life - usually short-term lovers that seemed not to satisfy him for long.
A fellow well-known photographer of the time period, Peter Gowland, recalled,
"Many times André and I were shooting different girls at opposite ends of
the same beach. The only difference between us was that André always left
with the girl, a loaf of bread, and a bottle of wine — while I went home
to my wife and family."

Seeking artistic autonomy and independence from assigned image making,
André built a career of photographing women. It would give him great
excitement and cause him great torment for many years. Los Angeles allowed

him to live out his fantasy like no other city would. The constant flow of aspiring actresses and models seemed to be endless, and all wanted to be recognized and put on film. André carved out a life for himself, and built a home by hand on a lot he purchased high in the Hollywood hills above Sunset Boulevard. During these years his life moved quickly — aided by his Hollywood locale and the famous people he photographed.

The André de Dienes of the 1950s was a bit older and wiser — and suddenly a well-known photographic commodity. As a European, he pushed himself into a medium that was still considered taboo in many parts of postwar America. He clearly stood out as a major photographer of the female form in that time period. In 1953, the front cover of a brand new magazine called Playboy led with the headline "At home with André de Dienes". André had made it — and would ride the new trend of "girlie" magazines that would start to proliferate on American newsstands. Publishers from Europe and America sought his material, and he had a wealth of monographs published that are highly sought after and collectible to this day.

In his latter years, André became a recluse in his hillside home. The last decade of his life included little picture taking. Instead, he sequestered himself in his darkroom and printed and reprinted his life of negatives in all subject matter. After his death, André's estate and photograph collection were upset by legal battles for many years.

Despite his long absence from publication, the recent resurgence of his work is refreshing and his images are vital once again.

In the coming years, André de Dienes will undoubtedly be rediscovered as a significant contributor to the medium of photography. As an individual, he will always be remembered as an independent, passionate and emotionally charged man, inseparable from his association with Marilyn Monroe.

The Hollywood version of the photographer and model romance story has been told many times over. Indeed, André was the first of many photographers with whom Marilyn would become romantically involved. Despite this, the story of André and Marilyn is most poignant as it took place during a time of rare innocence in the life of Marilyn. As André commented many times, Norma Jeane was not Marilyn Monroe back in 1945! She was simply a girl that possessed an unexplainable, almost mystical ingredient that propelled her to a level of fame almost incomparable to that of any other celebrity. To a great extent, many will always consider André and Marilyn inseparable. Appropriately, André's and Marilyn's graves lie very near each other in Westwood Memorial Cemetery in Los Angeles.

Steve Crist
Los Angeles, April 2002

16

A Note about the Text   André de Dienes wrote his memoirs in the last days of his life, typing them and making additions and corrections by hand. The complete Marilyn Monroe section of these memoirs is reproduced in facsimile in the accompanying volume. The text contained in the present volume comprises edited excerpts from the memoirs, flowing chronologically alongside the photographs, for ease of navigation.

N.B. That Marilyn Monroe's name was originally spelled "Norma Jean" is a common misconception. The correct spelling, and the one she herself used, was "Norma Jeane."

Love, Norma Jeane

134

Norma Jeane   Reality can be stranger than fiction. Soon after I got
myself installed in a bungalow at the Garden of Allah in Hollywood, I phoned
Emmeline Snively, who had the Blue Book Model Agency at the Ambassador Hotel,
and I explained to her that I was back in Hollywood again and that I needed
models for photos of nudes, artistic nudes, for a new project I had in mind.
Miss Snively said there was a very pretty girl in her office, waiting for her
first modeling assignment, a model who just started in the profession, and
perhaps she would pose for nudes. Miss Snively said she would send the young
lady to see me right away and that her name was Norma Jeane Baker.

When Norma Jeane arrived at my bungalow later in the afternoon, it was
as if a miracle had happened to me. Norma Jeane seemed to be like an angel.
I could hardly believe it for a few moments. An earthly, sexy-looking angel!
Sent expressly for me! The impact Norma Jeane had on me was tremendous.
As minutes passed, I fell more and more in love with Norma Jeane; there was
an immediate rapport between us. She responded to everything I said. She
started to look around in my room, examining all the pictures I put on the
walls, and began asking questions. I had the immediate feeling that she was
something special, something different from most girls and models I had met
before her, mainly because she was so eager to ask questions about me and
the pictures I put on the walls. She wanted to know many things right away,
she was interested in me! She was utterly sincere; she did not wish to speak

Memo:
Year. 1945.

about herself, except when I asked her my own questions. She was sincere in
wanting to know who I was and what I was doing with my life, and I began to
amuse her exceedingly with all sorts of stories that ran through my mind and
I just kept dishing them out to her. I still remember it as clearly as if
it happened just recently.

Norma Jeane wore a pale pink sweater, tight to her body, and her curly
ash-blonde hair was tied around her head with pink ribbon; her rosy pinkish
face and her blue eyes reminded me of a pretty Easter bunny. I told her
I had bought two large rabbit dolls in a toy shop in New York, which I intended
to photograph for a new magazine I was planning to start (to be financed by
a wealthy literary agent), and how sorry I was not to have brought them with
me to Hollywood, because I would have loved to photograph her with the
rabbits for my new magazine. Norma Jeane loved the idea, and laughed heartily.

(Thinking back to all that, I find it a bizarre coincidence, or a
premonition, that I told Norma Jeane in 1945 about wanting to start a new
kind of magazine, the picture of the rabbit as the emblem of the magazine
and pictures of her nude inside the magazine. Eight years later, Hugh Hefner,
a genius businessman, made it a reality! Norma Jeane was going to be the
cover star of the first issue of my magazine; correspondingly, the first
issue of Playboy featured my darling Norma Jeane, but as Marilyn Monroe,
on the cover, and nude on the inside.)

THIS IS SHARP PER...

I noticed Norma Jeane had a wedding ring on her finger. She informed me she was married, but separated from her husband and no longer in love with him. He was a merchant marine away at sea, and she was free and modeling was her new goal. She mentioned nothing about wanting to become an actress. The few words of explanation she gave me freed my mind from inhibition. The truth was that I wanted to photograph her very much, but I wanted her more than anything else in the world! I was completely love struck from the moment she appeared at the door.

While we were talking, Norma Jeane took a good look at one of several old engravings I had on the wall — a nude Indian girl sitting on a rock, surrounded by mountainous scenery and animals, sort of an allegorical representation of the vision of America, the way Europeans figured life was like in America a few centuries ago. Norma Jeane was very interested in the picture and I told her I brought the pictures with me all the way from Transylvania. I went into a long story, telling her that in Spain in the 16th century, it was believed that California was an island inhabited by beautiful and strong native women — who lived in the nude. And that the entire continent of the West was rumored to be rich with gold, so Cortes, the famous Spanish explorer, outfitted ships and came to explore and conquer California, driven by the lust for gold and women. She laughed like crazy when I told her that I had the same thing in mind coming here to Hollywood, and my intentions were to photograph beautiful

girls in the nude all throughout the West, but at the same time to explore old forgotten gold mines and look for gold in the mountains too. I came straight to the point in our conversation, asking her whether she would like to come travel with me. We would go by car to explore the vast West and take pictures everywhere — glamour photos for magazine covers, and nudes too!

I had a stack of large enlargements of photos I took of movie stars the year before, and some nudes, and Norma Jeane looked through them with great approval. She was excited and wanted to pose for me. She asked, "Would you like to see my figure?" In a jiffy, she grabbed her hatbox, went to the adjoining room (the bedroom), put on a bathing suit, and, smiling, beaming with happiness, she swirled around the center of the living room, happy to be able to show me her beautiful figure.

A day later, I took her to the beach to take pictures of her. Again and again, I photographed her each day. My mind was made up for sure — I wanted to take her away from Hollywood right away on a long trip. Just go with her, everywhere! I felt completely enamored by her!

I offered to pay her 100 dollars per week for posing plus all expenses, and that I would buy all sorts of things for her to wear for pictures (jeans, blouses, sweaters, bathing suits) and promised she could eat as much and as well as she pleased, because I noticed she loved food. She was young and she had a good appetite!

23

25

25

26

29

34

36

42

46

SHE STARTED
HERE

1945

The Journey Begins   In the days that followed, I bought Norma Jeane various clothes to wear for my pictures and to keep her warm because it was December and my plans were to visit the desert, the mountains, everywhere in California, Nevada, Arizona, anywhere my fancy would dictate going. I removed the back seat of my big Buick Roadmaster automobile and laid down a sheet of thick foam rubber with blankets on top and pillows all around, so Norma Jeane could sleep whenever she wished during the long drives I was planning. That was her little "cage" as I called it. She laughed like crazy when I told her she would become my little slave and prisoner, that I might even buy a long thin chain to attach one end of to her ankle and the other end to the car! Her hatbox full of her things and a small suitcase were also placed in her "cage," plus a basketful of food and thermos bottles for milk and coffee, etc. The trunk of the car was for my equipment and the front seat was also for her, with pillows against the door to give her as much comfort as possible. And thus the long journey began.

We were hardly on the outskirts of Los Angeles when the police patrol stopped me for faulty driving. Norma Jeane was sitting close to me and the policeman might have felt jealous! She felt very indignant. In her sweet voice she riposted to the policeman that he was a crook and that we had done nothing wrong. The man, part seriously and part joking, said to Norma Jeane that if she cared to stay there for the night he would not make us pay the fine.

I paid twenty dollars and we continued the trip. That was only the first
proposal she got on that trip. Amazingly, at various places we stopped,
people began proposing to her. A garage mechanic said he would give his left
arm if she would stay and become his wife. A miner in the mountains said he
wanted her and would give her everything he had. A young farmer said he was
looking for a woman of her beauty! The owner of a motel proposed to her! And
the haberdasher where I stopped to buy her jeans went nearly out of his mind
wanting to see Norma Jeane try on various garments in the little dressing
closet. Like a magnet, she attracted all men! I became reluctant, even
cautious, stopping wherever there were men around. She good-humoredly laughed
every time and gently apologized to the men that she was unable to stay….
She did not tell me so, but I knew she was very pleased. So that's how
the legend of Marilyn Monroe began — every man was crazy about her!

　　After we left the police station, I asked her to stand on the highway,
barefoot, fixing her hair in pigtails. While taking her picture like that,
in a sudden, strange, psychic revelation, I began pointing at the small white
stars on her red skirt, prognosticating that those stars meant that some day
she would become a very famous movie star! For a while I was talking,
babbling about a future fabulous life, foretelling almost incoherently that
the road behind her symbolized life, and that those were the first photos of
her future successes to come!

53

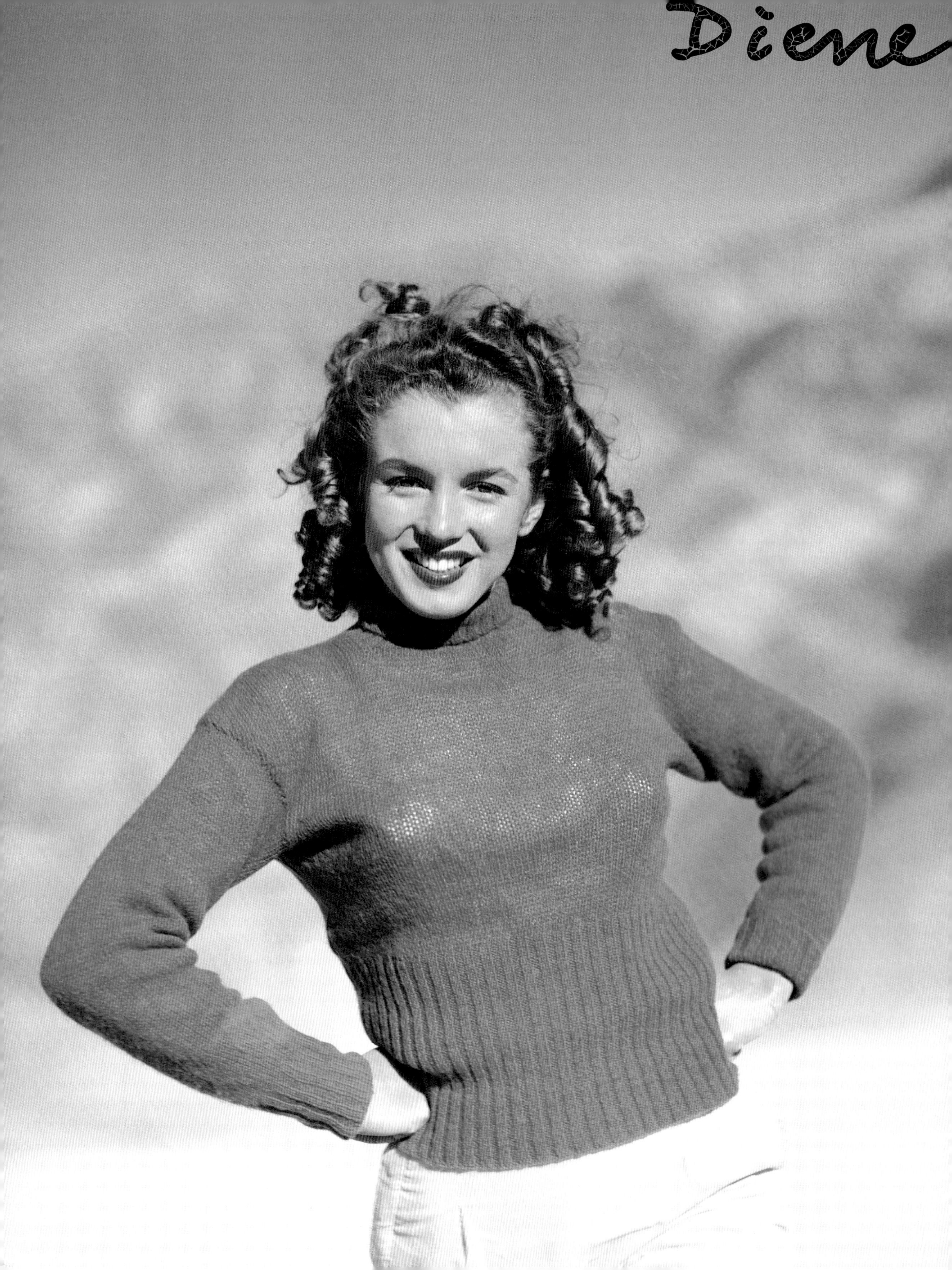
Diene

in Death Valley, Calif.

COLOR

Death Valley   My first destination was Death Valley, California, where
I wanted to visit places connected to finding gold. Also, I had in mind to
take nude photos of Norma Jeane at a place called "Darwin Falls" in the
western region of Death Valley, which I imagined to be a large, beautiful
waterfall. As it turns out, imagination and reality are two different things.
After a long drive, and some hiking, we found only a small waterfall with a
little bit of water coming down, and even if I could have taken nudes against
that, I simply could not go through with it. I was too much in love with her
to ask her crudely to undress and expose herself. I knew that if I really
asked her to undress, or insisted on it, she would have done it, but it
seemed to me a heartless, tactless procedure to make her shed all of her
clothes all of a sudden. I could not go through with it! I just began
adoring her; I did not want her to show herself to me in the bright
sunlight, I was too idealistic and shy!

In the evening when we got to Furnace Creek Inn, in the heart of Death
Valley, I asked Norma Jeane whether she would like to sleep in the same cabin
with me or whether she would prefer a separate one. Sweet, darling Norma
Jeane calmly explained her sentiments to me — that she liked me very much,
but she was only separated, not divorced, and she would feel far better if
she had her own cabin. Besides, she loved to sleep well, and if we were
together, she would not be able to get her rest. She got her wish!

TRAVELLING THROUGH CALIFORNIA

MT. WHITNEY , WEST OF DEATH VALLY, CAL.
THE HIGHEST PEEK IN THE U.S.

We had separate cabins. But I could hardly sleep all night — I felt the torment of wanting her! Toward dawn, I ventured to knock on her door. She opened it, and laughingly, like someone who is accustomed to handling men in those kinds of situations, she asked me to remain a "good boy" and to return to my cabin. I did.

A few hours later, when I woke up, the sun was just rising from behind the mountains. I was ready to start on the trip again, and to my great surprise, when I went to knock on her door again, she was already made up and taking the curlers out of her hair. The sunlight shone right into her cabin and she was cheerful, exuberant, and eager to go to the dining room for her breakfast. It was a very chilly morning and still, she was eager to pose for pictures as soon as she got dressed. Any other model would have still been in bed, or would have wiped her sleepy eyes, complaining about having to get up, saying what a "sadist" I was to wake her up so early… to "slave" for me for pictures! But not Norma Jeane! She was the sweetest darling I have ever met!

Again, instead of photographing her nude, I took pictures of her dressed, sitting on rocks. Since the desert seemed so beautiful, so tranquil to both of us, I spread out a blanket and I was reading to her from a quotation book I had brought along with quotations about most everything that touches spiritual life. Norma Jeane listened attentively, and then she took from her handbag her Christian Science prayer book and she, too, read for me.

61

63

68

We were parking right here

Cathedral Gorge   I decided to visit a scenic wonder, far north of
Las Vegas, called Cathedral Gorge State Park. It turned out to be a fantastic
place, an incredible maze of mountains eroded by thousands if not millions
of years of rainfalls and windstorms, eroded in such a curious way that only
the photographic camera can prove. There I thought I might take nudes of
Norma Jeane, because that unusual scenery fascinated my imagination. But it
turned out otherwise.

As I was unloading my photo equipment, two hoodlum-looking characters
approached us, offering us guidance to some of the most unusual and remote
places there, that few visitors would ever be able to visit otherwise. But
I was no fool; I sensed danger. I declined the offer, saying I came to take
a few pictures and that I loved photographing the morning sunlight, and that
I did not need any guides. The two fellows were examining Norma Jeane with
envious eyes while directing jealous and hostile glances at me, but they
walked away to a nearby outhouse.

Since we had parked in the very center of that amazing canyon, I did
venture to take a few photos. For protection, I always had a sharp old
sword underneath the front seat of the car, and I handed it to Norma Jeane
to carry. In my camera case, I also had an Indian hunting knife, so with
those in our possession I felt somewhat protected while I was snapping a few
pictures. But then we saw the two fellows coming toward us. Norma Jeane and

I ran to the car as fast as we could. I pushed her in, threw my equipment in, and we took off just in time to escape from something frightening — rape, or murder! The men were running toward us when we escaped. Even now, I shudder thinking of it.

Norma Jeane did not think much of the incident. As usual, she just laughed with lots of humor, from her heart, and she said I just worried too much. I insisted that we had escaped being murdered, and I made her swear she would never tell her Aunt Ana that I had exposed her to such danger.

I really laugh now, thinking how, all of a sudden, I took off from Hollywood with a pretty girl and engaged into facing the most rugged desert territory of the western part of the U.S., where I was a total stranger and my automobile tires were all worn and gas was not easy to find. Yet I adore laughing about it because when one is in love, one can be nearly insane! I am astonished now, while thinking back to all that: me, a young man, under some hypnotic influence, enamored of a 19-year-old pretty young girl, traveling, driving around, willy-nilly in the wilderness, having not the slightest sure idea of what he wants to do, where he is traveling to, and for what purpose!

THE OLD LADY AT
THE GAS STATION,
IN THE DESERT

<u>A Change in Plans</u>   In the next twenty-four hours, I drove hundreds
of miles south, all the way along the Colorado River, sometimes on terrible
roads where only foolhardy people travel. But the desert was absolutely
magnificent everywhere! A tire blew out on the main highway to Yuma, just
before we would have driven through many miles of sand dunes.

To our great surprise, the person who owned the gas station was an old
woman, very western looking, with a cigarette in her mouth. When I told her
I planned to visit Picacho Camp, north of Yuma, and explore Superstition
Mountain up in Arizona to look for gold, she said I was insane! Furthermore,
she said the weather was changing; the windstorm would create a fantastic
dust storm across the sand dunes, and if I tried to go across, we would
never emerge alive!

While I was installing an old, recapped tire I purchased (World War II
had just ended and new tires were still almost impossible to find), the two
ladies got acquainted. She was interrogating Norma Jeane about who she was,
where from, etc. and Norma Jeane divulged to her that she had a mother who
was just released from a sanatorium for mental disorders, who was staying
in a hotel in Portland, Oregon. At that, the old lady began lecturing me:
"Never mind the childish, foolish ideas to search for gold" — I had the gold
right there with me (Norma Jeane) and she instructed me: "Young man, take
your girl up to Portland to see her mother!"

71

Norma Jeane was looking at me with questioning eyes, as if to ask me if I would drive up to Oregon to see her mother. But I said, "No, let's not chicken out! Let's go to Arizona!" Then she confessed that she was scared to go, and she was scared the day before, too, when the two hoodlums were running after us. But she did not want to spoil my happy, adventurous plans, so she kept silent.

I decided we would not go to Arizona to roam the mountains, but we would take pictures in the sand dunes which were just a few miles from the gas station. And then, afterward, we would go to Oregon. The old lady was right: we had hardly entered the region of the sand dunes when the wind began to blow stronger and stronger. The road was just a one-lane, unpaved road, winding like a snake. Luckily, I could make a U-turn and we returned before the wind created an immense dust storm!

I had consumed a few bottles of beer after we left the old lady and rented a motel room, begging Norma Jeane to take a shower and to relax. And there she was, stark naked, reclining on the bed, reading a newspaper, but our thoughts were extremely perplexing. Neither she nor I wished to start out on a sexual venture. There was a short period of silence, mute nervousness in us both, and I asked her to get dressed. I did not want her to do any favors for me! Love ought to be mutual!

Yosemite   From the lowest part of Southern California, where we started the trip, to Portland, Oregon is easily at least 1200 miles of driving; for the love of Norma Jeane, and to earn her respect, I was driving day and night toward the north. Fantastic what one can endure when young and enthusiastic! I drove all night long in steady pouring rain toward Yosemite, and at daybreak it was snowing very hard as we were slowly driving down into the Yosemite Valley. The large hotel and the lodge in Yosemite were all filled with skiers; no rooms were available. No beds in the dormitory either. Not even cabins nearby; the only cabins available were unheated log cabins, much further away in the woods. Of course, I rented two. I had no choice; we were exhausted. The cabins were simple, small, with just a bed and a small table, but everything was very clean. No bathroom. Her cabin was a few feet away from mine. The outhouses were a few hundred feet away. It was very cold, and although it was only afternoon, we went to bed fully clothed.

During the night, I was awakened by banging on the cabin door. She had something to ask me. She said she was afraid to go to the "john" by herself; she was afraid of the bears, and would I please accompany her there? I remembered my uncle telling me, when I was a child in Transylvania, that wolves, bears, and all wild animals hated loud noises, so I emptied a large can of tomato juice and while Norma Jeane walked with the flashlight to the outhouse, I walked behind her, beating the empty can furiously with a spoon to make as much noise as I could. I chuckle every time I think of that funny "procession" through the snow to the "john" and back to the cabins!

The next morning, she told me she felt very embarrassed. I took her in my arms, hugged her, kissed her, and promised I would make up for it, make her forget that awful night. We went to the lodge and while she took a shower in the dormitory, I bought her a complete winter sports outfit at the gift shop. Two sweaters, ski pants, bright red woolies for undergarments, several kinds of ski bonnets to keep her ears warm, wool socks, ski boots, ski gloves, and a beautiful Indian silver and turquoise concho belt, the kind you only find in the Indian trading posts, way out on the reservations.

By the time she was back from the shower, there was a heap of merchandise on the counter, all for her. There were nearly tears in her eyes, she was so happy! As soon as she put those things on, in her cabin, we left Yosemite. It was much too cold there. Her hands were purple from the cold. It was a great adventure, and funny. I love to reminisce about it.

RUSSIAN CHURCH, NORTHERN CALIF.

Your Crazy Hungarian   A very funny thing happened on the seacoast, somewhere north of San Francisco. I was going to photograph Norma Jeane against an old church built of unpainted wood, but by the time she got ready with her makeup, an old woman ran to us screaming that we were on Russian territory! I could not believe what she was talking about, yet she was dead serious. I thought she must have been drunk or crazy. She was going to whack at me and at Norma Jeane.

The unpleasant behavior of the furious old woman did not abash us for too long. Norma Jeane was laughing in disbelief; I felt I needed some wine to calm myself, and by the time we stopped at a motel, I was rather tipsy. I asked the lady manager in the office for a pair of adjoining single cabins, connected! The lady looked at me, surprised. She looked out the window where my car was parked, and she saw Norma Jeane waiting in it. And she asked me, "Are you two married?" I could not lie, I said, "No". Domineering like a mother, she yelled at me, "Separate cabins!" And she handed me the keys and asked me to register our names. The cabins were five dollars each.

And again, from wanting her, I felt tormented all night and I could hardly sleep. During the night, I sprang to my feet and wrote Norma Jeane a letter, and went to slip it under her door. It amazes me how vividly my mind can remember certain details; I think these were almost the exact words I wrote to her:

In the dead of night, December 1945

Dear sweet Norma Jeane:

It is so painful for a man to stay away from making love, especially when the beloved is right nearby! And maybe she, too, suffers from the same self-denial. But she is too shy to let herself go….

What a pity we are created so shy! What a pleasurable, glorious night we could spend if only we would dare!

The cemeteries are full of corpses and bones who were once alive, and also too shy, too strict, too religious, too morally inclined, even with themselves, to please and to satisfy their true instincts. And they spent perhaps even a lifetime tormenting themselves with lack of loving! Something Nature did not wish them to do! Billions of people have died without having had enough earthly pleasures!

Norma Jeane, love is the only real thing in life. The only thing which really matters! Please come to knock on my door. Please let me love you! I shall never forsake you! I shall always love you!

Your crazy Hungarian, [André]

I pushed the note under her door, knocked a few times to wake her up, and I rushed back to my cabin. But she did not come to knock on my door. The good providence arranged it differently, two nights later.

Inner Norma Jeane   We stopped in Sacramento for an hour to pay a fast
visit to a relative of her Aunt Ana and then we headed north to Eureka and
into Oregon. Norma Jeane was completely awed, spellbound, when we made stops
in the various redwood forests in northern California. There in the forests,
that pretty Hollywood model's Nordic ancestral instinct awoke. I noticed a
great change in her there; she became alive to the surroundings. It seemed
to me as if those were the places where she belonged. She noticed and pointed
out to me the smallest details, like miniature bugs she picked up or the
smallest little flowers hardly visible in the vegetation and the patterns of
the ferns and little brown mushrooms growing at the feet of the giant Sequoia
trees. She went to take a long, solitary walk among the giant trees, despite
the fact that it was raining. Her hands turned blue and purple. She walked
away so far, I was worried she would get lost. By late afternoon I found her
sitting at the base of a giant tree, praying.

Norma Jeane did not pretend to be spiritual — she did not have to; she
was absolutely nobody at that time, just a 19-year-old girl who had just
started out modeling a few weeks before that trip. She was completely sincere
and natural. And it was there, in the forest, that I really fell in love
with her. I saw the perfect kind of wife to last for a lifetime. She was
easy to get along with! She was a delight to travel with! It was wintertime
and daytime was short; I told her we must start early each morning, so she

77

had an alarm clock and she was up before me every morning! She was constantly
in a good mood, very cheerful. She was completely content having just a
basketful of food in the back of the automobile, where she slept sometimes.
Her happiest moments were when she ate cottage cheese with pineapples right
out of the container. The food basket was her little kitchen and if I did not
feel like stopping in a restaurant, it was completely okay with her.
She was a completely uncomplicated young lady!

Alternately, she was quiet and reserved, sometimes very serious, but
never pretentious, never trying to impose her ego on me. And certain little
things impressed her, struck her so funny that she could hardly stop
laughing. She was no movie star at that time, and never even dreamed she
would be some day.

In the forest, I started singing loudly "I love you as I have never loved
before, since first I met you at the village green." Norma Jeane took over
the song from me and sang loud. She had a rather lovely, natural voice. It
became like our team-song, from then on. Ever since, when I sing it, I think
of her and get tears in my eyes each time. When I am in the mood to get sad,
I start singing the song and the vision of sweet Norma Jeane comes back to
me, walking through the cathedral-like beautiful forests in northern
California. And from that afternoon on, I called her "Little Mushroom,"
a nickname for her admiring the mushrooms on the bark of the trees.

HELL'S BELLS !

<u>Hell's Bells!</u>   The idyll in the forest with my "Little Mushroom" turned into a small disaster a couple of hours later. We were both soaking when we resumed the drive, and soon we got to a large group of cabins in the midst of a forest grove. I promptly rented two cabins, side by side, as usual, and unloaded part of the luggage and told Norma Jeane to stay there while I would drive to the nearby service station to take care of the car.

It was already dark when I got back and Norma Jeane wasn't there. The luggage was gone from both cabins, except her toothbrush and a few things in the bathroom. The man in the office could not tell me anything. He said that no dishonesty ever happened there and that they did not even have locks on the cabin doors, only to bolt the lock from the inside!

I was nearly out of my mind. How could she desert me after such a beautiful afternoon in the forest? I was about to drive to the sheriff's when a car drove up, driven by a young fellow, and out hopped Norma Jeane with a large paper bag on her arm, from which she pulled out one of the two bottles of red wine she'd bought. I was shouting at her angrily, asking where she was and why the hell she had left the cabins. And she looked at me horrified as she saw my angry and rude disposition. Then she explained that she walked to the village to buy me wine, cheese, and salami and the grocery clerk drove her back.

The fact was that part of my photo equipment and part of our luggage was stolen from our cabins, the negatives of the beautiful photos I took of her in the forest were gone — forever! And other lovely photos of her — all gone! And one of my valuable cameras also! It seemed like a disaster. I was angry at her for not staying in the cabin until I returned. I spent a tormented night; I did not even think of trying to sleep with her. But in the morning, she greeted me with a cheerful disposition. She never seemed sweeter; she was telling me not to be concerned with the value of the camera lost, nor about the negatives gone, or anything. She kept emphasizing that only half of the luggage was unloaded and stolen, so I still had the rest in the car! And she shouted at me, "Hell's bells, André, cheer up!" I loved hearing her cheerful loud shout, "Hell's bells!" She laughed, because she knew her exclamation seemed funny (otherwise, she would not have used the word "hell"). She was enjoying her own wit, and her laugh was beautiful!

The sheriff took down the case, but the questioning was too embarrassing to answer! I knew the case was hopeless, so there was nothing else to do but leave and not to worry about the loss anymore, nor to blame Norma Jeane. She had nice intentions when she walked to the store to buy me the wine…. The love letter I left under her cabin door the night before must have done something to her mind; the wine she brought back must have been an invitation to something! And fate arranged it that the two bottles of wine she bought were mighty nice to have the next night, and the night after…. Her intuitions were right! We needed the wine; days and days of driving were beginning to be too much.

<u>Portland</u>   Anticipating a happy reunion between Norma Jeane and her mother, we bought various presents (for which I paid, of course), but the actual meeting was a let-down — a dull, rather gloomy event. The hotel was an old mediocre place in the center of Portland. We found her mother in a small room on the top floor. She greeted Norma Jeane with a sad expression, then she sat in the chair near the window and they carried on a slow-paced conversation in a very low, monotonous tone. The lady was aged, thin, expressionless, and void of any emotions while the conversation went on. Norma Jeane was in good spirits and she tried to cheer up her mother, unsuccessfully. Before we went to visit her, I'd failed to question Norma Jeane about her mother, so I had no idea why she was just released from some institution for her mental problems. I recall that during the conversation, her mother put her head into her hands and bent down; there were many rather painful moments like that. It was a dark, cloudy afternoon, the room seemed very gloomy to me, and Norma Jeane looked at me with painful embarrassment. Then, since there was little else to do, we departed. My mind was on my trip and I was eager to reach Timberline Lodge, a wonderful big hotel east of Portland at the foot of Mount Hood.

I am sorry I did not take any pictures of Norma Jeane with her mother, but since I have never liked to get mixed up in other people's relationships, I did not even think of snapping pictures of them in that darkly lit, sad room. I was a young, amorous man! I wanted to be with Norma Jeane; I wanted to be happy!

AT MOUNT HOOD,

IN OREGON,
DEC. 1945

Marry Me!   It was raining while we drove to Mount Hood, Oregon, and the
rain turned into snow when we got to the Timberline Lodge. I went to inquire
for accommodations and there was only one room available, with a double bed.
I went out to the car where Norma Jeane was waiting; she was in a rather
serious mood. She said she could prefer it if we would drive on and find
cabins somewhere in the woods… separate cabins. I felt disappointed, because
I liked that hotel and wanted the comfort there. The opportunity would have
been extraordinary to take pictures of Mount Hood — a beautiful, extinct
volcano — and it's a fantastic place for good skiing. But I obeyed Norma
Jeane and drove down on the narrow, curving road while it was snowing really
hard and dusk was coming. At the junction of that narrow road and the main
highway, there was a place called Government Lodge. The snow was already too
deep and my car could not go any further. We got stuck right in front of the
hotel, as if fate's hand had guided us there purposefully. And in that hotel,
too, there was only one room left available — a room with one double bed
and a bathroom at the end of a long corridor. I came out to inform Norma
Jeane that we had to stay there! It was already darkening. Norma Jeane
smiled at me. She said, "Okay, let's take the room. Let's not worry anymore
about anything!"

A funny thing happened there almost as soon as I registered. On the
ground floor there were slot machines everywhere. I pointed at one slot

machine out of the many and told Norma Jeane in a loud voice that she needed pocket money for Jergen's lotion (that she loved for her skin) and I commanded the slot machine to provide a jackpot for it. The bartender and everybody at the bar were staring at us, perhaps thinking I had gone nuts. I told Norma Jeane to stretch out the bottom of her sweater under the machine. I put the quarter in and pulled the handle, and out gushed a flood of quarters! Everybody cheered.

We had a good dinner and afterward we flipped a coin to decide who would occupy the bathroom first. It wasn't much of a bathroom, just a lousy shower and a toilet. Then we went to bed without the slightest nervousness, as if what was happening was the most natural thing in the world. It was a strange contrast to all the days of amorous emotions I had to fight, and the frustration I went through every night. Finally, we spent the night together, in the same bed! When the lovemaking was over with, Norma Jeane cried in my arms. She was happy, satisfied. And I was holding her, and she was holding me as if I were her child.

You might say, "André, let's hear what it was really like to make love with the future Marilyn Monroe!" But to respect Marilyn's memory, I prefer not to discuss sex. She was a divine, lovely young woman. And said she was never as happy before! She was crying. It was a fantastic, almost supernatural feeling when I fell asleep in bed with Norma Jeane.

84

85

She was hugging me, I was kissing her tears; she said she had never had an orgasm before in her life. And I felt greatly satisfied also, having waited for at least two weeks to make love with her — more than I could possibly endure! Why didn't or couldn't I have made her pregnant? I've asked myself ever since….

Next, when we went down for lunch, it was still snowing hard, and my car was covered with snow. The wife of the owner of the hotel took us for honeymooners, and offered us the best room they had, on the first floor — a wood-paneled wonderful cozy room. We stayed in there for two days while it was still snowing relentlessly. Our short stay there was like being in paradise!

A bizarre event happened there in that room during the first day of our stay. Norma Jeane was manicuring and putting nail polish on her toenails and she lifted her hands in the air to show me her palms, observing how curious it was that in each palm there was a large M. Somewhat childishly, we compared our palms, looking at the lines in them. And there, I told Norma Jeane the story of an old bell-ringer in Transylvania who, in my childhood, had predicted that the two letters "MM" would mean a great deal to me when I grew up. And I told Norma Jeane the story about my meeting the old man while reading a strange old book, and how the old man was preoccupied with one of the pages where the writing began with the two words "memento mori."

FAMILY CIRCLE 1946
MAGAZINE COVER

170

Norma Jeane was fascinated by my story, and we discussed again and again the two Ms in our palms. I told her jovially that the Ms had nothing to do with death — to the contrary, they meant "marry me!" And we pressed our palms together. We hugged and kissed and decided we shall get married as soon as she would get a divorce from her husband. We decided she would go to Las Vegas to get the divorce and we would get married there, right after. From those moments onward, we felt we were engaged. I told Norma Jeane about my wanderings through Transylvania on foot, and having carved many times in the bark of trees the two initials "M.M." I promised her that when we got married, I would buy her a thick, heavy, gold wedding ring, and have the two initials engraved inside the ring, as a memento to remember the prediction of the old bell-ringer. I even took a picture of her palm.

While it was snowing, we stayed in the room all day long, except for a brief hour when I took her out to photograph her in the snow, reading. She was pampering herself, combing her curly hair out again and again at the mirror, and draping herself in the bed sheet, while examining the results in the mirror. A sexy little "vampire" she was, glamorizing herself with the bed sheet, as if it were an expensive evening gown! If only I had the foresight to photograph her in that room as she was glamorizing herself on the bed naked, quite uninhibited. The future Marilyn Monroe was there, in that room! A sex symbol was incubating that afternoon!

<u>Idyll Interrupted</u>   I had the strong urge to call my fortuneteller friend in New York, to tell him about Norma Jeane — that I got all of a sudden engaged to that girl he predicted I would meet and fall in love with in Hollywood! I called and called my studio all night, without luck. When I called him at his other place, I got the shocking news, the surprise of my life. The man at the desk told me that my friend was killed in an automobile accident while speeding on a rainy night. He died instantly.

The idyll, the romance between Norma Jeane and me was drastically interrupted, even severed. If I had not phoned New York, who knows where else I could have taken Norma Jeane and where the trip would have ended. If only I hadn't made that phone call so soon, I could have continued photographing and loving Norma Jeane!

The last thing I remember of her in that hotel room is that while I was on the phone to New York, she was painting her fingernails and her toenails bright red. And she was showing me her beautiful legs in a very enticing way, not like a girl who is ready to get married to a man who loved the rugged outdoors and shunned the phony façade of Hollywood.

The news about the death of my friend changed my plans immediately. I was worried about leaving my studio in New York unattended. It was fortunate that the snow stopped, the road got cleared by the big snowplows, and we were on our way back to Los Angeles, to take Norma Jeane home. The trip was long and

Norma Jeane was often carsick and dizzy. She had to sleep a lot to fight it! Later in her life, when she became Marilyn Monroe, constantly in demand for work or to give interviews, and was late to show up to work at Fox, she used the excuse that she was ill. Nobody believed her. I did believe it! Because I remember and still remember, that despite her cheerful, enthusiastic attitude to life, sometimes her moods changed. The long drives tired her mind; she said she was carsick and needed sleep.

I suppose I must have confused Norma Jeane on that trip. Sometimes the issue was that we would get married, travel and do things together, and other times it was my boasting that I would find gold and become very rich, and then I contradicted all that with my predictions that she would become famous and successful in the movies. So all that must have been confusing to her. Then, on occasion, when we discussed the future, I asked her what she would really like to become. To my surprise, she said a lawyer! I asked why, and she said she would like to do good, to defend the helpless and victimized! That was a beautiful statement.

We discussed that she would come to live with me in New York, in my studio on 58th Street and 5th Avenue which I would decorate beautifully starting as soon as I returned to New York, and she would go to Columbia University to study law. This wasn't just talk — we meant it!

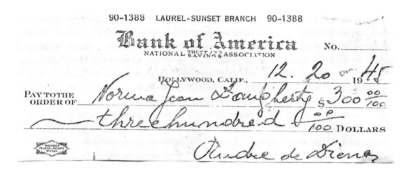

<u>Hollywood</u>   As I look back, indeed it was confusing, sort of making plans for our future marriage. But what happened an hour later gave a good blow to it all. We were approaching Los Angeles and entered Hollywood by Laurel Canyon. It was evening, and we reached Sunset Boulevard at the 8000 block, where the Garden of Allah was, where we had first met a month before. I suggested having coffee at Schwab's Pharmacy, a famous drugstore which was like a landmark in Hollywood. For nearly fifty years, it was the gathering place of a potpourri of movie personalities in Hollywood, and show biz people who came here to try their luck in Hollywood; movie extras, male and female, young actors and actresses, talent scouts, agents, handsome wolves, etc. Even the famous columnist Sidney Skolsky stopped by every day; the place was his information-gathering source for several decades. To Norma Jeane, I suggested going to Schwab's, because I was going to write out a check for the two weeks she traveled with me, a hundred dollars a week, plus I added a hundred dollars more to be nice to her. And she would sign the usual model's release. That way of doing business was a routine, customary thing for me. Even with my new fiancée it had to be so!

Norma Jeane didn't know anything about Schwab's drugstore, as she had never been there before, and I thought it was be nice to take her there. But it turned out that I took my darling little "lamb" right into a lion's den. Hardly a few moments passed after I gave her the check and she signed

94

the release, when a photographer I knew came over to us saying something like this: "André, I must congratulate you! You know how to pick pretty girls! Who is this delightful creature, would you please introduce me to her? I would like to photograph her someday." And the photographer and Norma Jeane engaged in conversation. The photographer started bragging about what a great photographer he was and what beautiful photographs he would take of her. The truth was that as a photographer, he was just okay, but as a seducer of women he had a great reputation in Hollywood. Norma Jeane was smiling, happy, very nice to him, and willingly wrote down her phone number for him. She told him she would call him in a few days and would be very happy to pose for him!

It was like a thunderbolt had struck me. I got a fantastic shock, seeing my beloved Norma Jeane nearly flirting and giving her phone number to the photographer so willingly. Of course, I felt jealous, but controlled my rage and revulsion. I was shocked that my newfound sweetheart, my future wife, was so delighted to give her phone number to a total stranger! The shock awakened me from the dream, from the illusion… from the puppy-love we built on the trip…. We were back in Hollywood! And the reality was that she was just a model whom I hired to pose for me! And then, at the drugstore, she was free again to pursue her career, to do as she pleased! Indeed, even though she had said nothing to me about wanting to be in the movies, Norma Jeane was just another pretty girl in Hollywood who wanted to make it in the movies, and I was just a girl-crazy photographer who fell in love with her!

Suddenly, my mind got illuminated by the truth, that certain relationships are like castles of cards, collapsing at any moment, by the slightest touch. But now, thinking of it, I realize that the trip home was a long ordeal and we were both tired from driving a thousand miles without interruption, so Norma Jeane found it refreshing to be greeted by a man who flattered her so strongly! Besides, I know it was meant to be so. She was nice to me, too, from the first moment she met me. So she was nice to that photographer, and nice to many, many people she met afterward. That is the natural course of life! It was a good thing I did not show my jealousy. I took her home to Aunt Ana in West Los Angeles, and we parted in good spirits, agreed to write, and planned to get married after her divorce sometime in the middle of the following year, 1946.

<u>Nothing Would Stop Her</u>   During the months that followed my engagement
with Norma Jeane, through the first part of 1946, she and I corresponded
regularly and spoke on the phone also. But it was she who phoned most of
the time — collect, of course — and usually the conversation ended with
her letting me know that she was broke. I remember her crying in the phone,
loudly enough for me to hear, about being broke, and the conversation always
ended with me promising to wire her by Western Union — right away — twenty-
five or fifty dollar sums. I did that quite a few times. Poor thing, she
had a hard time getting started in her career as a model.

Then summer 1946 was approaching, and Norma Jeane went to Las Vegas to
get divorced from her husband, James Dougherty. I contributed some money
to her expenses, and it was agreed that we would get married in that little
chapel she liked in Las Vegas.

I phoned Norma Jeane in Los Angeles to tell her she could leave for Las
Vegas and instructed her in which hotel to meet me. I told her how wonderfully
happy I felt that at last we were getting married. Disaster struck me in
those moments: in a sweet, apologetic voice, Norma Jeane said, "André, please
don't come, I can't marry you! I want to become an actress!" She said she had
thought it over and her career was more important! She wanted to get into the
movies! The news shocked me, but I took it calmly and told her I would come
to Los Angeles anyway and that I would phone her when I arrived.

I drove hundreds of miles without rest to reach Hollywood and when I arrived, I phoned Norma Jeane again. She said she would meet me at Sunset and Vine, in front of the NBC studios, at 1 p.m. I waited there at least 2 hours but she didn't show up. Then, jealous, enraged, disillusioned, and feeling cheated and betrayed, I drove to her apartment on South 3rd Street in Santa Monica. As I was parking the car in front of the building, I saw a man coming out and I had a strong, intuitive feeling that he had just left Norma Jeane's apartment. I backed my car away a short distance and watched the man drive away, then I waited a few minutes or so and then went to ring her doorbell. Norma Jeane opened the door and gazed at me, ashen white and speechless. She wore a black lacy sort of nightgown — somewhat torn — and there were empty wine bottles and empty glasses on the table behind her, movie scripts, phonograph records in confusion, the bed all messed up, and a large bouquet of flowers in a vase. I stood there, smiling, sizing up the delightfully disorderly room and sensing what must have been going on there during the previous hours. Norma Jeane was extremely embarrassed. I took her tenderly in my arms, kissed her cheeks, pressed my cheek against hers, and I consoled her, asking her not to be so embarrassed….

I felt guilty for surprising her. She was sniffling for a while, her cheeks were wet with tears, but she regained her composure and soon she was in her usual cheerful mood. We agreed that our marriage was over with.

But so what? We would remain friends! I promised that I would never be jealous or possessive in any way from then on, and that I would never come to visit her unannounced! My sweet Norma Jeane was smiling again. I even made her laugh, when I told her she made the right decision not to marry a domineering sex-maniac Hungarian like me!

I remained in California for a few more months after that afternoon in 1946. I remember I did ask Norma Jeane whether that man who left her apartment when I arrived was any use to her, to advance her career. And she said, "YES!" I knew who the man was, someone very important in Hollywood who slept with many beautiful girls. So I asked Norma Jeane what he had done for her. She handed me a clipping from the newspaper. In the photo, she sat at his side in a nightclub. It was then that I felt nothing would stop Norma Jeane from getting ahead in her career. It became clear to me that she was a true product of Hollywood; her mother worked for the movie studios, she was born and raised there and she had no other culture than what she absorbed in her childhood from the atmosphere of Hollywood. Her destiny was not at all with me.

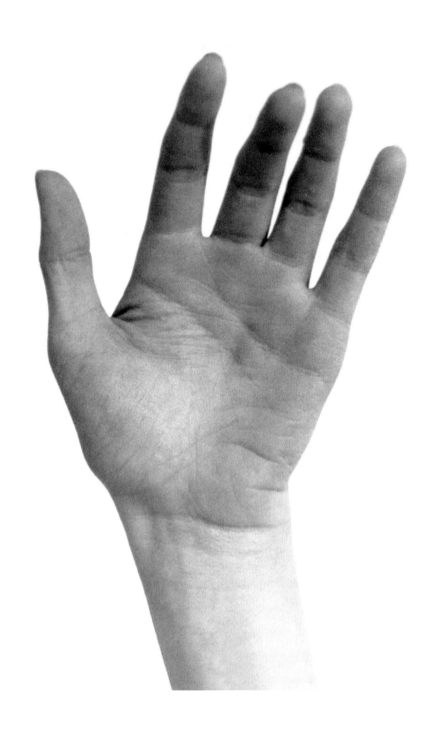

100

M. M.

<u>M.M.</u>   During the summer of 1946, just at the onset of Labor Day, again, Norma Jeane called me to say she had important news to tell me, and she asked me to come to her apartment. When I got there, she came right to the subject: "Guess what, I have a new name!" With a pencil, slowly, carefully, she wrote her new name on a sheet of paper: MARILYN MONROE. And she emphasized the two M initials in an almost calligraphic way! I have never forgotten, through all these years, my big surprise when I stood there, behind her, watching her writing her name…. There was something almost supernatural about how beautifully she wrote the large capital Ms. How much I've regretted since that day when Norma Jeane, or rather Marilyn, wrote down her name for me, that I did not have the foresight to keep that sheet of paper.

From now on, I shall refer to Norma Jeane as Marilyn. I had to get used to her new name right away. After she signed her new name, the conversation went on for a while about the certain mysteries of life one cannot explain, like she so cleverly finding a name with two Ms, especially the name "Marilyn," because in Portland, Oregon, just a half year previously, I'd told her that the two large Ms in her palm meant "Marry Me," and now, even that resembles her new name — "Marry" became "Marilyn!" We were discussing how amazingly the subconscious mind goes to work and concocts decisions, because of previous impressions or suggestions!

1946

214

I remembered that there was a long weekend ahead, and I suggested that we visit a few of the beautiful California Missions. Marilyn had nothing better to do for the weekend. So we took off in my car to visit, first, the Mission in San Juan Capistrano, and afterward others, further down, and one in San Diego.

Marilyn loved the missions. She got exalted everywhere, and whenever we passed by a small cell, where padres once slept on primitive wooden beds with just a thin mattress, jokingly I remarked to Marilyn that we should remain in the mission after it closed, and we could bathe in the fountains outside and sleep in the beds the padres slept in a hundred or more years before! And I said to Marilyn rather loudly, "Let's stay, let's go to bed here tonight!" People around heard me and smiled, making some funny remarks; but sweet Marilyn did not get angry at me, she laughed goodheartedly and remarked, indeed, how lovely it might be to spend a night in an old adobe room by candlelight.

That evening, all the way down to San Diego, all the motel cabins were filled up. None available! Marilyn, exhausted, was sleeping in the backseat of the car. She did not care where she slept; she always trusted me, and I never failed to take good care of her.

102

    <u>Hollywood Memorial</u>   One day, still in 1946, I was driving through Hollywood, taking Marilyn to a movie studio on Gower Street and as we passed the Hollywood Memorial Cemetery on Santa Monica Boulevard, I suggested we ought to make a quick tour inside the cemetery where many famous movie personalities were buried, such as Rudolph Valentino, Norma Talmadge, Marion Davies, Douglas Fairbanks, Sr., and many others. Marilyn didn't particularly care for the suggestion, but when I told her that the cemetery was just behind Paramount Studios on Melrose Avenue and that Rudolph Valentino was resting in his coffin just a few hundred feet away from where she might be making a film someday, her interest was aroused.

    Marilyn became very silent when I guided her through the marble corridors of the vast mausoleum to the place where Rudolph Valentino was resting entombed in the wall behind a white marble slab. And we discussed what fantastic fame he achieved and what a fantastic event his sudden death became in 1926. I remarked to Marilyn that she was born the same year, 1926, and maybe she was born to replace and continue his legendary career! And maybe she, too, will become famous!

    I recall Marilyn answering something to the effect that since he died so young, it wasn't worth it at all! And I said to her, "What more can you ask? He became immortal!" And Marilyn responded that she would prefer a long, happy life. Then she lifted a rose out from one of the urns on both sides of the bronze plaque bearing his name, and I recall having chided her that it wasn't a nice thing to steal flowers from the dead…. And Marilyn answered something like: "I am sure he would be very pleased to know that a lonesome girl took the flower home to keep it next to her bed." (Strange thing is, now I'm the one who goes to visit Marilyn's remains in the cemetery, and steals flowers from her to bring home and have them in a glass next to my bed.)

After we went out, I suggested that she ought not to go to her appointment at the studio, but instead I would read to her from a large quotation book which was always with me in the trunk of my car. We sat on the lawn, right at the spot where Tyrone Power is buried. We read about life, love, happiness, fame, vanity, women, death, and other things, but it was the word "fame" that caught her attention the most. She made me underline some quotes she liked most. I still have the book, and I copy out a few she liked and include them here:

"A woman's fame is the tomb of her happiness." - L.E. Landon

"Live for something! Be good and leave behind you a monument of virtue that the storm of time can never destroy. Write your name in kindness, love, and mercy on the hearts of the thousands you come in contact with, year by year, and you will never be forgotten. Your name, your deeds will be as legible on the hearts you leave behind as the stars on the brow of evening. Good deeds will shine as the stars of heaven." - Chalmers

"What is fame? The advantage of being known by people of whom you yourself know nothing, and for whom you care as little." - Stanislaus

Then she suddenly decided that she'd had enough poetry and philosophy and she should go to her appointment, even if she was already very late. I'm sure it was the word "fame" that prompted her to leave me! A pang of jealousy gripped me, and I yelled at her something like, "Are you going to lay that producer?!" And she angrily answered, "Yes! Why not?" And we hurled at each other a few more angry words. But the bad mood was over soon and I dropped her on Gower Street. It was agreed maybe we'd go to the seashore some day, and read some more…. She said she needed to educate herself and that I ought to bring along some unusual books.

But in my mind it was otherwise. I was thinking of going back to New York to mind my business…. I was still in love with her, but I felt the relationship became hopeless for me. She just liked me to sustain her ego, to feed her with my constant enthusiasm for life, and for all the pep talks I gave her.

226

"THE SPRINGTINE OF
LIFE "

<u>The End of Everything</u>   Soon after that day in the cemetery, I entered
a second-hand bookshop I passed by. I suppose I reacted to Marilyn's
suggestion that I ought to bring an <u>unusual</u> kind of book! I was browsing from
shelf to shelf, having absolutely no fixed idea of what I wanted. I was about
to leave when my eyes fell on an old leather-bound volume. I pulled it out.
The cover looked worn and torn, and handwritten pages were loose and about to
fall out. There were small, very old engravings pasted on the pages here and
there of famous people, like Pascal, Boccaccio, Tennyson, Edgar Allan Poe,
and small engravings of landscapes from Italy and Germany and Scotland. The
book dealer, with a gesture of nonchalance and lack of concern, said that I
could have the book for fifteen dollars. I paid and hurriedly left, fearing
he might change his mind, declaring he had made a mistake; the book was worth
far more!

I went to a restaurant to sit and sit and study what I had bought. I
read the beautiful, handwritten poems and studied the pictures. It was an
album a lady started in Scotland around 1830. In it, she wrote her thoughts,
her own poems, and poems she'd copied of famous people. I called Marilyn to
tell her I'd found something very unusual, a book I must show her, share with
her, so we can read it together. That agreement we had made in the cemetery
that we would go out to the seashore and read some more could come through,
due to the book I'd found. A few days later, Marilyn and I were far out at

" *TIME* "

the seashore, north of Malibu on a deserted beach, where we read the pages
of the book with a magnifier to decipher the small but beautiful handwriting.

I remember so well which poems Marilyn loved. She was nearly in tears
several times. Marilyn wasn't the kind of person who would have tears in
her eyes easily, no matter how deep the emotion. But the poems touched her
immensely. She was holding herself back from bursting into sobs while she
was reading a poem entitled, "Lines on the Death of Mary." She told me that
it fit her, but the lady who wrote it forgot to put the "lyn" after the name
"Mary!" I remarked that a few days before in the cemetery she told me she
preferred a long, happy life and now she was saying she would not live long….
The poem we were reading about the death of Mary was a prediction for her
that she would die young!

The reading ended and I began taking pictures of her, one by one,
depicting the moods she interpreted for me. An entire spectrum of life,
depicting happiness, pensiveness, introspection, serenity, sadness,
torment, distress — I even asked her to show me what "death" looked like
in her imagination. She threw a blanket over her head; that was how she
interpreted it.

The photo that followed was her own idea. She told me to get ready with
my camera because she was going to show me what her own death would look
like — someday. She looked down with a very sordid expression, pointing out

112

" THE END OF EVERYTHING ! "

to me that the picture's meaning would be "THE END OF EVERYTHING." I quickly snapped the photo. I asked her why she pictured her death so sordid, so gloomy, instead of giving me an expression of calm smile as if dying was nothing more than going from one world into another, a beautiful transfiguration. But Marilyn insisted that was the way she imagined her death.

The next photo was my idea. I asked her to lie down on the ground to show me what she would look like when dead and again, I snapped the photo. It was already late afternoon; we were taking photos on the top of a cliff, overlooking the ocean. The scenery and the light of the setting sun were magnificent; I was in the mood to take many more poetic photos of her, but after I took the photo of her face simulating death, suddenly she sprang to her feet and, part seriously, part wittily, she began shouting, screaming at me, "Hell's bells, look what you've made me do to my hair! I have a date tonight!" And she was shaking her head and taking out the pieces of straw that stuck in her hair. I calmed her down by promising that someday I would do a beautiful album with her pictures, accompanied by all kinds of lovely quotations from my book, and even some of the poems she liked in that album we'd just read together. She made a strange remark, saying, "André, do not publish those photos now, wait until I die!" And I asked her, how does she know she will die before me? After all, I was 12 years older than her. And in a sad, low-toned voice, she said she thought she would die before me.

"HAPPINESS"

But that took only moments; soon she was gay and cheerful again, looking forward to her dinner date, and she was urging me to hurry, hurry, pack everything into the car and leave!

I can't forget how sad I felt that evening while driving back to Hollywood — to be on time for <u>her</u> dinner date. Marilyn was no longer the lovely Norma Jeane I once knew, only a few months before! She was going out to have dinner at Romanoff's in Beverly Hills, and I felt terribly, terribly put down, belittled, and left behind.

I was packing my bags that night to return to New York, when the phone rang. It was her! She said she had a miserable evening with a lousy guy — a swindler, someone who wanted <u>her</u> to pay for the dinner! But we reasoned that since she had exposed herself to a career in Hollywood, she ought to be strong enough to cope with everything that comes along — good or bad. But I did not inquire as to what happened. Instead, she suggested we ought to go out the following night and that I ought to photograph her during the night. In a vindictive mood, I told her, "No. I am leaving for New York," and that I wasn't interested in her anymore! I did go back to New York the next day.

114

118

Tobey Beach   After a long time away from Marilyn, I suddenly spent an extremely happy and productive day with her during the summer of 1949. This is what happened:

I was driving from New York to Binghamton, NY to see a client. Before I reached Binghamton, I drove through a lovely wooded section of Pennsylvania and decided to stay the night at a motel near the woods. But for some reason, I did not sleep well; bizarre dreams woke me up in the middle of the night and I simply could not go back to sleep. After a while I said to myself "heck, I'll get up and drive to Binghamton where I can continue to sleep in a hotel."

When I stepped out from my cabin in the dead of night, thick fog shrouded everything around me. I started to drive, and drove and drove slowly and cautiously. After a couple of hours I realized I was driving in the wrong direction — back to New York! Tired and exasperated by my mistake, I found the excuse that it was fate's will! And I drove home to New York, thinking I would make the trip again soon.

Was that just a coincidence, or was it a premonition or telepathic communication with Marilyn back in New York? No sooner than I woke up from a good long sleep, the phone was ringing, and without any preliminary greetings of any kind, Marilyn was shouting on the phone, "André, let's take pictures again! Let's make history!" And she explained that she had just arrived,

her first ever trip to New York. She was on a nationwide trip to publicize "Love Happy," in which she had a small but nice part with Groucho Marx (who liked her very much), and now, at long last, her career as an actress was really, really going to begin the right way! I could tell by her voice that she was happy, very excited, exhilarated! She was shouting, "Let's take pictures tomorrow! I give you my entire day!" And she asked me, "Do you have a nice bathing suit I can wear?"

She was staying at the Hotel Pierre, only a few blocks from my studio. The Pierre is one of the classiest hotels in New York. I knew she could not afford such an expensive place; she had a small contract guaranteeing about 100 dollars per week, and she'd only had two bit parts in movies…. So whom did she come to New York with, to stay at the Pierre? But I wasn't nosy, I could not have cared less who she stayed with at the Pierre or who she made love with! The important thing was that she asked me to photograph her again — in a bathing suit. It was, in fact, bathing suit pictures of pretty girls that I had been going to sell in Binghamton! The coincidence was amazing! Marilyn had arrived just in time! And she insisted I photograph her! And my sweet darling love, Norma Jeane, because of whom I once almost killed myself, was on the telephone, almost ordering me to spend the day with her on her first day in New York City! We agreed to spend the following day at the seashore out on Long Island on a deserted beach.

© . ANDRE DE Dienes

I rushed to the department stores and bought two bathing suits (one white, one pink), two parasols (one white, the other red with white polka dots), and several silk scarves, with the express idea that after we were through with the bathing suit pictures, I would make her take off the bathing suit and cover herself with the scarf and dance for me with the scarf tight against her body in the wind; while shooting the fast action pictures, the wind would blow the scarf away and I could capture a few fantastic action shots of her in the nude! I also prepared a basketful of food and included a bottle of brandy which was strictly for me — to calm my nerves after the picture-taking session was over.

It was only 6 or 7 o'clock in the morning when she called again the next day, saying she'd slept really well and was full of energy and ready to go! I can never forget those moments when my sweet, innocent Norma Jeane stepped out of the elevator at the Pierre that morning. She was transformed into a magnificent, elegant young woman, with great poise! Sophisticated like I had never seen her before, her eyes were sparkling with happiness. She was the most dazzling beauty in the world! And I could feel that she wanted me to know that the magical times of her life were about to begin.

It was a really hot, humid summer day and Jones Beach was already crowded when we got there. I always hated taking pictures of models when there were people around, but to work among a crowd, that was impossible for me! I felt

125

335

dismayed and we drove on further to a place called Tobey Beach, which was also full of people. I was pondering what to do when luck came to my help. The wind began to blow, clouds were billowing, lightning struck, and the crowd, fearing the coming of an immense storm, hastily packed up and left the beach. Honestly, it was as if God had swept the beach clean just for Marilyn and me. Hardly anybody remained, yet it hardly rained at all, then the storm calmed down and disappeared completely and by mid-afternoon the entire beach was nearly deserted. It was like a miracle! Nobody came back. I could take pictures in peace for a few hours in the late afternoon sunlight I loved so much for my photography.

I had taken along my small, gray Persian cat because Marilyn had insisted the kitty cat would be lonesome in my studio. The little cat was roaming around on the wet sand, amused by the waves of the ocean, and Marilyn was dancing gaily for the cat. I directed her to pretend the cat was a handsome young man and she was to entice him. And to look right into my lens, because the whole world would be looking at her later! When I photograph somebody, I talk a great deal, almost continuously; I give directions, I relentlessly invent stories to keep up the interest of my subject. With Marilyn, I asked her to flirt with my camera, to entice me with all her sex appeal and to move as fast as possible, without any posing, while I was clicking the shutter over and over. And I spoke to Marilyn about she being a new Lillian Russell

and I began teaching her how to walk onto a stage. She was holding the parasol and I told her that she was Lillian, the great stage actress, and over and over I made Marilyn walk towards me with more and more self-assurance and sex appeal, pretending she was walking onstage! I took at least two dozen shots of her like that. Marilyn was extremely cooperative, patient, eager to please me and eager to learn! Out of a little idea and imagination I created an enormous enthusiasm for both of us that afternoon, and repeatedly we told each other that we were going to make history! And I told her my pictures of her would last forever. It was a happy afternoon for both of us.

There was only one minor little problem — the cup of the bathing suit had wire in it and it was badly scratching Marilyn's bosoms. Her skin was all red on her breasts. She suffered a lot, but did not complain at all, and she danced in the scarf too, as I had planned it, but the wind did not blow it away from her body. I did not mind not taking nudes of her; I knew I could find plenty of other models for that purpose. We felt happy; there was no way I would have wanted to change the mood of that gloriously happy day — by wanting to photograph her nude. I had love and respect for my beautiful Marilyn. I felt fortunate and grateful that she chose me to be with, for a full day, before she began her publicity appearance in New York City.

The photographs I took of her that day in 1949 represent a young Marilyn. The poses are casual, because that was the kind of photography I was very

129

active in creating in those years. I did not care how the wind blew her hair; I even liked her hair to be all messed up. But her image as movie star became different. It became how the public had seen her on the screen, in her movies. That image was created at the Hollywood studios, done by hairdressers, make-up men, etc. A far more glamorized kind of photography, sometimes too artificial for my taste. I preferred — for my pictures — a very casual Marilyn.

The next day Marilyn gave the first and most important interview of her career. The press literally mobbed her, adored her! And from that day onward, her name was mentioned almost every day in the newspapers all over the world — the craze for Marilyn Monroe had started!

Dienes

134

ANDRE DE DIEN...

138

141

147

148

153

154

Dienes

157

158

AT THE ICE CREAM PARLOR

Unexpected Visitor   During the latter part of 1950, I decided to give
up living in New York for good. The paintings, art and antiques that had
taken me years to accumulate brought me a few thousand dollars at auction,
and with a new Cadillac, my cameras, books, and my gray Persian cat, I left
New York. After I got to Los Angeles, I went to see a real estate agent
and explained frankly that I had eight thousand dollars to put down on
a small house, somewhere on the hillside, not too far from Sunset Strip.
I was shown only three houses and for a very peculiar reason I decided on
one immediately. My choice was swift and final. The house was new, not even
finished, a small modern ranch-type house with a long carport. I could see
the city below from the small yard in front of the house. I told the agent
that as soon as I gave him the down payment, he should let me move in right
away, before the deal even went through escrow.

It sounds glamorous that I bought a house in Hollywood with Marilyn
living not too far from me, but I hastily inform the reader that much of the
adjacent hills were undeveloped land, covered with tall brush, which provided
refuge to all kinds of rodents, lizards, spiders, scorpions, and snakes
of several varieties. Every night small foxes and coyotes came to my yard
looking for food. I lived only a few hundred feet from Sunset Boulevard,
where famous movie stars gathered every night, but the hillside around me
was dark and undeveloped!

AT FOX STUDIO'S MAKEUP DEPT. 604
WITH "GLORIA" THE HAIRDRESSER

I got busy photographing nudes, because I had an immediate market for
them. Meanwhile, Marilyn was busy with her career. Occasionally, she visited
me unexpectedly. I respected and treasured the joyful, occasional visits
Marilyn paid me during her stardom. Usually, when she felt unhappy, very
low in morale, unexpectedly she rang at my door. She came by taxi and left
by taxi.

She came to complain and to discuss some of her problems and even to ask
my advice about trifles. Then, she cooked a meal and washed the dishes. Each
of her sporadic visits was like a little present to me. Usually, as soon as
she arrived, I opened a bottle of French Beaujolais wine and I drank,
purposely, because I did not want to continue cerebral conversations for
too long, or to engage in any of my jealous outbursts. I became exhilarated,
intoxicated, because I wanted her to listen to my favorite operatic arias
from the stacks of records I had of Puccini - Tosca, La Bohème, Madame
Butterfly, Manon Lescaut - and many others. I shed tears of joy and sadness,
and one time I poured red wine on her feet and kissed them passionately,
aroused by the gloriously happy music from the first part of Verdi's La
Traviata. And later, when in the last act Violetta was dying, I was crying
and kept pouring red wine on her feet and messed up the rug with the wine.
She laughed and said I was completely mad! But she was happy, pleased,
contented, satisfied! Nobody in the world knew where she was during those

162

few hours. But only rarely could she escape her reality. Here, with me, it was as if she were on a desert island, in complete isolation from the outside.

Only once did the phone ring while she was with me, and an angry female voice I immediately recognized was asking for her. It was Marilyn's acting coach, Natasha Lytess, who dominated Marilyn's career in those years. I said Marilyn wasn't with me, but she shouted at me not to lie! She said she knew she was in my house! I can never forget that occasion. Marilyn and I were lying side by side on the living room rug, both of us transfixed, spellbound by the beautiful soprano voice singing Mimi's aria, "Si, mi chiamano Mimi" from the first act of La Bohème. And I was telling Marilyn in my wonderfully delirious state of mind that not in a thousand years, in fact, never again will there be another composer like Puccini. Marilyn herself was in tears, moved by the music, when the ringing of the phone and the harsh voice of Natasha interrupted us. I screamed at Marilyn for having been so stupid as to let the woman know where she was that afternoon. Marilyn left me in haste, greatly worried.

163

165

166

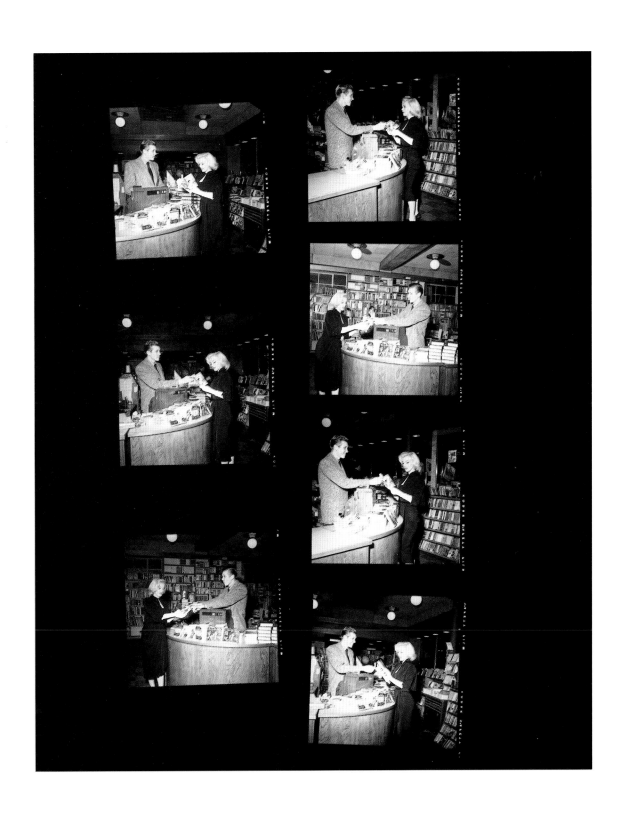

169

Bel Air Hotel   In 1949, Marilyn had posed nude for photographer Tom Kelley, because she needed the fifty dollars he paid for it. She never told me about it, but the truth came out three years later, in 1952. Ironically, I was with her when the story appeared in the newspapers that Marilyn had posed in the nude. Here I shall reminisce about it:

By late 1952, Marilyn had become an extremely successful actress. She was making one picture after another. I got a phone call from my agent in New York that Pageant magazine wanted a photo layout of the "Blonde Heat," as they called her. Roy Craft, the clever publicity man who had done a great deal to make Marilyn's fame an immense phenomenon, arranged for the sitting. Marilyn told him she and I were bosom friends and we wanted to be alone the day I would photograph her, that we didn't want any hairdressers, wardrobe ladies, or make-up men around us while we photographed. Marilyn's wish was a command — we had our privacy. I went to her bungalow at the Bel Air Hotel in Stone Canyon, an exclusive, beautiful place in a secluded canyon west of Beverly Hills. We started photographing about ten in the morning. Marilyn looked extremely lovely. She was in the happiest mood I had ever seen her. Then the phone rang.

I rushed to it and asked Marilyn not to touch it. We were going to take photographs all day and didn't want to be disturbed by anybody. I took many photos of her all morning and the phone kept ringing but she did not answer.

She was extremely cooperative and greatly stimulated. I had a delightful time photographing her and it was a rather unusual experience for me and for her, too, I guess, because she knew she was a great movie star and no longer my little Norma Jeane, not a girl whom I almost married! Yet we felt excessively comfortable with each other. She knew I respected and admired her and she had complete faith in my photography. No matter how I wished to pose her, she obeyed and all the pictures we took were delightful. There was absolutely no nervousness for any reason whatsoever. Only the phone's ringing bugged me, but I ordered her not to touch it!

I took pictures of her inside the bungalow and out on the patio, and by late afternoon she was taking a bubble bath. Afterward I began photographing her with a towel at the fireplace. She was in a bewitching mood! She had nothing on under the white towel, and mischievously she was opening and closing the towel, letting me see her nude for a split second, as if signaling to me that this was the occasion for me to photograph her nude — if I wanted to. These photos at the fireplace were to be the last photos of the day and we were planning to go out afterward to the most fancy restaurant, the most expensive place in Hollywood — Chasen's. Marilyn began insisting that she pay for dinner and for once I should let her be the boss! I told her we'd flip a coin. The phone rang again and rang and rang, and finally Marilyn picked it up. She kept listening and listening and gradually

172

173

her expression turned frightened, practically horrified. She said something like, "Yes, I will, I will," and hung up the receiver. The change in her mood was incredible. She was staggering away from the phone like someone who is ill, dizzy, ready to faint. I asked her what was wrong and she said she couldn't tell me. She said I had to leave her alone as she had to go to the studio at once to explain something. Even in those moments of distress she was so nice to me,she said I ought to order drinks for myself, and dinner, and charge it to her. I felt sad for her, and confused. I packed my equipment and left.

Days later, I found out what was the cause of her great distress. It was her studio that had called all afternoon; it was one of the executives at Fox who wanted her to come in at once, to explain the nude calendar which she had posed for. The story had just come out in the newspapers and the executives at Fox were worried her career might be totally ruined! A few evenings later, she came over to my house to look over the photos and I showed her all the lovely shots I had taken that day. She loved all the photos, she crossed out only one, and to reassure her I took the scissors and cut that negative to bits.

The nude calendar did not ruin her career. To the contrary! The write-ups about it in the newspapers coast-to-coast gave her even more publicity! And the public sympathized with her, thus her future fame was even more assured. In fact, I always suspected that all the brouhaha about the nude photo was a clever publicity stunt; Marilyn's publicity was always a stunning thing.

179

183

184

188

192

"Sadness"

<u>Beverly Hills at Night</u>   One late night, Marilyn phoned me and said she couldn't sleep. She proposed that we go take pictures of her somewhere in a dark alley in Beverly Hills. She would pose sad and lonely! I hopped out of bed, gathered my equipment, and we went to take pictures all night long. I had no flashlight, but as they say, necessity is the mother of invention; I lit Marilyn with the headlights of my car! Was she just playing a melodrama in those pictures, or was she conscious that something was wrong in her life, or that something tragic would happen to her?

196

199

200

44S

44·5

WITH
NATASHA
LYTESS,

<u>LIFE Magazine Assignment</u>   I would be lying if I gave the impression
to the reader that my involvement with Marilyn was just a lovey-dovey affair.
Far from it — I had quite a few clashes with her. What comes to me most
readily goes back to the early 50s while she was rising to great fame.
I had an acting assignment from LIFE magazine to photograph Marilyn with
her drama coach, Natasha Lytess. The scene was to be an acting lesson in
Marilyn's house in the heart of Beverly Hills. No sooner had I started
taking pictures when everything went wrong.

First, Natasha had a good fight with Marilyn about something I did not
know of. Then the bad mood they had created influenced me and I started
complaining that I simply hated the ensemble Marilyn was wearing. That
blouse, which covered her completely, and that long, unattractive skirt
which went almost down to her ankles — Marilyn was all covered up! And
I even hated her formal hairdo. I wanted to photograph her sexy, very
glamorous, provocative, very desirable to the minds of men who love women
with sex appeal. I wasn't shy at all about my opinions, and suggested that
Marilyn take off all her clothes and stand there, facing Natasha, wearing
only her short black slip, with her hair messed up. There should be action
going on for my pictures! Marilyn should make real dramatic movements! But
Natasha had other thoughts. She was a cultured and very serious European
woman and a domineering sort of person. She wanted to impose all her ego

on Marilyn, and Marilyn was also, deep in her instincts, a very serious person, so she responded to Natasha's wishes and suggestions.

Marilyn would have been willing to take off her clothes and pose in her slip, but Natasha did not like my ideas. She was shouting that Marilyn should become a dramatic actress and not a sex-bobble! And I yelled back, reminding her that Marilyn was becoming famous because of her sex appeal! For once, I became a raging mad photographer. I packed my equipment and left, screaming that I did not want to associate with hypocrites and that I would never see any of them ever again! Of course, I was wrong; I should have continued photographing and I could have taken any kind of photos I wanted of Marilyn later that day. Instead, I got Marilyn angry at me!

That was just the beginning of other incidents between Marilyn and me of a very personal nature. Once, during a discussion, I shouted at her that she had ruined my life, that I could have continued to be a very successful commercial photographer had it not been that I fell in love with her so stupidly! And Marilyn shouted back something like, "Who asked you to fall in love with me? I wanted to become an actress, not your maid, not your whore!" And the whole thing became a terrible fight. She got dressed and left my house by foot, but by the time I went down by car to pick her up and take her home, she had vanished.

<u>Later Years</u>   From 1953 on, my encounters with Marilyn became sparser
and sparser. She became extremely famous, extremely busy, and in January
1954 she married Joe DiMaggio. But by October of that year, she had filed for
divorce. In 1956 she married Arthur Miller and four years later she divorced
him. While she was reaping success and glory, I photographed a couple hundred
young, beautiful women — dressed and undressed. During the mid- and late-
fifties I remember only a few things concerning Marilyn and me.

Once, when she was in the Cedars of Lebanon Hospital here in Hollywood,
I sent her flowers. A few weeks after she came out of the hospital, she
phoned me to thank me for the flowers and she said she thought of me when
she entered the hospital, because they had asked the question "Who is your
nearest relative?" and for a few moments she did not know what to answer,
whose name to give, because she had nobody. She was divorced; she had a
thousand friends, ten thousand acquaintances, and yet she felt all alone.
She paid me a compliment by saying that she even thought to give <u>my</u> name
as a reference at the hospital. Why? Because my case was like hers. I, too,
was all alone in the world! Strange, how a person can be world-famous and
still feel absolutely and completely alone.

The second incident was something humorous yet tragic. She phoned,
I don't remember for what reason, and complained about a number of her
problems. I was just in a very high-spirited, cocky mood, and I told her

"GEMINI" (HER ZODIAC)
QUICK THIN-
KER, STIMU-
LATING,
GENIAL,
ETC.

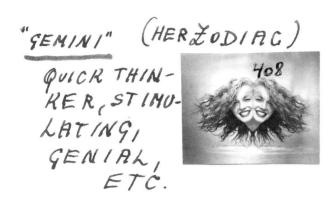

if she came over, I had a "cure for all ills" for her. I said she could
leave all her cares behind and come to hear about my cure. But she did not
come that day. A few weeks later a mysteriously dressed lady got out from
a taxicab at the bottom of my driveway. Marilyn was so bundled up in things
I did not recognize her until she walked up the driveway to my garage, where
I was working on something. Her head was covered with a scarf, she wore dark
eyeglasses, jeans, sandals, and a coat, looking completely unrecognizable.

I never forgot those first moments after she took off her eyeglasses and
I recognized her from ten feet away. I was thinking, "What on earth happened
to my lovely, happy, laughing-all-the-time Norma Jeane? How can she look so
unglamorous, so unhappy?" She said she had come to find out what my "cure
for all ills" was. The conversation that followed went something like this:

Me: What's bothering you?
Her: I didn't sleep all night!
Me: Did you drink much coffee yesterday?
Her: No.
Me: Are you broke?
Her: No.
Me: Are you worried about many things?
Her: Yes, quite a few things! I am being swindled!

And I snapped at her, "Well, that's cause number one for sleeplessness! You are angry, because you feel used!" Then I asked her whether she was physically tired when she went to bed. She said no. I told her that was cause number two for sleeplessness. Then I asked her: "Are you lonesome? Tell me the truth, Marilyn, the absolute truth! Are you lonesome?" And she said yes, she was! So that was the third cause for sleeplessness. The next questions (quite frank and straight to the point, as I usually am): "When did you last make love? When did you have your last orgasm?" She answered that it had been weeks and weeks! And I asserted that that was one of the most important reasons why she couldn't sleep all night.

I was going to remind her that when she used to travel with me in the car in 1945 and 1946, she used to need a great deal of sleep! After we would have transplanted a tree, I would have fixed her a drink or given her the red wine I loved (very healthy, in moderation!). She was about to respond, agreeing with me, when unfortunately our conversation got interrupted by an unexpected visitor, just like her, coming out of the blue…. A young beautiful model came to see me, sent by the model agent. In great contrast to Marilyn's disguise that did not show any of her sex appeal, the model wore a pink skin-tight silk dress to emphasize her sexy contour and dainty high-heeled shoes, her long hair flowing down on her shoulders splendidly. The young lady put on her best smile and all her charms as she entered my house, and as she

749

was walking through the long corridor, I could see she was imitating the famous Marilyn Monroe walk! For a few seconds the entire event became like an incredibly ironical confrontation with fate's trickery! The model who was willing to pose nude for fifty dollars was sexier than Marilyn!

She exposed all her sex appeal, but Marilyn, in great contrast to the girl, looked worn out, worried, and sad. She turned her head away to avoid being recognized by the young lady and while I was chatting with the girl, Marilyn disappeared to call a taxi. She locked herself in the bathroom until the cab arrived, then she asked me not to let the model see her on her way out of the house. Fortunately she was cheered up; her pride must have pepped her up! As she was entering the taxi she remembered to ask me what the "cure for all ills" was. But I was too embarrassed to talk about it in the presence of the taxi driver. I asked her to wait a few seconds, and dashed into my office to grab a copy of a little trifle I had copied from that old album from Scotland, the one I had so unexpectedly found in a bookshop a few years before. I handed the copy to her, then the cab left. That was the last time I saw her for quite a long time.

209

674

"SHE DIED IN BEAUTY"

(TO ILLUSTRATE A POEM
I LIKE) "SHE DIED
IN BEAUTY"

Incredible Paradox   In the latter part of 1960, on a Friday afternoon,
Marilyn came to my house unexpectedly. She was dressed in a black suit,
modest but elegant; she looked very beautiful. I noticed she was no more
the youngish type I used to know, she had entered into womanhood (at age 34).
She was calm, even sad. We were hardly over the first moments of greetings
and hugs when she came right out saying, "André, take pictures of me again!
Tonight, and tomorrow, too…. I'll stay with you."

I had just spent a long day working, selecting photos for a book I was
putting together with glamour photos. My mind was tired when Marilyn arrived;
the weekend was coming — time for fun, romance, lovemaking, anything except
for taking pictures. Marilyn's request gave a good jolt to my mind — here
we go again, I have to work! No matter how beautiful a woman is, photography
is always hard work. I pointed to the hundreds of photos on my long
worktable, and almost angrily I said to Marilyn that I was constantly
oversaturated with "glamour" and I didn't care how beautiful or famous she
was, I didn't care to take pictures of her at all! I went into a neurotic
outburst stemming from sheer frustration. I needed to make love more than
anything else in the world, not to work on capturing her beauty.

What I said must have hurt her feelings because soon after she decided
to go back to her apartment at the Chateau Marmont, on Sunset Boulevard, just
a few blocks away from my house. While I walked her home, she said she had

Beautiful!

just finished filming "The Misfits" and her marriage with Arthur Miller was over with.

At her two-room apartment, there were a good number of suitcases and two large wardrobe trunks, so I asked her whether she was leaving or had just arrived. She answered that she was going back to New York… maybe. But she wasn't sure whether she wanted to go, or where else to go, or, for that matter, where her home was. She was undecided, and perplexed as to where she belonged!

She put down her purse on a wardrobe trunk and sat down on one of the suitcases, and the scene seemed to me the most incomprehensible sight in the world, the most incredible paradox. I was looking at the world's most publicized, most glamorous, most adulated beauty, in that musty-smelling old lousy apartment; she was alone and had no place to go. What an incredible, sad sight!

I asked her about the farm she had bought in Connecticut, where she lived with Arthur Miller, wasn't that her home? Marilyn calmly answered that she had given the farm to Arthur. I blew up! I shouted, "Are you crazy? You gave away the only home you ever owned! Having a home is the most important thing in life, and you let yourself be out in nowhere, due to your stupidity, to your damned kind heart! Oh, Norma Jeane, what are you doing to yourself?" She only looked at me, vaguely smiling… saying nothing. I began to feel guilty for not accepting her offer to come to stay at my house and to take pictures of her. How absurd I had acted! How stupid I had been!

While she was occupying herself in the kitchenette to pour me a drink from the half-empty champagne bottle, I was asking myself what could have been the real purpose of her coming to my house that afternoon. What did she want from me that she could not get elsewhere, from somebody else? Why ask me to take pictures of her when she had just finished a film and had her pictures in magazines and newspapers all over the world? My ego began fantasizing…. Perhaps she came over to tell me, "André, I've had it, I quit! Take me away! Now you can have me!"

For a couple of minutes there was silence. I had the chance to sit in a big, old, comfortable armchair, wondering what famous movie star might have once sat there, maybe as unhappy as Marilyn Monroe…. She felt just as alone in the world as I felt, as I was…. While thinking that, suddenly it occurred to me that I was a damned fool! Perhaps Marilyn came to see me because she wanted to make love! Taking pictures was just an excuse to come to my house! Women are more shy than men in expressing their desires. She did not dare to come out with it so frankly, and I was a stupid fool not to realize it right away.

I emptied the second glass Marilyn handed me, and on an empty stomach, on a tired mind; the alcohol became like a magic sorcerer. I became exuberant, completely revived. Just off the cuff, I started a completely unmeditated scenario, saying, "Marilyn, let's quit everything! Let's elope! Let's go to live in North Africa or on Bora Bora in the South Pacific or in the Andes mountains in Peru! Or let's live in the forests of my native Transylvania and I shall rebuild a crumbling medieval castle just for you!" By then, Marilyn began to smile and she was chuckling when I was telling her the headlines in the newspapers the world over: "MARILYN MONROE DISAPPEARS…."

Suddenly, the telephone was ringing, and it rang and rang until she finally picked up the receiver. She kept listening, and talked back in a low, monotonous voice and her expression turned sad, sordid; after talking for a while she was wiping her tears while still listening on the phone.

I was never the snoopy kind of person who listens to other people's phone conversations, so I went into the bathroom. When I returned I heard Marilyn's last few words: "Yes, I am coming! I will be there tomorrow." Then she hung up the receiver and turned to me, saying, "André, please go home, I have to go back to New York tomorrow." She looked very strange; the mascara from her eyes was running down on her cheeks.

While I was walking home, a few blocks away, suddenly, I thought what a fool I was. I could have photographed Marilyn all night long at my house and made love to her afterwards! What an enormous blunder! I stopped and kept slapping my face with both hands, as hard as I could, to punish myself.

It's a good thing it was dark and nobody saw me doing it! Quite suddenly,
I turned around and rushed back to her apartment to tell her how stupid and
sorry I was….

I did not even ring the doorbell or knock, I just charged in. She was
still on the sofa, talking on the phone, crying. She wasn't at all surprised
to see me again. She hung up the receiver; I knelt down and kissed her
hands, asking her to come back to my house. I said, "Norma Jeane, we will
take fantastic photos! I will fill the bathtub with flowers, and you will
take a bubble bath among them. Please, Norma Jeane, don't go to New York yet!
Come with me, let's go to my house!"

But my pleading was useless. She said I must go home and that people
were waiting for her. That's how that Friday evening ended. The next morning
when I phoned, the switchboard operator told me Marilyn had checked out.
I felt sick from remorse and regret. And I shall regret it for the rest of
my life, because sentiments can vanish like smoke, talk is cheap, but
<u>photographs remain</u>.

My Last Visit with Norma Jeane   It was on June 1, 1961, on her
birthday, that I last saw Norma Jeane alive. On that day, I was working in
my garden and in the afternoon suddenly it came to my mind that this day
was Marilyn's birthday. It was a most amazing telepathic experience, because
without the slightest knowledge of where Marilyn was, I went inside my house,
picked up the telephone and asked Information to give me the number of the
Beverly Hills Hotel. Yet I did not know she would be staying there! I knew
at least ten different places where she lived or stayed during those sixteen
years I had known her, but why I suddenly chose the Beverly Hills Hotel is
absolutely baffling to me! Then the hotel operator answered my call. Just like
that, I asked for Miss Marilyn Monroe and got connected with her immediately!
It was an extraordinary experience. I started by singing "Happy birthday" to
Marilyn. She recognized my voice, and jubilantly asked me to come over right
away. She said she was alone in bungalow ten. I was thinking, "Hurray, the
weekend is coming and maybe I can persuade her to stay with me for a few days!"

Marilyn was very cheerful when I arrived. She took out a small jar of
caviar and two bottles of champagne from the small refrigerator at the side
of the bungalow living room and she kept refilling my glass. The same, sweet,
considerate, good-hearted Norma Jeane! The same soul, like years before….

We had a long discussion about many things, but the conversation became
somber. She began complaining about her problems with her studio, 20th

Century Fox. They had given her a birthday party that day at the studio, but she was tired and left early; she wanted to be alone. She felt unhappy and exploited by them. And she was glad to go back to New York.

Then, I asked her about her highly publicized habit of being last on the set when she was filming: "Why did you let, so often, a big crew of hundreds of people wait for you to appear on the set? Didn't you realize that every hour of delay was costing the studio thousands of dollars? When we were traveling together in 1945, you were always up early in the morning, at daybreak, putting on your make-up, doing your hair… so why the hell did you let an entire crew wait and wait for you to appear on the set day after day? What the hell got into you, acting difficult when you were never like that before with me? What kind of snob have you become?"

And then Marilyn, Norma Jeane, answered me in a sort of pleading, painful way: "André, many times I could not help it! I was too tired, too exhausted to get up so early in the day. You remember how I used to get carsick during those long rides, when we were touring the West? You were driving endlessly, all day and night, and I just slumped over and went to sleep because I felt so tired…. So during all the filming at Fox, I was feeling the same way, just tired and needing rest! Sometimes I was drinking a little, with men I liked, and the nights were far too short, far too delightful, to go to work so early in the morning. Isn't that all very human? I was simply too

exhausted and it became almost impossible to cope with all that hard work. And now the studio is mocking me, saying openly that I am going insane!"

That struck me as strange, because with me, Marilyn was always rational, or almost always; she made good sense and she was correct, normal, never erratic or going into hysterics. But I observed that while she was talking, she became more and more downcast, bitter, and sad. She let herself go, telling me the bad things life had dealt her. She said people were swindling her and treated her rotten.

She looked so lovely, but so sad also, as she stood near the usual large pile of suitcases, everything all packed for her return to New York. This was just another of the many trips she made through the years between Hollywood and New York. I was thinking, what an amazing contrast, this meeting with her compared to when we had first met a little over fifteen years before. Now my darling little Norma Jeane's soul was very worn out. During the short hours we were conversing, she smiled very little and kept complaining about her problems with various people. She tried hard to conceal everything that was perturbing her, but she could not withhold her tears as she spoke. What a contrast her sad mood was to the flippant, flirtatious mood she was in when she first showed herself to me in her bathing suit in the center of my living room at the Garden of Allah in 1945! What a price we all pay sometimes for what we get in life.

I tried to cheer her up, to reassure her that she was now lovelier and more beautiful than ever. An intelligent, experienced, mature woman with the whole world at her feet, and that the best was just beginning for her. The talk helped her a little, we toasted to that. I could not help it, I was in a happy, jovial mood, so happy to see her again. My previous meeting with her at the Chateau Marmont had haunted me for months and now here I was again with the girl I used to love so much! I got quite intoxicated with champagne. I saw the bed in the adjoining room, uncovered, so I began hugging her, kissing her, like old times in years before, and I suggested we should make love because it would make her feel better. I had the right to suggest it — after all, we had nearly been married! But she said I should behave myself, and that she'd had an operation recently. She exclaimed, "You want to kill me! I need rest, André, please forgive me!" These were almost the last words I heard from Norma Jeane's lips, that June evening, a year before she died. Then, she handed me my jacket, walked me to the door of her bungalow, and bid me good night.

After she closed the door, I walked away a hundred feet, then removed my shoes and tiptoed back to her veranda, about twenty feet away from her bedroom window, and sat for a long while in the balmy, deliciously cool dark of the evening. I wanted to see what would happen later. Would she get up and leave, or would someone come to visit her? Instead, she turned out the

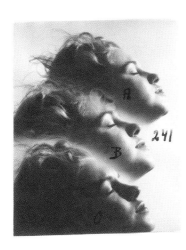

lights in the bedroom. Through the open windows, the nylon curtains were
blowing in the breeze, looking, in the darkness, like some kind of ghosts….
After that apparition, I left the scene.

The next day, I rushed to Beverly Hills and bought a beautiful Italian
ceramic fruit bowl. I filled it with oranges and bought flowers and wrote
a letter to her to apologize for having been so "fresh" and wanting to make
love with her. At the hotel, I gave a generous tip to the bellboy and
instructed him to be sure to hand the things to Marilyn personally.

I know she received it, because a day later, I found one of the flowers
at the front door of my house, and she had slipped an envelope full of
studio stills of herself under my door. She must have passed by before going
to the airport.

I never saw or talked with her again… only in my dreams.

Premonitions   Intuition and precognition can become an amazing and baffling experience. Marilyn's death was foretold to me in the most peculiar way; a very strange thing happened to me in June 1962, about two months before Marilyn's sudden death.

In 1952, when a big storm very badly damaged my house, my photo laboratory, and a large quantity of photos, letters, and negatives that were stored in cardboard boxes, instead of sorting anything, I dug a huge hole in the yard and threw everything in it, covering the hole with earth. It was somewhat like a burial. Ten years later, in June 1962, I was preparing a set of never-seen photos of Marilyn, showing her without makeup, that I had taken in 1946. I was going to propose that set of photos to LIFE magazine with the title "Who is she?" because I thought no one would recognize her. All of a sudden, a strong urge dictated to me to take a shovel and dig up my yard, hoping that perhaps I might find new negatives of Marilyn. While digging the hole, I had morbid thoughts; it felt as if I were digging a grave.

All the things made of paper had completely disintegrated, but the negatives protected each other and to my surprise, I found a few of Marilyn in a rather undamaged state — two negatives in particular. One was of Marilyn looking down at the ground, with a very sordid expression on her face. When I took that picture, Marilyn gave it a title. She said, "André, I am looking at my grave." This one is called "The End of Everything." The other negative I found was of her lying on the ground, eyes shut, pretending that she was dead. What was most particular about my preparing this unusual set of photos, and especially that I found these two negatives dealing with death, was that I didn't have the faintest idea that Marilyn was going through the most distressful period in her life that June. I was so involved with my work that I did not read any newspapers and did not know what was going on with Marilyn.

Early in July, while working with Marilyn's strange photos, I was having a mixture of very peculiar, disturbing nightmares. I saw my mother's coffin underneath my bed, and Marilyn, too, was intermingled in these nightmares. Right after I woke up one morning from one of these bizarre dreams, I had the strong urge to go to the nearest Western Union telegraph office, on Sunset Boulevard, to send a telegram to Marilyn. I addressed it to her studio where she was filming her last picture. The telegram said: TURKEY FOOT, I HAD VERY BAD DREAMS ABOUT YOU LAST NIGHT. PLEASE CALL ME. LOVE W.W.

I am sure the reader wonders what "Turkey Foot" and "W.W." are all about so I will explain briefly: in 1945, when I photographed Norma Jeane in the mountains, her hands often turned purple from the cold, and that color reminded me of the dark purplish color of turkey feet, hence I nicknamed her "Turkey Foot." And "W.W." stood for "Worry Wart." Norma Jeane had nicknamed me that because she thought I was always too cautious, too worried about things, especially about the state of my car, during that trip we took

225

225

together. She laughed gaily whenever she called me W.W. instead of André. Those two names were our secrets. On some occasions, I used to send her notes or letters and nobody could have made any sense out of my funny messages except her….

I didn't receive a phone call or any response to that telegram. On August 4, Saturday evening, the night of her death, I went to the movies. When I came home, at the entrance door, I heard the phone ring and ring, while I was trying to find the key. After I rushed in and grabbed the receiver, the caller had just hung up. It was wishful thinking, but I thought perhaps she was the one who had called. One does not know whom one might call in moments of intoxication. Under the influence of alcohol or drugs, the mind goes berserk….

Nobody knows how many telephone calls she might have made during that fatal night, nor to whom. Several people who knew her closely thought, like me, that it might have been them she was calling. Much has been written about how she spent her last day alive, and why and how she might have died. Was she murdered? Did she commit suicide? Nobody knows for sure and perhaps it will remain a mystery forever. Accidental suicide is probably the best logical explanation.

I was shaving when I heard on the radio that Marilyn had died during the night. Of course, I was astounded, shocked, during the first few minutes, but after a while, while looking at her photos all laid out on my long worktable,

I took it quite calmly. My mind was prepared. I looked at the first photo of Norma Jeane smiling, then at the next photos in which she looked more serious, and then at the last series of photos where she was… dead. I had worked for several weeks preparing those photos! It was a clear case of precognition!

Only some people can comprehend what Marilyn went through during her busy career, or the pressures she had to endure from the time when she gave her first important interview in 1949 until her last day, August 4, 1962. Probably, she didn't have a peaceful day during those thirteen years — and that's probably what killed her.

MRS. EUNICE
MURRAY;
HOUSEKEEPER
TO MARILYN

BEDROOM WINDOW, WHERE MARILYN
DIED. AUG. 5. 1962

<u>Remembrance</u>   The day she died, August 5, 1962, a reporter named Jack
Smith from the Los Angeles Times came over to my house to interview me.
The long article appeared in the paper three days later with the headline:
"'I LOVED MARILYN, STARTED CAREER,' MOURNS HOLLYWOOD PHOTOGRAPHER." From
the day that newspaper article appeared, my telephone started ringing and
I received call after call from all over the USA for days afterward.
Journalists wanted to interview me, magazine editors were inquiring as to
whether I had nude photos of Marilyn, and people wanted to tape interviews
which would be made into phonographic records. Also, quite a few women
called, saying they were as pretty as Marilyn, or even more so, and wished
I would take pictures of them.

   I gave only three interviews, to a reporter from France, another from
Germany, and the third from New York, but after those interviews I felt
completely exhausted and I had the guilty feeling that I had said the wrong
things, that I might have said things not too complimentary about Marilyn.
During those hours of being interviewed, I was so nervous, I could hardly
remember what I had said to the previous reporter. I phoned later to one of
the reporters and asked him to please not print anything I had said. I know
I did not say anything untrue, but I was angry at myself for saying things
that were far too personal. I got so fed up that I refused any further
interviews. I could well imagine what Marilyn endured year after year!

WESTWOOD MEMORIAL CEMETERY

649

650

Marilyn is entombed in an outdoor mausoleum crypt, behind a marble slab, well protected by a shield of thick concrete to ensure that no one will steal her remains. The cemetery is on Wilshire Boulevard in the heart of Westwood. It's like a small park, just a square block. It's all green in there, with flowers everywhere and a few beautiful trees. I never fail to drive in, park the car, and say hello to her whenever I am in that neighborhood; and I always visit her on June 1, her birthday, and August 5, the anniversary of her death. Usually, there are only a few people in there, while outside there are tall office and apartment buildings, and the neighborhood is jammed with traffic and often there is a long line of people waiting to get into the movie theater, which is near where Marilyn is resting. It always strikes me as strange that the people are in there, watching a film, but perhaps only a few know that Marilyn Monroe's coffin is right behind the movie screen, only fifty feet away!

I always meet visitors who, like me, come to see her, and I am amazed by the variety of people who come from the world over… from Europe, the Orient, Australia, and from all over the U.S. They bring flowers; they leave her letters and sentimental notes and poems. Her mother, too, an old lady in her eighties, is still alive and sends her flowers and brief messages, delivered by a florist.

Darryl Francis Zanuck (1902 — 1979), President of 20th Century Fox, is also buried there, just 200 feet away from Marilyn. How fantastic this life of ours is! Marilyn had so much trouble and unhappiness during her career because of her various problems with Fox studios… yet now, both of them are there, resting in peace forever.

Once, while I was photographing Marilyn, we went into a discussion about reincarnation. We were outdoors and it was a beautiful sunny day with lots of clouds in the sky. Marilyn was happy and laughing; she said in her next life she wanted to be a butterfly. I looked at the clouds and said to her, "Look, Norma Jeane, of course, there is a certain kind of reincarnation — most of the weight of our bodies is water, and when we die, that water evaporates and becomes clouds! Clouds create rain, rain fertilizes the soil, and from the soil grow things for animals and humans to eat. So the process of life keeps repeating itself!" Marilyn said to me, "You want me to become a cloud? Take pictures of it!" With her arms outstretched, she ran towards me with her head upward, her hair blowing out in the wind….

André de Dienes, November 1983

Epilogue   It rained last night, but the sun was shining already when I went to the cemetery early this morning. Everything looked so clean, and green, and beautiful. The roses and all the other flowers were full of raindrops, and the sunshine created many sparkling diamonds for Marilyn. The birds were singing, and I could not help thinking how beautiful life is. Then, a butterfly flew over, right to Marilyn. I took pictures of Marilyn's initials reflecting in the golden sunlight. When I left the cemetery, instead of having gloomy thoughts about death, I started to amuse myself thinking up words which begin with two Ms, even silly words, like: Merry Making, Many Moods, Mystical Memories, Monroe Memorabilia, Masochistic Misfits, Magic Moments… and I was thinking that while I developed my film and made prints I would listen to Marvelous Music! I felt so good! Los Angeles is a Marvelous, Magic place to live in. It's endless what one can see and do here each day!

233

Acknowledgements   Late in 1999, I had the opportunity to see the documentary film "Let's Get Lost" by photographer Bruce Weber. Somewhere in the film, Bruce showed a book of nude photographs to the musician Chet Baker, remarking how beautiful the unnamed artist's work was. Intrigued, I slowed down the videotape many times until I caught a brief glimpse of the photos and the name André de Dienes on the spine. Who was this unknown photographer? Why had his work slipped past me? I began to search. What had become of this photographer and his pictures? Perhaps I could purchase a print or an old book for my collection.

Eventually, with patience and a lot of luck, I tracked down André's widow less than a few hours away from my home. She reluctantly agreed to meet me, and we had our first encounter at a roadside diner in the middle of the California desert. She wore dark glasses and asked to see my driver's license to verify my identity. Satisfied, she produced a small box of André's photographs from underneath the table. Instead of the nudes I expected, she told a tale of Marilyn Monroe... lost images... and unpublished diaries. Right then, I knew I had stumbled upon a treasure and there was much more to this story than I ever imagined.

The weeks and months that followed were a blur of unboxing photographs, reading scribbled notes, and unfolding the actual umbrellas that a young Marilyn had held on the beach all those years before. In one box lay André's camera, with the letters MM inscribed on the case. Carefully tucked away in a bedroom closet were André's original diaries. I began to read, and the story started to come together...

Unknown to me at the time was the fact that Benedikt Taschen had been seeking out André's work in hopes of publishing it. Our mutual friend, the noted photographer William Claxton, had just introduced us around the time I was tracking down André — just another of the many coincidences in this project. I suppose now that all of this was simply fate unfolding before our eyes. Clearly, the resurrection of these photographs and diaries has been a series of strange coincidences and connections. Collecting, archiving, and piecing together this long overdue book has been a wonderful experience — equal parts photography, history, and mystery. Finally, the whole story can now be told as I know André would have wanted. It may well be the last untold story in the life of Marilyn Monroe, published exactly forty years after her death.

Thank you to the many people who have contributed to the creation of this book: Shirley de Dienes and family, Benedikt and Angelika Taschen and all at TASCHEN, William Claxton, Peggy Moffitt, Stephen Cohen and the staff of Stephen Cohen Gallery, Eric Ruffing at 13th Floor, Peter Shurkin, Monika Reynolds, Don Weinstein and the staff of Photo Impact Hollywood, Anita Teckemeyer, Horst Neuzner, Kim Goodwin, and Clark Kidder.

Most importantly, much love and gratitude to Gloria, Miles, and Lola.

Steve Crist

This book would never have come into being had I not had the good fortune to meet with Mr. Benedikt Taschen. To him, I owe my first debt of gratitude.

My greatest appreciation and love to my late husband, André de Dienes. Without his love and trust in me this beautiful material may well have never been preserved for you, the reader, to share. His genius in photography is unsurpassed. I love you, André, and thank you for your belief in me.

My deepest admiration and respect to Norma Jeane/Marilyn Monroe, whose beauty in body and soul touched our lives forever. Love is patient, love is kind, and love trusts always, hopes and has faith. The greatest of these you followed eagerly and made an indelible mark on history forever. Thank you Norma Jeane for leaving us with this beautiful gift.

No book can be published without the editor. My heartfelt appreciation and special thanks to Mr. Steve Crist, whose devotion and hard work made it possible for this project to succeed. Thank you Steve and your beautiful wife Gloria, who had to put up with both of us!

To the millions of fans all over the world, I salute and love you all, for without you, our Marilyn would not be alive today.

I thank my companion and my friend, Dennis E. Twohy, for sharing my journey of many trials and tribulations for the past fourteen years. Most of all, for putting up with all the highs and lows which I have encountered in trying to honor André's memory, his work, and in fighting to keep his archive intact. I love you, Den Den. Thank you!

I thank my mother and father for their loving efforts to raise a family of five children. I thank my sisters, Irene Ellis Lynn and Mary Ellis Flory, for their love, support and understanding. I thank my deceased brother William (Billy), whose spirit has always guided me through many tough times.

Last, but most importantly, I'd like to express a very special thanks to my beloved sister, Charlotte, who was and remains my mentor, my teacher and my friend! Sweet sister Charl, you are my role model and without your endless understanding, faith and love where would I be? I love you and shall be eternally grateful for the special friendship we shared.

To all who made this beautiful book come together, I shall be forever indebted to you. Thank you!

Ms. Shirley T. Ellis de Dienes

Selected Bibliography

1949	Études de Nus	Éditions du Chêne / Paris
1950s	André de Dienes	publisher and date unknown / Tokyo
1950s	Nus	Société Parisienne d'Éditions Artistiques / Paris
1956	The Nude	The Bodley Head Ltd. / London
1958	Nude Pattern	The Bodley Head Ltd. / London
1960	Impression	Fravex / Frankfurt
1962	Best Nudes	The Bodley Head Ltd. / London
1965	Sun Warmed Nudes	Elysium Inc. / Los Angeles
1965	Beauty and Nature III	Editions Die Neue Zeit / Thielle
1966	Natural Nudes	Amphoto / New York
1967	Western Art	Fravex / Flensburg
1967	The Glory of de Dienes Women	Elysium Inc. / Los Angeles
1970	Die 64 besten Sexfotos	Stephenson Verlag / Flensburg
1972	Heiße Sexfotos	Stephenson Verlag / Flensburg
1973	Nudes, My Camera and I	Focal Press Ltd. / London
1974	Exotic Nudes	Panu Publishing Co. / Los Angeles
1977	Nude Variations	Amphoto / New York
1985	Marilyn Mon Amour	E.P.I. Filipacchi / Paris

© 2007 TASCHEN GmbH

This 2007 edition published by Barnes & Noble, Inc.,
by arrangement with TASCHEN GmbH.

© 2004 for the images and original diary pages
The Estate of André de Dienes
www.AndredeDienes.com

Licensed by OneWest Publishing Inc. Worldwide
9461 Charleville Blvd. #500, Beverly Hills,
CA 90121, USA
www.OneWestPublishing.com

© 2002 Steve Crist for the introductory essay

Art direction and design: Richard Allan, Sydney
Design assistance: Rebecca Anderson, Sydney
Text editor: Alison Castle, Paris
Production: Horst Neuzner, Cologne

ISBN-13: 978-1-4351-0051-0
ISBN-10: 1-4351-0051-4

Printed in China

1 3 5 7 9 10 8 6 4 2 1

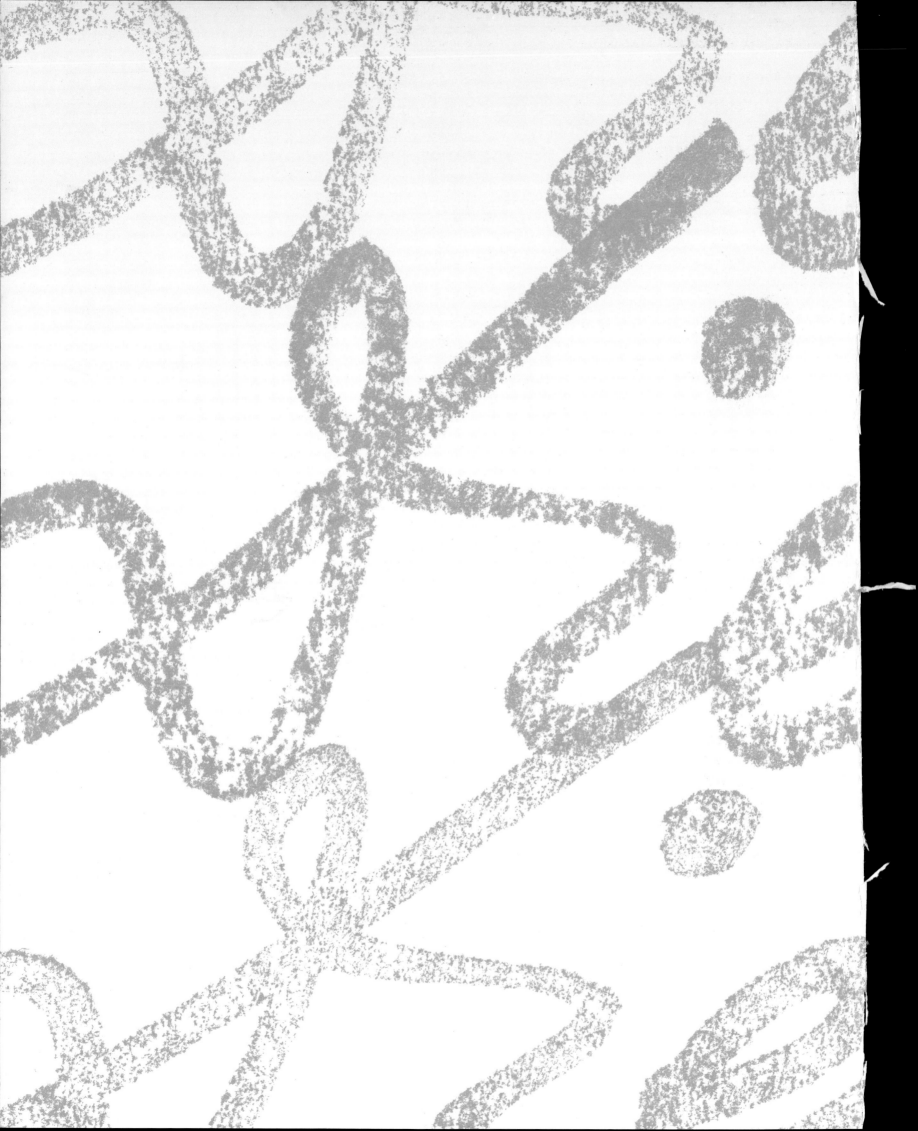